14TH EDITION

Doing Business 2017

Equal Opportunity for All

COMPARING BUSINESS REGULATION FOR DOMESTIC FIRMS IN **190** ECONOMIES

A World Bank Group Flagship Report

Doing Business 2017

Resources on the *Doing Business* website

Current features
News on the *Doing Business* project
http://www.doingbusiness.org

Rankings
How economies rank—from 1 to 190
http://www.doingbusiness.org/rankings

Data
All the data for 190 economies—topic rankings, indicator values, lists of regulatory procedures and details underlying indicators
http://www.doingbusiness.org/data

Reports
Access to *Doing Business* reports as well as subnational and regional reports, case studies and customized economy and regional profiles
http://www.doingbusiness.org/reports

Methodology
The methodologies and research papers underlying *Doing Business*
http://www.doingbusiness.org/methodology

Research
Abstracts of papers on *Doing Business* topics and related policy issues
http://www.doingbusiness.org/research

***Doing Business* reforms**
Short summaries of DB2017 business regulation reforms and lists of reforms since DB2006
http://www.doingbusiness.org/reforms

Historical data
Customized data sets since DB2004
http://www.doingbusiness.org/custom-query

Law library
Online collection of business laws and regulations relating to business
http://www.doingbusiness.org/law-library

Contributors
More than 12,500 specialists in 190 economies who participate in *Doing Business*
http://www.doingbusiness.org/contributors/doing-business

Entrepreneurship data
Data on new business density (number of newly registered companies per 1,000 working-age people) for 136 economies
http://www.doingbusiness.org/data/exploretopics/entrepreneurship

Distance to frontier
Data benchmarking 190 economies to the frontier in regulatory practice and a distance to frontier calculator
http://www.doingbusiness.org/data/distance-to-frontier

Information on good practices
Showing where the many good practices identified by *Doing Business* have been adopted
http://www.doingbusiness.org/data/good-practice

Contents

Case studies

Doing Business 2017

- *Doing Business 2017* is the 14th in a series of annual reports investigating the regulations that enhance business activity and those that constrain it. *Doing Business* presents quantitative indicators on business regulation and the protection of property rights that can be compared across 190 economies—from Afghanistan to Zimbabwe—and over time.
- *Doing Business* measures aspects of regulation affecting 11 areas of the life of a business. Ten of these areas are included in this year's ranking on the ease of doing business: starting a business, dealing with construction permits, getting electricity, registering property, getting credit, protecting minority investors, paying taxes, trading across borders, enforcing contracts, and resolving insolvency. *Doing Business* also measures features of labor market regulation, which is not included in the ranking.
- Data in *Doing Business 2017* are current as of June 1, 2016. The indicators are used to analyze economic outcomes and identify what reforms of business regulation have worked, where and why.

Foreword

Now in its 14th edition, the *Doing Business* report demonstrates the power of a simple idea: measure and report the actual effect of a government policy.

In the summer of 1983, a group of researchers working with Hernando de Soto got all the permits required to open a small garment business on the outskirts of Lima, Peru. Their goal was to measure how long this took. I read de Soto's book, *The Other Path*, decades ago, but I was so astonished by the answer it reported that I remember it today: 289 days.

De Soto's conjecture, which turned out to be right, was that measuring and reporting would create pressure for improvements in the efficiency of government. In the foreword to the revised edition of his book that he wrote in 2002, de Soto reports that because of changes to regulations and procedures, the same business could get all the required permits in a single day.

In a letter published in the Winter 2006 issue of the *Journal of Economic Perspectives*, Simeon Djankov describes how de Soto's idea grew into this report. When Joseph Stiglitz was the World Bank Chief Economist, he selected the topic and picked the team for *The World Development Report 2002: Building Institutions for Markets*. Djankov, who was a member of this team, reached out to Andrei Shleifer, a professor at Harvard, who had done research on the effects that different legal systems had on market development. Shleifer and co-authors agreed to work on some background papers for the *World Development Report* that would examine new data on such processes as getting the permits to start a new business that could be compared across countries. In 2003, this data collection effort yielded the first *Doing Business* report, which presented five indicators for 133 countries.

The *Doing Business* report has had the same effect on policy in many economies that de Soto's initial effort had in Peru. In 2005, it was possible to get the permits to start a business in less than 20 days in only 41 economies. In 2016, this is possible in 130 economies. This history should give us the optimism and impatience to keep launching new ideas and to keep striving for better results. The progress to date should give us optimism. The large amount that remains to be done should make us impatient.

Doing Business 2017 highlights the large disparities between high- and low-income economies and the higher barriers that women face to starting a business or getting a job compared to men. In 155 economies women do not have the same legal rights as men, much less the supporting environment that is vital to promote entrepreneurship.[1] *Doing Business 2017* gives prominence to these issues, expanding three indicators—starting a business, registering property and enforcing contracts—to account for gender discriminatory practices. But why the gender focus?

Research shows that gender gaps exist in women's access to economic opportunities. While women represent 49.6% of the world's population, they account for only 40.8% of the formal workforce. In emerging markets between 31 and 38% of formal small and medium-size enterprises have at least one woman owner, but their average growth rate is significantly lower than that of male-owned firms.[2] Gender gaps in women's entrepreneurship and labor force participation account for an estimated total income loss of 27% in the Middle East and North Africa, a 19% loss in South Asia, a 14% loss in Latin America and the Caribbean and a 10% loss in Europe.[3] Globally, if all women were to be excluded from the labor force income per capita would be reduced by almost 40%.[4]

To capture ways in which governments set additional hurdles for women entrepreneurs, *Doing Business 2017* considers for the first time a number of gender-specific scenarios. The area of company incorporation, for example, now explores whether companies owned by women have the same registration requirements as companies owned by men. It finds that in some economies women must submit additional paperwork or authorizations from their husbands. In the case of property transfers there is a new focus on property ownership and how different sets of rights between men and women affect female entrepreneurs' access to credit. Finally, when it comes to gender equality in court, the enforcing contracts indicator now highlights places where a woman's testimony is given less weight in court than a man's, thereby putting her at a fundamental disadvantage in commercial dealings. *Doing Business* now incorporates these considerations to better reflect the ease of doing business for the widest range of entrepreneurs in a given economy, female entrepreneurs included. The adjustments build on several years of methodology development and cross-country data collection by the *Women, Business and the Law* project, housed in the Global Indicators Group.

Doing Business 2017 also contains a discussion of the role business regulatory reform may play in the global goal to reduce income inequality. Of course there are many determinants of income inequality, including economic growth patterns, the levels and the quality of investments in human capital and the prevalence of bribery and corruption, among many others. Yet some are linked to the regulatory environment for entrepreneurship. Potential entrepreneurs are often discouraged from setting up businesses if the requirements to do so are overly burdensome. When this is the case entrepreneurs often resort to operating within the informal sector which has less protection for labor conditions and is more vulnerable to economic shocks. Having simple, transparent rules for registering a business, paying taxes, getting credit and registering property helps create a level playing field for doing business. Evidence from 175 economies reveals that economies with more stringent entry regulations often experience higher levels of income inequality as measured by the Gini index.[5]

At its core, *Doing Business* seeks to provide quantitative measures of business regulation in 11 regulatory areas that are central to how the private sector functions. A growing body of literature shows that government action to create a sound, predictable regulatory environment is central to whether or not economies perform well and whether that performance is sustainable in the long run.[6] Regulation can aid to correct and prevent traditional types of market failures, such as negative externalities, incomplete markets and information asymmetries. However, regulation can also be used as an intervention when market transactions have led to socially unacceptable outcomes such as improper wealth distribution and inequality.[7] Governments have the ability to design and enforce regulation to help ensure the existence of a level playing field for citizens and economic actors within a society.[8]

Business regulations are a specific type of regulation that can encourage growth and protect individuals in the private sector. The role of the private sector is now almost universally recognized as a key driver of economic growth and development. Nearly 90% of employment (including formal and informal jobs) occurs within the private sector—this sector has abundant potential that should be harnessed.[9] Governments can work together with the private sector to create a thriving business environment. More specifically, effective business regulation can encourage firm start-up and growth as well as minimize the chance for market distortions or failures. Of course, a discussion of the benefits of business regulation must be accompanied by a parallel discussion of its costs. Many businesses complain about the negative impacts of excessive regulation—or as it is more commonly known, "red tape." The answer is not always more regulation; rather, the more effective answer advocated by *Doing Business* is smarter regulation, that aims to strike a balance between the need to facilitate the activities of the private sector while providing adequate safeguards for the interests of consumers and other social groups.

More economies are taking up the challenge for reform. New Zealand is the economy with the highest ranking this year, taking over from Singapore. Sub-Saharan African economies are also improving their *Doing Business* scores at a rate that is three times that of OECD high-income economies. This rate of improvement reflects a low base, but is nonetheless encouraging. Indeed, over the past decade there has been more than a doubling in the number of countries in Sub-Saharan Africa that are engaged in one or more business regulatory reforms—a total of 37 economies in this year's report. The overarching goal of *Doing Business* is to help entrepreneurs in low-income economies face the easier business conditions of their counterparts in high-income economies. The data show persuasively that it is facilitating that convergence, and for that we should celebrate.

The story I told above about an idea launched in 1983 in Peru by Hernando de Soto reminds us that ideas gain power as they pass from person to person, each of whom improves, extends, or challenges the contributions of others. In the best case, this process of exchange and improvement connects professors in universities, employees of organizations such as the World Bank, government officials, members of civil society organizations, business owners and ordinary citizens. Ideas about improving our institutions will themselves improve only if they keep circulating through this network of people.

We welcome your continued feedback on the *Doing Business* project. As I start in the role of the World Bank's Chief Economist, I am astonished by how much room for improvement there is in everything that people do. This heightens my sense of impatient optimism about the potential for meeting the Bank's two goals: ending extreme poverty and promoting shared prosperity. *Doing Business* helps us make progress on one crucial strategy for meeting these goals—offering market opportunities to everyone. It should also inspire us to be more ambitious about how to carry out other complementary strategies. We depend on you, the reader, to help us shape, improve, extend and replicate this project. You keep its ideas in motion. You give them power.

Paul Romer

Paul M. Romer
Chief Economist and
Senior Vice President
The World Bank
Washington, DC

NOTES

1. World Bank 2015a.
2. World Bank Group 2011.
3. Cuberes and Teignier 2014.
4. Cuberes and Teignier 2014.
5. McLaughlin and Stanley 2016.
6. Hall and Jones 1999; Rodrick 1998; Jalilian, Kirkpatrick and Parker 2006.
7. Parker and Kirkpatrick 2012.
8. Bufford 2006.
9. World Bank Group 2013.

Overview

The opportunity to find a job or develop one's business idea is crucial for most people's personal satisfaction. It creates a sense of belonging and purpose and can provide an income that delivers financial stability. It can raise people out of poverty or prevent them from falling into it.

But what does one need to find a job or to start a business, especially if that job or business is in the private sector? Many things are needed, but well-functioning markets—that are properly regulated so that distortions are minimized—are crucial. Governments play a pivotal role in establishing these well-functioning markets through regulation. If the land registry is not required to provide reliable information on who owns what, for example, the efficacy of the property market is undermined making it difficult for entrepreneurs to acquire property, put their ideas to practice and create new jobs. Without well-regulated credit information sharing systems it is difficult for credit markets to thrive and be more inclusive. A properly functioning tax system is also key. Where the burden of tax administration is heavy—making it difficult to comply with tax obligations—firms will have an incentive to avoid paying all taxes due or may opt for informality, thereby eroding the tax base.

To start a business, entrepreneurs need a business registration system that is efficient and accessible to all. *Doing Business* data on Argentina, for example, show that it takes 14 procedures to start a new business, double the global average of just seven. So it is perhaps unsurprising that there are only 0.43 formal new businesses per 1,000 adults in Argentina. By contrast, in Georgia—where three procedures are sufficient to start a business—there are over 5.65 formal new businesses per 1,000 adults.

Failure is part of taking risks and innovating. For people to be willing to start a new business there needs to be a well-developed system in place for closing businesses that do not succeed. In addition to the complicated entry process in Argentina, if the business fails only 23 cents on the dollar are recovered after going through an insolvency proceeding. By contrast, in the Czech Republic the same business failure would have a recovery rate of 67 cents on the dollar. This higher recovery rate also helps to explain the larger number of new businesses in Prague (at 3.42 formal new businesses per 1,000 adults) than in Buenos Aires.

OLD AND NEW FACTORS COVERED IN *DOING BUSINESS*

Doing Business focuses on regulation that affects small and medium-size enterprises, operating in the largest business city of an economy, across 11 areas.[1] Ten of these areas—starting a business, dealing with construction permits, getting electricity, registering property, getting credit, protecting minority investors, paying taxes, trading across borders, enforcing contracts and resolving insolvency—are included in the distance to frontier score

- ***Doing Business* measures aspects of regulation that enable or prevent private sector businesses from starting, operating and expanding. These regulations are measured using 11 indicator sets: starting a business, dealing with construction permits, getting electricity, registering property, getting credit, protecting minority investors, paying taxes, trading across borders, enforcing contracts, resolving insolvency and labor market regulation.**
- ***Doing Business 2017* expands the paying taxes indicators to cover postfiling processes—tax audits, tax refunds and tax appeals—and presents analysis of pilot data on selling to the government which measures public procurement regulations.**
- **Using the data originally developed by *Women, Business and the Law*, this year for the first time *Doing Business* adds a gender component to three indicators—starting a business, registering property, and enforcing contracts—and finds that those economies which limit women's access in these areas have fewer women working in the private sector both as employers and employees.**
- **New data show that there has been an increase in the pace of reform—more economies are reforming and implementing more reforms.**
- ***Doing Business* has recorded over 2,900 regulatory reforms across 186 economies since 2004. Europe and Central Asia has consistently been the region with the highest average number of reforms per economy; the region is now close to having the same good practices in place as the OECD high-income economies. A number of countries in the region—Georgia, Latvia, Lithuania, and the former Yugoslav Republic of Macedonia—are now ranked among the top 30 economies in *Doing Business*.**
- **Better performance in *Doing Business* is on average associated with lower levels of income inequality. This is particularly the case regarding the starting a business and resolving insolvency indicator sets.**

and ease of doing business ranking. *Doing Business* also publishes indicators on labor market regulation which are not included in the distance to frontier score or ease of doing business ranking. The economic literature has shown the importance of such regulations for firm and job creation, international trade and financial inclusion. For more discussion on this literature, see the chapter About *Doing Business*.

Over time, *Doing Business* has evolved from focusing mainly on the efficiency of regulatory processes to also measure the quality of business regulation. *Doing Business* not only measures whether there is, for example, a fast, simple and affordable process for transferring property but also whether the land administration has systems in place that ensure the accuracy of the information about that transfer.

This year *Doing Business* expands further by adding postfiling processes to the paying taxes indicators, including a gender component in three of the indicators and developing a new pilot indicator set on selling to the government (figure 1.1). Also for the first time this year *Doing Business* collects data on Somalia, bringing the total number of economies covered to 190.

Although conceptually important, these changes have a small impact on the distance to frontier and the overall doing business ranking. In paying taxes, the new postfiling processes component accounts for only 25% of the overall indicator set and, furthermore, there is a positive correlation between the old and new part of the indicator.[2] Economies that have efficient processes for paying taxes during the regular filing period also tend to have efficient processes in the postfiling period. For the most part, the formal regulatory environment as measured by *Doing Business* does not differentiate procedures according to the gender of the business owner. The addition of gender components to three separate indicators has a small impact on each of them and therefore a small impact overall. However, even if business regulation as measured by *Doing Business* is gender blind in the majority of economies, this does not mean that in practice men and women have equal opportunities as business owners. Firms owned by women, for example, tend to be smaller and less profitable than firms owned by men.[3]

FIGURE 1.1 What is changing in *Doing Business*?

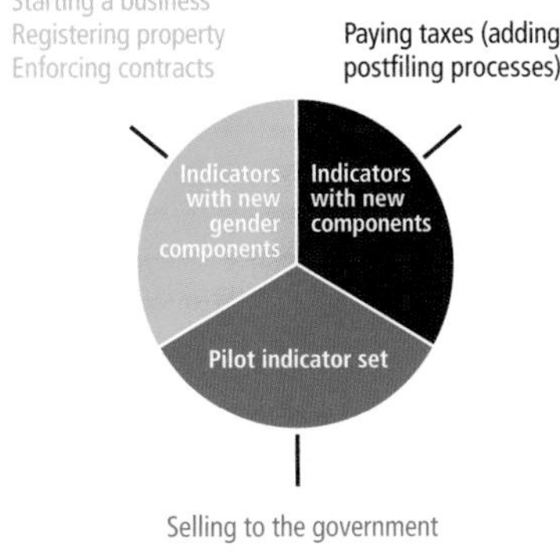

Source: Doing Business database.

While economies that do well in the existing dimensions of the regulatory environment covered by *Doing Business* also tend to do well in the new aspects measured this year, it nevertheless is important to document regulatory practices in these new areas. Doing so helps to document standards of good practices in new areas of regulation which policy makers can use to chart out reforms and set benchmarks. For more information on the *Doing Business* methodology, see the data notes.

Taxes

The paying taxes indicator set is expanded this year to include postfiling processes—those processes that occur after a firm complies with its regular tax obligations. These include tax refunds, tax audits and tax appeals. In particular *Doing Business* measures the time it takes to get a value added tax (VAT) refund, deal with a simple mistake on a corporate income tax return that can potentially trigger an audit and good practices in administrative appeal processes.

The VAT refund is an integral component of a modern VAT system. The VAT has statutory incidence on the final consumer, not on businesses. According to the tax policy guidelines set out by the Organisation for Economic Co-operation and Development (OECD) a VAT system should be neutral and efficient.[4] Some businesses will incur more VAT on their purchases than they collect on their taxable sales in a given tax period and therefore should be entitled to claim the difference from the tax authorities. *Doing Business* data show that OECD high-income economies process VAT refunds the most efficiently with an average of 14.4 weeks to issue a reimbursement (even including some economies where an audit is likely to be conducted).

To analyze tax audits the *Doing Business* case study scenario was expanded to assume that a company made a simple error in the calculation of its income tax liability, leading to an incorrect corporate income tax return and consequently an underpayment of due income tax liability. The firm discovered the error and voluntarily notified the tax authority. In 74 economies—even following immediate notification by the taxpayer—the error in the income tax return is likely to trigger an audit. And in 38 economies this error will lead to a comprehensive audit of the tax return. OECD high-income economies as well as Europe and Central Asia economies have the simplest processes in place to correct a minor mistake in the income tax return. For an analysis of the data for the indicators, see the case study on paying taxes.

Gender

This year for the first time *Doing Business* adds gender components to three indicator sets included in the distance to frontier score and ease of doing business ranking. These are starting a business, registering property and enforcing contracts. This addition is based on data originally collected by *Women, Business and the Law*[5] and updated by *Doing Business*.

Why is it important to incorporate a measure of gender differences? First, around half of the world's population is female and therefore it is important that *Doing Business* measures aspects of regulation that specifically impact this large group. For some years now the *Women, Business and the Law* data have shown, for example, that in some economies a female entrepreneur faces more obstacles than her male counterpart for a variety of economic and business activities. To the extent that these obstacles are ignored, the *Doing Business* data will be incomplete. More importantly, over the last two decades we have learned a great deal about the relationship between various dimensions of gender inequality and economic growth.[6]

There is ample evidence that those economies that have integrated women more rapidly into the workforce have improved their international competitiveness by developing export-oriented manufacturing industries that tend to favor the employment of women. For the most part, legal gender disparities have been shown to have a strong link with female labor force participation.[7] Studies have also shown a clear link between economic growth and development and female labor force participation.[8]

Gender discrimination limits choices and creates distortions that can lead to less efficient outcomes. An employer's decision not to hire a woman based solely on her gender can lead to lower productivity for that particular firm. Where this practice is widespread it can have negative effects at the macro level—an economy's output and growth potential can be lower because of gender discrimination.[9]

The *Women, Business and the Law* team has documented and measured the legal disparities that are relevant to a woman's economic empowerment. Economies where there are more gender differences (as measured by *Women, Business and the Law*) perform worse on average on several important economic and social development variables: formal years of education for women compared to men are lower, labor force participation rates for women compared to men are lower, the proportion of top managers who are women is lower, the proportion of women in parliament is lower, the percentage of women that borrow from financial institutions relative to men is lower and child mortality rates are higher.[10]

Doing Business builds on the work of *Women, Business and the Law* by adding gender components to three indicator sets this year. Starting a business now includes two case studies—one where the entrepreneurs are men and one where the entrepreneurs are women—in order to address a previous lack of data on those economies where women face a higher number of procedures. Registering property now measures legal gender differentiations in property rights for ownership, use and transfer. And enforcing contracts was expanded to measure whether women's and men's testimony have the same evidentiary weight in civil courts. These three areas were selected because there is enough evidence to show their relevance for economic development and because they fit well within the *Doing Business* methodology. One new area—quotas for women in corporate boards—was studied but not included in this year's report because the evidence in this area has been mixed so far (box 1.1).

Several studies highlight the importance of equal opportunities for women entrepreneurs, creating the need to measure the differences faced by women entrepreneurs when starting a new business.[11] Research also shows the importance of equal rules regarding property rights for men and women. One study finds that after a reform to the family law in Ethiopia that established more equitable property rights over marital property between spouses, there was an increase in female labor force participation and in more productive sectors.[12] Another study finds that after changes were made to the Hindu Succession Act improving inheritance rights for women in India, there was an increase in education for girls.[13] Improving land tenure security benefits all, but a study of Rwanda's land tenure regularization program showed that women benefit the most.[14]

Twenty-three economies impose more procedures for women than men to start a business. Sixteen limit women's ability to own, use and transfer property. And in 17 economies, the civil courts do not value a woman's testimony the same way as a man's.

Three gender-related measures were added to the starting a business indicator set—whether a woman requires permission to leave the house, whether there are gender-specific identification procedures and whether a married woman requires her husband's permission to start a business. In 17 economies a married woman cannot leave the house without her husband's permission by law. Although in practice this law may not be enforced, it still reduces women's bargaining power within the household and can undermine their ability to pursue a business venture. In three economies the process of obtaining official identification is different for men and women. The official identification document is a pre-requisite to starting a business. *Doing Business* has not traditionally captured the process of obtaining identification in starting a business; it is assumed that the entrepreneur has identification before deciding to create a new business. However, when capturing gender-specific procedures it is crucial to include female-specific requirements. In Benin, for example, a married woman must present a marriage certificate when applying for identification but the same requirement does not apply to a married man. In four economies a woman requires her husband's explicit permission to start a business. This is the case in the Democratic Republic of

BOX 1.1 Women in corporate boards

Building on *Women, Business and the Law* data, this year *Doing Business* collected data on regulation that imposes quotas for women in corporate boards as well as sanctions and incentives for meeting those quotas. The data show that nine economies have such provisions. Seven of the nine economies that define quotas for women in corporate boards or impose penalties for noncompliance are OECD high-income economies—namely Belgium, France, Germany, Iceland, Israel, Italy and Norway. This type of regulation exists in other regions of the world but it is less common. The law in India, for example, requires that publicly-listed companies have at least one director that is a woman. Any business appointing a woman to a management position in Sierra Leone is now eligible for a tax credit equal to 6.5% of that female manager's compensation.

Although the data were collected, they were not included in the *Doing Business* indicators because the empirical evidence on the value of quotas for women in corporate boards is mixed. For example, some studies have questioned the link between women in the boardroom and firm performance, finding either no relationship between gender diversity and performance or even a negative relationship.[a] A Norwegian law mandating 40% representation of women in corporate boards is probably the most researched regulation in this area. One study finds that there were no significant reductions in gender wage gaps.[b] Another study of the same regulation reports a significant drop in stock prices when the law was made public and a deterioration in operating performance.[c] Nevertheless, another study found that firms with women in corporate boards undertake fewer workforce reductions than firms with only male board members.[d]

However, there are patterns of positive firm outcomes connected to the presence of women in important decision-making positions. Quoting a broad range of studies, the World Bank argues that low gender diversity in corporate boards "is seen by many as undermining a company's potential value and growth. Higher diversity is often thought to improve the board's functioning by increasing its monitoring capacity, broadening its access to information on its potential customer base, and enhancing its creativity by multiplying viewpoints. Greater diversity implies that board directors can be selected from a broader talent pool."[e] Indeed, there is evidence that companies benefit from fostering an increase in the number of women board directors. A study comparing the top and bottom quartiles of women board directors at *Fortune 500* companies found that where there were higher numbers of women on the board the companies thrived.[f] Analyzing financial measures such as return on equity, return on sales, and return on invested capital, this study established that companies with more women board directors were able to outperform those with fewer by between 42 and 66%.

There is also evidence that companies with greater participation of women in boards tend to have stronger ethical foundations. According to a report from the index provider MSCI, bribery, fraud or other corporate governance scandals are less common in corporations with more women on their boards. The dataset used in this analysis included 6,500 boards globally.[g]

a. van Dijk and others 2012; Adams and Ferreira 2009.
b. Bertrand and others 2014.
c. Ahern and Dittmar 2012.
d. Matsa and Miller 2013.
e. World Bank 2011.
f. Joy and others 2007.
g. Lee and others 2015.

Congo, where by law a married woman needs the authorization of her husband to incorporate a business.

The registering property indicators now include two aspects regarding ownership rights. *Doing Business* measures whether unmarried men and unmarried women have equal ownership rights to property. Only two economies—Swaziland and Tonga—grant fewer rights to unmarried women. However, when the same question is used to compare the property rights of married men with married women, differences arise in 16 economies. Restrictions on property ownership are far more common for married women because these are normally linked to family and marriage codes.

Restrictions for women on starting a business are more frequent in economies in both the Middle East and North Africa and Sub-Saharan Africa. The restrictions measured in registering property are more prevalent in Sub-Saharan Africa, while those measured in enforcing contracts are more present in the Middle East and North Africa. However, these types of restrictions are present in every region except Europe and Central Asia. Only one OECD high-income economy still has a restriction—in Chile the law provides fewer property rights to married women than to married men.

Economies with more restrictions for women tend to have on average lower female labor force participation and a lower percentage of female labor force relative to male. The same relationship applies to women's participation in firm ownership and management (figure 1.2). In fact, the new gender components added to the distance to frontier have a

FIGURE 1.2 Less equal business regulation is associated with fewer women running firms

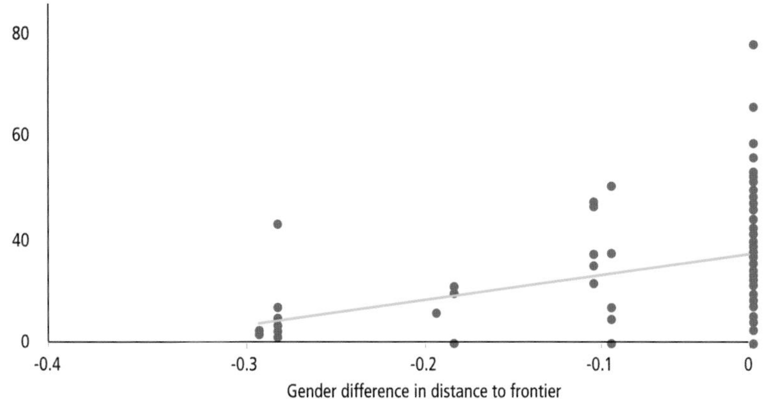

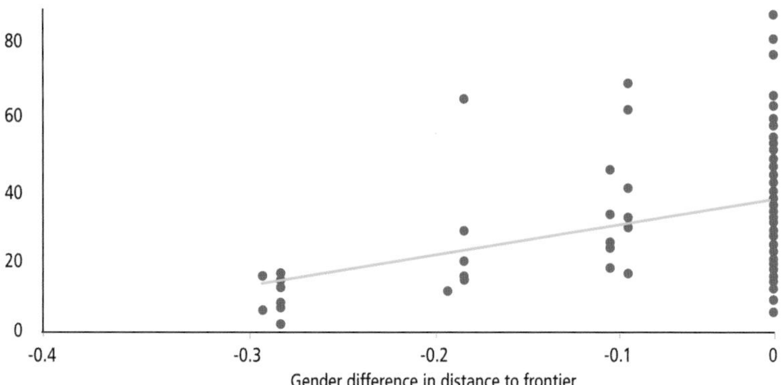

Sources: Doing Business database; Enterprise Surveys database (http://www.enterprisesurveys.org), World Bank.
Note: The relationship between the percentage of firms with female participation in ownership and the difference in distance to frontier due to the addition of gender components in three topics is significant at the 1% level after controlling for income per capita. The same applies when the analysis is done using the percentage of firms with a female top manager.

strong association with outcomes that represent women's economic empowerment. These results are associations and cannot be interpreted in a causal fashion.

Procurement

Public procurement is the process of purchasing goods, services or works by the public sector from the private sector. Overall, public procurement represents on average 10 to 25% of GDP, making the procurement market a unique pool of business opportunities for the private sector.[15] This year *Doing Business* includes an annex with analysis of a pilot indicator set on public procurement regulation called "selling to the government." The procurement process is studied across five main areas: accessibility and transparency, bid security, payment delays, incentives for small and medium-size enterprises and complaints mechanisms. For accessibility and transparency, the annex discusses data on whether information is accessible to prospective bidders and how that information can be accessed. For bid security, the indicators measure the amount that prospective bidders need to pay upfront in order to be considered in the bidding process and the form of the security deposit. For payment delays, the annex discusses data on the time it takes for the firm to receive payment from the government after the contract is completed and the service has been delivered. The incentives for small and medium-size enterprises component measures whether economies have set up specific legal provisions or policies to promote fair access for small and medium-size enterprises to government contracts. And for the complaints mechanism component, the indicators measure the process to file a grievance regarding a public procurement project including who can file a complaint, where to file a complaint and the independence of the review body as well as what remedies are granted.

The data show that 97% of the 78 economies analyzed have at least one or more online portals dedicated to public procurement and that close to 90% of economies impose a bid security deposit requirement that suppliers must fulfill for their bid to be considered. In 37% of the economies included in the selling to the government indicators, payment occurs on average within 30 days while in 48% of the economies suppliers can expect to receive payments between 31 and 90 days following completion of the contract. This analysis is presented in the annex on selling to the government and the data are available on the *Doing Business* website.

ECONOMIES WITH MORE BUSINESS-FRIENDLY REGULATIONS

Doing Business scores economies based on how business friendly their regulatory systems are using the distance to frontier score and the ease of doing business ranking. The distance to frontier score measures the distance of each economy to the "frontier," which represents the best performance observed on each of the indicators across all economies in the *Doing Business* sample since 2005 or the third year in which data were collected for the indicator. For the getting electricity indicators, for example, the frontier is set at three procedures, 18 days and no cost to obtain a new electricity connection in the economy's largest business city. The worst for the same group of indicators is set at

9 procedures, 248 days and 81 times the economy's income per capita as the cost. In addition, the getting electricity indicators measure the reliability of electricity supply and transparency of tariffs through an index ranging from 0 to 8; in this case 8 is the frontier score. For example, in the case of reliability and transparency, an economy with a score of 6 would be considered to be 75% of the way to the frontier and would have a distance to frontier score of that value. The ease of doing business ranking is based on economies' relative positions on the distance to frontier scores on ten different *Doing Business* indicator sets. For more details, see the chapter on the distance to frontier and ease of doing business ranking.

There was some change in the 20 economies with the top scores due mainly to the implementation of business regulatory reforms (table 1.1) and, to a much lesser extent, on account of the methodology changes mentioned above. Austria, Georgia and Latvia join the top 20 economies this year. Georgia implemented five reforms as measured by *Doing Business*. And Latvia implemented two - it improved access to credit information (by launching a private credit bureau) and made it easier to file taxes (electronically). Although the top 20 economies already have simple, effective and accessible business regulations, they continued to implement reforms this year with a total of 20 reforms implemented among them. Hong Kong SAR, China, for example, made starting a business less costly by reducing the business registration fee while Sweden made it easier to transfer property and Norway made enforcing contracts easier by introducing an electronic filing system.

OECD high-income economies have on average the most business-friendly regulatory systems, followed by Europe and Central Asia (figure 1.3). There is, however, a large variation within those two regions. New Zealand has a ranking of 1 while Greece has a ranking of 61; FYR Macedonia stands at 10 while Tajikistan is at 128. The Sub-Saharan Africa region continues to be home to the economies with the least business-friendly regulations on average. However, this year the regional improvement in the distance to frontier score for Sub-Saharan Africa was almost three times as high as the average improvement for OECD high-income economies. Nevertheless, there is still a long way for Sub-Saharan Africa to go: it takes 60 days on average to transfer property in that region, for example, compared to only 22 days for the same transaction in OECD high-income economies.

Following the expansion of the scope of the indicators in last year's report, *Doing Business* now provides further clarity on the differences between well-designed and badly designed regulation. New data on the quality of regulation make it easier to identify where regulation is enabling businesses to thrive and where it is enabling rent seeking. *Doing Business* measures the quality of regulation by focusing on whether an economy has in place the rules and processes that can lead to good outcomes, linked in each case to *Doing Business* measures of efficiency. Scores are higher for economies that, for example, have a land administration system that maintains a dependable database and produces credible titles that are respected as reliable by the legal system. Another way that *Doing Business* measures regulatory quality is through the building quality control index, which evaluates the quality of building regulations, the strength of quality control and safety mechanisms, liability and insurance regimes and professional certification requirements that ultimately

FIGURE 1.3 The biggest gaps between regulatory efficiency and regulatory quality are in the Middle East and North Africa and in Sub-Saharan Africa

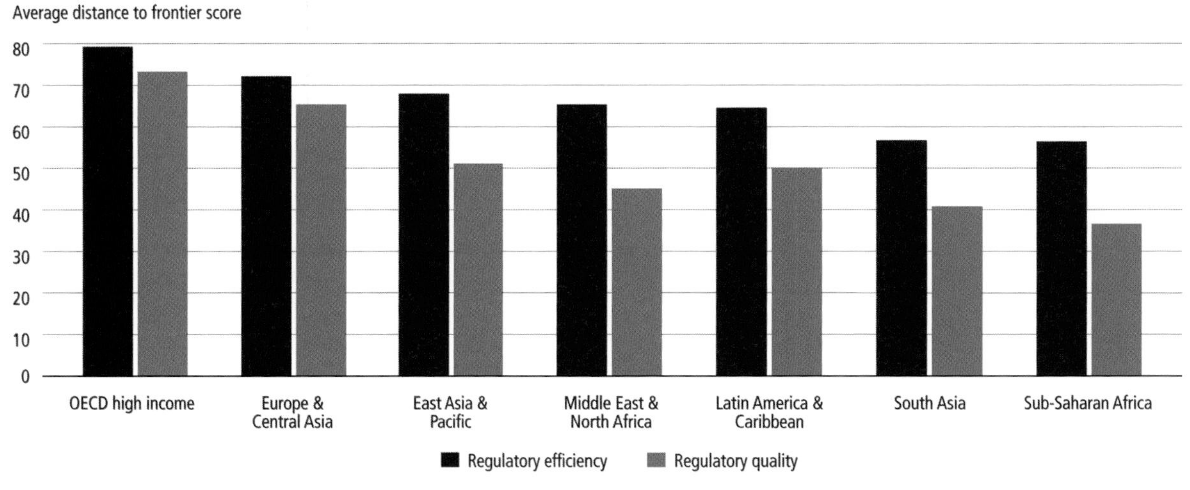

Source: Doing Business database.

Note: The distance to frontier score for regulatory efficiency is the aggregate score for the procedures (where applicable), time and cost indicators from the following indicator sets: starting a business (also including the minimum capital requirement indicator), dealing with construction permits, getting electricity, registering property, paying taxes (also including the postfiling index), trading across borders, enforcing contracts and resolving insolvency. The distance to frontier score for regulatory quality is the aggregate score for getting credit and protecting minority investors as well as the regulatory quality indices from the indicator sets on dealing with construction permits, getting electricity, registering property, enforcing contracts and resolving insolvency.

TABLE 1.1 Ease of doing business ranking

Rank	Economy	DTF score
1	New Zealand	87.01 ↑
2	Singapore	85.05 ↑
3	Denmark	84.87 ↑
4	Hong Kong SAR, China	84.21 ↑
5	Korea, Rep.	84.07 ↑
6	Norway	82.82 ↑
7	United Kingdom	82.74 ↑
8	United States	82.45
9	Sweden	82.13 ↑
10	Macedonia, FYR	81.74 ↑
11	Taiwan, China	81.09 ↑
12	Estonia	81.05 ↑
13	Finland	80.84
14	Latvia	80.61 ↑
15	Australia	80.26 ↑
16	Georgia	80.20 ↑
17	Germany	79.87
18	Ireland	79.53 ↑
19	Austria	78.92 ↑
20	Iceland	78.91 ↑
21	Lithuania	78.84 ↑
22	Canada	78.57
23	Malaysia	78.11
24	Poland	77.81 ↑
25	Portugal	77.40 ↑
26	United Arab Emirates	76.89 ↑
27	Czech Republic	76.71 ↑
28	Netherlands	76.38 ↑
29	France	76.27 ↑
30	Slovenia	76.14 ↑
31	Switzerland	76.06
32	Spain	75.73 ↑
33	Slovak Republic	75.61 ↑
34	Japan	75.53 ↑
35	Kazakhstan	75.09 ↑
36	Romania	74.26 ↑
37	Belarus	74.13 ↑
38	Armenia	73.63 ↑
39	Bulgaria	73.51 ↑
40	Russian Federation	73.19
41	Hungary	73.07 ↑
42	Belgium	73.00
43	Croatia	72.99 ↑
44	Moldova	72.75 ↑
45	Cyprus	72.65 ↑
46	Thailand	72.53 ↑
47	Mexico	72.29 ↑
47	Serbia	72.29 ↑
49	Mauritius	72.27 ↑
50	Italy	72.25 ↑
51	Montenegro	72.08 ↑
52	Israel	71.65 ↑
53	Colombia	70.92 ↑
54	Peru	70.25 ↑
55	Puerto Rico (U.S.)	69.82 ↑
56	Rwanda	69.81 ↑
57	Chile	69.56 ↑
58	Albania	68.90 ↑
59	Luxembourg	68.81 ↑
60	Kosovo	68.79 ↑
61	Greece	68.67
62	Costa Rica	68.50 ↑
63	Bahrain	68.44 ↑
64	Mongolia	68.15 ↑
65	Azerbaijan	67.99 ↑
66	Oman	67.73 ↑
67	Jamaica	67.54 ↑
68	Morocco	67.50 ↑
69	Turkey	67.19
70	Panama	66.19
71	Botswana	65.55 ↑
72	Brunei Darussalam	65.51 ↑
73	Bhutan	65.37 ↑
74	South Africa	65.20
75	Kyrgyz Republic	65.17 ↑
76	Malta	65.01 ↑
77	Tunisia	64.89 ↑
78	China	64.28 ↑
79	San Marino	64.11 ↑
80	Ukraine	63.90 ↑
81	Bosnia and Herzegovina	63.87 ↑
82	Vietnam	63.83 ↑
83	Qatar	63.66
83	Vanuatu	63.66 ↑
85	Tonga	63.58
86	St. Lucia	63.13
87	Uzbekistan	63.03 ↑
88	Guatemala	62.93 ↑
89	Samoa	62.17 ↑
90	Uruguay	61.85 ↑
91	Indonesia	61.52 ↑
92	Kenya	61.22 ↑
93	Seychelles	61.21 ↑
94	Saudi Arabia	61.11 ↑
95	El Salvador	61.02
96	Trinidad and Tobago	60.99
97	Fiji	60.71
98	Zambia	60.54
99	Philippines	60.40 ↑
100	Lesotho	60.37 ↑
101	Dominica	60.27
102	Kuwait	59.55
103	Dominican Republic	59.35 ↑
104	Solomon Islands	59.17 ↑
105	Honduras	59.09
106	Paraguay	59.03
107	Nepal	58.88
108	Ghana	58.82 ↑
108	Namibia	58.82
110	Sri Lanka	58.79 ↑
111	Swaziland	58.34 ↑
112	Belize	58.06
113	Antigua and Barbuda	58.04
114	Ecuador	57.97 ↑
115	Uganda	57.77 ↑
116	Argentina	57.45 ↑
117	Barbados	57.42 ↑
118	Jordan	57.30 ↑
119	Papua New Guinea	57.29 ↑
120	Iran, Islamic Rep.	57.26 ↑
121	Bahamas, The	56.65
122	Egypt, Arab Rep.	56.64 ↑
123	Brazil	56.53
124	Guyana	56.26 ↑
125	St. Vincent and the Grenadines	55.91
126	Lebanon	55.90
127	Nicaragua	55.75 ↑
128	Tajikistan	55.34 ↑
129	Cabo Verde	55.28
130	India	55.27 ↑
131	Cambodia	54.79 ↑
132	Tanzania	54.48 ↑
133	Malawi	54.39 ↑
134	St. Kitts and Nevis	53.96
135	Maldives	53.94
136	Palau	53.81 ↑
137	Mozambique	53.78
138	Grenada	53.75
139	Lao PDR	53.29 ↑
140	West Bank and Gaza	53.21 ↑
141	Mali	52.96 ↑
142	Côte d'Ivoire	52.31 ↑
143	Marshall Islands	51.92 ↑
144	Pakistan	51.77 ↑
145	Gambia, The	51.70 ↑
146	Burkina Faso	51.33 ↑
147	Senegal	50.68 ↑
148	Sierra Leone	50.23 ↑
149	Bolivia	49.85 ↑
150	Niger	49.57 ↑
151	Micronesia, Fed. Sts.	49.48
152	Kiribati	49.19 ↑
153	Comoros	48.69 ↑
154	Togo	48.57 ↑
155	Benin	48.52 ↑
156	Algeria	47.76 ↑
157	Burundi	47.37 ↑
158	Suriname	47.28 ↑
159	Ethiopia	47.25 ↑
160	Mauritania	47.21 ↑
161	Zimbabwe	47.10 ↑
162	São Tomé and Príncipe	46.75 ↑
163	Guinea	46.23 ↑
164	Gabon	45.88
165	Iraq	45.61 ↑
166	Cameroon	45.27 ↑
167	Madagascar	45.10 ↑
168	Sudan	44.76
169	Nigeria	44.63 ↑
170	Myanmar	44.56 ↑
171	Djibouti	44.50 ↑
172	Guinea-Bissau	41.63 ↑
173	Syrian Arab Republic	41.43
174	Liberia	41.41
175	Timor-Leste	40.88
176	Bangladesh	40.84 ↑
177	Congo, Rep.	40.58
178	Equatorial Guinea	39.83
179	Yemen, Rep.	39.57
180	Chad	39.07 ↑
181	Haiti	38.66 ↑
182	Angola	38.41
183	Afghanistan	38.10
184	Congo, Dem. Rep.	37.57 ↑
185	Central African Republic	36.25
186	South Sudan	33.48
187	Venezuela, RB	33.37
188	Libya	33.19
189	Eritrea	28.05 ↑
190	Somalia	20.29 ↑

Source: Doing Business database.

Note: The rankings are benchmarked to June 2016 and based on the average of each economy's distance to frontier (DTF) scores for the 10 topics included in this year's aggregate ranking. For the economies for which the data cover two cities, scores are a population-weighted average for the two cities. An arrow indicates an improvement in the score between 2015 and 2016 (and therefore an improvement in the overall business environment as measured by *Doing Business*), while the absence of one indicates either no improvement or a deterioration in the score. The score for both years is based on the new methodology.

lead to safe buildings. Efficient business regulatory systems allow entrepreneurs to achieve business-related tasks simply, quickly and inexpensively. Therefore, an economy scores better on the metric for regulatory efficiency if it has a system in place that allows entrepreneurs to start a business through a small number of steps, in short time and at lower cost.

Regulatory efficiency and regulatory quality go hand in hand. Economies that have efficient regulatory processes as measured by *Doing Business* also tend to have good regulatory quality. However, the gap between the two measures varies significantly by region. In OECD high-income economies, the average distance to the frontier score for regulatory efficiency is 79.4 while regulatory quality lags at 73.4. In the Middle East and North Africa and Sub-Saharan Africa the gap between efficiency and quality is larger: on efficiency these regions score 65.4 and 56.5 while on quality they score 45.2 and 36.7, respectively.

ECONOMIES WITH THE LARGEST IMPROVEMENTS IN BUSINESS REGULATION IN 2015/16

In 2015/16, 137 economies worldwide implemented 283 business regulatory reforms. This represents an increase of more than 20% compared to last year. In fact, the number of economies that implemented at least one reform increased from 122 to 137, indicating that there are more economies trying to improve in the areas measured in *Doing Business*. And 139 economies made an improvement in the distance to frontier score; doing business is now easier and less costly in those economies compared to last year. With 49 reforms, starting a business continues to be the indicator set with the highest number of reforms followed by paying taxes with 46. Of the economies in Europe and Central Asia, 96% implemented at least one *Doing Business* reform. Sub-Saharan Africa is the region with the second-highest incidence of reforms, with 77% of economies implementing at least one reform captured by *Doing Business*.

Ten economies are highlighted this year for making the biggest improvements in their business regulations—Brunei Darussalam, Kazakhstan, Kenya, Belarus, Indonesia, Serbia, Georgia, Pakistan, the United Arab Emirates and Bahrain. The ease of doing business ranking for these economies ranges from 144 in Pakistan to 16 in Georgia; on average it is 62. Compared to previous years there is a lower number of top improvers from Sub-Saharan Africa even though this region accounts for over a quarter of all reforms globally.

There are several possible explanations for the increase in reform intensity. One is that economies are increasingly interested in improving business regulatory conditions and therefore are reforming more. Another is that there are more areas where reforms can be captured following the expansion of the *Doing Business* methodology. The data indicate that both factors have contributed. A substantial number of the reforms implemented this year are in areas that were added since *Doing Business 2015* (figure 1.4). Around 26% of the reforms implemented in the expanded indicator sets were only made in these new areas. And another 17% concern both the new and old indicators. Indeed, over 40% of all reforms affected at least one of the components added since *Doing Business 2015*. The frequency of reform in the new areas varies substantially by topic, with the most reforms occurring within the enforcing contracts and registering property indicators. In registering property, for example, this year the cadastral maps have been digitized and made available online in Jakarta and Surabaya, Indonesia. The online application provides customers with access to a spatial database that allows them to check property boundaries. And in enforcing contracts, the government of Rwanda introduced the Integrated Electronic Case Management

FIGURE 1.4 *Doing Business* reforms in 2015/16 in the areas added since *Doing Business 2015*

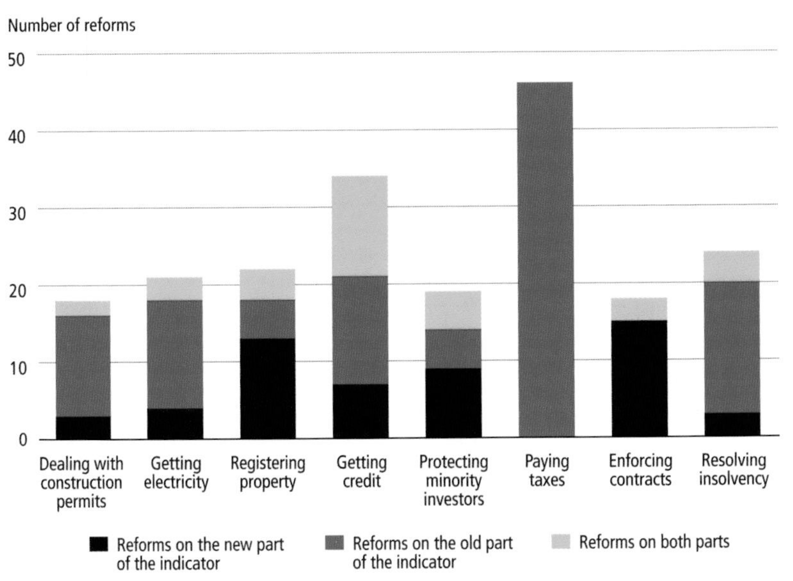

Source: Doing Business database.

Note: The new components added since *Doing Business* 2015 are: the building quality control index in dealing with construction permits, the reliability of supply and transparency of tariffs index in getting electricity, the quality of land administration index in registering property, 3 points in the strength of legal rights index and 2 points in the depth of credit information index in getting credit, extent of shareholder governance index in protecting minority investors, post-filing in paying taxes, quality of judicial processes index in enforcing contracts and strength of insolvency framework index in resolving insolvency.

System in Kigali city courts and all commercial courts.

For a full discussion of the 283 reforms implemented in 2015/16 and more information on the top improvers, see the chapter on reforming the business environment.

ECONOMIES WITH THE LARGEST IMPROVEMENTS IN BUSINESS REGULATION SINCE 2003

Each year *Doing Business* captures substantive reforms implemented by economies across all ten indicator sets included in the ease of doing business ranking. Since *Doing Business 2005* over 2,900 business regulatory reforms have been implemented in 186 economies. Only Kiribati, Libya, Somalia and South Sudan have not implemented a reform captured by the *Doing Business* indicators. The majority of these reforms have been made in low-income and middle-income economies, leading to more significant improvements in business regulation compared to high-income economies. The gap between high-income economies and low-income economies is therefore narrowing when it comes to the quality and efficiency of business regulation (figure 1.5).

The reform intensity varies considerably across regions. With over 26 reforms per economy since 2004, Europe and Central Asia is the region that has reformed the most intensely since *Doing Business* began gathering data on business regulation. The global average is around 15 reforms per economy. These reforms have produced significant improvements in business regulation. Since 2004, economies in Europe and Central Asia have improved over 20 points on average in the distance to frontier score, moving into second position in the regional rankings behind the OECD high-income economies for the most business-friendly regulations (figure 1.6).

FIGURE 1.5 Low-income economies have made bigger improvements over time in the quality and efficiency of business regulation

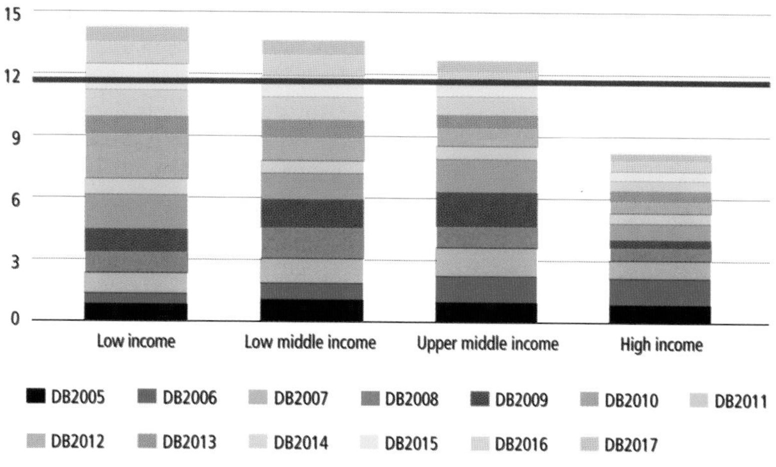

Source: Doing Business database.

Note: The red line shows the average global improvement in the distance to frontier score since 2004. The measure is normalized to range from 0 to 100, with 100 representing the frontier. Because of changes over the years in methodology and in the economies and indicators included, the improvements are measured year on year using pairs of consecutive years with comparable data.

How did Europe and Central Asia accomplish this? The most reformed *Doing Business* areas in Europe and Central Asia are starting a business, paying taxes and getting credit. Georgia, FYR Macedonia, Kazakhstan, Belarus, Armenia, and the Russian Federation have made the most reforms in Europe and Central Asia, implementing over 30 reforms each since 2004. Moreover, seven countries in the region—Armenia, Belarus, Georgia, Kazakhstan, Lithuania, FYR Macedonia

FIGURE 1.6 Europe and Central Asia has made a substantially bigger improvement in business regulation over time than any other region

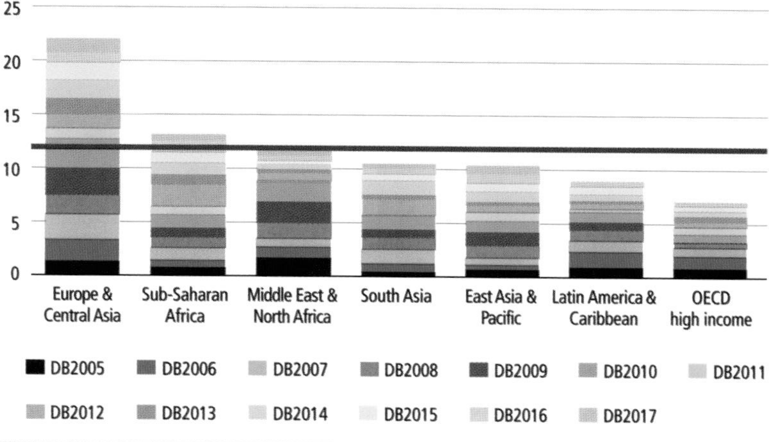

Source: Doing Business database.

Note: The red line shows the average global improvement in the distance to frontier score since 2004. The measure is normalized to range from 0 to 100, with 100 representing the frontier. Because of changes over the years in methodology and in the economies and indicators included, the improvements are measured year on year using pairs of consecutive years with comparable data.

and Ukraine—reformed across all *Doing Business* indicators. Another 13 economies implemented reforms in eight to 10 areas measured by *Doing Business*. This shows that economies tend to expand their reform efforts to encompass multiple business regulatory environments rather than choosing a narrow reform path.

The region with the lowest average number of reforms per economy is East Asia and the Pacific with 13 reforms per economy since 2004. This is partly due to the fact that the Pacific islands have been slow to reform. The OECD high-income economies have the lowest average improvement, mainly because of reduced room for progress. It is hard to advance by much when you are already close to the top.

Reforming the requirements for starting a business is by far the most common area for reform—586 reforms have been captured by the starting a business indicator set since 2004 (figure 1.7). Only 14 economies have not improved their business registration processes. One of these economies is República Bolivariana de Venezuela, where it takes 230 days to start a new business, significantly higher than the global average of 21 days (down from 51 days in 2003). In the past year, República Bolivariana de Venezuela has actually made the process more time consuming—an increase of 44 days—by limiting the work schedule of the public sector amidst an energy crisis.

The indicator set with the second highest number of reforms is paying taxes, with 443 reforms implemented since 2004. But reforms captured within the getting credit indicators—although there were only 400 recorded—have resulted in a bigger improvement in the distance to frontier score. The data also show that court systems, as captured in both the enforcing contracts and resolving insolvency indicator sets, are the institutions reformed least frequently.

THE RELATIONSHIP BETWEEN BUSINESS REGULATION AND INCOME INEQUALITY

A recent World Bank report focusing on poverty and shared prosperity provides new evidence on the status of income inequality worldwide. Domestic income inequality has fallen in more economies than it has risen since 2008 (across a sample of 81 economies). However, the global average for domestic income inequality is larger today than 25 years ago.[16] Indeed, income inequality is an important concern. Excessive income inequality can have many negative effects, including political instability and civil unrest. The determinants of income inequality have been widely studied in the economic literature—what increases it, what can reduce it and its negative consequences. For example, policies such as early childhood development, universal education and health care

FIGURE 1.7 Economies have improved regulatory processes the most in the area of starting a business

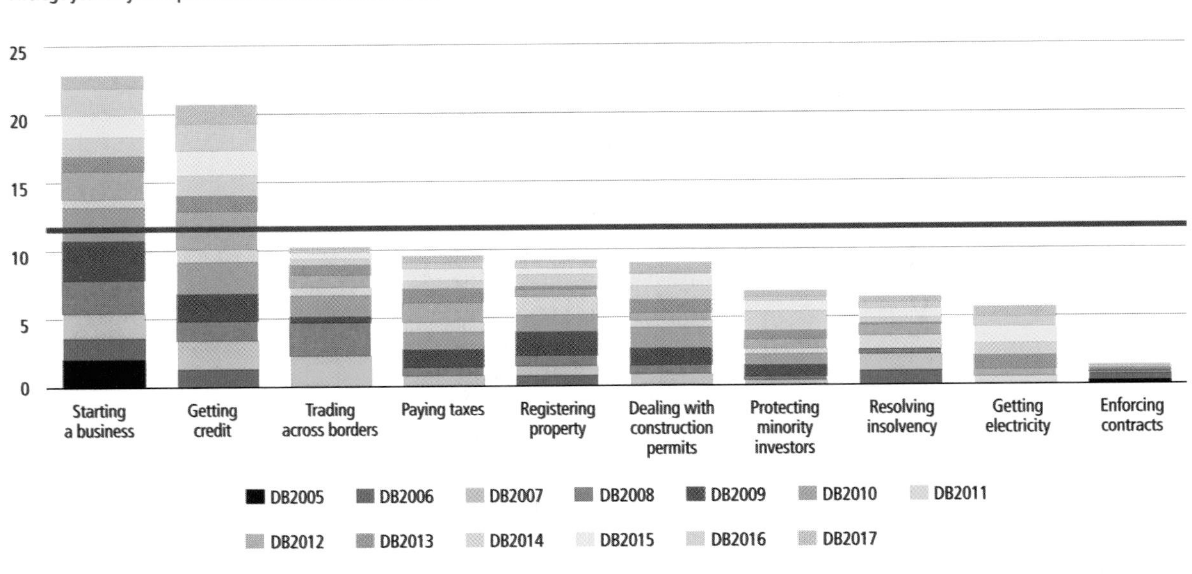

Source: Doing Business database.

Note: The red line shows the average global improvement in the distance to frontier score since 2004. The measure is normalized to range from 0 to 100, with 100 representing the frontier. Because of changes over the years in methodology and in the economies and indicators included, the improvements are measured year on year using pairs of consecutive years with comparable data.

and infrastructure investments in roads and electrification have been shown to have positive effects in reducing income inequality.[17]

Several recent studies link weaker economic growth to higher income inequality, although there is a debate on the validity of these results.[18] Growth analysis is typically based on cross-country data across multiple years. These data tend to have statistical characteristics that make it harder to identify causality and understand the links between variables. Furthermore, the data on inequality in a large cross-country setting and over time is very limited and often may be imputed between years. With that caveat in mind, studies linking economic growth and inequality find that, for example, higher income inequality is associated with a smaller tax base and therefore lower tax collection and more indebtedness by governments.[19] There is also a gender component to income disparity; the data show that where there are higher levels of gender inequality, there are also higher levels of income inequality.[20] Gender inequality exists at various levels: educational, access to assets and overall low investment in girls and women.[21]

A considerable body of evidence confirms that cross-country differences in the quality of business regulation are strongly correlated with differences in income per capita across economies.[22] But can business regulation also be a factor in understanding income differences across individuals within an economy? Business regulation that is transparent and accessible makes it easier for people of all income levels to access markets, develop their businesses and navigate the bureaucratic world. People of low income are more likely to benefit from transparent regulation because, unlike wealthy individuals, they cannot afford experts to help them navigate the system and are more likely to be excluded from economic opportunities when business regulation is cumbersome. In fact, research shows that where business regulation is simpler and more accessible, firms start smaller and firm size can be a proxy for the income of the entrepreneur.[23] *Doing Business* data confirms this notion. There is a negative association between the Gini index, which measures income inequality within an economy, and the distance to frontier score, which measures the quality and efficiency of business regulation when the data are compared over time (figure 1.8).

FIGURE 1.8 Economies with more business-friendly regulation tend to have lower levels of income inequality on average

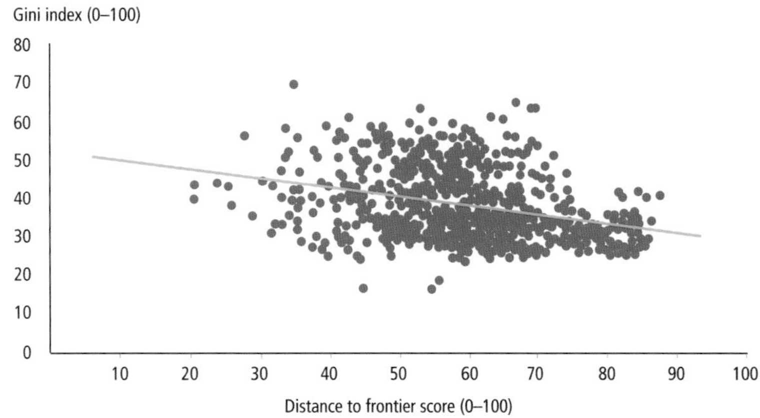

Sources: Doing Business database; PovcalNet (http://iresearch.worldbank.org/PovcalNet/index.htm), World Bank.
Note: The figure compares distance to frontier score to the Gini index as calculated in PovcalNet. The data ranges from 2003 to 2013 and includes 713 observations. The correlation between the Gini index and the distance to frontier score is -0.33. The relationship is significant at the 1% level after controlling for income per capita and government expenditure.

Data across multiple years and economies show that as economies improve business regulation, income inequality tends to decrease in parallel. Although these results are associations and do not imply causality, it is important to see such relation. The results differ by regulatory area. Facilitating entry and exit in and out of the market—as measured by the starting a business and resolving insolvency

FIGURE 1.9 Economies where it is easier to start a business tend to have lower levels of income inequality on average

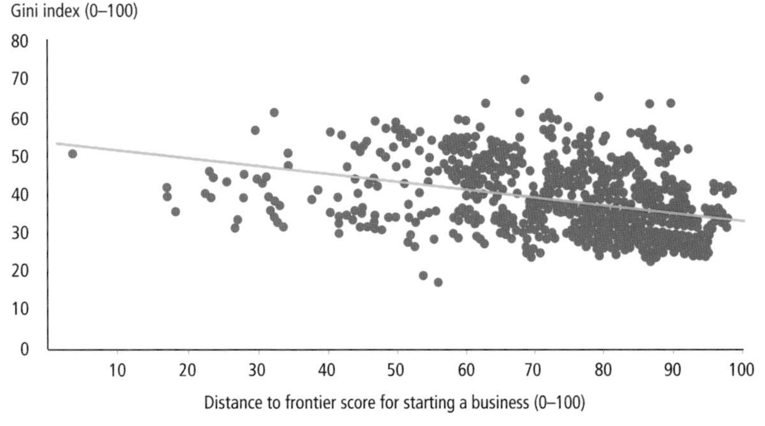

Sources: Doing Business database; PovcalNet (http://iresearch.worldbank.org/PovcalNet/index.htm), World Bank.
Note: The figure compares the starting a business indicator distance to frontier score to the Gini index as calculated in PovcalNet. The data ranges from 2003 to 2013 and includes 713 observations. The correlation between the Gini index and the distance to frontier score is -0.35. The relationship is significant at the 1% level after controlling for income per capita and government expenditure.

FIGURE 1.10 Economies where it is easier to close a business tend to have lower levels of income inequality on average

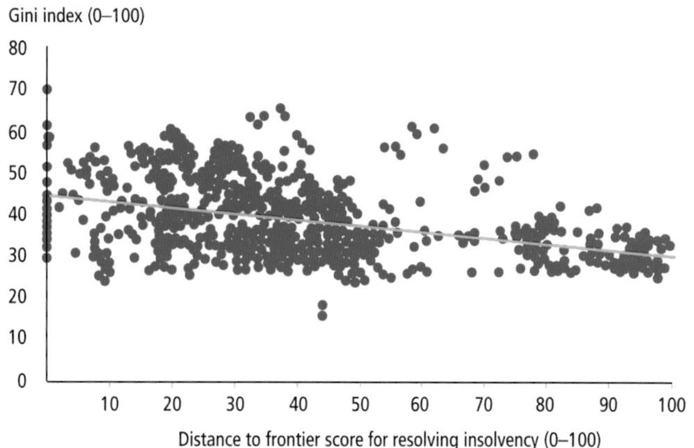

Sources: Doing Business database; PovcalNet (http://iresearch.worldbank.org/PovcalNet/index.htm), World Bank.
Note: The figure compares the resolving insolvency indicator distance to frontier score to the Gini index as calculated in PovcalNet. The data ranges from 2003 to 2013 and includes 713 observations. The correlation between the Gini index and the distance to frontier score is -0.40. The relationship is significant at the 5% level after controlling for income per capita and government expenditure.

indicators—have the strongest link with income inequality reduction (figures 1.9 and 1.10). These two *Doing Business* indicators are focused on equalizing opportunities and access to markets.

CONTENTS OF THIS YEAR'S REPORT

This year's report presents six case studies and two annexes. The case studies focus on the areas that are included in the ease of doing business ranking while the annexes cover areas not included in the ranking. The case studies and annexes either present new indicators or provide further insights from the data collected through methodology changes implemented in the past two years.

The getting electricity case study highlights the importance of a reliable power supply for business and discusses the challenges and successes of four very different economies—Cameroon, Guatemala, Indonesia and Pakistan. This year, two case studies on getting credit are presented, one focusing on the strength of legal rights index and one focusing on the depth of credit information. The case study on the strength of legal rights index discusses two approaches to the reform process, one where the economy completely discards the existing laws and regulation and creates a new overarching framework for secured transactions and another where the economy makes piecemeal reforms while preserving the existing overarching framework. The case study on the depth of credit information highlights the importance of a well-functioning credit bureau or registry for financial inclusion and discusses how they can increase their coverage by broadening the sources of information. The case study on protecting minority investors analyzes the reforms that focus on the newest parts of the indicator. Reforms implemented in India and Switzerland are discussed in detail. The case study on paying taxes presents and analyzes the new data on postfiling processes. Finally, the case study on trading across borders discusses the importance of single windows and electronic systems for simplifying trade logistics and reducing corruption.

The two annexes present the data analysis for two topics, labor market regulation and selling to the government. Selling to the government is a pilot indicator this year, covering 78 economies.

NOTES

1. For 11 economies the data are also collected for the second largest business city (see table 12A.1 in the data notes).
2. The correlation between the old part and the new part of the paying taxes indicator set is 0.92.
3. Amin 2010; Bruhn 2009.
4. OECD 2014a.
5. World Bank Group 2015a.
6. Klasen 1999; Duflo 2012.
7. Gonzales and others 2015.
8. Elborgh-Woytek and others 2013; Duflo 2012; Revenga and Shetty 2012; World Bank 2011.
9. Esteve-Volart 2000 and 2004.
10. Iqbal and others 2016.
11. OECD 2012.
12. Hallward-Driemeier and Hasan 2012.
13. Deininger and others 2010.
14. Ali and others 2014.
15. The European Union estimates that public procurement amounts to between 10 and 25% of GDP globally (see http://ec.europa.eu/trade/policy/accessing-markets/public-procurement/). The WTO estimates that public procurement represents between 10 and 15% of GDP (https://www.wto.org/english/tratop_e/gproc_e/gproc_e.htm).
16. World Bank 2016a.
17. World Bank 2016a.
18. Kraay 2015.
19. Aizenman and Jinjarak 2012.
20. Gonzales and others 2015.
21. Dollar and Gatti 1999; World Bank 2011.
22. Marimon and Quadrini 2008; Barseghyan 2008; Freund and Bolaky 2008.
23. Klapper and others 2006.

About *Doing Business*

The foundation of *Doing Business* is the notion that economic activity, particularly private sector development, benefits from clear and coherent rules: Rules that set out and clarify property rights and facilitate the resolution of disputes. And rules that enhance the predictability of economic interactions and provide contractual partners with essential protections against arbitrariness and abuse. Such rules are much more effective in shaping the incentives of economic agents in ways that promote growth and development where they are reasonably efficient in design, are transparent and accessible to those for whom they are intended and can be implemented at a reasonable cost. The quality of the rules also has a crucial bearing on how societies distribute the benefits and finance the costs of development strategies and policies.

Good rules are a key to social inclusion. Enabling growth—and ensuring that all people, regardless of income level, can participate in its benefits—requires an environment where new entrants with drive and good ideas can get started in business and where good firms can invest and expand. The role of government policy in the daily operations of domestic small and medium-size firms is a central focus of the *Doing Business* data. The objective is to encourage regulation that is designed to be efficient, accessible to all and simple to implement. Onerous regulation diverts the energies of entrepreneurs away from developing their businesses. But regulation that is efficient, transparent and implemented in a simple way facilitates business expansion and innovation, and makes it easier for aspiring entrepreneurs to compete on an equal footing.

Doing Business measures aspects of business regulation for domestic firms through an objective lens. The focus of the project is on small and medium-size companies in the largest business city of an economy. Based on standardized case studies, *Doing Business* presents quantitative indicators on the regulations that apply to firms at different stages of their life cycle. The results for each economy can be compared with those for 189 other economies and over time.

FACTORS *DOING BUSINESS* MEASURES

Doing Business captures several important dimensions of the regulatory environment as it applies to local firms. It provides quantitative indicators on regulation for starting a business, dealing with construction permits, getting electricity, registering property, getting credit, protecting minority investors, paying taxes, trading across borders, enforcing contracts and resolving insolvency (table 2.1). *Doing Business* also measures features of labor market regulation. Although *Doing Business* does not present rankings of economies on the labor market regulation indicators or include the topic in the aggregate distance to frontier score or ranking on the ease of doing business, it does present the data for these indicators.

- **_Doing Business_ measures aspects of business regulation affecting domestic small and medium-size firms defined based on standardized case scenarios and located in the largest business city of each economy. In addition, for 11 economies a second city is covered.**
- **_Doing Business_ covers 11 areas of business regulation across 190 economies. Ten of these areas—starting a business, dealing with construction permits, getting electricity, registering property, getting credit, protecting minority investors, paying taxes, trading across borders, enforcing contracts and resolving insolvency—are included in the distance to frontier score and ease of doing business ranking. _Doing Business_ also measures features of labor market regulation, which is not included in these two measures.**
- **_Doing Business_ relies on four main sources of information: the relevant laws and regulations, _Doing Business_ respondents, the governments of the economies covered and the World Bank Group regional staff.**
- **More than 39,000 professionals in 190 economies have assisted in providing the data that inform the _Doing Business_ indicators over the past 14 years.**
- **This year's report expands the paying taxes indicator set to cover postfiling processes—what happens after a firm pays taxes—such as tax refunds, tax audits and administrative tax appeals.**
- **_Doing Business_ includes a gender dimension in four of the 11 indicator sets. Starting a business, registering property and enforcing contracts present a gender dimension for the first time this year. Labor market regulation already captured gender disaggregated data in last year's report.**

TABLE 2.1 What *Doing Business* measures—11 areas of business regulation

Indicator set	What is measured
Starting a business	Procedures, time, cost and paid-in minimum capital to start a limited liability company
Dealing with construction permits	Procedures, time and cost to complete all formalities to build a warehouse and the quality control and safety mechanisms in the construction permitting system
Getting electricity	Procedures, time and cost to get connected to the electrical grid, the reliability of the electricity supply and the transparency of tariffs
Registering property	Procedures, time and cost to transfer a property and the quality of the land administration system
Getting credit	Movable collateral laws and credit information systems
Protecting minority investors	Minority shareholders' rights in related-party transactions and in corporate governance
Paying taxes	Payments, time and total tax rate for a firm to comply with all tax regulations as well as post-filing processes
Trading across borders	Time and cost to export the product of comparative advantage and import auto parts
Enforcing contracts	Time and cost to resolve a commercial dispute and the quality of judicial processes
Resolving insolvency	Time, cost, outcome and recovery rate for a commercial insolvency and the strength of the legal framework for insolvency
Labor market regulation	Flexibility in employment regulation and aspects of job quality

How the indicators are selected

The choice of the 11 sets of *Doing Business* indicators has been guided by economic research and firm-level data, specifically data from the World Bank Enterprise Surveys.[1] These surveys provide data highlighting the main obstacles to business activity as reported by entrepreneurs in more than 130,000 firms in 139 economies. Access to finance and access to electricity, for example, are among the factors identified by the surveys as important to businesses—inspiring the design of the *Doing Business* indicators on getting credit and getting electricity.

The design of the *Doing Business* indicators has also been informed by theoretical insights gleaned from extensive research and the literature on the role of institutions in enabling economic development. In addition, the background papers developing the methodology for each of the *Doing Business* indicator sets have established the importance of the rules and regulations that *Doing Business* focuses on for such economic outcomes as trade volumes, foreign direct investment, market capitalization in stock exchanges and private credit as a percentage of GDP.[2]

Some *Doing Business* indicators give a higher score for more regulation and better-functioning institutions (such as courts or credit bureaus). Higher scores are given for stricter disclosure requirements for related-party transactions, for example, in the area of protecting minority investors. Higher scores are also given for a simplified way of applying regulation that keeps compliance costs for firms low—such as by easing the burden of business start-up formalities with a one-stop shop or through a single online portal. Finally, *Doing Business* scores reward economies that apply a risk-based approach to regulation as a way to address social and environmental concerns—such as by imposing a greater regulatory burden on activities that pose a high risk to the population and a lesser one on lower-risk activities. Thus the economies that rank highest on the ease of doing business are not those where there is no regulation—but those where governments have managed to create rules that facilitate interactions in the marketplace without needlessly hindering the development of the private sector.

The distance to frontier and ease of doing business ranking

To provide different perspectives on the data, *Doing Business* presents data both for individual indicators and for two aggregate measures: the distance to frontier score and the ease of doing business ranking. The distance to frontier score aids in assessing the absolute level of regulatory performance and how it improves over time. This measure shows the distance of each economy to the "frontier," which represents the best performance observed on each of the indicators across all economies in the *Doing Business* sample since 2005 or the third year in which data were collected for the indicator. The frontier is set at the highest possible value for indicators calculated as scores, such as the strength of legal rights index or the quality of land administration index. This underscores the gap between a particular economy's performance and the best performance at any point in time and to assess the absolute change in the economy's regulatory environment over time as measured by *Doing Business*. The distance to frontier is first computed for each topic and then averaged across all topics to compute the aggregate distance to frontier score. The ranking on the ease of doing business complements the distance to frontier score by providing information about an economy's performance in business regulation relative to the performance of other economies as measured by *Doing Business*.

Doing Business uses a simple averaging approach for weighting component indicators, calculating rankings and determining the distance to frontier score.[3] Each topic covered by *Doing Business* relates to a different aspect of the business regulatory environment. The distance to frontier scores and rankings of each economy vary, often considerably, across topics, indicating that a strong performance by an economy in one area of regulation can coexist with weak performance in another (figure 2.1). One way to assess the variability of an economy's regulatory performance is to look at its distance to frontier scores across topics (see the country tables). Morocco, for example, has an overall distance to frontier score of 67.50, meaning that it is two-thirds of the way from the worst to the best performance. Its distance to frontier score is 92.34 for starting a business, 83.51 for paying taxes and 81.12 for trading across borders. At the same time, it has a distance to frontier score of 33.89 for resolving insolvency, 45 for getting credit and 53.33 for protecting minority investors.

TABLE 2.2 What *Doing Business* does not cover

Examples of areas not covered
Macroeconomic stability
Development of the financial system
Quality of the labor force
Incidence of bribery and corruption
Market size
Lack of security
Examples of aspects not included within the areas covered
In paying taxes, personal income tax rates
In getting credit, the monetary policy stance and the associated ease or tightness of credit conditions for firms
In trading across borders, export or import tariffs and subsidies
In resolving insolvency, personal bankruptcy rules

FACTORS *DOING BUSINESS* DOES NOT MEASURE

Many important policy areas are not covered by *Doing Business;* even within the areas it covers its scope is narrow (table 2.2). *Doing Business* does not measure the full range of factors, policies and institutions that affect the quality of an economy's business environment or its national competitiveness. It does not, for example, capture aspects of macroeconomic stability, development of the financial system, market size, the incidence of bribery and corruption or the quality of the labor force.

The focus is deliberately narrow even within the relatively small set of indicators included in *Doing Business*. The time and cost required for the logistical process of exporting and importing goods is captured in the trading across borders indicators, for example, but they do not measure the cost of tariffs or of international transport. *Doing Business* provides a narrow perspective on the infrastructure challenges that firms face, particularly in the developing world, through these indicators. It does not address the extent to which inadequate roads, rail, ports and communications may add to firms' costs and undermine competitiveness (except to the extent that the trading across borders indicators indirectly measure the quality of ports and border connections). Similar to the

FIGURE 2.1 An economy's regulatory environment may be more business-friendly in some areas than in others

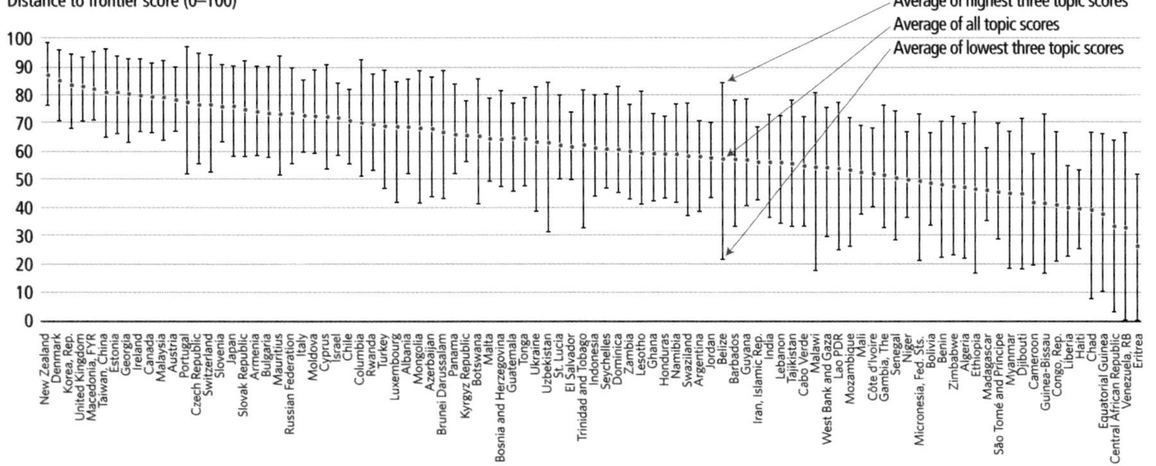

Source: Doing Business database.

Note: The distance to frontier scores reflected are those for the 10 *Doing Business* topics included in this year's aggregate distance to frontier score. The figure is illustrative only; it does not include all 190 economies covered by this year's report. See the country tables for the distance to frontier scores for each *Doing Business* topic for all economies.

indicators on trading across borders, all aspects of commercial legislation are not covered by those on starting a business or protecting minority investors. And while *Doing Business* measures only a few aspects within each area that it covers, business regulation reforms should not focus only on these aspects, because those that it does not measure are also important.

Doing Business does not attempt to quantify all costs and benefits of a particular law or regulation to society as a whole. The paying taxes indicators measure the total tax rate, which, in isolation, is a cost to businesses. However, the indicators do not measure—nor are they intended to measure—the benefits of the social and economic programs funded with tax revenues. Measuring the quality and efficiency of business regulation provides only one input into the debate on the regulatory burden associated with achieving regulatory objectives, which can differ across economies. *Doing Business* provides a starting point for this discussion and should be used in conjunction with other data sources.

TABLE 2.3 Advantages and limitations of the *Doing Business* methodology

Feature	Advantages	Limitations
Use of standardized case scenarios	Makes data comparable across economies and methodology transparent, using case scenarios that are common globally	Reduces scope of data; only regulatory reforms in areas measured can be systematically tracked; the case scenarios may not be the most common in a particular economy
Focus on largest business city[a]	Makes data collection manageable (cost-effective) and data comparable	Reduces representativeness of data for an economy if there are significant differences across locations
Focus on domestic and formal sector	Keeps attention on formal sector—where regulations are relevant and firms are most productive	Unable to reflect reality for informal sector—important where that is large—or for foreign firms facing a different set of constraints
Reliance on expert respondents	Ensures that data reflect knowledge of those with most experience in conducting types of transactions measured	Indicators less able to capture variation in experiences among entrepreneurs
Focus on the law	Makes indicators "actionable"—because the law is what policy makers can change	Where systematic compliance with the law is lacking, regulatory changes will not achieve full results desired

Source: Doing Business database.

a. In economies with a population of more than 100 million as of 2013, *Doing Business* covers business regulation in both the largest and second largest business city.

ADVANTAGES AND LIMITATIONS OF THE METHODOLOGY

The *Doing Business* methodology is designed to be an easily replicable way to benchmark specific aspects of business regulation. Its advantages and limitations should be understood when using the data (table 2.3).

Ensuring comparability of the data across a global set of economies is a central consideration for the *Doing Business* indicators, which are developed around standardized case scenarios with specific assumptions. One such assumption is the location of a standardized business—the subject of the *Doing Business* case study—in the largest business city of the economy. The reality is that business regulations and their enforcement may differ within a country, particularly in federal states and large economies. But gathering data for every relevant jurisdiction in each of the 190 economies covered by *Doing Business* is infeasible. Nevertheless, where policy makers are interested in generating data at the local level, beyond the largest business city, *Doing Business* has complemented its global indicators with subnational studies (box 2.1). Coverage was extended to the second largest business city in economies with a population of more than 100 million (as of 2013) in *Doing Business 2015*.

Doing Business recognizes the limitations of the standardized case scenarios and assumptions. But while such assumptions come at the expense of generality, they also help to ensure the comparability of data. Some *Doing Business* topics are complex, and so it is important that the standardized cases are defined carefully. For example, the standardized case scenario usually involves a limited liability company or its legal equivalent. There are two reasons for this assumption. First, private, limited liability companies are the most prevalent business form (for firms with more than one owner) in many economies around the world. Second, this choice reflects the focus of *Doing Business* on expanding opportunities for entrepreneurship: investors are encouraged to venture into business when potential losses are limited to their capital participation.

Another assumption underlying the *Doing Business* indicators is that entrepreneurs have knowledge of and comply with applicable regulations. In practice, entrepreneurs may not be aware of what needs to be done or how to comply with regulations and may lose considerable time trying to find out. Alternatively, they may intentionally avoid compliance—by not registering for social security, for example. Firms may opt for bribery and other informal arrangements intended to bypass the rules where regulation is particularly onerous—an aspect that helps explain differences between the de jure data provided by *Doing Business* and the de facto insights offered by the World Bank Enterprise Surveys.[4] Levels of informality tend to be higher in economies with particularly burdensome regulation. Compared with their formal sector counterparts, firms in the informal sector typically grow more slowly, have poorer access to credit and employ fewer

BOX 2.1 Comparing regulation at the local level: subnational *Doing Business* studies

Subnational *Doing Business* studies, which are undertaken at the request of governments, expand the *Doing Business* analysis beyond an economy's largest business city. They measure variation in regulations or in the implementation of national laws across locations within an economy (as in Poland) or a region (as in South East Europe).

Data collected by subnational studies over the past three years show that there can be substantial variation within an economy (see figure). In Mexico, for example, in 2016 registering a property transfer took as few as 9 days in Puebla and as many as 78 in Oaxaca. Indeed, within the same economy one can find locations that perform as well as economies ranking in the top 20 on the ease of registering property and locations that perform as poorly as economies ranking in the bottom 40 on that indicator.

Different locations, different regulatory processes, same economy

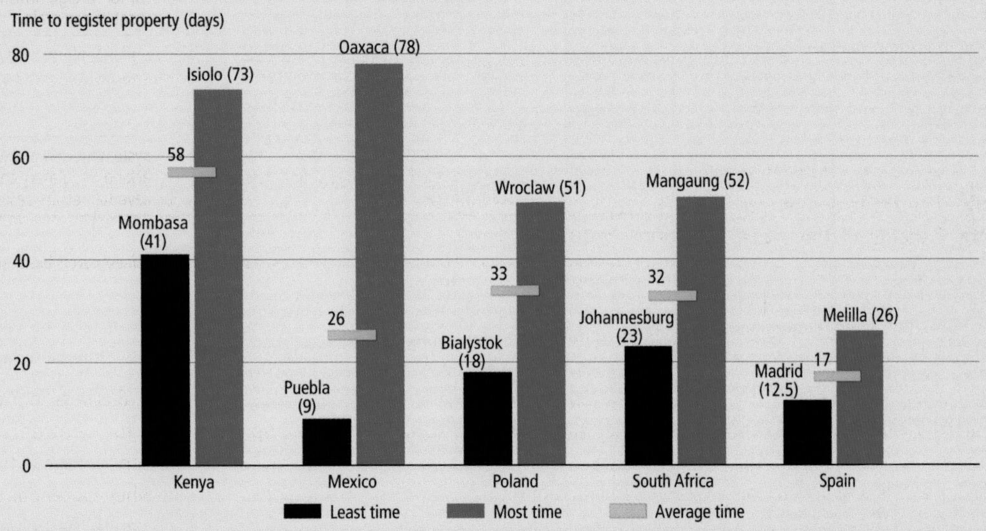

Source: Subnational *Doing Business* database.
Note: The average time shown for each economy is based on all locations covered by the data: 11 cities in Kenya in 2016, 32 states in Mexico in 2016, 18 cities in Poland in 2015, 9 cities in South Africa in 2015 and 19 cities in Spain in 2015.

While subnational *Doing Business* studies generate disaggregated data on business regulation, they go beyond a data collection exercise. They have been shown to be strong motivators for regulatory reform at the local level:

- Results can be benchmarked both locally and globally because the data produced are comparable across locations within the economy and internationally. Comparing locations within the same economy—which share the same legal and regulatory framework—can be revealing: local officials struggle to explain why doing business is more challenging in their jurisdiction than in a neighboring one.

- Highlighting good practices that exist in some locations but not others within an economy helps policy makers recognize the potential for replicating these good practices. This can yield discussions about regulatory reform across different levels of government, providing opportunities for local governments and agencies to learn from one another and resulting in local ownership and capacity building.

Since 2005 subnational reports have covered 438 locations in 65 economies (see map). Seventeen economies—including the Arab Republic of Egypt, Mexico, Nigeria, the Philippines, and the Russian Federation—have undertaken two or more rounds of subnational data collection to measure progress over time. This year subnational studies were completed in Kenya, Mexico and the United Arab Emirates. Ongoing studies include those in Afghanistan (5 cities), Colombia (32 cities), three EU member states (22 cities in Bulgaria, Hungary and Romania) and Kazakhstan (8 cities).

Subnational reports are available on the Doing Business website at http://www.doingbusiness.org/subnational.

(continued)

BOX 2.1 Comparing regulation at the local level: subnational *Doing Business* studies *(continued)*

Subnational studies cover a large number of cities across all regions of the world

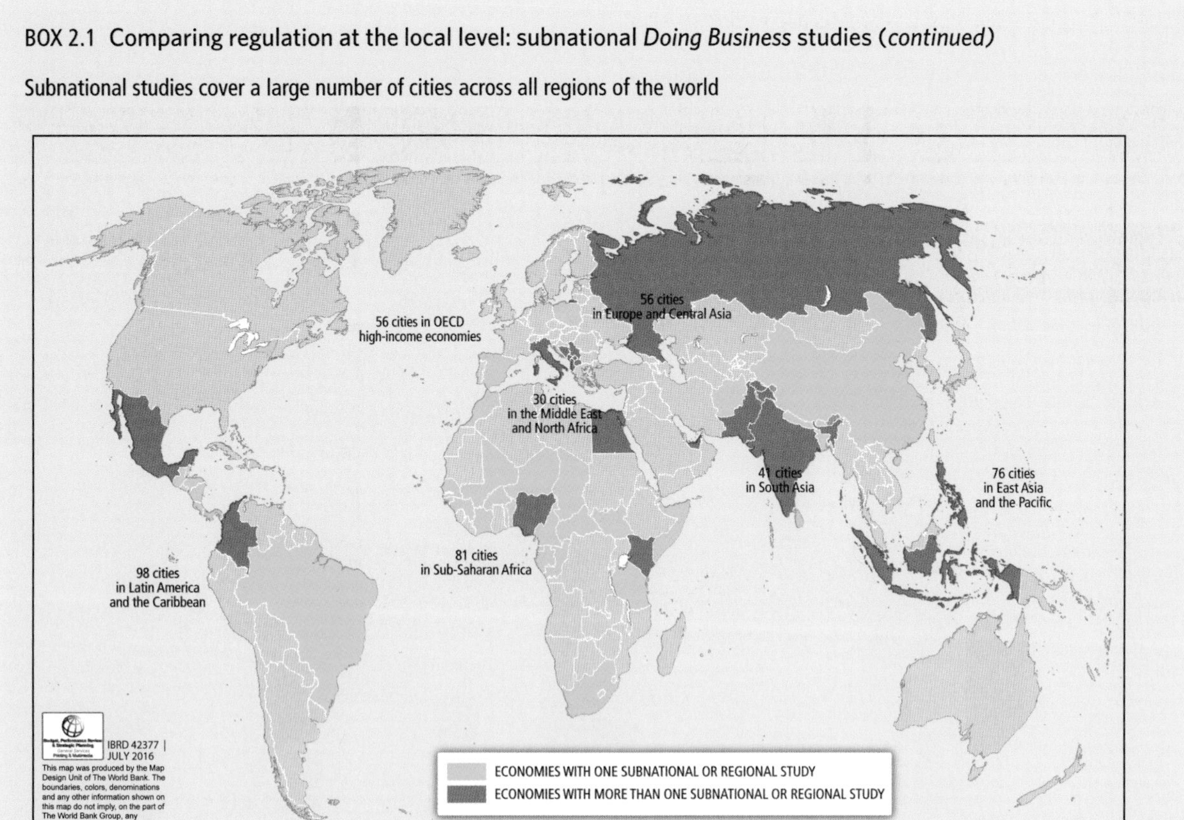

Source: Subnational *Doing Business* database.

workers—and these workers remain outside the protections of labor law and, more generally, other legal protections embedded in the law.[5] Firms in the informal sector are also less likely to pay taxes. *Doing Business* measures one set of factors that help explain the occurrence of informality and give policy makers insights into potential areas of regulatory reform.

DATA COLLECTION IN PRACTICE

The *Doing Business* data are based on a detailed reading of domestic laws and regulations as well as administrative requirements. The report covers 190 economies—including some of the smallest and poorest economies, for which little or no data are available from other sources. The data are collected through several rounds of communication with expert respondents (both private sector practitioners and government officials), through responses to questionnaires, conference calls, written correspondence and visits by the team. *Doing Business* relies on four main sources of information: the relevant laws and regulations, *Doing Business* respondents, the governments of the economies covered and the World Bank Group regional staff (figure 2.2). For a detailed explanation of the *Doing Business* methodology, see the data notes.

Relevant laws and regulations

The *Doing Business* indicators are based mostly on laws and regulations: around 60% of the data embedded in the *Doing Business* indicators are based on a reading of the law. In addition to filling out questionnaires, *Doing Business* respondents submit references to the relevant laws, regulations and fee schedules. The *Doing Business* team collects the texts of the relevant laws and regulations and checks the questionnaire responses for accuracy. The team will examine the civil procedure code, for example, to check the maximum number of adjournments in a commercial court dispute, and read the insolvency code to identify if the debtor can initiate liquidation or reorganization proceeding. These and other types of laws are available on the *Doing Business* law library website.[6] Since the data collection process involves an annual update of an established database, having a very large sample of respondents is not strictly necessary. In principle, the role of the contributors

FIGURE 2.2 How *Doing Business* collects and verifies the data

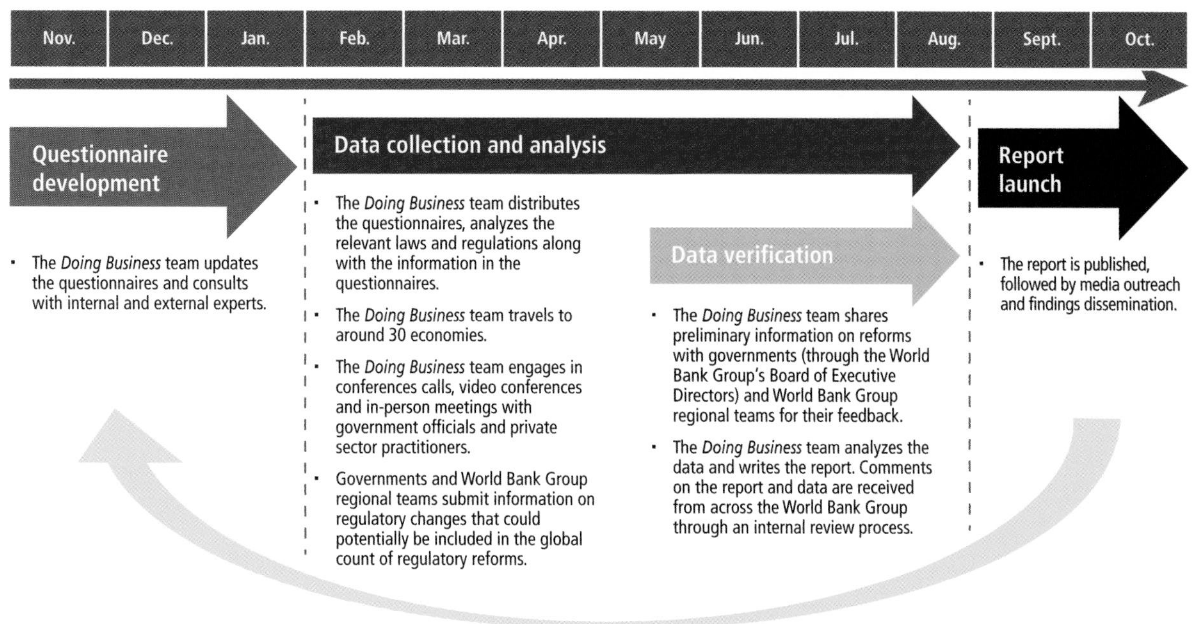

is largely advisory—helping the *Doing Business* team to locate and understand the laws and regulations. There are quickly diminishing returns to an expanded pool of contributors. This notwithstanding, the number of contributors rose by 58% between 2010 and 2016.

Extensive consultations with multiple contributors are conducted by the team to minimize measurement error for the rest of the data. For some indicators—for example, those on dealing with construction permits, enforcing contracts and resolving insolvency—the time component and part of the cost component (where fee schedules are lacking) are based on actual practice rather than the law on the books. This introduces a degree of judgment by respondents on what actual practice looks like. When respondents disagree, the time indicators reported by *Doing Business* represent the median values of several responses given under the assumptions of the standardized case.

Doing Business respondents

More than 39,000 professionals in 190 economies have assisted in providing the data that inform the *Doing Business* indicators over the past 14 years.[7] This year's report draws on the inputs of more than 12,500 professionals.[8] Table 12.2 in the data notes lists the number of respondents for each indicator set. The *Doing Business* website shows the number of respondents for each economy and each indicator set.

Selected on the basis of their expertise in these areas, respondents are professionals who routinely administer or advise on the legal and regulatory requirements in the specific areas covered by *Doing Business*. Because of the focus on legal and regulatory arrangements, most of the respondents are legal professionals such as lawyers, judges or notaries. In addition, officials of the credit bureau or registry complete the credit information questionnaire. Accountants, architects, engineers, freight forwarders and other professionals answer the questionnaires related to paying taxes, dealing with construction permits, trading across borders and getting electricity. Information that is incorporated into the indicators is also provided by certain public officials (such as registrars from the company or property registry).

The *Doing Business* approach is to work with legal practitioners or other professionals who regularly undertake the transactions involved. Following the standard methodological approach for time-and-motion studies, *Doing Business* breaks down each process or transaction, such as starting a business or registering a building, into separate steps to ensure a better estimate of time. The time estimate for each step is given by practitioners with significant and routine experience in the transaction.

There are two main reasons that *Doing Business* does not survey firms. The first relates to the frequency with which firms engage in the transactions captured by the indicators, which is generally low. For example, a firm goes through the start-up process once in its existence, while an incorporation lawyer may carry out 10 such transactions each month. The incorporation lawyers and other experts providing information to *Doing Business* are therefore better able to assess the process of starting a business than are individual firms. They also have access to current regulations and practices, while a firm may have faced a different set of rules when incorporating years before. The second reason is that the *Doing Business* questionnaires mostly gather legal information, which firms are unlikely to be fully familiar with. For example, few firms will know about all the many legal procedures involved in resolving a commercial dispute through the courts, even if they have gone through the process themselves. But a litigation lawyer should have little difficulty in providing the requested information on all the processes.

Governments and World Bank Group regional staff

After receiving the completed questionnaires from the *Doing Business* respondents, verifying the information against the law and conducting follow-up inquiries to ensure that all relevant information is captured, the *Doing Business* team shares the preliminary descriptions of regulatory reforms with governments (through the World Bank Group's Board of Executive Directors) and with regional staff of the World Bank Group. Through this process government authorities and World Bank Group staff working on most of the economies covered can alert the team about, for example, regulatory reforms not included by the respondents or additional achievements of regulatory reforms already captured in the database. The *Doing Business* team can then turn to the local private sector experts for further consultation and, as needed, corroboration. In addition, the team responds formally to the comments of governments or regional staff and provides explana ions of the scoring decisions.

Data adjustments

Information on data corrections is provided in the data notes and on the *Doing Business* website. A transparent complaint procedure allows anyone to challenge the data. From November 2015 to October 2016 the team received and responded to more than 240 queries on the data. If changes in data are confirmed, they are immediately reflected on the website.

USES OF THE *DOING BUSINESS* DATA

Doing Business was designed with two main types of users in mind: policy makers and researchers.[9] It is a tool that governments can use to design sound business regulatory policies. Nevertheless, the *Doing Business* data are limited in scope and should be complemented with other sources of information. *Doing Business* focuses on a few specific rules relevant to the specific case studies analyzed. These rules and case studies are chosen to be illustrative of the business regulatory environment, but they are not a comprehensive description of that environment. By providing a unique data set that enables analysis aimed at better understanding the role of business regulation in economic development, *Doing Business* is also an important source of information for researchers.

Governments and policy makers

Doing Business offers policy makers a benchmarking tool useful in stimulating policy debate, both by exposing potential challenges and by identifying good practices and lessons learned. Despite the narrow focus of the indicators, the initial debate in an economy on the results they highlight typically turns into a deeper discussion on areas where business regulatory reform is needed, including areas well beyond those measured by *Doing Business*.

Many *Doing Business* indicators can be considered actionable. For example, governments can set the minimum capital requirement for new firms, invest in company and property registries to increase their efficiency, or improve the efficiency of tax administration by adopting the latest technology to facilitate the preparation, filing and payment of taxes by the business community. And they can undertake court reforms to shorten delays in the enforcement of contracts. But some *Doing Business* indicators capture procedures, time and costs that involve private sector participants, such as lawyers, notaries, architects, electricians or freight forwarders. Governments may have little influence in the short run over the fees these professions charge, though much can be achieved by strengthening professional licensing regimes and preventing anticompetitive behavior. And governments have no control over the geographic location of their economy, a factor that can adversely affect businesses.

While many *Doing Business* indicators are actionable, this does not necessarily mean that they are all "action-worthy" in a particular context. Business regulatory reforms are only one element of a strategy aimed at improving competitiveness and establishing a solid foundation for sustainable economic growth. There are many other important goals to pursue—such as effective management of public finances, adequate attention to education and training, adoption of the latest technologies to boost economic productivity and the quality of public services, and appropriate regard for air and water quality to safeguard public health. Governments must decide what set of priorities best suits their needs. To say that governments should work toward a sensible set of rules for private sector activity (as embodied, for example, in the *Doing Business* indicators) does not suggest that doing so should come at the expense of other worthy policy goals.

Over the past decade governments have increasingly turned to *Doing Business* as a repository of actionable, objective data providing unique insights into good practices worldwide as they have come to understand the importance of business regulation as a driving force of competitiveness. To ensure the coordination of efforts across agencies, economies such as Colombia, Malaysia and Russia have formed regulatory reform committees. These committees use the *Doing Business* indicators as one input to inform their programs for improving the business environment. More than 40 other economies have also formed such committees. In East Asia and the Pacific they include: Brunei Darussalam; Indonesia; the Republic of Korea; the Philippines; Taiwan, China; and Thailand. In the Middle East and North Africa: the Arab Republic of Egypt, Kuwait, Morocco, Saudi Arabia and the United Arab Emirates. In South Asia: India and Pakistan. In Europe and Central Asia: Albania, Croatia, Georgia, Kazakhstan, Kosovo, the Kyrgyz Republic, the former Yugoslav Republic of Macedonia, Moldova, Montenegro, Poland, Tajikistan, Ukraine and Uzbekistan. In Sub-Saharan Africa: the Democratic Republic of Congo, the Republic of Congo, Côte d'Ivoire, Burundi, Guinea, Kenya, Liberia, Malawi, Mali, Mauritius, Nigeria, Rwanda, Sierra Leone, Togo, Zambia and Zimbabwe. And in Latin America: Chile, Costa Rica, the Dominican Republic, Guatemala, Mexico, Panama and Peru. Governments have reported more than 2,900 regulatory reforms, 777 of which have been informed by *Doing Business* since 2003.[10]

Many economies share knowledge on the regulatory reform process related to the areas measured by *Doing Business*. Among the most common venues for this knowledge sharing are peer-to-peer learning events—workshops where officials from different governments across a region or even across the globe meet to discuss the challenges of regulatory reform and to share their experiences.

Think tanks and other research organizations

Doing Business data are widely used by think tanks and other research organizations, both for the development of new indexes and to produce research papers.

Many research papers have shown the importance of business regulation and how it relates to different economic outcomes.[11] One of the most cited theoretical mechanisms on how excessive business regulation affects economic performance and development is that it makes it too costly for firms to engage in the formal economy, causing them not to invest or to move to the informal economy. Recent studies have conducted extensive empirical testing of this proposition using *Doing Business* and other related indicators. According to one study, for example, a reform that simplified business registration in Mexican municipalities increased registration by 5% and wage employment by 2.2%—and, as a result of increased competition, reduced the income of incumbent businesses by 3%.[12] Business registration reforms in Mexico also resulted in 14.9% of informal business owners shifting to the formal economy.[13]

Considerable effort has been devoted to studying the link between government regulation of firm entry and employment growth. In Portugal business reforms resulted in a reduction of the time and cost needed for company formalization, increasing the number of business start-ups by 17% and creating 7 new jobs per 100,000 inhabitants per month. But although these start-ups were smaller and more likely to be female-owned than before the reform, they were also headed by less experienced and poorly-educated entrepreneurs with lower sales per worker.[14]

In many economies companies engaged in international trade struggle with high trade costs arising from transport, logistics and regulations, impeding their competitiveness and preventing them from taking full advantage of their productive capacity. With the availability of *Doing Business* indicators on trading across borders—which measure the time, procedural and monetary costs of exporting and importing—several empirical studies have assessed how trade costs affect the export and import performance of economies. A rich body of empirical research shows that efficient infrastructure and a healthy business environment are positively linked to export performance.[15]

Improving infrastructure efficiency and trade logistics bring documented benefits to an economy's balance of trade and individual traders but delays in transit time can reduce exports: a study analyzing the importance of trade logistics found that a 1-day increase in transit time reduces exports by an average of 7% in Sub-Saharan Africa.[16] Another study found that a 1-day delay in transport time for landlocked economies and for time-sensitive agricultural and manufacturing products has a particularly large negative impact, reducing trade by more than 1% for each day of delay.[17] Delays while clearing customs procedures also negatively impact a firm's ability to export, particularly when goods are destined for new clients.[18] And in economies with flexible entry regulations, a 1% increase in trade is associated with an increase of more than 0.5% in income per capita, but has no positive income effects in economies with more rigid regulation.[19] Research has also found that—although domestic buyers benefit from having goods of varying quality and price to choose from—import competition only results in minimal quality upgrading in OECD high-income economies with cumbersome regulation while it has no effect on quality upgrading in non-OECD economies with cumbersome regulation.[20] Therefore, the potential gains for consumers from import competition are reduced where regulations are cumbersome.

Doing Business measures aspects of business regulation affecting domestic firms. However, research shows that better business regulation—as measured by

Doing Business—is associated with higher levels of foreign direct investment.[21] Furthermore, foreign direct investment can either impede or promote domestic investment depending on how business friendly entry regulations are in the host economy. In fact, foreign direct investment has been shown to crowd out domestic investment in economies with costly processes for starting a business.[22] Another study showed that economies with higher international market integration have, on average, easier and simpler processes for starting a business.[23]

Recent empirical work shows the importance of well-designed credit market regulations and well-functioning court systems for debt recovery. For example, a reform making bankruptcy laws more efficient significantly improved the recovery rate of viable firms in Colombia.[24] In a multi-economy study, the introduction of collateral registries for movable assets was shown to increase firms' access to finance by approximately 8%.[25] In India the establishment of debt recovery tribunals reduced non-performing loans by 28% and lowered interest rates on larger loans, suggesting that faster processing of debt recovery cases cut the cost of credit.[26] An in-depth review of global bank flows revealed that firms in economies with better credit information sharing systems and higher branch penetration evade taxes to a lesser degree.[27] Strong shareholder rights have been found to lower financial frictions, especially for firms with large external finance relative to their capital stock (such as small firms or firms in distress).[28]

There is also a large body of theoretical and empirical work investigating the distortionary effects of high tax rates and cumbersome tax codes and procedures. According to one study, business licensing among retail firms rose 13% after a tax reform in Brazil.[29] Another showed that a 10% reduction in tax complexity is comparable to a 1% reduction in effective corporate tax rates.[30]

Labor market regulation—as measured by *Doing Business*—has been shown to have important implications for the labor market. According to one study, graduating from school during a time of adverse economic conditions has a persistent, harmful effect on workers' subsequent employment opportunities. The persistence of this negative effect is stronger in countries with stricter employment protection legislation.[31] Rigid employment protection legislation can also have negative distributional consequences. A study on Chile, for example, found that the tightening of job security rules was associated with lower employment rates for youth, unskilled workers and women.[32]

Indexes

Doing Business identified 17 different data projects or indexes that use *Doing Business* as one of its sources of data.[33] Most of these projects or institutions use indicator level data and not the aggregate ease of doing business ranking. Starting a business is the indicator set most widely used, followed by labor market regulation and paying taxes. These indexes typically combine *Doing Business* data with data from other sources to assess an economy along a particular aggregate dimension such as competitiveness or innovation. The Heritage Foundation's Index of Economic Freedom, for example, has used six *Doing Business* indicators to measure the degree of economic freedom in the world.[34] Economies that score better in these six areas also tend to have a high degree of economic freedom.

Similarly, the World Economic Forum uses *Doing Business* data in its Global Competitiveness Index to demonstrate how competitiveness is a global driver of economic growth. The organization also uses *Doing Business* indicators in four other indexes that measure technological readiness, human capital development, travel and tourism sector competitiveness and trade facilitation. These publicly accessible sources expand the general business environment data generated by *Doing Business* by incorporating it into the study of other important social and economic issues across economies and regions. They prove that, taken individually, *Doing Business* indicators remain a useful starting point for a rich body of analysis across different areas and dimensions in the research world.

Doing Business has contributed substantially to the debate on the importance of business regulation for economic development. By expanding the time series and the scope of the data with the recent methodology expansion, *Doing Business* hopes to continue being a key reference going forward.

NEW AREAS INCLUDED IN THIS YEAR'S REPORT

This year's *Doing Business* report includes data for one new economy, Somalia, expands the paying taxes indicators, includes gender dimensions in four indicator sets and adds a new annex on selling to the government.

For any new indicators or economies added to the distance to frontier score and the ease of doing business ranking, the data are presented for the last two consecutive years to ensure that there are at least two years of comparable data.

Paying taxes

The paying taxes indicator set is the last to be expanded as part of the methodology improvement process started three years ago that affects 9 of the 10 areas covered in the ease of doing business ranking. Only the starting a business indicators remain under the original methodology.

The paying taxes indicator set assesses the number of payments, time and total tax rate for a firm to comply with all tax regulations. This year's report adds a new indicator to include postfiling processes. Under postfiling processes,

Doing Business measures value added tax refund, corporate income tax audits and administrative tax appeals. Under value added tax refunds, *Doing Business* measures how long it takes to comply and to obtain back the value added tax paid on a capital purchase (including any value added tax audits associated with it). Under the corporate income tax audits, *Doing Business* focuses on the time it takes and the process to complete a tax audit when a firm mistakenly declares a lower tax liability than it should have. *Doing Business* also measures good practices in the tax appeals process, such as independence from the tax collecting agency, but those are not scored. In this year's report there is a case study dedicated to analyzing the results of this methodology expansion.

Adding gender components

This year's *Doing Business* report presents a gender dimension in four of the indicator sets: starting a business, registering property, enforcing contracts and labor market regulation. Three of these areas are included in the distance to frontier score and in the ease of doing business ranking, while the fourth—labor market regulation—is not.

Doing Business has traditionally assumed that the entrepreneurs or workers discussed in the case studies were men. This was incomplete by not reflecting correctly the *Doing Business* processes as applied to women—which in some economies may be different from the processes applied to men. Starting this year, *Doing Business* measures the starting a business process for two case scenarios: one where all entrepreneurs are men and one where all entrepreneurs are women. In economies where the processes are more onerous if the entrepreneur is a woman, *Doing Business* now counts the extra procedures applied to roughly half of the population that is female (for example, obtaining a husband's consent or gender-specific requirements for opening a personal bank account when starting a business).

Within the registering property indicators, a gender component has been added to the quality of land administration index. This component measures women's ability to use, own, and transfer property according to the law. Finally, within the enforcing contracts indicator set, economies will be scored on having equal evidentiary weight of women's and men's testimony in court.

The labor market regulation indicators have included data on gender components for the past two years. These data include: whether nonpregnant and nonnursing women can work the same night hours as men; whether the law mandates equal remuneration for work of equal value; whether the law mandates nondiscrimination based on gender in hiring; whether the law mandates paid or unpaid maternity leave; the minimum length of paid maternity leave; and whether employees on maternity leave receive 100% of wages.

Selling to the government

The analysis uses a new pilot indicator set, selling to the government, which measures public procurement regulation and is presented as an annex to this year's report. The procurement process is analyzed across five main areas: accessibility and transparency, bid security, payment delays, incentives for small and medium-size enterprises and complaints mechanisms. Accessibility and transparency covers whether information is accessible to prospective bidders and how that information can be accessed. The analysis on bid security discusses the amount that prospective bidders need to pay upfront in order to be considered in the bidding process and the form of the security deposit. For payment delays, the annex presents the time it takes for the firm to receive payment from the government after the contract is completed and the service has been delivered. The incentives for small and medium-size enterprises component measures whether economies have set up specific legal provisions or policies to promote fair access for small and medium-size firms to government contracts. And for the complaints mechanism component, the annex discusses the process to file a grievance regarding a public procurement project, including who can file a complaint, where to file a complaint and the independence of the review body and what remedies are granted.

NOTES

1. Data from the World Bank Enterprise Surveys and *Doing Business* complement each other as two sides of the same coin. They both provide useful information on the business environment of an economy, but in significantly different ways. The scope of *Doing Business* is narrower than the Enterprise Surveys. However, by focusing on actionable indicators related to business regulation, *Doing Business* provides a clear roadmap for governments to improve. *Doing Business* uses standardized case scenarios while the Enterprise Surveys use representative samples. For more on the Enterprise Surveys and the differences between the Enterprise Surveys and *Doing Business*, see the website at http://www.enterprisesurveys.org.
2. These papers are available on the *Doing Business* website at http://www.doingbusiness.org/methodology.
3. For getting credit, indicators are weighted proportionally, according to their contribution to the total score, with a weight of 60% assigned to the strength of legal rights index and 40% to the depth of credit information index. In this way each point included in these indexes has the same value independent of the component it belongs to. Indicators for all other topics are assigned equal weights. For more details, see the chapter on the distance to frontier and ease of doing business ranking.
4. Hallward-Driemeier and Pritchett 2015.
5. Schneider 2005; La Porta and Shleifer 2008.
6. For the law library, see the website at http://www.doingbusiness.org/law-library.
7. The annual data collection exercise is an update of the database. The *Doing Business* team and the contributors examine the extent to which the regulatory framework has changed in ways relevant for the features captured by the indicators. The data collection process should therefore be seen as adding each year to an existing stock of knowledge reflected in the previous year's report, not as creating an entirely new data set.
8. While about 12,500 contributors provided data for this year's report, many of them completed a questionnaire for more than one *Doing Business* indicator set. Indeed, the total number of contributions received for this year's report is more than 15,700, which represents a true measure of the inputs

received. The average number of contributions per indicator set and economy is more than seven. For more details, see http://www.doingbusiness.org/contributors/doing-business.

9. The focus of the *Doing Business* indicators remains the regulatory regime faced by domestic firms engaging in economic activity in the largest business city of an economy. *Doing Business* was not initially designed to inform decisions by foreign investors, though investors may in practice find the data useful as a proxy for the quality of the national investment climate. Analysis done in the World Bank Group's Global Indicators Group has shown that countries that have sensible rules for domestic economic activity also tend to have good rules for the activities of foreign subsidiaries engaged in the local economy.
10. These are reforms for which *Doing Business* is aware that information provided by *Doing Business* was used in shaping the reform agenda.
11. The papers cited here are just a few examples of research done in the areas measured by *Doing Business*. Since 2003, when the *Doing Business* report was first published, 2,182 research articles discussing how regulation in the areas measured by *Doing Business* influences economic outcomes have been published in peer-reviewed academic journals. Another 6,296 working papers have been posted online.
12. Bruhn 2011.
13. Bruhn 2013.
14. Branstetter and others 2013.
15. Portugal-Perez and Wilson 2011.
16. Freund and Rocha 2011.
17. Djankov, Freund and Pham 2010.
18. Martincus, Carballo and Graziano 2015.
19. Freund and Bolaky 2008.
20. Amiti and Khandelwal 2011.
21. Corcoran and Gillanders 2015.
22. Munemo 2014.
23. Norbäck, Persson and Douhan 2014.
24. Giné and Love 2010.
25. Love, Martinez-Peria and Singh 2013.
26. Visaria 2009.
27. Beck, Lin and Ma 2014.
28. Claessens, Ueda and Yafeh 2014.
29. Monteiro and Assunção 2012.
30. Lawless 2013.
31. Kawaguchi and Murao 2014.
32. Montenegro and Pagés 2003.
33. The 17 indexes are: the Millennium Challenge Corporation's Open Data Catalog; the Heritage Foundation's Index of Economic Freedom (IEF); the World Economic Forum's Global Competitiveness Index (GCI), Networked Readiness Index (NRI, jointly with INSEAD), Human Capital Index (HCI), Enabling Trade Index (ETI) and Travel and Tourism Competitiveness Index (TTCI); INSEAD's Global Talent Competitiveness Index (GTCI) and Global Innovation Index (GII, jointly with Cornell University and the World Intellectual Property Organization); Fraser Institute's Economic Freedom of the World (EFW); KPMG's Change Readiness Index (CRI); Citi and Imperial College London's Digital Money Index; International Institute for Management Development's World Competitiveness Yearbook; DHL's Global Connectedness Index (GCI); PricewaterhouseCoopers' Paying Taxes 2016: The Global Picture; and Legatum Institute's Legatum Prosperity Index.
34. For more on the Heritage Foundation's Index of Economic Freedom, see the website at http://heritage.org/index.

Reforming the Business Environment in 2015/16

Efficient business regulation leads to greater market entry, job creation, higher productivity and improved levels of overall economic development.[1] Even though the scope of the *Doing Business* indicators is limited by necessity, there is well-established evidence that moving from the lowest quartile of improvement in business regulation to the highest quartile is associated with significant increases in annual economic growth per capita.[2] A large body of literature indicates that the simplification of business entry regulation results in higher numbers of new businesses and an increased rate of employment.[3] Research covering 172 economies in the period from 2006 to 2010 shows that each additional business regulatory reform is associated with an average increase of 0.15% in economic growth. Indeed, business regulatory reforms might have helped to mitigate the effects of the 2008 global financial crisis since economies that undertook more reforms experienced higher economic growth rates.[4]

Regulation is necessary to maintain efficient, safe and orderly societies. *Doing Business* focuses on the development of streamlined, necessary and competent regulatory practices that facilitate private sector development rather than create unnecessary bureaucratic obstacles and opportunities for rent seeking. *Doing Business* advocates adherence to established good practices like free access to information, transparency of fees and the use of online services. Since the publication of the first *Doing Business* report, governments around the world have implemented over 2,900 reforms striving to align domestic business regulation with the good practices advocated by *Doing Business*. Many governments use *Doing Business* indicator sets to formulate and monitor their reform efforts. The Indian government, for example, has committed to improving its *Doing Business* ranking by steadily implementing reforms across all indicators (box 3.1).[5]

In Japan the government aims to improve the economy's *Doing Business* ranking from 19 (among 31 OECD high-income economies) to the top three. To achieve this goal, Haidar and Hoshi (2015) outlined 31 reform recommendations classified into six different categories depending on whether the reform was administrative or legal and on the level of potential political resistance.[6] Proposed administrative changes with low political resistance include the electronic submission and processing of export and import documents, fast-track procedures for property transfers and the consolidation of bureaucratic processes at the Legal Affairs Office. Administrative changes with medium political resistance focus on the reduction of the number of procedures to obtain a construction permit, development of specialized commercial courts and expansion of case management systems. An administrative change that will most likely face high political resistance is the introduction of performance measures for judges due to the division of power between the legal system, the government and the business environment.[7]

- In the year ending June 1, 2016, 137 economies implemented 283 total reforms across the different areas measured by *Doing Business*, an increase of over 20% from last year.
- *Doing Business* has recorded more than 2,900 regulatory reforms making it easier to do business since 2004.
- The economies showing the most notable improvement in performance on the *Doing Business* indicators in 2015/16 were Brunei Darussalam, Kazakhstan, Kenya, Belarus and Indonesia.
- Reforms inspired by *Doing Business* have been implemented by economies in all regions. But Europe and Central Asia continues to be the region with the highest share of economies implementing at least one reform—96% of economies in the region have implemented at least one business regulatory reform.
- Starting a business continues to be the most common reform area with 49 reforms, followed by paying taxes with 46.
- Increasingly, the competitiveness of cities is seen as an important driver of job creation and economic growth. By focusing on cities, subnational *Doing Business* studies contribute to the improvement of their competitiveness, providing information to policy makers on how to reform the business regulatory environment.

BOX 3.1 India has embarked on an ambitious reform path

The current government of India was elected in 2014 on a platform of increasing job creation, mostly through encouraging investment in the manufacturing sector. Soon after the elections policy makers realized that for this to occur substantial improvements would need to be made to the country's overall business regulatory environment. The *Doing Business* indicators have been employed as one of the main measures to monitor improvements in India's business climate. As a result of the election platform-driven reform agenda, over the past two years the *Doing Business* report has served as an effective tool to design and implement business regulatory reforms.

The data presented by the *Doing Business* indicators have led to a clear realization that India is in need of transformative reforms. The country has embarked on a fast-paced reform path, and the *Doing Business 2017* report acknowledges a number of substantial improvements. For example, India has achieved significant reductions in the time and cost to provide electricity connections to businesses. In 2015/16 the utility in Delhi streamlined the connection process for new commercial electricity connections by allowing consumers to obtain connections for up to 200 kilowatt capacity to low-tension networks. This reform led to the simplification of the commercial electricity connection process in two ways. First, it eliminated the need to purchase and install a distribution transformer and related connection materials, as the connection is now done directly to the distribution network, leading to a reduction in cost. Second, the time required to conduct external connection works by the utility has been greatly reduced due to the low-tension connection and there is no longer a need to install a distribution transformer. As a result, the time needed to connect to electricity was reduced from 138 days in 2013/14 to 45 days in 2015/16. And in the same period, the cost was reduced from 846% of income per capita to 187%.

Over the past three years, the utility in Delhi has substantially reduced the time and cost of obtaining an electricity connection

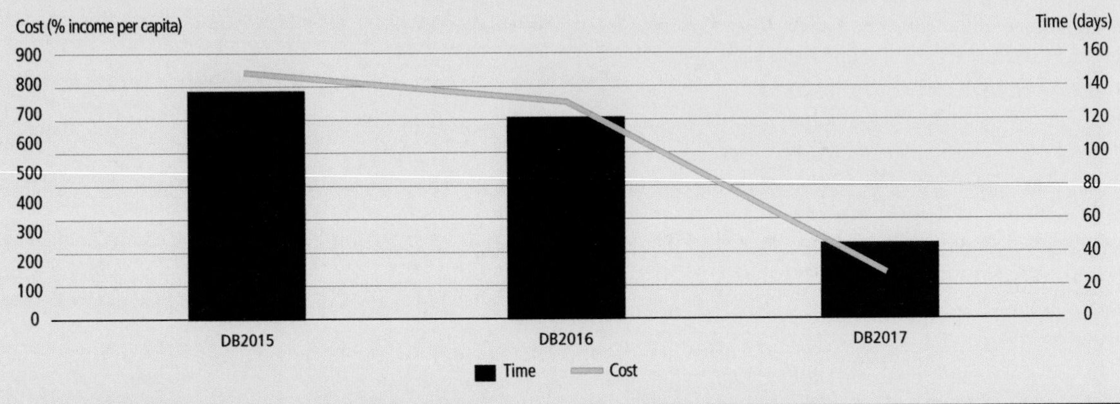

Source: Doing Business database.

Furthermore, India has made paying taxes easier by introducing an electronic system for paying employee state insurance contributions. In the area of trade, as of April 2016 the Customs Electronic Commerce Interchange Gateway portal allowed for the electronic filing (e-filing) of integrated customs declarations, bills of entry and shipping bills, reducing the time and cost for export and import documentary compliance. The portal also facilitates data and communication exchanges between applicants and customs, reducing the time for export and import border compliance. Additionally, an Integrated Risk Management System has become fully operational and ensured that all the consignments are selected based on the principles of risk management. Furthermore, the government of India adopted the Companies (Amendment) Act (No. 21) in May 2015. The amendments were published in the official gazette and immediately entered into force upon notification by the Ministry of Corporate Affairs. As a result, the minimum capital requirement for company incorporation was abolished and the requirement to obtain a certificate to commence business operations was eliminated. To improve court efficiency, the passage of the Commercial Courts, Commercial Divisions and Commercial Appellate Divisions Act of 2015 established effective mechanisms for addressing commercial cases. And in May 2016 the government of India enacted the Insolvency and Bankruptcy Code (IBC), which—when it comes into effect—will overhaul the 60-year-old framework for company liquidation and introduce new insolvency practices.

The experience of implementing reforms based on *Doing Business* data has demonstrated to the government the significance of establishing clear stakeholder feedback mechanisms to close the gaps between policy formulation and implementation. Finally, the government has also acknowledged the need to implement reforms across the country—not just in Mumbai and Delhi, which are the cities covered by *Doing Business*. Lawmakers have recommended the implementation of a large number of reforms across all states, going beyond the scope of *Doing Business*.

Regulatory reforms inspired by *Doing Business* have been implemented by economies in all regions. Rwanda, which ranks second in Africa in *Doing Business 2017*, is an example of an economy that used *Doing Business* as a guide to improve its business environment. From *Doing Business 2005* to *Doing Business 2017* Rwanda implemented a total of 47 reforms across all indicators. Rwanda is one of only 10 economies that have implemented reforms in all of the *Doing Business* indicators and every year since *Doing Business 2006*.[8] These reforms are in line with Rwanda's Vision 2020 development strategy, which aims to transform Rwanda from a low-income economy to a lower-middle-income economy by raising income per capita from $290 to $1,240 by 2020.[9]

Doing Business is widely used by policy makers in Sub-Saharan Africa to advance their reform agendas. Some of these economies have established units dedicated to specific reform action plans targeting the *Doing Business* indicators. In Kenya, for example, the Ease of Doing Business Delivery Unit operates under the leadership of the Ministry of Industrialization and the Deputy President, meeting on average every two weeks to discuss progress on an established action plan. The meeting is chaired by either the Deputy President or the Minister of Industrialization, while several stakeholder agencies are responsible for implementing measures stated in the action plan.

In Burundi, the investment climate reform agenda is overseen by the Office of the Second Vice President. The dedicated Doing Business Intelligence Committee comprises several ministers and is supported by an executive secretariat, which assumes the day-to-day work and reform coordination as well as public-private dialogue and communication on current reforms. Nigeria's government, which came to power in 2015, has placed a strong emphasis on increasing the country's competitiveness. In early 2016 Nigeria established the Presidential Enabling Business Environment Council, which is chaired by the Vice President; the Federal Minister of Industry, Trade and Investment is the vice-chairman. The Council's main mandate is the supervision of the competitiveness and investment climate agenda at the federal and state levels, while the Enabling Business Environment Secretariat is charged with day-to-day reform implementation.

Similarly, the Prime Minister of Côte d'Ivoire is the champion of the investment climate reform agenda and chairs the National Interdepartmental Doing Business Committee. The prerogative of this committee, which includes public and private sector stakeholders, is to formulate the reform agenda and to ensure the high-level monitoring of its implementation. Its permanent secretariat assumes coordination and implementation of the established reform agenda. In Zimbabwe, the Office of the President and Cabinet oversees the *Doing Business* reform initiative using a Rapid Results Initiative approach. The Chief Secretary to the President and Cabinet is the strategic sponsor of the Initiative. Permanent Secretaries from more than 10 ministries are responsible for implementing measures outlined in the action plan for each of the *Doing Business* indicators.

Recently some reform efforts have advanced beyond the geographic boundaries of individual states. In 2015, 10 economies came together to form the Association of Southeast Asian Nations (ASEAN) Economic Community, a single market economy for goods, services, capital and labor, which—once it is realized—could result in a market larger than the European Union or North America. This year the 10 ASEAN economies implemented a total of 31 reforms across the *Doing Business* indicators—including six reforms in the area of paying taxes and six reforms in the area of getting credit. Malaysia, for example, introduced an online system for filing and paying goods and services tax and strengthened credit reporting by beginning to provide consumer credit scores.

ASEAN can also learn from other Asia-Pacific Economic Cooperation (APEC) economies how to reform and create a uniform business environment. The APEC Ease of Doing Business (EoDB) initiative set a goal of an APEC-wide improvement of 25% by 2015 in five *Doing Business* indicators: starting a business, dealing with construction permits, getting credit, trading across borders and enforcing contracts. This goal—of making doing business faster, cheaper and easier—was endorsed by APEC leaders in 2009. By 2015 APEC economies reached an improvement of 12.7% and launched the EoDB Action Plan (2016-2018) to further this effort. The new target was an improvement of 10% by 2018 in the existing five priority areas using the baseline data of 2015.[10] The main overarching objectives across the recommendations are simplifying and streamlining business processes, creating electronic platforms and establishing a single-interface service.

HIGHLIGHTS OF REFORMS MEASURED IN *DOING BUSINESS* IN 2015/16

The private sector is universally recognized as being a key driver of economic growth and development. Nearly 90% of employment, including formal and informal jobs, occurs within the private sector, which has an abundant potential that should be harnessed.[11] Governments in many economies work together with the private sector to create a thriving business environment. One way of doing this is through implementing effective business regulation that ensures that all actors have fair and equal opportunities to participate in a competitive market. More specifically, effective business regulation can encourage firm creation and growth and minimize market distortions or failures. *Doing Business* continues to capture dozens of reforms implemented through its 11 indicator sets.

BOX 3.2 Subnational *Doing Business* studies in Mexico and Colombia: reforming through competition and collaboration

In 2005 Mexico requested that the World Bank expand the *Doing Business* benchmarks beyond Mexico City to assess the business regulatory environment across states, arguing that the capital city was not representative of Mexico as a whole. A decade later subnational *Doing Business* studies have been replicated across the globe, measuring 438 locations in 65 economies and recording 583 regulatory reforms. The strong demand for subnational *Doing Business* studies proves that comparisons among locations within the same economy and the sharing of good practices are strong drivers of reform.

By leveraging the methodology of *Doing Business* and combining it with a strong engagement strategy with local authorities, subnational *Doing Business* studies increase ownership of the reform agenda at all levels of government. The results from repeated benchmarking exercises in Colombia and Mexico—three and six rounds, respectively—and the growing commitment from government partners in these countries provide examples of how subnational *Doing Business* studies can be used as a public policy tool to identify local differences, guide reform efforts and track progress over time.

Over the course of the subnational series in Mexico, the number of states reforming has increased considerably. Greater buy-in from different government institutions has also expanded the range of reforms. The first two rounds recorded reforms in the majority of the states, but not all. However, soon after the first study, competition and collaboration spurred the reform momentum and, since 2012, all the 32 states have embarked on an active path to reform. States and municipalities began to expand their reform efforts to a larger number of areas. They did this by strengthening intragovernmental collaboration—between state, municipal and national authorities—and reaching out to the judiciary. With the support of the judiciary, Mexico introduced legal reforms to facilitate contract enforcement. Between 2012 and 2016 the Mexican states of Colima, Estado de México, Puebla, San Luis Potosí and Sinaloa reformed in all four areas measured by the project. Subnational *Doing Business* has recorded a total of 252 regulatory improvements across all states in Mexico to date.

In Mexico the top improvers started out as the worst performers

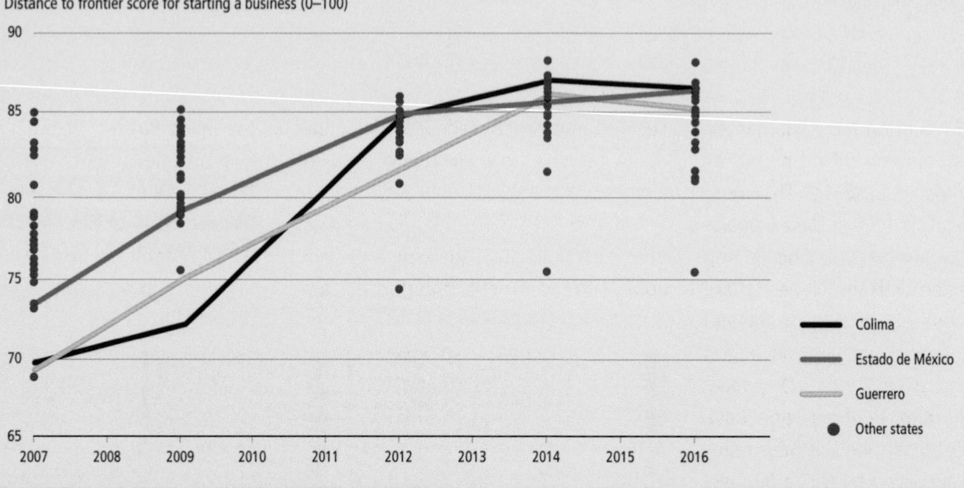

Source: Doing Business database.

Note: Among Mexican states Colima, Estado de México and Guerrero have made the most improvement on the starting a business indicator set since 2007.

In Colombia 100% of locations reformed after the first benchmark in 2008. The third round in 2012 covered 23 locations and recorded a total of 62 reforms across all indicators. Those locations that had initially ranked poorly—the large business centers such as Medellín, Bucaramanga and Cartagena—improved the most that year. The findings of the subnational studies spurred technical assistance programs implemented by the national government to support local reforms. The fourth round, in 2017, will expand the geographic coverage to measure all departments (states) in Colombia for the first time.

The findings of subnational *Doing Business* studies not only encourage competition but also inspire peer-to-peer learning initiatives by highlighting good practices in an economy. Peer-to-peer learning can be one of the most powerful drivers of reforms, particularly when good practices are replicated within the cities of the same economy. Cities with inefficient business regulation benefit the most from such practice, learning from a wealth of information available on national good practices. It is therefore not uncommon to see cities that performed poorly in a business regulatory area to show a steep improvement in the next round of measurement.

(continued)

BOX 3.2 Subnational *Doing Business* studies in Mexico and Colombia: reforming through competition and collaboration *(continued)*

In Colombia the cities of Neiva and Cartagena stand out. Neiva, which ranked last in Colombia's subnational *Doing Business* study in 2008, established an "anti-red tape" committee, bringing together the municipality, chamber of commerce, business associations and representatives of national agencies, such as the police and the tax authority. This committee met every month to propose changes to the regulatory environment and monitor progress. As a result, Neiva launched a one-stop shop for business registration which connected the municipal and state governments, eliminating 11 procedures required to start a business and speeding up the process by five weeks.

After finishing near the bottom of the ranking on the ease of starting a business twice in a row, the Mayor of Cartagena put forward an ambitious plan to eliminate the bottlenecks identified by subnational *Doing Business*. In a joint effort between the city and the private sector, Cartagena was able to implement reforms that reduced the time to register a company by half and costs by over 60%. As a result, Cartagena rose from a ranking of 21 on the ease of starting a business in 2008 to a ranking of 6 in 2012.

Mexican states have also made marked improvements in their performance in the subnational *Doing Business* studies. In 2007 Colima, Estado de México and Guerrero were several of the states where it was most challenging to start a business. It took on average two months and 18% of income per capita for entrepreneurs to formally start their business. In 2016 it takes entrepreneurs in Colima, Estado de Mexico and Guerrero no more than two weeks to start a business and on average their costs have been reduced by half.

Competitive cities can be drivers of job creation and economic growth. By focusing on cities, the subnational *Doing Business* studies contribute to the improvement of their competitiveness, providing information to policy makers on how to reform the business regulatory environment. Ultimately, competitive cities can help eliminate extreme poverty and promote prosperity for all citizens.[a]

a. Kilroy, Mukhim and Negri 2015.

In 2015/16, 137 economies implemented 283 reforms across different areas measured by *Doing Business*. The most reformed indicators this cycle are starting a business, paying taxes and getting credit. The region with the highest share of reforms across all topics is Europe and Central Asia, continuing a trend begun well over a decade ago (table 3.1). Indeed, 96% of economies in the region have implemented at least one business regulatory reform recorded by *Doing Business 2017*. Kazakhstan, Georgia and Belarus are regional leaders on the total count of reforms, implementing seven, five and four reforms, respectively.

In 2015/16, 29 economies implemented a net of at least three reforms improving their business regulatory systems or related institutions as measured by *Doing Business*. These 29 include economies from all income groups: low-income (seven economies), lower-middle-income (nine), upper-middle-income (eight) and high-income (five). Ten economies in Sub-Saharan Africa made a net of at least three reforms making it easier to do business in 2015/16.

The 10 economies showing the most notable improvement in performance on the *Doing Business* indicators in 2015/16 were Brunei Darussalam, Kazakhstan, Kenya, Belarus, Indonesia, Serbia, Georgia, Pakistan, the United Arab Emirates and Bahrain (table 3.2). These economies together implemented 48 business

TABLE 3.1 Economies in Europe and Central Asia have the highest share of reformers in 2015/16

Area of reform	Number of reforms in 2015/16	Region with the highest share of reformers in 2015/16
Starting a business	49	Middle East & North Africa
Dealing with construction permits	18	Europe & Central Asia
Getting electricity	21	Europe & Central Asia
Registering property	22	Europe & Central Asia
Getting credit	34	East Asia & Pacific
Protecting minority investors	19	Europe & Central Asia
Paying taxes	46	Europe & Central Asia
Trading across borders	32	South Asia
Enforcing contracts	18	Europe & Central Asia
Resolving insolvency	24	Sub-Saharan Africa

Source: Doing Business database.
Note: The labor market regulation indicators also recorded 21 regulatory changes in the *Doing Business 2017* report. These changes are not included in the total reform count.

TABLE 3.2 The 10 economies improving the most across three or more areas measured by *Doing Business* in 2015/16												
			Reforms making it easier to do business									
Economy	**Ease of doing business rank**	**Change in DTF score**	Starting a business	Dealing with construction permits	Getting electricity	Registering property	Getting credit	Protecting minority investors	Paying taxes	Trading across borders	Enforcing contracts	Resolving insolvency
Brunei Darussalam	72	5.28			✔		✔	✔	✔		✔	✔
Kazakhstan	35	4.71	✔	✔	✔			✔		✔	✔	✔
Kenya	92	3.52	✔		✔	✔		✔				✔
Belarus	37	3.22			✔	✔	✔	✔				
Indonesia	91	2.95	✔		✔	✔	✔		✔	✔	✔	
Serbia	47	2.59	✔	✔		✔						
Georgia	16	2.45			✔	✔		✔	✔	✔		
Pakistan	144	2.08				✔	✔			✔		
United Arab Emirates	26	2.07	✔	✔	✔	✔		✔				
Bahrain	63	2.05	✔				✔			✔		

Source: Doing Business database.

Note: Economies are selected on the basis of the number of reforms and ranked on how much their distance to frontier score improved. First, *Doing Business* selects the economies that implemented reforms making it easier to do business in 3 or more of the 10 areas included in this year's aggregate distance to frontier score. Regulatory changes making it more difficult to do business are subtracted from the number of those making it easier. Second, *Doing Business* ranks these economies on the increase in their distance to frontier score from the previous year. The improvement in their score is calculated not by using the data published in 2015 but by using comparable data that capture data revisions and methodology changes. The choice of the most improved economies is determined by the largest improvements in the distance to frontier score among those with at least three reforms.

regulatory reforms across all of the areas measured by *Doing Business*. Overall, the 10 top improvers implemented the most regulatory reforms in the areas of getting electricity and registering property—with seven reforms for each indicator set. These economies also actively reformed in the areas of starting a business and protecting minority investors, with six reforms in each area. Kazakhstan and Georgia joined the list of top improvers for the fourth time in the past 12 years.

Two economies from East Asia and the Pacific made it to the list of 10 top improvers. Brunei Darussalam made the biggest advance toward the regulatory frontier in 2015/16, thanks to six business regulatory reforms. Brunei Darussalam, for instance, increased the reliability of power supply by implementing an automatic energy management system to monitor outages and service restoration. To improve access to credit, it began distributing consumer data from utility companies. Brunei Darussalam also passed a new insolvency law, offering protections for secured creditors during an automatic stay in reorganization proceedings. In addition, Brunei Darussalam strengthened minority investor protections by making it easier to sue directors in case of prejudicial related-party transactions and by allowing the rescission of related-party transactions that harm companies.

Indonesia made starting a business easier by abolishing the paid-in minimum capital requirement for small and medium-size enterprises and encouraging the use of an online system for name reservation. In Jakarta, a single form to obtain company registration certificates and trading licenses was also created. Getting electricity was made easier in Indonesia by reducing the time for contractors to perform external work thanks to an increase in the stock of electrical material supplied by the utility. In Surabaya, getting electricity was also made easier after the utility streamlined the process for new connection requests. In addition, Indonesia digitalized its cadastral records and launched a fully automated geographic information system, making it easier to register a property. Moreover, Indonesia established a modern collateral registry and introduced a dedicated procedure for small claims for commercial litigation. In the area of trading across borders, it improved the customs services and document submission functions of the Indonesia National Single Window. Finally, Indonesia made paying taxes easier by introducing an online system for filing tax returns and paying health contributions.

Economies in Europe and Central Asia continued to reform actively in 2015/16. Kazakhstan and Georgia increased the reliability of the electricity supply by starting to penalize utilities for having poor power outage indicators. Both economies also strengthened minority investor protections by increasing shareholder rights in major decisions, clarifying ownership and control structures and requiring greater corporate transparency. In the area of trading across borders, Kazakhstan made exporting less costly by eliminating two documents previously required for customs clearance; Georgia made import and export documentary compliance faster by improving its electronic document processing system. Belarus improved its business climate by establishing a one-stop shop at the electricity utility, launching an electronic geographic information system for property registration, providing consumer credit scores to banks and regulated financial institutions and by introducing remedies in cases where related-party transactions are harmful to the company. Owing to streamlined processes and time limits, Serbia reduced the time needed to start a business, obtain a building permit and transfer property.

Pakistan and Bahrain improved access to credit information by adopting new regulations that guarantee by law borrowers' rights to inspect their credit data. Trading across borders also became easier by improving infrastructure and streamlining procedures in Bahrain and introducing a new electronic platform for customs clearance in Pakistan. Among other reforms, the United Arab Emirates made dealing with construction permits easier by implementing risk-based inspections and streamlining the final joint inspection with the process of obtaining a completion certificate. The United Arab Emirates also reduced the time required to obtain a new electricity connection by implementing a new program with strict deadlines for reviewing applications, carrying out inspections and installing meters. Additionally, the United Arab Emirates introduced compensation for power outages.

Removing obstacles to start up a business

Studies have shown that removing excessive bureaucratic formalities in the start-up process has numerous benefits for both economies and entrepreneurs. Some of these gains include higher levels of firm formalization, economic growth and greater profits.[12] Governments embark on various reform paths to improve business incorporation processes and encourage entrepreneurship. In 2015/16, 49 reforms were captured by the starting a business indicator set, ranging from removing redundant processes required to operate formally to expanding the use of modern technology and creating or improving one-stop shops.

Onerous incorporation processes cost entrepreneurs time and money. During 2015/16 one-third of the reforms captured by the starting a business indicators involved streamlining the formalities for registering a business. The government of Sri Lanka, for example, waived the stamp duty on issued shares. Similarly, by repealing a requirement to have registration documents signed before a commission of oaths Ireland, Kenya and Uganda significantly reduced the time needed by entrepreneurs to start a business. All of these actions have significantly reduced the number of interactions between entrepreneurs and government officials, thereby lowering opportunities for rent-seeking.

Governments continue to improve their efficiency through the use of technology. In the past year, *Doing Business* data show that economies that implement online procedures see a reduction in the time taken to start a business (figure 3.1). In 2015/16, 20% of economies reforming company startup processes either introduced or improved online portals. The Nigerian Corporate Affairs Commission, for example, launched an online registration portal allowing companies to reserve their names electronically. Rwanda now has a fully functioning electronic portal that combines company registration, information on tax obligations and duties and value added tax registration—saving entrepreneurs an average of two days and eliminating two interactions with government officials.

Several economies also reformed their one-stop shops for business registration in 2015/16. Cyprus merged the process of registration for value added tax and corporate income tax. Likewise, Malta's companies register and inland revenue department merged their operations to allow the automatic generation of tax identification numbers. The Arab Republic of Egypt created a unit inside its one-stop shop to facilitate and streamline interactions between entrepreneurs and various governmental agencies. Egyptian entrepreneurs now have fewer direct interactions with regulatory agencies when completing both registration and postregistration procedures.

Streamlining the process of obtaining a building permit

The construction industry is a vital sector of an economy. It stimulates growth by

FIGURE 3.1 Economies implementing online procedures in 2015/16 have reduced the time needed to start a business

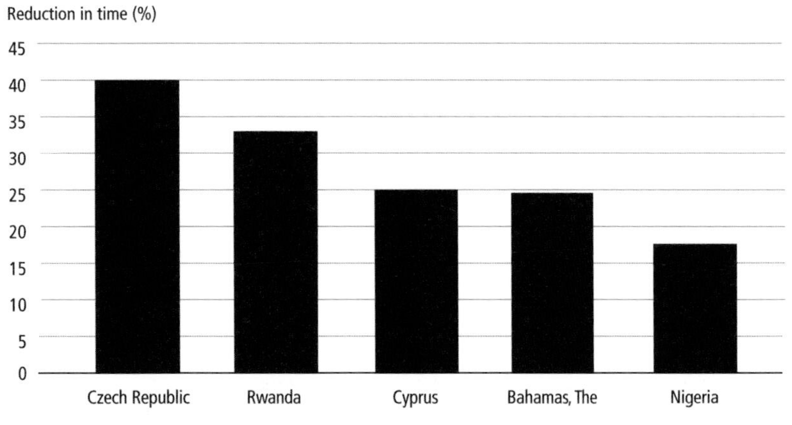

Source: Doing Business database.

attracting sizeable investments and supporting supply chains, thereby generating employment and contributing to the process of capital formation.[13] Research suggests that the construction industry is responsible for 6% of global GDP—or a 5% share of GDP in developed economies and an 8% share in developing economies.[14] Over the past three years economies have mostly focused their construction-permitting reforms on streamlining procedures and improving coordination among the various agencies involved in the process. Other common areas of improvement included reducing the time and cost incurred by builders, followed by improving electronic platforms and building quality control processes (figure 3.2).

FIGURE 3.2 Construction reforms have mostly focused on streamlining procedures over the past three years

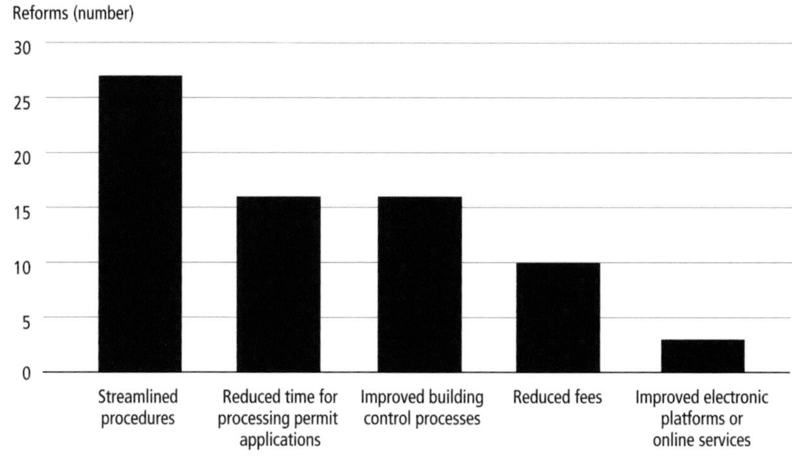

Source: Doing Business database.

In the area of construction, five of 18 economies reduced the time it takes to obtain a building permit in 2015/16. Algeria and Cameroon, for example, enforced the processing time limits prescribed by law. Similarly, the Democratic Republic of Congo improved building quality controls and compliance with legal time limits to obtain a building permit. Zimbabwe streamlined the approval process for construction permits by improving interagency coordination between the Harare City Council and architectural agencies.

Five economies—Cameroon, Côte d'Ivoire, Madagascar, the Philippines and the United Arab Emirates—improved their performance on the building quality control index by increasing the transparency of building regulations. In the Philippines, for example, the Department of Building Official Services of Quezon City updated its website to list the required preapprovals needed to obtain a construction permit. With respect to cost reduction, both France and San Marino reduced the fees for obtaining a building permit.

Botswana's Gaborone City Council abolished a requirement to present a rates clearance certificate when applying for a building permit, thereby easing bureaucratic requirements. Poland eliminated a requirement to obtain technical conditions for utilities and clearance from the public roads administrator. Kazakhstan introduced a single window portal to streamline the approvals process to obtain a building permit. The Russian Federation abolished the requirement to obtain an approval to fence construction sites in St. Petersburg. Capitalizing on advancements in modern technology, Serbia made it mandatory to request a building permit online through the e-permit system. Likewise, Singapore enhanced its electronic one-stop shop, making the process of obtaining approvals from different authorities easier. Finally, Albania's Constitutional Court lifted a moratorium on issuing construction permits. As a result, the issuance of building permits has been resumed.

Making access to electricity more efficient and reliable

A reliable electricity supply—as well as an efficient connection process—is linked to better firm performance, especially in industries that require a steady supply of electricity.[15] In fact, a reliable electricity supply is associated with higher firm production efficiency and higher levels of foreign direct investment.[16] A more efficient connection process is associated with positive electricity sector outcomes, such as higher rates of electrification and lower numbers of bribe payments.[17] Economies can substantially improve their business environment by investing in the electricity sector.

One index included in the getting electricity indicator set is the quality of supply and transparency of tariffs index. In 2015/16, seven economies—Algeria, Brunei Darussalam, Bulgaria, Georgia, Kazakhstan, the Lao People's Democratic Republic and the United Arab Emirates—implemented reforms in this capacity. To improve the reliability of the power supply the utility in Bulgaria is now using an automatic energy management system, SCADA (Supervisory Control and Data Acquisition), to monitor power outages and to restore the service. And the utility in Algeria improved the level of transparency in the electricity sector by publishing electricity tariffs online.

Of the 21 reforms captured by the getting electricity indicators, 17 economies implemented reforms improving the efficiency of the electricity connection process. Such reforms included the streamlining of connection procedures, the reduction of connection fees and the creation of one-stop shops. Belarus, for example, established a one-stop shop at the utility that fulfills

FIGURE 3.3 Kenya's reform led to a reduction in time and streamlined connection procedures

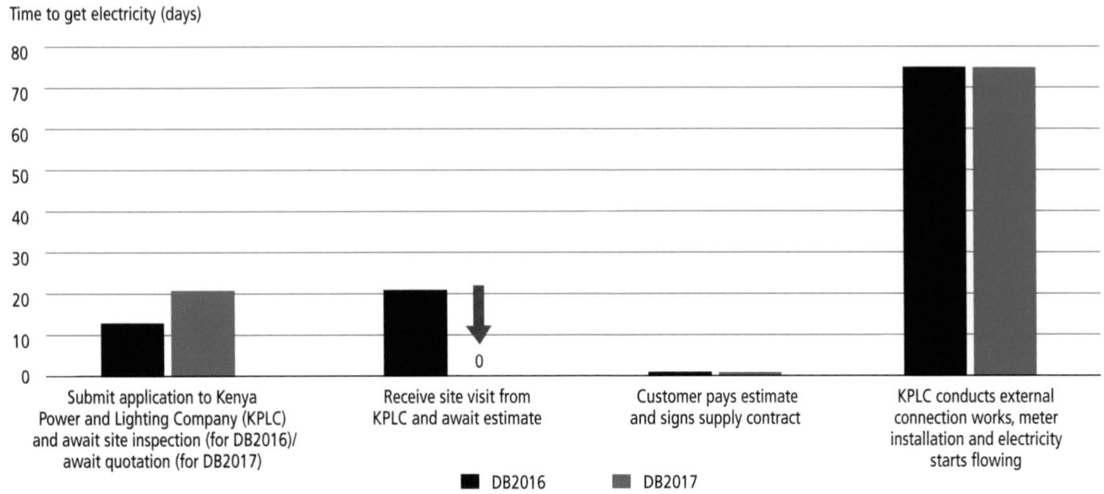

Source: Doing Business database.

all utility connection-related services, including the design and construction of the distribution line. Kenya streamlined the process of getting electricity by introducing the use of a geographic information system that allows the utility to provide price quotes to customers without conducting a site visit. Moreover, all substations, transformers and meters are now mapped on the system which is also linked to well-documented cadastral maps. Customers simply submit all required documentation and wait for quotes to be directly prepared by the utility office (figure 3.3).

Recent amendments to the Construction Law of Poland eliminated the need for an excavation permit, which previously was required for the utility to extend low voltage grids and build medium voltage transformer stations. The utility is now able to carry out external connection works without having to wait for an excavation permit to be issued. As a result of this reform Poland decreased the total time needed to obtain an electricity connection by 11 days.

Improving the quality of land administration

Registered property rights are necessary to support investment, productivity and growth.[18] Evidence from economies around the world suggests that property owners with registered titles are more likely to invest[19]—and they have a higher likelihood of getting credit when using property as collateral. It is essential that governments have reliable, up-to-date information in cadasters and land registries to correctly assess and collect taxes. In 2015/16, 22 economies made it easier for businesses to register property by increasing the efficiency of property transfers and improving the quality of land administration. In 17 of these economies, reforms improved the reliability of infrastructure and the transparency of information of land administration systems (figure 3.4).

Among the 190 economies included in *Doing Business*, Rwanda made the largest improvement on the registering property indicators in 2015/16. The Rwanda Natural Resources Authority introduced a fast track procedure for commercial property transfers, and improved the transparency of the land registry by establishing a land administration services complaints mechanism and by publishing statistics on property transfers. Mexico—another significant improver—modernized its land management infrastructure. Over the past two years, the Mexico City government acquired new information technology infrastructure which enabled it to digitize all recorded land titles and create an electronic database of land ownership.

Among all regions, Sub-Saharan Africa accounts for the largest number of reforms in 2015/16, a total of seven out of 22. Zambia, for example, decreased the property transfer tax. Senegal improved the transparency of information by publishing a list of all required documents, service standards and official fees needed to complete any type of property transaction. In Europe and Central Asia, four economies implemented changes pertinent to the registering property indicators. In 2015, Belarus introduced the new geographic information system which provides free access to information on land plot boundaries and technical information on geospatial location. Additionally, Serbia reduced the time required to transfer a property while Georgia increased coverage of all maps for privately held land plots in Tbilisi.

Indonesia implemented measures to digitize land plans and maps in both Jakarta and Surabaya. As a result of these efforts, the cadastral maps were made publicly available through an online portal. The new online platform provides open

FIGURE 3.4 Seventeen economies improved their score on the quality of land administration index in 2015/16

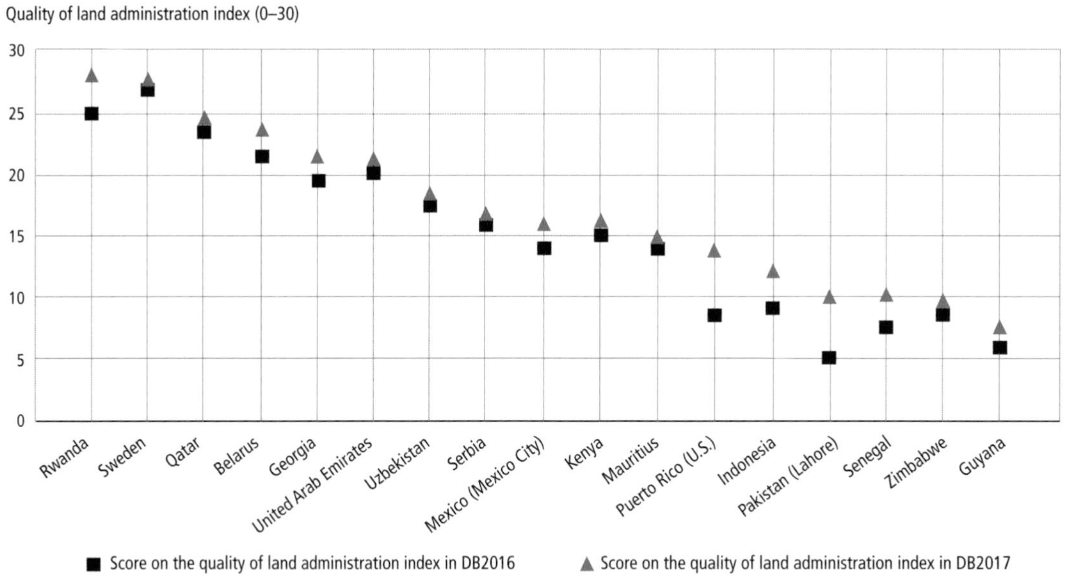

Quality of land administration index (0–30)

30 25 20 15 10 5 0

Rwanda Sweden Qatar Belarus Georgia United Arab Emirates Uzbekistan Serbia Mexico (Mexico City) Kenya Mauritius Puerto Rico (U.S.) Indonesia Pakistan (Lahore) Senegal Zimbabwe Guyana

■ Score on the quality of land administration index in DB2016 ▲ Score on the quality of land administration index in DB2017

Source: Doing Business database.

access to the geospatial information system, allowing clients to review and verify boundaries of land plots in Indonesia. Pakistan was the sole economy in South Asia to reform property transfers. Starting in 2007, the Punjab province of Pakistan launched the Land Records Management and Information Program to strengthen the capacity of land administration institutions in Lahore. During a five-year period, the project deployed an automated land records system and improved the quality of services provided by the land agency.

Strengthening access to credit

Nine economies—Armenia, Brunei Darussalam, The Gambia, Indonesia, the former Yugoslav Republic of Macedonia, Malawi, Nigeria, Papua New Guinea and Vanuatu—implemented reforms to strengthen access to credit by transforming and adopting new laws regarding secured transactions, including in some cases by creating an operational unified collateral registry. The parliament enacted a new law in Armenia which establishes a modern and unified collateral registry. Indonesia made registrations, amendments and cancellations at the collateral registry available to the general public through an online portal, Fidusia Online. The Gambia introduced a new law which established a centralized, notice-based collateral registry, a reform that increased The Gambia's legal rights index score by 4 points. Furthermore, Malawi and Papua New Guinea introduced new secured transactions legislation and established modern unified collateral registries. Both registries are now fully operational, resulting in an improvement in the ability of small businesses to obtain credit as they can now use firm assets as collateral.

Twenty-seven economies implemented reforms improving their credit information systems in 2015/16 (figure 3.5). Guyana and Tanzania made the largest improvements by expanding borrower coverage. Tanzania's credit bureau, Creditinfo, expanded its borrower coverage from 4.97% to 6.48% of the adult population, aided in part by signing agreements with retailers and merchants to share credit data on their customers. Similarly, Creditinfo Guyana, which became operational in May 2015, expanded its borrower coverage from 2.40% to 16.40% of the adult population through obtaining data from one microfinance institution, one trade creditor and one water utility company as well as from six private commercial banks.

Over the past *Doing Business* cycle, six economies established legal frameworks to improve the functioning of credit reporting markets, most of them in Sub-Saharan Africa. Mozambique, for example, enacted a new law that allows the establishment of a credit bureau. The national assemblies of Burkina Faso and Togo passed the Uniform Law,[20] providing the legal framework for the establishment, licensing, organization of activities and supervision of credit bureaus. This same law was previously adopted in Côte d'Ivoire, Mali, Niger and Senegal, where new credit bureaus became operational in February 2016.

Several other economies improved features of existing credit reporting systems. In six economies, credit bureaus and registries began offering credit scores to banks and other financial institutions to help them assess the creditworthiness of borrowers. In Thailand, for example, the National Credit Bureau started offering consumer and commercial credit scoring.

FIGURE 3.5 Main reform features in the area of getting credit—credit information

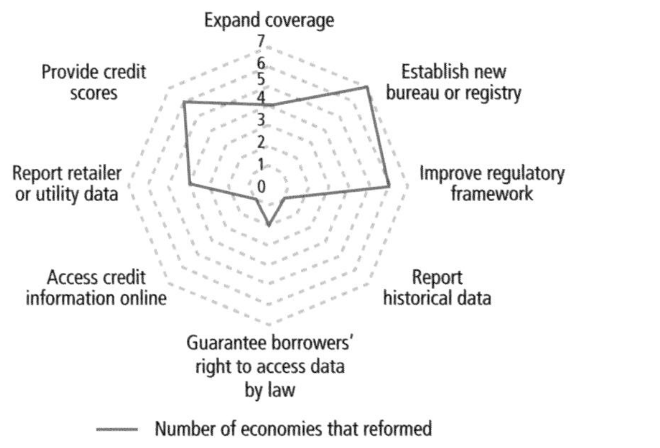

Source: Doing Business database.
Note: The scale represents the number of economies with the particular reform feature.

Credit scores pool information across many creditors as well as some public information sources. Such scores offer lenders information that is otherwise unavailable to any individual creditor, including total exposure, number of outstanding loans and previous defaults. This, in turn, aids the decision making of lenders when assessing loan applications.

Brunei Darussalam, China, Tanzania and Tunisia expanded the scope of information collected and reported by credit reporting service providers by distributing data from retailers or utility companies. Economies also enacted reforms guaranteeing borrowers' rights to access and inspect their data. In Bahrain, for example, clients of a credit bureau have the right to obtain a free credit report once every 12 months, to add information to their credit report and to file a complaint or objection related to the accuracy or limitation of the information contained in their credit report. In Pakistan there is a legal obligation for a credit bureau to provide a borrower with a copy of a credit report.

Strengthening the rights of minority shareholders

Firm-level research on a sample of nearly 1,000 firms in the United States shows a robust negative association between restrictions on shareholder rights and the market value of firms relative to the total value of their assets. The more shareholder rights are limited the more undervalued firms tend to be.[21] Moreover, an analysis of controlled companies—where ownership is concentrated typically in the hands of the founding family—highlights that sound corporate governance should be comprised of two strategies: enhancing the rights of minority shareholders and moderating the powers of the controlling shareholder.[22]

To comply with internationally-accepted good practices, in 2015/16 19 economies strengthened the rights of minority shareholders. Georgia enacted amendments to the Law on Securities Market and the Law on Entrepreneurs. These amendments directly address shareholders' rights with respect to preemptive rights, voting rights, ownership and control. As a result, Georgia's score increased from 6 to 7 on the extent of shareholder rights index and from 4 to 8 on the extent of ownership and control index.

Fiji, Morocco, Saudi Arabia and Vietnam introduced greater requirements for corporate transparency into their laws and regulations. Such laws promote detailed disclosure of primary employment, appointments and remuneration of directors, ensure detailed and advance notice of general meetings of shareholders, oblige members of limited liability companies to meet at least once per year and allow shareholders to add items to the meeting agenda. These reforms resulted in an improvement in the scores of these four economies on the corporate transparency index.

Croatia, Kenya, Mauritania, Niger, Sri Lanka and Ukraine introduced legal changes focused on mitigating the potential prejudicial effect of conflicts of interest, particularly in the context of related-party transactions. Croatia, for example, now requires that directors disclose in detail to the management board and supervisory board of their company all relevant facts about the nature, relationship and existence of their conflicts of interest before considering any proposed resolution to enter into a major transaction. Likewise, in Ukraine, interested directors and interested shareholders are now excluded from the vote approving the transaction in which they have a conflict of interest. Lastly, Sri Lanka introduced a Code of Best Practices on Related Party Transactions in 2013, at first on a voluntary basis. Since January 2016 all companies listed on the Colombo Stock Exchange must comply with its requirements, which include board approval of such transactions and detailed disclosure by board members.

Enhancing electronic tax filing systems

Properly developed, effective taxation systems are crucial for a well-functioning society. In most economies taxes are the main source of federal, state and local government revenues that are needed to fund projects related to health care, education, public transport and unemployment benefits, among others. The corporate tax burden has a direct impact on investment and growth. And tax administration efficiency is as important to businesses as effective tax rates.[23] A low cost of tax compliance and efficient tax-related procedures are advantageous for firms. Overly complicated tax systems are associated with high levels of tax evasion, large informal sectors, more corruption and less investment.[24] Tax compliance systems should be designed so as not to discourage businesses from participating in the formal economy. Modern tax administrations seek to optimize tax collections while minimizing administration costs and taxpayer compliance costs.

Of the 46 reforms captured by the paying taxes indicators, 26 economies either implemented new online systems for filing and paying taxes or improved the already existing online platforms in 2015 (figure 3.6). Italy, for example, introduced two improvements to its online system used by business taxpayers for filing labor taxes and mandatory contributions. Employers are now only required to enter personal information about employees once—at the beginning of employment and then it is carried forward automatically to future periods—and the payment process for labor taxes and mandatory contributions has been upgraded. The system now allows the previous period's payment request to be copied into the current one—it retains all relevant information such as taxpayer identification and the purpose and destination of the payment.

Singapore was one of the first economies to introduce an electronic system for public administration. In 1992 the Inland Revenue Authority of Singapore developed an integrated and computerized tax administration system, making internal processes more efficient by freeing staff from unproductive bureaucratic tasks. As a result, between 1992 and 2000 the time needed to issue tax assessments decreased from 12–18 months to 3–5 months.[25] Singapore continues to improve its tax compliance system even though it is among the best performers on the paying taxes indicators. In 2015 the online system underwent further upgrades, allowing for fewer delays in filing returns for corporate income tax and value added tax.

Other reforms were enacted to lower tax costs for businesses. Profit tax rates were reduced in nine economies while seven economies—Angola, Hungary, Italy, Jamaica, Jordan, Kosovo and Spain—either allowed more corporate expense deductions or higher fixed asset tax depreciation. The Dominican Republic decreased its corporate income tax rate while Jordan increased the depreciation rates for certain fixed assets. And eight economies abolished certain taxes. Azerbaijan, for instance, abolished vehicle tax for residents.

FIGURE 3.6 Electronic systems for filing and paying taxes save compliance time worldwide

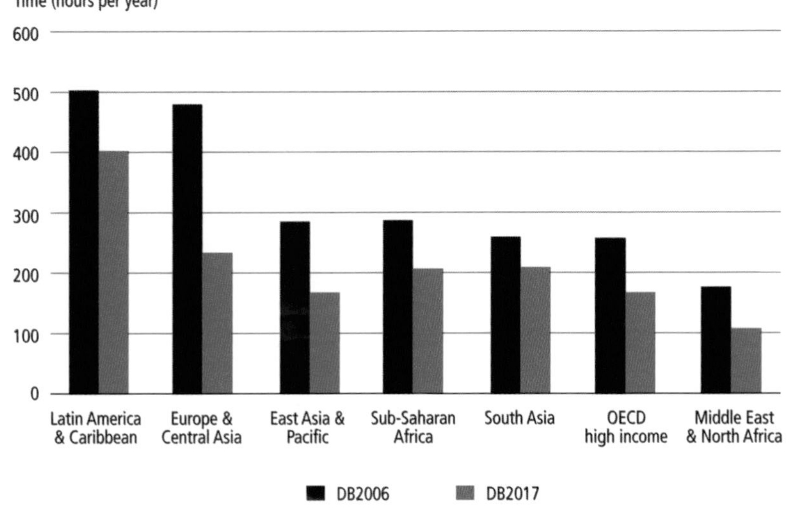

Source: Doing Business database.

Facilitating international trade through electronic solutions

Largely because of the progress made in tariff reduction over the last several decades, the focus of global trade policy and reforms has now shifted from trade tariffs to trade facilitation. A better logistics performance in the trade sector is strongly associated with trade growth, export diversification and economic growth.[26] In 2013, World Trade Organization (WTO) member countries signed the Trade Facilitation Agreement (TFA) committing to implement border management policies that make it easier to export and import goods across borders. A recent study suggests that, if the TFA is fully implemented by all member countries, the time spent in customs would be reduced by an average of 1.6 days for imports and 2 days for exports. By the time of the TFA's full implementation the estimated global welfare gain is expected to be $210 billion per year, with estimates ranging from $16 to $33 annually for each resident of WTO member countries.[27]

Among trade reformers, many economies made trading across borders easier by improving their existing electronic systems for both imports and exports, reducing the cost and time of documentary and border compliance (figure 3.7). Argentina, for example, introduced a new Import Monitoring System for products qualified for automatic licenses which is less restrictive and faster than the one previously used. Georgia reduced document processing times by enhancing its electronic document processing system as well as introducing an advanced electronic document submission option. The latter allows electronic registration of containers shipped by sea, eliminating the outdated process of manual registration of containers. Kosovo reduced the time and cost of documentary and border compliance for exporting by advancing its automated customs data management

FIGURE 3.7 Implementation of electronic systems had the most significant impact on time reduction among those economies reforming in trade in 2015/16

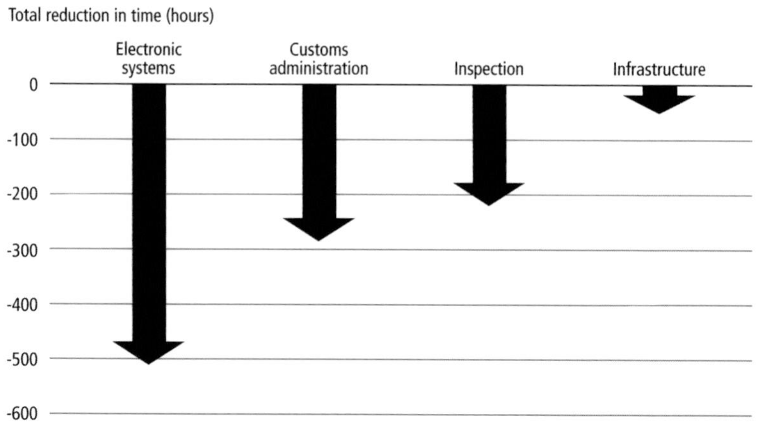

Source: Doing Business database.

Note: The time reduction captures reforms that were implemented and had a positive impact on time for the trading across borders indicators from from June 2015 to June 2016. The reforms recorded during this period can be aggregated into four wide-ranging categories: electronic systems, customs administration, inspections and infrastructure.

system, streamlining customs clearance processes and implementing the Albania-Kosovo Transit Corridor.

Another common feature of trade reforms in 2015/16 is the introduction of—and for some economies, the advancement of—the ASYCUDA (Automated System for Customs Data) World system, an automated customs data management system that facilitates both export and import processes. In Afghanistan the customs department introduced a series of technical improvements to the online document processing system. Both Grenada and Jamaica made significant upgrades to their electronic platforms, resulting in a substantial decrease in the time required for international trade processes. Their systems allow for the electronic submission of customs declarations and supporting trade documents. As a result, customs brokers no longer need to go to several customs clearance officers or government agencies to validate documents. Kosovo, Nepal and St. Lucia also eliminated the use of paper documents by upgrading their ASYCUDA World systems, allowing for payments and submissions of export declarations to be done electronically.

Enhancing judicial efficiency

Efficient contract enforcement is essential to economic development and sustainable growth.[28] Economies with an efficient judiciary in which courts can effectively enforce contractual obligations have more developed credit markets and a higher level of overall development.[29] A stronger judiciary is also associated with more rapid growth of small firms[30] and enhanced judicial system efficiency can improve the business climate, foster innovation, attract foreign direct investment and secure tax revenues.[31] Conscious of the important role played by judicial efficiency, governments have been active in reforming different aspects measured by the *Doing Business* enforcing contracts indicators. Worldwide, revisions of alternative dispute resolution legislation and applicable civil procedure rules was the most common reform feature in 2015/16. However, none of the low-income economies made reforms in this area (figure 3.8).

Low-income and middle-income economies, predominantly in Sub-Saharan Africa and East Asia, have focused their reform efforts on strengthening judicial infrastructure. Côte d'Ivoire and Indonesia, for example, introduced dedicated simplified procedures for the resolution of small claims. Similarly, India and Niger strengthened their institutions by introducing dedicated venues to resolve commercial disputes. The presence of specialized commercial courts or divisions can make a significant difference in the effectiveness of a judiciary. Specialized courts can reduce the number of cases pending before main first-instance courts, leading to shorter resolution times within the main trial court. Commercial courts and divisions also tend to promote consistency in the application of the law, increasing predictability for court users.

Other economies, mainly high-income economies, have focused their reform efforts on attaining a higher level of court automation. Brunei Darussalam, Hungary, Norway and Spain have introduced an electronic system to file initial complaints with the competent court. Electronic filing streamlines and accelerates the process of commencing a lawsuit. Reducing in-person interactions with court officers also minimizes potential opportunities for corruption and results in speedier trials, better access to courts and more reliable service of process. These features also reduce the cost to enforce a contract—court users save in reproduction costs and courthouse visits while courts save in storage, archiving and court officers' costs.

Some economies have pushed their automation efforts even further by introducing sophisticated and comprehensive electronic case management systems. In January 2016, for example, Rwanda implemented the Integrated Electronic Case Management System, a web-based application that integrates five main institutions of the justice sector, throughout Kigali's courts.[32] Among other features, the system allows for the automatic registration of lawsuits, electronic organization and scheduling of cases and automated claims processing. Rwandan authorities expect the system to result in considerable cost and time savings along with

FIGURE 3.8 Revisions of applicable civil procedure rules and ADR rules has been the most common reform feature in 2015/16

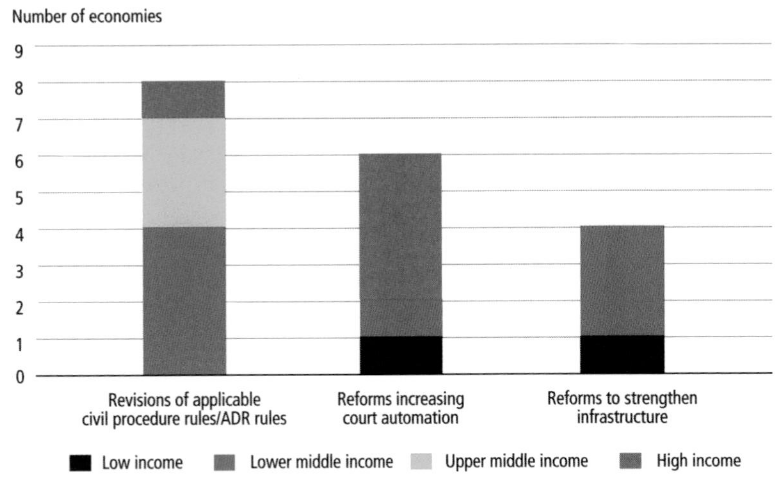

Source: Doing Business database.

increased transparency and more reliable statistical data on court operations.

Many economies have concentrated their reform efforts on making complex revisions of their civil procedure laws. A third of reforms in 2015/16 entailed approvals of entirely new codes of civil procedure. Bolivia, Brazil, Ecuador, Kazakhstan, Niger and the Syrian Arab Republic are among the economies that implemented such reforms. Several economies, mainly in the Europe and Central Asia region, have approved changes to their mediation laws in an attempt to strengthen alternative dispute resolution mechanisms.

Promoting efficient bankruptcy regimes

Bankruptcy laws are strongly linked to collateral eligibility requirements, access of firms to loans and long-term debt and the level of firms' financing relative to their size.[33] When it comes to bankruptcy reforms, speeding up the resolution of debt disputes may improve the likelihood of timely repayment. Increasing the protection of creditors and their participation in bankruptcy proceedings may lower the cost of debt and lead to a higher aggregate credit level. Moreover, economies that introduce new reorganization mechanisms may reduce failure rates among firms.[34] Efficient bankruptcy regimes with orderly procedures for the sale and distribution of assets can improve loan terms, leverage ratios and bank recovery rates.[35]

Doing Business recorded 24 reforms in the area of resolving insolvency, mainly in Sub-Saharan African economies, in 2015/16. Substantial regulatory reform efforts have been undertaken by the 17 member states of the Organization for the Harmonization of Business Law in Africa, known by its French acronym OHADA. The organization adopted a revised Uniform Act Organizing Collective Proceedings for Wiping Off Debts in 2015, which introduced a simplified preventive settlement procedure for small companies and a new conciliation procedure for companies facing financial difficulties, encouraging an agreement between a debtor and main creditors. The OHADA Uniform Act also introduced provisions on cross-border insolvency that were implemented in all 17 OHADA member states. Similarly, Kenya adopted a new Insolvency Act which closely follows the insolvency framework of the United Kingdom. The new law introduced the mechanism of administration—a form of reorganization that allows insolvent companies to continue operating while negotiating a settlement with creditors.

Another region with active reformers in the area of insolvency is East Asia and the Pacific, where Brunei Darussalam, Thailand and Vanuatu made notable progress. Brunei Darussalam completely overhauled its insolvency framework. Prior to the reform, insolvency provisions for liquidation of corporate entities were included in the Companies Act and some rules were incorporated in the Bankruptcy Act, which applied to individuals. The latest reform created a designated legal act encompassing all provisions related to corporate insolvency and reflecting many modern good practices. Companies in Brunei Darussalam now have access to reorganization proceedings in the form of judicial management. Although the insolvency reform in Thailand was less comprehensive it represented a significant achievement in line with initiatives implemented in other economies in East Asia and the Pacific. Thailand expanded the application of its reorganization framework so that not only large companies—but also small and medium-size enterprises—can take advantage of this mechanism. This step is expected to provide relief to many viable companies which otherwise would be forced to cease operations.

Changing labor market regulation

Regulation is important to ensure efficient functioning of labor markets and adequate protection for workers. Studies have shown that labor market regulation can have an impact on aggregate job flows, productivity and informality.[36] The challenge for governments is to strike the right balance between flexibility of employment regulation and worker protection.[37] In 2015/16, 21 economies changed labor rules. Some made their labor regulation more flexible, others more stringent and in some economies the changes were in both directions. Most of the reforms were implemented in Sub-Saharan Africa and EU member states.

Nine economies changed regulation of fixed-term contracts. Norway amended the legislation to allow the use of fixed-term contracts for permanent tasks for a 12-month period. Angola permitted the use of fixed-term contracts for permanent tasks and extended their maximum duration to 120 months. Kazakhstan reformed the legislation to allow for two extensions of fixed-term contracts. By contrast, several economies made regulation of fixed-term contracts more rigid. In Zambia fixed-term contracts can no longer be used for permanent tasks. The Netherlands, Poland, Portugal and the United Arab Emirates reduced the maximum duration of fixed-term contracts and in Zimbabwe the maximum duration of fixed-term contracts was left to the discretion of the Employment Council.

Two economies introduced minimum wages in 2015/16. Myanmar established the first national minimum wage and São Tomé and Príncipe introduced the first minimum wage for the private sector. In addition, Mexico eliminated geographic differences related to minimum wages.

Several economies changed regulation of working hours. Cyprus and Hungary, for example, amended the legislation to allow stores to be open on Sundays. Kazakhstan reduced the premium for work on weekly holidays and Angola changed the premiums for overtime and night work as well as work on weekly holidays.

Moreover, seven economies changed the legislation governing redundancy rules and costs. In Kazakhstan, employers are no longer required to reassign an employee to a different position within the company before making the employee redundant. The Netherlands introduced severance pay for redundancy dismissals for employees with at least two years of continuous employment. Zimbabwe significantly reduced the severance package for redundancy dismissals, which was previously among the highest in the world. Angola and Myanmar increased severance pay requirements for some workers and decreased for others, depending on the length of job tenure. The Comoros reduced the length of notice period and the amount of severance pay for redundancy dismissals and Saudi Arabia increased the notice period for redundancy dismissals.

Finally, in 2015/16 four economies reformed legislation in the area of job quality. The Democratic Republic of Congo enacted a law that prohibits gender discrimination in hiring and Liberia adopted a Decent Work Act that establishes equal remuneration for work of equal value. Cabo Verde introduced unemployment insurance while Brazil expanded eligibility for unemployment benefits.

NOTES

1. Barseghyan 2008; Bruhn 2013; Dabla-Norris, Ho and Kyobe 2016; Deininger and others 2015; Haidar 2012; Kaplan, Piedra and Seira 2011; Monteiro and Assunção 2012.
2. Divanbeigi and Ramalho 2015.
3. Bertrand and Kramarz 2002; Klapper and others 2006; Ciccone and Papaioannou 2007; Bjørnskov and Foss 2008; Dreher and Gassebner 2013.
4. Haidar 2012.
5. Mishra, Nair and Vishwanath 2016.
6. Haidar and Hoshi 2015.
7. Haidar and Hoshi 2015.
8. World Bank 2016b.
9. Rwanda, Ministry of Finance and Economic Planning 2000.
10. Asia-Pacific Economic Association 2015.
11. World Bank Group 2013.
12. Motta, Oviedo and Santini 2010; Klapper and Love 2011; Fritsch and Noseleit 2013.
13. Ozkan, Ozkan and Gunduz 2012.
14. World Economic Forum 2016; Lewis 2009.
15. Geginat and Ramalho 2015.
16. Abotsi (2016) finds that the number of power outages experienced in a typical month has a negative impact on the production efficiency of firms in Africa. He also finds that the number of power outages experienced in a typical month has a negative and significant impact on foreign ownership of firms in Africa.
17. Geginat and Ramalho 2015.
18. Deininger 2003.
19. Galiani and Schargrodsky 2009.
20. The Uniform Law on the Regulation of Credit Information Bureaus (BICs) in the member states of the West African Economic and Monetary Union (UEMOA).
21. Cremers and Ferrell 2014.
22. Lan and Varottil 2015.
23. For more on the World Bank Enterprise Surveys, see the website at http://www.enterprisesurveys.org.
24. Djankov and others 2010.
25. Bird and Oldman 2000.
26. Arvis and others 2010.
27. Hillberry and Zhang 2015.
28. Esposito, Lanau and Pompe 2014; Dakolias 1999; Ball and Kesan 2010; Klerman 2006; Dam 2006.
29. Dam 2006.
30. Islam 2003.
31. Esposito, Lanau and Pompe 2014.
32. These include the Rwanda National Police, National Public Prosecution Authority, the judiciary, Civil Litigation, Rwanda Correctional Services, the bar association and all citizens who interface with justice institutions.
33. Araujo, Ferreira and Funchal 2012.
34. Klapper and Love 2011.
35. Cirmizi, Klapper and Uttamchandani 2010.
36. See World Bank 2012a; Martin and Scarpetta 2011; Loayza and others 2005.
37. World Bank 2012a.

TABLE 3.3 Who reduced regulatory complexity and cost or strengthened legal institutions in 2015/16—and what did they do?

Feature	Economies	Some highlights
Making it easier to start a business		
Simplified preregistration and registration formalities (publication, notarization, inspection, other requirements)	Barbados; Benin; Bolivia; Equatorial Guinea; Fiji; Hong Kong SAR, China; Ireland; Kenya; Myanmar; Niger; Papua New Guinea; Saudi Arabia; Sierra Leone; Sri Lanka; Thailand; Uganda; Vanuatu	Benin eliminated the need to notarize company bylaws. Equatorial Guinea made the process of starting a business easier by eliminating the need to obtain a copy of the business founders' criminal records. Ireland made starting a business easier by removing the requirement for a founder to swear before a commissioner of oaths when incorporating a company. Thailand made starting a business easier by creating a single window for registration payment.
Abolished or reduced paid-in minimum capital requirement	Algeria; Angola; Bahrain; Bosnia and Herzegovina; Burkina Faso; Chad; Indonesia; Mali; Oman; Qatar	Mali reduced the cost of starting a business by reducing the paid-in minimum capital required to register a company. Oman made starting a business easier by removing the requirement to pay the minimum capital within three months of incorporation.
Cut or simplified postregistration procedures (tax registration, social security registration, licensing)	Brazil; China; Colombia; Cyprus; Ecuador; Israel; Kazakhstan; Republic of Korea; Lao PDR; Madagascar; Malawi; Malta; Oman; Rwanda; Serbia; Turkey	Brazil made starting a business faster by implementing an online portal for business licenses in Rio de Janeiro. Lao People's Democratic Republic made starting a business faster by implementing simplified procedures for obtaining a license and registered company seal.
Introduced or improved online procedures	The Bahamas; Cyprus; Czech Republic; Indonesia; Republic of Korea; Morocco; Nigeria; Rwanda; South Africa	The Bahamas made starting a business easier by allowing local limited liability companies to register online. Indonesia made starting a business easier by allowing the use of the online system for name reservation.
Introduced or improved one-stop shop	Arab Republic of Egypt; Indonesia; Malta; Niger; Rwanda; United Arab Emirates	The Arab Republic of Egypt and Niger made starting a business easier by merging procedures at the one-stop shop.
Making it easier to deal with construction permits		
Reduced time for processing permit applications	Algeria; Cameroon; Democratic Republic of Congo; Iraq; Zimbabwe	Algeria enforced legal time limits to process building permit applications. Cameroon put in place a reception desk to check for the completeness of building permit applications upon submission to reduce processing times.
Streamlined procedures	Albania; Botswana; Kazakhstan; Poland; Russian Federation; Serbia; Singapore; United Arab Emirates	Botswana abolished the requirement to submit a rates clearance certificate. Poland eliminated the requirements to obtain technical conditions for utilities, as well as the clearance from the administrator of the public road.
Adopted new building regulations	Albania	Albania lifted the moratorium on issuing construction permits in June 2015.
Improved building control process	Cameroon; Côte d'Ivoire; Madagascar; Philippines; United Arab Emirates	Côte d'Ivoire made procedural information concerning the process of obtaining a building permit openly accessible. The Philippines increased the transparency of building regulations by publishing the required pre-approvals to obtain a building permit.
Reduced fees	France; San Marino	France adopted a fixed fee schedule for warehouses and slightly reduced the tariff per square meter for building fees. San Marino set a fixed fee for building permits.
Introduced or improved one-stop shop	Serbia; Singapore	Serbia made it mandatory to request a building permit online through the e-permit system. Singapore improved its one-stop shop, CORENET (Construction and Real Estate Network) e-submission system.
Making it easier to get electricity		
Improved regulation of connection processes and costs	Belarus; Lithuania	Belarus made it cheaper to obtain a new electricity connection by setting fixed prices for connections to electric networks and revising the connection fee structure.
Improved process efficiency	Albania; Azerbaijan; Belarus; Czech Republic; Dominican Republic; Hong Kong SAR, China; India; Indonesia; Iraq; Kazakhstan; Lithuania; Moldova; Poland; Portugal; United Arab Emirates	Lithuania introduced time limits for the utility to connect clients. The Dominican Republic made getting an electricity connection faster by enacting time limits for the utility to approve electrical connection plans. Portugal made getting an electricity connection faster by reducing the time required to approve electrical connection requests.
Streamlined approval process	Brunei Darussalam; Hong Kong SAR, China; Kenya	Hong Kong SAR, China, streamlined the processes of reviewing applications as site inspections can now be conducted without involving the customer. Kenya introduced the use of a geographic information system which eliminated the need to conduct a site visit.
Facilitated more reliable power supply and transparency of tariff information	Algeria; Brunei Darussalam; Bulgaria; Georgia; Kazakhstan; Lao PDR; United Arab Emirates	The utility in Lao PDR started fully recording the duration and frequency of outages to compute annual SAIDI and SAIFI. Algeria made getting electricity more transparent by publishing electricity tariffs on the websites of the utility and the energy regulator.

TABLE 3.3 Who reduced regulatory complexity and cost or strengthened legal institutions in 2015/16—and what did they do?

Feature	Economies	Some highlights
Making it easier to register property		
Increased reliability of infrastructure	Belarus; Indonesia; Mauritius; Mexico; Pakistan; Puerto Rico (U.S.)	Indonesia digitized its cadastral records and set up a geographic information system. In Pakistan the Punjab province launched the Land Records Management and Information Program in order to strengthen the capacity of land administration institutions in Lahore. In Puerto Rico (U.S.), the Registry of Immovable Property was digitized and the majority of land records became accessible in digital format.
Increased transparency of information	Guyana; Kenya; Qatar; Senegal; Singapore; United Arab Emirates; Uzbekistan; Zimbabwe	Senegal made the list of documents, service standards and official fees to complete a property transaction available online and also updated the cadastral map. The United Arab Emirates published the list of service standards for any operation at the Dubai Land Department.
Reduced taxes or fees	The Bahamas; Comoros; Zambia	The Bahamas decreased the property transfer tax from 10% to 2.5% of the property value. Zambia reduced the property transfer tax from 10% to 5% of the property value.
Increased administrative efficiency	Morocco; Rwanda; Sweden	Sweden introduced a new administrative process for automatic registration of mortgages and renewal of ownership.
Setting up effective time limits	Serbia	Serbia introduced effective time limits for the registration of property rights at the real estate cadaster.
Increased geographic coverage	Georgia	Georgia reached full coverage of all maps for privately held land plots in the main business city.
Strengthening legal rights of borrowers and lenders		
Created a unified and/or modern collateral registry for movable property	Armenia; The Gambia; Indonesia; FYR Macedonia; Malawi; Nigeria; Papua New Guinea	Armenia strengthened access to credit by adopting a new law on secured transactions that establishes a modern and centralized collateral registry.
Introduced a functional and secured transactions system	The Gambia; FYR Macedonia; Malawi; Papua New Guinea	The Gambia strengthened access to credit by adopting the Security Interests in Moveable Property Act. The new law on secured transactions implements a functional secured transactions system. The law regulates functional equivalents to loans secured with movable property, such as financial leases and sales with retention of title.
Allowed for general description of assets that can be used as collateral	FYR Macedonia	The former Yugoslav Republic of Macedonia implemented new laws which allow for the general description of assets granted as collateral.
Expanded range of movable assets that can be used as collateral	Papua New Guinea	Papua New Guinea introduced a new law that broadens the scope of assets which can be used as collateral to secure a loan.
Granted absolute priority to secured creditors or allowed out-of-court enforcement	The Gambia; Papua New Guinea; Vanuatu	The Gambia introduced a new law that allows out-of-court enforcement.
Granted exemptions to secured creditors from automatic stay in insolvency proceedings	Brunei Darussalam	Brunei Darussalam adopted a new insolvency law that contemplates protections for secured creditors during an automatic stay in reorganization proceedings.
Improving the sharing of credit information		
Expanded scope of information collected and reported by credit bureau or registry	Brunei Darussalam; China; Tanzania; Tunisia	In Brunei Darussalam the credit registry began distributing data from two utility companies in its credit reports with information on their clients' payment histories.
Improved regulatory framework for credit reporting	Armenia; Burkina Faso; Mozambique; Myanmar; Togo; Zimbabwe	Zimbabwe strengthened its credit reporting system by amending an act to allow for the establishment of a credit registry.
Established a new credit bureau or registry	Côte d'Ivoire; Latvia; Mali; Malta; Niger; Senegal; Solomon Islands	Côte d'Ivoire, Mali, Niger and Senegal established a new credit bureau, Creditinfo VoLo, which banks can consult to assess the creditworthiness of consumer and commercial borrowers.
Guaranteed by law borrowers' right to inspect data	Bahrain; Pakistan	Bahrain introduced amendments to the Central Bank of Bahrain and Financial Institutions Law guaranteeing borrowers' right to inspect their own data.
Introduced bureau or registry credit scores as a value added service	Belarus; Cambodia; China; Malaysia; Morocco; Thailand	In Cambodia the credit bureau began offering credit scoring in June 2015 to facilitate the assessment of the repayment capacity of borrowers.
Introduced online access to the credit information	Mauritania	Mauritania provided banks and financial institutions online access to the data of the credit registry.
Expanded borrower coverage by credit bureau or registry	Guyana; Lesotho; Pakistan; Tanzania	Guyana expanded the number of borrowers listed by its credit bureau with information on their borrowing history from the past five years to more than 5% of the adult population.

TABLE 3.3 Who reduced regulatory complexity and cost or strengthened legal institutions in 2015/16—and what did they do?		
Feature	**Economies**	**Some highlights**
Strengthening minority investor protections		
Increased disclosure requirements for related-party transactions	Croatia; Kenya; Mauritania; Sri Lanka; Ukraine	Croatia amended its companies act to require that directors disclose in detail all relevant facts about the nature, relationship and existence of their conflicts of interest in a proposed transaction.
Enhanced access to information in shareholder actions	FYR Macedonia; Niger	Niger amended its civil procedure code and addressed the allocation of legal expenses at the conclusion of a civil action.
Expanded shareholders' role in company management	Belarus; Arab Republic of Egypt; Fiji; Georgia; Kazakhstan; FYR Macedonia; Morocco; Saudi Arabia; Ukraine; United Arab Emirates; Uzbekistan; Vanuatu; Vietnam	Vanuatu's new companies act stipulates that the sale of 50% of the assets of a company must be approved by the shareholders and that changes to their rights must be approved by the affected shareholders.
Increased director liability	Belarus; Brunei Darussalam; Kenya; Mauritania; Ukraine; Vietnam	Vietnam adopted a law that mandates that liable directors repay profits derived from a transaction in which they had a conflict of interest.
Making it easier to pay taxes		
Introduced or enhanced electronic systems	Albania; Argentina; Brunei Darussalam; Cyprus; El Salvador; Georgia; India; Indonesia; Italy; Jamaica; Japan; Kosovo; Latvia; Malaysia; Moldova; Mongolia; Montenegro; Netherlands; Philippines; Portugal; Singapore; Spain; Tajikistan; Turkey; Uganda; Uruguay	Albania launched an upgraded online platform for filing corporate income tax, value added tax and labor contributions as of January 1, 2015. One consolidated online return for mandatory contributions and payroll taxes was integrated within the online system. The Philippines introduced online filing and payment of health contributions as of April 1, 2015.
Reduced profit tax rate	Dominica; Dominican Republic; Guatemala; Peru; Portugal; San Marino; Senegal; Tajikistan; Uzbekistan	Portugal reduced the corporate income tax rate from 23% to 21% as of January 1, 2015. Senegal reduced the maximum corporate income tax collectable. San Marino allowed companies incorporated after January 1, 2014, to benefit from a 50% corporate income tax reduction for the first six years of activity.
Reduced labor taxes and mandatory contributions	Japan (Osaka); Netherlands; New Zealand; Uzbekistan	The Netherlands reduced the rates for health insurance contribution, special unemployment contribution and unemployment insurance contribution as of January 1, 2015.
Reduced taxes other than profit tax and labor taxes	Algeria; Angola; Argentina; Cyprus; Italy; Montenegro; Netherlands; Singapore; Slovak Republic; Spain; Tajikistan	Algeria reduced tax on professional activity from 2% to 1% of turnover as of July 1, 2015. Cyprus increased the discount rate for immovable property tax from 15% to 20% in 2015.
Merged or eliminated taxes other than profit tax	Azerbaijan; Bosnia and Herzegovina; Jamaica; Japan; New Zealand; Puerto Rico (U.S.); Singapore; Spain; Vietnam	Bosnia and Herzegovina abolished the tourist fee at the end of January 2015. Puerto Rico (U.S.) abolished the national gross receipt tax in 2015.
Allowed for more deductible expenses or depreciation	Angola; Hungary; Italy; Jamaica; Jordan; Kosovo; Spain	Angola increased the tax deduction for bad debt provisions from 2% to 4%. Italy increased the rate of the notional interest deduction from 4% to 4.5% in 2015.
Simplified tax compliance processes or decreased number of tax filings or payments	Algeria; Angola; Burundi; Georgia; Mauritania; Portugal; Senegal; Slovak Republic; Togo; Vietnam	Burundi introduced a new unique tax return and eliminated the personalized value added tax declaration form. Mauritania reduced the frequency of filing and payment of value added tax returns.
Making it easier to trade across borders		
Introduced or improved electronic submission and processing of documents for exports	Afghanistan; Azerbaijan; Georgia; Haiti; India; Indonesia; Islamic Republic of Iran; Jamaica; Jordan; Kosovo; Kuwait; Madagascar; Mauritania; Nepal; Oman; Pakistan; Paraguay; St. Lucia; Togo; Uganda; Vietnam	Georgia reduced export document processing time from 48 hours to 2 hours by improving its document processing system. Jamaica and Nepal reduced export documentary compliance time. Kosovo introduced electronic payments electronic submission of export declarations and reduced export documentary compliance time. Oman and Paraguay introduced a new online single window that decreased export border compliance time.
Introduced or improved electronic submission and processing of documents for imports	Afghanistan; Argentina; Azerbaijan; Brazil; Georgia; Ghana; Grenada; Haiti; India; Indonesia; Islamic Republic of Iran; Jordan; Kosovo; Kuwait; Madagascar; Mauritania; Morocco; Nepal; Niger; Oman; Pakistan; Rwanda; St. Lucia; Togo; Vietnam	Argentina introduced a new Import Monitoring System, which reduced the time for import documentary compliance from 336 hours to 192 hours. Ghana, Niger and Rwanda removed the pre-arrival assessment inspection for imports which reduced import documentary compliance time.
Entered a customs union or signed a trade agreement with major trade partner for exports and imports	Kosovo; Kyrgyz Republic	The Kyrgyz Republic reduced time for exporting by 10 hours and the cost of exporting by $85 by becoming a member of the Eurasian Economic Union. Albania and Kosovo launched an Albania-Kosovo Transit Corridor that decreased the export compliance time by 15 hours.
Strengthened transport or port infrastructure for exports	Jordan	Infrastructure improvements in Jordan decreased border compliance time by 2.1 hours for exports.
Strengthened transport or port infrastructure for imports	Bahrain; Haiti; Jordan	Bahrain, Jordan and Haiti improved infrastructure and streamlined procedures which decreased export border compliance.
Reduced documentary burden for exports and imports	Antigua and Barbuda; Kazakhstan	Antigua and Barbuda removed the tax compliance certificate for import customs clearance, which decreased the time and costs for import documentation. Kazakhstan removed two documents required for customs clearance, which reduced the export documentary compliance time.

TABLE 3.3 Who reduced regulatory complexity and cost or strengthened legal institutions in 2015/16—and what did they do?

Feature	Economies	Some highlights
Making it easier to enforce contracts		
Expanded the alternative dispute resolution framework	Armenia; Brazil; Moldova	Armenia, Brazil and Moldova introduced laws regulating voluntary mediation and setting incentives for the parties to attempt mediation.
Introduced a small claims court or a dedicated procedure for small claims	Côte d'Ivoire; Indonesia	Côte d'Ivoire and Indonesia each introduced a fast-track procedure to be used for the resolution of small claims. Both allow litigants to represent themselves during this procedure.
Introduced or expanded specialized commercial court	India; Niger	India and Niger each introduced dedicated venues to resolve commercial disputes.
Introduced significant changes to the applicable civil procedure rules	Bolivia; Brazil; Ecuador; Greece; Kazakhstan; Niger; Syrian Arab Republic	Bolivia and Ecuador each introduced a new Code of Civil Procedure regulating pre-trial conference. Kazakhstan and Niger each added measures of case management to their new rules on civil procedure.
Introduced electronic filing	Brunei Darussalam; Hungary; Norway; Spain	Brunei Darussalam, Hungary, Norway and Spain introduced an electronic filing system for commercial cases, allowing attorneys to submit the initial summons online.
Expanded court automation	Brunei Darussalam; Rwanda; Ukraine	Brunei Darussalam and Ukraine introduced a system allowing court users to pay court fees electronically. Rwanda introduced an electronic case management system for the use of judges and lawyers.
Making it easier to resolve insolvency		
Introduced a new restructuring procedure	Benin; Brunei Darussalam; Burkina Faso; Cameroon; Central African Republic; Chad; Comoros; Democratic Republic of Congo; Republic of Congo; Côte d'Ivoire; Equatorial Guinea; Gabon; Guinea; Guinea-Bissau; Kenya; Mali; Niger; Poland; Senegal; Togo	Poland introduced new restructuring mechanisms and established a centralized restructuring and bankruptcy register.
Improved the likelihood of successful reorganization	Brunei Darussalam; Kenya; Thailand	Brunei Darussalam made changes to its insolvency framework, including provisions authorizing post-commencement credit during insolvency proceedings and establishing rules for priority repayment of post-commencement creditors.
Improved provisions on treatment of contracts during insolvency	Brunei Darussalam; Kenya; Vanuatu	Vanuatu allowed avoidance of undervalued transactions concluded prior to commencement of insolvency proceedings.
Regulated the profession of insolvency administrators	Brunei Darussalam; Kenya	Kenya updated its insolvency framework, including stricter requirements for qualifications of insolvency administrators.
Strengthened creditors' rights	Kazakhstan; FYR Macedonia	Kazakhstan provided additional protections to creditors in the process of voting on the reorganization plan.
Changing labor legislation		
Altered hiring rules	Angola; Kazakhstan; Mexico; Myanmar; Netherlands; Norway; Poland; Portugal; São Tomé and Príncipe; United Arab Emirates; Zambia; Zimbabwe	Norway amended the legislation to allow the use of fixed-term contracts for permanent tasks. Myanmar introduced a national minimum wage and São Tomé and Príncipe introduced a minimum wage for the private sector.
Amended regulation of working hours	Angola; Cyprus; France; Hungary; Kazakhstan; Liberia	Cyprus and Hungary changed the legislation to allow stores to be open on Sundays. Kazakhstan reduced the premium for work on weekly holidays.
Changed redundancy rules and cost	Angola; Comoros; Kazakhstan; Myanmar; Netherlands; Saudi Arabia; Zimbabwe	Kazakhstan eliminated the requirement to reassign an employee to a different position before making the employee redundant. The Netherlands introduced severance pay for redundancy dismissals for employees with at least two years of continuous employment. Zimbabwe significantly reduced the severance package for redundancy dismissals.
Reformed legislation regulating worker protection and social benefits	Brazil; Cabo Verde; Democratic Republic of Congo; Liberia	The Democratic Republic of Congo enacted a law that prohibits gender discrimination in hiring. Liberia established equal remuneration for work of equal value. Cabo Verde introduced an unemployment insurance scheme.

Source: Doing Business database.

Note: Reforms affecting the labor market regulation indicators are included here but do not affect the ranking on the ease of doing business.

Getting Electricity

Factors affecting the reliability of electricity supply

- The getting electricity indicators measure the reliability of electricity supply using data on the duration and frequency of power outages, among other metrics.
- A broad range of variables impact the reliability of electricity supply. These include the electricity generation adequacy, the condition of power system infrastructure, utility financial and operational performance and energy sector regulation.
- Evidence from four lower-middle-income economies with varying levels of reliability suggests that continuous investment in infrastructure is essential to ensure a reliable electricity supply.
- Indonesia implemented structural changes to its energy sector, increased investment in infrastructure and introduced regulatory initiatives to improve overall power reliability.
- Guatemala liberalized its energy sector and adopted different tariff strategies while maintaining incentives to enable cost recovery. These measures, coupled with the presence of an overarching regulatory body, fostered a high level of power reliability in Guatemala City.
- In the cases of Cameroon and Pakistan, inadequate end-user tariff levels and high transmission and distribution losses had an impact on the overall financial standing of utilities—and, in turn, on the reliability of supply.
- The experience of these economies suggests that utilities must ensure a healthy financial position so they can invest the necessary resources to increase the reliability of electricity supply.

Since 2011 *Doing Business*, through its getting electricity indicator set, has recorded the time, cost and number of procedures required for a small to medium-size business to legally connect a commercial warehouse to the electrical grid. Starting in 2015, the reliability of supply and the price of electricity have also been measured. Reliability is measured through quantitative data on the duration and frequency of power outages as well as through qualitative information, which includes—among other things—the mechanisms put in place by the utility for monitoring power outages. These measures are important because a reliable electricity supply is critical for enterprises to operate and grow. According to 2016 World Bank Enterprise Survey data, business owners in around 30% of developing economies perceive unreliable electricity services as a major obstacle to their activities. In Sub-Saharan Africa, where economies suffered an average of 690 hours of outages in 2015,[1] the annual economic growth drag of a weak power infrastructure is estimated to be about two percentage points.[2] In addition to negatively affecting business operations, an unreliable supply can compromise an economy's overall well-being. For example, Beirut residents cope with an average of three hours with no electricity every day. Residents in other areas of the country must endure 12 hours of daily power outages. The average Lebanese household must then resort to generator usage, spending $1,300 on electricity each year—equivalent to almost 15% of income per capita.[3]

Minimizing the number and the duration of power outages is critical for societies at large. Although electricity is ultimately provided by a distribution utility (the "last step" in the supply chain), it is not the only entity responsible for providing a stable supply, as many other actors play an important role throughout the process of generation, transmission and distribution of electricity. This case study focuses on lower-middle-income economies with varying levels of electricity supply reliability. By comparing different aspects of their energy sectors, this chapter highlights some key elements and actors that can drive, or prevent, a reliable electricity supply.[4]

FACTORS AFFECTING THE PROVISION OF ELECTRICITY

A power system consists of three main components: generation power plants, which use resources like hydropower, coal or renewables to produce electricity; the transmission network, consisting of a high voltage network (usually above 35 kilo-volts) used to transmit electricity from the generation station to the distribution network; and the distribution network, a low-to-medium-voltage network that is used to deliver electricity to customers (figure 4.1).

The reliability of electricity supply is determined by multiple interdependent factors. This case study focuses on four main areas which directly impact the power sector: electricity generation adequacy, power system infrastructure,

FIGURE 4.1 *Doing Business* measures the connection process at the level of distribution utilities

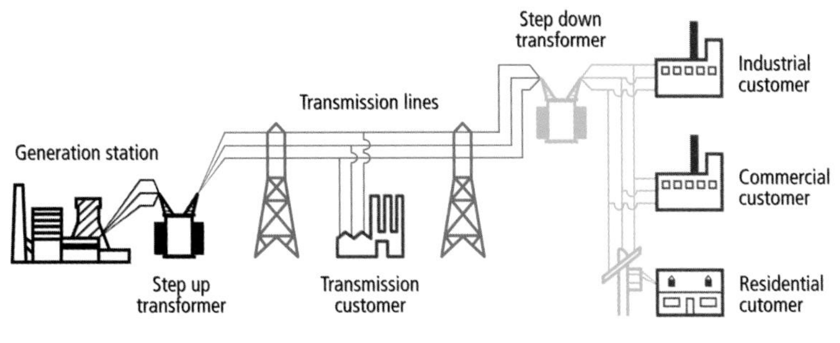

Source: U.S.-Canada Power System Outage Task Force 2004.

utility financial and operational performance, and energy sector regulation (figure 4.2).

Electricity generation is the basis of any power system, and generation adequacy is determined by the availability of resources as well as by their cost. If an economy has sufficient domestic energy resources and the necessary technological conditions, generation may be assured at a lower cost compared to economies that rely on imported fossil fuels. Additionally, energy self-reliance may ensure a higher reliability of supply as it reduces an economy's vulnerability to supply shortages in the global commodity markets.

The upkeep and the technical condition of a power system's infrastructure directly affect its operation and, therefore, the duration and frequency of power cuts. Poor upkeep is further exacerbated when an economy faces exogenous shocks or inclement weather. In Zambia, for example, poorly maintained distribution lines coupled with insufficient rainfall due to the El Niño weather phenomenon resulted in electricity shortages in 2015—with Lusaka experiencing 137 hours of outages per customer. Such power cuts undermine the economy; each minute of outage costs $9,000 to the Zambian mining sector.[5]

FIGURE 4.2 Various factors affect the reliability of electricity supply

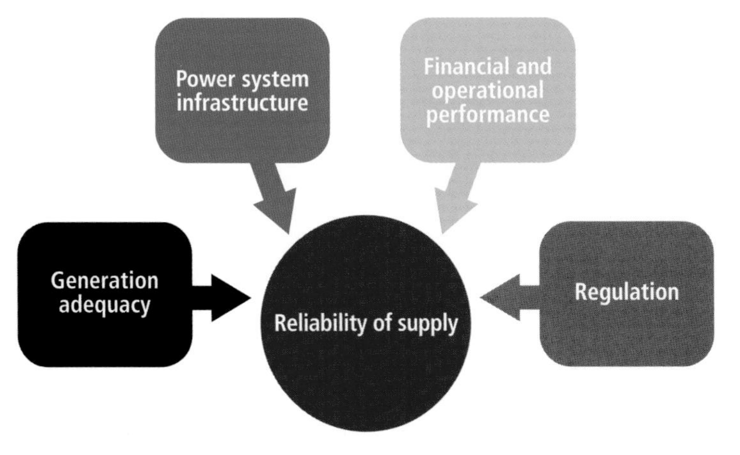

The financial performance of a utility depends on its ability to generate sufficient revenue to cover the costs of providing electricity and to ensure the profitability of its operations. End-user tariffs are a central aspect of the sector's financial performance because the revenues of all market players in an energy system—including the generation, transmission and distribution companies—come from electricity bills. In principle, tariffs take into account the costs involved in the operation of the power system. However, when tariffs do not allow for full cost recovery, insufficient revenues accrued by distribution utilities can create financial constraints across the power system. This may force cutbacks on maintenance spending and capital investments, resulting in increased production costs and a deterioration of power system reliability. In addition to tariff pricing, a utility's operational performance is crucial for the electricity sector as without proper attention to market factors, its ability to ensure electricity provision can be compromised. Ownership structure in the power sector varies greatly across economies, including purely public, private, or mixed partnership. Regardless of a utility's ownership type, having an efficient management structure is essential.

Finally, it is the role of the energy regulator to set the "rules of the game" for all players. Since the electricity market is often monopolistic, only an independent regulator is in a position to supervise the price of electricity and ensure consumer protection. In terms of electricity reliability, the regulator may set objectives regarding utilities' performance as well as deterrents to reduce the duration and frequency of outages. An example of a financial deterrent can be setting a threshold for the number and/or duration of power outages. In that case, when outages surpass a certain threshold, the regulator can impose penalties or allow for customers to receive compensation. *Doing Business* data reveal that low- and lower-middle-income economies using such financial deterrents had 53 power cuts on average in 2015, while economies in the same income group without financial deterrents to limit outages had three times more outages.

RELIABILITY ACROSS FOUR ECONOMIES

To assess the power reliability in different economies across the dimensions highlighted, this study looks at four lower-middle-income economies. Guatemala and Indonesia are examples of economies that provide a reliable electricity supply in the main business cities, having registered low levels of outages in 2015, according to *Doing Business* data (table 4.1.). Cameroon and Pakistan, however, have outages on a regular basis and are examples of economies providing an unreliable supply for customers (table 4.2.).[6] For the other aspects analyzed, the majority of the data are from 2014. In some cases, newer data were available but the same base year was chosen for cross-comparability purposes.

Reliable electricity supply

Indonesia

From an energy perspective, Indonesia faces considerable challenges: it has the fourth largest population globally, a complex geography and falling oil reserves. Nevertheless, Indonesia has achieved a high level of electrification with 96% of the total population having access to electricity in 2012, up from 67% in 1990.[7] Furthermore, the frequency and duration of power outages in Jakarta and Surabaya today are low compared to other economies in East Asia and the Pacific. System average interruption duration index (SAIFI) data suggest that a business in Jakarta only suffered two outages in 2015, almost nine times less than the regional average. As electricity outages and tariff levels are relatively low in Java,[8] where over half of Indonesians live, it is then not surprising to observe that the World Bank Enterprise Surveys report that less than 1% of firms in Indonesia see electricity as their "biggest obstacle"—compared to almost 10% of firms worldwide. This reflects a well-performing power sector in Indonesia's largest municipalities, yet major investments had to be made to overcome several challenges.

In the 1990s, power outages were a common occurrence in Jakarta. Rising electricity demand coupled with the 1997 Asian financial crisis placed a heavy strain on the system. Generation activities—as well as transmission and distribution—were conducted exclusively by Perusahaan Listrik Negara (PLN), the state-owned, vertically-integrated utility. However, the 1999 electricity law opened up the electricity generation market to the private sector. With the entrance of new actors, installed generation capacity was able to expand substantially. At the end of 2014, independent power producers and private utilities accounted for approximately 30% of Indonesia's installed generation capacity.[9]

In parallel to the partial liberalization of the sector, the government of Indonesia also devised ambitious infrastructure investment plans to meet rising electricity demand.[10] Between 2004 and 2014, generation capacity doubled from 26.4 gigawatts to 53.0 gigawatts[11] through a mix of private and public investments. These investments allowed the country to diversify electricity production and reduce reliance on oil, of which Indonesia is a net importer, increasing the share of natural gas (21%), hydropower (7%) and geothermal power (5%) in its generation mix.[12]

While Indonesia's success vis-à-vis power reliability is largely attributed to infrastructure development, regulatory deterrents to prevent utility underperformance may also have contributed to minimizing power cuts. Per government regulation, customers experiencing outages beyond certain levels are eligible for compensation from PLN. And *Doing Business* data now suggest that PLN in Jakarta is a good performer if the time needed to get a new permanent electricity connection is used as a proxy to gauge utility efficiency.[13] It took 59 days to get a new electrical connection in Jakarta in 2016 compared to 101 days in 2009. This improvement is the result of better customer engagement and the streamlining of administrative processes as highlighted by several reforms recorded by *Doing Business*.

A stable electricity supply in Indonesia has been achieved over the past decades mostly by supply-side initiatives. On the demand side, the country has not sought to limit consumption through tariffs. In fact, the pricing policy pursued by the government aims to balance the financial standing of the utility with the affordability of electricity tariffs. Tariffs are, therefore, set below market levels, but PLN is compensated through subsidies that allow for a profit margin of 7%.[14] Tariffs are also routinely reviewed by the regulator. End-user tariffs were raised by 15% in 2013, for example, to help improve PLN's financial performance in the wake of rising energy prices.

Even though access to reliable electricity has improved in Java, Indonesia still faces considerable challenges going forward. According to the Indonesian Ministry of Energy and Mineral Resources, over 12,000 villages in the country are still without electricity and approximately 65% of them are in six provinces in eastern Indonesia.[15] In the coming years, it will be crucial for the country to pursue its *Indonesia Terang* (Bright Indonesia) plan by building island-based generation capacity infrastructure and expanding access to electricity across the archipelago.

Guatemala

Substantial improvements to the reliability of electricity supply have been achieved in Guatemala, particularly in the capital. Although some regions still struggle to provide a reliable electricity supply, residents of Guatemala City had, on average, less than three outages in

2015 compared to an average 13 power cuts in the other main business cities of Latin America and the Caribbean. This is quite a feat considering concerns two decades ago about potential shortfalls in generation capacity due to rising demand—which increased by 7% annually on average between 1986 and 2012.[16] As in Indonesia, Guatemala's first push to boost capacity involved opening the energy sector to private participation.

Unlike its Southeast Asian counterpart, however, Guatemala unbundled the entire energy sector in 1996 through a general electricity law. Competition was introduced, with private and public players entering the generation, transmission, electricity trading and distribution segments. As a result, the Instituto Nacional de Electrificación (INDE), which previously controlled all assets from generation to distribution, now operates 15% of Guatemala's installed generation capacity. The remaining 85% is operated by a variety of private companies.[17] The private sector is also present in the electricity transmission sector and in the distribution sector, where the privately-owned Energuate controls 60% of the market share.[18]

Within two decades of its adoption, the electricity law spurred a series of investments which have more than tripled Guatemala's installed capacity from 1.0 gigawatts to 3.7 gigawatts.[19] This increase in capacity was accompanied by a diversification of the energy mix, notably through tariff and tax incentives, thereby encouraging the use of renewable resources. In 1996, 31% of Guatemalan electricity was generated from oil, and biofuel accounted for 13%.[20] Twenty years later, biofuel's share has grown to 38% and the share of oil-based generation has fallen to 12%.[21] Furthermore, the Central American regional electricity market has provided some flexibility to Guatemala, allowing it to export its excess supply of electricity (or to import it when needed).[22]

Following the liberalization program, the government recognized the need to create a regulatory framework to oversee the new competitive market. The national electricity commission, an independent regulatory body, was established in 1996. The commission sets the market rules, monitors power outages and imposes financial penalties on utilities when excessive service interruptions occur. End-user tariffs are also regulated by the commission and are classified into two categories: a "regular rate"—which is determined based on the blended costs of supply from generation companies, as well as transmission and distribution costs—and a subsidized "social rate" for consumers with monthly demand of up to 300 kilowatt-hours.[23] Utilities can thus recuperate their capital investments while, at the same time, consumers are protected from price gouging.[24]

Doing Business data also suggest that the improved reliability in Guatemala City may be partly attributed to effective utility management. *Doing Business* ranks Guatemala among the highest in Latin America and the Caribbean for utility performance; it takes just 39 days to get a new connection to the electrical grid in Guatemala compared to the regional average of 66 days.

TABLE 4.1 Reliability of supply and transparency of tariff index for Guatemala and Indonesia

	Guatemala	Indonesia
Reliability of supply and transparency of tariff index (0–8)	**7**	**6**
Total duration and frequency of outages per customer a year (0–3)	2	2
System average interruption duration index (SAIDI) in 2015	3.7	2.6
System average interruption frequency index (SAIFI) in 2015	2.6	1.7
Mechanisms for monitoring outages (0–1)	1	1
Does the distribution utility use automated tools to monitor outages?	Yes	Yes
Mechanisms for restoring service (0–1)	1	1
Does the distribution utility use automated tools to restore service?	Yes	Yes
Regulatory monitoring (0–1)	1	1
Does a regulator monitor the utility's performance on reliability of supply?	Yes	Yes
Financial deterrents aimed at limiting outages (0–1)	1	1
Does the utility either pay compensation to customers or face fines by the regulator (or both) if outages exceed a certain cap?	Yes	Yes
Communication of tariffs and tariff changes (0–1)	1	0
Are effective tariffs available online?	Yes	Yes
Are customers notified of tariff changes at least 1 month ahead of time?	Yes	No

Source: Doing Business database.

Note: SAIDI is the average total duration of outages over the course of a year for each customer served, while SAIFI is the average number of service interruptions experienced by a customer in a year. For Indonesia, SAIDI/SAIFI data are for Jakarta only.

Unreliable electricity supply

Cameroon

Cameroon was one of the first Sub-Saharan African economies to liberalize its energy sector. The adoption of the 1998 Electricity Sector Law led to the privatization of the vertically-integrated and state-owned utility, the Société Nationale d'Electricité (SONEL).[25] Nonetheless, the total installed generation capacity remained largely stagnant between 2000 (0.8 gigawatts) and 2012 (1.0 gigawatts)[26] in view of Cameroon's rising energy needs and population growth. As a result, Cameroon faces a severe electricity supply deficit—even though about half of the population is not connected to the grid.[27] Douala residents experienced on average almost two hours of outages each week in 2015. This has likely impacted business behavior; approximately 35% of firms in Cameroon own a generator.[28]

Cameroon's privatization program has not resulted in a sharp rise in installed capacity nor has it established a fully competitive market. Power generation is open to independent private sector participation, yet the sector remains largely dominated by one company, ENEO Cameroon (formerly SONEL). Because the power sector is not fully unbundled, the transmission and distribution sectors are also operated by ENEO Cameroon, which struggles with transmission losses. For example, 35% of the electricity generated from hydro-powered and gas plants is lost through electricity transmission.[29] In this context, the government recently announced the establishment of a new state-owned entity, the Société Nationale de Transport de l'Electricité (Sonatrel), which will take over the transmission sector with the goal of upgrading the power infrastructure.

Cameroon relies entirely on domestically-sourced resources, with hydropower accounting for 71% of generated electricity, and oil and gas making up the balance.[30] While it could export electricity to neighboring economies thanks to an abundance of natural resources, that potential is under-exploited.[31] Cameroon's heavy reliance on hydroelectricity has also meant that droughts often result in prolonged outages. This was the case in 2015 as power outages brought activities at the Douala port to a standstill for several days.[32] To prevent such scenarios in the future, Cameroon is aiming to diversify its energy mix and boost generation capacity through a series of tax-based incentives for renewable electricity generation projects.

The electricity sector law of 1998 created the Agence de Régulation du Secteur de l'Electricité (ARSEL), a regulatory agency responsible for setting end-user tariffs. The agency's duties also include the monitoring of power outages and the levying of penalties on utilities for non-compliance with outage limits. Nevertheless, such penalties were not imposed between 2012 and 2015 as ARSEL opted instead to hold tariffs steady, thereby providing customers with lower tariffs in real terms in "compensation" for excessive outages.[33]

Cameroon's energy sector faces considerable challenges. However, *Doing Business* data suggest that reliability issues in Douala stem more from the generation mix and infrastructure than from utility management. Obtaining a new electricity connection, for example, takes on average 64 days in Cameroon, about half the average time in the Sub-Saharan Africa region.

Pakistan

Pakistan is in the midst of an energy crisis. The rapid expansion of the economy in recent decades has led to increased energy demand. In 2011, electricity shortages exceeded 7.0 gigawatts, equal to about one-third of peak demand.[34] And while Pakistan was able to increase its level of electrification from 60% in 1990 to 94% in 2012,[35] the frequency and duration of outages remain high in its two largest cities. *Doing Business* data show that Karachi and Lahore were among the cities that experienced the most outages globally in 2015. Indeed, World Bank Enterprise Survey data report that for 45% of enterprises in Pakistan, a lack of reliable electricity supply is the largest obstacle to the operation of their business.

After three decades of energy sector expansion, privatization in Pakistan began in 1994 with the unbundling of the Water and Power Development Authority and the opening of power generation to independent producers. Subsequent reforms, such as the provision of incentives for private investments, were pursued in the late 1990s leading to an inflow of private capital and an increase in generation capacity.[36] However, declining investment following the 1997 Asian financial crisis coupled with surging local demand resulted in a severe electricity deficit. Between

TABLE 4.2 Reliability of supply and transparency of tariff index for Cameroon and Pakistan

	Cameroon	Pakistan
Reliability of supply and transparency of tariff index (0–8)	**3**	**0**
Total duration and frequency of outages per customer a year (0–3)	0	0
System average interruption duration index (SAIDI) in 2015	89	861.7
System average interruption frequency index (SAIFI) in 2015	23.3	387.2
Mechanisms for monitoring outages (0–1)	0	1
Does the distribution utility use automated tools to monitor outages?	No	Yes
Mechanisms for restoring service (0–1)	0	1
Does the distribution utility use automated tools to restore service?	No	Yes
Regulatory monitoring (0–1)	1	1
Does a regulator monitor the utility's performance on reliability of supply?	Yes	Yes
Financial deterrents aimed at limiting outages (0–1)	1	1
Does the utility either pay compensation to customers or face fines by the regulator (or both) if outages exceed a certain cap?	Yes	Yes
Communication of tariffs and tariff changes (0–1)	1	0
Are effective tariffs available online?	Yes	Yes
Are customers notified of tariff changes at least 1 month ahead of time?	Yes	No

Source: Doing Business database.

Note: Under the getting electricity methodology if SAIDI/SAIFI is 100 or more then the economy is not eligible to score on the reliability of supply and transparency of tariff index. For Pakistan, SAIDI/SAIFI data are for Karachi only.

2004 and 2008, commercial electricity consumption increased by approximately 8% per year. In addition, the electricity sector's share of total public investment fell from 51% in the mid-1990s to 26% by 2010.[37] As a result, generation capacity was not able to keep up with demand.

Pakistan's generation sector is comprised of different players with private power producers providing about 30% of the total generation capacity. On the distribution end, the sector is operated by 10 state-owned regional utilities and a private company, K-Electric, which serves Karachi. Almost all of the utilities, however, experience the same sets of challenges: shortfalls in electricity supply, chronic transmission and distribution losses[38] and insufficient exploitation of existing capacity.

Pakistan's electricity generation mix consists mainly of thermal power (69%) and hydropower (28%).[39] Gas is sourced domestically but the economy is a net importer of oil, which makes the electricity sector reliant on imports and exposed to market fluctuations. Repeated hikes in global oil prices have at times strained the public—and utility—finances, but the oil share of electricity generation has grown since the 1990s.[40] Considering this situation, Pakistan has undertaken a power sector reform agenda to address its generation shortfall by further developing its hydropower potential. In this context, hydropower investment projects supported by multilateral institutions such as the World Bank Group have recently been announced.[41]

The regulator, the National Electric Power Regulatory Authority (NEPRA), was established in 1998 as an autonomous body without any government administrative control. However, while NEPRA has jurisdiction on tariffs, all decisions need to be approved by the state, which has led successive governments to set tariff levels in a discretionary manner. Consequently, end-user prices have been set below the cost of supply with the difference being paid to the utility through extensive government subsidies[42]—which are sizeable both in relation to GDP and total general government expenditures.[43] Delays in disbursing these subsidies have at times contributed to debts that have strained the finances of generation companies, undermining investments and the upkeep of the distribution network.

The unreliability of the electricity sector in Pakistan may also be attributed to the state of utility financial and operational performance. According to *Doing Business* data, it takes well over 100 days for a business to connect to electricity in Lahore and Karachi and a new connection costs about 1,770% of the national income per capita, a cost that is among the highest in South Asia.

DRIVERS OF SUPPLY RELIABILITY

Evidence suggests that adequate investment in electricity generation is essential to ensure a reliable electricity supply. Without investment, generation capacity can quickly be overtaken by rising demand, as occurred in Cameroon and Pakistan. The experiences of Guatemala and Indonesia show that investment can be implemented through a strategy pursuing sectoral liberalization or with a vertically-integrated public utility continuing to play a major role in the energy sector, so long as there are incentives to ensure generation adequacy (figure 4.3).

The highlighted good performers underscore the importance of not only investing in productive capacity but also of maintaining the power system infrastructure. Aging infrastructure results in increased losses and a deterioration in the reliability of supply. It is also useful to diversify the energy mix to decrease the dependence on a given resource. A country that is over-reliant on hydropower, for example, might be particularly exposed to droughts, while a country that strongly relies on imported oil may be vulnerable to fluctuations in global crude prices.

Other factors impacting the reliability of supply are tariff levels, bill collection rates and transmission and distribution losses. In many economies, tariffs are calculated taking into account all costs associated with the generation, transmission and distribution of electricity, as well as profit margins and infrastructure maintenance costs. Subsidies, if needed, typically target certain groups of customers for

FIGURE 4.3 Generation capacity from 2000 to 2012

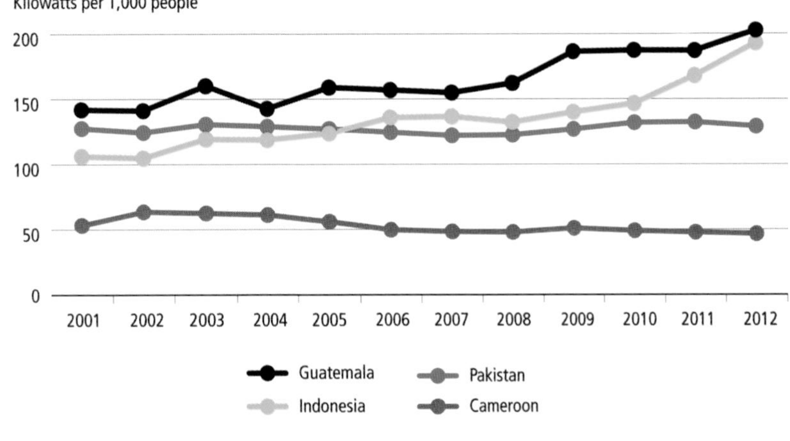

Sources: International Energy Agency database (http://www.iea.org/statistics/); World Bank country data (http://data.worldbank.org/country).

In turn, this poses challenges to the ability of utilities to pay their suppliers.

Pakistan's power sector also grapples with financial challenges. In 2014 electricity tariffs were charged at 20.8 cents per kilowatt-hour,[44] but the bill collection rate was below 80%.[45] Because tariffs were set at below cost-recovery level, generation costs were not entirely recuperated through end-user tariffs. This resulted in chronic debt for the power system.[46]

Transmission and distribution losses, which serve as a metric of operational efficiency for a utility, also affect the financial performance and the reliability of electricity supply. In Cameroon and Pakistan, transmission and distribution losses stand at approximately 30%, compared to 10% or less in Guatemala and Indonesia (figure 4.4). These losses can be divided into technical and commercial losses. Technical losses are due to the natural resistance of the electric cables to the flow of the electric current. They depend on the distance from generators to customers, on the voltage level and the quality of infrastructure, among other factors. Commercial losses are caused by non-payment due to theft, non-registered consumption or improper metering. In OECD high-income economies, commercial losses are minimal and stood at 6.5% in 2012.[47] By contrast, the majority of losses in Cameroon and Pakistan are commercial, considering that—based on World Bank Group energy sector experience—technical losses usually do not exceed 12%. Such high numbers can compromise utilities' financial standing.

FIGURE 4.4 Electric power transmission and distribution losses in 2012

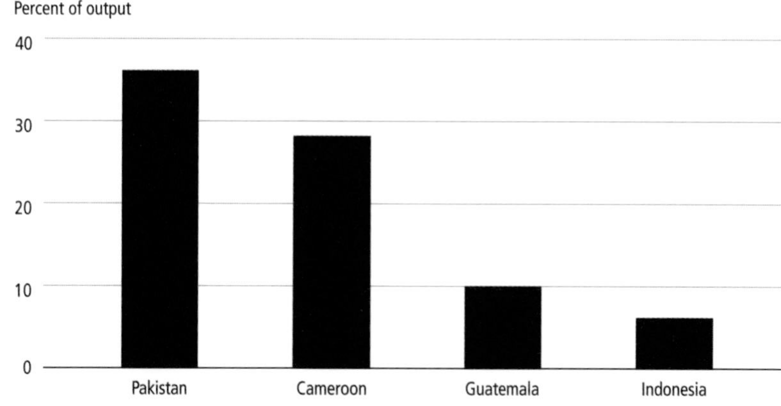

Source: International Energy Agency database (http://www.iea.org/statistics/).

Another key driver of supply reliability is a proper, overarching regulatory framework, as it can ensure adequate tariffs for each customer group and hold utilities accountable for the frequency and duration of power outages. All four economies analyzed have regulatory bodies in place and impose financial deterrents aimed at limiting outages. However, energy regulation cannot by itself ensure a high level of reliability of supply—the frequency and duration of power outages recorded in Guatemala and Indonesia are significantly lower than in Cameroon and Pakistan.

CONCLUSION

The reliability of electricity supply is critical for the development of the private sector—as well as for societies at large. There are multiple interdependent factors that directly affect reliability. Some are beyond the control of policy makers (such as inclement weather or commodity prices) yet many factors are, in fact, actionable if a long-term and comprehensive approach is adopted. Therefore, adequate generation capacity, financial performance, the operational efficiency of the utilities and the overarching regulatory framework need not be treated separately. All of these levers are integral to ensuring that electricity supply meets demand in a sustainable fashion.

With adequate planning and foresight, different strategies can be used to ensure a constant flow of electricity, as policy makers must cope with local market factors and other development objectives such as "greening" the energy mix and making electricity affordable for subsets of the population. The cases of Indonesia and Guatemala are interesting for this reason: growing demand was met through different investment strategies and varying degrees of sectoral liberalization. And while liberalization helped spur investment in these two economies, it has been less of a success in Pakistan and Cameroon where some factors—such as sustainable tariff pricing, sound financial management, high operational performance and balanced energy mix—were partly neglected in the past. As these cases suggest, having a multipronged approach is necessary to ensure the reliability of electricity supply.

NOTES

This case study was written by Jean Arlet, Diane Davoine, Tigran Parvanyan, Jayashree Srinivasan, and Erick Tjong.

1. Average excludes Sub-Saharan African economies for which SAIDI/SAIFI data was unavailable. These economies are: Angola, Benin, Botswana, Burundi, the Central African Republic, Chad, the Republic of Congo, Equatorial Guinea, Ethiopia, The Gambia, Ghana, Guinea-Bissau, Lesotho, Madagascar, Malawi, Mauritius, Mozambique, Namibia, Rwanda, São Tomé and Príncipe, Senegal, Sierra Leone, Somalia, South Africa, South Sudan and Togo. Averages are for the primary business city of each economy and exclude data from Kano, Nigeria.
2. Andersen and Dalgaard 2012.
3. Westall, Sylvia. 2015. "No light at end of tunnel for Lebanon's power crisis." Reuters, October 26. http://www.reuters.com/article/us-lebanon-electricity-idUSKCN0SK1LH20151026/.
4. Exogenous factors, such as natural cataclysms, are not considered in the case study.

5. Mutale, Alexander. 2015. "Zambia: Hello darkness." Financial Mail. May 21. http://www.financialmail.co.za/features/2015/05/21/zambia-hello-darkness; Botah, Tozya. 2016. "How El Nino is affecting Zambia." Zambia Daily Mail. January 14. https://www.daily-mail.co.zm/?p=56004.
6. *Doing Business* collects data on the average frequency and duration of power outages per customer in the main business city of each economy over the course of one year.
7. Data in this section are from the Sustainable Energy for All (SE4ALL) database, World Bank, Washington, DC, http://data.worldbank.org/data-catalog/sustainable-energy-for-all.
8. According to *Doing Business* data commercial tariffs stand at 11 cents per kilowatt-hour in Indonesia in 2016 compared to an average of 23 cents per kilowatt-hour globally.
9. PwC 2015.
10. Electricity demand is rising rapidly in Indonesia (up by 6% in 2014 and forecast by PwC to rise by 9% annually between 2015 and 2019). https://www.pwc.com/id/en/publications/assets/eumpublications/utilities/power-guide-2015.pdf.
11. Indonesia, Ministry of Energy and Mineral Resources 2015.
12. Tharakan 2015.
13. Geginat and Ramalho 2015.
14. Tharakan 2015.
15. The six regions are Maluku, North Maluku, East Nusa Tenggara (NTT), West Nusa Tenggara (NTB), Papua and West Papua.
16. Guatemala, Ministry of Energy and Mines 2013.
17. Guatemala, Ministry of Energy and Mines 2016.
18. Bolaños, Rosa María. 2016. "IC Power compra a Deocsa y Deorsa." Prensa Libre, January 1. http://www.prensalibre.com/economia/energuate-cambiaria-de-dueo-firma-estadounidense-acuerda-compra/.
19. Data in this section are from the international energy statistics database of the U.S. Energy Information Administration, Washington, DC, http://www.eia.gov/cfapps/ipdbproject/IEDIndex3.cfm.
20. According to IEA data, in 2013 the generation mix was: 15.8% coal, 17% oil, 18.1% biomass, 46.9% hydro and 2.1% geothermal.
21. Guatemala, Ministry of Energy and Mines 2016.
22. Although electricity imports and exports have both increased since 2010, Guatemala remains a net energy exporter. Guatemala, Ministry of Energy and Mines 2013.
23. IDB 2013.
24. Guatemala, National Electric Energy Commission 2015.
25. In 2001 SONEL was acquired by the US-based AES Corporation, thereby becoming AES SONEL, and granted a 20-year monopoly over generation, transmission and distribution. In 2014 AES SONEL was acquired by a British group, ACTIS, and renamed ENEO Cameroon.
26. These data are from the Electricity Installed Capacity 1980-2012 section of the Cameroon Data Portal (database), Yaoundé, Cameroon, http://cameroon.opendataforafrica.org/sdjsclb/cameroon-electricity-installed-capacity-1980-2012.
27. Data on access to electricity are for 2012 and are from the World Development Indicators database (http://data.worldbank.org/indicator), World Bank.
28. Enterprise Surveys database (http://www.enterprisesurveys.org/), World Bank.
29. World Bank 2014a.
30. These data are for 2013 and are from the statistical database of the International Energy Agency, Paris, France, http://www.iea.org/statistics/.
31. According to the World Bank, Cameroon has the third largest hydropower potential in Sub-Saharan Africa with an estimated capacity of 12,000 megawatts.
32. Kindzeka, Moki Edwin. 2015. "Cameroon economy suffers through power failures." VOA News. June 19. http://www.voanews.com/content/cameroon-economy-suffers-through-power-failures/2829060.html.
33. Investingincameroon.com. 2015. "The electricity regulator in Cameroon announced a heavy penalty against Eneo." July 9. http://www.investiraucameroun.com/energie/0907-6527-pour-2015-le-regulateur-de-l-electricite-au-cameroun-annonce-une-lourde-penalite-contre-eneo.
34. Aziz and Ahmad 2015.
35. Data in this section are from the Sustainable Energy for All (SE4ALL) database, World Bank, Washington, DC, http://data.worldbank.org/data-catalog/sustainable-energy-for-all.
36. Installed capacity rose from 7,700 megawatts to 19,300 megawatts and production from 37.7 terawatt hours to 93.8 terawatt hours.
37. Aziz and Ahmad 2015.
38. These are estimated at 23% to 25% in 2016 according to data from the United States Institute of Peace.
39. Kessides 2012.
40. Aziz and Ahmad 2015.
41. World Bank Group 2016.
42. Mills 2012.
43. Kugelman 2013.
44. These data are from the *Doing Business* database and are for 2014.
45. Jamal, Nasir. 2014. "Amount of Unpaid Power Bills Increases to Rs286bn." April 16. http://www.dawn.com/news/1100237.
46. USAID 2016.
47. These data are from the statistical database of the International Energy Agency, Paris, France, http://www.iea.org/statistics/.

Getting Credit: Legal Rights

Two approaches to developing an integrated secured transactions regime

- Modern secured transactions regimes can be regulated either by a piecemeal approach, where various existing laws are amended, or by the passage of a new comprehensive law that encompasses all types of security interests.
- An integrated approach to secured transactions enlarges the scope of assets that small and medium-size enterprises can use as collateral, thus expanding their access to finance. This approach allows the borrower to maintain possession of the collateralized asset for use in its business operations.
- A modern collateral registry—centralized, notice-based and with online public access—is a key ingredient of a well-functioning modern economy. The registry should be unified for all types of movable assets, searchable and accessible online for verifications, registrations, amendments and renewals. By mid-2016, 26 economies had operational, notice-based and modern collateral registries, including Australia, Colombia, the Lao People's Democratic Republic and most recently Costa Rica, El Salvador, Liberia and Malawi.

Secured transactions regimes are designed to make it easier for small and medium-size enterprises to obtain credit and other types of funding from both traditional and nontraditional financial institutions. However, these systems should be supported by effective enforcement mechanisms. The most traditional component of an effective secured transactions system is a guarantee over assets (nonpossessory security interests) where a debtor is authorized to continue operating by using the secured asset for the benefit of their business. In addition to the traditional nonpossessory pledge, other guarantee equivalents have emerged in an effort to increase business capital. For example, with a financial lease, a business can use a leased machine in exchange for monthly payments. However, had this debt not been recorded, future lenders would not have a clear view of the business standing and who has priority over its assets, especially if the business becomes insolvent. The registration of assets in a well-running collateral registry is crucial for the efficient operation of financial institutions.

Reforms to legal frameworks governing secured transactions have increased worldwide in the past decade, benefitting creditors and businesses alike. The enactment of laws that cover all types of lending contracts using movable assets as collateral can expand the scope of assets available to secure repayment of a loan. The capital stock of businesses in most developing economies is typically in movable assets.[1] The ability to use movable assets as collateral is therefore central to improving access to credit and, in a broad sense, to funding. Such collateral can be created on a range of assets. Further, there are many equivalents to traditional collateral where the borrower keeps use of the collateral—often referred to as functional equivalents—including fiduciary transfer of title, financial lease, assignment of receivables and retention-of-title sales (table 5.1). Funding can be achieved not only through traditional bank financing and credit but also through financial lease agreements, for example, that can benefit small and medium-size enterprises unable to raise money directly in the capital markets. Such agreements allow these firms to access funding, thereby preserving their cash flow and increasing their potential for growth.[2]

Creditors are more willing to provide funding when it can be guaranteed with a security interest, meaning property interests created by agreement or by law over the debtor's assets. A good practice associated with collaterals that remain in the possession of the debtor so that the company can continue to use them (that is, the company that received the loan keeps using machines that serve as collateral in order to generate profit for its business and pay back the loan) is for the law to allow for a general description of the collateral. Rather than being specific—300 XYZ laptops, serial number 1234, metal colored, 14-inch screen, for example—a general description of

TABLE 5.1 Examples of functional equivalents

Functional equivalents	Possession (usage of assets)	Ownership title (to asset)	Example
Fiduciary transfer of title (of a movable asset)	Borrower	Lender (Borrower after full loan is paid)	Borrower transfers title of movable asset (for example, a sewing machine) to lender (creditor), but keeps and uses machine. Title of machine is returned to debtor when loan is fully repaid.
Financial lease agreement	Lessee	Lessor (Lessee after full lease is repaid)	Lessor (creditor) owns leased asset which he leases to lessee. Lessee makes payments that amortize full or substantial part of cost of leased asset.
Assignment of receivables	Creditor	Debtor	Debtor assigns right to receive payments from specific account receivables to creditor (lender) but remains owner of accounts.
Sale with retention of title	Debtor	Seller (Debtor upon full repayment of price)	Debtor buys movable asset from seller (creditor), but seller keeps ownership title until debtor repays full price.

"all laptop inventories" would be acceptable. Credit markets also tend to operate better when the law stipulates that all such interests be registered in a collateral registry so as to be enforceable against third parties.

It is essential that national legislation allows for a nonpossessory security interest. A financial lease on a company's machine does not, for example, imply that the machine will be handed over to the lessor but rather that the firm may use the machine to carry on business and generate profits to pay off the debt. A modern collateral registry should protect the nonpossessory security rights of creditors against third parties by ensuring transparency. Legislation should also allow for collateral to cover any assets obtained in the future or acquired after the collateral was created as well as products, proceeds and replacements of the original assets (for example, wood in stock is guaranteed for a loan used to produce furniture that is automatically collateralized).[3] The law should allow for a general description of the assets subject to security, without requiring detailed descriptions or serial numbers, within the scope of the value of the loan. The description should provide enough detail to simply allow the identification of the collateral. Permitting a wide range of assets to be used as collateral provides security for all types of obligations, present and future, including one-time loans and revolving credit lines.

COLLATERAL REGISTRIES

A centralized collateral registry—which encompasses all types of collateral, security interests and their functional equivalents—should support the secured transactions legal and institutional regime at the national level. This registry is distinct from a serial number collateral registry which serves for registration of assets such as motor vehicles, sea-going vessels and aircraft, for example. A modern secured transactions system allows secured creditors to establish their priority to the collateral, in case of business liquidation or default, in an efficient and transparent manner. The collateral registry needs to be centralized nationally, unified for all types of movable assets, accessible online for verifications, registrations, amendments and renewals, searchable by debtor's identifiers and accessible to the general public. The registration process needs to be simple, requiring only the basic information related to the collateral, such as identifiers of the parties, description of the collateral and the secured amount without need for specification. The law should not have as a registration requirement that the underlying security documentation—such as loan agreements, security agreements, and the terms and conditions of the loan—be reported to the collateral registry for the simple reason that the purpose of the registry is only to "give notice" of a security interest and to establish a priority scheme. Also, a notice-based system eliminates the risk of human error by registry employees and reduces the cost of operating the collateral registry. Policy makers should encourage a modest registration fee be charged to offset the operational costs of running the registry.

The introduction of a collateral registry increases the share of firms with access to a line of credit, loan or overdraft (figure 5.1). One study showed that the number of firms with access to finance increased by approximately 8% on average in the period following the introduction of the registry for movable collateral; interest rates also fell and loan maturities were extended. Introducing a new registry for movable collateral has stronger benefits for small firms, which are often more constrained in their access to finance and do not have many fixed assets that can serve as collateral but which, on the other hand, are often the primary generators of new jobs and make a substantial contribution to economic growth, particularly in the developing world.[4]

A ground-breaking property law was approved in China in 2007 and a modern collateral registry was set up in the same year. More than a dozen government policies and regulations concerning movable asset finance have been issued since. As a result, a majority of lending institutions have rolled out various credit products based on movable assets benefiting mostly small and medium-size enterprises but also agribusiness

FIGURE 5.1 The introduction of a collateral registry increases access to finance for businesses

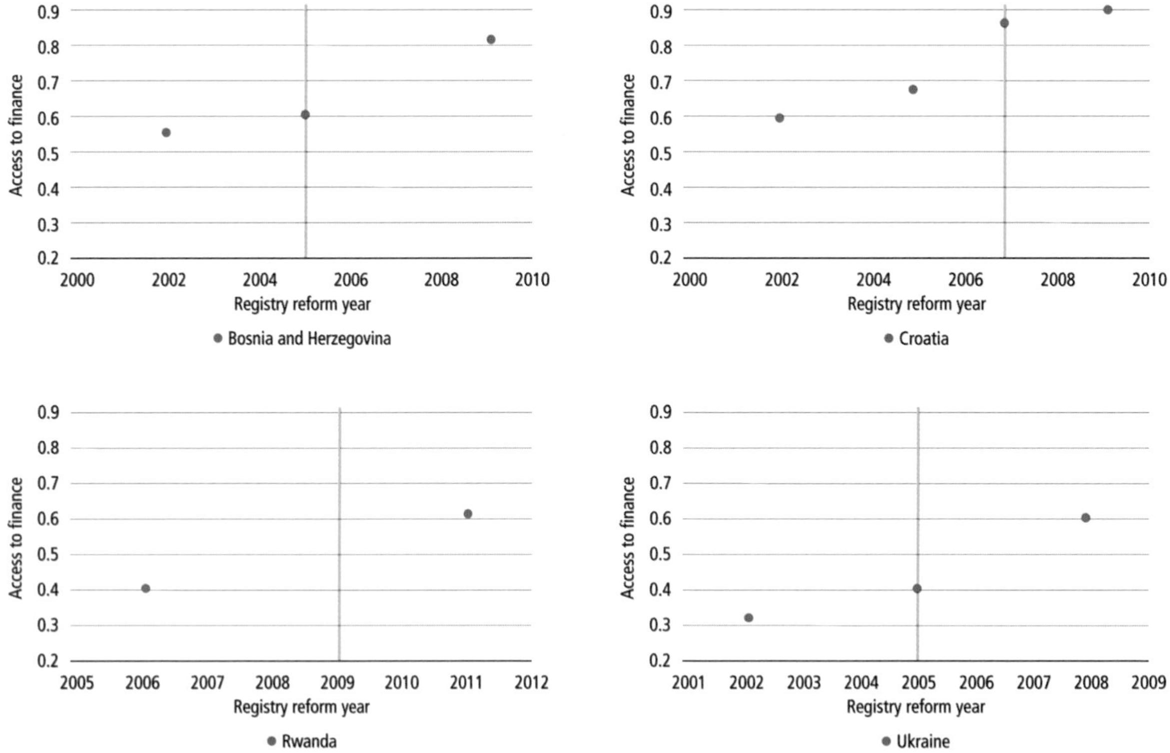

Source: Adapted from Love, Martínez Pería and Singh (2013, figure 1).
Note: The vertical line indicates the year of introduction of a collateral registry for movable assets.

operators and domestic and international traders. A digital accounts receivable finance platform under the central bank has been running since the end of 2013 with a cumulative financing volume of about $400 billion. The share of commercial credit involving movable assets has been raised from 12% in 2004 to around 40% currently. Cumulatively since the end of 2007—and for accounts receivable and lease finance only—over 2.2 million transactions have been registered at the collateral registry with a financing volume of at least $10 trillion. Annual disbursements of debt finance involving movable assets is around $3 trillion, including large but important infrastructure deals and the issuance of bonds backed by receivables.

Besides achieving impressive results, Ghana's collateral registry reform project from 2008 to 2014 enabled the design and implementation of the first modern collateral registry in Africa, opening the market for secured transactions and collateral registry reforms in the region. Between its establishment in 2010 and the end of 2015, the registry facilitated $1.3 billion in financing for small-scale businesses and $12 billion in total financing for the business sector overall using only movable assets as collateral for loans. Women entrepreneurs have played an important role in this scheme—women borrowers account for 40% of total registrations and more than $100 million in financing for this sector.

As in most fragile and conflict-affected economies, the lack of access to credit remains a key challenge to enterprise development in Liberia. A collateral registry was officially launched in Liberia on June 18, 2014. It was widely expected that the Ebola crisis, which had a negative impact on commercial bank financing, would have reduced the use of the collateral registry as well. By June 2016, however—only two years after its launch—the registry had recorded 527 security interest registrations, over 94% of which went to individuals (51% of which were women), facilitating financing of more than $237 million.[5]

TWO WAYS TO REFORM

Eighty two economies have reformed their legislation governing secured transactions over the past decade.[6] During that period two approaches have emerged in the way these economies have made the adjustments to their national laws to expand coverage to all traditional security interests on movable assets and their functional equivalents. The *Doing*

FIGURE 5.2 Legal rights of secured creditors in several economies that reformed in 2014-2016

New law and collateral registry reforms

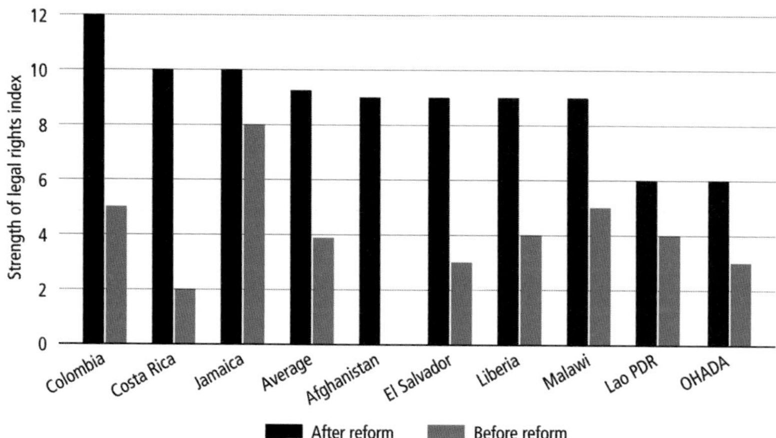

Piecemeal reforms

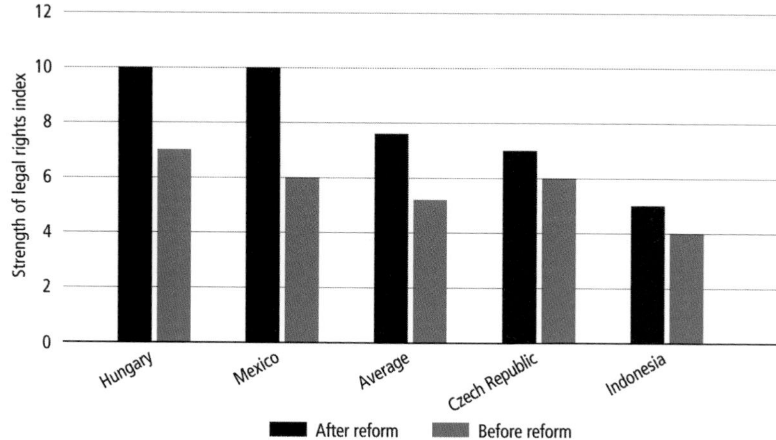

Sources: Doing Business database; Enterprise Surveys database (http://www.enterprisesurveys.org), World Bank.
Note: This figure captures economies with reforms between *Doing Business 2014* and *Doing Business 2017*. Reforms that took place earlier or prior to the inception of *Doing Business 2003* are not reflected in this figure. The score for Indonesia and Mexico is the average for both cities measured in each case.

Business getting credit indicators capture some of these reforms (figure 5.2).

The first approach is to introduce one comprehensive law covering secured transactions that regulates all types of security interests available to both incorporated and non-incorporated entities. An example of this approach is the new secured transactions law in Colombia, which entered into force in August 2014. A follow-up regulation established the terms for the implementation of a centralized collateral registry. Together these established a modern legal regime for secured transactions wherein all types of movable assets, present or future, may be used as collateral to secure a loan. Functional equivalents of loans secured with movable property, such as assignment of receivables or sales with retention of title, were brought under regulation. The law also provides for priority rules outside bankruptcy and establishes the rights of secured creditors during a reorganization procedure, thereby assuring lenders that they can recover payments due ahead of any other claims. Finally, the law permits out-of-court enforcement of collateral allowing for both public tender and private sale.

The new legal framework in Colombia allows borrowers to obtain loans by using collateral resources such as inventory, machinery and crops. Since the registry went live in March 2015, there have been over one million registrations valued at more than $93 billion. Over 10% of these loans represent new credits. More than 100 financial institutions are participating in the registry of lenders. Some of Colombia's largest banks have provided loans secured by movable collateral including embroidery machines, milking equipment and rice crops.[7] According to data from the World Bank Enterprise Surveys, almost one third of Colombian entrepreneurs cited access to credit as the most pressing constraint to the growth of their enterprise before the law was enacted.[8] This is nearly double the average for the rest of Latin America and the Caribbean.[9]

Costa Rica is one of the most recent examples of introducing a secured transactions system which allows entrepreneurs to leverage movable assets for a loan. More than 40% of small and medium-size enterprises consider the lack of funding a barrier to their economic activity.[10] Proper implementation was the main challenge in introducing a new secured transactions system in Costa Rica, as is commonly the case when such a reform is introduced. The reformed system requires a paradigm shift in various perceptions and lending practices, such as raising the awareness of all users and providing training so that they can use the system more efficiently. Costa Rica's system was launched in May 2015 and by December 2015 registrations totaled 5,334, including over 2,900 small and medium-size firms receiving loans secured with movable property.

In Jamaica, a law which came into force in January 2014 established a modern legal framework for secured transactions wherein all types of movable assets, present or future, can be used as collateral to secure a loan. The law also regulates functional equivalents of loans secured with movable property such as financial leases or sales with retention of title and also allows out-of-court enforcement of the collateral through public auction or private sale. The same law also established the regulation for the implementation of a centralized collateral registry.

Afghanistan introduced a law in 2009 establishing a comprehensive secured transactions regime with a functional approach. The law regulates both present and future collateral and its proceeds and contains clear rules of enforcement through public auction or private sale. With the support of the Afghanistan secured lending project, which aimed to increase private sector credit access by strengthening lenders' rights in movable assets, a fully-operational, modern, centralized collateral registry was created in March 2013. The registry, which is hosted by the central bank, allows for online registrations, searches, modifications and cancellations. Establishing the secured transactions system in Afghanistan was accomplished in three stages. First, careful planning of legislative reform led to the enactment of the law in 2009 as well as amendments to existing laws and regulations aimed at enhancing the rights of creditors in movable assets. Second, the movable assets registry was established to enable lenders to effectively file a notice related to their proprietary rights. Third, a public awareness and capacity building program was launched in March 2013 to educate government and private sector participants about the benefits of a well-functioning secured transactions system. Following the training of officers at the central bank, the institution has taken the lead in raising public awareness in Afghanistan on the use of the collateral registry. This new legal and institutional framework has resulted in more than 4,500 loans registered by all 16 commercial banks and 2 microfinance institutions since the registry's launch. The majority of clients (85%) are micro, small and medium-size enterprises. The value of financing using movable assets was estimated at $910 million as of August 2015, including various lending products where accounts receivable and tangible assets are used as securities. Furthermore, over 10,000 online searches have been conducted, highlighting the widespread use of the system.

In all of the above cases the law foresees the extension of the original collateral to future assets. Many jurisdictions only permit grantors to create security rights in assets that are in existence and that they own when the security right is created (that is, they are not able to grant security in assets not yet in existence or that they have not yet acquired). This restriction is to protect debtors from over-committing their assets—in particular, their future assets—to one secured creditor. Nevertheless, because businesses may not always have available existing assets to secure credit, this limitation prevents them from obtaining various types of credit that are predicated upon a stream of future assets, such as inventory and receivables. Thus it is a good practice that, except to the extent that consumer protection legislation provides otherwise, a security right should be created in future assets. Also, the cost of secured credit depends in part on the cost associated with obtaining security rights. An efficient secured transactions regime will establish streamlined procedures for obtaining security rights. Transaction costs will be reduced notably by: minimizing formalities, providing for a single method for creating security rights rather than a multiplicity of security devices for different types of encumbered asset, and providing a mechanism that permits the creation of security rights in future assets and securing future advances of credit without the need for any additional documentation or action by the parties.[11]

The application of new legislation often reveals areas for improvement of the law or the supporting institutions. A law in Bosnia and Herzegovina, which adopted the functional approach, established the same regime for possessory pledges (when the debtor must transfer the collateral to the creditor or a third party), nonpossessory pledges, leases and other security rights. A pledge can include tangible property, like machinery or inventory, bank accounts, account receivables, or shares in a company with limited liability. The law permits great freedom to define both the object of the security (specifically or generally, including as a pool of fluctuating assets) and also the secured debt (including revolving loans, credit lines), thereby providing companies with significant flexibility with respect to their collateralized assets.

The 17 member states of the Organization for the Harmonization of Business Law in Africa, known by its French acronym OHADA,[12] have also reformed existing legislation in recent years. These changes have broadened the range of assets that can be used as collateral (to include future assets), extended security interests to the proceeds of the original asset and introduced the possibility of out-of-court enforcement. However, the establishment of a centralized, modern, notice-based collateral registry—available online for the registration of lending contracts, searches by debtor's name, modification and cancellations—remains a challenge in these economies.

The second approach for creating a modern secured transactions legal system is by introducing specific provisions to existing legislation. Hungary, for example, amended its civil code in 2014 to include new rules and principles for the creation, publicity and enforcement of pledges over movable assets by specifically extending the pledge to include its products and proceeds. Such pledges can now be registered online directly by the contracting parties. Similarly, Poland has amended numerous laws to allow for rights in movable assets to be created for security purposes by agreement. A bill, once approved by the Parliament, will allow for electronic auctions of debtors' movable assets through an electronic system provided by the district courts and the exchange of legal correspondence through electronic means. Electronic auctions are expected to reduce the need to hold multiple physical auctions by reaching out to a wider market of potential buyers.[13] Amendments to existing laws have also been implemented in the Czech Republic. The definition of receivables, which are now considered movable assets, was modified in 2014 following a change to the civil code. As a result, legal provisions related to security interests and the pledge registry are now applicable to receivables. In addition, the law allows secured creditors to enforce their security interests out of court, through a public auction, and to execute a security as stipulated in the security agreement.

In jurisdictions where multiple laws regulate various types of security interests and their functional equivalents, the requirement to register all types of collateral in a unified collateral registry can act as a catalyst. In 2013, Indonesia operationalized a national movable collateral registry, through which registration of all types of security rights over movable assets are processed and managed. However, fiduciary transfer registrations were only allowed to be completed by notaries and other functional equivalents were not recorded in the registry database. In 2015 the online registry for fiduciary transfer in Indonesia—which centralized all fiduciary transfer registrations since 2013—expanded its database to be searchable online by debtor's name, among other unique search elements. The search function is accessible to the public through the online portal.[14]

CONCLUSION

Policy makers in some economies choose to enact a comprehensive and completely new law while others amend existing legislation to govern secured transactions. Some of the economies that chose to replace various incomplete laws governing the security interest with a single piece of updated legislation also followed up with the creation of a modern collateral registry, resulting in a higher average score on the strength of legal rights index. However, those economies that chose to amend their existing laws to create a unified secured transactions regime scored significantly lower on average. This suggests that multiple good practices were already included in the existing provisions. Complementing existing legislation with new legal and regulatory reform works well in economies where legislation is relatively solid and functional. Many economies in Europe and Central Asia, Sub-Saharan Africa and Latin America and the Caribbean have followed this approach by introducing laws unifying the regulation and registration of security interests including functional equivalents.

NOTES

This case study was written by Maria Magdalena Chiquier, Selima Daadouche Crum and Magdalini Konidari.

1. Typical examples of movable assets are machines, inventory and furniture, among others.
2. Kraemer-Eis and Lang 2012.
3. Pursuant to good practices promoted by the United Nations Commission on International Trade Law (UNCITRAL) Legislative Guide on Secured Transactions.
4. Love, Martínez Pería and Singh 2013.
5. The data cited for registries in China, Ghana and Liberia were provided by World Bank Group staff that obtained them for the respective registries.
6. *Doing Business* data.
7. For more on loans secured by movable collateral, see the IFC's website at http://www.ifc.org/wps/wcm/connect/news_ext_content/ifc_external_corporate_site/news+and+events/news/breaking+down+barriers+to+finance.
8. For more on the World Bank Enterprise Surveys, see the website at http://www.enterprisesurveys.org.
9. Barsky 2014.
10. Costa Rica, Ministry of Economy, Industry and Commerce 2015.
11. United Nations Commission on International Trade Law (UNCITRAL) Legislative Guide on Secured Transactions. Available online from https://www.uncitral.org/pdf/english/texts/security-lg/e/09-82670_Ebook-Guide_09-04-10English.pdf.
12. The 17 members of OHADA are Benin, Burkina Faso, Cameroon, Central African Republic, Chad, the Comoros, the Democratic Republic of Congo, the Republic of Congo, Côte d'Ivoire, Equatorial Guinea, Gabon, Guinea, Guinea-Bissau, Mali, Niger, Senegal and Togo; OHADA 2012.
13. World Bank 2015b.
14. See Indonesia's online fiduciary registry website at http://ahu.go.id/pencarian/fidusia/.

Getting Credit: Credit Information

Casting a wide net to expand financial inclusion

- A comprehensive credit reporting system that includes credit history data from alternative sources—in addition to banks—is critical to the establishment of a well-developed and inclusive financial infrastructure.
- In economies where credit bureaus or registries include data from retailers, utility companies and trade creditors, the average coverage of the credit reporting system tends to be higher than in those where such information is not available.
- OECD high-income economies and Latin America and the Caribbean have the largest proportion of economies where the main credit reporting service provider distributes data from non-regulated entities.
- In 50 out of 190 economies measured by *Doing Business* the main credit reporting service provider distributes data from utility companies in its reports. At least one credit reporting service provider reports repayment history from financing corporations or leasing companies in 110 economies worldwide.
- Reporting microfinance data benefits borrowers (by establishing repayment histories that help them obtain loans) and microloan lenders (by helping them assess the repayment capacity of their clients).

The ability to access affordable credit is a critical element of private sector-led growth. While factors such as interest rates and collateral requirements play an important role in access to finance for firms and individuals, underdeveloped financial infrastructure increases the cost and risk of lending to both borrowers and financial services providers. A comprehensive credit reporting system that includes credit history data not only from banks but from other institutions—such as trade creditors, leasing and factoring companies, retailers and utilities and microfinance institutions—is critical in the establishment of a well-developed and inclusive financial infrastructure.[1] This can be of special importance for developing economies where lower levels of institutional development—reflected in weak judicial systems and creditor rights—are associated with greater financing constraints and less developed credit markets.[2]

Around 2.5 billion people currently lack access to formal financial services.[3] Globally, 42% of adults reported having borrowed money in the previous 12 months in the 2014 Global Findex survey.[4] Although the overall share of adults with a new loan—formal or informal—was fairly consistent across regions and economies, the source of new loans varied widely. In OECD high-income economies financial institutions were the main source of financing, with 18% of adults reporting borrowing from one in the past year. By contrast, in developing economies nearly a third (29%) of adults reported borrowing from family or friends, while only 9% reported borrowing from a financial institution. In the Middle East, South Asia and Sub-Saharan Africa more people reported borrowing from a store (using installment credit or buying on credit) than from a financial institution. The gap in the Middle East was the largest, with close to 20% of borrowers having a retail store credit and less than 10% having a loan from a financial institution.[5]

Access to finance is a fundamental factor affecting the growth opportunities of small businesses. Globally, 27% of firms identify access to finance as a major constraint.[6] While a quarter of firms use banks to finance investments, only 15% of these firms' total investments are financed by banks, with 71% of investments being financed internally, 5% by supplier credit and 5% by equity or stock sales.[7] Compared to large firms, smaller firms finance a lesser share of their investment from formal sources, relying instead on informal sources such as borrowing from family and friends or from unregulated moneylenders.[8] Around 70% of formal small and medium-size enterprises in developing economies are estimated to be either unserved or underserved by the formal financial sector.[9] The total credit gap that they face amounts to $1.3 to $1.6 trillion, or $700 to $850 billion if firms in OECD high-income economies are excluded.[10] A credit reporting system that accounts for the diverse sources of finance for small and medium-size firms can contribute to a reduction of the credit gap and the promotion of private sector growth.

FIGURE 6.1 In economies where borrower coverage is higher, the share of adults with credit cards and borrowing from financial institutions is larger

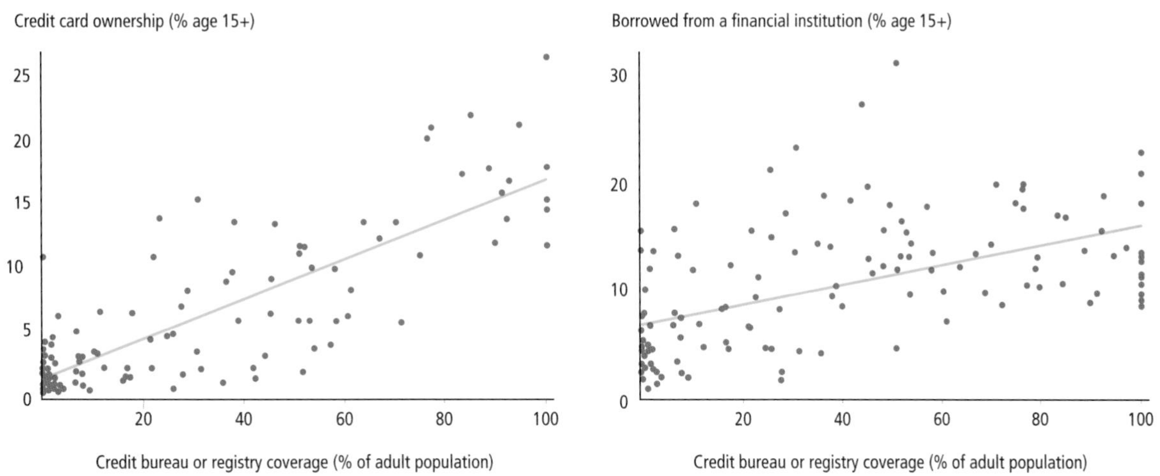

Sources: Doing Business database; Global Findex database (http://www.worldbank.org/en/programs/globalfindex), World Bank.
Note: The samples include 106 and 130 economies covered by both *Doing Business* database and Global Findex database. Both relationships are significant at the 1% level after controlling for income per capita.

EXPANDING CREDIT ACCESS THROUGH COMPREHENSIVE CREDIT REPORTING

Lenders and borrowers—both individuals and firms—benefit from sharing credit information with credit reporting service providers (CRSPs). In economies where a larger share of the adult population is covered by CRSPs, more adults have a credit card, borrow from a bank or other financial institution (figure 6.1) and formal private sector lending is higher (figure 6.2). This is consistent with earlier studies indicating that credit reporting institutions are associated with higher ratios of private credit to GDP across economies and that an improvement in information sharing increases credit levels over time.[11] Higher economic growth rates and a lower likelihood of financial crisis are additional benefits associated with greater credit reporting.[12] It is important to note that the figures presented here describe an association between variables measuring credit reporting systems and credit market outcomes. No causality is implied given the cross-economy nature of the data.

More firms tend to have bank loans or lines of credit (figure 6.3) and fewer rejections of loan applications (figure 6.4) in economies where credit bureaus and credit registries have higher commercial borrower coverage. This finding is consistent with recent analysis using firm-level surveys of 63 economies covering more than 75,000 firms over the period from 2002 to 2013. Its results reveal that the

FIGURE 6.2 In economies where borrower coverage is higher, the levels of formal private sector lending are higher

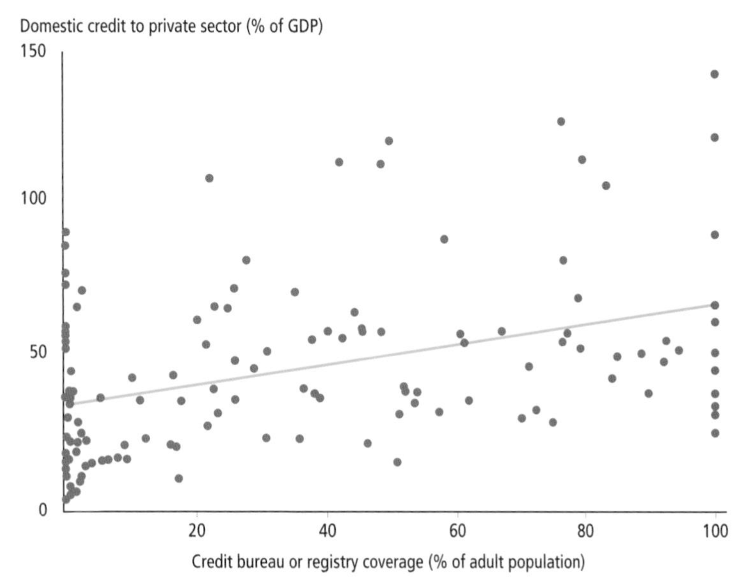

Sources: Doing Business database; World Development Indicators database (http://data.worldbank.org/data-catalog/world-development-indicators), World Bank.
Note: The sample includes 129 economies covered by both the *Doing Business* database and World Development Indicators database. The relationship is significant at the 10% level after controlling for income per capita.

FIGURE 6.3 Higher borrower coverage is associated with higher percentage of firms with a bank loan/line of credit

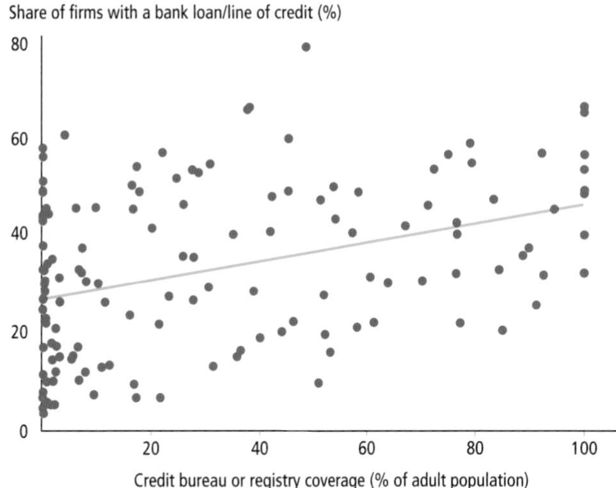

Sources: Doing Business database; Enterprise Surveys database (http://www.enterprisesurveys.org), World Bank.
Note: The sample includes 138 economies covered by both *Doing Business* database and World Bank Enterprise Surveys database. The relationship is significant at the 5% level after controlling for income per capita.

introduction of a credit bureau improves the firms' likelihood of access to finance, with longer-term loans, lower interest rates and higher share of working capital financed by banks. The study also finds that the greater the coverage of the credit bureau and the scope and accessibility of the credit information, the more profound its impact is on firm financing.[13]

By sharing credit information credit reporting helps to reduce information asymmetries between creditors and borrowers. Borrowers typically know their financial abilities and investment opportunities much better than lenders do. The inability of lenders to accurately assess the creditworthiness of borrowers contributes to higher default rates and smaller loan portfolios. Lenders are also more likely to lend to larger firms, which may be more transparent as a result of more elaborate legal and accounting rules and the regular publication of certified financial reports.

Credit reporting has been shown to decrease contract delinquencies and defaults, especially when firms are informationally opaque, without loosening lending standards.[14] Studies suggest that, following the introduction of credit reporting systems, repayment rates have risen when lending is for a single transaction and repayment is not enforceable by a third party, mainly because borrowers believe that a good credit record improves their access to credit. Credit reporting also affects market outcomes by weakening lenders' ability to extract rents[15] while leading to higher profits and lowering the risks to banks.[16] In addition, more advanced credit reporting systems and greater financial sector outreach are associated with a lower degree of tax evasion by firms.[17]

For an individual without an established credit history, securing a loan from a formal financial institution can become a vicious circle. Lenders are typically reluctant to provide financing with limited client credit information. This credit information asymmetry could be mitigated by casting a wide net across various credit sources—beyond just banks—to collect valuable information about the repayment history of borrowers and potential borrowers. Even if individuals and firms do not have a traditional banking relationship, they are likely to have a credit history with other types of credit providers. For individuals, these could include utility companies that have records of clients' payment histories. Trade creditors—that effectively extend unsecured, short-term lines of credit—could attest to how well a firm fulfills its commitments.

FIGURE 6.4 Fewer loan applications are rejected when commercial borrower coverage is higher

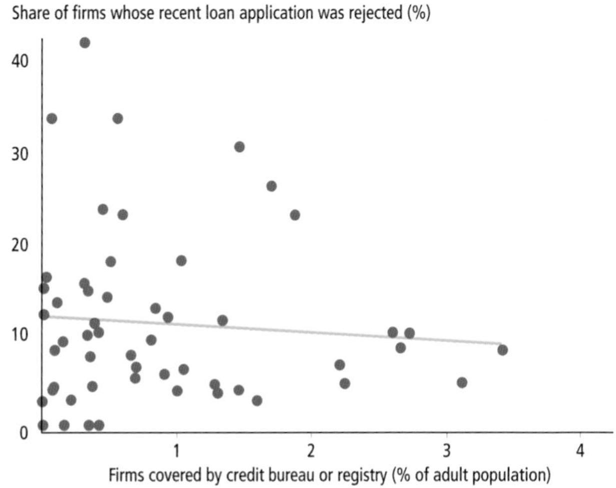

Sources: Doing Business database; Enterprise Surveys database (http://www.enterprisesurveys.org), World Bank.
Note: The sample includes 53 economies covered by both *Doing Business* database and World Bank Enterprise Surveys database. The relationship is significant at the 10% level after controlling for income per capita.

In contrast to segmented credit reporting, which is based on the collection and distribution of information from/to a limited number of sources,[18] comprehensive credit reporting is based on the collection and distribution of information from a wide array of sources and sectors, including retail, small business, microfinance, corporate credit cards, insurance, telecoms and utility companies, among others. Those credit bureaus and credit registries that collect and distribute data from a larger number of sources also have higher coverage rate (figure 6.5). These "non-traditional" sources of data—such as data on payments associated with utilities or telecom services—bolster information on "thin file" clients who are not typically covered by traditional sources. As a result, comprehensive credit reporting increases the ability of creditors to assess and monitor credit risk, creditworthiness and credit capacity.

FIGURE 6.5 More varieties of data providers are associated with a higher level of borrower coverage

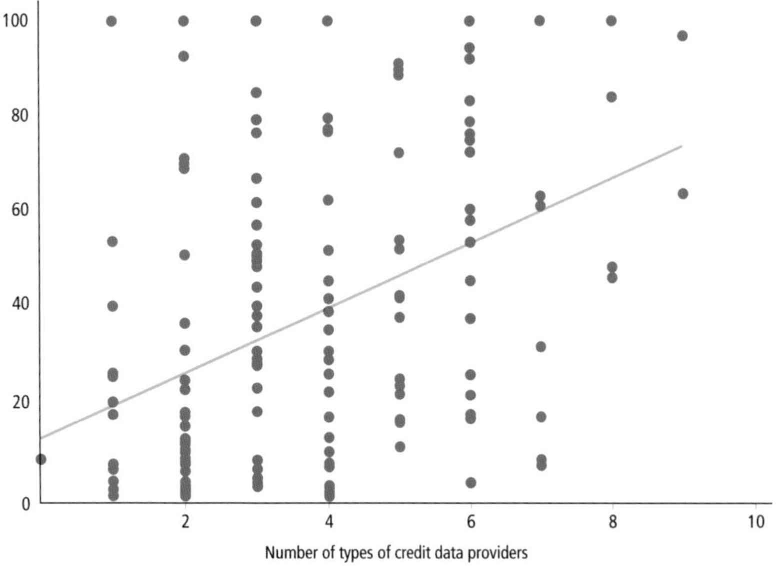

Source: Doing Business database.
Note: The sample includes 177 credit bureaus and credit registries. The relationship is significant at the 1% level after controlling for income per capita.

CASTING A WIDE NET

Economies that adopt a more comprehensive approach and report repayment histories from non-regulated entities tend to include higher numbers of individuals and firms with different income levels and backgrounds in their credit reporting system (figure 6.6). The following sections describe how the use of data from these entities enhances the coverage of consumers and firms with a limited borrowing history.

Trade creditors

Trade credit, where goods or services are provided before payment, typically consists of an open, unsecured line of credit. Through their provision of trade credit, business suppliers are among the most important non-financial institutions for businesses, particularly small and medium-size firms. The use of trade credit data in credit reporting can help firms without a loan or other credit facility with a regulated financial institution to develop a credit history. However, this information is rarely reported. The main credit bureau or credit registry collects data from trade creditors in only 36 economies measured by *Doing Business* (figure 6.7). These are mainly concentrated in Latin America and the Caribbean (10) and OECD high-income economies (9). On average, the coverage of the credit reporting systems that collect and report data from trade creditors is 29% higher than those systems that do not report such data.

Trade credit data can play a positive role in increasing access to traditional sources of finance, such as banks, as they are a

FIGURE 6.6 Economies reporting non-financial credit data tend to have higher coverage of the adult population

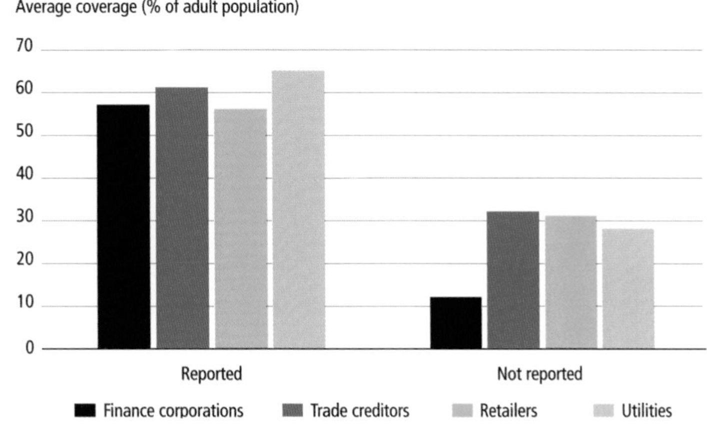

Source: Doing Business database.
Note: Data include 190 economies. For the definition of coverage, see the data notes.

FIGURE 6.7 Share of economies with an operating credit bureau or credit registry that report various types of data, by region

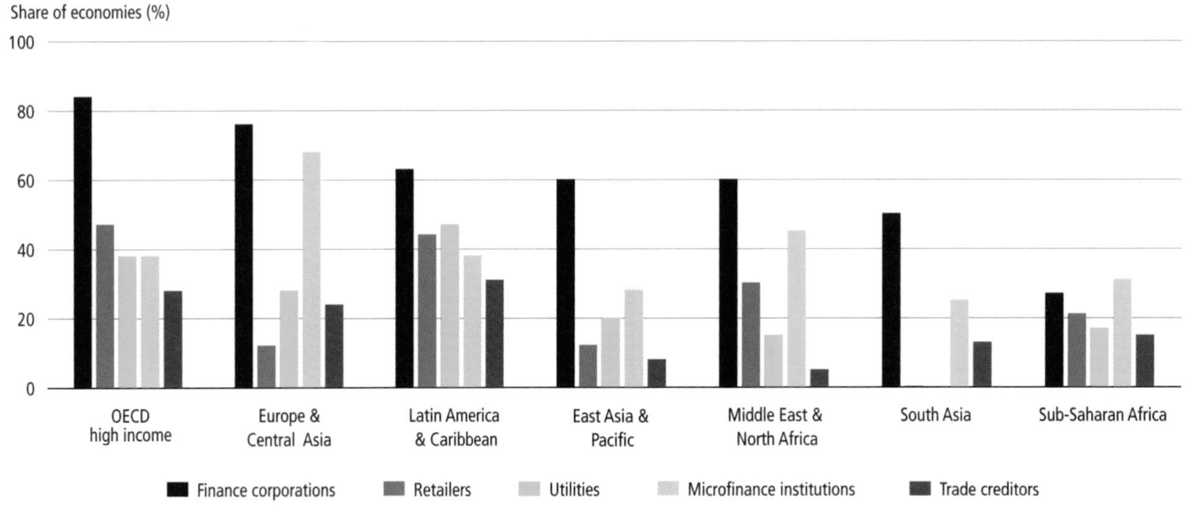

Source: Doing Business database.

reliable source of information on a firm's financial health. Ratings based on trade credit payment information can more reliably predict firm failure compared to other types of information that are available to lenders, such as firm financial statements.[19] Trade credit is also associated with higher access to bank financing for firms, with trade credit information acting as a signal of the quality of the firm. The impact of such data is even stronger in the case of younger firms in the early stages of the banking relationship when banks have not accumulated enough soft information on them to support their reputation.[20]

A stronger participation of trade creditors in the credit reporting system through increased information sharing can also expand access to trade credit for small and medium-size firms. A recent study in the United Kingdom found that if trade creditors had access to credit reports and credit scores based not only on data from public sources but also data from banks and other financial intermediaries, the credit scores of 50% of firms in the sample would improve and 21% of these would see their credit limits increase.[21] In the United States, Dun and Bradstreet used trade payment data to develop the *Paydex* score for millions of firms in its database. The score provides information on the likelihood that a business will meet its payment obligations to suppliers and vendors.

Finance corporations and leasing companies

Leasing and factoring companies are also important sources of finance for firms and can be valuable data providers to credit bureaus and registries. When leasing, a firm makes a small down payment and subsequent monthly payments on the equipment—usually for a period of five years or less. At the end of the lease term the firm can purchase the equipment by making a minimal buyout payment. Factoring is a transaction where a business sells its account receivables to a third-party financial company in order to raise funds. Through factoring businesses can boost their cash receipts while also outsourcing credit and collections, thereby freeing up owners to spend more time concentrating on core competencies. In practice, however, the majority of factoring companies do not share their data with credit bureaus.

Leasing presents an important financing opportunity for young firms and enables them to preserve cash for profit-generating activities. In economies where weak collateral laws hinder bank lending, leasing typically offers the advantage of not requiring collateral beyond the security of the leased asset itself.[22] Because the leasing company purchases the equipment directly from the supplier, little opportunity exists for the firm to use the funds for other purposes.[23] The separation of ownership and control of leased assets also facilitates a simpler recovery procedure, even in weak legal and institutional environments.[24] In many economies firms can offset their lease payments against income before taxes, compared to just the interest on bank loans in buying equipment. The leasing companies may also pass on tax benefits associated with their depreciation to the firms through lower financing cost.[25]

Leasing activities are not equally developed across all emerging market economies. There are nascent leasing industries in low-income economies in Africa and Asia and maturing leasing markets in the more advanced economies of Latin America and Eastern Europe.[26] In the euro area,[27] leasing, hire-purchase and factoring are the third most important financing source for small and medium-size enterprises, preceded by bank overdrafts, credit lines, credit card overdrafts and bank loans.[28] Between October 2014 and March 2015, 44% of small and medium-size firms in the euro area reported using leasing in the previous six months or considering it as a relevant source of finance.[29]

There are 110 economies worldwide that have at least one CRSP that reports repayment history from financing corporations and leasing companies. OECD high-income economies have the highest proportion of such economies (84%), followed by Europe and Central Asia (76%), Latin America and the Caribbean (63%), East Asia and the Pacific (60%), Middle East and North Africa (60%), South Asia (50%) and Sub-Saharan Africa (27%). The Czech Republic's credit bureau, CRIF, set up a non-banking bureau in 2005, covering leasing and sales data that were not available in the banking registers. The price for using these data varies according to the type of company—for example, different prices apply to providers of small consumer credits and car leasing companies. In Taiwan, China, a new product, "R04 Finance Leasing Information," was released by the Joint Credit Information Center (JCIC) in February 2014, after an agreement with the finance leasing association. This provides JCIC's member institutions access to borrowers' leasing transaction information from finance leasing companies. The JCIC also benefits finance leasing companies by offering them an electronic credit report on borrowers.

Utility companies

More than half of adults in the poorest 40% of households worldwide do not have a bank account at a financial institution.[30] This represents an obstacle for borrowers who are unable to build credit histories that would increase their chances of obtaining loans. Collecting credit data from utility companies, such as electricity providers and mobile phone companies, is particularly important for the poor. A recent study by the *DataCrédito* credit bureau in Colombia—which distributes information from utilities in its credit reports—showed that the telecommunications sector is the channel through which the majority of new borrowers, without previous credit relationships, enter the credit market.[31] In the United States research has found that the acceptance rate for new loans can increase by up to 10% for those borrowers with "thin files" once data from non-traditional sources such as utilities and telecoms are included in the credit reports.[32]

In economies where credit bureaus or registries include data from utility companies, the average coverage of the credit reporting system tends to be higher (65%) than in those where such information is not available (28%). The main CRSP in 50 economies distributes these data in its reports. The majority of these are in Latin America and the Caribbean (15) and in OECD high-income economies (12). In the United States, DTE Energy—an electricity and natural gas company—began fully reporting customer payment data to credit bureaus in August 2006. DTE customers with no prior credit history (8.1% of the total) gained either a credit file or a credit score and began to prioritize making payments to DTE.[33] Within six months DTE had 80,000 fewer accounts in arrears. This good practice is also being implemented in developing economies. In Rwanda, for example, shortly after the launch in 2010 of the country's first credit bureau, two telecommunications companies and one utility began providing credit information to the bureau. This has contributed to increasing the coverage of the credit reporting system from less than 1% of the adult population in 2010 to 16.6% in 2016. In Mongolia, MobiCom Corporation—a telecommunications company—began providing credit data to the credit registry in March 2015. As a result, credit reports in Mongolia now include negative payment information for telecommunication services and full payment history for mobile phone leasing.

Microfinance institutions

Microfinance institutions that offer financial services to low-income populations help bridge the gap in access to credit from traditional lenders by providing small loans—usually with collateral substitutes such as group guarantees—that can gradually increase based on good repayment patterns. Microcredit benefits low-income populations and enterprises that are typically small, labor intensive and growing. The Grameen Bank in Bangladesh, for example, provided credit for the purchase of capital inputs and promoted productive self-employment among the poor and women, while participation in the program had a significant impact on female empowerment.[34] Microcredit clients' enterprises have been found to perform better than non-client enterprises in terms of profits, fixed assets and employment.[35]

Over the past 30 years, the microfinance industry has grown to reach an estimated 200 million clients.[36] While having positive impacts on assets and income levels, microfinance institution services may increase vulnerability if borrowers over-leverage and pose risks to the financial systems.[37] A 2011 survey found that credit risk is the top concern for microfinance professionals in 86 economies.[38] The inability of lenders to accurately assess the risk of default contributes to relationship-based lending. By submitting microcredit data to credit reporting service providers microfinance institutions can minimize problems of asymmetric information. Reporting microfinance data benefits borrowers (by establishing repayment histories that help them obtain loans), micro-loan lenders (by helping them assess the repayment capacity of their clients) and regulators (by monitoring credit markets and trends).

Microcredit reporting is expanding. In 2015/16 68% of economies in Europe and Central Asia have an operational credit bureau or credit registry that reports micro-credit information; 45% in the Middle East and North Africa; 38% in Latin America and the Caribbean; 31% in Sub-Saharan Africa; 28% in East Asia and the Pacific and 25% in South Asia. In India the growing microfinance market is concentrated in just a few states, leading to multiple cases of lending and over-indebtedness within the same borrower base. Since 2010 IFC has helped India's fastest growing credit bureau, CRIF High Mark, to expand its services to microfinance lenders, ensuring informed lending and promoting financial inclusion.[39] In Bolivia, in the three years following the establishment of a microfinance credit reporting system, microcredit lending more than doubled (outpacing a 23% rise in traditional bank lending), and the percentage of nonperforming loans decreased.[40] Similarly in Bosnia and Herzegovina, the inclusion of microfinance institutions in the credit reporting system contributed to a higher level of financial discipline and a significantly lower level of nonperforming loans.[41]

CONCLUSION

The lack of access to formal banking continues to represent a hurdle for millions of individuals and firms as the problem of asymmetric information excludes them from traditional credit markets. Casting a wide net of sources of data in the credit reporting system can help to address this problem by making it easier for borrowers to develop a credit history.

Alternative sources of data include leasing and financial corporations, trade creditors, utility companies and microfinance institutions. The credit information that these institutions have on their customers can be used to expand the coverage of the credit reporting systems by providing information on individuals and firms with limited recorded borrowing history. Coverage is higher in those economies where data from these entities are actively collected and distributed by the credit reporting service providers. Additional sources of data can improve the accuracy and scope of the credit reports produced by credit bureaus and credit registries and generate incentives to improve borrower discipline, particularly in economies with weak legal enforcement mechanisms. When more information is available to lenders they can evaluate more clearly the creditworthiness of their potential clients, which ultimately translates into increased access to finance and cheaper loans.

Comprehensive credit reporting is expanding as economies adopt strategies and solutions according to their particular needs.[42] Although CRSPs have made stronger progress in this area in OECD high-income economies and, to a lesser extent, in Latin America and the Caribbean, several emerging economies are adopting innovative approaches to improve the quality and scope of their credit reporting systems. By including data from trade creditors, finance corporations, utility companies and microfinance institutions, these types of initiatives have the potential to improve the chances of getting credit for millions of low-income individuals and firms.

NOTES

This case study was written by Edgar Chavez, Charlotte Nan Jiang and Khrystyna Kushnir.

1. World Bank Group 2012.
2. Beck and others 2006; Djankov and others 2007.
3. World Bank Group 2015a.
4. Demirgüç-Kunt and others 2015.
5. Demirgüç-Kunt and others 2015.
6. Enterprise Surveys database (http://www.enterprisesurveys.org/), World Bank.
7. Enterprise Surveys database (http://www.enterprisesurveys.org/), World Bank.
8. Beck and Demirgüç-Kunt 2006.
9. Stein and others 2013.
10. Stein and others 2010.
11. Djankov and others 2007.
12. Houston and others 2010.
13. Martinez Peria and Singh 2014.
14. Doblas-Madrid and Minetti 2013.
15. Brown and Zehnder 2007.
16. Houston and others 2010.
17. Beck and others 2010.
18. A typical example of segmented credit reporting would be information that is collected from banks and is distributed only to such banks.
19. Kallberg and Udell 2003. The authors analyze the capacity to correctly predict firm failure of Dun and Bradstreet's Paydex score—which is based on the number of days past due for a firm's last year of trade experiences—in contrast with financial statement information of the firm including leverage, quick and net liquid balance ratios.
20. Agostino and Trivieri 2014.
21. Bank of England 2015.
22. World Bank Group 1996; World Bank Group 2009.
23. World Bank Group 1996.
24. Eisfeldt and Rampini 2009; Beck and Demirgüç-Kunt 2006; Berger and Udell 2006.
25. World Bank Group 1996.
26. World Bank Group 2009.
27. Austria, Belgium, Finland, France, Greece, Germany, the Netherlands, Ireland, Italy, Portugal, Slovakia and Spain.
28. Kraemer-Eis and Lang 2012.
29. European Central Bank 2015.
30. World Bank, Global Findex Database, 2014.
31. El Tiempo. 2015. "Gracias a la compra de celulares, jóvenes entran al mundo del crédito." March 26. http://app.eltiempo.com/economia/sectores/gracias-a-la-compra-de-celulares-j-venes-entran-al-mundo-del-cr-dito/15470719.
32. Turner and others 2006.
33. World Bank Conference. Financial Infrastructure Week. Brazil, March 15-17, 2010.
34. McKernan 2002; Schuler and Hashemi 1994; Steele, Amin and Naved 2001.
35. Dunn and Arbuckle 2001.
36. World Bank Group 2015a.
37. Mosley 2001.
38. Lascelles and Mendelson 2009.
39. While comprehensive credit reporting helps to promote financial inclusion, the main motivation was to address the problem of multiple lending and over-indebtedness among microfinance clients in India.
40. Bustelo 2009.
41. Lyman and others 2011.
42. Economies must address many challenges to enable comprehensive reporting, including integrating unregulated sectors in the regulatory regime and identifying microfinance borrowers.

Protecting Minority Investors

Achieving sound corporate governance

Investment is key to private sector development. Yet business risk, political risk and other exogenous factors can turn a seemingly well-calculated investment decision into a loss. The one factor, however, that can be mitigated through adequate regulation is legal risk.[1] *Doing Business*, through the protecting minority investors indicator set, measures aspects such as the protection of shareholders against directors' misuse of corporate assets for personal gain and the rights and role of shareholders in corporate governance.

When it comes to private sector and capital market development, shareholder protection and empowerment are increasingly elevated to policy goals—even more so following the 2008 global financial crisis.[2] Policy makers around the world are implementing reforms aimed at increasing the involvement of minority shareholders in corporate decisions. In fact, *Doing Business* has recorded and documented 166 reforms to aspects of corporate governance in 100 economies since 2005 (figure 7.1).[3]

The legal implications of shareholder empowerment have been studied extensively.[4] The literature has been scarcer, however, on the effect of shareholder empowerment on economic indicators, such as firm value, profitability, cost of capital, or capital market size.[5] One of the objectives of *Doing Business* is to provide standardized, comparable measurements on the adoption of corporate governance practices across 190 economies that can be tested against economic indicators. Using *Doing Business* data and existing literature, this case study presents empirical evidence on the economic benefits

FIGURE 7.1 Protecting minority investors reforms over time

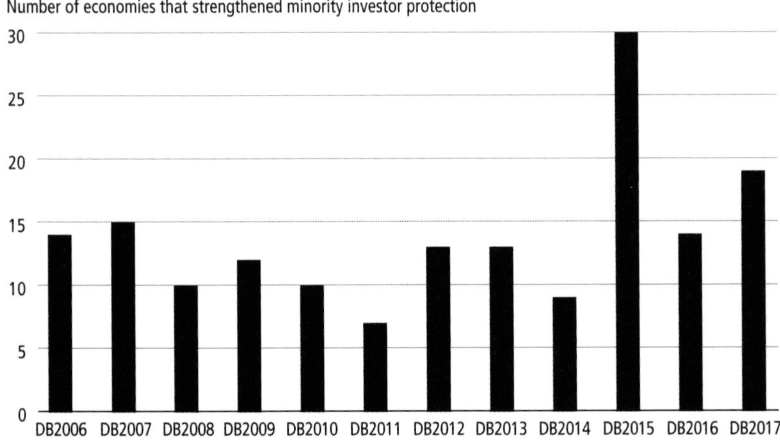

Source: Doing Business database.

Note: The number for *Doing Business 2015* includes an amendment to the OHADA (Organization for the Harmonization of Business Law in Africa) Uniform Act on companies, which is applicable in its 17 member states.

- *Doing Business* has recorded and documented 166 reforms to aspects of corporate governance in 100 economies since 2005.
- Since 2013, 54 economies introduced 63 legislative changes strengthening minority shareholder protections: 38 on the extent of conflict of interest regulation index, 17 on the extent of shareholder governance index and eight on both.
- *Doing Business* data confirm the positive relationship between greater protection of minority shareholders on the one hand and capital market development and access to equity finance on the other.
- India carried out an ambitious, multi-year overhaul of its Companies Act, bringing Indian companies in line with global standards—particularly regarding accountability and corporate governance practices—while ensuring that businesses contribute more to shared prosperity through a quantified and legislated corporate social responsibility requirement.
- When tackling what they referred to as "excessive remuneration in publicly listed companies" Swiss lawmakers opted for a comprehensive reform that also regulated the election and term of board members, their organization in subcommittees and their reporting obligations.

of corporate governance practices that promote shareholder protection and empowerment. The study also contributes to defining the concept of sound corporate governance.

WHAT ARE SOUND CORPORATE GOVERNANCE PRACTICES?

Sound corporate governance is the optimal balance between controlling shareholders, minority shareholders, company managers and market regulators. Many studies provide evidence that achieving sound corporate governance promotes economic development through higher returns on equity, efficiency of investment allocation, firm performance and valuation, lower cost of capital and easier access to external financing.[6]

That growing attention is being devoted to corporate governance is neither new nor surprising. Today the Organisation for Economic Co-operation and Development (OECD) principles of corporate governance,[7] originally developed in 1999 and last updated in 2015, constitute a cornerstone. The American Law Institute, whose corporate governance project was formally initiated in 1978[8] and materialized into principles in 1992,[9] is another foundational reference.

Corporate governance and development

Introducing corporate governance principles —as opposed to giving each company complete discretion in determining its internal rules—guarantees a minimum standard through which companies must be directed and controlled.[10] When these rules are violated these principles also provide shareholders with judicial recourse.[11] Investors become more willing to finance the business ventures of others without exerting direct control over the affairs of the company.[12] As a result, entrepreneurs can tap into broader sources of financing. With easier access to capital, companies are more likely to grow, generate tax revenues and create jobs.[13]

The benefits extend beyond greater access to finance. Corporate governance also contributes to value maximization throughout the life of a company.[14] Properly executed, it ensures that companies are run in the best interest of their owners.[15] Executives and managers are given authority to do so efficiently, with sufficient discretion to apply their skills and business acumen.[16] Internal structures and processes are clearly laid out.[17] The risk of mismanagement and abuse is mitigated thanks to increased accountability, predictability and transparency.

The aggregate effect of all companies following sound corporate governance promises significant positive outcomes for the economy overall. Research shows how sound corporate governance can lead to higher returns on equity and greater efficiency.[18] In deciding the rules and practices that individual companies must follow, legal scholars and legislators have traditionally relied on concepts such as legal certainty,[19] predictability, equity and enforceability. To empirically assess the relevance of these concepts to the overall performance of an economy, scholars increasingly started to use quantitative analysis tools. The so-called law and economics approach, and its subsequent branching into law and finance, have become an integral part of modern policymaking.[20]

What does the protecting minority investors indicator set measure?

The protecting minority investors dataset provides data for 38 aspects of corporate governance in 190 economies, grouped into two sets of three indices each (table 7.1).

The first set of indices focuses on the regulation of conflicts of interest, specifically self-dealing in the context of related-party transactions. A related-party transaction refers to a case where a person has an economic or personal interest in both parties to the transaction. A company executive entering into a supply contract with another company that is wholly owned by his or her spouse is an example of a related-party transaction. Although related-party transactions are not inherently harmful, they are more likely to result in self-dealing—a type of abuse—and therefore require specific regulation. Self-dealing consists of benefiting oneself while under the duty to serve the interests of someone else. In this example, self-dealing would occur if the supply contract were priced above market so as to benefit the spouse at the expense of the company's owners. Unsurprisingly, research shows that protecting against self-dealing is positively associated with capital market development.[21]

The second set of indices provide a more general view of corporate governance practices, ranging from shareholder rights, protection from share dilution, ownership structure and control of the company to managerial compensation and audit transparency. They are derived from recent comparative law and economics research that has analyzed these practices separately in detail, some of which are described hereafter.[22]

Overall, these two sets of indices present a positive correlation with stock

TABLE 7.1 Indicators of minority investor protection

Extent of conflict of interest regulation index	Extent of disclosure index Extent of director liability index Ease of shareholder suits index	Measured since 2004
Extent of shareholder governance index	Extent of shareholder rights index Extent of ownership and control index Extent of corporate transparency index	Measured since 2014

market development as measured by market capitalization as a percentage of GDP (figure 7.2).[23] *Doing Business* data confirm the existing research on the positive relationship between greater protection of minority shareholders, capital market development and access to equity finance.[24] Subsequent sections provide more evidence from recent research regarding the effects of various corporate governance practices on economic indicators.

FIGURE 7.2 Stronger minority investor protection is associated with greater market capitalization

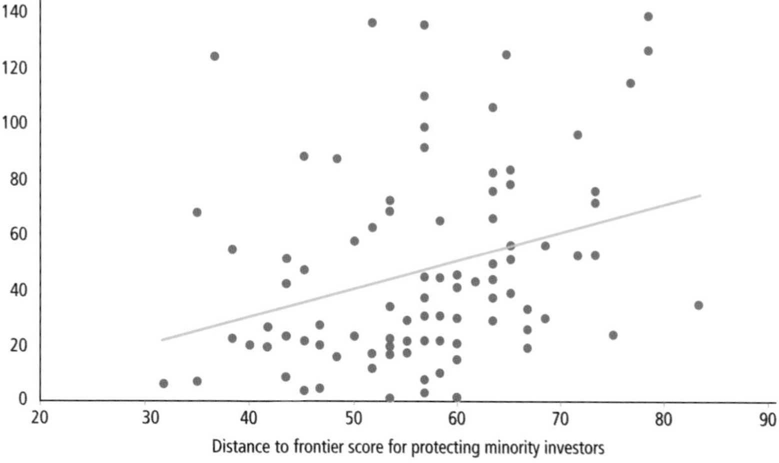

Sources: Doing Business database; Bloomberg; World Federation of Exchanges database.
Note: The correlation between market capitalization as a percentage of GDP and the distance to frontier score for protecting minority investors is 0.23. The relationship is significant at the 5% level after controlling for income per capita. The sample includes 91 economies for which data on market capitalization are available for the past 5 years.

How have economies enhanced corporate governance?

Since 2013, 54 economies introduced 63 legislative changes strengthening minority shareholder protections. Twenty-two of these economies did so by introducing practices and requirements measured by the extent of shareholder governance index introduced in *Doing Business 2015* (table 7.2). These economies have used a variety of different legislative approaches to strengthen their minority shareholder protections. As part of an ambitious multi-year overhaul of its Companies Act, for example, India enhanced corporate governance by affirming the right of shareholders of privately held companies to approve the issuance of new shares and their priority thereon. The new version of the Companies Act was enacted in 2013 and its provisions progressively entered into force over the following two years.

While India chose to reform the legal foundation applicable to all companies (its Companies Act), the Dominican Republic chose a different approach, focusing instead on companies that offer securities to the public. Among the changes introduced in 2013 to its Regulations of the Securities Market Law, it granted minority shareholders the right to request an extraordinary meeting and required an external audit of the financial statements of listed companies.

Ecuador and Kazakhstan elected to introduce one piece of legislation containing amendments to several other legislative instruments. Ecuador's 2014 Law to Strengthen and Optimize the Corporate Sector and the Stock Market, for example, introduced changes to the Securities Market Law, the Commercial Code, the Company Law, the General Law of Financial Institutions and the Code of Civil Procedure, among others. The new law also guarantees a way out for minority shareholders when their company changes hands: if a new investor acquires a majority, he or she must make an offer to purchase the shares of all remaining shareholders. Although Swiss lawmakers had one specific area in mind—excessive remuneration in publicly listed companies—when they issued a federal ordinance in 2013, to tackle the problem effectively they chose a comprehensive response. The result was an ordinance that also regulated the election and term of board members, their organization in subcommittees and their reporting obligations. Similar objectives led the Republic of Korea to enact the Financial Investment Business and Capital Markets Act in 2013. One of its features is the requirement that listed corporations disclose the remuneration of chief officers on an individual basis.

Different rulemaking approaches—whether a series of targeted amendments or a one-time complete revision of a code—aimed at different aspects of corporate governance—such as increasing minority shareholder rights or regulating directors and majority shareholders—contribute to better corporate governance practices. Because *Doing Business* captures outcomes on legal equivalents, these different approaches have a similar impact on its indicators. In other words, to ensure a positive impact on their economy, rather than on benchmarking exercises, policy makers should introduce sounder corporate governance practices in a manner that is consistent with their legal system and tradition. In doing so, policy makers should ensure that different company forms exist, each with different levels of regulatory requirements. Sound corporate governance adapts the compliance burden to company size and revenue. It contributes to creating a "regulatory pyramid," in which companies at the top in terms of market size, turnover, cash flow and systemic importance are also at the top of the regulatory requirements.

TABLE 7.2 Twenty-two economies introduced regulatory changes impacting the extent of shareholder governance index since its inception

		Extent of shareholder governance index		
Year	**Economy**	**Extent of shareholder rights index**	**Extent of ownership and control index**	**Extent of corporate transparency index**
2015/16	Belarus			✓
	Brunei Darussalam		✓	
	Egypt, Arab Rep.	✓	✓	
	Fiji			✓
	Georgia	✓	✓	
	Kazakhstan	✓	✓	✓
	Macedonia, FYR	✓	✓	
	Mauritania	✓		
	Morocco		✓	✓
	Saudi Arabia		✓	✓
	United Arab Emirates	✓	✓	✓
	Uzbekistan		✓	
	Vanuatu	✓	✓	
	Vietnam		✓	✓
2014/15	Egypt, Arab Rep.		✓	
	Kazakhstan		✓	
	Lithuania	✓	✓	✓
	Rwanda	✓		✓
	Spain	✓		
	United Arab Emirates		✓	
2013/14	Dominican Republic	✓		
	Ecuador		✓	
	India	✓		
	Korea, Rep.			✓
	Switzerland		✓	✓

Source: Doing Business database.

THE CASE OF SWITZERLAND

How would a typical business owner react if employees could set their own salaries and not necessarily inform the owner what amount they have decided to pay themselves? This is essentially how companies in many economies determine the remuneration of board members and senior executives vis-à-vis shareholders. In 2014 Switzerland decided that a different model was necessary and enacted an ordinance introducing checks and balances on senior executive compensation.[25] Its purpose was to address concerns both from the public at large and for firm performance.[26] The Swiss experience is an example of public opinion-induced corporate governance reform following the 2008 global financial crisis.[27] The first step occurred on March 3, 2013, when the Swiss voted in favor of a public consultation initiative best translated as "against remuneration rip-off." It passed with 68% of the votes.[28] The Federal Council—the seven-member head of the Swiss government—then drafted a regulation reflecting the consultation's outcome. The Federal Council's ordinance was published on November 20, 2013, and the new requirements entered into force on January 1, 2014.[29]

A closer look at the legal instruments used by Swiss policy makers illustrates how sound corporate governance improves outcomes. There are two primary mechanisms—disclosure and shareholder vote—through which the ordinance affects corporate governance and therefore firm behavior.[30] The disclosure component requires the board of directors to issue a compensation report annually that shows all compensation awarded by the company, directly or indirectly, to members of the board of directors, the executive management and the advisory board.[31] It also stipulates an annual disclosure to the public by annexing the compensation report to the financial statements.[32] Items to be disclosed include fees, salaries, bonuses, profit sharing, services and benefits in kind. It must also be reviewed by an auditor.[33]

The policy objective of disclosure is to provide information that would not otherwise be obtainable and on which informed decisions can be made. In practice, however, shareholders rarely read all the information presented to them, be it before deciding to invest in a company or when participating in a general meeting. Thus the primary effect of disclosure is to guide the decisions made by insiders, knowing in advance that they will have to reveal the information later.

The beneficiary of the disclosure also matters. When the intended beneficiary is broad—that is, the public—the primary concern is the reputation and the image of the company. By contrast, where the disclosure is targeted—to the regulator or stock exchange authority—the concern is compliance. In this case, the goal is to be accurate and avoid sanctions by the authorities. These two options have practical policy implications: in particular cases, disclosure to the regulator is preferable. Complex financial and legal submissions, for example, are effective only if reviewed by experts. In other cases, companies should disclose to the public or shareholders at large rather than to the regulator. For regulatory agencies, the only concern would be that the figures are accurate and provide a complete picture of all benefits and incentives in accordance with applicable accounting standards. Shareholders, on the other hand, would decide on the somewhat subjective concept of excessive compensation. Switzerland, therefore, opted for public disclosure. The reform was captured in the 2015 edition of the *Doing Business* report (figure 7.3).

In addition to disclosure, Switzerland also mandated shareholder vote. The so-called "say on pay" mechanism of the ordinance applies to proposed compensation, which must be put to a vote and approved by the majority of shareholders to be valid. Unequivocally this results in increased shareholder control. But once again, and similar to disclosure, giving shareholders more say is a means rather than an end. The primary goal is to affect firm behavior. When company insiders know in advance that a decision will be subject to shareholder approval, this changes the nature and content of the decision itself.

Two years after the ordinance entered into force practitioners reported that all listed corporations had implemented the new rules without serious issues. So far, shareholders have approved all compensation proposals, which is unsurprising: firms have adjusted their behavior in anticipation to avoid disapproval.[34]

Asking shareholders more interesting questions—such as whether or not they agree with the remuneration of their directors and executives—reaps other benefits. For one, it increases the likelihood that shareholders will actively exercise their voting rights at general meetings. According to a survey of 107 investors, the exercise of voting rights in Switzerland increased from 62.9% to 86.1% after the ordinance passed. And 13.9% of investors who actively used their voting rights did so only on compensation.[35] At the same time, vote outcomes have been mostly positive. Swiss companies continue to operate normally, managers have not found themselves hindered (contrary to initial concerns) and shareholders have been broadly supportive of the proposals put before them. What has changed following the empowerment of shareholders is the increase in accountability and the sense of having a say in major decisions. This has in turn generated trust and confidence, a crucial commodity for the Swiss Exchange or any other capital market.[36]

FIGURE 7.3 Switzerland strengthened shareholder governance as measured by *Doing Business*

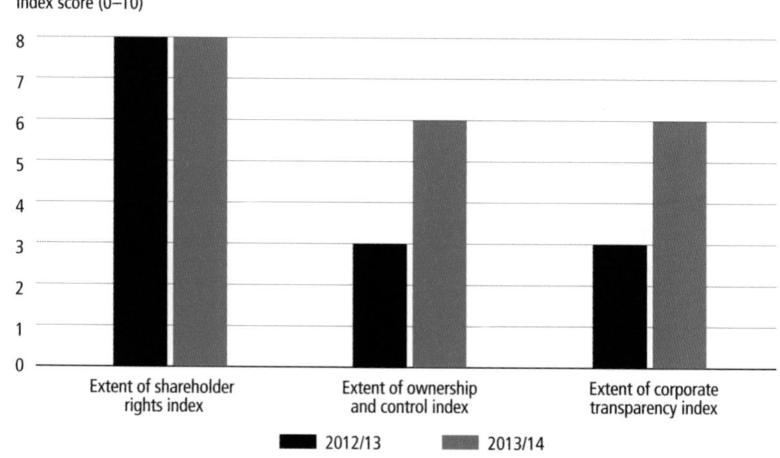

Source: Doing Business database.

THE CASE OF INDIA

India's experience was unique to that of Switzerland. But the goals—trust and economic growth—were similar. Rather than a popular initiative focused on managerial compensation—albeit a central issue with multiple ramifications—the government of India took on the task of completely overhauling its Companies Act, its primary set of rules governing how businesses are incorporated, owned, managed, rehabilitated or closed when insolvent, and challenged in court. The previous version dated from 1956.

Ambitious and comprehensive legislation takes time. India's lawmaking process started in 2004[37] and was followed by years of drafting, redrafting and consultations on the bill. It was finally submitted to parliament in 2012 and passed by the upper house on August 8, 2013. It received the assent of the president shortly after, on August 29. The date of entry into force is less straightforward. India follows an unusual system whereby provisions are not applicable until the Ministry of Corporate Affairs notifies each section; notification typically happens in waves. The first took place in September 2013 with the notification of 98 sections followed by another series of notifications in April 2014. As of June 2016, 282 of the 470 total sections were notified and eight provisions of the 1956 Act remain applicable. Despite this piecemeal introduction, it has paid off both in economic terms and in India's performance in *Doing Business*: India's score increased in three of the six indices of the protecting minority investors indicator set (figure 7.4).[38]

Four objectives guided the drafting of the reformed Companies Act. First, administrative requirements weighing on companies had to be simplified. Second, more transparency had to be instilled in their operations and decision-making structures. Third, the competitiveness of Indian firms had to be increased by bringing them in line with global standards, particularly regarding accountability and corporate governance practices. Lastly, it had to advance all of the above while ensuring that businesses contribute more to shared prosperity in an economy where demographics and income inequality pose stark challenges.

To simplify administrative requirements the minimum paid-in capital was abolished. To instill greater transparency the Act increased disclosure requirements, particularly regarding related-party transactions.[39] To bring Indian firms in line with global standards the Act added requirements to disclose managerial compensation and to have one-third independent directors and at least one woman on the board.[40] The fourth objective, however—contributing to greater shared prosperity—garnered the most attention by aspiring that all companies allocate 2% of their net profits to socially responsible projects. In effect, India became the first economy in the world with a quantified and legislated corporate social responsibility (CSR) requirement. However, it is enforceable on a "comply or explain" basis and goes beyond the scope of areas measured by *Doing Business*.[41] In practice, this means that companies who fail to meet the target must simply state so in their annual report and provide a justification. The Act provides a statutory definition of CSR as activities relating to hunger and poverty eradication, education, women empowerment, and health and environmental sustainability, among others.[42]

Company regulation is an ongoing process. Since the enactment of the Companies Act, 2013, the Ministry of Corporate Affairs has issued clarifications, notifications and circulars on a regular basis to address ambiguities in the law. Most notably, two sets of amendments were released in August 2014 and in May 2015, highlighting the Indian government's ongoing commitment to reform. On June 4, 2015, it set up a committee tasked with identifying and recommending further amendments to the Act and with centralizing recommendations and concerns from private sector stakeholders and regulatory agencies.[43] The case of India serves as a reminder of the time it takes and the challenges inherent to a holistic legislative overhaul. Piecemeal fixes can be a time- and cost-effective approach, but only a full-fledged legislative reform gives policy makers the opportunity to innovate and sends a strong signal to the business community.

CONCLUSION

Achieving sound corporate governance is not a simple task. It is a specialized and technical area of regulation. Its impact is not as immediate as, for example, facilitating business incorporation or streamlining tax compliance. But thanks to the analytical tools provided by the law and economics approach, research shows that gains for the economy are tangible. At the outset, it increases investor confidence. With easier access to finance, companies can grow and, in so doing, pay more taxes and employ more workers. It is also shown to increase the returns on equity, efficiency of investment allocation and to decrease the cost of capital.

FIGURE 7.4 India's Companies Act 2013 made strides in three indices

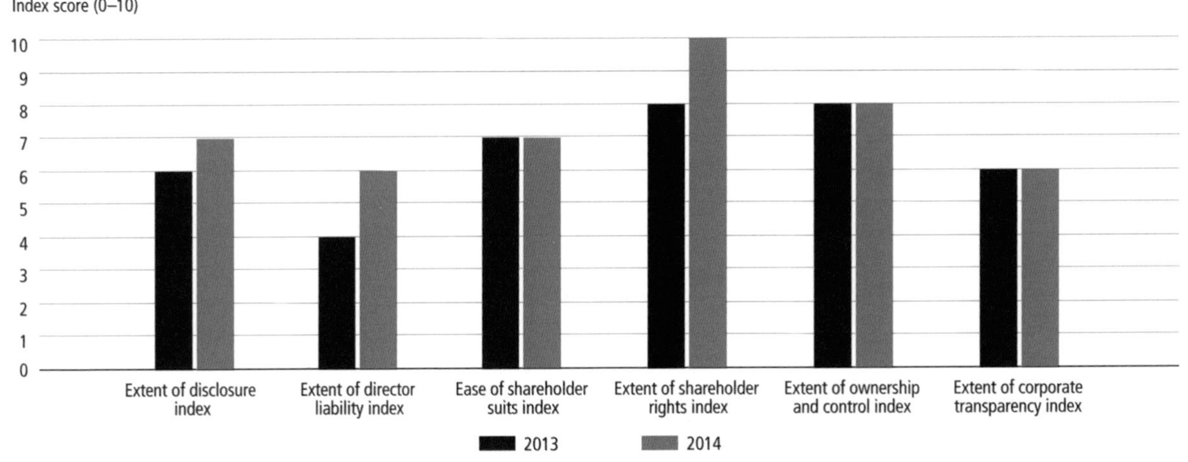

Source: Doing Business database.

The growing body of research on achieving sound corporate governance is also having an impact. Lessons learned from other economies adopting these practices and constant new research—including those using *Doing Business* data—confirm their economic benefit. Although performance on this indicator set is very highly correlated with the stage of economic development, policy makers in developing economies now have a clearer path to introduce effective corporate governance and maximize the potential of their firms.

The majority of the 54 economies that made strides in minority investor protection in the past three years are the ones that have the furthest to go: 44 of them are low- or middle-income economies. To contribute to this effort, *Doing Business* has doubled the areas of corporate governance included in the protecting minority investors indicator set and expanded it to include regulatory frameworks that are relevant for small and medium-size enterprises. The immediate result is that more strengths, weaknesses and therefore potential improvements can be identified from its annual findings. In addition, researchers, lawyers and policy makers now have a more comprehensive baseline when working toward introducing sounder corporate governance practices.

NOTES

This case study was written by Nadine Abi Chakra, Varun Eknath, Albina Gasanbekova and Hervé Kaddoura.

1. Legal risk refers to the risk of loss arising from insufficient, improperly applied or unfavorable legislation and the resulting lawsuits.
2. Mukwiri and Siems 2014; Dignam 2013; Reisberg 2013; Cheffins 2009.
3. A corporate governance reform is a legislative or regulatory change that increases the level of protection of minority investors as measured by the *Doing Business* protecting minority investors indicators. See the data notes for more details.
4. Katelouzou and Siems 2015.
5. Bebchuk 2005.
6. Asker and others 2015; Claessens 2006; Klapper and Love 2004; Kutan 2015.
7. OECD 2015.
8. Eisenberg 1993.
9. American Law Institute 1992.
10. The OECD summarizes corporate governance as a set of relationships between a company's management, its board, its shareholders and other stakeholders. Corporate governance also provides the structure through which the objectives of the company are set, and the means of attaining those objectives and monitoring performance are determined.
11. For a discussion on the importance of effective enforcement see Okpara 2011.
12. Dyck and Zingales 2004; Holderness 2003; La Porta and others 2000; Shleifer and Vishny 1986.
13. Arora 2014; Rupeika-Apoga 2014.
14. Ammann and others 2011; Brown and Caylor 2009; Gompers and others 2003.
15. Bebchuk and others 1999.
16. Aggarwal and others 2009; Denis and Serrano 1996; Grossman and Hart 1982.
17. Bebchuk 2013.
18. Ates and others 2014; Lan and others 2015; Liljeblom and others 2015.
19. Legal certainty may be defined as the consistent application of a rule—the same facts invariably resulting in the same clear, definite and binding decisions.
20. Posner 1983; La Porta and others 1996.
21. Djankov and others 2008.
22. See "Going beyond related-party transactions" in *Doing Business 2015*. See also Black and others 2010; Cremers and Ferrell 2014; Dharmapala and Khanna 2013; McLean and others 2012; Lima and Zoratto 2013; Chen and others 2011; Malhotra and others 2013; Guo and Masulis 2013; Lang and others 2012; Martynova and Renneboog 2011.
23. The data for market capitalization as a percentage of GDP are from Bloomberg. The market capitalization figures are calculated from "all shares outstanding." The data do not include exchange traded funds (ETFs) and American depository receipts (ADRs) as they do not directly represent companies. They include only actively traded, primary securities on national exchanges to avoid double counting. Therefore the values will be significantly lower than market capitalization values of an economy's exchanges from other sources. Bloomberg standardizes the figures by dividing market capitalization by GDP to be able to make comparisons among economies. See also Pagano and Volpin 2006; Ali and Aamir 2014.
24. Dahya and others 2008.
25. Swiss Federal Justice and Police Department. 2013. "Initiative populaire 'contre les rémunérations abusives'." Press release, March 3. Available at http://www.ejpd.admin.ch/ejpd/fr/home/aktuell/abstimmungen/2013-03-03.html/.
26. Core and others 1999, for example, find that firms with weaker governance structures have greater agency problems, that CEOs at firms with greater agency problems receive greater compensation and that firms with greater agency problems perform worse.
27. Barthold and others 2014.
28. Swiss Federal Justice and Police Department 2013.
29. Roberts 2014.
30. The ordinance also contains other important features. Only the general meeting of shareholders can now elect the chairman of the board of directors and the members of the compensation committee. The establishment of a compensation committee became mandatory, and provisions on proxies and pension fund schemes were also introduced.
31. Disclosure of managerial compensation is one of the practices that are measured by the protecting minority investors indicator set. It was added when the methodology was expanded in 2014.
32. Article 13 of the ordinance against excessive compensation in listed companies and Articles 696 and 958e of the Swiss Federal Code of Obligations.
33. Articles 13-16 of the ordinance against excessive compensation in listed companies.
34. Daeniker and others 2014.
35. Swiss Proxy Advisor 2014.
36. Over the two-year period after the ordinance against excessive compensation in listed companies became effective, the Swiss Market Index rose by 6.6%.
37. Venkateshwaran 2013.
38. World Development Indicators database (http://data.worldbank.org/indicator), World Bank; *Doing Business* database.
39. Section 188, Indian Companies Act, 2013.
40. Section 149, Indian Companies Act, 2013.
41. Section 135, Indian Companies Act, 2013.
42. Schedule VII, Indian Companies Act, 2013.
43. India, Ministry of Corporate Affairs. 2016. Report of the Companies Law Committee. February. http://www.mca.gov.in/Ministry/pdf/Report_Companies_Law_Committee_01022016.pdf/.

Paying Taxes

Assessing postfiling processes

- Up until *Doing Business 2016*, the paying taxes indicator set measured the cost of complying with tax obligations up to the filing of tax returns and the payment of taxes due. Filing the return with the tax authority, however, does not imply agreement with the final tax liability. Postfiling processes—such as claiming a value added tax (VAT) refund, undergoing a tax audit or appealing a tax assessment—can be the most challenging interactions that a business has with a tax authority. *Doing Business 2017* expands the paying taxes indicators to include a new measure on postfiling.
- *Doing Business* data shows that OECD high-income economies process VAT refunds the most efficiently with an average of 14.4 weeks to reimburse the VAT refund. Economies in Europe and Central Asia also perform well with an average refund time of 16 weeks.
- On average, businesses spend six hours correcting an error in an income tax return and preparing any additional documents, submitting the files and making additional payment. Even following immediate voluntary notification by the taxpayer, in 74 economies an error in the income tax return is likely to trigger an audit. In 38 economies this error will lead to a comprehensive audit of the tax return.
- OECD high-income economies as well as Europe and Central Asia economies have the easiest and simplest processes in place to correct a minor mistake in the corporate income tax return.
- An internal administrative review process should be based on a transparent legal framework. This process should be independent and resolve disputes in a timely manner.

Taxes are important to the proper functioning of an economy. They are the main source of federal, state and local government revenues used to fund health care, education, public transport, unemployment benefits and pensions, among others. While the size of the tax cost imposed on businesses has implications for their ability to invest and grow, the efficiency of the tax administration system is also critical for businesses.[1] A low cost of tax compliance and efficient tax-related procedures are advantageous for firms. Overly complicated tax systems are associated with high levels of tax evasion, large informal sectors, more corruption and less investment.[2] Tax compliance systems should be designed so as not to discourage businesses from participating in the formal economy.

Modern tax systems seek to optimize tax collections while minimizing administrative and taxpayer compliance costs. The most cost-effective tax collection systems are those that encourage the vast majority of taxpayers to meet their tax obligations voluntarily, thereby allowing tax officials to concentrate their efforts on non-compliant taxpayers and other services provided by tax administrations.[3] Taxpayers are more likely to comply voluntarily when a tax administration has established a transparent system that is regarded by taxpayers as being honest and fair.

Total tax compliance costs include all major transactions that generate external costs to the taxpayer. Up until *Doing Business 2016*, the paying taxes indicator set measured only the cost of complying with tax obligations up until the filing of tax returns and the payment of taxes due. However, filing the tax return with the tax authority does not imply agreement with the final tax liability. Postfiling processes—such as claiming a value added tax (VAT) refund, undergoing a tax audit or appealing a tax assessment—can be the most challenging interactions that a business has with a tax authority.

Doing Business 2017 expands the paying taxes indicators to include a new measure of the time businesses spend complying with two postfiling processes: claiming a VAT refund and correcting a mistake in the corporate income tax return. This case study examines these two postfiling procedures across 190 economies and shows where postfiling processes and practices work efficiently and what drives the differences in the overall tax compliance cost across economies. This case study also includes a section on the structure of a first level administrative appeal process. The data on first level administrative appeal process is not included in the distance to frontier score for paying taxes.

VAT REFUNDS

The VAT refund is an integral component of a modern VAT system. In principle, the statutory incidence of VAT is on the final consumer, not on businesses. According to tax policy guidelines set out by the Organisation for Economic Co-operation and Development (OECD) a value added tax system should be neutral and efficient.[4] Some businesses will incur more VAT on their purchases than they collect on their taxable sales in a given tax period and therefore should be entitled to claim the difference from the tax authorities. When businesses incur VAT which is not refunded at all—or reclaimed with delays and large compliance costs—then the principles of neutrality and efficiency are undermined. This alters the nature of VAT by effectively making it a tax on production. Any tax that cannot be recovered by the business could have a distortionary effect on market prices and competition and consequently constrain economic growth.[5]

Refund processes can be a major weakness of VAT systems. This was the finding of a study that examined the VAT administration refund mechanism in 36 economies around the world.[6] Even in economies where refund procedures are in place, businesses often find the complexity of the process challenging. The study examined the tax authorities' treatment of excess VAT credits, the size of refund claims, the procedures followed by refund claimants and the time needed for the tax authorities to process refunds. The results showed that statutory time limits for making refunds are crucial but often not applied in practice.

Most VAT systems allow credit to be carried-forward for a specific period of time and offset against future net liabilities to reduce the number of refunds processed. The rationale is that excess VAT credits in one tax period would be followed by periods when net liabilities would absorb the credit brought forward, especially for businesses producing and selling in the domestic market. A refund is paid only if an amount of excess credit remains to be recovered by the taxpayer at the end of the carry-forward period. Some systems also allow a VAT credit in a given tax period to be offset against other current tax liabilities such as income tax. While the option of carry-forward is allowed in most VAT systems, it is good practice for economies to put in place an adequate VAT refund system. Because considerable differences in the efficiency of processing VAT cash refunds exist between economies, the paying taxes indicators focus on assessing VAT refund systems.

The IMF's Tax Administration Diagnostic Assessment Tool (TADAT) provides an integrated monitoring framework to measure the performance of an economy's tax administration system across different functions, including the adequacy of its VAT refund system. It does this by measuring the time taken to pay (or offset) refunds.[7]

Like any tax, VAT is prone to fraud and its refund mechanism may be open to abuse by taxpayers.[8] Delays in processing refunds, therefore, may be the result of concerns over potential fraud. Even when claims reach the finance division responsible for approving them and making payment, there can be delays in transmission. Additional procedural checks at this stage—prompted by a fear of the system being abused—are common.

In some economies a claim for a VAT refund can automatically trigger a costly audit, undermining the overall effectiveness of the system.[9] Effective audit programs and VAT refund payment systems are inextricably linked. Tax audits (direct and indirect) vary in their scope and complexity, ranging from a full audit—which typically entails a comprehensive examination of all information relevant to the calculation of a taxpayer's tax liability in a given period—to a limited scope audit that is restricted to specific issues on the tax return or a single issue audit that is limited to one item.[10]

The transactions that lead to substantial VAT refund claims typically include exports, capital expenses, extraordinary losses and startup operations.[11] Through its paying taxes indicators, *Doing Business* measures the efficiency of VAT refunds by analyzing the case of capital expenses. The *Doing Business* case study company, TaxpayerCo., is a domestic business that does not participate in foreign trade. It performs a general industrial and commercial activity in the domestic market and is in its second year of operation. TaxpayerCo. meets the VAT threshold for registration and its monthly sales and monthly operating expenses are fixed throughout the year resulting in a positive output VAT payable to the tax authorities within each accounting period. The case study scenario has been expanded to include a capital purchase of a machine in the month of June; this substantial capital expenditure results in input VAT exceeding output VAT in the month of June.

Compliance with VAT refunds

In principle, when input VAT exceeds output VAT the amount should be paid as a refund to a registered business within the time period stipulated in the legislation. In practice, however, only 93 of the economies covered by *Doing Business* allow for a VAT cash refund in this scenario. Some economies restrict the right to receive an immediate cash refund to specific types of taxpayers such as exporters, embassies and non-profit organizations. This is the case in 43 economies including Belarus, Bolivia, Colombia, the Dominican Republic, Ecuador, Kazakhstan, Kenya, Mali and the Philippines. In Ecuador VAT refunds are limited to exporters, embassies, diplomatic missions, some specific non-government entities and international cargo companies. In Armenia cash refunds are only allowed when zero-rated VAT transactions (primarily exports) exceed 20% of all transactions.

In some economies businesses are only allowed to claim a cash refund after rolling over the excess credit for a specified period of time (for example, four months). The net VAT balance is refunded to the business only when this period ends. This is the case in 21 economies included in *Doing Business*.[12] In Albania, Azerbaijan, Cambodia, The Gambia, Lesotho, Malawi and St. Lucia, businesses must carry forward the excess input VAT for three months before a cash refund can be given. In other economies—typically those with a weaker administrative or financial capacity to handle cash refunds—the legislation may not permit refunds outright. Instead, tax authorities require businesses to carry forward the claim and offset the excess amount against future output VAT. This is the case in Grenada, Guinea-Bissau, Sudan and República Bolivariana de Venezuela. In these two groups of economies it is common to make exceptions for exporters in relation to domestic supply. Twenty-eight economies do not levy VAT.

In 68 of the 93 economies that allow for VAT cash refunds (as in the *Doing Business* case scenario) the legal framework includes a time limit to repay the VAT refund starting from the moment the refund was requested. These time limits are always applied in practice in only 29 economies (21 of these economies are high-income economies). In only 28 of the 93 economies, a claim for a VAT refund does not ordinarily lead to an audit being conducted.[13]

In 46 economies the VAT refund due is calculated and requested within the standard VAT return, which is submitted for each accounting period and without additional work. The main purpose of filing a VAT return is to provide a summary of the output and input VAT activities that result in the net VAT payable or due (as credit or refund). For these economies the compliance time to prepare and request a VAT refund is minimal because it simply requires ticking a box. Twenty-one of these economies are OECD high-income economies. Furthermore eight of the 14 economies where taxpayers will not face an audit—and therefore will not spend additional time complying with the requirements of the auditor—are OECD high-income economies. This partly explains the average low compliance time in the region (figure 8.1).

In Germany, the Republic of Korea and the Netherlands, taxpayers request a VAT refund by simply checking a box on the standard VAT return. Taxpayers do not need to submit any additional documents to substantiate the claim and it is unlikely that this specific case study scenario of a domestic capital purchase would trigger an audit. In all three economies, the standard VAT return is submitted electronically.

FIGURE 8.1 Complying with VAT refund processes is most challenging in Latin America and the Caribbean, followed closely by Sub-Saharan Africa

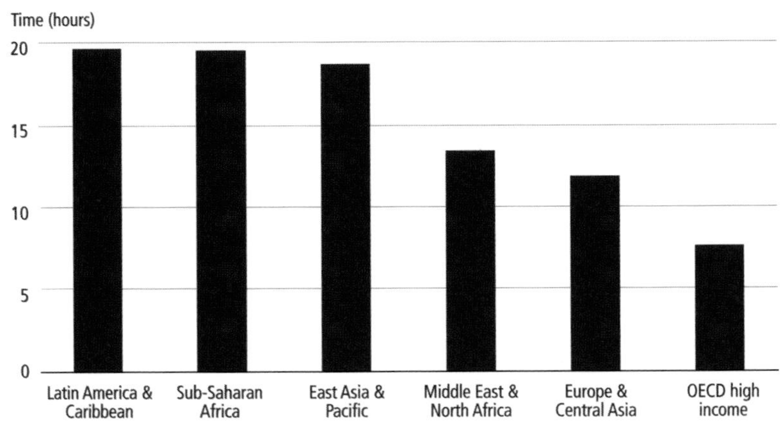

Source: Doing Business database.
Note: South Asia is not included in the figure because VAT refunds are available in only one economy (Bangladesh).

However, some economies require businesses to file a separate application, letter or form for a VAT refund or to complete a specific section in the VAT return as well as to prepare some additional documentation to substantiate the claim (for example, the contract with the supplier of the machine). This is the case in Azerbaijan, Bangladesh, Costa Rica, Cyprus, Mexico, Senegal, St. Lucia and Sweden, among others. In these economies businesses spend on average 5.2 hours gathering the required information, calculating the claim and preparing the refund application and other documentation before submitting them to the relevant authority.

The requirements in these cases vary from simply completing a specific section of the standard VAT return to submitting a specific refund application. In Switzerland, for example, taxpayers would need to complete a section of the VAT return. It takes taxpayers in Switzerland 1.5 hours to gather the necessary information from internal sources and to complete the relevant section. The VAT return is submitted electronically. In Moldova, however, taxpayers must submit a specific VAT refund form and it is highly likely that a field audit would be triggered by the refund request.

Completing a VAT refund process

A request for a VAT cash refund is likely to trigger an audit in 65 economies covered by *Doing Business*. As a general rule the refunds are paid upon completion of the audit and not at the end of the statutory period. This adds time and costs for businesses to comply with auditor requests and the payment of the cash refund is further delayed. Businesses in these economies spend on average 14.7 hours complying with the requirements of the auditor in terms of document preparation, engage in several rounds of interactions with the auditor that last on average 7.9 weeks and wait an additional 5.6 weeks until the final audit decision is made. Of the 65 economies, businesses are likely to undergo a field audit in 34, a correspondence audit in 22 and an office audit in nine. Businesses subjected to a field audit would spend on average an additional

7.7 hours complying with the auditor's requirements compared to businesses subjected to a correspondence audit.

In Canada, Denmark, Estonia and Norway the request for a VAT refund is likely to trigger a correspondence audit, which requires less interaction with the auditor and less paperwork. By contrast, in most of the economies in Sub-Saharan Africa where an audit is likely to take place, taxpayers are exposed to a field audit in which the auditor visits the premises of the taxpayer. This is the case in Botswana, The Gambia, Malawi, Niger, Zambia and Zimbabwe.

The OECD high-income economies process VAT refunds most efficiently with an average of 14.4 weeks to reimburse a VAT refund (including some economies where an audit is likely to be conducted). Economies in Europe and Central Asia also perform well with an average refund processing time of 16 weeks (figure 8.2). This implies that those economies provide refunds in a manner that is less likely to expose businesses to unnecessary administrative costs and detrimental cash flow impacts.

From the moment a taxpayer submits a VAT refund request in Austria, it takes only one week for the tax authority to issue a refund. And it is unlikely that the request would trigger an audit. The refund is processed electronically through online banking. In Estonia, despite the fact that the claim for a VAT refund per the case scenario is highly likely to trigger a correspondence audit, the process is efficient. The VAT refund is reimbursed in 1.7 weeks on average assuming the refund is approved. This includes the time spent by the taxpayer engaging with the auditor and the time waiting until the final tax assessment is issued.

The experience in economies in other regions is less favorable. Obtaining a VAT refund in Latin America and the Caribbean takes on average 35 weeks. In the Middle East and North Africa and Sub-Saharan Africa it takes on average 28.8 and 27.5 weeks, respectively, to obtain a VAT refund. The sample for Latin America and the Caribbean includes only nine economies (the other economies do not allow for VAT cash refund per the case study scenario). The Middle East and North Africa sample consists of only six economies as most economies in the region do not levy any type of consumption tax. However, in Sub-Saharan Africa the story is different: the refund waiting time is longer because in most of the economies in the region where cash refund is allowed, taxpayers are likely to be audited before the refund is approved.

FIGURE 8.2 The process of obtaining a VAT refund is most efficient in OECD high-income economies

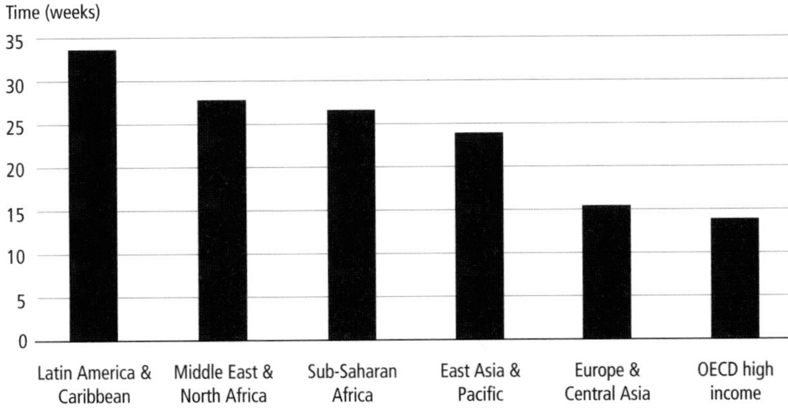

Source: Doing Business database.
Note: South Asia is not included in the figure because VAT refunds are available in only one economy (Bangladesh).

The efficiency of the VAT refund process in OECD high-income economies is partly attributable to the commitment of all OECD members to apply the OECD International VAT Guidelines.[14] Furthermore, the binding nature of the 2010 European Union (EU) Directives on VAT implementation ensures that refunds are processed fully and efficiently.

A major determinant of the ability of revenue authorities to provide good standards of service for the repayment of VAT refund claims is the availability and use of modern electronic services (such as electronic filing, pre-population and direct crediting of VAT refunds). VAT refunds are paid electronically in only 30 economies covered by *Doing Business*. Delays in VAT refund payments may arise if, for example, the finance division that is tasked with checking and approving the claim is forced to make additional procedural checks to guard against fraud before payment is made.[15]

Laws provide for interest to be paid on late VAT refunds by the tax authorities in 70 economies covered by *Doing Business*. However, the payment of interest is always applied in practice in only 32 economies. The prescribed interest period typically begins when the tax authority fails to refund VAT within the prescribed statutory deadlines.

There is a positive correlation between the time to comply with a VAT refund process and the time to comply with filing the standard VAT return and payment of VAT liabilities (figure 8.3). This suggests that spending time up front to comply with the requirements of the tax system does not necessarily translate into an easier time postfiling. Indeed, in economies with tax systems that are more difficult to comply with when filing taxes, the entire process is more likely to be challenging.

FIGURE 8.3 Economies with complex VAT postfiling processes also tend to have high compliance times for VAT prefiling

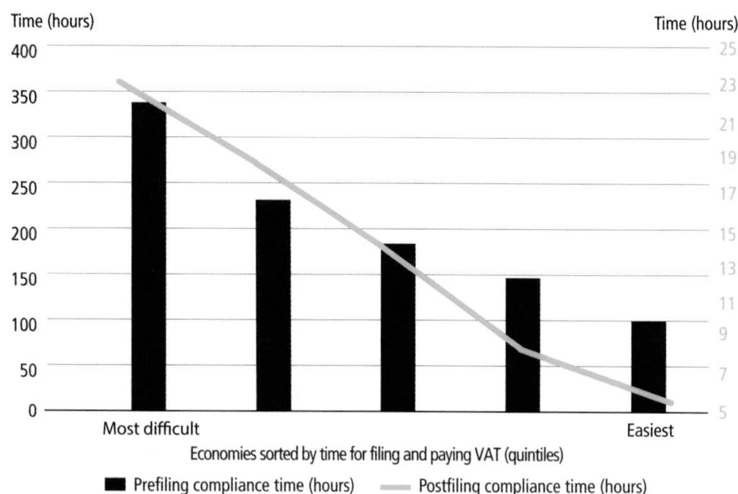

Source: Doing Business database.

TAX AUDITS

A tax audit is one of the most sensitive interactions between a taxpayer and a tax authority. Although tax audits have a role in ensuring tax compliance, they impose a burden on the taxpayer to a greater or lesser extent depending on the number and type of interactions (field visit by the auditor or office visit by the taxpayer) and the level of documentation requested by the auditor. It is therefore essential that the right legal framework is in place to ensure integrity in the way tax authorities carry out audits.[16] Additionally, an audit must have defined start and end points and the taxpayer must be notified once the audit process is completed.

A risk-based approach takes into consideration different aspects of a business such as historical compliance, industry characteristics, debt-credit ratios for VAT-registered businesses and firm size. Characteristics of firms are also used to better assess which businesses are most prone to tax evasion. One study showed that data-mining techniques for auditing, regardless of the technique, captured more noncompliant taxpayers than random audits.[17] In a risk-based approach the exact criteria used to capture noncompliant firms, however, should be concealed to prevent taxpayers from purposefully planning how to avoid detection and to allow for a degree of uncertainty to drive voluntary compliance.[18] Most economies have risk assessment systems in place to select companies for tax audits and the basis on which these companies are selected is not disclosed. Despite being a postfiling procedure, audit strategies set by tax authorities can have a fundamental impact on the way businesses file and pay taxes.

To analyze audits of direct taxes the *Doing Business* case study scenario was expanded to assume that TaxpayerCo. made a simple error in the calculation of its income tax liability, leading to an incorrect corporate income tax return and consequently an underpayment of income tax liability due. TaxpayerCo. discovered the error and voluntarily notified the tax authority. In all economies that levy corporate income tax—only 10 out of 190 do not—taxpayers can notify the authorities of the error, submit an amended return and any additional documentation (typically a letter explaining the error and, in some cases, amended financial statements) and pay the difference immediately. On average, businesses spend six hours preparing the amended return and any additional documents, submitting the files and making payment. In 74 economies—even following immediate notification by the taxpayer—the error in the income tax return is likely to trigger an audit. On average taxpayers will spend 24.7 hours complying with the requirements of the auditor, spend 10.6 weeks going through several rounds of interactions with the auditor and wait 6.7 weeks for the auditor to issue the final decision on the tax assessment.

In 38 economies this error will lead to a comprehensive audit of the income tax return, requiring that additional time be spent by businesses. And in the majority of cases the auditor will visit the taxpayer's premises. OECD high-income economies as well as Europe and Central Asia economies have the easiest and simplest processes in place to correct a minor mistake in the income tax return (figure 8.4). A mistake in the income tax return does not automatically trigger an audit by the tax authorities in 25 OECD high-income economies. Taxpayers need only to submit an amended return and, in some cases, additional documentation and pay the difference in balance of tax due. In Latin America and the Caribbean taxpayers suffer the most from a lengthy process to correct a minor mistake in an income tax return. In most cases this process will involve an audit imposing a waiting time on taxpayers until the final assessment is issued (figure 8.5).

In Portugal and Estonia, taxpayers must only submit an amended tax return and make the necessary payment at the moment of submission. It takes taxpayers half an hour to prepare the amended return and another half an hour to submit it electronically. The payment is also made online. In these economies, the case study scenario of a minor mistake in the income tax return is not likely to

FIGURE 8.4 Correcting an income tax return is easiest in OECD high-income economies, followed closely by Europe and Central Asia economies

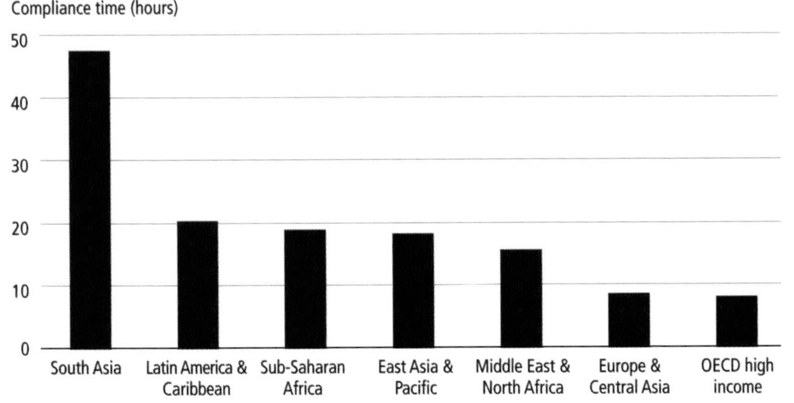

Source: Doing Business database.

trigger an audit. In New Zealand, taxpayers must submit a specific voluntary disclosure form—which takes on average three hours to prepare—with the submission and payment being made electronically. Similarly, taxpayers are unlikely to be exposed to an audit in the case measured in *Doing Business*.

In Brazil, Honduras, Nicaragua and Peru the fact that taxpayers erroneously declared and underpaid their income tax liability would likely trigger a field audit by the tax authorities. In Peru taxpayers will undergo a comprehensive audit of all items on the income tax return, requiring interaction with the auditor for around six weeks and waiting an additional seven weeks for the auditor to issue the final assessment.

ADMINISTRATIVE TAX APPEALS

Tax disputes are common in any tax system. Disputes between a tax authority and taxpayers must be resolved in a fair, timely and efficient manner.[19] In the first instance, taxpayers should attempt to settle their final tax assessment with the tax authority. If a dispute continues, however, taxpayers should have the opportunity—within a prescribed period of time—to seek resolution from a special administrative appeal board or department. The creation of boards of appeal within tax administrations is considered by the OECD as an effective tool for addressing and resolving complaints and avoiding the overburdening of the courts.[20] A serious backlog of tax cases threatens revenue collection.[21]

FIGURE 8.5 The audit time resulting from a simple mistake in an income tax return is the longest in Latin America and the Caribbean

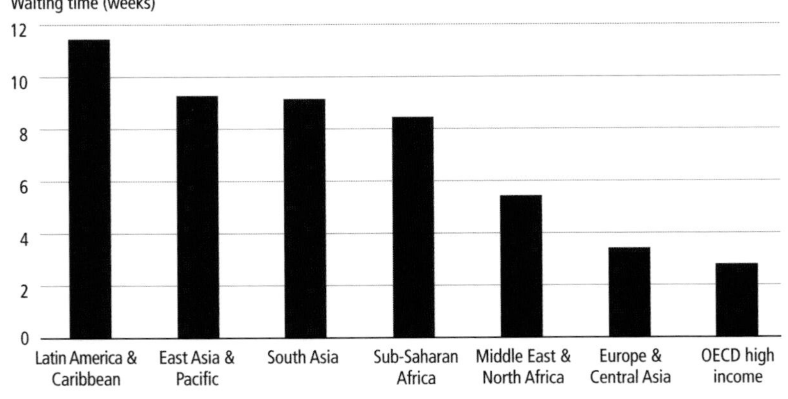

Source: Doing Business database.

Resolving tax disputes in a way that is independent, fast and fair is important. The IMF's TADAT tool also assesses the adequacy of tax dispute resolution by looking at whether an appropriately graduated mechanism of administrative and judicial review is available, whether the administrative review mechanism is independent of the audit process and whether information on the appeal process is published. An internal administrative review process must safeguard a taxpayer's right to challenge an assessment resulting from a tax audit. The process should be based on a legal framework that is known by taxpayers, is easily accessible and independent and resolves disputed matters in a timely manner. Internal reviews can be achieved through a separate appeals division, a senior official that does not directly supervise the original case auditor or a new auditor with no previous knowledge of the case. Operational manuals should be developed, decisions should be published and annual appeal statistics should be reported—helping to create a positive public perception of the tax administration's integrity.

Through the paying taxes indicators, *Doing Business* conducts research on what kind of first level administrative appeal process exists in an economy following a corporate income tax audit where a taxpayer disagrees with the tax authority's final decision. The data on first level administrative appeal process are not included in the distance to frontier score for paying taxes. In 123 economies the first level administrative appeal authority is an independent department within the tax office (figure 8.6).

FIGURE 8.6 Most economies have an independent department within the tax office for taxpayer appeals

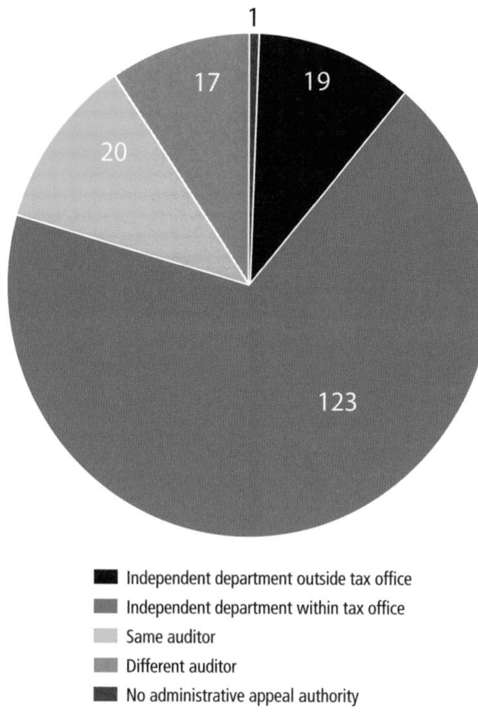

Source: Doing Business database.

Appeal guidelines are available to taxpayers either through a printed publication, online or in person at the tax office in the 171 of the 180 economies covered by *Doing Business* that levy corporate income tax. In 102 economies the legal framework imposes timeframes on the taxpayer and the appeal authority for each stage of the appeal process. In only 47 economies, however, respondents reported that the time limits are consistently applied in practice.

In Chile a taxpayer can appeal to the regional director of the Chilean Internal Revenue Service (SII) following a corporate income tax audit where the taxpayer disagrees with the tax authority's final decision. Guidelines on how to appeal the decision and the timeframe to conclude the process are easily accessible to the public through the SII's website. By law, the Chilean Tax Code sets a time limit of 50 days for the SII's regional director to issue a decision on the appeal. This time limit is applied in practice.

CONCLUSION

Little is known about the tax compliance cost of postfiling procedures. This analysis is therefore intended to generate new research to better understand firms' decisions and the dynamics in developing economies, to highlight which processes and practices work—and which do not—and, eventually, to induce governments to reform and enhance their postfiling processes.

The new indicator on the adequacy of postfiling processes provides policy makers who are dealing with the challenge of designing an optimal tax system with a broader dataset that allows them to benchmark their economy against others on the administrative burden of complying with postfiling procedures.

NOTES

This case study was written by Emily Jane Bourke, Joanna Nasr, Nadia Novik and Rodrigo A. Sarmento de Beires.

1. For more on the World Bank Enterprise Surveys, see the website at http://www.enterprisesurveys.org.
2. Djankov and others 2010.
3. IMF 2015a.
4. OECD 2014c.
5. OECD 2014c.
6. Harrison and Krelove 2005.
7. For more information on the Tax Administration Diagnostic Assessment Tool (TADAT), see the website at http://www.tadat.org/.
8. Keen and Smith 2007.
9. Harrison and Krelove 2005.
10. OECD 2006a.
11. The key point for exports is that the supplies are taxable but zero-rated as they are taxed at the destination economy leading to input VAT being offset against zero output VAT. The notion of claiming a VAT refund immediately for substantial capital expenditure in an accounting period is that the recoverable amount of input VAT in that period could be large and result in excess input tax credit or a refund claim for the period. Extraordinary events—such as fire, flood or seasonal trends—may lower sales activities over periods of time or even halt sales while the business continues filing regular VAT returns. Lastly, new businesses would register for VAT based on the sales that they expect to make even before they start making actual sales. This means that new businesses could offset input VAT on start-up expenses against a minimal output VAT, resulting in a VAT refund claim.
12. These economies are Albania; Antigua and Barbuda; Azerbaijan; Bulgaria; Cambodia; Dominica; The Gambia; Guyana; Jordan; Kiribati; Lesotho; Malawi; Nepal; Pakistan; Seychelles; St. Kitts and Nevis; St. Lucia; Tanzania; Tonga; Tunisia; and Vietnam.
13. These economies are Austria; Barbados; Belize; Costa Rica; Croatia; Cyprus; Ethiopia; Finland; France; Germany; the Islamic Republic of Iran; Ireland; the Republic of Korea; Latvia; Lithuania; Malta; Netherlands; New Zealand; Papua New Guinea; Portugal; Samoa; Seychelles; Slovenia; Spain; Sweden; Switzerland; Taiwan, China; and the Republic of Yemen.
14. OECD 2014c.
15. Child 2008.
16. OECD 2006a.
17. Gupta and Nagadevara 2007.
18. Alm and McKee 2006; Khwaja, Awasthi and Loeprick 2011.
19. Thuronyi 2003.
20. OECD 2010.
21. Gordon 1996.

Trading Across Borders

Technology gains in trade facilitation

In the era of digital advancement and constant innovation, international trade has greatly benefitted from the development and integration of various electronic interfaces. Aspiring to advance cross-border trade through the use of digital technologies and electronic services, the World Customs Organization (WCO) declared 2016 the Year of Digital Customs. The WCO placed a special emphasis on the coordination of customs activities such as automated customs clearance systems, the implementation of single windows as well as improvement of electronic information exchanges. The goal of these activities is to promote the free flow of information and increase transparency while improving the efficiency of day-to-day trade processes.[1] Adding to this effort, the *Doing Business* trading across borders indicator set measures technological advancement in the area of trade facilitation by collecting data on the time and cost of customs clearance and inspections procedures.[2] For the first time this year, the indicators collect data on the use and advancement of single windows around the world. For this purpose, *Doing Business* defines a single window as a system that receives trade-related information and disseminates it to all the relevant governmental authorities, thus systematically coordinating controls throughout trade processes. The new data on single windows capture the different levels of their integration and digitalization.[3]

THE ADVANCEMENT OF SINGLE WINDOWS

International trade has evolved into a complex network of actors, both within and outside sovereign borders. Trade processes involve not only government authorities and private firms but also customs brokers, commercial banks, vendors, insurance companies and freight forwarders.[4] For example, at least nine institutions play a role in the process of exporting coffee from Colombia to the United States. First, the National Institute of Food and Drug Monitoring issues a phytosanitary certificate, which ensures that the coffee meets current sanitary standards. The Colombia Coffee Growers Federation then issues a certificate that attests to the quality of the shipment.[5] The Colombian Agricultural Institute then conducts a phytosanitary inspection while the antinarcotics police perform security inspections and customs clears the freight. The exporter must obtain a certificate of origin from the Colombian Chamber of Commerce to comply with the U.S.-Colombia Trade Promotion Agreement. And these are only the steps that must be completed in Colombia. Once the shipment of coffee reaches the United States, it has to go through clearance with the U.S. Customs and Border Protection, Food and Drug Administration and the U.S. Department of Agriculture. Remarkably, the Colombian example is a relatively simple one compared to most

- Increased national trade digitalization leads to efficiency gains for exporters and importers.
- Many single windows have a high level of sophistication and consist of complex networks of regulatory agencies and private actors. This is the case of the Ventanilla Única de Comercio Exterior (VUCE) in Colombia, which connects multiple public agencies and several private companies with exporters, importers, customs agents and brokers.
- Sweden was one of the first economies to introduce a national single window in 1989. Since then, the system has evolved from an export statistics platform to a comprehensive trade facilitation tool.
- Seaports maintain their competitive edge through the automation and modernization of port infrastructure.
- Economies that perform well on the trading across borders indicators also tend to have lower levels of corruption.

other trade-related interactions worldwide. To ensure effective coordination, Colombia developed a single window system for foreign trade—the Ventanilla Única de Comercio Exterior (VUCE)—in the early 2000s. The single window connects 21 public agencies and three private companies (that provide e-signature certificates and legal information) with importers, exporters, customs agents and brokers through an online platform that allows users to request approvals, authorizations and other certifications needed to import and export goods. In addition, tax identification and business registration records are available to the agencies integrated into the system.

In the early 1980s governments and international organizations recognized the need to facilitate the coordination of multiple trade actors to make cross-border trade more cost effective and time efficient. Trade processes gradually began to shift from physical to electronic platforms. One of the first attempts to create a trade electronic platform took place when the United Nations Conference on Trade and Development (UNCTAD) launched an automated customs data management system, the Automated System for Customs Data (ASYCUDA).[6] Following a request from the Economic Community of West African States (ECOWAS) in 1981 for technical assistance to collect foreign trade statistics from its member states, UNCTAD developed customs software covering most foreign trade procedures. The focus of the ASYCUDA software is trade facilitation, customs clearance, fiscal control and operational capacity, allowing for the replicability and adaptability of its software in a cost-effective manner. The program, which is implemented free of charge by UNCTAD, currently is installed or being installed in over 90 economies worldwide.

In most cases, ASYCUDA yields positive results for all parties involved. Traders benefit from faster customs formalities and governments report an increase in customs revenue.[7] As a result of the introduction of ASYCUDA in the Philippines in 1996 and Sri Lanka in 1994, in the first year of implementation customs revenues increased by more than $215 million and $100 million, respectively.[8] Similarly, St. Lucia has benefited from the implementation of ASYCUDA. Customs brokers no longer need to visit multiple customs clearance officers or government agencies to verify and obtain documents as most of the paperwork is verified automatically. By enabling the rapid electronic submission of documents, the overall customs clearance process in St. Lucia has been reduced by 24 hours since implementation. However, not all of the economies that adopted the ASYCUDA program managed to achieve the desired results. The Comoros, for example, introduced the ASYCUDA software in 2010 but it was not used widely by local traders. Electricity cuts and shortages made the system unreliable during regular business hours; the private sector did not experience the expected positive impact from the implementation of the program.

As trade chains have become increasingly globalized, the demand for the coordination of diverse trade actors has continued to rise.[9] Many economies have needed to move beyond relatively simple customs electronic data interchange systems, such as ASYCUDA, and toward a more inclusive and sophisticated platform: the single window. The importance of the adoption and integration of single windows in trade has been highlighted by the Bali Agreement of the World Trade Organization (WTO), particularly in the context of developing economies.[10]

The level of national digitalization, specifically regarding cross-border trade, has been shown to have a significant impact on economic growth.[11] Specifically, studies have found that an increase of an economy's digitalization score by just 10% leads to a 0.75% growth in GDP.[12] Research also demonstrates the positive impact of single window systems on increasing the number of exporting firms and on improving international trade flows.[13] In Costa Rica, for example, the implementation of streamlined procedures to process export permits through a single window resulted in an increase in the number of exporters by 22.4%.[14] Moreover, *Doing Business* data show that traders in economies with fully operational electronic systems (that allow for export and import customs declarations to be submitted and processed online) spend considerably less time on customs clearance (figure 9.1). Recognizing the positive impact of digitalization, governments and international institutions worldwide have dedicated significant resources to modernizing border compliance processes.

Challenges of establishing single windows

In 2005, the United Nations Centre for Trade Facilitation and Electronic Business defined a single window as a platform that enables trade stakeholders to submit documentation and other relevant information through a single point of entry in a standardized way in order to complete export, import and transit procedures.[15] However, over the past decade, the concept of a single window has expanded to include the entire evolution of electronic systems, including customs automation, trade point portals, electronic data interchange techniques, agency-specific single windows, national single windows, and even regional and global single windows (figure 9.2).[16] Due to the multifaceted nature of electronic interchange systems, national governments and international development organizations face numerous obstacles in coordinating the implementation of comprehensive single window platforms. Furthermore, cross-country comparability is complicated by the fact that different economies choose to introduce single windows of varying complexity. Mauritius' single window, TradeNet, is mostly focused on customs procedures and currently the system only includes the Mauritius Revenue Authority,

FIGURE 9.1 Trade digitalization leads to efficiency gains for both exporters and importers

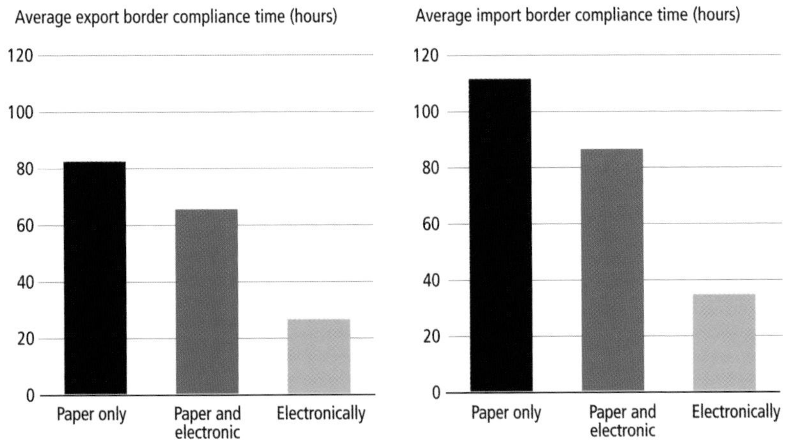

Source: Doing Business database.

Note: The relationship is significant at the 1% level after controlling for income per capita. The three categories are: only paper submission of customs declaration is possible; both paper and electronic submissions are in use; and only electronic submission is possible. The sample includes 165 economies.

the Mauritius Port Authority and the Mauritius Chamber of Commerce and Industry.[17] In Australia, by contrast, the Customs and Border Protection Service Integrated Cargo System incorporates a broad range of government agencies. The Australian single window connects customs authorities, quarantine authorities and meat producers. These actors work closely throughout the production and trade processes, conducting sanitary inspections and issuing sanitary certificates.[18]

Single windows may suffer from various institutional and regulatory limitations that stem from conflicting interests related to technical standards, data harmonization and information sharing.[19] Border operations, especially those managed by customs authorities, are legislated at the national level. As such, governments and development organizations must first convince different political actors of the need to integrate and modernize trade operations.[20] Moreover, because the information technology suppliers of the electronic systems are third parties with complex contractual relationships with governments, change can be slow. Beyond agreeing on the scope of work and bringing together different stakeholders, implementation of a single window can entail a number of organizational complexities. The cost may also vary depending on the parties involved and the level of integration. The

FIGURE 9.2 Some single windows have a high level of sophistication, encompassing complex networks of regulatory agencies and private actors

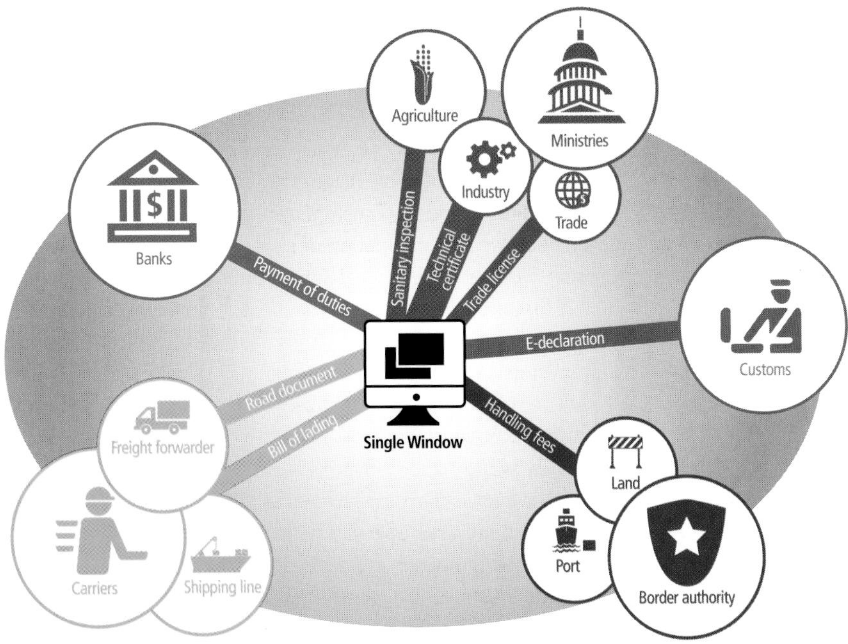

Source: Doing Business database.

single window for exports in Guatemala, for example, was developed by the private sector for less than $1 million, with ongoing operational costs of $1.2 million per year. Users of the Guatemalan single window pay a fee for each transaction in addition to a flat monthly fee. Conversely, the single window in Malaysia, which covers both exports and imports, was established through a public-private partnership and cost about $3.5 million.[21]

One study shows that among 12 selected trade facilitation mechanisms, single windows generate one of the largest long-term cost savings despite having some of the highest setup and operating costs and an average implementation time of about four years.[22] Despite the different uses and applications of single windows, the benefits outweigh the costs of developing a comprehensive framework integrating multiple trade actors. These benefits include improved revenue yields and the adoption of control risk management techniques for governments, as well as enhanced predictability, reduced costs and fewer delays for traders.[23] As a result of implementing an electronic data interchange system in the Philippines, customs custody time was reduced to 4–6 hours for "green channel" shipments (from 6–8 days previously).[24] Albania also significantly reduced the time spent in customs by adopting a digital risk-based border inspection process. Between 2007 and 2012, this process reduced the days goods spent in Albanian customs by 7% and boosted the value of imports also by 7%.[25] The implementation of this electronic facility, based on ASYCUDA modules for risk management, was recognized as a positive reform in the *Doing Business 2016* report.

The implementation of a single window in Singapore yielded positive results. Following a recession in the 1980s, Singapore's government set up a high-level committee to improve economic competitiveness. One of the committee's recommendations was to increase the use of information technology in trade. Singapore's single window for trade, TradeNet, one of the first such systems put in place in the world, began operating in 1989 as an electronic data interchange system that allowed the computer-to-computer exchange of structured messages between the government and members of Singapore's trading community.[26] TradeNet now handles more than 30,000 declarations a day, processes 99% of permits in just 10 minutes and receives all monetary collections through interbank transactions.[27] Regarding cost, trading firms report savings of between 25% and 30% in document processing.[28]

Sweden was also one of the first countries to introduce a national single window. The first steps toward the implementation of the Swedish single window were taken in 1989 with the development of the Customs Information System (CIS) by the Swedish customs authorities. During this initial stage, the CIS was an online platform that recorded export statistics electronically to the statistics bureau. The system gradually evolved from an export data exchange to a comprehensive single window that encompasses exports, imports and transit goods' procedures. Currently, the Swedish single window connects customs not only to the statistics bureau but also to other important international trade actors.[29] Clearing goods in Sweden is easy and straightforward. The trader or representative submits the customs declaration online; even though paper copies are still allowed, they are rarely used. Customs processes the relevant information and if a license or a permit from other agencies is required it is requested automatically through the single window.[30] Even though the use of the online system is not compulsory, 94% of customs declarations are submitted electronically, and approximately 12,000 companies and 7,000 citizens use it.[31] The platform operates 24 hours a day, seven days a week and is free of charge.

Over time single windows have moved beyond national boundaries, encompassing entire geographic regions. In synchronization with national single window efforts, electronically integrated regional systems are on the rise. The Association of South East Asian Nations (ASEAN)[32] Single Window (ASW) initiative, which was adopted and endorsed during the Ninth ASEAN Summit in 2003, aims to integrate the national single windows of ASEAN countries by allowing the electronic exchange of customs information and expediting cargo clearance. The regional single window is expected to reduce the overall cost of trading by 8%, with the largest savings arising from a reduction in documentation dispatch costs.[33] The implementation of the ASW is being carried out gradually; member states are currently in the process of implementing their respective domestic ratifications. A significant challenge has been the fact that most ASEAN member states have their own customs regimes and relevant legislation in place, which can be difficult to reconcile with new regional legislation.

Efforts toward electronic regional integration are also underway in Latin America and the Caribbean. The Inter-American Network of International Trade Single Windows (Red VUCE) initiative was launched in 2011 as a forum to promote cooperation and peer-to-peer learning among national single windows in Latin America and the Caribbean, with the goal of reducing the time and cost of trading in the region.[34] During its fifth meeting in 2014, Red VUCE representatives agreed to launch a pilot project that will allow interoperability of single windows in the region with the primary objective of eliminating paper copies of documents and interconnecting the single windows of Chile, Colombia, Mexico and Peru, the four founding members of the Pacific Alliance, by 2016.[35]

Economies that trade through seaports maintain their competitive edge not only through the use of electronic services and single windows but also through the automation and modernization of port infrastructure (box 9.1).

BOX 9.1 Improving trade efficiency through port and customs automation

The ability of ports to ensure timely cargo transfers is a vital dimension of their competitiveness. Efficient ports are not only technologically advanced—using robots and automated container handling—but also employ digital platforms, such as port community systems, to ensure the smooth and reliable transfer of information between all members of the seaport network. Efficient ports generate many economic benefits, including increased trade volume, lower trade costs, and higher employment and foreign investment. Port quality impacts entire supply chains and even the economies of nearby cities.

Studies show the importance of port efficiency for trade facilitation and regional development. According to one study, port efficiency is a crucial determinant of shipping costs: improving port efficiency from the 25th to the 75th percentile reduces shipping costs by around 12%. Furthermore, reductions in inefficiencies associated with transport costs from the 25th to 75th percentile imply an increase in bilateral trade of around 25%.[a] Another study, on the economic impact of the port cluster in Rotterdam, suggests that the value added of the port accounts for approximately 10% of regional GDP.[b] The Le Havre/Rouen port cluster had an even higher share of regional GDP (21%).[c] Going beyond port automation, data show that, on average, economies with full-time automated processing systems for customs agencies—as well as electronic data exchange platforms—take significantly less time to move exported goods compared to ones where full-time automation is not implemented (see figure). Port and customs automation make the exporting process more efficient. Moreover, data suggest that around-the-clock automated processing systems are a key factor for making border compliance more efficient.

Customs automation at ports/borders allows exporters to save time when dealing with trade logistics

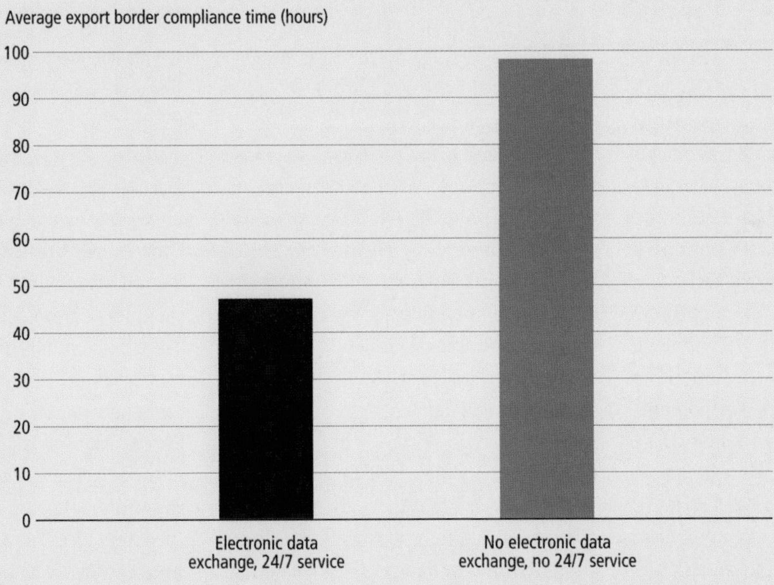

Sources: Doing Business database; OECD 2015 database.
Note: The sample consists of 75 economies. The relationship is significant at the 1% level after controlling for income per capita.

Automation improves reliability, predictability, safety and competitiveness of operations. Ports are land-intensive; automated cranes and vehicles in ports improve the productivity of stacking crane interchange zones, which allows for more efficient land allocation and use. Furthermore, modern automated machinery is fast, economical and low-maintenance and it helps to avoid collisions and other physical damage. Better technology and automation also improves worker safety.[c] In April 2015 the Patrick terminal at Sydney's Port Botany optimized the use of AutoStrad, a single piece of equipment that combines stacking and transportation capabilities without any human engagement. This technology has made the port safer, more predictable and efficient, ultimately benefiting both users and customers.[d]

In the global trade logistics environment, where the number of containers is rapidly increasing due to higher international trade volumes, competition among ports to dominate the container market continues to intensify. Ports are complex constructions and changes are not easy to implement. Ports are communities composed of numerous players, both public and private.[e] Usually port authorities and customs constitute the core of these communities. Other entities include shipping lines, freight forwarders, customs brokers, importers and exporters, all involved in conducting trade.

(continued)

BOX 9.1 Improving trade efficiency through port and customs automation *(continued)*

Location is no longer an important differentiator among ports. Now the services ports offer and the added economic value ports provide determine their competitive advantage.[f] Port efficiency is an integral prerequisite for surviving in the competitive world of trade. Container automation and port community systems can be leveraged to improve efficiency. Given that information sharing is a key element within the port community, information technology capabilities—and port community systems in particular—serve as important differentiators among ports. But container automation can be costly and cause workforce optimization and therefore its implementation should be carefully weighed. Yet port community systems generate multiple first-hand benefits, including reduced paperwork, better information quality and reliability and safeguarded access to information by all members of the port community.

a. Clark, Dollar and Micco 2004.
b. Port cluster means port with multiple functions.
c. OECD 2011a.
d. Sydney Morning Herald 2015.
e. Wrigley, Wagenaar and Clarke 1994.
f. van Baalen, Zuidwijk and van Nunen 2008.

INFORMATION TECHNOLOGY TO FIGHT CORRUPTION

Research shows a negative relationship between corruption and investment, which constrains economic growth.[36] Corruption is particularly damaging for international trade.[37] Through advocating for adherence to international trade laws, international organizations have been actively combating corruption in the area of trade.[38] Intra-regional trade, especially in developing economies, remains highly vulnerable to fraudulent and corrupt practices. In economies with weak institutions and inefficient governments, the negative effects of corruption on growth are even more pronounced.[39] Recent studies on intra-regional trade in Africa demonstrate that corruption coupled with weak institutional frameworks poses major obstacles to the development of trade flows within the Economic and Monetary Community of Central Africa.[40] Corruption can alter natural trade flows and cause various market distortions by, for example, causing substantial delays in the delivery of goods. To extract bribes, corrupt civil servants create additional interruptions and constraints in an otherwise well-functioning system.[41] The literature suggests that even when businesses pay bribes, they still face high time delays and experience greater capital costs.[42]

In the realm of international trade, and particularly in customs clearance procedures, corruption can flourish because customs officials control something that firms greatly value—access to international markets.[43] Research shows that customs officials are particularly prone to accepting bribes and are more likely to engage in corruption compared to other sectors of the economy.[44] Import and export processes are equally affected by corruption. Customs officials can fraudulently overlook import regulations and exonerate goods from inspections while importing, or abuse their roles of gatekeepers during export procedures.[45]

Doing Business data show that economies that perform well on the trading across borders indicators tend to have lower levels of corruption (figure 9.3). For example, there is a strong positive association between the economies' distance to frontier score in the trading across borders indicators and their score in Transparency International's Corruption Perceptions Index.[46] Similarly, the distance to frontier score on the trading across borders indicators is strongly and negatively correlated with the percentage of firms that are expected to give gifts to obtain an import license. The distance to frontier score tends to be higher in economies where fewer firms need to offer a bribe to get things done. Performance on the trading across borders indicators is also strongly and significantly correlated with the Worldwide Governance Indicators' rule of law and control of corruption variables.[47]

Economies worldwide have spent decades trying to eradicate corruption in international trade, with varying levels of success. Many East African economies are signatories of the World Customs Organization (WCO) Arusha Declaration, which is a recognized focal tool of an effective approach to tackling corruption and increasing integrity in customs for WCO members. Nevertheless, corruption and dominance of non-official fees and charges remain an important challenge in the region. To enhance integrity in East African economies, Kenya, for example, created an anti-corruption commission tasked with implementing good practices proposed by the Revised Arusha Declaration and the WCO Integrity Development Guide and Compendium of Integrity Best Practices. The Arusha Declaration explicitly recognizes the automation of trade processes, including electronic data interchange, as powerful anti-corruption tools.[48]

Increased trade digitalization, which minimizes human interactions, creates fewer opportunities for bribery and fraud. The Philippines successfully fought corruption in its customs services by adopting systems that limit in-person interactions and by imposing heavy penalties on corrupt officials. Its approach relied on the use of modern technology to reengineer the customs services operating environment.[49]

FIGURE 9.3 A good performance on the trading across borders indicators is associated with lower levels of corruption

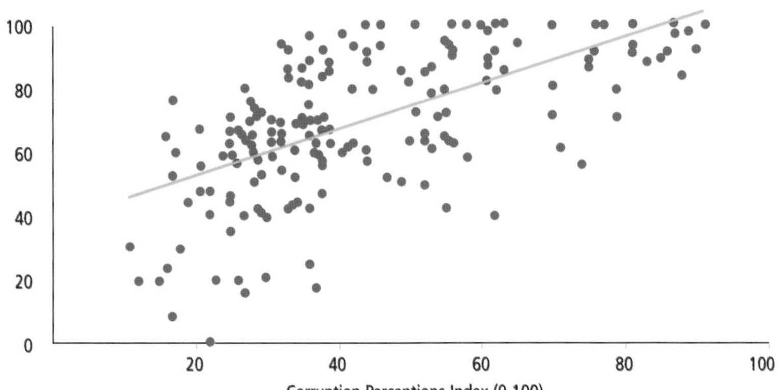

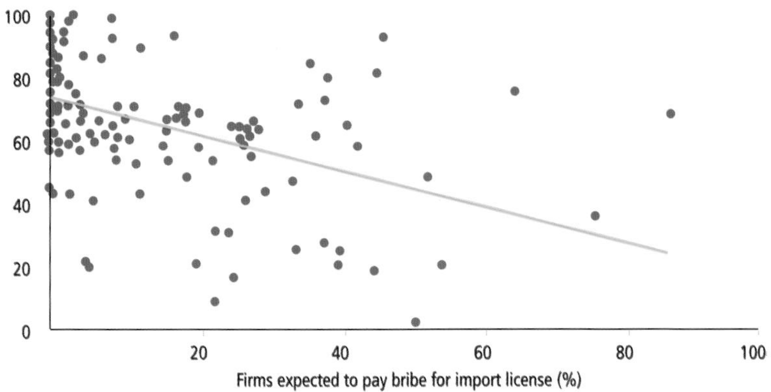

Sources: Doing Business database; Enterprise Surveys database (http://www.enterprisesurveys.org), World Bank; Transparency International data (https://www.transparency.org/cpi2015/results).

Note: The results are significant at the 1% level after controlling for income per capita. A higher score on Transparency International's Corruption Perceptions Index indicates a lower level of perceived corruption. Data for the Corruption Perceptions Index are for 2015. The samples include 146 economies covered by both Transparency International and *Doing Business* and 121 economies covered by the Enterprise Surveys and *Doing Business*.

As a result of the anti-corruption reforms, about 70% of imports to the Philippines are now processed through the "green channel" within just two hours.[50] Similarly, single window systems—which limit the monopoly power of customs agents—can be implemented to deter corruption in customs services.[51] The automation and digitalization of administrative systems largely eliminates the monopolistic power of customs officials.[52] Similarly to the case of the Philippines, prior to 2003 the customs department as well as other administrations and agencies in Georgia faced a rampant corruption problem. A key step to tackling corruption in the Georgian customs was the introduction of a one-stop shop system that reduced face-to-face interactions between entrepreneurs and customs officials.[53]

The introduction of computerized solutions for processing customs documents—and the general automation of customs clearance—leaves little to the discretion of customs officials, thereby reducing opportunities for corruption.[54] However, despite myriad efforts to implement good practices, corruption is still prevalent in many customs departments in Sub-Saharan Africa. In economies where anti-corruption reforms have failed, customs officials are often torn between bureaucratic norms and the expectations of their networks and surroundings. In some African economies, a kinship-based social organization that combines moral obligation and attachment is strong, making corruption more present and acceptable.[55]

Mozambique launched an extensive customs reform program in 1995 to modernize the customs department and tackle corruption. Customs operations did not have any substantial information technology support before the reform was implemented. Despite considerable progress, Mozambique still needs to develop further its existing information technology infrastructure to deal effectively with corruption and smuggling. Corruption is also a challenge in the customs administration in Uganda. The Uganda Revenue Authority has been implementing various solutions to fight corruption, such as requiring officials to declare their assets, increasing salaries and providing training on integrity.[56] Uganda recently introduced a modernized version of the ASYCUDA World system, but its impact on fighting corruption remains to be seen.

CONCLUSION

Implementing a single window is not an easy undertaking. The complex process requires extensive cooperation and coordination among multiple players, and it can take several years for new electronic platforms to become fully operational and used by the majority of traders. However, the long-term benefits substantially outweigh the costs and the actual integration of single windows or similar systems can be done in phases. Most economies start with relatively simple electronic exchange solutions and progressively make systemic upgrades and expansions. Port automation and modernization is an important milestone that economies can work toward to improve their competitiveness.

The integration of single windows into international trade processes and improved port automation can aid economies in combating corruption. Corruption remains a major problem in international trade. It perpetuates delays and inefficiencies, increases costs and ultimately has a negative impact on economic growth and development. Customs departments are especially prone to corruption, as customs officials often hold important decision-making powers in the international trade process. The digitalization of customs procedures is an efficient tool for tackling corruption; it is most effective when integrated into larger anti-corruption campaigns. Modern information technology infrastructure not only reduces opportunities for corruption but also has a generally positive impact on the entire trade process, thereby benefitting economic development overall.

NOTES

This case study was written by Cécile Ferro, Marilyne Florence Mafoboue Youbi, Dorina Peteva Georgieva, Valentina Saltane and Inés Zabalbeitia Múgica.

1. World Customs Organization 2015.
2. WTO 1998a. Trade facilitation is defined by the WTO as "The simplification and harmonization of international trade procedures, where trade procedures are the activities, practices, and formalities involved in collecting, presenting, communicating, and processing data and other information required for the movement of goods in international trade."
3. In *Doing Business 2017* the trading across borders indicators collect data on the status of implementation of the following components of single window systems in 190 economies: physical one-stop shop; customs electronic data interchange system; port or border integration; other governmental agencies integration; national single window; regional single window.
4. UNCTAD, "Saving one hundred billion dollars annually by the year 2000." United Nations International Symposium on Trade Efficiency, Columbus, Ohio, Fact Sheet # 5. 1994.
5. See the website of Colombia's Superintendencia de Industria y Comercio available at http://www.sic.gov.co/drupal/.
6. UNCTAD, "The ASYCUDA Programme."
7. For more information on the Automated System for Customs Data (ASYCUDA), see its website at http://www.asycuda.org/.
8. WTO 1998b.
9. Elms and Low 2013.
10. WTO 2013a.
11. Wilson, Mann and Otsuki 2003. Engman 2005.
12. Sabbagh and others 2013. Booz & Company's Digitization Index is a composite score that calculates the level of an economy's digitization using 23 indicators to measure six attributes: ubiquity, affordability, reliability, speed, usability and speed. The Digitization Index measures an economy's level of digitization on a scale of 0 to 100, with 100 signifying the most advanced, to identify its distinct stage of digital development: constrained, emerging, transitional or advanced.
13. Sá Porto, Morini and Canuto 2015.
14. Carballo, Schaur and Volpe Martincus 2015.
15. UN/CEFACT 2005.
16. Tsen 2011.
17. Tsen 2011.
18. World Bank 2015c.
19. Macedo and Scorza 2013.
20. Grainger 2008.
21. UNECE 2005. The costs of establishing a single window can vary greatly depending on the information technology interface, the level of sophistication, the number of adopted modules and overall trade volumes.
22. Duval 2006; Moise, Orliac and Minor 2011. The Duval 2006 study lists the following 12 common trade facilitation measures: alignment of trade documents according to the UN Layout Key for trade documents; online publication of relevant trade data; establishment of enquiry points and single national focal points for trade regulations and other trade facilitation issues; establishment of a national trade facilitation committee; provision of advance rulings; establishment of an effective appeal procedure for customs; establishment of a single window system; establishment and systematic use of pre-arrival clearance mechanism; implementation of modern risk management systems; establishment and wider use of audit-based customs; expedited clearance of goods and expedited procedures for express shipments and qualified traders/companies.
23. UNECE 2005.
24. Maniego 1999. "Green channel" clearance of goods refers to the process of customs clearance without routine examination of the goods. "Green channel" status is provided only to certain traders and products that meet the eligibility requirements set by customs authorities. Eligibility requirements may include, but are not limited to: government-approved list of companies and products, top importers in terms of duty payment and traders who have an impeccable record. Moving goods through the "green channel" that are not part of an economy's list of "green channel" products constitutes a customs offense that carries administrative and in some cases criminal liability.
25. Fernandes, Hillberry and Mendoza Alcantara 2015.
26. World Bank 2013a.
27. Neo and Leong 1994.
28. OECD 2009.
29. The Swedish single window also connects customs to the National Board of Trade, the Swedish Board of Agriculture, the National Inspectorate of Strategic Products, the National Board of Taxation, the National Debt Office, the Swedish police, Norwegian customs, Russian customs and the European Commission.
30. See the website of the Swedish customs service at http://www.tullverket.se/.
31. UNECE 2005.
32. The members of the Association of Southeast Asian Nations are: Brunei Darussalam, Cambodia, Indonesia, the Lao People's Democratic Republic, Malaysia, Myanmar, the Philippines, Singapore, Thailand, and Vietnam.
33. USAID 2012.
34. The members of Red VUCE (Inter-American Network of International Trade Single Windows) are: Argentina, The Bahamas, Barbados, Belize, Bolivia, Brazil, Chile, Colombia, Costa Rica, Dominican Republic, Ecuador, El Salvador, Guatemala, Guyana, Haiti, Honduras, Jamaica, Mexico, Nicaragua, Panama, Paraguay, Peru, Suriname, Trinidad and Tobago, Uruguay and República Bolivariana de Venezuela.
35. Red VUCE 2014. Inter-American Network of International Trade Single Windows meeting in Cusco, Peru.
36. Mauro 1995.
37. Dreher and Herzfeld 2005.
38. Parisi and Rinoldi 2004.
39. Meon and Sekkat 2003 and Lopez-Claros 2015.
40. Avom and Fankem 2014. The members of the Central African Economic and Monetary Community (CEMAC) are Cameroon, the Central African Republic, Chad, Equatorial Guinea, Gabon and the Republic of Congo.
41. Myrdal 1968.
42. Kaufmann and Wei 2000 and Freund, Hallward-Driemeier and Rijkers 2014.
43. Dutt and Traca 2010.
44. Rose-Ackerman 1997.
45. Dutt and Traca 2010.
46. A higher score on the Corruption Perceptions Index indicates a lower level of perceived corruption.
47. World Bank 2015c. The rule of law variable "reflects perceptions of the extent to which agents have confidence in and abide by the rules of society, and in particular the quality of contract enforcement, property rights, the police, and the courts, as well as the likelihood of crime and violence." The control of corruption variable "reflects perceptions of the extent to which public power is exercised for private gain, including both petty and grand forms of corruption, as well as "capture" of the state by elites and private interests."
48. World Customs Organization 1998.
49. Parayno 2013.
50. Parayno 2004.
51. Ndonga 2013.
52. McLinden 2005.
53. World Bank 2012b.
54. Crotty 2010.
55. Fjeldstad 2009.
56. de Wulf and Sokol 2004.

Annex: Labor Market Regulation

What can we learn from Doing Business *data?*

Labor market regulation can protect workers' rights, reduce the risk of job loss and support equity and social cohesion. However, overregulation of the labor market can discourage job creation and constrain the movement of workers from low to high productivity jobs. Stringent labor regulation has also been associated with labor market segmentation and reduced employment of women and youth. Laws that restrict women's access to certain jobs, for example in mining or manufacturing, often with the goal of protecting women's interests, may contribute to occupational segregation and a larger gender wage gap.[1] By contrast, weak labor market rules can exacerbate problems of unequal power and inadequate risk management.[2] The challenge in developing labor policies is to avoid the extremes of over and under-regulation by reaching a balance between worker protection and flexibility.[3]

Doing Business measures several aspects of labor market regulation—hiring, working hours, redundancy rules and cost—as well as a number of job quality aspects (such as the availability of unemployment protection, maternity leave and gender nondiscrimination at the workplace) for 190 economies worldwide. This helps benchmark an economy's labor rules and examine the relationship between labor market regulation and economic outcomes. For example, economies with more flexible labor regulation tend to have a higher share of formally registered firms. Furthermore, flexible employment regulation is associated with a larger share of active contributors to a pension scheme in the labor force—a measure that can be used as a proxy for formal employment (figure 10.1).

Employment protection legislation (EPL)—the rules governing hiring and dismissal of workers—is designed to enhance worker welfare and prevent discrimination. However, its impact on labor market outcomes is a contentious subject. Proponents of strict EPL argue that it provides stability by moderating employment fluctuations over the business cycle and increases worker effort and firm investments in human capital. Critics have linked stringent employment protection legislation to the proliferation of dual labor markets, whereby a labor force becomes segmented into formal versus informal sector workers (in developing economies) and permanent versus contingent workers (in high-income economies). Several studies point to the association between strict labor market regulation and higher levels of informality,[4] which negatively impacts productivity and welfare. On average, firms in the informal sector have less value added per worker and pay lower salaries than formal sector enterprises. Informal firms also offer little job security and few fringe benefits to their employees. Rigid labor rules have also been linked to the decreased ability of vulnerable groups—women, youth and the low skilled—to find jobs.[5] Some studies have found that strict employment regulation reduces aggregate job flows and hinders productivity.[6] The overall

- **Regulation is essential for the efficient functioning of labor markets and worker protection. Labor market rules can also potentially have an impact on economic outcomes. *Doing Business* data show that rigid employment regulation is associated with higher levels of informality. By contrast, weak labor market rules can result in discrimination and poor treatment of workers.**
- **The challenge for governments in developing labor policies is to strike the right balance between worker protection and flexibility.**
- **Regulation of labor markets differs significantly by income group. Low- and lower-middle-income economies tend to have stricter employment protection regulation than more developed economies.**
- **One reason for more rigid employment protection legislation in low- and lower-middle-income economies is the lack of unemployment insurance. None of the low-income economies and only 23% of lower-middle-income economies have unemployment protection stipulated in the law.**
- **Most economies do not have laws mandating gender nondiscrimination in hiring and equal remuneration for work of equal value. Such laws are most common in OECD high-income economies.**
- **There is no blueprint for the optimal mix of employment protection rules. Regulation should be tailored to national circumstances and designed in collaboration with social partners.**

FIGURE 10.1 Stringent labor regulation is associated with higher informality

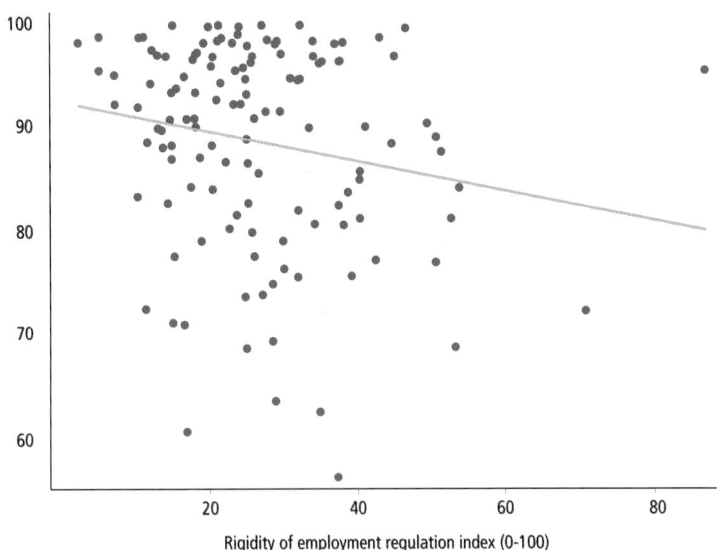

Sources: Doing Business database; World Bank Enterprise Surveys database (http://www.enterprisesurveys.org).
Note: The rigidity of employment regulation index is the average of four sub-indices: hiring, working hours, redundancy rules and cost. The relationship is significant at the 5% level after controlling for GDP per capita.

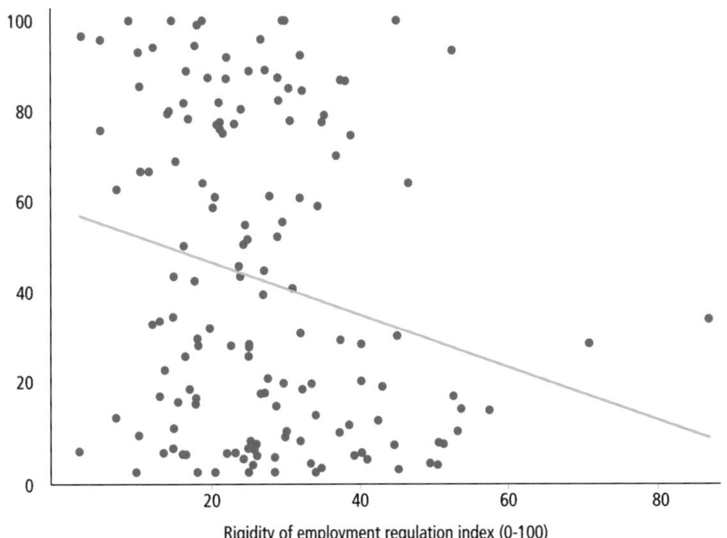

Sources: Doing Business database; ILO 2014.
Note: The rigidity of employment regulation index is the average of four sub-indices: hiring, working hours, redundancy rules and cost. The relationship is significant at the 10% level after controlling for GDP per capita.

impact of strict EPL on productivity is unclear, however, as firms may choose to invest in capital and skills deepening in response to stricter legislation.[7]

Balancing employment protection legislation to ensure adequate worker protection as well as efficient labor allocation is an important priority for governments as they strive to create more and better jobs. Measuring labor market regulation is a key step in formulating informed public policy. This year *Doing Business,* which has measured aspects of labor market regulation since 2003, includes information on about 40 aspects of labor laws in 190 economies.

WHO REGULATES HIRING AND REDUNDANCY RULES THE MOST?

Doing Business data show that low- and lower-middle-income economies tend to have more rigid employment protection legislation compared to more developed economies (figure 10.2). The narrative below discusses differences in selected labor market regulations, such as availability of fixed-term contracts, redundancy rules, severance pay and unemployment insurance across different groups of economies.[8]

Hiring

As economies develop, several types of contracts may be required to satisfy business needs. *Doing Business* measures the availability of fixed-term contracts[9] for a task relating to a permanent activity of the firm. Fixed-term contracts allow firms to better respond to seasonal fluctuations in demand, temporarily replace workers on maternity leave and reduce the risks associated with starting an innovative activity with uncertain returns on investment. Fixed-term contracts also have the potential to increase the employability of first time labor market entrants, particularly the youth, by providing them with experience and access to professional networks, which may eventually enable

FIGURE 10.2 Low-income economies tend to have more rigid employment protection legislation

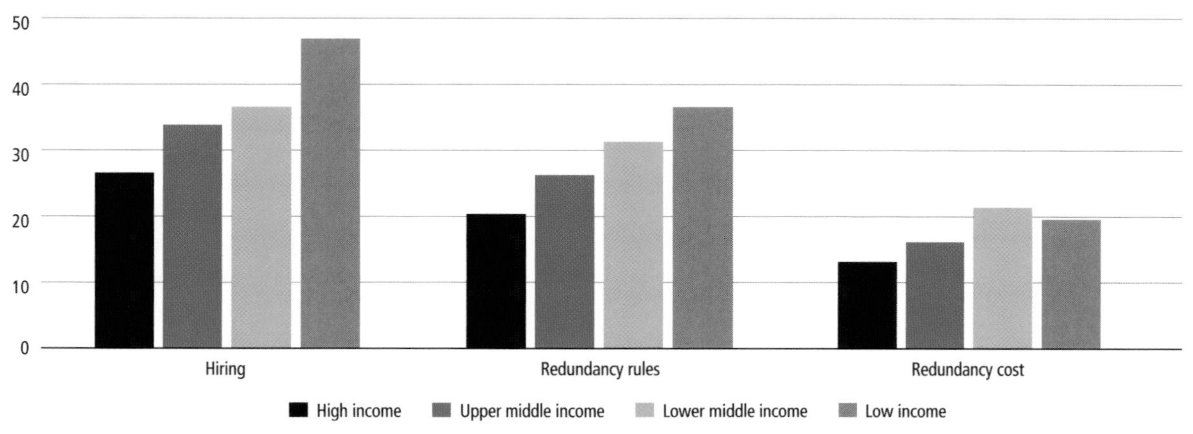

Source: Doing Business database.
Note: Higher scores indicate more rigid regulation.

them to find permanent jobs.[10] Evidence from the Organisation for Economic Co-operation and Development (OECD) shows that fixed-term contracts are more common among the youth than older workers, suggesting that many young people manage to transition to permanent jobs after an initial fixed-term contract.[11] For example, in the EU-10[12] only 50% of young workers hold a permanent contract one year after leaving school but 73% are in permanent employment five years after completing their education.[13] These numbers are higher in the Republic of Korea and the United Kingdom where 86% and 81% of young workers, respectively, are in permanent employment one year after leaving school and more than 90% five years after graduation.[14]

Fixed-term contracts are currently available in 64% of economies but there is a significant regional variation: 84% of economies in East Asia and the Pacific compared to 44% in Europe and Central Asia allow the use of fixed-term contracts for permanent tasks (figure 10.3). Low-income economies are less likely to allow fixed-term contracts than middle-income and high-income economies (figure 10.4).

The impact of the use of fixed-term contracts on labor market outcomes depends on the rigidity of employment protection

FIGURE 10.3 The use of fixed-term contracts varies widely by region

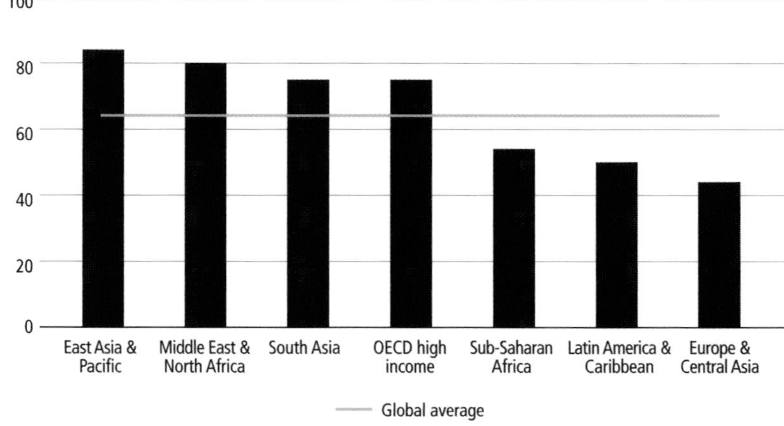

Source: Doing Business database.

FIGURE 10.4 Low-income economies are most likely to limit the use of fixed-term contracts

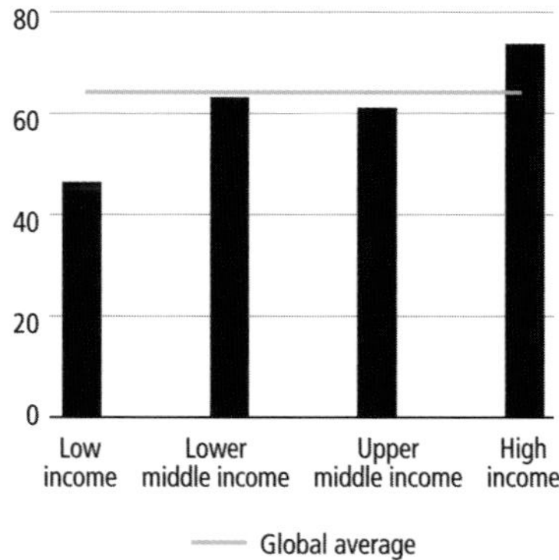

Source: Doing Business database.

BOX 10.1 Flexibility at the margin: The perils of the dual labor market in Spain

Spain has the highest level of labor market segmentation in the EU-15,[a] with around a quarter of its population and almost 90% of new hires employed on fixed-term contracts.[b] The conversion rate from fixed-term to permanent employment hovers around 6%.[c] Nearly all fixed-term employees in Spain (96%) accepted contracts of limited duration because they could not find a permanent job.[d]

The origin of Spain's labor market duality dates back to a 1984 reform. The Spanish economy was hit hard by the second oil crisis and the unemployment rate surged. To boost employment, the government removed most restrictions on the use of fixed-term contracts while the dismissal rules for regular contracts remained unchanged. After the reform, fixed-term contracts could be used for any economic activity for up to three years. These contracts entailed a relatively low dismissal cost (with severance pay of up to 12 days per year of service) and their termination could not be appealed in labor courts.[e] For permanent contracts, dismissal costs depended on the reason for the layoff and the seniority of the employee: fair dismissals required mandatory severance pay of 20 days of salary per year of service with a maximum of 12 monthly wages; unfair dismissals mandated payment of 45 days of salary per year of service with a maximum of 42 monthly wages.[f] Economic reasons for fair dismissals included in the law were limited and the courts had a very narrow reading of those reasons. Given the large difference in dismissal costs, it is not surprising that soon after the reform almost all new hires were made on fixed-term contracts.

Although reforms have been introduced since 1994 to encourage permanent employment, these have had little impact on the prevalence of fixed-term contracts. Around 35% of employees in Spain were on a fixed-term contract in 2006. This figure declined to 24.5% in 2011/12 following the global economic crisis as temporary workers were the first to be dismissed.[g]

The dual labor market has resulted in a number of negative equity and efficiency outcomes. Fixed-term workers in Spain experience frequent job turnover and face a higher risk of unemployment. The probability of being unemployed one year after being in fixed-term employment in Spain is 6.2 percentage points higher for men and 7.3 percentage points for women compared to permanent employees.[h] Furthermore, firms are much less likely to invest in training for temporary workers in economies with dual labor markets compared to those where transitions from fixed-term to permanent employment are easier.[i] In Spain, the probability of receiving employer sponsored on-the-job training is 18% lower for fixed-term workers relative to permanent employees.[j] This contributes to skill gaps between employees on different types of contracts and makes the transition to regular employment more difficult for fixed-term workers. Furthermore, a wide gap in the dismissal costs for fixed-term and permanent contracts—and consequently, low conversion rates—have been linked to poor total factor productivity growth in Spain.[k]

The government of Spain introduced several reforms between 2012 and 2015 to increase flexibility, reduce labor market duality and improve employment outcomes of young people. Measures included: (i) increasing flexibility in wage bargaining and work scheduling by prioritizing firm level agreements over those at the sectoral or regional level (to allow for labor market adjustments through wages and hours worked rather than dismissals); (ii) eliminating administrative authorization for collective dismissals while maintaining the requirement of negotiation with the unions before giving the worker notice of dismissal; (iii) reducing severance payments for unfair dismissals (compensation for fair and unfair dismissals in Spain remains larger than the average in OECD countries even after the reform); (iv) creating tax incentives for new permanent hires; and (v) establishing active labor market programs for the youth and the long-term unemployed.[l] The preliminary assessments showed that these reforms were associated with increased hiring on permanent contracts and reduced separations of workers on temporary contracts.[m] The impacts were small, however, and it will take time and a sustained reform effort to reduce labor market duality.[n]

a. EU-15 consists of 15 economies that were members of the EU before the May 1, 2004, enlargement (Austria, Belgium, Denmark, Finland, France, Germany, Greece, Ireland, Italy, Luxembourg, the Netherlands, Portugal, Spain, Sweden, and the United Kingdom).
b. OECD 2014b.
c. Cabrales, Dolado and Mora 2014.
d. OECD 2014b.
e. Bentolila, Dolado and Jimeno 2011.
f. Bentolila, Dolado and Jimeno 2011.
g. OECD 2014b.
h. OECD 2014b.
i. Cabrales, Dolado and Mora 2014.
j. OECD 2014b.
k. Dolado, Ortigueira and Stucchi 2012.
l. IMF 2015b; OECD 2014c.
m. IMF 2015b; OECD 2014c.
n. IMF 2015b; OECD 2014c

legislation for regular workers. Evidence from the OECD shows that in economies with significant differences in regulation governing permanent and fixed-term contracts, firms tend to exploit the latter arrangement.[15] Substantial variations in employment protection legislation for different types of contracts incentivizes companies to substitute fixed-term for permanent workers with no overall increase in employment.[16] It also reduces the conversion rate of temporary to permanent employment, turning fixed-term contracts into a trap rather than a stepping stone toward an open-ended job.[17] Indeed, in almost all EU economies on which data are available, less than 50% of the workers that were hired on a temporary contract in a given year are employed on a permanent contract three years later.[18] Furthermore, if dismissing permanent employees is costly, workers on fixed-term contracts will bear a disproportionate burden of labor market adjustments.[19] Evidence from the OECD also shows that firms are less likely to invest in training for temporary workers compared to permanent workers (by 14%, on average, for economies on which data are available) with negative implications for professional development and earnings as well as overall firm productivity.[20] The resulting duality of labor markets can have a number of negative outcomes (box 10.1).

Redundancy rules

Modification of the size and composition of the workforce is essential to ensure that firms can respond to changing economic conditions and technological developments. However, job destruction negatively impacts dismissed workers through income loss and skill deterioration if the search for a new job is protracted. Large-scale dismissals can also have high social costs. The challenge for governments is to avoid overregulation of redundancy rules, which constrains labor reallocation to more productive activities and, at the same time, to protect workers against discrimination and minimize the costs of job loss through effective unemployment insurance, and active labor market and social assistance programs.

Doing Business data on redundancy rules show that while the majority of economies have relatively flexible legislation, pockets of rigidity remain for certain types of regulation. Redundancy is allowed as a ground for dismissal in all but three economies, namely Bolivia, República Bolivariana de Venezuela and Oman. However, a number of economies limit the firms' freedom to decide which workers they want to employ and which to dismiss. In particular, 40% of economies have priority rules for redundancies (such as the requirement that the person hired most recently be dismissed first) and 37% for reemployment (the provision that new jobs first be offered to the previously dismissed workers). Low-income economies are more likely to have such rules than middle-income and high-income economies (figure 10.5). Priority rules for dismissals and reemployment benefit the incumbents disproportionately at the expense of young and potentially more productive workers. Given the rising share of youth in the working population and the high rates of youth unemployment in low-income

FIGURE 10.5 Priority rules for redundancies and reemployment are more common in low-income economies

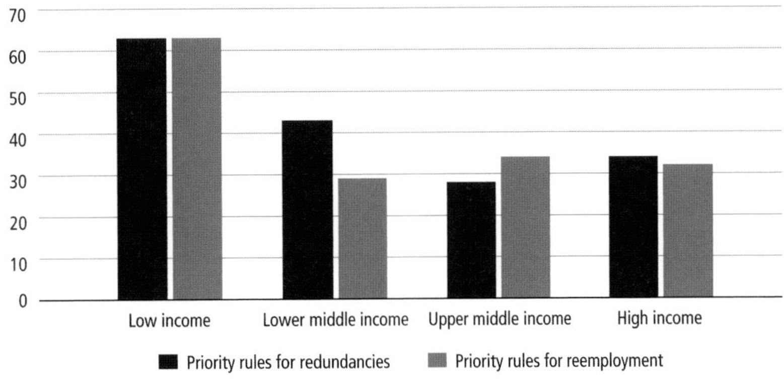

Source: Doing Business database.

FIGURE 10.6 Notification and approval requirements are more common for collective dismissals

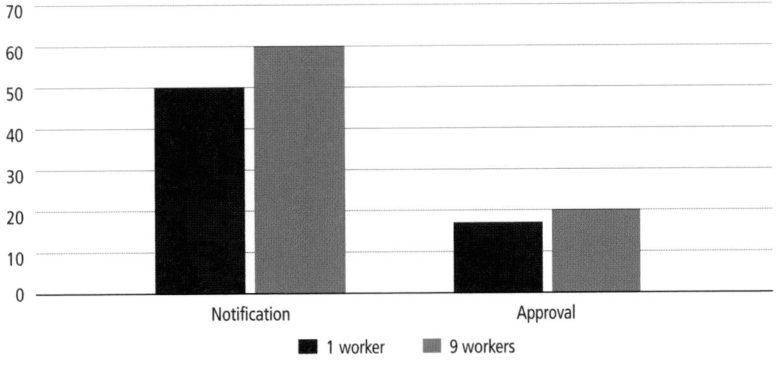

Source: Doing Business database.

BOX 10.2 India's labor regulation has been associated with a number of economic distortions*

Labor market issues in India are regulated by 45 central government laws and more than 100 state statutes. One of the most controversial laws, the Industrial Dispute Resolution Act (IDA) of 1947, requires factories with more than 100 employees to receive government approval to dismiss workers and close down. Obtaining such approvals entails a lengthy and difficult process and illegal worker dismissals can result in significant fines and a prison sentence. Industrial establishments also have to observe many other laws that regulate every aspect of their operations from the frequency of wall painting to working hours and employee benefits. Compliance with labor regulation also entails a considerable amount of paperwork and filing requirements.

Indian states have the freedom to amend labor laws. Besley and Burgess[a] found that states with rigid employment regulation had lower output, employment and productivity in formal manufacturing than they would have had if their regulations were more flexible. Sharma[b] applied Besley and Burgess' methodology to assess the impact of delicensing reform on informality. The paper finds that following this reform, the informal sector contracted to a greater extent in states with more flexible labor laws; these states also experienced a larger increase in value added per worker compared to states with more rigid regulation. The author concludes that entry deregulation can lead to productivity-enhancing labor reallocation from the informal to the formal sector, if labor laws are flexible. Ahsan and Pages[c] modified the Besley and Burgess methodology and evaluated the effects of employment protection legislation and the cost of labor disputes on economic outcomes. They found that in states that raised the rigidity of labor regulations above the IDA requirements, employment, output and value added per worker in registered manufacturing decreased compared to states that did not introduce such amendments. Hasan and Jandoc[d] studied the impact of labor regulation on firm size and found that there is a much greater prevalence of larger firms in labor-intensive industries in states with more flexible labor regulation.

Although Indian labor laws aim to increase employment security and worker welfare, they often have negative impacts by creating incentives to use less labor and encouraging informality and small firm size. Indeed, Indian firms are more capital-intensive relative to the economy's factor endowments. High labor costs in formal manufacturing have also contributed to India's specialization in the production and export of capital-intensive and knowledge-intensive goods despite the country's comparative advantage in low-skilled, labor-intensive manufacturing. To circumvent labor laws and other regulations, most Indian firms do not register and about 85% of non-agricultural employment is in the informal sector.[e] Informality is associated with low productivity: value added per worker in India's manufacturing sector averages about one-eighth of the formal sector.[f] Furthermore, only 9.8 million workers out of a total estimated workforce of 470 million were employed in private sector firms with 10 or more workers in 2007-2008.[g] This pattern of employment distribution has important welfare implications as small enterprises in India and globally are on average less productive and pay lower wages.[h]

The Indian government recently announced plans for major reforms to labor regulation aimed at increasing job creation and encouraging compliance. The planned legislative amendments include the consolidation of central labor laws, facilitating the retrenchment and closing down of factories by allowing firms employing less than 300 workers to dismiss them without seeking government approval, and increasing compensation to retrenched workers. Broad consultation with a wide range of stakeholders is essential to inform the design and ensure support for reform implementation. Evaluating the impact of the reform will be important.

a. Besley and Burgess 2004.
b. Sharma 2009.
c. Ahsan and Pagés 2009.
d. Hasan and Jandoc 2012.
e. World Development Indicators database (http://worldbank.org/indicator), World Bank.
f. World Bank 2010.
g. Bhagwati and Panagariya 2013.
h. Hasan and Jandoc 2012.
* Many of the findings presented in this box were also discussed in the World Bank's "World Development Report 2014: Risk and Opportunity."

economies, measures that limit the ability of new labor market entrants to find jobs can be particularly damaging.

Many economies require notification of a third-party (for example, the government employment office) for redundancy dismissals. These requirements are more common for collective dismissals involving a group of at least nine redundant workers. By contrast, third-party approval requirements for redundancy dismissals are less common (figure 10.6). The legislation tends to be more rigid in low-income economies—30% of low-income economies require third-party approval for collective dismissals while only 7% of high-income economies do so. In economies with well-functioning employment services, notification requirements for collective dismissals can help government officials prepare for an increase in the number of unemployed, including through the design of targeted job search assistance and training programs. By contrast, there is little justification for mandating third-party approval for redundancy dismissals. In some economies, obtaining such approval entails a lengthy process or the approval is hardly ever granted, making dismissals de facto impossible. This is the case in India, where cumbersome redundancy rules—combined with rigidities in other labor regulations—have been linked to a number of economic distortions (box 10.2).

Severance pay, unemployment insurance and social assistance

Most economies (79%) mandate severance payments for redundancy dismissals. This requirement can be justified by the need to provide some income protection for redundant workers. However, severance payments are a weak mechanism for income loss mitigation and are no substitute for unemployment insurance.[21] On the income protection front, there is no connection between the benefits and workers' financial situation—the same amount is paid regardless of the duration of unemployment. Despite legal entitlement, many workers fail to obtain their benefits as liabilities often arise when the firm is least capable of paying them.[22] Severance pay may also contribute to labor market duality as the increase in dismissal costs can reduce access to jobs for vulnerable groups.[23] Furthermore, given that severance payments tend to increase with tenure, redundancy decisions may be biased against young workers.[24]

Severance payments may be damaging for domestic small and medium-size enterprises struggling with economic difficulties or going out of business. In some economies, severance payments approximate or exceed one year of salary. Table 10.1 provides a snapshot of the economies with the highest legally-mandated severance pay for workers with 10 years of tenure. Overall, the magnitude of severance payments tends to decrease as the income levels of economies increase. *Doing Business* data show that severance payments for workers with 10 years of tenure are significantly higher in low- and lower-middle-income economies compared to high-income economies (table 10.2). However, in developing economies the capacity to enforce the law is poor,[25] leaving the majority of workers outside the public sector unprotected against job loss risks.

Lack of unemployment insurance (and social assistance programs more generally) is one reason behind the sizeable severance pay in low- and lower-middle-income economies (table 10.2). Globally, 60% of economies do not have any unemployment benefit schemes stipulated by law; the situation is particularly dire in low-income economies. Unemployment insurance is a more effective mechanism for income protection than severance pay because it pools risk, allowing resources to be accumulated in good times and released in times of hardship. However, the introduction of unemployment insurance in economies with large informal sectors is challenging as many workers have both formal and informal jobs, which makes it difficult to establish their eligibility for unemployment insurance.[26] Furthermore, open unemployment is not common in low-income economies, where the majority of the population is engaged in agriculture or self-employment. In this context, income loss is more common than job loss, making social assistance programs critically important.[27] However, only one quarter of the poorest quintile are covered by some type of social assistance programs in low- and lower-middle-income economies compared to 64% in upper-middle-income economies.[28]

In developing economies that have introduced unemployment insurance, such programs are often characterized by low coverage (due to large informal sectors and strict eligibility criteria) as well as low benefits.[29] Similarly, the outreach and quality of active labor market programs like job search assistance, training, and public work programs in the developing economies is inadequate.[30]

TABLE 10.1 Top 10 economies with the highest severance pay

Economy	Severance pay (in weeks of salary) for a worker with 10 years of tenure
Sierra Leone	132.0
Sri Lanka	97.5
Indonesia	95.3
Ghana	86.7
Zambia	86.7
Mozambique	65.0
Equatorial Guinea	64.3
Ecuador	54.2
Egypt, Arab Rep.	54.2
Lao PDR	52.0

Source: Doing Business database.

TABLE 10.2 Availability of unemployment protection and magnitude of severance pay

Income group	Availability of unemployment protection (% of economies)	Severance pay for a worker with 10 years of tenure (in weeks of salary)
Low income	0	24
Lower middle income	23	28
Upper middle income	44	20
High income	81	13
Global average	40	21

Source: Doing Business database.

Evidence from evaluations shows that, when well designed, active labor market programs in developing economies can be cost effective and have a positive impact on employment outcomes.[31] Job search assistance and training programs can help workers find jobs and improve earnings provided that job openings exist. Such programs can also be effective in reaching vulnerable groups. For example, in Latin American economies and economies in transition, youth and women record significantly better outcomes from training than do middle-aged men.[32] There is also evidence from a number of developing economies that public employment programs can be used effectively to provide workers with temporary jobs and a source of income.[33]

FIGURE 10.7 Laws on gender nondiscrimination in hiring and equal remuneration for work of equal value are most common in OECD high-income economies

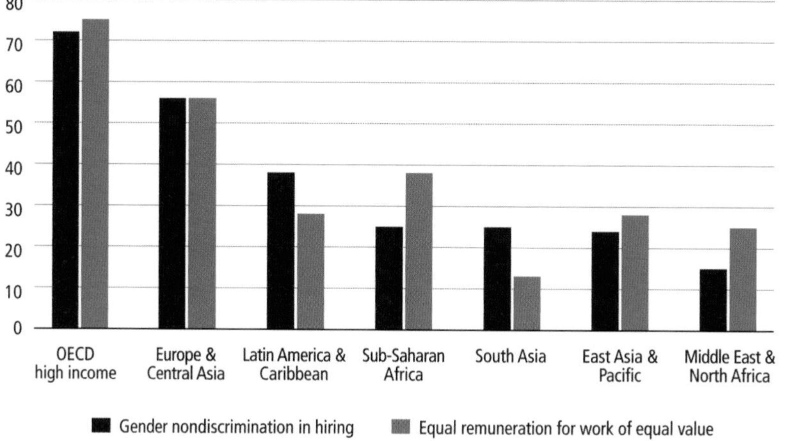

Source: Doing Business database.

HOW ARE GENDER RELATIONS REGULATED IN THE WORKPLACE?

Gender equality can make institutions more representative, improve social cohesion and increase productivity. Women constitute approximately 40% of the global labor force and over 50% of university students.[34] Removing regulatory barriers to women's access to the labor market can generate broad productivity gains and improve socioeconomic outcomes.

Doing Business data show that approximately 60% of economies do not have laws mandating gender nondiscrimination in hiring and equal remuneration for work of equal value (figure 10.7). Such laws are more common in OECD high-income economies, followed by economies in Europe and Central Asia. Women's earnings globally are estimated to be on average 77% of men's earnings[35] and the magnitude of the wage gap varies significantly by economy, sector and occupation. The establishment of nondiscrimination laws can provide a legal framework for action on women's rights and is an important step toward reducing gender inequality in the labor market.

Some economies regulate the types of jobs women can take through restrictions on working at night or in certain industries and occupations. Restrictions on working hours for nonpregnant and nonnursing women are present in 18% of economies and are most common in the Middle East and North Africa (figure 10.8). Legal barriers to women's work in certain industries and occupations are much more common—100 out of 173 economies for which data are available prohibit women's participation in certain economic activities.[36] For example, in the Kyrgyz Republic women cannot enter approximately 400 professions[37] and in the Russian Federation women are barred from 456 specified jobs.[38] Such legislation is often meant to protect women's interests but has been associated with occupational segregation and larger wage gaps as many of these jobs

FIGURE 10.8 Restrictions on women's night work are most common in the Middle East and North Africa

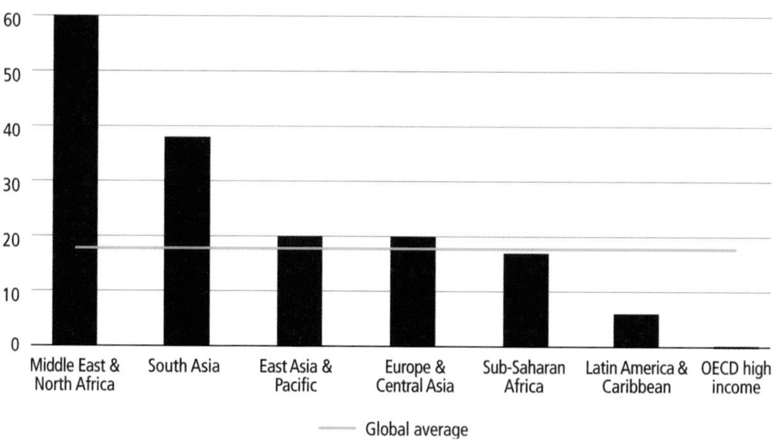

Source: Doing Business database.

are in well-paid sectors such as mining and manufacturing.[39] Furthermore, economies with work hour or industry restrictions also have, on average, lower female labor force participation—45%, compared with 60% in economies with no restrictions.[40]

Women, Business and the Law provides quantitative measures of regulations that affect women's economic opportunities and offers useful insights on the impact of legal gender disparities on women's economic outcomes. The analysis shows that lower legal gender equality is associated with a larger gender gap in secondary school attendance as families may decide that it is not worthwhile to invest in girls' education in economies where women face legal barriers to labor market access. Furthermore, in economies with larger legal gender disparities, a woman is less likely than a man to be employed, run a business or advance to management positions. Economies with lower legal gender equality also tend to have a larger wage gap compared to economies where laws are more gender equal.

CONCLUSION

Low- and middle-income economies tend to have stricter hiring and redundancy rules. This tendency may be partially explained by the lack of effective mechanisms to protect the income of workers in case of job loss. However, strict EPL may not be an optimal mechanism to support workers and improve the functioning of labor markets. Rules on severance pay, for example, may be difficult to enforce when firms are struggling with economic difficulties or going out of business. Despite stringent employment protection legislation, workers in low-income economies are vulnerable to arbitrary treatment by employers and job loss risks due to weak law enforcement and large informal sectors.

Labor policies aimed at protecting workers rather than jobs may carry bigger promise. Strengthening social protection systems—through the development of unemployment insurance, active labor market programs and social safety nets—is instrumental to support workers that have lost their jobs or experienced a decline in earnings.[41] Expanding coverage of social assistance programs to the informal sector is important for economies where the informal sector is large. One way to do it is through the establishment of integrated cash transfer programs, which could be linked to requirements to participate in training or public work programs, and provide income support while improving worker employability. It is also important to strengthen labor inspectorates, both to enforce worker rights and to provide advisory services to enterprises to improve their compliance with core labor standards.

Preserving jobs that are no longer economically viable—whether due to technological change or domestic or international competitive pressures—may result in an inefficient allocation of resources and hinder productivity. There is no blueprint for the optimal mix of employment protection rules and such regulation should be tailored to national circumstances and designed or reformed in collaboration with social partners. Care should be taken to avoid policies that discourage job creation and increase the level of informality in the economy.

Governments around the world can do more to improve access to economic opportunities for women. Establishment and enforcement of legislation that levels the playing field in access to jobs and remuneration for men and women can strengthen women's economic status and reduce gender inequality in the labor market. Instead of creating impediments for women's access to certain jobs, governments can work with employers' organizations and social partners to promote health and safety standards for men and women. This approach can help reduce occupational injuries and support women in realization of their professional aspirations.

NOTES

This case study was written by Anna Reva and Margarida Rodrigues.

1. World Bank 2015a.
2. World Bank 2012a.
3. World Bank 2012a.
4. Djankov and Ramalho 2009; Sharma 2009; Loayza, Oviedo and Serven 2005.
5. Montenegro and Pages 2003; Kahn 2010; Kugler, Jimeno and Hernanz 2005.
6. Martin and Scarpetta, 2011; Bassanini, Nunizata and Venn 2008.
7. Betcherman 2012.
8. More detailed and economy disaggregated data on these and other aspects of labor regulation are available in the annex to the report and on the *Doing Business* website.
9. A fixed-term contract refers to a contract with a specified end date. Fixed-term contracts can be used for permanent as well as for temporary and seasonal activities.
10. OECD 2014b.
11. OECD 2014b.
12. The EU-10 consists of Austria, Belgium, Denmark, Finland, Germany, Greece, Ireland, Italy, Portugal, and Spain.
13. OECD 2008.
14. OECD 2008.
15. OECD 2014b.
16. OECD 2013a.
17. OECD 2014b.
18. OECD 2014b.
19. OECD 2014b.
20. OECD 2014b.
21. Holzmann and Vodopivec 2012.
22. A study on Peru found that only half of all workers legally entitled to severance payments are likely to receive them. In 2000 one-third of the total severance pay obligations in Slovenia were not honored; Holzmann and Vodopivec 2012.
23. Holzmann and Vodopivec 2012.
24. Holzmann and Vodopivec 2012.
25. Holzmann and Vodopivec 2012.
26. See the discussion of possible models to adjust the classic unemployment insurance schemes to developing economy contexts in Vodopivec 2013 and Robalino, Vodopivec and Bodor 2009.
27. World Bank 2012a.
28. World Bank 2015a.
29. Kuddo, Robalino and Weber 2015.
30. Banerji and others 2014.
31. World Bank 2012a.
32. World Bank 2012a.
33. Subbarao and others 2013.
34. World Bank 2011.
35. ILO 2016.
36. World Bank 2015a.
37. Sakhonchik 2016.
38. World Bank 2015a.
39. World Bank 2015a.
40. World Bank 2011.
41. World Bank 2012a; Kuddo, Robalino and Weber 2015; Vodopivec 2013; Grosh and others 2008.

Annex: Selling to the Government

Why public procurement matters

- The selling to the government indicators aim to assess the ease of accessing and navigating public procurement markets across 78 economies, based on consistent and objective data that can inform policy makers in their procurement reform agenda.
- The selling to the government indicators measure aspects that are relevant to improving the ease with which companies can do business with governments across economies: access to electronic procurement, bid security, payment delays, incentives for small and medium-size enterprises and complaint mechanisms.
- There is a clear move toward the use of electronic public procurement systems. Indeed, 97% of the economies analyzed have one or more online portals dedicated to public procurement.
- Of the economies included in the selling to the government indicators close to 90% impose a bid security deposit requirement that suppliers must fulfill for their bid to be accepted.
- In 37% of the economies included in the selling to the government indicators payment occurs within 30 days on average while in 47% of the economies suppliers can expect to receive payments between 31 and 90 days following completion of the contract.

Public procurement is the process of purchasing goods, services or works by the public sector from the private sector. The range of industries involved in public procurement is therefore as wide as what a government needs to function properly and to deliver public services to its citizens. Whether for the construction of a school or to purchase hospital supplies, to secure information technology services in public buildings or renew a fleet of city buses, governments must constantly turn to the private sector to supply goods and services. Overall, public procurement represents on average 10 to 25% of GDP, making procurement markets a unique pool of business opportunities for the private sector.[1]

Given its significant size, public procurement can impact the structure and functioning of the market beyond the mere quantities of goods and services purchased.[2] For instance, through its procurement policies, the public sector can affect the incentives of firms to compete in a number of ways.[3] In the short-term, public procurement can impact competition among potential suppliers; in the long-term, public procurement can affect investment, innovation and the competitiveness of the market.[4] Indeed, research has shown that where entry barriers to procurement markets are kept to a minimum and the competitive process can play its role, the private sector thrives and tends to compete and innovate more.[5] In fact, where businesses—particularly small and medium-size enterprises—have a fair chance to compete for government contracts, it can give them the necessary boost to further develop their activity, and even propose innovative goods and services that will meet demand in other markets.[6] Competition in procurement markets is therefore critical on many levels and procurement policy may be used to shape the longer term effects on competition in an industry or sector.[7]

BUILDING NEW INDICATORS: SELLING TO THE GOVERNMENT

Public procurement laws and regulations—and their implementation in practice—can encourage competition by increasing suppliers' confidence in the integrity and efficiency of the procurement process.[8] That will, in turn, allow government agencies to deliver better services and give the public more confidence in the way public funds are spent.[9] To build and maintain a reputation as a trustworthy and efficient business partner, which can increase competition in later procurements, the purchasing entity has to pay promptly when payment is due in return for adequate performance. The legal framework should specify a timeframe for making payments and provide additional compensation when the procuring entity fails to pay on time. Indeed, delays in payment can have severe consequences for private sector suppliers, particularly small and medium-size enterprises which typically do not have large cash flows.[10] Companies may also be deterred from responding to public calls for tender if it is difficult to access the relevant information in a timely fashion, if delays and extraordinary costs are expected to be incurred throughout the procurement process and if unpredictable regulations create additional burdensome hurdles.

The selling to the government indicators aim to assess the ease of accessing and navigating public procurement markets across 78 economies, based on consistent and objective data that can inform policy makers in their procurement reform agenda. The indicators have been developed by the Benchmarking Public Procurement project, an initiative developed at the request of the G20 Anti-Corruption Working Group, in order to measure transaction costs of public procurement contracts.[11] The Benchmarking Public Procurement data for indicators selected for the analysis presented here are available on the *Doing Business* website.

There is a recognized need for more research on good practices and challenges in the public procurement sector.[12] Due to the lack of comparable global statistics there has been limited research analyzing how legal frameworks and government policies in public procurement enhance competition and private sector development.[13]

The most comprehensive tool that exists in the field of public procurement is the Use of Country Procurement Systems—an initiative led by the Organisation for Economic Co-operation and Development (OECD) with the cooperation of other international financial institutions including the World Bank Group—which aims to increase reliance on domestic procurement systems through donor-funded projects. In 2008 the World Bank launched a program for the use of country systems in bank-supported operations. Through this program a number of economies have been selected to be assessed in a comprehensive manner. Tools like the Country Procurement Assessment Reports (CPAR)—which review the legal and institutional framework for procurement and recommend reforms—and the Methodology for Assessing Procurement Systems (MAPS) were used to assess the systems for public procurement, public financial management and governance in these economies.[14] Other integrated diagnostic tools such as the Public Expenditure and Financial Accountability (PEFA) instrument were also created.[15]

The selling to the government indicator set will generate data that will directly support national priorities and help economies to strengthen their procurement systems and ultimately achieve sustainable development outcomes. The data will also help economies to promote private sector competition by addressing the constraints to competition in public procurement. The selling to the government indicators measure aspects that are relevant to improving the ease with which companies can do business with governments across economies: access to electronic procurement, bid security, payment delays, incentives for small and medium-size enterprises and complaint mechanisms (figure 11.1).

To ensure that the data are comparable across the 78 economies covered, several assumptions about the bidding company, the procuring entity and the type of services being procured were used during the data collection process and analysis. In particular, a procuring entity which is a local authority in the main business city is planning to resurface a road for a value equivalent to 91 times the economy's income per capita or $2 million, whichever value is higher. It initiates a public call for tender following an open and competitive procedure. BidCo, a private, domestically-owned limited liability company, is a bidder.

FIGURE 11.1 What is measured

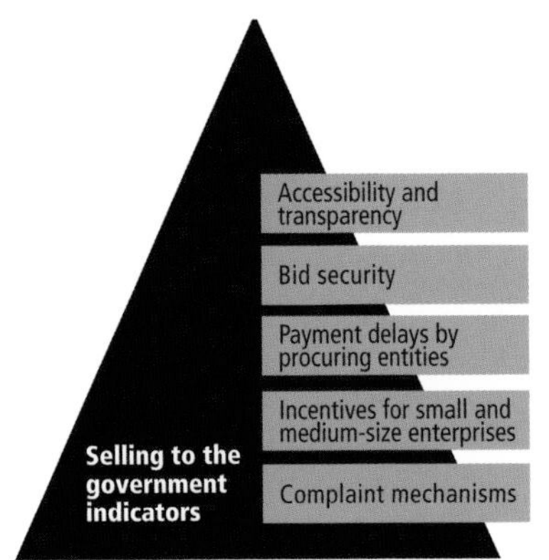

WHERE SELLING TO THE GOVERNMENT IS EASIER AND WHY

Accessing information and services online: accessibility and transparency

By streamlining the procurement process and supporting virtual access to information, the digitalization of public procurement—or e-procurement—lowers costs, reduces delays, maximizes efficiency and increases transparency. Research has shown that increased publicity requirements reduce government spending and maximize the effectiveness of their public procurement systems.[16] As a result, the procurement process becomes much simpler and cost-efficient, especially for companies with limited resources. In the past 10 years e-procurement has developed rapidly as more and more economies have recognized its added value and engaged in a transition toward digitalization.[17] The selling to the government indicators examine which materials can be accessed online and whether a supplier can submit a bid, sign the procurement contract and request payments through an online platform.

A well-functioning e-procurement portal which serves as a one-stop shop to access all public procurement opportunities and associated information increases the participation of small and medium-size enterprises in public calls for tender.[18] In Chile, for example, 10 years after the ChileCompra portal was implemented the share of contracts awarded to small and medium-size enterprises had risen from 24% to 44%.[19] The Korean e-procurement system, KONEPS, is another example of how a well-functioning portal can enhance efficiency, effectiveness and integrity of public procurement and act as a driver for investment and economic growth.[20] E-procurement also lowers the risk of fraud and corruption by limiting one-on-one interactions between buyers and sellers[21] and as such is recognized as an effective tool in combating corruption.[22] An e-procurement system increases transparency by collecting and publishing public procurement information and enhancing access for suppliers and other stakeholders through standardized and simplified processes. Research has shown that e-procurement improves service quality by facilitating entry for higher quality suppliers and reducing delays to public works projects.[23]

Procurement portals should support interactions between bidders and public buyers. Accessing information and interacting with public buyers—whether to ask questions or submit a bid—can be a costly and lengthy process for bidders. Having the option to do this online will save significant time and money.

There is a clear move toward the use of electronic public procurement systems. Indeed, 97% of the economies analyzed have one or more online portals dedicated to public procurement. Where economies have made measurable progress in implementing online procurement platforms, some are more advanced than others when it comes to the services offered to the users. Across economies the electronic platforms range from simple websites—that do not support interactions but allow users to merely access tendering information—to sophisticated platforms offering a range of services for conducting the procurement process online. In countries like Australia, Italy, the Republic of Korea, New Zealand and Singapore bidders can access notices of calls for tender and tender documents online as well as submit their bids through an electronic platform. Because of these options bidders in such economies spend less time performing necessary procedures than a prospective bidder in an economy where tender documents have to be obtained in hard copies and bids have to be submitted in person or via regular mail, as is the case in Angola and The Gambia.

Award notices should also be available online. In economies like Sweden the online publication of awards is mandated by law but in other economies such as Burundi, Jamaica and Myanmar bidders are still unable to access the outcome of the tendering process online (figure 11.2).

Guaranteeing the seriousness of bids through bid security instruments

When a company submits a bid in response to a call for tender it is often required to post bid security, either in the form of monies or a bank or insurance guarantee. The procuring entity typically holds the security deposit until the procurement contract is signed, after which all deposits are returned to the bidders. Bid security is a valuable instrument for procuring entities because it helps avoid the unnecessary use of resources. The selling to the government indicators measure the legal framework for bid security, the amount and the time for the procuring entity to return the deposit.

Requiring bidders to secure a guarantee or put together a substantial amount of money discourages those firms that may be tempted to approach the bidding process in a manner that is not serious. However, for bid security to fulfill its purpose and not act as a deterrent to companies it should be regulated and of a reasonable amount. A bid security that is too high can prohibit companies with limited resources from participating in the public market. To prevent this from occurring the maximum amount that procuring entities can request as bid security should not be left to their discretion—it should be regulated by law to prevent excessive amounts and guarantee equal treatment. The timeframe for purchasing entities to return a deposit—as well as the decision to cash it—should also be regulated.

Of the economies included in the selling to the government indicators close

FIGURE 11.2 E-mail submission of bids is an area where many economies can improve

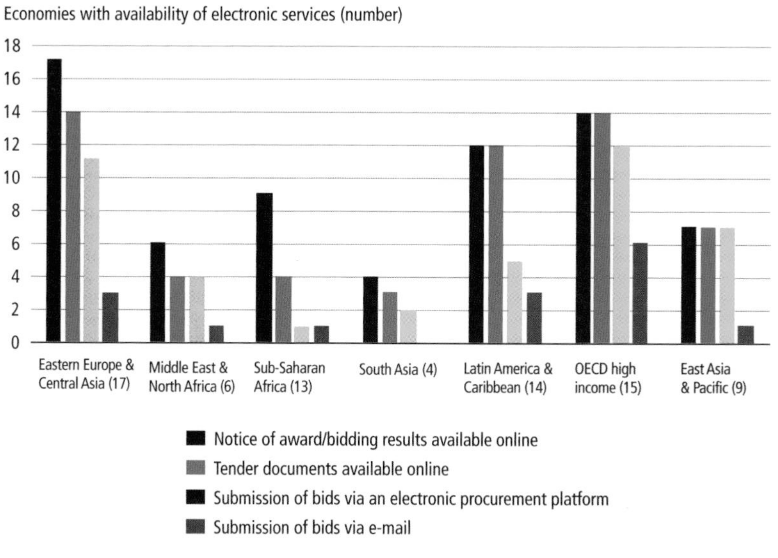

Source: Doing Business database.

to 90% impose a bid security deposit requirement that suppliers must fulfill for their bid to be accepted (figure 11.3). However in 16 of these economies the legal framework does not stipulate a maximum amount that the procuring entity can request bidders to deposit,[24] leaving it to the discretion of the procuring entity. This is the case in Morocco, among others.

Obtaining payment following the performance of contractual obligations

Obtaining payment in due time is of critical importance for businesses, especially small and medium-size ones. Research has shown that delays in government payments directly impact small enterprises as they often need to increase borrowing to offset the shortage of cash.[25] Increased delays in public payments have a direct impact on private sector liquidity and profits, thereby reducing economic growth.[26] When a supplier is not paid for its good, work or service, it can run into a cash flow

FIGURE 11.3 The bid security is regulated in the majority of economies

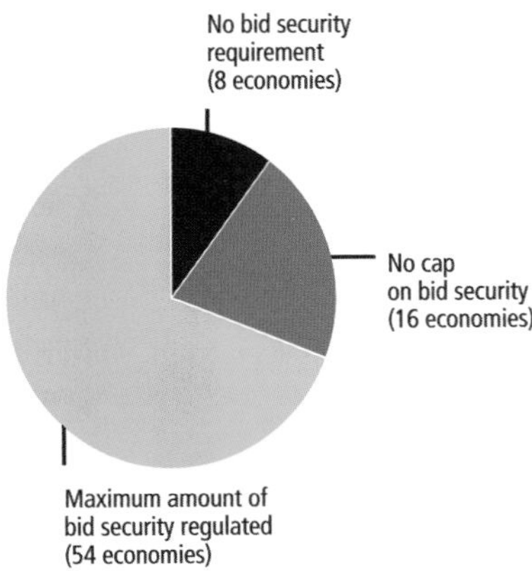

Source: Doing Business database.

Note: In Chile the procuring entity will include the amount of the bid security in the tender documents. In the case that the procuring entity fails to include the amount of the bid security in the tender documents, and a bid security is required as part of the offer, the bid security amount will automatically be 2% of the estimated contract price.

problem that will significantly impact its business. Therefore, where public buyers are known to pay their suppliers late and provide no financial compensation for the delay, companies might refrain from doing business with them.

The selling to the government indicators focus on the legal and actual timeframe to process payments. The recognized good practice is that suppliers should be paid within 30 days following the performance of the contract.[27] In practice, however, payment delays are frequent in public procurement markets. In 37% of the economies included in the selling to the government indicators payment occurs within 30 days on average (figure 11.4) while in 48% of the economies suppliers can expect to receive payments between 31 and 90 days following completion of the contract. It takes between 91 and 180 days for the supplier to obtain payment in only 14% of economies.[28]

Payment delays are positively correlated with Transparency International's Corruption Perceptions Index (CPI) in the sample of 76 economies. Indeed, the average CPI is higher (less corruption) in economies with shorter payment time periods (figure 11.5).

Increasing the participation of small and medium-size enterprises in the public procurement market

With small and medium-size enterprises constituting a large proportion of businesses, governments around the world are seeking ways to encourage these firms to participate in the public procurement market. Findings from the selling to the government indicators show that 62% of economies measured have set up specific legal provisions or policies to promote fair access for small and medium-size enterprises to government contracts.

The new European Union directives on public procurement seek to expand access for small and medium-size enterprises to

FIGURE 11.4 Payments are received within 30 days in around a third of economies

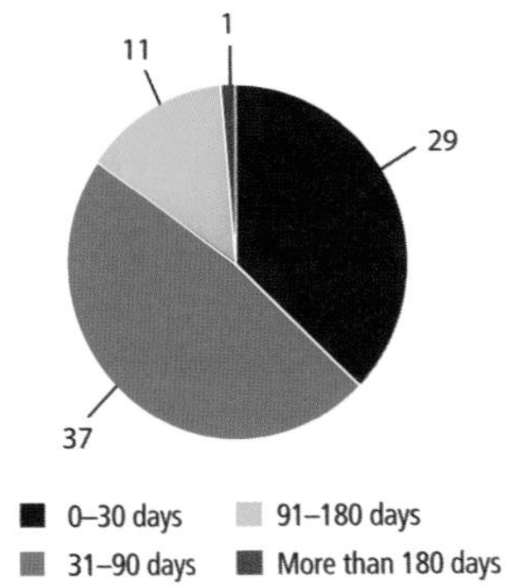

Source: Doing Business database.

public procurement markets. Large public contracts are divided into smaller batches, thereby allowing small and medium-size enterprises to participate in large tenders. Furthermore, preferential treatment is given to small and medium-size enterprises by limiting their turnover requirement to twice the contract value. Other regions are also establishing incentives aimed at facilitating access by small and medium-size firms to public tenders. In Angola, Côte d'Ivoire, the Dominican Republic, India and Morocco, for example, procuring entities

FIGURE 11.5 Shorter payment delays are associated with less corruption

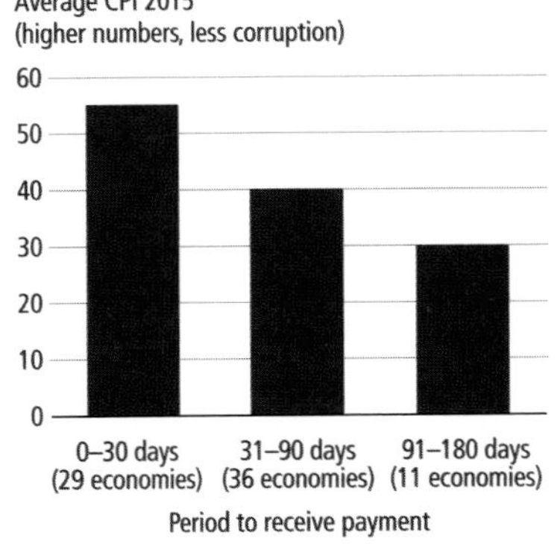

Sources: Doing Business database; Transparency International (https://www.transparency.org/cpi2015/results).

Note: Two economies were excluded from the sample: the Marshall Islands, for which CPI data was not available, and the Dominican Republic, the only economy in which payment delays exceed 181 days.

are required to allocate around 20% of the total value of government contracts to small and medium-size enterprises. That "set aside" ratio increases to 25% in Angola and Kenya and 40% in Taiwan, China. In some economies, the incentive takes a different form: projects below a certain threshold value are earmarked to small and medium-size enterprises. That threshold is equivalent to $190,000 in Indonesia, $125,000 in Colombia and $24,650 in Brazil (applicable only to micro and small enterprises). In economies such as Bolivia and the Arab Republic of Egypt, incentives for small and medium-size enterprises include an exemption from a portion or the full amount of a bid security. Additionally, in the Russian Federation the maximum amount of bid security cannot exceed 2% of the maximum price of the contract when the bid is submitted by a small or medium-size enterprise. Incentives pertaining to expedited payments are also in place in some economies. Public entities in Angola, for example, are required to pay small and medium-size enterprises within 45 days following the receipt of an invoice.

Having access to a fair and efficient complaint system

A well-functioning complaint system in the context of public procurement serves many purposes. For bidders a fair and impartial complaint mechanism is critical as it guarantees that they can file a complaint and that their complaint will be examined in a timely fashion. A robust complaint mechanism also serves as a deterrent to improper conduct by procuring officials,[29] making it paramount to the very integrity of a procurement system. The selling to the government indicators examine elements such as who has standing to file, time limits for review bodies to render decisions, remedies available to suppliers and standstill periods.[30]

Standing to file a complaint differs depending on the stage of the procurement process. During the pre-award stage (that is, when the government purchase is being prepared) standing should not be limited to suppliers who actually submitted a bid. Standing should also be accessible to potential bidders provided they can show an interest in the tender. Once the award decision is taken, then only actual bidders should be allowed to contest the decision in order to deter potentially frivolous complaints. Data show that during the pre-award stage 66 of the economies included in the selling to government indicators allow both actual bidders and potential bidders to file a complaint. In economies where the post-award stage is different, only Burkina Faso grants the right to file a complaint to potential bidders.

Delays in the resolution of complaints can deter potential bidders as they increase the costs for both governments and suppliers—particularly for companies which cannot afford the cost of contesting a flaw in the tendering process or the award itself. A time limit should be set in the law so that when a complaint is submitted the complaining party knows when it will receive a response. This time limit should be long enough to allow for an in-depth review of the complaint but not too long to disrupt the procurement process, especially in economies where a complaint leads to a suspension of the process. But having a regulatory time limit does not guarantee prompt review of complaints. The data show that the time to render a decision by the first-tier review body during the pre-award phase varies greatly across economies depending on whether the first-tier review body is the procuring entity or not. In economies where the first-tier review body is the procuring entity, the complaining party is likely to obtain a timely resolution.

When it comes to second-tier review, the time taken to render a decision also varies considerably depending on the economy. Companies may be reluctant to resort to the complaint mechanism in economies like Bolivia, where it can take up to four years to receive a decision, or India, where a decision can take up to three years. In Colombia, Uruguay and República Bolivariana de Venezuela, decisions on appeals are rendered within two years. However, in economies where the second-tier review body is not a court but an independent review body (such as, for example, an administrative review committee within the national procurement agency), the decision on the appeal is rendered more quickly. This is the case in Albania, Burkina Faso and Senegal, where firms receive a decision from the second-tier review body in less than 10 days.

FIGURE 11.6 Complaints lodged with the procuring entity are decided faster

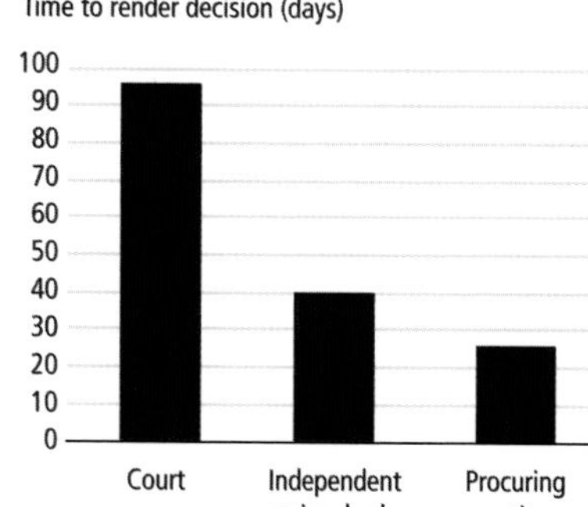

Source: Doing Business database.

Effective remedies should be available in the law to suppliers that can demonstrate that the violation of a particular procurement rule has harmed them. During the pre-award stage, such remedies should include the modification of tender documents, the payment of damages and the overturn in whole or in part of an act or a decision of the procuring entity. The legal framework allows first-tier and second-tier review bodies to overturn in whole or in part an act or a decision of the procuring entity in about half of the economies. Furthermore, damages are more frequently awarded by second-tier review bodies (26 economies) than first-tier review bodies (6 economies).

Once the procuring entity announces its award decision it is important that it allows for a standstill period. A minimum of 10 days is recognized as a good practice by judgments of the European Court of Justice and the World Trade Organization's Government Procurement Agreement.[31] Twenty-nine economies do not provide for a standstill period and 12 economies allow for a period shorter than 16 days. In Bolivia and Georgia, for example, the standstill period is three calendar days, which does not leave sufficient time for suppliers to file a complaint.

CONCLUSION

The selling to the government indicators expose significant disparities among the 78 economies measured. Although there is a clear move toward enhancing the transparency and efficiency of public procurement systems, impediments such as a lack of access to information, payment delays, unforeseen bid security requirements and inefficient complaint mechanisms remain prevalent across economies of various income groups.

The benefits of well-functioning electronic procurement portals have been widely recognized. In addition to enhancing transparency, they provide equal access to markets and reduce in-person interactions that offer opportunities for corruption. Similarly, predictable and regulated bid security requirements deter suppliers from submitting frivolous offers, while allowing serious bidders to anticipate the amount needed for deposit. Timely payments encourage suppliers, particularly small and medium-size enterprises which typically do not have large cash flows, to participate in the procurement market. Finally, efficient complaint mechanisms increase the confidence of private suppliers in the fairness of the procurement process and their willingness to file a complaint.

By exposing prevailing practices and highlighting obstacles that hinder private suppliers' access to the public market, the indicators have the potential to influence governments to undertake reforms that are necessary to promote more transparent, competitive and efficient public procurement systems. Ultimately, the objective is to create a more favorable environment for private suppliers, notably small and medium-size enterprises, by granting them a fair opportunity to access the public marketplace.

NOTES

This case study was written by Elisabeth Danon, Tania Ghossein, Maria Paula Gutierrez Casadiego and Sophie Pouget.

1. EU 2014. The European Union estimates that public procurement amounts to between 10% and 25% of GDP globally (see http://ec.europa.eu/trade/policy/accessing-markets/public-procurement/). The WTO estimates that public procurement represents between 10% and 15% of GDP. (see https://www.wto.org/english/tratop_e/gproc_e/gproc_e.htm).
2. OECD 2013b.
3. OECD 2016a; Cernat and Zornitsa 2015; World Bank Group 2014.
4. OECD 2011b.
5. Uyarra and others 2014.
6. Caldwell and others 2005.
7. OECD 2011b.
8. OECD 2016a.
9. Mahacek and Turkalj 2015; Tabarcea 2014.
10. Connell 2014.
11. For more information on the Benchmarking Public Procurement project, see the website at http://bpp.worldbank.org/.
12. Sánchez-Rodríguez and others 2003.
13. Arrowsmith and Hartley 2002.
14. World Bank Group 2014.
15. For more information on the PEFA methodology see the website at https://pefa.org/.
16. Coviello and Mariniello 2014.
17. World Bank Group 2015b.
18. Beauvallet and Boughzala 2011.
19. Chile 2013.
20. OECD 2016a.
21. Clare and others 2016.
22. Kashta 2014.
23. Lewis-Faupel and others 2014; Shingal 2015.
24. The bid security deposit is either a flat amount or a percentage of the value of the procurement contract or the bidder's proposal.
25. Nayak 2014.
26. Checherita-Westphal and others 2015.
27. OECD 2006b.
28. The data for payment delays was collected in four categories: payment delays of 0 to 30 calendar days, 31 to 90 calendar days, 91 to 180 calendar days and above 181 calendar days. This captured economies where payment delays are non-existent or reasonable (0 to 30 or 31 to 90 calendar days) or long (91 to 180 or more than 181 calendar days).
29. Gordon 2006.
30. The standstill period is the period of time between the announcement of the award and the signing of the contract during which bidders have the time to review the award decision and file a complaint if needed.
31. WTO 1994.

Doing Business 2017

References

Adams, Renée, and Daniel Ferreira. 2009. "Women in the Boardroom and Their Impact on Governance and Performance." *Journal of Financial Economics* 94 (2): 291-309.

Aggarwal, Reena, Isil Erel, Rene Stulz and Rohan Williamson. 2009. "Differences in Governance Practice between U.S. and Foreign Firms: Measurement, Causes, and Consequences." *Review of Financial Studies* 22: 3131-69.

Agostino, Mariarosaria, and Francesco Trivieri. 2014. "Does Trade Credit Play a Signaling Role? Some Evidence from SMEs Microdata." *Small Business Economics* 42 (1): 131-51.

Ahern, Kenneth, and Amy Dittmar, 2012. "The Changing of the Boards: The Impact on Firm Valuation of Mandated Female Board Representation." *Quarterly Journal of Economics* 127 (1): 137-97.

Ahsan, Ahmad and Carmen Pagés. 2009. "Are All Labor Regulations Equal? Evidence from Indian Manufacturing." *Journal of Comparative Economics* 37 (1): 62-75.

Aizenman, Joshua and Yothin Jinjarak. 2012. "Income Inequality, Tax Base and Sovereign Spreads." NBER Working Paper 18176. National Bureau of Economic Research, Cambridge, MA. Available at Social Science Research Network (SSRN). http://ssrn.com/abstract=2089248.

Ali, Daniel Ayalew, Klaus Deininger and Marcus Goldstein. 2014. "Environmental and Gender Impacts of Land Tenure Regularization in Africa: Pilot Evidence from Rwanda," *Journal of Development Economics* 110: 262-75.

Ali, Muhammad Aamir and Nazish Aamir. 2014. "Stock Market Development and Economic Growth: Evidence from India, Pakistan, China, Malaysia and Singapore." *International Journal of Economics, Finance and Management Sciences* 2 (3): 220-26.

Alm, James and Michael McKee. 2006. "Audit Certainty, Audit Productivity, and Taxpayer Compliance." Andrew Young School of Policy Studies Research Paper 2006-43. Available at Social Science Research Network (SSRN). http://ssrn.com/abstract=897341.

American Law Institute. 1992. *Principles of Corporate Governance: Analysis and Recommendations*. Philadelphia: American Law Institute.

Amin, Mohammad. 2010. "Gender and Firm-size: Evidence from Africa." *World Bank Economics Bulletin* 30 (1): 663-668.

Amiti, Mary, and Amit K. Khandelwal. 2011. "Import Competition and Quality Upgrading." *Review of Statistics and Economics* 95 (2): 476-90.

Ammann, Manuel, David Oesch and Markus Schmid. 2011. "Corporate Governance and Firm Value: International Evidence." *Journal of Empirical Finance* 18 (1): 36-55.

Andersen, Thomas Barnebeck and Carl-Johan Dalgaard. 2013. "Power Outages and Economic Growth in Africa." *Energy Economics*, Elsevier, 38 (C): 19-23.

Angel-Urdinola, Diego and Arvo Kuddo. 2010. "Key Characteristics of Employment Regulation in the Middle East and North Africa." Social Protection Discussion Paper 1006. World Bank, Washington, DC.

Araujo, Aloisio P., Rafael V. X. Ferreira and Bruno Funchal. 2012. "The Brazilian Bankruptcy Law Experience." *Journal of Corporate Finance* 18 (4): 994-1004.

Arora, Rashmi U. 2014. "Access to Finance: An Empirical Analysis." *European Journal of Development Research* 26: 798-814.

Arrowsmith, Sue, ed. 2011. *EU Public Procurement Regulations: An Introduction*. England: Nottingham University.

Arrowsmith, Sue and Keith Hartley, eds. 2002. *Public Procurement*. Northampton, Massachusetts: Edward Edgar Publishing Limited.

Arvis, Jean-Francois, Monica Alina Mustra, Mona Haddad, Bernard Hoekman, Lauri Ojala, Daniel Saslavsky and Ben Shepherd. 2010. "Connecting to Compete 2010: Trade Logistics in the Global Economy." Working Paper 55852. World Bank, Washington, DC.

Asia-Pacific Economic Association. 2015. "2015 Leaders Declaration." Manila, Philippines. November 19. Available at http://www.apec.org/Meeting-Papers/Leaders Declarations/2015/2015_aelm.aspx.

Asker, John, Joan Farre-Mensa and Alexander Ljungqvist. 2015. "Corporate Investment and Stock Market Listing: A Puzzle?" *Review of Financial Studies* 28 (2): 342-90.

Ates, Abidin, Sevin Gurarda and Emre Ozsoz. 2014. "Ownership Structure and Corporate Governance in the Case of Turkey." MPRA Paper 58293. Available at http://mpra.ub.uni-muenchen.de/58293/.

Avom, Désiré, and Gislain Stephane Gandjon Fankem. 2014. "Qualité du cadre juridique, corruption et commerce international: le cas de la CEMAC." *Revue d'economie politique* 124: 101-28.

Aziz, Rashid and Munawar Baseer Ahmad. 2015. "Pakistan's Power Crisis, The Way Forward." United States Institute of Peace, Special Report 375, June. Available at https://www.usip.org/sites/default/files/SR375-Pakistans-Power-Crisis-The-Way-Forward.pdf.

Ball, Gwendolyn G., and Jay P. Kesan. 2010. "Judges, Courts and Economic Development: The Impact of Judicial Human Capital on the Efficiency and Accuracy of the Court System." Paper presented at the 15th Annual Conference of the International Society for New Institutional Economics, Stanford University, Stanford, CA, June 16-18. Available at http://papers.isnie.org/paper/716.html.

Banerji, Arup, David Newhouse, Pierella Paci, and David Robalino, eds. 2014. *Working through the Crisis: Jobs and Policies in Developing Countries During the Great Recession*. Directions in Development. Washington, DC: World Bank.

Barseghyan, Levon. 2008. "Entry Costs and Cross-Country Differences in Productivity and Output." *Journal of Economic Growth* 13(2): 145-67.

Barsky, Jennifer. 2014. International Finance Corporation Press Release, May 19, Bogota, Colombia.

Barthold, Beat, Marco Rizzi and Mark Montanari. 2014. "Swiss Ordinance Against Excessive Compensation in Listed Stock Companies—First Experiences After the Shareholder's Meeting Season 2014." Available at http://www.lexology.com/219/author / Dr_Beat_M_Barthold/.

Bassanini, Andrea, Luca Nunizata, and Danielle Venn. 2008. "Job Protection Legislation and Productivity Growth in OECD Countries." IZA Discussion Paper 3555. Institute for the Study of Labor (IZA), Germany.

Beauvallet, Godefroy, Younès Boughzala and Said Assar. 2011. "E-Procurement, from Project to Practice: Empirical Evidence from the French Public Sector." In *Practical Studies in E-Government: Best Practices from Around the World*. 2011:13-27.

Bebchuk, Lucian. 2013. "The Myth that Insulating Boards Serves Long-Term Value." *Columbia Law Review* 113 (6): 1637-94.

Bebchuk, Lucian. 2005. "The Case for Increasing Shareholder Power." *Harvard Law Review* 118 (3): 833-914.

Bebchuk, Lucian, Reinier Kraakman and George Triantis. 1999. "Stock Pyramids, Cross-Ownership and Dual Class Equity: The Creation and Agency Costs of Separating Control from Cash Flow Rights." Discussion Paper 249, Harvard Law School, Cambridge, MA.

Beck, Thorsten, and Asli Demirgüç-Kunt. 2006. "Small and Medium-Size Enterprises: Access to Finance as a Growth Constraint." *Journal of Banking and Finance* 30 (11): 2931-43.

Beck, Thorsten, Asli Demirgüc-Kunt, Luc Laeven and Vojislav Maksimovic. 2006. "The determinants of financing obstacles." *Journal of International Money and Finance* 25 (6), 932-95.

Beck, Thorsten, Asli Demirgüç-Kunt and María Soledad Martínez Peria. 2008. "Bank Financing for SMEs around the World: Drivers, Obstacles, Business Models, and Lending Practices." Policy Research Working Paper 4785. World Bank, Washington, DC.

Beck, Thorsten, Chen Lin and Yue Ma. 2014. "Why Do Firms Evade Taxes? The Role of Information Sharing and Financial Sector Outreach." *Journal of Finance* 69: 763-817.

Bentolila, Samuel, Juan Dolado and Juan Jimeno. 2011. "Reforming an Insider-Outsider Labor Market: The Spanish Experience." IZA Discussion Paper 6186. Institute for the Study of Labor (IZA), Germany.

Berger, Allen N., and Gregory F. Udell. 2006. "A More Complete Conceptual Framework for SME Finance." *Journal of Banking and Finance* 30 (11): 2945-66.

Bertrand, Marianne and Francis Kramarz. 2002. "Does Entry Regulation Hinder Job Creation? Evidence from the French Retail Industry." *Quarterly Journal of Economics* 117 (4): 1369-1413.

Bertrand, Marianne, Sandra E. Black, Sissel Jensen and Adriana Lleras-Muney. 2014."Breaking the Glass Ceiling? The Effect of Board Quotas on Female Labor Market Outcomes in Norway." National Bureau of Economic Research Working Paper Series, NBER, Cambridge, MA.

Besley, Timothy, and Robin Burgess. 2004. "Can Labor Regulation Hinder Economic Performance? Evidence from India." *Quarterly Journal of Economics* 119 (1): 91-134.

Betcherman, Gordon. 2012. "Labor Market Institutions: A Review of the Literature." Policy Research Working Paper 6272. World Bank, Washington, DC.

Bhagwati, Jagdish, and Arvind Panagariya. 2013. *Why Growth Matters: How Economic Growth in India Reduced Poverty and the*

Lessons for Other Developing Countries. New York, NY: Public Affairs.

Bird, R., and O. Oldman. 2000. "Improving Taxpayer Service and Facilitating Compliance in Singapore." The World Bank PREM Notes, Public Sector. December. 48: 1-4.

Bjørnskov, C., and N.J. Foss. 2008. "Economic Freedom and Entrepreneurial Activity: Some Cross-Country Evidence." *Public Choice* 134 (3): 307-28.

Black, Bernard, Woochan Kim, Hasung Jang and Kyung Suh Park. 2010. "How Corporate Governance Affects References Firm Value: Evidence on Channels from Korea." Finance Working Paper 103/2005, European Corporate Governance Institute, Brussels.

Botero, Juan Carlos, Simeon Djankov, Rafael La Porta, Florencio López-de-Silanes and Andrei Shleifer. 2004. "The Regulation of Labor." *Quarterly Journal of Economics* 119 (4): 1339-82.

Branstetter, Lee G., Francisco Lima, Lowell J. Taylor and Ana Venâncio. 2013. "Do Entry Regulations Deter Entrepreneurship and Job Creation? Evidence from Recent Reforms in Portugal." *Economic Journal.* Published electronically July 16, 2013. doi:10.1111//ecoj.12044.

Brown, Lawrence and Marcus Caylor. 2009. "Corporate Governance and Firm Operating Performance." *Review of Quantitative Finance and Accounting* 32 (2): 129-44.

Brown, Martin, and Christian Zehnder. 2007. "Credit Registries, Relationship Banking, and Loan Repayment." *Journal of Money, Credit and Banking* 39 (8): 1883-918.

Bruhn, Miriam. 2009. "Female-Owned Firms in Latin America: Characteristics, Performance, and Obstacles to Growth." Policy Research Working Paper 5122, World Bank, Washington, DC.

_______. 2011. "License to Sell: The Effect of Business Registration Reform on Entrepreneurial Activity in Mexico." *Review of Economics and Statistics* 93 (1): 382-86.

_______. 2013. "A Tale of Two Species: Revisiting the Effect of Registration Reform on Informal Business Owners in Mexico." *Journal of Development Economics* 103: 275-83.

Bufford, Samuel. 2006. "International Rule of Law and the Market Economy—An Outline." *Southwestern Journal of Law and Trade in the Americas* 303 (12).

Business World. 2013. "Ghana Unveils Ultra-Modern Collateral Registry." May 10. Available at http://www.businessworldghana.com/ghana-unveils-ultra-modern-collateral-registry/

Bustelo, Frederic. 2009. "Finance for All: Integrating Microfinance to Credit Information Sharing in Bolivia." *Celebrating Reforms 2009.* Washington, DC: International Finance Corporation.

Cabrales, Antonio, Juan Dolado and Ricardo Mora. 2014. "Dual Labour Markets and (Lack of) On-the-Job Training: PIAAC Evidence from Spain and Other EU Countries." IZA Discussion Paper 8649. Institute for the Study of Labor (IZA), Germany.

Caldwell, N., H. Walker, C. Harland, L. Knight, J. Zheng and T. Wakeley. 2005. "Promoting Competitive Markets: The Role of Public Procurement." *Journal of Purchasing and Supply Management,* 11 (5-6): 242-51.

Carballo, Jerónimo, Georg Schaur, and Christian Volpe Martincus. 2015. "The Border Labyrinth: Information Technologies and Trade in the Presence of Multiple Agencies." University of Maryland, University of Tennessee, and Inter-American Development Bank.

Cernat, Lucien and Zornitsa Kutlina-Dimitrova. 2015. "International Public Procurement: From Scant Facts to Hard Data" European Union TRADE Chief Economist Note. April. European Commission, Brussels. Available at http://trade.ec.europa.eu/doclib/docs/2015/april/tradoc_153347.pdf.

Checherita-Westphal, Cristina, Alexander Klemm and Paul Viefers. 2015. "Governments' Payment Discipline: The Macroeconomic Impact of Public Payment Delays and Arrears." IMF Working Papers 1771, International Monetary Fund, Washington, DC.

Cheffins, Brian. 2009. "Did Corporate Governance 'Fail' During the 2008 Stock Market Meltdown? The Case of the S&P 500." *Business Lawyer* 65 (1).

Chen, Kevin, Zhihong Chen and John Wei. 2011. "Agency Costs of Free Cash Flows and the Effect of Shareholder Rights on the Implied Cost of Capital." *Journal of Financial and Quantitative Analysis* 46: 171-207.

Child, David. 2008. "VAT Administration: Addressing Private Sector Concerns." In *VAT in Africa,* edited by Richard Krever. Pretoria: Pretoria University Law Press.

Chile, Ministry of the Treasury, ChileCompra. 2013. "MIPE informe proveedores micro y pequeños empresarios." September. http://www.chilecompra.cl/index.php?option=com_content&view=article&id=1579&Itemid=1090.

Ciccone, Antonio, and Elias Papaioannou. 2007. "Red Tape and Delayed Entry." *Journal of the European Economic Association* 5 (2-3): 444-58.

Cirmizi, Elena, Leora Klapper and Mahesh Uttamchandani. 2010. "The Challenges of Bankruptcy Reform." Policy Research Working Paper 5448, World Bank, Washington, DC.

Claessens, Stijn, Kenichi Ueda and Yishay Yafeh. 2014. "Institutions and Financial Frictions: Estimating with Structural Restrictions on Firm Value and Investment." *Journal of Development Economics* 110: 107-22.

Claessens, Stijn. 2006. "Corporate Governance and Development." *The World Bank Research Observer* 21 (1): 91-122.

Clare, Ali, David Sangokoya, Stefaan Verhulst and Andrew Young. 2016. "Open Contracting and Procurement in Slovakia." Open Data's Impact. New York, NY. Available at http://odimpact.org/static/files/case-study-slovakia.pdf.

Clark, Ximena, David Dollar, and Alejandro Micco. 2004. "Port Efficiency, Maritime Transport Costs, and Bilateral Trade." *Journal of Development Economics* 75: 417-50.

Connell, William. 2014. "The Economic Impact of Late Payments." European Commission, Economic Papers 531, September, European Commission, Brussels. Available at http://ec.europa.eu/economy_finance/publications/

economic_paper/2014/pdf/ecp531_en.pdf

Corcoran, Adrian, and Robert Gillanders. 2015. "Foreign Direct Investment and the Ease of Doing Business." *Review of World Economics* 151 (1): 103-26.

Core, John, Robert Holthausen and David Larcker. 1999, "Corporate Governance, Chief Executive Officer Compensation, and Firm Performance." *Journal of Financial Economics* 51(3): 371-406.

Costa Rica, Ministry of Economy, Industry and Commerce. 2015. "Ley de garantias mobiliarias es una realidad para MIPYMES." Press Release, May 11.

Coviello, Decio, and Mario Mariniello. 2014. "Publicity Requirements in Public Procurement: Evidence from a Regression Discontinuity Design." *Journal of Public Economics* 109: 76-100.

Cremers, Martijn, and Allen Ferrell. 2014. "Thirty Years of Shareholder Rights and Firm Value." *The Journal of Finance* 69: 1167-96.

Crotty, John. 2010. "Practical Measures to Promote Integrity in Customs Administrations." Paper presented at the Eight International Anti-Corruption Conference, Prague, Czech Republic, September 7-11.

Cuberes, David, and Marc Teignier. 2014. "Aggregate Costs of Gender Gaps in the Labor Market: A Quantitative Estimate." UB Economics Working Papers E14/308.

Dabla-Norris, Era, Giang Ho, and Anette Kyobe. 2016. "Structural Reforms and Productivity Growth in Emerging Market and Developing Economies." IMF Working Paper WP/16/15, International Monetary Fund, Washington, DC.

Dabla-Norris, Era, Kalpana Kochhar, Nujin Suphaphiphat, Frantisek Ricka and Evridiki Tsounta. 2015. "Causes and Consequences of Income Inequality: A Global Perspective." IMF Staff Discussion Notes 15/33, International Monetary Fund, Washington, DC.

Dam, Kenneth. 2006. "The Judiciary and Economic Development." University of Chicago Law & Economics, Olin Working Paper 287. Available at Social Science Research Network (SSRN). http://ssrn.com/abstract=892030.

Daeniker, Daniel, Claude Lambert, David Oser and Andreas Muller. 2014. "Say on Pay in Switzerland." Homburger, July 7. Available at http://www.homburger.ch/.

Dahya, Jay, Orlin Dimitrov and John McConnell. 2008. "Dominant Shareholders, Corporate Boards, and Corporate Value: A Cross-Country Analysis." *Journal of Financial Economics* 87 (1): 73-100.

Dakolias, Maria. 1999. "Court Performance around the World: A Comparative Perspective." World Bank Technical Paper 430, World Bank, Washington, DC.

De Mel, Suresh, David McKenzie and Christopher Woodruff. 2013. "The Demand for, and Consequences of, Formalization Among Informal Firms in Sri Lanka." *American Economic Journal: Applied Economics* 5 (2): 122-50.

De Soto, Hernando. 1989. *The Other Path*. New York, New York: Harper & Row Publishers, Inc.

De Wulf, Luc, and José Sokol. 2004. "Customs Modernization Initiatives: Case Studies." Washington, DC: World Bank and Oxford University Press.

Deininger, Klaus. 2003. "Land Policies for Growth and Poverty Reduction." World Bank Policy Research Report. New York: Oxford University Press.

Deininger, Klaus, Aparajita Goyal and Hari Nagarajan. 2010. "Inheritance Law Reform and Women's Access to Capital: Evidence from India's Hindu Succession Act." Policy Research Working Paper 5338, World Bank, Washington, DC.

Deininger, Klaus W., Songqing Jin, Shouying Liu and Fang Xia. 2015. "Impact of Property Rights Reform to Support China's Rural-Urban Integration: Household-Level Evidence from the Chengdu National Experiment." Policy Research Working Paper 7388, World Bank, Washington, DC.

Demirgüç-Kunt, Asli, Leora Klapper, Dorothe Singer and Peter Van Oudheusden. 2015. "The Global Findex Database 2014: Measuring Financial Inclusion Around the World." World Bank Policy Research Working Paper 7255. World Bank, Washington, DC.

Denis, David, and Jan Serrano. 1996. "Active Investors and Management Turnover Following Unsuccessful Control Contests." *Journal of Financial Economics* 40 (2): 239.

Dharmapala, Dhammika, and Vikramaditya Khanna. 2013. "Corporate Governance, Enforcement, and Firm Value." *Journal of Law, Economics and Organization* 29 (5): 1056-84.

Dignam, Alan. 2013. "The Future of Shareholder Democracy in the Shadow of the Financial Crisis." *Seattle University Law Review* 36: 639-94.

Divanbeigi, Raian, and Rita Ramalho. 2015. "Business Regulations and Growth." Policy Research Working Paper 7299, World Bank, Washington, DC.

Djankov, Simeon, Caralee McLiesh and Andrei Shleifer. 2007. "Private Credit in 129 Countries." *Journal of Financial Economics* 84 (2): 299-329.

Djankov, Simeon, Caroline Freund and Cong S. Pham. 2010. "Trading on Time." *Review of Economics and Statistics* 92 (1): 166-73.

Djankov, Simeon, Oliver Hart, Caralee McLiesh and Andrei Shleifer. 2008. "Debt Enforcement Around the World." *Journal of Political Economy* 116 (6): 1105-49.

Djankov, Simeon, Rafael La Porta, Florencio López-de-Silanes and Andrei Shleifer. 2002. "The Regulation of Entry." *Quarterly Journal of Economics* 117 (1): 1-37.

Djankov, Simeon, Rafael La Porta, Florencio López-de-Silanes and Andrei Shleifer. 2003. "Courts." *Quarterly Journal of Economics* 118 (2): 453-517.

Djankov, Simeon, Rafael La Porta, Florencio López-de-Silanes and Andrei Shleifer. 2008. "The Law and Economics of Self-Dealing." *Journal of Financial Economics* 88 (3): 430-65.

Djankov, Simeon, and Rita Ramalho. 2009. "Employment Laws in Developing Countries." *Journal of Comparative Economics* 37 (2009) 3-13.

Djankov, Simeon, Tim Ganser, Caralee McLiesh, Rita Ramalho and Andrei Shleifer. 2010. "The Effect of Corporate Taxes on Investment and Entrepreneurship." *American Economic Journal: Macroeconomics* 2 (3): 31-64.

Djankov, Simeon. 2016. "The *Doing Business* Project: How It Started: Correspondence." *Journal of Economic Perspectives* 30 (1): 247-48.

Doblas-Madrid, Antonio, and Raoul Minetti. 2013. "Sharing Information in the Credit Market: Contract-Level evidence from U.S. firms." *Journal of Financial Economics* 109 (1): 198.

Dolado, Juan, Salvador Ortigueira and Rodolfo Stucchi. 2012. "Does Dual Employment Protection Affect TFP? Evidence from Spanish Manufacturing Firms." CEPR Discussion Paper 8763. Centre for Economic Policy Research, London.

Dollar, David, and Roberta Gatti. 1999. "Gender Inequality, Income and Growth: Are Good Times Good for Women?" World Bank Policy Research Report on Gender and Development Working Paper Series No 1, World Bank, Washington, DC.

Dreher, A., and M. Gassebner. 2013. "Greasing the Wheels? The Impact of Regulations and Corruption on Firm Entry." *Public Choice* 155(3-4): 413-32.

Dreher, Axel, and Thomas Herzfeld. 2005. "The Economic Costs of Corruption: A Survey and New Evidence." Available at Social Science Research Network (SSRN). http://ssrn.com/abstract=734184.

Duflo, Esther. 2012. "Women Empowerment and Economic Development." *Journal of Economic Literature* 50 (4) 1051-79.

Dunn, Elizabeth, and J. Gordon Arbuckle. 2001. "Microcredit and Microenterprise Performance: Impact Evidence from Peru." *Small Enterprise Development* 12 (4): 22-33.

Dutt, Pushan, and Daniel Traca. 2010. "Corruption and Bilateral Trade Flows: Extortion or Evasion?" *The Review of Economics and Statistics* 92 (4): 843-60.

Duval, Yann. 2006. "Cost and Benefits of Implementing Trade Facilitation Measures under Negotiations at the WTO: An Exploratory Survey." Working Paper 3, Asia-Pacific Research and Training Network on Trade, January.

Dyck, Alexander, and Luigi Zingales. 2004. "Private Benefits of Control: An International Comparison." *Journal of Finance* 59 (2): 537-600.

ECB (European Central Bank). 2015. "Survey on the Access to Finance of Enterprises in the Euro Area: October 2014 to March 2015." Frankfurt.: European Central Bank.

Eisenberg, Melvin. 1993. "An Overview of the Principles of Corporate Governance." *Business Lawyer* 48 (1993): 1271.

Eisfeldt, Andrea L., and Adriano A. Rampini. 2009. "Leasing, Ability to Repossess, and Debt Capacity." *Review of Financial Studies* 22 (4): 1621-57.

Elborgh-Woytek, Katrin, Monique Newiak, Kalpana Kochhar, Stefania Fabrizio, Kangni Kpodar, Philippe Wingender, Benedict J. Clements and Gerd Schwartz. 2013. "Women, Work, and the Economy: Macroeconomic Gains from Gender Equity." IMF Staff Discussion Notes 13/10, International Monetary Fund, Washington, DC.

Elms, Deborah, and Patric Low. 2013. *Global Value Chains in a Changing World*. Geneva, Switzerland: World Trade Organization.

Engman, Michael. 2005. "The Economic Impact of Trade Facilitation." OECD Trade Policy Working Paper 21. Paris, France: OECD.

Esposito, Gianluca, Sergi Lanau and Sebastiaan Pompe. 2014. "Judicial System Reform in Italy: A Key to Growth." IMF Working Paper 14/32, International Monetary Fund, Washington, DC.

Esteve-Volart, Berta. 2000. "Sex Discrimination and Growth." IMF Working Paper 00/84, International Monetary Fund, Washington, DC. Available at Social Science Research Network (SSRN). http://ssrn.com/abstract=1127011.

———. 2004. "Gender Discrimination and Growth. Theory and Evidence from India." LSE STICERD Research Paper No. DEDPS42. York University, Department of Economics. Available at Social Science Research Network (SSRN). http://ssrn.com/abstract=1127011.

European Commission, DG Enterprise and Industry. 2014. "Evaluation of SMEs' Access to Public Procurement Markets in the EU: Final Report." European Commission, Brussels. Available at http://www.vergabebrief.de/wp-content/uploads/2014/07/EU_sme_public_procurement_annex.pdf.

Fernandes, Ana Margarida, Russell Henry Hillberry, and Alejandra Mendoza Alcantara. 2015. "Trade Effects of Customs Reform: Evidence from Albania." Policy Research Working Paper 7210, World Bank, Washington, DC.

Fjeldstad, Odd-Helge. 2009. "The Pursuit of Integrity in Customs: Experiences from Sub-Saharan Africa." Working Paper WP 2009: 8, Chr. Michelsen Institute, Bergen, Norway.

Freund, Caroline, and Bineswaree Bolaky. 2008. "Trade, Regulations, and Income." *Journal of Development Economics* 87: 309-21.

Freund, Caroline, and Nadia Rocha. 2011. "What Constrains Africa's Exports?" *The World Bank Economic Review* 25 (3): 361-86.

Freund, Caroline, Mary Hallward-Driemeier and Bob Rijkers. 2014. "Deal and Delays: Firm-level Evidence on Corruption and Policy Implementation Times." Policy Research Working Paper 6949, World Bank, Washington, DC.

Fritsch, Michael, and Florian Noseleit. 2013. "Investigating the Anatomy of the Employment Effect of New Business Formation." *Cambridge Journal of Economics* 37(2): 349-77.

Galiani, Sebastian, and Ernesto Schargrodsky. 2009. "Property Rights for the Poor: Effects of Land Titling." Working Paper 7 (revised), Ronald Coase Institute, St. Louis, MO.

Geginat, Carolin, and Rita Ramalho. 2015. "Electricity Connections and Firm Performance in 183 Countries." Policy Research Working Paper 7460, World Bank, Washington, DC.

Giné, Xavier, and Inessa Love. 2010. "Do Reorganization Costs Matter for Efficiency? Evidence from a Bankruptcy Reform in Colombia." *Journal of Law and Economics* 53 (4): 833-64.

Gompers, Paul, Joy Ishii and Andrew Metrick. 2003. "Corporate Governance and Equity Prices." *The Quarterly Journal of Economics* 118 (1): 107-55.

Gonzales, Christian, Sonali Jain-Chandra, Kalpana Kochhar, Monique Newiak. 2015. "Fair Play: More Equal Laws Boost Female Labor Force Participation." IMF Staff Discussion Notes 15/2, International Monetary Fund, Washington, DC.

Gonzales, Christian, Sonali Jain-Chandra, Kalpana Kochhar, Monique Newiak, and Tlek Zeinullayev. 2015. "Catalyst for Change; Empowering Women and Tackling Income Inequality." IMF Staff Discussion Notes 15/20, International Monetary Fund, Washington, DC.

Gordon, Daniel. 2006. "Constructing a Bid Protest Process: Choices Every Procurement Challenge System Must Make." *Public Contract Law Journal* 35(3). 427-55.

Gordon, Richard. 1996. "Chapter 4: Law of Tax Administration and Procedure." In *Tax Law Design and Drafting*, edited by Victor Thuronyi. Washington, DC: International Monetary Fund.

Grainger, Andrew. 2008. "Customs and Trade Facilitation: From Concepts to Implementation." *World Customs Journal* 2 (1): 17-30.

Grosh, Margaret, Carlo del Ninno, Emil Tesliuc and Azedine Ouerghi. 2008. *For Protection and Promotion: The Design and Implementation of Effective Safety Nets.* Washington, DC: World Bank.

Grossman, Sanford and Oliver Hart. 1982. "Corporate Financial Structure and Managerial Incentive." In *The Economics of Information and Uncertainty*, 107-140. Chicago: University of Chicago Press.

Guatemala, Ministry of Energy and Mines. 2013. "Energy Policy 2013-2027: Energy for Development." Available at http://www.mem.gob.gt/wp-content/uploads/2015/07/Energy-Policy-2013-2027.pdf.

Guatemala, Ministry of Energy and Mines. 2016. "Statistics on Electric Subsector." Available at http://www.mem.gob.gt/wp-content/uploads/2015/06/Subsector-El%C3%A9ctrico-en-Guatemala.pdf.

Guatemala, National Electric Energy Commission. 2015. "Metodología para la Elaboración del Estudio del Valor Agregado—EVAD." June. Available at http://www.cnee.gob.gt/xhtml/estadisti/tarifas/VAD/MetodologiaEVAD.pdf.

Guo, Lixiong, and Ronald W. Masulis. 2013. "Board Structure and Monitoring: New Evidence from CEO Turnovers." Finance Working Paper 351/2013, European Corporate Governance Institute, Brussels.

Gupta, Sanjeev, Hamid Davoodi and Rosa Alonso-Terme. 2002. "Does Corruption Affect Income Inequality and Poverty?" *Economics of Governance* (3): 23-45.

Gupta, M., and V. Nagadevara. 2007. "Audit Selection Strategy for Improving Tax Compliance-Application of Data Mining Techniques." In *Foundations of E-government*, edited by A. Agarwal and V. Venkata Ramana. Hyderabad, India: Computer Society of India.

Gutierrez Ossio, José E. 2001. "Customs Reform and Modernisation Program." Statement draft contributed to the WTO Workshop on Technical Assistance and Capacity Building in Trade Facilitation. Geneva, Switzerland, May 10-11.

Haidar, Jamal Ibrahim. 2012. "The Impact of Business Regulatory Reforms on Economic Growth." *Journal of the Japanese and International Economies* 26(3): 285-307.

Haider, Jamal Ibrahim and Takeo Hoshi. 2015. "Implementing Structural Reforms in Abenomics: How to Reduce the Cost of Doing Business in Japan." NBER Working Paper 21507. National Bureau of Economic Research, Cambridge, MA.

Hall, Robert, and Charles Jones. 1999. "Why Do Some Countries Produce So Much More Output Per Worker Than Others?" *The Quarterly Journal of Economics* 114 (1): 83-116.

Hallward-Driemeier, Mary, and Ousman Gajigo. 2010. "Strengthening Economic Rights and Women's Occupational Choice: The Impact of Reforming Ethiopia's Family Law." Development Economics, World Bank, Washington, DC.

Hallward-Driemeier, Mary, and Tazeen Hasan. 2012. *Empowering Women: Legal Rights and Economic Opportunities in Africa.* World Bank, Washington, DC.

Hallward-Driemeier, Mary, and Lant Pritchett. 2015. "How Business Is Done in the Developing World: Deals versus Rules." *Journal of Economic Perspectives* 29 (3): 121-40.

Harrison, Graham and Russell Krelove. 2005. "VAT Refunds: A Review of Country Experience," IMF Working Paper 05/218, International Monetary Fund, Washington, DC.

Hasan, Rana, and Karl Jandoc. 2012. "Labor Regulations and the Firm Size Distribution in Indian Manufacturing." Working Paper 1118, School of International and Public Affairs, Columbia University, New York.

Hillberry, Russell, and Xiaohui Zhang. 2015. "Policy and Performance in Customs. Evaluating the Trade Facilitation Agreement." World Bank Policy Research Working Paper 7211. World Bank, Washington, DC.

Holderness, Clifford. 2003. "A Survey of Blockholders and Corporate Control." *Economic Policy Review* 9 (1): 51-63.

Holzmann, Robert, and Milan Vodopivec, eds. 2012. *Reforming Severance Pay.* Washington, DC: World Bank.

Houston, Joel F., Ping Lin, Chen Lin and Yue Ma. 2010. "Creditor Rights, Information Sharing, and Bank Risk Taking." *Journal of Financial Economics* 96 (3): 485-512.

IDB (Inter-American Development Bank). 2013. "Energy Dossier, Guatemala." Washington, DC: IDB.

ILO (International Labor Organization). 2014. "World Social Protection Report 2014-15: Building Economic Recovery, Inclusive Development and Social Justice." Geneva: ILO.

———. 2016. "Women at Work: Trends 2016." Geneva: ILO.

IMF (International Monetary Fund). 2015a. "Current Challenges in Revenue Mobilization: Improving Tax Compliance." IMF Staff Report. IMF: Washington DC.

———. 2015b. "Spain: Selected Issues." IMF Country Report No 15/233. IMF: Washington DC.

Indonesia, Ministry of Energy and Mineral Resources. 2015. "Handbook of Energy and Economic Statistics of Indonesia." Available at http://prokum.esdm.go.id/Publikasi/Handbook%20of%20Energy%20&%20Economic%20Statistics%20of%20Indonesia%20/Buku%20Handbook%202015.pdf.

Islam, Roumeen. 2003. "Do More Transparent Governments Govern Better?" Policy Research Working Paper 3077, World Bank, Washington, DC.

Iqbal, Sarah, Asif Islam, Rita Ramalho, Alena Sakhonchik. 2016. "Unequal before the Law: Measuring Legal Gender Disparities across the World." Policy Research Working Paper, World Bank, Washington, DC.

Jalilian, Hossein, Colin Kirkpatrick and David Parker. 2006. "The Impact of Regulation on Economic Growth in Developing Countries: A Cross-Country Analysis." *World Development* 35 (1): 87-103.

Joy, Lois, Nancy Carter, Harvey Wagner, and Sriram Narayanan. 2007. "The Bottom Line: Corporate Performance and Women's Representation on Boards." Catalyst, Inc. Available at http://www.catalyst.org/knowledge/bottom-line-corporate-performance-and-womens-representation-boards.

Kahn, Lawrence. 2010. "Labor Market Policy: A Comparative View on the Costs and Benefits of Labor Market Flexibility." IZA Discussion Paper 5100. Institute for the Study of Labor (IZA), Germany.

Kallberg, Jarl G., and Gregory F. Udell. 2003. "The Value of Private Sector Business Credit Information Sharing: The U.S. Case." *Journal of Banking and Finance* 27 (3): 449-69.

Kaplan, David. 2008. "Job Creation and Labor Reform in Latin America." Policy Research Working Paper 4708, World Bank, Washington, DC.

Kaplan, David, Eduardo Piedra and Enrique Seira. 2011. "Entry Regulation and Business Start-ups: Evidence from Mexico." *Journal of Development Economics* 95: 1501-15.

Kashta, Reida. 2014. "Corruption and Innovation in the Albanian Public Procurement System." *Academicus International Scientific Journal* 10: 212-25.

Katelouzou, Dionysia and Mathias Siems. 2015. "Disappearing Paradigms in Shareholder Protection: Leximetric Evidence for 30 Countries, 1990-2013." *Journal of Corporate Law Studies* 15: 127-60.

Kaufmann, Daniel, and Shang-Jin Wei. 2000. "Does 'Grease Money' Speed Up the Wheels of Commerce?" IMF Working Paper 00/64, International Monetary Fund, Washington, DC.

Kawaguchi, Daiji, and Tetsushi Murao. 2014. "Labor-Market Institutions and Long-Term Effects of Youth Unemployment." *Journal of Money Credit and Banking* 46 (S2): 95-116.

Keen, Michael, and Stephen Smith. 2007. "VAT Fraud and Evasion: What Do We Know, and What Can Be Done?" IMF Working Paper 07/31, International Monetary Fund, Washington, DC.

Kessides, Ioannis N. 2012. "Chaos in Power: Pakistan's Electricity Crisis." *Energy Policy* 55: 271-85.

Khwaja, Munawer Sultan, Rajul Awasthi and Jan Loeprick. 2011. *Risk-Based Tax Audits: Approaches and Country Experiences.* Washington DC: World Bank.

Kilroy, Austin Francis Louis, Megha Mukim and Stefano Negri. "Competitive Cities for Jobs and Growth: What, Who and How." Working Paper 101546, World Bank, Washington, DC.

Klapper, Leora. 2011. "Saving Viable Businesses." Public Policy Journal Note 328, World Bank Group, Washington, DC.

Klapper, Leora, and Inessa Love. 2004. "Corporate Governance, Investor Protection, and Performance in Emerging Markets." *Journal of Corporate Finance* 10 (5): 703-28.

Klapper, Leora, Luc Laeven and Raghuram Rajan. 2006. "Entry Regulation as a Barrier to Entrepreneurship." *Journal of Financial Economics* 82 (3): 591-629.

Klapper, Leora, and Inessa Love. 2011. "The Impact of Business Environment Reforms on New Firm Registration." World Bank Policy Research Working Paper 5493, World Bank, Washington, DC.

Klasen, Stephan. 1999. "Does Gender Inequality Reduce Growth and Development? Evidence from Cross-Country Regressions." Working Paper 7, Policy Research Report on Gender and Development, World Bank, Washington, DC.

Klerman, Daniel. 2006. "Legal Infrastructure, Judicial Independence, and Economic Development." Law and Economics Working Paper Series, University of Southern California Law School, Los Angeles.

Kraemer-Eis, Helmut, and Frank Lang. 2012. "The Importance of Leasing for SME Finance." Research and Market Analysis Working Paper 2012/15, European Investment Fund, Luxembourg.

Kraay, Aart. 2015. "Weak Instruments in Growth Regressions: Implications for Recent Cross-Country Evidence on Inequality and Growth." Policy Research Working Paper 7494. World Bank, Washington, DC.

Kuddo, Arvo, David Robalino and Michael Weber. 2015. *Balancing Regulations to Promote Jobs.* Washington, DC: World Bank.

Kugelman, Michael. 2013. "Pakistan's Energy Crisis: From Conundrum to Crisis." The National Bureau of Asian Research, NBR Commentary, April 13. Available at http://www.nbr.org/downloads/pdfs/eta/Kugelman_ commentary_03132013.pdf.

Kugler, Adriana, Juan F. Jimeno and Virginia Hernanz. 2005. "Employment Consequences of Restrictive Permanent Contracts: Evidence from Spanish Labor Market Reforms." University of Houston.

Kutan, Ali M. 2015. "Finance, Development, and Corporate Governance." *Emerging Economies, Emerging Markets Finance and Trade* 51 (S1).

Lan, Luh Luh, and Umakanth Varottil. 2015. "Shareholder Empowerment in Controlled Companies: The Case of Singapore." In *The Research Handbook of Shareholder Power*, edited by Randall Thomas and Jennifer Hill. Cheltenham: Edward Elgar. Available at Social Science Research Network (SSRN). http://ssrn.com/abstract=2695702.

Lang, Mark, Karl Lins and Mark Maffett. 2012. "Transparency, Liquidity, and Valuation: International Evidence on When Transparency Matters Most." *Journal of Accounting Research* 50 (3): 729-74.

La Porta, Rafael, and Andrei Shleifer. 2008. "The Unofficial Economy and Economic Development." Tuck School of Business Working Paper 2009-57, Dartmouth College, Hanover, NH. Available at Social Science Research Network (SSRN). http://ssrn.com/abstract=1304760.

La Porta, Rafael, Florencio Lopez-de-Silanes, Andrei Shleifer and Robert Vishny. 1996. "Law and Finance." Harvard Institute of Economic Research Working Paper 1768, Harvard University Institute of Economic Research, Cambridge, MA.

_______. 2000. "Investor Protection and Corporate Governance." *Journal of Financial Economics* 58, 3-27.

Lascelles, David, and Sam Mendelson. 2009. "Microfinance Banana Skins 2009: Confronting Crisis and Change." New York: Center of the Study of Financial Innovation.

Lawless, Martina. 2013. "Do Complicated Tax Systems Prevent Foreign Direct Investment?" *Economica* 80 (317): 1-22.

Lee, Linda-Eling, Ric Marshall, Damion Rallis and Matt Moscardi. 2015. "Women on Boards: Global Trends in Gender Diversity on Corporate Boards." MSCI ESG Research, Inc. November.

Léon de Mariz, Christine, Claude Ménard and Bernard Abeillé. 2014. *Public Procurement Reforms in Africa: Challenges in Institutions and Governance*. Oxford: Oxford University Press.

Lewis, Timothy Michael. 2009. "Quantifying the GDP-Construction Relationship." In *Economics for the Modern Built Environment*, edited by Les Ruddock. New York, New York: Taylor and Francis: 34-59.

Lewis-Faupel, Sean, Yusuf Neggers, Benjamin A. Olken and Rohini Pande. 2014. "Can Electronic Procurement Improve Infrastructure Provision? Evidence from Public Works in India and Indonesia." NBER Working Paper 20344. National Bureau of Economic Research, Cambridge, MA.

Lilienfeld-Toal, Ulf von, Dilip Mookherjee, and SujataVisaria. 2012. "The Distributive Impact of Reforms in Credit enforcement: Evidence from Indian Debt Recovery Tribunals." *Econometrica* 80 (2): 497-558.

Liljeblom, Eva, and Benjamin Maury. 2015. "Shareholder Protection, Ownership, and Dividends: Russian Evidence." *Emerging Markets Finance and Trade.*

Lima, Bruno Faustino, and Antonio Zoratto Sanvicente. 2013. "Quality of Corporate Governance and Cost of Equity in Brazil." *Journal of Applied Corporate Finance* 25 (1): 72-80.

Lindstädt, Hagen, Michael Wolff, and Kerstin Fehre. 2011. *Frauen in Führungspositionen Auswirkungen auf den Unternehmenserfolg.* Bundesministerium für Familie, Senioren, Frauen und Jugend, Berlin, Germany.

Loayza, Norman, Ana Maria Oviedo and Luis Serven. 2005. "The Impact of Regulation on Growth and Informality: Cross-Country Evidence." Policy Research Working Paper 3623. World Bank, Washington, DC.

Lopez-Claros, Augusto. 2015. "Removing Impediments to Sustainable Economic Development: The Case of Corruption." *Journal of International Commerce, Economics and Policy* 6 (1): 1-35.

Love, Inessa, María Soledad Martínez Pería and Sandeep Singh. 2013. "Collateral Registries for Movable Assets: Does Their Introduction Spur Firms' Access to Bank Finance?" Policy Research Working Paper 6477, World Bank, Washington, DC.

Luoto, Jill, Craig McIntosh and Bruce Wydick. 2007. "Credit Information Systems in Less Developed Countries: A Test with Microfinance in Guatemala." *Economic Development and Cultural Change* 55 (2): 313-34.

Lyman, Timothy, Tony Lythgoe, Margaret Miller, Xavier Reille and Shalini Sankaranarayan, 2011. "Credit Reporting at the Base of the Pyramid: Key Issues and Success Factors." CGAP Access to Finance Forum No. 1 (September). Washington, DC: World Bank Group.

Macedo, Leonardo C. L., and Flavio Augusto Trevisan Scorza. 2013. "Guichê Único (Single Window) e as negociações da OMC sobre Facilitação do Comércio." In *Organização Mundial do Comércio – Temas Contemporâneos*. Santos, Brazil: Leopoldianum.

Mahacek, Dubravka, and Zeljko Turkalj. 2015. "Procurement Procedures in the Function of Improving Company Business Conduct." *Business Logistics in Modern Management* 15: 67-78.

Malhotra, D. K., Raymond Poteau and Joseph Fritz. 2013. "Does Corporate Governance Impact Performance? An Analysis of Dow Thirty Stocks." *International Journal of Business & Economics Perspectives* 8 (1): 62-75.

Maniego, Buenaventura. 1999. "The Role of Information Technology in Customs Modernisation." In *Simplification of Customs Procedures—Reducing Transaction Costs for Efficiency, Integrity and Trade Facilitation*, edited by Salvatore Schiavo-Campo, 65-72. Asian Development Bank.

Marimon, Ramon, and Vincenzo Quadrini. 2008. "Competition, Human Capital and Income Inequality with Limited Commitment." *Journal of Economic Theory* 146 (3): 976-1008.

Martin, John, and Stefano Scarpetta. 2011. "Setting It Right: Employment Protection, Labour Reallocation and Productivity." IZA Policy Paper 27. Institute for the Study of Labor (IZA), Germany.

Martincus, Christian Volpe, Jeronimo Carballo and Alejandro Graziano 2015. "Customs." *Journal of International Economics* 96 (2015): 119-37.

Martínez Peria, María Soledad and Sandeep Singh. 2014. "The Impact of Credit Information Sharing Reforms on Firm Financing?" World Bank Policy Research Working Paper 7013. World Bank: Washington, DC.

Martynova, Marina, and Luc Renneboog. 2011. "Evidence on the International Evolution and Convergence of Corporate Governance Regulations." *Journal of Corporate Finance* 17: 1531-57.

Matsa, David A., and Amalia R. Miller, 2013. "A Female Style in Corporate Leadership? Evidence from Quotas." *American Economic Journal: Applied Economics* 5(3): 136-69.

Mauro, Paolo. 1995. "Corruption and Growth." *The Quarterly Journal of Economics* (110)3: 681-712.

McKernan, Signe-Mary. 2002. "The Impact of Microcredit Programs on Self-Employment Profits: Do Noncredit Program Aspects Matter?" *Review of Economics and Statistics* 84 (1): 93-115.

McLaughlin, Patrick, and Laura Stanley. 2016. "Regulation and Income Inequality: The Regressive Effects of Entry Regulation." Mercatus Working Paper, George Mason University, Arlington, VA.

McLean, David, Tianyu Zhang and Mengxin Zhao. 2012. "Why Does the Law Matter? Investor Protection and Its Effects on Investment, Finance, and Growth." *Journal of Finance* 67 (1): 313-50.

McLinden, Gerard. 2005. "Integrity in Customs." In *Customs Modernization Handbook*, edited by Luc De Wulf and José Sokol. Washington, DC: World Bank.

Meon, Pierre-Guillaume, and Khalid Sekkat. 2003. "Does Corruption Grease or Sand the Wheels of Growth?" *Public Choice* 122 (2005): 69-97.

Merk, Olaf, Cesar Ducruet, Patrick Dubarle, Elvira Haezendonck, and Michael Dooms. 2011. "The Competitiveness of Global Port-Cities: The Case of the Seine Axis (Le Havre, Rouen, Paris, Caen)- France." OECD Regional Development Working Papers, 2011/07. Paris, France: OECD Publishing.

Mills, Elizabeth. 2012. "Pakistan's Energy Crisis." Washington, DC: United States Institute of Peace.

Mishra, Asit, Remya Nair and Apurva Vishwanath. 2016. "Two Years of NDA: Reforms, Transparency Aid Ease of Doing Business." *LiveMint*, May 23. Available at http://www.livemint.com/Politics/XIkeuleENLr9gLJGphosJO/Two-years-of-NDA-Reforms-transparency-aid-ease-of-doing-bu.html.

Moïsé, Evdokia, Thomas Orliac and Peter Minor. 2011. "Trade Facilitation Indicators: The Impact on Trade Costs." OECD Trade Policy Working Paper 118. Paris, France: OECD.

Monteiro, Joana, and Juliano J. Assunção. 2012. "Coming Out of the Shadows? Estimating the Impact of Bureaucracy Simplification and Tax Cut on Formality in Brazilian Microenterprises." *Journal of Development Economics* 99: 105-15.

Montenegro, Claudio, and Carmen Pagés. 2003. "Who Benefits from Labor Market Regulations?" Policy Research Working Paper 3143. World Bank, Washington DC.

Mosley, Paul. 2001. "Microfinance and Poverty in Bolivia." *Journal of Development Studies* 37 (4): 101-32.

Motta, Marialisa, Ana Maria Oviedo and Massimiliano Santini. 2010. "An Open Door for Firms: The Impact of Business Entry Reforms." Viewpoint Series Note 323, World Bank, Washington, DC.

Mukwiri, Jonathan, and Mathias Siems. 2014. "The Financial Crisis: A Reason to Improve Shareholder Protection in the EU?" *Journal of Law and Society* 41 (51): 51-72.

Munemo, Jonathan. 2014. "Business Start-Up Regulations and The Complementarity Between Foreign and Domestic Investment" *Review of World Economics* 150 (4): 745-61.

Myrdal, Gunnar. 1968. "Asian Drama: An Enquiry into the Poverty of Nations," vol 2. New York: The Twentieth Century Fund. Reprint in *Political corruption: A handbook*, edited by Arnold J. Heidenheimer, Michael Johnston and Victor T. LeVine. 1989. Oxford, United Kingdom: Transaction Books: 953-61.

Nayak, Gayatri. 2014. "Government Delays Payments, Forces Small Businesses to Take Additional Loans!" The Economic Times, January 3. http://articles.economictimes.indiatimes.com/2014-01-03/news/45836993_1_fiscal-deficit-target-rating-downgrade-delayed-payments

Ndonga, Dennis. 2013. "Managing the Risk of Corruption in Customs Through Single Window Systems." *World Customs Journal* 7(2): 23-38.

Neo, Boon Siong, and Kwong Sin Leong. 1994. "Managing Risks in Information Technology Projects: A Case Study of TradeNet." *Journal of Information Technology Management* 5 (3): 29-45.

Norbäck, Pehr-Johan, Lars Persson, and Robin Douhan. 2014. "Entrepreneurship Policy and Globalization." *Journal of Development Economics* 110: 22-38.

OECD (Organisation for Economic Co-operation and Development).2006a. "Strengthening Tax Audit Capabilities: General Principles and Approaches." OECD, Center for Tax Policy and Administration, Paris, France: OECD.

_______. 2006b. *Methodology for Assessment of National Procurement Systems*. Paris, France: OECD.

_______. 2008. "OECD Employment Outlook 2008." Paris, France: OECD.

_______. 2009. "Overcoming Border Bottlenecks: The Costs and Benefits of Trade Facilitation." OECD Trade Policy Studies. Paris, France: OECD.

_______. 2010. "Chapter 6: Compliance, Enforcement, Appeals." *In Better Regulation in Europe*. Paris, France: OECD.

_______. 2011a. "Competitiveness of Port-Cities: The Case of the Seine Axis (Le Havre, Rouen, Paris, Caen)-France." OECD Regional Development Working Papers 2011/07. Paris, France: OECD.

_______. 2011b. "Competition and Procurement." In *Competition Committee Key Findings*. Paris, France: OECD.

_______. 2012. "Women in Business: Policies to Support Women's Entrepreneurship Development in the MENA Region." Paris, France: OECD.

_______. 2013a. "OECD Employment Outlook 2013." Paris, France: OECD.

_______. 2013b. "Implementing the OECD Principles for Integrity in Public Procurement: Progress since 2008." OECD Public Governance Reviews. Paris, France: OECD.

_______. 2014a. "International VAT/GST Guidelines." Global Forum on VAT. 17-18 April. OECD, Paris. Available at: http://drtp.ca/wp-content/uploads/2015/09/oecd-international-vat-gst-guidelines.pdf.

_______. 2014b. "OECD Employment Outlook 2014." Paris, France: OECD.

_______. 2014c. "The 2012 Labor Market Reform in Spain: A Preliminary Assessment." Paris, France: OECD.

_______. 2015. "Principles of Corporate Governance." Paris, France: OECD.

_______. 2016a. "Corruption in Public Procurement." Paris, France: OECD. Available at http://www.oecd.org/gov/ethics/Corruption-in-Public-Procurement-Brochure.pdf.

_______. 2016b. "The Korean Public Service. Innovating for effectiveness." OECD Public Governance Reviews. Paris, France: OECD.

OECD and the European Commission. 2010. *Better Regulation in Europe: Finland*. Paris, France: OECD.

OHADA (Organization for the Harmonization of Business Law in Africa). 2012. *Uniform Act on Secured Transactions* (adopted on April 17, 1997).

Okpara, John. 2011. "Corporate Governance in a Developing Economy: Barriers, Issues, and Implications for Firms." *Corporate*

Governance: The International Journal of Business in Society 11 (2): 184-99.

Ostry, Jonathan David, and Andrew Berg. 2013. "Inequality and Unsustainable Growth: Two Sides of the Same Coin?" *International Research Journal* 8 (4): 77-99.

Ouedraogo, Alice, Isabel Caruana, Elsa Rodriguez and Susann Tischendorf, Susann. 2012. "It Started in Ghana: Implementing Africa's First Collateral Registry." IFC Smart Lessons Brief. The World Bank, Washington DC.

Ozkan, Filiz, Omer Ozkan and Murat Gunduz. 2012. "Causal Relationship between Construction Investment Policy and Economic Growth in Turkey. *Technological Forecasting and Social Change* 79(2): 362-370.

Pagano, Marco, and Paolo Volpin. 2006. "Shareholder Protection, Stock Market Development, and Politics." *Journal of the European Economic Association* 4: 315-41.

Pakistan, Ministry of Finance. 2014. "Economic Survey 2013-14." Available at http://finance.gov.pk/survey_1314.html/.

Parayno, Guillermo. 2004. "The Philippines." In *Customs Modernization Initiatives: Case Studies*, edited by Luc De Wulf and José Sokol. Washington, DC: World Bank.

Parayno, Guillermo. 2013. "Combatting Corruption in the Philippine Customs Service." In *Corruption and Anti-Corruption*, edited by Peter Larmour and Nick Wolanin. Canberra, Australia: ANU Press.

Parisi, Nicoletta, and Dino Rinoldi. 2004. "Recent Evolutions in the Fight against Corruption in International Trade Law." International Business Law (2004): 345.

Parker, David, and Colin Kirkpatrick. 2012. "Measuring Regulatory Performance—The Economic Impact of Regulatory Policy: A Literature Review of Quantitative Evidence." OECD Expert Paper 3. Paris, France: OECD Publishing.

Portugal-Perez, Alberto, and John S. Wilson. 2011. "Export Performance and Trade Facilitation Reform: Hard and Soft Infrastructure." *World Development* 40 (7): 1295-1307.

Posner, Richard. 1983. *The Economics of Justice*. Cambridge: Harvard University Press.

PwC. 2015. "Power in Indonesia, Investment and Taxation Guide." August, Third Edition. Available at https://www.pwc.com/id/en/energy-utilities-mining/assets/Power%20Guide%202015%20(final-octL).pdf

Reisberg, Arad. 2013. "Shareholder Value after the Financial Crisis: A Dawn of a New Era?" *International Corporate Rescue* 10 (143).

Revenga, A., and S. Shetty. 2012. "Empowering Women is Smart Economics," *Finance and Development* 49 (1): 40-43.

Robalino, David, Milan Vodopivec, and András Bodor. 2009. "Savings for Unemployment in Good or Bad Times: Options for Developing Countries." Social Protection Discussion Paper 417. World Bank, Washington, DC.

Roberts, Matthew. 2014. "FAQ: Switzerland Excessive Remuneration Ordinance." Institutional Shareholder Services. Available at http://www.issgovernance.com/.

Rodrick, Dani. 1998. "Where Did All the Growth Go? External Shocks, Social Conflict, and Growth Collapses." *Journal of Economic Growth* 4: 358-412.

Rose-Ackerman, Susan. 1997. "The Political Economy of Corruption." In *Corruption and the Global Economy*, edited by K.A. Elliot. Washington DC.: Institute for International Economics.

Rupeika-Apoga, Ramona. 2014. "Access to Finance: Baltic Financial Markets." *Procedia Economics and Finance* 9: 181-92.

Russian Federation. 2012. Executive Order on Long-Term State Economic Policy. Office of the President, Moscow. Available at http://en.kremlin.ru/acts/news/15232.

Rwanda, Ministry of Finance and Economic Planning. 2000. Rwanda Vision 2020. Available at http://www.gesci.org/.

Sabbagh, Karim, Roman Friedrich, Bahjat El-Darwiche, Miling Singh, and Alex Koster. 2013. "Digitalization for Economic Growth and Job Creation: Regional and Industry Perspectives." The Global Technology Report: 36.

Sakhonchik, Alena. 2016. "Remnants of the Soviet Past: Restrictions on Women's Employment in the Commonwealth of Independent States." *Voices: Perspectives on Development* (blog), April 28. World Bank, Washington, DC. Available at http://blogs.worldbank.org/voices/remnants-soviet-past-restrictions-womens-employment-commonwealth-independent-states.

Sánchez-Rodríguez, C., A.R. Martínez-Lorente and J.J. García-Clavel. 2003. "Benchmarking in the Purchasing Function and its Impact on Purchasing and Business Performance." *Benchmarking: An International Journal* 10(5): 457-71.

Sá Porto, Paulo C., Cristiano Morini and Otaviano Canuto. 2015. "The Impacts of Trade Facilitation Measures on International Trade Flows." Policy Research Working Paper 7367, World Bank, Washington, DC.

Shleifer, Andrei, and Robert Vishny. 1986. "Large Shareholders and Corporate Control." *Journal of Political Economy* 94: 461-88.

Schneider, Friedrich. 2005. "The Informal Sector in 145 Countries." Department of Economics, University Linz.

Schuler, Sidney Ruth, and Syed M. Hashemi. 1994. "Credit Programs, Women's Empowerment, and Contraceptive Use in Rural Bangladesh." *Studies in Family Planning* 25 (2): 65-76.

Sharma, Siddharth. 2009. "Entry Regulation, Labor Laws and Informality." Working Paper 48927. World Bank, Washington, DC.

Shingal, Anirudh. 2015. "Internationalization of Government Procurement Regulation: The Case of India." European University Institute, Robert Schuman Centre for Advanced Studies Research Paper 86, San Domenico di Fiesole, Italy.

Steele, Fiona, Sajeda Amin and Ruchira T. Naved. 2001. "Savings/Credit Group Formation and Change in Contraception." *Demography* 38 (2): 267-82.

Stein, Peer, Oya Pinar Ardic and Martin Hommes. 2013. *Closing the Credit Gap for Formal and Informal Micro, Small and Medium Enterprises*. Washington, DC: International Finance Corporation.

Stein, Peer, Tony Goland and Robert Schiff. 2010. "Two Trillion and Counting: Assessing the Credit Gap for Micro, Small, and Medium-Size Enterprises in the Developing World."

McKinsey & Company and International Finance Corporation, World Bank, Washington, DC.

Subbarao, Kalanidhi, Carlo del Ninno, Colin Andrews, and Claudia Rodríguez-Alas. 2013. "Public Works as a Safety Net: Design, Evidence, and Implementation." Working Paper 73824. World Bank, Washington, DC.

Swiss Proxy Advisor. 2014. "Year one after the Ordinance against Excessive Compensation, Insights and Challenges, A Survey by SWIPRA." Zurich: Swiss Proxy Advisor.

Sydney Morning Herald. 2015. "Sydney's Patrick Terminal Goes Automated, with Fewer Staff but Dancing Robots." June 18. Available at http://www.smh.com.au/nsw/sydneys-patrick-terminal-goes-automated-with-fewer-staff-but-dancing-robots-20150617-ghqc24.html.

Tabarcea, Andrei. 2014. "Quantifying the Moral Development of Public Procurement Experts." The Yearbook of the *"Gh. Zhane" Institute of Economic and Social Researches* 23 (1): 19-26.

Tajti, Tibor. 2013. "Post-1990 Secured Transactions Law Reforms in Central and Eastern Europe." *Szegedi Közjegyzői Közlöny* 2 (3): 14-21; 2 (4): 18-26.

Tharakan, Pradeep. 2015. "Summary of Indonesia's Energy Sector Assessment." Papers On Indonesia, Asian Development Bank, Jakarta.

Thuronyi, Victor. 2003. "How Can an Excessive Volume of Tax Disputes Be Dealt With?" Legal Department, International Monetary Fund, Washington, DC.

Transparency International. 2014. "Curbing Corruption in Public Procurement." Berlin, Germany. Available at http://www.acec.ca/source/2014/november/pdf/2014_AntiCorruption_PublicProcurement_Guide_EN.pdf

Tsen, Jonathan Koh Tat. 2011. "Ten Years of Single Window Implementation: Lessons Learned for the Future." Global Trade Facilitation Conference on Single Window and Supply Chains in the Next Decade. Geneva, Switzerland, December 12-13.

Turner, Michael A., Alyssa S. Lee, Ann Schnare, Robin Varghese and Patrick D. Walker. 2006. *Give Credit Where Credit Is Due*. Washington, DC: Political and Economics Research Council and The Brookings Institution Urban Markets Initiative.

UN/CEFACT (United Nations Centre for Trade Facilitation and Electronic Business). 2005. *Recommendations and Guidelines on Establishing a Single Window*. New York: United Nations.

UNCITRAL (United Nations Commission on International Trade Law). 1994. *Model Law on the Procurement of Goods, Construction and Services*. New York: United Nations.

———. 2004. *Legislative Guide on Insolvency Law*. New York: United Nations.

———. 2010. *Legislative Guide on Secured Transactions*. New York: United Nations.

———. 2011. *Model Law on Public Procurement*. New York: United Nations.

UNCTAD (United Nations Conference for Trade and Development). "The ASYCUDA Programme." Available at http://www.asycuda.org/PDF%20DOCS%5Cprogramme.pdf.

UNECE (United Nations Economic Commission for Europe). 2005. "Case Studies on Implementing a Single Window." Geneva, Switzerland. Available at http://www.unece.org/fileadmin/DAM/cefact/single_window/draft_160905.pdf.

United Kingdom, Bank of England. 2015. "Report on Enhancing the Use of Commercial Credit Data by Trade Creditors." December. London, England.

USAID (United States Agency for International Development). 2016. "Pakistan Energy Factsheet 2016". Available at https://www.usaid.gov/sites/default/files/Factsheet-Energy-June-2016.pdf

———. 2012. "Asean Single Window-Potential Impact Survey." Washington, DC: United States Agency for International Development.

U.S.-Canada Power System Outage Task Force. 2004. *Final Report on the August 14, 2003 Blackout in the United States and Canada: Causes and Recommendations*. Available online from http://www.ferc.gov/industries/electric/indus-act/reliability/blackout/ch1-3.pdf.

Uyarra, Elvira, Jakob Edler, Javier Garcia-Estevez, Luke Georghioua and Jillian Yeow. 2014. "Barriers to Innovation through Public Procurement: A Supplier Perspective." *Technovation* 34 (10): 631-45.

Van Baalen, Peter, Rob Zuidwijk, and Jo van Nunen. 2008. "Port Inter-Organizational Information Systems: Capabilities to Service Global Supply Chains." *Foundations and Trends in Technology, Information and Operations Management*, 2 (2-3): 81-241.

Van Dijk, H., M.L. van Engen, and D. van Knippenberg. 2012. "Defying Conventional Wisdom: A Meta-Analytical Examination of the Differences between Demographic and Job-related Diversity Relationships with Performance." *Organizational Behavior and Human Decision Processes* (119) 38-53. doi:10.1016/j.obhdp.2012.06.003.

Venkateshwaran, Sai. 2013. *Companies Act 2013 New Rules of the Game*. Mumbai: KPMG.

Visaria, Sujata. 2009. "Legal Reform and Loan Repayment: The Microeconomic Impact of Debt Recovery Tribunals in India." *American Economic Journal: Applied Economics* 1 (3): 59-81.

Vodopivec, Milan. 2013. "Introducing Unemployment Insurance to Developing Countries." *IZA Journal of Labor Policy* 2:1.

Wilson, John, Catherine Mann and Tsunehiro Otsuki. 2003. "Trade Facilitation and Economic Development: A New Approach to Quantifying the Impact." *World Bank Economic Review* 17 (3): 367-89.

World Bank. 2010. *India's Employment Challenge: Creating Jobs, Helping Workers*. Oxford University Press for the World Bank.

———. 2011. "World Development Report 2012: Gender Equality and Development." Washington, DC: World Bank.

———. 2012a. "World Development Report 2013: Jobs." Washington DC: World Bank.

———. 2012b. "Fighting Corruption in Public Services: Chronicling Georgia's Reforms." Washington DC: World Bank.

_______. 2012. *Financial Inclusion Strategies Reference Framework*. Washington, DC: World Bank.

_______. 2013a. *Doing Business 2014*. Washington DC: World Bank.

_______. 2013b. "World Development Report 2014: Risk and Opportunity: Managing Risk for Development" Washington, DC: World Bank.

_______. 2014a. *Readiness for Investment in Sustainable Energy: A Tool for Policy Makers*. Washington DC: World Bank.

_______. 2014b. *Doing Business 2015*. Washington DC: World Bank.

_______. 2015a. *Women, Business and the Law 2016: Getting to Equal*. Washington DC: World Bank.

_______. 2015b. *Doing Business in Poland 2015*. Washington DC: World Bank.

_______. 2015c. *Doing Business 2016*. Washington DC: World Bank.

_______. 2015d. *The State of Social Safety Nets 2015*. Washington, DC: World Bank.

_______. 2016a. *Poverty and Shared Prosperity 2016: Taking on Inequality*. Washington, DC: World Bank.

_______. 2016b. *Doing Business 2016: Historical Reform Count DB05-DB16*. Washington, DC: World Bank.

World Bank Group. 1996. *Leasing in Emerging Markets. Lessons of Experience Series*. Washington DC: International Finance Corporation.

_______. 2009. *Leasing in Development: Guidelines for Emerging Economies*. Washington, DC: International Finance Corporation.

_______. 2011. *Strengthening Access to Finance for Women-Owned SMEs in Developing Countries*. Washington, DC: International Finance Corporation.

_______. 2013. *IFC Jobs Study: Assessing Private Sector Contributions to Job Creation and Poverty Reduction*. Washington, DC: International Finance Corporation.

_______. 2014. *The World Bank Group and Public Procurement–An Independent Evaluation*. Washington, DC: World Bank.

_______. 2015a. *Small beginnings for great opportunities: Lessons learned from 20 years of microfinance projects in IFC*. IFC Smart Lessons Book. Washington, DC: World Bank.

_______. 2015b. *World Development Indicators 2016, Digital Dividends*. Washington, DC: World Bank.

_______. 2016. "IFC Works to Improve Hydropower Sector in Pakistan." Press Release, April 18.

World Customs Organization. 1998. "The Arusha Declaration. Declaration of the Customs Co-operation Council Concerning Good Governance and Integrity in Customs."

_______. 2015. "World Customs Organization Declares 2016 to be the Year of Digital Customs." Press release, November.

World Economic Forum. 2016. *Shaping the Future of Construction–A Landscape in Transformation: An Introduction*. Geneva, Switzerland.

Wrigley, Clive, Rene Wagenaar, and Roger Clarke. 1994. "Electronic Data Interchange in International Trade: Frameworks for the Strategic Analysis of Ocean Port Communities." *Journal of Strategic Information Systems* 3(3): 211-234.

WTO (World Trade Organization). 1994. *Agreement on Government Procurement*. Geneva: WTO.

_______. 1998a. WTO: *A Training Package: What Is Trade Facilitation*. Geneva: WTO.

_______. 1998. "WTO Trade Facilitation Symposium." Report by the Secretariat. March 9-10. Geneva: WTO.

_______. 2013. *Bali Agreement on Trade Facilitation*. Geneva: WTO.

_______. 2013. "Global Value Chains in a Changing World." Geneva: WTO.

Data Notes

The indicators presented and analyzed in *Doing Business* measure business regulation and the protection of property rights—and their effect on businesses, especially small and medium-size domestic firms. First, the indicators document the complexity of regulation, such as the number of procedures to start a business or to register a transfer of commercial property. Second, they gauge the time and cost to achieve a regulatory goal or comply with regulation, such as the time and cost to enforce a contract, go through bankruptcy or trade across borders. Third, they measure the extent of legal protections of property, for example, the protections of minority investors against looting by company directors or the range of assets that can be used as collateral according to secured transactions laws. Fourth, a set of indicators documents the tax burden on businesses. Finally, a set of data covers different aspects of employment regulation. The 11 sets of indicators measured in *Doing Business* were added over time, and the sample of economies and cities expanded (table 12.1).

METHODOLOGY

The *Doing Business* data are collected in a standardized way. To start, the *Doing Business* team, with academic advisers, designs a questionnaire. The questionnaire uses a simple business case to ensure comparability across economies and over time—with assumptions about the legal form of the business, its size, its location and the nature of its operations. Questionnaires are administered to more than 12,500 local experts, including lawyers, business consultants, accountants, freight forwarders, government officials and other professionals routinely administering or advising on legal and regulatory requirements (table 12.2). These experts have several rounds of interaction with the *Doing Business* team, involving conference calls, written correspondence and visits by the team. For *Doing Business 2017* team members visited 34 economies to verify data and recruit respondents. The data from questionnaires are subjected to numerous rounds of verification, leading to revisions or expansions of the information collected.

The *Doing Business* methodology offers several advantages. It is transparent, using factual information about what laws and regulations say and allowing multiple interactions with local respondents to clarify potential misinterpretations of questions. Having representative samples of respondents is not an issue; *Doing Business* is not a statistical survey, and the texts of the relevant laws and regulations are collected and answers checked for accuracy. The methodology is inexpensive and easily replicable, so data can be collected in a large sample of economies. Because standard assumptions are used in the data collection, comparisons and benchmarks are valid across economies. Finally, the data not only highlight the extent of specific regulatory obstacles to business but also identify their source and point to what might be reformed.

TABLE 12.1 Topics and economies covered by each *Doing Business* report

Topic	DB 2004	DB 2005	DB 2006	DB 2007	DB 2008	DB 2009	DB 2010	DB 2011	DB 2012	DB 2013	DB 2014	DB 2015	DB 2016	DB 2017
Getting electricity														
Dealing with construction permits														
Trading across borders														
Paying taxes														
Protecting minority investors														
Registering property														
Getting credit														
Resolving insolvency														
Enforcing contracts														
Labor market regulation														
Starting a business														
Number of economies	**133**	**145**	**155**	**175**	**178**	**181**	**183**	**183**	**183**	**185**	**189**	**189**	**189**	**190**

Note: Data for the economies added to the sample each year are back-calculated to the previous year. The exceptions are Kosovo and Montenegro, which were added to the sample after they became members of the World Bank Group. Eleven cities (though no additional economies) were added to the sample starting in *Doing Business 2015*. The data for all sets of indicators in *Doing Business 2017* are for June 2016.[1]

LIMITS TO WHAT IS MEASURED

The *Doing Business* methodology has five limitations that should be considered when interpreting the data. First, for most economies the collected data refer to businesses in the largest business city (which in some economies differs from the capital) and may not be representative of regulation in other parts of the economy. (The exceptions are 11 economies with a population of more than 100 million as of 2013, where *Doing Business* now also collects data for the second largest business city.)[2] To address this limitation, subnational *Doing Business* indicators were created (box 12.1). Second, the data often focus on a specific business form—generally a limited liability company (or its legal equivalent) of a specified size—and may not be representative of the regulation on other businesses (for example, sole proprietorships). Third, transactions described in a standardized case scenario refer to a specific set of issues and may not represent the full set of issues that a business encounters. Fourth, the measures of time involve an element of judgment by the expert respondents. When sources indicate different estimates, the time indicators reported in *Doing Business* represent the median values of several responses given under the assumptions of the standardized case.

TABLE 12.2 How many experts does *Doing Business* consult?

Indicator set	Respondents	Economies with given number of respondents (%)		
		1–2	3–5	5+
Starting a business	2,120	7	23	70
Dealing with construction permits	1,368	15	38	47
Getting electricity	1,154	18	39	43
Registering property	1,363	18	32	50
Getting credit	1,815	4	25	71
Protecting minority investors	1,305	14	41	45
Paying taxes	1,467	11	34	55
Enforcing contracts	1,600	17	36	47
Trading across borders	1,063	22	45	33
Resolving insolvency	1,196	23	39	38
Labor market regulation	1,293	17	40	43
Total	**15,744**	**15**	**36**	**49**

Finally, the methodology assumes that a business has full information on what is required and does not waste time when completing procedures. In practice, completing a procedure may take longer if the business lacks information or is unable to follow up promptly. Alternatively, the business may choose to disregard some burdensome procedures. For both reasons the time delays reported in *Doing Business 2017* would differ from the recollection of entrepreneurs reported in the World Bank Enterprise Surveys or other firm-level surveys.

Economy characteristics

Gross national income per capita

Doing Business 2017 reports 2015 income per capita as published in the World Bank's *World Development Indicators 2016*. Income is calculated using the Atlas method (in current U.S. dollars). For cost indicators expressed as a percentage of income per capita, 2015 gross national income (GNI) per capita in current U.S. dollars is used as the denominator. GNI data based on the Atlas method were not available for Argentina; Brunei Darussalam; the Comoros; Djibouti; Eritrea; The Gambia; the Islamic Republic of Iran; Lesotho; Malta; the Marshall Islands; Mauritania; the Federated States of Micronesia; Myanmar; Papua New Guinea; Puerto Rico (territory of the United States); San Marino; São Tomé and Príncipe; Somalia; the Syrian Arab Republic; Taiwan, China; Tonga; Vanuatu; República Bolivariana de Venezuela; West Bank and Gaza; the Republic of Yemen. In these cases GDP or GNP per capita data and growth rates from other sources, such as the International Monetary Fund's World Economic Outlook database and the Economist Intelligence Unit, were used.

Region and income group

Doing Business uses the World Bank regional and income group classifications, available at https://datahelpdesk.worldbank.org/knowledgebase/articles/906519. Regional averages presented in figures and tables in the *Doing Business* report include economies from all income groups (low, lower middle, upper middle and high income), though high-income OECD economies are assigned the "regional" classification *OECD high income*.

Population

Doing Business 2017 reports midyear 2015 population statistics as published in the World Bank's *World Development Indicators 2016*.

BOX 12.1 Subnational *Doing Business* indicators

Subnational *Doing Business* studies point to differences in business regulations and their implementation—as well as in the pace of regulatory reform—across cities in the same economy or region. For several economies subnational studies are now periodically updated to measure change over time or expand geographic coverage to additional cities.

This year subnational studies were completed in Kenya, Mexico, and the United Arab Emirates. In addition, ongoing studies are updating the data for locations in Colombia and expanding the geographic coverage to cities in Afghanistan, Kazakhstan as well as three European Union member states—Bulgaria, Hungary and Romania. And for the first time, the Mexico subnational study—now in its sixth round of benchmarking—expanded on the *Doing Business* methodology to examine in greater depth the process of connecting a small business to the water and sewerage networks.

CHANGES IN WHAT IS MEASURED

Doing Business 2017 has three major innovations. First it expands the paying taxes indicator set to also cover postfiling processes. Paying taxes is the final indicator set to be changed as part of the methodology update initiated in *Doing Business 2015*. Second, three indicator sets (starting a business, registering property and enforcing contracts) were expanded to cover a gender dimension, in addition to labor markets regulation which was expanded last year. Starting a business was expanded to also measure the process of starting a business when all shareholders are women. Registering property now also measures equality in ownership rights to property. And enforcing contracts was expanded to measure equality in evidentiary weight for men and women.

Despite the changes in methodology introduced this year, the data under the old and new methodologies are highly correlated. Comparing the ease of doing business rankings as calculated using the *Doing Business 2016* data and methodology with the rankings as calculated using the *Doing Business 2016* data but the *Doing Business 2017* methodology shows a correlation very close to 1 (table 12.3). In previous years the correlations between same-year data under the methodology for that year and the methodology for the subsequent year were even stronger.

DATA CHALLENGES AND REVISIONS

Most laws and regulations underlying the *Doing Business* data are available on the *Doing Business* website at http://www.doingbusiness.org. All the sample questionnaires and the details underlying the indicators are also published on the website. Questions on the methodology and challenges to data can be submitted through email at rru@worldbank.org.

Doing Business publishes 24,120 indicators (120 indicators per economy) each year. To create these indicators, the team measures more than 115,000 data points, each of which is made available

TABLE 12.3 Correlation between rankings under old and new methodologies after each set of changes in methodology

	DB2017	DB2016	DB2015	DB2014	DB2013	DB2012	DB2011	DB2010
DB2016	0.999							
DB2015		0.974						
DB2014			0.980					
DB2013				0.996				
DB2012					0.995			
DB2011						0.987		
DB2010							0.989	
DB2009								0.998

Source: Doing Business database.
Note: The correlation in each case is based on data for the same year but methodologies for consecutive years (for the same year as for the data and for the subsequent year). 0.999 refers to the correlation coefficient between the methodology of *Doing Business* 2016 and the methodology of *Doing Business* 2017.

on the *Doing Business* website. Historical data for each indicator and economy are available on the website, beginning with the first year the indicator or economy was included in the report. To provide a comparable time series for research, the data set is back-calculated to adjust for changes in methodology and any revisions in data due to corrections. The website also makes available all original data sets used for background papers. The correction rate between *Doing Business 2016* and *Doing Business 2017* is 7.1%.[3]

Governments submit queries on the data and provide new information to *Doing Business*. During the *Doing Business 2017* production cycle the team received 110 such queries from governments. In addition, the team held multiple video conferences with government representatives in 46 economies and in-person meetings with government representatives in 34 economies.

STARTING A BUSINESS

Doing Business records all procedures officially required, or commonly done in practice, for an entrepreneur to start up and formally operate an industrial or commercial business, as well as the time and cost to complete these procedures and the paid-in minimum capital requirement (figure 12.1). These procedures include the processes entrepreneurs undergo when obtaining all necessary approvals, licenses, permits and completing any required notifications, verifications or inscriptions for the company and employees with relevant authorities. The ranking of economies on the ease of starting a business is determined by sorting their distance to frontier scores for starting a business. These scores are the simple average of the distance to frontier scores for each of the component indicators (figure 12.2). The distance to frontier score shows the distance of an economy to the "frontier," which is derived from the most efficient practice or highest score achieved on each indicator.

Two types of local liability companies are considered under the starting a business methodology. They are identical in all aspects, except that one company is owned by five married women and other by five married men. The distance to frontier score for each indicator is the average of the scores obtained for each of the component indicators for both of these standardized companies.

After a study of laws, regulations and publicly available information on business entry, a detailed list of procedures is developed, along with the time and cost to comply with each procedure under normal circumstances and the paid-in minimum capital requirement. Subsequently, local incorporation lawyers, notaries and government officials complete and verify the data.

Information is also collected on the sequence in which procedures are to be completed and whether procedures may be carried out simultaneously. It is assumed that any required information is readily available and that the entrepreneur will pay no bribes. If answers by local experts differ, inquiries continue until the data are reconciled.

To make the data comparable across economies, several assumptions about the businesses and the procedures are used.

FIGURE 12.1 What are the time, cost, paid-in minimum capital and number of procedures to get a local limited liability company up and running?

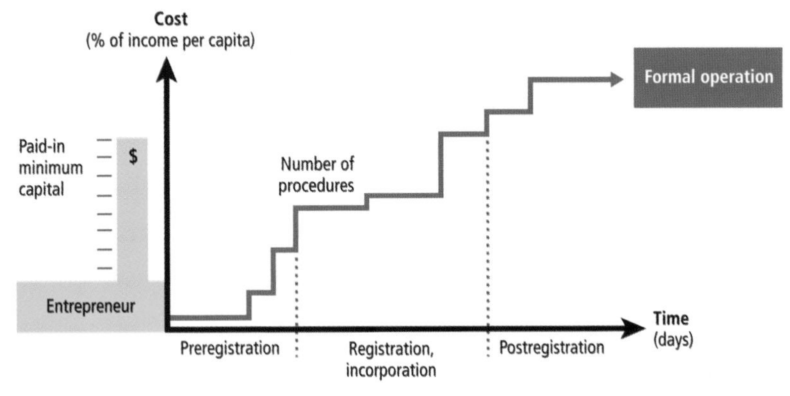

FIGURE 12.2 Starting a business: getting a local limited liability company up and running

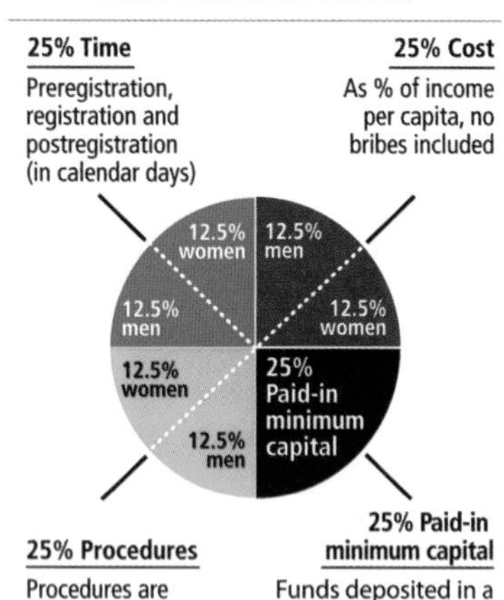

Assumptions about the business

The business:

- Is a limited liability company (or its legal equivalent). If there is more than one type of limited liability company in the economy, the limited liability form most common among domestic firms is chosen. Information on the most common form is obtained from incorporation lawyers or the statistical office.
- Operates in the economy's largest business city. For 11 economies the data are also collected for the second largest business city (table 12A.1 at the end of the data notes).
- Is 100% domestically owned and has five owners, none of whom is a legal entity.
- Has start-up capital of 10 times income per capita.
- Performs general industrial or commercial activities, such as the production or sale to the public of products or services. The business does not perform foreign trade activities and does not handle products subject to a special tax regime, for example, liquor or tobacco. It is not using heavily polluting production processes.
- Leases the commercial plant or offices and is not a proprietor of real estate.
- The amount of the annual lease for the office space is equivalent to 1 times income per capita.
- The size of the entire office space is approximately 929 square meters (10,000 square feet).
- Does not qualify for investment incentives or any special benefits.
- Has at least 10 and up to 50 employees one month after the commencement of operations, all of them domestic nationals.
- Has a turnover of at least 100 times income per capita.
- Has a company deed 10 pages long.

The owners:

- Have reached the legal age of majority and are capable of making decisions as an adult. If there is no legal age of majority, they are assumed to be 30 years old.
- Are sane, competent, in good health and have no criminal record.
- Are married, the marriage is monogamous and registered with the authorities.
- Where the answer differs according to the legal system applicable to the woman or man in question (as may be the case in economies where there is legal plurality), the answer used will be the one that applies to the majority of the population.

Procedures

A procedure is defined as any interaction of the company founders with external parties (for example, government agencies, lawyers, auditors or notaries) or spouses (if legally required). Interactions between company founders or company officers and employees are not counted as procedures. Procedures that must be completed in the same building but in different offices or at different counters are counted as separate procedures. If founders have to visit the same office several times for different sequential procedures, each is counted separately. The founders are assumed to complete all procedures themselves, without middlemen, facilitators, accountants or lawyers, unless the use of such a third party is mandated by law or solicited by the majority of entrepreneurs. If the services of professionals are required, procedures conducted by such professionals on behalf of the company are counted as separate procedures. Each electronic procedure is counted as a separate procedure. Approval from spouses to own a business or leave the home are considered procedures if required by law or if by failing to do he or she will suffer consequences under the law, such as the loss of right to financial maintenance. Documents or permission required by only one gender for company registration and operation, opening a bank account or obtaining a national identification card are considered additional procedures. Only procedures that are required for one spouse but not the other are counted.

Both pre- and post-incorporation procedures that are officially required or commonly done in practice for an entrepreneur to formally operate a business are recorded (table 12.4). Any interaction with an external party within three months of registration will be considered a procedure, except value added tax or goods and services tax registration which will be counted whenever the assumed turnover exceeds the determined threshold.

Procedures required for official correspondence or transactions with public agencies are also included. For example, if a company seal or stamp is required on official documents, such as tax declarations, obtaining the seal or stamp is counted. Similarly, if a company must open a bank account in order to complete any subsequent procedure—such as registering for value added tax or showing proof of minimum capital deposit—this transaction is included as a procedure. Shortcuts are counted only if they fulfill four criteria: they are legal, they are available to the general public, they are used by the majority of companies, and avoiding them causes delays.

Only procedures required of all businesses are covered. Industry-specific procedures are excluded. For example, procedures to comply with environmental regulations are included only when they apply to all businesses conducting general commercial or industrial activities. Procedures that the company undergoes to connect to electricity, water, gas and waste disposal services are not included in the starting a business indicators.

Time

Time is recorded in calendar days. The measure captures the median duration that incorporation lawyers or notaries indicate is necessary in practice to complete a procedure with minimum follow-up with government agencies and no unofficial payments. It is assumed that the minimum time required for each procedure is one day, except for procedures that can be fully completed online, for which the time required is recorded as half a day. Although procedures may take place simultaneously, they cannot start on the same day (that is, simultaneous procedures start on consecutive days), again with the exception of procedures that can be fully completed online. A registration process is considered completed once the company has received the final incorporation document or can officially commence business operations. If a procedure can be accelerated legally for an additional cost, the fastest procedure is chosen if that option is more beneficial to the economy's ranking. When obtaining spouse's approval, it is assumed that permission is granted at no additional cost unless the permission needs to be notarized. It is assumed that the entrepreneur does not waste time and commits to completing each remaining procedure without delay. The time that the entrepreneur spends on gathering information is ignored. It is assumed that the entrepreneur is aware of all entry requirements and their sequence from the beginning but has had no prior contact with any of the officials involved.

TABLE 12.4 What do the starting a business indicators measure?

Procedures to legally start and formally operate a company (number)
Preregistration (for example, name verification or reservation, notarization)
Registration in the economy's largest business city[a]
Postregistration (for example, social security registration, company seal)
Obtaining approval from spouse to start a business, to leave the home to register the company or open a bank account.
Obtaining any gender specific document for company registration and operation, national identification card or opening a bank account.
Time required to complete each procedure (calendar days)
Does not include time spent gathering information
Each procedure starts on a separate day (two procedures cannot start on the same day)—though procedures that can be fully completed online are an exception to this rule
Registration process considered completed once final incorporation document is received or company can officially start operating
No prior contact with officials takes place
Cost required to complete each procedure (% of income per capita)
Official costs only, no bribes
No professional fees unless services required by law or commonly used in practice
Paid-in minimum capital (% of income per capita)
Funds deposited in a bank or with a notary before registration (or up to three months after incorporation)

a. For 11 economies the data are also collected for the second largest business city.

Cost

Cost is recorded as a percentage of the economy's income per capita. It includes all official fees and fees for legal or professional services if such services are required by law or commonly used in practice. Fees for purchasing and legalizing company books are included if these transactions are required by law. Although value added tax registration can be counted as a separate procedure, value added tax is not part of the incorporation cost. The company law, the commercial code and specific regulations and fee schedules are used as sources for calculating costs. In the absence of fee schedules, a government officer's estimate is taken as an official source. In the absence of a government officer's estimate, estimates by incorporation lawyers are used. If several incorporation lawyers provide different estimates, the median reported value is applied. In all cases the cost excludes bribes.

Paid-in minimum capital

The paid-in minimum capital requirement reflects the amount that the entrepreneur needs to deposit in a bank or with a notary before registration or up to three months after incorporation and is recorded as a percentage of the economy's income per capita. The amount is typically specified in the commercial code or the company law. Many economies require minimum capital but allow businesses to pay only a part of it before registration, with the rest to be paid after the first year of operation. In Turkey in June 2015, for example, the minimum capital requirement was 10,000 Turkish liras, of which one-fourth needed to be paid before registration. The paid-in minimum capital recorded for Turkey is therefore 2,500 Turkish liras, or 10.2% of income per capita.

REFORMS

The starting a business indicator set tracks changes related to the ease of incorporating and formally operating a limited liability company every year. Depending on the impact on the data, certain changes are classified as reforms and listed in the summaries of *Doing Business* reforms in the 2015/2016 section of the report in order to acknowledge the implementation of significant changes. Reforms are divided into two types: those that make it easier to do business and those changes that make it more difficult to do business. The starting a business indicator set uses one criterion to recognize a reform.

The aggregate gap on the overall distance to frontier of the indicator set is used to assess the impact of data changes. Any data update that leads to a change of two or more percentage points on the relative distance to frontier gap is classified as a reform (for more details on the relative gap see the chapter on the distance to frontier and ease of doing business ranking). For example if the implementation of a new one-stop shop for company registration reduces time and procedures in a way that the overall relative gap decreases by two percentage points or more, the change is classified as a reform. On the contrary, minor fee updates or other small changes in the indicators that have an aggregate impact of less than two percentage points on the relative gap are not classified as a reform, but their impact is still reflected in the most updated indicators for this indicator set.

The data details on starting a business can be found for each economy at http://www.doingbusiness.org. This methodology was developed by Djankov and others (2002) and is adopted here with minor changes.

DEALING WITH CONSTRUCTION PERMITS

Doing Business records all procedures required for a business in the construction industry to build a warehouse, along with the time and cost to complete each procedure. In addition, *Doing Business* measures the building quality control index, evaluating the quality of building regulations, the strength of quality control and safety mechanisms, liability and insurance regimes, and professional certification requirements. Information is collected through a questionnaire administered to experts in construction licensing, including architects, civil engineers, construction lawyers, construction firms, utility service providers, and public officials who deal with building regulations, including approvals, permit issuance, and inspections.

The ranking of economies on the ease of dealing with construction permits is determined by sorting their distance to frontier scores for dealing with construction permits. These scores are the simple average of the distance to frontier scores for each of the component indicators (figure 12.3).

EFFICIENCY OF CONSTRUCTION PERMITTING

Doing Business divides the process of building a warehouse into distinct procedures in the questionnaire and solicits data for calculating the time and cost to complete each procedure (figure 12.4). These procedures include, but are not limited to:

- Obtaining and submitting all relevant project-specific documents (for example, building plans, site maps and certificates of urbanism) to the authorities.
- Hiring external third-party supervisors, consultants, engineers or inspectors (if necessary).
- Obtaining all necessary clearances, licenses, permits and certificates.
- Submitting all required notifications.
- Requesting and receiving all necessary inspections (unless completed by a hired private, third-party inspector).

Doing Business also records procedures for obtaining connections for water and sewerage. Procedures necessary to register the warehouse so that it can be used as collateral or transferred to another entity are also counted.

To make the data comparable across economies, several assumptions about the construction company, the warehouse project and the utility connections are used.

FIGURE 12.3 Dealing with construction permits: efficiency and quality of building regulation

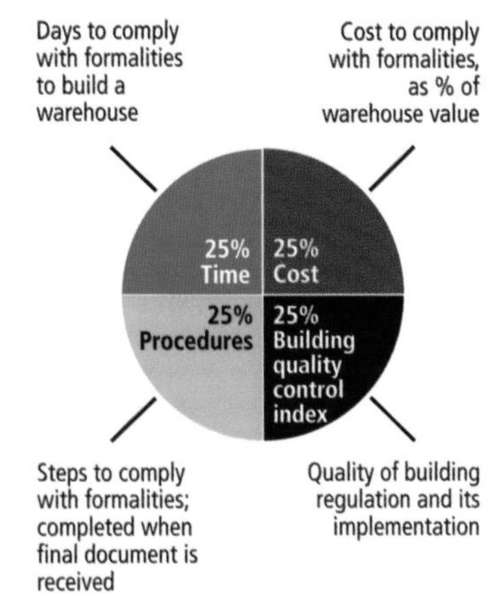

Assumptions about the construction company

The construction company (BuildCo):

- Is a limited liability company (or its legal equivalent);
- Operates in the economy's largest business city. For 11 economies the data are also collected for the second largest business city (table 12A.1);
- Is 100% domestically and privately owned;
- Has five owners, none of whom is a legal entity;

FIGURE 12.4 What are the time, cost and number of procedures to comply with formalities to build a warehouse?

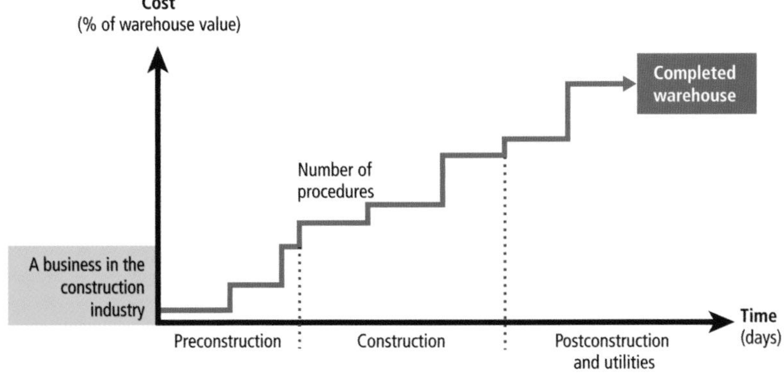

- Is fully licensed and insured to carry out construction projects, such as building warehouses;
- Has 60 builders and other employees, all of them nationals with the technical expertise and professional experience necessary to obtain construction permits and approvals;
- Has a licensed architect and a licensed engineer, both registered with the local association of architects or engineers. BuildCo is not assumed to have any other employees who are technical or licensed specialists, such as geological or topographical experts;
- Has paid all taxes and taken out all necessary insurance applicable to its general business activity (for example, accidental insurance for construction workers and third-person liability);
- Owns the land on which the warehouse will be built and will sell the warehouse upon its completion.

Assumptions about the warehouse

The warehouse:

- Will be used for general storage activities, such as storage of books or stationery. The warehouse will not be used for any goods requiring special conditions, such as food, chemicals, or pharmaceuticals;
- Will have two stories, both above ground, with a total constructed area of approximately 1,300.6 square meters (14,000 square feet). Each floor will be 3 meters (9 feet, 10 inches) high;
- Will have road access and be located in the periurban area of the economy's largest business city (that is, on the fringes of the city but still within its official limits). For 11 economies the data are also collected for the second largest business city;
- Will not be located in a special economic or industrial zone;
- Will be located on a land plot of approximately 929 square meters (10,000 square feet) that is 100% owned by BuildCo and is accurately registered in the cadastre and land registry;
- Is valued at 50 times income per capita;
- Will be a new construction (with no previous construction on the land), with no trees, natural water sources, natural reserves, or historical monuments of any kind on the plot;
- Will have complete architectural and technical plans prepared by a licensed architect. If preparation of the plans requires such steps as obtaining further documentation or getting prior approvals from external agencies, these are counted as procedures;
- Will include all technical equipment required to be fully operational;
- Will take 30 weeks to construct (excluding all delays due to administrative and regulatory requirements);

Assumptions about the utility connections

The water and sewerage connections:

- Will be 150 meters (492 feet) from the existing water source and sewer tap. If there is no water delivery infrastructure in the economy, a borehole will be dug. If there is no sewerage infrastructure, a septic tank in the smallest size available will be installed or built;
- Will not require water for fire protection reasons; a fire extinguishing system (dry system) will be used instead. If a wet fire protection system is required by law, it is assumed that the water demand specified below also covers the water needed for fire protection;
- Will have an average water use of 662 liters (175 gallons) a day and an average wastewater flow of 568 liters (150 gallons) a day. Will have a peak water use of 1,325 liters (350 gallons) a day and a peak wastewater flow of 1,136 liters (300 gallons) a day;
- Will have a constant level of water demand and wastewater flow throughout the year;
- Will be 1 inch in diameter for the water connection and 4 inches in diameter for the sewerage connection.

Procedures

A procedure is any interaction of the building company's employees, managers, or any party acting on behalf of the company with external parties, including government agencies, notaries, the land registry, the cadastre, utility companies, and public inspectors—and the hiring of external private inspectors and technical experts where needed. Interactions between company employees, such as development of the warehouse plans and internal inspections, are not counted as procedures. However, interactions with external parties that are required for the architect to prepare the plans and drawings (such as obtaining topographic or geological surveys), or to have such documents approved or stamped by external parties, are counted as procedures. Procedures that the company undergoes to connect the warehouse to water and sewerage are included. All procedures that are legally required and that are done in practice by the majority of companies to build a warehouse are counted, even if they may be avoided in exceptional cases. This includes obtaining technical conditions for electricity or clearance of the electrical plans only if they are required to obtain a building permit (table 12.5).

Time

Time is recorded in calendar days. The measure captures the median duration that local experts indicate is necessary to complete a procedure in practice. It is assumed that the minimum time required for each procedure is one day, except for procedures that can be fully completed online, for which the time required is recorded as half a day. Although procedures may take place simultaneously, they cannot start on the same day (that is, simultaneous procedures start on consecutive days), again with the exception of procedures that can be fully completed online. If a procedure can be accelerated legally for an additional cost and the accelerated procedure is used by the majority of companies, the fastest time to complete a procedure is chosen. It is

TABLE 12.5 What do the indicators on the efficiency of construction permitting measure?
Procedures to legally build a warehouse (number)
Submitting all relevant documents and obtaining all necessary clearances, licenses, permits and certificates
Submitting all required notifications and receiving all necessary inspections
Obtaining utility connections for water and sewerage
Registering the warehouse after its completion (if required for use as collateral or for transfer of the warehouse)
Time required to complete each procedure (calendar days)
Does not include time spent gathering information
Each procedure starts on a separate day—though procedures that can be fully completed online are an exception to this rule
Procedure considered completed once final document is received
No prior contact with officials
Cost required to complete each procedure (% of warehouse value)
Official costs only, no bribes

assumed that BuildCo does not waste time and commits to completing each remaining procedure without delay. The time that BuildCo spends on gathering information is not taken into account. It is assumed that BuildCo is aware of all building requirements and their sequence from the beginning.

Cost

Cost is recorded as a percentage of the warehouse value (assumed to be 50 times income per capita). Only official costs are recorded. All fees associated with completing the procedures to legally build a warehouse are recorded, including those associated with obtaining land use approvals and preconstruction design clearances; receiving inspections before, during and after construction; obtaining utility connections; and registering the warehouse at the property registry. Nonrecurring taxes required for the completion of the warehouse project are also recorded. Sales taxes (such as value added tax) or capital gains taxes are not recorded. Nor are deposits that must be paid up front and are later refunded. The building code, information from local experts, and specific regulations and fee schedules are used as sources for costs. If several local partners provide different estimates, the median reported value is used.

BUILDING QUALITY CONTROL

The building quality control index is based on six other indices—the quality of building regulations, quality control before, during and after construction, liability and insurance regimes, and professional certifications indices (table 12.6). The indicator is based on the same case study assumptions as the measures of efficiency.

Quality of building regulations index

The quality of building regulations index has two components:

- Whether building regulations are easily accessible. A score of 1 is assigned if building regulations (including the building code) or regulations dealing with construction permits are available on a website that is updated as new regulations are passed; 0.5 if the building regulations are available free of charge (or for a nominal fee) at the relevant permit-issuing authority; 0 if the building regulations must be purchased or if they are not made easily accessible anywhere.
- Whether the requirements for obtaining a building permit are clearly specified. A score of 1 is assigned if the building regulations (including the building code) or any accessible website, brochure, or pamphlet clearly specifies the list of required documents to submit, the fees to be paid, and all required preapprovals of the drawings or plans by the relevant agencies; 0 if none of these sources specify any of these requirements or if these sources specify fewer than the three requirements mentioned above.

The index ranges from 0 to 2, with higher values indicating clearer and more transparent building regulations. In the United Kingdom, for example, all relevant legislation can be found on an official government website (a score of 1). The legislation specifies the list of required documents to submit, the fees to be paid, and all required preapprovals of the drawings or plans by the relevant agencies (a score of 1). Adding these numbers gives the United Kingdom a score of 2 on the quality of building regulations index.

Quality control before construction index

The quality control before construction index has one component:

- Whether by law, a licensed architect or licensed engineer is part of the

TABLE 12.6 What do the indicators on building quality control measure?
Quality of building regulations index (0–2)
Accessibility of building regulations
Clarity of requirements for obtaining a building permit
Quality control before construction index (0–1)
Whether licensed or technical experts approve building plans
Quality control during construction index (0–3)
Types of inspections legally mandated during construction
Implementation of legally mandated inspections in practice
Quality control after construction index (0–3)
Final inspection legally mandated after construction
Implementation of legally mandated final inspection in practice
Liability and insurance regimes index (0–2)
Parties held legally liable for structural flaws after building occupancy
Parties legally mandated to obtain insurance to cover structural flaws after building occupancy or insurance is commonly obtained in practice
Professional certifications index (0–4)
Qualification requirements for individual who approves building plans
Qualification requirements for individual who supervises construction or conducts inspections
Building quality control index (0–15)
Sum of the quality of building regulations, quality control before construction, quality control during construction, quality control after construction, liability and insurance regimes, and professional certifications indices

committee or team that reviews and approves building permit applications and whether that person has the authority to refuse an application if the plans are not in conformity with regulations. A score of 1 is assigned if the national association of architects or engineers (or its equivalent) must review the building plans, if an independent firm or expert who is a licensed architect or engineer must review the plans, if the architect or engineer who prepared the plans must submit an attestation to the permit-issuing authority stating that the plans are in compliance with the building regulations or if a licensed architect or engineer is part of the committee or team that approves the plans at the relevant permit-issuing authority; 0 if no licensed architect or engineer is involved in the review of the plans to ensure their compliance with building regulations.

The index ranges from 0 to 1, with higher values indicating better quality control in the review of the building plans. In Rwanda, for example, the city hall in Kigali must review the building permit application, including the plans and drawings, and both a licensed architect and a licensed engineer are part of the team that reviews the plans and drawings. Rwanda therefore receives a score of 1 on the quality control before construction index.

Quality control during construction index

The quality control during construction index has two components:

- Whether inspections are mandated by law during the construction process. A score of 2 is assigned if an in-house supervising engineer (for example, an employee of the building company), an external supervising engineer or a government agency is legally mandated to conduct risk-based inspections during construction. A score of 1 is assigned if an in-house engineer (that is, an employee of the building company), an external supervising engineer or an external inspections firm is legally mandated to conduct technical inspections at different stages during the construction of the building or if a government agency is legally mandated to conduct only technical inspections at different stages during the construction. A score of 0 is assigned if a government agency is legally mandated to conduct unscheduled inspections, or if no technical inspections are mandated by law.
- Whether inspections during construction are implemented in practice. A score of 1 is assigned if the legally mandated inspections during construction always occur in practice; 0 if the legally mandated inspections do not occur in practice, if the inspections occur most of the time but not always, if inspections are not mandated by law regardless of whether or not they commonly occur in practice.

The index ranges from 0 to 3, with higher values indicating better quality control during the construction process. In Antigua and Barbuda, for example, the Development Control Authority is legally mandated to conduct phased inspections under the Physical Planning Act of 2003 (a score of 1). However, the Development Control Authority rarely conducts these inspections in practice (a score of 0). Adding these numbers gives Antigua and Barbuda a score of 1 on the quality control during construction index.

Quality control after construction index

The quality control after construction index has two components:

- Whether a final inspection is mandated by law in order to verify that the building was built in compliance with the approved plans and existing building regulations. A score of 2 is assigned if an in-house supervising engineer (that is, an employee of the building company), an external supervising engineer or an external inspections firm is legally mandated to verify that the building has been built in accordance with the approved plans and existing building regulations, or if a government agency is legally mandated to conduct a final inspection upon completion of the building; 0 if no final inspection is mandated by law after construction and no third party is required to verify that the building has been built in accordance with the approved plans and existing building regulations.
- Whether the final inspection is implemented in practice. A score of 1 is assigned if the legally mandated final inspection after construction always occurs in practice or if a supervising engineer or firm attests that the building has been built in accordance with the approved plans and existing building regulations; 0 if the legally mandated final inspection does not occur in practice, if the legally mandated final inspection occurs most of the time but not always, or if a final inspection is not mandated by law regardless of whether or not it commonly occurs in practice.

The index ranges from 0 to 3, with higher values indicating better quality control after the construction process. In Haiti, for example, the Municipality of Port-au-Prince is legally mandated to conduct a final inspection under the National Building Code of 2012 (a score of 2). However, the final inspection does not occur in practice (a score of 0). Adding these numbers gives Haiti a score of 2 on the quality control after construction index.

Liability and insurance regimes index

The liability and insurance regimes index has two components:

- Whether any parties involved in the construction process are held legally liable for latent defects such as structural flaws or problems in the building once it is in use. A score of 1 is assigned if at least two of the following parties are held legally liable for structural flaws or problems in the building once it is in use: the architect or engineer who designed the plans for the building, the professional or agency that conducted technical inspections, or the construction company; 0.5 if only one of the parties is held legally liable for structural flaws or problems in the building once it is in use; 0 if no party is held legally liable for structural flaws or problems in the building once it is in use, if the project owner or investor is the only party held liable, if liability is determined in court, or if liability is stipulated in a contract.

- Whether any parties involved in the construction process is legally required to obtain a latent defect liability—or decennial (10 years) liability—insurance policy to cover possible structural flaws or problems in the building once it is in use. A score of 1 is assigned if the architect or engineer who designed the plans for the building, the professional or agency that conducted the technical inspections, the construction company, or the project owner or investor is required by law to obtain either a decennial liability insurance policy or a latent defect liability insurance to cover possible structural flaws or problems in the building once it is in use or if a decennial liability insurance policy or a latent defect liability insurance is commonly obtained in practice by the majority of any of these parties even if not required by law; a score of 0 is assigned if no party is required by law to obtain either a decennial liability insurance or a latent defect liability insurance and such insurance is not commonly obtained in practice by any party, if the requirement to obtain an insurance policy is stipulated in a contract, if any party must obtain a professional insurance or an all risk insurance to cover the safety of workers or any other defects during construction but not a decennial liability insurance or a latent defect liability insurance that would cover defects after the building is in use, or if any party is required to pay for any damages caused on their own without having to obtain an insurance policy.

The index ranges from 0 to 2, with higher values indicating more stringent latent defect liability and insurance regimes. In Madagascar, for example, under article 1792 of the Civil Code both the architect who designed the plans and the construction company are legally held liable for latent defects for a period of 10 years after the completion of the building (a score of 1). However, there is no legal requirement for any party to obtain a decennial liability insurance policy to cover structural defects, nor do most parties obtain such insurance in practice (a score of 0). Adding these numbers gives Madagascar a score of 1 on the liability and insurance regimes index.

Professional certifications index

The professional certifications index has two components:

- The qualification requirements of the professional responsible for verifying that the architectural plans or drawings are in compliance with the building regulations. A score of 2 is assigned if this professional must have a minimum number of years of practical experience, must have a university degree (a minimum of a bachelor's) in architecture or engineering, and must also either be a registered member of the national order (association) of architects or engineers or pass a qualification exam. A score of 1 is assigned if the professional must have a university degree (a minimum of a bachelor's) in architecture or engineering and must also *either* have a minimum number of years of practical experience *or* be a registered member of the national order (association) of architects or engineers or pass a qualification exam. A score of 0 is assigned if the professional must meet only one of the above requirements, if the professional must meet two of the requirements but neither of the two is to have a university degree, or if the professional is subject to no qualification requirements.
- The qualification requirements of the professional who conducts the technical inspections during construction. A score of 2 is assigned if this professional must have a minimum number of years of practical experience, must have a university degree (a minimum of a bachelor's) in engineering, and must also either be a registered member of the national order of engineers or pass a qualification exam. A score of 1 is assigned if the professional must have a university degree (a minimum of a bachelor's) in engineering and must also *either* have a minimum number of years of practical experience *or* be a registered member of the national order (association) of engineers or pass a qualification exam. A score of 0 is assigned if the professional must meet only one of the requirements, if the professional must meet two of the requirements but neither of the two is to have a university degree, or if the professional is subject to no qualification requirements.

The index ranges from 0 to 4, with higher values indicating greater professional certification requirements. In Cambodia, for example, the professional responsible for verifying that the architectural plans or drawings are in compliance with the building regulations must have a relevant university degree and must pass a qualification exam (a score of 1). However, the professional conducting technical inspections during construction must only have a university degree (a score of 0). Adding these numbers gives Cambodia a score of 1 on the professional certifications index.

Building quality control index

The building quality control index is the sum of the scores on the quality of building regulations, quality control before construction, quality control during construction, quality control after construction, liability and insurance regimes, and professional certifications indices. The index ranges from 0 to 15, with higher values indicating better quality control and safety mechanisms in the construction regulatory system.

If an economy issued no building permits between June 2015 and June 2016 or if the applicable building legislation in the economy is not being implemented, the economy receives a "no practice" mark on the procedures, time and cost indicators. In addition, a "no practice" economy receives a score of 0 on the building quality control index even if its legal framework includes provisions related to building quality control and safety mechanisms.

REFORMS

The dealing with construction permits indicator set tracks changes related to the efficiency and quality of construction permitting systems every year. Depending on the impact on the data certain changes are classified as reforms and listed in the summaries of *Doing Business* reforms in 2015/2016 section of the report in order to acknowledge the implementation of significant changes. Reforms are divided into two types: those that make it easier to do business and those changes that make it more difficult to do business. The dealing with construction permits indicator set uses only one criterion to recognize a reform.

The aggregate gap on the overall distance to frontier of the indicator set is used to assess the impact of data changes. Any data update that leads to a change of 2 or more percentage points on the relative distance to frontier gap is classified as a reform (for more details on the relative gap, see the chapter on the distance to frontier and ease of doing business ranking). For example if the implementation of a new electronic permitting system reduces time in a way that the overall relative gap decreases by 2 percentage points or more, such a change is classified as a reform. On the contrary, minor fee updates or other smaller changes in the indicators that have an aggregate impact of less than 2 percentage points on the relative gap are not classified as a reform, but their impact is still reflected on the most updated indicators for this indicator set.

The data details on dealing with construction permits can be found for each economy at http://www.doingbusiness.org.

GETTING ELECTRICITY

Doing Business records all procedures required for a business to obtain a permanent electricity connection and supply for a standardized warehouse (figure 12.5). These procedures include applications and contracts with electricity utilities, all necessary inspections and clearances from the distribution utility and other agencies, and the external and final connection works. The questionnaire divides the process of getting an electricity connection into distinct procedures and solicits data for calculating the time and cost to complete each procedure.

In addition, *Doing Business* also measures the reliability of supply and transparency of tariffs index (included in the aggregate distance to frontier score and ranking on the ease of doing business) and the price of electricity (omitted from these aggregate measures). The reliability of supply and transparency of tariffs index encompasses quantitative data on the duration and frequency of power outages as well as qualitative information on the mechanisms put in place by the utility for monitoring power outages and restoring power supply, the reporting relationship between the utility and the regulator for power outages, the transparency and accessibility of tariffs and whether the utility faces a financial deterrent aimed at limiting outages (such as a requirement to compensate customers or pay fines when outages exceed a certain cap).

The ranking of economies on the ease of getting electricity is determined by sorting their distance to frontier scores for getting electricity. These scores are the simple average of the distance to frontier scores for all the component indicators except the price of electricity (figure 12.6).

Data on reliability of supply are collected from the electricity distribution utilities or regulators, depending upon the specific technical nature of the data. The rest of the data, including data on transparency of tariffs and procedures for obtaining electricity connection, are collected from all market players—the electricity distribution utility, electricity regulatory agencies and independent professionals such as electrical engineers, electrical contractors and construction companies. The electricity distribution utility consulted is the one serving the area (or areas) where warehouses are located. If there is a choice of distribution utilities, the one serving the largest number of customers is selected.

FIGURE 12.5 *Doing Business* measures the connection process at the level of distribution utilities

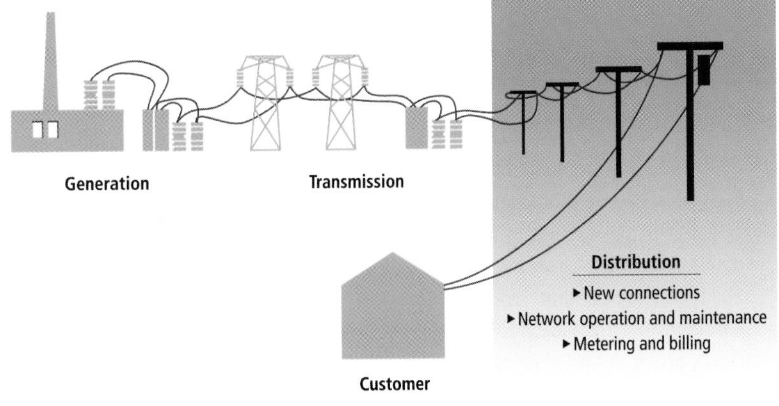

To make the data comparable across economies, several assumptions about the warehouse, the electricity connection and the monthly consumption are used.

Assumptions about the warehouse

The warehouse:

- Is owned by a local entrepreneur.
- Is located in the economy's largest business city. For 11 economies the data are also collected for the second largest business city (table 12A.1).
- Is located in an area where similar warehouses are typically located. In this area a new electricity connection is not eligible for a special investment promotion regime (offering special subsidization or faster service, for example).
- Is located in an area with no physical constraints. For example, the property is not near a railway.
- Is a new construction and is being connected to electricity for the first time.
- Has two stories, both above ground, with a total surface area of approximately 1,300.6 square meters (14,000 square feet). The plot of land on which it is built is 929 square meters (10,000 square feet).
- Is used for storage of goods.

FIGURE 12.6 Getting electricity: efficiency, reliability and transparency

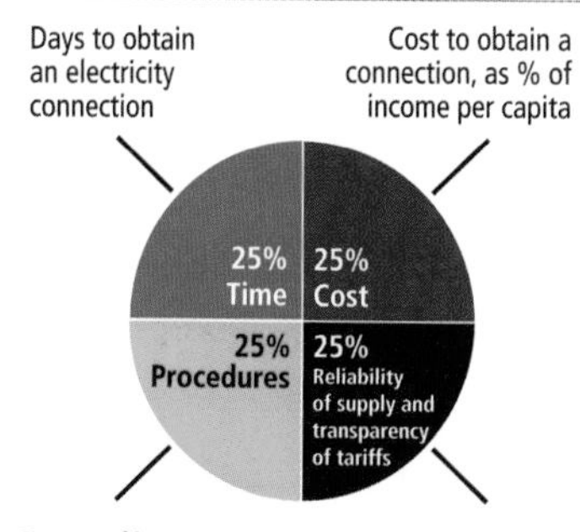

Note: The price of electricity is measured but does not count for the rankings.

Assumptions about the electricity connection

The electricity connection:

- Is a permanent one.
- Is a three-phase, four-wire Y connection with a subscribed capacity of 140-kilo-volt-ampere (kVA) with a power factor of 1, when 1 kVA = 1 kilowatt (kW).
- Has a length of 150 meters. The connection is to either the low- or medium-voltage distribution network and is either overhead or underground, whichever is more common in the area where the warehouse is located.
- Requires works that involve the crossing of a 10-meter wide road (by excavation, overhead lines) but are all carried out on public land. There is no crossing of other owners' private property because the warehouse has access to a road.
- Includes only negligible length in the customer's private domain.
- Does not require work to install the internal wiring of the warehouse. This has already been completed up to and including the customer's service panel or switchboard and the meter base.

Assumptions about the monthly consumption for March

- It is assumed that the warehouse operates 30 days a month from 9:00 a.m. to 5:00 p.m. (8 hours a day), with equipment utilized at 80% of capacity on average and that there are no electricity cuts (assumed for simplicity reasons).
- The monthly energy consumption is 26,880 kilowatt-hours (kWh); hourly consumption is 112 kWh.
- If multiple electricity suppliers exist, the warehouse is served by the cheapest supplier.
- Tariffs effective in March of the current year are used for calculation of the price of electricity for the warehouse. Although March has 31 days, for calculation purposes only 30 days are used.

Procedures

A procedure is defined as any interaction of the company's employees or its main electrician or electrical engineer (that is, the one who may have done the internal wiring) with external parties, such as the electricity distribution utility, electricity supply utilities, government agencies, electrical contractors and electrical firms. Interactions between company employees and steps related to the internal electrical wiring, such as the design and execution of the internal electrical installation plans, are not counted as procedures. Procedures that must be completed with the same utility but with different departments are counted as separate procedures (table 12.7).

The company's employees are assumed to complete all procedures themselves unless the use of a third party is mandated (for example, if only an electrician registered with the utility is allowed to submit an application). If the company can, but is not required to, request the services of professionals (such as a private firm rather than the utility for the external works), these procedures are recorded if they are commonly done. For all procedures only the most likely cases (for example, more than 50% of the time the utility has the material) and those followed in practice for connecting a warehouse to electricity are counted.

Time

Time is recorded in calendar days. The measure captures the median duration that the electricity utility and experts indicate is necessary in practice, rather than required by law, to complete a procedure with minimum follow-up and no extra payments. It is assumed that the minimum time required for each procedure is one day. Although procedures may take place simultaneously, they cannot start on the same day (that is, simultaneous procedures start on consecutive days). It is assumed that the company does not waste time and commits to completing each remaining procedure without delay. The time that the company spends on

TABLE 12.7 What do the getting electricity indicators measure?

Procedures to obtain an electricity connection (number)
Submitting all relevant documents and obtaining all necessary clearances and permits
Completing all required notifications and receiving all necessary inspections
Obtaining external installation works and possibly purchasing material for these works
Concluding any necessary supply contract and obtaining final supply
Time required to complete each procedure (calendar days)
Is at least one calendar day
Each procedure starts on a separate day
Does not include time spent gathering information
Reflects the time spent in practice, with little follow-up and no prior contact with officials
Cost required to complete each procedure (% of income per capita)
Official costs only, no bribes
Value added tax excluded
Reliability of supply and transparency of tariffs index (0–8)
Duration and frequency of power outages
Tools to monitor power outages
Tools to restore power supply
Regulatory monitoring of utilities' performance
Financial deterrents aimed at limiting outages
Transparency and accessibility of tariffs
Price of electricity (cents per kilowatt-hour)
Price based on monthly bill for commercial warehouse in case study

Note: While *Doing Business* measures the price of electricity, it does not include these data when calculating the distance to frontier score for getting electricity or the ranking on the ease of getting electricity.

gathering information is not taken into account. It is assumed that the company is aware of all electricity connection requirements and their sequence from the beginning.

Cost

Cost is recorded as a percentage of the economy's income per capita. Costs are recorded exclusive of value added tax. All the fees and costs associated with completing the procedures to connect a warehouse to electricity are recorded, including those related to obtaining clearances from government agencies, applying for the connection, receiving inspections of both the site and the internal wiring, purchasing material, getting the actual connection works and paying a security deposit. Information from local experts and specific regulations and fee schedules are used as sources for costs. If several local partners provide different estimates, the median reported value is used. In all cases the cost excludes bribes.

Security deposit

Utilities may require security deposits as a guarantee against the possible failure of customers to pay their consumption bills. For this reason the security deposit for a new customer is most often calculated as a function of the customer's estimated consumption.

Doing Business does not record the full amount of the security deposit. If the deposit is based on the customer's actual consumption, this basis is the one assumed in the case study. Rather than the full amount of the security deposit, *Doing Business* records the present value of the losses in interest earnings experienced by the customer because the utility holds the security deposit over a prolonged period, in most cases until the end of the contract (assumed to be after five years). In cases where the security deposit is used to cover the first monthly consumption bills, it is not recorded. To calculate the present value of the lost interest earnings, the end-2015 lending rates from the International Monetary Fund's *International Financial Statistics* are used. In cases where the security deposit is returned with interest, the difference between the lending rate and the interest paid by the utility is used to calculate the present value.

In some economies the security deposit can be put up in the form of a bond: the company can obtain from a bank or an insurance company a guarantee issued on the assets it holds with that financial institution. In contrast to the scenario in which the customer pays the deposit in cash to the utility, in this scenario the company does not lose ownership control over the full amount and can continue using it. In return the company will pay the bank a commission for obtaining the bond. The commission charged may vary depending on the credit standing of the company. The best possible credit standing and thus the lowest possible commission are assumed. Where a bond can be put up, the value recorded for the deposit is the annual commission times the five years assumed to be the length of the contract. If both options exist, the cheaper alternative is recorded.

In Honduras in June 2016 a customer requesting a 140-kVA electricity connection would have had to put up a security deposit of 126,894 Honduran lempiras ($5,616) in cash or check, and the deposit would have been returned only at the end of the contract. The customer could instead have invested this money at the prevailing lending rate of 20.66%. Over the five years of the contract this would imply a present value of lost interest earnings of 77,273 lempiras ($3,420). In contrast, if the customer chose to settle the deposit with a bank guarantee at an annual rate of 2.5%, the amount lost over the five years would be just 15,862 lempiras ($702).

Reliability of supply and transparency of tariffs index

Doing Business uses the system average interruption duration index (SAIDI) and the system average interruption frequency index (SAIFI) to measure the duration and frequency of power outages in the largest business city of each economy (for 11 economies the data are also collected for the second largest business city; table 12A.1). SAIDI is the average total duration of outages over the course of a year for each customer served, while SAIFI is the average number of service interruptions experienced by a customer in a year. Annual data (covering the calendar year) are collected from distribution utility companies and national regulators on SAIDI and SAIFI. Both SAIDI and SAIFI estimates include load shedding.

An economy is eligible to obtain a score on the reliability of supply and transparency of tariffs index if the utility collects data on electricity outages (measuring the average total duration of outages per customer and the average number of outages per customer) and the SAIDI value is below a threshold of 100 hours and the SAIFI value below a threshold of 100 outages.

Because the focus is on measuring the reliability of the electricity supply in each economy's largest business city (and, in 11 economies, also in the second largest business city), an economy is not eligible to obtain a score if outages are too frequent or long-lasting for the electricity supply to be considered reliable—that is, if the SAIDI value exceeds the threshold of 100 hours or the SAIFI value exceeds the threshold of 100 outages.[4] An economy is also not eligible to obtain a score on the index if data on power outages are not collected.

For all economies that meet the criteria as determined by *Doing Business*, a score on the reliability of supply and transparency of tariffs index is calculated on the basis of the following six components:

- What the SAIDI and SAIFI values are. If SAIDI and SAIFI are 12 (equivalent to an outage of one hour each month) or below, a score of 1 is assigned. If SAIDI and SAIFI are 4 (equivalent to an outage of one hour each quarter) or below, 1 additional point is assigned. Finally, if SAIDI and SAIFI are 1 (equivalent to an outage of one hour per year) or below, 1 more point is assigned.
- What tools are used by the distribution utility to monitor power outages. A score of 1 is assigned if the utility uses automated tools, such as the Supervisory Control and Data Acquisition (SCADA) system; 0 if it relies solely on calls from customers and records and monitors outages manually.
- What tools are used by the distribution utility to restore power supply. A score of 1 is assigned if the utility uses automated tools, such as the SCADA system; 0 if it relies solely on manual resources for service restoration, such as field crews or maintenance personnel.
- Whether a regulator—that is, an entity separate from the utility—monitors the utility's performance on reliability of supply. A score of 1 is assigned if the regulator performs periodic or real-time reviews; 0 if it does not monitor power outages and does not require the utility to report on reliability of supply.
- Whether financial deterrents exist to limit outages. A score of 1 is assigned if the utility compensates customers when outages exceed a certain cap, if the utility is fined by the regulator when outages exceed a certain cap or if both these conditions are met; 0 if no compensation mechanism of any kind is available.
- Whether electricity tariffs are transparent and easily available. A score of 1 is assigned if effective tariffs are available online and customers are notified of a change in tariff a full billing cycle (that is, one month) ahead of time; 0 if not.

The index ranges from 0 to 8, with higher values indicating greater reliability of electricity supply and greater transparency of tariffs. In the Czech Republic, for example, the distribution utility company PREdistribuce uses SAIDI and SAIFI metrics to monitor and collect data on power outages. In 2015 the average total duration of power outages in Prague was 0.49 hours per customer and the average number of outages experienced by a customer was 0.33. Both SAIDI and SAIFI are below the threshold and indicate that there was less than one outage a year per customer, for a total duration of less than one hour. So the economy not only meets the eligibility criteria for obtaining a score on the index, it also receives a score of 3 on the first component of the index. The utility uses an automated system (SCADA) to identify faults in the network (a score of 1) and restore electricity service (a score of 1). The national regulator actively reviews the utility's performance in providing reliable electricity service (a score of 1) and requires the utility to compensate customers if outages last longer than a maximum period defined by the regulator (a score of 1). Customers are notified of a change in tariffs ahead of the next billing cycle and can easily check effective tariffs online (a score of 1). Adding these numbers gives the Czech Republic a score of 8 on the reliability of supply and transparency of tariffs index.

On the other hand, several economies receive a score of 0 on the reliability of supply and transparency of tariffs index. The reason may be that outages occur more than once a month and none of the mechanisms and tools measured by the index are in place. An economy may also receive a score of 0 if either the SAIDI or SAIFI value (or both) exceeds the threshold of 100. For Papua New Guinea, for example, the SAIDI value (211) exceeds the threshold. Based on the criteria established, Papua New Guinea cannot receive a score on the index even though the country has regulatory monitoring of outages and there is a compensation mechanism for customers.

If an economy issued no new electricity connections to an electrical grid between June 2015 and June 2016, or if electricity is not provided during that period, the economy receives a "no practice" mark on the procedures, time and cost indicators. In addition, a "no practice" economy receives a score of 0 on the reliability of supply and transparency of tariff index even if the utility has in place automated systems for monitoring and restoring outages; there is regulatory oversight of utilities on power interruptions, and public availability of tariffs.

Price of electricity

Doing Business measures the price of electricity but does not include these data when calculating the distance to frontier score for getting electricity or the ranking on the ease of getting electricity. (The data are available on the *Doing Business* website, at http://www.doingbusiness.org.) The data on electricity prices are based on standardized assumptions to ensure comparability across economies.

The price of electricity is measured in U.S. cents per kilowatt-hour. On the basis of the assumptions about monthly consumption, a monthly bill for a commercial warehouse in the largest business city of the economy is computed for the month of March (for 11 economies the data are also collected for the second largest business city; table 12A.1). As noted, the warehouse uses electricity 30 days a month, from 9:00 a.m. to 5:00 p.m., so different tariff schedules may apply if a time-of-use tariff is available.

REFORMS

The getting electricity indicator set tracks changes related to the efficiency of the connection process, as well as the reliability of power supply and transparency of tariffs. Depending on the impact on the data, certain changes are classified as reforms and listed in the summaries of *Doing Business* reforms in 2015/2016 section of the report in order to acknowledge the implementation of significant changes. Reforms are divided in two types: those that make it easier to do business and those changes that make it more difficult to do business. The getting electricity indicator set uses two criteria to recognize a reform.

First, the aggregate gap on the overall distance to frontier of the indicator set is used to assess the impact of data changes. Any data update that leads to a change of 2 or more percentage points on the relative distance to frontier gap is classified as a reform (for more details on the relative gap, see the chapter on the distance to frontier and ease of doing business ranking). For example if the implementation of a new single window at the utility reduces the time to process new connection requests in a way that the overall relative gap decreases by 2 percentage points or more, such a change is classified as a reform. On the other hand, minor fee updates from the utility or other small changes that have an aggregate impact of less than 2 percentage points on the relative gap are not classified as a reform, but their impact is still reflected on the most updated indicators for this topic.

Second, to be considered a reform, changes in the data must be tied to an initiative led by the utility or by the government—and not an exogenous event. For example if outages increase considerably from one year to the next due to inclement weather, this cannot be considered a reform that makes doing business harder. Similarly, if the cost of electricity-related materials (such as cabling or transformers) decreases due to a currency appreciation, this cannot be considered a reform that makes doing business easier. However, if a utility establishes a one-stop shop to streamline the connection process or if it installs an automated system to improve monitoring of power outages and restoration of electricity services, these actions would be considered reforms that made doing business easier.

The data details on getting electricity can be found for each economy at http://www.doingbusiness.org. The initial methodology was developed by Geginat and Ramalho (2015) and is adopted here with minor changes.

REGISTERING PROPERTY

Doing Business records the full sequence of procedures necessary for a business (the buyer) to purchase a property from another business (the seller) and to transfer the property title to the buyer's name so that the buyer can use the property for expanding its business, use the property as collateral in taking new loans or, if necessary, sell the property to another business. It also measures the time and cost to complete each of these procedures. *Doing Business* also measures the quality of the land administration system in each economy. The quality of land administration index has five dimensions: reliability of infrastructure, transparency of information, geographic coverage, land dispute resolution and equal access to property rights.

The ranking of economies on the ease of registering property is determined by sorting their distance to frontier scores for registering property. These scores are the simple average of the distance to frontier scores for each of the component indicators (figure 12.7).

EFFICIENCY OF TRANSFERRING PROPERTY

As recorded by *Doing Business*, the process of transferring property starts with obtaining the necessary documents, such as a copy of the seller's title if necessary, and conducting due diligence if required. The transaction is considered complete when it is opposable to third parties and when the buyer

FIGURE 12.7 Registering property: efficiency and quality of land administration system

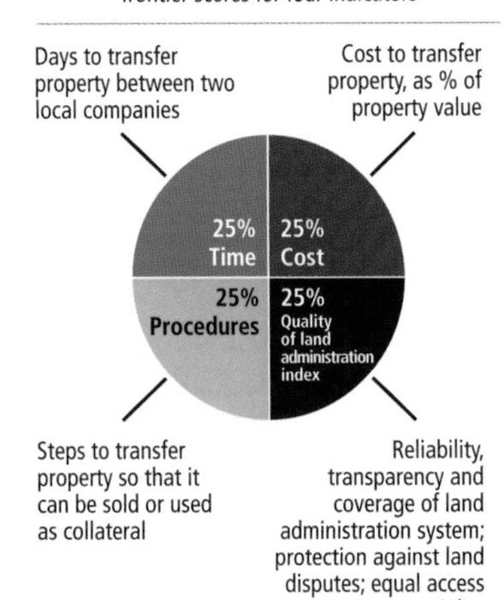

can use the property, use it as collateral for a bank loan or resell it (figure 12.8). Every procedure required by law or necessary in practice is included, whether it is the responsibility of the seller or the buyer or must be completed by a third party on their behalf. Local property lawyers, notaries and property registries provide information on procedures as well as the time and cost to complete each of them.

To make the data comparable across economies, several assumptions about the parties to the transaction, the property and the procedures are used.

FIGURE 12.8 What are the time, cost and number of procedures required to transfer property between two local companies?

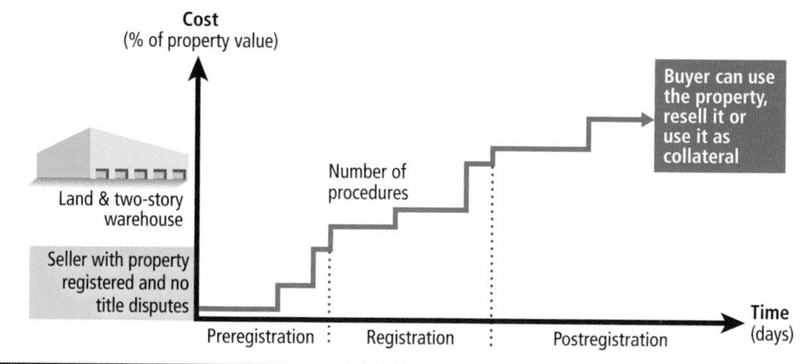

Assumptions about the parties

The parties (buyer and seller):

- Are limited liability companies (or the legal equivalent).
- Are located in the periurban area of the economy's largest business city. For 11 economies the data are also collected for the second largest business city (table 12A.1).
- Are 100% domestically and privately owned.
- Have 50 employees each, all of whom are nationals.
- Perform general commercial activities.

Assumptions about the property

The property:

- Has a value of 50 times income per capita. The sale price equals the value.
- Is fully owned by the seller.
- Has no mortgages attached and has been under the same ownership for the past 10 years.
- Is registered in the land registry or cadastre, or both, and is free of title disputes.
- Is located in a periurban commercial zone, and no rezoning is required.
- Consists of land and a building. The land area is 557.4 square meters (6,000 square feet). A two-story warehouse of 929 square meters (10,000 square feet) is located on the land. The warehouse is 10 years old, is in good condition and complies with all safety standards, building codes and other legal requirements. It has no heating system. The property of land and building will be transferred in its entirety.
- Will not be subject to renovations or additional building following the purchase.
- Has no trees, natural water sources, natural reserves or historical monuments of any kind.
- Will not be used for special purposes, and no special permits, such as for residential use, industrial plants, waste storage or certain types of agricultural activities, are required.
- Has no occupants, and no other party holds a legal interest in it.

Procedures

A procedure is defined as any interaction of the buyer or the seller, their agents (if an agent is legally or in practice required) with external parties, including government agencies, inspectors, notaries and lawyers. Interactions between company officers and employees are not considered. All procedures that are legally or in practice required for registering property are recorded, even if they may be avoided in exceptional cases (table 12.8). It is assumed that the buyer follows the fastest legal option available and used by the majority of property owners. Although the buyer may use lawyers or other professionals where necessary in the registration process, it is assumed that the buyer does not employ an outside facilitator in the registration process unless legally or in practice required to do so.

Time

Time is recorded in calendar days. The measure captures the median duration that property lawyers, notaries or registry officials indicate is necessary to complete a procedure. It is assumed that the minimum time required for each procedure is one day, except for procedures that can be fully completed online, for which the time required is recorded as half a day. Although procedures may

TABLE 12.8 What do the indicators on the efficiency of transferring property measure?
Procedures to legally transfer title on immovable property (number)
Preregistration procedures (for example, checking for liens, notarizing sales agreement, paying property transfer taxes)
Registration procedures in the economy's largest business city[a]
Postregistration procedures (for example, filing title with municipality)
Time required to complete each procedure (calendar days)
Does not include time spent gathering information
Each procedure starts on a separate day—though procedures that can be fully completed online are an exception to this rule
Procedure considered completed once final document is received
No prior contact with officials
Cost required to complete each procedure (% of property value)
Official costs only, no bribes
No value added or capital gains taxes included

a. For 11 economies the data are also collected for the second largest business city.

take place simultaneously, they cannot start on the same day, again with the exception of procedures that can be fully completed online. It is assumed that the buyer does not waste time and commits to completing each remaining procedure without delay. If a procedure can be accelerated for an additional cost, the fastest legal procedure available and used by the majority of property owners is chosen. If procedures can be undertaken simultaneously, it is assumed that they are. It is assumed that the parties involved are aware of all requirements and their sequence from the beginning. Time spent on gathering information is not considered.

Cost

Cost is recorded as a percentage of the property value, assumed to be equivalent to 50 times income per capita. Only official costs required by law are recorded, including fees, transfer taxes, stamp duties and any other payment to the property registry, notaries, public agencies or lawyers. Other taxes, such as capital gains tax or value added tax, are excluded from the cost measure. Both costs borne by the buyer and those borne by the seller are included. If cost estimates differ among sources, the median reported value is used.

QUALITY OF LAND ADMINISTRATION

The quality of land administration index is composed of five other indices: the reliability of infrastructure, transparency of information, geographic coverage, land dispute resolution and equal access to property rights indices (table 12.9). Data are collected for each economy's largest business city. For 11 economies the data are also collected for the second largest business city.

TABLE 12.9 What do the indicators on the quality of land administration measure?

Reliability of infrastructure index (0–8)
Type of system for archiving information on land ownership
Availability of electronic database to check for encumbrances
Type of system for archiving maps
Availability of geographic information system
Link between property ownership registry and mapping system
Transparency of information index (0–6)
Accessibility of information on land ownership
Accessibility of maps of land plots
Publication of fee schedules, lists of registration documents, service standards
Availability of a specific and separate mechanism for complaints
Publication of statistics about the number of property transactions
Geographic coverage index (0–8)
Coverage of land registry at the level of the largest business city and the economy[a]
Coverage of mapping agency at the level of the largest business city and the economy[a]
Land dispute resolution index (0–8)
Legal framework for immovable property registration
Mechanisms to prevent and resolve land disputes
Equal access to property rights (-2–0)
Unequal ownership rights to property between unmarried men and women
Unequal ownership rights to property between married men and women
Quality of land administration index (0–30)
Sum of the reliability of infrastructure, transparency of information, geographic coverage, land dispute resolution indices and equal access to property rights

a. For 11 economies the data are also collected for the second largest business city.

Reliability of infrastructure index

The reliability of infrastructure index has six components:

- How land titles are kept at the registry of the largest business city of the economy. A score of 2 is assigned if the majority of land titles are fully digital; 1 if the majority are scanned; 0 if the majority are kept in paper format.
- Whether there is an electronic database for checking for encumbrances. A score of 1 is assigned if yes; 0 if no.
- How maps of land plots are kept at the mapping agency of the largest business city of the economy. A score of 2 is assigned if the majority of maps are fully digital; 1 if the majority are scanned; 0 if the majority are kept in paper format.
- Whether there is a geographic information system—an electronic database for recording boundaries, checking plans and providing cadastral information. A score of 1 is assigned if yes; 0 if no.
- How the land ownership registry and mapping agency are linked. A score of 1 is assigned if information about land ownership and maps are kept in a single database or in linked databases; 0 if there is no connection between the different databases.
- How immovable property is identified. A score of 1 is assigned if there is a unique number to identify properties for the majority of land plots; 0 if there are multiple identifiers.

The index ranges from 0 to 8, with higher values indicating a higher quality of infrastructure for ensuring the reliability of information on property titles and boundaries. In Turkey, for example, the land registry offices in Istanbul maintain titles in a fully digital format (a score of 2) and have a fully electronic database to check for encumbrances (a score of 1). The Cadastral Directorate offices in Istanbul have digital maps (a score of 2), and the Geographical Information Directorate has a public portal allowing users to check the plans and cadastral information on parcels along with satellite images (a score of 1). Databases about land ownership and maps are linked to each other through the TAKBIS system, an integrated information system for the land registry offices and cadastral offices (a score of 1). Finally, there is a unique identifying number for properties (a score of 1). Adding these numbers gives Turkey a score of 8 on the reliability of infrastructure index.

Transparency of information index

The transparency of information index has 10 components:

- Whether information on land ownership is made publicly available. A score of 1 is assigned if information on land ownership is accessible by anyone; 0 if access is restricted.
- Whether the list of documents required for completing any type of property transaction is made publicly available. A score of 0.5 is assigned if the list of documents is accessible online or on a public board; 0 if it is not made available to the public or if it can be obtained only in person.
- Whether the fee schedule for completing any type of property transaction is made publicly available. A score of 0.5 is assigned if the fee schedule is accessible online or on a public board or is free of charge; 0 if it is not made available to the public or if it can be obtained only in person.
- Whether the agency in charge of immovable property registration commits to delivering a legally binding document that proves property ownership within a specific time frame. A score of 0.5 is assigned if the service standard is accessible online or on a public board; 0 if it is not made available to the public or if it can be obtained only in person.
- Whether there is a specific and separate mechanism for filing complaints about a problem that occurred at the agency in charge of immovable property registration. A score of 1 is assigned if there is a specific and separate mechanism for filing a complaint; 0 if there is only a general mechanism or no mechanism.
- Whether there are publicly available official statistics tracking the number of transactions at the immovable property registration agency. A score of 0.5 is assigned if statistics are published about property transfers in the largest business city in the past calendar year at the latest on June 1st of the following year; 0 if no such statistics are made publicly available.
- Whether maps of land plots are made publicly available. A score of 0.5 is assigned if maps are accessible by anyone; 0 if access is restricted.
- Whether the fee schedule for accessing maps is made publicly available. A score of 0.5 is assigned if the fee schedule is accessible online or on a public board or free of charge; 0 if it is not made available to the public or if it can be obtained only in person.
- Whether the mapping agency commits to delivering an updated map within a specific time frame. A score of 0.5 is assigned if the service standard is accessible online or on a public board; 0 if it is not made available to the public or if it can be obtained only in person.
- Whether there is a specific and separate mechanism for filing complaints about a problem that occurred at the mapping agency. A score of 0.5 is assigned if there is a specific and separate mechanism for filing a complaint; 0 if there is only a general mechanism or no mechanism.

The index ranges from 0 to 6, with higher values indicating greater transparency in the land administration system. In the Netherlands, for example, anyone who pays a fee can consult the land ownership database (a score of 1). Information can be obtained at the office, by mail or online using the Kadaster website (http://www.kadaster.nl). Anyone can also get information online about the list of documents to submit for property registration (a score of 0.5), the fee schedule for registration (a score of 0.5) and the service standards (a score of 0.5). And anyone facing a problem at the land registry can file a complaint or report an error by filling in a specific form online (a score of 1). In addition, the Kadaster makes statistics about land transactions available to the public, reporting a total of 178,293 property transfers in Amsterdam in 2015 (a score of 0.5). Moreover, anyone who pays a fee can consult online cadastral maps (a score of 0.5). It is also possible to get public access to the fee schedule for map consultation (a score of 0.5), the service standards for delivery of an updated plan (a score of 0.5) and a specific mechanism for filing a complaint about a map (a score of 0.5). Adding these numbers gives the Netherlands a score of 6 on the transparency of information index.

Geographic coverage index

The geographic coverage index has four components:

- How complete the coverage of the land registry is at the level of the largest business city. A score of 2 is assigned if all privately held land plots in the city are formally registered at the land registry; 0 if not.
- How complete the coverage of the land registry is at the level of the economy. A score of 2 is assigned if all privately held land plots in the economy are formally registered at the land registry; 0 if not.
- How complete the coverage of the mapping agency is at the level of the largest business city. A score of 2 is assigned if all privately held land plots in the city are mapped; 0 if not.
- How complete the coverage of the mapping agency is at the level of the economy. A score of 2 is assigned if all privately held land plots in the economy are mapped; 0 if not.

The index ranges from 0 to 8, with higher values indicating greater geographic coverage in land ownership registration and cadastral mapping. In the Republic of Korea, for example, all privately held land plots are formally registered at the land registry in Seoul (a score of 2) and in the economy as a whole (a score of 2). In addition, all privately held land plots are mapped in Seoul (a score of 2) and in the economy as a whole (a score of 2). Adding these numbers gives Korea a score of 8 on the geographic coverage index.

Land dispute resolution index

The land dispute resolution index assesses the legal framework for immovable property registration and the accessibility of dispute resolution mechanisms. The index has eight components:

- Whether the law requires that all property sale transactions be registered at the immovable property registry to make them opposable to third parties. A score of 1.5 is assigned if yes; 0 if no.
- Whether the formal system of immovable property registration is subject to a guarantee. A score of 0.5 is assigned if either a state or private guarantee over immovable property registration is required by law; 0 if no such guarantee is required.
- Whether there is a specific compensation mechanism to cover for losses incurred by parties who engaged in good faith in a property transaction based on erroneous information certified by the immovable property registry. A score of 0.5 is assigned if yes; 0 if no.
- Whether the legal system requires verification of the legal validity of the documents necessary for a property transaction. A score of 0.5 is assigned if there is a review of legal validity, either by the registrar or by a professional (such as a notary or lawyer); 0 if there is no review.
- Whether the legal system requires verification of the identity of the parties to a property transaction. A score of 0.5 is assigned if there is verification of identity, either by the registrar or by a professional (such as a notary or lawyer); 0 if there is no verification.
- Whether there is a national database to verify the accuracy of identity documents. A score of 1 is assigned if such a national database is available; 0 if not.
- How much time it takes to obtain a decision from a court of first instance (without appeal) in a standard land dispute between two local businesses over tenure rights worth 50 times income per capita and located in the largest business city. A score of 3 is assigned if it takes less than one year; 2 if it takes between one and two years; 1 if it takes between two and three years; 0 if it takes more than three years.
- Whether there are publicly available statistics on the number of land disputes in the first instance. A score of 0.5 is assigned if statistics are published about land disputes in the economy in the past calendar year; 0 if no such statistics are made publicly available.

The index ranges from 0 to 8, with higher values indicating greater protection against land disputes. In Lithuania, for example, according to the Civil Code and the Law on the Real Property Register, property transactions must be registered at the land registry to make them opposable to third parties (a score of 1.5). The property transfer system is guaranteed by the state (a score of 0.5) and has a compensation mechanism to cover for losses incurred by parties who engaged in good faith in a property transaction based on an error by the registry (a score of 0.5). A notary verifies the legal validity of the documents in a property transaction (a score of 0.5) and the identity of the parties (a score of 0.5), in accordance with the Law on the Notary Office (Law I-2882). Lithuania has a national database to verify the accuracy of identity documents (a score of 1). In a land dispute between two Lithuanian companies over the tenure rights of a property worth $750,000, the Vilnius District Court gives a decision in less than one year (a score of 3). Finally, statistics about land disputes are collected and published; there were a total of 7 land disputes in the country in 2015 (a score of 0.5). Adding these numbers gives Lithuania a score of 8 on the land dispute resolution index.

Equal access to property rights index

The equal access to property rights index has two components:

- Whether unmarried men and unmarried women have equal ownership rights to property. A score of -1 is assigned if there are unequal ownership rights to property; 0 if there is equality.
- Whether married men and married women have equal ownership rights to property. A score of -1 is assigned if there are unequal ownership rights to property; 0 if there is equality.

Ownership rights cover the ability to manage, control, administer, access, encumber, receive, dispose of and transfer property. Each restriction is considered if there is a differential treatment for men and women in the law considering the default marital property regime. For customary land systems, equality is assumed unless there is a general legal provision stating a differential treatment.

The index ranges from -2 to 0, with higher values indicating greater inclusiveness of property rights. In Mali, for example, unmarried men and unmarried women have equal ownership rights to property (a score of 0). The same applies to married men and women who can use their property in the same way (a score of 0). Adding these numbers gives Mali a score of 0 on the equal access to property rights index—which indicates equal property rights between men and women. On the contrary in Swaziland, unmarried men and unmarried women do not have equal ownership rights to property according to the Deeds Registry Act of 1968, Article 16 (a score of -1). The same applies to married men and women who are not permitted to use their property in the same way according to the Deeds Registry Act of 1968, Articles 16 and 45 (a score of -1). Adding these numbers gives Swaziland a score of -2 on the equal access to property rights index—which indicates unequal property rights between men and women.

Quality of land administration index

The quality of land administration index is the sum of the scores on the reliability of infrastructure, transparency of information, geographic coverage, land dispute resolution and equal access to property indices. The index ranges from 0 to 30 with higher values indicating better quality of the land administration system.

If private sector entities were unable to register property transfers in an economy between June 2015 and June 2016, the economy receives a "no practice" mark on the procedures, time and cost indicators. A "no practice" economy receives a score of 0 on the quality of land administration index even if its legal framework includes provisions related to land administration.

REFORMS

The registering property indicator set tracks changes related to the efficiency and quality of land administration systems every year. Depending on the impact on the data, certain changes are classified as reforms and listed in the summaries of *Doing Business* reforms in 2015/2016 section of the report in order to acknowledge the implementation of significant changes. Reforms are divided into two types: those that make it easier to do business and those changes that make it more difficult to do business. The registering property indicator set uses two criteria to recognize a reform.

First, the aggregate gap on the overall distance to frontier of the indicator set is used to assess the impact of data changes. Any data update that leads to a change of 2 or more percentage points on the relative distance to frontier gap is classified as a reform (for more details on the relative gap, see the chapter on the distance to frontier and ease of doing business ranking). For example if the implementation of a new electronic property registration system reduces time in a way that the overall relative gap decreases by 2 percentage points or more, such change is classified as a reform. On the contrary, minor fee updates or other smaller changes in the indicators that have an aggregate impact of less than 2 percentage points on the relative gap are not classified as a reform, but their impact is still reflected on the most updated indicators for this indicator set.

Second, the overall score on the quality of land administration is also considered as a criterion. Any change of 1 point or more on the overall quality score is acknowledged as a reform. For instance, the completion of the geographic coverage of the land registry of the business city (2 points) is considered as a reform. However, the publication of statistics about property transfers (0.5 point) is not significant enough to be classified as a reform.

The data details on registering property can be found for each economy at http:// www.doingbusiness.org.

GETTING CREDIT

Doing Business measures the legal rights of borrowers and lenders with respect to secured transactions through one set of indicators and the reporting of credit information through another. The first set of indicators measures whether certain features that facilitate lending exist within the applicable collateral and bankruptcy laws. The second set measures the coverage, scope and accessibility of credit information available through credit reporting service providers such as credit bureaus or credit registries (figure 12.9). The ranking of economies on the ease of getting credit is determined by sorting their distance to frontier scores for getting credit. These scores are the distance to frontier score for the sum of the strength of legal rights index and the depth of credit information index (figure 12.10).

LEGAL RIGHTS OF BORROWERS AND LENDERS

The data on the legal rights of borrowers and lenders are gathered through a questionnaire administered to financial lawyers and verified through analysis of laws and regulations as well as public sources of information on collateral and bankruptcy laws. Questionnaire responses are verified through several rounds of follow-up communication with respondents as well as by contacting third parties and consulting public sources. The questionnaire data are confirmed through teleconference calls or on-site visits in all economies.

Strength of legal rights index

The strength of legal rights index measures the degree to which collateral and bankruptcy laws protect the rights of borrowers and lenders and thus facilitate lending (table 12.10). For each economy it is first determined whether a unitary secured transactions system exists. Then two case scenarios, case A and case B, are used to determine how a

FIGURE 12.9 Do lenders have credit information on entrepreneurs seeking credit? Is the law favorable to borrowers and lenders using movable assets as collateral?

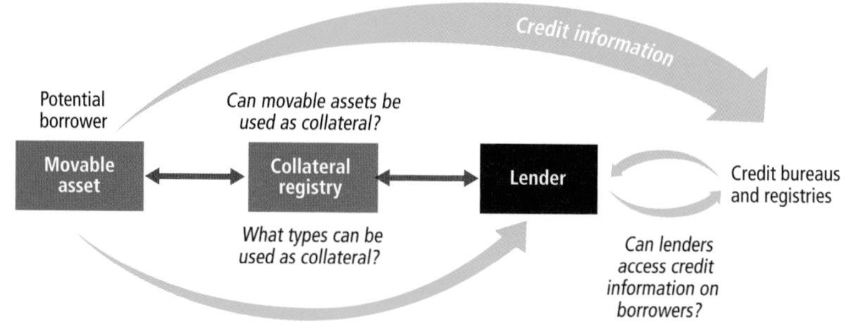

FIGURE 12.10 Getting credit: collateral rules and credit information

Rankings are based on distance to frontier scores for the sum of two indicators

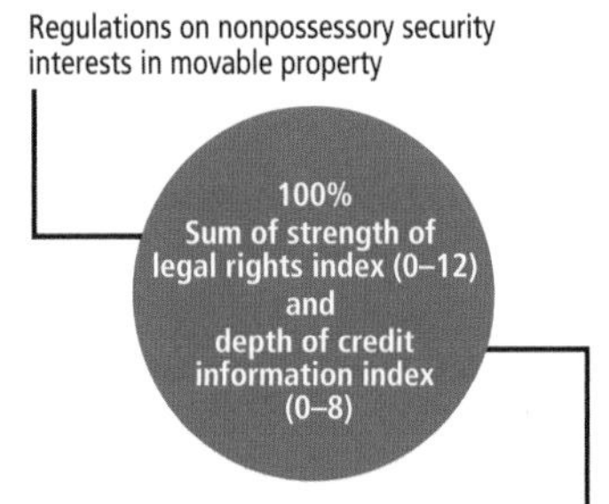

Note: Credit bureau coverage and credit registry coverage are measured but do not count for the rankings.

nonpossessory security interest is created, publicized and enforced according to the law. Special emphasis is given to how the collateral registry operates (if registration of security interests is possible). The case scenarios involve a secured borrower, company ABC, and a secured lender, BizBank.

In some economies the legal framework for secured transactions will allow only case A or case B (not both) to apply. Both cases examine the same set of legal provisions relating to the use of movable collateral.

TABLE 12.10 What do the getting credit indicators measure?
Strength of legal rights index (0–12)
Protection of rights of borrowers and lenders through collateral laws
Protection of secured creditors' rights through bankruptcy laws
Depth of credit information index (0–8)
Scope and accessibility of credit information distributed by credit bureaus and credit registries
Credit bureau coverage (% of adults)
Number of individuals and firms listed in the largest credit bureau as percentage of adult population
Credit registry coverage (% of adults)
Number of individuals and firms listed in a credit registry as percentage of adult population

Several assumptions about the secured borrower (ABC) and lender (BizBank) are used:

- ABC is a domestic limited liability company (or its legal equivalent).
- ABC has up to 50 employees.
- ABC has its headquarters and only base of operations in the economy's largest business city. For 11 economies the data are also collected for the second largest business city (table 12A.1).
- Both ABC and BizBank are 100% domestically owned.

The case scenarios also involve assumptions. In case A, as collateral for the loan, ABC grants BizBank a nonpossessory security interest in one category of movable assets, for example, its machinery or its inventory. ABC wants to keep both possession and ownership of the collateral. In economies where the law does not allow nonpossessory security interests in movable property, ABC and BizBank use a fiduciary transfer-of-title arrangement (or a similar substitute for nonpossessory security interests).

In case B, ABC grants BizBank a business charge, enterprise charge, floating charge or any charge that gives BizBank a security interest over ABC's combined movable assets (or as much of ABC's movable assets as possible). ABC keeps ownership and possession of the assets.

The strength of legal rights index covers functional equivalents to security interests in movable assets (such as financial leases and sales with retention of title) only in its first component, to assess how integrated or unified the economy's legal framework for secured transactions is.

The strength of legal rights index includes 10 aspects related to legal rights in collateral law and 2 aspects in bankruptcy law. A score of 1 is assigned for each of the following features of the laws:

- The economy has an integrated or unified legal framework for secured transactions that extends to the creation, publicity and enforcement of four functional equivalents to security interests in movable assets: fiduciary transfers of title; financial leases; assignments or transfers of receivables; and sales with retention of title.
- The law allows a business to grant a nonpossessory security right in a single category of movable assets (such as machinery or inventory), without requiring a specific description of the collateral.
- The law allows a business to grant a nonpossessory security right in substantially all its movable assets, without requiring a specific description of the collateral.
- A security right can be given over future or after-acquired assets and extends automatically to the products, proceeds or replacements of the original assets.
- A general description of debts and obligations is permitted in the collateral agreement and in registration documents, all types of debts and obligations can be secured between the parties, and the collateral agreement can include a maximum amount for which the assets are encumbered.
- A collateral registry or registration institution for security interests granted over movable property by incorporated and nonincorporated entities is in operation, unified geographically and with an electronic database indexed by debtors' names.
- The collateral registry is a notice-based registry—a registry that files only a notice of the existence of a security interest (not the underlying documents) and does not perform a legal review of the transaction. The registry also publicizes functional equivalents to security interests.
- The collateral registry has modern features such as those that allow secured creditors (or their representatives) to register, search, amend or cancel security interests online.
- Secured creditors are paid first (for example, before tax claims

and employee claims) when a debtor defaults outside an insolvency procedure.

- Secured creditors are paid first (for example, before tax claims and employee claims) when a business is liquidated.
- Secured creditors are subject to an automatic stay on enforcement procedures when a debtor enters a court-supervised reorganization procedure, but the law protects secured creditors' rights by providing clear grounds for relief from the automatic stay (for example, if the movable property is in danger) or setting a time limit for it.
- The law allows parties to agree in the collateral agreement that the lender may enforce its security right out of court; the law allows public and private auctions and also permits the secured creditor to take the asset in satisfaction of the debt.

The index ranges from 0 to 12, with higher scores indicating that collateral and bankruptcy laws are better designed to expand access to credit.

REFORMS

The strength of legal rights index tracks changes related to secured transactions and insolvency every year. Depending on the impact on the data, certain changes are classified as reforms and listed in the summaries of *Doing Business* reforms in 2015/2016 section of the report in order to acknowledge the implementation of significant changes. Reforms are divided in two types: those that make it easier to do business and those changes that make it more difficult to do business. The strength of legal rights index uses the following criteria to recognize a reform.

All changes in laws and regulations that have any impact on the economy's score on the existence of a secured transaction legal framework which regulates the creation, publicity and enforcement of nonpossessory security interests and their functional equivalents. Each year, new laws and amendments are evaluated to see if they facilitate obtaining credit by small and medium enterprises, allowing for maximum flexibility in the choice of assets which can be used as collateral. Guidelines, model rules, principles, recommendations and case law are excluded.

Reforms impacting the strength of legal rights index include amendments to or the introduction of a secured transactions act, insolvency code, or civil code as well as the establishment or modernization of any of the features of a collateral registry as measured by the indicators. For example, introducing a law which provides for a collateral registry and actually establishing that collateral registry—which is geographically centralized, unified for all types of movable assets and for both incorporated and non-incorporated entities searchable by debtor's name—would represent a reform with a 1-point increase and would therefore be acknowledged in the report.

CREDIT INFORMATION

The data on the reporting of credit information are built in two stages. First, banking supervision authorities and public information sources are surveyed to confirm the presence of a credit reporting service provider, such as a credit bureau or credit registry. Second, when applicable, a detailed questionnaire on the credit bureau's or credit registry's structure, laws and associated rules is administered to the entity itself. Questionnaire responses are verified through several rounds of follow-up communication with respondents as well as by contacting third parties and consulting public sources. The questionnaire data are confirmed through teleconference calls or on-site visits in all economies.

Depth of credit information index

The depth of credit information index measures rules and practices affecting the coverage, scope and accessibility of credit information available through either a credit bureau or a credit registry. A score of 1 is assigned for each of the following eight features of the credit bureau or credit registry (or both):

- Data on firms and individuals are distributed.
- Both positive credit information (for example, original loan amounts, outstanding loan amounts and a pattern of on-time repayments) and negative information (for example, late payments and the number and amount of defaults) are distributed.
- Data from retailers or utility companies are distributed in addition to data from financial institutions.
- At least two years of historical data are distributed. Credit bureaus and registries that erase data on defaults as soon as they are repaid or distribute negative information more than 10 years after defaults are repaid receive a score of 0 for this component.
- Data on loan amounts below 1% of income per capita are distributed.
- By law, borrowers have the right to access their data in the largest credit bureau or registry in the economy. Credit bureaus and registries that charge more than 1% of income per capita for borrowers to inspect their data receive a score of 0 for this component.
- Banks and other financial institutions have online access to the credit information (for example, through a web interface, a system-to-system connection or both).
- Bureau or registry credit scores are offered as a value added service to help banks and other financial institutions assess the creditworthiness of borrowers.

The index ranges from 0 to 8, with higher values indicating the availability of more credit information, from either a credit bureau or a credit registry, to facilitate lending decisions. If the credit bureau or registry is not operational or covers less than 5% of the adult population, the score on the depth of credit information index is 0.

In Lithuania, for example, both a credit bureau and a credit registry operate. Both distribute data on firms and individuals (a score of 1). Both distribute positive and negative information (a score of 1). Although the credit registry does not distribute data from retailers or utilities, the credit bureau does (a score of 1). Both distribute at least two years of historical data (a score of 1). Although the credit registry has a threshold of €290, the credit bureau distributes data on loans of any value (a score of 1). Borrowers have the right to access their data in both the credit bureau and the credit registry free of charge once a year (a score of 1). Both entities provide data users access to databases through a web interface (a score of 1). Although the credit registry does not provide credit scores, the credit bureau does (a score of 1). Adding these numbers gives Lithuania a score of 8 on the depth of credit information index.

Credit bureau coverage

Credit bureau coverage reports the number of individuals and firms listed in a credit bureau's database as of January 1, 2016, with information on their borrowing history within the past five years, plus the number of individuals and firms that have had no borrowing history in the past five years but for which a lender requested a credit report from the bureau in the period between January 2, 2015, and January 1, 2016. The number is expressed as a percentage of the adult population (the population age 15 and above in 2015 according to the World Bank's *World Development Indicators*). A credit bureau is defined as a private firm or nonprofit organization that maintains a database on the creditworthiness of borrowers (individuals or firms) in the financial system and facilitates the exchange of credit information among creditors. (Many credit bureaus support banking and overall financial supervision activities in practice, though this is not their primary objective.) Credit investigative bureaus that do not directly facilitate information exchange among banks and other financial institutions are not considered. If no credit bureau operates, the coverage value is 0.0%.

Credit registry coverage

Credit registry coverage reports the number of individuals and firms listed in a credit registry's database as of January 1, 2016, with information on their borrowing history within the past five years, plus the number of individuals and firms that have had no borrowing history in the past five years but for which a lender requested a credit report from the registry in the period between January 2, 2015, and January 1, 2016. The number is expressed as a percentage of the adult population (the population age 15 and above in 2015 according to the World Bank's *World Development Indicators*). A credit registry is defined as a database managed by the public sector, usually by the central bank or the superintendent of banks, that collects information on the creditworthiness of borrowers (individuals or firms) in the financial system and facilitates the exchange of credit information among banks and other regulated financial institutions (while their primary objective is to assist banking supervision). If no credit registry operates, the coverage value is 0.0%.

REFORMS

The depth of credit information index tracks changes related to the coverage, scope and accessibility of credit information available through either a credit bureau or a credit registry every year. Depending on the impact on the data, certain changes are classified as reforms and listed in the summaries of *Doing Business* reforms in 2015/2016 section of the report in order to acknowledge the implementation of significant changes. Reforms are divided into two types: those that make it easier to do business and those changes that make it more difficult to do business. The credit information index uses three criteria to recognize a reform.

First, all changes in laws, regulations and practices that have any impact on the economy's score on the credit information index are classified as reforms. Examples of reforms impacting the index include measures to distribute positive credit data in addition to negative data, the distribution of credit data from utilities or retailers or the introduction of credit scores as a value-added service. Any change that improves the score of a given economy in any of the eight features of the index is considered a reform. Some reforms can have an impact in more than one feature. For example the introduction of a new credit bureau covering more than 5% of the adult population that distributes information on firms and individuals, as well as positive and negative data and provides online access to data users, represents a 3 point increase in the index. In contrast, the introduction of legislation that guarantees borrowers' rights to access their data in the largest credit bureau or registry in the economy represents a reform with a 1 point increase in the index.

Second, changes that increase the coverage of the largest credit bureau or registry in an economy above 5% of the adult population may also be classified as reforms. According to the getting credit methodology, if the credit bureau or registry is not operational or covers less than 5% of the adult population, the score on the depth of credit information index is 0. The impact of the reform will depend on the characteristics of the economy's credit reporting system as it relates to the eight features of the index. Expanded coverage that does not reach 5% of the adult population is not classified as a reform but the impact is still reflected on the most updated statistics.

Third, occasionally the credit information index will acknowledge legislative changes with no current impact on the data as reforms. This option is typically reserved to legislative changes of exceptional magnitude, such as the introduction of laws allowing the operation of credit bureaus or laws on personal data protection.

The data details on getting credit can be found for each economy at http://www.doingbusiness.org. The initial methodology was developed by Djankov, McLiesh and Shleifer (2007) and is adopted here with minor changes.

PROTECTING MINORITY INVESTORS

Doing Business measures the protection of minority investors from conflicts of interest through one set of indicators and shareholders' rights in corporate governance through another (table 12.11). The data come from a questionnaire administered to corporate and securities lawyers and are based on securities regulations, company laws, civil procedure codes and court rules of evidence. The ranking of economies on the strength of minority investor protections is determined by sorting their distance to frontier scores for protecting minority investors. These scores are the simple average of the distance to frontier scores for the extent of conflict of interest regulation index and the extent of shareholder governance index (figure 12.11).

TABLE 12.11 What do the protecting minority investors indicators measure?

Extent of disclosure index (0–10)	Extent of shareholder rights index (0–10)
Review and approval requirements for related-party transactions	Shareholders' rights and role in major corporate decisions
Internal, immediate and periodic disclosure requirements for related-party transactions	
Extent of director liability index (0–10)	**Extent of ownership and control index (0–10)**
Minority shareholders' ability to sue and hold interested directors liable for prejudicial related-party transactions	Governance safeguards protecting shareholders from undue board control and entrenchment
Available legal remedies (damages, disgorgement of profits, fines, imprisonment, rescission of transactions)	
Ease of shareholder suits index (0–10)	**Extent of corporate transparency index (0–10)**
Access to internal corporate documents	Corporate transparency on significant owners, executive compensation, annual meetings and audits
Evidence obtainable during trial	
Allocation of legal expenses	
Extent of conflict of interest regulation index (0–10)	**Extent of shareholder governance index (0–10)**
Simple average of the extent of disclosure, extent of director liability and ease of shareholder suits indices	Simple average of the extent of shareholder rights, extent of ownership and control and extent of corporate transparency indices
Strength of minority investor protection index (0–10)	
Simple average of the extent of conflict of interest regulation and extent of shareholder governance indices	

PROTECTION OF SHAREHOLDERS FROM CONFLICTS OF INTEREST

The extent of conflict of interest regulation index measures the protection of shareholders against directors' misuse of corporate assets for personal gain by distinguishing three dimensions of regulation that address conflicts of interest: transparency of related-party transactions (extent of disclosure index), shareholders' ability to sue and hold directors liable for self-dealing (extent of director liability index) and access to evidence and allocation of legal expenses in shareholder litigation (ease of shareholder suits index). To make the data comparable across economies, several assumptions about the business and the transaction are used (figure 12.12).

Assumptions about the business

The business (Buyer):

- Is a publicly traded corporation listed on the economy's most important stock exchange. If the number of publicly traded companies listed on that exchange is less than 10, or if there is no stock exchange in the economy, it is assumed that Buyer is a large private company with multiple shareholders.
- Has a board of directors and a chief executive officer (CEO) who may legally act on behalf of Buyer where permitted, even if this is not specifically required by law.
- Has a supervisory board (applicable to economies with a two-tier board system) on which 60% of the shareholder-elected members have been appointed by Mr. James, who is Buyer's

FIGURE 12.11 Protecting minority investors: shareholders' rights in conflicts of interest and corporate governance

Rankings are based on distance to frontier scores for two indicators

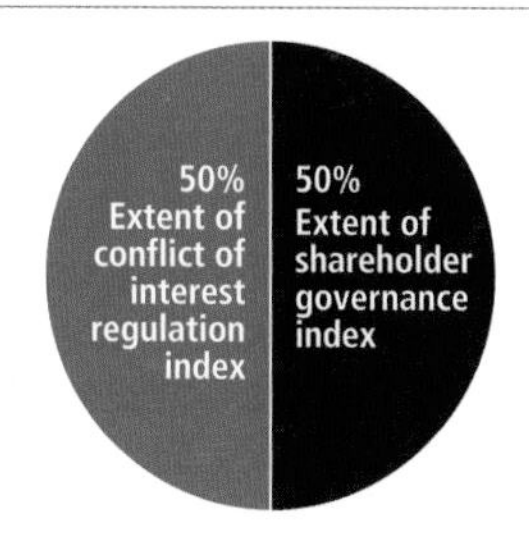

FIGURE 12.12 How well are minority shareholders protected from conflicts of interest?

Extent of disclosure
Disclosure and approval requirements

Extent of director liability
Ability to sue directors for damages

Ease of shareholder suits
Access by shareholders to documents plus other evidence for trial

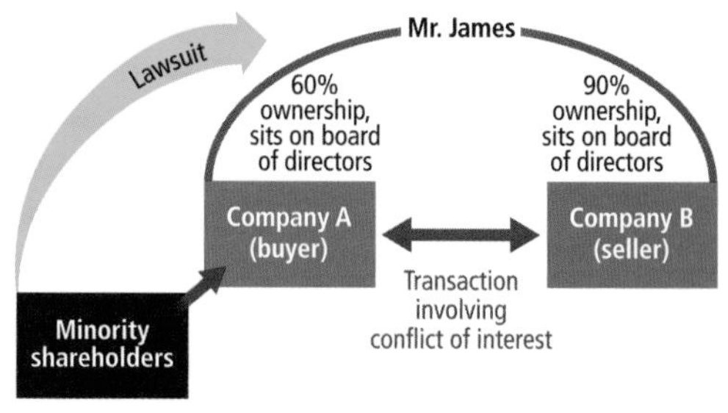

controlling shareholder and a member of Buyer's board of directors.
- Has not adopted any bylaws or articles of association that differ from default minimum standards and does not follow any nonmandatory codes, principles, recommendations or guidelines relating to corporate governance.
- Is a manufacturing company with its own distribution network.

Assumptions about the transaction

- Mr. James owns 60% of Buyer and elected two directors to Buyer's five-member board.
- Mr. James also owns 90% of Seller, a company that operates a chain of retail hardware stores. Seller recently closed a large number of its stores.
- Mr. James proposes that Buyer purchase Seller's unused fleet of trucks to expand Buyer's distribution of its food products, a proposal to which Buyer agrees. The price is equal to 10% of Buyer's assets and is higher than the market value.
- The proposed transaction is part of the company's ordinary course of business and is not outside the authority of the company.
- Buyer enters into the transaction. All required approvals are obtained, and all required disclosures made (that is, the transaction is not fraudulent).
- The transaction causes damages to Buyer. Shareholders sue Mr. James and the other parties that approved the transaction.

Extent of disclosure index

The extent of disclosure index has five components:

- Which corporate body can provide legally sufficient approval for the transaction. A score of 0 is assigned if it is the CEO or the managing director alone; 1 if the board of directors, the supervisory board or shareholders must vote and Mr. James is permitted to vote; 2 if the board of directors or the supervisory board must vote and Mr. James is not permitted to vote; 3 if shareholders must vote and Mr. James is not permitted to vote.
- Whether it is required that an external body, for example, an external auditor, review the transaction before it takes place. A score of 0 is assigned if no; 1 if yes.
- Whether disclosure by Mr. James to the board of directors or the supervisory board is required.[5] A score of 0 is assigned if no disclosure is required; 1 if a general disclosure of the existence of a conflict of interest is required without any specifics; 2 if full disclosure of all material facts relating to Mr. James's interest in the Buyer-Seller transaction is required.
- Whether immediate disclosure of the transaction to the public, the regulator or the shareholders is required. A score of 0 is assigned if no disclosure is required; 1 if disclosure on the terms of the transaction is required but not on Mr. James's conflict of interest; 2 if disclosure on both the terms and Mr. James's conflict of interest is required.
- Whether disclosure in the annual report is required. A score of 0 is assigned if no disclosure on the transaction is required; 1 if disclosure on the terms of the transaction is required but not on Mr. James's conflict of interest; 2 if disclosure on both the terms and Mr. James's conflict of interest is required.

The index ranges from 0 to 10, with higher values indicating greater disclosure. In Poland, for example, the board of directors must approve the transaction and Mr. James is not allowed to vote (a score of 2). Poland does not require an external body to review the transaction (a score of 0). Before the transaction Mr. James must disclose his conflict of interest to the other directors, but he is not required to provide specific information about it (a score of 1). Buyer is required to disclose immediately all information affecting the stock price, including the conflict of interest (a score of 2). In its annual report Buyer must also disclose the terms of the transaction and Mr. James's ownership in Buyer and Seller (a score of 2). Adding these numbers gives Poland a score of 7 on the extent of disclosure index.

Extent of director liability index

The extent of director liability index has seven components:[6]

- Whether shareholder plaintiffs are able to sue directly or derivatively for the damage the transaction causes to the company. A score of 0 is assigned if suits are unavailable or are available only for shareholders holding more than 10% of the company's share capital; 1 if direct or derivative suits are available for shareholders holding 10% of share capital.
- Whether a shareholder plaintiff is able to hold Mr. James liable for the damage the Buyer-Seller transaction causes to the company. A score of 0 is assigned if Mr. James cannot be held liable or can be held liable only for fraud, bad faith or gross negligence; 1 if Mr. James can be held liable only if he influenced the approval of the transaction or was negligent; 2 if Mr. James can be held liable when the transaction is unfair or prejudicial to the other shareholders.
- Whether a shareholder plaintiff is able to hold the approving body (the CEO, members of the board of directors or members of the supervisory board) liable for the damage the transaction causes to the company. A score of 0 is assigned if the approving body cannot be held liable or can be held liable only for fraud, bad faith or gross negligence; 1 if the approving body can be held liable for negligence; 2 if the approving body can be held liable when the transaction is unfair or prejudicial to the other shareholders.
- Whether Mr. James pays damages for the harm caused to the company upon a successful claim by the shareholder plaintiff. A score of 0 is assigned if no; 1 if yes.
- Whether Mr. James repays profits made from the transaction upon a successful claim by the shareholder plaintiff. A score of 0 is assigned if no; 1 if yes.

- Whether Mr. James is fined and imprisoned or disqualified upon a successful claim by the shareholder plaintiff. A score of 0 is assigned if no; 1 if he is fined and imprisoned or if he is disqualified—that is, disallowed from representing or holding a managerial position in any company for a year or more.
- Whether a court can void the transaction upon a successful claim by a shareholder plaintiff. A score of 0 is assigned if rescission is unavailable or is available only in case of fraud, bad faith or gross negligence; 1 if rescission is available when the transaction is oppressive or prejudicial to the other shareholders; 2 if rescission is available when the transaction is unfair or entails a conflict of interest.

The index ranges from 0 to 10, with higher values indicating greater liability of directors. In Panama, for example, direct or derivative suits are available for shareholders holding 10% of share capital (a score of 1). Assuming that the prejudicial transaction was duly approved and disclosed, in order to hold Mr. James liable a plaintiff must prove that Mr. James influenced the approving body or acted negligently (a score of 1). To hold the other directors liable, a plaintiff must prove that they acted negligently (a score of 1). If Mr. James is found liable, he must pay damages (a score of 1) but he is not required to disgorge his profits (a score of 0). Mr. James can be neither fined and imprisoned nor disqualified (a score of 0). The prejudicial transaction cannot be voided (a score of 0). Adding these numbers gives Panama a score of 4 on the extent of director liability index.

Ease of shareholder suits index

The ease of shareholder suits index has six components:

- Whether shareholders owning 10% of the company's share capital have the right to inspect the transaction documents before filing suit or request that a government inspector investigate the Buyer-Seller transaction without filing suit. A score of 0 is assigned if no; 1 if yes.
- What range of documents is available to the shareholder plaintiff from the defendant and witnesses during trial. A score of 1 is assigned for each of the following types of documents available: information that the defendant has indicated he intends to rely on for his defense; information that directly proves specific facts in the plaintiff's claim; and any information relevant to the subject matter of the claim.
- Whether the plaintiff can obtain categories of relevant documents from the defendant without identifying each document specifically. A score of 0 is assigned if no; 1 if yes.
- Whether the plaintiff can directly examine the defendant and witnesses during trial. A score of 0 is assigned if no; 1 if yes, with prior approval of the questions by the judge; 2 if yes, without prior approval.
- Whether the standard of proof for civil suits is lower than that for a criminal case. A score of 0 is assigned if no; 1 if yes.
- Whether shareholder plaintiffs can recover their legal expenses from the company. A score of 0 is assigned if no; 1 if plaintiffs can recover their legal expenses from the company only upon a successful outcome of their legal action or if payment of their attorney fees is contingent on a successful outcome; 2 if plaintiffs can recover their legal expenses from the company regardless of the outcome of their legal action.

The index ranges from 0 to 10, with higher values indicating greater powers of shareholders to challenge the transaction. In Croatia, for example, a shareholder holding 10% of Buyer's shares can request that a government inspector review suspected mismanagement by Mr. James and the CEO without filing suit in court (a score of 1). The plaintiff can access documents that the defendant intends to rely on for his defense (a score of 1). The plaintiff must specifically identify the documents being sought (for example, the Buyer-Seller purchase agreement of July 15, 2015) and cannot simply request categories (for example, all documents related to the transaction) (a score of 0). The plaintiff can examine the defendant and witnesses during trial, without prior approval of the questions by the court (a score of 2). The standard of proof for civil suits is preponderance of the evidence, while the standard for a criminal case is beyond a reasonable doubt (a score of 1). The plaintiff can recover legal expenses from the company only upon a successful outcome of the legal action (a score of 1). Adding these numbers gives Croatia a score of 6 on the ease of shareholder suits index.

Extent of conflict of interest regulation index

The extent of conflict of interest regulation index is the average of the extent of disclosure index, the extent of director liability index and the ease of shareholder suits index. The index ranges from 0 to 10, with higher values indicating stronger regulation of conflicts of interest.

SHAREHOLDERS' RIGHTS IN CORPORATE GOVERNANCE

The extent of shareholder governance index measures shareholders' rights in corporate governance by distinguishing three dimensions of good governance: shareholders' rights and role in major corporate decisions (extent of shareholder rights index), governance safeguards protecting shareholders from undue board control and entrenchment (extent of ownership and control index) and corporate transparency on ownership stakes, compensation, audits and financial prospects (extent of corporate transparency index). The index also measures whether a subset of relevant rights and safeguards are available in limited companies.

Extent of shareholder rights index

For each component of the extent of shareholder rights index, a score of 0 is assigned if the answer is no; 1 if yes. The index has 10 components:

- Whether the sale of 51% of Buyer's assets requires shareholder approval.
- Whether shareholders representing 10% of Buyer's share capital have the right to call for an extraordinary meeting of shareholders.
- Whether Buyer must obtain its shareholders' approval every time it issues new shares.
- Whether shareholders automatically receive preemption or subscription rights every time Buyer issues new shares.
- Whether the election and dismissal of the external auditor must be approved by the shareholders.
- Whether changes to rights associated with a class of shares are only possible if the holders of the affected shares approve those changes.
- Assuming that Buyer is a limited company, whether the sale of 51% of Buyer's assets requires member approval.
- Assuming that Buyer is a limited company, whether members representing 10% have the right to call for a meeting of members.
- Assuming that Buyer is a limited company, whether all members must consent to add a new member.[7]
- Assuming that Buyer is a limited company, whether a member must first offer to sell his or her interest to the existing members before selling to a non-member.

Extent of ownership and control index

For each component of the extent of ownership and control index, a score of 0 is assigned if the answer is no; 1 if yes. The index has 10 components:

- Whether the same individual cannot be appointed CEO and chair of the board of directors.
- Whether the board of directors must include independent and nonexecutive board members.
- Whether shareholder can remove members of the board of directors without cause before the end of their term.
- Whether the board of directors must include a separate audit committee.
- Whether a potential acquirer must make a tender offer to all shareholders upon acquiring 50% of Buyer.
- Whether Buyer must pay dividends within a maximum period set by law after the declaration date.
- Whether a subsidiary is prohibited from acquiring shares issued by its parent company.
- Assuming that Buyer is a limited company, whether there is a management deadlock breaking mechanism.[8]
- Assuming that Buyer is a limited company, whether a potential acquirer must make a tender offer to all members upon acquiring 50% of Buyer.
- Assuming that Buyer is a limited company, whether Buyer must distribute profits within a maximum period set by law after the declaration date.

Extent of corporate transparency index

For each component of the extent of corporate transparency index, a score of 0 is assigned if the answer is no; 1 if yes. The index has 10 components:

- Whether Buyer must disclose direct and indirect beneficial ownership stakes representing 5%.
- Whether Buyer must disclose information about board members' other directorships as well as basic information on their primary employment.
- Whether Buyer must disclose the compensation of individual managers.
- Whether a detailed notice of general meeting must be sent 21 calendar days before the meeting.[9]
- Whether shareholders representing 5% of Buyer's share capital can put items on the agenda for the general meeting.
- Whether Buyer's annual financial statements must be audited by an external auditor.
- Whether Buyer must disclose its audit reports to the public.
- Assuming that Buyer is a limited company, whether members must meet at least once a year.[10]
- Assuming that Buyer is a limited company, whether members representing 5% can put items on the meeting agenda.
- Assuming that Buyer is a limited company larger than a threshold set by law, whether its annual financial statements must be audited by an external auditor.

Extent of shareholder governance index

The extent of shareholder governance index is the average of the extent of shareholder rights index, the extent of ownership and control index and the extent of corporate transparency index. The index ranges from 0 to 10, with higher values indicating stronger rights of shareholders in corporate governance.

REFORMS

The protecting minority investors indicator set captures changes related to the regulation of related-party transactions as well as corporate governance every year. Depending on the impact on the data, certain changes are listed in the summaries of *Doing Business* reforms in 2015/2016 section of the report in order to acknowledge the implementation of significant changes. They are divided into two types: reforms that make it easier to do business and changes that make it more difficult to do business. The protecting minority investors indicator set uses the following criteria to recognize a reform:

All legislative and regulatory changes that impact the score assigned to a given economy on any of the 48 questions comprising the six indicators on minority investor protection are classified as a reform. The change must be mandatory, meaning that failure to comply allows shareholders to sue in court or for sanctions to be leveled by a regulatory body such as the company registrar, the capital market authority or the securities and exchange commission. Guidelines, model rules, principles, recommendations and duties to explain in case of non-compliance are excluded. When a change exclusively affects companies that are listed on the stock exchange, it will be captured only if the stock exchange has 10 or more equity listings. If the economy has no stock exchange or a stock exchange with less than 10 equity listings, the change is taken into account only if it affects companies irrespective of whether their shares are listed or not.

Reforms impacting the protecting minority investors indicator set include amendments to or the introduction of a new companies act, commercial code, securities regulation, code of civil procedure, court rules, law, decree, order, supreme court decision, or stock exchange listing rule. The changes must affect the rights and duties of issuers, company managers, directors and shareholders in connection with related-party transactions or, more generally, the aspects of corporate governance measured by the indicators. For example in a given economy, related-party transactions have to be approved by the board of directors including board members who have a personal financial interest in seeing the transaction succeed. This economy introduces a law requiring that related-party transactions be approved instead by a general meeting of shareholders and that excludes shareholders with conflicting interests from participating in the vote. This law would result in a 2-point increase on the corresponding question in the extent of disclosure index and would therefore be acknowledged in the report.

The data details on protecting minority investors can be found for each economy at http://www.doingbusiness.org. The initial methodology was developed by Djankov, La Porta and others (2008).

PAYING TAXES

Doing Business records the taxes and mandatory contributions that a medium-size company must pay in a given year as well as measures of the administrative burden of paying taxes and contributions and complying with postfiling procedures (figure 12.13). The project was developed and implemented in cooperation with PwC.[11] Taxes and contributions measured include the profit or corporate income tax, social contributions and labor taxes paid by the employer, property taxes, property transfer taxes, dividend tax, capital gains tax, financial transactions tax, waste collection taxes, vehicle and road taxes, and any other small taxes or fees.

The ranking of economies on the ease of paying taxes is determined by sorting their distance to frontier scores for paying taxes. These scores are the simple average of the distance to frontier scores for each of the component indicators (figure 12.14), with a threshold and a nonlinear transformation applied to one of the component indicators, the total tax rate.[12] The threshold is defined as the total tax rate at the 15th percentile of the overall distribution for all years included in the analysis up to and including *Doing Business 2015*, which is 26.1%. All economies with a total tax rate below this threshold receive the same score as the economy at the threshold.

The threshold is not based on any economic theory of an "optimal tax rate" that minimizes distortions or maximizes efficiency in an economy's overall tax system. Instead, it is mainly empirical in nature, set at the lower end of the distribution of tax rates levied on medium-size enterprises in the manufacturing sector as observed through the paying taxes indicators. This reduces the bias in the total tax rate indicator toward economies that do not need to levy significant taxes on companies like the *Doing Business* standardized case study company because they raise public revenue in other ways—for example, through taxes on foreign companies, through taxes on sectors other than manufacturing or from natural resources (all of which are outside the scope of the methodology).

FIGURE 12.13 What are the time, total tax rate and number of payments necessary for a local medium-size company to pay all taxes and how efficient is it for a local medium-size company to comply with postfiling processes?

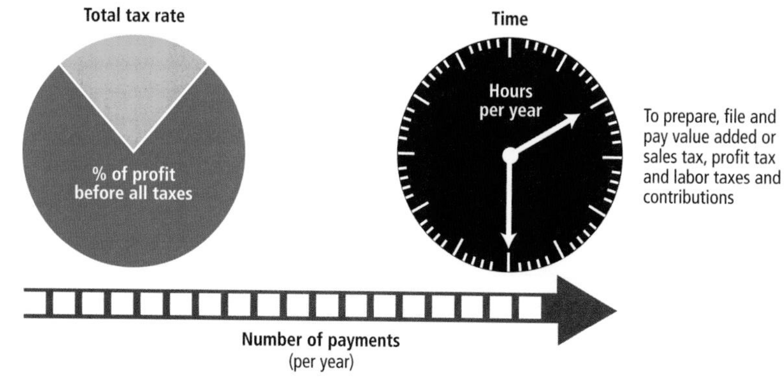

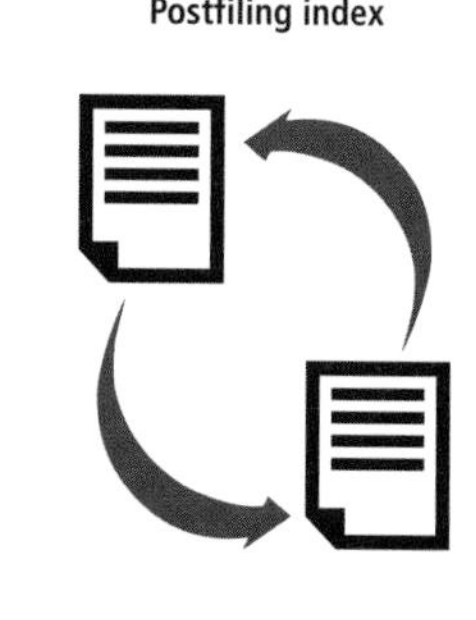

FIGURE 12.14 Paying taxes: tax compliance for a local manufacturing company

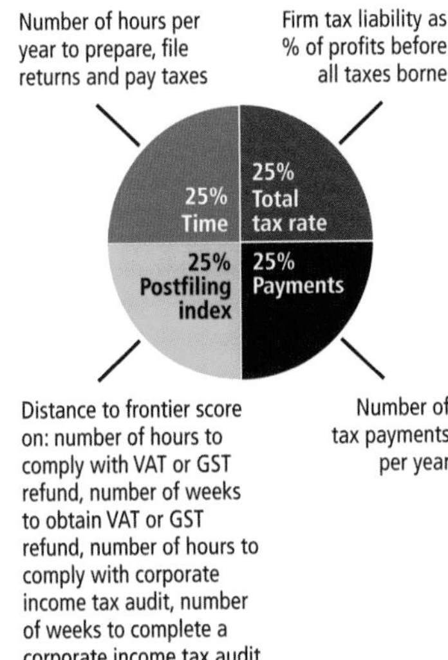

Note: All economies below the threshold receive the same score in the total tax rate component as the economies at the threshold. If both VAT (or GST) and corporate income tax apply, the postfiling index is the simple average of the distance to frontier scores for each of the four components: time to comply with VAT or GST refund, time to obtain VAT or GST refund, time to comply with corporate income tax audit and time to complete a corporate income tax audit. If only VAT (or GST) or corporate income tax applies, the postfiling index is the simple average of the scores for only the two components pertaining to the applicable tax. If neither VAT (or GST) nor corporate income tax applies, the postfiling index is not included in the ranking of the ease of paying taxes.

Doing Business measures all taxes and contributions that are government mandated (at any level—federal, state or local) and that apply to the standardized business and have an impact in its financial statements. In doing so, *Doing Business* goes beyond the traditional definition of a tax. As defined for the purposes of government national accounts, taxes include only compulsory, unrequited payments to general government. *Doing Business* departs from this definition because it measures imposed charges that affect business accounts, not government accounts. One main difference relates to labor contributions. The *Doing Business* measure includes government-mandated contributions paid by the employer to a requited private pension fund or workers' insurance fund. It includes, for example, Australia's compulsory superannuation guarantee and workers' compensation insurance. For the purpose of calculating the total tax rate (defined below), only taxes borne are included. For example, value added taxes (VAT) are generally excluded (provided that they are not irrecoverable) because they do not affect the accounting profits of the business—that is, they are not reflected in the income statement. They are, however, included for the purpose of the compliance measures (time and payments), as they add to the burden of complying with the tax system.

Doing Business uses a case scenario to measure the taxes and contributions paid by a standardized business and the complexity of an economy's tax compliance system. This case scenario uses a set of financial statements and assumptions about transactions made over the course of the year. In each economy tax experts from a number of different firms (in many economies these include PwC) compute the taxes and mandatory contributions due in their jurisdiction based on the standardized case study facts. Information is also compiled on the frequency of filing and payments, the time taken to comply with tax laws in an economy, the time taken to request and process a VAT refund claim and the time taken to comply with and complete a corporate income tax audit. To make the data comparable across economies, several assumptions about the business and the taxes and contributions are used.

Assumptions about the business

The business:

- Is a limited liability, taxable company. If there is more than one type of limited liability company in the economy, the limited liability form most common among domestic firms is chosen. The most common form is reported by incorporation lawyers or the statistical office.
- Started operations on January 1, 2014. At that time the company purchased all the assets shown in its balance sheet and hired all its workers.
- Operates in the economy's largest business city. For 11 economies the data are also collected for the second largest business city (table 12A.1).
- Is 100% domestically owned and has five owners, all of whom are natural persons.
- At the end of 2014, has a start-up capital of 102 times income per capita.
- Performs general industrial or commercial activities. Specifically, it produces ceramic flowerpots and sells them at retail. It does not participate in foreign trade (no import or export) and does not handle products subject to a special tax regime, for example, liquor or tobacco.
- At the beginning of 2015, owns two plots of land, one building, machinery, office equipment, computers and one truck and leases one truck.
- Does not qualify for investment incentives or any benefits apart from those related to the age or size of the company.
- Has 60 employees—4 managers, 8 assistants and 48 workers. All are nationals, and one manager is also an owner. The company pays for additional medical insurance for employees (not mandated by any law) as an additional benefit. In addition, in some economies reimbursable business travel and client entertainment expenses are considered fringe benefits. When applicable, it is assumed that the company pays the fringe benefit tax on this expense or that the benefit becomes taxable income for the employee. The case study assumes no additional salary additions for meals, transportation, education or others. Therefore, even when such benefits are frequent, they are not added to or removed from the taxable gross salaries to arrive at the labor tax or contribution calculation.
- Has a turnover of 1,050 times income per capita.
- Makes a loss in the first year of operation.

- Has a gross margin (pretax) of 20% (that is, sales are 120% of the cost of goods sold).
- Distributes 50% of its net profits as dividends to the owners at the end of the second year.
- Sells one of its plots of land at a profit at the beginning of the second year.
- Is subject to a series of detailed assumptions on expenses and transactions to further standardize the case. For example, the owner who is also a manager spends 10% of income per capita on traveling for the company (20% of this owner's expenses are purely private, 20% are for entertaining customers, and 60% are for business travel). All financial statement variables are proportional to 2012 income per capita (this is an update from *Doing Business 2013* and previous years' reports, where the variables were proportional to 2005 income per capita). For some economies a multiple of two or three times income per capita has been used to estimate the financial statement variables.[13] The 2012 income per capita was not sufficient to bring the salaries of all the case study employees up to the minimum wage thresholds that exist in these economies.

Assumptions about the taxes and contributions

- All the taxes and contributions recorded are those paid in the second year of operation (calendar year 2015). A tax or contribution is considered distinct if it has a different name or is collected by a different agency. Taxes and contributions with the same name and agency, but charged at different rates depending on the business, are counted as the same tax or contribution.
- The number of times the company pays taxes and contributions in a year is the number of different taxes or contributions multiplied by the frequency of payment (or withholding) for each tax. The frequency of payment includes advance payments (or withholding) as well as regular payments (or withholding).

Tax payments

The tax payments indicator reflects the total number of taxes and contributions paid, the method of payment, the frequency of payment, the frequency of filing and the number of agencies involved for the standardized case study company during the second year of operation (table 12.12). It includes taxes withheld by the company, such as sales tax, VAT and employee-borne labor taxes. These taxes are traditionally collected by the company from the consumer or employee on behalf of the tax agencies. Although they do not affect the income statements of the company, they add to the administrative burden of complying with the tax system and so are included in the tax payments measure.

The number of payments takes into account electronic filing. Where full electronic filing and payment is allowed and it is used by the majority of medium-size businesses, the tax is counted as paid once a year even if filings and payments are more frequent. For payments made through third parties, such as tax on interest paid by a financial institution or fuel tax paid by a fuel distributor, only one payment is included even if payments are more frequent.

Where two or more taxes or contributions are filed for and paid jointly using the same form, each of these joint payments is counted once. For example, if mandatory health insurance contributions and mandatory pension contributions are filed for and paid together, only one of these contributions would be included in the number of payments.

Time

Time is recorded in hours per year. The indicator measures the time taken to prepare, file and pay three major types of taxes and contributions: the corporate income tax, value added or sales tax, and labor taxes, including payroll taxes and social contributions. Preparation time includes the time to collect all information necessary to compute the tax payable and to calculate the amount payable. If separate accounting books must be kept for tax purposes—or separate calculations made—the time associated with these processes is included. This extra time is included only if the regular accounting work is not enough to fulfill the tax accounting requirements. Filing time includes the time to complete all necessary tax return forms and file the relevant returns at the tax authority. Payment time considers the hours needed to make the payment online or in person. Where taxes and contributions are paid in person, the time includes delays while waiting.

TABLE 12.12 What do the paying taxes indicators measure?

Tax payments for a manufacturing company in 2015 (number per year adjusted for electronic and joint filing and payment)
Total number of taxes and contributions paid, including consumption taxes (value added tax, sales tax or goods and service tax)
Method and frequency of filing and payment
Time required to comply with three major taxes (hours per year)
Collecting information and computing the tax payable
Completing tax return forms, filing with proper agencies
Arranging payment or withholding
Preparing separate mandatory tax accounting books, if required
Total tax rate (% of profit before all taxes)
Profit or corporate income tax
Social contributions and labor taxes paid by the employer
Property and property transfer taxes
Dividend, capital gains and financial transactions taxes
Waste collection, vehicle, road and other taxes
Postfiling index
Compliance time of a VAT or GST refund process
Time to receive a VAT or GST refund
Compliance time of correcting an error in the corporate income tax return including compliance with an audit process if applicable
Time to complete a corporate income tax audit

Total tax rate

The total tax rate measures the amount of taxes and mandatory contributions borne by the business in the second year of operation, expressed as a share of commercial profit. *Doing Business 2017* reports the total tax rate for calendar year 2015. The total amount of taxes borne is the sum of all the different taxes and contributions payable after accounting for allowable deductions and exemptions. The taxes withheld (such as personal income tax) or collected by the company and remitted to the tax authorities (such as VAT, sales tax or goods and service tax) but not borne by the company are excluded. The taxes included can be divided into five categories: profit or corporate income tax, social contributions and labor taxes paid by the employer (for which all mandatory contributions are included, even if paid to a private entity such as a requited pension fund), property taxes, turnover taxes and other taxes (such as municipal fees and vehicle taxes). Fuel taxes are no longer included in the total tax rate because of the difficulty of computing these taxes in a consistent way for all economies covered. The fuel tax amounts are in most cases very small, and measuring these amounts is often complicated because they depend on fuel consumption. Fuel taxes continue to be counted in the number of payments.

The total tax rate is designed to provide a comprehensive measure of the cost of all the taxes a business bears. It differs from the statutory tax rate, which merely provides the factor to be applied to the tax base. In computing the total tax rate, the actual tax payable is divided by commercial profit. Data for Iraq are provided as an example (table 12.13).

TABLE 12.13 Computing the total tax rate for Iraq

Type of tax (tax base)	Statutory rate r (%)	Statutory tax base b (ID)	Actual tax payable $a = r \times b$ (ID)	Commercial profit* c (ID)	Total tax rate $t = a/c$ (%)
Corporate income tax (taxable income)	15	432,461,855	64,869,278	453,188,210	14.3
Employer-paid social security contributions (taxable wages)	12	511,191,307	61,342,957	453,188,210	13.5
Total			**126,212,235**		**27.8**

Source: Doing Business database.
Note: Commercial profit is assumed to be 59.4 times income per capita. ID is Iraqi dinar.
* Profit before all taxes borne.

Commercial profit is essentially net profit before all taxes borne. It differs from the conventional profit before tax, reported in financial statements. In computing profit before tax, many of the taxes borne by a firm are deductible. In computing commercial profit, these taxes are not deductible. Commercial profit therefore presents a clear picture of the actual profit of a business before any of the taxes it bears in the course of the fiscal year.

Commercial profit is computed as sales minus cost of goods sold, minus gross salaries, minus administrative expenses, minus other expenses, minus provisions, plus capital gains (from the property sale) minus interest expense, plus interest income and minus commercial depreciation. To compute the commercial depreciation, a straight-line depreciation method is applied, with the following rates: 0% for the land, 5% for the building, 10% for the machinery, 33% for the computers, 20% for the office equipment, 20% for the truck and 10% for business development expenses. Commercial profit amounts to 59.4 times income per capita.

The methodology for calculating the total tax rate is broadly consistent with the Total Tax Contribution framework developed by PwC and the calculation within this framework for taxes borne. But while the work undertaken by PwC is usually based on data received from the largest companies in the economy, *Doing Business* focuses on a case study for a standardized medium-size company.

Postfiling index

The postfiling index is based on four components—time to comply with VAT or GST refund, time to obtain VAT or GST refund, time to comply with corporate income tax audit and time to complete a corporate income tax audit. If both VAT (or GST) and corporate income tax apply, the postfiling index is the simple average of the distance to frontier scores for each of the four components. If only VAT (or GST) or corporate income tax applies, the postfiling index is the simple average of the scores for only the two components pertaining to the applicable tax. If neither VAT (or GST) nor corporate income tax applies, the postfiling index is not included in the ranking of the ease of paying taxes.

The indicators are based on expanded case study assumptions.

Assumptions about the VAT refund process

- In June 2015, TaxpayerCo. makes a large capital purchase: one additional machine for manufacturing pots.
- The value of the machine is 65 times income per capita of the economy.
- Sales are equally spread per month (that is, 1,050 times income per capita divided by 12).
- Cost of goods sold are equally expensed per month (that is, 875 times income per capita divided by 12).
- The seller of the machinery is registered for VAT or general sales tax (GST).
- Excess input VAT incurred in June will be fully recovered after four consecutive months if the VAT or GST rate is the same for inputs, sales and the machine and the tax reporting period is every month.

Assumptions about the corporate income tax audit process

- An error in the calculation of the income tax liability (for example, use of incorrect tax depreciation rates, or incorrectly treating an expense as tax deductible) leads to an incorrect income tax return and consequently an underpayment of corporate income tax.
- TaxpayerCo. discovered the error and voluntarily notified the tax authority of the error in the corporate income tax return.
- The value of the underpaid income tax liability is 5% of the corporate income tax liability due.
- TaxpayerCo. submits the corrected information after the deadline for submitting the annual tax return, but within the tax assessment period.

Time to comply with VAT refund

Time is recorded in hours. The indicator has two parts:

- The process of claiming a VAT or GST refund. Time includes: time spent by TaxpayerCo. on gathering VAT information from internal sources, including time spent on any additional analysis of accounting information and calculating the VAT refund amount; time spent by TaxpayerCo. on preparing the VAT refund claim; time spent by TaxpayerCo. preparing any additional documents that are needed to substantiate the claim for the VAT refund; time spent making representation at the tax office if required and time spent by TaxpayerCo. completing any other mandatory activities or tasks associated with the VAT or GST refund. Input VAT will exceed Output VAT in June 2015 (table 12.14).
- The process of an audit if the case scenario is likely to trigger an audit. Time includes: time spent by TaxpayerCo. on gathering information and preparing any documentation (information such as receipts, financial statements, pay stubs) as required by the tax auditor; time spent by TaxpayerCo. in submitting the documents requested by the auditor.

A total estimate of zero hours is recorded if the process of claiming a VAT or GST refund is done automatically within the standard VAT or GST return without the need to complete any additional section or part of the return, no additional documents or tasks are required as a result of the input tax credit and the case scenario is unlikely to trigger an audit. It is assumed that in cases where taxpayers are required to submit a specific form for a VAT refund request and additional documents these are submitted at the same time as the VAT return.

An estimate of half an hour is recorded for submission of documents requested during an audit in the case of an audit taking place if the submission is done electronically and takes a matter of minutes. An estimate of zero hours is recorded in the case of a field audit if documents are submitted in person and at the taxpayer's premises.

In Kosovo, for example, taxpayers spend 30 hours complying with the process of claiming a VAT refund. Taxpayers must submit a special form for a VAT refund request in addition to the standard VAT return. Taxpayers spend two hours gathering information from internal sources and accounting records and 1 hour to prepare the form. Taxpayers must also prepare and have available for review all purchase and sales invoices for the past three months, a business explanation of VAT overpayment for large purchases or investments, bank statements, any missing tax declaration and a copy of fiscal and VAT certificates. Taxpayers spend four hours preparing these additional documents. Taxpayers must also appear in person at the tax office to explain the VAT refund claim and the reasons for the excess input VAT in the month of June. This takes three hours. Additionally, the claim for a VAT refund would trigger a full audit at the taxpayer's premises. Taxpayers spend 20 hours preparing the documents requested by the auditor including purchase and sales invoices, bills, bank transactions, records on accounting software, tax returns and contracts. Taxpayers submit the documents to the auditor in person at their premises (zero hours for submission).

Time to obtain VAT refund

Time is recorded in weeks. Time measures the total waiting time to receive a VAT or GST refund from the moment the request has been submitted. If the case scenario is likely to trigger an audit, time includes time spent by TaxpayerCo. interacting with the auditor from the moment an audit begins until there are no further interactions between TaxpayerCo. and the auditor (including the various rounds of interactions between TaxpayerCo. and the auditor) and the time spent waiting for the tax auditor to issue the final tax assessment from the moment TaxpayerCo. has submitted all relevant information and documents and there are no further interactions between TaxpayerCo. and the auditor.

TABLE 12.14 Computing the value of the VAT/GST input tax credit for Albania

	VAT rate *R*	Output VAT *R x Sales*	Input VAT *(R x A + R x B)*
Sales = ALL 37,398,864.84	20%	ALL 7,479,772.97	
Capital purchase (A) = ALL 27,782,013.88	20%		ALL 5,556,402.78
Raw material expenses (B) = ALL 31,165,720.70	20%		ALL 6,233,144.14
VAT refund *(R x A + R x B) – (R x Sales)*			ALL 4,309,773.95

Source: Doing Business database.

Time includes an average waiting time to submit the refund claim. The average waiting time to submit the refund claim is half a month if the VAT or GST refund claim is filed monthly. The average waiting time to submit the refund claim is one month if the VAT or GST refund claim is filed bimonthly. The average waiting time to submit the refund claim is one and a half months if the VAT or GST refund claim is filed quarterly. The average waiting time to submit the refund claim is three months if the VAT or GST refund claim is filed semi-annually. The average waiting time to submit the refund claim is six months if the VAT or GST refund claim is filed annually.

Time includes the mandatory carry forward time before a VAT refund in cash can be paid. The carry forward time is zero if there is no mandatory carry forward period.

In Albania, for example, it takes 27.7 weeks to receive a VAT refund. The request for a VAT refund triggers an audit by the tax authorities. Taxpayers spend 8.6 weeks interacting with the auditor and wait four weeks until the final assessment is issued. Taxpayers only receive the VAT refund after the audit is completed. In Albania the taxpayers must carry forward the VAT refund for three consecutive VAT accounting periods (three months in the case of Albania) before a refund in cash is requested. The three months (13 weeks) carry forward period is included in the total time to receive a VAT refund. The VAT return is filed monthly and thus 0.5 month (2.1 weeks) is included in the total time to receive a VAT refund.

If an economy does not have a VAT or GST, the economy will not be scored on the two indicators for a VAT or GST refund process—time to comply with VAT refund and time to obtain VAT refund. This is the case in Bahrain. If an economy has a VAT or GST and the purchase of a machine is not subject to VAT, the economy will not be scored on time to comply with VAT refund and time to obtain VAT refund. This is the case in Sierra Leone. If an economy has a VAT or GST that was introduced in calendar year 2015 and there is not sufficient data to assess the refund process, the economy will not be scored on time to comply with VAT refund and time to obtain VAT refund. This is the case in Malaysia, which replaced sales tax with GST on April 1, 2015.

If an economy has a VAT or GST but the ability to claim a refund is restricted to specific categories of taxpayers that do not include the case study company, the economy is assigned a score of 0 on the distance to frontier score for time to comply with VAT refund and time to obtain VAT refund. In Bolivia, for example, only exporters are eligible to request a VAT refund. As a result, Bolivia receives a score of 0 on the distance to frontier score for time to comply with VAT refund and time to obtain VAT refund. If an economy has a VAT or GST and the case study company is eligible to claim a refund but cash refunds do not occur in practice, the economy is assigned a score of 0 on the distance to frontier score for time to comply with VAT refund and time to obtain VAT refund. This is the case in Central African Republic. If an economy has a VAT or GST but there is no refund mechanism in place, the economy is assigned a score of 0 on the distance to frontier score for time to comply with VAT refund and time to obtain VAT refund. This is the case in Grenada. If an economy has a VAT or GST but input tax on a capital purchase is a cost on the business, the economy is scored 0 on the distance to frontier score for time to comply with VAT refund and time to obtain VAT refund. This is the case in Myanmar. If an economy has a VAT or GST and legislation mandates that taxpayers carry forward the excess input tax for four months or more before a cash refund can be requested, the economy is scored 0 on the distance to frontier score for time to comply with VAT refund and time to obtain VAT refund. This is the case in Antigua and Barbuda.

Time to comply with corporate income tax audit

Time is recorded in hours. The indicator has two parts:

- The process of notifying the tax authorities of the error, amending the return and making additional payment. Time includes: time spent by TaxpayerCo. gathering information and preparing the documents required to notify the tax authorities; time spent by TaxpayerCo. in submitting the documents; and time spent by TaxpayerCo. in making the additional tax payment.
- The process of an audit if the case scenario is likely to trigger an audit. Time includes: time spent by TaxpayerCo. on gathering information and preparing any documentation (information such as receipts, financial statements, pay stubs) as required by the tax auditor; and time spent by TaxpayerCo. in submitting the documents requested by the auditor.

An estimate of half an hour is recorded for submission of documents or payment of the income tax liability due if the submission or payment is done electronically and takes several minutes. An estimate of zero hours is recorded in the case of a field audit if documents are submitted in person and at the taxpayer's premises.

In the Slovak Republic, for example, taxpayers would submit an amended corporate income tax return electronically. It takes taxpayers one hour to correct the error in the return, half an hour to submit the amended return online and half an hour to make the additional payment online. Amending a corporate income tax return per the case study scenario in the Slovak Republic would not trigger an audit. This brings the total compliance time to two hours.

Time to complete a corporate income tax audit

Time is recorded in weeks. Time includes the time spent by TaxpayerCo. interacting with the auditor from the moment an audit begins until there are no further interactions between TaxpayerCo. and the auditor (including the various rounds of interactions between TaxpayerCo. and the auditor). Time also includes the time spent waiting for the tax auditor to issue the final tax assessment—from the moment TaxpayerCo. has submitted all relevant information and documents and there are no further interactions between TaxpayerCo. and the auditor.

Time to complete a corporate income tax audit is recorded as zero if the case study scenario is unlikely to trigger an audit.

In Switzerland, for example, taxpayers are subject to a single issue audit conducted at the taxpayer's premises as a result of amending a corporate income tax return per the case study scenario. Taxpayers interact for a total of four days (0.6 weeks) with the auditor and wait for four weeks until the final assessment is issued by the auditor, resulting in a total of 4.6 weeks to complete a corporate income tax audit.

If an economy does not levy corporate income tax, the economy will not be scored on the two indicators: time to comply with corporate income tax audit and time to complete a corporate income tax audit. This is the case in Vanuatu.

REFORMS

The paying taxes indicator set tracks changes related to the different taxes and mandatory contributions that a medium-size company must pay in a given year, the administrative burden of paying taxes and contributions and the administrative burden of complying with two postfiling processes (VAT refund, and tax audit) per calendar year. Depending on the impact on the data, certain changes are classified as reforms and listed in the summaries of *Doing Business* reforms in 2015/2016 section of the report in order to acknowledge the implementation of significant changes. Reforms are divided into two types: those that make it easier to do business and those changes that make it more difficult to do business. The paying taxes indicator set uses one criterion to recognize a reform.

The aggregate gap on the overall distance to frontier of the indicator set is used to assess the impact of data changes. Any data update that leads to a change of 2 or more percentage points on the relative distance to frontier gap is classified as a reform (for more details on the relative gap, see the chapter on the distance to frontier and ease of doing business ranking). For example if the implementation of a new electronic system for filing or paying one of the three major taxes (corporate income tax, VAT or GST, labor taxes and mandatory contributions) reduces time and/or the number of payments in a way that the overall relative gap decreases by 2 percentage points or more, such change is classified as a reform. Alternatively, minor updates to tax rates or fixed charges or other smaller changes in the indicators that have an aggregate impact less than 2 percentage points on the relative gap are not classified as a reform, but their impact is still reflected on the most updated indicators for this indicator set.

The data details on paying taxes can be found for each economy at http://www.doingbusiness.org. This methodology was developed by Djankov and others (2010).

TRADING ACROSS BORDERS

Doing Business records the time and cost associated with the logistical process of exporting and importing goods. *Doing Business* measures the time and cost (excluding tariffs) associated with three sets of procedures—documentary compliance, border compliance and domestic transport—within the overall process of exporting or importing a shipment of goods. Figure 12.15, using the example of Brazil (as exporter) and China (as importer), shows the process of exporting a shipment from a warehouse in the origin economy to a warehouse in an overseas trading partner through a port. Figure 12.16, using the example of Kenya

FIGURE 12.15 What makes up the time and cost to export to an overseas trading partner?

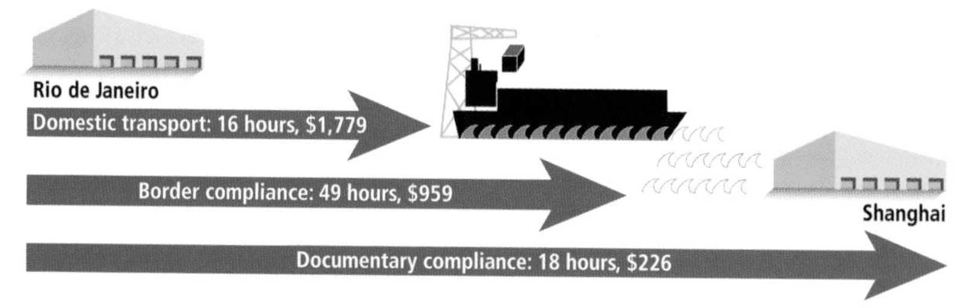

Source: Doing Business database.

FIGURE 12.16 What makes up the time and cost to export to a regional trading partner?

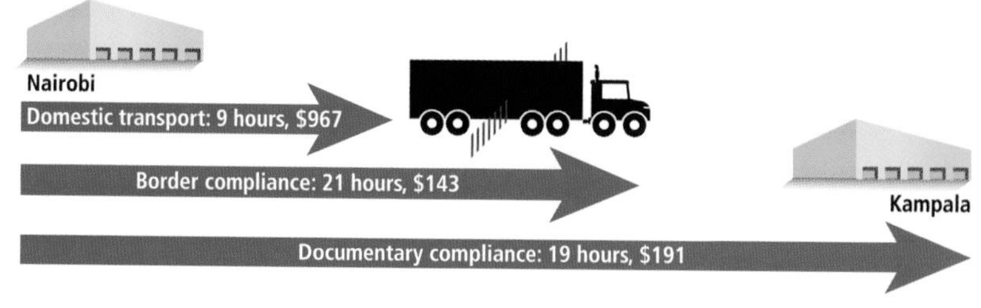

Source: Doing Business database.

(as exporter) and Uganda (as importer), shows the process of exporting a shipment from a warehouse in the origin economy to a warehouse in a regional trading partner through a land border. The ranking of economies on the ease of trading across borders is determined by sorting their distance to frontier scores for trading across borders. These scores are the simple average of the distance to frontier scores for the time and cost for documentary compliance and border compliance to export and import (figure 12.17).

Although *Doing Business* collects and publishes data on the time and cost for domestic transport, it does not use these data in calculating the distance to frontier score for trading across borders or the ranking on the ease of trading across borders. The main reason for this is that the time and cost for domestic transport are affected by many external factors—such as the geography and topography of the transit territory, road capacity and general infrastructure, proximity to the nearest port or border, and the location of warehouses where the traded goods are stored—and so are not directly influenced by an economy's trade policies and reforms.

FIGURE 12.17 Trading across borders: time and cost to export and import

Rankings are based on distance to frontier scores for eight indicators

Time for documentary compliance and border compliance when exporting the product of comparative advantage

Cost for documentary compliance and border compliance when exporting the product of comparative advantage

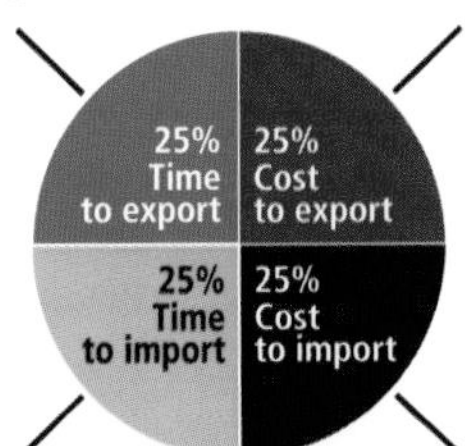

Time for documentary compliance and border compliance when importing auto parts

Cost for documentary compliance and border compliance when importing auto parts

Note: The time and cost for domestic transport and the number of documents to export and import are measured but do not count for the rankings.

The data on trading across borders are gathered through a questionnaire administered to local freight forwarders, customs brokers, port authorities and traders. Questionnaire responses are verified through several rounds of follow-up communication with respondents as well as by contacting third parties and consulting public sources. The questionnaire data are confirmed through teleconference calls or on-site visits in most economies.

If an economy has no formal, large-scale, private sector cross-border trade taking place as a result of government restrictions, armed conflict or a natural disaster, it is considered a "no practice" economy. A "no practice" economy receives a distance to frontier score of 0 for all the trading across borders indicators.

Assumptions of the case study

To make the data comparable across economies, several assumptions are made about the traded goods and the transactions:

- For each of the 190 economies covered by *Doing Business*, it is assumed that a shipment travels from a warehouse in the largest business city of the exporting economy to a warehouse in the largest business city of the importing economy. For 11 economies the data are also collected, under the same case study assumptions, for the second largest business city (table 12A.1).
- The import and export case studies assume different traded products. It is assumed that each economy imports a standardized shipment of 15 metric tons of containerized auto parts (HS 8708) from its natural import partner—the economy from which it imports the largest value (price times quantity) of auto parts. It is assumed that each economy exports the product of its comparative advantage (defined by the largest export value) to its natural export partner—the economy that is the largest purchaser of this product. Precious metal and gems, mineral fuels, oil products, live animals, residues and waste of foods and products as well as pharmaceuticals are excluded from the list of possible export products, however, and in these cases the second largest product category is considered as needed.[14]
- A shipment is a unit of trade. Export shipments do not necessarily need to be containerized, while import shipments of auto parts are assumed to be containerized.
- If government fees are determined by the value of the shipment, the value is assumed to be $50,000.
- The product is new, not secondhand or used merchandise.
- The exporting/importing firm hires and pays for a freight forwarder or customs broker (or both) and pays for all costs related to international shipping, domestic transport, clearance and mandatory inspections by customs and other government agencies, port or border handling, documentary compliance fees and the like.
- The mode of transport is the one most widely used for the chosen export or import product and the trading partner, as is the seaport or land border crossing.
- All electronic submissions of information requested by any government agency in connection with the shipment are considered to be documents obtained, prepared and submitted during the export or import process.
- A port or border is defined as a place (seaport or land border crossing) where merchandise can enter or leave an economy.
- Government agencies considered relevant are agencies such as customs, port authorities, road police, border guards, standardization agencies, ministries or departments of agriculture or industry, national security agencies, central banks and any other government authorities.

Time

Time is measured in hours, and 1 day is 24 hours (for example, 22 days are recorded as 22 × 24 = 528 hours). If customs clearance takes 7.5 hours, the data are recorded as is. Alternatively, suppose that documents are submitted to a customs agency at 8:00 a.m., are processed overnight and can be picked up at 8:00 a.m. the next day. In this case the time for customs clearance would be recorded as 24 hours because the actual procedure took 24 hours.

Cost

Insurance cost and informal payments for which no receipt is issued are excluded from the costs recorded. Costs are reported in U.S. dollars. Contributors are asked to convert local currency into U.S. dollars based on the exchange rate prevailing on the day they answer the questionnaire. Contributors are private sector experts in international trade logistics and are informed about exchange rates and their movements.

TABLE 12.15 What do the indicators on the time and cost to export and import cover?

Documentary compliance
Obtaining, preparing and submitting documents during transport, clearance, inspections and port or border handling in origin economy
Obtaining, preparing and submitting documents required by destination economy and any transit economies
Covers all documents required by law and in practice, including electronic submissions of information as well as non-shipment-specific documents necessary to complete the trade
Border compliance
Customs clearance and inspections by customs
Inspections by other agencies (if applied to more than 10% of shipments)
Port or border handling at most widely used port or border of economy
Domestic transport
Loading and unloading of shipment at warehouse, dry port or border
Transport by most widely used mode between warehouse and terminal or dry port
Transport by most widely used mode between terminal or dry port and most widely used border or port
Traffic delays and road police checks while shipment is en route

Documentary compliance

Documentary compliance captures the time and cost associated with compliance with the documentary requirements of all government agencies of the origin economy, the destination economy and any transit economies (table 12.15). The aim is to measure the total burden of preparing the bundle of documents that will enable completion of the international trade for the product and partner pair assumed in the case study. As a shipment moves from Mumbai to New York City, for example, the freight forwarder must prepare and submit documents to the customs agency in India, to the port authorities in Mumbai and to the customs agency in New York City.

The time and cost for documentary compliance include the time and cost for obtaining documents (such as time spent to get the document issued and stamped); preparing documents (such as time spent gathering information to complete the customs declaration or certificate of origin); processing documents (such as time spent waiting for the relevant authority to issue a phytosanitary certificate); presenting documents (such as time spent showing a port terminal receipt to port authorities); and submitting documents (such as time spent submitting a customs declaration to the customs agency in person or electronically).

All electronic or paper submissions of information requested by any government agency in connection with the shipment are considered to be documents obtained, prepared and submitted during the export or import process. All documents prepared by the freight forwarder or customs broker for the product and partner pair assumed in the case study are included regardless of whether they are required by law or in practice. Any documents prepared and submitted so as to get access to preferential treatment—for example, a certificate of origin—are included in the calculation of the time and cost for documentary compliance. Any documents prepared and submitted because of a perception that they ease the passage of the shipment are also included (for example, freight forwarders may prepare a packing list because in their experience this reduces the probability of physical or other intrusive inspections).

In addition, any documents that are mandatory for exporting or importing are included in the calculation of time and cost. Documents that need to be obtained only once are not counted, however. And *Doing Business* does not include documents needed to produce and sell in the domestic market—such as certificates of third-party safety standards testing that may be required to sell toys domestically—unless a government agency needs to see these documents during the export process.

Border compliance

Border compliance captures the time and cost associated with compliance with the economy's customs regulations and with regulations relating to other inspections that are mandatory in order for the shipment to cross the economy's border, as well as the time and cost for handling that takes place at its port or border. The time and cost for this segment include time and cost for customs clearance and inspection procedures conducted by other government agencies. For example, the time and cost for conducting a phytosanitary inspection would be included here.

The computation of border compliance time and cost depends on where the border compliance procedures take place, who requires and conducts the procedures and what is the probability that inspections will be conducted. If all customs clearance and other inspections take place at the port or border, the time estimate for border compliance takes this simultaneity into account. It is entirely possible that the border compliance time and cost could be negligible or zero, as in the case of trade between members of the European Union or other customs unions.

If some or all customs or other inspections take place at other locations, the time and cost for these procedures are added to the time and cost for those that take place at the port or border. In Kazakhstan, for example, all customs clearance and inspections take place at a customs post in Almaty that is not at the land border between Kazakhstan and China. In this case border compliance time is the sum of the time spent at the terminal in Almaty and the handling time at the border.

Doing Business asks contributors to estimate the time and cost for clearance and inspections by customs agencies—defined as documentary and physical inspections for the purpose of calculating duties by verifying product classification, confirming quantity, determining origin and checking the veracity of other information on the customs declaration. (This category includes all inspections aimed at preventing smuggling.) These are clearance and inspection procedures that take place in the majority of cases and thus are considered the "standard" case. The time and cost estimates capture the efficiency of the customs agency of the economy.

Doing Business also asks contributors to estimate the total time and cost for clearance and inspections by customs and all other government agencies for the specified product. These estimates account for inspections related to health, safety, phytosanitary standards, conformity and the like, and thus capture the efficiency of agencies that require and conduct these additional inspections.

If inspections by agencies other than customs are conducted in 20% or fewer cases, the border compliance time and cost measures take into account only clearance and inspections by customs (the standard case). If inspections by other agencies take place in more than 20% of cases, the time and cost measures account for clearance and inspections by all agencies. Different types of inspections may take place with different probabilities—for example, scanning may take place in 100% of cases while physical inspection occurs in 5% of cases. In situations like this, *Doing Business* would count the time only for scanning because it happens in more than 20% of cases while physical inspection does not. The border compliance time and cost for an economy do not include the time and cost for compliance with the regulations of any other economy.

Domestic transport

Domestic transport captures the time and cost associated with transporting the shipment from a warehouse in the largest business city of the economy to the most widely used seaport, airport or land border of the economy. For 11 economies the data are also collected for the second largest business city (table 12A.1). This set of procedures captures the time for (and cost of) the actual transport; any traffic delays and road police checks; as well as time spent on loading or unloading at the warehouse or border. For a coastal economy with an overseas trading partner, domestic transport captures the time and cost from the loading of the shipment at the warehouse until the shipment reaches the economy's port (figure 12.15). For an economy trading through a land border, domestic transport captures the time and cost from the loading of the shipment at the warehouse until the shipment reaches the economy's land border (figure 12.16).

The time and cost estimates are based on the most widely used mode of transport (truck, train, riverboat) and the most widely used route (road, border posts) as reported by contributors. In the overwhelming majority of cases all contributors in an economy agree on the mode and route. In the few remaining cases *Doing Business* consulted additional contributors to get a sense of why there was disagreement. In these cases time and cost estimates are based on the mode and route chosen by the majority of contributors. For the 11 economies for which data are collected for both the largest and the second largest business city, *Doing Business* allows the most widely used route and the most widely used mode of transport to be different for the two cities. For example, shipments from Delhi are transported by train to Mundra port for export, while shipments from Mumbai travel by truck to Nhava Sheva port to be exported.

In the export case study, as noted, *Doing Business* does not assume a containerized shipment, and time and cost estimates may be based on the transport of 15 tons of noncontainerized products. In the import case study auto parts are assumed to be containerized. In the cases where cargo is containerized, the time and cost for transport and other procedures are based on a shipment consisting of homogeneous cargo belonging to a single Harmonized System (HS) classification code. This assumption is particularly important for inspections, because shipments of homogeneous products are often subject to fewer and shorter inspections than shipments of products belonging to various HS codes.

In some cases the shipment travels from the warehouse to a customs post or terminal for clearance or inspections and then travels onward to the port or border. In these cases the domestic transport time is the sum of the time for both transport segments. The time and cost for clearance or inspections are included in the measures for border compliance, however, not in those for domestic transport.

REFORMS

The trading across borders indicator set records the time and cost associated with the logistical process of exporting and importing goods every year. Depending on the impact on the data, certain changes are classified as reforms and listed in the summaries of *Doing Business* reforms in 2015/16 section of the report in order to acknowledge the implementation of significant changes. Reforms are divided into two types: those that make it easier to do business and those that make it more difficult to do business. The trading across borders indicator uses a standard criterion to recognize a reform.

The aggregate gap on the overall distance to frontier of the indicator set is used to assess the impact of data changes. Any data update that leads to a change of 2 or more percentage points on the relative distance to frontier gap is classified as a reform (for more details on the relative gap, see the chapter on the distance to frontier and ease of doing business ranking). For example if the implementation of a single window system reduces time or cost in a way that the overall relative gap decreases by 2 percentage points or more, such change is classified as a reform. Minor shipping fee updates or other small changes on the indicators that have an aggregate impact of less than 2 percentage points on the relative gap are not classified as a reform, yet, but their impact is still reflected on the most updated indicators for this indicator set.

The data details on trading across borders can be found for each economy at http://www.doingbusiness.org.

ENFORCING CONTRACTS

Doing Business measures the time and cost for resolving a commercial dispute through a local first-instance court (table 12.16) and the quality of judicial processes index, evaluating whether each economy has adopted a series of good practices that promote quality and efficiency in the court system. The data are collected through study of the codes of civil procedure and other court regulations as well as questionnaires completed by local litigation lawyers and judges. The ranking of economies on the ease of enforcing contracts is determined by sorting their distance to frontier scores for enforcing contracts. These scores are the simple average of the distance to frontier scores for each of the component indicators (figure 12.18).

EFFICIENCY OF RESOLVING A COMMERCIAL DISPUTE

The data on time and cost are built by following the step-by-step evolution of a commercial sale dispute (figure 12.19). The data are collected for a specific court for each city covered, under the assumptions about the case described below. The court is the one with jurisdiction over disputes worth 200% of income per capita or $5,000, whichever is greater. The name of the relevant court in each economy is published on the *Doing Business* website at http://www.doingbusiness.org/data/exploretopics/enforcing-contracts. For the 11 economies for which the data are also collected for the second largest business city, the name of the relevant court in that city is given as well.

Assumptions about the case

- The value of the claim is equal to 200% of the economy's income per capita or $5,000, whichever is greater.
- The dispute concerns a lawful transaction between two businesses (Seller and Buyer), both located in the economy's largest business city. For 11 economies the data are also collected for the second largest business city (table 12A.1). Pursuant to a contract between the businesses, Seller sells some custom-made furniture to Buyer worth 200% of the economy's income per capita or $5,000, whichever is greater. After Seller delivers the goods

TABLE 12.16 What do the indicators on the efficiency of resolving a commercial dispute measure?

Time required to enforce a contract through the courts (calendar days)
Time to file and serve the case
Time for trial and to obtain the judgment
Time to enforce the judgment
Cost required to enforce a contract through the courts (% of claim)
Average attorney fees
Court costs
Enforcement costs

FIGURE 12.18 Enforcing contracts: efficiency and quality of commercial dispute resolution

FIGURE 12.19 What are the time and cost to resolve a commercial dispute through a local first-instance court?

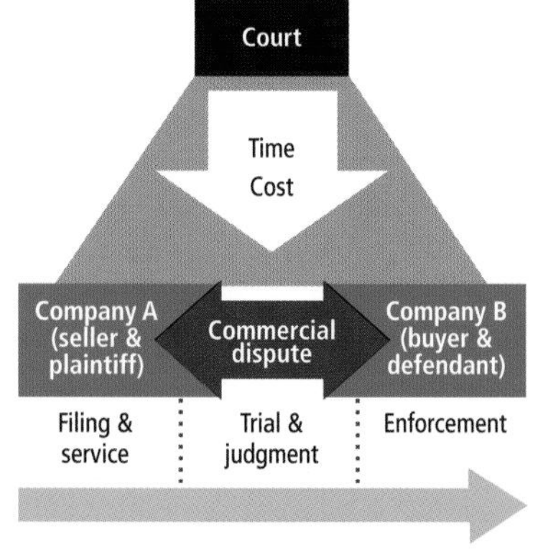

to Buyer, Buyer refuses to pay the contract price, alleging that the goods are not of adequate quality. Because they were custom-made, Seller is unable to sell them to anyone else.

- Seller (the plaintiff) sues Buyer (the defendant) to recover the amount under the sales agreement. The dispute is brought before the court located in the economy's largest business city with jurisdiction over commercial cases worth 200% of income per capita or $5,000, whichever is greater. As noted, for 11 economies the data are also collected for the second largest business city.
- At the outset of the dispute, Seller decides to attach Buyer's movable assets (for example, office equipment and vehicles) because Seller fears that Buyer may hide its assets or otherwise become insolvent.
- The claim is disputed on the merits because of Buyer's allegation that the quality of the goods was not adequate. Because the court cannot decide the case on the basis of documentary evidence or legal title alone, an expert opinion is given on the quality of the goods. If it is standard practice in the economy for each party to call its own expert witness, the parties each call one expert witness. If it is standard practice for the judge to appoint an independent expert, the judge does so. In this case the judge does not allow opposing expert testimony.
- Following the expert opinion, the judge decides that the goods delivered by Seller were of adequate quality and that Buyer must pay the contract price. The judge thus renders a final judgment that is 100% in favor of Seller.
- Buyer does not appeal the judgment. Seller decides to start enforcing the judgment as soon as the time allocated by law for appeal lapses.
- Seller takes all required steps for prompt enforcement of the judgment. The money is successfully collected through a public sale of Buyer's movable assets (for example, office equipment and vehicles).

Time

Time is recorded in calendar days, counted from the moment the plaintiff decides to file the lawsuit in court until payment. This includes both the days when actions take place and the waiting periods in between. The average duration of three different stages of dispute resolution is recorded: the completion of service of process (time to file and serve the case), the issuance of judgment (time for trial and to obtain the judgment) and the recovery of the claim value through a public sale (time for enforcement of the judgment).

Cost

Cost is recorded as a percentage of the claim value, assumed to be equivalent to 200% of income per capita or $5,000, whichever is greater. Three types of costs are recorded: court costs, enforcement costs and average attorney fees.

Court costs include all costs that Seller (plaintiff) must advance to the court, regardless of the final cost borne by Seller. Court costs include the fees that must be paid to obtain an expert opinion. Enforcement costs are all costs that Seller (plaintiff) must advance to enforce the judgment through a public sale of Buyer's movable assets, regardless of the final cost borne by Seller. Average attorney fees are the fees that Seller (plaintiff) must advance to a local attorney to represent Seller in the standardized case, regardless of final reimbursement. Bribes are not taken into account.

QUALITY OF JUDICIAL PROCESSES

The quality of judicial processes index measures whether each economy has adopted a series of good practices in its court system in four areas: court structure and proceedings, case management, court automation and alternative dispute resolution (table 12.17).

Court structure and proceedings index

The court structure and proceedings index has five components:

- Whether a specialized commercial court or a section dedicated solely to hearing commercial cases is in place. A score of 1.5 is assigned if yes; 0 if no.
- Whether a small claims court or a fast-track procedure for small claims is in place. A score of 1 is assigned if such a court or procedure is in place, it is applicable to all civil cases and the law sets a cap on the value of cases that can be handled through this court or procedure. If small claims are handled by a stand-alone court, the point is assigned only if this court applies a simplified procedure. An additional score of 0.5 is assigned if parties can represent themselves before this court or during this procedure. If no small claims court or simplified procedure is in place, a score of 0 is assigned.
- Whether plaintiffs can obtain pretrial attachment of the defendant's movable assets if they fear the assets may be moved out of the jurisdiction or otherwise dissipated. A score of 1 is assigned if yes; 0 if no.
- Whether cases are assigned randomly and automatically to judges throughout the competent court. A score of 1 is assigned if the assignment of cases is random and automated; 0.5 if it is random but not automated; 0 if it is neither random nor automated.
- Whether a woman's testimony carries the same evidentiary weight in court as a man's. A score of -1 is assigned if the law differentiates between the evidentiary value of a woman's testimony and that of a man; 0 if it does not.

The index ranges from 0 to 5, with higher values indicating a more sophisticated and streamlined court structure. In Bosnia and Herzegovina, for example, a specialized commercial court is in place (a score of 1.5), and small claims can be resolved through a dedicated court in which self-representation is allowed (a score of 1.5). Plaintiffs can obtain pretrial attachment of the defendant's movable assets if they fear dissipation during trial (a score of 1). Cases are assigned randomly through an electronic case management system (a score of 1). A woman's testimony carries the same evidentiary weight in court as a man's (a score of 0). Adding these numbers gives Bosnia and Herzegovina a score of 5 on the court structure and proceedings index.

TABLE 12.17 What do the indicators on the quality of judicial processes measure?
Court structure and proceedings index (0–5)
Availability of specialized commercial court, division or section
Availability of small claims court and/or simplified procedure for small claims
Availability of pretrial attachment
Criteria used to assign cases to judges
Evidentiary weight of woman's testimony
Case management index (0–6)
Regulations setting time standards for key court events
Regulations on adjournments and continuances
Availability of performance measurement mechanisms
Availability of pretrial conference
Availability of electronic case management system for judges
Availability of electronic case management system for lawyers
Court automation index (0–4)
Ability to file initial complaint electronically
Ability to serve initial complaint electronically
Ability to pay court fees electronically
Publication of judgments
Alternative dispute resolution index (0–3)
Arbitration
Voluntary mediation and/or conciliation
Quality of judicial processes index (0–18)
Sum of the court structure and proceedings, case management, court automation and alternative dispute resolution indices

Case management index

The case management index has six components:

- Whether any of the applicable laws or regulations on civil procedure contain time standards for at least three of the following key court events: (i) service of process; (ii) first hearing; (iii) filing of the statement of defense; (iv) completion of the evidence period; (v) filing of testimony by expert; and (vi) submission of the final judgment. A score of 1 is assigned if such time standards are available and respected in more than 50% of cases; 0.5 if they are available but not respected in more than 50% of cases; 0 if there are time standards for less than three of these key court events or for none.
- Whether there are any laws regulating the maximum number of adjournments or continuances that can be granted, whether adjournments are limited by law to unforeseen and exceptional circumstances and whether these rules are respected in more than 50% of cases. A score of 1 is assigned if all three conditions are met; 0.5 if only two of the three conditions are met; 0 if only one of the conditions is met or if none are.
- Whether there are any performance measurement reports that can be generated about the competent court to monitor the court's performance, to track the progress of cases through the court and to ensure compliance with established time standards. A score of 1 is assigned if at least two of the following four reports are made publicly available: (i) time to disposition report; (ii) clearance rate report; (iii) age of pending cases report; and (iv) single case progress report. A score of 0 is assigned if only one of these reports is available or if none are.
- Whether a pretrial conference is among the case management techniques used before the competent court and at least three of the following issues are discussed during the pretrial conference: (i) scheduling (including the time frame for filing motions and other documents with the court); (ii) case complexity and projected length of trial; (iii) possibility of settlement or alternative dispute resolution; (iv) exchange of witness lists; (v) evidence; (vi) jurisdiction and other procedural issues; and (vii) narrowing down of contentious issues. A score of 1 is assigned if a pretrial conference in which at least three of these events are discussed is held within the competent court; 0 if not.
- Whether judges within the competent court can use an electronic case management system for at least four of the following purposes: (i) to access laws, regulations and case law; (ii) to automatically generate a hearing schedule for all cases on their docket; (iii) to send notifications (for example, e-mails) to lawyers; (iv) to track the status of a case on their docket; (v) to view and manage case documents (briefs, motions); (vi) to assist in writing judgments; (vii) to semiautomatically generate court orders; and (viii) to view court orders and judgments in a particular case. A score of 1 is assigned if an electronic case management system is available that judges can use for at least four of these purposes; 0 if not.

- Whether lawyers can use an electronic case management system for at least four of the following purposes: (i) to access laws, regulations and case law; (ii) to access forms to be submitted to the court; (iii) to receive notifications (for example, e-mails); (iv) to track the status of a case; (v) to view and manage case documents (briefs, motions); (vi) to file briefs and documents with the court; and (vii) to view court orders and decisions in a particular case. A score of 1 is assigned if an electronic case management system is available that lawyers can use for at least four of these purposes; 0 if not.

The index ranges from 0 to 6, with higher values indicating a more qualitative and efficient case management system. In Croatia, for example, time standards for at least three key court events are established in applicable civil procedure instruments and are respected in more than 50% of cases (a score of 1). The law stipulates that adjournments can be granted only for unforeseen and exceptional circumstances and this rule is respected in more than 50% of cases (a score of 0.5). A time to disposition report and a clearance rate report can be generated about the competent court (a score of 1). A pretrial conference is among the case management techniques used before the Zagreb Commercial Court (a score of 1). An electronic case management system satisfying the criteria outlined above is available to judges (a score of 1) and to lawyers (a score of 1). Adding these numbers gives Croatia a score of 5.5 on the case management index, the highest score attained by any economy on this index.

Court automation index

The court automation index has four components:

- Whether the initial complaint can be filed electronically through a dedicated platform (not e-mail or fax) within the relevant court. A score of 1 is assigned if yes; 0 if no.
- Whether the initial complaint can be served on the defendant electronically, through a dedicated system or by e-mail, fax or SMS (short message service). A score of 1 is assigned if yes; 0 if no.
- Whether court fees can be paid electronically, either through a dedicated platform or through online banking. A score of 1 is assigned if yes; 0 if no.
- Whether judgments rendered by local courts are made available to the general public through publication in official gazettes, in newspapers or on the internet. A score of 1 is assigned if judgments rendered in commercial cases at all levels are made available to the general public; 0.5 if only judgments rendered at the appeal and supreme court level are made available to the general public; 0 in all other instances.

The index ranges from 0 to 4, with higher values indicating a more automated, efficient and transparent court system. In Korea, for example, the initial summons can be filed online (a score of 1), it can be served on the defendant electronically (a score of 1), and court fees can be paid electronically as well (a score of 1). In addition, judgments in commercial cases at all levels are made publicly available through the internet (a score of 1). Adding these numbers gives Korea a score of 4 on the court automation index.

Alternative dispute resolution index

The alternative dispute resolution index has six components:

- Whether domestic commercial arbitration is governed by a consolidated law or consolidated chapter or section of the applicable code of civil procedure encompassing substantially all its aspects. A score of 0.5 is assigned if yes; 0 if no.
- Whether commercial disputes of all kinds—aside from those dealing with public order, public policy, bankruptcy, consumer rights, employment issues or intellectual property—can be submitted to arbitration. A score of 0.5 is assigned if yes; 0 if no.
- Whether valid arbitration clauses or agreements are enforced by local courts in more than 50% of cases. A score of 0.5 is assigned if yes; 0 if no.
- Whether voluntary mediation, conciliation or both are a recognized way of resolving commercial disputes. A score of 0.5 is assigned if yes; 0 if no.
- Whether voluntary mediation, conciliation or both are governed by a consolidated law or consolidated chapter or section of the applicable code of civil procedure encompassing substantially all their aspects. A score of 0.5 is assigned if yes; 0 if no.
- Whether there are any financial incentives for parties to attempt mediation or conciliation (for example, if mediation or conciliation is successful, a refund of court filing fees, an income tax credit or the like). A score of 0.5 is assigned if yes; 0 if no.

The index ranges from 0 to 3, with higher values associated with greater availability of alternative dispute resolution mechanisms. In Israel, for example, arbitration is regulated through a dedicated statute (a score of 0.5), all relevant commercial disputes can be submitted to arbitration (a score of 0.5), and valid arbitration clauses are usually enforced by the courts (a score of 0.5). Voluntary mediation is a recognized way of resolving commercial disputes (a score of 0.5), it is regulated through a dedicated statute (a score of 0.5), and part of the filing fees is reimbursed if the process is successful (a score of 0.5). Adding these numbers gives Israel a score of 3 on the alternative dispute resolution index.

Quality of judicial processes index

The quality of judicial processes index is the sum of the scores on the court structure and proceedings, case management, court automation and alternative dispute resolution indices. The index ranges from 0 to 18, with higher values indicating better and more efficient judicial processes.

REFORMS

The enforcing contracts indicator set tracks changes related to the efficiency and quality of commercial dispute resolution systems every year. Depending on the impact on the data, certain changes are classified as reforms and listed in the summaries of *Doing Business* reforms in 2015/2016 section of the report in order to acknowledge the implementation of significant changes. Reforms are divided into two types: those that make it easier to do business and those changes that make it more difficult to do business. The enforcing contracts indicator set uses three criteria to recognize a reform.

First, all changes in laws and regulations that have any impact on the economy's score on the quality of judicial processes index are classified as reforms. Examples of reforms impacting the quality of judicial processes index include measures to introduce electronic filing of the initial complaint, the creation of a commercial court or division, or the introduction of dedicated systems to resolve small claims. Changes affecting the quality of judicial processes index can be different in magnitude and scope and still be considered a reform. For example, implementing a new electronic case management system for the use of judges and lawyers represents a reform with a 2-point increase in the index, while introducing incentives for the parties to use mediation represents a reform with a 0.5-point increase in the index.

Second, changes that have an impact on the time and cost to resolve a dispute may also be classified as reforms depending on the magnitude of the changes. According to the enforcing contracts methodology, any updates in legislation leading to a change of 2 or more percentage points on the relative distance to frontier gap (for more details, see the chapter on the distance to frontier and ease of doing business ranking) of the time and cost indicators is classified as a reform. Changes with lower impact are not classified as reforms but they are still reflected on the most updated indicators.

Third, occasionally the enforcing contracts indicator set will acknowledge legislative changes with no current impact on the data as reforms. This option is typically reserved to legislative changes of exceptional magnitude such as sizeable revisions of the applicable civil procedure laws.

The data details on enforcing contracts can be found for each economy at http://www.doingbusiness.org. This methodology was initially developed by Djankov and others (2003) and is adopted here with several changes. The quality of judicial processes index was introduced in Doing Business 2016. *The good practices tested in this index were developed on the basis of internationally recognized good practices promoting judicial efficiency.*

RESOLVING INSOLVENCY

Doing Business studies the time, cost and outcome of insolvency proceedings involving domestic entities as well as the strength of the legal framework applicable to judicial liquidation and reorganization proceedings. The data for the resolving insolvency indicators are derived from questionnaire responses by local insolvency practitioners and verified through a study of laws and regulations as well as public information on insolvency systems. The ranking of economies on the ease of resolving insolvency is determined by sorting their distance to frontier scores for resolving insolvency. These scores are the simple average of the distance to frontier scores for the recovery rate and the strength of insolvency framework index (figure 12.20).

RECOVERY OF DEBT IN INSOLVENCY

The recovery rate is calculated based on the time, cost and outcome of insolvency proceedings in each economy. To make the data on the time, cost and outcome of insolvency proceedings comparable across economies, several assumptions about the business and the case are used.

Assumptions about the business

The business:

- Is a limited liability company.
- Operates in the economy's largest business city. For 11 economies the data are also collected for the second largest business city (table 12A.1).
- Is 100% domestically owned, with the founder, who is also chairman of the supervisory board, owning 51% (no other shareholder holds more than 5% of shares).
- Has downtown real estate, where it runs a hotel, as its major asset.
- Has a professional general manager.
- Has 201 employees and 50 suppliers, each of which is owed money for the last delivery.
- Has a 10-year loan agreement with a domestic bank secured by a mortgage over the hotel's real estate property. A universal business charge (an enterprise charge) is also assumed in economies where such collateral is recognized. If the laws of the economy do not specifically provide for an enterprise charge but contracts commonly use some other provision to that effect, this provision is specified in the loan agreement.

FIGURE 12.20 Resolving insolvency: recovery rate and strength of insolvency framework

Rankings are based on distance to frontier scores for two indicators

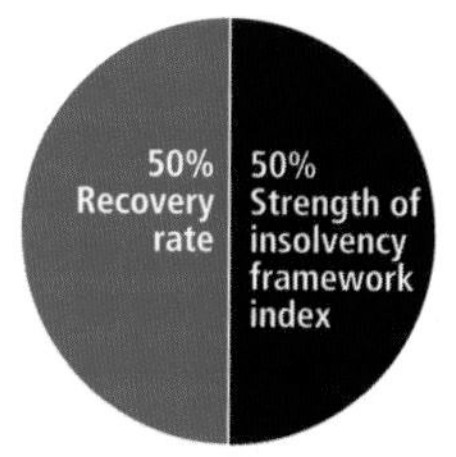

- Has observed the payment schedule and all other conditions of the loan up to now.
- Has a market value, operating as a going concern, of 100 times income per capita or $200,000, whichever is greater. The market value of the company's assets, if sold piecemeal, is 70% of the market value of the business.

Assumptions about the case

The business is experiencing liquidity problems. The company's loss in 2015 reduced its net worth to a negative figure. It is January 1, 2016. There is no cash to pay the bank interest or principal in full, due the next day, January 2. The business will therefore default on its loan. Management believes that losses will be incurred in 2016 and 2017 as well. But it expects 2016 cash flow to cover all operating expenses, including supplier payments, salaries, maintenance costs and taxes, though not principal or interest payments to the bank.

The amount outstanding under the loan agreement is exactly equal to the market value of the hotel business and represents 74% of the company's total debt. The other 26% of its debt is held by unsecured creditors (suppliers, employees, tax authorities).

The company has too many creditors to negotiate an informal out-of-court workout. The following options are available: a judicial procedure aimed at the rehabilitation or reorganization of the company to permit its continued operation; a judicial procedure aimed at the liquidation or winding-up of the company; or a judicial debt enforcement procedure (foreclosure or receivership) against the company.

Assumptions about the parties

The bank wants to recover as much as possible of its loan, as quickly and cheaply as possible. The unsecured creditors will do everything permitted under the applicable laws to avoid a piecemeal sale of the assets. The majority shareholder wants to keep the company operating and under his control. Management wants to keep the company operating and preserve its employees' jobs. All the parties are local entities or citizens; no foreign parties are involved.

Time

Time for creditors to recover their credit is recorded in calendar years (table 12.18). The period of time measured by *Doing Business* is from the company's default until the payment of some or all of the money owed to the bank. Potential delay tactics by the parties, such as the filing of dilatory appeals or requests for extension, are taken into consideration.

Cost

The cost of the proceedings is recorded as a percentage of the value of the debtor's estate. The cost is calculated on the basis of questionnaire responses and includes court fees and government levies; fees of insolvency administrators, auctioneers, assessors and lawyers; and all other fees and costs.

Outcome

Recovery by creditors depends on whether the hotel business emerges from the proceedings as a going concern or the company's assets are sold piecemeal. If the business continues operating, 100% of the hotel value is preserved. If the assets are sold piecemeal, the maximum amount that can be recovered is 70% of the value of the hotel.

Recovery rate

The recovery rate is recorded as cents on the dollar recovered by secured creditors through judicial reorganization, liquidation or debt enforcement (foreclosure or receivership) proceedings (figure 12.21). The calculation takes into account the outcome: whether the business emerges from the proceedings as a going concern or the assets are sold piecemeal. Then the costs of the proceedings are deducted (1 cent for each percentage point of the value of the debtor's estate). Finally, the value lost as a result of the time the money remains tied up in insolvency proceedings is taken into account, including the loss of value due to depreciation

TABLE 12.18 What do the indicators on debt recovery in insolvency measure?

Time required to recover debt (years)
Measured in calendar years
Appeals and requests for extension are included
Cost required to recover debt (% of debtor's estate)
Measured as percentage of estate value
Court fees
Fees of insolvency administrators
Lawyers' fees
Assessors' and auctioneers' fees
Other related fees
Outcome
Whether the business continues operating as a going concern or whether its assets are sold piecemeal
Recovery rate for secured creditors (cents on the dollar)
Measures the cents on the dollar recovered by secured creditors
Present value of debt recovered
Official costs of the insolvency proceedings are deducted
Depreciation of furniture is taken into account
Outcome for the business (survival or not) affects the maximum value that can be recovered

FIGURE 12.21 Recovery rate is a function of the time, cost and outcome of insolvency proceedings against a local company

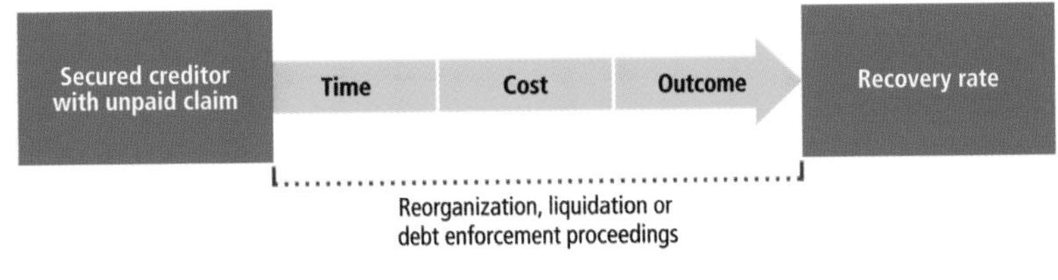

of the hotel furniture. Consistent with international accounting practice, the annual depreciation rate for furniture is taken to be 20%. The furniture is assumed to account for a quarter of the total value of assets. The recovery rate is the present value of the remaining proceeds, based on end-2015 lending rates from the International Monetary Fund's *International Financial Statistics*, supplemented with data from central banks and the Economist Intelligence Unit.

If an economy had zero completed cases a year over the past five years involving a judicial reorganization, judicial liquidation or debt enforcement procedure (foreclosure or receivership), the economy receives a "no practice" mark on the time, cost and outcome indicators. This means that creditors are unlikely to recover their money through a formal legal process. The recovery rate for "no practice" economies is zero. In addition, a "no practice" economy receives a score of 0 on the strength of insolvency framework index even if its legal framework includes provisions related to insolvency proceedings (liquidation or reorganization).

STRENGTH OF INSOLVENCY FRAMEWORK

The strength of insolvency framework index is based on four other indices: commencement of proceedings index, management of debtor's assets index, reorganization proceedings index and creditor participation index (figure 12.22; table 12.19).

Commencement of proceedings index

The commencement of proceedings index has three components:

- Whether debtors can initiate both liquidation and reorganization proceedings. A score of 1 is assigned if debtors can initiate both types of proceedings; 0.5 if they can initiate only one of these types (either liquidation or reorganization); 0 if they cannot initiate insolvency proceedings.

FIGURE 12.22 Strength of insolvency framework index measures the quality of insolvency laws that govern relations between debtors, creditors and the court

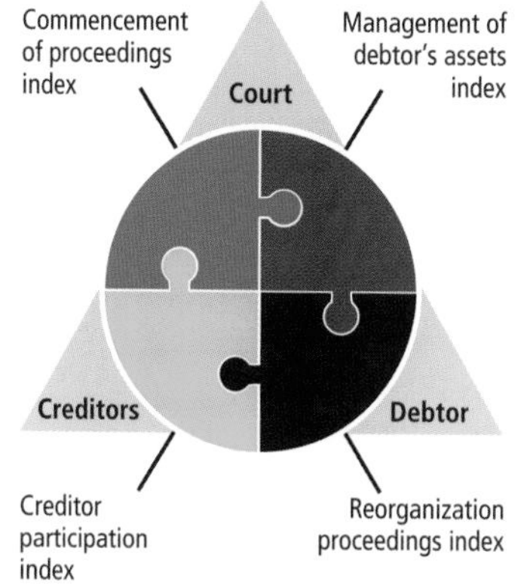

- Whether creditors can initiate both liquidation and reorganization proceedings. A score of 1 is assigned if creditors can initiate both types of proceedings; 0.5 if they can initiate only one of these types (either liquidation or reorganization); 0 if they cannot initiate insolvency proceedings.
- What standard is used for commencement of insolvency proceedings. A score of 1 is assigned if a liquidity test (the debtor is generally unable to pay its debts as they mature) is used; 0.5 if the balance sheet test (the liabilities of the debtor exceed its assets) is used; 1 if both the liquidity and balance sheet tests are available but only one is required to initiate insolvency proceedings; 0.5 if both tests are required; 0 if a different test is used.

The index ranges from 0 to 3, with higher values indicating greater access to insolvency proceedings. In Bulgaria, for example, debtors can initiate both liquidation and reorganization proceedings (a score of 1), but creditors can initiate only liquidation proceedings (a score of 0.5). Either the liquidity test or the balance sheet test can be used to commence insolvency proceedings (a score of 1). Adding these numbers gives Bulgaria a score of 2.5 on the commencement of proceedings index.

TABLE 12.19 What do the indicators on the strength of the insolvency framework measure?

Commencement of proceedings index (0–3)
Availability of liquidation and reorganization to debtors and creditors
Standards for commencement of insolvency proceedings
Management of debtor's assets index (0–6)
Continuation and rejection of contracts during insolvency
Avoidance of preferential and undervalued transactions
Post-commencement finance
Reorganization proceedings index (0–3)
Approval and content of reorganization plan
Creditor participation index (0–4)
Creditors' participation in and rights during liquidation and reorganization proceedings
Strength of insolvency framework index (0–16)
Sum of the commencement of proceedings, management of debtor's assets, reorganization proceedings and creditor participation indices

Management of debtor's assets index

The management of debtor's assets index has six components:

- Whether the debtor (or an insolvency representative on its behalf) can continue performing contracts essential to the debtor's survival. A score of 1 is assigned if yes; 0 if continuation of contracts is not possible or if the law contains no provisions on this subject.
- Whether the debtor (or an insolvency representative on its behalf) can reject overly burdensome contracts. A score of 1 is assigned if yes; 0 if rejection of contracts is not possible or if the law contains no provisions on this subject.
- Whether transactions entered into before commencement of insolvency proceedings that give preference to one or several creditors can be avoided after proceedings are initiated. A score of 1 is assigned if yes; 0 if avoidance of such transactions is not possible or if the law contains no provisions on this subject.
- Whether undervalued transactions entered into before commencement

of insolvency proceedings can be avoided after proceedings are initiated. A score of 1 is assigned if yes; 0 if avoidance of such transactions is not possible or if the law contains no provisions on this subject.

- Whether the insolvency framework includes specific provisions that allow the debtor (or an insolvency representative on its behalf), after commencement of insolvency proceedings, to obtain financing necessary to function during the proceedings. A score of 1 is assigned if yes; 0 if obtaining post-commencement finance is not possible or if the law contains no provisions on this subject.
- Whether post-commencement finance receives priority over ordinary unsecured creditors during distribution of assets. A score of 1 is assigned if yes; 0.5 if post-commencement finance is granted superpriority over all creditors, secured and unsecured; 0 if no priority is granted to post-commencement finance or if the law contains no provisions on this subject.

The index ranges from 0 to 6, with higher values indicating more advantageous treatment of the debtor's assets from the perspective of the company's stakeholders. In Mozambique, for example, debtors can continue essential contracts (a score of 1) and reject burdensome ones (a score of 1) during insolvency proceedings. The insolvency framework allows avoidance of preferential transactions (a score of 1) and undervalued ones (a score of 1). But the insolvency framework contains no provisions allowing post-commencement finance (a score of 0) or granting priority to such finance (a score of 0). Adding these numbers gives Mozambique a score of 4 on the management of debtor's assets index.

Reorganization proceedings index

The reorganization proceedings index has three components:

- Whether the reorganization plan is voted on only by the creditors whose rights are modified or affected by the plan. A score of 1 is assigned if yes; 0.5 if all creditors vote on the plan, regardless of its impact on their interests; 0 if creditors do not vote on the plan or if reorganization is not available.
- Whether creditors entitled to vote on the plan are divided into classes, each class votes separately and the creditors within each class are treated equally. A score of 1 is assigned if the voting procedure has these three features; 0 if the voting procedure does not have these three features or if reorganization is not available.
- Whether the insolvency framework requires that dissenting creditors receive as much under the reorganization plan as they would have received in liquidation. A score of 1 is assigned if yes; 0 if no such provisions exist or if reorganization is not available.

The index ranges from 0 to 3, with higher values indicating greater compliance with internationally accepted practices. Nicaragua, for example, has no judicial reorganization proceedings and therefore receives a score of 0 on the reorganization proceedings index. In Estonia, another example, only creditors whose rights are affected by the reorganization plan are allowed to vote (a score of 1). The reorganization plan divides creditors into classes, each class votes separately and creditors within the same class are treated equally (a score of 1). But there are no provisions requiring that the return to dissenting creditors be equal to what they would have received in liquidation (a score of 0). Adding these numbers gives Estonia a score of 2 on the reorganization proceedings index.

Creditor participation index

The creditor participation index has four components:

- Whether creditors participate in the selection of an insolvency representative. A score of 1 is assigned if yes; 0 if no.
- Whether creditors are required to approve the sale of substantial assets of the debtor in the course of insolvency proceedings. A score of 1 is assigned if yes; 0 if no.
- Whether an individual creditor has the right to access financial information about the debtor during insolvency proceedings. A score of 1 is assigned if yes; 0 if no.
- Whether an individual creditor can object to a decision of the court or of the insolvency representative to approve or reject claims against the debtor brought by the creditor itself and by other creditors. A score of 1 is assigned if yes; 0 if no.

The index ranges from 0 to 4, with higher values indicating greater participation of creditors. In Iceland, for example, the court appoints the insolvency representative, without creditors' approval (a score of 0). The insolvency representative decides unilaterally on the sale of the debtor's assets (a score of 0). Any creditor can inspect the records kept by the insolvency representative (a score of 1). And any creditor is allowed to challenge a decision of the insolvency representative to approve all claims if this decision affects the creditor's rights (a score of 1). Adding these numbers gives Iceland a score of 2 on the creditor participation index.

Strength of insolvency framework index

The strength of insolvency framework index is the sum of the scores on the commencement of proceedings index, management of debtor's assets index, reorganization proceedings index and creditor participation index. The index ranges from 0 to 16, with higher values indicating insolvency legislation that is better designed for rehabilitating viable firms and liquidating nonviable ones.

REFORMS

The resolving insolvency indicator set tracks changes related to the efficiency and quality of insolvency framework every year. Depending on the impact on the data, certain changes are classified as reforms and listed in the summaries of *Doing Business* reforms in 2015/2016 section of the report in order to acknowledge the implementation of significant changes. Reforms are divided into two types: those that make it easier to do business and those changes that make it more difficult to do business. The resolving insolvency indicator set uses three criteria to recognize a reform.

First, all changes to laws and regulations that have any impact on the economy's score on the strength of insolvency framework index are classified as reforms. Examples of reforms impacting the strength of insolvency framework index include changes in the commencement standard for insolvency proceedings, the introduction of reorganization procedures for the first time and measures to regulate post-commencement credit and its priority. Changes affecting the strength of insolvency framework index can be different in magnitude and scope and still be considered a reform. For example implementing a post-commencement credit provision and designating it with certain priorities represents a reform with a potential 2 point increase in the index, while changing the commencement standard from the balance sheet test to the liquidity test represents a reform with a 0.5 points increase in the index.

Second, changes that have an impact on the time, cost or outcome of insolvency proceedings may also be classified as reforms depending on the magnitude of the changes. According to the resolving insolvency methodology any update in legislation leading to a change of 2 or more percentage points on the relative distance to frontier gap (for more details, see the chapter on the distance to frontier and ease of doing business ranking) of the time, cost and outcome indicators is classified as a reform. Changes with lower impact are not classified as reforms but their impact is still reflected on the most updated indicators.

Third, occasionally the resolving insolvency indicator set will acknowledge legislative changes with no current impact on the data as reforms. This option is typically reserved to legislative changes of exceptional magnitude such as sizeable revisions of corporate insolvency laws.

This methodology was developed by Djankov, Hart and others (2008) and is adopted here with several changes. The strength of insolvency framework index was introduced in Doing Business 2015. *The good practices tested in this index were developed on the basis of the World Bank's* Principles for Effective Insolvency and Creditor/Debtor Regimes *(World Bank 2011) and the United Nations Commission on International Trade Law's* Legislative Guide on Insolvency Law *(UNCITRAL 2004a)*

LABOR MARKET REGULATION

Doing Business studies the flexibility of regulation of employment, specifically as it relates to the areas of hiring, working hours and redundancy. *Doing Business* also measures several aspects of job quality such as the availability of maternity leave, paid sick leave and the equal treatment of men and women at the workplace (figure 12.23).

Doing Business 2017 presents the data for the labor market regulation indicators in an annex. The report does not present rankings of economies on these indicators or include this indicator set in the aggregate distance to frontier score or ranking on the ease of doing business. Detailed data collected on labor market regulation are available on the *Doing Business* website (http://www.doingbusiness.org). The data on labor market regulation are based on a detailed questionnaire on employment regulations that is completed by local lawyers and public officials. Employment laws and regulations as well as secondary sources are reviewed to ensure accuracy.

To make the data comparable across economies, several assumptions about the worker and the business are used.

Assumptions about the worker

The worker:

- Is a cashier in a supermarket or grocery store, age 19, with one year of work experience.[15]
- Is a full-time employee.
- Is not a member of the labor union, unless membership is mandatory

Assumptions about the business

The business:

- Is a limited liability company (or the equivalent in the economy).

FIGURE 12.23 What do the labor market regulation indicators cover?

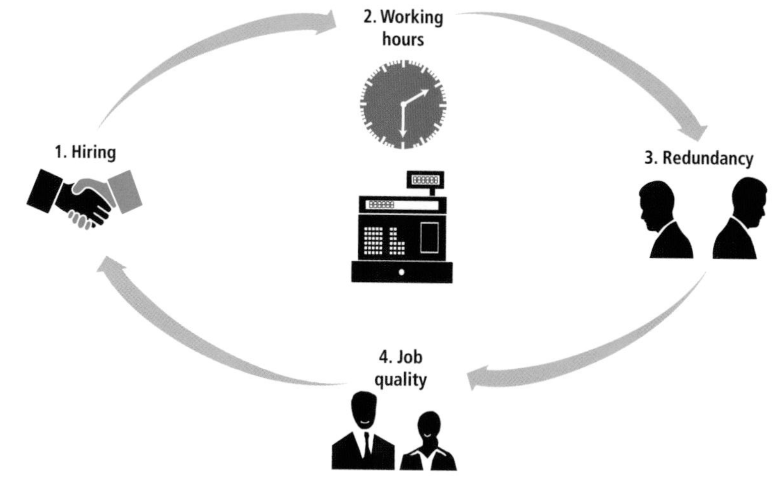

- Operates a supermarket or grocery store in the economy's largest business city. For 11 economies the data are also collected for the second largest business city (table 12A.1).
- Has 60 employees.
- Is subject to collective bargaining agreements if such agreements cover more than 50% of the food retail sector and apply even to firms that are not party to them.
- Abides by every law and regulation but does not grant workers more benefits than those mandated by law, regulation or (if applicable) collective bargaining agreements.

Employment

Data on employment cover three areas: hiring, working hours and redundancy (table 12.20).

Data on hiring cover four questions: (i) whether fixed-term contracts are prohibited for permanent tasks; (ii) the maximum cumulative duration of fixed-term contracts; (iii) the minimum wage for a cashier, age 19, with one year of work experience and (iv) the ratio of the minimum wage to the average value added per worker.[16]

Data on working hours cover nine questions: (i) the maximum number of working days allowed per week; (ii) the premium for night work (as a percentage of hourly pay); (iii) the premium for work on a weekly rest day (as a percentage of hourly pay); (iv) the premium for overtime work (as a percentage of hourly pay); (v) whether there are restrictions on night work; (vi) whether nonpregnant and nonnursing women can work the same night hours as men; (vii) whether there are restrictions on weekly holiday work; (viii) whether there are restrictions on overtime work; and (ix) the average paid annual leave for workers with 1 year of tenure, 5 years of tenure and 10 years of tenure.

Data on redundancy cover nine questions: (i) the length of the maximum probationary period (in months) for permanent employees; (ii) whether redundancy is allowed as a basis for terminating workers; (iii) whether the employer needs to notify a third party (such as a government agency) to terminate one redundant worker; (iv) whether the employer needs to notify a third party to terminate a group of nine redundant workers; (v) whether the employer needs approval from a third party to terminate one redundant worker; (vi) whether the employer needs approval from a third party to terminate a group of nine redundant workers; (vii) whether the law requires the employer to reassign or retrain a worker before making the worker redundant; (viii) whether priority rules apply for redundancies; and (ix) whether priority rules apply for reemployment.

TABLE 12.20 What do the labor market regulation indicators measure?

Employment
Hiring
Whether fixed-term contracts are prohibited for permanent tasks
Maximum duration of fixed-term contracts (in months), including renewals
Minimum wage for a cashier, age 19, with one year of work experience (US$/month)
Ratio of minimum wage to value added per worker
Working hours
Maximum number of working days per week
Premium for night work, work on weekly rest day and overtime work (% of hourly pay)
Whether there are restrictions on night work, weekly holiday work and overtime work
Whether nonpregnant and nonnursing women can work the same night hours as men
Paid annual vacation days for workers with 1 year of tenure, 5 years of tenure and 10 years of tenure.
Redundancy
Length of maximum probationary period (in months) for permanent employees
Whether redundancy is allowed as grounds for termination
Whether third-party notification is required for termination of a redundant worker or group of workers
Whether third-party approval is required for termination of a redundant worker or group of workers
Whether employer is obligated to reassign or retrain workers prior to making them redundant and to follow priority rules for redundancy and reemployment
Redundancy cost (weeks of salary)
Notice requirements and severance payments due when terminating a redundant worker, expressed in weeks of salary
Job quality
Whether the law mandates equal remuneration for work of equal value
Whether the law mandates nondiscrimination based on gender in hiring
Whether the law mandates paid or unpaid maternity leave
Minimum length of paid maternity leave (calendar days)
Whether employees on maternity leave receive 100% of wages
Availability of five fully paid days of sick leave a year
Whether unemployment protection is available after one year of employment
Minimum duration of contribution period (in months) required for unemployment protection

Redundancy cost

Redundancy cost measures the cost of advance notice requirements and severance payments due when terminating a redundant worker, expressed in weeks of salary. The average value of notice requirements and severance payments applicable to a worker with 1 year of tenure, a worker with 5 years and a worker with 10 years is considered. One month is recorded as 4 and 1/3 weeks.

Job quality

Doing Business introduced new data on job quality in 2015. *Doing Business 2017* covers eight questions on job quality (i) whether the law mandates equal remuneration for work of equal value; (ii) whether the law mandates nondiscrimination based on gender in hiring; (iii) whether the law mandates paid or unpaid maternity leave;[17] (iv) the minimum length of paid maternity leave (in calendar days);[18] (v) whether employees on maternity leave receive 100% of wages;[19] (vi) the availability of five fully paid days of sick leave a year; (vii) whether a worker is eligible for an unemployment protection scheme after one year of service; and (viii) the minimum duration of the contribution period (in months) required for unemployment protection.

REFORMS

The labor market regulation indicator set tracks changes in labor rules every year. Depending on the impact on the data, certain changes are classified as reforms and listed in the summaries of *Doing Business* reforms in 2015/2016 section of the report in order to acknowledge the implementation of significant changes. Examples include a change in the maximum duration of fixed-term contracts, regulation of weekly holiday work, redundancy rules, notice requirements and severance payments for redundant workers, introduction of unemployment insurance and laws that mandate gender nondiscrimination in hiring and equal remuneration for work of equal value in line with ILO standards. The introduction of a minimum wage in the private sector is recognized as a major reform and acknowledged in the reform summary. Changes in minimum wages are reflected in the *Doing Business* data but not acknowledged in the reform summary. Similarly, the introduction of maternity leave would be acknowledged in the reform summary but not an increase in the duration of maternity leave. Occasionally the labor market regulation indicator set will acknowledge legislative changes in areas not directly measured by the indicators. This option is reserved for legislative changes of exceptional magnitude, such as the introduction of a new labor code.

The data details on labor market regulation can be found for each economy at http://www.doingbusiness.org. The Doing Business *website also provides historical data sets. The methodology was developed by Botero and others (2004).* Doing Business 2017 *does not present rankings of economies on the labor market regulation indicators.*

NOTES

1. The data for paying taxes refer to January-December 2015.
2. These are Bangladesh, Brazil, China, India, Indonesia, Japan, Mexico, Nigeria, Pakistan, the Russian Federation and the United States.
3. This correction rate reflects changes that exceed 5% up or down.
4. According to a study by Chakravorty, Pelli and Marchand (2014) based on evidence from India between 1994 and 2005, a higher-quality electricity supply, with no more than two outages a week (or no more than about 100 a year), leads to higher nonagricultural incomes.
5. This matter is usually regulated by stock exchange or securities laws. Points are awarded only to economies with more than 10 listed firms in their most important stock exchange.
6. When evaluating the regime of liability for company directors for a prejudicial related-party transaction, *Doing Business* assumes that the transaction was duly disclosed and approved. *Doing Business* does not measure director liability in the event of fraud.
7. This component is revised in *Doing Business 2017*.
8. This component is revised in *Doing Business 2017*.
9. This component is revised in *Doing Business 2017*.
10. This component is revised in *Doing Business 2017*.
11. PwC refers to the network of member firms of PricewaterhouseCoopers International Limited (PwCIL) or, as the context requires, individual member firms of the PwC network. Each member firm is a separate legal entity and does not act as agent of PwCIL or any other member firm. PwCIL does not provide any services to clients. PwCIL is not responsible or liable for the acts or omissions of any of its member firms nor can it control the exercise of their professional judgment or bind them in any way. No member firm is responsible or liable for the acts or omissions of any other member firm nor can it control the exercise of another member firm's professional judgment or bind another member firm or PwCIL in any way.
12. The nonlinear distance to frontier score for the total tax rate is equal to the distance to frontier score for the total tax rate to the power of 0.8.
13. The economies for which a multiple of three times income per capita has been used are Honduras, Mozambique, West Bank and Gaza, and Zimbabwe. Those for which a multiple of two times income per capita has been used are Belize, Benin, Bosnia and Herzegovina, Burkina Faso, the Central African Republic, Chad, Fiji, Guatemala, Haiti, Kenya, Lesotho, Madagascar, the Federated States of Micronesia, Morocco, Nepal, Nicaragua, Niger, Nigeria, the Philippines, the Solomon Islands, South Africa, South Sudan, Tanzania, Togo, Vanuatu and Zambia.
14. To identify the trading partners and export product for each economy, *Doing Business* collected data on trade flows for the most recent four-year period from international databases such as the United Nations Commodity Trade Statistics Database (UN Comtrade). For economies for which trade flow data were not available, data from ancillary government sources (various ministries and departments) and World Bank Group country offices were used to identify the export product and natural trading partners.
15. The case study assumption that the worker is 19 years old with one year of work experience is considered only for the calculation of the minimum wage. For all other questions where the tenure of the worker is relevant, *Doing Business* collects data for workers with 1, 5 and 10 years of tenure.
16. The average value added per worker is the ratio of an economy's GNI per capita to the working-age population as a percentage of the total population.
17. If no maternity leave is mandated by law, parental leave is measured if applicable.
18. The minimum number of days that legally have to be paid by the government, the employer or both. If no maternity leave is mandated by law, parental leave is measured if applicable.
19. If no maternity leave is mandated by law, parental leave is measured if applicable.

TABLE 12A.1 Cities covered in each economy by the *Doing Business* report

Economy	City or cities	Economy	City or cities	Economy	City or cities	Economy	City or cities	Economy	City or cities
Afghanistan	Kabul	**Congo, Rep.**	Brazzaville	**Iran, Islamic Rep.**	Tehran	**Morocco**	Casablanca	**Somalia**	Mogadishu
Albania	Tirana	**Costa Rica**	San José	**Iraq**	Baghdad	**Mozambique**	Maputo	**South Africa**	Johannesburg
Algeria	Algiers	**Côte d'Ivoire**	Abidjan	**Ireland**	Dublin	**Myanmar**	Yangon	**South Sudan**	Juba
Angola	Luanda	**Croatia**	Zagreb	**Israel**	Tel Aviv	**Namibia**	Windhoek	**Spain**	Madrid
Antigua and Barbuda	St. John's	**Cyprus**	Nicosia	**Italy**	Rome	**Nepal**	Kathmandu	**Sri Lanka**	Colombo
Argentina	Buenos Aires	**Czech Republic**	Prague	**Jamaica**	Kingston	**Netherlands**	Amsterdam	**St. Kitts and Nevis**	Basseterre
Armenia	Yerevan	**Denmark**	Copenhagen	**Japan**	Tokyo, Osaka	**New Zealand**	Auckland	**St. Lucia**	Castries
Australia	Sydney	**Djibouti**	Djibouti Ville	**Jordan**	Amman	**Nicaragua**	Managua	**St. Vincent and the Grenadines**	Kingstown
Austria	Vienna	**Dominica**	Roseau	**Kazakhstan**	Almaty	**Niger**	Niamey	**Sudan**	Khartoum
Azerbaijan	Baku	**Dominican Republic**	Santo Domingo	**Kenya**	Nairobi	**Nigeria**	Lagos, Kano	**Suriname**	Paramaribo
Bahamas, The	Nassau	**Ecuador**	Quito	**Kiribati**	Tarawa	**Norway**	Oslo	**Swaziland**	Mbabane
Bahrain	Manama	**Egypt, Arab Rep.**	Cairo	**Korea, Rep.**	Seoul	**Oman**	Muscat	**Sweden**	Stockholm
Bangladesh	Dhaka, Chittagong	**El Salvador**	San Salvador	**Kosovo**	Pristina	**Pakistan**	Karachi, Lahore	**Switzerland**	Zurich
Barbados	Bridgetown	**Equatorial Guinea**	Malabo	**Kuwait**	Kuwait City	**Palau**	Koror	**Syrian Arab Republic**	Damascus
Belarus	Minsk	**Eritrea**	Asmara	**Kyrgyz Republic**	Bishkek	**Panama**	Panama City	**Taiwan, China**	Taipei
Belgium	Brussels	**Estonia**	Tallinn	**Lao PDR**	Vientiane	**Papua New Guinea**	Port Moresby	**Tajikistan**	Dushanbe
Belize	Belize City	**Ethiopia**	Addis Ababa	**Latvia**	Riga	**Paraguay**	Asunción	**Tanzania**	Dar es Salaam
Benin	Cotonou	**Fiji**	Suva	**Lebanon**	Beirut	**Peru**	Lima	**Thailand**	Bangkok
Bhutan	Thimphu	**Finland**	Helsinki	**Lesotho**	Maseru	**Philippines**	Quezon City	**Timor-Leste**	Dili
Bolivia	La Paz	**France**	Paris	**Liberia**	Monrovia	**Poland**	Warsaw	**Togo**	Lomé
Bosnia and Herzegovina	Sarajevo	**Gabon**	Libreville	**Libya**	Tripoli	**Portugal**	Lisbon	**Tonga**	Nuku'alofa
Botswana	Gaborone	**Gambia, The**	Banjul	**Lithuania**	Vilnius	**Puerto Rico (U.S.)**	San Juan	**Trinidad and Tobago**	Port of Spain
Brazil	São Paulo, Rio de Janeiro	**Georgia**	Tbilisi	**Luxem-bourg**	Luxembourg	**Qatar**	Doha	**Tunisia**	Tunis
Brunei Darussalam	Bandar Seri Begawan	**Germany**	Berlin	**Macedonia, FYR**	Skopje	**Romania**	Bucharest	**Turkey**	Istanbul
Bulgaria	Sofia	**Ghana**	Accra	**Madagascar**	Antananarivo	**Russian Federation**	Moscow, St. Petersburg	**Uganda**	Kampala
Burkina Faso	Ouagadougou	**Greece**	Athens	**Malawi**	Blantyre	**Rwanda**	Kigali	**Ukraine**	Kiev
Burundi	Bujumbura	**Grenada**	St. George's	**Malaysia**	Kuala Lumpur	**Samoa**	Apia	**United Arab Emirates**	Dubai
Cabo Verde	Praia	**Guatemala**	Guatemala City	**Maldives**	Malé	**San Marino**	San Marino	**United Kingdom**	London
Cambodia	Phnom Penh	**Guinea**	Conakry	**Mali**	Bamako	**São Tomé and Prín-cipe**	São Tomé	**United States**	New York City, Los Angeles
Cameroon	Douala	**Guinea-Bissau**	Bissau	**Malta**	Valletta	**Saudi Arabia**	Riyadh	**Uruguay**	Montevideo
Canada	Toronto	**Guyana**	Georgetown	**Marshall Islands**	Majuro	**Senegal**	Dakar	**Uzbekistan**	Tashkent
Central African Republic	Bangui	**Haiti**	Port-au-Prince	**Mauritania**	Nouakchott	**Serbia**	Belgrade	**Vanuatu**	Port-Vila
Chad	N'Djamena	**Honduras**	Tegucigalpa	**Mauritius**	Port Louis	**Seychelles**	Victoria	**Venezuela, RB**	Caracas
Chile	Santiago	**Hong Kong SAR, China**	Hong Kong SAR	**Mexico**	Mexico City, Monterrey	**Sierra Leone**	Freetown	**Vietnam**	Ho Chi Minh City
China	Shanghai, Beijing	**Hungary**	Budapest	**Micronesia, Fed. Sts.**	Island of Pohnpei	**Singapore**	Singapore	**West Bank and Gaza**	Ramallah
Colombia	Bogotá	**Iceland**	Reykjavik	**Moldova**	Chişinău	**Slovak Republic**	Bratislava	**Yemen, Rep.**	Sana'a
Comoros	Moroni	**India**	Mumbai, Delhi	**Mongolia**	Ulaanbaatar	**Slovenia**	Ljubljana	**Zambia**	Lusaka
Congo, Dem. Rep.	Kinshasa	**Indonesia**	Jakarta, Surabaya	**Montene-gro**	Podgorica	**Solomon Islands**	Honiara	**Zimbabwe**	Harare

Distance to Frontier and Ease of Doing Business Ranking

The *Doing Business* report presents results for two aggregate measures: the distance to frontier score and the ease of doing business ranking, which is based on the distance to frontier score. The ease of doing business ranking compares economies with one another; the distance to frontier score benchmarks economies with respect to regulatory best practice, showing the absolute distance to the best performance on each *Doing Business* indicator. When compared across years, the distance to frontier score shows how much the regulatory environment for local entrepreneurs in an economy has changed over time in absolute terms, while the ease of doing business ranking can show only how much the regulatory environment has changed relative to that in other economies.

DISTANCE TO FRONTIER

The distance to frontier score captures the gap between an economy's performance and a measure of best practice across the entire sample of 41 indicators for 10 *Doing Business* topics (the labor market regulation indicators are excluded). For starting a business, for example, New Zealand has the smallest number of procedures required (1) and the shortest time to fulfill them (0.5 days). Slovenia has the lowest cost (0.0), and Australia, Colombia and 111 other economies have no paid-in minimum capital requirement (table 14.1).

Calculation of the distance to frontier score

Calculating the distance to frontier score for each economy involves two main steps. In the first step individual component indicators are normalized to a common unit where each of the 41 component indicators *y* (except for the total tax rate) is rescaled using the linear transformation *(worst−y)/(worst−frontier)*. In this formulation the frontier represents the best performance on the indicator across all economies since 2005 or the third year in which data for the indicator were collected. Both the best performance and the worst performance are established every five years based on the *Doing Business* data for the year in which they are established, and remain at that level for the five years regardless of any changes in data in interim years. Thus an economy may set the frontier for an indicator even though it is no longer at the frontier in a subsequent year.

For scores such as those on the strength of legal rights index or the quality of land administration index, the frontier is set at the highest possible value. For the total tax rate, consistent with the use of a threshold in calculating the rankings on this indicator, the frontier is defined as the total tax rate at the 15th percentile of the overall distribution for all years included in the analysis up to and including *Doing Business 2015*. For the time to pay taxes the frontier is defined as the lowest time recorded among all economies that levy the three major taxes: profit tax, labor

TABLE 14.1 What is the frontier in regulatory practice?

Topic and indicator	Who set the frontier	Frontier	Worst performance
Starting a business			
Procedures (number)	New Zealand	1	18[a]
Time (days)	New Zealand	0.5	100[b]
Cost (% of income per capita)	Slovenia	0.0	200.0[b]
Minimum capital (% of income per capita)	Australia; Colombia[c]	0.0	400.0[b]
Dealing with construction permits			
Procedures (number)	No economy was at the frontier as of June 1, 2016.	5	30[a]
Time (days)	Singapore	26	373[b]
Cost (% of warehouse value)	No economy was at the frontier as of June 1, 2016.	0.0	20.0[b]
Building quality control index (0–15)	Luxembourg; New Zealand	15	0[d]
Getting electricity			
Procedures (number)	Germany; Republic of Korea[e]	3	9[a]
Time (days)	Republic of Korea; St. Kitts and Nevis	18	248[b]
Cost (% of income per capita)	Japan	0.0	8,100.0[b]
Reliability of supply and transparency of tariffs index (0–8)	Belgium; Ireland; Malaysia[f]	8	0[d]
Registering property			
Procedures (number)	Georgia; Norway; Portugal; Sweden	1	13[a]
Time (days)	Georgia; New Zealand; Portugal	1	210[b]
Cost (% of property value)	Saudi Arabia	0.0	15.0[b]
Quality of land administration index (0–30)	No economy has attained the frontier yet.	30	0[d]
Getting credit			
Strength of legal rights index (0–12)	Colombia; Montenegro; New Zealand	12	0[d]
Depth of credit information index (0–8)	Ecuador; United Kingdom[g]	8	0[d]
Protecting minority investors			
Extent of disclosure index (0–10)	China; Malaysia[h]	10	0[d]
Extent of director liability index (0–10)	Cambodia	10	0[d]
Ease of shareholder suits index (0–10)	No economy has attained the frontier yet.	10	0[d]
Extent of shareholder rights index (0–10)	Chile; India[i]	10	0[d]
Extent of ownership and control index (0–10)	No economy has attained the frontier yet.	10	0[d]
Extent of corporate transparency index (0–10)	No economy has attained the frontier yet.	10	0[d]
Paying taxes			
Payments (number per year)	Hong Kong SAR, China; Saudi Arabia	3	63[b]
Time (hours per year)	Singapore	49[j]	696[b]
Total tax rate (% of profit)	Singapore[k]	26.1[l]	84.0[b]
Postfiling index (0–100)	No economy has attained the frontier yet.	100	0
Time to comply with VAT refund (hours)	Croatia; Netherlands[m]	0	50[b]
Time to obtain VAT refund (weeks)	Austria	3.2	55[b]
Time to comply with corporate income tax audit (hours)	Lithuania; Portugal[n]	1.5	56[b]
Time to complete a corporate income tax audit (weeks)	Sweden; United States[o]	0	32[b]

(continued)

TABLE 14.1 What is the frontier in regulatory practice? *(continued)*

Topic and indicator	Who set the frontier	Frontier	Worst performance
Trading across borders			
Time to export			
Documentary compliance (hours)	Canada; Poland; Spain[p]	1[q]	170[b]
Border compliance (hours)	Austria; Belgium; Denmark[r]	1[q]	160[b]
Cost to export			
Documentary compliance (US$)	Hungary; Luxembourg; Norway[s]	0	400[b]
Border compliance (US$)	France; Netherlands; Portugal[t]	0	1,060[b]
Time to import			
Documentary compliance (hours)	Republic of Korea; Latvia; New Zealand[u]	1[q]	240[b]
Border compliance (hours)	Estonia; France; Germany[v]	1[q]	280[b]
Cost to import			
Documentary compliance (US$)	Iceland; Latvia; United Kingdom[w]	0	700[b]
Border compliance (US$)	Belgium; Denmark; Estonia[x]	0	1,200[b]
Enforcing contracts			
Time (days)	Singapore	120	1,340[b]
Cost (% of claim)	Bhutan	0.1	89.0[b]
Quality of judicial processes index (0–18)	No economy has attained the frontier yet.	18	0[d]
Resolving insolvency			
Recovery rate (cents on the dollar)	Norway	92.9	0[d]
Strength of insolvency framework index (0–16)	No economy has attained the frontier yet.	16	0[d]

Source: Doing Business database.

a. Worst performance is defined as the 99th percentile among all economies in the *Doing Business* sample.
b. Worst performance is defined as the 95th percentile among all economies in the *Doing Business* sample.
c. Another 111 economies also have a paid-in minimum capital requirement of 0.
d. Worst performance is the worst value recorded.
e. In 14 other economies it also takes only 3 procedures to get an electricity connection.
f. Another 23 economies also have a score of 8 on the reliability of supply and transparency of tariffs index.
g. Another 28 economies also have a score of 8 on the depth of credit information index.
h. Another 10 economies also have a score of 10 on the extent of disclosure index.
i. Another 4 economies also have a score of 10 on the extent of shareholder rights index.
j. Defined as the lowest time recorded among all economies in the *Doing Business* sample that levy the three major taxes: profit tax, labor taxes and mandatory contributions, and VAT or sales tax.
k. Another 31 economies also have a total tax rate equal to or lower than 26.1% of profit.
l. Defined as the highest total tax rate among the 15% of economies with the lowest total tax rate in the *Doing Business* sample for all years included in the analysis up to and including *Doing Business 2015*.
m. Another 7 economies also have a compliance time for VAT refund of 0 hours.
n. Another 3 economies also have a compliance time for corporate income tax audit of 1.5 hours.
o. Another 104 economies also have a completion time for corporate income tax audit of 0 weeks.
p. Another 22 economies also have a documentary compliance time to export of no more than 1 hour.
q. Defined as 1 hour even though in many economies the time is less than that.
r. Another 15 economies also have a border compliance time to export of no more than 1 hour.
s. Another 16 economies also have a documentary compliance cost to export of 0.00.
t. Another 15 economies also have a border compliance cost to export of 0.00.
u. Another 26 economies also have a documentary compliance time to import of no more than 1 hour.
v. Another 22 economies also have a border compliance time to import of no more than 1 hour.
w. Another 27 economies also have a documentary compliance cost to import of 0.00.
x. Another 25 economies also have a border compliance cost to import of 0.00.

taxes and mandatory contributions, and value added tax (VAT) or sales tax. For the different times to trade across borders, the frontier is defined as 1 hour even though in many economies the time is less than that.

In the same formulation, to mitigate the effects of extreme outliers in the distributions of the rescaled data for most component indicators (very few economies need 700 days to complete the procedures to start a business, but many need 9 days), the worst performance is calculated after the removal of outliers. The definition of outliers is based on the distribution for each component indicator. To simplify the process two rules were defined: the 95th percentile is used for the indicators with the most dispersed distributions (including minimum capital, number of payments to pay taxes, and the time and cost indicators), and the 99th percentile is used for the number of procedures. No outlier is removed for component indicators bound by definition or construction, including legal index scores (such as the depth of credit information index, extent of conflict of interest regulation index and strength of insolvency framework index) and the recovery rate (figure 14.1).

In the second step for calculating the distance to frontier score, the scores obtained for individual indicators for each economy are aggregated through simple averaging into one distance to frontier score, first for each topic and then across all 10 topics: starting a business, dealing with construction permits, getting electricity, registering property, getting credit, protecting minority investors, paying taxes, trading across borders, enforcing contracts and resolving insolvency. More complex aggregation methods—such as principal components and unobserved components—yield a ranking nearly identical to the simple average used by *Doing Business*.[1] Thus *Doing Business* uses the simplest method: weighting all topics equally and, within each topic, giving equal weight to each of the topic components.[2]

An economy's distance to frontier score is indicated on a scale from 0 to 100, where 0 represents the worst performance and 100 the frontier. All distance to frontier calculations are based on a maximum of five decimals. However, indicator ranking calculations and the ease of doing business ranking calculations are based on two decimals.

The difference between an economy's distance to frontier score in any previous year and its score in 2016 illustrates the extent to which the economy has closed the gap to the regulatory frontier over time. And in any given year the score measures how far an economy is from the best performance at that time.

FIGURE 14.1 How are distance to frontier scores calculated for indicators? Two examples

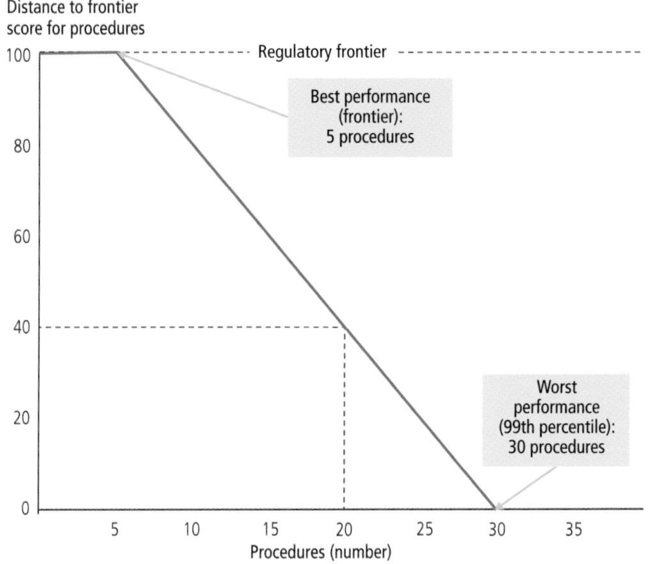

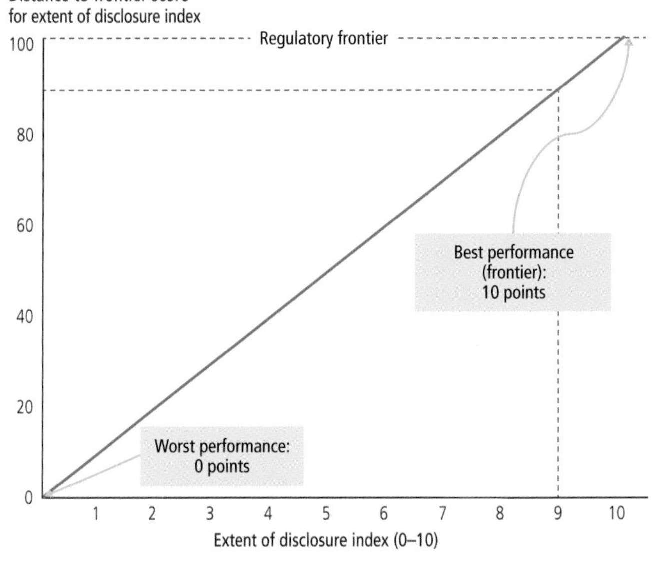

Source: Doing Business database.

Treatment of the total tax rate

The total tax rate component of the paying taxes indicator set enters the distance to frontier calculation in a different way than any other indicator. The distance to frontier score obtained for the total tax rate is transformed in a nonlinear fashion before it enters the distance to frontier score for paying taxes. As a result of the nonlinear transformation, an increase in the total tax rate has a smaller impact on the distance to frontier score for the total tax rate—and therefore on the distance to frontier score for paying taxes—for economies with a below-average total tax rate than it would have had before this approach was adopted in *Doing Business 2015* (line B is smaller than line A in figure 14.2). And for economies with an extreme total tax rate (a rate that is very high relative to the average), an increase has a greater impact on both these distance to frontier scores than it would have had before (line D is bigger than line C in figure 14.2).

The nonlinear transformation is not based on any economic theory of an "optimal tax rate" that minimizes distortions or maximizes efficiency in an economy's overall tax system. Instead, it is mainly empirical in nature. The nonlinear transformation along with the threshold reduces the bias in the indicator toward economies that do not need to levy significant taxes on companies like the *Doing Business* standardized case study company because they raise public revenue in other ways—for example, through taxes on foreign companies, through taxes on sectors other than manufacturing or from natural resources (all of which are outside the scope of the methodology). In addition, it acknowledges the need of economies to collect taxes from firms.

Calculation of scores for economies with two cities covered

For each of the 11 economies in which *Doing Business* collects data for the second largest business city as well as the largest one, the distance to frontier score is calculated as the population-weighted average of the distance to frontier scores for these two cities (table 14.2). This is done for the aggregate score, the scores for each topic and the scores for all the component indicators for each topic.

Variability of economies' scores across topics

Each indicator set measures a different aspect of the business regulatory environment. The distance to frontier scores and associated rankings of an economy can vary, sometimes significantly, across indicator sets. The average correlation coefficient between the 10 indicator sets included in the aggregate distance to frontier score is 0.48, and the coefficients between 2 sets of indicators range from 0.32 (between getting credit and paying taxes) to 0.61 (between registering property and enforcing contracts). These correlations suggest that economies rarely score universally well or universally badly on the indicators (table 14.3).

Consider the example of Portugal. Its aggregate distance to frontier score is 77.40. Its score is 92.85 for starting a business and 100.00 for trading across borders. But its score is only 56.67 for protecting minority investors and 45.00 for getting credit.

Figure 2.1 in the chapter "About *Doing Business*" illustrates the degree of variability for each economy's performance across the different areas of business regulation covered by *Doing Business*. The figure draws attention to economies

FIGURE 14.2 How the nonlinear transformation affects the distance to frontier score for the total tax rate

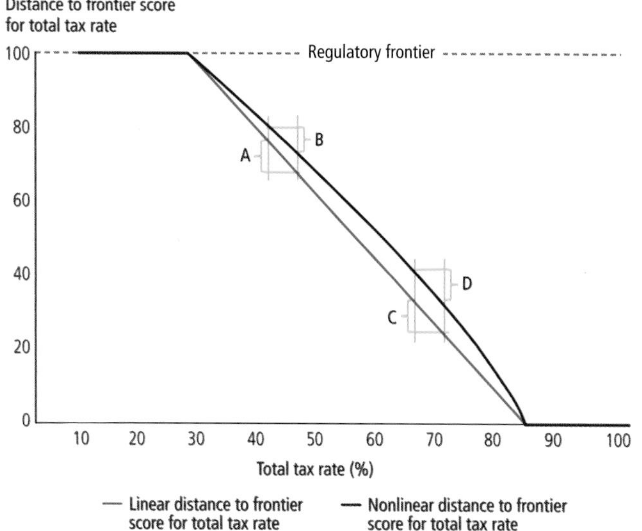

Source: Doing Business database.
Note: The nonlinear distance to frontier score for the total tax rate is equal to the distance to frontier score for the total tax rate to the power of 0.8.

TABLE 14.2 Weights used in calculating the distance to frontier scores for economies with two cities covered

Economy	City	Weight (%)
Bangladesh	Dhaka	78
	Chittagong	22
Brazil	São Paulo	61
	Rio de Janeiro	39
China	Shanghai	55
	Beijing	45
India	Mumbai	47
	Delhi	53
Indonesia	Jakarta	78
	Surabaya	22
Japan	Tokyo	65
	Osaka	35
Mexico	Mexico City	83
	Monterrey	17
Nigeria	Lagos	77
	Kano	23
Pakistan	Karachi	65
	Lahore	35
Russian Federation	Moscow	70
	St. Petersburg	30
United States	New York City	60
	Los Angeles	40

Source: United Nations, Department of Economic and Social Affairs, Population Division, World Urbanization Prospects, 2014 Revision, "File 12: Population of Urban Agglomerations with 300,000 Inhabitants or More in 2014, by Country, 1950–2030 (thousands)," http://esa.un.org/unpd/wup/CD-ROM/Default.aspx.

TABLE 14.3 Correlations between economy distance to frontier scores for *Doing Business* topics

	Dealing with construction permits	Getting electricity	Registering property	Getting credit	Protecting minority investors	Paying taxes	Trading across borders	Enforcing contracts	Resolving insolvency
Starting a business	0.47	0.48	0.45	0.41	0.52	0.53	0.45	0.40	0.47
Dealing with construction permits		0.48	0.50	0.37	0.46	0.48	0.44	0.37	0.40
Getting electricity			0.49	0.42	0.51	0.54	0.60	0.51	0.55
Registering property				0.50	0.53	0.50	0.49	0.61	0.51
Getting credit					0.57	0.32	0.43	0.39	0.54
Protecting minority investors						0.46	0.49	0.49	0.61
Paying taxes							0.52	0.44	0.45
Trading across borders								0.49	0.59
Enforcing contracts									0.46

Source: Doing Business database.

with a particularly uneven performance by showing, for each economy, the distance between the average of its highest three distance to frontier scores and the average of its lowest three across the 10 topics included in this year's aggregate distance to frontier score. While a relatively small distance between these two averages suggests a broadly consistent approach across the areas of business regulation measured by *Doing Business*, a relatively large distance suggests a more uneven approach, with greater room for improvements in some areas than in others.

Variation in performance across the indicator sets is not at all unusual. It reflects differences in the degree of priority that government authorities give to particular areas of business regulation reform and in the ability of different government agencies to deliver tangible results in their area of responsibility.

Economies improving the most across three or more *Doing Business* topics in 2015/16

Doing Business 2017 uses a simple method to calculate which economies improved the ease of doing business the most. First, it selects the economies that in 2015/16 implemented regulatory reforms making it easier to do business in 3 or more of the 10 topics included in this year's aggregate distance to frontier score.[3] Twenty-nine economies meet this criterion: Algeria; Azerbaijan; Bahrain; Belarus; Brazil; Brunei Darussalam; Burkina Faso; Côte d'Ivoire; Georgia; India; Indonesia; Kazakhstan; Kenya; Madagascar; Mali; Mauritania; Morocco; Niger; Pakistan; Poland; Senegal; Serbia; Singapore; Thailand; Togo; Uganda; the United Arab Emirates; Uzbekistan and Vanuatu. Second, *Doing Business* sorts these economies on the increase in their distance to frontier score from the previous year using comparable data.

Selecting the economies that implemented regulatory reforms in at least three topics and had the biggest improvements in their distance to frontier scores is intended to highlight economies with ongoing, broad-based reform programs. The improvement in the distance to frontier score is used to identify the top improvers because this allows a focus on the absolute improvement—in contrast with the relative improvement shown by a change in rankings—that economies have made in their regulatory environment for business.

EASE OF DOING BUSINESS RANKING

The ease of doing business ranking ranges from 1 to 190. The ranking of economies is determined by sorting the aggregate distance to frontier scores, rounded to two decimals.

NOTES

1. See Djankov, Manraj and others (2005). Principal components and unobserved components methods yield a ranking nearly identical to that from the simple average method because both these methods assign roughly equal weights to the topics, since the pairwise correlations among indicators do not differ much. An alternative to the simple average method is to give different weights to the topics, depending on which are considered of more or less importance in the context of a specific economy.
2. For getting credit, indicators are weighted proportionally, according to their contribution to the total score, with a weight of 60% assigned to the strength of legal rights index and 40% to the depth of credit information index. Indicators for all other topics are assigned equal weights.
3. Changes making it more difficult to do business are subtracted from the total number of those making it easier to do business.

Summaries of *Doing Business* Reforms in 2015/16

Doing Business reforms affecting all sets of indicators included in this year's report, implemented from June 2015 to June 2016.

✔ Reform making it easier to do business
✘ Change making it more difficult to do business

Afghanistan

✔ **Trading across borders**
Afghanistan made exporting and importing easier by introducing a number of technical, human resource and infrastructure improvements to ASYCUDA World, an electronic data interchange system.

✘ **Paying taxes**
Afghanistan made paying taxes more costly by increasing the business receipts tax rate.

Albania

✔ **Dealing with construction permits**
Albania made dealing with construction permits easier by reintroducing the issuance of building permits and streamlining the process of receiving the final inspection and compliance certificate.

✔ **Getting electricity**
Albania made getting electricity easier by speeding up the process for obtaining a new connection.

✘ **Trading across borders**
Albania made trading across borders more difficult by introducing mandatory scanning inspections for exports and imports, which increased the time and cost for border compliance.

✔ **Paying taxes**
Albania made paying taxes easier by introducing an online system for filing and paying taxes.

Algeria

✔ **Starting a business**
Algeria made starting a business easier by eliminating the minimum capital requirement for business incorporation.

✔ **Dealing with construction permits**
Algeria made dealing with construction permits faster by reducing the time to obtain a construction permit.

✔ **Getting electricity**
Algeria made getting electricity more transparent by publishing electricity tariffs on the websites of the utility and the energy regulator.

✔ **Paying taxes**
Algeria made paying taxes less costly by decreasing the tax on professional activities rate. The introduction of advanced accounting systems also made paying taxes easier.

Angola

✔ **Starting a business**
Angola made starting a business easier by eliminating the paid-in minimum capital requirement.

Reforms affecting the labor market regulation indicators are included here but do not affect the ranking on the ease of doing business.

✔ **Paying taxes**
Angola made paying taxes easier and less costly by reducing the frequency of advance payments of corporate income tax and increasing the allowable deductions for bad debt provisions. At the same time, Angola made interest income tax a final tax that is not deductible for the calculation of corporate income tax.

Labor market regulation
Angola adopted a new labor law that decreased the wage premium for overtime and night work and increased the wage premium for work on weekly holidays. The law also extended the maximum duration of fixed-term contracts and made fixed-term contracts able to be used for permanent tasks, reduced severance pay for redundancy dismissals of employees with five and ten years of continuous employment and increased severance pay for employees with one continuous year of service.

Antigua and Barbuda

✔ **Trading across borders**
Antigua and Barbuda made trading across borders easier by eliminating the tax compliance certificate required for import customs clearance.

Argentina

✘ **Dealing with construction permits**
Argentina made dealing with construction permits more difficult by increasing municipal fees.

✔ **Trading across borders**
Argentina made trading across borders easier by introducing a new licensing system for importing, which reduced the time required for documentary compliance.

✔ **Paying taxes**
Argentina made paying taxes less costly by increasing the threshold for the 5% turnover tax. Argentina also made paying taxes easier by introducing improvements to the online portal for filing taxes.

Armenia

✔ **Getting credit**
Armenia strengthened access to credit by adopting a new law on secured transactions that establishes a modern and centralized collateral registry. Armenia improved its credit information system by adopting a new law on personal data protection.

✔ **Enforcing contracts**
Armenia made enforcing contracts easier by introducing a consolidated chapter regulating voluntary mediation and by establishing financial incentives for the parties to attempt mediation.

Azerbaijan

✔ **Getting electricity**
Azerbaijan streamlined the process of obtaining a new electricity connection by introducing an electronic capacity/availability of connection map, which reduced the time needed to determine new customer connection points.

✔ **Trading across borders**
Azerbaijan made trading across borders easier by introducing an electronic system for submitting export and import declarations.

✔ **Paying taxes**
Azerbaijan made paying taxes easier by abolishing vehicle tax for residents.

Bahamas, The

✔ **Starting a business**
The Bahamas made starting a business easier by allowing local limited liability companies to register online. On the other hand, The Bahamas made starting a business more costly by increasing the fees for registering a company name and incorporation.

✔ **Registering property**
The Bahamas made registering property easier by reducing the cost of transferring a property.

✘ **Paying taxes**
The Bahamas made paying taxes more complicated by introducing a value added tax (VAT).

Bahrain

✔ **Starting a business**
Bahrain made starting a business easier by reducing the minimum capital requirement.

✔ **Getting credit**
Bahrain improved access to credit information by guaranteeing by law borrowers' right to inspect their own data.

✔ **Trading across borders**
Bahrain made exporting easier by improving infrastructure and streamlining procedures at the King Fahad Causeway.

Bangladesh

✘ **Paying taxes**
Bangladesh made paying taxes more complicated for companies by increasing the time it takes to prepare VAT and corporate income tax returns. This reform applies to both Chittagong and Dhaka.

Barbados

✔ **Starting a business**
Barbados made starting a business easier by reducing the time needed to register a company.

Belarus

✔ **Getting electricity**
Belarus streamlined the process of obtaining an electricity connection by establishing a one-stop shop at the utility that fulfills all connection-related services, including the design and construction of the distribution line.

✔ **Registering property**
Belarus made it easier to transfer a property by improving the transparency and reliability of the land administration system.

✔ **Getting credit**
In Belarus the credit bureau started to provide credit scores, strengthening the credit reporting system.

✔ **Protecting minority investors**
Belarus strengthened minority investor protections by introducing remedies in cases where related-party transactions are harmful to the company and requiring greater corporate transparency.

Benin

✔ **Starting a business**
Benin made starting a business easier by eliminating the need to notarize company bylaws to activate a bank account after incorporation.

✔ **Resolving insolvency**
Benin made resolving insolvency easier by introducing a new conciliation procedure for companies in financial difficulties and a simplified preventive settlement procedure for small companies.

Bolivia

✔ **Starting a business**
Bolivia made starting a business easier by decreasing the time needed to register a company.

✘ **Dealing with construction permits**
Bolivia made dealing with construction permits more difficult by implementing a new requirement to pay for land registry certificates at the Judicial Council.

✔ **Enforcing contracts**
Bolivia made enforcing contracts easier by adopting a new code of civil procedure that introduces pre-trial conferences.

Bosnia and Herzegovina

✔ **Starting a business**
Bosnia and Herzegovina made starting a business easier by reducing the paid-in minimum capital requirement for limited liability companies and increasing the efficiency of the notary system.

✔ **Paying taxes**
Bosnia and Herzegovina made paying taxes easier by abolishing the tourist community fee.

Botswana

✔ **Dealing with construction permits**
Botswana made dealing with construction permits easier by eliminating the requirement to submit a rates clearance certificate to obtain a building permit.

Brazil

✔ **Starting a business**
Brazil reduced the time needed to start a business by implementing an online portal for business licenses in Rio de Janeiro. However, Brazil also made starting a business more difficult by shortening the opening hours of the business registry in Rio de Janeiro.

✔ **Trading across borders**
Brazil made trading across borders easier by implementing an electronic system for importing, which reduced the time required for documentary compliance. This reform applies to both Rio de Janeiro and São Paulo.

✔ **Enforcing contracts**
Brazil made enforcing contracts easier through a new mediation law—that includes financial incentives for parties to attempt mediation—and a new code of civil procedure. These reforms apply to both Rio de Janeiro and São Paulo.

Labor market regulation
Brazil expanded eligibility for unemployment benefits to employees with one year of continuous work experience. This reform applies to both Rio de Janeiro and São Paulo.

Brunei Darussalam

✔ **Getting electricity**
The utility in Brunei Darussalam streamlined the processes of reviewing applications, and the time to issue an excavation permit was reduced. In addition, Brunei Darussalam increased the reliability of power supply by rolling out a Supervisory Control and Data Acquisition (SCADA) automatic energy management system for the monitoring of outages and the restoration of service.

✔ **Getting credit**
Brunei Darussalam improved access to credit information by beginning to distribute data from two utility companies. In addition, Brunei Darussalam strengthened access to credit by adopting a new insolvency law that contemplates protections for secured creditors during an automatic stay in reorganization proceedings.

✔ **Protecting minority investors**
Brunei Darussalam strengthened minority investor protections by clarifying ownership and control structures, making it easier to sue directors in case of prejudicial related-party transactions and allowing the rescission of related-party transactions that harm the company.

✔ **Paying taxes**
Brunei Darussalam made paying taxes easier by fully implementing an electronic system for filing and paying corporate income tax.

✔ **Enforcing contracts**
Brunei Darussalam made enforcing contracts easier by introducing an electronic filing system as well as a platform that allows users to pay court fees electronically.

✔ **Resolving insolvency**
Brunei Darussalam made resolving insolvency easier by adopting a new insolvency law that introduced a reorganization procedure and facilitated continuation of the debtor's business during insolvency proceedings. Brunei Darussalam also introduced regulations for insolvency practitioners.

Bulgaria

✔ **Getting electricity**
Bulgaria increased the reliability of power supply by implementing an automatic energy management system, the Supervisory Control and Data Acquisition (SCADA), to monitor outages and service restoration.

Burkina Faso

✔ **Starting a business**

Burkina Faso made starting a business easier by reducing the paid-in minimum capital required to register a company.

✔ **Getting credit**

Burkina Faso improved access to credit information by introducing regulations that govern the licensing and functioning of credit bureaus in West African Economic and Monetary Union (UEMOA) member states.

✔ **Resolving insolvency**

Burkina Faso made resolving insolvency easier by introducing a new conciliation procedure for companies in financial difficulties and a simplified preventive settlement procedure for small companies.

Burundi

✔ **Paying taxes**

Burundi made paying taxes easier by introducing a new tax return and eliminating the personalized VAT declaration form.

Cabo Verde

Labor market regulation

Cabo Verde introduced unemployment insurance for workers with a contribution period of at least six months.

Cambodia

✘ **Starting a business**

Cambodia made starting a business more difficult by increasing the time required to register and by requiring companies to submit evidence of capital deposit after registration.

✔ **Getting credit**

In Cambodia the credit bureau started to provide credit scores to banks and financial institutions, improving access to credit information.

Cameroon

✔ **Dealing with construction permits**

Cameroon made dealing with construction permits easier by reducing the time it takes to obtain the building permit and strengthen the Building Quality Control Index by increasing transparency.

✘ **Paying taxes**

Cameroon made paying taxes more costly by increasing the minimum tax rate for companies.

✔ **Resolving insolvency**

Cameroon made resolving insolvency easier by introducing a new conciliation procedure for companies in financial difficulties and a simplified preventive settlement procedure for small companies.

Central African Republic

✔ **Resolving insolvency**

The Central African Republic made resolving insolvency easier by introducing a new conciliation procedure for companies in financial difficulties and a simplified preventive settlement procedure for small companies.

Chad

✔ **Starting a business**

Chad made starting a business easier by reducing the paid-in minimum capital required to register a company.

✔ **Resolving insolvency**

Chad made resolving insolvency easier by introducing a new conciliation procedure for companies in financial difficulties and a simplified preventive settlement procedure for small companies.

China

✔ **Starting a business**

China made starting a business easier by introducing a single form to obtain a business license, organization code and tax registration. This reform applies to both Shanghai and Beijing.

✔ **Getting credit**

China improved access to credit information by starting to report payment histories from utility companies and providing credit scores to banks and financial institutions. This reform applies to both Shanghai and Beijing.

Colombia

✔ **Starting a business**

Colombia made starting a business easier by streamlining registration procedures.

Comoros

✔ **Registering property**

The Comoros made transferring a property less expensive by reducing transfer costs.

✔ **Resolving insolvency**

The Comoros made resolving insolvency easier by introducing a new conciliation procedure for companies in financial difficulties and a simplified preventive settlement procedure for small companies.

Labor market regulation

The Comoros reduced the length of notice period and amount of severance payment for redundancy dismissals.

Congo, Dem. Rep.

✔ **Dealing with construction permits**

The Democratic Republic of Congo made dealing with construction permits easier by improving building quality control and reducing the time it takes to obtain the building permit.

✘ **Registering property**

The Democratic Republic of Congo made it more expensive to transfer property by increasing the property transfer tax.

✔ **Resolving insolvency**

The Democratic Republic of Congo made resolving insolvency easier by introducing a new conciliation procedure for companies in financial difficulties and a simplified preventive settlement procedure for small companies.

Labor market regulations

The Democratic Republic of Congo adopted legislation that prohibits discrimination in hiring on the basis of gender.

Congo, Rep.

✔ **Resolving insolvency**

The Republic of Congo made resolving insolvency easier by introducing a new conciliation procedure for companies in financial difficulties and a simplified preventive settlement procedure for small companies.

Côte d'Ivoire

✔ **Dealing with construction permits**

Côte d'Ivoire made dealing with construction permits more transparent by making building regulations accessible online.

✔ **Getting credit**

Côte d'Ivoire improved access to credit information by establishing a new credit bureau.

✔ **Enforcing contracts**

Côte d'Ivoire made enforcing contracts easier by introducing a simplified fast-track procedure for small claims that allows for parties' self-representation.

✔ **Resolving insolvency**

Côte d'Ivoire made resolving insolvency easier by introducing a new conciliation procedure for companies in financial difficulties and a simplified preventive settlement procedure for small companies.

Croatia

✘ **Starting a business**

Croatia made starting a business more difficult by increasing notary fees.

✔ **Protecting minority investors**

Croatia strengthened minority investor protections by requiring detailed internal disclosure of conflicts of interest by directors.

✘ **Paying taxes**

Croatia made paying taxes more complicated by introducing a radio and television fee, and eliminating the reduction of the Chamber of Economy fee for new companies.

Cyprus

✔ **Starting a business**

Cyprus made starting a business easier by merging the procedures to register for taxes and VAT, and making company name search and reservation faster.

✘ **Getting credit**

Cyprus made access to credit information more difficult by stopping the distribution of historical credit data.

✔ **Paying taxes**

Cyprus made paying taxes easier by introducing improvements to its internal processes and to the electronic tax filing system. Cyprus also made paying taxes less costly by increasing the discount rate applied on immovable property tax.

Labor market regulation

Cyprus amended its legislation to allow shops and supermarkets to operate seven days a week.

Czech Republic

✔ **Starting a business**

The Czech Republic made starting a business easier by reducing the cost and the time required to register a company in commercial courts by allowing notaries to directly register companies through an online system.

✔ **Getting electricity**

The Czech Republic made getting electricity faster by designating personnel to deal with all incoming connection applications.

Dominica

✔ **Paying taxes**

Dominica made paying taxes less costly by reducing the corporate income tax rate.

Dominican Republic

✔ **Getting electricity**

The Dominican Republic made getting an electricity connection faster by reducing the time required to approve electrical connection plans.

✔ **Paying taxes**

The Dominican Republic made paying taxes less costly by decreasing the corporate income tax rate.

Ecuador

✔ **Starting a business**

Ecuador made starting a business easier by eliminating the publication of company charters in local newspapers.

✔ **Enforcing contracts**

Ecuador adopted a new code of civil procedure that made enforcing contracts easier by introducing a pre-trial conference. The new code also made enforcing contracts more difficult by eliminating a dedicated procedure for the resolution of small claims.

Egypt, Arab Rep.

✔ **Starting a business**

The Arab Republic of Egypt made starting a business easier by merging procedures at the one-stop shop by introducing a follow-up unit in charge of liaising with the tax and labor authority on behalf of the company.

✔ **Protecting minority investors**

The Arab Republic of Egypt strengthened minority investor protections by increasing shareholder rights and role in major corporate decisions and by clarifying ownership and control structures.

✘ **Trading across borders**

The Arab Republic of Egypt made trading across borders more difficult by making the process of obtaining and processing documents more complex and by imposing a cap on foreign exchange deposits and withdrawals for imports.

El Salvador

✘ **Getting credit**

El Salvador made access to credit information more difficult by reducing the coverage of the credit bureau.

✔ **Paying taxes**

El Salvador made paying taxes easier by encouraging the use of the electronic system for filing taxes.

Equatorial Guinea

✔ **Starting a business**

Equatorial Guinea made starting a business easier by eliminating the requirement to obtain company founders' criminal records.

✘ **Paying taxes**

Equatorial Guinea made paying taxes more costly by increasing the minimum tax.

✔ **Resolving insolvency**

Equatorial Guinea made resolving insolvency easier by introducing a new conciliation procedure for companies in financial difficulties and a simplified preventive settlement procedure for small companies.

Fiji

✔ **Starting a business**

Fiji made starting a business easier by reducing the time required to start a business. Fiji also made starting a business less costly by reducing fees at the business registry.

✘ **Getting credit**

The credit bureau in Fiji suspended operations making it more difficult to gain access to credit information.

✔ **Protecting minority investors**

Fiji strengthened minority investor protections by introducing greater disclosure requirements for related-party transactions.

France

✔ **Dealing with construction permits**

France made dealing with construction permits less expensive by reducing the cost of obtaining a building permit.

✘ **Registering property**

France made transferring property more expensive by increasing property transfer tax rate and introducing an additional tax for businesses in Paris.

Labor market regulation

France reformed its labor legislation by introducing changes to the administration of labor tribunals, extending Sunday and evening work in areas designated as international tourist zones and facilitating employee-employer dialogue.

Gabon

✔ **Resolving insolvency**

Gabon made resolving insolvency easier by introducing a new conciliation procedure for companies in financial difficulties and a simplified preventive settlement procedure for small companies.

Gambia, The

✔ **Getting credit**

The Gambia strengthened access to credit by adopting a new law on secured transactions that implements a functional secured transactions system and establishes a centralized, notice-based collateral registry.

Georgia

✔ **Getting electricity**

Georgia improved the reliability of electricity supply by introducing penalties for the utility for having worse scores on the annual system average interruption duration index (SAIDI) and system average interruption frequency index (SAIFI) than the previous year. Georgia also mandated the notification of customers by the utility of planned electricity outages.

✔ **Registering property**

Georgia improved the quality of land administration by increasing coverage of all maps for privately held land plots in the main business city.

✔ **Protecting minority investors**

Georgia strengthened minority investor protections by increasing shareholder rights and role in major corporate decisions and by clarifying ownership and control structures.

✔ **Trading across borders**

Georgia made export and import documentary compliance faster by improving its electronic document processing system. It also introduced an advanced electronic document submission option.

✔ **Paying taxes**

Georgia made paying taxes easier by abolishing additional annex to corporate income tax returns and by improving the efficiency of the online system used for filing VAT returns.

Ghana

✘ **Starting a business**

Ghana made starting a business more costly by increasing registration and authentication fees.

✘ **Dealing with construction permits**

Ghana made dealing with construction permits more expensive by increasing the cost of obtaining a building permit.

✔ **Trading across borders**

Ghana made trading across borders easier by removing the mandatory pre-arrival assessment inspection at origin for imported goods.

Greece

✘ **Paying taxes**

Greece made paying taxes more costly by increasing the corporate income tax rate.

✔ **Enforcing contracts**

Greece made enforcing contracts easier by amending its rules of civil procedure to introduce tighter rules on adjournments, impose deadlines for key court events and limit the recourses that can be lodged during enforcement proceedings.

Grenada

✔ **Trading across borders**

Grenada made trading across borders easier by streamlining import document submission procedures, reducing the time required for documentary compliance.

Guatemala

✔ **Paying taxes**

Guatemala made paying taxes less costly by reducing the rate of corporate income tax.

Guinea

✔ **Resolving insolvency**

Guinea made resolving insolvency easier by introducing a new conciliation procedure for companies in financial difficulties and a simplified preventive settlement procedure for small companies.

Guinea-Bissau

✔ **Resolving insolvency**

Guinea-Bissau made resolving insolvency easier by introducing a new conciliation procedure for companies in financial difficulties and a simplified preventive settlement procedure for small companies.

Guyana

✔ **Registering property**

Guyana made registering property easier by increasing the transparency of the Lands and Survey Commission.

✔ **Getting credit**

Guyana improved access to credit information by expanding the coverage of the credit bureau.

Haiti

✔ **Trading across borders**

Haiti made trading across borders easier by improving port infrastructure and further implementing the ASYCUDA World electronic data interchange system by allowing the online submission of supporting documents.

Honduras

✘ **Trading across borders**

Honduras made trading across borders more difficult by increasing the number of intrusive inspections for importing, which increased the border compliance time.

Hong Kong SAR, China

✔ **Starting a business**

Hong Kong SAR, China, made starting a business less costly by reducing the business registration fee.

✔ **Getting electricity**

Hong Kong SAR, China, streamlined the processes of reviewing applications for new electrical connections and also reduced the time needed to issue an excavation permit.

Hungary

✔ **Paying taxes**

Hungary made paying taxes less costly for small and medium-size businesses by allowing tax relief by means of an additional deduction for new acquisitions of land and buildings.

✔ **Enforcing contracts**

Hungary made enforcing contracts easier by introducing an electronic filing system.

Labor market regulation

Hungary amended legislation to remove restrictions limiting the operating hours for retail shops.

India

✔ **Getting electricity**

India made getting electricity faster and cheaper by streamlining the process of getting a new commercial electricity connection. This reform impacts Delhi.

✔ **Paying taxes**

India made paying taxes easier by introducing an electronic system for paying employee state insurance contributions. This reform applies to both Mumbai and Delhi.

✔ **Trading across borders**

India made exporting and importing easier by launching the ICEGATE portal and simplifying border and documentary procedures. This reform applies to both Mumbai and Delhi.

✔ **Enforcing contracts**

India made enforcing contracts easier by creating dedicated divisions to resolve commercial cases. This reform applies to both Mumbai and Delhi.

Indonesia

✔ **Starting a business**

Indonesia made starting a business easier by creating a single form to apply for the company registration certificate and trading license. This reform applies to Jakarta. Indonesia also made starting a business easier by abolishing the minimum capital requirement for small and medium-size enterprises and by encouraging the use of an online system to reserve company names. This reform applies to both Jakarta and Surabaya.

✔ **Getting electricity**

Indonesia made the process for getting an electricity connection faster by reducing the time for contractors to perform external work thanks to an increase in the stock of electrical material supplied by the utility. In Surabaya, getting electricity was also made easier after the utility streamlined the process for new connection requests.

✔ **Registering property**

Indonesia made it easier to register property by digitizing its cadastral records and setting up a geographic information system. This reform applies to both Jakarta and Surabaya.

✔ **Getting credit**

Indonesia strengthened access to credit by establishing a modern collateral registry. This reform applies to both Jakarta and Surabaya.

✔ **Paying taxes**

Indonesia made paying taxes easier by introducing an online system for filing and paying health contributions. Indonesia also made paying taxes more costly by levying a new pension contribution at a rate of 2% paid by employers. These reforms apply to both Jakarta and Surabaya.

✔ **Trading across borders**

Indonesia made exporting and importing easier by improving the customs services and document submission functions of the national single window. This reform applies to both Jakarta and Surabaya.

✔ **Enforcing contracts**

Indonesia made enforcing contracts easier by introducing a dedicated procedure for small claims that allows for parties' self-representation. This reform applies to both Jakarta and Surabaya.

Iran, Islamic Rep.

✔ **Trading across borders**

The Islamic Republic of Iran made exporting and importing easier by improving and expanding the services offered by the national single window.

Iraq

✔ **Dealing with construction permits**

Iraq made dealing with construction permits easier by allowing the simultaneous processing of utility clearances and building permit applications.

✔ **Getting electricity**

The Ministry of Electricity made getting electricity faster by enforcing tighter deadlines on electricity connections.

Ireland

✔ **Starting a business**

Ireland made starting a business easier by removing the requirement that a founder seeking to incorporate a company swear before a commissioner of oaths.

Israel

✔ **Starting a business**

Israel made starting a business easier by merging registration for tax and social security.

Italy

✔ **Paying taxes**

Italy made paying taxes easier by allowing full cost of labor to be deductible for regional tax on productive activities (IRAP) purposes, as well as updating coefficients used for calculation of tax on real estate (IMU) and municipal service tax (TASI). Furthermore the electronic system for preparing and paying labor taxes was improved.

Jamaica

✘ **Starting a business**

Jamaica made starting a business more difficult by removing the ability to complete next-day company incorporation.

✔ **Paying taxes**

Jamaica made paying taxes less costly by increasing tax depreciation rates and the initial capital allowance for assets acquired on or after January 1, 2014. Furthermore, companies incorporated for less than 24 months are exempted from paying the minimum business tax. Jamaica also made paying taxes easier by implementing an electronic system for filing of corporate income tax, VAT and social security contributions.

✔ **Trading across borders**

Jamaica reduced the time of documentary compliance for exporting by implementing ASYCUDA World, an automated customs data management system.

Japan

✔ **Paying taxes**

Japan made paying taxes easier by disclosing the technical specifications of the eTax platform and allowing the upload of additional information in comma separated value (CSV) format. The restoration surtax was also abolished. However, a local corporation tax was introduced and the rates of special local corporation tax, inhabitants tax and enterprise tax were raised. Welfare pension premiums were also raised. These reforms apply to both Tokyo and Osaka. However, the rate for health insurance contributions paid by employers was reduced only in Osaka.

Jordan

✔ **Paying taxes**

Jordan made paying taxes less costly by increasing the depreciation rates for some fixed assets.

✔ **Trading across borders**

Jordan made exporting and importing easier by streamlining customs clearance processes, advancing the use of a single window and improving infrastructure at the Port of Aqaba.

Kazakhstan

✔ **Starting a business**

Kazakhstan simplified the process of starting a business by abolishing the requirement to notarize company documents and founders' signatures.

✔ **Dealing with construction permits**

Kazakhstan made dealing with construction permits easier by introducing a single window and streamlining procedures.

✔ **Getting electricity**

Kazakhstan streamlined the process of obtaining an electricity connection by eliminating the need for an official excavation permit and an inspection by the State Energy Supervision Committee. Kazakhstan also reduced the time needed to fulfill utility technical requirements and to sign supply contracts. The reliability of the power supply in Kazakhstan was also improved following the establishment of normative levels for the annual system average interruption duration index (SAIDI) and system average interruption frequency index (SAIFI).

✔ **Protecting minority investors**

Kazakhstan strengthened minority investor protections by introducing greater requirements for immediate disclosure of related-party transactions to the public, increasing shareholder rights and role in major corporate decisions, clarifying ownership and control structures and requiring greater corporate transparency.

✔ **Trading across borders**
Kazakhstan made exporting less costly by removing two export documents required for customs clearance.

✔ **Enforcing contracts**
Kazakhstan made enforcing contracts easier by adopting a new code of civil procedure and by regulating the maximum number of adjournments that can be granted by a judge in a given case.

✔ **Resolving insolvency**
Kazakhstan made resolving insolvency easier by changing voting procedures for reorganization plans and providing protections to creditors who vote against such plans. Additionally, creditors were granted greater access to information about the debtor during insolvency proceedings and allowed to challenge decisions affecting their rights.

Labor market regulation
Kazakhstan adopted a new labor code that decreased the wage premium for work on weekly holidays, eliminated the requirement to reassign employees before making them redundant, extended the maximum duration of probationary periods and introduced mandatory out-of-court mediation procedures before parties can file claims in court.

Kenya

✔ **Starting a business**
Kenya made starting a business easier by removing the stamp duty fees required for the nominal capital, memorandum and articles of association. Kenya also eliminated requirements to sign the declaration of compliance before a commissioner of oaths. However, Kenya also made starting a business more expensive by introducing a flat fee for company incorporation.

✔ **Getting electricity**
Kenya streamlined the process of getting electricity by introducing the use of a geographic information system which eliminates the need to conduct a site visit, thereby reducing the time and interactions needed to obtain an electricity connection.

✔ **Registering property**
Kenya made registering property easier by increasing the transparency at its land registry and cadaster.

✔ **Protecting minority investors**
Kenya strengthened minority investor protections by introducing greater requirements for disclosure of related-party transactions to the board of directors, by making it easier to sue directors in cases of prejudicial related-party transactions and by allowing the rescission of related-party transactions that are shown to harm the company.

✔ **Resolving insolvency**
Kenya made resolving insolvency easier by introducing a reorganization procedure, facilitating continuation of the debtor's business during insolvency proceedings and by introducing regulations for insolvency practitioners.

Korea, Rep.

✔ **Starting a business**
Korea made starting a business faster by eliminating post-registration procedures.

Kosovo

✔ **Paying taxes**
Kosovo made paying taxes easier by introducing an online system for filing and paying VAT and social security contributions, and it made paying taxes less costly by allowing more types of expenses to be deducted for the calculation of corporate income tax.

✔ **Trading across borders**
Kosovo reduced the time and cost of documentary compliance and the time of border compliance for exporting by improving its automated customs data management system, streamlining customs clearance processes and implementing the Albania-Kosovo Transit Corridor.

Kuwait

✘ **Starting a business**
Kuwait made starting a business more difficult by increasing the time needed to register by requiring companies to submit the original documents both online and in person.

✔ **Trading across borders**
Kuwait made exporting and importing easier by introducing customs electronic links and facilitating the electronic exchange of information among various agencies.

Kyrgyz Republic

✔ **Trading across borders**
The Kyrgyz Republic decreased the time and cost needed for exporting by becoming a member of the Eurasian Economic Union.

Lao PDR

✔ **Starting a business**
The Lao People's Democratic Republic made the process of starting a business faster by implementing simplified procedures for obtaining a license and a registered company seal.

✔ **Getting electricity**
Lao PDR improved the regulation of outages by beginning to record data for the annual system average interruption duration index (SAIDI) and system average interruption frequency index (SAIFI).

Latvia

✔ **Getting credit**
Latvia improved access to credit information by launching a private credit bureau.

✔ **Paying taxes**
Latvia made paying taxes less complicated by improving its online systems for filing corporate income tax returns and mandatory labor contributions.

Lesotho

✔ **Getting credit**

Lesotho improved access to credit information by expanding the coverage of its credit bureau.

Liberia

Labor market regulation

Liberia shortened the workweek by increasing the mandatory number of weekly rest hours to 36 consecutive hours with Sunday designated as the weekly holiday. It also mandated a maximum of five overtime hours per week. Liberia also introduced paid annual leave entitlements to employees after one year of employment, extended the duration of paid maternity leave and mandated equal remuneration for work of equal value.

Lithuania

✔ **Getting electricity**

Lithuania made getting electricity faster by introducing time limits on the utility to conduct necessary connection procedures and lowering the connection tariff.

Macedonia, FYR

✔ **Getting credit**

The former Yugoslav Republic of Macedonia improved access to credit by amending its laws to implement a functional secured transactions system, provide modern features for the collateral registry and allow parties to grant nonpossessory security rights in a single category of assets with general descriptions.

✔ **Protecting minority investors**

FYR Macedonia strengthened minority investor protections by increasing shareholder rights and role in major corporate decisions, allowing greater access to corporate information during trial and clarifying ownership and control structures.

✘ **Enforcing contracts**

FYR Macedonia made enforcing contracts more difficult by adopting amendments to the Law on Civil Procedure that mandate mediation before filing a claim, thus lengthening the initial phase of judicial proceedings.

✔ **Resolving insolvency**

FYR Macedonia made resolving insolvency easier by changing voting procedures for the reorganization plans and allowing creditors greater participation in insolvency proceedings.

Madagascar

✔ **Starting a business**

Madagascar made starting a business easier by reducing the number of procedures needed to register a company.

✔ **Dealing with construction permits**

Madagascar increased the transparency of dealing with construction permits by publishing construction-related regulations online and free of charge.

✔ **Trading across borders**

Madagascar made trading across borders easier by simplifying and streamlining customs procedures and implementing an electronic data interchange system, reducing the time for preparation and submission of trade documents for exporting and importing.

Malawi

✔ **Starting a business**

Malawi made starting a business easier by eliminating the legal requirement to use a company seal.

✔ **Getting credit**

Malawi strengthened access to credit by adopting a new law on secured transactions that implements a functional secured transactions system and establishes a centralized, notice-based, online collateral registry.

Malaysia

✘ **Starting a business**

Malaysia made starting a business more difficult by requiring that companies with an annual revenue of more than MYR 500,000 register as a GST payer.

✔ **Getting credit**

In Malaysia the credit bureau began to provide consumer credit scores.

✔ **Paying taxes**

Malaysia made paying taxes easier by introducing an online system for filing and paying goods and services tax (GST) while also making it more complex by replacing sales tax with GST.

Mali

✔ **Starting a business**

Mali made starting a business easier by reducing the paid-in minimum capital required to register a company.

✔ **Getting credit**

Mali improved access to credit information by establishing a new credit bureau.

✔ **Resolving insolvency**

Mali made resolving insolvency easier by introducing a new conciliation procedure for companies in financial difficulties and a simplified preventive settlement procedure for small companies.

Malta

✔ **Starting a business**

Malta made starting a business easier by offering automatic registration with the Inland Revenue Department following the receipt of the company registration number.

✔ **Getting credit**

Malta improved access to credit information by launching a new credit registry.

✘ **Paying taxes**

Malta made paying taxes more costly by replacing the capital gains tax with a property transfer tax, and increasing the maximum social security contribution paid by employers.

Mauritania

✔ **Getting credit**

Mauritania improved access to credit information by providing banks and financial institutions with online access to credit registry data.

✔ **Protecting minority investors**

Mauritania strengthened minority investor protections by requiring prior external review of related-party transactions, by increasing director liability and by expanding shareholders' role in major transactions.

✔ **Paying taxes**

Mauritania made paying taxes easier by reducing the frequency of both tax filing and payment of social security contributions.

✔ **Trading across borders**

Mauritania made trading across borders easier by upgrading to the ASYCUDA World electronic data interchange system, which reduced the time for preparation and submission of customs declarations for both exports and imports.

Mauritius

✔ **Registering property**

Mauritius made registering property easier by digitizing its land records.

Mexico

✘ **Starting a business**

Mexico made starting a business more difficult by discontinuing the use of an online portal for tax and business registration. This reform applies to Mexico City.

✔ **Registering property**

Mexico made registering property easier by digitizing its land records, improving the quality of the land registry infrastructure and making the registration process more efficient. This reform applies to Mexico City.

Labor market regulation

Mexico adopted a resolution that eliminated geographic differences in national minimum wages. Prior to the reform Mexico was divided into two zones—zone A and zone B—with different applicable minimum wages. This reform applies to both Mexico City and Monterrey.

Moldova

✘ **Starting a business**

Moldova made starting a business more costly by increasing the cost of company registration.

✔ **Getting electricity**

Moldova streamlined the process of obtaining a new electricity connection by eliminating the need for new customers with a capacity of less than 200 kilowatts to obtain an inspection from the State Energy Inspectorate.

✔ **Paying taxes**

Moldova made paying taxes easier by eliminating a requirement to submit social security documents in hard copy. However, Moldova also made paying taxes more costly by raising rates for road tax, environmental levy and health insurance contributions paid by employers.

✔ **Enforcing contracts**

Moldova made enforcing contracts easier by adopting a new mediation law establishing financial incentives for the parties to attempt mediation.

Mongolia

✔ **Paying taxes**

Mongolia made paying taxes easier by introducing an electronic system for filing and payment of taxes.

Montenegro

✔ **Paying taxes**

Montenegro made paying taxes less costly by reducing the personal income tax rate. Montenegro made paying taxes easier by providing an electronic system for filing and paying VAT. At the same time, Montenegro made paying taxes more costly by increasing the health contribution rate paid by employers.

Morocco

✔ **Starting a business**

Morocco made the process of starting a business easier by introducing an online platform to reserve a company name and reducing registration fees.

✔ **Registering property**

Morocco made registering property easier by streamlining the property registration process.

✔ **Getting credit**

In Morocco the credit bureau began to provide credit scores.

✔ **Protecting minority investors**

Morocco strengthened minority investor protections by clarifying ownership and control structures and by requiring greater corporate transparency.

✔ **Trading across borders**

Morocco reduced the time for border compliance for importing by further developing its single window system.

Mozambique

✘ **Starting a business**

Mozambique made starting a business more difficult by increasing registration and notary fees.

✔ **Getting credit**

Mozambique improved access to credit information by enacting a law that allows the establishment of a new credit bureau.

Myanmar

✔ **Starting a business**

Myanmar made starting a business easier by reducing the cost to register a company. It also simplified the process by removing the requirement to submit a reference letter and a criminal history certificate in order to incorporate a company.

✔ **Getting credit**

Myanmar improved its credit information system by enacting a law that allows the establishment of a new credit bureau.

✘ **Trading across borders**

Myanmar made trading across borders more difficult for traders as they experience higher cost and time delays due to congestion at the port of Yangon.

Labor market regulation

Myanmar introduced a minimum wage and changed the regulation of severance pay.

Nepal

✘ **Dealing with construction permits**

Nepal made dealing with construction permits more difficult by increasing the cost of obtaining a building permit.

✔ **Trading across borders**

Nepal made exporting and importing easier by implementing ASYCUDA World, an electronic data interchange system.

Netherlands

✔ **Paying taxes**

The Netherlands made paying taxes less costly by lowering the rates paid by employers for health insurance contributions, special unemployment insurance, unemployment insurance and real estate taxes. The Netherlands also made paying taxes easier by improving the online system for paying corporate income tax. However, the Netherlands made paying taxes more costly by increasing the rates for disablement insurance contribution paid by employers, polder board tax and motor tax.

Labor market regulation

The Netherlands reduced the maximum duration of fixed-term contracts from 36 to 24 months. Severance pay was introduced for redundancy dismissals for employees with at least 2 years of continuous employment.

New Zealand

✔ **Paying taxes**

New Zealand made paying taxes easier by abolishing the cheque levy. New Zealand made paying less costly by decreasing the rate of accident compensation levy paid by employers. At the same time, New Zealand made paying taxes more costly by raising property tax and road user levy rates.

Nicaragua

✘ **Trading across borders**

Nicaragua made trading across borders more expensive by introducing a new security fee, increasing the cost of border compliance for exporting and importing.

Niger

✔ **Starting a business**

Niger made starting a business easier by reducing the time and cost needed to register a company. Niger also eliminated the requirement to notarize a company's bylaws.

✔ **Getting credit**

Niger improved access to credit information by establishing a new credit bureau.

✔ **Protecting minority investors**

Niger strengthened minority investor protections by introducing a provision that requires the winning party's legal expenses be reimbursed by the losing party.

✔ **Trading across borders**

Niger made trading across borders easier by removing the mandatory pre-shipment inspection for imported products.

✔ **Enforcing contracts**

Niger made enforcing contracts easier by creating a specialized commercial court in Niamey and by adopting a new code of civil procedure that establishes time standards for key court events.

✔ **Resolving insolvency**

Niger made resolving insolvency easier by introducing a new conciliation procedure for companies in financial difficulties and a simplified preventive settlement procedure for small companies.

Nigeria

✔ **Starting a business**

Nigeria made starting a business easier by improving online government portals. This reform applies to both Kano and Lagos.

✔ **Getting credit**

Nigeria strengthened access to credit by creating a centralized collateral registry. This reform applies to both Kano and Lagos.

Norway

✔ **Enforcing contracts**

Norway made enforcing contracts easier by introducing an electronic filing system for court users.

Labor market regulation

Norway allowed the use of fixed-term contracts for permanent tasks for 12 months.

Oman

✔ **Starting a business**

Oman made starting a business easier by removing the requirement to pay the minimum capital within three months of incorporation and streamlining the registration of employees.

✔ **Trading across borders**

Oman reduced the time for border and documentary compliance by introducing a new online single window that allows for rapid electronic clearance of goods.

Pakistan

✔ **Registering property**

Pakistan improved the quality of land administration by digitizing ownership and land records. This reform applies to Lahore.

✔ **Getting credit**

Pakistan improved access to credit information guaranteeing by law borrowers' rights to inspect their own data. The credit bureau also expanded its borrower coverage. This reform applies to both Lahore and Karachi.

✔ **Trading across borders**

Pakistan made exporting and importing easier by enhancing its electronic customs platform. This reform applies to both Lahore and Karachi.

Papua New Guinea

✔ **Starting a business**

Papua New Guinea reduced the time required to start a business by streamlining business registration at the Investment Promotion Agency (IPA).

✔ **Getting credit**

Papua New Guinea strengthened access to credit by adopting a new law on secured transactions that implemented a functional secured transactions system and established a centralized, notice-based collateral registry. The new law broadens the scope of assets that can be used as collateral and allows out-of-court enforcement of collateral.

Paraguay

✘ **Getting credit**

Paraguay reduced access to credit information by limiting the distribution of historical data on borrowers.

✔ **Trading across borders**

Paraguay made trading across borders easier by introducing a single window for exporting, which reduced the time required of border and documentary compliance.

Peru

✔ **Paying taxes**

Peru made paying taxes less costly by decreasing the corporate income tax rate.

Philippines

✔ **Dealing with construction permits**

The Philippines made dealing with construction permits easier by increasing the transparency of its building regulations.

✔ **Paying taxes**

The Philippines made paying taxes easier by introducing an online system for filing and paying health contributions and by allowing for the online corporate income tax and VAT returns to be completed offline.

Poland

✔ **Dealing with construction permits**

Poland made dealing with construction permits simpler by streamlining the process of obtaining a building permit.

✔ **Getting electricity**

Poland made getting an electricity connection faster by eliminating the need to secure an excavation permit for external connection works, which reduced the time of mentioned works.

✔ **Resolving insolvency**

Poland made resolving insolvency easier by introducing new restructuring mechanisms, changing voting procedures for restructuring plans and allowing creditors greater participation in insolvency proceedings. It also established a central restructuring and bankruptcy register and released guidelines for the remuneration of insolvency representatives.

Labor market regulation

Poland reduced the maximum duration of fixed term contracts to 33 months and limited the total number of fixed-term contracts between the same employer and employee to three.

Portugal

✔ **Getting electricity**

Portugal made getting an electricity connection faster by reducing the time required to approve electrical connection requests.

✔ **Paying taxes**

Portugal made paying taxes easier and less costly by using better accounting software and enhancing the online filing system of taxes and decreasing the corporate income tax rate.

Labor market regulation

Portugal reduced the maximum duration of fixed-term contracts.

Puerto Rico (U.S.)

✔ **Registering property**

Puerto Rico (U.S.) made registering property easier by digitizing its land records and improving the quality of infrastructure and transparency of its land administration system.

✔ **Paying taxes**

Puerto Rico (U.S.) made paying taxes less costly by abolishing gross receipts tax. However, the capital gains tax rate was increased.

Qatar

✔ **Starting a business**

Qatar made starting a business easier by abolishing the paid-in minimum capital requirement for limited liability companies.

✔ **Registering property**

Qatar made registering property easier by increasing the transparency at its land registry.

✘ **Protecting minority investors**

Qatar weakened minority investor protections by decreasing the rights of shareholders in major decisions, by diminishing ownership and control structures, by reducing requirements for approval of related-party transactions and their disclosure to the board of directors and by limiting the liability of interested directors and board of directors in the event of prejudicial related-party transactions.

Romania

✘ **Starting a business**

Romania made starting a business more difficult by increasing the time needed to register for VAT.

Russian Federation

✔ **Dealing with construction permits**

The Russian Federation made dealing with construction permits easier by removing the requirements to obtain permission to fence the construction site and to obtain approval of the architectural and urban planning design for non-residential buildings. This reform only applies to the city of St. Petersburg.

✘ **Enforcing contracts**

Russia made enforcing contracts more difficult by mandating pre-trial resolution before filing a claim, thereby lengthening the initial phase of judicial proceedings. This reform applies to both Moscow and St. Petersburg.

Rwanda

✔ **Starting a business**

Rwanda made starting a business easier by improving the online registration one-stop shop and streamlining post-registration procedures.

✘ **Dealing with construction permits**

Rwanda made dealing with construction permits more cumbersome and expensive by introducing new requirements to obtain a building permit. At the same time, Rwanda also strengthened quality control by establishing required qualifications for architects and engineers.

✔ **Registering property**

Rwanda made it easier to register property by introducing effective time limits and increasing the transparency of the land administration system.

✘ **Paying taxes**

Rwanda made paying taxes more complicated by introducing a requirement that companies file and pay social security contributions monthly instead of quarterly.

✔ **Trading across borders**

Rwanda made trading across borders easier by removing the mandatory pre-shipment inspection for imported products.

✔ **Enforcing contracts**

Rwanda made enforcing contracts easier by introducing an electronic case management system for judges and lawyers.

San Marino

✔ **Dealing with construction permits**

San Marino made dealing with construction permits easier and cheaper by reducing the cost and streamlining the process of obtaining a building permit.

✔ **Paying taxes**

San Marino made paying taxes less costly by introducing a 50% reduction of corporate income tax for new companies.

São Tomé and Príncipe

Labor market regulation

São Tomé and Príncipe adopted a minimum wage for the private sector.

Saudi Arabia

✔ **Starting a business**

Saudi Arabia made starting a business easier by reducing the time to notarize a company's articles of association.

✔ **Protecting minority investors**

Saudi Arabia strengthened minority investor protections by strengthening ownership and control structures of companies and by increasing corporate transparency requirements.

✘ **Paying taxes**

Saudi Arabia made paying taxes more difficult by introducing a more complex income tax return.

Labor market regulation

Saudi Arabia increased the length of the notice period for redundancy dismissals.

Senegal

✔ **Registering property**

Senegal made registering property easier by increasing transparency at its land registry and cadaster.

✔ **Getting credit**

Senegal improved access to credit information by establishing a new credit bureau.

✔ **Paying taxes**

Senegal made paying taxes less costly by reducing the maximum cap for corporate income tax and implementing more efficient accounting systems and software.

✔ **Resolving insolvency**

Senegal made resolving insolvency easier by introducing a new conciliation procedure for companies in financial difficulties and a simplified preventive settlement procedure for small companies.

Serbia

✔ **Starting a business**

Serbia simplified the process of starting a business by reducing the time to register a company.

✔ **Dealing with construction permits**

Serbia made dealing with construction permits faster by implementing an online system and streamlining the process of obtaining building permits.

✔ **Registering property**

Serbia simplified property transfer process by introducing effective time limits.

Sierra Leone

✔ **Starting a business**

Sierra Leone made starting a business easier by reducing registration fees.

Singapore

✔ **Dealing with construction permits**
Singapore made dealing with construction permits easier by streamlining procedures and improving the online one-stop shop.

✔ **Registering property**
Singapore made it easier to transfer a property by introducing an independent mechanism for reporting errors on titles and maps.

✔ **Paying taxes**
Singapore made paying taxes easier by introducing improvements to the online system for filing corporate income tax returns and VAT returns. At the same, the social security contribution rate paid by employers increased and the rebate of 30% on vehicle tax expired.

Slovak Republic

✔ **Paying taxes**
The Slovak Republic made paying taxes less costly and easier by reducing the motor vehicle tax and the number of property tax payments.

Solomon Islands

✔ **Getting credit**
The Solomon Islands improved access to credit information by establishing a credit bureau.

South Africa

✔ **Starting a business**
South Africa made starting a business easier by introducing an online portal to search for a company name.

✘ **Registering property**
South Africa made it more expensive to transfer property by increasing the property transfer tax.

✘ **Paying taxes**
South Africa made paying taxes more costly by increasing the rates of vehicle tax and property tax. At the same time the rate of social security contributions paid by employers was reduced. South Africa made paying taxes more complicated by increasing the time it takes to prepare VAT returns.

Spain

✔ **Paying taxes**
Spain made paying taxes less costly by reducing the property tax rate, vehicle tax rate, tax on property transfer, and abolishing the environmental fee. Spain made paying taxes easier by introducing a new electronic system for filing social security contributions.

✔ **Enforcing contracts**
Spain made enforcing contracts easier by introducing a mandatory electronic filing system for court users.

Sri Lanka

✔ **Starting a business**
Sri Lanka made starting a business easier by removing the stamp duty on newly issued shares.

✔ **Protecting minority investors**
Sri Lanka strengthened minority investor protections by requiring board and in some cases shareholder approval of related-party transactions and by requiring that such transactions undergo external review.

St. Kitts and Nevis

✘ **Registering property**
Saint Kitts and Nevis made it more difficult to transfer property due to a backlog of registration of property transfers at the Supreme Court Registry. Hovever, the stamp duty was reduced for transferring property.

St. Lucia

✘ **Getting electricity**
The utility made getting electricity more difficult by introducing a requirement to obtain a current land registry extract to get a new connection.

✔ **Trading across borders**
St. Lucia made exporting and importing easier by upgrading its electronic data interchange system and linking the customs and port authorities through a common online platform.

Sudan

✘ **Starting a business**
Sudan made starting a business more difficult by increasing the cost of a company seal.

✘ **Protecting minority investors**
Sudan strengthened minority investor protections by introducing greater requirements for disclosure of related-party transactions to the board of directors and granting shareholders preemption rights in limited liability companies. However, Sudan weakened minority investor protections by making it more difficult to sue directors in case of prejudicial related-party transactions, decreasing shareholder rights and role in major corporate decisions and undermining ownership and control structures.

Sweden

✔ **Registering property**
Sweden made it easier to transfer a property by increasing administrative efficiency and introducing an independent and separate mechanism for reporting errors on maps.

Syrian Arab Republic

✘ **Starting a business**
The Syrian Arab Republic made starting a business more difficult by increasing the time for company registration and more costly by increasing fees for post-registration procedures.

✘ **Registering property**
Syria made registering property more complex by requiring a security clearance prior to transferring the property.

✔ **Enforcing contracts**

Syria made enforcing contracts easier by adopting a new code of civil procedure.

Tajikistan

✘ **Starting a business**

Tajikistan made starting a business more difficult by requiring that companies with annual revenue of more than SM 500,000 register as a VAT payer.

✔ **Paying taxes**

Tajikistan made paying taxes easier by introducing electronic invoices and expanding the electronic system for filing and paying taxes to include road tax. It also made paying taxes less costly by reducing road tax rates. On the other hand, land tax rates were increased.

Tanzania

✔ **Getting credit**

The credit bureau in Tanzania expanded credit bureau borrower coverage and began to distribute credit data from retailers.

✘ **Paying taxes**

Tanzania made paying taxes more complicated by increasing the frequency of filing of the skills development levy and more costly by introducing a workers' compensation tariff paid by employers.

Thailand

✔ **Starting a business**

Thailand made starting a business easier by creating a single window for registration payment and reducing the time needed to obtain a company seal.

✔ **Getting credit**

Thailand improved access to credit information by starting to provide credit scores to banks and financial institutions.

✔ **Resolving insolvency**

Thailand made resolving insolvency easier by introducing new restructuring for small and medium-size companies and by streamlining provisions related to company liquidation.

Togo

✔ **Getting credit**

Togo improved access to credit information by introducing regulations that govern the licensing and functioning of credit bureaus in UEMOA member states.

✔ **Paying taxes**

Togo made paying taxes easier by streamlining the administrative process of complying with tax obligations.

✔ **Trading across borders**

Togo made trading across borders easier by implementing an electronic single window system, which reduced the time for border and documentary compliance for both exporting and importing.

✔ **Resolving insolvency**

Togo made resolving insolvency easier by introducing a new conciliation procedure for companies in financial difficulties and a simplified preventive settlement procedure for small companies.

Tonga

✘ **Dealing with construction permits**

Tonga made dealing with construction permits more complex by introducing two new procedures.

Tunisia

✔ **Getting credit**

Tunisia strengthened credit reporting by starting to distribute historical credit information and credit information from a telecommunications company.

Turkey

✔ **Starting a business**

Turkey made starting a business easier by allowing new companies to automatically receive potential tax identification number online through the Central Registration Recording System.

✔ **Paying taxes**

Turkey made paying taxes easier by introducing electronic invoicing and electronic bookkeeping. At the same time, however, Turkey also increased the rate of transaction tax applicable on checks.

Uganda

✔ **Starting a business**

Uganda made starting a business easier by eliminating the requirement that a commissioner of oaths must sign compliance declarations.

✔ **Paying taxes**

Uganda made paying taxes easier by eliminating a requirement for tax returns to be submitted in paper copy following online submission. At the same time, Uganda increased the stamp duty for insurance contracts.

✔ **Trading across borders**

Uganda made trading across borders easier by constructing the Malaba One-Stop Border Post, which reduced border compliance time for exports.

Ukraine

✔ **Protecting minority investors**

Ukraine strengthened minority investor protections by requiring interested director or shareholder to be excluded from the vote, by requiring that proposed related-party transactions undergo external review, by introducing remedies in cases where related-party transactions are harmful to the company and also clarifying ownership and control structures.

✔ **Enforcing contracts**

Ukraine made enforcing contracts easier by introducing a system that allows users to pay court fees electronically.

United Arab Emirates

✔ **Starting a business**

The United Arab Emirates made it easier to start a business by streamlining name reservation and articles of association notarization and merging registration procedures with the Ministry of Human Resources and General Pensions and Social Security Authority.

✔ **Dealing with construction permits**
The United Arab Emirates made dealing with construction permits easier by implementing risk-based inspections and merging the final inspection into the process of obtaining a completion certificate.

✔ **Getting electricity**
The United Arab Emirates reduced the time required to obtain a new electricity connection by implementing a new program with strict deadlines for reviewing applications, carrying out inspections and meter installations. The United Arab Emirates also introduced compensation for power outages.

✔ **Registering property**
The United Arab Emirates made registering property easier by increasing the transparency at its land registry.

✔ **Protecting minority investors**
The United Arab Emirates strengthened minority investor protections by increasing shareholder rights and role in major corporate decisions, clarifying ownership and control structures and requiring greater corporate transparency.

Labor market regulation
The United Arab Emirates reduced the duration of a single fixed-term contract from 48 to 24 month.

Uruguay

✘ **Starting a business**
Uruguay made starting a business more costly by increasing the value of the official fiscal unit used for the payment of government fees.

✔ **Paying taxes**
Uruguay made paying taxes easier by introducing an electronic system for paying social security contributions. Online filing was already in place.

Uzbekistan

✔ **Registering property**
Uzbekistan made transferring a property easier by increasing transparency of information.

✔ **Protecting minority investors**
Uzbekistan strengthened minority investor protections by clarifying ownership and control structures.

✔ **Paying taxes**
Uzbekistan made paying taxes less costly by reducing the unified social payment rate paid by employers and the corporate income tax rate. However, the land tax rates in city of Tashkent increased.

Vanuatu

✔ **Starting a business**
Vanuatu made starting a business easier by removing registration requirements and digitizing the company register.

✔ **Getting credit**
Vanuatu improved access to credit by passing a law that allows secured creditors to realize their assets without being subject to priorities of other creditors.

✔ **Protecting minority investors**
Vanuatu strengthened minority investor protections by increasing shareholder rights and role in major corporate decisions and clarifying ownership and control structures.

✔ **Resolving insolvency**
Vanuatu made resolving insolvency easier by strengthening and modernizing its legal framework in relation to liquidation and receivership proceedings.

Venezuela, RB

✘ **Starting a business**
República Bolivariana de Venezuela made starting a business more expensive by raising the value of the tributary unit and lawyers' fees. It also made the process more time consuming by limiting the work schedule of the public sector.

Vietnam

✘ **Starting a business**
Vietnam made starting a business more difficult by requiring entrepreneurs to receive approval of the seal sample before using it.

✔ **Protecting minority investors**
Vietnam strengthened minority investor protections by making it easier to sue directors in cases of prejudicial transactions between interested parties, by increasing shareholder rights and role in major corporate decisions, by strengthening the ownership and control structures of companies and by increasing corporate transparency requirements.

✔ **Paying taxes**
Vietnam made paying taxes easier and less costly by streamlining the administrative process of complying with tax obligations and abolishing environmental protection fees.

✔ **Trading across borders**
Vietnam made trading across borders easier by implementing an electronic customs clearance system.

Zambia

✘ **Dealing with construction permits**
Zambia made dealing with construction permits more costly by raising the costs associated with submitting a brief to the environmental agency.

✔ **Registering property**
Zambia made it more affordable to transfer property by decreasing the property transfer tax.

Labor market regulation
Zambia eliminated fixed-term contracts for permanent tasks.

Zimbabwe

✔ **Dealing with construction permits**

Zimbabwe made dealing with construction permits faster by streamlining the building plan approval process.

✔ **Registering property**

Zimbabwe made registering property easier by launching an official website containing information on the list of documents and fees for completing a property transaction, as well as, a specific time frame for delivering a legally binding document that proves property ownership.

✔ **Getting credit**

Zimbabwe improved access to credit information by allowing the establishment of a credit registry.

✘ **Trading across borders**

Zimbabwe made trading across borders more difficult by introducing a mandatory pre-shipment inspection for imported products.

Labor market regulation

Zimbabwe reduced severance payments and introduced stricter rules governing fixed-term contracts.

Country Tables

✔ Reform making it easier to do business ✘ Change making it more difficult to do business

AFGHANISTAN

AFGHANISTAN		South Asia		GNI per capita (US$)	630
Ease of doing business rank (1–190)	183	Overall distance to frontier (DTF) score (0–100)	38.10	Population	32,526,562
Starting a business (rank)	42	**Getting credit** (rank)	101	✔ **Trading across borders** (rank)	175
DTF score for starting a business (0–100)	92.08	DTF score for getting credit (0–100)	45.00	DTF score for trading across borders (0–100)	30.63
Procedures (number)	3.5	Strength of legal rights index (0–12)	9	*Time to export*	
Time (days)	7.5	Depth of credit information index (0–8)	0	Documentary compliance (hours)	228
Cost (% of income per capita)	19.9	Credit bureau coverage (% of adults)	0.0	Border compliance (hours)	48
Minimum capital (% of income per capita)	0.0	Credit registry coverage (% of adults)	0.8	*Cost to export*	
				Documentary compliance (US$)	344
Dealing with construction permits (rank)	186	**Protecting minority investors** (rank)	189	Border compliance (US$)	453
DTF score for dealing with construction permits (0–100)	22.39	DTF score for protecting minority investors (0–100)	11.67	*Time to import*	
Procedures (number)	13	Extent of disclosure index (0–10)	1	Documentary compliance (hours)	324
Time (days)	356	Extent of director liability index (0–10)	1	Border compliance (hours)	96
Cost (% of warehouse value)	82.7	Ease of shareholder suits index (0–10)	3	*Cost to import*	
Building quality control index (0–15)	2.5	Extent of shareholder rights index (0–10)	0	Documentary compliance (US$)	900
		Extent of ownership and control index (0–10)	0	Border compliance (US$)	750
Getting electricity (rank)	159	Extent of corporate transparency index (0–10)	2		
DTF score for getting electricity (0–100)	45.04			**Enforcing contracts** (rank)	180
Procedures (number)	6	✘ **Paying taxes** (rank)	163	DTF score for enforcing contracts (0–100)	31.76
Time (days)	114	DTF score for paying taxes (0–100)	51.29	Time (days)	1,642
Cost (% of income per capita)	2,274.7	Payments (number per year)	20	Cost (% of claim)	29.0
Reliability of supply and transparency of tariffs index (0–8)	0	Time (hours per year)	275	Quality of judicial processes index (0–18)	5.0
		Total tax rate (% of profit)	48.3		
Registering property (rank)	186	Postfiling index (0–100)	0.45	**Resolving insolvency** (rank)	159
DTF score for registering property (0–100)	27.50			DTF score for resolving insolvency (0–100)	23.62
Procedures (number)	9			Time (years)	2.0
Time (days)	250			Cost (% of estate)	25.0
Cost (% of property value)	5.0			Recovery rate (cents on the dollar)	26.5
Quality of land administration index (0–30)	3.0			Strength of insolvency framework index (0–16)	3.0

ALBANIA

ALBANIA		Europe & Central Asia		GNI per capita (US$)	4,290
Ease of doing business rank (1–190)	58	Overall distance to frontier (DTF) score (0–100)	68.90	Population	2,889,167
Starting a business (rank)	46	**Getting credit** (rank)	44	✘ **Trading across borders** (rank)	24
DTF score for starting a business (0–100)	91.73	DTF score for getting credit (0–100)	65.00	DTF score for trading across borders (0–100)	96.29
Procedures (number)	5	Strength of legal rights index (0–12)	7	*Time to export*	
Time (days)	5	Depth of credit information index (0–8)	6	Documentary compliance (hours)	6
Cost (% of income per capita)	10.1	Credit bureau coverage (% of adults)	0.0	Border compliance (hours)	9
Minimum capital (% of income per capita)	0.0	Credit registry coverage (% of adults)	38.9	*Cost to export*	
				Documentary compliance (US$)	10
✔ **Dealing with construction permits** (rank)	106	**Protecting minority investors** (rank)	19	Border compliance (US$)	55
DTF score for dealing with construction permits (0–100)	67.61	DTF score for protecting minority investors (0–100)	71.67	*Time to import*	
Procedures (number)	16	Extent of disclosure index (0–10)	9	Documentary compliance (hours)	8
Time (days)	220	Extent of director liability index (0–10)	7	Border compliance (hours)	10
Cost (% of warehouse value)	3.3	Ease of shareholder suits index (0–10)	7	*Cost to import*	
Building quality control index (0–15)	13.0	Extent of shareholder rights index (0–10)	7	Documentary compliance (US$)	10
		Extent of ownership and control index (0–10)	6	Border compliance (US$)	77
✔ **Getting electricity** (rank)	156	Extent of corporate transparency index (0–10)	7		
DTF score for getting electricity (0–100)	48.30			**Enforcing contracts** (rank)	116
Procedures (number)	6	✔ **Paying taxes** (rank)	97	DTF score for enforcing contracts (0–100)	53.66
Time (days)	134	DTF score for paying taxes (0–100)	70.96	Time (days)	525
Cost (% of income per capita)	515.5	Payments (number per year)	34	Cost (% of claim)	34.9
Reliability of supply and transparency of tariffs index (0–8)	0	Time (hours per year)	261	Quality of judicial processes index (0–18)	6.0
		Total tax rate (% of profit)	36.5		
Registering property (rank)	106	Postfiling index (0–100)	82.97	**Resolving insolvency** (rank)	43
DTF score for registering property (0–100)	58.77			DTF score for resolving insolvency (0–100)	64.96
Procedures (number)	6			Time (years)	2.0
Time (days)	19			Cost (% of estate)	10.0
Cost (% of property value)	9.9			Recovery rate (cents on the dollar)	42.3
Quality of land administration index (0–30)	15.5			Strength of insolvency framework index (0–16)	13.5

Note: Most indicator sets refer to a case scenario in the largest business city of an economy, though for 11 economies the data are a population-weighted average for the two largest business cities. For some indicators a result of "no practice" may be recorded for an economy; see the data notes for more details. In starting a business, procedures (number), time (days) and cost (% of income per capita) are calculated as the average of both men and women. For the postfiling index, a result of "not applicable" may be recorded for an economy.

✔ Reform making it easier to do business ✘ Change making it more difficult to do business

ALGERIA

ALGERIA		Middle East & North Africa		GNI per capita (US$)	4,870
Ease of doing business rank (1–190)	156	Overall distance to frontier (DTF) score (0–100)	47.76	Population	39,666,519

✔ Starting a business (rank)	142
DTF score for starting a business (0–100)	77.54
Procedures (number)	12
Time (days)	20
Cost (% of income per capita)	11.1
Minimum capital (% of income per capita)	0.0

✔ Dealing with construction permits (rank)	77
DTF score for dealing with construction permits (0–100)	71.02
Procedures (number)	17
Time (days)	130
Cost (% of warehouse value)	0.9
Building quality control index (0–15)	10.0

✔ Getting electricity (rank)	118
DTF score for getting electricity (0–100)	60.58
Procedures (number)	5
Time (days)	180
Cost (% of income per capita)	1,330.4
Reliability of supply and transparency of tariffs index (0–8)	5

Registering property (rank)	162
DTF score for registering property (0–100)	43.83
Procedures (number)	10
Time (days)	55
Cost (% of property value)	7.1
Quality of land administration index (0–30)	7.0

Getting credit (rank)	175
DTF score for getting credit (0–100)	10.00
Strength of legal rights index (0–12)	2
Depth of credit information index (0–8)	0
Credit bureau coverage (% of adults)	0.0
Credit registry coverage (% of adults)	3.0

Protecting minority investors (rank)	173
DTF score for protecting minority investors (0–100)	33.33
Extent of disclosure index (0–10)	4
Extent of director liability index (0–10)	1
Ease of shareholder suits index (0–10)	5
Extent of shareholder rights index (0–10)	3
Extent of ownership and control index (0–10)	5
Extent of corporate transparency index (0–10)	2

✔ Paying taxes (rank)	155
DTF score for paying taxes (0–100)	53.99
Payments (number per year)	27
Time (hours per year)	265
Total tax rate (% of profit)	65.6
Postfiling index (0–100)	49.31

Trading across borders (rank)	178
DTF score for trading across borders (0–100)	24.15
Time to export	
Documentary compliance (hours)	149
Border compliance (hours)	118
Cost to export	
Documentary compliance (US$)	374
Border compliance (US$)	593
Time to import	
Documentary compliance (hours)	249
Border compliance (hours)	327
Cost to import	
Documentary compliance (US$)	400
Border compliance (US$)	466

Enforcing contracts (rank)	102
DTF score for enforcing contracts (0–100)	55.49
Time (days)	630
Cost (% of claim)	19.9
Quality of judicial processes index (0–18)	5.5

Resolving insolvency (rank)	74
DTF score for resolving insolvency (0–100)	47.67
Time (years)	1.3
Cost (% of estate)	7.0
Recovery rate (cents on the dollar)	50.8
Strength of insolvency framework index (0–16)	6.5

ANGOLA

ANGOLA		Sub-Saharan Africa		GNI per capita (US$)	4,180
Ease of doing business rank (1–190)	182	Overall distance to frontier (DTF) score (0–100)	38.41	Population	25,021,974

✔ Starting a business (rank)	144
DTF score for starting a business (0–100)	77.34
Procedures (number)	8
Time (days)	36
Cost (% of income per capita)	27.5
Minimum capital (% of income per capita)	0.0

Dealing with construction permits (rank)	111
DTF score for dealing with construction permits (0–100)	66.51
Procedures (number)	10
Time (days)	203
Cost (% of warehouse value)	0.6
Building quality control index (0–15)	6.0

Getting electricity (rank)	171
DTF score for getting electricity (0–100)	40.84
Procedures (number)	7
Time (days)	145
Cost (% of income per capita)	1,195.7
Reliability of supply and transparency of tariffs index (0–8)	0

Registering property (rank)	170
DTF score for registering property (0–100)	40.64
Procedures (number)	7
Time (days)	190
Cost (% of property value)	3.0
Quality of land administration index (0–30)	7.0

Getting credit (rank)	181
DTF score for getting credit (0–100)	5.00
Strength of legal rights index (0–12)	1
Depth of credit information index (0–8)	0
Credit bureau coverage (% of adults)	0.0
Credit registry coverage (% of adults)	1.9

Protecting minority investors (rank)	81
DTF score for protecting minority investors (0–100)	55.00
Extent of disclosure index (0–10)	4
Extent of director liability index (0–10)	6
Ease of shareholder suits index (0–10)	6
Extent of shareholder rights index (0–10)	7
Extent of ownership and control index (0–10)	6
Extent of corporate transparency index (0–10)	4

✔ Paying taxes (rank)	157
DTF score for paying taxes (0–100)	53.23
Payments (number per year)	31
Time (hours per year)	287
Total tax rate (% of profit)	48.0
Postfiling index (0–100)	27.96

Trading across borders (rank)	183
DTF score for trading across borders (0–100)	19.27
Time to export	
Documentary compliance (hours)	169
Border compliance (hours)	240
Cost to export	
Documentary compliance (US$)	240
Border compliance (US$)	735
Time to import	
Documentary compliance (hours)	180
Border compliance (hours)	276
Cost to import	
Documentary compliance (US$)	460
Border compliance (US$)	935

Enforcing contracts (rank)	186
DTF score for enforcing contracts (0–100)	26.26
Time (days)	1,296
Cost (% of claim)	44.4
Quality of judicial processes index (0–18)	4.5

Resolving insolvency (rank)	169
DTF score for resolving insolvency (0–100)	0.00
Time (years)	NO PRACTICE
Cost (% of estate)	NO PRACTICE
Recovery rate (cents on the dollar)	0.0
Strength of insolvency framework index (0–16)	0.0

ANTIGUA AND BARBUDA

ANTIGUA AND BARBUDA		Latin America & Caribbean		GNI per capita (US$)	13,390
Ease of doing business rank (1–190)	113	Overall distance to frontier (DTF) score (0–100)	58.04	Population	91,818

Starting a business (rank)	124
DTF score for starting a business (0–100)	81.66
Procedures (number)	9
Time (days)	22
Cost (% of income per capita)	9.4
Minimum capital (% of income per capita)	0.0

Dealing with construction permits (rank)	107
DTF score for dealing with construction permits (0–100)	67.41
Procedures (number)	16
Time (days)	110
Cost (% of warehouse value)	0.4
Building quality control index (0–15)	6.0

Getting electricity (rank)	35
DTF score for getting electricity (0–100)	83.49
Procedures (number)	4
Time (days)	42
Cost (% of income per capita)	117.6
Reliability of supply and transparency of tariffs index (0–8)	5

Registering property (rank)	150
DTF score for registering property (0–100)	47.51
Procedures (number)	7
Time (days)	108
Cost (% of property value)	10.8
Quality of land administration index (0–30)	19.0

Getting credit (rank)	157
DTF score for getting credit (0–100)	25.00
Strength of legal rights index (0–12)	5
Depth of credit information index (0–8)	0
Credit bureau coverage (% of adults)	0.0
Credit registry coverage (% of adults)	0.0

Protecting minority investors (rank)	87
DTF score for protecting minority investors (0–100)	53.33
Extent of disclosure index (0–10)	4
Extent of director liability index (0–10)	8
Ease of shareholder suits index (0–10)	8
Extent of shareholder rights index (0–10)	4
Extent of ownership and control index (0–10)	5
Extent of corporate transparency index (0–10)	3

Paying taxes (rank)	160
DTF score for paying taxes (0–100)	53.03
Payments (number per year)	57
Time (hours per year)	207
Total tax rate (% of profit)	41.9
Postfiling index (0–100)	49.08

✔ Trading across borders (rank)	110
DTF score for trading across borders (0–100)	65.76
Time to export	
Documentary compliance (hours)	51
Border compliance (hours)	85
Cost to export	
Documentary compliance (US$)	121
Border compliance (US$)	546
Time to import	
Documentary compliance (hours)	48
Border compliance (hours)	85
Cost to import	
Documentary compliance (US$)	100
Border compliance (US$)	546

Enforcing contracts (rank)	35
DTF score for enforcing contracts (0–100)	68.11
Time (days)	476
Cost (% of claim)	27.1
Quality of judicial processes index (0–18)	11.5

Resolving insolvency (rank)	124
DTF score for resolving insolvency (0–100)	35.12
Time (years)	3.0
Cost (% of estate)	7.0
Recovery rate (cents on the dollar)	36.2
Strength of insolvency framework index (0–16)	5.0

Note: Most indicator sets refer to a case scenario in the largest business city of an economy, though for 11 economies the data are a population-weighted average for the two largest business cities. For some indicators a result of "no practice" may be recorded for an economy; see the data notes for more details. In starting a business, procedures (number), time (days) and cost (% of income per capita) are calculated as the average of both men and women. For the postfiling index, a result of "not applicable" may be recorded for an economy.

✔ Reform making it easier to do business ✘ Change making it more difficult to do business

ARGENTINA

Ease of doing business rank (1–190)	116	Latin America & Caribbean Overall distance to frontier (DTF) score (0–100)	57.45	GNI per capita (US$) Population	14,510 43,416,755

Starting a business (rank)	157
DTF score for starting a business (0–100)	73.56
Procedures (number)	14
Time (days)	25
Cost (% of income per capita)	9.3
Minimum capital (% of income per capita)	0.0

✘ Dealing with construction permits (rank)	173
DTF score for dealing with construction permits (0–100)	51.17
Procedures (number)	21
Time (days)	341
Cost (% of warehouse value)	2.8
Building quality control index (0–15)	11.0

Getting electricity (rank)	91
DTF score for getting electricity (0–100)	69.98
Procedures (number)	6
Time (days)	92
Cost (% of income per capita)	32.2
Reliability of supply and transparency of tariffs index (0–8)	5

Registering property (rank)	114
DTF score for registering property (0–100)	56.32
Procedures (number)	7
Time (days)	51.5
Cost (% of property value)	6.6
Quality of land administration index (0–30)	13.0

Getting credit (rank)	82
DTF score for getting credit (0–100)	50.00
Strength of legal rights index (0–12)	2
Depth of credit information index (0–8)	8
Credit bureau coverage (% of adults)	100.0
Credit registry coverage (% of adults)	41.6

Protecting minority investors (rank)	51
DTF score for protecting minority investors (0–100)	61.67
Extent of disclosure index (0–10)	7
Extent of director liability index (0–10)	2
Ease of shareholder suits index (0–10)	6
Extent of shareholder rights index (0–10)	9
Extent of ownership and control index (0–10)	6
Extent of corporate transparency index (0–10)	7

✔ Paying taxes (rank)	178
DTF score for paying taxes (0–100)	39.76
Payments (number per year)	9
Time (hours per year)	359
Total tax rate (% of profit)	106.0
Postfiling index (0–100)	16.97

✔ Trading across borders (rank)	111
DTF score for trading across borders (0–100)	65.36
Time to export	
Documentary compliance (hours)	30
Border compliance (hours)	21
Cost to export	
Documentary compliance (US$)	60
Border compliance (US$)	150
Time to import	
Documentary compliance (hours)	192
Border compliance (hours)	60
Cost to import	
Documentary compliance (US$)	120
Border compliance (US$)	1,200

Enforcing contracts (rank)	50
DTF score for enforcing contracts (0–100)	64.81
Time (days)	660
Cost (% of claim)	22.5
Quality of judicial processes index (0–18)	11.5

Resolving insolvency (rank)	98
DTF score for resolving insolvency (0–100)	41.87
Time (years)	2.8
Cost (% of estate)	14.5
Recovery rate (cents on the dollar)	22.6
Strength of insolvency framework index (0–16)	9.5

ARMENIA

Ease of doing business rank (1–190)	38	Europe & Central Asia Overall distance to frontier (DTF) score (0–100)	73.63	GNI per capita (US$) Population	3,880 3,017,712

Starting a business (rank)	9
DTF score for starting a business (0–100)	96.07
Procedures (number)	3
Time (days)	4
Cost (% of income per capita)	0.9
Minimum capital (% of income per capita)	0.0

Dealing with construction permits (rank)	81
DTF score for dealing with construction permits (0–100)	70.03
Procedures (number)	18
Time (days)	84
Cost (% of warehouse value)	0.9
Building quality control index (0–15)	8.0

Getting electricity (rank)	76
DTF score for getting electricity (0–100)	73.17
Procedures (number)	4
Time (days)	138
Cost (% of income per capita)	80.3
Reliability of supply and transparency of tariffs index (0–8)	5

Registering property (rank)	13
DTF score for registering property (0–100)	87.36
Procedures (number)	3
Time (days)	7
Cost (% of property value)	0.2
Quality of land administration index (0–30)	21.0

✔ Getting credit (rank)	20
DTF score for getting credit (0–100)	75.00
Strength of legal rights index (0–12)	7
Depth of credit information index (0–8)	8
Credit bureau coverage (% of adults)	71.1
Credit registry coverage (% of adults)	0.0

Protecting minority investors (rank)	53
DTF score for protecting minority investors (0–100)	60.00
Extent of disclosure index (0–10)	5
Extent of director liability index (0–10)	6
Ease of shareholder suits index (0–10)	8
Extent of shareholder rights index (0–10)	8
Extent of ownership and control index (0–10)	2
Extent of corporate transparency index (0–10)	7

Paying taxes (rank)	88
DTF score for paying taxes (0–100)	72.49
Payments (number per year)	14
Time (hours per year)	313
Total tax rate (% of profit)	18.5
Postfiling index (0–100)	49.08

Trading across borders (rank)	48
DTF score for trading across borders (0–100)	86.45
Time to export	
Documentary compliance (hours)	2
Border compliance (hours)	39
Cost to export	
Documentary compliance (US$)	150
Border compliance (US$)	100
Time to import	
Documentary compliance (hours)	2
Border compliance (hours)	41
Cost to import	
Documentary compliance (US$)	100
Border compliance (US$)	100

✔ Enforcing contracts (rank)	28
DTF score for enforcing contracts (0–100)	69.71
Time (days)	570
Cost (% of claim)	16.0
Quality of judicial processes index (0–18)	11.5

Resolving insolvency (rank)	78
DTF score for resolving insolvency (0–100)	46.06
Time (years)	1.9
Cost (% of estate)	11.0
Recovery rate (cents on the dollar)	36.2
Strength of insolvency framework index (0–16)	8.5

AUSTRALIA

Ease of doing business rank (1–190)	15	OECD high income Overall distance to frontier (DTF) score (0–100)	80.26	GNI per capita (US$) Population	60,070 23,781,169

Starting a business (rank)	7
DTF score for starting a business (0–100)	96.47
Procedures (number)	3
Time (days)	2.5
Cost (% of income per capita)	0.7
Minimum capital (% of income per capita)	0.0

Dealing with construction permits (rank)	2
DTF score for dealing with construction permits (0–100)	86.56
Procedures (number)	10
Time (days)	112
Cost (% of warehouse value)	0.5
Building quality control index (0–15)	14.0

Getting electricity (rank)	41
DTF score for getting electricity (0–100)	82.31
Procedures (number)	5
Time (days)	75
Cost (% of income per capita)	12.6
Reliability of supply and transparency of tariffs index (0–8)	7

Registering property (rank)	45
DTF score for registering property (0–100)	74.22
Procedures (number)	5
Time (days)	4.5
Cost (% of property value)	5.2
Quality of land administration index (0–30)	20.0

Getting credit (rank)	5
DTF score for getting credit (0–100)	90.00
Strength of legal rights index (0–12)	11
Depth of credit information index (0–8)	7
Credit bureau coverage (% of adults)	100.0
Credit registry coverage (% of adults)	0.0

Protecting minority investors (rank)	63
DTF score for protecting minority investors (0–100)	58.33
Extent of disclosure index (0–10)	8
Extent of director liability index (0–10)	2
Ease of shareholder suits index (0–10)	8
Extent of shareholder rights index (0–10)	5
Extent of ownership and control index (0–10)	4
Extent of corporate transparency index (0–10)	8

Paying taxes (rank)	25
DTF score for paying taxes (0–100)	85.60
Payments (number per year)	11
Time (hours per year)	105
Total tax rate (% of profit)	47.6
Postfiling index (0–100)	95.35

Trading across borders (rank)	91
DTF score for trading across borders (0–100)	70.65
Time to export	
Documentary compliance (hours)	7
Border compliance (hours)	36
Cost to export	
Documentary compliance (US$)	264
Border compliance (US$)	749
Time to import	
Documentary compliance (hours)	4
Border compliance (hours)	39
Cost to import	
Documentary compliance (US$)	100
Border compliance (US$)	525

Enforcing contracts (rank)	3
DTF score for enforcing contracts (0–100)	79.72
Time (days)	395
Cost (% of claim)	21.8
Quality of judicial processes index (0–18)	15.5

Resolving insolvency (rank)	21
DTF score for resolving insolvency (0–100)	78.73
Time (years)	1.0
Cost (% of estate)	8.0
Recovery rate (cents on the dollar)	82.4
Strength of insolvency framework index (0–16)	11.0

Note: Most indicator sets refer to a case scenario in the largest business city of an economy, though for 11 economies the data are a population-weighted average for the two largest business cities. For some indicators a result of "no practice" may be recorded for an economy; see the data notes for more details. In starting a business, procedures (number), time (days) and cost (% of income per capita) are calculated as the average of both men and women. For the postfiling index, a result of "not applicable" may be recorded for an economy.

✔ Reform making it easier to do business ✘ Change making it more difficult to do business

AUSTRIA

AUSTRIA		OECD high income		GNI per capita (US$)	47,120
Ease of doing business rank (1–190)	19	Overall distance to frontier (DTF) score (0–100)	78.92	Population	8,611,088

Starting a business (rank)	111
DTF score for starting a business (0–100)	83.72
Procedures (number)	8
Time (days)	21
Cost (% of income per capita)	0.3
Minimum capital (% of income per capita)	12.8
Dealing with construction permits (rank)	49
DTF score for dealing with construction permits (0–100)	74.96
Procedures (number)	11
Time (days)	222
Cost (% of warehouse value)	1.3
Building quality control index (0–15)	13.0
Getting electricity (rank)	20
DTF score for getting electricity (0–100)	87.70
Procedures (number)	5
Time (days)	23
Cost (% of income per capita)	95.7
Reliability of supply and transparency of tariffs index (0–8)	7
Registering property (rank)	30
DTF score for registering property (0–100)	79.97
Procedures (number)	3
Time (days)	20.5
Cost (% of property value)	4.6
Quality of land administration index (0–30)	23.0
Getting credit (rank)	62
DTF score for getting credit (0–100)	60.00
Strength of legal rights index (0–12)	5
Depth of credit information index (0–8)	7
Credit bureau coverage (% of adults)	53.6
Credit registry coverage (% of adults)	2.3
Protecting minority investors (rank)	32
DTF score for protecting minority investors (0–100)	65.00
Extent of disclosure index (0–10)	5
Extent of director liability index (0–10)	5
Ease of shareholder suits index (0–10)	6
Extent of shareholder rights index (0–10)	8
Extent of ownership and control index (0–10)	8
Extent of corporate transparency index (0–10)	7
Paying taxes (rank)	42
DTF score for paying taxes (0–100)	83.39
Payments (number per year)	12
Time (hours per year)	131
Total tax rate (% of profit)	51.6
Postfiling index (0–100)	98.45
Trading across borders (rank)	1
DTF score for trading across borders (0–100)	100.00
Time to export	
Documentary compliance (hours)	1
Border compliance (hours)	0
Cost to export	
Documentary compliance (US$)	0
Border compliance (US$)	0
Time to import	
Documentary compliance (hours)	1
Border compliance (hours)	0
Cost to import	
Documentary compliance (US$)	0
Border compliance (US$)	0
Enforcing contracts (rank)	10
DTF score for enforcing contracts (0–100)	75.49
Time (days)	397
Cost (% of claim)	20.6
Quality of judicial processes index (0–18)	13.0
Resolving insolvency (rank)	20
DTF score for resolving insolvency (0–100)	78.93
Time (years)	1.1
Cost (% of estate)	10.0
Recovery rate (cents on the dollar)	82.8
Strength of insolvency framework index (0–16)	11.0

AZERBAIJAN

AZERBAIJAN		Europe & Central Asia		GNI per capita (US$)	6,560
Ease of doing business rank (1–190)	65	Overall distance to frontier (DTF) score (0–100)	67.99	Population	9,651,349

Starting a business (rank)	5
DTF score for starting a business (0–100)	97.74
Procedures (number)	2
Time (days)	3
Cost (% of income per capita)	1.3
Minimum capital (% of income per capita)	0.0
Dealing with construction permits (rank)	127
DTF score for dealing with construction permits (0–100)	63.63
Procedures (number)	18
Time (days)	203
Cost (% of warehouse value)	4.5
Building quality control index (0–15)	12.0
✔ **Getting electricity** (rank)	105
DTF score for getting electricity (0–100)	64.83
Procedures (number)	7
Time (days)	69
Cost (% of income per capita)	150.4
Reliability of supply and transparency of tariffs index (0–8)	4
Registering property (rank)	22
DTF score for registering property (0–100)	82.52
Procedures (number)	3
Time (days)	8.5
Cost (% of property value)	0.2
Quality of land administration index (0–30)	15.5
Getting credit (rank)	118
DTF score for getting credit (0–100)	40.00
Strength of legal rights index (0–12)	2
Depth of credit information index (0–8)	6
Credit bureau coverage (% of adults)	0.0
Credit registry coverage (% of adults)	36.4
Protecting minority investors (rank)	32
DTF score for protecting minority investors (0–100)	65.00
Extent of disclosure index (0–10)	10
Extent of director liability index (0–10)	5
Ease of shareholder suits index (0–10)	8
Extent of shareholder rights index (0–10)	7
Extent of ownership and control index (0–10)	3
Extent of corporate transparency index (0–10)	6
✔ **Paying taxes** (rank)	40
DTF score for paying taxes (0–100)	83.52
Payments (number per year)	6
Time (hours per year)	195
Total tax rate (% of profit)	39.8
Postfiling index (0–100)	81.00
✔ **Trading across borders** (rank)	83
DTF score for trading across borders (0–100)	72.28
Time to export	
Documentary compliance (hours)	33
Border compliance (hours)	29
Cost to export	
Documentary compliance (US$)	300
Border compliance (US$)	214
Time to import	
Documentary compliance (hours)	38
Border compliance (hours)	30
Cost to import	
Documentary compliance (US$)	200
Border compliance (US$)	423
Enforcing contracts (rank)	44
DTF score for enforcing contracts (0–100)	65.66
Time (days)	277
Cost (% of claim)	18.5
Quality of judicial processes index (0–18)	5.5
Resolving insolvency (rank)	86
DTF score for resolving insolvency (0–100)	44.77
Time (years)	1.5
Cost (% of estate)	12.0
Recovery rate (cents on the dollar)	39.6
Strength of insolvency framework index (0–16)	7.5

BAHAMAS, THE

BAHAMAS, THE		Latin America & Caribbean		GNI per capita (US$)	21,310
Ease of doing business rank (1–190)	121	Overall distance to frontier (DTF) score (0–100)	56.65	Population	388,019

✔ **Starting a business** (rank)	118
DTF score for starting a business (0–100)	82.71
Procedures (number)	8
Time (days)	21.5
Cost (% of income per capita)	13.8
Minimum capital (% of income per capita)	0.0
Dealing with construction permits (rank)	110
DTF score for dealing with construction permits (0–100)	66.64
Procedures (number)	16
Time (days)	180
Cost (% of warehouse value)	1.0
Building quality control index (0–15)	9.0
Getting electricity (rank)	116
DTF score for getting electricity (0–100)	60.89
Procedures (number)	5
Time (days)	67
Cost (% of income per capita)	146.8
Reliability of supply and transparency of tariffs index (0–8)	0
✔ **Registering property** (rank)	166
DTF score for registering property (0–100)	42.74
Procedures (number)	7
Time (days)	122
Cost (% of property value)	4.7
Quality of land administration index (0–30)	3.0
Getting credit (rank)	139
DTF score for getting credit (0–100)	30.00
Strength of legal rights index (0–12)	6
Depth of credit information index (0–8)	0
Credit bureau coverage (% of adults)	0.0
Credit registry coverage (% of adults)	0.0
Protecting minority investors (rank)	118
DTF score for protecting minority investors (0–100)	46.67
Extent of disclosure index (0–10)	2
Extent of director liability index (0–10)	5
Ease of shareholder suits index (0–10)	8
Extent of shareholder rights index (0–10)	8
Extent of ownership and control index (0–10)	3
Extent of corporate transparency index (0–10)	2
✘ **Paying taxes** (rank)	95
DTF score for paying taxes (0–100)	71.39
Payments (number per year)	31
Time (hours per year)	233
Total tax rate (% of profit)	33.8
Postfiling index (0–100)	NOT APPLICABLE
Trading across borders (rank)	152
DTF score for trading across borders (0–100)	53.07
Time to export	
Documentary compliance (hours)	12
Border compliance (hours)	36
Cost to export	
Documentary compliance (US$)	550
Border compliance (US$)	512
Time to import	
Documentary compliance (hours)	6
Border compliance (hours)	51
Cost to import	
Documentary compliance (US$)	550
Border compliance (US$)	1,385
Enforcing contracts (rank)	75
DTF score for enforcing contracts (0–100)	59.43
Time (days)	532
Cost (% of claim)	28.9
Quality of judicial processes index (0–18)	8.0
Resolving insolvency (rank)	59
DTF score for resolving insolvency (0–100)	52.93
Time (years)	3.0
Cost (% of estate)	12.0
Recovery rate (cents on the dollar)	63.5
Strength of insolvency framework index (0–16)	6.0

Note: Most indicator sets refer to a case scenario in the largest business city of an economy, though for 11 economies the data are a population-weighted average for the two largest business cities. For some indicators a result of "no practice" may be recorded for an economy; see the data notes for more details. In starting a business, procedures (number), time (days) and cost (% of income per capita) are calculated as the average of both men and women. For the postfiling index, a result of "not applicable" may be recorded for an economy.

✔ Reform making it easier to do business ✘ Change making it more difficult to do business

BAHRAIN

BAHRAIN		Middle East & North Africa		GNI per capita (US$)	20,350
Ease of doing business rank (1–190)	63	Overall distance to frontier (DTF) score (0–100)	68.44	Population	1,377,237

✔ **Starting a business** (rank)	73
DTF score for starting a business (0–100)	87.82
Procedures (number)	7.5
Time (days)	9.5
Cost (% of income per capita)	1.2
Minimum capital (% of income per capita)	3.4
Dealing with construction permits (rank)	19
DTF score for dealing with construction permits (0–100)	79.56
Procedures (number)	9
Time (days)	146
Cost (% of warehouse value)	2.2
Building quality control index (0–15)	12.0
Getting electricity (rank)	72
DTF score for getting electricity (0–100)	74.80
Procedures (number)	5
Time (days)	85
Cost (% of income per capita)	66.8
Reliability of supply and transparency of tariffs index (0–8)	5
Registering property (rank)	25
DTF score for registering property (0–100)	81.07
Procedures (number)	2
Time (days)	31
Cost (% of property value)	1.7
Quality of land administration index (0–30)	17.5
✔ **Getting credit** (rank)	101
DTF score for getting credit (0–100)	45.00
Strength of legal rights index (0–12)	1
Depth of credit information index (0–8)	8
Credit bureau coverage (% of adults)	25.7
Credit registry coverage (% of adults)	0.0
Protecting minority investors (rank)	106
DTF score for protecting minority investors (0–100)	50.00
Extent of disclosure index (0–10)	8
Extent of director liability index (0–10)	4
Ease of shareholder suits index (0–10)	4
Extent of shareholder rights index (0–10)	6
Extent of ownership and control index (0–10)	4
Extent of corporate transparency index (0–10)	4
Paying taxes (rank)	4
DTF score for paying taxes (0–100)	94.44
Payments (number per year)	13
Time (hours per year)	27
Total tax rate (% of profit)	13.5
Postfiling index (0–100)	NOT APPLICABLE
✔ **Trading across borders** (rank)	82
DTF score for trading across borders (0–100)	72.50
Time to export	
Documentary compliance (hours)	24
Border compliance (hours)	71
Cost to export	
Documentary compliance (US$)	211
Border compliance (US$)	47
Time to import	
Documentary compliance (hours)	84
Border compliance (hours)	54
Cost to import	
Documentary compliance (US$)	130
Border compliance (US$)	397
Enforcing contracts (rank)	110
DTF score for enforcing contracts (0–100)	54.53
Time (days)	635
Cost (% of claim)	14.7
Quality of judicial processes index (0–18)	4.0
Resolving insolvency (rank)	88
DTF score for resolving insolvency (0–100)	44.66
Time (years)	2.5
Cost (% of estate)	9.5
Recovery rate (cents on the dollar)	42.3
Strength of insolvency framework index (0–16)	7.0

BANGLADESH

BANGLADESH		South Asia		GNI per capita (US$)	1,190
Ease of doing business rank (1–190)	176	Overall distance to frontier (DTF) score (0–100)	40.84	Population	160,995,642

Starting a business (rank)	122
DTF score for starting a business (0–100)	81.74
Procedures (number)	9
Time (days)	19.5
Cost (% of income per capita)	13.8
Minimum capital (% of income per capita)	0.0
Dealing with construction permits (rank)	138
DTF score for dealing with construction permits (0–100)	61.60
Procedures (number)	14.2
Time (days)	269
Cost (% of warehouse value)	2.7
Building quality control index (0–15)	10.0
Getting electricity (rank)	187
DTF score for getting electricity (0–100)	16.17
Procedures (number)	9
Time (days)	428.9
Cost (% of income per capita)	2,860.9
Reliability of supply and transparency of tariffs index (0–8)	0
Registering property (rank)	185
DTF score for registering property (0–100)	27.58
Procedures (number)	8
Time (days)	244
Cost (% of property value)	7.0
Quality of land administration index (0–30)	4.5
Getting credit (rank)	157
DTF score for getting credit (0–100)	25.00
Strength of legal rights index (0–12)	5
Depth of credit information index (0–8)	0
Credit bureau coverage (% of adults)	0.0
Credit registry coverage (% of adults)	0.9
Protecting minority investors (rank)	70
DTF score for protecting minority investors (0–100)	56.67
Extent of disclosure index (0–10)	6
Extent of director liability index (0–10)	7
Ease of shareholder suits index (0–10)	6
Extent of shareholder rights index (0–10)	4
Extent of ownership and control index (0–10)	5
Extent of corporate transparency index (0–10)	6
✘ **Paying taxes** (rank)	151
DTF score for paying taxes (0–100)	55.56
Payments (number per year)	33
Time (hours per year)	435
Total tax rate (% of profit)	34.4
Postfiling index (0–100)	43.57
Trading across borders (rank)	173
DTF score for trading across borders (0–100)	34.86
Time to export	
Documentary compliance (hours)	147
Border compliance (hours)	99.7
Cost to export	
Documentary compliance (US$)	225
Border compliance (US$)	408.2
Time to import	
Documentary compliance (hours)	144
Border compliance (hours)	183
Cost to import	
Documentary compliance (US$)	370
Border compliance (US$)	1,293.8
Enforcing contracts (rank)	189
DTF score for enforcing contracts (0–100)	22.21
Time (days)	1,442
Cost (% of claim)	66.8
Quality of judicial processes index (0–18)	7.5
Resolving insolvency (rank)	151
DTF score for resolving insolvency (0–100)	27.02
Time (years)	4.0
Cost (% of estate)	8.0
Recovery rate (cents on the dollar)	27.0
Strength of insolvency framework index (0–16)	4.0

BARBADOS

BARBADOS		Latin America & Caribbean		GNI per capita (US$)	14,800
Ease of doing business rank (1–190)	117	Overall distance to frontier (DTF) score (0–100)	57.42	Population	284,215

✔ **Starting a business** (rank)	101
DTF score for starting a business (0–100)	85.10
Procedures (number)	8
Time (days)	15
Cost (% of income per capita)	7.7
Minimum capital (% of income per capita)	0.0
Dealing with construction permits (rank)	161
DTF score for dealing with construction permits (0–100)	54.96
Procedures (number)	9
Time (days)	442
Cost (% of warehouse value)	0.2
Building quality control index (0–15)	5.5
Getting electricity (rank)	93
DTF score for getting electricity (0–100)	69.38
Procedures (number)	7
Time (days)	87
Cost (% of income per capita)	64.7
Reliability of supply and transparency of tariffs index (0–8)	6
Registering property (rank)	130
DTF score for registering property (0–100)	52.35
Procedures (number)	6
Time (days)	105
Cost (% of property value)	5.6
Quality of land administration index (0–30)	11.5
Getting credit (rank)	133
DTF score for getting credit (0–100)	35.00
Strength of legal rights index (0–12)	7
Depth of credit information index (0–8)	0
Credit bureau coverage (% of adults)	0.0
Credit registry coverage (% of adults)	0.0
Protecting minority investors (rank)	165
DTF score for protecting minority investors (0–100)	35.00
Extent of disclosure index (0–10)	2
Extent of director liability index (0–10)	2
Ease of shareholder suits index (0–10)	7
Extent of shareholder rights index (0–10)	4
Extent of ownership and control index (0–10)	2
Extent of corporate transparency index (0–10)	4
Paying taxes (rank)	85
DTF score for paying taxes (0–100)	72.70
Payments (number per year)	28
Time (hours per year)	237
Total tax rate (% of profit)	34.7
Postfiling index (0–100)	73.62
Trading across borders (rank)	125
DTF score for trading across borders (0–100)	61.88
Time to export	
Documentary compliance (hours)	54
Border compliance (hours)	41
Cost to export	
Documentary compliance (US$)	109
Border compliance (US$)	350
Time to import	
Documentary compliance (hours)	74
Border compliance (hours)	104
Cost to import	
Documentary compliance (US$)	146
Border compliance (US$)	1,585
Enforcing contracts (rank)	167
DTF score for enforcing contracts (0–100)	38.02
Time (days)	1,340
Cost (% of claim)	19.7
Quality of judicial processes index (0–18)	6.5
Resolving insolvency (rank)	36
DTF score for resolving insolvency (0–100)	69.78
Time (years)	1.8
Cost (% of estate)	15.0
Recovery rate (cents on the dollar)	65.8
Strength of insolvency framework index (0–16)	11.0

Note: Most indicator sets refer to a case scenario in the largest business city of an economy, though for 11 economies the data are a population-weighted average for the two largest business cities. For some indicators a result of "no practice" may be recorded for an economy; see the data notes for more details. In starting a business, procedures (number), time (days) and cost (% of income per capita) are calculated as the average of both men and women. For the postfiling index, a result of "not applicable" may be recorded for an economy.

✔ Reform making it easier to do business ✘ Change making it more difficult to do business

BELARUS

Ease of doing business rank (1–190)	**37**	**Europe & Central Asia**		**GNI per capita (US$)**	**6,460**
		Overall distance to frontier (DTF) score (0–100)	**74.13**	**Population**	**9,513,000**
Starting a business (rank)	31	✔ **Getting credit** (rank)	101	**Trading across borders** (rank)	30
DTF score for starting a business (0–100)	92.91	DTF score for getting credit (0–100)	45.00	DTF score for trading across borders (0–100)	93.71
Procedures (number)	5	Strength of legal rights index (0–12)	2	*Time to export*	
Time (days)	5	Depth of credit information index (0–8)	7	Documentary compliance (hours)	4
Cost (% of income per capita)	0.6	Credit bureau coverage (% of adults)	0.0	Border compliance (hours)	5
Minimum capital (% of income per capita)	0.0	Credit registry coverage (% of adults)	70.1	*Cost to export*	
				Documentary compliance (US$)	140
Dealing with construction permits (rank)	28	✔ **Protecting minority investors** (rank)	42	Border compliance (US$)	108
DTF score for dealing with construction permits (0–100)	78.32	DTF score for protecting minority investors (0–100)	63.33	*Time to import*	
Procedures (number)	16	Extent of disclosure index (0–10)	7	Documentary compliance (hours)	4
Time (days)	115	Extent of director liability index (0–10)	2	Border compliance (hours)	1
Cost (% of warehouse value)	0.7	Ease of shareholder suits index (0–10)	8	*Cost to import*	
Building quality control index (0–15)	13.0	Extent of shareholder rights index (0–10)	6	Documentary compliance (US$)	0
		Extent of ownership and control index (0–10)	8	Border compliance (US$)	0
✔ **Getting electricity** (rank)	24	Extent of corporate transparency index (0–10)	7		
DTF score for getting electricity (0–100)	86.01			**Enforcing contracts** (rank)	27
Procedures (number)	4	**Paying taxes** (rank)	99	DTF score for enforcing contracts (0–100)	70.36
Time (days)	105	DTF score for paying taxes (0–100)	70.40	Time (days)	275
Cost (% of income per capita)	119.3	Payments (number per year)	7	Cost (% of claim)	23.4
Reliability of supply and transparency of tariffs index (0–8)	8	Time (hours per year)	176	Quality of judicial processes index (0–18)	9.0
		Total tax rate (% of profit)	54.8		
✔ **Registering property** (rank)	5	Postfiling index (0–100)	50.00	**Resolving insolvency** (rank)	69
DTF score for registering property (0–100)	92.19			DTF score for resolving insolvency (0–100)	49.08
Procedures (number)	2			Time (years)	1.5
Time (days)	3			Cost (% of estate)	20.0
Cost (% of property value)	0.0			Recovery rate (cents on the dollar)	33.1
Quality of land administration index (0–30)	23.5			Strength of insolvency framework index (0–16)	10.0

BELGIUM

Ease of doing business rank (1–190)	**42**	**OECD high income**		**GNI per capita (US$)**	**44,360**
		Overall distance to frontier (DTF) score (0–100)	**73.00**	**Population**	**11,285,721**
Starting a business (rank)	17	**Getting credit** (rank)	101	**Trading across borders** (rank)	1
DTF score for starting a business (0–100)	94.49	DTF score for getting credit (0–100)	45.00	DTF score for trading across borders (0–100)	100.00
Procedures (number)	3	Strength of legal rights index (0–12)	4	*Time to export*	
Time (days)	4	Depth of credit information index (0–8)	5	Documentary compliance (hours)	1
Cost (% of income per capita)	5.0	Credit bureau coverage (% of adults)	0.0	Border compliance (hours)	0
Minimum capital (% of income per capita)	17.0	Credit registry coverage (% of adults)	95.3	*Cost to export*	
				Documentary compliance (US$)	0
Dealing with construction permits (rank)	44	**Protecting minority investors** (rank)	63	Border compliance (US$)	0
DTF score for dealing with construction permits (0–100)	75.34	DTF score for protecting minority investors (0–100)	58.33	*Time to import*	
Procedures (number)	10	Extent of disclosure index (0–10)	8	Documentary compliance (hours)	1
Time (days)	212	Extent of director liability index (0–10)	6	Border compliance (hours)	0
Cost (% of warehouse value)	1.0	Ease of shareholder suits index (0–10)	7	*Cost to import*	
Building quality control index (0–15)	12.0	Extent of shareholder rights index (0–10)	4	Documentary compliance (US$)	0
		Extent of ownership and control index (0–10)	4	Border compliance (US$)	0
Getting electricity (rank)	60	Extent of corporate transparency index (0–10)	6		
DTF score for getting electricity (0–100)	79.58			**Enforcing contracts** (rank)	52
Procedures (number)	6	**Paying taxes** (rank)	66	DTF score for enforcing contracts (0–100)	64.25
Time (days)	88	DTF score for paying taxes (0–100)	77.31	Time (days)	505
Cost (% of income per capita)	102.4	Payments (number per year)	11	Cost (% of claim)	18.0
Reliability of supply and transparency of tariffs index (0–8)	8	Time (hours per year)	161	Quality of judicial processes index (0–18)	8.0
		Total tax rate (% of profit)	58.7		
Registering property (rank)	131	Postfiling index (0–100)	88.28	**Resolving insolvency** (rank)	10
DTF score for registering property (0–100)	51.43			DTF score for resolving insolvency (0–100)	84.32
Procedures (number)	8			Time (years)	0.9
Time (days)	56			Cost (% of estate)	3.5
Cost (% of property value)	12.7			Recovery rate (cents on the dollar)	89.9
Quality of land administration index (0–30)	22.5			Strength of insolvency framework index (0–16)	11.5

BELIZE

Ease of doing business rank (1–190)	**112**	**Latin America & Caribbean**		**GNI per capita (US$)**	**4,420**
		Overall distance to frontier (DTF) score (0–100)	**58.06**	**Population**	**359,287**
Starting a business (rank)	158	**Getting credit** (rank)	167	**Trading across borders** (rank)	101
DTF score for starting a business (0–100)	73.22	DTF score for getting credit (0–100)	20.00	DTF score for trading across borders (0–100)	68.13
Procedures (number)	9	Strength of legal rights index (0–12)	4	*Time to export*	
Time (days)	43	Depth of credit information index (0–8)	0	Documentary compliance (hours)	38
Cost (% of income per capita)	34.6	Credit bureau coverage (% of adults)	0.0	Border compliance (hours)	96
Minimum capital (% of income per capita)	0.1	Credit registry coverage (% of adults)	0.0	*Cost to export*	
				Documentary compliance (US$)	28
Dealing with construction permits (rank)	100	**Protecting minority investors** (rank)	118	Border compliance (US$)	710
DTF score for dealing with construction permits (0–100)	68.17	DTF score for protecting minority investors (0–100)	46.67	*Time to import*	
Procedures (number)	15	Extent of disclosure index (0–10)	3	Documentary compliance (hours)	36
Time (days)	109	Extent of director liability index (0–10)	4	Border compliance (hours)	48
Cost (% of warehouse value)	2.0	Ease of shareholder suits index (0–10)	7	*Cost to import*	
Building quality control index (0–15)	7.0	Extent of shareholder rights index (0–10)	7	Documentary compliance (US$)	75
		Extent of ownership and control index (0–10)	2	Border compliance (US$)	688
Getting electricity (rank)	79	Extent of corporate transparency index (0–10)	5		
DTF score for getting electricity (0–100)	72.96			**Enforcing contracts** (rank)	134
Procedures (number)	5	**Paying taxes** (rank)	44	DTF score for enforcing contracts (0–100)	50.11
Time (days)	66	DTF score for paying taxes (0–100)	83.03	Time (days)	892
Cost (% of income per capita)	319.9	Payments (number per year)	29	Cost (% of claim)	27.5
Reliability of supply and transparency of tariffs index (0–8)	4	Time (hours per year)	147	Quality of judicial processes index (0–18)	8.0
		Total tax rate (% of profit)	31.1		
Registering property (rank)	126	Postfiling index (0–100)	97.60	**Resolving insolvency** (rank)	81
DTF score for registering property (0–100)	52.84			DTF score for resolving insolvency (0–100)	45.48
Procedures (number)	9			Time (years)	2.0
Time (days)	60			Cost (% of estate)	22.5
Cost (% of property value)	4.8			Recovery rate (cents on the dollar)	55.5
Quality of land administration index (0–30)	11.5			Strength of insolvency framework index (0–16)	5.0

Note: Most indicator sets refer to a case scenario in the largest business city of an economy, though for 11 economies the data are a population-weighted average for the two largest business cities. For some indicators a result of "no practice" may be recorded for an economy; see the data notes for more details. In starting a business, procedures (number), time (days) and cost (% of income per capita) are calculated as the average of both men and women. For the postfiling index, a result of "not applicable" may be recorded for an economy.

✔ Reform making it easier to do business ✘ Change making it more difficult to do business

BENIN

BENIN		Sub-Saharan Africa		GNI per capita (US$)	860
Ease of doing business rank (1–190)	155	Overall distance to frontier (DTF) score (0–100)	48.52	Population	10,879,829

✔ Starting a business (rank)	57
DTF score for starting a business (0–100)	90.56
Procedures (number)	5.5
Time (days)	8.5
Cost (% of income per capita)	3.7
Minimum capital (% of income per capita)	5.4

Dealing with construction permits (rank)	74
DTF score for dealing with construction permits (0–100)	71.29
Procedures (number)	13
Time (days)	88
Cost (% of warehouse value)	3.0
Building quality control index (0–15)	7.5

Getting electricity (rank)	174
DTF score for getting electricity (0–100)	33.84
Procedures (number)	5
Time (days)	90
Cost (% of income per capita)	12,581.5
Reliability of supply and transparency of tariffs index (0–8)	0

Registering property (rank)	173
DTF score for registering property (0–100)	39.96
Procedures (number)	4
Time (days)	120
Cost (% of property value)	11.5
Quality of land administration index (0–30)	5.5

Getting credit (rank)	139
DTF score for getting credit (0–100)	30.00
Strength of legal rights index (0–12)	6
Depth of credit information index (0–8)	0
Credit bureau coverage (% of adults)	0.0
Credit registry coverage (% of adults)	0.6

Protecting minority investors (rank)	145
DTF score for protecting minority investors (0–100)	40.00
Extent of disclosure index (0–10)	7
Extent of director liability index (0–10)	1
Ease of shareholder suits index (0–10)	5
Extent of shareholder rights index (0–10)	5
Extent of ownership and control index (0–10)	4
Extent of corporate transparency index (0–10)	2

Paying taxes (rank)	173
DTF score for paying taxes (0–100)	44.61
Payments (number per year)	57
Time (hours per year)	270
Total tax rate (% of profit)	57.4
Postfiling index (0–100)	48.85

Trading across borders (rank)	133
DTF score for trading across borders (0–100)	59.89
Time to export	
Documentary compliance (hours)	48
Border compliance (hours)	78
Cost to export	
Documentary compliance (US$)	80
Border compliance (US$)	487
Time to import	
Documentary compliance (hours)	59
Border compliance (hours)	82
Cost to import	
Documentary compliance (US$)	529
Border compliance (US$)	599

Enforcing contracts (rank)	169
DTF score for enforcing contracts (0–100)	36.34
Time (days)	750
Cost (% of claim)	64.7
Quality of judicial processes index (0–18)	6.0

✔ Resolving insolvency (rank)	115
DTF score for resolving insolvency (0–100)	38.72
Time (years)	4.0
Cost (% of estate)	21.5
Recovery rate (cents on the dollar)	19.7
Strength of insolvency framework index (0–16)	9.0

BHUTAN

BHUTAN		South Asia		GNI per capita (US$)	2,370
Ease of doing business rank (1–190)	73	Overall distance to frontier (DTF) score (0–100)	65.37	Population	774,830

Starting a business (rank)	94
DTF score for starting a business (0–100)	85.59
Procedures (number)	8
Time (days)	15
Cost (% of income per capita)	3.8
Minimum capital (% of income per capita)	0.0

Dealing with construction permits (rank)	97
DTF score for dealing with construction permits (0–100)	68.47
Procedures (number)	21
Time (days)	151
Cost (% of warehouse value)	1.2
Building quality control index (0–15)	12.0

Getting electricity (rank)	54
DTF score for getting electricity (0–100)	80.16
Procedures (number)	4
Time (days)	61
Cost (% of income per capita)	525.4
Reliability of supply and transparency of tariffs index (0–8)	5

Registering property (rank)	51
DTF score for registering property (0–100)	73.40
Procedures (number)	3
Time (days)	77
Cost (% of property value)	5.0
Quality of land administration index (0–30)	24.0

Getting credit (rank)	82
DTF score for getting credit (0–100)	50.00
Strength of legal rights index (0–12)	4
Depth of credit information index (0–8)	6
Credit bureau coverage (% of adults)	26.0
Credit registry coverage (% of adults)	0.0

Protecting minority investors (rank)	114
DTF score for protecting minority investors (0–100)	48.33
Extent of disclosure index (0–10)	4
Extent of director liability index (0–10)	4
Ease of shareholder suits index (0–10)	6
Extent of shareholder rights index (0–10)	6
Extent of ownership and control index (0–10)	4
Extent of corporate transparency index (0–10)	5

Paying taxes (rank)	19
DTF score for paying taxes (0–100)	88.11
Payments (number per year)	18
Time (hours per year)	85
Total tax rate (% of profit)	35.3
Postfiling index (0–100)	95.95

Trading across borders (rank)	26
DTF score for trading across borders (0–100)	94.25
Time to export	
Documentary compliance (hours)	9
Border compliance (hours)	5
Cost to export	
Documentary compliance (US$)	50
Border compliance (US$)	59
Time to import	
Documentary compliance (hours)	8
Border compliance (hours)	5
Cost to import	
Documentary compliance (US$)	50
Border compliance (US$)	110

Enforcing contracts (rank)	47
DTF score for enforcing contracts (0–100)	65.36
Time (days)	225
Cost (% of claim)	23.1
Quality of judicial processes index (0–18)	5.5

Resolving insolvency (rank)	169
DTF score for resolving insolvency (0–100)	0.00
Time (years)	NO PRACTICE
Cost (% of estate)	NO PRACTICE
Recovery rate (cents on the dollar)	0.0
Strength of insolvency framework index (0–16)	0.0

BOLIVIA

BOLIVIA		Latin America & Caribbean		GNI per capita (US$)	3,080
Ease of doing business rank (1–190)	149	Overall distance to frontier (DTF) score (0–100)	49.85	Population	10,724,705

✔ Starting a business (rank)	177
DTF score for starting a business (0–100)	62.94
Procedures (number)	14
Time (days)	45
Cost (% of income per capita)	54.1
Minimum capital (% of income per capita)	0.0

✘ Dealing with construction permits (rank)	152
DTF score for dealing with construction permits (0–100)	57.18
Procedures (number)	12
Time (days)	322
Cost (% of warehouse value)	0.9
Building quality control index (0–15)	7.0

Getting electricity (rank)	99
DTF score for getting electricity (0–100)	68.19
Procedures (number)	8
Time (days)	42
Cost (% of income per capita)	686.8
Reliability of supply and transparency of tariffs index (0–8)	6

Registering property (rank)	139
DTF score for registering property (0–100)	49.90
Procedures (number)	7
Time (days)	90
Cost (% of property value)	4.7
Quality of land administration index (0–30)	7.0

Getting credit (rank)	133
DTF score for getting credit (0–100)	35.00
Strength of legal rights index (0–12)	0
Depth of credit information index (0–8)	7
Credit bureau coverage (% of adults)	45.2
Credit registry coverage (% of adults)	15.4

Protecting minority investors (rank)	137
DTF score for protecting minority investors (0–100)	41.67
Extent of disclosure index (0–10)	1
Extent of director liability index (0–10)	5
Ease of shareholder suits index (0–10)	6
Extent of shareholder rights index (0–10)	7
Extent of ownership and control index (0–10)	2
Extent of corporate transparency index (0–10)	4

Paying taxes (rank)	186
DTF score for paying taxes (0–100)	21.41
Payments (number per year)	42
Time (hours per year)	1,025
Total tax rate (% of profit)	83.7
Postfiling index (0–100)	49.08

Trading across borders (rank)	98
DTF score for trading across borders (0–100)	68.41
Time to export	
Documentary compliance (hours)	192
Border compliance (hours)	48
Cost to export	
Documentary compliance (US$)	25
Border compliance (US$)	65
Time to import	
Documentary compliance (hours)	96
Border compliance (hours)	114
Cost to import	
Documentary compliance (US$)	30
Border compliance (US$)	315

✔ Enforcing contracts (rank)	128
DTF score for enforcing contracts (0–100)	51.57
Time (days)	591
Cost (% of claim)	33.2
Quality of judicial processes index (0–18)	5.5

Resolving insolvency (rank)	96
DTF score for resolving insolvency (0–100)	42.28
Time (years)	1.8
Cost (% of estate)	14.5
Recovery rate (cents on the dollar)	40.8
Strength of insolvency framework index (0–16)	6.5

Note: Most indicator sets refer to a case scenario in the largest business city of an economy, though for 11 economies the data are a population-weighted average for the two largest business cities. For some indicators a result of "no practice" may be recorded for an economy; see the data notes for more details. In starting a business, procedures (number), time (days) and cost (% of income per capita) are calculated as the average of both men and women. For the postfiling index, a result of "not applicable" may be recorded for an economy.

✔ Reform making it easier to do business ✘ Change making it more difficult to do business

BOSNIA AND HERZEGOVINA

Europe & Central Asia	
GNI per capita (US$)	4,680
Ease of doing business rank (1–190)	81
Overall distance to frontier (DTF) score (0–100)	63.87
Population	3,810,416

✔ **Starting a business** (rank)	174
DTF score for starting a business (0–100)	65.09
Procedures (number)	12
Time (days)	65
Cost (% of income per capita)	13.5
Minimum capital (% of income per capita)	13.4
Dealing with construction permits (rank)	170
DTF score for dealing with construction permits (0–100)	52.54
Procedures (number)	15
Time (days)	179
Cost (% of warehouse value)	18.5
Building quality control index (0–15)	13.0
Getting electricity (rank)	123
DTF score for getting electricity (0–100)	60.05
Procedures (number)	8
Time (days)	125
Cost (% of income per capita)	400.2
Reliability of supply and transparency of tariffs index (0–8)	6
Registering property (rank)	99
DTF score for registering property (0–100)	61.54
Procedures (number)	7
Time (days)	24
Cost (% of property value)	5.2
Quality of land administration index (0–30)	12.5
Getting credit (rank)	44
DTF score for getting credit (0–100)	65.00
Strength of legal rights index (0–12)	7
Depth of credit information index (0–8)	6
Credit bureau coverage (% of adults)	10.4
Credit registry coverage (% of adults)	37.6
Protecting minority investors (rank)	81
DTF score for protecting minority investors (0–100)	55.00
Extent of disclosure index (0–10)	3
Extent of director liability index (0–10)	6
Ease of shareholder suits index (0–10)	5
Extent of shareholder rights index (0–10)	7
Extent of ownership and control index (0–10)	6
Extent of corporate transparency index (0–10)	6
✔ **Paying taxes** (rank)	133
DTF score for paying taxes (0–100)	60.08
Payments (number per year)	34
Time (hours per year)	411
Total tax rate (% of profit)	22.6
Postfiling index (0–100)	47.94
Trading across borders (rank)	36
DTF score for trading across borders (0–100)	91.87
Time to export	
Documentary compliance (hours)	4
Border compliance (hours)	5
Cost to export	
Documentary compliance (US$)	92
Border compliance (US$)	106
Time to import	
Documentary compliance (hours)	8
Border compliance (hours)	6
Cost to import	
Documentary compliance (US$)	97
Border compliance (US$)	109
Enforcing contracts (rank)	64
DTF score for enforcing contracts (0–100)	60.60
Time (days)	595
Cost (% of claim)	36.0
Quality of judicial processes index (0–18)	11.0
Resolving insolvency (rank)	41
DTF score for resolving insolvency (0–100)	66.93
Time (years)	3.3
Cost (% of estate)	9.0
Recovery rate (cents on the dollar)	37.3
Strength of insolvency framework index (0–16)	15.0

BOTSWANA

Sub-Saharan Africa	
GNI per capita (US$)	6,510
Ease of doing business rank (1–190)	71
Overall distance to frontier (DTF) score (0–100)	65.55
Population	2,262,485

Starting a business (rank)	153
DTF score for starting a business (0–100)	76.21
Procedures (number)	9
Time (days)	48
Cost (% of income per capita)	0.8
Minimum capital (% of income per capita)	0.0
✔ **Dealing with construction permits** (rank)	50
DTF score for dealing with construction permits (0–100)	74.81
Procedures (number)	17
Time (days)	100
Cost (% of warehouse value)	0.3
Building quality control index (0–15)	10.5
Getting electricity (rank)	125
DTF score for getting electricity (0–100)	59.25
Procedures (number)	5
Time (days)	77
Cost (% of income per capita)	323.7
Reliability of supply and transparency of tariffs index (0–8)	0
Registering property (rank)	70
DTF score for registering property (0–100)	67.27
Procedures (number)	4
Time (days)	12
Cost (% of property value)	5.1
Quality of land administration index (0–30)	10.0
Getting credit (rank)	75
DTF score for getting credit (0–100)	55.00
Strength of legal rights index (0–12)	5
Depth of credit information index (0–8)	6
Credit bureau coverage (% of adults)	53.5
Credit registry coverage (% of adults)	0.0
Protecting minority investors (rank)	81
DTF score for protecting minority investors (0–100)	55.00
Extent of disclosure index (0–10)	7
Extent of director liability index (0–10)	8
Ease of shareholder suits index (0–10)	3
Extent of shareholder rights index (0–10)	6
Extent of ownership and control index (0–10)	3
Extent of corporate transparency index (0–10)	6
Paying taxes (rank)	55
DTF score for paying taxes (0–100)	80.58
Payments (number per year)	34
Time (hours per year)	152
Total tax rate (% of profit)	25.1
Postfiling index (0–100)	89.89
Trading across borders (rank)	51
DTF score for trading across borders (0–100)	85.93
Time to export	
Documentary compliance (hours)	24
Border compliance (hours)	8
Cost to export	
Documentary compliance (US$)	179
Border compliance (US$)	317
Time to import	
Documentary compliance (hours)	3
Border compliance (hours)	4
Cost to import	
Documentary compliance (US$)	67
Border compliance (US$)	98
Enforcing contracts (rank)	132
DTF score for enforcing contracts (0–100)	50.95
Time (days)	625
Cost (% of claim)	39.8
Quality of judicial processes index (0–18)	7.0
Resolving insolvency (rank)	64
DTF score for resolving insolvency (0–100)	50.53
Time (years)	1.7
Cost (% of estate)	18.0
Recovery rate (cents on the dollar)	64.8
Strength of insolvency framework index (0–16)	5.0

BRAZIL

Latin America & Caribbean	
GNI per capita (US$)	9,850
Ease of doing business rank (1–190)	123
Overall distance to frontier (DTF) score (0–100)	56.53
Population	207,847,528

✔ **Starting a business** (rank)	175
DTF score for starting a business (0–100)	65.04
Procedures (number)	11
Time (days)	79.5
Cost (% of income per capita)	5.2
Minimum capital (% of income per capita)	0.0
Dealing with construction permits (rank)	172
DTF score for dealing with construction permits (0–100)	51.28
Procedures (number)	18.2
Time (days)	425.7
Cost (% of warehouse value)	0.4
Building quality control index (0–15)	9.0
Getting electricity (rank)	47
DTF score for getting electricity (0–100)	81.23
Procedures (number)	4
Time (days)	64.4
Cost (% of income per capita)	58.0
Reliability of supply and transparency of tariffs index (0–8)	5
Registering property (rank)	128
DTF score for registering property (0–100)	52.62
Procedures (number)	13.6
Time (days)	31.4
Cost (% of property value)	3.1
Quality of land administration index (0–30)	13.8
Getting credit (rank)	101
DTF score for getting credit (0–100)	45.00
Strength of legal rights index (0–12)	2
Depth of credit information index (0–8)	7
Credit bureau coverage (% of adults)	78.9
Credit registry coverage (% of adults)	53.4
Protecting minority investors (rank)	32
DTF score for protecting minority investors (0–100)	65.00
Extent of disclosure index (0–10)	5
Extent of director liability index (0–10)	8
Ease of shareholder suits index (0–10)	4
Extent of shareholder rights index (0–10)	7
Extent of ownership and control index (0–10)	7
Extent of corporate transparency index (0–10)	8
Paying taxes (rank)	181
DTF score for paying taxes (0–100)	33.03
Payments (number per year)	9.6
Time (hours per year)	2,038
Total tax rate (% of profit)	68.4
Postfiling index (0–100)	8.03
✔ **Trading across borders** (rank)	149
DTF score for trading across borders (0–100)	55.57
Time to export	
Documentary compliance (hours)	18
Border compliance (hours)	49
Cost to export	
Documentary compliance (US$)	226.4
Border compliance (US$)	958.7
Time to import	
Documentary compliance (hours)	120
Border compliance (hours)	63.1
Cost to import	
Documentary compliance (US$)	106.9
Border compliance (US$)	969.6
✔ **Enforcing contracts** (rank)	37
DTF score for enforcing contracts (0–100)	67.41
Time (days)	731
Cost (% of claim)	20.7
Quality of judicial processes index (0–18)	13.6
Resolving insolvency (rank)	67
DTF score for resolving insolvency (0–100)	49.15
Time (years)	4.0
Cost (% of estate)	12.0
Recovery rate (cents on the dollar)	15.8
Strength of insolvency framework index (0–16)	13.0

Note: Most indicator sets refer to a case scenario in the largest business city of an economy, though for 11 economies the data are a population-weighted average for the two largest business cities. For some indicators a result of "no practice" may be recorded for an economy; see the data notes for more details. In starting a business, procedures (number), time (days) and cost (% of income per capita) are calculated as the average of both men and women. For the postfiling index, a result of "not applicable" may be recorded for an economy.

✔ Reform making it easier to do business ✘ Change making it more difficult to do business

BRUNEI DARUSSALAM

Ease of doing business rank (1–190)	72	East Asia & Pacific		GNI per capita (US$)	24,892
		Overall distance to frontier (DTF) score (0–100)	65.51	Population	423,188

Starting a business (rank)	84
DTF score for starting a business (0–100)	86.72
Procedures (number)	7.5
Time (days)	14.5
Cost (% of income per capita)	1.6
Minimum capital (% of income per capita)	0.0
Dealing with construction permits (rank)	37
DTF score for dealing with construction permits (0–100)	76.06
Procedures (number)	18
Time (days)	75
Cost (% of warehouse value)	1.9
Building quality control index (0–15)	12.0
✔ **Getting electricity** (rank)	21
DTF score for getting electricity (0–100)	87.57
Procedures (number)	4
Time (days)	35
Cost (% of income per capita)	54.2
Reliability of supply and transparency of tariffs index (0–8)	6
Registering property (rank)	134
DTF score for registering property (0–100)	50.65
Procedures (number)	6
Time (days)	298
Cost (% of property value)	0.6
Quality of land administration index (0–30)	14.5
✔ **Getting credit** (rank)	62
DTF score for getting credit (0–100)	60.00
Strength of legal rights index (0–12)	5
Depth of credit information index (0–8)	7
Credit bureau coverage (% of adults)	0.0
Credit registry coverage (% of adults)	61.8
✔ **Protecting minority investors** (rank)	102
DTF score for protecting minority investors (0–100)	51.67
Extent of disclosure index (0–10)	4
Extent of director liability index (0–10)	8
Ease of shareholder suits index (0–10)	8
Extent of shareholder rights index (0–10)	5
Extent of ownership and control index (0–10)	1
Extent of corporate transparency index (0–10)	5
✔ **Paying taxes** (rank)	89
DTF score for paying taxes (0–100)	72.43
Payments (number per year)	16
Time (hours per year)	76.5
Total tax rate (% of profit)	8.7
Postfiling index (0–100)	15.63
Trading across borders (rank)	142
DTF score for trading across borders (0–100)	57.69
Time to export	
Documentary compliance (hours)	163
Border compliance (hours)	117
Cost to export	
Documentary compliance (US$)	90
Border compliance (US$)	340
Time to import	
Documentary compliance (hours)	140
Border compliance (hours)	48
Cost to import	
Documentary compliance (US$)	50
Border compliance (US$)	395
✔ **Enforcing contracts** (rank)	93
DTF score for enforcing contracts (0–100)	57.25
Time (days)	540
Cost (% of claim)	36.6
Quality of judicial processes index (0–18)	8.5
✔ **Resolving insolvency** (rank)	57
DTF score for resolving insolvency (0–100)	55.11
Time (years)	2.5
Cost (% of estate)	3.5
Recovery rate (cents on the dollar)	47.2
Strength of insolvency framework index (0–16)	9.5

BULGARIA

Ease of doing business rank (1–190)	39	Europe & Central Asia		GNI per capita (US$)	7,220
		Overall distance to frontier (DTF) score (0–100)	73.51	Population	7,177,991

Starting a business (rank)	82
DTF score for starting a business (0–100)	86.82
Procedures (number)	6
Time (days)	23
Cost (% of income per capita)	1.3
Minimum capital (% of income per capita)	0.0
Dealing with construction permits (rank)	48
DTF score for dealing with construction permits (0–100)	75.06
Procedures (number)	16
Time (days)	105
Cost (% of warehouse value)	3.9
Building quality control index (0–15)	13.0
✔ **Getting electricity** (rank)	104
DTF score for getting electricity (0–100)	64.97
Procedures (number)	6
Time (days)	130
Cost (% of income per capita)	318.3
Reliability of supply and transparency of tariffs index (0–8)	5
Registering property (rank)	60
DTF score for registering property (0–100)	70.19
Procedures (number)	8
Time (days)	11
Cost (% of property value)	2.9
Quality of land administration index (0–30)	19.0
Getting credit (rank)	32
DTF score for getting credit (0–100)	70.00
Strength of legal rights index (0–12)	9
Depth of credit information index (0–8)	5
Credit bureau coverage (% of adults)	0.0
Credit registry coverage (% of adults)	66.9
Protecting minority investors (rank)	13
DTF score for protecting minority investors (0–100)	73.33
Extent of disclosure index (0–10)	10
Extent of director liability index (0–10)	2
Ease of shareholder suits index (0–10)	8
Extent of shareholder rights index (0–10)	9
Extent of ownership and control index (0–10)	6
Extent of corporate transparency index (0–10)	9
Paying taxes (rank)	83
DTF score for paying taxes (0–100)	72.81
Payments (number per year)	14
Time (hours per year)	453
Total tax rate (% of profit)	27.0
Postfiling index (0–100)	73.30
Trading across borders (rank)	21
DTF score for trading across borders (0–100)	97.41
Time to export	
Documentary compliance (hours)	2
Border compliance (hours)	4
Cost to export	
Documentary compliance (US$)	52
Border compliance (US$)	55
Time to import	
Documentary compliance (hours)	1
Border compliance (hours)	1
Cost to import	
Documentary compliance (US$)	0
Border compliance (US$)	0
Enforcing contracts (rank)	49
DTF score for enforcing contracts (0–100)	65.09
Time (days)	564
Cost (% of claim)	23.8
Quality of judicial processes index (0–18)	10.5
Resolving insolvency (rank)	48
DTF score for resolving insolvency (0–100)	59.38
Time (years)	3.3
Cost (% of estate)	9.0
Recovery rate (cents on the dollar)	34.9
Strength of insolvency framework index (0–16)	13.0

BURKINA FASO

Ease of doing business rank (1–190)	146	Sub-Saharan Africa		GNI per capita (US$)	660
		Overall distance to frontier (DTF) score (0–100)	51.33	Population	18,105,570

✔ **Starting a business** (rank)	72
DTF score for starting a business (0–100)	88.06
Procedures (number)	3
Time (days)	13
Cost (% of income per capita)	43.4
Minimum capital (% of income per capita)	7.0
Dealing with construction permits (rank)	61
DTF score for dealing with construction permits (0–100)	72.87
Procedures (number)	14
Time (days)	121
Cost (% of warehouse value)	5.0
Building quality control index (0–15)	12.0
Getting electricity (rank)	181
DTF score for getting electricity (0–100)	29.42
Procedures (number)	4
Time (days)	169
Cost (% of income per capita)	10,028.1
Reliability of supply and transparency of tariffs index (0–8)	0
Registering property (rank)	136
DTF score for registering property (0–100)	50.26
Procedures (number)	4
Time (days)	67
Cost (% of property value)	12.1
Quality of land administration index (0–30)	11.5
✔ **Getting credit** (rank)	139
DTF score for getting credit (0–100)	30.00
Strength of legal rights index (0–12)	6
Depth of credit information index (0–8)	0
Credit bureau coverage (% of adults)	0.0
Credit registry coverage (% of adults)	0.3
Protecting minority investors (rank)	145
DTF score for protecting minority investors (0–100)	40.00
Extent of disclosure index (0–10)	7
Extent of director liability index (0–10)	1
Ease of shareholder suits index (0–10)	5
Extent of shareholder rights index (0–10)	5
Extent of ownership and control index (0–10)	4
Extent of corporate transparency index (0–10)	2
Paying taxes (rank)	150
DTF score for paying taxes (0–100)	55.77
Payments (number per year)	45
Time (hours per year)	270
Total tax rate (% of profit)	41.3
Postfiling index (0–100)	48.85
Trading across borders (rank)	104
DTF score for trading across borders (0–100)	66.58
Time to export	
Documentary compliance (hours)	84
Border compliance (hours)	75
Cost to export	
Documentary compliance (US$)	86
Border compliance (US$)	261
Time to import	
Documentary compliance (hours)	96
Border compliance (hours)	102
Cost to import	
Documentary compliance (US$)	197
Border compliance (US$)	265
Enforcing contracts (rank)	161
DTF score for enforcing contracts (0–100)	41.05
Time (days)	446
Cost (% of claim)	81.7
Quality of judicial processes index (0–18)	7.5
✔ **Resolving insolvency** (rank)	112
DTF score for resolving insolvency (0–100)	39.25
Time (years)	4.0
Cost (% of estate)	21.0
Recovery rate (cents on the dollar)	20.7
Strength of insolvency framework index (0–16)	9.0

Note: Most indicator sets refer to a case scenario in the largest business city of an economy, though for 11 economies the data are a population-weighted average for the two largest business cities. For some indicators a result of "no practice" may be recorded for an economy; see the data notes for more details. In starting a business, procedures (number), time (days) and cost (% of income per capita) are calculated as the average of both men and women. For the postfiling index, a result of "not applicable" may be recorded for an economy.

✔ Reform making it easier to do business ✘ Change making it more difficult to do business

BURUNDI

Sub-Saharan Africa	GNI per capita (US$) 260
Ease of doing business rank (1–190) 157	Overall distance to frontier (DTF) score (0–100) 47.37
Population	11,178,921

Starting a business (rank)	18
DTF score for starting a business (0–100)	94.45
Procedures (number)	3
Time (days)	4
Cost (% of income per capita)	13.9
Minimum capital (% of income per capita)	0.0
Dealing with construction permits (rank)	169
DTF score for dealing with construction permits (0–100)	52.72
Procedures (number)	14
Time (days)	99
Cost (% of warehouse value)	10.4
Building quality control index (0–15)	3.0
Getting electricity (rank)	183
DTF score for getting electricity (0–100)	26.45
Procedures (number)	5
Time (days)	158
Cost (% of income per capita)	16,917.5
Reliability of supply and transparency of tariffs index (0–8)	0
Registering property (rank)	94
DTF score for registering property (0–100)	62.52
Procedures (number)	5
Time (days)	23
Cost (% of property value)	3.2
Quality of land administration index (0–30)	4.5
Getting credit (rank)	175
DTF score for getting credit (0–100)	10.00
Strength of legal rights index (0–12)	2
Depth of credit information index (0–8)	0
Credit bureau coverage (% of adults)	0.0
Credit registry coverage (% of adults)	4.0
Protecting minority investors (rank)	137
DTF score for protecting minority investors (0–100)	41.67
Extent of disclosure index (0–10)	8
Extent of director liability index (0–10)	7
Ease of shareholder suits index (0–10)	2
Extent of shareholder rights index (0–10)	6
Extent of ownership and control index (0–10)	1
Extent of corporate transparency index (0–10)	1
✔ **Paying taxes** (rank)	123
DTF score for paying taxes (0–100)	62.20
Payments (number per year)	25
Time (hours per year)	232
Total tax rate (% of profit)	40.3
Postfiling index (0–100)	33.99
Trading across borders (rank)	160
DTF score for trading across borders (0–100)	47.38
Time to export	
Documentary compliance (hours)	120
Border compliance (hours)	59
Cost to export	
Documentary compliance (US$)	150
Border compliance (US$)	106
Time to import	
Documentary compliance (hours)	180
Border compliance (hours)	154
Cost to import	
Documentary compliance (US$)	1,025
Border compliance (US$)	444
Enforcing contracts (rank)	149
DTF score for enforcing contracts (0–100)	45.74
Time (days)	832
Cost (% of claim)	38.6
Quality of judicial processes index (0–18)	7.0
Resolving insolvency (rank)	141
DTF score for resolving insolvency (0–100)	30.52
Time (years)	5.0
Cost (% of estate)	30.0
Recovery rate (cents on the dollar)	7.4
Strength of insolvency framework index (0–16)	8.5

CABO VERDE

Sub-Saharan Africa	GNI per capita (US$) 3,290
Ease of doing business rank (1–190) 129	Overall distance to frontier (DTF) score (0–100) 55.28
Population	520,502

Starting a business (rank)	100
DTF score for starting a business (0–100)	85.24
Procedures (number)	8
Time (days)	11
Cost (% of income per capita)	14.7
Minimum capital (% of income per capita)	0.0
Dealing with construction permits (rank)	108
DTF score for dealing with construction permits (0–100)	67.28
Procedures (number)	16
Time (days)	140
Cost (% of warehouse value)	4.1
Building quality control index (0–15)	10.0
Getting electricity (rank)	142
DTF score for getting electricity (0–100)	53.81
Procedures (number)	7
Time (days)	88
Cost (% of income per capita)	1,026.9
Reliability of supply and transparency of tariffs index (0–8)	2
Registering property (rank)	73
DTF score for registering property (0–100)	66.63
Procedures (number)	6
Time (days)	22
Cost (% of property value)	2.3
Quality of land administration index (0–30)	10.0
Getting credit (rank)	118
DTF score for getting credit (0–100)	40.00
Strength of legal rights index (0–12)	2
Depth of credit information index (0–8)	6
Credit bureau coverage (% of adults)	0.0
Credit registry coverage (% of adults)	20.0
Protecting minority investors (rank)	162
DTF score for protecting minority investors (0–100)	36.67
Extent of disclosure index (0–10)	1
Extent of director liability index (0–10)	5
Ease of shareholder suits index (0–10)	6
Extent of shareholder rights index (0–10)	3
Extent of ownership and control index (0–10)	5
Extent of corporate transparency index (0–10)	2
Paying taxes (rank)	86
DTF score for paying taxes (0–100)	72.64
Payments (number per year)	30
Time (hours per year)	180
Total tax rate (% of profit)	36.6
Postfiling index (0–100)	70.62
Trading across borders (rank)	113
DTF score for trading across borders (0–100)	64.74
Time to export	
Documentary compliance (hours)	48
Border compliance (hours)	90
Cost to export	
Documentary compliance (US$)	125
Border compliance (US$)	630
Time to import	
Documentary compliance (hours)	48
Border compliance (hours)	60
Cost to import	
Documentary compliance (US$)	125
Border compliance (US$)	588
Enforcing contracts (rank)	43
DTF score for enforcing contracts (0–100)	65.76
Time (days)	425
Cost (% of claim)	19.8
Quality of judicial processes index (0–18)	8.0
Resolving insolvency (rank)	169
DTF score for resolving insolvency (0–100)	0.00
Time (years)	NO PRACTICE
Cost (% of estate)	NO PRACTICE
Recovery rate (cents on the dollar)	0.0
Strength of insolvency framework index (0–16)	0.0

CAMBODIA

East Asia & Pacific	GNI per capita (US$) 1,070
Ease of doing business rank (1–190) 131	Overall distance to frontier (DTF) score (0–100) 54.79
Population	15,577,899

✘ **Starting a business** (rank)	180
DTF score for starting a business (0–100)	54.93
Procedures (number)	9
Time (days)	99
Cost (% of income per capita)	57.2
Minimum capital (% of income per capita)	22.5
Dealing with construction permits (rank)	183
DTF score for dealing with construction permits (0–100)	38.64
Procedures (number)	20
Time (days)	652
Cost (% of warehouse value)	5.8
Building quality control index (0–15)	6.5
Getting electricity (rank)	136
DTF score for getting electricity (0–100)	56.00
Procedures (number)	4
Time (days)	179
Cost (% of income per capita)	2,172.3
Reliability of supply and transparency of tariffs index (0–8)	3
Registering property (rank)	120
DTF score for registering property (0–100)	54.96
Procedures (number)	7
Time (days)	56
Cost (% of property value)	4.3
Quality of land administration index (0–30)	7.5
✔ **Getting credit** (rank)	7
DTF score for getting credit (0–100)	85.00
Strength of legal rights index (0–12)	11
Depth of credit information index (0–8)	6
Credit bureau coverage (% of adults)	44.0
Credit registry coverage (% of adults)	0.0
Protecting minority investors (rank)	114
DTF score for protecting minority investors (0–100)	48.33
Extent of disclosure index (0–10)	5
Extent of director liability index (0–10)	10
Ease of shareholder suits index (0–10)	4
Extent of shareholder rights index (0–10)	1
Extent of ownership and control index (0–10)	4
Extent of corporate transparency index (0–10)	5
Paying taxes (rank)	124
DTF score for paying taxes (0–100)	61.97
Payments (number per year)	40
Time (hours per year)	173
Total tax rate (% of profit)	21.0
Postfiling index (0–100)	28.73
Trading across borders (rank)	102
DTF score for trading across borders (0–100)	67.28
Time to export	
Documentary compliance (hours)	132
Border compliance (hours)	48
Cost to export	
Documentary compliance (US$)	100
Border compliance (US$)	375
Time to import	
Documentary compliance (hours)	132
Border compliance (hours)	8
Cost to import	
Documentary compliance (US$)	120
Border compliance (US$)	240
Enforcing contracts (rank)	178
DTF score for enforcing contracts (0–100)	32.67
Time (days)	483
Cost (% of claim)	103.4
Quality of judicial processes index (0–18)	5.0
Resolving insolvency (rank)	72
DTF score for resolving insolvency (0–100)	48.10
Time (years)	6.0
Cost (% of estate)	18.0
Recovery rate (cents on the dollar)	13.9
Strength of insolvency framework index (0–16)	13.0

Note: Most indicator sets refer to a case scenario in the largest business city of an economy, though for 11 economies the data are a population-weighted average for the two largest business cities. For some indicators a result of "no practice" may be recorded for an economy; see the data notes for more details. In starting a business, procedures (number), time (days) and cost (% of income per capita) are calculated as the average of both men and women. For the postfiling index, a result of "not applicable" may be recorded for an economy.

✔ Reform making it easier to do business ✘ Change making it more difficult to do business

CAMEROON

CAMEROON		Sub-Saharan Africa		GNI per capita (US$)	1,330
Ease of doing business rank (1–190)	166	Overall distance to frontier (DTF) score (0–100)	45.27	Population	23,344,179

Starting a business (rank)	149
DTF score for starting a business (0–100)	76.99
Procedures (number)	5.5
Time (days)	15.5
Cost (% of income per capita)	32.2
Minimum capital (% of income per capita)	137.6

✔ Dealing with construction permits (rank)	141
DTF score for dealing with construction permits (0–100)	61.18
Procedures (number)	15
Time (days)	135
Cost (% of warehouse value)	14.1
Building quality control index (0–15)	13.0

Getting electricity (rank)	89
DTF score for getting electricity (0–100)	70.28
Procedures (number)	4
Time (days)	64
Cost (% of income per capita)	1,597.4
Reliability of supply and transparency of tariffs index (0–8)	3

Registering property (rank)	177
DTF score for registering property (0–100)	37.33
Procedures (number)	5
Time (days)	86
Cost (% of property value)	18.8
Quality of land administration index (0–30)	7.0

Getting credit (rank)	133
DTF score for getting credit (0–100)	35.00
Strength of legal rights index (0–12)	6
Depth of credit information index (0–8)	1
Credit bureau coverage (% of adults)	0.0
Credit registry coverage (% of adults)	8.0

Protecting minority investors (rank)	137
DTF score for protecting minority investors (0–100)	41.67
Extent of disclosure index (0–10)	7
Extent of director liability index (0–10)	1
Ease of shareholder suits index (0–10)	6
Extent of shareholder rights index (0–10)	5
Extent of ownership and control index (0–10)	4
Extent of corporate transparency index (0–10)	2

✘ Paying taxes (rank)	180
DTF score for paying taxes (0–100)	35.87
Payments (number per year)	44
Time (hours per year)	630
Total tax rate (% of profit)	57.7
Postfiling index (0–100)	48.39

Trading across borders (rank)	186
DTF score for trading across borders (0–100)	15.99
Time to export	
Documentary compliance (hours)	66
Border compliance (hours)	202
Cost to export	
Documentary compliance (US$)	306
Border compliance (US$)	983
Time to import	
Documentary compliance (hours)	163
Border compliance (hours)	271
Cost to import	
Documentary compliance (US$)	849
Border compliance (US$)	1,407

Enforcing contracts (rank)	160
DTF score for enforcing contracts (0–100)	41.76
Time (days)	800
Cost (% of claim)	46.6
Quality of judicial processes index (0–18)	6.0

✔ Resolving insolvency (rank)	122
DTF score for resolving insolvency (0–100)	36.63
Time (years)	2.8
Cost (% of estate)	33.5
Recovery rate (cents on the dollar)	15.8
Strength of insolvency framework index (0–16)	9.0

CANADA

CANADA		OECD high income		GNI per capita (US$)	47,500
Ease of doing business rank (1–190)	22	Overall distance to frontier (DTF) score (0–100)	78.57	Population	35,851,774

Starting a business (rank)	2
DTF score for starting a business (0–100)	98.23
Procedures (number)	2
Time (days)	1.5
Cost (% of income per capita)	0.4
Minimum capital (% of income per capita)	0.0

Dealing with construction permits (rank)	57
DTF score for dealing with construction permits (0–100)	73.66
Procedures (number)	12
Time (days)	249
Cost (% of warehouse value)	1.3
Building quality control index (0–15)	14.0

Getting electricity (rank)	108
DTF score for getting electricity (0–100)	63.76
Procedures (number)	7
Time (days)	137
Cost (% of income per capita)	125.8
Reliability of supply and transparency of tariffs index (0–8)	6

Registering property (rank)	43
DTF score for registering property (0–100)	75.40
Procedures (number)	6
Time (days)	16.5
Cost (% of property value)	3.1
Quality of land administration index (0–30)	21.5

Getting credit (rank)	7
DTF score for getting credit (0–100)	85.00
Strength of legal rights index (0–12)	9
Depth of credit information index (0–8)	8
Credit bureau coverage (% of adults)	100.0
Credit registry coverage (% of adults)	0.0

Protecting minority investors (rank)	7
DTF score for protecting minority investors (0–100)	76.67
Extent of disclosure index (0–10)	8
Extent of director liability index (0–10)	9
Ease of shareholder suits index (0–10)	9
Extent of shareholder rights index (0–10)	6
Extent of ownership and control index (0–10)	8
Extent of corporate transparency index (0–10)	6

Paying taxes (rank)	17
DTF score for paying taxes (0–100)	88.86
Payments (number per year)	8
Time (hours per year)	131
Total tax rate (% of profit)	21.0
Postfiling index (0–100)	76.44

Trading across borders (rank)	46
DTF score for trading across borders (0–100)	88.36
Time to export	
Documentary compliance (hours)	1
Border compliance (hours)	2
Cost to export	
Documentary compliance (US$)	156
Border compliance (US$)	167
Time to import	
Documentary compliance (hours)	1
Border compliance (hours)	2
Cost to import	
Documentary compliance (US$)	163
Border compliance (US$)	172

Enforcing contracts (rank)	112
DTF score for enforcing contracts (0–100)	54.35
Time (days)	910
Cost (% of claim)	22.3
Quality of judicial processes index (0–18)	9.5

Resolving insolvency (rank)	15
DTF score for resolving insolvency (0–100)	81.43
Time (years)	0.8
Cost (% of estate)	7.0
Recovery rate (cents on the dollar)	87.4
Strength of insolvency framework index (0–16)	11.0

CENTRAL AFRICAN REPUBLIC

CENTRAL AFRICAN REPUBLIC		Sub-Saharan Africa		GNI per capita (US$)	320
Ease of doing business rank (1–190)	185	Overall distance to frontier (DTF) score (0–100)	36.25	Population	4,900,274

Starting a business (rank)	190
DTF score for starting a business (0–100)	31.36
Procedures (number)	10
Time (days)	22
Cost (% of income per capita)	209.4
Minimum capital (% of income per capita)	556.6

Dealing with construction permits (rank)	154
DTF score for dealing with construction permits (0–100)	56.88
Procedures (number)	15
Time (days)	200
Cost (% of warehouse value)	4.5
Building quality control index (0–15)	6.0

Getting electricity (rank)	184
DTF score for getting electricity (0–100)	24.64
Procedures (number)	7
Time (days)	98
Cost (% of income per capita)	15,810.3
Reliability of supply and transparency of tariffs index (0–8)	0

Registering property (rank)	167
DTF score for registering property (0–100)	41.87
Procedures (number)	5
Time (days)	75
Cost (% of property value)	11.1
Quality of land administration index (0–30)	3.0

Getting credit (rank)	139
DTF score for getting credit (0–100)	30.00
Strength of legal rights index (0–12)	6
Depth of credit information index (0–8)	0
Credit bureau coverage (% of adults)	0.0
Credit registry coverage (% of adults)	3.1

Protecting minority investors (rank)	145
DTF score for protecting minority investors (0–100)	40.00
Extent of disclosure index (0–10)	7
Extent of director liability index (0–10)	1
Ease of shareholder suits index (0–10)	5
Extent of shareholder rights index (0–10)	5
Extent of ownership and control index (0–10)	4
Extent of corporate transparency index (0–10)	2

Paying taxes (rank)	187
DTF score for paying taxes (0–100)	20.56
Payments (number per year)	56
Time (hours per year)	483
Total tax rate (% of profit)	73.3
Postfiling index (0–100)	11.83

Trading across borders (rank)	138
DTF score for trading across borders (0–100)	58.64
Time to export	
Documentary compliance (hours)	48
Border compliance (hours)	141
Cost to export	
Documentary compliance (US$)	60
Border compliance (US$)	280
Time to import	
Documentary compliance (hours)	120
Border compliance (hours)	98
Cost to import	
Documentary compliance (US$)	500
Border compliance (US$)	209

Enforcing contracts (rank)	182
DTF score for enforcing contracts (0–100)	30.46
Time (days)	660
Cost (% of claim)	82.0
Quality of judicial processes index (0–18)	5.0

✔ Resolving insolvency (rank)	146
DTF score for resolving insolvency (0–100)	28.13
Time (years)	4.8
Cost (% of estate)	76.0
Recovery rate (cents on the dollar)	0.0
Strength of insolvency framework index (0–16)	9.0

Note: Most indicator sets refer to a case scenario in the largest business city of an economy, though for 11 economies the data are a population-weighted average for the two largest business cities. For some indicators a result of "no practice" may be recorded for an economy; see the data notes for more details. In starting a business, procedures (number), time (days) and cost (% of income per capita) are calculated as the average of both men and women. For the postfiling index, a result of "not applicable" may be recorded for an economy.

✔ Reform making it easier to do business ✘ Change making it more difficult to do business

CHAD

CHAD		Sub-Saharan Africa		GNI per capita (US$)	880
Ease of doing business rank (1–190)	**180**	**Overall distance to frontier (DTF) score (0–100)**	**39.07**	**Population**	**14,037,472**

✔ **Starting a business** (rank)	182
DTF score for starting a business (0–100)	51.91
Procedures (number)	9
Time (days)	60
Cost (% of income per capita)	159.8
Minimum capital (% of income per capita)	22.4
Dealing with construction permits (rank)	133
DTF score for dealing with construction permits (0–100)	62.00
Procedures (number)	13
Time (days)	221
Cost (% of warehouse value)	8.1
Building quality control index (0–15)	11.5
Getting electricity (rank)	179
DTF score for getting electricity (0–100)	32.17
Procedures (number)	6
Time (days)	67
Cost (% of income per capita)	8,526.9
Reliability of supply and transparency of tariffs index (0–8)	0
Registering property (rank)	157
DTF score for registering property (0–100)	44.74
Procedures (number)	6
Time (days)	44
Cost (% of property value)	12.8
Quality of land administration index (0–30)	8.0
Getting credit (rank)	139
DTF score for getting credit (0–100)	30.00
Strength of legal rights index (0–12)	6
Depth of credit information index (0–8)	0
Credit bureau coverage (% of adults)	0.0
Credit registry coverage (% of adults)	2.3
Protecting minority investors (rank)	158
DTF score for protecting minority investors (0–100)	38.33
Extent of disclosure index (0–10)	7
Extent of director liability index (0–10)	1
Ease of shareholder suits index (0–10)	4
Extent of shareholder rights index (0–10)	5
Extent of ownership and control index (0–10)	4
Extent of corporate transparency index (0–10)	2
Paying taxes (rank)	189
DTF score for paying taxes (0–100)	18.76
Payments (number per year)	54
Time (hours per year)	766
Total tax rate (% of profit)	63.5
Postfiling index (0–100)	16.42
Trading across borders (rank)	171
DTF score for trading across borders (0–100)	40.12
Time to export	
Documentary compliance (hours)	87
Border compliance (hours)	106
Cost to export	
Documentary compliance (US$)	188
Border compliance (US$)	319
Time to import	
Documentary compliance (hours)	172
Border compliance (hours)	242
Cost to import	
Documentary compliance (US$)	500
Border compliance (US$)	669
Enforcing contracts (rank)	154
DTF score for enforcing contracts (0–100)	44.58
Time (days)	743
Cost (% of claim)	45.7
Quality of judicial processes index (0–18)	6.5
✔ **Resolving insolvency** (rank)	146
DTF score for resolving insolvency (0–100)	28.13
Time (years)	4.0
Cost (% of estate)	60.0
Recovery rate (cents on the dollar)	0.0
Strength of insolvency framework index (0–16)	9.0

CHILE

CHILE		OECD high income		GNI per capita (US$)	14,060
Ease of doing business rank (1–190)	**57**	**Overall distance to frontier (DTF) score (0–100)**	**69.56**	**Population**	**17,948,141**

Starting a business (rank)	59
DTF score for starting a business (0–100)	89.84
Procedures (number)	7
Time (days)	5.5
Cost (% of income per capita)	0.7
Minimum capital (% of income per capita)	0.0
Dealing with construction permits (rank)	26
DTF score for dealing with construction permits (0–100)	78.83
Procedures (number)	13
Time (days)	152
Cost (% of warehouse value)	0.6
Building quality control index (0–15)	13.0
Getting electricity (rank)	64
DTF score for getting electricity (0–100)	78.31
Procedures (number)	6
Time (days)	43
Cost (% of income per capita)	70.5
Reliability of supply and transparency of tariffs index (0–8)	6
Registering property (rank)	58
DTF score for registering property (0–100)	70.89
Procedures (number)	6
Time (days)	28.5
Cost (% of property value)	1.2
Quality of land administration index (0–30)	14.0
Getting credit (rank)	82
DTF score for getting credit (0–100)	50.00
Strength of legal rights index (0–12)	4
Depth of credit information index (0–8)	6
Credit bureau coverage (% of adults)	12.4
Credit registry coverage (% of adults)	48.4
Protecting minority investors (rank)	32
DTF score for protecting minority investors (0–100)	65.00
Extent of disclosure index (0–10)	8
Extent of director liability index (0–10)	6
Ease of shareholder suits index (0–10)	7
Extent of shareholder rights index (0–10)	10
Extent of ownership and control index (0–10)	6
Extent of corporate transparency index (0–10)	2
Paying taxes (rank)	120
DTF score for paying taxes (0–100)	63.85
Payments (number per year)	7
Time (hours per year)	291
Total tax rate (% of profit)	30.5
Postfiling index (0–100)	5.58
Trading across borders (rank)	65
DTF score for trading across borders (0–100)	80.56
Time to export	
Documentary compliance (hours)	24
Border compliance (hours)	60
Cost to export	
Documentary compliance (US$)	50
Border compliance (US$)	290
Time to import	
Documentary compliance (hours)	36
Border compliance (hours)	54
Cost to import	
Documentary compliance (US$)	50
Border compliance (US$)	290
Enforcing contracts (rank)	56
DTF score for enforcing contracts (0–100)	62.81
Time (days)	480
Cost (% of claim)	28.6
Quality of judicial processes index (0–18)	9.0
Resolving insolvency (rank)	55
DTF score for resolving insolvency (0–100)	55.51
Time (years)	3.2
Cost (% of estate)	14.5
Recovery rate (cents on the dollar)	33.5
Strength of insolvency framework index (0–16)	12.0

CHINA

CHINA		East Asia & Pacific		GNI per capita (US$)	7,820
Ease of doing business rank (1–190)	**78**	**Overall distance to frontier (DTF) score (0–100)**	**64.28**	**Population**	**1,371,220,000**

✔ **Starting a business** (rank)	127
DTF score for starting a business (0–100)	81.02
Procedures (number)	9
Time (days)	28.9
Cost (% of income per capita)	0.7
Minimum capital (% of income per capita)	0.0
Dealing with construction permits (rank)	177
DTF score for dealing with construction permits (0–100)	48.52
Procedures (number)	22
Time (days)	244.3
Cost (% of warehouse value)	7.0
Building quality control index (0–15)	9.0
Getting electricity (rank)	97
DTF score for getting electricity (0–100)	68.73
Procedures (number)	5.5
Time (days)	143.2
Cost (% of income per capita)	390.4
Reliability of supply and transparency of tariffs index (0–8)	6
Registering property (rank)	42
DTF score for registering property (0–100)	76.15
Procedures (number)	4
Time (days)	19.5
Cost (% of property value)	3.4
Quality of land administration index (0–30)	18.3
✔ **Getting credit** (rank)	62
DTF score for getting credit (0–100)	60.00
Strength of legal rights index (0–12)	4
Depth of credit information index (0–8)	8
Credit bureau coverage (% of adults)	21.3
Credit registry coverage (% of adults)	91.1
Protecting minority investors (rank)	123
DTF score for protecting minority investors (0–100)	45.00
Extent of disclosure index (0–10)	10
Extent of director liability index (0–10)	1
Ease of shareholder suits index (0–10)	4
Extent of shareholder rights index (0–10)	1
Extent of ownership and control index (0–10)	2
Extent of corporate transparency index (0–10)	9
Paying taxes (rank)	131
DTF score for paying taxes (0–100)	60.46
Payments (number per year)	9
Time (hours per year)	259
Total tax rate (% of profit)	68.0
Postfiling index (0–100)	48.62
Trading across borders (rank)	96
DTF score for trading across borders (0–100)	69.13
Time to export	
Documentary compliance (hours)	21.2
Border compliance (hours)	25.9
Cost to export	
Documentary compliance (US$)	84.6
Border compliance (US$)	522.4
Time to import	
Documentary compliance (hours)	65.7
Border compliance (hours)	92.3
Cost to import	
Documentary compliance (US$)	170.9
Border compliance (US$)	776.6
Enforcing contracts (rank)	5
DTF score for enforcing contracts (0–100)	77.98
Time (days)	452.8
Cost (% of claim)	16.2
Quality of judicial processes index (0–18)	14.3
Resolving insolvency (rank)	53
DTF score for resolving insolvency (0–100)	55.82
Time (years)	1.7
Cost (% of estate)	22.0
Recovery rate (cents on the dollar)	36.9
Strength of insolvency framework index (0–16)	11.5

Note: Most indicator sets refer to a case scenario in the largest business city of an economy, though for 11 economies the data are a population-weighted average for the two largest business cities. For some indicators a result of "no practice" may be recorded for an economy; see the data notes for more details. In starting a business, procedures (number), time (days) and cost (% of income per capita) are calculated as the average of both men and women. For the postfiling index, a result of "not applicable" may be recorded for an economy.

✔ Reform making it easier to do business ✘ Change making it more difficult to do business

COLOMBIA

COLOMBIA		Latin America & Caribbean		GNI per capita (US$)	7,130
Ease of doing business rank (1–190)	53	Overall distance to frontier (DTF) score (0–100)	70.92	Population	48,228,704

✔ **Starting a business** (rank)	61
DTF score for starting a business (0–100)	89.57
Procedures (number)	6
Time (days)	9
Cost (% of income per capita)	7.5
Minimum capital (% of income per capita)	0.0

Dealing with construction permits (rank)	34
DTF score for dealing with construction permits (0–100)	76.54
Procedures (number)	10
Time (days)	73
Cost (% of warehouse value)	6.7
Building quality control index (0–15)	11.0

Getting electricity (rank)	74
DTF score for getting electricity (0–100)	73.73
Procedures (number)	5
Time (days)	109
Cost (% of income per capita)	581.4
Reliability of supply and transparency of tariffs index (0–8)	6

Registering property (rank)	53
DTF score for registering property (0–100)	73.29
Procedures (number)	6
Time (days)	16
Cost (% of property value)	2.0
Quality of land administration index (0–30)	16.5

Getting credit (rank)	2
DTF score for getting credit (0–100)	95.00
Strength of legal rights index (0–12)	12
Depth of credit information index (0–8)	7
Credit bureau coverage (% of adults)	92.1
Credit registry coverage (% of adults)	0.0

Protecting minority investors (rank)	13
DTF score for protecting minority investors (0–100)	73.33
Extent of disclosure index (0–10)	9
Extent of director liability index (0–10)	7
Ease of shareholder suits index (0–10)	8
Extent of shareholder rights index (0–10)	6
Extent of ownership and control index (0–10)	8
Extent of corporate transparency index (0–10)	6

Paying taxes (rank)	139
DTF score for paying taxes (0–100)	58.91
Payments (number per year)	12
Time (hours per year)	239
Total tax rate (% of profit)	69.8
Postfiling index (0–100)	47.48

Trading across borders (rank)	121
DTF score for trading across borders (0–100)	62.83
Time to export	
Documentary compliance (hours)	60
Border compliance (hours)	112
Cost to export	
Documentary compliance (US$)	90
Border compliance (US$)	545
Time to import	
Documentary compliance (hours)	64
Border compliance (hours)	112
Cost to import	
Documentary compliance (US$)	50
Border compliance (US$)	545

Enforcing contracts (rank)	174
DTF score for enforcing contracts (0–100)	34.29
Time (days)	1,288
Cost (% of claim)	45.8
Quality of judicial processes index (0–18)	9.0

Resolving insolvency (rank)	33
DTF score for resolving insolvency (0–100)	71.74
Time (years)	1.7
Cost (% of estate)	8.5
Recovery rate (cents on the dollar)	69.4
Strength of insolvency framework index (0–16)	11.0

COMOROS

COMOROS		Sub-Saharan Africa		GNI per capita (US$)	647
Ease of doing business rank (1–190)	153	Overall distance to frontier (DTF) score (0–100)	48.69	Population	788,474

Starting a business (rank)	161
DTF score for starting a business (0–100)	71.59
Procedures (number)	8
Time (days)	15
Cost (% of income per capita)	98.4
Minimum capital (% of income per capita)	34.8

Dealing with construction permits (rank)	92
DTF score for dealing with construction permits (0–100)	68.88
Procedures (number)	10
Time (days)	108
Cost (% of warehouse value)	1.5
Building quality control index (0–15)	4.0

Getting electricity (rank)	135
DTF score for getting electricity (0–100)	56.35
Procedures (number)	3
Time (days)	120
Cost (% of income per capita)	2,451.0
Reliability of supply and transparency of tariffs index (0–8)	0

✔ **Registering property** (rank)	90
DTF score for registering property (0–100)	63.47
Procedures (number)	4
Time (days)	30
Cost (% of property value)	4.6
Quality of land administration index (0–30)	7.0

Getting credit (rank)	118
DTF score for getting credit (0–100)	40.00
Strength of legal rights index (0–12)	6
Depth of credit information index (0–8)	2
Credit bureau coverage (% of adults)	0.0
Credit registry coverage (% of adults)	7.9

Protecting minority investors (rank)	145
DTF score for protecting minority investors (0–100)	40.00
Extent of disclosure index (0–10)	7
Extent of director liability index (0–10)	1
Ease of shareholder suits index (0–10)	5
Extent of shareholder rights index (0–10)	5
Extent of ownership and control index (0–10)	4
Extent of corporate transparency index (0–10)	2

Paying taxes (rank)	168
DTF score for paying taxes (0–100)	48.41
Payments (number per year)	33
Time (hours per year)	100
Total tax rate (% of profit)	216.5
Postfiling index (0–100)	51.53

Trading across borders (rank)	107
DTF score for trading across borders (0–100)	66.18
Time to export	
Documentary compliance (hours)	57
Border compliance (hours)	51
Cost to export	
Documentary compliance (US$)	124
Border compliance (US$)	651
Time to import	
Documentary compliance (hours)	29
Border compliance (hours)	70
Cost to import	
Documentary compliance (US$)	93
Border compliance (US$)	765

Enforcing contracts (rank)	179
DTF score for enforcing contracts (0–100)	32.05
Time (days)	506
Cost (% of claim)	89.4
Quality of judicial processes index (0–18)	5.0

✔ **Resolving insolvency** (rank)	169
DTF score for resolving insolvency (0–100)	0.00
Time (years)	NO PRACTICE
Cost (% of estate)	NO PRACTICE
Recovery rate (cents on the dollar)	0.0
Strength of insolvency framework index (0–16)	0.0

CONGO, DEM. REP.

CONGO, DEM. REP.		Sub-Saharan Africa		GNI per capita (US$)	410
Ease of doing business rank (1–190)	184	Overall distance to frontier (DTF) score (0–100)	37.57	Population	77,266,814

Starting a business (rank)	96
DTF score for starting a business (0–100)	85.49
Procedures (number)	6.5
Time (days)	11.5
Cost (% of income per capita)	29.3
Minimum capital (% of income per capita)	0.0

✔ **Dealing with construction permits** (rank)	114
DTF score for dealing with construction permits (0–100)	65.89
Procedures (number)	12
Time (days)	122
Cost (% of warehouse value)	6.2
Building quality control index (0–15)	7.5

Getting electricity (rank)	175
DTF score for getting electricity (0–100)	33.59
Procedures (number)	6
Time (days)	54
Cost (% of income per capita)	15,264.0
Reliability of supply and transparency of tariffs index (0–8)	0

✘ **Registering property** (rank)	156
DTF score for registering property (0–100)	46.60
Procedures (number)	7
Time (days)	44
Cost (% of property value)	11.5
Quality of land administration index (0–30)	10.0

Getting credit (rank)	139
DTF score for getting credit (0–100)	30.00
Strength of legal rights index (0–12)	6
Depth of credit information index (0–8)	0
Credit bureau coverage (% of adults)	0.0
Credit registry coverage (% of adults)	0.7

Protecting minority investors (rank)	162
DTF score for protecting minority investors (0–100)	36.67
Extent of disclosure index (0–10)	7
Extent of director liability index (0–10)	1
Ease of shareholder suits index (0–10)	3
Extent of shareholder rights index (0–10)	5
Extent of ownership and control index (0–10)	4
Extent of corporate transparency index (0–10)	2

Paying taxes (rank)	177
DTF score for paying taxes (0–100)	40.12
Payments (number per year)	52
Time (hours per year)	346
Total tax rate (% of profit)	54.6
Postfiling index (0–100)	29.97

Trading across borders (rank)	188
DTF score for trading across borders (0–100)	1.26
Time to export	
Documentary compliance (hours)	698
Border compliance (hours)	515
Cost to export	
Documentary compliance (US$)	2,500
Border compliance (US$)	2,223
Time to import	
Documentary compliance (hours)	216
Border compliance (hours)	588
Cost to import	
Documentary compliance (US$)	875
Border compliance (US$)	3,039

Enforcing contracts (rank)	171
DTF score for enforcing contracts (0–100)	36.06
Time (days)	610
Cost (% of claim)	80.6
Quality of judicial processes index (0–18)	7.0

✔ **Resolving insolvency** (rank)	169
DTF score for resolving insolvency (0–100)	0.00
Time (years)	NO PRACTICE
Cost (% of estate)	NO PRACTICE
Recovery rate (cents on the dollar)	0.0
Strength of insolvency framework index (0–16)	0.0

Note: Most indicator sets refer to a case scenario in the largest business city of an economy, though for 11 economies the data are a population-weighted average for the two largest business cities. For some indicators a result of "no practice" may be recorded for an economy; see the data notes for more details. In starting a business, procedures (number), time (days) and cost (% of income per capita) are calculated as the average of both men and women. For the postfiling index, a result of "not applicable" may be recorded for an economy.

✔ Reform making it easier to do business ✘ Change making it more difficult to do business

CONGO, REP.

CONGO, REP.		Sub-Saharan Africa		GNI per capita (US$)	2,540
Ease of doing business rank (1–190)	**177**	**Overall distance to frontier (DTF) score (0–100)**	**40.58**	**Population**	**4,620,330**

Starting a business (rank)	178
DTF score for starting a business (0–100)	59.44
Procedures (number)	11
Time (days)	50
Cost (% of income per capita)	61.2
Minimum capital (% of income per capita)	92.2
Dealing with construction permits (rank)	124
DTF score for dealing with construction permits (0–100)	64.16
Procedures (number)	12
Time (days)	164
Cost (% of warehouse value)	7.1
Building quality control index (0–15)	9.0
Getting electricity (rank)	178
DTF score for getting electricity (0–100)	32.90
Procedures (number)	6
Time (days)	135
Cost (% of income per capita)	5,469.1
Reliability of supply and transparency of tariffs index (0–8)	0
Registering property (rank)	171
DTF score for registering property (0–100)	40.52
Procedures (number)	6
Time (days)	55
Cost (% of property value)	12.3
Quality of land administration index (0–30)	3.5

Getting credit (rank)	118
DTF score for getting credit (0–100)	40.00
Strength of legal rights index (0–12)	6
Depth of credit information index (0–8)	2
Credit bureau coverage (% of adults)	0.0
Credit registry coverage (% of adults)	12.2
Protecting minority investors (rank)	145
DTF score for protecting minority investors (0–100)	40.00
Extent of disclosure index (0–10)	7
Extent of director liability index (0–10)	1
Ease of shareholder suits index (0–10)	5
Extent of shareholder rights index (0–10)	5
Extent of ownership and control index (0–10)	4
Extent of corporate transparency index (0–10)	2
Paying taxes (rank)	183
DTF score for paying taxes (0–100)	27.39
Payments (number per year)	50
Time (hours per year)	602
Total tax rate (% of profit)	54.3
Postfiling index (0–100)	14.72

Trading across borders (rank)	182
DTF score for trading across borders (0–100)	19.68
Time to export	
Documentary compliance (hours)	120
Border compliance (hours)	276
Cost to export	
Documentary compliance (US$)	165
Border compliance (US$)	1,975
Time to import	
Documentary compliance (hours)	208
Border compliance (hours)	397
Cost to import	
Documentary compliance (US$)	310
Border compliance (US$)	1,581
Enforcing contracts (rank)	155
DTF score for enforcing contracts (0–100)	43.99
Time (days)	560
Cost (% of claim)	53.2
Quality of judicial processes index (0–18)	5.0
✔ **Resolving insolvency** (rank)	117
DTF score for resolving insolvency (0–100)	37.75
Time (years)	3.3
Cost (% of estate)	25.0
Recovery rate (cents on the dollar)	17.9
Strength of insolvency framework index (0–16)	9.0

COSTA RICA

COSTA RICA		Latin America & Caribbean		GNI per capita (US$)	10,210
Ease of doing business rank (1–190)	**62**	**Overall distance to frontier (DTF) score (0–100)**	**68.50**	**Population**	**4,807,850**

Starting a business (rank)	125
DTF score for starting a business (0–100)	81.57
Procedures (number)	9
Time (days)	22.5
Cost (% of income per capita)	9.1
Minimum capital (% of income per capita)	0.0
Dealing with construction permits (rank)	53
DTF score for dealing with construction permits (0–100)	74.63
Procedures (number)	15
Time (days)	118
Cost (% of warehouse value)	1.7
Building quality control index (0–15)	11.0
Getting electricity (rank)	27
DTF score for getting electricity (0–100)	85.04
Procedures (number)	5
Time (days)	45
Cost (% of income per capita)	182.3
Reliability of supply and transparency of tariffs index (0–8)	7
Registering property (rank)	52
DTF score for registering property (0–100)	73.39
Procedures (number)	5
Time (days)	19
Cost (% of property value)	3.4
Quality of land administration index (0–30)	17.5

Getting credit (rank)	7
DTF score for getting credit (0–100)	85.00
Strength of legal rights index (0–12)	10
Depth of credit information index (0–8)	7
Credit bureau coverage (% of adults)	100.0
Credit registry coverage (% of adults)	30.5
Protecting minority investors (rank)	165
DTF score for protecting minority investors (0–100)	35.00
Extent of disclosure index (0–10)	2
Extent of director liability index (0–10)	5
Ease of shareholder suits index (0–10)	3
Extent of shareholder rights index (0–10)	4
Extent of ownership and control index (0–10)	5
Extent of corporate transparency index (0–10)	2
Paying taxes (rank)	62
DTF score for paying taxes (0–100)	78.98
Payments (number per year)	10
Time (hours per year)	151
Total tax rate (% of profit)	58.3
Postfiling index (0–100)	91.11

Trading across borders (rank)	71
DTF score for trading across borders (0–100)	79.32
Time to export	
Documentary compliance (hours)	24
Border compliance (hours)	20
Cost to export	
Documentary compliance (US$)	80
Border compliance (US$)	375
Time to import	
Documentary compliance (hours)	26
Border compliance (hours)	80
Cost to import	
Documentary compliance (US$)	75
Border compliance (US$)	420
Enforcing contracts (rank)	125
DTF score for enforcing contracts (0–100)	52.41
Time (days)	852
Cost (% of claim)	24.3
Quality of judicial processes index (0–18)	8.0
Resolving insolvency (rank)	107
DTF score for resolving insolvency (0–100)	39.62
Time (years)	3.0
Cost (% of estate)	14.5
Recovery rate (cents on the dollar)	27.2
Strength of insolvency framework index (0–16)	8.0

CÔTE D'IVOIRE

CÔTE D'IVOIRE		Sub-Saharan Africa		GNI per capita (US$)	1,410
Ease of doing business rank (1–190)	**142**	**Overall distance to frontier (DTF) score (0–100)**	**52.31**	**Population**	**22,701,556**

Starting a business (rank)	50
DTF score for starting a business (0–100)	91.38
Procedures (number)	4
Time (days)	7
Cost (% of income per capita)	18.9
Minimum capital (% of income per capita)	3.3
✔ **Dealing with construction permits** (rank)	182
DTF score for dealing with construction permits (0–100)	44.36
Procedures (number)	23
Time (days)	347
Cost (% of warehouse value)	0.9
Building quality control index (0–15)	7.0
Getting electricity (rank)	132
DTF score for getting electricity (0–100)	57.78
Procedures (number)	8
Time (days)	55
Cost (% of income per capita)	2,589.5
Reliability of supply and transparency of tariffs index (0–8)	5
Registering property (rank)	113
DTF score for registering property (0–100)	57.24
Procedures (number)	6
Time (days)	30
Cost (% of property value)	7.6
Quality of land administration index (0–30)	10.5

✔ **Getting credit** (rank)	139
DTF score for getting credit (0–100)	30.00
Strength of legal rights index (0–12)	6
Depth of credit information index (0–8)	0
Credit bureau coverage (% of adults)	2.3
Credit registry coverage (% of adults)	0.3
Protecting minority investors (rank)	145
DTF score for protecting minority investors (0–100)	40.00
Extent of disclosure index (0–10)	7
Extent of director liability index (0–10)	1
Ease of shareholder suits index (0–10)	5
Extent of shareholder rights index (0–10)	5
Extent of ownership and control index (0–10)	4
Extent of corporate transparency index (0–10)	2
Paying taxes (rank)	175
DTF score for paying taxes (0–100)	43.35
Payments (number per year)	63
Time (hours per year)	270
Total tax rate (% of profit)	51.3
Postfiling index (0–100)	44.27

Trading across borders (rank)	150
DTF score for trading across borders (0–100)	54.15
Time to export	
Documentary compliance (hours)	120
Border compliance (hours)	110
Cost to export	
Documentary compliance (US$)	136
Border compliance (US$)	387
Time to import	
Documentary compliance (hours)	89
Border compliance (hours)	125
Cost to import	
Documentary compliance (US$)	267
Border compliance (US$)	456
✔ **Enforcing contracts** (rank)	101
DTF score for enforcing contracts (0–100)	55.74
Time (days)	525
Cost (% of claim)	41.7
Quality of judicial processes index (0–18)	8.5
✔ **Resolving insolvency** (rank)	68
DTF score for resolving insolvency (0–100)	49.13
Time (years)	2.2
Cost (% of estate)	18.0
Recovery rate (cents on the dollar)	39.0
Strength of insolvency framework index (0–16)	9.0

Note: Most indicator sets refer to a case scenario in the largest business city of an economy, though for 11 economies the data are a population-weighted average for the two largest business cities. For some indicators a result of "no practice" may be recorded for an economy; see the data notes for more details. In starting a business, procedures (number), time (days) and cost (% of income per capita) are calculated as the average of both men and women. For the postfiling index, a result of "not applicable" may be recorded for an economy.

✔ Reform making it easier to do business ✘ Change making it more difficult to do business

CROATIA

CROATIA		Europe & Central Asia		GNI per capita (US$)	12,690
Ease of doing business rank (1–190)	43	Overall distance to frontier (DTF) score (0–100)	72.99	Population	4,224,404

✘ **Starting a business** (rank)	95
DTF score for starting a business (0–100)	85.56
Procedures (number)	8
Time (days)	7
Cost (% of income per capita)	7.3
Minimum capital (% of income per capita)	25.5

Dealing with construction permits (rank)	128
DTF score for dealing with construction permits (0–100)	63.41
Procedures (number)	19
Time (days)	127
Cost (% of warehouse value)	8.3
Building quality control index (0–15)	12.0

Getting electricity (rank)	68
DTF score for getting electricity (0–100)	76.25
Procedures (number)	5
Time (days)	65
Cost (% of income per capita)	303.2
Reliability of supply and transparency of tariffs index (0–8)	5

Registering property (rank)	62
DTF score for registering property (0–100)	69.77
Procedures (number)	5
Time (days)	62
Cost (% of property value)	5.0
Quality of land administration index (0–30)	22.5

Getting credit (rank)	75
DTF score for getting credit (0–100)	55.00
Strength of legal rights index (0–12)	5
Depth of credit information index (0–8)	6
Credit bureau coverage (% of adults)	100.0
Credit registry coverage (% of adults)	0.0

✔ **Protecting minority investors** (rank)	27
DTF score for protecting minority investors (0–100)	66.67
Extent of disclosure index (0–10)	5
Extent of director liability index (0–10)	6
Ease of shareholder suits index (0–10)	6
Extent of shareholder rights index (0–10)	8
Extent of ownership and control index (0–10)	9
Extent of corporate transparency index (0–10)	6

✘ **Paying taxes** (rank)	49
DTF score for paying taxes (0–100)	81.74
Payments (number per year)	31
Time (hours per year)	206
Total tax rate (% of profit)	20.9
Postfiling index (0–100)	97.88

Trading across borders (rank)	1
DTF score for trading across borders (0–100)	100.00
Time to export	
Documentary compliance (hours)	1
Border compliance (hours)	0
Cost to export	
Documentary compliance (US$)	0
Border compliance (US$)	0
Time to import	
Documentary compliance (hours)	1
Border compliance (hours)	0
Cost to import	
Documentary compliance (US$)	0
Border compliance (US$)	0

Enforcing contracts (rank)	7
DTF score for enforcing contracts (0–100)	75.87
Time (days)	572
Cost (% of claim)	16.7
Quality of judicial processes index (0–18)	15.0

Resolving insolvency (rank)	54
DTF score for resolving insolvency (0–100)	55.62
Time (years)	3.1
Cost (% of estate)	14.5
Recovery rate (cents on the dollar)	33.7
Strength of insolvency framework index (0–16)	12.0

CYPRUS

CYPRUS		Europe & Central Asia		GNI per capita (US$)	25,930
Ease of doing business rank (1–190)	45	Overall distance to frontier (DTF) score (0–100)	72.65	Population	1,165,300

✔ **Starting a business** (rank)	53
DTF score for starting a business (0–100)	91.21
Procedures (number)	5
Time (days)	6
Cost (% of income per capita)	12.2
Minimum capital (% of income per capita)	0.0

Dealing with construction permits (rank)	125
DTF score for dealing with construction permits (0–100)	64.01
Procedures (number)	8
Time (days)	507
Cost (% of warehouse value)	1.1
Building quality control index (0–15)	11.0

Getting electricity (rank)	63
DTF score for getting electricity (0–100)	78.33
Procedures (number)	5
Time (days)	137
Cost (% of income per capita)	130.4
Reliability of supply and transparency of tariffs index (0–8)	8

Registering property (rank)	91
DTF score for registering property (0–100)	63.43
Procedures (number)	7
Time (days)	9
Cost (% of property value)	10.4
Quality of land administration index (0–30)	23.0

✘ **Getting credit** (rank)	62
DTF score for getting credit (0–100)	60.00
Strength of legal rights index (0–12)	7
Depth of credit information index (0–8)	5
Credit bureau coverage (% of adults)	68.9
Credit registry coverage (% of adults)	0.0

Protecting minority investors (rank)	27
DTF score for protecting minority investors (0–100)	66.67
Extent of disclosure index (0–10)	8
Extent of director liability index (0–10)	4
Ease of shareholder suits index (0–10)	8
Extent of shareholder rights index (0–10)	6
Extent of ownership and control index (0–10)	7
Extent of corporate transparency index (0–10)	7

✔ **Paying taxes** (rank)	34
DTF score for paying taxes (0–100)	84.45
Payments (number per year)	28
Time (hours per year)	127
Total tax rate (% of profit)	24.7
Postfiling index (0–100)	91.53

Trading across borders (rank)	45
DTF score for trading across borders (0–100)	88.44
Time to export	
Documentary compliance (hours)	2
Border compliance (hours)	18
Cost to export	
Documentary compliance (US$)	50
Border compliance (US$)	300
Time to import	
Documentary compliance (hours)	2
Border compliance (hours)	15
Cost to import	
Documentary compliance (US$)	50
Border compliance (US$)	335

Enforcing contracts (rank)	139
DTF score for enforcing contracts (0–100)	48.59
Time (days)	1,100
Cost (% of claim)	16.4
Quality of judicial processes index (0–18)	8.0

Resolving insolvency (rank)	16
DTF score for resolving insolvency (0–100)	81.38
Time (years)	1.5
Cost (% of estate)	14.5
Recovery rate (cents on the dollar)	72.8
Strength of insolvency framework index (0–16)	13.5

CZECH REPUBLIC

CZECH REPUBLIC		OECD high income		GNI per capita (US$)	18,050
Ease of doing business rank (1–190)	27	Overall distance to frontier (DTF) score (0–100)	76.71	Population	10,551,219

✔ **Starting a business** (rank)	81
DTF score for starting a business (0–100)	86.86
Procedures (number)	8
Time (days)	9
Cost (% of income per capita)	5.7
Minimum capital (% of income per capita)	0.0

Dealing with construction permits (rank)	130
DTF score for dealing with construction permits (0–100)	62.76
Procedures (number)	21
Time (days)	247
Cost (% of warehouse value)	0.3
Building quality control index (0–15)	12.0

✔ **Getting electricity** (rank)	13
DTF score for getting electricity (0–100)	90.32
Procedures (number)	4
Time (days)	68
Cost (% of income per capita)	25.0
Reliability of supply and transparency of tariffs index (0–8)	8

Registering property (rank)	31
DTF score for registering property (0–100)	79.68
Procedures (number)	4
Time (days)	28
Cost (% of property value)	4.0
Quality of land administration index (0–30)	25.0

Getting credit (rank)	32
DTF score for getting credit (0–100)	70.00
Strength of legal rights index (0–12)	7
Depth of credit information index (0–8)	7
Credit bureau coverage (% of adults)	79.2
Credit registry coverage (% of adults)	6.8

Protecting minority investors (rank)	53
DTF score for protecting minority investors (0–100)	60.00
Extent of disclosure index (0–10)	2
Extent of director liability index (0–10)	5
Ease of shareholder suits index (0–10)	9
Extent of shareholder rights index (0–10)	8
Extent of ownership and control index (0–10)	7
Extent of corporate transparency index (0–10)	5

Paying taxes (rank)	53
DTF score for paying taxes (0–100)	80.69
Payments (number per year)	8
Time (hours per year)	234
Total tax rate (% of profit)	50.0
Postfiling index (0–100)	94.29

Trading across borders (rank)	1
DTF score for trading across borders (0–100)	100.00
Time to export	
Documentary compliance (hours)	1
Border compliance (hours)	0
Cost to export	
Documentary compliance (US$)	0
Border compliance (US$)	0
Time to import	
Documentary compliance (hours)	1
Border compliance (hours)	0
Cost to import	
Documentary compliance (US$)	0
Border compliance (US$)	0

Enforcing contracts (rank)	68
DTF score for enforcing contracts (0–100)	60.36
Time (days)	611
Cost (% of claim)	33.0
Quality of judicial processes index (0–18)	10.5

Resolving insolvency (rank)	26
DTF score for resolving insolvency (0–100)	76.42
Time (years)	2.1
Cost (% of estate)	17.0
Recovery rate (cents on the dollar)	66.5
Strength of insolvency framework index (0–16)	13.0

Note: Most indicator sets refer to a case scenario in the largest business city of an economy, though for 11 economies the data are a population-weighted average for the two largest business cities. For some indicators a result of "no practice" may be recorded for an economy; see the data notes for more details. In starting a business, procedures (number), time (days) and cost (% of income per capita) are calculated as the average of both men and women. For the postfiling index, a result of "not applicable" may be recorded for an economy.

✔ Reform making it easier to do business ✘ Change making it more difficult to do business

DENMARK

DENMARK		OECD high income		GNI per capita (US$)	58,590
Ease of doing business rank (1–190)	3	Overall distance to frontier (DTF) score (0–100)	84.87	Population	5,676,002

Starting a business (rank)	24
DTF score for starting a business (0–100)	94.07
Procedures (number)	4
Time (days)	3
Cost (% of income per capita)	0.2
Minimum capital (% of income per capita)	13.9
Dealing with construction permits (rank)	6
DTF score for dealing with construction permits (0–100)	84.69
Procedures (number)	7
Time (days)	64
Cost (% of warehouse value)	1.8
Building quality control index (0–15)	10.0
Getting electricity (rank)	14
DTF score for getting electricity (0–100)	90.20
Procedures (number)	4
Time (days)	38
Cost (% of income per capita)	109.4
Reliability of supply and transparency of tariffs index (0–8)	7
Registering property (rank)	12
DTF score for registering property (0–100)	89.88
Procedures (number)	3
Time (days)	4
Cost (% of property value)	0.6
Quality of land administration index (0–30)	24.5
Getting credit (rank)	32
DTF score for getting credit (0–100)	70.00
Strength of legal rights index (0–12)	8
Depth of credit information index (0–8)	6
Credit bureau coverage (% of adults)	7.4
Credit registry coverage (% of adults)	0.0
Protecting minority investors (rank)	19
DTF score for protecting minority investors (0–100)	71.67
Extent of disclosure index (0–10)	7
Extent of director liability index (0–10)	5
Ease of shareholder suits index (0–10)	8
Extent of shareholder rights index (0–10)	8
Extent of ownership and control index (0–10)	6
Extent of corporate transparency index (0–10)	9
Paying taxes (rank)	7
DTF score for paying taxes (0–100)	92.11
Payments (number per year)	10
Time (hours per year)	130
Total tax rate (% of profit)	25.0
Postfiling index (0–100)	92.63
Trading across borders (rank)	1
DTF score for trading across borders (0–100)	100.00
Time to export	
Documentary compliance (hours)	1
Border compliance (hours)	0
Cost to export	
Documentary compliance (US$)	0
Border compliance (US$)	0
Time to import	
Documentary compliance (hours)	1
Border compliance (hours)	0
Cost to import	
Documentary compliance (US$)	0
Border compliance (US$)	0
Enforcing contracts (rank)	24
DTF score for enforcing contracts (0–100)	71.23
Time (days)	380
Cost (% of claim)	23.3
Quality of judicial processes index (0–18)	11.0
Resolving insolvency (rank)	8
DTF score for resolving insolvency (0–100)	84.86
Time (years)	1.0
Cost (% of estate)	4.0
Recovery rate (cents on the dollar)	88.0
Strength of insolvency framework index (0–16)	12.0

DJIBOUTI

DJIBOUTI		Middle East & North Africa		GNI per capita (US$)	1,789
Ease of doing business rank (1–190)	171	Overall distance to frontier (DTF) score (0–100)	44.50	Population	887,861

Starting a business (rank)	172
DTF score for starting a business (0–100)	66.91
Procedures (number)	7
Time (days)	14
Cost (% of income per capita)	167.0
Minimum capital (% of income per capita)	0.0
Dealing with construction permits (rank)	120
DTF score for dealing with construction permits (0–100)	64.87
Procedures (number)	17
Time (days)	111
Cost (% of warehouse value)	6.9
Building quality control index (0–15)	10.0
Getting electricity (rank)	172
DTF score for getting electricity (0–100)	39.49
Procedures (number)	4
Time (days)	125
Cost (% of income per capita)	6,386.8
Reliability of supply and transparency of tariffs index (0–8)	0
Registering property (rank)	168
DTF score for registering property (0–100)	41.34
Procedures (number)	6
Time (days)	39
Cost (% of property value)	12.7
Quality of land administration index (0–30)	3.0
Getting credit (rank)	181
DTF score for getting credit (0–100)	5.00
Strength of legal rights index (0–12)	1
Depth of credit information index (0–8)	0
Credit bureau coverage (% of adults)	0.0
Credit registry coverage (% of adults)	0.4
Protecting minority investors (rank)	178
DTF score for protecting minority investors (0–100)	30.00
Extent of disclosure index (0–10)	4
Extent of director liability index (0–10)	3
Ease of shareholder suits index (0–10)	0
Extent of shareholder rights index (0–10)	6
Extent of ownership and control index (0–10)	3
Extent of corporate transparency index (0–10)	2
Paying taxes (rank)	106
DTF score for paying taxes (0–100)	68.96
Payments (number per year)	36
Time (hours per year)	82
Total tax rate (% of profit)	37.6
Postfiling index (0–100)	52.18
Trading across borders (rank)	155
DTF score for trading across borders (0–100)	51.87
Time to export	
Documentary compliance (hours)	72
Border compliance (hours)	109
Cost to export	
Documentary compliance (US$)	95
Border compliance (US$)	944
Time to import	
Documentary compliance (hours)	50
Border compliance (hours)	78
Cost to import	
Documentary compliance (US$)	100
Border compliance (US$)	1,209
Enforcing contracts (rank)	184
DTF score for enforcing contracts (0–100)	28.39
Time (days)	1,225
Cost (% of claim)	34.0
Quality of judicial processes index (0–18)	2.5
Resolving insolvency (rank)	71
DTF score for resolving insolvency (0–100)	48.20
Time (years)	2.3
Cost (% of estate)	11.0
Recovery rate (cents on the dollar)	37.3
Strength of insolvency framework index (0–16)	9.0

DOMINICA

DOMINICA		Latin America & Caribbean		GNI per capita (US$)	6,760
Ease of doing business rank (1–190)	101	Overall distance to frontier (DTF) score (0–100)	60.27	Population	72,680

Starting a business (rank)	64
DTF score for starting a business (0–100)	89.26
Procedures (number)	5
Time (days)	12
Cost (% of income per capita)	15.7
Minimum capital (% of income per capita)	0.0
Dealing with construction permits (rank)	90
DTF score for dealing with construction permits (0–100)	69.09
Procedures (number)	10
Time (days)	175
Cost (% of warehouse value)	0.1
Building quality control index (0–15)	6.0
Getting electricity (rank)	61
DTF score for getting electricity (0–100)	79.26
Procedures (number)	5
Time (days)	61
Cost (% of income per capita)	479.7
Reliability of supply and transparency of tariffs index (0–8)	6
Registering property (rank)	164
DTF score for registering property (0–100)	43.39
Procedures (number)	5
Time (days)	42
Cost (% of property value)	13.3
Quality of land administration index (0–30)	4.5
Getting credit (rank)	139
DTF score for getting credit (0–100)	30.00
Strength of legal rights index (0–12)	6
Depth of credit information index (0–8)	0
Credit bureau coverage (% of adults)	0.0
Credit registry coverage (% of adults)	0.0
Protecting minority investors (rank)	70
DTF score for protecting minority investors (0–100)	56.67
Extent of disclosure index (0–10)	4
Extent of director liability index (0–10)	8
Ease of shareholder suits index (0–10)	8
Extent of shareholder rights index (0–10)	6
Extent of ownership and control index (0–10)	5
Extent of corporate transparency index (0–10)	3
✔ **Paying taxes** (rank)	111
DTF score for paying taxes (0–100)	67.38
Payments (number per year)	37
Time (hours per year)	117
Total tax rate (% of profit)	35.2
Postfiling index (0–100)	49.54
Trading across borders (rank)	80
DTF score for trading across borders (0–100)	74.26
Time to export	
Documentary compliance (hours)	12
Border compliance (hours)	36
Cost to export	
Documentary compliance (US$)	50
Border compliance (US$)	625
Time to import	
Documentary compliance (hours)	24
Border compliance (hours)	39
Cost to import	
Documentary compliance (US$)	50
Border compliance (US$)	906
Enforcing contracts (rank)	79
DTF score for enforcing contracts (0–100)	59.17
Time (days)	681
Cost (% of claim)	36.0
Quality of judicial processes index (0–18)	11.5
Resolving insolvency (rank)	128
DTF score for resolving insolvency (0–100)	34.19
Time (years)	4.0
Cost (% of estate)	10.0
Recovery rate (cents on the dollar)	28.7
Strength of insolvency framework index (0–16)	6.0

Note: Most indicator sets refer to a case scenario in the largest business city of an economy, though for 11 economies the data are a population-weighted average for the two largest business cities. For some indicators a result of "no practice" may be recorded for an economy; see the data notes for more details. In starting a business, procedures (number), time (days) and cost (% of income per capita) are calculated as the average of both men and women. For the postfiling index, a result of "not applicable" may be recorded for an economy.

✔ Reform making it easier to do business ✘ Change making it more difficult to do business

DOMINICAN REPUBLIC

Ease of doing business rank (1–190)	103
Latin America & Caribbean	
Overall distance to frontier (DTF) score (0–100)	59.35
GNI per capita (US$)	6,130
Population	10,528,391

Starting a business (rank)	115
DTF score for starting a business (0–100)	83.34
Procedures (number)	7
Time (days)	14.5
Cost (% of income per capita)	16.3
Minimum capital (% of income per capita)	36.5
Dealing with construction permits (rank)	45
DTF score for dealing with construction permits (0–100)	75.20
Procedures (number)	13
Time (days)	184
Cost (% of warehouse value)	1.7
Building quality control index (0–15)	13.0
✔ **Getting electricity** (rank)	148
DTF score for getting electricity (0–100)	52.18
Procedures (number)	7
Time (days)	67
Cost (% of income per capita)	267.1
Reliability of supply and transparency of tariffs index (0–8)	0
Registering property (rank)	82
DTF score for registering property (0–100)	65.61
Procedures (number)	6
Time (days)	45
Cost (% of property value)	3.5
Quality of land administration index (0–30)	14.5
Getting credit (rank)	101
DTF score for getting credit (0–100)	45.00
Strength of legal rights index (0–12)	1
Depth of credit information index (0–8)	8
Credit bureau coverage (% of adults)	74.9
Credit registry coverage (% of adults)	25.2
Protecting minority investors (rank)	87
DTF score for protecting minority investors (0–100)	53.33
Extent of disclosure index (0–10)	5
Extent of director liability index (0–10)	4
Ease of shareholder suits index (0–10)	7
Extent of shareholder rights index (0–10)	9
Extent of ownership and control index (0–10)	2
Extent of corporate transparency index (0–10)	5
✔ **Paying taxes** (rank)	129
DTF score for paying taxes (0–100)	60.70
Payments (number per year)	7
Time (hours per year)	317
Total tax rate (% of profit)	42.4
Postfiling index (0–100)	14.06
Trading across borders (rank)	58
DTF score for trading across borders (0–100)	83.51
Time to export	
Documentary compliance (hours)	10
Border compliance (hours)	16
Cost to export	
Documentary compliance (US$)	15
Border compliance (US$)	488
Time to import	
Documentary compliance (hours)	14
Border compliance (hours)	24
Cost to import	
Documentary compliance (US$)	40
Border compliance (US$)	579
Enforcing contracts (rank)	131
DTF score for enforcing contracts (0–100)	51.03
Time (days)	505
Cost (% of claim)	40.9
Quality of judicial processes index (0–18)	5.5
Resolving insolvency (rank)	160
DTF score for resolving insolvency (0–100)	23.55
Time (years)	3.5
Cost (% of estate)	38.0
Recovery rate (cents on the dollar)	8.9
Strength of insolvency framework index (0–16)	6.0

ECUADOR

Ease of doing business rank (1–190)	114
Latin America & Caribbean	
Overall distance to frontier (DTF) score (0–100)	57.97
GNI per capita (US$)	6,010
Population	16,144,363

✔ **Starting a business** (rank)	166
DTF score for starting a business (0–100)	70.61
Procedures (number)	11
Time (days)	48.5
Cost (% of income per capita)	21.0
Minimum capital (% of income per capita)	0.0
Dealing with construction permits (rank)	76
DTF score for dealing with construction permits (0–100)	71.03
Procedures (number)	15
Time (days)	114
Cost (% of warehouse value)	0.8
Building quality control index (0–15)	8.0
Getting electricity (rank)	95
DTF score for getting electricity (0–100)	69.13
Procedures (number)	7
Time (days)	74
Cost (% of income per capita)	606.3
Reliability of supply and transparency of tariffs index (0–8)	6
Registering property (rank)	69
DTF score for registering property (0–100)	67.53
Procedures (number)	7
Time (days)	38
Cost (% of property value)	2.1
Quality of land administration index (0–30)	15.5
Getting credit (rank)	101
DTF score for getting credit (0–100)	45.00
Strength of legal rights index (0–12)	1
Depth of credit information index (0–8)	8
Credit bureau coverage (% of adults)	58.3
Credit registry coverage (% of adults)	0.0
Protecting minority investors (rank)	118
DTF score for protecting minority investors (0–100)	46.67
Extent of disclosure index (0–10)	2
Extent of director liability index (0–10)	5
Ease of shareholder suits index (0–10)	6
Extent of shareholder rights index (0–10)	8
Extent of ownership and control index (0–10)	5
Extent of corporate transparency index (0–10)	2
Paying taxes (rank)	137
DTF score for paying taxes (0–100)	59.25
Payments (number per year)	8
Time (hours per year)	664
Total tax rate (% of profit)	32.5
Postfiling index (0–100)	49.31
Trading across borders (rank)	97
DTF score for trading across borders (0–100)	68.65
Time to export	
Documentary compliance (hours)	24
Border compliance (hours)	96
Cost to export	
Documentary compliance (US$)	140
Border compliance (US$)	560
Time to import	
Documentary compliance (hours)	120
Border compliance (hours)	24
Cost to import	
Documentary compliance (US$)	75
Border compliance (US$)	250
✔ **Enforcing contracts** (rank)	96
DTF score for enforcing contracts (0–100)	56.68
Time (days)	588
Cost (% of claim)	27.2
Quality of judicial processes index (0–18)	7.0
Resolving insolvency (rank)	157
DTF score for resolving insolvency (0–100)	25.17
Time (years)	5.3
Cost (% of estate)	18.0
Recovery rate (cents on the dollar)	17.7
Strength of insolvency framework index (0–16)	5.0

EGYPT, ARAB REP.

Ease of doing business rank (1–190)	122
Middle East & North Africa	
Overall distance to frontier (DTF) score (0–100)	56.64
GNI per capita (US$)	3,340
Population	91,508,084

✔ **Starting a business** (rank)	39
DTF score for starting a business (0–100)	92.43
Procedures (number)	4.5
Time (days)	6.5
Cost (% of income per capita)	7.4
Minimum capital (% of income per capita)	0.0
Dealing with construction permits (rank)	64
DTF score for dealing with construction permits (0–100)	72.46
Procedures (number)	17
Time (days)	145
Cost (% of warehouse value)	1.6
Building quality control index (0–15)	12.0
Getting electricity (rank)	88
DTF score for getting electricity (0–100)	70.33
Procedures (number)	6
Time (days)	54
Cost (% of income per capita)	244.9
Reliability of supply and transparency of tariffs index (0–8)	4
Registering property (rank)	109
DTF score for registering property (0–100)	58.30
Procedures (number)	8
Time (days)	60
Cost (% of property value)	0.5
Quality of land administration index (0–30)	7.0
Getting credit (rank)	82
DTF score for getting credit (0–100)	50.00
Strength of legal rights index (0–12)	2
Depth of credit information index (0–8)	8
Credit bureau coverage (% of adults)	21.6
Credit registry coverage (% of adults)	7.1
✔ **Protecting minority investors** (rank)	114
DTF score for protecting minority investors (0–100)	48.33
Extent of disclosure index (0–10)	8
Extent of director liability index (0–10)	3
Ease of shareholder suits index (0–10)	3
Extent of shareholder rights index (0–10)	3
Extent of ownership and control index (0–10)	7
Extent of corporate transparency index (0–10)	5
Paying taxes (rank)	162
DTF score for paying taxes (0–100)	51.96
Payments (number per year)	29
Time (hours per year)	392
Total tax rate (% of profit)	43.5
Postfiling index (0–100)	29.05
✘ **Trading across borders** (rank)	168
DTF score for trading across borders (0–100)	42.23
Time to export	
Documentary compliance (hours)	88
Border compliance (hours)	48
Cost to export	
Documentary compliance (US$)	100
Border compliance (US$)	258
Time to import	
Documentary compliance (hours)	265
Border compliance (hours)	240
Cost to import	
Documentary compliance (US$)	1,000
Border compliance (US$)	554
Enforcing contracts (rank)	162
DTF score for enforcing contracts (0–100)	40.9
Time (days)	1,010
Cost (% of claim)	26.2
Quality of judicial processes index (0–18)	4.5
Resolving insolvency (rank)	109
DTF score for resolving insolvency (0–100)	39.51
Time (years)	2.5
Cost (% of estate)	22.0
Recovery rate (cents on the dollar)	27.0
Strength of insolvency framework index (0–16)	8.0

Note: Most indicator sets refer to a case scenario in the largest business city of an economy, though for 11 economies the data are a population-weighted average for the two largest business cities. For some indicators a result of "no practice" may be recorded for an economy; see the data notes for more details. In starting a business, procedures (number), time (days) and cost (% of income per capita) are calculated as the average of both men and women. For the postfiling index, a result of "not applicable" may be recorded for an economy.

✔ Reform making it easier to do business ✘ Change making it more difficult to do business

EL SALVADOR

Ease of doing business rank (1–190)	95
Latin America & Caribbean	
Overall distance to frontier (DTF) score (0–100)	61.02
GNI per capita (US$)	3,940
Population	6,126,583

Starting a business (rank)	129
DTF score for starting a business (0–100)	80.70
Procedures (number)	8
Time (days)	15.5
Cost (% of income per capita)	40.7
Minimum capital (% of income per capita)	2.5
Dealing with construction permits (rank)	156
DTF score for dealing with construction permits (0–100)	56.29
Procedures (number)	24
Time (days)	111
Cost (% of warehouse value)	4.2
Building quality control index (0–15)	7.0
Getting electricity (rank)	109
DTF score for getting electricity (0–100)	63.75
Procedures (number)	8
Time (days)	59
Cost (% of income per capita)	513.0
Reliability of supply and transparency of tariffs index (0–8)	5
Registering property (rank)	71
DTF score for registering property (0–100)	67.09
Procedures (number)	5
Time (days)	31
Cost (% of property value)	3.8
Quality of land administration index (0–30)	12.5
✘ **Getting credit** (rank)	44
DTF score for getting credit (0–100)	65.00
Strength of legal rights index (0–12)	9
Depth of credit information index (0–8)	4
Credit bureau coverage (% of adults)	3.0
Credit registry coverage (% of adults)	28.7
Protecting minority investors (rank)	158
DTF score for protecting minority investors (0–100)	38.33
Extent of disclosure index (0–10)	3
Extent of director liability index (0–10)	0
Ease of shareholder suits index (0–10)	7
Extent of shareholder rights index (0–10)	6
Extent of ownership and control index (0–10)	2
Extent of corporate transparency index (0–10)	5
✔ **Paying taxes** (rank)	166
DTF score for paying taxes (0–100)	49.51
Payments (number per year)	41
Time (hours per year)	248
Total tax rate (% of profit)	38.8
Postfiling index (0–100)	10.09
Trading across borders (rank)	44
DTF score for trading across borders (0–100)	88.49
Time to export	
Documentary compliance (hours)	9
Border compliance (hours)	38
Cost to export	
Documentary compliance (US$)	50
Border compliance (US$)	128
Time to import	
Documentary compliance (hours)	13
Border compliance (hours)	40
Cost to import	
Documentary compliance (US$)	67
Border compliance (US$)	128
Enforcing contracts (rank)	104
DTF score for enforcing contracts (0–100)	55.2
Time (days)	786
Cost (% of claim)	19.2
Quality of judicial processes index (0–18)	7.5
Resolving insolvency (rank)	80
DTF score for resolving insolvency (0–100)	45.83
Time (years)	3.5
Cost (% of estate)	12.0
Recovery rate (cents on the dollar)	32.9
Strength of insolvency framework index (0–16)	9.0

EQUATORIAL GUINEA

Ease of doing business rank (1–190)	178
Sub-Saharan Africa	
Overall distance to frontier (DTF) score (0–100)	39.83
GNI per capita (US$)	7,790
Population	845,060

✔ **Starting a business** (rank)	187
DTF score for starting a business (0–100)	36.90
Procedures (number)	17
Time (days)	134
Cost (% of income per capita)	102.7
Minimum capital (% of income per capita)	27.8
Dealing with construction permits (rank)	160
DTF score for dealing with construction permits (0–100)	54.97
Procedures (number)	13
Time (days)	144
Cost (% of warehouse value)	4.2
Building quality control index (0–15)	1.0
Getting electricity (rank)	143
DTF score for getting electricity (0–100)	53.75
Procedures (number)	5
Time (days)	106
Cost (% of income per capita)	1,085.4
Reliability of supply and transparency of tariffs index (0–8)	0
Registering property (rank)	160
DTF score for registering property (0–100)	44.45
Procedures (number)	6
Time (days)	23
Cost (% of property value)	12.5
Quality of land administration index (0–30)	4.0
Getting credit (rank)	118
DTF score for getting credit (0–100)	40.00
Strength of legal rights index (0–12)	6
Depth of credit information index (0–8)	2
Credit bureau coverage (% of adults)	0.0
Credit registry coverage (% of adults)	9.0
Protecting minority investors (rank)	137
DTF score for protecting minority investors (0–100)	41.67
Extent of disclosure index (0–10)	7
Extent of director liability index (0–10)	1
Ease of shareholder suits index (0–10)	6
Extent of shareholder rights index (0–10)	5
Extent of ownership and control index (0–10)	4
Extent of corporate transparency index (0–10)	2
✘ **Paying taxes** (rank)	179
DTF score for paying taxes (0–100)	39.25
Payments (number per year)	46
Time (hours per year)	492
Total tax rate (% of profit)	79.4
Postfiling index (0–100)	83.94
Trading across borders (rank)	174
DTF score for trading across borders (0–100)	32.05
Time to export	
Documentary compliance (hours)	154
Border compliance (hours)	132
Cost to export	
Documentary compliance (US$)	85
Border compliance (US$)	760
Time to import	
Documentary compliance (hours)	240
Border compliance (hours)	240
Cost to import	
Documentary compliance (US$)	70
Border compliance (US$)	985
Enforcing contracts (rank)	103
DTF score for enforcing contracts (0–100)	55.25
Time (days)	475
Cost (% of claim)	19.5
Quality of judicial processes index (0–18)	3.0
✔ **Resolving insolvency** (rank)	169
DTF score for resolving insolvency (0–100)	0.00
Time (years)	NO PRACTICE
Cost (% of estate)	NO PRACTICE
Recovery rate (cents on the dollar)	0.0
Strength of insolvency framework index (0–16)	0.0

ERITREA

Ease of doing business rank (1–190)	189
Sub-Saharan Africa	
Overall distance to frontier (DTF) score (0–100)	28.05
GNI per capita (US$)	591
Population	5,227,791

Starting a business (rank)	186
DTF score for starting a business (0–100)	46.36
Procedures (number)	13
Time (days)	84
Cost (% of income per capita)	37.6
Minimum capital (% of income per capita)	165.1
Dealing with construction permits (rank)	187
DTF score for dealing with construction permits (0–100)	0.00
Procedures (number)	NO PRACTICE
Time (days)	NO PRACTICE
Cost (% of warehouse value)	NO PRACTICE
Building quality control index (0–15)	0.0
Getting electricity (rank)	141
DTF score for getting electricity (0–100)	54.33
Procedures (number)	5
Time (days)	59
Cost (% of income per capita)	2,553.0
Reliability of supply and transparency of tariffs index (0–8)	0
Registering property (rank)	178
DTF score for registering property (0–100)	35.26
Procedures (number)	11
Time (days)	78
Cost (% of property value)	9.1
Quality of land administration index (0–30)	6.5
Getting credit (rank)	185
DTF score for getting credit (0–100)	0.00
Strength of legal rights index (0–12)	0
Depth of credit information index (0–8)	0
Credit bureau coverage (% of adults)	0.0
Credit registry coverage (% of adults)	0.0
Protecting minority investors (rank)	165
DTF score for protecting minority investors (0–100)	35.00
Extent of disclosure index (0–10)	3
Extent of director liability index (0–10)	0
Ease of shareholder suits index (0–10)	5
Extent of shareholder rights index (0–10)	6
Extent of ownership and control index (0–10)	3
Extent of corporate transparency index (0–10)	4
Paying taxes (rank)	147
DTF score for paying taxes (0–100)	56.82
Payments (number per year)	30
Time (hours per year)	216
Total tax rate (% of profit)	83.7
Postfiling index (0–100)	96.79
Trading across borders (rank)	189
DTF score for trading across borders (0–100)	0.00
Time to export	
Documentary compliance (hours)	NO PRACTICE
Border compliance (hours)	NO PRACTICE
Cost to export	
Documentary compliance (US$)	NO PRACTICE
Border compliance (US$)	NO PRACTICE
Time to import	
Documentary compliance (hours)	NO PRACTICE
Border compliance (hours)	NO PRACTICE
Cost to import	
Documentary compliance (US$)	NO PRACTICE
Border compliance (US$)	NO PRACTICE
Enforcing contracts (rank)	121
DTF score for enforcing contracts (0–100)	52.75
Time (days)	490
Cost (% of claim)	22.6
Quality of judicial processes index (0–18)	2.5
Resolving insolvency (rank)	169
DTF score for resolving insolvency (0–100)	0.00
Time (years)	NO PRACTICE
Cost (% of estate)	NO PRACTICE
Recovery rate (cents on the dollar)	0.0
Strength of insolvency framework index (0–16)	0.0

Note: Most indicator sets refer to a case scenario in the largest business city of an economy, though for 11 economies the data are a population-weighted average for the two largest business cities. For some indicators a result of "no practice" may be recorded for an economy; see the data notes for more details. In starting a business, procedures (number), time (days) and cost (% of income per capita) are calculated as the average of both men and women. For the postfiling index, a result of "not applicable" may be recorded for an economy.

✔ Reform making it easier to do business ✘ Change making it more difficult to do business

ESTONIA

Ease of doing business rank (1–190)	12	**OECD high income**		**GNI per capita (US$)**	18,480
		Overall distance to frontier (DTF) score (0–100)	81.05	**Population**	1,311,998

Starting a business (rank)	14
DTF score for starting a business (0–100)	95.13
Procedures (number)	3
Time (days)	3.5
Cost (% of income per capita)	1.2
Minimum capital (% of income per capita)	16.4
Dealing with construction permits (rank)	9
DTF score for dealing with construction permits (0–100)	82.57
Procedures (number)	10
Time (days)	102
Cost (% of warehouse value)	0.2
Building quality control index (0–15)	11.0
Getting electricity (rank)	38
DTF score for getting electricity (0–100)	83.20
Procedures (number)	5
Time (days)	91
Cost (% of income per capita)	173.0
Reliability of supply and transparency of tariffs index (0–8)	8
Registering property (rank)	6
DTF score for registering property (0–100)	91.02
Procedures (number)	3
Time (days)	17.5
Cost (% of property value)	0.5
Quality of land administration index (0–30)	27.5
Getting credit (rank)	32
DTF score for getting credit (0–100)	70.00
Strength of legal rights index (0–12)	7
Depth of credit information index (0–8)	7
Credit bureau coverage (% of adults)	35.1
Credit registry coverage (% of adults)	0.0
Protecting minority investors (rank)	53
DTF score for protecting minority investors (0–100)	60.00
Extent of disclosure index (0–10)	8
Extent of director liability index (0–10)	3
Ease of shareholder suits index (0–10)	6
Extent of shareholder rights index (0–10)	9
Extent of ownership and control index (0–10)	4
Extent of corporate transparency index (0–10)	6
Paying taxes (rank)	21
DTF score for paying taxes (0–100)	88.04
Payments (number per year)	8
Time (hours per year)	84
Total tax rate (% of profit)	48.7
Postfiling index (0–100)	98.55
Trading across borders (rank)	17
DTF score for trading across borders (0–100)	99.92
Time to export	
Documentary compliance (hours)	1
Border compliance (hours)	2
Cost to export	
Documentary compliance (US$)	0
Border compliance (US$)	0
Time to import	
Documentary compliance (hours)	1
Border compliance (hours)	0
Cost to import	
Documentary compliance (US$)	0
Border compliance (US$)	0
Enforcing contracts (rank)	11
DTF score for enforcing contracts (0–100)	75.16
Time (days)	425
Cost (% of claim)	21.9
Quality of judicial processes index (0–18)	13.5
Resolving insolvency (rank)	42
DTF score for resolving insolvency (0–100)	65.46
Time (years)	3.0
Cost (% of estate)	9.0
Recovery rate (cents on the dollar)	40.3
Strength of insolvency framework index (0–16)	14.0

ETHIOPIA

Ease of doing business rank (1–190)	159	**Sub-Saharan Africa**		**GNI per capita (US$)**	590
		Overall distance to frontier (DTF) score (0–100)	47.25	**Population**	99,390,750

Starting a business (rank)	179
DTF score for starting a business (0–100)	55.96
Procedures (number)	14
Time (days)	35
Cost (% of income per capita)	69.3
Minimum capital (% of income per capita)	121.5
Dealing with construction permits (rank)	176
DTF score for dealing with construction permits (0–100)	48.83
Procedures (number)	12
Time (days)	130
Cost (% of warehouse value)	18.7
Building quality control index (0–15)	7.0
Getting electricity (rank)	127
DTF score for getting electricity (0–100)	58.64
Procedures (number)	4
Time (days)	95
Cost (% of income per capita)	1,238.8
Reliability of supply and transparency of tariffs index (0–8)	0
Registering property (rank)	133
DTF score for registering property (0–100)	51.30
Procedures (number)	7
Time (days)	52
Cost (% of property value)	6.1
Quality of land administration index (0–30)	6.0
Getting credit (rank)	170
DTF score for getting credit (0–100)	15.00
Strength of legal rights index (0–12)	3
Depth of credit information index (0–8)	0
Credit bureau coverage (% of adults)	0.0
Credit registry coverage (% of adults)	0.2
Protecting minority investors (rank)	175
DTF score for protecting minority investors (0–100)	31.67
Extent of disclosure index (0–10)	3
Extent of director liability index (0–10)	0
Ease of shareholder suits index (0–10)	3
Extent of shareholder rights index (0–10)	6
Extent of ownership and control index (0–10)	3
Extent of corporate transparency index (0–10)	4
Paying taxes (rank)	90
DTF score for paying taxes (0–100)	72.06
Payments (number per year)	30
Time (hours per year)	306
Total tax rate (% of profit)	38.6
Postfiling index (0–100)	90.57
Trading across borders (rank)	167
DTF score for trading across borders (0–100)	42.39
Time to export	
Documentary compliance (hours)	91
Border compliance (hours)	57
Cost to export	
Documentary compliance (US$)	175
Border compliance (US$)	144
Time to import	
Documentary compliance (hours)	209
Border compliance (hours)	203
Cost to import	
Documentary compliance (US$)	750
Border compliance (US$)	668
Enforcing contracts (rank)	80
DTF score for enforcing contracts (0–100)	59.06
Time (days)	530
Cost (% of claim)	15.2
Quality of judicial processes index (0–18)	5.0
Resolving insolvency (rank)	120
DTF score for resolving insolvency (0–100)	37.60
Time (years)	3.0
Cost (% of estate)	14.5
Recovery rate (cents on the dollar)	29.2
Strength of insolvency framework index (0–16)	7.0

FIJI

Ease of doing business rank (1–190)	97	**East Asia & Pacific**		**GNI per capita (US$)**	4,800
		Overall distance to frontier (DTF) score (0–100)	60.71	**Population**	892,145

✔ **Starting a business** (rank)	159
DTF score for starting a business (0–100)	73.13
Procedures (number)	11
Time (days)	40
Cost (% of income per capita)	17.9
Minimum capital (% of income per capita)	0.0
Dealing with construction permits (rank)	101
DTF score for dealing with construction permits (0–100)	67.88
Procedures (number)	15
Time (days)	141
Cost (% of warehouse value)	0.4
Building quality control index (0–15)	7.0
Getting electricity (rank)	82
DTF score for getting electricity (0–100)	71.92
Procedures (number)	4
Time (days)	81
Cost (% of income per capita)	1,477.7
Reliability of supply and transparency of tariffs index (0–8)	4
Registering property (rank)	55
DTF score for registering property (0–100)	71.86
Procedures (number)	4
Time (days)	69
Cost (% of property value)	3.0
Quality of land administration index (0–30)	19.5
✘ **Getting credit** (rank)	157
DTF score for getting credit (0–100)	25.00
Strength of legal rights index (0–12)	5
Depth of credit information index (0–8)	0
Credit bureau coverage (% of adults)	0.0
Credit registry coverage (% of adults)	0.0
✔ **Protecting minority investors** (rank)	106
DTF score for protecting minority investors (0–100)	50.00
Extent of disclosure index (0–10)	2
Extent of director liability index (0–10)	8
Ease of shareholder suits index (0–10)	7
Extent of shareholder rights index (0–10)	6
Extent of ownership and control index (0–10)	4
Extent of corporate transparency index (0–10)	3
Paying taxes (rank)	110
DTF score for paying taxes (0–100)	67.55
Payments (number per year)	38
Time (hours per year)	247
Total tax rate (% of profit)	33.1
Postfiling index (0–100)	68.91
Trading across borders (rank)	75
DTF score for trading across borders (0–100)	77.57
Time to export	
Documentary compliance (hours)	56
Border compliance (hours)	56
Cost to export	
Documentary compliance (US$)	76
Border compliance (US$)	317
Time to import	
Documentary compliance (hours)	34
Border compliance (hours)	42
Cost to import	
Documentary compliance (US$)	58
Border compliance (US$)	320
Enforcing contracts (rank)	86
DTF score for enforcing contracts (0–100)	58.44
Time (days)	397
Cost (% of claim)	38.9
Quality of judicial processes index (0–18)	7.5
Resolving insolvency (rank)	90
DTF score for resolving insolvency (0–100)	43.75
Time (years)	1.8
Cost (% of estate)	10.0
Recovery rate (cents on the dollar)	46.4
Strength of insolvency framework index (0–16)	6.0

Note: Most indicator sets refer to a case scenario in the largest business city of an economy, though for 11 economies the data are a population-weighted average for the two largest business cities. For some indicators a result of "no practice" may be recorded for an economy; see the data notes for more details. In starting a business, procedures (number), time (days) and cost (% of income per capita) are calculated as the average of both men and women. For the postfiling index, a result of "not applicable" may be recorded for an economy.

✔ Reform making it easier to do business ✘ Change making it more difficult to do business

FINLAND

FINLAND		OECD high income		GNI per capita (US$)	46,360
Ease of doing business rank (1–190)	13	Overall distance to frontier (DTF) score (0–100)	80.84	Population	5,482,013

Starting a business (rank)	28
DTF score for starting a business (0–100)	93.13
Procedures (number)	3
Time (days)	14
Cost (% of income per capita)	1.0
Minimum capital (% of income per capita)	6.6
Dealing with construction permits (rank)	40
DTF score for dealing with construction permits (0–100)	75.72
Procedures (number)	17
Time (days)	65
Cost (% of warehouse value)	0.9
Building quality control index (0–15)	10.0
Getting electricity (rank)	18
DTF score for getting electricity (0–100)	88.97
Procedures (number)	5
Time (days)	42
Cost (% of income per capita)	28.0
Reliability of supply and transparency of tariffs index (0–8)	8
Registering property (rank)	20
DTF score for registering property (0–100)	82.94
Procedures (number)	3
Time (days)	32
Cost (% of property value)	4.0
Quality of land administration index (0–30)	27.0
Getting credit (rank)	44
DTF score for getting credit (0–100)	65.00
Strength of legal rights index (0–12)	7
Depth of credit information index (0–8)	6
Credit bureau coverage (% of adults)	20.7
Credit registry coverage (% of adults)	0.0
Protecting minority investors (rank)	70
DTF score for protecting minority investors (0–100)	56.67
Extent of disclosure index (0–10)	6
Extent of director liability index (0–10)	4
Ease of shareholder suits index (0–10)	8
Extent of shareholder rights index (0–10)	7
Extent of ownership and control index (0–10)	3
Extent of corporate transparency index (0–10)	6
Paying taxes (rank)	13
DTF score for paying taxes (0–100)	90.23
Payments (number per year)	8
Time (hours per year)	93
Total tax rate (% of profit)	38.1
Postfiling index (0–100)	93.09
Trading across borders (rank)	33
DTF score for trading across borders (0–100)	92.44
Time to export	
Documentary compliance (hours)	2
Border compliance (hours)	36
Cost to export	
Documentary compliance (US$)	70
Border compliance (US$)	213
Time to import	
Documentary compliance (hours)	1
Border compliance (hours)	2
Cost to import	
Documentary compliance (US$)	0
Border compliance (US$)	0
Enforcing contracts (rank)	30
DTF score for enforcing contracts (0–100)	69.40
Time (days)	375
Cost (% of claim)	16.2
Quality of judicial processes index (0–18)	8.5
Resolving insolvency (rank)	1
DTF score for resolving insolvency (0–100)	93.89
Time (years)	0.9
Cost (% of estate)	3.5
Recovery rate (cents on the dollar)	90.3
Strength of insolvency framework index (0–16)	14.5

FRANCE

FRANCE		OECD high income		GNI per capita (US$)	40,580
Ease of doing business rank (1–190)	29	Overall distance to frontier (DTF) score (0–100)	76.27	Population	66,808,385

Starting a business (rank)	27
DTF score for starting a business (0–100)	93.27
Procedures (number)	5
Time (days)	3.5
Cost (% of income per capita)	0.7
Minimum capital (% of income per capita)	0.0
✔ **Dealing with construction permits** (rank)	20
DTF score for dealing with construction permits (0–100)	79.23
Procedures (number)	9
Time (days)	183
Cost (% of warehouse value)	3.0
Building quality control index (0–15)	14.0
Getting electricity (rank)	25
DTF score for getting electricity (0–100)	85.78
Procedures (number)	5
Time (days)	71
Cost (% of income per capita)	40.8
Reliability of supply and transparency of tariffs index (0–8)	8
✘ **Registering property** (rank)	100
DTF score for registering property (0–100)	61.09
Procedures (number)	8
Time (days)	64
Cost (% of property value)	7.3
Quality of land administration index (0–30)	24.5
Getting credit (rank)	82
DTF score for getting credit (0–100)	50.00
Strength of legal rights index (0–12)	4
Depth of credit information index (0–8)	6
Credit bureau coverage (% of adults)	0.0
Credit registry coverage (% of adults)	46.7
Protecting minority investors (rank)	32
DTF score for protecting minority investors (0–100)	65.00
Extent of disclosure index (0–10)	8
Extent of director liability index (0–10)	3
Ease of shareholder suits index (0–10)	6
Extent of shareholder rights index (0–10)	6
Extent of ownership and control index (0–10)	8
Extent of corporate transparency index (0–10)	8
Paying taxes (rank)	63
DTF score for paying taxes (0–100)	78.72
Payments (number per year)	8
Time (hours per year)	139
Total tax rate (% of profit)	62.8
Postfiling index (0–100)	92.42
Trading across borders (rank)	1
DTF score for trading across borders (0–100)	100.00
Time to export	
Documentary compliance (hours)	1
Border compliance (hours)	0
Cost to export	
Documentary compliance (US$)	0
Border compliance (US$)	0
Time to import	
Documentary compliance (hours)	1
Border compliance (hours)	0
Cost to import	
Documentary compliance (US$)	0
Border compliance (US$)	0
Enforcing contracts (rank)	18
DTF score for enforcing contracts (0–100)	73.04
Time (days)	395
Cost (% of claim)	17.4
Quality of judicial processes index (0–18)	11.0
Resolving insolvency (rank)	24
DTF score for resolving insolvency (0–100)	76.62
Time (years)	1.9
Cost (% of estate)	9.0
Recovery rate (cents on the dollar)	78.5
Strength of insolvency framework index (0–16)	11.0

GABON

GABON		Sub-Saharan Africa		GNI per capita (US$)	9,210
Ease of doing business rank (1–190)	164	Overall distance to frontier (DTF) score (0–100)	45.88	Population	1,725,292

Starting a business (rank)	152
DTF score for starting a business (0–100)	76.28
Procedures (number)	7
Time (days)	50
Cost (% of income per capita)	14.3
Minimum capital (% of income per capita)	10.8
Dealing with construction permits (rank)	167
DTF score for dealing with construction permits (0–100)	53.33
Procedures (number)	12
Time (days)	329
Cost (% of warehouse value)	0.9
Building quality control index (0–15)	5.0
Getting electricity (rank)	158
DTF score for getting electricity (0–100)	47.05
Procedures (number)	7
Time (days)	148
Cost (% of income per capita)	1,101.7
Reliability of supply and transparency of tariffs index (0–8)	2
Registering property (rank)	175
DTF score for registering property (0–100)	37.80
Procedures (number)	6
Time (days)	103
Cost (% of property value)	10.5
Quality of land administration index (0–30)	3.5
Getting credit (rank)	118
DTF score for getting credit (0–100)	40.00
Strength of legal rights index (0–12)	6
Depth of credit information index (0–8)	2
Credit bureau coverage (% of adults)	0.0
Credit registry coverage (% of adults)	50.8
Protecting minority investors (rank)	158
DTF score for protecting minority investors (0–100)	38.33
Extent of disclosure index (0–10)	7
Extent of director liability index (0–10)	1
Ease of shareholder suits index (0–10)	4
Extent of shareholder rights index (0–10)	5
Extent of ownership and control index (0–10)	4
Extent of corporate transparency index (0–10)	2
Paying taxes (rank)	161
DTF score for paying taxes (0–100)	53.00
Payments (number per year)	26
Time (hours per year)	488
Total tax rate (% of profit)	45.2
Postfiling index (0–100)	45.56
Trading across borders (rank)	166
DTF score for trading across borders (0–100)	43.94
Time to export	
Documentary compliance (hours)	60
Border compliance (hours)	96
Cost to export	
Documentary compliance (US$)	200
Border compliance (US$)	1,633
Time to import	
Documentary compliance (hours)	120
Border compliance (hours)	84
Cost to import	
Documentary compliance (US$)	170
Border compliance (US$)	1,320
Enforcing contracts (rank)	177
DTF score for enforcing contracts (0–100)	32.84
Time (days)	1,160
Cost (% of claim)	34.3
Quality of judicial processes index (0–18)	4.0
✔ **Resolving insolvency** (rank)	123
DTF score for resolving insolvency (0–100)	36.18
Time (years)	5.0
Cost (% of estate)	14.5
Recovery rate (cents on the dollar)	15.0
Strength of insolvency framework index (0–16)	9.0

Note: Most indicator sets refer to a case scenario in the largest business city of an economy, though for 11 economies the data are a population-weighted average for the two largest business cities. For some indicators a result of "no practice" may be recorded for an economy; see the data notes for more details. In starting a business, procedures (number), time (days) and cost (% of income per capita) are calculated as the average of both men and women. For the postfiling index, a result of "not applicable" may be recorded for an economy.

✔ Reform making it easier to do business ✘ Change making it more difficult to do business

GAMBIA, THE

Ease of doing business rank (1–190)	145
Sub-Saharan Africa	
Overall distance to frontier (DTF) score (0–100)	51.70
GNI per capita (US$)	485
Population	1,990,924

Starting a business (rank)	168
DTF score for starting a business (0–100)	69.37
Procedures (number)	7
Time (days)	25
Cost (% of income per capita)	125.2
Minimum capital (% of income per capita)	0.0
Dealing with construction permits (rank)	122
DTF score for dealing with construction permits (0–100)	64.27
Procedures (number)	12
Time (days)	144
Cost (% of warehouse value)	2.2
Building quality control index (0–15)	4.5
Getting electricity (rank)	154
DTF score for getting electricity (0–100)	49.13
Procedures (number)	5
Time (days)	78
Cost (% of income per capita)	3,569.1
Reliability of supply and transparency of tariffs index (0–8)	0
Registering property (rank)	124
DTF score for registering property (0–100)	53.27
Procedures (number)	5
Time (days)	66
Cost (% of property value)	7.6
Quality of land administration index (0–30)	8.5
✔ **Getting credit** (rank)	118
DTF score for getting credit (0–100)	40.00
Strength of legal rights index (0–12)	8
Depth of credit information index (0–8)	0
Credit bureau coverage (% of adults)	0.0
Credit registry coverage (% of adults)	0.0
Protecting minority investors (rank)	165
DTF score for protecting minority investors (0–100)	35.00
Extent of disclosure index (0–10)	2
Extent of director liability index (0–10)	5
Ease of shareholder suits index (0–10)	5
Extent of shareholder rights index (0–10)	4
Extent of ownership and control index (0–10)	1
Extent of corporate transparency index (0–10)	4
Paying taxes (rank)	171
DTF score for paying taxes (0–100)	48.08
Payments (number per year)	49
Time (hours per year)	326
Total tax rate (% of profit)	51.3
Postfiling index (0–100)	48.43
Trading across borders (rank)	112
DTF score for trading across borders (0–100)	65.27
Time to export	
Documentary compliance (hours)	61
Border compliance (hours)	109
Cost to export	
Documentary compliance (US$)	183
Border compliance (US$)	381
Time to import	
Documentary compliance (hours)	32
Border compliance (hours)	87
Cost to import	
Documentary compliance (US$)	152
Border compliance (US$)	326
Enforcing contracts (rank)	107
DTF score for enforcing contracts (0–100)	54.84
Time (days)	407
Cost (% of claim)	37.9
Quality of judicial processes index (0–18)	5.5
Resolving insolvency (rank)	117
DTF score for resolving insolvency (0–100)	37.75
Time (years)	2.0
Cost (% of estate)	14.5
Recovery rate (cents on the dollar)	26.6
Strength of insolvency framework index (0–16)	7.5

GEORGIA

Ease of doing business rank (1–190)	16
Europe & Central Asia	
Overall distance to frontier (DTF) score (0–100)	80.20
GNI per capita (US$)	4,160
Population	3,679,000

Starting a business (rank)	8
DTF score for starting a business (0–100)	96.13
Procedures (number)	3
Time (days)	3
Cost (% of income per capita)	2.4
Minimum capital (% of income per capita)	0.0
Dealing with construction permits (rank)	8
DTF score for dealing with construction permits (0–100)	82.84
Procedures (number)	7
Time (days)	48
Cost (% of warehouse value)	0.2
Building quality control index (0–15)	7.0
✔ **Getting electricity** (rank)	39
DTF score for getting electricity (0–100)	82.73
Procedures (number)	4
Time (days)	71
Cost (% of income per capita)	354.0
Reliability of supply and transparency of tariffs index (0–8)	6
✔ **Registering property** (rank)	3
DTF score for registering property (0–100)	92.85
Procedures (number)	1
Time (days)	1
Cost (% of property value)	0.0
Quality of land administration index (0–30)	21.5
Getting credit (rank)	7
DTF score for getting credit (0–100)	85.00
Strength of legal rights index (0–12)	9
Depth of credit information index (0–8)	8
Credit bureau coverage (% of adults)	88.6
Credit registry coverage (% of adults)	0.0
✔ **Protecting minority investors** (rank)	7
DTF score for protecting minority investors (0–100)	76.67
Extent of disclosure index (0–10)	9
Extent of director liability index (0–10)	6
Ease of shareholder suits index (0–10)	8
Extent of shareholder rights index (0–10)	7
Extent of ownership and control index (0–10)	8
Extent of corporate transparency index (0–10)	8
✔ **Paying taxes** (rank)	22
DTF score for paying taxes (0–100)	87.43
Payments (number per year)	5
Time (hours per year)	270
Total tax rate (% of profit)	16.4
Postfiling index (0–100)	87.22
✔ **Trading across borders** (rank)	54
DTF score for trading across borders (0–100)	85.15
Time to export	
Documentary compliance (hours)	2
Border compliance (hours)	14
Cost to export	
Documentary compliance (US$)	35
Border compliance (US$)	383
Time to import	
Documentary compliance (hours)	2
Border compliance (hours)	15
Cost to import	
Documentary compliance (US$)	189
Border compliance (US$)	396
Enforcing contracts (rank)	16
DTF score for enforcing contracts (0–100)	73.21
Time (days)	285
Cost (% of claim)	29.9
Quality of judicial processes index (0–18)	12.0
Resolving insolvency (rank)	106
DTF score for resolving insolvency (0–100)	40.02
Time (years)	2.0
Cost (% of estate)	10.0
Recovery rate (cents on the dollar)	39.5
Strength of insolvency framework index (0–16)	6.0

GERMANY

Ease of doing business rank (1–190)	17
OECD high income	
Overall distance to frontier (DTF) score (0–100)	79.87
GNI per capita (US$)	45,790
Population	81,413,145

Starting a business (rank)	114
DTF score for starting a business (0–100)	83.42
Procedures (number)	9
Time (days)	10.5
Cost (% of income per capita)	1.9
Minimum capital (% of income per capita)	32.9
Dealing with construction permits (rank)	12
DTF score for dealing with construction permits (0–100)	81.45
Procedures (number)	8
Time (days)	96
Cost (% of warehouse value)	1.1
Building quality control index (0–15)	9.5
Getting electricity (rank)	5
DTF score for getting electricity (0–100)	98.79
Procedures (number)	3
Time (days)	28
Cost (% of income per capita)	40.8
Reliability of supply and transparency of tariffs index (0–8)	8
Registering property (rank)	79
DTF score for registering property (0–100)	65.72
Procedures (number)	6
Time (days)	52
Cost (% of property value)	6.7
Quality of land administration index (0–30)	22.0
Getting credit (rank)	32
DTF score for getting credit (0–100)	70.00
Strength of legal rights index (0–12)	6
Depth of credit information index (0–8)	8
Credit bureau coverage (% of adults)	100.0
Credit registry coverage (% of adults)	1.9
Protecting minority investors (rank)	53
DTF score for protecting minority investors (0–100)	60.00
Extent of disclosure index (0–10)	5
Extent of director liability index (0–10)	5
Ease of shareholder suits index (0–10)	5
Extent of shareholder rights index (0–10)	8
Extent of ownership and control index (0–10)	6
Extent of corporate transparency index (0–10)	7
Paying taxes (rank)	48
DTF score for paying taxes (0–100)	82.10
Payments (number per year)	9
Time (hours per year)	218
Total tax rate (% of profit)	48.9
Postfiling index (0–100)	97.45
Trading across borders (rank)	38
DTF score for trading across borders (0–100)	91.77
Time to export	
Documentary compliance (hours)	1
Border compliance (hours)	36
Cost to export	
Documentary compliance (US$)	45
Border compliance (US$)	345
Time to import	
Documentary compliance (hours)	1
Border compliance (hours)	0
Cost to import	
Documentary compliance (US$)	0
Border compliance (US$)	0
Enforcing contracts (rank)	17
DTF score for enforcing contracts (0–100)	73.17
Time (days)	499
Cost (% of claim)	14.4
Quality of judicial processes index (0–18)	12.0
Resolving insolvency (rank)	3
DTF score for resolving insolvency (0–100)	92.28
Time (years)	1.2
Cost (% of estate)	8.0
Recovery rate (cents on the dollar)	84.4
Strength of insolvency framework index (0–16)	15.0

Note: Most indicator sets refer to a case scenario in the largest business city of an economy, though for 11 economies the data are a population-weighted average for the two largest business cities. For some indicators a result of "no practice" may be recorded for an economy; see the data notes for more details. In starting a business, procedures (number), time (days) and cost (% of income per capita) are calculated as the average of both men and women. For the postfiling index, a result of "not applicable" may be recorded for an economy.

✔ Reform making it easier to do business ✘ Change making it more difficult to do business

GHANA

GHANA		Sub-Saharan Africa		GNI per capita (US$)	1,480
Ease of doing business rank (1–190)	108	Overall distance to frontier (DTF) score (0–100)	58.82	Population	27,409,893

✘ **Starting a business** (rank)	110
DTF score for starting a business (0–100)	83.73
Procedures (number)	8
Time (days)	14
Cost (% of income per capita)	19.7
Minimum capital (% of income per capita)	2.0
✘ **Dealing with construction permits** (rank)	117
DTF score for dealing with construction permits (0–100)	65.34
Procedures (number)	14
Time (days)	170
Cost (% of warehouse value)	2.9
Building quality control index (0–15)	8.0
Getting electricity (rank)	120
DTF score for getting electricity (0–100)	60.30
Procedures (number)	4
Time (days)	79
Cost (% of income per capita)	1,265.8
Reliability of supply and transparency of tariffs index (0–8)	0
Registering property (rank)	77
DTF score for registering property (0–100)	65.99
Procedures (number)	5
Time (days)	46
Cost (% of property value)	1.2
Quality of land administration index (0–30)	8.0
Getting credit (rank)	44
DTF score for getting credit (0–100)	65.00
Strength of legal rights index (0–12)	7
Depth of credit information index (0–8)	6
Credit bureau coverage (% of adults)	16.0
Credit registry coverage (% of adults)	0.0
Protecting minority investors (rank)	87
DTF score for protecting minority investors (0–100)	53.33
Extent of disclosure index (0–10)	7
Extent of director liability index (0–10)	5
Ease of shareholder suits index (0–10)	8
Extent of shareholder rights index (0–10)	7
Extent of ownership and control index (0–10)	3
Extent of corporate transparency index (0–10)	2
Paying taxes (rank)	122
DTF score for paying taxes (0–100)	62.91
Payments (number per year)	33
Time (hours per year)	224
Total tax rate (% of profit)	32.7
Postfiling index (0–100)	37.92
✔ **Trading across borders** (rank)	154
DTF score for trading across borders (0–100)	52.32
Time to export	
Documentary compliance (hours)	89
Border compliance (hours)	108
Cost to export	
Documentary compliance (US$)	155
Border compliance (US$)	490
Time to import	
Documentary compliance (hours)	76
Border compliance (hours)	89
Cost to import	
Documentary compliance (US$)	474
Border compliance (US$)	553
Enforcing contracts (rank)	114
DTF score for enforcing contracts (0–100)	54.00
Time (days)	710
Cost (% of claim)	23.0
Quality of judicial processes index (0–18)	6.5
Resolving insolvency (rank)	155
DTF score for resolving insolvency (0–100)	25.27
Time (years)	1.9
Cost (% of estate)	22.0
Recovery rate (cents on the dollar)	23.7
Strength of insolvency framework index (0–16)	4.0

GREECE

GREECE		OECD high income		GNI per capita (US$)	20,290
Ease of doing business rank (1–190)	61	Overall distance to frontier (DTF) score (0–100)	68.67	Population	10,823,732

Starting a business (rank)	56
DTF score for starting a business (0–100)	90.70
Procedures (number)	5
Time (days)	13
Cost (% of income per capita)	2.2
Minimum capital (% of income per capita)	0.0
Dealing with construction permits (rank)	58
DTF score for dealing with construction permits (0–100)	73.63
Procedures (number)	17
Time (days)	124
Cost (% of warehouse value)	1.8
Building quality control index (0–15)	12.0
Getting electricity (rank)	52
DTF score for getting electricity (0–100)	80.57
Procedures (number)	6
Time (days)	51
Cost (% of income per capita)	69.9
Reliability of supply and transparency of tariffs index (0–8)	7
Registering property (rank)	141
DTF score for registering property (0–100)	49.67
Procedures (number)	10
Time (days)	20
Cost (% of property value)	4.8
Quality of land administration index (0–30)	4.5
Getting credit (rank)	82
DTF score for getting credit (0–100)	50.00
Strength of legal rights index (0–12)	3
Depth of credit information index (0–8)	7
Credit bureau coverage (% of adults)	79.6
Credit registry coverage (% of adults)	0.0
Protecting minority investors (rank)	42
DTF score for protecting minority investors (0–100)	63.33
Extent of disclosure index (0–10)	7
Extent of director liability index (0–10)	4
Ease of shareholder suits index (0–10)	5
Extent of shareholder rights index (0–10)	8
Extent of ownership and control index (0–10)	7
Extent of corporate transparency index (0–10)	7
✘ **Paying taxes** (rank)	64
DTF score for paying taxes (0–100)	78.22
Payments (number per year)	8
Time (hours per year)	193
Total tax rate (% of profit)	50.7
Postfiling index (0–100)	79.27
Trading across borders (rank)	29
DTF score for trading across borders (0–100)	93.72
Time to export	
Documentary compliance (hours)	1
Border compliance (hours)	24
Cost to export	
Documentary compliance (US$)	30
Border compliance (US$)	300
Time to import	
Documentary compliance (hours)	1
Border compliance (hours)	1
Cost to import	
Documentary compliance (US$)	0
Border compliance (US$)	0
✔ **Enforcing contracts** (rank)	133
DTF score for enforcing contracts (0–100)	50.19
Time (days)	1,580
Cost (% of claim)	14.4
Quality of judicial processes index (0–18)	12.0
Resolving insolvency (rank)	52
DTF score for resolving insolvency (0–100)	56.66
Time (years)	3.5
Cost (% of estate)	9.0
Recovery rate (cents on the dollar)	35.6
Strength of insolvency framework index (0–16)	12.0

GRENADA

GRENADA		Latin America & Caribbean		GNI per capita (US$)	8,430
Ease of doing business rank (1–190)	138	Overall distance to frontier (DTF) score (0–100)	53.75	Population	106,825

Starting a business (rank)	77
DTF score for starting a business (0–100)	87.02
Procedures (number)	6
Time (days)	15
Cost (% of income per capita)	15.8
Minimum capital (% of income per capita)	0.0
Dealing with construction permits (rank)	105
DTF score for dealing with construction permits (0–100)	67.64
Procedures (number)	13
Time (days)	128
Cost (% of warehouse value)	0.3
Building quality control index (0–15)	5.0
Getting electricity (rank)	66
DTF score for getting electricity (0–100)	76.40
Procedures (number)	5
Time (days)	38
Cost (% of income per capita)	191.1
Reliability of supply and transparency of tariffs index (0–8)	4
Registering property (rank)	137
DTF score for registering property (0–100)	50.15
Procedures (number)	8
Time (days)	32
Cost (% of property value)	7.4
Quality of land administration index (0–30)	7.0
Getting credit (rank)	139
DTF score for getting credit (0–100)	30.00
Strength of legal rights index (0–12)	6
Depth of credit information index (0–8)	0
Credit bureau coverage (% of adults)	0.0
Credit registry coverage (% of adults)	0.0
Protecting minority investors (rank)	123
DTF score for protecting minority investors (0–100)	45.00
Extent of disclosure index (0–10)	4
Extent of director liability index (0–10)	8
Ease of shareholder suits index (0–10)	8
Extent of shareholder rights index (0–10)	3
Extent of ownership and control index (0–10)	3
Extent of corporate transparency index (0–10)	1
Paying taxes (rank)	132
DTF score for paying taxes (0–100)	60.44
Payments (number per year)	42
Time (hours per year)	140
Total tax rate (% of profit)	45.3
Postfiling index (0–100)	48.39
✔ **Trading across borders** (rank)	126
DTF score for trading across borders (0–100)	61.52
Time to export	
Documentary compliance (hours)	13
Border compliance (hours)	101
Cost to export	
Documentary compliance (US$)	40
Border compliance (US$)	1,034
Time to import	
Documentary compliance (hours)	24
Border compliance (hours)	37
Cost to import	
Documentary compliance (US$)	50
Border compliance (US$)	1,745
Enforcing contracts (rank)	76
DTF score for enforcing contracts (0–100)	59.33
Time (days)	688
Cost (% of claim)	32.6
Quality of judicial processes index (0–18)	11.0
Resolving insolvency (rank)	169
DTF score for resolving insolvency (0–100)	0.00
Time (years)	NO PRACTICE
Cost (% of estate)	NO PRACTICE
Recovery rate (cents on the dollar)	0.0
Strength of insolvency framework index (0–16)	0.0

Note: Most indicator sets refer to a case scenario in the largest business city of an economy, though for 11 economies the data are a population-weighted average for the two largest business cities. For some indicators a result of "no practice" may be recorded for an economy; see the data notes for more details. In starting a business, procedures (number), time (days) and cost (% of income per capita) are calculated as the average of both men and women. For the postfiling index, a result of "not applicable" may be recorded for an economy.

✔ Reform making it easier to do business ✘ Change making it more difficult to do business

GUATEMALA

GUATEMALA		Latin America & Caribbean		GNI per capita (US$)	3,590
Ease of doing business rank (1–190)	88	Overall distance to frontier (DTF) score (0–100)	62.93	Population	16,342,897

Starting a business (rank)	119
DTF score for starting a business (0–100)	82.31
Procedures (number)	7
Time (days)	19.5
Cost (% of income per capita)	24.1
Minimum capital (% of income per capita)	17.2
Dealing with construction permits (rank)	89
DTF score for dealing with construction permits (0–100)	69.30
Procedures (number)	11
Time (days)	158
Cost (% of warehouse value)	6.8
Building quality control index (0–15)	11.0
Getting electricity (rank)	19
DTF score for getting electricity (0–100)	88.95
Procedures (number)	4
Time (days)	39
Cost (% of income per capita)	477.6
Reliability of supply and transparency of tariffs index (0–8)	7
Registering property (rank)	74
DTF score for registering property (0–100)	66.47
Procedures (number)	6
Time (days)	24
Cost (% of property value)	3.7
Quality of land administration index (0–30)	13.0
Getting credit (rank)	16
DTF score for getting credit (0–100)	80.00
Strength of legal rights index (0–12)	9
Depth of credit information index (0–8)	7
Credit bureau coverage (% of adults)	7.9
Credit registry coverage (% of adults)	17.7
Protecting minority investors (rank)	173
DTF score for protecting minority investors (0–100)	33.33
Extent of disclosure index (0–10)	3
Extent of director liability index (0–10)	2
Ease of shareholder suits index (0–10)	5
Extent of shareholder rights index (0–10)	5
Extent of ownership and control index (0–10)	2
Extent of corporate transparency index (0–10)	3
✔ **Paying taxes** (rank)	93
DTF score for paying taxes (0–100)	71.55
Payments (number per year)	8
Time (hours per year)	256
Total tax rate (% of profit)	35.2
Postfiling index (0–100)	39.27
Trading across borders (rank)	77
DTF score for trading across borders (0–100)	75.31
Time to export	
Documentary compliance (hours)	48
Border compliance (hours)	36
Cost to export	
Documentary compliance (US$)	105
Border compliance (US$)	310
Time to import	
Documentary compliance (hours)	32
Border compliance (hours)	72
Cost to import	
Documentary compliance (US$)	140
Border compliance (US$)	405
Enforcing contracts (rank)	173
DTF score for enforcing contracts (0–100)	34.55
Time (days)	1,402
Cost (% of claim)	26.5
Quality of judicial processes index (0–18)	6.0
Resolving insolvency (rank)	149
DTF score for resolving insolvency (0–100)	27.52
Time (years)	3.0
Cost (% of estate)	14.5
Recovery rate (cents on the dollar)	27.9
Strength of insolvency framework index (0–16)	4.0

GUINEA

GUINEA		Sub-Saharan Africa		GNI per capita (US$)	470
Ease of doing business rank (1–190)	163	Overall distance to frontier (DTF) score (0–100)	46.23	Population	12,608,590

Starting a business (rank)	133
DTF score for starting a business (0–100)	80.20
Procedures (number)	6
Time (days)	8
Cost (% of income per capita)	77.7
Minimum capital (% of income per capita)	13.6
Dealing with construction permits (rank)	164
DTF score for dealing with construction permits (0–100)	54.26
Procedures (number)	27
Time (days)	173
Cost (% of warehouse value)	1.9
Building quality control index (0–15)	8.5
Getting electricity (rank)	160
DTF score for getting electricity (0–100)	44.81
Procedures (number)	4
Time (days)	69
Cost (% of income per capita)	6,636.4
Reliability of supply and transparency of tariffs index (0–8)	0
Registering property (rank)	140
DTF score for registering property (0–100)	49.81
Procedures (number)	6
Time (days)	44
Cost (% of property value)	8.5
Quality of land administration index (0–30)	5.5
Getting credit (rank)	139
DTF score for getting credit (0–100)	30.00
Strength of legal rights index (0–12)	6
Depth of credit information index (0–8)	0
Credit bureau coverage (% of adults)	0.0
Credit registry coverage (% of adults)	0.0
Protecting minority investors (rank)	145
DTF score for protecting minority investors (0–100)	40.00
Extent of disclosure index (0–10)	7
Extent of director liability index (0–10)	1
Ease of shareholder suits index (0–10)	5
Extent of shareholder rights index (0–10)	5
Extent of ownership and control index (0–10)	4
Extent of corporate transparency index (0–10)	2
Paying taxes (rank)	184
DTF score for paying taxes (0–100)	24.28
Payments (number per year)	57
Time (hours per year)	440
Total tax rate (% of profit)	68.3
Postfiling index (0–100)	12.31
Trading across borders (rank)	162
DTF score for trading across borders (0–100)	46.24
Time to export	
Documentary compliance (hours)	139
Border compliance (hours)	72
Cost to export	
Documentary compliance (US$)	128
Border compliance (US$)	778
Time to import	
Documentary compliance (hours)	156
Border compliance (hours)	91
Cost to import	
Documentary compliance (US$)	180
Border compliance (US$)	909
Enforcing contracts (rank)	115
DTF score for enforcing contracts (0–100)	53.87
Time (days)	311
Cost (% of claim)	45.0
Quality of judicial processes index (0–18)	5.0
✔ **Resolving insolvency** (rank)	113
DTF score for resolving insolvency (0–100)	38.84
Time (years)	3.8
Cost (% of estate)	8.0
Recovery rate (cents on the dollar)	19.9
Strength of insolvency framework index (0–16)	9.0

GUINEA-BISSAU

GUINEA-BISSAU		Sub-Saharan Africa		GNI per capita (US$)	590
Ease of doing business rank (1–190)	172	Overall distance to frontier (DTF) score (0–100)	41.63	Population	1,844,325

Starting a business (rank)	176
DTF score for starting a business (0–100)	63.86
Procedures (number)	8.5
Time (days)	8.5
Cost (% of income per capita)	36.9
Minimum capital (% of income per capita)	295.7
Dealing with construction permits (rank)	155
DTF score for dealing with construction permits (0–100)	56.55
Procedures (number)	11
Time (days)	116
Cost (% of warehouse value)	13.4
Building quality control index (0–15)	6.5
Getting electricity (rank)	182
DTF score for getting electricity (0–100)	28.64
Procedures (number)	7
Time (days)	455
Cost (% of income per capita)	1,519.8
Reliability of supply and transparency of tariffs index (0–8)	0
Registering property (rank)	149
DTF score for registering property (0–100)	47.81
Procedures (number)	8
Time (days)	51
Cost (% of property value)	5.5
Quality of land administration index (0–30)	3.0
Getting credit (rank)	139
DTF score for getting credit (0–100)	30.00
Strength of legal rights index (0–12)	6
Depth of credit information index (0–8)	0
Credit bureau coverage (% of adults)	0.0
Credit registry coverage (% of adults)	0.1
Protecting minority investors (rank)	137
DTF score for protecting minority investors (0–100)	41.67
Extent of disclosure index (0–10)	7
Extent of director liability index (0–10)	1
Ease of shareholder suits index (0–10)	6
Extent of shareholder rights index (0–10)	5
Extent of ownership and control index (0–10)	4
Extent of corporate transparency index (0–10)	2
Paying taxes (rank)	149
DTF score for paying taxes (0–100)	56.08
Payments (number per year)	46
Time (hours per year)	208
Total tax rate (% of profit)	45.5
Postfiling index (0–100)	48.39
Trading across borders (rank)	153
DTF score for trading across borders (0–100)	52.86
Time to export	
Documentary compliance (hours)	60
Border compliance (hours)	67
Cost to export	
Documentary compliance (US$)	316
Border compliance (US$)	677
Time to import	
Documentary compliance (hours)	36
Border compliance (hours)	72
Cost to import	
Documentary compliance (US$)	384
Border compliance (US$)	755
Enforcing contracts (rank)	164
DTF score for enforcing contracts (0–100)	38.81
Time (days)	1,715
Cost (% of claim)	25.0
Quality of judicial processes index (0–18)	8.0
✔ **Resolving insolvency** (rank)	169
DTF score for resolving insolvency (0–100)	0.00
Time (years)	NO PRACTICE
Cost (% of estate)	NO PRACTICE
Recovery rate (cents on the dollar)	0.0
Strength of insolvency framework index (0–16)	0.0

Note: Most indicator sets refer to a case scenario in the largest business city of an economy, though for 11 economies the data are a population-weighted average for the two largest business cities. For some indicators a result of "no practice" may be recorded for an economy; see the data notes for more details. In starting a business, procedures (number), time (days) and cost (% of income per capita) are calculated as the average of both men and women. For the postfiling index, a result of "not applicable" may be recorded for an economy.

✔ Reform making it easier to do business ✘ Change making it more difficult to do business

GUYANA

GUYANA		Latin America & Caribbean		GNI per capita (US$)	4,090
Ease of doing business rank (1–190)	124	Overall distance to frontier (DTF) score (0–100)	56.26	Population	767,085

Starting a business (rank)	99
DTF score for starting a business (0–100)	85.45
Procedures (number)	7
Time (days)	18
Cost (% of income per capita)	10.7
Minimum capital (% of income per capita)	0.0
Dealing with construction permits (rank)	148
DTF score for dealing with construction permits (0–100)	59.28
Procedures (number)	15
Time (days)	188
Cost (% of warehouse value)	0.6
Building quality control index (0–15)	4.0
Getting electricity (rank)	129
DTF score for getting electricity (0–100)	58.46
Procedures (number)	8
Time (days)	82
Cost (% of income per capita)	404.6
Reliability of supply and transparency of tariffs index (0–8)	4
✔ **Registering property** (rank)	122
DTF score for registering property (0–100)	54.31
Procedures (number)	6
Time (days)	75
Cost (% of property value)	4.6
Quality of land administration index (0–30)	7.5
✔ **Getting credit** (rank)	82
DTF score for getting credit (0–100)	50.00
Strength of legal rights index (0–12)	3
Depth of credit information index (0–8)	7
Credit bureau coverage (% of adults)	16.4
Credit registry coverage (% of adults)	0.0
Protecting minority investors (rank)	87
DTF score for protecting minority investors (0–100)	53.33
Extent of disclosure index (0–10)	5
Extent of director liability index (0–10)	5
Ease of shareholder suits index (0–10)	8
Extent of shareholder rights index (0–10)	6
Extent of ownership and control index (0–10)	3
Extent of corporate transparency index (0–10)	5
Paying taxes (rank)	136
DTF score for paying taxes (0–100)	59.27
Payments (number per year)	35
Time (hours per year)	256
Total tax rate (% of profit)	32.3
Postfiling index (0–100)	31.01
Trading across borders (rank)	135
DTF score for trading across borders (0–100)	59.33
Time to export	
Documentary compliance (hours)	200
Border compliance (hours)	72
Cost to export	
Documentary compliance (US$)	78
Border compliance (US$)	378
Time to import	
Documentary compliance (hours)	156
Border compliance (hours)	84
Cost to import	
Documentary compliance (US$)	63
Border compliance (US$)	265
Enforcing contracts (rank)	91
DTF score for enforcing contracts (0–100)	57.62
Time (days)	581
Cost (% of claim)	25.2
Quality of judicial processes index (0–18)	7.0
Resolving insolvency (rank)	154
DTF score for resolving insolvency (0–100)	25.55
Time (years)	3.0
Cost (% of estate)	28.5
Recovery rate (cents on the dollar)	18.4
Strength of insolvency framework index (0–16)	5.0

HAITI

HAITI		Latin America & Caribbean		GNI per capita (US$)	820
Ease of doing business rank (1–190)	181	Overall distance to frontier (DTF) score (0–100)	38.66	Population	10,711,067

Starting a business (rank)	188
DTF score for starting a business (0–100)	33.61
Procedures (number)	12
Time (days)	97
Cost (% of income per capita)	219.3
Minimum capital (% of income per capita)	15.5
Dealing with construction permits (rank)	166
DTF score for dealing with construction permits (0–100)	53.76
Procedures (number)	12
Time (days)	80
Cost (% of warehouse value)	14.9
Building quality control index (0–15)	5.0
Getting electricity (rank)	139
DTF score for getting electricity (0–100)	54.82
Procedures (number)	4
Time (days)	60
Cost (% of income per capita)	3,708.5
Reliability of supply and transparency of tariffs index (0–8)	0
Registering property (rank)	180
DTF score for registering property (0–100)	32.10
Procedures (number)	5
Time (days)	312
Cost (% of property value)	7.0
Quality of land administration index (0–30)	2.5
Getting credit (rank)	175
DTF score for getting credit (0–100)	10.00
Strength of legal rights index (0–12)	2
Depth of credit information index (0–8)	0
Credit bureau coverage (% of adults)	0.0
Credit registry coverage (% of adults)	1.6
Protecting minority investors (rank)	188
DTF score for protecting minority investors (0–100)	20.00
Extent of disclosure index (0–10)	2
Extent of director liability index (0–10)	3
Ease of shareholder suits index (0–10)	4
Extent of shareholder rights index (0–10)	2
Extent of ownership and control index (0–10)	1
Extent of corporate transparency index (0–10)	0
Paying taxes (rank)	159
DTF score for paying taxes (0–100)	53.10
Payments (number per year)	47
Time (hours per year)	184
Total tax rate (% of profit)	40.3
Postfiling index (0–100)	26.79
✔ **Trading across borders** (rank)	76
DTF score for trading across borders (0–100)	76.69
Time to export	
Documentary compliance (hours)	22
Border compliance (hours)	28
Cost to export	
Documentary compliance (US$)	48
Border compliance (US$)	368
Time to import	
Documentary compliance (hours)	28
Border compliance (hours)	83
Cost to import	
Documentary compliance (US$)	150
Border compliance (US$)	583
Enforcing contracts (rank)	123
DTF score for enforcing contracts (0–100)	52.49
Time (days)	530
Cost (% of claim)	42.6
Quality of judicial processes index (0–18)	7.0
Resolving insolvency (rank)	169
DTF score for resolving insolvency (0–100)	0.00
Time (years)	NO PRACTICE
Cost (% of estate)	NO PRACTICE
Recovery rate (cents on the dollar)	0.0
Strength of insolvency framework index (0–16)	0.0

HONDURAS

HONDURAS		Latin America & Caribbean		GNI per capita (US$)	2,270
Ease of doing business rank (1–190)	105	Overall distance to frontier (DTF) score (0–100)	59.09	Population	8,075,060

Starting a business (rank)	148
DTF score for starting a business (0–100)	77.02
Procedures (number)	11
Time (days)	13
Cost (% of income per capita)	41.1
Minimum capital (% of income per capita)	0.0
Dealing with construction permits (rank)	84
DTF score for dealing with construction permits (0–100)	69.57
Procedures (number)	15
Time (days)	89
Cost (% of warehouse value)	6.0
Building quality control index (0–15)	10.0
Getting electricity (rank)	144
DTF score for getting electricity (0–100)	53.66
Procedures (number)	7
Time (days)	39
Cost (% of income per capita)	775.1
Reliability of supply and transparency of tariffs index (0–8)	0
Registering property (rank)	85
DTF score for registering property (0–100)	64.26
Procedures (number)	6
Time (days)	22
Cost (% of property value)	5.7
Quality of land administration index (0–30)	14.0
Getting credit (rank)	7
DTF score for getting credit (0–100)	85.00
Strength of legal rights index (0–12)	9
Depth of credit information index (0–8)	8
Credit bureau coverage (% of adults)	60.5
Credit registry coverage (% of adults)	22.8
Protecting minority investors (rank)	132
DTF score for protecting minority investors (0–100)	43.33
Extent of disclosure index (0–10)	3
Extent of director liability index (0–10)	8
Ease of shareholder suits index (0–10)	6
Extent of shareholder rights index (0–10)	5
Extent of ownership and control index (0–10)	2
Extent of corporate transparency index (0–10)	2
Paying taxes (rank)	152
DTF score for paying taxes (0–100)	54.97
Payments (number per year)	48
Time (hours per year)	224
Total tax rate (% of profit)	44.4
Postfiling index (0–100)	48.07
✘ **Trading across borders** (rank)	109
DTF score for trading across borders (0–100)	65.85
Time to export	
Documentary compliance (hours)	48
Border compliance (hours)	88
Cost to export	
Documentary compliance (US$)	80
Border compliance (US$)	601
Time to import	
Documentary compliance (hours)	72
Border compliance (hours)	96
Cost to import	
Documentary compliance (US$)	70
Border compliance (US$)	483
Enforcing contracts (rank)	151
DTF score for enforcing contracts (0–100)	45.54
Time (days)	920
Cost (% of claim)	35.2
Quality of judicial processes index (0–18)	7.5
Resolving insolvency (rank)	139
DTF score for resolving insolvency (0–100)	31.66
Time (years)	3.8
Cost (% of estate)	14.5
Recovery rate (cents on the dollar)	18.2
Strength of insolvency framework index (0–16)	7.0

Note: Most indicator sets refer to a case scenario in the largest business city of an economy, though for 11 economies the data are a population-weighted average for the two largest business cities. For some indicators a result of "no practice" may be recorded for an economy; see the data notes for more details. In starting a business, procedures (number), time (days) and cost (% of income per capita) are calculated as the average of both men and women. For the postfiling index, a result of "not applicable" may be recorded for an economy.

✔ Reform making it easier to do business ✘ Change making it more difficult to do business

HONG KONG SAR, CHINA

HONG KONG SAR, CHINA		East Asia & Pacific		GNI per capita (US$)	41,000
Ease of doing business rank (1–190)	**4**	**Overall distance to frontier (DTF) score (0–100)**	**84.21**	**Population**	**7,305,700**

✔ **Starting a business** (rank)	3
DTF score for starting a business (0–100)	98.20
Procedures (number)	2
Time (days)	1.5
Cost (% of income per capita)	0.6
Minimum capital (% of income per capita)	0.0
Dealing with construction permits (rank)	5
DTF score for dealing with construction permits (0–100)	84.82
Procedures (number)	11
Time (days)	72
Cost (% of warehouse value)	0.7
Building quality control index (0–15)	12.0
✔ **Getting electricity** (rank)	3
DTF score for getting electricity (0–100)	99.02
Procedures (number)	3
Time (days)	27
Cost (% of income per capita)	1.4
Reliability of supply and transparency of tariffs index (0–8)	8
Registering property (rank)	61
DTF score for registering property (0–100)	69.79
Procedures (number)	5
Time (days)	27.5
Cost (% of property value)	7.7
Quality of land administration index (0–30)	23.0

Getting credit (rank)	20
DTF score for getting credit (0–100)	75.00
Strength of legal rights index (0–12)	8
Depth of credit information index (0–8)	7
Credit bureau coverage (% of adults)	100.0
Credit registry coverage (% of adults)	0.0
Protecting minority investors (rank)	3
DTF score for protecting minority investors (0–100)	80.00
Extent of disclosure index (0–10)	10
Extent of director liability index (0–10)	8
Ease of shareholder suits index (0–10)	9
Extent of shareholder rights index (0–10)	9
Extent of ownership and control index (0–10)	4
Extent of corporate transparency index (0–10)	8
Paying taxes (rank)	3
DTF score for paying taxes (0–100)	98.69
Payments (number per year)	3
Time (hours per year)	74
Total tax rate (% of profit)	22.9
Postfiling index (0–100)	98.62

Trading across borders (rank)	42
DTF score for trading across borders (0–100)	88.94
Time to export	
Documentary compliance (hours)	1
Border compliance (hours)	19
Cost to export	
Documentary compliance (US$)	57
Border compliance (US$)	282
Time to import	
Documentary compliance (hours)	1
Border compliance (hours)	19
Cost to import	
Documentary compliance (US$)	57
Border compliance (US$)	266
Enforcing contracts (rank)	21
DTF score for enforcing contracts (0–100)	72.57
Time (days)	360
Cost (% of claim)	21.2
Quality of judicial processes index (0–18)	11.0
Resolving insolvency (rank)	28
DTF score for resolving insolvency (0–100)	75.06
Time (years)	0.8
Cost (% of estate)	5.0
Recovery rate (cents on the dollar)	87.2
Strength of insolvency framework index (0–16)	9.0

HUNGARY

HUNGARY		OECD high income		GNI per capita (US$)	12,990
Ease of doing business rank (1–190)	**41**	**Overall distance to frontier (DTF) score (0–100)**	**73.07**	**Population**	**9,844,686**

Starting a business (rank)	75
DTF score for starting a business (0–100)	87.28
Procedures (number)	6
Time (days)	7
Cost (% of income per capita)	7.1
Minimum capital (% of income per capita)	45.5
Dealing with construction permits (rank)	69
DTF score for dealing with construction permits (0–100)	71.70
Procedures (number)	17
Time (days)	202
Cost (% of warehouse value)	0.2
Building quality control index (0–15)	13.0
Getting electricity (rank)	121
DTF score for getting electricity (0–100)	60.13
Procedures (number)	5
Time (days)	257
Cost (% of income per capita)	93.9
Reliability of supply and transparency of tariffs index (0–8)	6
Registering property (rank)	28
DTF score for registering property (0–100)	80.08
Procedures (number)	4
Time (days)	17.5
Cost (% of property value)	5.0
Quality of land administration index (0–30)	26.0

Getting credit (rank)	20
DTF score for getting credit (0–100)	75.00
Strength of legal rights index (0–12)	10
Depth of credit information index (0–8)	5
Credit bureau coverage (% of adults)	89.8
Credit registry coverage (% of adults)	0.0
Protecting minority investors (rank)	81
DTF score for protecting minority investors (0–100)	55.00
Extent of disclosure index (0–10)	2
Extent of director liability index (0–10)	4
Ease of shareholder suits index (0–10)	6
Extent of shareholder rights index (0–10)	8
Extent of ownership and control index (0–10)	6
Extent of corporate transparency index (0–10)	7
✔ **Paying taxes** (rank)	77
DTF score for paying taxes (0–100)	74.46
Payments (number per year)	11
Time (hours per year)	277
Total tax rate (% of profit)	46.5
Postfiling index (0–100)	75.79

Trading across borders (rank)	1
DTF score for trading across borders (0–100)	100.00
Time to export	
Documentary compliance (hours)	1
Border compliance (hours)	0
Cost to export	
Documentary compliance (US$)	0
Border compliance (US$)	0
Time to import	
Documentary compliance (hours)	1
Border compliance (hours)	0
Cost to import	
Documentary compliance (US$)	0
Border compliance (US$)	0
✔ **Enforcing contracts** (rank)	8
DTF score for enforcing contracts (0–100)	75.79
Time (days)	395
Cost (% of claim)	15.0
Quality of judicial processes index (0–18)	12.0
Resolving insolvency (rank)	63
DTF score for resolving insolvency (0–100)	51.25
Time (years)	2.0
Cost (% of estate)	14.5
Recovery rate (cents on the dollar)	43.0
Strength of insolvency framework index (0–16)	9.0

ICELAND

ICELAND		OECD high income		GNI per capita (US$)	49,730
Ease of doing business rank (1–190)	**20**	**Overall distance to frontier (DTF) score (0–100)**	**78.91**	**Population**	**330,823**

Starting a business (rank)	34
DTF score for starting a business (0–100)	92.64
Procedures (number)	5
Time (days)	3.5
Cost (% of income per capita)	2.0
Minimum capital (% of income per capita)	7.6
Dealing with construction permits (rank)	70
DTF score for dealing with construction permits (0–100)	71.66
Procedures (number)	17
Time (days)	84
Cost (% of warehouse value)	0.4
Building quality control index (0–15)	8.0
Getting electricity (rank)	9
DTF score for getting electricity (0–100)	92.24
Procedures (number)	4
Time (days)	22
Cost (% of income per capita)	10.6
Reliability of supply and transparency of tariffs index (0–8)	7
Registering property (rank)	15
DTF score for registering property (0–100)	86.61
Procedures (number)	3
Time (days)	3.5
Cost (% of property value)	3.6
Quality of land administration index (0–30)	26.5

Getting credit (rank)	62
DTF score for getting credit (0–100)	60.00
Strength of legal rights index (0–12)	5
Depth of credit information index (0–8)	7
Credit bureau coverage (% of adults)	100.0
Credit registry coverage (% of adults)	0.0
Protecting minority investors (rank)	22
DTF score for protecting minority investors (0–100)	70.00
Extent of disclosure index (0–10)	7
Extent of director liability index (0–10)	5
Ease of shareholder suits index (0–10)	8
Extent of shareholder rights index (0–10)	8
Extent of ownership and control index (0–10)	7
Extent of corporate transparency index (0–10)	7
Paying taxes (rank)	29
DTF score for paying taxes (0–100)	84.88
Payments (number per year)	21
Time (hours per year)	140
Total tax rate (% of profit)	30.1
Postfiling index (0–100)	89.15

Trading across borders (rank)	66
DTF score for trading across borders (0–100)	80.27
Time to export	
Documentary compliance (hours)	2
Border compliance (hours)	36
Cost to export	
Documentary compliance (US$)	40
Border compliance (US$)	655
Time to import	
Documentary compliance (hours)	3
Border compliance (hours)	24
Cost to import	
Documentary compliance (US$)	0
Border compliance (US$)	655
Enforcing contracts (rank)	32
DTF score for enforcing contracts (0–100)	69.10
Time (days)	417
Cost (% of claim)	9.0
Quality of judicial processes index (0–18)	7.5
Resolving insolvency (rank)	14
DTF score for resolving insolvency (0–100)	81.70
Time (years)	1.0
Cost (% of estate)	3.5
Recovery rate (cents on the dollar)	85.0
Strength of insolvency framework index (0–16)	11.5

Note: Most indicator sets refer to a case scenario in the largest business city of an economy, though for 11 economies the data are a population-weighted average for the two largest business cities. For some indicators a result of "no practice" may be recorded for an economy; see the data notes for more details. In starting a business, procedures (number), time (days) and cost (% of income per capita) are calculated as the average of both men and women. For the postfiling index, a result of "not applicable" may be recorded for an economy.

✔ Reform making it easier to do business ✘ Change making it more difficult to do business

INDIA

Ease of doing business rank (1–190)	**130**
South Asia	
Overall distance to frontier (DTF) score (0–100)	**55.27**
GNI per capita (US$)	**1,590**
Population	**1,311,050,527**
Starting a business (rank)	155
DTF score for starting a business (0–100)	74.31
Procedures (number)	12.9
Time (days)	26
Cost (% of income per capita)	13.8
Minimum capital (% of income per capita)	0.0
Dealing with construction permits (rank)	185
DTF score for dealing with construction permits (0–100)	32.83
Procedures (number)	35.1
Time (days)	190
Cost (% of warehouse value)	25.9
Building quality control index (0–15)	11.5
✔ **Getting electricity** (rank)	26
DTF score for getting electricity (0–100)	85.09
Procedures (number)	5
Time (days)	45.9
Cost (% of income per capita)	133.2
Reliability of supply and transparency of tariffs index (0–8)	7
Registering property (rank)	138
DTF score for registering property (0–100)	50.00
Procedures (number)	7
Time (days)	46.8
Cost (% of property value)	7.7
Quality of land administration index (0–30)	7.0
Getting credit (rank)	44
DTF score for getting credit (0–100)	65.00
Strength of legal rights index (0–12)	6
Depth of credit information index (0–8)	7
Credit bureau coverage (% of adults)	21.4
Credit registry coverage (% of adults)	0.0
Protecting minority investors (rank)	13
DTF score for protecting minority investors (0–100)	73.33
Extent of disclosure index (0–10)	7
Extent of director liability index (0–10)	6
Ease of shareholder suits index (0–10)	7
Extent of shareholder rights index (0–10)	10
Extent of ownership and control index (0–10)	8
Extent of corporate transparency index (0–10)	6
✔ **Paying taxes** (rank)	172
DTF score for paying taxes (0–100)	46.58
Payments (number per year)	25
Time (hours per year)	241
Total tax rate (% of profit)	60.6
Postfiling index (0–100)	4.27
✔ **Trading across borders** (rank)	143
DTF score for trading across borders (0–100)	57.61
Time to export	
Documentary compliance (hours)	38.4
Border compliance (hours)	106.1
Cost to export	
Documentary compliance (US$)	91.9
Border compliance (US$)	413.1
Time to import	
Documentary compliance (hours)	61.3
Border compliance (hours)	283.3
Cost to import	
Documentary compliance (US$)	134.8
Border compliance (US$)	574
✔ **Enforcing contracts** (rank)	172
DTF score for enforcing contracts (0–100)	35.19
Time (days)	1,420
Cost (% of claim)	39.6
Quality of judicial processes index (0–18)	9.0
Resolving insolvency (rank)	136
DTF score for resolving insolvency (0–100)	32.75
Time (years)	4.3
Cost (% of estate)	9.0
Recovery rate (cents on the dollar)	26.0
Strength of insolvency framework index (0–16)	6.0

INDONESIA

Ease of doing business rank (1–190)	**91**
East Asia & Pacific	
Overall distance to frontier (DTF) score (0–100)	**61.52**
GNI per capita (US$)	**3,440**
Population	**257,563,815**
✔ **Starting a business** (rank)	151
DTF score for starting a business (0–100)	76.43
Procedures (number)	11.2
Time (days)	24.9
Cost (% of income per capita)	19.4
Minimum capital (% of income per capita)	0.0
Dealing with construction permits (rank)	116
DTF score for dealing with construction permits (0–100)	65.73
Procedures (number)	17
Time (days)	200.2
Cost (% of warehouse value)	5.1
Building quality control index (0–15)	13.0
✔ **Getting electricity** (rank)	49
DTF score for getting electricity (0–100)	80.92
Procedures (number)	4.8
Time (days)	57.7
Cost (% of income per capita)	357.0
Reliability of supply and transparency of tariffs index (0–8)	6
✔ **Registering property** (rank)	118
DTF score for registering property (0–100)	55.72
Procedures (number)	5
Time (days)	27.4
Cost (% of property value)	10.8
Quality of land administration index (0–30)	12.3
✔ **Getting credit** (rank)	62
DTF score for getting credit (0–100)	60.00
Strength of legal rights index (0–12)	6
Depth of credit information index (0–8)	6
Credit bureau coverage (% of adults)	0.0
Credit registry coverage (% of adults)	51.8
Protecting minority investors (rank)	70
DTF score for protecting minority investors (0–100)	56.67
Extent of disclosure index (0–10)	10
Extent of director liability index (0–10)	5
Ease of shareholder suits index (0–10)	2
Extent of shareholder rights index (0–10)	6
Extent of ownership and control index (0–10)	6
Extent of corporate transparency index (0–10)	5
✔ **Paying taxes** (rank)	104
DTF score for paying taxes (0–100)	69.25
Payments (number per year)	43
Time (hours per year)	221
Total tax rate (% of profit)	30.6
Postfiling index (0–100)	76.49
✔ **Trading across borders** (rank)	108
DTF score for trading across borders (0–100)	65.87
Time to export	
Documentary compliance (hours)	61.3
Border compliance (hours)	53.3
Cost to export	
Documentary compliance (US$)	138.8
Border compliance (US$)	253.7
Time to import	
Documentary compliance (hours)	132.9
Border compliance (hours)	99.4
Cost to import	
Documentary compliance (US$)	164.4
Border compliance (US$)	382.6
✔ **Enforcing contracts** (rank)	166
DTF score for enforcing contracts (0–100)	38.15
Time (days)	471
Cost (% of claim)	115.7
Quality of judicial processes index (0–18)	7.8
Resolving insolvency (rank)	76
DTF score for resolving insolvency (0–100)	46.46
Time (years)	1.9
Cost (% of estate)	21.6
Recovery rate (cents on the dollar)	31.2
Strength of insolvency framework index (0–16)	9.5

IRAN, ISLAMIC REP.

Ease of doing business rank (1–190)	**120**
Middle East & North Africa	
Overall distance to frontier (DTF) score (0–100)	**57.26**
GNI per capita (US$)	**6,019**
Population	**79,109,272**
Starting a business (rank)	102
DTF score for starting a business (0–100)	85.06
Procedures (number)	8.5
Time (days)	15.5
Cost (% of income per capita)	1.1
Minimum capital (% of income per capita)	0.0
Dealing with construction permits (rank)	27
DTF score for dealing with construction permits (0–100)	78.50
Procedures (number)	15
Time (days)	99
Cost (% of warehouse value)	1.7
Building quality control index (0–15)	12.5
Getting electricity (rank)	94
DTF score for getting electricity (0–100)	69.15
Procedures (number)	6
Time (days)	77
Cost (% of income per capita)	828.6
Reliability of supply and transparency of tariffs index (0–8)	5
Registering property (rank)	86
DTF score for registering property (0–100)	64.17
Procedures (number)	7
Time (days)	12
Cost (% of property value)	5.7
Quality of land administration index (0–30)	15.0
Getting credit (rank)	101
DTF score for getting credit (0–100)	45.00
Strength of legal rights index (0–12)	2
Depth of credit information index (0–8)	7
Credit bureau coverage (% of adults)	50.5
Credit registry coverage (% of adults)	51.0
Protecting minority investors (rank)	165
DTF score for protecting minority investors (0–100)	35.00
Extent of disclosure index (0–10)	7
Extent of director liability index (0–10)	4
Ease of shareholder suits index (0–10)	1
Extent of shareholder rights index (0–10)	4
Extent of ownership and control index (0–10)	3
Extent of corporate transparency index (0–10)	2
Paying taxes (rank)	100
DTF score for paying taxes (0–100)	69.79
Payments (number per year)	20
Time (hours per year)	344
Total tax rate (% of profit)	44.1
Postfiling index (0–100)	78.81
✔ **Trading across borders** (rank)	170
DTF score for trading across borders (0–100)	40.66
Time to export	
Documentary compliance (hours)	152
Border compliance (hours)	101
Cost to export	
Documentary compliance (US$)	143
Border compliance (US$)	565
Time to import	
Documentary compliance (hours)	270
Border compliance (hours)	141
Cost to import	
Documentary compliance (US$)	197
Border compliance (US$)	660
Enforcing contracts (rank)	70
DTF score for enforcing contracts (0–100)	60.00
Time (days)	505
Cost (% of claim)	17.0
Quality of judicial processes index (0–18)	5.5
Resolving insolvency (rank)	156
DTF score for resolving insolvency (0–100)	25.25
Time (years)	4.5
Cost (% of estate)	15.0
Recovery rate (cents on the dollar)	17.9
Strength of insolvency framework index (0–16)	5.0

Note: Most indicator sets refer to a case scenario in the largest business city of an economy, though for 11 economies the data are a population-weighted average for the two largest business cities. For some indicators a result of "no practice" may be recorded for an economy; see the data notes for more details. In starting a business, procedures (number), time (days) and cost (% of income per capita) are calculated as the average of both men and women. For the postfiling index, a result of "not applicable" may be recorded for an economy.

✔ Reform making it easier to do business ✘ Change making it more difficult to do business

IRAQ

Ease of doing business rank (1–190)	165	**Middle East & North Africa** Overall distance to frontier (DTF) score (0–100)	45.61	**GNI per capita (US$)**	5,550
				Population	36,423,395
Starting a business (rank)	164	**Getting credit** (rank)	181	**Trading across borders** (rank)	179
DTF score for starting a business (0–100)	71.32	DTF score for getting credit (0–100)	5.00	DTF score for trading across borders (0–100)	23.51
Procedures (number)	9.5	Strength of legal rights index (0–12)	1	*Time to export*	
Time (days)	34.5	Depth of credit information index (0–8)	0	Documentary compliance (hours)	504
Cost (% of income per capita)	51.9	Credit bureau coverage (% of adults)	0.0	Border compliance (hours)	69
Minimum capital (% of income per capita)	18.6	Credit registry coverage (% of adults)	0.0	*Cost to export*	
				Documentary compliance (US$)	1,800
✔ **Dealing with construction permits** (rank)	104	**Protecting minority investors** (rank)	123	Border compliance (US$)	1,018
DTF score for dealing with construction permits (0–100)	67.66	DTF score for protecting minority investors (0–100)	45.00	*Time to import*	
Procedures (number)	11	Extent of disclosure index (0–10)	4	Documentary compliance (hours)	176
Time (days)	167	Extent of director liability index (0–10)	5	Border compliance (hours)	131
Cost (% of warehouse value)	0.3	Ease of shareholder suits index (0–10)	5	*Cost to import*	
Building quality control index (0–15)	5.5	Extent of shareholder rights index (0–10)	8	Documentary compliance (US$)	900
		Extent of ownership and control index (0–10)	3	Border compliance (US$)	644
✔ **Getting electricity** (rank)	133	Extent of corporate transparency index (0–10)	2		
DTF score for getting electricity (0–100)	57.51			**Enforcing contracts** (rank)	138
Procedures (number)	6	**Paying taxes** (rank)	52	DTF score for enforcing contracts (0–100)	48.94
Time (days)	56	DTF score for paying taxes (0–100)	80.86	Time (days)	520
Cost (% of income per capita)	279.2	Payments (number per year)	14	Cost (% of claim)	28.1
Reliability of supply and transparency of tariffs index (0–8)	0	Time (hours per year)	312	Quality of judicial processes index (0–18)	2.0
		Total tax rate (% of profit)	27.8		
Registering property (rank)	115	Postfiling index (0–100)	84.86	**Resolving insolvency** (rank)	169
DTF score for registering property (0–100)	56.28			DTF score for resolving insolvency (0–100)	0.00
Procedures (number)	5			Time (years)	NO PRACTICE
Time (days)	51			Cost (% of estate)	NO PRACTICE
Cost (% of property value)	7.9			Recovery rate (cents on the dollar)	0.0
Quality of land administration index (0–30)	10.5			Strength of insolvency framework index (0–16)	0.0

IRELAND

Ease of doing business rank (1–190)	18	**OECD high income** Overall distance to frontier (DTF) score (0–100)	79.53	**GNI per capita (US$)**	46,680
				Population	4,640,703
✔ **Starting a business** (rank)	10	**Getting credit** (rank)	32	**Trading across borders** (rank)	47
DTF score for starting a business (0–100)	95.91	DTF score for getting credit (0–100)	70.00	DTF score for trading across borders (0–100)	87.25
Procedures (number)	3	Strength of legal rights index (0–12)	7	*Time to export*	
Time (days)	5	Depth of credit information index (0–8)	7	Documentary compliance (hours)	1
Cost (% of income per capita)	0.2	Credit bureau coverage (% of adults)	100.0	Border compliance (hours)	24
Minimum capital (% of income per capita)	0.0	Credit registry coverage (% of adults)	0.0	*Cost to export*	
				Documentary compliance (US$)	75
Dealing with construction permits (rank)	38	**Protecting minority investors** (rank)	13	Border compliance (US$)	305
DTF score for dealing with construction permits (0–100)	76.01	DTF score for protecting minority investors (0–100)	73.33	*Time to import*	
Procedures (number)	10	Extent of disclosure index (0–10)	9	Documentary compliance (hours)	1
Time (days)	149.5	Extent of director liability index (0–10)	8	Border compliance (hours)	24
Cost (% of warehouse value)	5.4	Ease of shareholder suits index (0–10)	9	*Cost to import*	
Building quality control index (0–15)	13.0	Extent of shareholder rights index (0–10)	7	Documentary compliance (US$)	75
		Extent of ownership and control index (0–10)	4	Border compliance (US$)	253
Getting electricity (rank)	33	Extent of corporate transparency index (0–10)	7		
DTF score for getting electricity (0–100)	84.19			**Enforcing contracts** (rank)	90
Procedures (number)	5	**Paying taxes** (rank)	5	DTF score for enforcing contracts (0–100)	57.88
Time (days)	85	DTF score for paying taxes (0–100)	94.40	Time (days)	650
Cost (% of income per capita)	61.9	Payments (number per year)	9	Cost (% of claim)	26.9
Reliability of supply and transparency of tariffs index (0–8)	8	Time (hours per year)	82	Quality of judicial processes index (0–18)	8.5
		Total tax rate (% of profit)	26.0		
Registering property (rank)	41	Postfiling index (0–100)	92.70	**Resolving insolvency** (rank)	17
DTF score for registering property (0–100)	76.28			DTF score for resolving insolvency (0–100)	80.01
Procedures (number)	5			Time (years)	0.4
Time (days)	31.5			Cost (% of estate)	9.0
Cost (% of property value)	2.5			Recovery rate (cents on the dollar)	87.7
Quality of land administration index (0–30)	21.0			Strength of insolvency framework index (0–16)	10.5

ISRAEL

Ease of doing business rank (1–190)	52	**OECD high income** Overall distance to frontier (DTF) score (0–100)	71.65	**GNI per capita (US$)**	35,440
				Population	8,380,400
✔ **Starting a business** (rank)	41	**Getting credit** (rank)	44	**Trading across borders** (rank)	59
DTF score for starting a business (0–100)	92.28	DTF score for getting credit (0–100)	65.00	DTF score for trading across borders (0–100)	82.85
Procedures (number)	4	Strength of legal rights index (0–12)	6	*Time to export*	
Time (days)	12	Depth of credit information index (0–8)	7	Documentary compliance (hours)	13
Cost (% of income per capita)	3.3	Credit bureau coverage (% of adults)	72.5	Border compliance (hours)	36
Minimum capital (% of income per capita)	0.0	Credit registry coverage (% of adults)	0.0	*Cost to export*	
				Documentary compliance (US$)	73
Dealing with construction permits (rank)	71	**Protecting minority investors** (rank)	9	Border compliance (US$)	150
DTF score for dealing with construction permits (0–100)	71.61	DTF score for protecting minority investors (0–100)	75.00	*Time to import*	
Procedures (number)	15	Extent of disclosure index (0–10)	7	Documentary compliance (hours)	44
Time (days)	209	Extent of director liability index (0–10)	9	Border compliance (hours)	64
Cost (% of warehouse value)	1.5	Ease of shareholder suits index (0–10)	9	*Cost to import*	
Building quality control index (0–15)	13.0	Extent of shareholder rights index (0–10)	7	Documentary compliance (US$)	70
		Extent of ownership and control index (0–10)	4	Border compliance (US$)	307
Getting electricity (rank)	71	Extent of corporate transparency index (0–10)	9		
DTF score for getting electricity (0–100)	75.20			**Enforcing contracts** (rank)	89
Procedures (number)	6	**Paying taxes** (rank)	96	DTF score for enforcing contracts (0–100)	57.93
Time (days)	102	DTF score for paying taxes (0–100)	71.00	Time (days)	975
Cost (% of income per capita)	14.7	Payments (number per year)	33	Cost (% of claim)	25.3
Reliability of supply and transparency of tariffs index (0–8)	7	Time (hours per year)	235	Quality of judicial processes index (0–18)	13.0
		Total tax rate (% of profit)	28.1		
Registering property (rank)	126	Postfiling index (0–100)	65.53	**Resolving insolvency** (rank)	31
DTF score for registering property (0–100)	52.84			DTF score for resolving insolvency (0–100)	72.75
Procedures (number)	6			Time (years)	2.0
Time (days)	81			Cost (% of estate)	23.0
Cost (% of property value)	8.3			Recovery rate (cents on the dollar)	62.6
Quality of land administration index (0–30)	14.0			Strength of insolvency framework index (0–16)	12.5

Note: Most indicator sets refer to a case scenario in the largest business city of an economy, though for 11 economies the data are a population-weighted average for the two largest business cities. For some indicators a result of "no practice" may be recorded for an economy; see the data notes for more details. In starting a business, procedures (number), time (days) and cost (% of income per capita) are calculated as the average of both men and women. For the postfiling index, a result of "not applicable" may be recorded for an economy.

✔ Reform making it easier to do business ✘ Change making it more difficult to do business

ITALY

ITALY		OECD high income		GNI per capita (US$)	32,790
Ease of doing business rank (1–190)	50	Overall distance to frontier (DTF) score (0–100)	72.25	Population	60,802,085

Starting a business (rank)	63
DTF score for starting a business (0–100)	89.40
Procedures (number)	6
Time (days)	6.5
Cost (% of income per capita)	13.9
Minimum capital (% of income per capita)	0.0
Dealing with construction permits (rank)	86
DTF score for dealing with construction permits (0–100)	69.41
Procedures (number)	10
Time (days)	227.5
Cost (% of warehouse value)	3.5
Building quality control index (0–15)	11.0
Getting electricity (rank)	51
DTF score for getting electricity (0–100)	80.70
Procedures (number)	4
Time (days)	124
Cost (% of income per capita)	158.0
Reliability of supply and transparency of tariffs index (0–8)	7
Registering property (rank)	24
DTF score for registering property (0–100)	81.69
Procedures (number)	4
Time (days)	16
Cost (% of property value)	4.4
Quality of land administration index (0–30)	26.5
Getting credit (rank)	101
DTF score for getting credit (0–100)	45.00
Strength of legal rights index (0–12)	2
Depth of credit information index (0–8)	7
Credit bureau coverage (% of adults)	100.0
Credit registry coverage (% of adults)	29.0
Protecting minority investors (rank)	42
DTF score for protecting minority investors (0–100)	63.33
Extent of disclosure index (0–10)	7
Extent of director liability index (0–10)	4
Ease of shareholder suits index (0–10)	7
Extent of shareholder rights index (0–10)	8
Extent of ownership and control index (0–10)	5
Extent of corporate transparency index (0–10)	7
✔ **Paying taxes** (rank)	126
DTF score for paying taxes (0–100)	61.65
Payments (number per year)	14
Time (hours per year)	240
Total tax rate (% of profit)	62.0
Postfiling index (0–100)	48.39
Trading across borders (rank)	1
DTF score for trading across borders (0–100)	100.00
Time to export	
Documentary compliance (hours)	1
Border compliance (hours)	0
Cost to export	
Documentary compliance (US$)	0
Border compliance (US$)	0
Time to import	
Documentary compliance (hours)	1
Border compliance (hours)	0
Cost to import	
Documentary compliance (US$)	0
Border compliance (US$)	0
Enforcing contracts (rank)	108
DTF score for enforcing contracts (0–100)	54.79
Time (days)	1,120
Cost (% of claim)	23.1
Quality of judicial processes index (0–18)	13.0
Resolving insolvency (rank)	25
DTF score for resolving insolvency (0–100)	76.59
Time (years)	1.8
Cost (% of estate)	22.0
Recovery rate (cents on the dollar)	63.9
Strength of insolvency framework index (0–16)	13.5

JAMAICA

JAMAICA		Latin America & Caribbean		GNI per capita (US$)	5,010
Ease of doing business rank (1–190)	67	Overall distance to frontier (DTF) score (0–100)	67.54	Population	2,725,941

✘ **Starting a business** (rank)	12
DTF score for starting a business (0–100)	95.61
Procedures (number)	2
Time (days)	10
Cost (% of income per capita)	4.3
Minimum capital (% of income per capita)	0.0
Dealing with construction permits (rank)	75
DTF score for dealing with construction permits (0–100)	71.15
Procedures (number)	17
Time (days)	129.5
Cost (% of warehouse value)	0.8
Building quality control index (0–15)	10.0
Getting electricity (rank)	101
DTF score for getting electricity (0–100)	68.00
Procedures (number)	7
Time (days)	95
Cost (% of income per capita)	231.6
Reliability of supply and transparency of tariffs index (0–8)	6
Registering property (rank)	123
DTF score for registering property (0–100)	53.70
Procedures (number)	8
Time (days)	18
Cost (% of property value)	9.8
Quality of land administration index (0–30)	14.0
Getting credit (rank)	16
DTF score for getting credit (0–100)	80.00
Strength of legal rights index (0–12)	9
Depth of credit information index (0–8)	7
Credit bureau coverage (% of adults)	23.3
Credit registry coverage (% of adults)	0.0
Protecting minority investors (rank)	63
DTF score for protecting minority investors (0–100)	58.33
Extent of disclosure index (0–10)	4
Extent of director liability index (0–10)	8
Ease of shareholder suits index (0–10)	5
Extent of shareholder rights index (0–10)	6
Extent of ownership and control index (0–10)	6
Extent of corporate transparency index (0–10)	6
✔ **Paying taxes** (rank)	116
DTF score for paying taxes (0–100)	65.18
Payments (number per year)	11
Time (hours per year)	268
Total tax rate (% of profit)	34.3
Postfiling index (0–100)	19.45
✔ **Trading across borders** (rank)	131
DTF score for trading across borders (0–100)	60.70
Time to export	
Documentary compliance (hours)	47
Border compliance (hours)	58
Cost to export	
Documentary compliance (US$)	90
Border compliance (US$)	876
Time to import	
Documentary compliance (hours)	72
Border compliance (hours)	80
Cost to import	
Documentary compliance (US$)	90
Border compliance (US$)	906
Enforcing contracts (rank)	117
DTF score for enforcing contracts (0–100)	53.60
Time (days)	550
Cost (% of claim)	45.6
Quality of judicial processes index (0–18)	8.5
Resolving insolvency (rank)	38
DTF score for resolving insolvency (0–100)	69.15
Time (years)	1.1
Cost (% of estate)	18.0
Recovery rate (cents on the dollar)	64.6
Strength of insolvency framework index (0–16)	11.0

JAPAN

JAPAN		OECD high income		GNI per capita (US$)	36,680
Ease of doing business rank (1–190)	34	Overall distance to frontier (DTF) score (0–100)	75.53	Population	126,958,472

Starting a business (rank)	89
DTF score for starting a business (0–100)	86.09
Procedures (number)	8
Time (days)	11.2
Cost (% of income per capita)	7.5
Minimum capital (% of income per capita)	0.0
Dealing with construction permits (rank)	60
DTF score for dealing with construction permits (0–100)	73.33
Procedures (number)	12
Time (days)	197
Cost (% of warehouse value)	0.5
Building quality control index (0–15)	11.0
Getting electricity (rank)	15
DTF score for getting electricity (0–100)	89.88
Procedures (number)	3.4
Time (days)	97.7
Cost (% of income per capita)	0.0
Reliability of supply and transparency of tariffs index (0–8)	8
Registering property (rank)	49
DTF score for registering property (0–100)	73.91
Procedures (number)	6
Time (days)	13
Cost (% of property value)	5.8
Quality of land administration index (0–30)	24.5
Getting credit (rank)	82
DTF score for getting credit (0–100)	50.00
Strength of legal rights index (0–12)	4
Depth of credit information index (0–8)	6
Credit bureau coverage (% of adults)	100.0
Credit registry coverage (% of adults)	0.0
Protecting minority investors (rank)	53
DTF score for protecting minority investors (0–100)	60.00
Extent of disclosure index (0–10)	7
Extent of director liability index (0–10)	6
Ease of shareholder suits index (0–10)	8
Extent of shareholder rights index (0–10)	7
Extent of ownership and control index (0–10)	3
Extent of corporate transparency index (0–10)	5
✔ **Paying taxes** (rank)	70
DTF score for paying taxes (0–100)	77.03
Payments (number per year)	14
Time (hours per year)	175
Total tax rate (% of profit)	48.9
Postfiling index (0–100)	78.91
Trading across borders (rank)	49
DTF score for trading across borders (0–100)	86.43
Time to export	
Documentary compliance (hours)	2.4
Border compliance (hours)	22.6
Cost to export	
Documentary compliance (US$)	60.4
Border compliance (US$)	264.9
Time to import	
Documentary compliance (hours)	3.4
Border compliance (hours)	39.6
Cost to import	
Documentary compliance (US$)	100
Border compliance (US$)	299.2
Enforcing contracts (rank)	48
DTF score for enforcing contracts (0–100)	65.26
Time (days)	360
Cost (% of claim)	23.4
Quality of judicial processes index (0–18)	7.5
Resolving insolvency (rank)	2
DTF score for resolving insolvency (0–100)	93.34
Time (years)	0.6
Cost (% of estate)	4.2
Recovery rate (cents on the dollar)	92.1
Strength of insolvency framework index (0–16)	14.0

Note: Most indicator sets refer to a case scenario in the largest business city of an economy, though for 11 economies the data are a population-weighted average for the two largest business cities. For some indicators a result of "no practice" may be recorded for an economy; see the data notes for more details. In starting a business, procedures (number), time (days) and cost (% of income per capita) are calculated as the average of both men and women. For the postfiling index, a result of "not applicable" may be recorded for an economy.

✔ Reform making it easier to do business ✘ Change making it more difficult to do business

JORDAN

JORDAN		Middle East & North Africa		GNI per capita (US$)	4,680
Ease of doing business rank (1–190)	118	Overall distance to frontier (DTF) score (0–100)	57.30	Population	7,594,547

Starting a business (rank)	106
DTF score for starting a business (0–100)	84.62
Procedures (number)	7.5
Time (days)	12.5
Cost (% of income per capita)	22.4
Minimum capital (% of income per capita)	0.1
Dealing with construction permits (rank)	109
DTF score for dealing with construction permits (0–100)	67.19
Procedures (number)	16
Time (days)	63
Cost (% of warehouse value)	10.0
Building quality control index (0–15)	11.0
Getting electricity (rank)	48
DTF score for getting electricity (0–100)	80.93
Procedures (number)	5
Time (days)	50
Cost (% of income per capita)	325.3
Reliability of supply and transparency of tariffs index (0–8)	6
Registering property (rank)	96
DTF score for registering property (0–100)	62.18
Procedures (number)	7
Time (days)	21
Cost (% of property value)	9.0
Quality of land administration index (0–30)	20.5
Getting credit (rank)	185
DTF score for getting credit (0–100)	0.00
Strength of legal rights index (0–12)	0
Depth of credit information index (0–8)	0
Credit bureau coverage (% of adults)	0.0
Credit registry coverage (% of adults)	2.5
Protecting minority investors (rank)	165
DTF score for protecting minority investors (0–100)	35.00
Extent of disclosure index (0–10)	4
Extent of director liability index (0–10)	4
Ease of shareholder suits index (0–10)	2
Extent of shareholder rights index (0–10)	1
Extent of ownership and control index (0–10)	5
Extent of corporate transparency index (0–10)	5
✔ **Paying taxes** (rank)	79
DTF score for paying taxes (0–100)	73.94
Payments (number per year)	25
Time (hours per year)	145
Total tax rate (% of profit)	27.6
Postfiling index (0–100)	49.31
✔ **Trading across borders** (rank)	50
DTF score for trading across borders (0–100)	86.39
Time to export	
Documentary compliance (hours)	2
Border compliance (hours)	38
Cost to export	
Documentary compliance (US$)	16
Border compliance (US$)	131
Time to import	
Documentary compliance (hours)	55
Border compliance (hours)	75
Cost to import	
Documentary compliance (US$)	30
Border compliance (US$)	181
Enforcing contracts (rank)	124
DTF score for enforcing contracts (0–100)	52.42
Time (days)	689
Cost (% of claim)	31.2
Quality of judicial processes index (0–18)	7.0
Resolving insolvency (rank)	142
DTF score for resolving insolvency (0–100)	30.38
Time (years)	3.0
Cost (% of estate)	20.0
Recovery rate (cents on the dollar)	27.4
Strength of insolvency framework index (0–16)	5.0

KAZAKHSTAN

KAZAKHSTAN		Europe & Central Asia		GNI per capita (US$)	11,580
Ease of doing business rank (1–190)	35	Overall distance to frontier (DTF) score (0–100)	75.09	Population	17,544,126

✔ **Starting a business** (rank)	45
DTF score for starting a business (0–100)	91.94
Procedures (number)	5
Time (days)	9
Cost (% of income per capita)	0.3
Minimum capital (% of income per capita)	0.0
✔ **Dealing with construction permits** (rank)	22
DTF score for dealing with construction permits (0–100)	79.05
Procedures (number)	13
Time (days)	68
Cost (% of warehouse value)	1.3
Building quality control index (0–15)	10.0
✔ **Getting electricity** (rank)	75
DTF score for getting electricity (0–100)	73.64
Procedures (number)	7
Time (days)	77
Cost (% of income per capita)	50.6
Reliability of supply and transparency of tariffs index (0–8)	7
Registering property (rank)	18
DTF score for registering property (0–100)	83.72
Procedures (number)	3
Time (days)	3.5
Cost (% of property value)	0.1
Quality of land administration index (0–30)	16.0
Getting credit (rank)	75
DTF score for getting credit (0–100)	55.00
Strength of legal rights index (0–12)	4
Depth of credit information index (0–8)	7
Credit bureau coverage (% of adults)	52.0
Credit registry coverage (% of adults)	0.0
✔ **Protecting minority investors** (rank)	3
DTF score for protecting minority investors (0–100)	80.00
Extent of disclosure index (0–10)	10
Extent of director liability index (0–10)	6
Ease of shareholder suits index (0–10)	8
Extent of shareholder rights index (0–10)	9
Extent of ownership and control index (0–10)	7
Extent of corporate transparency index (0–10)	8
Paying taxes (rank)	60
DTF score for paying taxes (0–100)	79.54
Payments (number per year)	7
Time (hours per year)	178
Total tax rate (% of profit)	29.2
Postfiling index (0–100)	49.08
✔ **Trading across borders** (rank)	119
DTF score for trading across borders (0–100)	63.19
Time to export	
Documentary compliance (hours)	128
Border compliance (hours)	133
Cost to export	
Documentary compliance (US$)	320
Border compliance (US$)	574
Time to import	
Documentary compliance (hours)	6
Border compliance (hours)	2
Cost to import	
Documentary compliance (US$)	0
Border compliance (US$)	0
✔ **Enforcing contracts** (rank)	9
DTF score for enforcing contracts (0–100)	75.70
Time (days)	370
Cost (% of claim)	22.0
Quality of judicial processes index (0–18)	13.0
✔ **Resolving insolvency** (rank)	37
DTF score for resolving insolvency (0–100)	69.17
Time (years)	1.5
Cost (% of estate)	15.0
Recovery rate (cents on the dollar)	41.4
Strength of insolvency framework index (0–16)	15.0

KENYA

KENYA		Sub-Saharan Africa		GNI per capita (US$)	1,340
Ease of doing business rank (1–190)	92	Overall distance to frontier (DTF) score (0–100)	61.22	Population	46,050,302

✔ **Starting a business** (rank)	116
DTF score for starting a business (0–100)	83.13
Procedures (number)	7
Time (days)	22
Cost (% of income per capita)	21.1
Minimum capital (% of income per capita)	0.0
Dealing with construction permits (rank)	152
DTF score for dealing with construction permits (0–100)	57.18
Procedures (number)	17
Time (days)	160
Cost (% of warehouse value)	6.3
Building quality control index (0–15)	7.0
✔ **Getting electricity** (rank)	106
DTF score for getting electricity (0–100)	64.43
Procedures (number)	3
Time (days)	97
Cost (% of income per capita)	642.0
Reliability of supply and transparency of tariffs index (0–8)	0
✔ **Registering property** (rank)	121
DTF score for registering property (0–100)	54.40
Procedures (number)	9
Time (days)	61
Cost (% of property value)	6.1
Quality of land administration index (0–30)	16.0
Getting credit (rank)	32
DTF score for getting credit (0–100)	70.00
Strength of legal rights index (0–12)	7
Depth of credit information index (0–8)	7
Credit bureau coverage (% of adults)	25.8
Credit registry coverage (% of adults)	0.0
✔ **Protecting minority investors** (rank)	87
DTF score for protecting minority investors (0–100)	53.33
Extent of disclosure index (0–10)	6
Extent of director liability index (0–10)	5
Ease of shareholder suits index (0–10)	9
Extent of shareholder rights index (0–10)	4
Extent of ownership and control index (0–10)	4
Extent of corporate transparency index (0–10)	4
Paying taxes (rank)	125
DTF score for paying taxes (0–100)	61.72
Payments (number per year)	31
Time (hours per year)	195.5
Total tax rate (% of profit)	37.4
Postfiling index (0–100)	32.12
Trading across borders (rank)	105
DTF score for trading across borders (0–100)	66.38
Time to export	
Documentary compliance (hours)	19
Border compliance (hours)	21
Cost to export	
Documentary compliance (US$)	191
Border compliance (US$)	143
Time to import	
Documentary compliance (hours)	84
Border compliance (hours)	180
Cost to import	
Documentary compliance (US$)	115
Border compliance (US$)	833
Enforcing contracts (rank)	87
DTF score for enforcing contracts (0–100)	58.27
Time (days)	465
Cost (% of claim)	41.8
Quality of judicial processes index (0–18)	9.0
✔ **Resolving insolvency** (rank)	92
DTF score for resolving insolvency (0–100)	43.39
Time (years)	4.5
Cost (% of estate)	22.0
Recovery rate (cents on the dollar)	28.4
Strength of insolvency framework index (0–16)	9.0

Note: Most indicator sets refer to a case scenario in the largest business city of an economy, though for 11 economies the data are a population-weighted average for the two largest business cities. For some indicators a result of "no practice" may be recorded for an economy; see the data notes for more details. In starting a business, procedures (number), time (days) and cost (% of income per capita) are calculated as the average of both men and women. For the postfiling index, a result of "not applicable" may be recorded for an economy.

✔ Reform making it easier to do business ✘ Change making it more difficult to do business

KIRIBATI

KIRIBATI		East Asia & Pacific		GNI per capita (US$)	3,230
Ease of doing business rank (1–190)	**152**	**Overall distance to frontier (DTF) score (0–100)**	**49.19**	**Population**	**112,423**

Starting a business (rank)	140
DTF score for starting a business (0–100)	78.17
Procedures (number)	7
Time (days)	31
Cost (% of income per capita)	36.3
Minimum capital (% of income per capita)	13.0
Dealing with construction permits (rank)	119
DTF score for dealing with construction permits (0–100)	65.13
Procedures (number)	14
Time (days)	149
Cost (% of warehouse value)	0.3
Building quality control index (0–15)	5.0
Getting electricity (rank)	164
DTF score for getting electricity (0–100)	43.95
Procedures (number)	6
Time (days)	97
Cost (% of income per capita)	3,228.7
Reliability of supply and transparency of tariffs index (0–8)	0
Registering property (rank)	144
DTF score for registering property (0–100)	49.13
Procedures (number)	5
Time (days)	513
Cost (% of property value)	0.0
Quality of land administration index (0–30)	9.0
Getting credit (rank)	167
DTF score for getting credit (0–100)	20.00
Strength of legal rights index (0–12)	4
Depth of credit information index (0–8)	0
Credit bureau coverage (% of adults)	0.0
Credit registry coverage (% of adults)	0.0
Protecting minority investors (rank)	123
DTF score for protecting minority investors (0–100)	45.00
Extent of disclosure index (0–10)	6
Extent of director liability index (0–10)	5
Ease of shareholder suits index (0–10)	8
Extent of shareholder rights index (0–10)	5
Extent of ownership and control index (0–10)	2
Extent of corporate transparency index (0–10)	1
Paying taxes (rank)	73
DTF score for paying taxes (0–100)	75.08
Payments (number per year)	11
Time (hours per year)	168
Total tax rate (% of profit)	32.7
Postfiling index (0–100)	41.30
Trading across borders (rank)	124
DTF score for trading across borders (0–100)	62.08
Time to export	
Documentary compliance (hours)	24
Border compliance (hours)	72
Cost to export	
Documentary compliance (US$)	310
Border compliance (US$)	420
Time to import	
Documentary compliance (hours)	48
Border compliance (hours)	96
Cost to import	
Documentary compliance (US$)	120
Border compliance (US$)	685
Enforcing contracts (rank)	118
DTF score for enforcing contracts (0–100)	53.39
Time (days)	660
Cost (% of claim)	25.8
Quality of judicial processes index (0–18)	6.0
Resolving insolvency (rank)	169
DTF score for resolving insolvency (0–100)	0.00
Time (years)	NO PRACTICE
Cost (% of estate)	NO PRACTICE
Recovery rate (cents on the dollar)	0.0
Strength of insolvency framework index (0–16)	0.0

KOREA, REP.

KOREA, REP.		OECD high income		GNI per capita (US$)	27,440
Ease of doing business rank (1–190)	**5**	**Overall distance to frontier (DTF) score (0–100)**	**84.07**	**Population**	**50,617,045**

✔ **Starting a business** (rank)	11
DTF score for starting a business (0–100)	95.83
Procedures (number)	2
Time (days)	4
Cost (% of income per capita)	14.6
Minimum capital (% of income per capita)	0.0
Dealing with construction permits (rank)	31
DTF score for dealing with construction permits (0–100)	77.84
Procedures (number)	10
Time (days)	28
Cost (% of warehouse value)	4.3
Building quality control index (0–15)	8.0
Getting electricity (rank)	1
DTF score for getting electricity (0–100)	99.88
Procedures (number)	3
Time (days)	18
Cost (% of income per capita)	38.3
Reliability of supply and transparency of tariffs index (0–8)	8
Registering property (rank)	39
DTF score for registering property (0–100)	76.34
Procedures (number)	7
Time (days)	5.5
Cost (% of property value)	5.1
Quality of land administration index (0–30)	27.5
Getting credit (rank)	44
DTF score for getting credit (0–100)	65.00
Strength of legal rights index (0–12)	5
Depth of credit information index (0–8)	8
Credit bureau coverage (% of adults)	100.0
Credit registry coverage (% of adults)	0.0
Protecting minority investors (rank)	13
DTF score for protecting minority investors (0–100)	73.33
Extent of disclosure index (0–10)	7
Extent of director liability index (0–10)	6
Ease of shareholder suits index (0–10)	8
Extent of shareholder rights index (0–10)	7
Extent of ownership and control index (0–10)	7
Extent of corporate transparency index (0–10)	9
Paying taxes (rank)	23
DTF score for paying taxes (0–100)	86.56
Payments (number per year)	12
Time (hours per year)	188
Total tax rate (% of profit)	33.1
Postfiling index (0–100)	92.58
Trading across borders (rank)	32
DTF score for trading across borders (0–100)	92.52
Time to export	
Documentary compliance (hours)	1
Border compliance (hours)	13
Cost to export	
Documentary compliance (US$)	11
Border compliance (US$)	185
Time to import	
Documentary compliance (hours)	1
Border compliance (hours)	6
Cost to import	
Documentary compliance (US$)	27
Border compliance (US$)	315
Enforcing contracts (rank)	1
DTF score for enforcing contracts (0–100)	84.15
Time (days)	290
Cost (% of claim)	12.7
Quality of judicial processes index (0–18)	14.5
Resolving insolvency (rank)	4
DTF score for resolving insolvency (0–100)	89.22
Time (years)	1.5
Cost (% of estate)	3.5
Recovery rate (cents on the dollar)	84.5
Strength of insolvency framework index (0–16)	14.0

KOSOVO

KOSOVO		Europe & Central Asia		GNI per capita (US$)	3,950
Ease of doing business rank (1–190)	**60**	**Overall distance to frontier (DTF) score (0–100)**	**68.79**	**Population**	**1,797,151**

Starting a business (rank)	13
DTF score for starting a business (0–100)	95.54
Procedures (number)	3
Time (days)	6
Cost (% of income per capita)	1.1
Minimum capital (% of income per capita)	0.0
Dealing with construction permits (rank)	129
DTF score for dealing with construction permits (0–100)	63.31
Procedures (number)	15
Time (days)	152
Cost (% of warehouse value)	6.1
Building quality control index (0–15)	9.0
Getting electricity (rank)	114
DTF score for getting electricity (0–100)	61.85
Procedures (number)	7
Time (days)	36
Cost (% of income per capita)	253.1
Reliability of supply and transparency of tariffs index (0–8)	2
Registering property (rank)	33
DTF score for registering property (0–100)	78.11
Procedures (number)	6
Time (days)	27
Cost (% of property value)	0.3
Quality of land administration index (0–30)	20.5
Getting credit (rank)	20
DTF score for getting credit (0–100)	75.00
Strength of legal rights index (0–12)	9
Depth of credit information index (0–8)	6
Credit bureau coverage (% of adults)	0.0
Credit registry coverage (% of adults)	38.1
Protecting minority investors (rank)	63
DTF score for protecting minority investors (0–100)	58.33
Extent of disclosure index (0–10)	6
Extent of director liability index (0–10)	6
Ease of shareholder suits index (0–10)	4
Extent of shareholder rights index (0–10)	10
Extent of ownership and control index (0–10)	4
Extent of corporate transparency index (0–10)	5
✔ **Paying taxes** (rank)	43
DTF score for paying taxes (0–100)	83.24
Payments (number per year)	10
Time (hours per year)	155
Total tax rate (% of profit)	15.2
Postfiling index (0–100)	61.00
✔ **Trading across borders** (rank)	51
DTF score for trading across borders (0–100)	85.93
Time to export	
Documentary compliance (hours)	38
Border compliance (hours)	42
Cost to export	
Documentary compliance (US$)	127
Border compliance (US$)	137
Time to import	
Documentary compliance (hours)	6
Border compliance (hours)	16
Cost to import	
Documentary compliance (US$)	42
Border compliance (US$)	83
Enforcing contracts (rank)	44
DTF score for enforcing contracts (0–100)	65.66
Time (days)	330
Cost (% of claim)	34.4
Quality of judicial processes index (0–18)	9.5
Resolving insolvency (rank)	163
DTF score for resolving insolvency (0–100)	20.88
Time (years)	2.0
Cost (% of estate)	15.0
Recovery rate (cents on the dollar)	38.8
Strength of insolvency framework index (0–16)	0.0

Note: Most indicator sets refer to a case scenario in the largest business city of an economy, though for 11 economies the data are a population-weighted average for the two largest business cities. For some indicators a result of "no practice" may be recorded for an economy; see the data notes for more details. In starting a business, procedures (number), time (days) and cost (% of income per capita) are calculated as the average of both men and women. For the postfiling index, a result of "not applicable" may be recorded for an economy.

✔ Reform making it easier to do business ✘ Change making it more difficult to do business

KUWAIT

KUWAIT		Middle East & North Africa		GNI per capita (US$)	40,930
Ease of doing business rank (1–190)	102	Overall distance to frontier (DTF) score (0–100)	59.55	Population	3,892,115

✘ **Starting a business** (rank)	173
DTF score for starting a business (0–100)	66.77
Procedures (number)	12.5
Time (days)	61.5
Cost (% of income per capita)	2.8
Minimum capital (% of income per capita)	10.2
Dealing with construction permits (rank)	144
DTF score for dealing with construction permits (0–100)	60.72
Procedures (number)	23
Time (days)	216
Cost (% of warehouse value)	0.7
Building quality control index (0–15)	11.0
Getting electricity (rank)	115
DTF score for getting electricity (0–100)	61.47
Procedures (number)	8
Time (days)	64
Cost (% of income per capita)	64.6
Reliability of supply and transparency of tariffs index (0–8)	4
Registering property (rank)	67
DTF score for registering property (0–100)	68.37
Procedures (number)	8
Time (days)	49
Cost (% of property value)	0.5
Quality of land administration index (0–30)	17.5
Getting credit (rank)	118
DTF score for getting credit (0–100)	40.00
Strength of legal rights index (0–12)	2
Depth of credit information index (0–8)	6
Credit bureau coverage (% of adults)	31.0
Credit registry coverage (% of adults)	14.5
Protecting minority investors (rank)	81
DTF score for protecting minority investors (0–100)	55.00
Extent of disclosure index (0–10)	4
Extent of director liability index (0–10)	9
Ease of shareholder suits index (0–10)	4
Extent of shareholder rights index (0–10)	3
Extent of ownership and control index (0–10)	5
Extent of corporate transparency index (0–10)	8
Paying taxes (rank)	6
DTF score for paying taxes (0–100)	92.48
Payments (number per year)	12
Time (hours per year)	98
Total tax rate (% of profit)	13.0
Postfiling index (0–100)	NOT APPLICABLE
✔ **Trading across borders** (rank)	157
DTF score for trading across borders (0–100)	50.57
Time to export	
Documentary compliance (hours)	32
Border compliance (hours)	72
Cost to export	
Documentary compliance (US$)	191
Border compliance (US$)	602
Time to import	
Documentary compliance (hours)	120
Border compliance (hours)	215
Cost to import	
Documentary compliance (US$)	332
Border compliance (US$)	646
Enforcing contracts (rank)	66
DTF score for enforcing contracts (0–100)	60.51
Time (days)	566
Cost (% of claim)	18.6
Quality of judicial processes index (0–18)	7.0
Resolving insolvency (rank)	108
DTF score for resolving insolvency (0–100)	39.58
Time (years)	4.2
Cost (% of estate)	10.0
Recovery rate (cents on the dollar)	32.9
Strength of insolvency framework index (0–16)	7.0

KYRGYZ REPUBLIC

KYRGYZ REPUBLIC		Europe & Central Asia		GNI per capita (US$)	1,170
Ease of doing business rank (1–190)	75	Overall distance to frontier (DTF) score (0–100)	65.17	Population	5,957,000

Starting a business (rank)	30
DTF score for starting a business (0–100)	92.95
Procedures (number)	4
Time (days)	10
Cost (% of income per capita)	2.0
Minimum capital (% of income per capita)	0.0
Dealing with construction permits (rank)	32
DTF score for dealing with construction permits (0–100)	76.74
Procedures (number)	11
Time (days)	142
Cost (% of warehouse value)	1.8
Building quality control index (0–15)	11.0
Getting electricity (rank)	163
DTF score for getting electricity (0–100)	44.05
Procedures (number)	7
Time (days)	125
Cost (% of income per capita)	858.1
Reliability of supply and transparency of tariffs index (0–8)	0
Registering property (rank)	8
DTF score for registering property (0–100)	90.60
Procedures (number)	3
Time (days)	3.5
Cost (% of property value)	0.2
Quality of land administration index (0–30)	24.5
Getting credit (rank)	32
DTF score for getting credit (0–100)	70.00
Strength of legal rights index (0–12)	8
Depth of credit information index (0–8)	6
Credit bureau coverage (% of adults)	30.6
Credit registry coverage (% of adults)	0.0
Protecting minority investors (rank)	42
DTF score for protecting minority investors (0–100)	63.33
Extent of disclosure index (0–10)	7
Extent of director liability index (0–10)	5
Ease of shareholder suits index (0–10)	8
Extent of shareholder rights index (0–10)	4
Extent of ownership and control index (0–10)	7
Extent of corporate transparency index (0–10)	7
Paying taxes (rank)	148
DTF score for paying taxes (0–100)	56.43
Payments (number per year)	51
Time (hours per year)	225
Total tax rate (% of profit)	29.0
Postfiling index (0–100)	36.93
✔ **Trading across borders** (rank)	79
DTF score for trading across borders (0–100)	74.91
Time to export	
Documentary compliance (hours)	21
Border compliance (hours)	20
Cost to export	
Documentary compliance (US$)	145
Border compliance (US$)	445
Time to import	
Documentary compliance (hours)	36
Border compliance (hours)	37
Cost to import	
Documentary compliance (US$)	200
Border compliance (US$)	512
Enforcing contracts (rank)	141
DTF score for enforcing contracts (0–100)	48.57
Time (days)	410
Cost (% of claim)	47.0
Quality of judicial processes index (0–18)	4.0
Resolving insolvency (rank)	130
DTF score for resolving insolvency (0–100)	34.08
Time (years)	1.5
Cost (% of estate)	15.0
Recovery rate (cents on the dollar)	34.3
Strength of insolvency framework index (0–16)	5.0

LAO PDR

LAO PDR		East Asia & Pacific		GNI per capita (US$)	1,730
Ease of doing business rank (1–190)	139	Overall distance to frontier (DTF) score (0–100)	53.29	Population	6,802,023

✔ **Starting a business** (rank)	160
DTF score for starting a business (0–100)	72.42
Procedures (number)	8
Time (days)	67
Cost (% of income per capita)	4.6
Minimum capital (% of income per capita)	0.0
Dealing with construction permits (rank)	47
DTF score for dealing with construction permits (0–100)	75.11
Procedures (number)	11
Time (days)	83
Cost (% of warehouse value)	0.5
Building quality control index (0–15)	6.5
✔ **Getting electricity** (rank)	155
DTF score for getting electricity (0–100)	48.67
Procedures (number)	6
Time (days)	134
Cost (% of income per capita)	1,408.7
Reliability of supply and transparency of tariffs index (0–8)	1
Registering property (rank)	65
DTF score for registering property (0–100)	68.70
Procedures (number)	4
Time (days)	53
Cost (% of property value)	1.0
Quality of land administration index (0–30)	9.5
Getting credit (rank)	75
DTF score for getting credit (0–100)	55.00
Strength of legal rights index (0–12)	6
Depth of credit information index (0–8)	5
Credit bureau coverage (% of adults)	0.0
Credit registry coverage (% of adults)	10.9
Protecting minority investors (rank)	165
DTF score for protecting minority investors (0–100)	35.00
Extent of disclosure index (0–10)	6
Extent of director liability index (0–10)	1
Ease of shareholder suits index (0–10)	3
Extent of shareholder rights index (0–10)	5
Extent of ownership and control index (0–10)	5
Extent of corporate transparency index (0–10)	1
Paying taxes (rank)	146
DTF score for paying taxes (0–100)	56.98
Payments (number per year)	35
Time (hours per year)	362
Total tax rate (% of profit)	26.2
Postfiling index (0–100)	29.76
Trading across borders (rank)	120
DTF score for trading across borders (0–100)	62.98
Time to export	
Documentary compliance (hours)	216
Border compliance (hours)	12
Cost to export	
Documentary compliance (US$)	235
Border compliance (US$)	73
Time to import	
Documentary compliance (hours)	216
Border compliance (hours)	14
Cost to import	
Documentary compliance (US$)	115
Border compliance (US$)	153
Enforcing contracts (rank)	88
DTF score for enforcing contracts (0–100)	58.07
Time (days)	443
Cost (% of claim)	31.6
Quality of judicial processes index (0–18)	6.5
Resolving insolvency (rank)	169
DTF score for resolving insolvency (0–100)	0.00
Time (years)	NO PRACTICE
Cost (% of estate)	NO PRACTICE
Recovery rate (cents on the dollar)	0.0
Strength of insolvency framework index (0–16)	0.0

Note: Most indicator sets refer to a case scenario in the largest business city of an economy, though for 11 economies the data are a population-weighted average for the two largest business cities. For some indicators a result of "no practice" may be recorded for an economy; see the data notes for more details. In starting a business, procedures (number), time (days) and cost (% of income per capita) are calculated as the average of both men and women. For the postfiling index, a result of "not applicable" may be recorded for an economy.

✔ Reform making it easier to do business ✘ Change making it more difficult to do business

LATVIA

LATVIA		Europe & Central Asia		GNI per capita (US$)	14,900
Ease of doing business rank (1–190)	14	Overall distance to frontier (DTF) score (0–100)	80.61	Population	1,978,440

Starting a business (rank)	22
DTF score for starting a business (0–100)	94.15
Procedures (number)	4
Time (days)	5.5
Cost (% of income per capita)	1.5
Minimum capital (% of income per capita)	0.0
Dealing with construction permits (rank)	23
DTF score for dealing with construction permits (0–100)	78.93
Procedures (number)	12
Time (days)	147
Cost (% of warehouse value)	0.3
Building quality control index (0–15)	12.0
Getting electricity (rank)	42
DTF score for getting electricity (0–100)	82.14
Procedures (number)	4
Time (days)	107
Cost (% of income per capita)	289.6
Reliability of supply and transparency of tariffs index (0–8)	7
Registering property (rank)	23
DTF score for registering property (0–100)	81.87
Procedures (number)	4
Time (days)	16.5
Cost (% of property value)	2.0
Quality of land administration index (0–30)	22.0
✔ **Getting credit** (rank)	7
DTF score for getting credit (0–100)	85.00
Strength of legal rights index (0–12)	9
Depth of credit information index (0–8)	8
Credit bureau coverage (% of adults)	63.2
Credit registry coverage (% of adults)	84.9
Protecting minority investors (rank)	42
DTF score for protecting minority investors (0–100)	63.33
Extent of disclosure index (0–10)	5
Extent of director liability index (0–10)	4
Ease of shareholder suits index (0–10)	8
Extent of shareholder rights index (0–10)	10
Extent of ownership and control index (0–10)	4
Extent of corporate transparency index (0–10)	7
✔ **Paying taxes** (rank)	15
DTF score for paying taxes (0–100)	89.79
Payments (number per year)	7
Time (hours per year)	168.5
Total tax rate (% of profit)	35.9
Postfiling index (0–100)	98.11
Trading across borders (rank)	25
DTF score for trading across borders (0–100)	95.26
Time to export	
Documentary compliance (hours)	2
Border compliance (hours)	24
Cost to export	
Documentary compliance (US$)	35
Border compliance (US$)	150
Time to import	
Documentary compliance (hours)	1
Border compliance (hours)	0
Cost to import	
Documentary compliance (US$)	0
Border compliance (US$)	0
Enforcing contracts (rank)	23
DTF score for enforcing contracts (0–100)	71.66
Time (days)	469
Cost (% of claim)	23.1
Quality of judicial processes index (0–18)	12.5
Resolving insolvency (rank)	44
DTF score for resolving insolvency (0–100)	63.95
Time (years)	1.5
Cost (% of estate)	10.0
Recovery rate (cents on the dollar)	49.1
Strength of insolvency framework index (0–16)	12.0

LEBANON

LEBANON		Middle East & North Africa		GNI per capita (US$)	7,930
Ease of doing business rank (1–190)	126	Overall distance to frontier (DTF) score (0–100)	55.90	Population	5,850,743

Starting a business (rank)	139
DTF score for starting a business (0–100)	78.45
Procedures (number)	8
Time (days)	15
Cost (% of income per capita)	40.6
Minimum capital (% of income per capita)	40.7
Dealing with construction permits (rank)	135
DTF score for dealing with construction permits (0–100)	61.85
Procedures (number)	18
Time (days)	244
Cost (% of warehouse value)	4.9
Building quality control index (0–15)	13.0
Getting electricity (rank)	122
DTF score for getting electricity (0–100)	60.12
Procedures (number)	5
Time (days)	75
Cost (% of income per capita)	114.8
Reliability of supply and transparency of tariffs index (0–8)	0
Registering property (rank)	103
DTF score for registering property (0–100)	59.94
Procedures (number)	8
Time (days)	34
Cost (% of property value)	5.9
Quality of land administration index (0–30)	16.0
Getting credit (rank)	118
DTF score for getting credit (0–100)	40.00
Strength of legal rights index (0–12)	2
Depth of credit information index (0–8)	6
Credit bureau coverage (% of adults)	0.0
Credit registry coverage (% of adults)	22.0
Protecting minority investors (rank)	145
DTF score for protecting minority investors (0–100)	40.00
Extent of disclosure index (0–10)	9
Extent of director liability index (0–10)	1
Ease of shareholder suits index (0–10)	5
Extent of shareholder rights index (0–10)	3
Extent of ownership and control index (0–10)	1
Extent of corporate transparency index (0–10)	5
Paying taxes (rank)	67
DTF score for paying taxes (0–100)	77.17
Payments (number per year)	20
Time (hours per year)	181
Total tax rate (% of profit)	30.3
Postfiling index (0–100)	63.32
Trading across borders (rank)	134
DTF score for trading across borders (0–100)	59.71
Time to export	
Documentary compliance (hours)	48
Border compliance (hours)	96
Cost to export	
Documentary compliance (US$)	100
Border compliance (US$)	410
Time to import	
Documentary compliance (hours)	72
Border compliance (hours)	180
Cost to import	
Documentary compliance (US$)	135
Border compliance (US$)	695
Enforcing contracts (rank)	127
DTF score for enforcing contracts (0–100)	51.70
Time (days)	721
Cost (% of claim)	30.8
Quality of judicial processes index (0–18)	7.0
Resolving insolvency (rank)	143
DTF score for resolving insolvency (0–100)	30.03
Time (years)	3.0
Cost (% of estate)	15.0
Recovery rate (cents on the dollar)	32.6
Strength of insolvency framework index (0–16)	4.0

LESOTHO

LESOTHO		Sub-Saharan Africa		GNI per capita (US$)	1,214
Ease of doing business rank (1–190)	100	Overall distance to frontier (DTF) score (0–100)	60.37	Population	2,135,022

Starting a business (rank)	117
DTF score for starting a business (0–100)	83.00
Procedures (number)	7
Time (days)	29
Cost (% of income per capita)	8.1
Minimum capital (% of income per capita)	0.0
Dealing with construction permits (rank)	171
DTF score for dealing with construction permits (0–100)	52.39
Procedures (number)	11
Time (days)	179
Cost (% of warehouse value)	11.8
Building quality control index (0–15)	5.5
Getting electricity (rank)	150
DTF score for getting electricity (0–100)	51.84
Procedures (number)	5
Time (days)	114
Cost (% of income per capita)	1,421.7
Reliability of supply and transparency of tariffs index (0–8)	0
Registering property (rank)	108
DTF score for registering property (0–100)	58.42
Procedures (number)	4
Time (days)	43
Cost (% of property value)	8.2
Quality of land administration index (0–30)	10.0
✔ **Getting credit** (rank)	82
DTF score for getting credit (0–100)	50.00
Strength of legal rights index (0–12)	5
Depth of credit information index (0–8)	5
Credit bureau coverage (% of adults)	7.1
Credit registry coverage (% of adults)	0.0
Protecting minority investors (rank)	106
DTF score for protecting minority investors (0–100)	50.00
Extent of disclosure index (0–10)	3
Extent of director liability index (0–10)	4
Ease of shareholder suits index (0–10)	9
Extent of shareholder rights index (0–10)	6
Extent of ownership and control index (0–10)	3
Extent of corporate transparency index (0–10)	5
Paying taxes (rank)	91
DTF score for paying taxes (0–100)	72.03
Payments (number per year)	32
Time (hours per year)	324
Total tax rate (% of profit)	13.6
Postfiling index (0–100)	78.94
Trading across borders (rank)	39
DTF score for trading across borders (0–100)	91.60
Time to export	
Documentary compliance (hours)	3
Border compliance (hours)	4
Cost to export	
Documentary compliance (US$)	90
Border compliance (US$)	150
Time to import	
Documentary compliance (hours)	3
Border compliance (hours)	5
Cost to import	
Documentary compliance (US$)	90
Border compliance (US$)	150
Enforcing contracts (rank)	94
DTF score for enforcing contracts (0–100)	57.18
Time (days)	615
Cost (% of claim)	31.3
Quality of judicial processes index (0–18)	8.5
Resolving insolvency (rank)	121
DTF score for resolving insolvency (0–100)	37.26
Time (years)	2.6
Cost (% of estate)	20.0
Recovery rate (cents on the dollar)	28.6
Strength of insolvency framework index (0–16)	7.0

Note: Most indicator sets refer to a case scenario in the largest business city of an economy, though for 11 economies the data are a population-weighted average for the two largest business cities. For some indicators a result of "no practice" may be recorded for an economy; see the data notes for more details. In starting a business, procedures (number), time (days) and cost (% of income per capita) are calculated as the average of both men and women. For the postfiling index, a result of "not applicable" may be recorded for an economy.

✔ Reform making it easier to do business ✘ Change making it more difficult to do business

LIBERIA

LIBERIA		Sub-Saharan Africa		GNI per capita (US$)	380
Ease of doing business rank (1–190)	**174**	**Overall distance to frontier (DTF) score (0–100)**	**41.41**	**Population**	**4,503,438**

Starting a business (rank)	37
DTF score for starting a business (0–100)	92.49
Procedures (number)	4
Time (days)	4.5
Cost (% of income per capita)	16.7
Minimum capital (% of income per capita)	0.0
Dealing with construction permits (rank)	175
DTF score for dealing with construction permits (0–100)	49.21
Procedures (number)	22
Time (days)	74
Cost (% of warehouse value)	6.9
Building quality control index (0–15)	2.0
Getting electricity (rank)	177
DTF score for getting electricity (0–100)	33.28
Procedures (number)	4
Time (days)	465
Cost (% of income per capita)	4,066.6
Reliability of supply and transparency of tariffs index (0–8)	0
Registering property (rank)	179
DTF score for registering property (0–100)	33.62
Procedures (number)	10
Time (days)	44
Cost (% of property value)	13.0
Quality of land administration index (0–30)	5.0
Getting credit (rank)	101
DTF score for getting credit (0–100)	45.00
Strength of legal rights index (0–12)	9
Depth of credit information index (0–8)	0
Credit bureau coverage (% of adults)	0.0
Credit registry coverage (% of adults)	1.7
Protecting minority investors (rank)	179
DTF score for protecting minority investors (0–100)	28.33
Extent of disclosure index (0–10)	4
Extent of director liability index (0–10)	1
Ease of shareholder suits index (0–10)	6
Extent of shareholder rights index (0–10)	3
Extent of ownership and control index (0–10)	2
Extent of corporate transparency index (0–10)	1
Paying taxes (rank)	72
DTF score for paying taxes (0–100)	76.07
Payments (number per year)	33
Time (hours per year)	139.5
Total tax rate (% of profit)	45.9
Postfiling index (0–100)	96.79
Trading across borders (rank)	185
DTF score for trading across borders (0–100)	17.64
Time to export	
Documentary compliance (hours)	186
Border compliance (hours)	193
Cost to export	
Documentary compliance (US$)	628
Border compliance (US$)	755
Time to import	
Documentary compliance (hours)	192
Border compliance (hours)	217
Cost to import	
Documentary compliance (US$)	528
Border compliance (US$)	660
Enforcing contracts (rank)	176
DTF score for enforcing contracts (0–100)	33.92
Time (days)	1,280
Cost (% of claim)	35.0
Quality of judicial processes index (0–18)	6.5
Resolving insolvency (rank)	168
DTF score for resolving insolvency (0–100)	4.59
Time (years)	3.0
Cost (% of estate)	42.5
Recovery rate (cents on the dollar)	8.5
Strength of insolvency framework index (0–16)	0.0

LIBYA

LIBYA		Middle East & North Africa		GNI per capita (US$)	6,030
Ease of doing business rank (1–190)	**188**	**Overall distance to frontier (DTF) score (0–100)**	**33.19**	**Population**	**6,278,438**

Starting a business (rank)	163
DTF score for starting a business (0–100)	71.48
Procedures (number)	10
Time (days)	35
Cost (% of income per capita)	31.2
Minimum capital (% of income per capita)	43.4
Dealing with construction permits (rank)	187
DTF score for dealing with construction permits (0–100)	0.00
Procedures (number)	NO PRACTICE
Time (days)	NO PRACTICE
Cost (% of warehouse value)	NO PRACTICE
Building quality control index (0–15)	0.0
Getting electricity (rank)	128
DTF score for getting electricity (0–100)	58.60
Procedures (number)	4
Time (days)	118
Cost (% of income per capita)	441.6
Reliability of supply and transparency of tariffs index (0–8)	0
Registering property (rank)	187
DTF score for registering property (0–100)	0.00
Procedures (number)	NO PRACTICE
Time (days)	NO PRACTICE
Cost (% of property value)	NO PRACTICE
Quality of land administration index (0–30)	NO PRACTICE
Getting credit (rank)	185
DTF score for getting credit (0–100)	0.00
Strength of legal rights index (0–12)	0
Depth of credit information index (0–8)	0
Credit bureau coverage (% of adults)	0.0
Credit registry coverage (% of adults)	0.5
Protecting minority investors (rank)	185
DTF score for protecting minority investors (0–100)	25.00
Extent of disclosure index (0–10)	4
Extent of director liability index (0–10)	1
Ease of shareholder suits index (0–10)	4
Extent of shareholder rights index (0–10)	4
Extent of ownership and control index (0–10)	1
Extent of corporate transparency index (0–10)	1
Paying taxes (rank)	121
DTF score for paying taxes (0–100)	63.78
Payments (number per year)	19
Time (hours per year)	889
Total tax rate (% of profit)	32.6
Postfiling index (0–100)	90.83
Trading across borders (rank)	114
DTF score for trading across borders (0–100)	64.66
Time to export	
Documentary compliance (hours)	72
Border compliance (hours)	72
Cost to export	
Documentary compliance (US$)	50
Border compliance (US$)	575
Time to import	
Documentary compliance (hours)	96
Border compliance (hours)	79
Cost to import	
Documentary compliance (US$)	60
Border compliance (US$)	637
Enforcing contracts (rank)	143
DTF score for enforcing contracts (0–100)	48.41
Time (days)	690
Cost (% of claim)	27.0
Quality of judicial processes index (0–18)	4.0
Resolving insolvency (rank)	169
DTF score for resolving insolvency (0–100)	0.00
Time (years)	NO PRACTICE
Cost (% of estate)	NO PRACTICE
Recovery rate (cents on the dollar)	0.0
Strength of insolvency framework index (0–16)	0.0

LITHUANIA

LITHUANIA		Europe & Central Asia		GNI per capita (US$)	15,000
Ease of doing business rank (1–190)	**21**	**Overall distance to frontier (DTF) score (0–100)**	**78.84**	**Population**	**2,910,199**

Starting a business (rank)	29
DTF score for starting a business (0–100)	92.99
Procedures (number)	4
Time (days)	5.5
Cost (% of income per capita)	0.6
Minimum capital (% of income per capita)	20.3
Dealing with construction permits (rank)	16
DTF score for dealing with construction permits (0–100)	80.44
Procedures (number)	12
Time (days)	103
Cost (% of warehouse value)	0.3
Building quality control index (0–15)	11.0
✔ **Getting electricity** (rank)	55
DTF score for getting electricity (0–100)	80.08
Procedures (number)	6
Time (days)	85
Cost (% of income per capita)	43.7
Reliability of supply and transparency of tariffs index (0–8)	8
Registering property (rank)	2
DTF score for registering property (0–100)	92.93
Procedures (number)	3
Time (days)	3.5
Cost (% of property value)	0.8
Quality of land administration index (0–30)	28.5
Getting credit (rank)	32
DTF score for getting credit (0–100)	70.00
Strength of legal rights index (0–12)	6
Depth of credit information index (0–8)	8
Credit bureau coverage (% of adults)	84.2
Credit registry coverage (% of adults)	37.8
Protecting minority investors (rank)	51
DTF score for protecting minority investors (0–100)	61.67
Extent of disclosure index (0–10)	7
Extent of director liability index (0–10)	4
Ease of shareholder suits index (0–10)	7
Extent of shareholder rights index (0–10)	7
Extent of ownership and control index (0–10)	6
Extent of corporate transparency index (0–10)	6
Paying taxes (rank)	27
DTF score for paying taxes (0–100)	85.44
Payments (number per year)	11
Time (hours per year)	171
Total tax rate (% of profit)	42.7
Postfiling index (0–100)	97.57
Trading across borders (rank)	19
DTF score for trading across borders (0–100)	97.70
Time to export	
Documentary compliance (hours)	3
Border compliance (hours)	9
Cost to export	
Documentary compliance (US$)	28
Border compliance (US$)	58
Time to import	
Documentary compliance (hours)	1
Border compliance (hours)	0
Cost to import	
Documentary compliance (US$)	0
Border compliance (US$)	0
Enforcing contracts (rank)	6
DTF score for enforcing contracts (0–100)	77.88
Time (days)	370
Cost (% of claim)	23.6
Quality of judicial processes index (0–18)	14.5
Resolving insolvency (rank)	66
DTF score for resolving insolvency (0–100)	49.23
Time (years)	2.3
Cost (% of estate)	10.0
Recovery rate (cents on the dollar)	45.0
Strength of insolvency framework index (0–16)	8.0

Note: Most indicator sets refer to a case scenario in the largest business city of an economy, though for 11 economies the data are a population-weighted average for the two largest business cities. For some indicators a result of "no practice" may be recorded for an economy; see the data notes for more details. In starting a business, procedures (number), time (days) and cost (% of income per capita) are calculated as the average of both men and women. For the postfiling index, a result of "not applicable" may be recorded for an economy.

✔ Reform making it easier to do business ✘ Change making it more difficult to do business

LUXEMBOURG

Ease of doing business rank (1–190)	**59**	**OECD high income**		**GNI per capita (US$)**	**77,000**
		Overall distance to frontier (DTF) score (0–100)	**68.81**	**Population**	**569,676**

Starting a business (rank)	67
DTF score for starting a business (0–100)	88.66
Procedures (number)	5
Time (days)	16.5
Cost (% of income per capita)	1.7
Minimum capital (% of income per capita)	19.5
Dealing with construction permits (rank)	7
DTF score for dealing with construction permits (0–100)	83.70
Procedures (number)	11
Time (days)	157
Cost (% of warehouse value)	0.7
Building quality control index (0–15)	15.0
Getting electricity (rank)	32
DTF score for getting electricity (0–100)	84.30
Procedures (number)	5
Time (days)	56
Cost (% of income per capita)	36.0
Reliability of supply and transparency of tariffs index (0–8)	7
Registering property (rank)	88
DTF score for registering property (0–100)	63.84
Procedures (number)	7
Time (days)	26.5
Cost (% of property value)	10.1
Quality of land administration index (0–30)	25.5
Getting credit (rank)	170
DTF score for getting credit (0–100)	15.00
Strength of legal rights index (0–12)	3
Depth of credit information index (0–8)	0
Credit bureau coverage (% of adults)	0.0
Credit registry coverage (% of adults)	0.0
Protecting minority investors (rank)	123
DTF score for protecting minority investors (0–100)	45.00
Extent of disclosure index (0–10)	6
Extent of director liability index (0–10)	4
Ease of shareholder suits index (0–10)	3
Extent of shareholder rights index (0–10)	5
Extent of ownership and control index (0–10)	3
Extent of corporate transparency index (0–10)	6
Paying taxes (rank)	16
DTF score for paying taxes (0–100)	88.92
Payments (number per year)	23
Time (hours per year)	55
Total tax rate (% of profit)	20.8
Postfiling index (0–100)	89.94
Trading across borders (rank)	1
DTF score for trading across borders (0–100)	100.00
Time to export	
Documentary compliance (hours)	1
Border compliance (hours)	0
Cost to export	
Documentary compliance (US$)	0
Border compliance (US$)	0
Time to import	
Documentary compliance (hours)	1
Border compliance (hours)	0
Cost to import	
Documentary compliance (US$)	0
Border compliance (US$)	0
Enforcing contracts (rank)	15
DTF score for enforcing contracts (0–100)	73.32
Time (days)	321
Cost (% of claim)	9.7
Quality of judicial processes index (0–18)	8.5
Resolving insolvency (rank)	82
DTF score for resolving insolvency (0–100)	45.40
Time (years)	2.0
Cost (% of estate)	14.5
Recovery rate (cents on the dollar)	43.7
Strength of insolvency framework index (0–16)	7.0

MACEDONIA, FYR

Ease of doing business rank (1–190)	**10**	**Europe & Central Asia**		**GNI per capita (US$)**	**5,140**
		Overall distance to frontier (DTF) score (0–100)	**81.74**	**Population**	**2,078,453**

Starting a business (rank)	4
DTF score for starting a business (0–100)	98.14
Procedures (number)	2
Time (days)	2
Cost (% of income per capita)	0.1
Minimum capital (% of income per capita)	0.0
Dealing with construction permits (rank)	11
DTF score for dealing with construction permits (0–100)	81.71
Procedures (number)	9
Time (days)	89
Cost (% of warehouse value)	5.1
Building quality control index (0–15)	13.0
Getting electricity (rank)	29
DTF score for getting electricity (0–100)	84.51
Procedures (number)	3
Time (days)	97
Cost (% of income per capita)	212.3
Reliability of supply and transparency of tariffs index (0–8)	6
Registering property (rank)	48
DTF score for registering property (0–100)	74.05
Procedures (number)	7
Time (days)	30
Cost (% of property value)	3.2
Quality of land administration index (0–30)	24.5
✔ **Getting credit** (rank)	16
DTF score for getting credit (0–100)	80.00
Strength of legal rights index (0–12)	9
Depth of credit information index (0–8)	7
Credit bureau coverage (% of adults)	94.5
Credit registry coverage (% of adults)	40.0
✔ **Protecting minority investors** (rank)	13
DTF score for protecting minority investors (0–100)	73.33
Extent of disclosure index (0–10)	8
Extent of director liability index (0–10)	9
Ease of shareholder suits index (0–10)	5
Extent of shareholder rights index (0–10)	8
Extent of ownership and control index (0–10)	7
Extent of corporate transparency index (0–10)	7
Paying taxes (rank)	9
DTF score for paying taxes (0–100)	91.67
Payments (number per year)	7
Time (hours per year)	119
Total tax rate (% of profit)	13.0
Postfiling index (0–100)	84.17
Trading across borders (rank)	27
DTF score for trading across borders (0–100)	93.87
Time to export	
Documentary compliance (hours)	2
Border compliance (hours)	9
Cost to export	
Documentary compliance (US$)	45
Border compliance (US$)	103
Time to import	
Documentary compliance (hours)	3
Border compliance (hours)	8
Cost to import	
Documentary compliance (US$)	50
Border compliance (US$)	150
✘ **Enforcing contracts** (rank)	36
DTF score for enforcing contracts (0–100)	67.79
Time (days)	634
Cost (% of claim)	28.8
Quality of judicial processes index (0–18)	14.0
✔ **Resolving insolvency** (rank)	32
DTF score for resolving insolvency (0–100)	72.38
Time (years)	1.5
Cost (% of estate)	10.0
Recovery rate (cents on the dollar)	47.4
Strength of insolvency framework index (0–16)	15.0

MADAGASCAR

Ease of doing business rank (1–190)	**167**	**Sub-Saharan Africa**		**GNI per capita (US$)**	**420**
		Overall distance to frontier (DTF) score (0–100)	**45.10**	**Population**	**24,235,390**

✔ **Starting a business** (rank)	113
DTF score for starting a business (0–100)	83.48
Procedures (number)	7
Time (days)	11
Cost (% of income per capita)	40.4
Minimum capital (% of income per capita)	0.0
✔ **Dealing with construction permits** (rank)	184
DTF score for dealing with construction permits (0–100)	36.88
Procedures (number)	15
Time (days)	185
Cost (% of warehouse value)	28.2
Building quality control index (0–15)	5.0
Getting electricity (rank)	185
DTF score for getting electricity (0–100)	19.91
Procedures (number)	6
Time (days)	450
Cost (% of income per capita)	5,699.2
Reliability of supply and transparency of tariffs index (0–8)	0
Registering property (rank)	159
DTF score for registering property (0–100)	44.56
Procedures (number)	6
Time (days)	100
Cost (% of property value)	9.2
Quality of land administration index (0–30)	8.5
Getting credit (rank)	170
DTF score for getting credit (0–100)	15.00
Strength of legal rights index (0–12)	3
Depth of credit information index (0–8)	0
Credit bureau coverage (% of adults)	0.0
Credit registry coverage (% of adults)	3.0
Protecting minority investors (rank)	114
DTF score for protecting minority investors (0–100)	48.33
Extent of disclosure index (0–10)	7
Extent of director liability index (0–10)	6
Ease of shareholder suits index (0–10)	5
Extent of shareholder rights index (0–10)	4
Extent of ownership and control index (0–10)	4
Extent of corporate transparency index (0–10)	3
Paying taxes (rank)	117
DTF score for paying taxes (0–100)	64.80
Payments (number per year)	23
Time (hours per year)	183
Total tax rate (% of profit)	38.1
Postfiling index (0–100)	30.21
✔ **Trading across borders** (rank)	129
DTF score for trading across borders (0–100)	60.95
Time to export	
Documentary compliance (hours)	49
Border compliance (hours)	70
Cost to export	
Documentary compliance (US$)	117
Border compliance (US$)	868
Time to import	
Documentary compliance (hours)	58
Border compliance (hours)	99
Cost to import	
Documentary compliance (US$)	150
Border compliance (US$)	595
Enforcing contracts (rank)	158
DTF score for enforcing contracts (0–100)	42.85
Time (days)	871
Cost (% of claim)	33.6
Quality of judicial processes index (0–18)	5.0
Resolving insolvency (rank)	127
DTF score for resolving insolvency (0–100)	34.24
Time (years)	3.0
Cost (% of estate)	8.5
Recovery rate (cents on the dollar)	11.4
Strength of insolvency framework index (0–16)	9.0

Note: Most indicator sets refer to a case scenario in the largest business city of an economy, though for 11 economies the data are a population-weighted average for the two largest business cities. For some indicators a result of "no practice" may be recorded for an economy; see the data notes for more details. In starting a business, procedures (number), time (days) and cost (% of income per capita) are calculated as the average of both men and women. For the postfiling index, a result of "not applicable" may be recorded for an economy.

✔ Reform making it easier to do business ✘ Change making it more difficult to do business

MALAWI

MALAWI		Sub-Saharan Africa		GNI per capita (US$)	350
Ease of doing business rank (1–190)	133	Overall distance to frontier (DTF) score (0–100)	54.39	Population	17,215,232

✔ **Starting a business** (rank)	150
DTF score for starting a business (0–100)	76.73
Procedures (number)	7
Time (days)	37
Cost (% of income per capita)	42.2
Minimum capital (% of income per capita)	0.0
Dealing with construction permits (rank)	65
DTF score for dealing with construction permits (0–100)	72.45
Procedures (number)	13
Time (days)	153
Cost (% of warehouse value)	1.0
Building quality control index (0–15)	9.5
Getting electricity (rank)	169
DTF score for getting electricity (0–100)	42.36
Procedures (number)	6
Time (days)	127
Cost (% of income per capita)	2,688.0
Reliability of supply and transparency of tariffs index (0–8)	0
Registering property (rank)	95
DTF score for registering property (0–100)	62.41
Procedures (number)	6
Time (days)	69
Cost (% of property value)	1.7
Quality of land administration index (0–30)	10.5
✔ **Getting credit** (rank)	101
DTF score for getting credit (0–100)	45.00
Strength of legal rights index (0–12)	9
Depth of credit information index (0–8)	0
Credit bureau coverage (% of adults)	0.0
Credit registry coverage (% of adults)	0.0
Protecting minority investors (rank)	132
DTF score for protecting minority investors (0–100)	43.33
Extent of disclosure index (0–10)	4
Extent of director liability index (0–10)	7
Ease of shareholder suits index (0–10)	6
Extent of shareholder rights index (0–10)	5
Extent of ownership and control index (0–10)	1
Extent of corporate transparency index (0–10)	3
Paying taxes (rank)	102
DTF score for paying taxes (0–100)	69.58
Payments (number per year)	35
Time (hours per year)	177.5
Total tax rate (% of profit)	34.5
Postfiling index (0–100)	63.35
Trading across borders (rank)	118
DTF score for trading across borders (0–100)	63.32
Time to export	
Documentary compliance (hours)	83
Border compliance (hours)	85
Cost to export	
Documentary compliance (US$)	342
Border compliance (US$)	243
Time to import	
Documentary compliance (hours)	63
Border compliance (hours)	64
Cost to import	
Documentary compliance (US$)	162
Border compliance (US$)	143
Enforcing contracts (rank)	148
DTF score for enforcing contracts (0–100)	46.48
Time (days)	522
Cost (% of claim)	69.1
Quality of judicial processes index (0–18)	9.0
Resolving insolvency (rank)	162
DTF score for resolving insolvency (0–100)	22.25
Time (years)	2.6
Cost (% of estate)	25.0
Recovery rate (cents on the dollar)	12.3
Strength of insolvency framework index (0–16)	5.0

MALAYSIA

MALAYSIA		East Asia & Pacific		GNI per capita (US$)	10,570
Ease of doing business rank (1–190)	23	Overall distance to frontier (DTF) score (0–100)	78.11	Population	30,331,007

✘ **Starting a business** (rank)	112
DTF score for starting a business (0–100)	83.67
Procedures (number)	8.5
Time (days)	18.5
Cost (% of income per capita)	6.2
Minimum capital (% of income per capita)	0.0
Dealing with construction permits (rank)	13
DTF score for dealing with construction permits (0–100)	81.10
Procedures (number)	15
Time (days)	79
Cost (% of warehouse value)	1.4
Building quality control index (0–15)	13.0
Getting electricity (rank)	8
DTF score for getting electricity (0–100)	94.34
Procedures (number)	4
Time (days)	31
Cost (% of income per capita)	26.6
Reliability of supply and transparency of tariffs index (0–8)	8
Registering property (rank)	40
DTF score for registering property (0–100)	76.29
Procedures (number)	8
Time (days)	13
Cost (% of property value)	3.4
Quality of land administration index (0–30)	27.5
✔ **Getting credit** (rank)	20
DTF score for getting credit (0–100)	75.00
Strength of legal rights index (0–12)	7
Depth of credit information index (0–8)	8
Credit bureau coverage (% of adults)	76.4
Credit registry coverage (% of adults)	62.4
Protecting minority investors (rank)	3
DTF score for protecting minority investors (0–100)	80.00
Extent of disclosure index (0–10)	10
Extent of director liability index (0–10)	9
Ease of shareholder suits index (0–10)	7
Extent of shareholder rights index (0–10)	8
Extent of ownership and control index (0–10)	7
Extent of corporate transparency index (0–10)	7
✔ **Paying taxes** (rank)	61
DTF score for paying taxes (0–100)	79.20
Payments (number per year)	9
Time (hours per year)	164
Total tax rate (% of profit)	40.0
Postfiling index (0–100)	64.31
Trading across borders (rank)	60
DTF score for trading across borders (0–100)	82.38
Time to export	
Documentary compliance (hours)	10
Border compliance (hours)	48
Cost to export	
Documentary compliance (US$)	45
Border compliance (US$)	321
Time to import	
Documentary compliance (hours)	10
Border compliance (hours)	72
Cost to import	
Documentary compliance (US$)	60
Border compliance (US$)	321
Enforcing contracts (rank)	42
DTF score for enforcing contracts (0–100)	66.61
Time (days)	425
Cost (% of claim)	37.3
Quality of judicial processes index (0–18)	12.0
Resolving insolvency (rank)	46
DTF score for resolving insolvency (0–100)	62.49
Time (years)	1.0
Cost (% of estate)	10.0
Recovery rate (cents on the dollar)	81.3
Strength of insolvency framework index (0–16)	6.0

MALDIVES

MALDIVES		South Asia		GNI per capita (US$)	6,670
Ease of doing business rank (1–190)	135	Overall distance to frontier (DTF) score (0–100)	53.94	Population	409,163

Starting a business (rank)	65
DTF score for starting a business (0–100)	88.98
Procedures (number)	6
Time (days)	12
Cost (% of income per capita)	5.2
Minimum capital (% of income per capita)	1.9
Dealing with construction permits (rank)	62
DTF score for dealing with construction permits (0–100)	72.80
Procedures (number)	10
Time (days)	140
Cost (% of warehouse value)	0.5
Building quality control index (0–15)	7.0
Getting electricity (rank)	145
DTF score for getting electricity (0–100)	53.57
Procedures (number)	6
Time (days)	91
Cost (% of income per capita)	321.7
Reliability of supply and transparency of tariffs index (0–8)	0
Registering property (rank)	172
DTF score for registering property (0–100)	39.97
Procedures (number)	6
Time (days)	57
Cost (% of property value)	15.9
Quality of land administration index (0–30)	8.5
Getting credit (rank)	133
DTF score for getting credit (0–100)	35.00
Strength of legal rights index (0–12)	2
Depth of credit information index (0–8)	5
Credit bureau coverage (% of adults)	0.0
Credit registry coverage (% of adults)	22.6
Protecting minority investors (rank)	123
DTF score for protecting minority investors (0–100)	45.00
Extent of disclosure index (0–10)	0
Extent of director liability index (0–10)	8
Ease of shareholder suits index (0–10)	8
Extent of shareholder rights index (0–10)	4
Extent of ownership and control index (0–10)	2
Extent of corporate transparency index (0–10)	5
Paying taxes (rank)	134
DTF score for paying taxes (0–100)	60.02
Payments (number per year)	30
Time (hours per year)	405.5
Total tax rate (% of profit)	30.2
Postfiling index (0–100)	45.87
Trading across borders (rank)	147
DTF score for trading across borders (0–100)	55.87
Time to export	
Documentary compliance (hours)	48
Border compliance (hours)	42
Cost to export	
Documentary compliance (US$)	300
Border compliance (US$)	596
Time to import	
Documentary compliance (hours)	61
Border compliance (hours)	100
Cost to import	
Documentary compliance (US$)	180
Border compliance (US$)	981
Enforcing contracts (rank)	105
DTF score for enforcing contracts (0–100)	55.07
Time (days)	760
Cost (% of claim)	16.5
Quality of judicial processes index (0–18)	6.5
Resolving insolvency (rank)	135
DTF score for resolving insolvency (0–100)	33.14
Time (years)	1.5
Cost (% of estate)	4.0
Recovery rate (cents on the dollar)	50.0
Strength of insolvency framework index (0–16)	2.0

Note: Most indicator sets refer to a case scenario in the largest business city of an economy, though for 11 economies the data are a population-weighted average for the two largest business cities. For some indicators a result of "no practice" may be recorded for an economy; see the data notes for more details. In starting a business, procedures (number), time (days) and cost (% of income per capita) are calculated as the average of both men and women. For the postfiling index, a result of "not applicable" may be recorded for an economy.

✔ Reform making it easier to do business ✘ Change making it more difficult to do business

MALI

MALI		Sub-Saharan Africa		GNI per capita (US$)	790
Ease of doing business rank (1–190)	141	Overall distance to frontier (DTF) score (0–100)	52.96	Population	17,599,694
✔ **Starting a business** (rank)	108	✔ **Getting credit** (rank)	139	**Trading across borders** (rank)	89
DTF score for starting a business (0–100)	84.12	DTF score for getting credit (0–100)	30.00	DTF score for trading across borders (0–100)	70.79
Procedures (number)	5	Strength of legal rights index (0–12)	6	*Time to export*	
Time (days)	8.5	Depth of credit information index (0–8)	0	Documentary compliance (hours)	48
Cost (% of income per capita)	61.0	Credit bureau coverage (% of adults)	0.0	Border compliance (hours)	48
Minimum capital (% of income per capita)	5.9	Credit registry coverage (% of adults)	0.1	*Cost to export*	
				Documentary compliance (US$)	33
Dealing with construction permits (rank)	142	**Protecting minority investors** (rank)	145	Border compliance (US$)	242
DTF score for dealing with construction permits (0–100)	61.02	DTF score for protecting minority investors (0–100)	40.00	*Time to import*	
Procedures (number)	13	Extent of disclosure index (0–10)	7	Documentary compliance (hours)	77
Time (days)	124	Extent of director liability index (0–10)	1	Border compliance (hours)	98
Cost (% of warehouse value)	6.5	Ease of shareholder suits index (0–10)	5	*Cost to import*	
Building quality control index (0–15)	5.5	Extent of shareholder rights index (0–10)	5	Documentary compliance (US$)	375
		Extent of ownership and control index (0–10)	4	Border compliance (US$)	298
Getting electricity (rank)	152	Extent of corporate transparency index (0–10)	2		
DTF score for getting electricity (0–100)	50.60			**Enforcing contracts** (rank)	156
Procedures (number)	4	**Paying taxes** (rank)	144	DTF score for enforcing contracts (0–100)	43.73
Time (days)	120	DTF score for paying taxes (0–100)	57.50	Time (days)	620
Cost (% of income per capita)	2,964.7	Payments (number per year)	35	Cost (% of claim)	52.0
Reliability of supply and transparency of tariffs index (0–8)	0	Time (hours per year)	270	Quality of judicial processes index (0–18)	5.5
		Total tax rate (% of profit)	48.3		
Registering property (rank)	135	Postfiling index (0–100)	49.54	✔ **Resolving insolvency** (rank)	99
DTF score for registering property (0–100)	50.37			DTF score for resolving insolvency (0–100)	41.46
Procedures (number)	5			Time (years)	3.6
Time (days)	29			Cost (% of estate)	18.0
Cost (% of property value)	11.8			Recovery rate (cents on the dollar)	24.8
Quality of land administration index (0–30)	8.0			Strength of insolvency framework index (0–16)	9.0

MALTA

MALTA		Middle East & North Africa		GNI per capita (US$)	19,687
Ease of doing business rank (1–190)	76	Overall distance to frontier (DTF) score (0–100)	65.01	Population	431,333
✔ **Starting a business** (rank)	132	✔ **Getting credit** (rank)	139	**Trading across borders** (rank)	40
DTF score for starting a business (0–100)	80.21	DTF score for getting credit (0–100)	30.00	DTF score for trading across borders (0–100)	91.01
Procedures (number)	9	Strength of legal rights index (0–12)	2	*Time to export*	
Time (days)	26	Depth of credit information index (0–8)	4	Documentary compliance (hours)	3
Cost (% of income per capita)	12.3	Credit bureau coverage (% of adults)	0.0	Border compliance (hours)	24
Minimum capital (% of income per capita)	1.3	Credit registry coverage (% of adults)	53.6	*Cost to export*	
				Documentary compliance (US$)	25
Dealing with construction permits (rank)	82	**Protecting minority investors** (rank)	32	Border compliance (US$)	325
DTF score for dealing with construction permits (0–100)	69.99	DTF score for protecting minority investors (0–100)	65.00	*Time to import*	
Procedures (number)	15	Extent of disclosure index (0–10)	3	Documentary compliance (hours)	1
Time (days)	167	Extent of director liability index (0–10)	6	Border compliance (hours)	2
Cost (% of warehouse value)	2.5	Ease of shareholder suits index (0–10)	8	*Cost to import*	
Building quality control index (0–15)	11.0	Extent of shareholder rights index (0–10)	8	Documentary compliance (US$)	0
		Extent of ownership and control index (0–10)	5	Border compliance (US$)	230
Getting electricity (rank)	77	Extent of corporate transparency index (0–10)	9		
DTF score for getting electricity (0–100)	73.00			**Enforcing contracts** (rank)	58
Procedures (number)	5	✘ **Paying taxes** (rank)	33	DTF score for enforcing contracts (0–100)	62.17
Time (days)	121	DTF score for paying taxes (0–100)	84.59	Time (days)	505
Cost (% of income per capita)	394.7	Payments (number per year)	8	Cost (% of claim)	35.9
Reliability of supply and transparency of tariffs index (0–8)	6	Time (hours per year)	139	Quality of judicial processes index (0–18)	10.5
		Total tax rate (% of profit)	43.8		
Registering property (rank)	147	Postfiling index (0–100)	85.95	**Resolving insolvency** (rank)	84
DTF score for registering property (0–100)	48.81			DTF score for resolving insolvency (0–100)	45.35
Procedures (number)	7			Time (years)	3.0
Time (days)	15			Cost (% of estate)	10.0
Cost (% of property value)	13.5			Recovery rate (cents on the dollar)	40.7
Quality of land administration index (0–30)	12.5			Strength of insolvency framework index (0–16)	7.5

MARSHALL ISLANDS

MARSHALL ISLANDS		East Asia & Pacific		GNI per capita (US$)	4,241
Ease of doing business rank (1–190)	143	Overall distance to frontier (DTF) score (0–100)	51.92	Population	52,993
Starting a business (rank)	70	**Getting credit** (rank)	82	**Trading across borders** (rank)	64
DTF score for starting a business (0–100)	88.41	DTF score for getting credit (0–100)	50.00	DTF score for trading across borders (0–100)	80.59
Procedures (number)	5	Strength of legal rights index (0–12)	10	*Time to export*	
Time (days)	17	Depth of credit information index (0–8)	0	Documentary compliance (hours)	24
Cost (% of income per capita)	12.5	Credit bureau coverage (% of adults)	0.0	Border compliance (hours)	60
Minimum capital (% of income per capita)	0.0	Credit registry coverage (% of adults)	0.0	*Cost to export*	
				Documentary compliance (US$)	20
Dealing with construction permits (rank)	79	**Protecting minority investors** (rank)	175	Border compliance (US$)	220
DTF score for dealing with construction permits (0–100)	70.77	DTF score for protecting minority investors (0–100)	31.67	*Time to import*	
Procedures (number)	7	Extent of disclosure index (0–10)	2	Documentary compliance (hours)	60
Time (days)	38	Extent of director liability index (0–10)	0	Border compliance (hours)	84
Cost (% of warehouse value)	2.4	Ease of shareholder suits index (0–10)	8	*Cost to import*	
Building quality control index (0–15)	1.0	Extent of shareholder rights index (0–10)	5	Documentary compliance (US$)	43
		Extent of ownership and control index (0–10)	2	Border compliance (US$)	220
Getting electricity (rank)	126	Extent of corporate transparency index (0–10)	2		
DTF score for getting electricity (0–100)	59.14			**Enforcing contracts** (rank)	99
Procedures (number)	5	**Paying taxes** (rank)	82	DTF score for enforcing contracts (0–100)	55.93
Time (days)	67	DTF score for paying taxes (0–100)	73.45	Time (days)	616
Cost (% of income per capita)	712.1	Payments (number per year)	9	Cost (% of claim)	32.1
Reliability of supply and transparency of tariffs index (0–8)	0	Time (hours per year)	120	Quality of judicial processes index (0–18)	8.0
		Total tax rate (% of profit)	64.8		
Registering property (rank)	187	Postfiling index (0–100)	NOT APPLICABLE	**Resolving insolvency** (rank)	167
DTF score for registering property (0–100)	0.00			DTF score for resolving insolvency (0–100)	9.19
Procedures (number)	NO PRACTICE			Time (years)	2.0
Time (days)	NO PRACTICE			Cost (% of estate)	38.0
Cost (% of property value)	NO PRACTICE			Recovery rate (cents on the dollar)	17.1
Quality of land administration index (0–30)	NO PRACTICE			Strength of insolvency framework index (0–16)	0.0

Note: Most indicator sets refer to a case scenario in the largest business city of an economy, though for 11 economies the data are a population-weighted average for the two largest business cities. For some indicators a result of "no practice" may be recorded for an economy; see the data notes for more details. In starting a business, procedures (number), time (days) and cost (% of income per capita) are calculated as the average of both men and women. For the postfiling index, a result of "not applicable" may be recorded for an economy.

✔ Reform making it easier to do business ✘ Change making it more difficult to do business

MAURITANIA

Ease of doing business rank (1–190)	160	Sub-Saharan Africa — Overall distance to frontier (DTF) score (0–100)	47.21	GNI per capita (US$)	1,200
				Population	4,067,564

Starting a business (rank)	80
DTF score for starting a business (0–100)	86.87
Procedures (number)	7
Time (days)	8
Cost (% of income per capita)	19.4
Minimum capital (% of income per capita)	0.0
Dealing with construction permits (rank)	118
DTF score for dealing with construction permits (0–100)	65.17
Procedures (number)	13
Time (days)	104
Cost (% of warehouse value)	4.3
Building quality control index (0–15)	5.5
Getting electricity (rank)	146
DTF score for getting electricity (0–100)	52.98
Procedures (number)	5
Time (days)	67
Cost (% of income per capita)	4,735.1
Reliability of supply and transparency of tariffs index (0–8)	2
Registering property (rank)	102
DTF score for registering property (0–100)	59.97
Procedures (number)	4
Time (days)	49
Cost (% of property value)	4.6
Quality of land administration index (0–30)	5.5
✔ **Getting credit** (rank)	157
DTF score for getting credit (0–100)	25.00
Strength of legal rights index (0–12)	2
Depth of credit information index (0–8)	3
Credit bureau coverage (% of adults)	0.0
Credit registry coverage (% of adults)	6.6
✔ **Protecting minority investors** (rank)	123
DTF score for protecting minority investors (0–100)	45.00
Extent of disclosure index (0–10)	6
Extent of director liability index (0–10)	3
Ease of shareholder suits index (0–10)	7
Extent of shareholder rights index (0–10)	4
Extent of ownership and control index (0–10)	4
Extent of corporate transparency index (0–10)	3
✔ **Paying taxes** (rank)	188
DTF score for paying taxes (0–100)	19.69
Payments (number per year)	45
Time (hours per year)	724
Total tax rate (% of profit)	71.3
Postfiling index (0–100)	18.98
✔ **Trading across borders** (rank)	137
DTF score for trading across borders (0–100)	58.82
Time to export	
Documentary compliance (hours)	51
Border compliance (hours)	72
Cost to export	
Documentary compliance (US$)	92
Border compliance (US$)	749
Time to import	
Documentary compliance (hours)	64
Border compliance (hours)	84
Cost to import	
Documentary compliance (US$)	400
Border compliance (US$)	582
Enforcing contracts (rank)	83
DTF score for enforcing contracts (0–100)	58.58
Time (days)	370
Cost (% of claim)	23.2
Quality of judicial processes index (0–18)	4.0
Resolving insolvency (rank)	169
DTF score for resolving insolvency (0–100)	0.00
Time (years)	NO PRACTICE
Cost (% of estate)	NO PRACTICE
Recovery rate (cents on the dollar)	0.0
Strength of insolvency framework index (0–16)	0.0

MAURITIUS

Ease of doing business rank (1–190)	49	Sub-Saharan Africa — Overall distance to frontier (DTF) score (0–100)	72.27	GNI per capita (US$)	9,610
				Population	1,262,605

Starting a business (rank)	48
DTF score for starting a business (0–100)	91.65
Procedures (number)	5.5
Time (days)	6.5
Cost (% of income per capita)	1.8
Minimum capital (% of income per capita)	0.0
Dealing with construction permits (rank)	33
DTF score for dealing with construction permits (0–100)	76.55
Procedures (number)	15
Time (days)	156
Cost (% of warehouse value)	0.6
Building quality control index (0–15)	13.0
Getting electricity (rank)	110
DTF score for getting electricity (0–100)	63.22
Procedures (number)	4
Time (days)	81
Cost (% of income per capita)	247.7
Reliability of supply and transparency of tariffs index (0–8)	0
✔ **Registering property** (rank)	98
DTF score for registering property (0–100)	61.99
Procedures (number)	4
Time (days)	14
Cost (% of property value)	10.6
Quality of land administration index (0–30)	15.0
Getting credit (rank)	44
DTF score for getting credit (0–100)	65.00
Strength of legal rights index (0–12)	6
Depth of credit information index (0–8)	7
Credit bureau coverage (% of adults)	0.0
Credit registry coverage (% of adults)	83.3
Protecting minority investors (rank)	32
DTF score for protecting minority investors (0–100)	65.00
Extent of disclosure index (0–10)	6
Extent of director liability index (0–10)	8
Ease of shareholder suits index (0–10)	9
Extent of shareholder rights index (0–10)	6
Extent of ownership and control index (0–10)	5
Extent of corporate transparency index (0–10)	5
Paying taxes (rank)	45
DTF score for paying taxes (0–100)	82.96
Payments (number per year)	8
Time (hours per year)	152
Total tax rate (% of profit)	21.8
Postfiling index (0–100)	56.08
Trading across borders (rank)	74
DTF score for trading across borders (0–100)	78.67
Time to export	
Documentary compliance (hours)	9
Border compliance (hours)	48
Cost to export	
Documentary compliance (US$)	128
Border compliance (US$)	303
Time to import	
Documentary compliance (hours)	9
Border compliance (hours)	51
Cost to import	
Documentary compliance (US$)	166
Border compliance (US$)	372
Enforcing contracts (rank)	34
DTF score for enforcing contracts (0–100)	68.65
Time (days)	519
Cost (% of claim)	25.0
Quality of judicial processes index (0–18)	12.0
Resolving insolvency (rank)	39
DTF score for resolving insolvency (0–100)	69.06
Time (years)	1.7
Cost (% of estate)	14.5
Recovery rate (cents on the dollar)	67.4
Strength of insolvency framework index (0–16)	10.5

MEXICO

Ease of doing business rank (1–190)	47	Latin America & Caribbean — Overall distance to frontier (DTF) score (0–100)	72.29	GNI per capita (US$)	9,710
				Population	127,017,224

✘ **Starting a business** (rank)	93
DTF score for starting a business (0–100)	85.74
Procedures (number)	7.8
Time (days)	8.4
Cost (% of income per capita)	17.8
Minimum capital (% of income per capita)	0.0
Dealing with construction permits (rank)	83
DTF score for dealing with construction permits (0–100)	69.79
Procedures (number)	13
Time (days)	86.4
Cost (% of warehouse value)	9.8
Building quality control index (0–15)	11.7
Getting electricity (rank)	98
DTF score for getting electricity (0–100)	68.32
Procedures (number)	6.8
Time (days)	100.4
Cost (% of income per capita)	336.7
Reliability of supply and transparency of tariffs index (0–8)	6.2
✔ **Registering property** (rank)	101
DTF score for registering property (0–100)	61.05
Procedures (number)	7.7
Time (days)	42.1
Cost (% of property value)	5.2
Quality of land administration index (0–30)	16.3
Getting credit (rank)	5
DTF score for getting credit (0–100)	90.00
Strength of legal rights index (0–12)	10
Depth of credit information index (0–8)	8
Credit bureau coverage (% of adults)	100.0
Credit registry coverage (% of adults)	0.0
Protecting minority investors (rank)	53
DTF score for protecting minority investors (0–100)	60.00
Extent of disclosure index (0–10)	8
Extent of director liability index (0–10)	5
Ease of shareholder suits index (0–10)	5
Extent of shareholder rights index (0–10)	8
Extent of ownership and control index (0–10)	6
Extent of corporate transparency index (0–10)	4
Paying taxes (rank)	114
DTF score for paying taxes (0–100)	65.81
Payments (number per year)	6
Time (hours per year)	286
Total tax rate (% of profit)	52.0
Postfiling index (0–100)	42.64
Trading across borders (rank)	61
DTF score for trading across borders (0–100)	82.09
Time to export	
Documentary compliance (hours)	8
Border compliance (hours)	20.4
Cost to export	
Documentary compliance (US$)	60
Border compliance (US$)	400
Time to import	
Documentary compliance (hours)	17.6
Border compliance (hours)	44.2
Cost to import	
Documentary compliance (US$)	100
Border compliance (US$)	450
Enforcing contracts (rank)	40
DTF score for enforcing contracts (0–100)	67.01
Time (days)	340.7
Cost (% of claim)	33.0
Quality of judicial processes index (0–18)	10.1
Resolving insolvency (rank)	30
DTF score for resolving insolvency (0–100)	73.11
Time (years)	1.8
Cost (% of estate)	18.0
Recovery rate (cents on the dollar)	69.1
Strength of insolvency framework index (0–16)	11.5

Note: Most indicator sets refer to a case scenario in the largest business city of an economy, though for 11 economies the data are a population-weighted average for the two largest business cities. For some indicators a result of "no practice" may be recorded for an economy; see the data notes for more details. In starting a business, procedures (number), time (days) and cost (% of income per capita) are calculated as the average of both men and women. For the postfiling index, a result of "not applicable" may be recorded for an economy.

✔ Reform making it easier to do business ✘ Change making it more difficult to do business

MICRONESIA, FED. STS.

MICRONESIA, FED. STS.		East Asia & Pacific		GNI per capita (US$)	3,201
Ease of doing business rank (1–190)	151	Overall distance to frontier (DTF) score (0–100)	49.48	Population	104,460

Starting a business (rank)	167
DTF score for starting a business (0–100)	69.73
Procedures (number)	7
Time (days)	16
Cost (% of income per capita)	140.4
Minimum capital (% of income per capita)	0.0
Dealing with construction permits (rank)	143
DTF score for dealing with construction permits (0–100)	60.92
Procedures (number)	14
Time (days)	86
Cost (% of warehouse value)	0.6
Building quality control index (0–15)	0.0
Getting electricity (rank)	107
DTF score for getting electricity (0–100)	64.32
Procedures (number)	3
Time (days)	105
Cost (% of income per capita)	397.1
Reliability of supply and transparency of tariffs index (0–8)	0
Registering property (rank)	187
DTF score for registering property (0–100)	0.00
Procedures (number)	NO PRACTICE
Time (days)	NO PRACTICE
Cost (% of property value)	NO PRACTICE
Quality of land administration index (0–30)	NO PRACTICE
Getting credit (rank)	75
DTF score for getting credit (0–100)	55.00
Strength of legal rights index (0–12)	11
Depth of credit information index (0–8)	0
Credit bureau coverage (% of adults)	0.0
Credit registry coverage (% of adults)	0.0
Protecting minority investors (rank)	185
DTF score for protecting minority investors (0–100)	25.00
Extent of disclosure index (0–10)	0
Extent of director liability index (0–10)	0
Ease of shareholder suits index (0–10)	8
Extent of shareholder rights index (0–10)	5
Extent of ownership and control index (0–10)	2
Extent of corporate transparency index (0–10)	0
Paying taxes (rank)	108
DTF score for paying taxes (0–100)	68.78
Payments (number per year)	21
Time (hours per year)	128
Total tax rate (% of profit)	60.5
Postfiling index (0–100)	NOT APPLICABLE
Trading across borders (rank)	57
DTF score for trading across borders (0–100)	84.00
Time to export	
Documentary compliance (hours)	26
Border compliance (hours)	36
Cost to export	
Documentary compliance (US$)	60
Border compliance (US$)	168
Time to import	
Documentary compliance (hours)	35
Border compliance (hours)	56
Cost to import	
Documentary compliance (US$)	80
Border compliance (US$)	180
Enforcing contracts (rank)	183
DTF score for enforcing contracts (0–100)	29.39
Time (days)	885
Cost (% of claim)	66.0
Quality of judicial processes index (0–18)	4.5
Resolving insolvency (rank)	119
DTF score for resolving insolvency (0–100)	37.65
Time (years)	5.3
Cost (% of estate)	38.0
Recovery rate (cents on the dollar)	3.2
Strength of insolvency framework index (0–16)	11.5

MOLDOVA

MOLDOVA		Europe & Central Asia		GNI per capita (US$)	2,220
Ease of doing business rank (1–190)	44	Overall distance to frontier (DTF) score (0–100)	72.75	Population	3,554,150

✘ **Starting a business** (rank)	44
DTF score for starting a business (0–100)	91.96
Procedures (number)	5
Time (days)	6
Cost (% of income per capita)	6.2
Minimum capital (% of income per capita)	0.0
Dealing with construction permits (rank)	165
DTF score for dealing with construction permits (0–100)	54.14
Procedures (number)	27
Time (days)	276
Cost (% of warehouse value)	0.7
Building quality control index (0–15)	12.0
✔ **Getting electricity** (rank)	73
DTF score for getting electricity (0–100)	74.60
Procedures (number)	6
Time (days)	87
Cost (% of income per capita)	738.4
Reliability of supply and transparency of tariffs index (0–8)	7
Registering property (rank)	21
DTF score for registering property (0–100)	82.92
Procedures (number)	5
Time (days)	5.5
Cost (% of property value)	0.9
Quality of land administration index (0–30)	22.0
Getting credit (rank)	32
DTF score for getting credit (0–100)	70.00
Strength of legal rights index (0–12)	8
Depth of credit information index (0–8)	6
Credit bureau coverage (% of adults)	11.4
Credit registry coverage (% of adults)	0.0
Protecting minority investors (rank)	42
DTF score for protecting minority investors (0–100)	63.33
Extent of disclosure index (0–10)	7
Extent of director liability index (0–10)	4
Ease of shareholder suits index (0–10)	8
Extent of shareholder rights index (0–10)	7
Extent of ownership and control index (0–10)	5
Extent of corporate transparency index (0–10)	7
✔ **Paying taxes** (rank)	31
DTF score for paying taxes (0–100)	84.76
Payments (number per year)	10
Time (hours per year)	181
Total tax rate (% of profit)	40.4
Postfiling index (0–100)	91.36
Trading across borders (rank)	34
DTF score for trading across borders (0–100)	92.32
Time to export	
Documentary compliance (hours)	48
Border compliance (hours)	3
Cost to export	
Documentary compliance (US$)	44
Border compliance (US$)	76
Time to import	
Documentary compliance (hours)	2
Border compliance (hours)	4
Cost to import	
Documentary compliance (US$)	41
Border compliance (US$)	83
✔ **Enforcing contracts** (rank)	62
DTF score for enforcing contracts (0–100)	60.87
Time (days)	585
Cost (% of claim)	28.6
Quality of judicial processes index (0–18)	9.5
Resolving insolvency (rank)	60
DTF score for resolving insolvency (0–100)	52.61
Time (years)	2.8
Cost (% of estate)	15.0
Recovery rate (cents on the dollar)	28.1
Strength of insolvency framework index (0–16)	12.0

MONGOLIA

MONGOLIA		East Asia & Pacific		GNI per capita (US$)	3,830
Ease of doing business rank (1–190)	64	Overall distance to frontier (DTF) score (0–100)	68.15	Population	2,959,134

Starting a business (rank)	36
DTF score for starting a business (0–100)	92.55
Procedures (number)	5
Time (days)	6
Cost (% of income per capita)	1.5
Minimum capital (% of income per capita)	0.0
Dealing with construction permits (rank)	29
DTF score for dealing with construction permits (0–100)	78.19
Procedures (number)	17
Time (days)	137
Cost (% of warehouse value)	0.1
Building quality control index (0–15)	14.0
Getting electricity (rank)	137
DTF score for getting electricity (0–100)	55.12
Procedures (number)	8
Time (days)	79
Cost (% of income per capita)	579.1
Reliability of supply and transparency of tariffs index (0–8)	3
Registering property (rank)	46
DTF score for registering property (0–100)	74.18
Procedures (number)	5
Time (days)	10.5
Cost (% of property value)	2.1
Quality of land administration index (0–30)	14.5
Getting credit (rank)	62
DTF score for getting credit (0–100)	60.00
Strength of legal rights index (0–12)	5
Depth of credit information index (0–8)	7
Credit bureau coverage (% of adults)	0.0
Credit registry coverage (% of adults)	42.2
Protecting minority investors (rank)	26
DTF score for protecting minority investors (0–100)	68.33
Extent of disclosure index (0–10)	6
Extent of director liability index (0–10)	8
Ease of shareholder suits index (0–10)	7
Extent of shareholder rights index (0–10)	4
Extent of ownership and control index (0–10)	8
Extent of corporate transparency index (0–10)	8
✔ **Paying taxes** (rank)	35
DTF score for paying taxes (0–100)	84.19
Payments (number per year)	19
Time (hours per year)	148
Total tax rate (% of profit)	24.7
Postfiling index (0–100)	78.73
Trading across borders (rank)	103
DTF score for trading across borders (0–100)	66.89
Time to export	
Documentary compliance (hours)	168
Border compliance (hours)	62
Cost to export	
Documentary compliance (US$)	64
Border compliance (US$)	191
Time to import	
Documentary compliance (hours)	115
Border compliance (hours)	48
Cost to import	
Documentary compliance (US$)	83
Border compliance (US$)	210
Enforcing contracts (rank)	85
DTF score for enforcing contracts (0–100)	58.48
Time (days)	374
Cost (% of claim)	30.6
Quality of judicial processes index (0–18)	5.5
Resolving insolvency (rank)	91
DTF score for resolving insolvency (0–100)	43.59
Time (years)	4.0
Cost (% of estate)	15.0
Recovery rate (cents on the dollar)	17.1
Strength of insolvency framework index (0–16)	11.0

Note: Most indicator sets refer to a case scenario in the largest business city of an economy, though for 11 economies the data are a population-weighted average for the two largest business cities. For some indicators a result of "no practice" may be recorded for an economy; see the data notes for more details. In starting a business, procedures (number), time (days) and cost (% of income per capita) are calculated as the average of both men and women. For the postfiling index, a result of "not applicable" may be recorded for an economy.

✔ Reform making it easier to do business ✘ Change making it more difficult to do business

MONTENEGRO

Ease of doing business rank (1–190)	51
Europe & Central Asia	
Overall distance to frontier (DTF) score (0–100)	72.08
GNI per capita (US$)	7,240
Population	622,388

Starting a business (rank)	58
DTF score for starting a business (0–100)	90.07
Procedures (number)	6
Time (days)	10
Cost (% of income per capita)	1.5
Minimum capital (% of income per capita)	0.0

Dealing with construction permits (rank)	93
DTF score for dealing with construction permits (0–100)	68.82
Procedures (number)	8
Time (days)	152
Cost (% of warehouse value)	11.3
Building quality control index (0–15)	12.0

Getting electricity (rank)	167
DTF score for getting electricity (0–100)	43.50
Procedures (number)	7
Time (days)	142
Cost (% of income per capita)	440.5
Reliability of supply and transparency of tariffs index (0–8)	0

Registering property (rank)	78
DTF score for registering property (0–100)	65.82
Procedures (number)	6
Time (days)	69
Cost (% of property value)	3.1
Quality of land administration index (0–30)	17.5

Getting credit (rank)	7
DTF score for getting credit (0–100)	85.00
Strength of legal rights index (0–12)	12
Depth of credit information index (0–8)	5
Credit bureau coverage (% of adults)	0.0
Credit registry coverage (% of adults)	30.8

Protecting minority investors (rank)	42
DTF score for protecting minority investors (0–100)	63.33
Extent of disclosure index (0–10)	5
Extent of director liability index (0–10)	8
Ease of shareholder suits index (0–10)	6
Extent of shareholder rights index (0–10)	6
Extent of ownership and control index (0–10)	4
Extent of corporate transparency index (0–10)	9

✔ **Paying taxes** (rank)	57
DTF score for paying taxes (0–100)	80.42
Payments (number per year)	18
Time (hours per year)	300
Total tax rate (% of profit)	22.2
Postfiling index (0–100)	85.48

Trading across borders (rank)	43
DTF score for trading across borders (0–100)	88.75
Time to export	
Documentary compliance (hours)	5
Border compliance (hours)	8
Cost to export	
Documentary compliance (US$)	67
Border compliance (US$)	158
Time to import	
Documentary compliance (hours)	10
Border compliance (hours)	23
Cost to import	
Documentary compliance (US$)	100
Border compliance (US$)	306

Enforcing contracts (rank)	41
DTF score for enforcing contracts (0–100)	66.75
Time (days)	545
Cost (% of claim)	25.7
Quality of judicial processes index (0–18)	11.5

Resolving insolvency (rank)	40
DTF score for resolving insolvency (0–100)	68.37
Time (years)	1.4
Cost (% of estate)	8.0
Recovery rate (cents on the dollar)	48.6
Strength of insolvency framework index (0–16)	13.5

MOROCCO

Ease of doing business rank (1–190)	68
Middle East & North Africa	
Overall distance to frontier (DTF) score (0–100)	67.50
GNI per capita (US$)	3,040
Population	34,377,511

✔ **Starting a business** (rank)	40
DTF score for starting a business (0–100)	92.34
Procedures (number)	4
Time (days)	9.5
Cost (% of income per capita)	7.9
Minimum capital (% of income per capita)	0.0

Dealing with construction permits (rank)	18
DTF score for dealing with construction permits (0–100)	79.77
Procedures (number)	13
Time (days)	88.5
Cost (% of warehouse value)	3.5
Building quality control index (0–15)	13.0

Getting electricity (rank)	57
DTF score for getting electricity (0–100)	79.71
Procedures (number)	5
Time (days)	49
Cost (% of income per capita)	1,770.2
Reliability of supply and transparency of tariffs index (0–8)	7

✔ **Registering property** (rank)	87
DTF score for registering property (0–100)	63.94
Procedures (number)	6
Time (days)	22
Cost (% of property value)	5.9
Quality of land administration index (0–30)	14.0

✔ **Getting credit** (rank)	101
DTF score for getting credit (0–100)	45.00
Strength of legal rights index (0–12)	2
Depth of credit information index (0–8)	7
Credit bureau coverage (% of adults)	24.6
Credit registry coverage (% of adults)	0.0

✔ **Protecting minority investors** (rank)	87
DTF score for protecting minority investors (0–100)	53.33
Extent of disclosure index (0–10)	9
Extent of director liability index (0–10)	2
Ease of shareholder suits index (0–10)	6
Extent of shareholder rights index (0–10)	5
Extent of ownership and control index (0–10)	4
Extent of corporate transparency index (0–10)	6

Paying taxes (rank)	41
DTF score for paying taxes (0–100)	83.51
Payments (number per year)	6
Time (hours per year)	211
Total tax rate (% of profit)	49.3
Postfiling index (0–100)	97.71

✔ **Trading across borders** (rank)	63
DTF score for trading across borders (0–100)	81.12
Time to export	
Documentary compliance (hours)	26
Border compliance (hours)	19
Cost to export	
Documentary compliance (US$)	107
Border compliance (US$)	156
Time to import	
Documentary compliance (hours)	26
Border compliance (hours)	106
Cost to import	
Documentary compliance (US$)	116
Border compliance (US$)	228

Enforcing contracts (rank)	57
DTF score for enforcing contracts (0–100)	62.34
Time (days)	510
Cost (% of claim)	25.2
Quality of judicial processes index (0–18)	8.5

Resolving insolvency (rank)	131
DTF score for resolving insolvency (0–100)	33.89
Time (years)	3.5
Cost (% of estate)	18.0
Recovery rate (cents on the dollar)	28.1
Strength of insolvency framework index (0–16)	6.0

MOZAMBIQUE

Ease of doing business rank (1–190)	137
Sub-Saharan Africa	
Overall distance to frontier (DTF) score (0–100)	53.78
GNI per capita (US$)	580
Population	27,977,863

✘ **Starting a business** (rank)	134
DTF score for starting a business (0–100)	79.86
Procedures (number)	10
Time (days)	19
Cost (% of income per capita)	18.0
Minimum capital (% of income per capita)	0.0

Dealing with construction permits (rank)	30
DTF score for dealing with construction permits (0–100)	77.85
Procedures (number)	10
Time (days)	111
Cost (% of warehouse value)	3.5
Building quality control index (0–15)	11.0

Getting electricity (rank)	168
DTF score for getting electricity (0–100)	42.65
Procedures (number)	7
Time (days)	91
Cost (% of income per capita)	2,509.0
Reliability of supply and transparency of tariffs index (0–8)	0

Registering property (rank)	107
DTF score for registering property (0–100)	58.76
Procedures (number)	6
Time (days)	40
Cost (% of property value)	5.4
Quality of land administration index (0–30)	9.5

✔ **Getting credit** (rank)	157
DTF score for getting credit (0–100)	25.00
Strength of legal rights index (0–12)	1
Depth of credit information index (0–8)	4
Credit bureau coverage (% of adults)	0.0
Credit registry coverage (% of adults)	5.3

Protecting minority investors (rank)	132
DTF score for protecting minority investors (0–100)	43.33
Extent of disclosure index (0–10)	5
Extent of director liability index (0–10)	4
Ease of shareholder suits index (0–10)	7
Extent of shareholder rights index (0–10)	6
Extent of ownership and control index (0–10)	3
Extent of corporate transparency index (0–10)	1

Paying taxes (rank)	112
DTF score for paying taxes (0–100)	67.11
Payments (number per year)	37
Time (hours per year)	200
Total tax rate (% of profit)	36.1
Postfiling index (0–100)	62.49

Trading across borders (rank)	106
DTF score for trading across borders (0–100)	66.31
Time to export	
Documentary compliance (hours)	70
Border compliance (hours)	78
Cost to export	
Documentary compliance (US$)	220
Border compliance (US$)	602
Time to import	
Documentary compliance (hours)	24
Border compliance (hours)	14
Cost to import	
Documentary compliance (US$)	171
Border compliance (US$)	354

Enforcing contracts (rank)	185
DTF score for enforcing contracts (0–100)	27.32
Time (days)	950
Cost (% of claim)	119.0
Quality of judicial processes index (0–18)	9.0

Resolving insolvency (rank)	65
DTF score for resolving insolvency (0–100)	49.61
Time (years)	1.5
Cost (% of estate)	20.5
Recovery rate (cents on the dollar)	34.1
Strength of insolvency framework index (0–16)	10.0

Note: Most indicator sets refer to a case scenario in the largest business city of an economy, though for 11 economies the data are a population-weighted average for the two largest business cities. For some indicators a result of "no practice" may be recorded for an economy; see the data notes for more details. In starting a business, procedures (number), time (days) and cost (% of income per capita) are calculated as the average of both men and women. For the postfiling index, a result of "not applicable" may be recorded for an economy.

✔ Reform making it easier to do business ✘ Change making it more difficult to do business

MYANMAR

MYANMAR		East Asia & Pacific		GNI per capita (US$)	1,293
Ease of doing business rank (1–190)	170	Overall distance to frontier (DTF) score (0–100)	44.56	Population	53,897,154

✔ **Starting a business** (rank)	146
DTF score for starting a business (0–100)	77.10
Procedures (number)	11
Time (days)	13
Cost (% of income per capita)	40.4
Minimum capital (% of income per capita)	0.0
Dealing with construction permits (rank)	66
DTF score for dealing with construction permits (0–100)	72.23
Procedures (number)	14
Time (days)	95
Cost (% of warehouse value)	3.0
Building quality control index (0–15)	9.0
Getting electricity (rank)	149
DTF score for getting electricity (0–100)	52.17
Procedures (number)	6
Time (days)	77
Cost (% of income per capita)	1,270.1
Reliability of supply and transparency of tariffs index (0–8)	0
Registering property (rank)	143
DTF score for registering property (0–100)	49.37
Procedures (number)	6
Time (days)	85
Cost (% of property value)	5.1
Quality of land administration index (0–30)	4.0
✔ **Getting credit** (rank)	175
DTF score for getting credit (0–100)	10.00
Strength of legal rights index (0–12)	2
Depth of credit information index (0–8)	0
Credit bureau coverage (% of adults)	0.0
Credit registry coverage (% of adults)	0.0
Protecting minority investors (rank)	179
DTF score for protecting minority investors (0–100)	28.33
Extent of disclosure index (0–10)	3
Extent of director liability index (0–10)	0
Ease of shareholder suits index (0–10)	3
Extent of shareholder rights index (0–10)	5
Extent of ownership and control index (0–10)	3
Extent of corporate transparency index (0–10)	3
Paying taxes (rank)	119
DTF score for paying taxes (0–100)	64.05
Payments (number per year)	31
Time (hours per year)	282
Total tax rate (% of profit)	31.3
Postfiling index (0–100)	46.10
✘ **Trading across borders** (rank)	159
DTF score for trading across borders (0–100)	47.40
Time to export	
Documentary compliance (hours)	144
Border compliance (hours)	144
Cost to export	
Documentary compliance (US$)	140
Border compliance (US$)	432
Time to import	
Documentary compliance (hours)	48
Border compliance (hours)	232
Cost to import	
Documentary compliance (US$)	210
Border compliance (US$)	457
Enforcing contracts (rank)	188
DTF score for enforcing contracts (0–100)	24.53
Time (days)	1,160
Cost (% of claim)	51.5
Quality of judicial processes index (0–18)	3.0
Resolving insolvency (rank)	164
DTF score for resolving insolvency (0–100)	20.39
Time (years)	5.0
Cost (% of estate)	18.0
Recovery rate (cents on the dollar)	14.7
Strength of insolvency framework index (0–16)	4.0

NAMIBIA

NAMIBIA		Sub-Saharan Africa		GNI per capita (US$)	5,210
Ease of doing business rank (1–190)	108	Overall distance to frontier (DTF) score (0–100)	58.82	Population	2,458,830

Starting a business (rank)	170
DTF score for starting a business (0–100)	68.87
Procedures (number)	10
Time (days)	66
Cost (% of income per capita)	11.5
Minimum capital (% of income per capita)	0.0
Dealing with construction permits (rank)	67
DTF score for dealing with construction permits (0–100)	72.22
Procedures (number)	10
Time (days)	137
Cost (% of warehouse value)	0.5
Building quality control index (0–15)	6.5
Getting electricity (rank)	124
DTF score for getting electricity (0–100)	59.36
Procedures (number)	6
Time (days)	37
Cost (% of income per capita)	349.4
Reliability of supply and transparency of tariffs index (0–8)	0
Registering property (rank)	174
DTF score for registering property (0–100)	38.35
Procedures (number)	8
Time (days)	52
Cost (% of property value)	13.8
Quality of land administration index (0–30)	8.5
Getting credit (rank)	62
DTF score for getting credit (0–100)	60.00
Strength of legal rights index (0–12)	5
Depth of credit information index (0–8)	7
Credit bureau coverage (% of adults)	61.2
Credit registry coverage (% of adults)	0.0
Protecting minority investors (rank)	81
DTF score for protecting minority investors (0–100)	55.00
Extent of disclosure index (0–10)	5
Extent of director liability index (0–10)	5
Ease of shareholder suits index (0–10)	7
Extent of shareholder rights index (0–10)	5
Extent of ownership and control index (0–10)	3
Extent of corporate transparency index (0–10)	8
Paying taxes (rank)	74
DTF score for paying taxes (0–100)	74.97
Payments (number per year)	27
Time (hours per year)	302
Total tax rate (% of profit)	20.7
Postfiling index (0–100)	78.99
Trading across borders (rank)	127
DTF score for trading across borders (0–100)	61.47
Time to export	
Documentary compliance (hours)	90
Border compliance (hours)	120
Cost to export	
Documentary compliance (US$)	348
Border compliance (US$)	745
Time to import	
Documentary compliance (hours)	3
Border compliance (hours)	6
Cost to import	
Documentary compliance (US$)	63
Border compliance (US$)	145
Enforcing contracts (rank)	98
DTF score for enforcing contracts (0–100)	56.03
Time (days)	460
Cost (% of claim)	35.8
Quality of judicial processes index (0–18)	6.5
Resolving insolvency (rank)	97
DTF score for resolving insolvency (0–100)	41.96
Time (years)	2.5
Cost (% of estate)	14.5
Recovery rate (cents on the dollar)	34.4
Strength of insolvency framework index (0–16)	7.5

NEPAL

NEPAL		South Asia		GNI per capita (US$)	730
Ease of doing business rank (1–190)	107	Overall distance to frontier (DTF) score (0–100)	58.88	Population	28,513,700

Starting a business (rank)	109
DTF score for starting a business (0–100)	83.77
Procedures (number)	7
Time (days)	17
Cost (% of income per capita)	26.1
Minimum capital (% of income per capita)	0.0
✘ **Dealing with construction permits** (rank)	123
DTF score for dealing with construction permits (0–100)	64.18
Procedures (number)	10
Time (days)	86
Cost (% of warehouse value)	13.2
Building quality control index (0–15)	9.0
Getting electricity (rank)	131
DTF score for getting electricity (0–100)	57.80
Procedures (number)	5
Time (days)	70
Cost (% of income per capita)	1,042.1
Reliability of supply and transparency of tariffs index (0–8)	0
Registering property (rank)	72
DTF score for registering property (0–100)	67.00
Procedures (number)	3
Time (days)	5
Cost (% of property value)	4.8
Quality of land administration index (0–30)	5.5
Getting credit (rank)	139
DTF score for getting credit (0–100)	30.00
Strength of legal rights index (0–12)	6
Depth of credit information index (0–8)	0
Credit bureau coverage (% of adults)	1.8
Credit registry coverage (% of adults)	0.0
Protecting minority investors (rank)	63
DTF score for protecting minority investors (0–100)	58.33
Extent of disclosure index (0–10)	6
Extent of director liability index (0–10)	1
Ease of shareholder suits index (0–10)	9
Extent of shareholder rights index (0–10)	8
Extent of ownership and control index (0–10)	6
Extent of corporate transparency index (0–10)	5
Paying taxes (rank)	142
DTF score for paying taxes (0–100)	58.05
Payments (number per year)	34
Time (hours per year)	339
Total tax rate (% of profit)	29.5
Postfiling index (0–100)	33.48
✔ **Trading across borders** (rank)	69
DTF score for trading across borders (0–100)	79.75
Time to export	
Documentary compliance (hours)	19
Border compliance (hours)	56
Cost to export	
Documentary compliance (US$)	85
Border compliance (US$)	288
Time to import	
Documentary compliance (hours)	48
Border compliance (hours)	61
Cost to import	
Documentary compliance (US$)	80
Border compliance (US$)	190
Enforcing contracts (rank)	152
DTF score for enforcing contracts (0–100)	45.26
Time (days)	910
Cost (% of claim)	26.8
Quality of judicial processes index (0–18)	5.5
Resolving insolvency (rank)	89
DTF score for resolving insolvency (0–100)	44.64
Time (years)	2.0
Cost (% of estate)	9.0
Recovery rate (cents on the dollar)	42.3
Strength of insolvency framework index (0–16)	7.0

Note: Most indicator sets refer to a case scenario in the largest business city of an economy, though for 11 economies the data are a population-weighted average for the two largest business cities. For some indicators a result of "no practice" may be recorded for an economy; see the data notes for more details. In starting a business, procedures (number), time (days) and cost (% of income per capita) are calculated as the average of both men and women. For the postfiling index, a result of "not applicable" may be recorded for an economy.

✔ Reform making it easier to do business ✘ Change making it more difficult to do business

NETHERLANDS

Ease of doing business rank (1–190)	28	OECD high income		GNI per capita (US$)	48,940
		Overall distance to frontier (DTF) score (0–100)	76.38	Population	16,936,520

Starting a business (rank)	22
DTF score for starting a business (0–100)	94.15
Procedures (number)	4
Time (days)	4
Cost (% of income per capita)	4.5
Minimum capital (% of income per capita)	0.0
Dealing with construction permits (rank)	87
DTF score for dealing with construction permits (0–100)	69.33
Procedures (number)	13
Time (days)	161
Cost (% of warehouse value)	3.7
Building quality control index (0–15)	10.0
Getting electricity (rank)	45
DTF score for getting electricity (0–100)	81.57
Procedures (number)	5
Time (days)	110
Cost (% of income per capita)	29.9
Reliability of supply and transparency of tariffs index (0–8)	8
Registering property (rank)	29
DTF score for registering property (0–100)	80.04
Procedures (number)	5
Time (days)	2.5
Cost (% of property value)	6.1
Quality of land administration index (0–30)	28.5
Getting credit (rank)	82
DTF score for getting credit (0–100)	50.00
Strength of legal rights index (0–12)	3
Depth of credit information index (0–8)	7
Credit bureau coverage (% of adults)	75.7
Credit registry coverage (% of adults)	0.0
Protecting minority investors (rank)	70
DTF score for protecting minority investors (0–100)	56.67
Extent of disclosure index (0–10)	4
Extent of director liability index (0–10)	4
Ease of shareholder suits index (0–10)	6
Extent of shareholder rights index (0–10)	7
Extent of ownership and control index (0–10)	6
Extent of corporate transparency index (0–10)	7
✔ **Paying taxes** (rank)	20
DTF score for paying taxes (0–100)	88.07
Payments (number per year)	9
Time (hours per year)	119
Total tax rate (% of profit)	40.4
Postfiling index (0–100)	93.40
Trading across borders (rank)	1
DTF score for trading across borders (0–100)	100.00
Time to export	
Documentary compliance (hours)	1
Border compliance (hours)	0
Cost to export	
Documentary compliance (US$)	0
Border compliance (US$)	0
Time to import	
Documentary compliance (hours)	1
Border compliance (hours)	0
Cost to import	
Documentary compliance (US$)	0
Border compliance (US$)	0
Enforcing contracts (rank)	71
DTF score for enforcing contracts (0–100)	59.94
Time (days)	514
Cost (% of claim)	23.9
Quality of judicial processes index (0–18)	7.0
Resolving insolvency (rank)	11
DTF score for resolving insolvency (0–100)	84.00
Time (years)	1.1
Cost (% of estate)	3.5
Recovery rate (cents on the dollar)	89.3
Strength of insolvency framework index (0–16)	11.5

NEW ZEALAND

Ease of doing business rank (1–190)	1	OECD high income		GNI per capita (US$)	40,080
		Overall distance to frontier (DTF) score (0–100)	87.01	Population	4,595,700

Starting a business (rank)	1
DTF score for starting a business (0–100)	99.96
Procedures (number)	1
Time (days)	0.5
Cost (% of income per capita)	0.3
Minimum capital (% of income per capita)	0.0
Dealing with construction permits (rank)	1
DTF score for dealing with construction permits (0–100)	87.40
Procedures (number)	10
Time (days)	93
Cost (% of warehouse value)	2.2
Building quality control index (0–15)	15.0
Getting electricity (rank)	34
DTF score for getting electricity (0–100)	83.96
Procedures (number)	5
Time (days)	58
Cost (% of income per capita)	76.0
Reliability of supply and transparency of tariffs index (0–8)	7
Registering property (rank)	1
DTF score for registering property (0–100)	94.46
Procedures (number)	2
Time (days)	1
Cost (% of property value)	0.1
Quality of land administration index (0–30)	26.0
Getting credit (rank)	1
DTF score for getting credit (0–100)	100.00
Strength of legal rights index (0–12)	12
Depth of credit information index (0–8)	8
Credit bureau coverage (% of adults)	100.0
Credit registry coverage (% of adults)	0.0
Protecting minority investors (rank)	1
DTF score for protecting minority investors (0–100)	83.33
Extent of disclosure index (0–10)	10
Extent of director liability index (0–10)	9
Ease of shareholder suits index (0–10)	9
Extent of shareholder rights index (0–10)	8
Extent of ownership and control index (0–10)	7
Extent of corporate transparency index (0–10)	7
✔ **Paying taxes** (rank)	11
DTF score for paying taxes (0–100)	90.71
Payments (number per year)	7
Time (hours per year)	152
Total tax rate (% of profit)	34.3
Postfiling index (0–100)	96.90
Trading across borders (rank)	55
DTF score for trading across borders (0–100)	84.55
Time to export	
Documentary compliance (hours)	3
Border compliance (hours)	38
Cost to export	
Documentary compliance (US$)	67
Border compliance (US$)	337
Time to import	
Documentary compliance (hours)	1
Border compliance (hours)	25
Cost to import	
Documentary compliance (US$)	80
Border compliance (US$)	367
Enforcing contracts (rank)	13
DTF score for enforcing contracts (0–100)	74.25
Time (days)	216
Cost (% of claim)	27.2
Quality of judicial processes index (0–18)	11.0
Resolving insolvency (rank)	34
DTF score for resolving insolvency (0–100)	71.43
Time (years)	1.3
Cost (% of estate)	3.5
Recovery rate (cents on the dollar)	83.4
Strength of insolvency framework index (0–16)	8.5

NICARAGUA

Ease of doing business rank (1–190)	127	Latin America & Caribbean		GNI per capita (US$)	1,940
		Overall distance to frontier (DTF) score (0–100)	55.75	Population	6,082,032

Starting a business (rank)	128
DTF score for starting a business (0–100)	81.00
Procedures (number)	6
Time (days)	13
Cost (% of income per capita)	68.0
Minimum capital (% of income per capita)	0.0
Dealing with construction permits (rank)	168
DTF score for dealing with construction permits (0–100)	52.97
Procedures (number)	16
Time (days)	207
Cost (% of warehouse value)	3.1
Building quality control index (0–15)	3.5
Getting electricity (rank)	99
DTF score for getting electricity (0–100)	68.19
Procedures (number)	6
Time (days)	55
Cost (% of income per capita)	904.2
Reliability of supply and transparency of tariffs index (0–8)	4
Registering property (rank)	146
DTF score for registering property (0–100)	48.86
Procedures (number)	9
Time (days)	56
Cost (% of property value)	5.0
Quality of land administration index (0–30)	6.5
Getting credit (rank)	101
DTF score for getting credit (0–100)	45.00
Strength of legal rights index (0–12)	1
Depth of credit information index (0–8)	8
Credit bureau coverage (% of adults)	53.9
Credit registry coverage (% of adults)	17.9
Protecting minority investors (rank)	145
DTF score for protecting minority investors (0–100)	40.00
Extent of disclosure index (0–10)	1
Extent of director liability index (0–10)	5
Ease of shareholder suits index (0–10)	6
Extent of shareholder rights index (0–10)	6
Extent of ownership and control index (0–10)	2
Extent of corporate transparency index (0–10)	4
Paying taxes (rank)	176
DTF score for paying taxes (0–100)	43.29
Payments (number per year)	42
Time (hours per year)	201
Total tax rate (% of profit)	60.8
Postfiling index (0–100)	13.62
✘ **Trading across borders** (rank)	73
DTF score for trading across borders (0–100)	78.99
Time to export	
Documentary compliance (hours)	48
Border compliance (hours)	60
Cost to export	
Documentary compliance (US$)	47
Border compliance (US$)	150
Time to import	
Documentary compliance (hours)	16
Border compliance (hours)	72
Cost to import	
Documentary compliance (US$)	86
Border compliance (US$)	400
Enforcing contracts (rank)	83
DTF score for enforcing contracts (0–100)	58.58
Time (days)	490
Cost (% of claim)	26.8
Quality of judicial processes index (0–18)	6.5
Resolving insolvency (rank)	103
DTF score for resolving insolvency (0–100)	40.66
Time (years)	2.2
Cost (% of estate)	14.5
Recovery rate (cents on the dollar)	34.9
Strength of insolvency framework index (0–16)	7.0

Note: Most indicator sets refer to a case scenario in the largest business city of an economy, though for 11 economies the data are a population-weighted average for the two largest business cities. For some indicators a result of "no practice" may be recorded for an economy; see the data notes for more details. In starting a business, procedures (number), time (days) and cost (% of income per capita) are calculated as the average of both men and women. For the postfiling index, a result of "not applicable" may be recorded for an economy.

✔ Reform making it easier to do business ✘ Change making it more difficult to do business

NIGER

NIGER		Sub-Saharan Africa		GNI per capita (US$)	390
Ease of doing business rank (1–190)	**150**	**Overall distance to frontier (DTF) score (0–100)**	**49.57**	**Population**	**19,899,120**
✔ **Starting a business** (rank)	88	✔ **Getting credit** (rank)	139	✔ **Trading across borders** (rank)	132
DTF score for starting a business (0–100)	86.16	DTF score for getting credit (0–100)	30.00	DTF score for trading across borders (0–100)	60.48
Procedures (number)	4	Strength of legal rights index (0–12)	6	*Time to export*	
Time (days)	10	Depth of credit information index (0–8)	0	Documentary compliance (hours)	51
Cost (% of income per capita)	32.4	Credit bureau coverage (% of adults)	0.0	Border compliance (hours)	48
Minimum capital (% of income per capita)	48.0	Credit registry coverage (% of adults)	0.3	*Cost to export*	
				Documentary compliance (US$)	39
Dealing with construction permits (rank)	179	✔ **Protecting minority investors** (rank)	145	Border compliance (US$)	543
DTF score for dealing with construction permits (0–100)	46.40	DTF score for protecting minority investors (0–100)	40.00	*Time to import*	
Procedures (number)	15	Extent of disclosure index (0–10)	7	Documentary compliance (hours)	156
Time (days)	112	Extent of director liability index (0–10)	1	Border compliance (hours)	78
Cost (% of warehouse value)	16.6	Ease of shareholder suits index (0–10)	5	*Cost to import*	
Building quality control index (0–15)	5.0	Extent of shareholder rights index (0–10)	5	Documentary compliance (US$)	457
		Extent of ownership and control index (0–10)	4	Border compliance (US$)	462
Getting electricity (rank)	166	Extent of corporate transparency index (0–10)	2		
DTF score for getting electricity (0–100)	43.54			✔ **Enforcing contracts** (rank)	150
Procedures (number)	4	**Paying taxes** (rank)	165	DTF score for enforcing contracts (0–100)	45.55
Time (days)	115	DTF score for paying taxes (0–100)	50.19	Time (days)	545
Cost (% of income per capita)	5,426.8	Payments (number per year)	41	Cost (% of claim)	52.6
Reliability of supply and transparency of tariffs index (0–8)	0	Time (hours per year)	270	Quality of judicial processes index (0–18)	5.5
		Total tax rate (% of profit)	48.2		
Registering property (rank)	125	Postfiling index (0–100)	30.16	✔ **Resolving insolvency** (rank)	105
DTF score for registering property (0–100)	52.98			DTF score for resolving insolvency (0–100)	40.36
Procedures (number)	4			Time (years)	5.0
Time (days)	35			Cost (% of estate)	18.0
Cost (% of property value)	9.0			Recovery rate (cents on the dollar)	22.7
Quality of land administration index (0–30)	4.0			Strength of insolvency framework index (0–16)	9.0

NIGERIA

NIGERIA		Sub-Saharan Africa		GNI per capita (US$)	2,820
Ease of doing business rank (1–190)	**169**	**Overall distance to frontier (DTF) score (0–100)**	**44.63**	**Population**	**182,201,962**
✔ **Starting a business** (rank)	138	✔ **Getting credit** (rank)	44	**Trading across borders** (rank)	181
DTF score for starting a business (0–100)	78.62	DTF score for getting credit (0–100)	65.00	DTF score for trading across borders (0–100)	19.93
Procedures (number)	8.7	Strength of legal rights index (0–12)	7	*Time to export*	
Time (days)	25.2	Depth of credit information index (0–8)	6	Documentary compliance (hours)	131.4
Cost (% of income per capita)	31.0	Credit bureau coverage (% of adults)	7.7	Border compliance (hours)	135.4
Minimum capital (% of income per capita)	0.0	Credit registry coverage (% of adults)	0.1	*Cost to export*	
				Documentary compliance (US$)	250
Dealing with construction permits (rank)	174	**Protecting minority investors** (rank)	32	Border compliance (US$)	785.7
DTF score for dealing with construction permits (0–100)	49.63	DTF score for protecting minority investors (0–100)	65.00	*Time to import*	
Procedures (number)	16.1	Extent of disclosure index (0–10)	7	Documentary compliance (hours)	172.7
Time (days)	106.3	Extent of director liability index (0–10)	7	Border compliance (hours)	283.7
Cost (% of warehouse value)	23.6	Ease of shareholder suits index (0–10)	7	*Cost to import*	
Building quality control index (0–15)	6.8	Extent of shareholder rights index (0–10)	6	Documentary compliance (US$)	564.3
		Extent of ownership and control index (0–10)	5	Border compliance (US$)	1,076.8
Getting electricity (rank)	180	Extent of corporate transparency index (0–10)	7		
DTF score for getting electricity (0–100)	29.43			**Enforcing contracts** (rank)	139
Procedures (number)	9	**Paying taxes** (rank)	182	DTF score for enforcing contracts (0–100)	48.59
Time (days)	195.2	DTF score for paying taxes (0–100)	28.09	Time (days)	509.8
Cost (% of income per capita)	422.8	Payments (number per year)	59	Cost (% of claim)	57.7
Reliability of supply and transparency of tariffs index (0–8)	0	Time (hours per year)	907.9	Quality of judicial processes index (0–18)	7.7
		Total tax rate (% of profit)	34.3		
Registering property (rank)	182	Postfiling index (0–100)	17.19	**Resolving insolvency** (rank)	140
DTF score for registering property (0–100)	31.44			DTF score for resolving insolvency (0–100)	30.60
Procedures (number)	12.1			Time (years)	2.0
Time (days)	69.6			Cost (% of estate)	22.0
Cost (% of property value)	10.5			Recovery rate (cents on the dollar)	27.8
Quality of land administration index (0–30)	6.3			Strength of insolvency framework index (0–16)	5.0

NORWAY

NORWAY		OECD high income		GNI per capita (US$)	93,820
Ease of doing business rank (1–190)	**6**	**Overall distance to frontier (DTF) score (0–100)**	**82.82**	**Population**	**5,195,921**
Starting a business (rank)	21	**Getting credit** (rank)	75	**Trading across borders** (rank)	22
DTF score for starting a business (0–100)	94.30	DTF score for getting credit (0–100)	55.00	DTF score for trading across borders (0–100)	96.97
Procedures (number)	4	Strength of legal rights index (0–12)	5	*Time to export*	
Time (days)	4	Depth of credit information index (0–8)	6	Documentary compliance (hours)	2
Cost (% of income per capita)	0.9	Credit bureau coverage (% of adults)	100.0	Border compliance (hours)	2
Minimum capital (% of income per capita)	4.7	Credit registry coverage (% of adults)	0.0	*Cost to export*	
				Documentary compliance (US$)	0
Dealing with construction permits (rank)	43	**Protecting minority investors** (rank)	9	Border compliance (US$)	125
DTF score for dealing with construction permits (0–100)	75.52	DTF score for protecting minority investors (0–100)	75.00	*Time to import*	
Procedures (number)	11	Extent of disclosure index (0–10)	7	Documentary compliance (hours)	2
Time (days)	110.5	Extent of director liability index (0–10)	5	Border compliance (hours)	2
Cost (% of warehouse value)	0.6	Ease of shareholder suits index (0–10)	8	*Cost to import*	
Building quality control index (0–15)	8.0	Extent of shareholder rights index (0–10)	8	Documentary compliance (US$)	0
		Extent of ownership and control index (0–10)	8	Border compliance (US$)	125
Getting electricity (rank)	12	Extent of corporate transparency index (0–10)	9		
DTF score for getting electricity (0–100)	90.58			✔ **Enforcing contracts** (rank)	4
Procedures (number)	4	**Paying taxes** (rank)	26	DTF score for enforcing contracts (0–100)	78.99
Time (days)	66	DTF score for paying taxes (0–100)	85.53	Time (days)	280
Cost (% of income per capita)	11.3	Payments (number per year)	4	Cost (% of claim)	9.9
Reliability of supply and transparency of tariffs index (0–8)	8	Time (hours per year)	83	Quality of judicial processes index (0–18)	11.0
		Total tax rate (% of profit)	39.5		
Registering property (rank)	14	Postfiling index (0–100)	67.99	**Resolving insolvency** (rank)	6
DTF score for registering property (0–100)	87.26			DTF score for resolving insolvency (0–100)	89.06
Procedures (number)	1			Time (years)	0.9
Time (days)	3			Cost (% of estate)	1.0
Cost (% of property value)	2.5			Recovery rate (cents on the dollar)	92.9
Quality of land administration index (0–30)	20.0			Strength of insolvency framework index (0–16)	12.5

Note: Most indicator sets refer to a case scenario in the largest business city of an economy, though for 11 economies the data are a population-weighted average for the two largest business cities. For some indicators a result of "no practice" may be recorded for an economy; see the data notes for more details. In starting a business, procedures (number), time (days) and cost (% of income per capita) are calculated as the average of both men and women. For the postfiling index, a result of "not applicable" may be recorded for an economy.

✔ Reform making it easier to do business ✘ Change making it more difficult to do business

OMAN

OMAN		Middle East & North Africa		GNI per capita (US$)	16,920
Ease of doing business rank (1–190)	66	Overall distance to frontier (DTF) score (0–100)	67.73	Population	4,490,541

✔ **Starting a business** (rank)	32
DTF score for starting a business (0–100)	92.85
Procedures (number)	4.5
Time (days)	6.5
Cost (% of income per capita)	4.0
Minimum capital (% of income per capita)	0.0
Dealing with construction permits (rank)	52
DTF score for dealing with construction permits (0–100)	74.64
Procedures (number)	12
Time (days)	157
Cost (% of warehouse value)	1.1
Building quality control index (0–15)	10.5
Getting electricity (rank)	69
DTF score for getting electricity (0–100)	76.22
Procedures (number)	6
Time (days)	62
Cost (% of income per capita)	80.7
Reliability of supply and transparency of tariffs index (0–8)	6
Registering property (rank)	35
DTF score for registering property (0–100)	76.95
Procedures (number)	2
Time (days)	16
Cost (% of property value)	3.0
Quality of land administration index (0–30)	13.0

Getting credit (rank)	133
DTF score for getting credit (0–100)	35.00
Strength of legal rights index (0–12)	1
Depth of credit information index (0–8)	6
Credit bureau coverage (% of adults)	0.0
Credit registry coverage (% of adults)	22.7
Protecting minority investors (rank)	118
DTF score for protecting minority investors (0–100)	46.67
Extent of disclosure index (0–10)	8
Extent of director liability index (0–10)	5
Ease of shareholder suits index (0–10)	3
Extent of shareholder rights index (0–10)	4
Extent of ownership and control index (0–10)	4
Extent of corporate transparency index (0–10)	4
Paying taxes (rank)	12
DTF score for paying taxes (0–100)	90.60
Payments (number per year)	15
Time (hours per year)	68
Total tax rate (% of profit)	23.9
Postfiling index (0–100)	85.32

✔ **Trading across borders** (rank)	67
DTF score for trading across borders (0–100)	80.17
Time to export	
Documentary compliance (hours)	22
Border compliance (hours)	52
Cost to export	
Documentary compliance (US$)	107
Border compliance (US$)	223
Time to import	
Documentary compliance (hours)	23
Border compliance (hours)	70
Cost to import	
Documentary compliance (US$)	20
Border compliance (US$)	354
Enforcing contracts (rank)	60
DTF score for enforcing contracts (0–100)	61.55
Time (days)	598
Cost (% of claim)	13.5
Quality of judicial processes index (0–18)	7.0
Resolving insolvency (rank)	94
DTF score for resolving insolvency (0–100)	42.65
Time (years)	4.0
Cost (% of estate)	3.5
Recovery rate (cents on the dollar)	38.6
Strength of insolvency framework index (0–16)	7.0

PAKISTAN

PAKISTAN		South Asia		GNI per capita (US$)	1,440
Ease of doing business rank (1–190)	144	Overall distance to frontier (DTF) score (0–100)	51.77	Population	188,924,874

Starting a business (rank)	141
DTF score for starting a business (0–100)	77.88
Procedures (number)	12
Time (days)	18
Cost (% of income per capita)	12.4
Minimum capital (% of income per capita)	0.0
Dealing with construction permits (rank)	150
DTF score for dealing with construction permits (0–100)	59.07
Procedures (number)	15
Time (days)	264.2
Cost (% of warehouse value)	7.0
Building quality control index (0–15)	12.0
Getting electricity (rank)	170
DTF score for getting electricity (0–100)	42.05
Procedures (number)	5.4
Time (days)	180.7
Cost (% of income per capita)	1,771.9
Reliability of supply and transparency of tariffs index (0–8)	0
✔ **Registering property** (rank)	169
DTF score for registering property (0–100)	40.70
Procedures (number)	7.7
Time (days)	154.8
Cost (% of property value)	4.6
Quality of land administration index (0–30)	6.8

✔ **Getting credit** (rank)	82
DTF score for getting credit (0–100)	50.00
Strength of legal rights index (0–12)	3
Depth of credit information index (0–8)	7
Credit bureau coverage (% of adults)	5.8
Credit registry coverage (% of adults)	9.4
Protecting minority investors (rank)	27
DTF score for protecting minority investors (0–100)	66.67
Extent of disclosure index (0–10)	6
Extent of director liability index (0–10)	6
Ease of shareholder suits index (0–10)	6
Extent of shareholder rights index (0–10)	8
Extent of ownership and control index (0–10)	9
Extent of corporate transparency index (0–10)	5
Paying taxes (rank)	156
DTF score for paying taxes (0–100)	53.40
Payments (number per year)	47
Time (hours per year)	311.5
Total tax rate (% of profit)	33.3
Postfiling index (0–100)	37.61

✔ **Trading across borders** (rank)	172
DTF score for trading across borders (0–100)	39.41
Time to export	
Documentary compliance (hours)	59
Border compliance (hours)	75
Cost to export	
Documentary compliance (US$)	307.1
Border compliance (US$)	426.4
Time to import	
Documentary compliance (hours)	147
Border compliance (hours)	129.3
Cost to import	
Documentary compliance (US$)	785.7
Border compliance (US$)	957.1
Enforcing contracts (rank)	157
DTF score for enforcing contracts (0–100)	43.49
Time (days)	1,071.2
Cost (% of claim)	20.5
Quality of judicial processes index (0–18)	5.7
Resolving insolvency (rank)	85
DTF score for resolving insolvency (0–100)	45.01
Time (years)	2.6
Cost (% of estate)	4.0
Recovery rate (cents on the dollar)	43.0
Strength of insolvency framework index (0–16)	7.0

PALAU

PALAU		East Asia & Pacific		GNI per capita (US$)	12,180
Ease of doing business rank (1–190)	136	Overall distance to frontier (DTF) score (0–100)	53.81	Population	21,291

Starting a business (rank)	120
DTF score for starting a business (0–100)	81.95
Procedures (number)	8
Time (days)	28
Cost (% of income per capita)	2.9
Minimum capital (% of income per capita)	7.7
Dealing with construction permits (rank)	98
DTF score for dealing with construction permits (0–100)	68.38
Procedures (number)	19
Time (days)	72
Cost (% of warehouse value)	0.8
Building quality control index (0–15)	7.0
Getting electricity (rank)	138
DTF score for getting electricity (0–100)	54.84
Procedures (number)	5
Time (days)	125
Cost (% of income per capita)	65.2
Reliability of supply and transparency of tariffs index (0–8)	0
Registering property (rank)	44
DTF score for registering property (0–100)	75.16
Procedures (number)	5
Time (days)	14
Cost (% of property value)	0.2
Quality of land administration index (0–30)	12.5

Getting credit (rank)	82
DTF score for getting credit (0–100)	50.00
Strength of legal rights index (0–12)	10
Depth of credit information index (0–8)	0
Credit bureau coverage (% of adults)	0.0
Credit registry coverage (% of adults)	0.0
Protecting minority investors (rank)	179
DTF score for protecting minority investors (0–100)	28.33
Extent of disclosure index (0–10)	0
Extent of director liability index (0–10)	0
Ease of shareholder suits index (0–10)	7
Extent of shareholder rights index (0–10)	5
Extent of ownership and control index (0–10)	3
Extent of corporate transparency index (0–10)	2
Paying taxes (rank)	118
DTF score for paying taxes (0–100)	64.65
Payments (number per year)	11
Time (hours per year)	142
Total tax rate (% of profit)	75.4
Postfiling index (0–100)	NOT APPLICABLE

Trading across borders (rank)	163
DTF score for trading across borders (0–100)	46.22
Time to export	
Documentary compliance (hours)	168
Border compliance (hours)	102
Cost to export	
Documentary compliance (US$)	200
Border compliance (US$)	505
Time to import	
Documentary compliance (hours)	168
Border compliance (hours)	84
Cost to import	
Documentary compliance (US$)	143
Border compliance (US$)	605
Enforcing contracts (rank)	126
DTF score for enforcing contracts (0–100)	52.21
Time (days)	810
Cost (% of claim)	35.3
Quality of judicial processes index (0–18)	9.5
Resolving insolvency (rank)	166
DTF score for resolving insolvency (0–100)	16.38
Time (years)	2.0
Cost (% of estate)	22.5
Recovery rate (cents on the dollar)	30.4
Strength of insolvency framework index (0–16)	0.0

Note: Most indicator sets refer to a case scenario in the largest business city of an economy, though for 11 economies the data are a population-weighted average for the two largest business cities. For some indicators a result of "no practice" may be recorded for an economy; see the data notes for more details. In starting a business, procedures (number), time (days) and cost (% of income per capita) are calculated as the average of both men and women. For the postfiling index, a result of "not applicable" may be recorded for an economy.

✔ Reform making it easier to do business ✘ Change making it more difficult to do business

PANAMA

PANAMA		Latin America & Caribbean		GNI per capita (US$)	12,050
Ease of doing business rank (1–190)	**70**	**Overall distance to frontier (DTF) score (0–100)**	**66.19**	**Population**	**3,929,141**

Starting a business (rank)	43
DTF score for starting a business (0–100)	92.01
Procedures (number)	5
Time (days)	6
Cost (% of income per capita)	5.8
Minimum capital (% of income per capita)	0.0
Dealing with construction permits (rank)	73
DTF score for dealing with construction permits (0–100)	71.31
Procedures (number)	16
Time (days)	98
Cost (% of warehouse value)	2.0
Building quality control index (0–15)	9.0
Getting electricity (rank)	23
DTF score for getting electricity (0–100)	86.67
Procedures (number)	5
Time (days)	35
Cost (% of income per capita)	8.9
Reliability of supply and transparency of tariffs index (0–8)	7
Registering property (rank)	84
DTF score for registering property (0–100)	65.17
Procedures (number)	7
Time (days)	22.5
Cost (% of property value)	2.4
Quality of land administration index (0–30)	11.0

Getting credit (rank)	20
DTF score for getting credit (0–100)	75.00
Strength of legal rights index (0–12)	7
Depth of credit information index (0–8)	8
Credit bureau coverage (% of adults)	58.1
Credit registry coverage (% of adults)	0.0
Protecting minority investors (rank)	70
DTF score for protecting minority investors (0–100)	56.67
Extent of disclosure index (0–10)	4
Extent of director liability index (0–10)	4
Ease of shareholder suits index (0–10)	8
Extent of shareholder rights index (0–10)	10
Extent of ownership and control index (0–10)	2
Extent of corporate transparency index (0–10)	6
Paying taxes (rank)	170
DTF score for paying taxes (0–100)	48.09
Payments (number per year)	52
Time (hours per year)	417
Total tax rate (% of profit)	37.2
Postfiling index (0–100)	46.56

Trading across borders (rank)	53
DTF score for trading across borders (0–100)	85.47
Time to export	
Documentary compliance (hours)	6
Border compliance (hours)	24
Cost to export	
Documentary compliance (US$)	60
Border compliance (US$)	270
Time to import	
Documentary compliance (hours)	6
Border compliance (hours)	24
Cost to import	
Documentary compliance (US$)	50
Border compliance (US$)	490
Enforcing contracts (rank)	145
DTF score for enforcing contracts (0–100)	48.10
Time (days)	686
Cost (% of claim)	38.0
Quality of judicial processes index (0–18)	6.0
Resolving insolvency (rank)	133
DTF score for resolving insolvency (0–100)	33.36
Time (years)	2.5
Cost (% of estate)	25.0
Recovery rate (cents on the dollar)	27.2
Strength of insolvency framework index (0–16)	6.0

PAPUA NEW GUINEA

PAPUA NEW GUINEA		East Asia & Pacific		GNI per capita (US$)	2,112
Ease of doing business rank (1–190)	**119**	**Overall distance to frontier (DTF) score (0–100)**	**57.29**	**Population**	**7,619,321**

✔ **Starting a business** (rank)	130
DTF score for starting a business (0–100)	80.53
Procedures (number)	6
Time (days)	41
Cost (% of income per capita)	15.6
Minimum capital (% of income per capita)	0.0
Dealing with construction permits (rank)	126
DTF score for dealing with construction permits (0–100)	63.89
Procedures (number)	17
Time (days)	217
Cost (% of warehouse value)	1.6
Building quality control index (0–15)	10.0
Getting electricity (rank)	103
DTF score for getting electricity (0–100)	65.50
Procedures (number)	4
Time (days)	66
Cost (% of income per capita)	38.0
Reliability of supply and transparency of tariffs index (0–8)	0
Registering property (rank)	119
DTF score for registering property (0–100)	55.27
Procedures (number)	4
Time (days)	72
Cost (% of property value)	5.2
Quality of land administration index (0–30)	4.5

✔ **Getting credit** (rank)	32
DTF score for getting credit (0–100)	70.00
Strength of legal rights index (0–12)	9
Depth of credit information index (0–8)	5
Credit bureau coverage (% of adults)	6.1
Credit registry coverage (% of adults)	0.0
Protecting minority investors (rank)	87
DTF score for protecting minority investors (0–100)	53.33
Extent of disclosure index (0–10)	4
Extent of director liability index (0–10)	5
Ease of shareholder suits index (0–10)	9
Extent of shareholder rights index (0–10)	7
Extent of ownership and control index (0–10)	4
Extent of corporate transparency index (0–10)	3
Paying taxes (rank)	94
DTF score for paying taxes (0–100)	71.40
Payments (number per year)	32
Time (hours per year)	207
Total tax rate (% of profit)	39.3
Postfiling index (0–100)	77.12

Trading across borders (rank)	164
DTF score for trading across borders (0–100)	44.64
Time to export	
Documentary compliance (hours)	96
Border compliance (hours)	42
Cost to export	
Documentary compliance (US$)	375
Border compliance (US$)	675
Time to import	
Documentary compliance (hours)	120
Border compliance (hours)	72
Cost to import	
Documentary compliance (US$)	425
Border compliance (US$)	810
Enforcing contracts (rank)	170
DTF score for enforcing contracts (0–100)	36.21
Time (days)	591
Cost (% of claim)	110.3
Quality of judicial processes index (0–18)	8.5
Resolving insolvency (rank)	137
DTF score for resolving insolvency (0–100)	32.15
Time (years)	3.0
Cost (% of estate)	23.0
Recovery rate (cents on the dollar)	24.9
Strength of insolvency framework index (0–16)	6.0

PARAGUAY

PARAGUAY		Latin America & Caribbean		GNI per capita (US$)	4,220
Ease of doing business rank (1–190)	**106**	**Overall distance to frontier (DTF) score (0–100)**	**59.03**	**Population**	**6,639,123**

Starting a business (rank)	143
DTF score for starting a business (0–100)	77.53
Procedures (number)	7
Time (days)	35
Cost (% of income per capita)	39.8
Minimum capital (% of income per capita)	0.0
Dealing with construction permits (rank)	56
DTF score for dealing with construction permits (0–100)	73.70
Procedures (number)	12
Time (days)	120
Cost (% of warehouse value)	0.7
Building quality control index (0–15)	8.0
Getting electricity (rank)	102
DTF score for getting electricity (0–100)	67.12
Procedures (number)	5
Time (days)	67
Cost (% of income per capita)	152.3
Reliability of supply and transparency of tariffs index (0–8)	2
Registering property (rank)	76
DTF score for registering property (0–100)	66.12
Procedures (number)	6
Time (days)	46
Cost (% of property value)	1.9
Quality of land administration index (0–30)	12.0

✘ **Getting credit** (rank)	101
DTF score for getting credit (0–100)	45.00
Strength of legal rights index (0–12)	2
Depth of credit information index (0–8)	7
Credit bureau coverage (% of adults)	45.3
Credit registry coverage (% of adults)	24.4
Protecting minority investors (rank)	137
DTF score for protecting minority investors (0–100)	41.67
Extent of disclosure index (0–10)	6
Extent of director liability index (0–10)	5
Ease of shareholder suits index (0–10)	6
Extent of shareholder rights index (0–10)	3
Extent of ownership and control index (0–10)	3
Extent of corporate transparency index (0–10)	2
Paying taxes (rank)	153
DTF score for paying taxes (0–100)	54.64
Payments (number per year)	20
Time (hours per year)	378
Total tax rate (% of profit)	35.0
Postfiling index (0–100)	10.22

✔ **Trading across borders** (rank)	116
DTF score for trading across borders (0–100)	64.03
Time to export	
Documentary compliance (hours)	24
Border compliance (hours)	120
Cost to export	
Documentary compliance (US$)	120
Border compliance (US$)	815
Time to import	
Documentary compliance (hours)	36
Border compliance (hours)	48
Cost to import	
Documentary compliance (US$)	135
Border compliance (US$)	500
Enforcing contracts (rank)	74
DTF score for enforcing contracts (0–100)	59.77
Time (days)	606
Cost (% of claim)	30.0
Quality of judicial processes index (0–18)	9.5
Resolving insolvency (rank)	102
DTF score for resolving insolvency (0–100)	40.70
Time (years)	3.9
Cost (% of estate)	9.0
Recovery rate (cents on the dollar)	20.5
Strength of insolvency framework index (0–16)	9.5

Note: Most indicator sets refer to a case scenario in the largest business city of an economy, though for 11 economies the data are a population-weighted average for the two largest business cities. For some indicators a result of "no practice" may be recorded for an economy; see the data notes for more details. In starting a business, procedures (number), time (days) and cost (% of income per capita) are calculated as the average of both men and women. For the postfiling index, a result of "not applicable" may be recorded for an economy.

✔ Reform making it easier to do business ✘ Change making it more difficult to do business

PERU

PERU		Latin America & Caribbean		GNI per capita (US$)	6,200
Ease of doing business rank (1–190)	54	Overall distance to frontier (DTF) score (0–100)	70.25	Population	31,376,670

Starting a business (rank)	103
DTF score for starting a business (0–100)	85.01
Procedures (number)	6
Time (days)	26
Cost (% of income per capita)	9.9
Minimum capital (% of income per capita)	0.0
Dealing with construction permits (rank)	51
DTF score for dealing with construction permits (0–100)	74.70
Procedures (number)	14
Time (days)	174
Cost (% of warehouse value)	0.5
Building quality control index (0–15)	12.0
Getting electricity (rank)	62
DTF score for getting electricity (0–100)	79.06
Procedures (number)	5
Time (days)	67
Cost (% of income per capita)	335.5
Reliability of supply and transparency of tariffs index (0–8)	6
Registering property (rank)	37
DTF score for registering property (0–100)	76.69
Procedures (number)	4
Time (days)	6.5
Cost (% of property value)	3.3
Quality of land administration index (0–30)	17.0
Getting credit (rank)	16
DTF score for getting credit (0–100)	80.00
Strength of legal rights index (0–12)	8
Depth of credit information index (0–8)	8
Credit bureau coverage (% of adults)	100.0
Credit registry coverage (% of adults)	37.4
Protecting minority investors (rank)	53
DTF score for protecting minority investors (0–100)	60.00
Extent of disclosure index (0–10)	9
Extent of director liability index (0–10)	6
Ease of shareholder suits index (0–10)	6
Extent of shareholder rights index (0–10)	9
Extent of ownership and control index (0–10)	3
Extent of corporate transparency index (0–10)	3
✔ **Paying taxes** (rank)	105
DTF score for paying taxes (0–100)	69.04
Payments (number per year)	9
Time (hours per year)	260
Total tax rate (% of profit)	35.6
Postfiling index (0–100)	32.17
Trading across borders (rank)	86
DTF score for trading across borders (0–100)	71.45
Time to export	
Documentary compliance (hours)	48
Border compliance (hours)	48
Cost to export	
Documentary compliance (US$)	50
Border compliance (US$)	460
Time to import	
Documentary compliance (hours)	72
Border compliance (hours)	72
Cost to import	
Documentary compliance (US$)	80
Border compliance (US$)	583
Enforcing contracts (rank)	63
DTF score for enforcing contracts (0–100)	60.70
Time (days)	426
Cost (% of claim)	35.7
Quality of judicial processes index (0–18)	8.5
Resolving insolvency (rank)	79
DTF score for resolving insolvency (0–100)	45.85
Time (years)	3.1
Cost (% of estate)	7.0
Recovery rate (cents on the dollar)	30.0
Strength of insolvency framework index (0–16)	9.5

PHILIPPINES

PHILIPPINES		East Asia & Pacific		GNI per capita (US$)	3,540
Ease of doing business rank (1–190)	99	Overall distance to frontier (DTF) score (0–100)	60.40	Population	100,699,395

Starting a business (rank)	171
DTF score for starting a business (0–100)	68.86
Procedures (number)	16
Time (days)	28
Cost (% of income per capita)	15.8
Minimum capital (% of income per capita)	3.1
✔ **Dealing with construction permits** (rank)	85
DTF score for dealing with construction permits (0–100)	69.45
Procedures (number)	24
Time (days)	98
Cost (% of warehouse value)	1.1
Building quality control index (0–15)	12.0
Getting electricity (rank)	22
DTF score for getting electricity (0–100)	86.90
Procedures (number)	4
Time (days)	42
Cost (% of income per capita)	25.7
Reliability of supply and transparency of tariffs index (0–8)	6
Registering property (rank)	112
DTF score for registering property (0–100)	57.54
Procedures (number)	9
Time (days)	35
Cost (% of property value)	4.3
Quality of land administration index (0–30)	12.5
Getting credit (rank)	118
DTF score for getting credit (0–100)	40.00
Strength of legal rights index (0–12)	3
Depth of credit information index (0–8)	5
Credit bureau coverage (% of adults)	10.2
Credit registry coverage (% of adults)	0.0
Protecting minority investors (rank)	137
DTF score for protecting minority investors (0–100)	41.67
Extent of disclosure index (0–10)	2
Extent of director liability index (0–10)	3
Ease of shareholder suits index (0–10)	7
Extent of shareholder rights index (0–10)	1
Extent of ownership and control index (0–10)	5
Extent of corporate transparency index (0–10)	7
✔ **Paying taxes** (rank)	115
DTF score for paying taxes (0–100)	65.74
Payments (number per year)	28
Time (hours per year)	185.6
Total tax rate (% of profit)	42.9
Postfiling index (0–100)	49.77
Trading across borders (rank)	95
DTF score for trading across borders (0–100)	69.39
Time to export	
Documentary compliance (hours)	72
Border compliance (hours)	42
Cost to export	
Documentary compliance (US$)	53
Border compliance (US$)	456
Time to import	
Documentary compliance (hours)	96
Border compliance (hours)	72
Cost to import	
Documentary compliance (US$)	50
Border compliance (US$)	580
Enforcing contracts (rank)	136
DTF score for enforcing contracts (0–100)	49.24
Time (days)	842
Cost (% of claim)	31.0
Quality of judicial processes index (0–18)	7.5
Resolving insolvency (rank)	56
DTF score for resolving insolvency (0–100)	55.24
Time (years)	2.7
Cost (% of estate)	32.0
Recovery rate (cents on the dollar)	21.3
Strength of insolvency framework index (0–16)	14.0

POLAND

POLAND		OECD high income		GNI per capita (US$)	13,370
Ease of doing business rank (1–190)	24	Overall distance to frontier (DTF) score (0–100)	77.81	Population	37,999,494

Starting a business (rank)	107
DTF score for starting a business (0–100)	84.22
Procedures (number)	4
Time (days)	37
Cost (% of income per capita)	12.1
Minimum capital (% of income per capita)	10.9
✔ **Dealing with construction permits** (rank)	46
DTF score for dealing with construction permits (0–100)	75.15
Procedures (number)	12
Time (days)	153
Cost (% of warehouse value)	0.3
Building quality control index (0–15)	10.0
✔ **Getting electricity** (rank)	46
DTF score for getting electricity (0–100)	81.35
Procedures (number)	4
Time (days)	122
Cost (% of income per capita)	19.0
Reliability of supply and transparency of tariffs index (0–8)	7
Registering property (rank)	38
DTF score for registering property (0–100)	76.49
Procedures (number)	6
Time (days)	33
Cost (% of property value)	0.3
Quality of land administration index (0–30)	19.5
Getting credit (rank)	20
DTF score for getting credit (0–100)	75.00
Strength of legal rights index (0–12)	7
Depth of credit information index (0–8)	8
Credit bureau coverage (% of adults)	92.5
Credit registry coverage (% of adults)	0.0
Protecting minority investors (rank)	42
DTF score for protecting minority investors (0–100)	63.33
Extent of disclosure index (0–10)	7
Extent of director liability index (0–10)	2
Ease of shareholder suits index (0–10)	9
Extent of shareholder rights index (0–10)	8
Extent of ownership and control index (0–10)	5
Extent of corporate transparency index (0–10)	7
Paying taxes (rank)	47
DTF score for paying taxes (0–100)	82.73
Payments (number per year)	7
Time (hours per year)	271
Total tax rate (% of profit)	40.4
Postfiling index (0–100)	92.18
Trading across borders (rank)	1
DTF score for trading across borders (0–100)	100.00
Time to export	
Documentary compliance (hours)	1
Border compliance (hours)	0
Cost to export	
Documentary compliance (US$)	0
Border compliance (US$)	0
Time to import	
Documentary compliance (hours)	1
Border compliance (hours)	0
Cost to import	
Documentary compliance (US$)	0
Border compliance (US$)	0
Enforcing contracts (rank)	55
DTF score for enforcing contracts (0–100)	63.44
Time (days)	685
Cost (% of claim)	19.4
Quality of judicial processes index (0–18)	10.5
✔ **Resolving insolvency** (rank)	27
DTF score for resolving insolvency (0–100)	76.37
Time (years)	3.0
Cost (% of estate)	15.0
Recovery rate (cents on the dollar)	60.6
Strength of insolvency framework index (0–16)	14.0

Note: Most indicator sets refer to a case scenario in the largest business city of an economy, though for 11 economies the data are a population-weighted average for the two largest business cities. For some indicators a result of "no practice" may be recorded for an economy; see the data notes for more details. In starting a business, procedures (number), time (days) and cost (% of income per capita) are calculated as the average of both men and women. For the postfiling index, a result of "not applicable" may be recorded for an economy.

✔ Reform making it easier to do business ✘ Change making it more difficult to do business

PORTUGAL

PORTUGAL		OECD high income		GNI per capita (US$)	20,530
Ease of doing business rank (1–190)	25	Overall distance to frontier (DTF) score (0–100)	77.40	Population	10,348,648

Starting a business (rank)	32
DTF score for starting a business (0–100)	92.85
Procedures (number)	5
Time (days)	4.5
Cost (% of income per capita)	2.1
Minimum capital (% of income per capita)	0.0
Dealing with construction permits (rank)	35
DTF score for dealing with construction permits (0–100)	76.47
Procedures (number)	14
Time (days)	113
Cost (% of warehouse value)	1.3
Building quality control index (0–15)	11.0
✔ **Getting electricity** (rank)	50
DTF score for getting electricity (0–100)	80.72
Procedures (number)	7
Time (days)	41
Cost (% of income per capita)	37.3
Reliability of supply and transparency of tariffs index (0–8)	8
Registering property (rank)	27
DTF score for registering property (0–100)	80.26
Procedures (number)	1
Time (days)	1
Cost (% of property value)	7.3
Quality of land administration index (0–30)	21.0

Getting credit (rank)	101
DTF score for getting credit (0–100)	45.00
Strength of legal rights index (0–12)	2
Depth of credit information index (0–8)	7
Credit bureau coverage (% of adults)	7.8
Credit registry coverage (% of adults)	100.0
Protecting minority investors (rank)	70
DTF score for protecting minority investors (0–100)	56.67
Extent of disclosure index (0–10)	6
Extent of director liability index (0–10)	5
Ease of shareholder suits index (0–10)	7
Extent of shareholder rights index (0–10)	4
Extent of ownership and control index (0–10)	6
Extent of corporate transparency index (0–10)	6
✔ **Paying taxes** (rank)	38
DTF score for paying taxes (0–100)	83.75
Payments (number per year)	8
Time (hours per year)	243
Total tax rate (% of profit)	39.8
Postfiling index (0–100)	92.71

Trading across borders (rank)	1
DTF score for trading across borders (0–100)	100.00
Time to export	
Documentary compliance (hours)	1
Border compliance (hours)	0
Cost to export	
Documentary compliance (US$)	0
Border compliance (US$)	0
Time to import	
Documentary compliance (hours)	1
Border compliance (hours)	0
Cost to import	
Documentary compliance (US$)	0
Border compliance (US$)	0
Enforcing contracts (rank)	19
DTF score for enforcing contracts (0–100)	73.01
Time (days)	547
Cost (% of claim)	13.8
Quality of judicial processes index (0–18)	12.5
Resolving insolvency (rank)	7
DTF score for resolving insolvency (0–100)	85.24
Time (years)	2.0
Cost (% of estate)	9.0
Recovery rate (cents on the dollar)	74.2
Strength of insolvency framework index (0–16)	14.5

PUERTO RICO (U.S.)

PUERTO RICO (U.S.)		Latin America & Caribbean		GNI per capita (US$)	19,149
Ease of doing business rank (1–190)	55	Overall distance to frontier (DTF) score (0–100)	69.82	Population	3,474,182

Starting a business (rank)	51
DTF score for starting a business (0–100)	91.23
Procedures (number)	6
Time (days)	5.5
Cost (% of income per capita)	1.3
Minimum capital (% of income per capita)	0.0
Dealing with construction permits (rank)	131
DTF score for dealing with construction permits (0–100)	62.17
Procedures (number)	20
Time (days)	165
Cost (% of warehouse value)	6.2
Building quality control index (0–15)	12.0
Getting electricity (rank)	65
DTF score for getting electricity (0–100)	76.55
Procedures (number)	5
Time (days)	32
Cost (% of income per capita)	354.1
Reliability of supply and transparency of tariffs index (0–8)	4
✔ **Registering property** (rank)	153
DTF score for registering property (0–100)	47.29
Procedures (number)	8
Time (days)	191
Cost (% of property value)	1.2
Quality of land administration index (0–30)	14.0

Getting credit (rank)	7
DTF score for getting credit (0–100)	85.00
Strength of legal rights index (0–12)	10
Depth of credit information index (0–8)	7
Credit bureau coverage (% of adults)	100.0
Credit registry coverage (% of adults)	0.0
Protecting minority investors (rank)	87
DTF score for protecting minority investors (0–100)	53.33
Extent of disclosure index (0–10)	7
Extent of director liability index (0–10)	6
Ease of shareholder suits index (0–10)	8
Extent of shareholder rights index (0–10)	3
Extent of ownership and control index (0–10)	2
Extent of corporate transparency index (0–10)	6
✔ **Paying taxes** (rank)	135
DTF score for paying taxes (0–100)	59.82
Payments (number per year)	16
Time (hours per year)	218
Total tax rate (% of profit)	62.3
Postfiling index (0–100)	41.42

Trading across borders (rank)	62
DTF score for trading across borders (0–100)	81.86
Time to export	
Documentary compliance (hours)	2
Border compliance (hours)	48
Cost to export	
Documentary compliance (US$)	75
Border compliance (US$)	386
Time to import	
Documentary compliance (hours)	2
Border compliance (hours)	48
Cost to import	
Documentary compliance (US$)	75
Border compliance (US$)	386
Enforcing contracts (rank)	97
DTF score for enforcing contracts (0–100)	56.13
Time (days)	630
Cost (% of claim)	25.6
Quality of judicial processes index (0–18)	7.0
Resolving insolvency (rank)	9
DTF score for resolving insolvency (0–100)	84.84
Time (years)	2.5
Cost (% of estate)	11.0
Recovery rate (cents on the dollar)	70.5
Strength of insolvency framework index (0–16)	15.0

QATAR

QATAR		Middle East & North Africa		GNI per capita (US$)	85,430
Ease of doing business rank (1–190)	83	Overall distance to frontier (DTF) score (0–100)	63.66	Population	2,235,355

✔ **Starting a business** (rank)	91
DTF score for starting a business (0–100)	86.06
Procedures (number)	8.5
Time (days)	9
Cost (% of income per capita)	6.2
Minimum capital (% of income per capita)	0.0
Dealing with construction permits (rank)	21
DTF score for dealing with construction permits (0–100)	79.16
Procedures (number)	16
Time (days)	58
Cost (% of warehouse value)	2.0
Building quality control index (0–15)	12.0
Getting electricity (rank)	44
DTF score for getting electricity (0–100)	81.72
Procedures (number)	4
Time (days)	90
Cost (% of income per capita)	10.8
Reliability of supply and transparency of tariffs index (0–8)	6
✔ **Registering property** (rank)	26
DTF score for registering property (0–100)	81.06
Procedures (number)	7
Time (days)	13
Cost (% of property value)	0.3
Quality of land administration index (0–30)	24.5

Getting credit (rank)	139
DTF score for getting credit (0–100)	30.00
Strength of legal rights index (0–12)	1
Depth of credit information index (0–8)	5
Credit bureau coverage (% of adults)	0.0
Credit registry coverage (% of adults)	30.5
✘ **Protecting minority investors** (rank)	183
DTF score for protecting minority investors (0–100)	26.67
Extent of disclosure index (0–10)	2
Extent of director liability index (0–10)	2
Ease of shareholder suits index (0–10)	2
Extent of shareholder rights index (0–10)	4
Extent of ownership and control index (0–10)	2
Extent of corporate transparency index (0–10)	4
Paying taxes (rank)	1
DTF score for paying taxes (0–100)	99.44
Payments (number per year)	4
Time (hours per year)	41
Total tax rate (% of profit)	11.3
Postfiling index (0–100)	NOT APPLICABLE

Trading across borders (rank)	128
DTF score for trading across borders (0–100)	61.41
Time to export	
Documentary compliance (hours)	10
Border compliance (hours)	30
Cost to export	
Documentary compliance (US$)	150
Border compliance (US$)	382
Time to import	
Documentary compliance (hours)	72
Border compliance (hours)	88
Cost to import	
Documentary compliance (US$)	617
Border compliance (US$)	754
Enforcing contracts (rank)	120
DTF score for enforcing contracts (0–100)	52.79
Time (days)	570
Cost (% of claim)	21.6
Quality of judicial processes index (0–18)	3.5
Resolving insolvency (rank)	116
DTF score for resolving insolvency (0–100)	38.23
Time (years)	2.8
Cost (% of estate)	22.0
Recovery rate (cents on the dollar)	30.4
Strength of insolvency framework index (0–16)	7.0

Note: Most indicator sets refer to a case scenario in the largest business city of an economy, though for 11 economies the data are a population-weighted average for the two largest business cities. For some indicators a result of "no practice" may be recorded for an economy; see the data notes for more details. In starting a business, procedures (number), time (days) and cost (% of income per capita) are calculated as the average of both men and women. For the postfiling index, a result of "not applicable" may be recorded for an economy.

✔ Reform making it easier to do business ✘ Change making it more difficult to do business

ROMANIA

ROMANIA		Europe & Central Asia		GNI per capita (US$)	9,500
Ease of doing business rank (1–190)	36	Overall distance to frontier (DTF) score (0–100)	74.26	Population	19,832,389

✘ **Starting a business** (rank)	62
DTF score for starting a business (0–100)	89.48
Procedures (number)	6
Time (days)	12
Cost (% of income per capita)	2.0
Minimum capital (% of income per capita)	0.6
Dealing with construction permits (rank)	95
DTF score for dealing with construction permits (0–100)	68.67
Procedures (number)	20
Time (days)	171
Cost (% of warehouse value)	2.0
Building quality control index (0–15)	13.0
Getting electricity (rank)	134
DTF score for getting electricity (0–100)	56.48
Procedures (number)	8
Time (days)	182
Cost (% of income per capita)	561.1
Reliability of supply and transparency of tariffs index (0–8)	7
Registering property (rank)	57
DTF score for registering property (0–100)	71.11
Procedures (number)	7
Time (days)	21
Cost (% of property value)	1.4
Quality of land administration index (0–30)	16.0
Getting credit (rank)	7
DTF score for getting credit (0–100)	85.00
Strength of legal rights index (0–12)	10
Depth of credit information index (0–8)	7
Credit bureau coverage (% of adults)	51.1
Credit registry coverage (% of adults)	16.8
Protecting minority investors (rank)	53
DTF score for protecting minority investors (0–100)	60.00
Extent of disclosure index (0–10)	9
Extent of director liability index (0–10)	4
Ease of shareholder suits index (0–10)	5
Extent of shareholder rights index (0–10)	6
Extent of ownership and control index (0–10)	5
Extent of corporate transparency index (0–10)	7
Paying taxes (rank)	50
DTF score for paying taxes (0–100)	81.64
Payments (number per year)	14
Time (hours per year)	161
Total tax rate (% of profit)	38.4
Postfiling index (0–100)	79.62
Trading across borders (rank)	1
DTF score for trading across borders (0–100)	100.00
Time to export	
Documentary compliance (hours)	1
Border compliance (hours)	0
Cost to export	
Documentary compliance (US$)	0
Border compliance (US$)	0
Time to import	
Documentary compliance (hours)	1
Border compliance (hours)	0
Cost to import	
Documentary compliance (US$)	0
Border compliance (US$)	0
Enforcing contracts (rank)	26
DTF score for enforcing contracts (0–100)	71.08
Time (days)	512
Cost (% of claim)	28.9
Quality of judicial processes index (0–18)	14.0
Resolving insolvency (rank)	49
DTF score for resolving insolvency (0–100)	59.16
Time (years)	3.3
Cost (% of estate)	10.5
Recovery rate (cents on the dollar)	34.4
Strength of insolvency framework index (0–16)	13.0

RUSSIAN FEDERATION

RUSSIAN FEDERATION		Europe & Central Asia		GNI per capita (US$)	11,400
Ease of doing business rank (1–190)	40	Overall distance to frontier (DTF) score (0–100)	73.19	Population	144,096,812

Starting a business (rank)	26
DTF score for starting a business (0–100)	93.57
Procedures (number)	3.7
Time (days)	9.8
Cost (% of income per capita)	1.0
Minimum capital (% of income per capita)	0.0
✔ **Dealing with construction permits** (rank)	115
DTF score for dealing with construction permits (0–100)	65.86
Procedures (number)	13.7
Time (days)	239.3
Cost (% of warehouse value)	1.4
Building quality control index (0–15)	10.0
Getting electricity (rank)	30
DTF score for getting electricity (0–100)	84.37
Procedures (number)	3
Time (days)	160.5
Cost (% of income per capita)	44.1
Reliability of supply and transparency of tariffs index (0–8)	8
Registering property (rank)	9
DTF score for registering property (0–100)	90.55
Procedures (number)	3
Time (days)	15
Cost (% of property value)	0.2
Quality of land administration index (0–30)	26
Getting credit (rank)	44
DTF score for getting credit (0–100)	65.00
Strength of legal rights index (0–12)	6
Depth of credit information index (0–8)	7
Credit bureau coverage (% of adults)	77.2
Credit registry coverage (% of adults)	0.0
Protecting minority investors (rank)	53
DTF score for protecting minority investors (0–100)	60.00
Extent of disclosure index (0–10)	6
Extent of director liability index (0–10)	2
Ease of shareholder suits index (0–10)	7
Extent of shareholder rights index (0–10)	8
Extent of ownership and control index (0–10)	5
Extent of corporate transparency index (0–10)	8
Paying taxes (rank)	45
DTF score for paying taxes (0–100)	82.96
Payments (number per year)	7
Time (hours per year)	168
Total tax rate (% of profit)	47.4
Postfiling index (0–100)	87.59
Trading across borders (rank)	140
DTF score for trading across borders (0–100)	57.96
Time to export	
Documentary compliance (hours)	25.4
Border compliance (hours)	96
Cost to export	
Documentary compliance (US$)	92
Border compliance (US$)	765
Time to import	
Documentary compliance (hours)	42.5
Border compliance (hours)	96
Cost to import	
Documentary compliance (US$)	152.5
Border compliance (US$)	1,125
✘ **Enforcing contracts** (rank)	12
DTF score for enforcing contracts (0–100)	74.96
Time (days)	337
Cost (% of claim)	16.5
Quality of judicial processes index (0–18)	11.0
Resolving insolvency (rank)	51
DTF score for resolving insolvency (0–100)	56.69
Time (years)	2.0
Cost (% of estate)	9.0
Recovery rate (cents on the dollar)	38.6
Strength of insolvency framework index (0–16)	11.5

RWANDA

RWANDA		Sub-Saharan Africa		GNI per capita (US$)	700
Ease of doing business rank (1–190)	56	Overall distance to frontier (DTF) score (0–100)	69.81	Population	11,609,666

✔ **Starting a business** (rank)	76
DTF score for starting a business (0–100)	87.17
Procedures (number)	5
Time (days)	4
Cost (% of income per capita)	48.5
Minimum capital (% of income per capita)	0.0
✘ **Dealing with construction permits** (rank)	158
DTF score for dealing with construction permits (0–100)	55.40
Procedures (number)	15
Time (days)	113
Cost (% of warehouse value)	42.4
Building quality control index (0–15)	13.0
Getting electricity (rank)	117
DTF score for getting electricity (0–100)	60.69
Procedures (number)	4
Time (days)	34
Cost (% of income per capita)	2,722.6
Reliability of supply and transparency of tariffs index (0–8)	0
✔ **Registering property** (rank)	4
DTF score for registering property (0–100)	92.67
Procedures (number)	3
Time (days)	12
Cost (% of property value)	0.1
Quality of land administration index (0–30)	28.0
Getting credit (rank)	2
DTF score for getting credit (0–100)	95.00
Strength of legal rights index (0–12)	11
Depth of credit information index (0–8)	8
Credit bureau coverage (% of adults)	16.6
Credit registry coverage (% of adults)	7.4
Protecting minority investors (rank)	102
DTF score for protecting minority investors (0–100)	51.67
Extent of disclosure index (0–10)	7
Extent of director liability index (0–10)	9
Ease of shareholder suits index (0–10)	3
Extent of shareholder rights index (0–10)	6
Extent of ownership and control index (0–10)	2
Extent of corporate transparency index (0–10)	4
✘ **Paying taxes** (rank)	59
DTF score for paying taxes (0–100)	79.69
Payments (number per year)	29
Time (hours per year)	124
Total tax rate (% of profit)	33.0
Postfiling index (0–100)	83.29
✔ **Trading across borders** (rank)	87
DTF score for trading across borders (0–100)	71.19
Time to export	
Documentary compliance (hours)	42
Border compliance (hours)	97
Cost to export	
Documentary compliance (US$)	110
Border compliance (US$)	183
Time to import	
Documentary compliance (hours)	72
Border compliance (hours)	86
Cost to import	
Documentary compliance (US$)	121
Border compliance (US$)	282
✔ **Enforcing contracts** (rank)	95
DTF score for enforcing contracts (0–100)	56.76
Time (days)	230
Cost (% of claim)	82.7
Quality of judicial processes index (0–18)	13.0
Resolving insolvency (rank)	73
DTF score for resolving insolvency (0–100)	47.85
Time (years)	2.5
Cost (% of estate)	29.0
Recovery rate (cents on the dollar)	19.2
Strength of insolvency framework index (0–16)	12.0

Note: Most indicator sets refer to a case scenario in the largest business city of an economy, though for 11 economies the data are a population-weighted average for the two largest business cities. For some indicators a result of "no practice" may be recorded for an economy; see the data notes for more details. In starting a business, procedures (number), time (days) and cost (% of income per capita) are calculated as the average of both men and women. For the postfiling index, a result of "not applicable" may be recorded for an economy.

✔ Reform making it easier to do business ✘ Change making it more difficult to do business

SAMOA

SAMOA		East Asia & Pacific		GNI per capita (US$)	3,930
Ease of doing business rank (1–190)	89	Overall distance to frontier (DTF) score (0–100)	62.17	Population	193,228
Starting a business (rank)	37	**Getting credit** (rank)	157	**Trading across borders** (rank)	141
DTF score for starting a business (0–100)	92.49	DTF score for getting credit (0–100)	25.00	DTF score for trading across borders (0–100)	57.81
Procedures (number)	4	Strength of legal rights index (0–12)	5	*Time to export*	
Time (days)	9	Depth of credit information index (0–8)	0	Documentary compliance (hours)	24
Cost (% of income per capita)	7.7	Credit bureau coverage (% of adults)	0.0	Border compliance (hours)	51
Minimum capital (% of income per capita)	0.0	Credit registry coverage (% of adults)	0.0	*Cost to export*	
				Documentary compliance (US$)	180
Dealing with construction permits (rank)	96	**Protecting minority investors** (rank)	63	Border compliance (US$)	1,400
DTF score for dealing with construction permits (0–100)	68.63	DTF score for protecting minority investors (0–100)	58.33	*Time to import*	
Procedures (number)	18	Extent of disclosure index (0–10)	5	Documentary compliance (hours)	25
Time (days)	58	Extent of director liability index (0–10)	6	Border compliance (hours)	84
Cost (% of warehouse value)	0.9	Ease of shareholder suits index (0–10)	9	*Cost to import*	
Building quality control index (0–15)	6.0	Extent of shareholder rights index (0–10)	8	Documentary compliance (US$)	230
		Extent of ownership and control index (0–10)	4	Border compliance (US$)	900
		Extent of corporate transparency index (0–10)	3		
Getting electricity (rank)	59			**Enforcing contracts** (rank)	67
DTF score for getting electricity (0–100)	79.61	**Paying taxes** (rank)	71	DTF score for enforcing contracts (0–100)	60.44
Procedures (number)	4	DTF score for paying taxes (0–100)	76.93	Time (days)	455
Time (days)	34	Payments (number per year)	37	Cost (% of claim)	24.4
Cost (% of income per capita)	641.9	Time (hours per year)	224	Quality of judicial processes index (0–18)	6.5
Reliability of supply and transparency of tariffs index (0–8)	4	Total tax rate (% of profit)	18.5		
Registering property (rank)	64	Postfiling index (0–100)	91.42	**Resolving insolvency** (rank)	134
DTF score for registering property (0–100)	69.12			DTF score for resolving insolvency (0–100)	33.33
Procedures (number)	5			Time (years)	2.0
Time (days)	15			Cost (% of estate)	38.0
Cost (% of property value)	3.8			Recovery rate (cents on the dollar)	18.4
Quality of land administration index (0–30)	12.5			Strength of insolvency framework index (0–16)	7.5

SAN MARINO

SAN MARINO		Europe & Central Asia		GNI per capita (US$)	48,162
Ease of doing business rank (1–190)	79	Overall distance to frontier (DTF) score (0–100)	64.11	Population	31,781
Starting a business (rank)	98	**Getting credit** (rank)	181	**Trading across borders** (rank)	20
DTF score for starting a business (0–100)	85.46	DTF score for getting credit (0–100)	5.00	DTF score for trading across borders (0–100)	97.48
Procedures (number)	7	Strength of legal rights index (0–12)	1	*Time to export*	
Time (days)	11.5	Depth of credit information index (0–8)	0	Documentary compliance (hours)	1
Cost (% of income per capita)	9.0	Credit bureau coverage (% of adults)	0.0	Border compliance (hours)	0
Minimum capital (% of income per capita)	29.4	Credit registry coverage (% of adults)	0.0	*Cost to export*	
				Documentary compliance (US$)	0
✔ **Dealing with construction permits** (rank)	72	**Protecting minority investors** (rank)	162	Border compliance (US$)	0
DTF score for dealing with construction permits (0–100)	71.43	DTF score for protecting minority investors (0–100)	36.67	*Time to import*	
Procedures (number)	15	Extent of disclosure index (0–10)	3	Documentary compliance (hours)	3
Time (days)	145.5	Extent of director liability index (0–10)	2	Border compliance (hours)	4
Cost (% of warehouse value)	5.3	Ease of shareholder suits index (0–10)	8	*Cost to import*	
Building quality control index (0–15)	13.0	Extent of shareholder rights index (0–10)	7	Documentary compliance (US$)	100
		Extent of ownership and control index (0–10)	2	Border compliance (US$)	50
Getting electricity (rank)	11	Extent of corporate transparency index (0–10)	0		
DTF score for getting electricity (0–100)	90.63			**Enforcing contracts** (rank)	78
Procedures (number)	3	✔ **Paying taxes** (rank)	14	DTF score for enforcing contracts (0–100)	59.25
Time (days)	45	DTF score for paying taxes (0–100)	90.02	Time (days)	575
Cost (% of income per capita)	58.8	Payments (number per year)	18	Cost (% of claim)	13.9
Reliability of supply and transparency of tariffs index (0–8)	6	Time (hours per year)	52	Quality of judicial processes index (0–18)	5.5
		Total tax rate (% of profit)	35.4		
Registering property (rank)	80	Postfiling index (0–100)	98.62	**Resolving insolvency** (rank)	110
DTF score for registering property (0–100)	65.66			DTF score for resolving insolvency (0–100)	39.48
Procedures (number)	9			Time (years)	2.3
Time (days)	42.5			Cost (% of estate)	5.0
Cost (% of property value)	4.1			Recovery rate (cents on the dollar)	47.2
Quality of land administration index (0–30)	23.0			Strength of insolvency framework index (0–16)	4.5

SÃO TOMÉ AND PRÍNCIPE

SÃO TOMÉ AND PRÍNCIPE		Sub-Saharan Africa		GNI per capita (US$)	1,534
Ease of doing business rank (1–190)	162	Overall distance to frontier (DTF) score (0–100)	46.75	Population	190,344
Starting a business (rank)	35	**Getting credit** (rank)	185	**Trading across borders** (rank)	122
DTF score for starting a business (0–100)	92.56	DTF score for getting credit (0–100)	0.00	DTF score for trading across borders (0–100)	62.78
Procedures (number)	4	Strength of legal rights index (0–12)	0	*Time to export*	
Time (days)	5	Depth of credit information index (0–8)	0	Documentary compliance (hours)	46
Cost (% of income per capita)	15.2	Credit bureau coverage (% of adults)	0.0	Border compliance (hours)	121
Minimum capital (% of income per capita)	0.0	Credit registry coverage (% of adults)	0.0	*Cost to export*	
				Documentary compliance (US$)	194
Dealing with construction permits (rank)	121	**Protecting minority investors** (rank)	183	Border compliance (US$)	426
DTF score for dealing with construction permits (0–100)	64.53	DTF score for protecting minority investors (0–100)	26.67	*Time to import*	
Procedures (number)	15	Extent of disclosure index (0–10)	3	Documentary compliance (hours)	17
Time (days)	104	Extent of director liability index (0–10)	1	Border compliance (hours)	156
Cost (% of warehouse value)	2.5	Ease of shareholder suits index (0–10)	6	*Cost to import*	
Building quality control index (0–15)	5.0	Extent of shareholder rights index (0–10)	3	Documentary compliance (US$)	75
		Extent of ownership and control index (0–10)	2	Border compliance (US$)	406
Getting electricity (rank)	119	Extent of corporate transparency index (0–10)	1		
DTF score for getting electricity (0–100)	60.56			**Enforcing contracts** (rank)	181
Procedures (number)	4	**Paying taxes** (rank)	127	DTF score for enforcing contracts (0–100)	31.21
Time (days)	89	DTF score for paying taxes (0–100)	61.22	Time (days)	1,065
Cost (% of income per capita)	827.2	Payments (number per year)	46	Cost (% of claim)	50.5
Reliability of supply and transparency of tariffs index (0–8)	0	Time (hours per year)	424	Quality of judicial processes index (0–18)	5.0
		Total tax rate (% of profit)	37.4		
Registering property (rank)	161	Postfiling index (0–100)	90.37	**Resolving insolvency** (rank)	158
DTF score for registering property (0–100)	44.04			DTF score for resolving insolvency (0–100)	23.98
Procedures (number)	7			Time (years)	6.2
Time (days)	62			Cost (% of estate)	22.0
Cost (% of property value)	9.0			Recovery rate (cents on the dollar)	9.7
Quality of land administration index (0–30)	4.5			Strength of insolvency framework index (0–16)	6.0

Note: Most indicator sets refer to a case scenario in the largest business city of an economy, though for 11 economies the data are a population-weighted average for the two largest business cities. For some indicators a result of "no practice" may be recorded for an economy; see the data notes for more details. In starting a business, procedures (number), time (days) and cost (% of income per capita) are calculated as the average of both men and women. For the postfiling index, a result of "not applicable" may be recorded for an economy.

✔ Reform making it easier to do business ✘ Change making it more difficult to do business

SAUDI ARABIA

SAUDI ARABIA		Middle East & North Africa		GNI per capita (US$)	23,550
Ease of doing business rank (1–190)	94	Overall distance to frontier (DTF) score (0–100)	61.11	Population	31,540,372

✔ **Starting a business** (rank)	147
DTF score for starting a business (0–100)	77.09
Procedures (number)	13.5
Time (days)	16.5
Cost (% of income per capita)	4.1
Minimum capital (% of income per capita)	0.0
Dealing with construction permits (rank)	15
DTF score for dealing with construction permits (0–100)	80.66
Procedures (number)	13
Time (days)	106
Cost (% of warehouse value)	0.5
Building quality control index (0–15)	12.0
Getting electricity (rank)	28
DTF score for getting electricity (0–100)	84.81
Procedures (number)	4
Time (days)	61
Cost (% of income per capita)	31.4
Reliability of supply and transparency of tariffs index (0–8)	6
Registering property (rank)	32
DTF score for registering property (0–100)	78.51
Procedures (number)	3
Time (days)	3
Cost (% of property value)	0.0
Quality of land administration index (0–30)	9.5
Getting credit (rank)	82
DTF score for getting credit (0–100)	50.00
Strength of legal rights index (0–12)	2
Depth of credit information index (0–8)	8
Credit bureau coverage (% of adults)	48.3
Credit registry coverage (% of adults)	0.0
✔ **Protecting minority investors** (rank)	63
DTF score for protecting minority investors (0–100)	58.33
Extent of disclosure index (0–10)	8
Extent of director liability index (0–10)	8
Ease of shareholder suits index (0–10)	4
Extent of shareholder rights index (0–10)	4
Extent of ownership and control index (0–10)	4
Extent of corporate transparency index (0–10)	7
✘ **Paying taxes** (rank)	69
DTF score for paying taxes (0–100)	77.04
Payments (number per year)	3
Time (hours per year)	67
Total tax rate (% of profit)	15.7
Postfiling index (0–100)	10.94
Trading across borders (rank)	158
DTF score for trading across borders (0–100)	49.62
Time to export	
Documentary compliance (hours)	90
Border compliance (hours)	69
Cost to export	
Documentary compliance (US$)	105
Border compliance (US$)	264
Time to import	
Documentary compliance (hours)	131
Border compliance (hours)	228
Cost to import	
Documentary compliance (US$)	390
Border compliance (US$)	779
Enforcing contracts (rank)	105
DTF score for enforcing contracts (0–100)	55.07
Time (days)	575
Cost (% of claim)	27.5
Quality of judicial processes index (0–18)	6.0
Resolving insolvency (rank)	169
DTF score for resolving insolvency (0–100)	0.00
Time (years)	NO PRACTICE
Cost (% of estate)	NO PRACTICE
Recovery rate (cents on the dollar)	0.0
Strength of insolvency framework index (0–16)	0.0

SENEGAL

SENEGAL		Sub-Saharan Africa		GNI per capita (US$)	1,000
Ease of doing business rank (1–190)	147	Overall distance to frontier (DTF) score (0–100)	50.68	Population	15,129,273

Starting a business (rank)	90
DTF score for starting a business (0–100)	86.07
Procedures (number)	4
Time (days)	6
Cost (% of income per capita)	62.7
Minimum capital (% of income per capita)	4.7
Dealing with construction permits (rank)	139
DTF score for dealing with construction permits (0–100)	61.47
Procedures (number)	13
Time (days)	202
Cost (% of warehouse value)	7.6
Building quality control index (0–15)	10.0
Getting electricity (rank)	162
DTF score for getting electricity (0–100)	44.51
Procedures (number)	6
Time (days)	75
Cost (% of income per capita)	3,822.3
Reliability of supply and transparency of tariffs index (0–8)	0
✔ **Registering property** (rank)	142
DTF score for registering property (0–100)	49.60
Procedures (number)	5
Time (days)	71
Cost (% of property value)	10.2
Quality of land administration index (0–30)	10.0
✔ **Getting credit** (rank)	139
DTF score for getting credit (0–100)	30.00
Strength of legal rights index (0–12)	6
Depth of credit information index (0–8)	0
Credit bureau coverage (% of adults)	0.6
Credit registry coverage (% of adults)	0.6
Protecting minority investors (rank)	137
DTF score for protecting minority investors (0–100)	41.67
Extent of disclosure index (0–10)	7
Extent of director liability index (0–10)	1
Ease of shareholder suits index (0–10)	6
Extent of shareholder rights index (0–10)	5
Extent of ownership and control index (0–10)	4
Extent of corporate transparency index (0–10)	2
✔ **Paying taxes** (rank)	174
DTF score for paying taxes (0–100)	43.70
Payments (number per year)	58
Time (hours per year)	441
Total tax rate (% of profit)	45.1
Postfiling index (0–100)	54.32
Trading across borders (rank)	130
DTF score for trading across borders (0–100)	60.85
Time to export	
Documentary compliance (hours)	26
Border compliance (hours)	61
Cost to export	
Documentary compliance (US$)	96
Border compliance (US$)	547
Time to import	
Documentary compliance (hours)	72
Border compliance (hours)	53
Cost to import	
Documentary compliance (US$)	545
Border compliance (US$)	702
Enforcing contracts (rank)	144
DTF score for enforcing contracts (0–100)	48.15
Time (days)	740
Cost (% of claim)	36.4
Quality of judicial processes index (0–18)	6.5
✔ **Resolving insolvency** (rank)	101
DTF score for resolving insolvency (0–100)	40.74
Time (years)	3.0
Cost (% of estate)	20.0
Recovery rate (cents on the dollar)	23.4
Strength of insolvency framework index (0–16)	9.0

SERBIA

SERBIA		Europe & Central Asia		GNI per capita (US$)	5,500
Ease of doing business rank (1–190)	47	Overall distance to frontier (DTF) score (0–100)	72.29	Population	7,098,247

✔ **Starting a business** (rank)	47
DTF score for starting a business (0–100)	91.67
Procedures (number)	5
Time (days)	7
Cost (% of income per capita)	6.5
Minimum capital (% of income per capita)	0.0
✔ **Dealing with construction permits** (rank)	36
DTF score for dealing with construction permits (0–100)	76.30
Procedures (number)	12
Time (days)	156
Cost (% of warehouse value)	3.2
Building quality control index (0–15)	13.0
Getting electricity (rank)	92
DTF score for getting electricity (0–100)	69.93
Procedures (number)	5
Time (days)	125
Cost (% of income per capita)	235.8
Reliability of supply and transparency of tariffs index (0–8)	5
✔ **Registering property** (rank)	56
DTF score for registering property (0–100)	71.31
Procedures (number)	6
Time (days)	21
Cost (% of property value)	2.8
Quality of land administration index (0–30)	16.5
Getting credit (rank)	44
DTF score for getting credit (0–100)	65.00
Strength of legal rights index (0–12)	6
Depth of credit information index (0–8)	7
Credit bureau coverage (% of adults)	100.0
Credit registry coverage (% of adults)	0.0
Protecting minority investors (rank)	70
DTF score for protecting minority investors (0–100)	56.67
Extent of disclosure index (0–10)	4
Extent of director liability index (0–10)	6
Ease of shareholder suits index (0–10)	5
Extent of shareholder rights index (0–10)	6
Extent of ownership and control index (0–10)	7
Extent of corporate transparency index (0–10)	6
Paying taxes (rank)	78
DTF score for paying taxes (0–100)	74.36
Payments (number per year)	33
Time (hours per year)	225.5
Total tax rate (% of profit)	39.7
Postfiling index (0–100)	94.00
Trading across borders (rank)	23
DTF score for trading across borders (0–100)	96.64
Time to export	
Documentary compliance (hours)	2
Border compliance (hours)	4
Cost to export	
Documentary compliance (US$)	35
Border compliance (US$)	47
Time to import	
Documentary compliance (hours)	3
Border compliance (hours)	4
Cost to import	
Documentary compliance (US$)	35
Border compliance (US$)	52
Enforcing contracts (rank)	61
DTF score for enforcing contracts (0–100)	61.41
Time (days)	635
Cost (% of claim)	40.8
Quality of judicial processes index (0–18)	13.0
Resolving insolvency (rank)	47
DTF score for resolving insolvency (0–100)	59.66
Time (years)	2.0
Cost (% of estate)	20.0
Recovery rate (cents on the dollar)	32.5
Strength of insolvency framework index (0–16)	13.5

Note: Most indicator sets refer to a case scenario in the largest business city of an economy, though for 11 economies the data are a population-weighted average for the two largest business cities. For some indicators a result of "no practice" may be recorded for an economy; see the data notes for more details. In starting a business, procedures (number), time (days) and cost (% of income per capita) are calculated as the average of both men and women. For the postfiling index, a result of "not applicable" may be recorded for an economy.

✔ Reform making it easier to do business ✘ Change making it more difficult to do business

SEYCHELLES

SEYCHELLES		Sub-Saharan Africa		GNI per capita (US$)	14,760
Ease of doing business rank (1–190)	93	Overall distance to frontier (DTF) score (0–100)	61.21	Population	92,900
Starting a business (rank)	137	**Getting credit** (rank)	118	**Trading across borders** (rank)	84
DTF score for starting a business (0–100)	78.64	DTF score for getting credit (0–100)	40.00	DTF score for trading across borders (0–100)	71.79
Procedures (number)	9	Strength of legal rights index (0–12)	2	*Time to export*	
Time (days)	32	Depth of credit information index (0–8)	6	Documentary compliance (hours)	44
Cost (% of income per capita)	13.4	Credit bureau coverage (% of adults)	0.0	Border compliance (hours)	82
Minimum capital (% of income per capita)	0.0	Credit registry coverage (% of adults)	100.0	*Cost to export*	
				Documentary compliance (US$)	115
Dealing with construction permits (rank)	146	**Protecting minority investors** (rank)	106	Border compliance (US$)	332
DTF score for dealing with construction permits (0–100)	60.22	DTF score for protecting minority investors (0–100)	50.00	*Time to import*	
Procedures (number)	17	Extent of disclosure index (0–10)	4	Documentary compliance (hours)	33
Time (days)	151	Extent of director liability index (0–10)	8	Border compliance (hours)	97
Cost (% of warehouse value)	0.4	Ease of shareholder suits index (0–10)	5	*Cost to import*	
Building quality control index (0–15)	4.0	Extent of shareholder rights index (0–10)	4	Documentary compliance (US$)	93
		Extent of ownership and control index (0–10)	5	Border compliance (US$)	341
Getting electricity (rank)	140	Extent of corporate transparency index (0–10)	4		
DTF score for getting electricity (0–100)	54.69			**Enforcing contracts** (rank)	129
Procedures (number)	6	**Paying taxes** (rank)	32	DTF score for enforcing contracts (0–100)	51.25
Time (days)	137	DTF score for paying taxes (0–100)	84.66	Time (days)	915
Cost (% of income per capita)	364.9	Payments (number per year)	29	Cost (% of claim)	15.4
Reliability of supply and transparency of tariffs index (0–8)	2	Time (hours per year)	85	Quality of judicial processes index (0–18)	6.5
		Total tax rate (% of profit)	30.1		
Registering property (rank)	66	Postfiling index (0–100)	93.19	**Resolving insolvency** (rank)	62
DTF score for registering property (0–100)	68.67			DTF score for resolving insolvency (0–100)	52.14
Procedures (number)	4			Time (years)	2.0
Time (days)	33			Cost (% of estate)	11.0
Cost (% of property value)	7.0			Recovery rate (cents on the dollar)	38.8
Quality of land administration index (0–30)	18.5			Strength of insolvency framework index (0–16)	10.0

SIERRA LEONE

SIERRA LEONE		Sub-Saharan Africa		GNI per capita (US$)	630
Ease of doing business rank (1–190)	148	Overall distance to frontier (DTF) score (0–100)	50.23	Population	6,453,184
✔ **Starting a business** (rank)	87	**Getting credit** (rank)	157	**Trading across borders** (rank)	169
DTF score for starting a business (0–100)	86.48	DTF score for getting credit (0–100)	25.00	DTF score for trading across borders (0–100)	42.07
Procedures (number)	6	Strength of legal rights index (0–12)	5	*Time to export*	
Time (days)	10	Depth of credit information index (0–8)	0	Documentary compliance (hours)	134
Cost (% of income per capita)	30.3	Credit bureau coverage (% of adults)	0.0	Border compliance (hours)	55
Minimum capital (% of income per capita)	0.0	Credit registry coverage (% of adults)	1.6	*Cost to export*	
				Documentary compliance (US$)	227
Dealing with construction permits (rank)	132	**Protecting minority investors** (rank)	87	Border compliance (US$)	552
DTF score for dealing with construction permits (0–100)	62.06	DTF score for protecting minority investors (0–100)	53.33	*Time to import*	
Procedures (number)	16	Extent of disclosure index (0–10)	6	Documentary compliance (hours)	137
Time (days)	166	Extent of director liability index (0–10)	8	Border compliance (hours)	182
Cost (% of warehouse value)	2.8	Ease of shareholder suits index (0–10)	6	*Cost to import*	
Building quality control index (0–15)	7.0	Extent of shareholder rights index (0–10)	5	Documentary compliance (US$)	387
		Extent of ownership and control index (0–10)	2	Border compliance (US$)	782
Getting electricity (rank)	176	Extent of corporate transparency index (0–10)	5		
DTF score for getting electricity (0–100)	33.58			**Enforcing contracts** (rank)	100
Procedures (number)	8	**Paying taxes** (rank)	87	DTF score for enforcing contracts (0–100)	55.92
Time (days)	82	DTF score for paying taxes (0–100)	72.63	Time (days)	515
Cost (% of income per capita)	4,417.3	Payments (number per year)	34	Cost (% of claim)	39.5
Reliability of supply and transparency of tariffs index (0–8)	0	Time (hours per year)	343	Quality of judicial processes index (0–18)	8.0
		Total tax rate (% of profit)	31.0		
Registering property (rank)	163	Postfiling index (0–100)	94.50	**Resolving insolvency** (rank)	148
DTF score for registering property (0–100)	43.47			DTF score for resolving insolvency (0–100)	27.76
Procedures (number)	7			Time (years)	2.3
Time (days)	56			Cost (% of estate)	42.0
Cost (% of property value)	10.7			Recovery rate (cents on the dollar)	10.9
Quality of land administration index (0–30)	6.5			Strength of insolvency framework index (0–16)	7.0

SINGAPORE

SINGAPORE		East Asia & Pacific		GNI per capita (US$)	52,090
Ease of doing business rank (1–190)	2	Overall distance to frontier (DTF) score (0–100)	85.05	Population	5,535,002
Starting a business (rank)	6	**Getting credit** (rank)	20	**Trading across borders** (rank)	41
DTF score for starting a business (0–100)	96.49	DTF score for getting credit (0–100)	75.00	DTF score for trading across borders (0–100)	89.30
Procedures (number)	3	Strength of legal rights index (0–12)	8	*Time to export*	
Time (days)	2.5	Depth of credit information index (0–8)	7	Documentary compliance (hours)	2
Cost (% of income per capita)	0.6	Credit bureau coverage (% of adults)	65.7	Border compliance (hours)	12
Minimum capital (% of income per capita)	0.0	Credit registry coverage (% of adults)	0.0	*Cost to export*	
				Documentary compliance (US$)	37
✔ **Dealing with construction permits** (rank)	10	**Protecting minority investors** (rank)	1	Border compliance (US$)	335
DTF score for dealing with construction permits (0–100)	81.75	DTF score for protecting minority investors (0–100)	83.33	*Time to import*	
Procedures (number)	9	Extent of disclosure index (0–10)	10	Documentary compliance (hours)	3
Time (days)	48	Extent of director liability index (0–10)	9	Border compliance (hours)	35
Cost (% of warehouse value)	6.1	Ease of shareholder suits index (0–10)	9	*Cost to import*	
Building quality control index (0–15)	12.0	Extent of shareholder rights index (0–10)	8	Documentary compliance (US$)	40
		Extent of ownership and control index (0–10)	6	Border compliance (US$)	220
Getting electricity (rank)	10	Extent of corporate transparency index (0–10)	8		
DTF score for getting electricity (0–100)	91.32			**Enforcing contracts** (rank)	2
Procedures (number)	4	✔ **Paying taxes** (rank)	8	DTF score for enforcing contracts (0–100)	83.61
Time (days)	30	DTF score for paying taxes (0–100)	91.85	Time (days)	164
Cost (% of income per capita)	25.8	Payments (number per year)	5	Cost (% of claim)	25.8
Reliability of supply and transparency of tariffs index (0–8)	7	Time (hours per year)	66.5	Quality of judicial processes index (0–18)	15.0
		Total tax rate (% of profit)	19.1		
✔ **Registering property** (rank)	19	Postfiling index (0–100)	73.43	**Resolving insolvency** (rank)	29
DTF score for registering property (0–100)	83.58			DTF score for resolving insolvency (0–100)	74.31
Procedures (number)	6			Time (years)	0.8
Time (days)	4.5			Cost (% of estate)	4.0
Cost (% of property value)	2.9			Recovery rate (cents on the dollar)	88.7
Quality of land administration index (0–30)	29.0			Strength of insolvency framework index (0–16)	8.5

Note: Most indicator sets refer to a case scenario in the largest business city of an economy, though for 11 economies the data are a population-weighted average for the two largest business cities. For some indicators a result of "no practice" may be recorded for an economy; see the data notes for more details. In starting a business, procedures (number), time (days) and cost (% of income per capita) are calculated as the average of both men and women. For the postfiling index, a result of "not applicable" may be recorded for an economy.

✔ Reform making it easier to do business ✘ Change making it more difficult to do business

SLOVAK REPUBLIC

Ease of doing business rank (1–190)	33	OECD high income		GNI per capita (US$)	17,310
		Overall distance to frontier (DTF) score (0–100)	75.61	Population	5,424,050

Starting a business (rank)	68
DTF score for starting a business (0–100)	88.62
Procedures (number)	6
Time (days)	11.5
Cost (% of income per capita)	1.2
Minimum capital (% of income per capita)	17.8
Dealing with construction permits (rank)	103
DTF score for dealing with construction permits (0–100)	67.82
Procedures (number)	10
Time (days)	286
Cost (% of warehouse value)	0.1
Building quality control index (0–15)	10.0
Getting electricity (rank)	53
DTF score for getting electricity (0–100)	80.31
Procedures (number)	5
Time (days)	121
Cost (% of income per capita)	52.6
Reliability of supply and transparency of tariffs index (0–8)	8
Registering property (rank)	7
DTF score for registering property (0–100)	91.00
Procedures (number)	3
Time (days)	16.5
Cost (% of property value)	0.0
Quality of land administration index (0–30)	26.5

Getting credit (rank)	44
DTF score for getting credit (0–100)	65.00
Strength of legal rights index (0–12)	7
Depth of credit information index (0–8)	6
Credit bureau coverage (% of adults)	76.4
Credit registry coverage (% of adults)	3.1
Protecting minority investors (rank)	87
DTF score for protecting minority investors (0–100)	53.33
Extent of disclosure index (0–10)	3
Extent of director liability index (0–10)	4
Ease of shareholder suits index (0–10)	7
Extent of shareholder rights index (0–10)	6
Extent of ownership and control index (0–10)	6
Extent of corporate transparency index (0–10)	6
✔ **Paying taxes** (rank)	56
DTF score for paying taxes (0–100)	80.57
Payments (number per year)	8
Time (hours per year)	192
Total tax rate (% of profit)	51.6
Postfiling index (0–100)	89.91

Trading across borders (rank)	1
DTF score for trading across borders (0–100)	100.00
Time to export	
Documentary compliance (hours)	1
Border compliance (hours)	0
Cost to export	
Documentary compliance (US$)	0
Border compliance (US$)	0
Time to import	
Documentary compliance (hours)	1
Border compliance (hours)	0
Cost to import	
Documentary compliance (US$)	0
Border compliance (US$)	0
Enforcing contracts (rank)	82
DTF score for enforcing contracts (0–100)	58.92
Time (days)	705
Cost (% of claim)	30.0
Quality of judicial processes index (0–18)	10.5
Resolving insolvency (rank)	35
DTF score for resolving insolvency (0–100)	70.53
Time (years)	4.0
Cost (% of estate)	18.0
Recovery rate (cents on the dollar)	55.6
Strength of insolvency framework index (0–16)	13.0

SLOVENIA

Ease of doing business rank (1–190)	30	OECD high income		GNI per capita (US$)	22,610
		Overall distance to frontier (DTF) score (0–100)	76.14	Population	2,063,768

Starting a business (rank)	49
DTF score for starting a business (0–100)	91.42
Procedures (number)	4
Time (days)	7
Cost (% of income per capita)	0.0
Minimum capital (% of income per capita)	40.6
Dealing with construction permits (rank)	80
DTF score for dealing with construction permits (0–100)	70.32
Procedures (number)	12
Time (days)	224.5
Cost (% of warehouse value)	2.7
Building quality control index (0–15)	12.0
Getting electricity (rank)	16
DTF score for getting electricity (0–100)	89.15
Procedures (number)	5
Time (days)	38
Cost (% of income per capita)	109.8
Reliability of supply and transparency of tariffs index (0–8)	8
Registering property (rank)	34
DTF score for registering property (0–100)	77.05
Procedures (number)	5
Time (days)	49.5
Cost (% of property value)	2.0
Quality of land administration index (0–30)	23.5

Getting credit (rank)	133
DTF score for getting credit (0–100)	35.00
Strength of legal rights index (0–12)	3
Depth of credit information index (0–8)	4
Credit bureau coverage (% of adults)	100.0
Credit registry coverage (% of adults)	3.1
Protecting minority investors (rank)	9
DTF score for protecting minority investors (0–100)	75.00
Extent of disclosure index (0–10)	5
Extent of director liability index (0–10)	9
Ease of shareholder suits index (0–10)	8
Extent of shareholder rights index (0–10)	9
Extent of ownership and control index (0–10)	8
Extent of corporate transparency index (0–10)	6
Paying taxes (rank)	24
DTF score for paying taxes (0–100)	86.55
Payments (number per year)	10
Time (hours per year)	245
Total tax rate (% of profit)	31.0
Postfiling index (0–100)	95.03

Trading across borders (rank)	1
DTF score for trading across borders (0–100)	100.00
Time to export	
Documentary compliance (hours)	1
Border compliance (hours)	0
Cost to export	
Documentary compliance (US$)	0
Border compliance (US$)	0
Time to import	
Documentary compliance (hours)	1
Border compliance (hours)	0
Cost to import	
Documentary compliance (US$)	0
Border compliance (US$)	0
Enforcing contracts (rank)	119
DTF score for enforcing contracts (0–100)	52.97
Time (days)	1,160
Cost (% of claim)	12.7
Quality of judicial processes index (0–18)	10.5
Resolving insolvency (rank)	12
DTF score for resolving insolvency (0–100)	83.97
Time (years)	0.8
Cost (% of estate)	4.0
Recovery rate (cents on the dollar)	89.2
Strength of insolvency framework index (0–16)	11.5

SOLOMON ISLANDS

Ease of doing business rank (1–190)	104	East Asia & Pacific		GNI per capita (US$)	1,940
		Overall distance to frontier (DTF) score (0–100)	59.17	Population	583,591

Starting a business (rank)	97
DTF score for starting a business (0–100)	85.48
Procedures (number)	7
Time (days)	9
Cost (% of income per capita)	28.5
Minimum capital (% of income per capita)	0.0
Dealing with construction permits (rank)	63
DTF score for dealing with construction permits (0–100)	72.76
Procedures (number)	13
Time (days)	98
Cost (% of warehouse value)	1.2
Building quality control index (0–15)	7.5
Getting electricity (rank)	80
DTF score for getting electricity (0–100)	72.53
Procedures (number)	4
Time (days)	53
Cost (% of income per capita)	1,253.7
Reliability of supply and transparency of tariffs index (0–8)	3
Registering property (rank)	152
DTF score for registering property (0–100)	47.38
Procedures (number)	10
Time (days)	86.5
Cost (% of property value)	4.7
Quality of land administration index (0–30)	11.0

✔ **Getting credit** (rank)	82
DTF score for getting credit (0–100)	50.00
Strength of legal rights index (0–12)	10
Depth of credit information index (0–8)	0
Credit bureau coverage (% of adults)	1.1
Credit registry coverage (% of adults)	0.0
Protecting minority investors (rank)	106
DTF score for protecting minority investors (0–100)	50.00
Extent of disclosure index (0–10)	3
Extent of director liability index (0–10)	7
Ease of shareholder suits index (0–10)	9
Extent of shareholder rights index (0–10)	6
Extent of ownership and control index (0–10)	4
Extent of corporate transparency index (0–10)	1
Paying taxes (rank)	39
DTF score for paying taxes (0–100)	83.58
Payments (number per year)	34
Time (hours per year)	80
Total tax rate (% of profit)	32.0
Postfiling index (0–100)	99.08

Trading across borders (rank)	151
DTF score for trading across borders (0–100)	53.45
Time to export	
Documentary compliance (hours)	60
Border compliance (hours)	110
Cost to export	
Documentary compliance (US$)	257
Border compliance (US$)	630
Time to import	
Documentary compliance (hours)	37
Border compliance (hours)	108
Cost to import	
Documentary compliance (US$)	215
Border compliance (US$)	740
Enforcing contracts (rank)	153
DTF score for enforcing contracts (0–100)	44.63
Time (days)	455
Cost (% of claim)	78.9
Quality of judicial processes index (0–18)	9.0
Resolving insolvency (rank)	138
DTF score for resolving insolvency (0–100)	31.90
Time (years)	1.0
Cost (% of estate)	38.0
Recovery rate (cents on the dollar)	24.4
Strength of insolvency framework index (0–16)	6.0

Note: Most indicator sets refer to a case scenario in the largest business city of an economy, though for 11 economies the data are a population-weighted average for the two largest business cities. For some indicators a result of "no practice" may be recorded for an economy; see the data notes for more details. In starting a business, procedures (number), time (days) and cost (% of income per capita) are calculated as the average of both men and women. For the postfiling index, a result of "not applicable" may be recorded for an economy.

✔ Reform making it easier to do business ✘ Change making it more difficult to do business

SOMALIA

Ease of doing business rank (1–190)	190
Sub-Saharan Africa	
Overall distance to frontier (DTF) score (0–100)	20.29
GNI per capita (US$)	510
Population	10,787,104

Starting a business (rank)	184
DTF score for starting a business (0–100)	48.71
Procedures (number)	9
Time (days)	70
Cost (% of income per capita)	176.5
Minimum capital (% of income per capita)	0.0
Dealing with construction permits (rank)	187
DTF score for dealing with construction permits (0–100)	0.00
Procedures (number)	NO PRACTICE
Time (days)	NO PRACTICE
Cost (% of warehouse value)	NO PRACTICE
Building quality control index (0–15)	0.0
Getting electricity (rank)	188
DTF score for getting electricity (0–100)	0.00
Procedures (number)	NO PRACTICE
Time (days)	NO PRACTICE
Cost (% of income per capita)	NO PRACTICE
Reliability of supply and transparency of tariffs index (0–8)	0
Registering property (rank)	148
DTF score for registering property (0–100)	47.97
Procedures (number)	5
Time (days)	188
Cost (% of property value)	1.5
Quality of land administration index (0–30)	7.5
Getting credit (rank)	185
DTF score for getting credit (0–100)	0.00
Strength of legal rights index (0–12)	0
Depth of credit information index (0–8)	0
Credit bureau coverage (% of adults)	0.0
Credit registry coverage (% of adults)	0.0
Protecting minority investors (rank)	190
DTF score for protecting minority investors (0–100)	0.00
Extent of disclosure index (0–10)	0
Extent of director liability index (0–10)	0
Ease of shareholder suits index (0–10)	0
Extent of shareholder rights index (0–10)	0
Extent of ownership and control index (0–10)	0
Extent of corporate transparency index (0–10)	0
Paying taxes (rank)	190
DTF score for paying taxes (0–100)	0.00
Payments (number per year)	NO PRACTICE
Time (hours per year)	NO PRACTICE
Total tax rate (% of profit)	NO PRACTICE
Postfiling index (0–100)	NO PRACTICE
Trading across borders (rank)	156
DTF score for trading across borders (0–100)	51.60
Time to export	
Documentary compliance (hours)	73
Border compliance (hours)	44
Cost to export	
Documentary compliance (US$)	350
Border compliance (US$)	495
Time to import	
Documentary compliance (hours)	76
Border compliance (hours)	85
Cost to import	
Documentary compliance (US$)	300
Border compliance (US$)	952
Enforcing contracts (rank)	109
DTF score for enforcing contracts (0–100)	54.58
Time (days)	575
Cost (% of claim)	21.4
Quality of judicial processes index (0–18)	4.5
Resolving insolvency (rank)	169
DTF score for resolving insolvency (0–100)	0.00
Time (years)	NO PRACTICE
Cost (% of estate)	NO PRACTICE
Recovery rate (cents on the dollar)	0.0
Strength of insolvency framework index (0–16)	0.0

SOUTH AFRICA

Ease of doing business rank (1–190)	74
Sub-Saharan Africa	
Overall distance to frontier (DTF) score (0–100)	65.20
GNI per capita (US$)	6,050
Population	54,956,920

✔ **Starting a business** (rank)	131
DTF score for starting a business (0–100)	80.47
Procedures (number)	7
Time (days)	43
Cost (% of income per capita)	0.2
Minimum capital (% of income per capita)	0.0
Dealing with construction permits (rank)	99
DTF score for dealing with construction permits (0–100)	68.21
Procedures (number)	19
Time (days)	141
Cost (% of warehouse value)	0.9
Building quality control index (0–15)	10.0
Getting electricity (rank)	111
DTF score for getting electricity (0–100)	63.18
Procedures (number)	4
Time (days)	84
Cost (% of income per capita)	156.1
Reliability of supply and transparency of tariffs index (0–8)	0
✘ **Registering property** (rank)	105
DTF score for registering property (0–100)	59.03
Procedures (number)	7
Time (days)	23
Cost (% of property value)	7.3
Quality of land administration index (0–30)	13.5
Getting credit (rank)	62
DTF score for getting credit (0–100)	60.00
Strength of legal rights index (0–12)	5
Depth of credit information index (0–8)	7
Credit bureau coverage (% of adults)	63.7
Credit registry coverage (% of adults)	0.0
Protecting minority investors (rank)	22
DTF score for protecting minority investors (0–100)	70.00
Extent of disclosure index (0–10)	8
Extent of director liability index (0–10)	8
Ease of shareholder suits index (0–10)	8
Extent of shareholder rights index (0–10)	8
Extent of ownership and control index (0–10)	6
Extent of corporate transparency index (0–10)	4
✘ **Paying taxes** (rank)	51
DTF score for paying taxes (0–100)	81.09
Payments (number per year)	7
Time (hours per year)	203
Total tax rate (% of profit)	28.8
Postfiling index (0–100)	58.61
Trading across borders (rank)	139
DTF score for trading across borders (0–100)	58.01
Time to export	
Documentary compliance (hours)	68
Border compliance (hours)	100
Cost to export	
Documentary compliance (US$)	170
Border compliance (US$)	428
Time to import	
Documentary compliance (hours)	36
Border compliance (hours)	144
Cost to import	
Documentary compliance (US$)	213
Border compliance (US$)	657
Enforcing contracts (rank)	113
DTF score for enforcing contracts (0–100)	54.10
Time (days)	600
Cost (% of claim)	33.2
Quality of judicial processes index (0–18)	7.0
Resolving insolvency (rank)	50
DTF score for resolving insolvency (0–100)	57.94
Time (years)	2.0
Cost (% of estate)	18.0
Recovery rate (cents on the dollar)	35.1
Strength of insolvency framework index (0–16)	12.5

SOUTH SUDAN

Ease of doing business rank (1–190)	186
Sub-Saharan Africa	
Overall distance to frontier (DTF) score (0–100)	33.48
GNI per capita (US$)	790
Population	12,339,812

Starting a business (rank)	181
DTF score for starting a business (0–100)	53.96
Procedures (number)	13
Time (days)	14
Cost (% of income per capita)	422.4
Minimum capital (% of income per capita)	0.0
Dealing with construction permits (rank)	178
DTF score for dealing with construction permits (0–100)	47.68
Procedures (number)	23
Time (days)	124
Cost (% of warehouse value)	11.1
Building quality control index (0–15)	7.0
Getting electricity (rank)	188
DTF score for getting electricity (0–100)	0.00
Procedures (number)	NO PRACTICE
Time (days)	NO PRACTICE
Cost (% of income per capita)	NO PRACTICE
Reliability of supply and transparency of tariffs index (0–8)	0
Registering property (rank)	181
DTF score for registering property (0–100)	31.64
Procedures (number)	9
Time (days)	50
Cost (% of property value)	15.9
Quality of land administration index (0–30)	5.0
Getting credit (rank)	175
DTF score for getting credit (0–100)	10.00
Strength of legal rights index (0–12)	2
Depth of credit information index (0–8)	0
Credit bureau coverage (% of adults)	0.0
Credit registry coverage (% of adults)	0.0
Protecting minority investors (rank)	179
DTF score for protecting minority investors (0–100)	28.33
Extent of disclosure index (0–10)	2
Extent of director liability index (0–10)	1
Ease of shareholder suits index (0–10)	5
Extent of shareholder rights index (0–10)	3
Extent of ownership and control index (0–10)	3
Extent of corporate transparency index (0–10)	3
Paying taxes (rank)	68
DTF score for paying taxes (0–100)	77.09
Payments (number per year)	37
Time (hours per year)	210
Total tax rate (% of profit)	29.1
Postfiling index (0–100)	94.04
Trading across borders (rank)	177
DTF score for trading across borders (0–100)	26.19
Time to export	
Documentary compliance (hours)	192
Border compliance (hours)	146
Cost to export	
Documentary compliance (US$)	194
Border compliance (US$)	763
Time to import	
Documentary compliance (hours)	360
Border compliance (hours)	179
Cost to import	
Documentary compliance (US$)	350
Border compliance (US$)	781
Enforcing contracts (rank)	73
DTF score for enforcing contracts (0–100)	59.91
Time (days)	228
Cost (% of claim)	30.0
Quality of judicial processes index (0–18)	4.0
Resolving insolvency (rank)	169
DTF score for resolving insolvency (0–100)	0.00
Time (years)	NO PRACTICE
Cost (% of estate)	NO PRACTICE
Recovery rate (cents on the dollar)	0.0
Strength of insolvency framework index (0–16)	0.0

Note: Most indicator sets refer to a case scenario in the largest business city of an economy, though for 11 economies the data are a population-weighted average for the two largest business cities. For some indicators a result of "no practice" may be recorded for an economy; see the data notes for more details. In starting a business, procedures (number), time (days) and cost (% of income per capita) are calculated as the average of both men and women. For the postfiling index, a result of "not applicable" may be recorded for an economy.

✔ Reform making it easier to do business ✘ Change making it more difficult to do business

SPAIN

SPAIN		OECD high income		GNI per capita (US$)	28,520
Ease of doing business rank (1–190)	32	Overall distance to frontier (DTF) score (0–100)	75.73	Population	46,418,269

Starting a business (rank)	85
DTF score for starting a business (0–100)	86.61
Procedures (number)	7
Time (days)	13
Cost (% of income per capita)	5.0
Minimum capital (% of income per capita)	12.9
Dealing with construction permits (rank)	113
DTF score for dealing with construction permits (0–100)	65.95
Procedures (number)	13
Time (days)	205
Cost (% of warehouse value)	5.2
Building quality control index (0–15)	11.0
Getting electricity (rank)	78
DTF score for getting electricity (0–100)	72.99
Procedures (number)	7
Time (days)	107
Cost (% of income per capita)	216.1
Reliability of supply and transparency of tariffs index (0–8)	8
Registering property (rank)	50
DTF score for registering property (0–100)	73.88
Procedures (number)	5
Time (days)	12.5
Cost (% of property value)	6.1
Quality of land administration index (0–30)	22.5
Getting credit (rank)	62
DTF score for getting credit (0–100)	60.00
Strength of legal rights index (0–12)	5
Depth of credit information index (0–8)	7
Credit bureau coverage (% of adults)	17.9
Credit registry coverage (% of adults)	49.6
Protecting minority investors (rank)	32
DTF score for protecting minority investors (0–100)	65.00
Extent of disclosure index (0–10)	5
Extent of director liability index (0–10)	6
Ease of shareholder suits index (0–10)	6
Extent of shareholder rights index (0–10)	10
Extent of ownership and control index (0–10)	4
Extent of corporate transparency index (0–10)	8
✔ **Paying taxes** (rank)	37
DTF score for paying taxes (0–100)	83.80
Payments (number per year)	8
Time (hours per year)	152
Total tax rate (% of profit)	49.0
Postfiling index (0–100)	92.55
Trading across borders (rank)	1
DTF score for trading across borders (0–100)	100.00
Time to export	
Documentary compliance (hours)	1
Border compliance (hours)	0
Cost to export	
Documentary compliance (US$)	0
Border compliance (US$)	0
Time to import	
Documentary compliance (hours)	1
Border compliance (hours)	0
Cost to import	
Documentary compliance (US$)	0
Border compliance (US$)	0
✔ **Enforcing contracts** (rank)	29
DTF score for enforcing contracts (0–100)	69.48
Time (days)	510
Cost (% of claim)	18.5
Quality of judicial processes index (0–18)	11.0
Resolving insolvency (rank)	18
DTF score for resolving insolvency (0–100)	79.62
Time (years)	1.5
Cost (% of estate)	11.0
Recovery rate (cents on the dollar)	78.3
Strength of insolvency framework index (0–16)	12.0

SRI LANKA

SRI LANKA		South Asia		GNI per capita (US$)	3,800
Ease of doing business rank (1–190)	110	Overall distance to frontier (DTF) score (0–100)	58.79	Population	20,966,000

✔ **Starting a business** (rank)	74
DTF score for starting a business (0–100)	87.52
Procedures (number)	7
Time (days)	9
Cost (% of income per capita)	12.2
Minimum capital (% of income per capita)	0.0
Dealing with construction permits (rank)	88
DTF score for dealing with construction permits (0–100)	69.31
Procedures (number)	13
Time (days)	115
Cost (% of warehouse value)	0.4
Building quality control index (0–15)	5.5
Getting electricity (rank)	86
DTF score for getting electricity (0–100)	71.12
Procedures (number)	5
Time (days)	100
Cost (% of income per capita)	732.1
Reliability of supply and transparency of tariffs index (0–8)	5
Registering property (rank)	155
DTF score for registering property (0–100)	46.76
Procedures (number)	9
Time (days)	51
Cost (% of property value)	5.1
Quality of land administration index (0–30)	3.5
Getting credit (rank)	118
DTF score for getting credit (0–100)	40.00
Strength of legal rights index (0–12)	2
Depth of credit information index (0–8)	6
Credit bureau coverage (% of adults)	57.2
Credit registry coverage (% of adults)	0.0
✔ **Protecting minority investors** (rank)	42
DTF score for protecting minority investors (0–100)	63.33
Extent of disclosure index (0–10)	8
Extent of director liability index (0–10)	5
Ease of shareholder suits index (0–10)	7
Extent of shareholder rights index (0–10)	6
Extent of ownership and control index (0–10)	6
Extent of corporate transparency index (0–10)	6
Paying taxes (rank)	158
DTF score for paying taxes (0–100)	53.16
Payments (number per year)	47
Time (hours per year)	179
Total tax rate (% of profit)	55.2
Postfiling index (0–100)	48.85
Trading across borders (rank)	90
DTF score for trading across borders (0–100)	70.70
Time to export	
Documentary compliance (hours)	76
Border compliance (hours)	43
Cost to export	
Documentary compliance (US$)	58
Border compliance (US$)	366
Time to import	
Documentary compliance (hours)	58
Border compliance (hours)	72
Cost to import	
Documentary compliance (US$)	283
Border compliance (US$)	300
Enforcing contracts (rank)	163
DTF score for enforcing contracts (0–100)	39.31
Time (days)	1,318
Cost (% of claim)	22.8
Quality of judicial processes index (0–18)	7.5
Resolving insolvency (rank)	75
DTF score for resolving insolvency (0–100)	46.73
Time (years)	1.7
Cost (% of estate)	10.0
Recovery rate (cents on the dollar)	46.2
Strength of insolvency framework index (0–16)	7.0

ST. KITTS AND NEVIS

ST. KITTS AND NEVIS		Latin America & Caribbean		GNI per capita (US$)	15,560
Ease of doing business rank (1–190)	134	Overall distance to frontier (DTF) score (0–100)	53.96	Population	55,572

Starting a business (rank)	92
DTF score for starting a business (0–100)	85.75
Procedures (number)	7
Time (days)	18.5
Cost (% of income per capita)	7.2
Minimum capital (% of income per capita)	0.0
Dealing with construction permits (rank)	41
DTF score for dealing with construction permits (0–100)	75.68
Procedures (number)	10
Time (days)	104
Cost (% of warehouse value)	0.3
Building quality control index (0–15)	7.0
Getting electricity (rank)	90
DTF score for getting electricity (0–100)	70.09
Procedures (number)	4
Time (days)	18
Cost (% of income per capita)	241.0
Reliability of supply and transparency of tariffs index (0–8)	0
✘ **Registering property** (rank)	184
DTF score for registering property (0–100)	28.79
Procedures (number)	6
Time (days)	224
Cost (% of property value)	11.0
Quality of land administration index (0–30)	9.0
Getting credit (rank)	157
DTF score for getting credit (0–100)	25.00
Strength of legal rights index (0–12)	5
Depth of credit information index (0–8)	0
Credit bureau coverage (% of adults)	0.0
Credit registry coverage (% of adults)	0.0
Protecting minority investors (rank)	102
DTF score for protecting minority investors (0–100)	51.67
Extent of disclosure index (0–10)	4
Extent of director liability index (0–10)	8
Ease of shareholder suits index (0–10)	8
Extent of shareholder rights index (0–10)	4
Extent of ownership and control index (0–10)	1
Extent of corporate transparency index (0–10)	6
Paying taxes (rank)	143
DTF score for paying taxes (0–100)	57.86
Payments (number per year)	39
Time (hours per year)	203
Total tax rate (% of profit)	49.7
Postfiling index (0–100)	49.54
Trading across borders (rank)	72
DTF score for trading across borders (0–100)	79.26
Time to export	
Documentary compliance (hours)	48
Border compliance (hours)	27
Cost to export	
Documentary compliance (US$)	100
Border compliance (US$)	335
Time to import	
Documentary compliance (hours)	33
Border compliance (hours)	37
Cost to import	
Documentary compliance (US$)	90
Border compliance (US$)	311
Enforcing contracts (rank)	46
DTF score for enforcing contracts (0–100)	65.51
Time (days)	578
Cost (% of claim)	26.6
Quality of judicial processes index (0–18)	11.5
Resolving insolvency (rank)	169
DTF score for resolving insolvency (0–100)	0.00
Time (years)	NO PRACTICE
Cost (% of estate)	NO PRACTICE
Recovery rate (cents on the dollar)	0.0
Strength of insolvency framework index (0–16)	0.0

Note: Most indicator sets refer to a case scenario in the largest business city of an economy, though for 11 economies the data are a population-weighted average for the two largest business cities. For some indicators a result of "no practice" may be recorded for an economy; see the data notes for more details. In starting a business, procedures (number), time (days) and cost (% of income per capita) are calculated as the average of both men and women. For the postfiling index, a result of "not applicable" may be recorded for an economy.

✔ Reform making it easier to do business ✘ Change making it more difficult to do business

ST. LUCIA

Ease of doing business rank (1–190)	86
Latin America & Caribbean	
Overall distance to frontier (DTF) score (0–100)	63.13
GNI per capita (US$)	7,390
Population	184,999

Starting a business (rank)	66
DTF score for starting a business (0–100)	88.80
Procedures (number)	5
Time (days)	11
Cost (% of income per capita)	21.4
Minimum capital (% of income per capita)	0.0

Dealing with construction permits (rank)	54
DTF score for dealing with construction permits (0–100)	74.54
Procedures (number)	14
Time (days)	116
Cost (% of warehouse value)	0.6
Building quality control index (0–15)	9.5

✘ **Getting electricity** (rank)	56
DTF score for getting electricity (0–100)	79.78
Procedures (number)	6
Time (days)	26
Cost (% of income per capita)	193.1
Reliability of supply and transparency of tariffs index (0–8)	6

Registering property (rank)	104
DTF score for registering property (0–100)	59.16
Procedures (number)	9
Time (days)	17
Cost (% of property value)	7.6
Quality of land administration index (0–30)	18.5

Getting credit (rank)	157
DTF score for getting credit (0–100)	25.00
Strength of legal rights index (0–12)	5
Depth of credit information index (0–8)	0
Credit bureau coverage (% of adults)	0.0
Credit registry coverage (% of adults)	0.0

Protecting minority investors (rank)	87
DTF score for protecting minority investors (0–100)	53.33
Extent of disclosure index (0–10)	4
Extent of director liability index (0–10)	8
Ease of shareholder suits index (0–10)	8
Extent of shareholder rights index (0–10)	4
Extent of ownership and control index (0–10)	5
Extent of corporate transparency index (0–10)	3

Paying taxes (rank)	65
DTF score for paying taxes (0–100)	78.09
Payments (number per year)	35
Time (hours per year)	110
Total tax rate (% of profit)	34.7
Postfiling index (0–100)	87.24

✔ **Trading across borders** (rank)	81
DTF score for trading across borders (0–100)	73.87
Time to export	
Documentary compliance (hours)	19
Border compliance (hours)	27
Cost to export	
Documentary compliance (US$)	63
Border compliance (US$)	718
Time to import	
Documentary compliance (hours)	14
Border compliance (hours)	27
Cost to import	
Documentary compliance (US$)	98
Border compliance (US$)	842

Enforcing contracts (rank)	71
DTF score for enforcing contracts (0–100)	59.94
Time (days)	635
Cost (% of claim)	37.3
Quality of judicial processes index (0–18)	11.5

Resolving insolvency (rank)	114
DTF score for resolving insolvency (0–100)	38.79
Time (years)	2.0
Cost (% of estate)	9.0
Recovery rate (cents on the dollar)	43.0
Strength of insolvency framework index (0–16)	5.0

ST. VINCENT AND THE GRENADINES

Ease of doing business rank (1–190)	125
Latin America & Caribbean	
Overall distance to frontier (DTF) score (0–100)	55.91
GNI per capita (US$)	6,670
Population	109,462

Starting a business (rank)	83
DTF score for starting a business (0–100)	86.78
Procedures (number)	7
Time (days)	10
Cost (% of income per capita)	16.1
Minimum capital (% of income per capita)	0.0

Dealing with construction permits (rank)	55
DTF score for dealing with construction permits (0–100)	74.42
Procedures (number)	14
Time (days)	92
Cost (% of warehouse value)	0.1
Building quality control index (0–15)	8.0

Getting electricity (rank)	85
DTF score for getting electricity (0–100)	71.13
Procedures (number)	3
Time (days)	52
Cost (% of income per capita)	56.6
Reliability of supply and transparency of tariffs index (0–8)	0

Registering property (rank)	165
DTF score for registering property (0–100)	43.10
Procedures (number)	7
Time (days)	47
Cost (% of property value)	11.8
Quality of land administration index (0–30)	7.0

Getting credit (rank)	157
DTF score for getting credit (0–100)	25.00
Strength of legal rights index (0–12)	5
Depth of credit information index (0–8)	0
Credit bureau coverage (% of adults)	0.0
Credit registry coverage (% of adults)	0.0

Protecting minority investors (rank)	87
DTF score for protecting minority investors (0–100)	53.33
Extent of disclosure index (0–10)	4
Extent of director liability index (0–10)	8
Ease of shareholder suits index (0–10)	8
Extent of shareholder rights index (0–10)	4
Extent of ownership and control index (0–10)	5
Extent of corporate transparency index (0–10)	3

Paying taxes (rank)	98
DTF score for paying taxes (0–100)	70.56
Payments (number per year)	36
Time (hours per year)	108
Total tax rate (% of profit)	39.3
Postfiling index (0–100)	65.07

Trading across borders (rank)	88
DTF score for trading across borders (0–100)	71.08
Time to export	
Documentary compliance (hours)	72
Border compliance (hours)	28
Cost to export	
Documentary compliance (US$)	80
Border compliance (US$)	425
Time to import	
Documentary compliance (hours)	24
Border compliance (hours)	48
Cost to import	
Documentary compliance (US$)	90
Border compliance (US$)	875

Enforcing contracts (rank)	53
DTF score for enforcing contracts (0–100)	63.66
Time (days)	595
Cost (% of claim)	30.3
Quality of judicial processes index (0–18)	11.5

Resolving insolvency (rank)	169
DTF score for resolving insolvency (0–100)	0.00
Time (years)	NO PRACTICE
Cost (% of estate)	NO PRACTICE
Recovery rate (cents on the dollar)	0.0
Strength of insolvency framework index (0–16)	0.0

SUDAN

Ease of doing business rank (1–190)	168
Sub-Saharan Africa	
Overall distance to frontier (DTF) score (0–100)	44.76
GNI per capita (US$)	1,840
Population	40,234,882

✘ **Starting a business** (rank)	156
DTF score for starting a business (0–100)	73.78
Procedures (number)	10.5
Time (days)	36.5
Cost (% of income per capita)	25.6
Minimum capital (% of income per capita)	0.0

Dealing with construction permits (rank)	145
DTF score for dealing with construction permits (0–100)	60.52
Procedures (number)	15
Time (days)	270
Cost (% of warehouse value)	2.2
Building quality control index (0–15)	9.5

Getting electricity (rank)	113
DTF score for getting electricity (0–100)	62.10
Procedures (number)	5
Time (days)	70
Cost (% of income per capita)	2,686.8
Reliability of supply and transparency of tariffs index (0–8)	3

Registering property (rank)	89
DTF score for registering property (0–100)	63.61
Procedures (number)	6
Time (days)	11
Cost (% of property value)	2.6
Quality of land administration index (0–30)	5.5

Getting credit (rank)	170
DTF score for getting credit (0–100)	15.00
Strength of legal rights index (0–12)	3
Depth of credit information index (0–8)	0
Credit bureau coverage (% of adults)	2.1
Credit registry coverage (% of adults)	0.0

✘ **Protecting minority investors** (rank)	187
DTF score for protecting minority investors (0–100)	21.67
Extent of disclosure index (0–10)	1
Extent of director liability index (0–10)	1
Ease of shareholder suits index (0–10)	5
Extent of shareholder rights index (0–10)	3
Extent of ownership and control index (0–10)	2
Extent of corporate transparency index (0–10)	1

Paying taxes (rank)	141
DTF score for paying taxes (0–100)	58.39
Payments (number per year)	42
Time (hours per year)	180
Total tax rate (% of profit)	45.4
Postfiling index (0–100)	46.56

Trading across borders (rank)	184
DTF score for trading across borders (0–100)	19.16
Time to export	
Documentary compliance (hours)	190
Border compliance (hours)	162
Cost to export	
Documentary compliance (US$)	428
Border compliance (US$)	950
Time to import	
Documentary compliance (hours)	132
Border compliance (hours)	144
Cost to import	
Documentary compliance (US$)	420
Border compliance (US$)	1,093

Enforcing contracts (rank)	147
DTF score for enforcing contracts (0–100)	46.91
Time (days)	810
Cost (% of claim)	19.8
Quality of judicial processes index (0–18)	3.5

Resolving insolvency (rank)	153
DTF score for resolving insolvency (0–100)	26.45
Time (years)	2.0
Cost (% of estate)	20.0
Recovery rate (cents on the dollar)	31.7
Strength of insolvency framework index (0–16)	3.0

Note: Most indicator sets refer to a case scenario in the largest business city of an economy, though for 11 economies the data are a population-weighted average for the two largest business cities. For some indicators a result of "no practice" may be recorded for an economy; see the data notes for more details. In starting a business, procedures (number), time (days) and cost (% of income per capita) are calculated as the average of both men and women. For the postfiling index, a result of "not applicable" may be recorded for an economy.

✔ Reform making it easier to do business ✘ Change making it more difficult to do business

SURINAME

SURINAME		Latin America & Caribbean		GNI per capita (US$)	9,300
Ease of doing business rank (1–190)	158	Overall distance to frontier (DTF) score (0–100)	47.28	Population	542,975

Starting a business (rank)	185
DTF score for starting a business (0–100)	47.82
Procedures (number)	13.5
Time (days)	84.5
Cost (% of income per capita)	101.4
Minimum capital (% of income per capita)	0.3
Dealing with construction permits (rank)	112
DTF score for dealing with construction permits (0–100)	66.43
Procedures (number)	10
Time (days)	223
Cost (% of warehouse value)	0.2
Building quality control index (0–15)	6.5
Getting electricity (rank)	84
DTF score for getting electricity (0–100)	71.51
Procedures (number)	4
Time (days)	113
Cost (% of income per capita)	484.4
Reliability of supply and transparency of tariffs index (0–8)	4
Registering property (rank)	176
DTF score for registering property (0–100)	37.52
Procedures (number)	6
Time (days)	106
Cost (% of property value)	13.7
Quality of land administration index (0–30)	10.0
Getting credit (rank)	175
DTF score for getting credit (0–100)	10.00
Strength of legal rights index (0–12)	2
Depth of credit information index (0–8)	0
Credit bureau coverage (% of adults)	0.0
Credit registry coverage (% of adults)	0.0
Protecting minority investors (rank)	165
DTF score for protecting minority investors (0–100)	35.00
Extent of disclosure index (0–10)	1
Extent of director liability index (0–10)	0
Ease of shareholder suits index (0–10)	6
Extent of shareholder rights index (0–10)	8
Extent of ownership and control index (0–10)	4
Extent of corporate transparency index (0–10)	2
Paying taxes (rank)	103
DTF score for paying taxes (0–100)	69.44
Payments (number per year)	30
Time (hours per year)	199
Total tax rate (% of profit)	27.9
Postfiling index (0–100)	48.39
Trading across borders (rank)	78
DTF score for trading across borders (0–100)	75.02
Time to export	
Documentary compliance (hours)	12
Border compliance (hours)	84
Cost to export	
Documentary compliance (US$)	40
Border compliance (US$)	468
Time to import	
Documentary compliance (hours)	24
Border compliance (hours)	48
Cost to import	
Documentary compliance (US$)	40
Border compliance (US$)	658
Enforcing contracts (rank)	187
DTF score for enforcing contracts (0–100)	25.94
Time (days)	1,715
Cost (% of claim)	37.1
Quality of judicial processes index (0–18)	3.5
Resolving insolvency (rank)	129
DTF score for resolving insolvency (0–100)	34.14
Time (years)	5.0
Cost (% of estate)	30.0
Recovery rate (cents on the dollar)	8.3
Strength of insolvency framework index (0–16)	9.5

SWAZILAND

SWAZILAND		Sub-Saharan Africa		GNI per capita (US$)	3,230
Ease of doing business rank (1–190)	111	Overall distance to frontier (DTF) score (0–100)	58.34	Population	1,286,970

Starting a business (rank)	154
DTF score for starting a business (0–100)	74.32
Procedures (number)	12
Time (days)	30
Cost (% of income per capita)	16.6
Minimum capital (% of income per capita)	0.3
Dealing with construction permits (rank)	91
DTF score for dealing with construction permits (0–100)	68.96
Procedures (number)	13
Time (days)	116
Cost (% of warehouse value)	2.6
Building quality control index (0–15)	7.0
Getting electricity (rank)	157
DTF score for getting electricity (0–100)	47.28
Procedures (number)	6
Time (days)	137
Cost (% of income per capita)	739.9
Reliability of supply and transparency of tariffs index (0–8)	0
Registering property (rank)	117
DTF score for registering property (0–100)	55.73
Procedures (number)	9
Time (days)	21
Cost (% of property value)	7.1
Quality of land administration index (0–30)	14.0
Getting credit (rank)	82
DTF score for getting credit (0–100)	50.00
Strength of legal rights index (0–12)	4
Depth of credit information index (0–8)	6
Credit bureau coverage (% of adults)	46.1
Credit registry coverage (% of adults)	0.0
Protecting minority investors (rank)	132
DTF score for protecting minority investors (0–100)	43.33
Extent of disclosure index (0–10)	2
Extent of director liability index (0–10)	5
Ease of shareholder suits index (0–10)	6
Extent of shareholder rights index (0–10)	6
Extent of ownership and control index (0–10)	4
Extent of corporate transparency index (0–10)	3
Paying taxes (rank)	76
DTF score for paying taxes (0–100)	74.65
Payments (number per year)	33
Time (hours per year)	122
Total tax rate (% of profit)	35.1
Postfiling index (0–100)	72.54
Trading across borders (rank)	31
DTF score for trading across borders (0–100)	92.68
Time to export	
Documentary compliance (hours)	4
Border compliance (hours)	3
Cost to export	
Documentary compliance (US$)	76
Border compliance (US$)	134
Time to import	
Documentary compliance (hours)	4
Border compliance (hours)	5
Cost to import	
Documentary compliance (US$)	76
Border compliance (US$)	134
Enforcing contracts (rank)	175
DTF score for enforcing contracts (0–100)	33.94
Time (days)	956
Cost (% of claim)	56.1
Quality of judicial processes index (0–18)	6.0
Resolving insolvency (rank)	95
DTF score for resolving insolvency (0–100)	42.47
Time (years)	2.0
Cost (% of estate)	14.5
Recovery rate (cents on the dollar)	38.3
Strength of insolvency framework index (0–16)	7.0

SWEDEN

SWEDEN		OECD high income		GNI per capita (US$)	57,810
Ease of doing business rank (1–190)	9	Overall distance to frontier (DTF) score (0–100)	82.13	Population	9,798,871

Starting a business (rank)	15
DTF score for starting a business (0–100)	94.64
Procedures (number)	3
Time (days)	7
Cost (% of income per capita)	0.5
Minimum capital (% of income per capita)	11.5
Dealing with construction permits (rank)	25
DTF score for dealing with construction permits (0–100)	78.85
Procedures (number)	7
Time (days)	116
Cost (% of warehouse value)	2.1
Building quality control index (0–15)	9.0
Getting electricity (rank)	6
DTF score for getting electricity (0–100)	96.20
Procedures (number)	3
Time (days)	52
Cost (% of income per capita)	32.3
Reliability of supply and transparency of tariffs index (0–8)	8
✔ **Registering property** (rank)	10
DTF score for registering property (0–100)	90.11
Procedures (number)	1
Time (days)	7
Cost (% of property value)	4.3
Quality of land administration index (0–30)	27.5
Getting credit (rank)	75
DTF score for getting credit (0–100)	55.00
Strength of legal rights index (0–12)	6
Depth of credit information index (0–8)	5
Credit bureau coverage (% of adults)	100.0
Credit registry coverage (% of adults)	0.0
Protecting minority investors (rank)	19
DTF score for protecting minority investors (0–100)	71.67
Extent of disclosure index (0–10)	8
Extent of director liability index (0–10)	4
Ease of shareholder suits index (0–10)	7
Extent of shareholder rights index (0–10)	9
Extent of ownership and control index (0–10)	8
Extent of corporate transparency index (0–10)	7
Paying taxes (rank)	28
DTF score for paying taxes (0–100)	85.28
Payments (number per year)	6
Time (hours per year)	122
Total tax rate (% of profit)	49.1
Postfiling index (0–100)	90.75
Trading across borders (rank)	18
DTF score for trading across borders (0–100)	98.04
Time to export	
Documentary compliance (hours)	1
Border compliance (hours)	2
Cost to export	
Documentary compliance (US$)	40
Border compliance (US$)	55
Time to import	
Documentary compliance (hours)	1
Border compliance (hours)	0
Cost to import	
Documentary compliance (US$)	0
Border compliance (US$)	0
Enforcing contracts (rank)	22
DTF score for enforcing contracts (0–100)	72.04
Time (days)	321
Cost (% of claim)	30.4
Quality of judicial processes index (0–18)	12.0
Resolving insolvency (rank)	19
DTF score for resolving insolvency (0–100)	79.44
Time (years)	2.0
Cost (% of estate)	9.0
Recovery rate (cents on the dollar)	77.9
Strength of insolvency framework index (0–16)	12.0

Note: Most indicator sets refer to a case scenario in the largest business city of an economy, though for 11 economies the data are a population-weighted average for the two largest business cities. For some indicators a result of "no practice" may be recorded for an economy; see the data notes for more details. In starting a business, procedures (number), time (days) and cost (% of income per capita) are calculated as the average of both men and women. For the postfiling index, a result of "not applicable" may be recorded for an economy.

✔ Reform making it easier to do business ✘ Change making it more difficult to do business

SWITZERLAND

SWITZERLAND		OECD high income		GNI per capita (US$)	84,180
Ease of doing business rank (1–190)	31	Overall distance to frontier (DTF) score (0–100)	76.06	Population	8,286,976

Starting a business (rank)	71
DTF score for starting a business (0–100)	88.39
Procedures (number)	6
Time (days)	10
Cost (% of income per capita)	2.3
Minimum capital (% of income per capita)	25.3
Dealing with construction permits (rank)	68
DTF score for dealing with construction permits (0–100)	71.74
Procedures (number)	13
Time (days)	156
Cost (% of warehouse value)	0.7
Building quality control index (0–15)	9.0
Getting electricity (rank)	7
DTF score for getting electricity (0–100)	94.41
Procedures (number)	3
Time (days)	39
Cost (% of income per capita)	58.9
Reliability of supply and transparency of tariffs index (0–8)	7
Registering property (rank)	16
DTF score for registering property (0–100)	86.12
Procedures (number)	4
Time (days)	16
Cost (% of property value)	0.3
Quality of land administration index (0–30)	23.5
Getting credit (rank)	62
DTF score for getting credit (0–100)	60.00
Strength of legal rights index (0–12)	6
Depth of credit information index (0–8)	6
Credit bureau coverage (% of adults)	25.8
Credit registry coverage (% of adults)	0.0
Protecting minority investors (rank)	106
DTF score for protecting minority investors (0–100)	50.00
Extent of disclosure index (0–10)	0
Extent of director liability index (0–10)	5
Ease of shareholder suits index (0–10)	5
Extent of shareholder rights index (0–10)	8
Extent of ownership and control index (0–10)	6
Extent of corporate transparency index (0–10)	6
Paying taxes (rank)	18
DTF score for paying taxes (0–100)	88.49
Payments (number per year)	19
Time (hours per year)	63
Total tax rate (% of profit)	28.8
Postfiling index (0–100)	86.56
Trading across borders (rank)	37
DTF score for trading across borders (0–100)	91.79
Time to export	
Documentary compliance (hours)	2
Border compliance (hours)	1
Cost to export	
Documentary compliance (US$)	75
Border compliance (US$)	201
Time to import	
Documentary compliance (hours)	2
Border compliance (hours)	1
Cost to import	
Documentary compliance (US$)	75
Border compliance (US$)	201
Enforcing contracts (rank)	39
DTF score for enforcing contracts (0–100)	67.10
Time (days)	420
Cost (% of claim)	24.0
Quality of judicial processes index (0–18)	9.5
Resolving insolvency (rank)	45
DTF score for resolving insolvency (0–100)	62.61
Time (years)	3.0
Cost (% of estate)	4.5
Recovery rate (cents on the dollar)	46.6
Strength of insolvency framework index (0–16)	12.0

SYRIAN ARAB REPUBLIC

SYRIAN ARAB REPUBLIC		Middle East & North Africa		GNI per capita (US$)	1,270
Ease of doing business rank (1–190)	173	Overall distance to frontier (DTF) score (0–100)	41.43	Population	18,502,413

✘ **Starting a business** (rank)	136
DTF score for starting a business (0–100)	78.93
Procedures (number)	7.5
Time (days)	15.5
Cost (% of income per capita)	8.9
Minimum capital (% of income per capita)	106.0
Dealing with construction permits (rank)	187
DTF score for dealing with construction permits (0–100)	0.00
Procedures (number)	NO PRACTICE
Time (days)	NO PRACTICE
Cost (% of warehouse value)	NO PRACTICE
Building quality control index (0–15)	0.0
Getting electricity (rank)	151
DTF score for getting electricity (0–100)	51.79
Procedures (number)	5
Time (days)	146
Cost (% of income per capita)	312.4
Reliability of supply and transparency of tariffs index (0–8)	0
✘ **Registering property** (rank)	154
DTF score for registering property (0–100)	46.88
Procedures (number)	4
Time (days)	48
Cost (% of property value)	27.9
Quality of land administration index (0–30)	10.5
Getting credit (rank)	170
DTF score for getting credit (0–100)	15.00
Strength of legal rights index (0–12)	1
Depth of credit information index (0–8)	2
Credit bureau coverage (% of adults)	0.0
Credit registry coverage (% of adults)	7.2
Protecting minority investors (rank)	87
DTF score for protecting minority investors (0–100)	53.33
Extent of disclosure index (0–10)	7
Extent of director liability index (0–10)	5
Ease of shareholder suits index (0–10)	3
Extent of shareholder rights index (0–10)	6
Extent of ownership and control index (0–10)	5
Extent of corporate transparency index (0–10)	6
Paying taxes (rank)	81
DTF score for paying taxes (0–100)	73.51
Payments (number per year)	20
Time (hours per year)	336
Total tax rate (% of profit)	42.7
Postfiling index (0–100)	90.37
Trading across borders (rank)	176
DTF score for trading across borders (0–100)	29.83
Time to export	
Documentary compliance (hours)	48
Border compliance (hours)	84
Cost to export	
Documentary compliance (US$)	725
Border compliance (US$)	1,113
Time to import	
Documentary compliance (hours)	149
Border compliance (hours)	141
Cost to import	
Documentary compliance (US$)	742
Border compliance (US$)	828
✔ **Enforcing contracts** (rank)	159
DTF score for enforcing contracts (0–100)	42.58
Time (days)	872
Cost (% of claim)	29.3
Quality of judicial processes index (0–18)	4.0
Resolving insolvency (rank)	161
DTF score for resolving insolvency (0–100)	22.44
Time (years)	4.1
Cost (% of estate)	16.0
Recovery rate (cents on the dollar)	12.7
Strength of insolvency framework index (0–16)	5.0

TAIWAN, CHINA

TAIWAN, CHINA		East Asia & Pacific		GNI per capita (US$)	22,267
Ease of doing business rank (1–190)	11	Overall distance to frontier (DTF) score (0–100)	81.09	Population	23,492,074

Starting a business (rank)	19
DTF score for starting a business (0–100)	94.42
Procedures (number)	3
Time (days)	10
Cost (% of income per capita)	2.1
Minimum capital (% of income per capita)	0.0
Dealing with construction permits (rank)	3
DTF score for dealing with construction permits (0–100)	86.30
Procedures (number)	10
Time (days)	93
Cost (% of warehouse value)	0.4
Building quality control index (0–15)	13.0
Getting electricity (rank)	2
DTF score for getting electricity (0–100)	99.44
Procedures (number)	3
Time (days)	22
Cost (% of income per capita)	41.3
Reliability of supply and transparency of tariffs index (0–8)	8
Registering property (rank)	17
DTF score for registering property (0–100)	83.89
Procedures (number)	3
Time (days)	4
Cost (% of property value)	6.2
Quality of land administration index (0–30)	28.5
Getting credit (rank)	62
DTF score for getting credit (0–100)	60.00
Strength of legal rights index (0–12)	4
Depth of credit information index (0–8)	8
Credit bureau coverage (% of adults)	97.1
Credit registry coverage (% of adults)	0.0
Protecting minority investors (rank)	22
DTF score for protecting minority investors (0–100)	70.00
Extent of disclosure index (0–10)	9
Extent of director liability index (0–10)	5
Ease of shareholder suits index (0–10)	6
Extent of shareholder rights index (0–10)	7
Extent of ownership and control index (0–10)	6
Extent of corporate transparency index (0–10)	9
Paying taxes (rank)	30
DTF score for paying taxes (0–100)	84.78
Payments (number per year)	11
Time (hours per year)	221
Total tax rate (% of profit)	34.5
Postfiling index (0–100)	90.82
Trading across borders (rank)	68
DTF score for trading across borders (0–100)	80.11
Time to export	
Documentary compliance (hours)	31
Border compliance (hours)	17
Cost to export	
Documentary compliance (US$)	84
Border compliance (US$)	335
Time to import	
Documentary compliance (hours)	41
Border compliance (hours)	47
Cost to import	
Documentary compliance (US$)	90
Border compliance (US$)	389
Enforcing contracts (rank)	14
DTF score for enforcing contracts (0–100)	73.49
Time (days)	510
Cost (% of claim)	17.7
Quality of judicial processes index (0–18)	13.0
Resolving insolvency (rank)	22
DTF score for resolving insolvency (0–100)	78.46
Time (years)	1.9
Cost (% of estate)	4.0
Recovery rate (cents on the dollar)	81.9
Strength of insolvency framework index (0–16)	11.0

Note: Most indicator sets refer to a case scenario in the largest business city of an economy, though for 11 economies the data are a population-weighted average for the two largest business cities. For some indicators a result of "no practice" may be recorded for an economy; see the data notes for more details. In starting a business, procedures (number), time (days) and cost (% of income per capita) are calculated as the average of both men and women. For the postfiling index, a result of "not applicable" may be recorded for an economy.

✔ Reform making it easier to do business ✘ Change making it more difficult to do business

TAJIKISTAN

Europe & Central Asia		GNI per capita (US$)	1,240
Ease of doing business rank (1–190)	128		
Overall distance to frontier (DTF) score (0–100)	55.34	Population	8,481,855

✘ **Starting a business** (rank)	85
DTF score for starting a business (0–100)	86.61
Procedures (number)	5
Time (days)	22
Cost (% of income per capita)	16.8
Minimum capital (% of income per capita)	0.0
Dealing with construction permits (rank)	162
DTF score for dealing with construction permits (0–100)	54.84
Procedures (number)	27
Time (days)	242
Cost (% of warehouse value)	2.1
Building quality control index (0–15)	12.0
Getting electricity (rank)	173
DTF score for getting electricity (0–100)	35.21
Procedures (number)	9
Time (days)	133
Cost (% of income per capita)	742.5
Reliability of supply and transparency of tariffs index (0–8)	0
Registering property (rank)	97
DTF score for registering property (0–100)	62.00
Procedures (number)	6
Time (days)	37
Cost (% of property value)	2.7
Quality of land administration index (0–30)	7.5
Getting credit (rank)	118
DTF score for getting credit (0–100)	40.00
Strength of legal rights index (0–12)	1
Depth of credit information index (0–8)	7
Credit bureau coverage (% of adults)	35.8
Credit registry coverage (% of adults)	0.0
Protecting minority investors (rank)	27
DTF score for protecting minority investors (0–100)	66.67
Extent of disclosure index (0–10)	8
Extent of director liability index (0–10)	6
Ease of shareholder suits index (0–10)	6
Extent of shareholder rights index (0–10)	9
Extent of ownership and control index (0–10)	4
Extent of corporate transparency index (0–10)	7
✔ **Paying taxes** (rank)	140
DTF score for paying taxes (0–100)	58.79
Payments (number per year)	12
Time (hours per year)	258
Total tax rate (% of profit)	65.2
Postfiling index (0–100)	41.75
Trading across borders (rank)	144
DTF score for trading across borders (0–100)	57.05
Time to export	
Documentary compliance (hours)	66
Border compliance (hours)	75
Cost to export	
Documentary compliance (US$)	330
Border compliance (US$)	313
Time to import	
Documentary compliance (hours)	126
Border compliance (hours)	108
Cost to import	
Documentary compliance (US$)	260
Border compliance (US$)	223
Enforcing contracts (rank)	54
DTF score for enforcing contracts (0–100)	63.49
Time (days)	430
Cost (% of claim)	25.5
Quality of judicial processes index (0–18)	8.0
Resolving insolvency (rank)	144
DTF score for resolving insolvency (0–100)	28.70
Time (years)	1.7
Cost (% of estate)	9.0
Recovery rate (cents on the dollar)	35.9
Strength of insolvency framework index (0–16)	3.0

TANZANIA

Sub-Saharan Africa		GNI per capita (US$)	910
Ease of doing business rank (1–190)	132		
Overall distance to frontier (DTF) score (0–100)	54.48	Population	53,470,420

Starting a business (rank)	135
DTF score for starting a business (0–100)	79.14
Procedures (number)	9
Time (days)	26
Cost (% of income per capita)	21.5
Minimum capital (% of income per capita)	0.0
Dealing with construction permits (rank)	136
DTF score for dealing with construction permits (0–100)	61.69
Procedures (number)	18
Time (days)	205
Cost (% of warehouse value)	5.3
Building quality control index (0–15)	11.5
Getting electricity (rank)	87
DTF score for getting electricity (0–100)	70.52
Procedures (number)	4
Time (days)	109
Cost (% of income per capita)	948.0
Reliability of supply and transparency of tariffs index (0–8)	4
Registering property (rank)	132
DTF score for registering property (0–100)	51.37
Procedures (number)	8
Time (days)	67
Cost (% of property value)	4.4
Quality of land administration index (0–30)	7.5
✔ **Getting credit** (rank)	44
DTF score for getting credit (0–100)	65.00
Strength of legal rights index (0–12)	5
Depth of credit information index (0–8)	8
Credit bureau coverage (% of adults)	6.5
Credit registry coverage (% of adults)	0.0
Protecting minority investors (rank)	145
DTF score for protecting minority investors (0–100)	40.00
Extent of disclosure index (0–10)	2
Extent of director liability index (0–10)	6
Ease of shareholder suits index (0–10)	8
Extent of shareholder rights index (0–10)	4
Extent of ownership and control index (0–10)	2
Extent of corporate transparency index (0–10)	2
✘ **Paying taxes** (rank)	154
DTF score for paying taxes (0–100)	54.13
Payments (number per year)	53
Time (hours per year)	195
Total tax rate (% of profit)	43.9
Postfiling index (0–100)	47.94
Trading across borders (rank)	180
DTF score for trading across borders (0–100)	20.21
Time to export	
Documentary compliance (hours)	96
Border compliance (hours)	96
Cost to export	
Documentary compliance (US$)	275
Border compliance (US$)	1,160
Time to import	
Documentary compliance (hours)	240
Border compliance (hours)	402
Cost to import	
Documentary compliance (US$)	375
Border compliance (US$)	1,350
Enforcing contracts (rank)	59
DTF score for enforcing contracts (0–100)	61.66
Time (days)	515
Cost (% of claim)	14.3
Quality of judicial processes index (0–18)	6.0
Resolving insolvency (rank)	100
DTF score for resolving insolvency (0–100)	41.04
Time (years)	3.0
Cost (% of estate)	22.0
Recovery rate (cents on the dollar)	21.1
Strength of insolvency framework index (0–16)	9.5

THAILAND

East Asia & Pacific		GNI per capita (US$)	5,620
Ease of doing business rank (1–190)	46		
Overall distance to frontier (DTF) score (0–100)	72.53	Population	67,959,359

✔ **Starting a business** (rank)	78
DTF score for starting a business (0–100)	87.01
Procedures (number)	5
Time (days)	25.5
Cost (% of income per capita)	6.6
Minimum capital (% of income per capita)	0.0
Dealing with construction permits (rank)	42
DTF score for dealing with construction permits (0–100)	75.65
Procedures (number)	17
Time (days)	103
Cost (% of warehouse value)	0.1
Building quality control index (0–15)	11.0
Getting electricity (rank)	37
DTF score for getting electricity (0–100)	83.22
Procedures (number)	5
Time (days)	37
Cost (% of income per capita)	42.5
Reliability of supply and transparency of tariffs index (0–8)	6
Registering property (rank)	68
DTF score for registering property (0–100)	68.34
Procedures (number)	4
Time (days)	6
Cost (% of property value)	7.4
Quality of land administration index (0–30)	15.0
✔ **Getting credit** (rank)	82
DTF score for getting credit (0–100)	50.00
Strength of legal rights index (0–12)	3
Depth of credit information index (0–8)	7
Credit bureau coverage (% of adults)	53.0
Credit registry coverage (% of adults)	0.0
Protecting minority investors (rank)	27
DTF score for protecting minority investors (0–100)	66.67
Extent of disclosure index (0–10)	10
Extent of director liability index (0–10)	7
Ease of shareholder suits index (0–10)	7
Extent of shareholder rights index (0–10)	4
Extent of ownership and control index (0–10)	5
Extent of corporate transparency index (0–10)	7
Paying taxes (rank)	109
DTF score for paying taxes (0–100)	68.68
Payments (number per year)	21
Time (hours per year)	266
Total tax rate (% of profit)	32.6
Postfiling index (0–100)	47.32
Trading across borders (rank)	56
DTF score for trading across borders (0–100)	84.10
Time to export	
Documentary compliance (hours)	11
Border compliance (hours)	51
Cost to export	
Documentary compliance (US$)	97
Border compliance (US$)	223
Time to import	
Documentary compliance (hours)	4
Border compliance (hours)	50
Cost to import	
Documentary compliance (US$)	43
Border compliance (US$)	233
Enforcing contracts (rank)	51
DTF score for enforcing contracts (0–100)	64.54
Time (days)	440
Cost (% of claim)	19.5
Quality of judicial processes index (0–18)	7.5
✔ **Resolving insolvency** (rank)	23
DTF score for resolving insolvency (0–100)	77.08
Time (years)	1.5
Cost (% of estate)	18.0
Recovery rate (cents on the dollar)	67.7
Strength of insolvency framework index (0–16)	13.0

Note: Most indicator sets refer to a case scenario in the largest business city of an economy, though for 11 economies the data are a population-weighted average for the two largest business cities. For some indicators a result of "no practice" may be recorded for an economy; see the data notes for more details. In starting a business, procedures (number), time (days) and cost (% of income per capita) are calculated as the average of both men and women. For the postfiling index, a result of "not applicable" may be recorded for an economy.

✔ Reform making it easier to do business ✘ Change making it more difficult to do business

TIMOR-LESTE

TIMOR-LESTE		East Asia & Pacific		GNI per capita (US$)	1,920
Ease of doing business rank (1–190)	**175**	**Overall distance to frontier (DTF) score (0–100)**	**40.88**	**Population**	**1,245,015**

Starting a business (rank)	145
DTF score for starting a business (0–100)	77.13
Procedures (number)	4
Time (days)	9
Cost (% of income per capita)	0.5
Minimum capital (% of income per capita)	260.1
Dealing with construction permits (rank)	159
DTF score for dealing with construction permits (0–100)	55.31
Procedures (number)	16
Time (days)	207
Cost (% of warehouse value)	0.5
Building quality control index (0–15)	3.0
Getting electricity (rank)	112
DTF score for getting electricity (0–100)	63.09
Procedures (number)	3
Time (days)	93
Cost (% of income per capita)	1,218.0
Reliability of supply and transparency of tariffs index (0–8)	0
Registering property (rank)	187
DTF score for registering property (0–100)	0.00
Procedures (number)	NO PRACTICE
Time (days)	NO PRACTICE
Cost (% of property value)	NO PRACTICE
Quality of land administration index (0–30)	NO PRACTICE
Getting credit (rank)	167
DTF score for getting credit (0–100)	20.00
Strength of legal rights index (0–12)	0
Depth of credit information index (0–8)	4
Credit bureau coverage (% of adults)	0.0
Credit registry coverage (% of adults)	5.6
Protecting minority investors (rank)	70
DTF score for protecting minority investors (0–100)	56.67
Extent of disclosure index (0–10)	5
Extent of director liability index (0–10)	4
Ease of shareholder suits index (0–10)	5
Extent of shareholder rights index (0–10)	8
Extent of ownership and control index (0–10)	7
Extent of corporate transparency index (0–10)	5
Paying taxes (rank)	130
DTF score for paying taxes (0–100)	60.55
Payments (number per year)	18
Time (hours per year)	276
Total tax rate (% of profit)	11.2
Postfiling index (0–100)	2.29
Trading across borders (rank)	94
DTF score for trading across borders (0–100)	69.90
Time to export	
Documentary compliance (hours)	33
Border compliance (hours)	96
Cost to export	
Documentary compliance (US$)	100
Border compliance (US$)	350
Time to import	
Documentary compliance (hours)	44
Border compliance (hours)	100
Cost to import	
Documentary compliance (US$)	115
Border compliance (US$)	410
Enforcing contracts (rank)	190
DTF score for enforcing contracts (0–100)	6.13
Time (days)	1,285
Cost (% of claim)	163.2
Quality of judicial processes index (0–18)	2.5
Resolving insolvency (rank)	169
DTF score for resolving insolvency (0–100)	0.00
Time (years)	NO PRACTICE
Cost (% of estate)	NO PRACTICE
Recovery rate (cents on the dollar)	0.0
Strength of insolvency framework index (0–16)	0.0

TOGO

TOGO		Sub-Saharan Africa		GNI per capita (US$)	540
Ease of doing business rank (1–190)	**154**	**Overall distance to frontier (DTF) score (0–100)**	**48.57**	**Population**	**7,304,578**

Starting a business (rank)	123
DTF score for starting a business (0–100)	81.71
Procedures (number)	5
Time (days)	6
Cost (% of income per capita)	71.2
Minimum capital (% of income per capita)	34.0
Dealing with construction permits (rank)	180
DTF score for dealing with construction permits (0–100)	45.09
Procedures (number)	11
Time (days)	163
Cost (% of warehouse value)	14.6
Building quality control index (0–15)	2.5
Getting electricity (rank)	147
DTF score for getting electricity (0–100)	52.78
Procedures (number)	3
Time (days)	66
Cost (% of income per capita)	5,508.3
Reliability of supply and transparency of tariffs index (0–8)	0
Registering property (rank)	183
DTF score for registering property (0–100)	31.40
Procedures (number)	5
Time (days)	283
Cost (% of property value)	9.2
Quality of land administration index (0–30)	6.0
✔ **Getting credit** (rank)	139
DTF score for getting credit (0–100)	30.00
Strength of legal rights index (0–12)	6
Depth of credit information index (0–8)	0
Credit bureau coverage (% of adults)	0.0
Credit registry coverage (% of adults)	0.5
Protecting minority investors (rank)	145
DTF score for protecting minority investors (0–100)	40.00
Extent of disclosure index (0–10)	7
Extent of director liability index (0–10)	1
Ease of shareholder suits index (0–10)	5
Extent of shareholder rights index (0–10)	5
Extent of ownership and control index (0–10)	4
Extent of corporate transparency index (0–10)	2
✔ **Paying taxes** (rank)	169
DTF score for paying taxes (0–100)	48.22
Payments (number per year)	49
Time (hours per year)	216
Total tax rate (% of profit)	48.5
Postfiling index (0–100)	27.79
✔ **Trading across borders** (rank)	117
DTF score for trading across borders (0–100)	63.66
Time to export	
Documentary compliance (hours)	11
Border compliance (hours)	67
Cost to export	
Documentary compliance (US$)	25
Border compliance (US$)	163
Time to import	
Documentary compliance (hours)	180
Border compliance (hours)	168
Cost to import	
Documentary compliance (US$)	252
Border compliance (US$)	612
Enforcing contracts (rank)	145
DTF score for enforcing contracts (0–100)	48.10
Time (days)	488
Cost (% of claim)	47.5
Quality of judicial processes index (0–18)	5.0
✔ **Resolving insolvency** (rank)	87
DTF score for resolving insolvency (0–100)	44.69
Time (years)	3.0
Cost (% of estate)	15.0
Recovery rate (cents on the dollar)	30.8
Strength of insolvency framework index (0–16)	9.0

TONGA

TONGA		East Asia & Pacific		GNI per capita (US$)	4,067
Ease of doing business rank (1–190)	**85**	**Overall distance to frontier (DTF) score (0–100)**	**63.58**	**Population**	**106,170**

Starting a business (rank)	55
DTF score for starting a business (0–100)	90.85
Procedures (number)	4
Time (days)	16
Cost (% of income per capita)	6.8
Minimum capital (% of income per capita)	0.0
✘ **Dealing with construction permits** (rank)	14
DTF score for dealing with construction permits (0–100)	80.96
Procedures (number)	13
Time (days)	77
Cost (% of warehouse value)	1.9
Building quality control index (0–15)	12.0
Getting electricity (rank)	67
DTF score for getting electricity (0–100)	76.29
Procedures (number)	5
Time (days)	42
Cost (% of income per capita)	85.9
Reliability of supply and transparency of tariffs index (0–8)	4
Registering property (rank)	158
DTF score for registering property (0–100)	44.64
Procedures (number)	4
Time (days)	112
Cost (% of property value)	15.1
Quality of land administration index (0–30)	17.0
Getting credit (rank)	44
DTF score for getting credit (0–100)	65.00
Strength of legal rights index (0–12)	10
Depth of credit information index (0–8)	3
Credit bureau coverage (% of adults)	17.3
Credit registry coverage (% of adults)	0.0
Protecting minority investors (rank)	123
DTF score for protecting minority investors (0–100)	45.00
Extent of disclosure index (0–10)	3
Extent of director liability index (0–10)	3
Ease of shareholder suits index (0–10)	9
Extent of shareholder rights index (0–10)	2
Extent of ownership and control index (0–10)	3
Extent of corporate transparency index (0–10)	7
Paying taxes (rank)	80
DTF score for paying taxes (0–100)	73.76
Payments (number per year)	30
Time (hours per year)	200
Total tax rate (% of profit)	30.1
Postfiling index (0–100)	68.90
Trading across borders (rank)	100
DTF score for trading across borders (0–100)	68.20
Time to export	
Documentary compliance (hours)	168
Border compliance (hours)	52
Cost to export	
Documentary compliance (US$)	70
Border compliance (US$)	201
Time to import	
Documentary compliance (hours)	72
Border compliance (hours)	26
Cost to import	
Documentary compliance (US$)	148
Border compliance (US$)	330
Enforcing contracts (rank)	92
DTF score for enforcing contracts (0–100)	57.32
Time (days)	350
Cost (% of claim)	30.5
Quality of judicial processes index (0–18)	4.5
Resolving insolvency (rank)	132
DTF score for resolving insolvency (0–100)	33.82
Time (years)	2.7
Cost (% of estate)	22.0
Recovery rate (cents on the dollar)	28.0
Strength of insolvency framework index (0–16)	6.0

Note: Most indicator sets refer to a case scenario in the largest business city of an economy, though for 11 economies the data are a population-weighted average for the two largest business cities. For some indicators a result of "no practice" may be recorded for an economy; see the data notes for more details. In starting a business, procedures (number), time (days) and cost (% of income per capita) are calculated as the average of both men and women. For the postfiling index, a result of "not applicable" may be recorded for an economy.

✔ Reform making it easier to do business ✘ Change making it more difficult to do business

TRINIDAD AND TOBAGO

Ease of doing business rank (1–190)	96	Latin America & Caribbean Overall distance to frontier (DTF) score (0–100)	60.99	GNI per capita (US$) Population	18,600 1,360,088

Starting a business (rank)	69
DTF score for starting a business (0–100)	88.59
Procedures (number)	7
Time (days)	10.5
Cost (% of income per capita)	0.6
Minimum capital (% of income per capita)	0.0
Dealing with construction permits (rank)	149
DTF score for dealing with construction permits (0–100)	59.21
Procedures (number)	16
Time (days)	253
Cost (% of warehouse value)	0.1
Building quality control index (0–15)	7.0
Getting electricity (rank)	31
DTF score for getting electricity (0–100)	84.36
Procedures (number)	4
Time (days)	61
Cost (% of income per capita)	177.4
Reliability of supply and transparency of tariffs index (0–8)	6
Registering property (rank)	150
DTF score for registering property (0–100)	47.51
Procedures (number)	9
Time (days)	77
Cost (% of property value)	7.0
Quality of land administration index (0–30)	12.0

Getting credit (rank)	44
DTF score for getting credit (0–100)	65.00
Strength of legal rights index (0–12)	7
Depth of credit information index (0–8)	6
Credit bureau coverage (% of adults)	72.3
Credit registry coverage (% of adults)	0.0
Protecting minority investors (rank)	53
DTF score for protecting minority investors (0–100)	60.00
Extent of disclosure index (0–10)	4
Extent of director liability index (0–10)	9
Ease of shareholder suits index (0–10)	8
Extent of shareholder rights index (0–10)	7
Extent of ownership and control index (0–10)	6
Extent of corporate transparency index (0–10)	2
Paying taxes (rank)	145
DTF score for paying taxes (0–100)	57.33
Payments (number per year)	39
Time (hours per year)	210
Total tax rate (% of profit)	32.2
Postfiling index (0–100)	22.67

Trading across borders (rank)	123
DTF score for trading across borders (0–100)	62.60
Time to export	
Documentary compliance (hours)	32
Border compliance (hours)	60
Cost to export	
Documentary compliance (US$)	250
Border compliance (US$)	499
Time to import	
Documentary compliance (hours)	44
Border compliance (hours)	78
Cost to import	
Documentary compliance (US$)	250
Border compliance (US$)	635
Enforcing contracts (rank)	168
DTF score for enforcing contracts (0–100)	36.55
Time (days)	1,340
Cost (% of claim)	33.5
Quality of judicial processes index (0–18)	8.5
Resolving insolvency (rank)	70
DTF score for resolving insolvency (0–100)	48.74
Time (years)	2.5
Cost (% of estate)	25.0
Recovery rate (cents on the dollar)	26.7
Strength of insolvency framework index (0–16)	11.0

TUNISIA

Ease of doing business rank (1–190)	77	Middle East & North Africa Overall distance to frontier (DTF) score (0–100)	64.89	GNI per capita (US$) Population	3,970 11,107,800

Starting a business (rank)	103
DTF score for starting a business (0–100)	85.01
Procedures (number)	9
Time (days)	11
Cost (% of income per capita)	4.7
Minimum capital (% of income per capita)	0.0
Dealing with construction permits (rank)	59
DTF score for dealing with construction permits (0–100)	73.34
Procedures (number)	17
Time (days)	93
Cost (% of warehouse value)	2.5
Building quality control index (0–15)	11.0
Getting electricity (rank)	40
DTF score for getting electricity (0–100)	82.32
Procedures (number)	4
Time (days)	65
Cost (% of income per capita)	696.6
Reliability of supply and transparency of tariffs index (0–8)	6
Registering property (rank)	92
DTF score for registering property (0–100)	63.22
Procedures (number)	4
Time (days)	39
Cost (% of property value)	6.1
Quality of land administration index (0–30)	11.0

✔ **Getting credit** (rank)	101
DTF score for getting credit (0–100)	45.00
Strength of legal rights index (0–12)	3
Depth of credit information index (0–8)	6
Credit bureau coverage (% of adults)	0.0
Credit registry coverage (% of adults)	27.5
Protecting minority investors (rank)	118
DTF score for protecting minority investors (0–100)	46.67
Extent of disclosure index (0–10)	4
Extent of director liability index (0–10)	7
Ease of shareholder suits index (0–10)	5
Extent of shareholder rights index (0–10)	3
Extent of ownership and control index (0–10)	3
Extent of corporate transparency index (0–10)	6
Paying taxes (rank)	106
DTF score for paying taxes (0–100)	68.96
Payments (number per year)	8
Time (hours per year)	144
Total tax rate (% of profit)	60.2
Postfiling index (0–100)	49.77

Trading across borders (rank)	92
DTF score for trading across borders (0–100)	70.50
Time to export	
Documentary compliance (hours)	3
Border compliance (hours)	50
Cost to export	
Documentary compliance (US$)	200
Border compliance (US$)	469
Time to import	
Documentary compliance (hours)	27
Border compliance (hours)	80
Cost to import	
Documentary compliance (US$)	144
Border compliance (US$)	596
Enforcing contracts (rank)	76
DTF score for enforcing contracts (0–100)	59.33
Time (days)	565
Cost (% of claim)	21.8
Quality of judicial processes index (0–18)	7.0
Resolving insolvency (rank)	58
DTF score for resolving insolvency (0–100)	54.53
Time (years)	1.3
Cost (% of estate)	7.0
Recovery rate (cents on the dollar)	52.0
Strength of insolvency framework index (0–16)	8.5

TURKEY

Ease of doing business rank (1–190)	69	Europe & Central Asia Overall distance to frontier (DTF) score (0–100)	67.19	GNI per capita (US$) Population	9,950 78,665,830

✔ **Starting a business** (rank)	79
DTF score for starting a business (0–100)	86.98
Procedures (number)	7
Time (days)	6.5
Cost (% of income per capita)	16.4
Minimum capital (% of income per capita)	10.2
Dealing with construction permits (rank)	102
DTF score for dealing with construction permits (0–100)	67.86
Procedures (number)	18
Time (days)	103
Cost (% of warehouse value)	3.5
Building quality control index (0–15)	9.5
Getting electricity (rank)	58
DTF score for getting electricity (0–100)	79.66
Procedures (number)	4
Time (days)	63
Cost (% of income per capita)	617.3
Reliability of supply and transparency of tariffs index (0–8)	5
Registering property (rank)	54
DTF score for registering property (0–100)	73.01
Procedures (number)	7
Time (days)	7
Cost (% of property value)	4.0
Quality of land administration index (0–30)	21.5

Getting credit (rank)	82
DTF score for getting credit (0–100)	50.00
Strength of legal rights index (0–12)	3
Depth of credit information index (0–8)	7
Credit bureau coverage (% of adults)	0.0
Credit registry coverage (% of adults)	76.6
Protecting minority investors (rank)	22
DTF score for protecting minority investors (0–100)	70.00
Extent of disclosure index (0–10)	9
Extent of director liability index (0–10)	5
Ease of shareholder suits index (0–10)	6
Extent of shareholder rights index (0–10)	8
Extent of ownership and control index (0–10)	7
Extent of corporate transparency index (0–10)	7
✔ **Paying taxes** (rank)	128
DTF score for paying taxes (0–100)	60.83
Payments (number per year)	11
Time (hours per year)	216.5
Total tax rate (% of profit)	41.1
Postfiling index (0–100)	3.90

Trading across borders (rank)	70
DTF score for trading across borders (0–100)	79.71
Time to export	
Documentary compliance (hours)	5
Border compliance (hours)	16
Cost to export	
Documentary compliance (US$)	87
Border compliance (US$)	376
Time to import	
Documentary compliance (hours)	11
Border compliance (hours)	41
Cost to import	
Documentary compliance (US$)	142
Border compliance (US$)	655
Enforcing contracts (rank)	33
DTF score for enforcing contracts (0–100)	68.87
Time (days)	580
Cost (% of claim)	24.9
Quality of judicial processes index (0–18)	13.0
Resolving insolvency (rank)	126
DTF score for resolving insolvency (0–100)	34.98
Time (years)	4.5
Cost (% of estate)	14.5
Recovery rate (cents on the dollar)	18.5
Strength of insolvency framework index (0–16)	8.0

Note: Most indicator sets refer to a case scenario in the largest business city of an economy, though for 11 economies the data are a population-weighted average for the two largest business cities. For some indicators a result of "no practice" may be recorded for an economy; see the data notes for more details. In starting a business, procedures (number), time (days) and cost (% of income per capita) are calculated as the average of both men and women. For the postfiling index, a result of "not applicable" may be recorded for an economy.

✔ Reform making it easier to do business ✘ Change making it more difficult to do business

UGANDA

UGANDA		Sub-Saharan Africa		GNI per capita (US$)	670
Ease of doing business rank (1–190)	115	Overall distance to frontier (DTF) score (0–100)	57.77	Population	39,032,383

✔ **Starting a business** (rank)	165
DTF score for starting a business (0–100)	71.30
Procedures (number)	13
Time (days)	26
Cost (% of income per capita)	37.1
Minimum capital (% of income per capita)	0.0
Dealing with construction permits (rank)	151
DTF score for dealing with construction permits (0–100)	57.19
Procedures (number)	18
Time (days)	122
Cost (% of warehouse value)	9.0
Building quality control index (0–15)	8.0
Getting electricity (rank)	161
DTF score for getting electricity (0–100)	44.78
Procedures (number)	6
Time (days)	66
Cost (% of income per capita)	8,449.0
Reliability of supply and transparency of tariffs index (0–8)	4
Registering property (rank)	116
DTF score for registering property (0–100)	55.81
Procedures (number)	10
Time (days)	42
Cost (% of property value)	2.6
Quality of land administration index (0–30)	10.5
Getting credit (rank)	44
DTF score for getting credit (0–100)	65.00
Strength of legal rights index (0–12)	6
Depth of credit information index (0–8)	7
Credit bureau coverage (% of adults)	6.6
Credit registry coverage (% of adults)	0.0
Protecting minority investors (rank)	106
DTF score for protecting minority investors (0–100)	50.00
Extent of disclosure index (0–10)	3
Extent of director liability index (0–10)	5
Ease of shareholder suits index (0–10)	7
Extent of shareholder rights index (0–10)	5
Extent of ownership and control index (0–10)	5
Extent of corporate transparency index (0–10)	5
✔ **Paying taxes** (rank)	75
DTF score for paying taxes (0–100)	74.71
Payments (number per year)	31
Time (hours per year)	195
Total tax rate (% of profit)	33.5
Postfiling index (0–100)	78.44
✔ **Trading across borders** (rank)	136
DTF score for trading across borders (0–100)	58.90
Time to export	
Documentary compliance (hours)	64
Border compliance (hours)	71
Cost to export	
Documentary compliance (US$)	102
Border compliance (US$)	287
Time to import	
Documentary compliance (hours)	138
Border compliance (hours)	154
Cost to import	
Documentary compliance (US$)	296
Border compliance (US$)	489
Enforcing contracts (rank)	64
DTF score for enforcing contracts (0–100)	60.60
Time (days)	490
Cost (% of claim)	31.3
Quality of judicial processes index (0–18)	8.5
Resolving insolvency (rank)	111
DTF score for resolving insolvency (0–100)	39.40
Time (years)	2.2
Cost (% of estate)	29.5
Recovery rate (cents on the dollar)	38.4
Strength of insolvency framework index (0–16)	6.0

UKRAINE

UKRAINE		Europe & Central Asia		GNI per capita (US$)	2,620
Ease of doing business rank (1–190)	80	Overall distance to frontier (DTF) score (0–100)	63.90	Population	45,198,200

Starting a business (rank)	20
DTF score for starting a business (0–100)	94.40
Procedures (number)	4
Time (days)	5
Cost (% of income per capita)	0.5
Minimum capital (% of income per capita)	0.0
Dealing with construction permits (rank)	140
DTF score for dealing with construction permits (0–100)	61.42
Procedures (number)	10
Time (days)	67
Cost (% of warehouse value)	15.2
Building quality control index (0–15)	8.0
Getting electricity (rank)	130
DTF score for getting electricity (0–100)	58.45
Procedures (number)	5
Time (days)	281
Cost (% of income per capita)	637.6
Reliability of supply and transparency of tariffs index (0–8)	6
Registering property (rank)	63
DTF score for registering property (0–100)	69.61
Procedures (number)	7
Time (days)	23
Cost (% of property value)	1.9
Quality of land administration index (0–30)	15.5
Getting credit (rank)	20
DTF score for getting credit (0–100)	75.00
Strength of legal rights index (0–12)	8
Depth of credit information index (0–8)	7
Credit bureau coverage (% of adults)	40.0
Credit registry coverage (% of adults)	0.0
✔ **Protecting minority investors** (rank)	70
DTF score for protecting minority investors (0–100)	56.67
Extent of disclosure index (0–10)	6
Extent of director liability index (0–10)	2
Ease of shareholder suits index (0–10)	6
Extent of shareholder rights index (0–10)	6
Extent of ownership and control index (0–10)	5
Extent of corporate transparency index (0–10)	9
Paying taxes (rank)	84
DTF score for paying taxes (0–100)	72.72
Payments (number per year)	5
Time (hours per year)	355.5
Total tax rate (% of profit)	51.9
Postfiling index (0–100)	79.26
Trading across borders (rank)	115
DTF score for trading across borders (0–100)	64.26
Time to export	
Documentary compliance (hours)	96
Border compliance (hours)	26
Cost to export	
Documentary compliance (US$)	292
Border compliance (US$)	75
Time to import	
Documentary compliance (hours)	168
Border compliance (hours)	72
Cost to import	
Documentary compliance (US$)	212
Border compliance (US$)	100
✔ **Enforcing contracts** (rank)	81
DTF score for enforcing contracts (0–100)	58.96
Time (days)	378
Cost (% of claim)	46.3
Quality of judicial processes index (0–18)	9.0
Resolving insolvency (rank)	150
DTF score for resolving insolvency (0–100)	27.50
Time (years)	2.9
Cost (% of estate)	42.0
Recovery rate (cents on the dollar)	7.5
Strength of insolvency framework index (0–16)	7.5

UNITED ARAB EMIRATES

UNITED ARAB EMIRATES		Middle East & North Africa		GNI per capita (US$)	43,170
Ease of doing business rank (1–190)	26	Overall distance to frontier (DTF) score (0–100)	76.89	Population	9,156,963

✔ **Starting a business** (rank)	53
DTF score for starting a business (0–100)	91.21
Procedures (number)	4.5
Time (days)	8.5
Cost (% of income per capita)	13.0
Minimum capital (% of income per capita)	0.0
✔ **Dealing with construction permits** (rank)	4
DTF score for dealing with construction permits (0–100)	86.15
Procedures (number)	11
Time (days)	49
Cost (% of warehouse value)	2.3
Building quality control index (0–15)	13.0
✔ **Getting electricity** (rank)	4
DTF score for getting electricity (0–100)	98.84
Procedures (number)	3
Time (days)	28
Cost (% of income per capita)	24.7
Reliability of supply and transparency of tariffs index (0–8)	8
✔ **Registering property** (rank)	11
DTF score for registering property (0–100)	90.04
Procedures (number)	2
Time (days)	1.5
Cost (% of property value)	0.2
Quality of land administration index (0–30)	21.0
Getting credit (rank)	101
DTF score for getting credit (0–100)	45.00
Strength of legal rights index (0–12)	2
Depth of credit information index (0–8)	7
Credit bureau coverage (% of adults)	53.8
Credit registry coverage (% of adults)	8.9
✔ **Protecting minority investors** (rank)	9
DTF score for protecting minority investors (0–100)	75.00
Extent of disclosure index (0–10)	10
Extent of director liability index (0–10)	9
Ease of shareholder suits index (0–10)	4
Extent of shareholder rights index (0–10)	6
Extent of ownership and control index (0–10)	9
Extent of corporate transparency index (0–10)	7
Paying taxes (rank)	1
DTF score for paying taxes (0–100)	99.44
Payments (number per year)	4
Time (hours per year)	12
Total tax rate (% of profit)	15.9
Postfiling index (0–100)	NOT APPLICABLE
Trading across borders (rank)	85
DTF score for trading across borders (0–100)	71.50
Time to export	
Documentary compliance (hours)	6
Border compliance (hours)	27
Cost to export	
Documentary compliance (US$)	178
Border compliance (US$)	462
Time to import	
Documentary compliance (hours)	12
Border compliance (hours)	54
Cost to import	
Documentary compliance (US$)	283
Border compliance (US$)	678
Enforcing contracts (rank)	25
DTF score for enforcing contracts (0–100)	71.14
Time (days)	495
Cost (% of claim)	20.1
Quality of judicial processes index (0–18)	12.0
Resolving insolvency (rank)	104
DTF score for resolving insolvency (0–100)	40.61
Time (years)	3.2
Cost (% of estate)	20.0
Recovery rate (cents on the dollar)	29.0
Strength of insolvency framework index (0–16)	8.0

Note: Most indicator sets refer to a case scenario in the largest business city of an economy, though for 11 economies the data are a population-weighted average for the two largest business cities. For some indicators a result of "no practice" may be recorded for an economy; see the data notes for more details. In starting a business, procedures (number), time (days) and cost (% of income per capita) are calculated as the average of both men and women. For the postfiling index, a result of "not applicable" may be recorded for an economy.

✔ Reform making it easier to do business ✘ Change making it more difficult to do business

UNITED KINGDOM

UNITED KINGDOM		OECD high income		GNI per capita (US$)	43,340
Ease of doing business rank (1–190)	7	Overall distance to frontier (DTF) score (0–100)	82.74	Population	65,138,232

Starting a business (rank)	16
DTF score for starting a business (0–100)	94.58
Procedures (number)	4
Time (days)	4.5
Cost (% of income per capita)	0.1
Minimum capital (% of income per capita)	0.0
Dealing with construction permits (rank)	17
DTF score for dealing with construction permits (0–100)	80.34
Procedures (number)	9
Time (days)	86
Cost (% of warehouse value)	1.1
Building quality control index (0–15)	9.0
Getting electricity (rank)	17
DTF score for getting electricity (0–100)	89.12
Procedures (number)	4
Time (days)	79
Cost (% of income per capita)	25.8
Reliability of supply and transparency of tariffs index (0–8)	8
Registering property (rank)	47
DTF score for registering property (0–100)	74.11
Procedures (number)	6
Time (days)	21.5
Cost (% of property value)	4.8
Quality of land administration index (0–30)	24.0
Getting credit (rank)	20
DTF score for getting credit (0–100)	75.00
Strength of legal rights index (0–12)	7
Depth of credit information index (0–8)	8
Credit bureau coverage (% of adults)	100.0
Credit registry coverage (% of adults)	0.0
Protecting minority investors (rank)	6
DTF score for protecting minority investors (0–100)	78.33
Extent of disclosure index (0–10)	10
Extent of director liability index (0–10)	7
Ease of shareholder suits index (0–10)	8
Extent of shareholder rights index (0–10)	8
Extent of ownership and control index (0–10)	6
Extent of corporate transparency index (0–10)	8
Paying taxes (rank)	10
DTF score for paying taxes (0–100)	90.74
Payments (number per year)	8
Time (hours per year)	110
Total tax rate (% of profit)	30.9
Postfiling index (0–100)	87.44
Trading across borders (rank)	28
DTF score for trading across borders (0–100)	93.76
Time to export	
Documentary compliance (hours)	4
Border compliance (hours)	24
Cost to export	
Documentary compliance (US$)	25
Border compliance (US$)	280
Time to import	
Documentary compliance (hours)	2
Border compliance (hours)	3
Cost to import	
Documentary compliance (US$)	0
Border compliance (US$)	0
Enforcing contracts (rank)	31
DTF score for enforcing contracts (0–100)	69.36
Time (days)	437
Cost (% of claim)	43.9
Quality of judicial processes index (0–18)	15.0
Resolving insolvency (rank)	13
DTF score for resolving insolvency (0–100)	82.04
Time (years)	1.0
Cost (% of estate)	6.0
Recovery rate (cents on the dollar)	88.6
Strength of insolvency framework index (0–16)	11.0

UNITED STATES

UNITED STATES		OECD high income		GNI per capita (US$)	54,960
Ease of doing business rank (1–190)	8	Overall distance to frontier (DTF) score (0–100)	82.45	Population	321,418,820

Starting a business (rank)	51
DTF score for starting a business (0–100)	91.23
Procedures (number)	6
Time (days)	5.6
Cost (% of income per capita)	1.1
Minimum capital (% of income per capita)	0.0
Dealing with construction permits (rank)	39
DTF score for dealing with construction permits (0–100)	75.74
Procedures (number)	15.8
Time (days)	80.6
Cost (% of warehouse value)	1.0
Building quality control index (0–15)	10.0
Getting electricity (rank)	36
DTF score for getting electricity (0–100)	83.39
Procedures (number)	4.8
Time (days)	89.6
Cost (% of income per capita)	24.4
Reliability of supply and transparency of tariffs index (0–8)	7.6
Registering property (rank)	36
DTF score for registering property (0–100)	76.80
Procedures (number)	4.4
Time (days)	15.2
Cost (% of property value)	2.4
Quality of land administration index (0–30)	17.6
Getting credit (rank)	2
DTF score for getting credit (0–100)	95.00
Strength of legal rights index (0–12)	11
Depth of credit information index (0–8)	8
Credit bureau coverage (% of adults)	100.0
Credit registry coverage (% of adults)	0.0
Protecting minority investors (rank)	41
DTF score for protecting minority investors (0–100)	64.67
Extent of disclosure index (0–10)	7.4
Extent of director liability index (0–10)	8.6
Ease of shareholder suits index (0–10)	9
Extent of shareholder rights index (0–10)	4
Extent of ownership and control index (0–10)	4.4
Extent of corporate transparency index (0–10)	5.4
Paying taxes (rank)	36
DTF score for paying taxes (0–100)	83.85
Payments (number per year)	10.6
Time (hours per year)	175
Total tax rate (% of profit)	44.0
Postfiling index (0–100)	93.12
Trading across borders (rank)	35
DTF score for trading across borders (0–100)	92.01
Time to export	
Documentary compliance (hours)	1.5
Border compliance (hours)	1.5
Cost to export	
Documentary compliance (US$)	60
Border compliance (US$)	175
Time to import	
Documentary compliance (hours)	7.5
Border compliance (hours)	1.5
Cost to import	
Documentary compliance (US$)	100
Border compliance (US$)	175
Enforcing contracts (rank)	20
DTF score for enforcing contracts (0–100)	72.61
Time (days)	420
Cost (% of claim)	30.5
Quality of judicial processes index (0–18)	13.8
Resolving insolvency (rank)	5
DTF score for resolving insolvency (0–100)	89.19
Time (years)	1.5
Cost (% of estate)	10.0
Recovery rate (cents on the dollar)	78.6
Strength of insolvency framework index (0–16)	15.0

URUGUAY

URUGUAY		Latin America & Caribbean		GNI per capita (US$)	15,720
Ease of doing business rank (1–190)	90	Overall distance to frontier (DTF) score (0–100)	61.85	Population	3,431,555

✘ **Starting a business** (rank)	60
DTF score for starting a business (0–100)	89.79
Procedures (number)	5
Time (days)	6.5
Cost (% of income per capita)	22.5
Minimum capital (% of income per capita)	0.0
Dealing with construction permits (rank)	163
DTF score for dealing with construction permits (0–100)	54.79
Procedures (number)	21
Time (days)	251
Cost (% of warehouse value)	1.1
Building quality control index (0–15)	8.0
Getting electricity (rank)	43
DTF score for getting electricity (0–100)	82.12
Procedures (number)	5
Time (days)	48
Cost (% of income per capita)	12.5
Reliability of supply and transparency of tariffs index (0–8)	6
Registering property (rank)	110
DTF score for registering property (0–100)	58.01
Procedures (number)	9
Time (days)	66
Cost (% of property value)	7.0
Quality of land administration index (0–30)	23.0
Getting credit (rank)	62
DTF score for getting credit (0–100)	60.00
Strength of legal rights index (0–12)	4
Depth of credit information index (0–8)	8
Credit bureau coverage (% of adults)	100.0
Credit registry coverage (% of adults)	100.0
Protecting minority investors (rank)	123
DTF score for protecting minority investors (0–100)	45.00
Extent of disclosure index (0–10)	3
Extent of director liability index (0–10)	4
Ease of shareholder suits index (0–10)	8
Extent of shareholder rights index (0–10)	5
Extent of ownership and control index (0–10)	6
Extent of corporate transparency index (0–10)	1
✔ **Paying taxes** (rank)	113
DTF score for paying taxes (0–100)	66.08
Payments (number per year)	20
Time (hours per year)	271
Total tax rate (% of profit)	41.8
Postfiling index (0–100)	49.31
Trading across borders (rank)	146
DTF score for trading across borders (0–100)	55.98
Time to export	
Documentary compliance (hours)	24
Border compliance (hours)	120
Cost to export	
Documentary compliance (US$)	231
Border compliance (US$)	1,095
Time to import	
Documentary compliance (hours)	72
Border compliance (hours)	13
Cost to import	
Documentary compliance (US$)	285
Border compliance (US$)	375
Enforcing contracts (rank)	111
DTF score for enforcing contracts (0–100)	54.44
Time (days)	725
Cost (% of claim)	23.2
Quality of judicial processes index (0–18)	7.0
Resolving insolvency (rank)	61
DTF score for resolving insolvency (0–100)	52.26
Time (years)	1.8
Cost (% of estate)	7.0
Recovery rate (cents on the dollar)	41.9
Strength of insolvency framework index (0–16)	9.5

Note: Most indicator sets refer to a case scenario in the largest business city of an economy, though for 11 economies the data are a population-weighted average for the two largest business cities. For some indicators a result of "no practice" may be recorded for an economy; see the data notes for more details. In starting a business, procedures (number), time (days) and cost (% of income per capita) are calculated as the average of both men and women. For the postfiling index, a result of "not applicable" may be recorded for an economy.

✔ Reform making it easier to do business ✘ Change making it more difficult to do business

UZBEKISTAN

UZBEKISTAN		Europe & Central Asia		GNI per capita (US$)	2,150
Ease of doing business rank (1–190)	87	Overall distance to frontier (DTF) score (0–100)	63.03	Population	31,299,500

Starting a business (rank)	25
DTF score for starting a business (0–100)	93.93
Procedures (number)	4
Time (days)	5.5
Cost (% of income per capita)	3.2
Minimum capital (% of income per capita)	0.0
Dealing with construction permits (rank)	147
DTF score for dealing with construction permits (0–100)	59.79
Procedures (number)	23
Time (days)	176
Cost (% of warehouse value)	3.8
Building quality control index (0–15)	11.0
Getting electricity (rank)	83
DTF score for getting electricity (0–100)	71.81
Procedures (number)	7
Time (days)	89
Cost (% of income per capita)	1,232.5
Reliability of supply and transparency of tariffs index (0–8)	8
✔ **Registering property** (rank)	75
DTF score for registering property (0–100)	66.23
Procedures (number)	9
Time (days)	46
Cost (% of property value)	1.3
Quality of land administration index (0–30)	18.5
Getting credit (rank)	44
DTF score for getting credit (0–100)	65.00
Strength of legal rights index (0–12)	6
Depth of credit information index (0–8)	7
Credit bureau coverage (% of adults)	27.8
Credit registry coverage (% of adults)	0.0
✔ **Protecting minority investors** (rank)	70
DTF score for protecting minority investors (0–100)	56.67
Extent of disclosure index (0–10)	8
Extent of director liability index (0–10)	3
Ease of shareholder suits index (0–10)	7
Extent of shareholder rights index (0–10)	6
Extent of ownership and control index (0–10)	5
Extent of corporate transparency index (0–10)	5
✔ **Paying taxes** (rank)	138
DTF score for paying taxes (0–100)	59.06
Payments (number per year)	46
Time (hours per year)	192.5
Total tax rate (% of profit)	38.1
Postfiling index (0–100)	47.02
Trading across borders (rank)	165
DTF score for trading across borders (0–100)	44.31
Time to export	
Documentary compliance (hours)	174
Border compliance (hours)	112
Cost to export	
Documentary compliance (US$)	292
Border compliance (US$)	278
Time to import	
Documentary compliance (hours)	174
Border compliance (hours)	111
Cost to import	
Documentary compliance (US$)	292
Border compliance (US$)	278
Enforcing contracts (rank)	38
DTF score for enforcing contracts (0–100)	67.26
Time (days)	225
Cost (% of claim)	20.5
Quality of judicial processes index (0–18)	6.0
Resolving insolvency (rank)	77
DTF score for resolving insolvency (0–100)	46.29
Time (years)	2.0
Cost (% of estate)	10.0
Recovery rate (cents on the dollar)	39.5
Strength of insolvency framework index (0–16)	8.0

VANUATU

VANUATU		East Asia & Pacific		GNI per capita (US$)	2,873
Ease of doing business rank (1–190)	83	Overall distance to frontier (DTF) score (0–100)	63.66	Population	264,652

✔ **Starting a business** (rank)	126
DTF score for starting a business (0–100)	81.24
Procedures (number)	7
Time (days)	18
Cost (% of income per capita)	44.3
Minimum capital (% of income per capita)	0.0
Dealing with construction permits (rank)	134
DTF score for dealing with construction permits (0–100)	61.91
Procedures (number)	14
Time (days)	64
Cost (% of warehouse value)	7.8
Building quality control index (0–15)	5.0
Getting electricity (rank)	81
DTF score for getting electricity (0–100)	72.00
Procedures (number)	4
Time (days)	120
Cost (% of income per capita)	1,091.0
Reliability of supply and transparency of tariffs index (0–8)	5
Registering property (rank)	81
DTF score for registering property (0–100)	65.63
Procedures (number)	4
Time (days)	58
Cost (% of property value)	7.0
Quality of land administration index (0–30)	18.5
✔ **Getting credit** (rank)	20
DTF score for getting credit (0–100)	75.00
Strength of legal rights index (0–12)	11
Depth of credit information index (0–8)	4
Credit bureau coverage (% of adults)	9.6
Credit registry coverage (% of adults)	0.0
✔ **Protecting minority investors** (rank)	106
DTF score for protecting minority investors (0–100)	50.00
Extent of disclosure index (0–10)	5
Extent of director liability index (0–10)	6
Ease of shareholder suits index (0–10)	5
Extent of shareholder rights index (0–10)	6
Extent of ownership and control index (0–10)	3
Extent of corporate transparency index (0–10)	5
Paying taxes (rank)	54
DTF score for paying taxes (0–100)	80.60
Payments (number per year)	31
Time (hours per year)	120
Total tax rate (% of profit)	8.5
Postfiling index (0–100)	80.04
Trading across borders (rank)	145
DTF score for trading across borders (0–100)	56.27
Time to export	
Documentary compliance (hours)	72
Border compliance (hours)	38
Cost to export	
Documentary compliance (US$)	282
Border compliance (US$)	709
Time to import	
Documentary compliance (hours)	48
Border compliance (hours)	126
Cost to import	
Documentary compliance (US$)	183
Border compliance (US$)	681
Enforcing contracts (rank)	130
DTF score for enforcing contracts (0–100)	51.13
Time (days)	430
Cost (% of claim)	56.0
Quality of judicial processes index (0–18)	7.5
✔ **Resolving insolvency** (rank)	93
DTF score for resolving insolvency (0–100)	42.85
Time (years)	2.6
Cost (% of estate)	38.0
Recovery rate (cents on the dollar)	44.8
Strength of insolvency framework index (0–16)	6.0

VENEZUELA, RB

VENEZUELA, RB		Latin America & Caribbean		GNI per capita (US$)	12,082
Ease of doing business rank (1–190)	187	Overall distance to frontier (DTF) score (0–100)	33.37	Population	31,108,083

✘ **Starting a business** (rank)	189
DTF score for starting a business (0–100)	32.94
Procedures (number)	20
Time (days)	230
Cost (% of income per capita)	136.4
Minimum capital (% of income per capita)	0.0
Dealing with construction permits (rank)	137
DTF score for dealing with construction permits (0–100)	61.65
Procedures (number)	9
Time (days)	434
Cost (% of warehouse value)	1.5
Building quality control index (0–15)	10.5
Getting electricity (rank)	186
DTF score for getting electricity (0–100)	16.85
Procedures (number)	6
Time (days)	208
Cost (% of income per capita)	18,867.2
Reliability of supply and transparency of tariffs index (0–8)	0
Registering property (rank)	129
DTF score for registering property (0–100)	52.36
Procedures (number)	9
Time (days)	52
Cost (% of property value)	2.7
Quality of land administration index (0–30)	5.5
Getting credit (rank)	118
DTF score for getting credit (0–100)	40.00
Strength of legal rights index (0–12)	1
Depth of credit information index (0–8)	7
Credit bureau coverage (% of adults)	27.9
Credit registry coverage (% of adults)	0.0
Protecting minority investors (rank)	175
DTF score for protecting minority investors (0–100)	31.67
Extent of disclosure index (0–10)	3
Extent of director liability index (0–10)	2
Ease of shareholder suits index (0–10)	3
Extent of shareholder rights index (0–10)	4
Extent of ownership and control index (0–10)	4
Extent of corporate transparency index (0–10)	3
Paying taxes (rank)	185
DTF score for paying taxes (0–100)	22.49
Payments (number per year)	70
Time (hours per year)	792
Total tax rate (% of profit)	64.7
Postfiling index (0–100)	48.39
Trading across borders (rank)	187
DTF score for trading across borders (0–100)	7.93
Time to export	
Documentary compliance (hours)	528
Border compliance (hours)	288
Cost to export	
Documentary compliance (US$)	375
Border compliance (US$)	1,250
Time to import	
Documentary compliance (hours)	1,090
Border compliance (hours)	240
Cost to import	
Documentary compliance (US$)	400
Border compliance (US$)	1,500
Enforcing contracts (rank)	137
DTF score for enforcing contracts (0–100)	48.97
Time (days)	610
Cost (% of claim)	43.7
Quality of judicial processes index (0–18)	6.5
Resolving insolvency (rank)	165
DTF score for resolving insolvency (0–100)	18.80
Time (years)	4.0
Cost (% of estate)	38.0
Recovery rate (cents on the dollar)	5.9
Strength of insolvency framework index (0–16)	5.0

Note: Most indicator sets refer to a case scenario in the largest business city of an economy, though for 11 economies the data are a population-weighted average for the two largest business cities. For some indicators a result of "no practice" may be recorded for an economy; see the data notes for more details. In starting a business, procedures (number), time (days) and cost (% of income per capita) are calculated as the average of both men and women. For the postfiling index, a result of "not applicable" may be recorded for an economy.

✔ Reform making it easier to do business ✘ Change making it more difficult to do business

VIETNAM

VIETNAM		East Asia & Pacific		GNI per capita (US$)	1,980
Ease of doing business rank (1–190)	82	Overall distance to frontier (DTF) score (0–100)	63.83	Population	91,703,800

✘ Starting a business (rank)	121
DTF score for starting a business (0–100)	81.76
Procedures (number)	9
Time (days)	24
Cost (% of income per capita)	4.6
Minimum capital (% of income per capita)	0.0

Dealing with construction permits (rank)	24
DTF score for dealing with construction permits (0–100)	78.89
Procedures (number)	10
Time (days)	166
Cost (% of warehouse value)	0.8
Building quality control index (0–15)	12.0

Getting electricity (rank)	96
DTF score for getting electricity (0–100)	69.11
Procedures (number)	5
Time (days)	46
Cost (% of income per capita)	1,261.3
Reliability of supply and transparency of tariffs index (0–8)	3

Registering property (rank)	59
DTF score for registering property (0–100)	70.61
Procedures (number)	5
Time (days)	57.5
Cost (% of property value)	0.6
Quality of land administration index (0–30)	14.0

Getting credit (rank)	32
DTF score for getting credit (0–100)	70.00
Strength of legal rights index (0–12)	7
Depth of credit information index (0–8)	7
Credit bureau coverage (% of adults)	14.8
Credit registry coverage (% of adults)	41.8

✔ Protecting minority investors (rank)	87
DTF score for protecting minority investors (0–100)	53.33
Extent of disclosure index (0–10)	7
Extent of director liability index (0–10)	4
Ease of shareholder suits index (0–10)	2
Extent of shareholder rights index (0–10)	7
Extent of ownership and control index (0–10)	5
Extent of corporate transparency index (0–10)	7

✔ Paying taxes (rank)	167
DTF score for paying taxes (0–100)	49.39
Payments (number per year)	31
Time (hours per year)	540
Total tax rate (% of profit)	39.4
Postfiling index (0–100)	38.94

✔ Trading across borders (rank)	93
DTF score for trading across borders (0–100)	69.92
Time to export	
Documentary compliance (hours)	50
Border compliance (hours)	58
Cost to export	
Documentary compliance (US$)	139
Border compliance (US$)	309
Time to import	
Documentary compliance (hours)	76
Border compliance (hours)	62
Cost to import	
Documentary compliance (US$)	183
Border compliance (US$)	392

Enforcing contracts (rank)	69
DTF score for enforcing contracts (0–100)	60.22
Time (days)	400
Cost (% of claim)	29.0
Quality of judicial processes index (0–18)	6.5

Resolving insolvency (rank)	125
DTF score for resolving insolvency (0–100)	35.08
Time (years)	5.0
Cost (% of estate)	14.5
Recovery rate (cents on the dollar)	21.6
Strength of insolvency framework index (0–16)	7.5

WEST BANK AND GAZA

WEST BANK AND GAZA		Middle East & North Africa		GNI per capita (US$)	3,105
Ease of doing business rank (1–190)	140	Overall distance to frontier (DTF) score (0–100)	53.21	Population	4,422,143

Starting a business (rank)	169
DTF score for starting a business (0–100)	69.36
Procedures (number)	10.5
Time (days)	43.5
Cost (% of income per capita)	46.9
Minimum capital (% of income per capita)	0.0

Dealing with construction permits (rank)	157
DTF score for dealing with construction permits (0–100)	55.98
Procedures (number)	20
Time (days)	108
Cost (% of warehouse value)	14.5
Building quality control index (0–15)	12.0

Getting electricity (rank)	70
DTF score for getting electricity (0–100)	75.25
Procedures (number)	5
Time (days)	47
Cost (% of income per capita)	1,259.3
Reliability of supply and transparency of tariffs index (0–8)	5

Registering property (rank)	93
DTF score for registering property (0–100)	62.71
Procedures (number)	7
Time (days)	51
Cost (% of property value)	3.0
Quality of land administration index (0–30)	13.5

Getting credit (rank)	118
DTF score for getting credit (0–100)	40.00
Strength of legal rights index (0–12)	0
Depth of credit information index (0–8)	8
Credit bureau coverage (% of adults)	0.0
Credit registry coverage (% of adults)	17.2

Protecting minority investors (rank)	158
DTF score for protecting minority investors (0–100)	38.33
Extent of disclosure index (0–10)	6
Extent of director liability index (0–10)	5
Ease of shareholder suits index (0–10)	6
Extent of shareholder rights index (0–10)	2
Extent of ownership and control index (0–10)	1
Extent of corporate transparency index (0–10)	3

Paying taxes (rank)	101
DTF score for paying taxes (0–100)	69.71
Payments (number per year)	28
Time (hours per year)	162
Total tax rate (% of profit)	15.3
Postfiling index (0–100)	37.99

Trading across borders (rank)	99
DTF score for trading across borders (0–100)	68.21
Time to export	
Documentary compliance (hours)	120
Border compliance (hours)	74
Cost to export	
Documentary compliance (US$)	288
Border compliance (US$)	196
Time to import	
Documentary compliance (hours)	45
Border compliance (hours)	2
Cost to import	
Documentary compliance (US$)	200
Border compliance (US$)	0

Enforcing contracts (rank)	122
DTF score for enforcing contracts (0–100)	52.51
Time (days)	540
Cost (% of claim)	27.0
Quality of judicial processes index (0–18)	4.0

Resolving insolvency (rank)	169
DTF score for resolving insolvency (0–100)	0.00
Time (years)	NO PRACTICE
Cost (% of estate)	NO PRACTICE
Recovery rate (cents on the dollar)	0.0
Strength of insolvency framework index (0–16)	0.0

YEMEN, REP.

YEMEN, REP.		Middle East & North Africa		GNI per capita (US$)	1,143
Ease of doing business rank (1–190)	179	Overall distance to frontier (DTF) score (0–100)	39.57	Population	26,832,215

Starting a business (rank)	161
DTF score for starting a business (0–100)	71.59
Procedures (number)	6.5
Time (days)	40.5
Cost (% of income per capita)	82.2
Minimum capital (% of income per capita)	0.0

Dealing with construction permits (rank)	94
DTF score for dealing with construction permits (0–100)	68.79
Procedures (number)	11
Time (days)	184
Cost (% of warehouse value)	1.1
Building quality control index (0–15)	7.5

Getting electricity (rank)	188
DTF score for getting electricity (0–100)	0.00
Procedures (number)	NO PRACTICE
Time (days)	NO PRACTICE
Cost (% of income per capita)	NO PRACTICE
Reliability of supply and transparency of tariffs index (0–8)	0

Registering property (rank)	83
DTF score for registering property (0–100)	65.20
Procedures (number)	6
Time (days)	19
Cost (% of property value)	1.8
Quality of land administration index (0–30)	7.0

Getting credit (rank)	185
DTF score for getting credit (0–100)	0.00
Strength of legal rights index (0–12)	0
Depth of credit information index (0–8)	0
Credit bureau coverage (% of adults)	0.0
Credit registry coverage (% of adults)	1.3

Protecting minority investors (rank)	132
DTF score for protecting minority investors (0–100)	43.33
Extent of disclosure index (0–10)	6
Extent of director liability index (0–10)	4
Ease of shareholder suits index (0–10)	3
Extent of shareholder rights index (0–10)	5
Extent of ownership and control index (0–10)	4
Extent of corporate transparency index (0–10)	4

Paying taxes (rank)	92
DTF score for paying taxes (0–100)	71.64
Payments (number per year)	44
Time (hours per year)	248
Total tax rate (% of profit)	33.1
Postfiling index (0–100)	95.42

Trading across borders (rank)	189
DTF score for trading across borders (0–100)	0.00
Time to export	
Documentary compliance (hours)	NO PRACTICE
Border compliance (hours)	NO PRACTICE
Cost to export	
Documentary compliance (US$)	NO PRACTICE
Border compliance (US$)	NO PRACTICE
Time to import	
Documentary compliance (hours)	NO PRACTICE
Border compliance (hours)	NO PRACTICE
Cost to import	
Documentary compliance (US$)	NO PRACTICE
Border compliance (US$)	NO PRACTICE

Enforcing contracts (rank)	142
DTF score for enforcing contracts (0–100)	48.52
Time (days)	645
Cost (% of claim)	30.0
Quality of judicial processes index (0–18)	4.0

Resolving insolvency (rank)	152
DTF score for resolving insolvency (0–100)	26.65
Time (years)	3.0
Cost (% of estate)	15.0
Recovery rate (cents on the dollar)	20.5
Strength of insolvency framework index (0–16)	5.0

Note: Most indicator sets refer to a case scenario in the largest business city of an economy, though for 11 economies the data are a population-weighted average for the two largest business cities. For some indicators a result of "no practice" may be recorded for an economy; see the data notes for more details. In starting a business, procedures (number), time (days) and cost (% of income per capita) are calculated as the average of both men and women. For the postfiling index, a result of "not applicable" may be recorded for an economy.

✔ Reform making it easier to do business ✘ Change making it more difficult to do business

ZAMBIA

ZAMBIA		Sub-Saharan Africa		GNI per capita (US$)	1,490
Ease of doing business rank (1–190)	**98**	**Overall distance to frontier (DTF) score (0–100)**	**60.54**	**Population**	**16,211,767**
Starting a business (rank)	105	**Getting credit** (rank)	20	**Trading across borders** (rank)	161
DTF score for starting a business (0–100)	84.95	DTF score for getting credit (0–100)	75.00	DTF score for trading across borders (0–100)	46.99
Procedures (number)	7	Strength of legal rights index (0–12)	7	*Time to export*	
Time (days)	8.5	Depth of credit information index (0–8)	8	Documentary compliance (hours)	130
Cost (% of income per capita)	33.7	Credit bureau coverage (% of adults)	16.8	Border compliance (hours)	148
Minimum capital (% of income per capita)	0.0	Credit registry coverage (% of adults)	0.0	*Cost to export*	
				Documentary compliance (US$)	200
✘ **Dealing with construction permits** (rank)	78	**Protecting minority investors** (rank)	87	Border compliance (US$)	370
DTF score for dealing with construction permits (0–100)	70.85	DTF score for protecting minority investors (0–100)	53.33	*Time to import*	
Procedures (number)	10	Extent of disclosure index (0–10)	4	Documentary compliance (hours)	134
Time (days)	189	Extent of director liability index (0–10)	6	Border compliance (hours)	163
Cost (% of warehouse value)	3.3	Ease of shareholder suits index (0–10)	7	*Cost to import*	
Building quality control index (0–15)	10.0	Extent of shareholder rights index (0–10)	6	Documentary compliance (US$)	175
		Extent of ownership and control index (0–10)	5	Border compliance (US$)	380
Getting electricity (rank)	153	Extent of corporate transparency index (0–10)	4		
DTF score for getting electricity (0–100)	49.86			**Enforcing contracts** (rank)	135
Procedures (number)	6	**Paying taxes** (rank)	58	DTF score for enforcing contracts (0–100)	49.89
Time (days)	117	DTF score for paying taxes (0–100)	80.16	Time (days)	611
Cost (% of income per capita)	609.6	Payments (number per year)	26	Cost (% of claim)	38.7
Reliability of supply and transparency of tariffs index (0–8)	0	Time (hours per year)	185.5	Quality of judicial processes index (0–18)	6.0
		Total tax rate (% of profit)	18.6		
✔ **Registering property** (rank)	145	Postfiling index (0–100)	80.06	**Resolving insolvency** (rank)	83
DTF score for registering property (0–100)	49.00			DTF score for resolving insolvency (0–100)	45.36
Procedures (number)	6			Time (years)	1.0
Time (days)	45			Cost (% of estate)	9.0
Cost (% of property value)	9.9			Recovery rate (cents on the dollar)	49.4
Quality of land administration index (0–30)	7.5			Strength of insolvency framework index (0–16)	6.0

ZIMBABWE

ZIMBABWE		Sub-Saharan Africa		GNI per capita (US$)	850
Ease of doing business rank (1–190)	**161**	**Overall distance to frontier (DTF) score (0–100)**	**47.10**	**Population**	**15,602,751**
Starting a business (rank)	183	✔ **Getting credit** (rank)	82	✘ **Trading across borders** (rank)	148
DTF score for starting a business (0–100)	49.13	DTF score for getting credit (0–100)	50.00	DTF score for trading across borders (0–100)	55.65
Procedures (number)	10	Strength of legal rights index (0–12)	5	*Time to export*	
Time (days)	91	Depth of credit information index (0–8)	5	Documentary compliance (hours)	99
Cost (% of income per capita)	119.2	Credit bureau coverage (% of adults)	31.4	Border compliance (hours)	72
Minimum capital (% of income per capita)	0.0	Credit registry coverage (% of adults)	0.0	*Cost to export*	
				Documentary compliance (US$)	170
✔ **Dealing with construction permits** (rank)	181	**Protecting minority investors** (rank)	102	Border compliance (US$)	285
DTF score for dealing with construction permits (0–100)	44.73	DTF score for protecting minority investors (0–100)	51.67	*Time to import*	
Procedures (number)	10	Extent of disclosure index (0–10)	8	Documentary compliance (hours)	81
Time (days)	238	Extent of director liability index (0–10)	2	Border compliance (hours)	228
Cost (% of warehouse value)	25.4	Ease of shareholder suits index (0–10)	5	*Cost to import*	
Building quality control index (0–15)	9.0	Extent of shareholder rights index (0–10)	7	Documentary compliance (US$)	150
		Extent of ownership and control index (0–10)	5	Border compliance (US$)	562
Getting electricity (rank)	165	Extent of corporate transparency index (0–10)	4		
DTF score for getting electricity (0–100)	43.81			**Enforcing contracts** (rank)	165
Procedures (number)	6	**Paying taxes** (rank)	164	DTF score for enforcing contracts (0–100)	38.73
Time (days)	106	DTF score for paying taxes (0–100)	51.15	Time (days)	410
Cost (% of income per capita)	2,957.9	Payments (number per year)	51	Cost (% of claim)	83.1
Reliability of supply and transparency of tariffs index (0–8)	0	Time (hours per year)	242	Quality of judicial processes index (0–18)	6.0
		Total tax rate (% of profit)	32.8		
✔ **Registering property** (rank)	111	Postfiling index (0–100)	23.78	**Resolving insolvency** (rank)	145
DTF score for registering property (0–100)	57.67			DTF score for resolving insolvency (0–100)	28.46
Procedures (number)	5			Time (years)	3.3
Time (days)	36			Cost (% of estate)	22.0
Cost (% of property value)	7.6			Recovery rate (cents on the dollar)	18.0
Quality of land administration index (0–30)	9.5			Strength of insolvency framework index (0–16)	6.0

Note: Most indicator sets refer to a case scenario in the largest business city of an economy, though for 11 economies the data are a population-weighted average for the two largest business cities. For some indicators a result of "no practice" may be recorded for an economy; see the data notes for more details. In starting a business, procedures (number), time (days) and cost (% of income per capita) are calculated as the average of both men and women. For the postfiling index, a result of "not applicable" may be recorded for an economy.

Labor Market Regulation Data

LABOR MARKET REGULATION DATA													
	Hiring				Working hours								
Economy	Fixed-term contracts prohibited for permanent tasks?	Maximum length of fixed-term contracts (months)[a]	Minimum wage for a full-time worker (US$/month)[b]	Ratio of minimum wage to value added per worker	Maximum number of working days per week	Premium for night work (% of hourly pay)	Premium for work on weekly rest day (% of hourly pay)	Premium for overtime work (% of hourly pay)	Restrictions on night work?	Nonpregnant and nonnursing women permitted to work same night hours as men?*	Restrictions on weekly holiday work?	Restrictions on overtime work?	Paid annual leave (working days)[c]
Afghanistan	No	No limit	0.00	0.00	6	25	50	25	Yes	No	No	Yes	20.0
Albania	Yes	No limit	191.60	0.37	5.5	50	25	25	Yes	Yes	No	No	20.0
Algeria	Yes	No limit	212.65	0.34	6	0	0	50	Yes	No	No	No	22.0
Angola	No	120	217.90	0.31	6	10	75	20	Yes	No	Yes	No	22.0
Antigua and Barbuda	No	No limit	618.72	0.38	6	0	0	50	No	Yes	No	No	12.0
Argentina	Yes	60	1,424.20	0.75	5.5	13	100	50	No	Yes	No	No	18.0
Armenia	Yes	No limit	122.88	0.27	6	30	100	50	No	Yes	No	No	20.0
Australia	No	No limit	2,266.32	0.30	6	25	100	50	No	Yes	No	No	20.0
Austria	No	No limit	1,674.51	0.29	5.5	67	100	50	Yes	Yes	No	No	25.0
Azerbaijan	No	60	126.66	0.17	6	40	150	100	Yes	No	No	No	17.0
Bahamas, The	No	No limit	878.85	0.35	5	0	0	50	No	Yes	No	No	11.7
Bahrain	No	60	0.00	0.00	6	50	50	38	No	No	No	No	30.0
Bangladesh (Chittagong)	No	No limit	0.00	0.00	5.5	0	0	100	No	Yes	No	No	17.0
Bangladesh (Dhaka)	No	No limit	0.00	0.00	5.5	0	0	100	No	Yes	No	No	17.0
Barbados	No	No limit	522.88	0.28	5	0	0	50	No	Yes	No	No	20.3
Belarus	No	No limit	170.35	0.22	6	20	100	100	No	Yes	No	No	18.0
Belgium	No	No limit	2,420.23	0.42	6	0	0	50	Yes	Yes	Yes	No	20.0
Belize	No	No limit	376.93	0.65	6	0	50	50	No	Yes	No	Yes	10.0
Benin	No	48	74.95	0.57	6	0	0	12	No	Yes	No	No	24.0

Redundancy rules									Redundancy cost		Job quality							
Maximum length of probationary period (months)[d]	Dismissal due to redundancy allowed by law?	Third-party notification if one worker is dismissed?	Third-party approval if one worker is dismissed?	Third-party notification if nine workers are dismissed?	Third-party approval if nine workers are dismissed?	Retraining or reassignment compulsory before redundancy?	Priority rules for redundancies?	Priority rules for reemployment?	Notice period for redundancy dismissal (weeks of salary)[c]	Severance pay for redundancy dismissal (weeks of salary)[c]	Equal remuneration for work of equal value?*	Gender nondiscrimination in hiring?*	Paid or unpaid maternity leave mandated by law?[e]*	Minimum length of maternity leave (calendar days)[f]*	Receive 100% of wages on maternity leave?*	Five fully paid days of sick leave a year?	Unemployment protection after one year of employment?	Minimum contribution period for unemployment protection (months)[g]
6.0	Yes	Yes	No	Yes	Yes	No	No	Yes	4.3	17.3	No	No	Yes	90	Yes	Yes	No	n.a.
3.0	Yes	No	No	No	No	No	No	Yes	10.1	10.7	No	Yes	Yes	365	No	No	Yes	12
6.0	Yes	Yes	No	Yes	No	Yes	Yes	No	4.3	13.0	Yes	No	Yes	98	Yes	No	No	36
3.0	Yes	Yes	Yes	Yes	Yes	No	No	Yes	4.3	13.6	Yes	No	Yes	90	Yes	No	No	n.a
3.0	Yes	No	No	No	No	Yes	Yes	No	3.4	12.8	No	Yes	Yes	91	No	Yes	No	n.a.
3.0	Yes	No	No	No	No	No	No	No	7.2	23.1	Yes	Yes	Yes	90	Yes	Yes	Yes	6
3.0	Yes	No	No	No	No	Yes	No	No	6.0	5.0	Yes	No	Yes	140	Yes	No	No	n.a
6.0	Yes	No	No	No	No	Yes	No	No	3.3	8.7	Yes	Yes	Yes	126	No	Yes	Yes	0
1.0	Yes	Yes	No	Yes	No	No	Yes	Yes	2.0	0.0	Yes	No	Yes	112	Yes	Yes	Yes	12
3.0	Yes	No	No	No	No	No	Yes	No	8.7	13.0	Yes	Yes	Yes	126	Yes	Yes	Yes	6
6.0	Yes	Yes	No	Yes	No	No	No	No	2.0	10.7	No	Yes	Yes	91	Yes	Yes	Yes	3
3.0	Yes	Yes	No	Yes	No	No	No	No	4.3	2.4	No	No	Yes	60	Yes	Yes	Yes	0
3.0	Yes	Yes	No	Yes	No	No	Yes	Yes	4.3	26.7	Yes	No	Yes	112	Yes	Yes	No	n.a.
3.0	Yes	Yes	No	Yes	No	No	Yes	Yes	4.3	26.7	Yes	No	Yes	112	Yes	Yes	No	n.a.
n.a.	Yes	No	No	No	No	No	No	Yes	2.7	13.3	No	No	Yes	84	Yes	Yes	Yes	12
3.0	Yes	No	No	No	No	Yes	Yes	No	8.7	13.0	Yes	No	Yes	126	Yes	Yes	Yes	0
0.0	Yes	No	No	No	No	No	No	No	19.7	0.0	Yes	Yes	Yes	105	No	Yes	No	14.4
2.0	Yes	Yes	No	Yes	No	No	No	No	4.7	8.3	No	No	Yes	98	No	Yes	No	n.a.
2.0	Yes	Yes	No	Yes	No	No	Yes	Yes	4.3	7.3	No	Yes	Yes	98	Yes	Yes	No	n.a.

LABOR MARKET REGULATION DATA

Economy	Hiring				Working hours								
	Fixed-term contracts prohibited for permanent tasks?	Maximum length of fixed-term contracts (months)[a]	Minimum wage for a full-time worker (US$/month)[b]	Ratio of minimum wage to value added per worker	Maximum number of working days per week	Premium for night work (% of hourly pay)	Premium for work on weekly rest day (% of hourly pay)	Premium for overtime work (% of hourly pay)	Restrictions on night work?	Nonpregnant and nonnursing women permitted to work same night hours as men?*	Restrictions on weekly holiday work?	Restrictions on overtime work?	Paid annual leave (working days)[c]
Bhutan	No	No limit	58.17	0.20	6	0	0	0	No	Yes	No	No	15.0
Bolivia[h]	Yes	24	239.85	0.57	6	25	100	100	No	No	No	No	21.7
Bosnia and Herzegovina	No	24	353.60	0.64	6	30	20	30	No	Yes	No	No	18.0
Botswana	No	No limit	100.58	0.12	6	0	100	50	No	Yes	No	No	15.0
Brazil (Rio de Janeiro)	Yes	24	418.98	0.35	6	20	100	50	Yes	Yes	No	No	26.0
Brazil (São Paulo)	Yes	24	383.99	0.32	6	20	100	50	Yes	Yes	No	No	26.0
Brunei Darussalam	No	No limit	0.00	0.00	6	0	50	50	No	Yes	No	No	13.3
Bulgaria	No	36	262.92	0.29	6	3	0	50	Yes	Yes	No	Yes	20.0
Burkina Faso	No	No limit	98.95	0.94	6	0	0	15	No	Yes	Yes	No	22.0
Burundi	No	No limit	2.40	0.06	6	35	0	35	No	Yes	No	No	21.0
Cabo Verde	Yes	60	121.69	0.29	6	25	100	50	No	Yes	No	No	22.0
Cambodia	No	24	0.00	0.00	6	130	0	50	No	Yes	No	No	19.3
Cameroon	No	48	66.36	0.32	6	0	0	20	No	Yes	No	No	25.0
Canada	No	No limit	1,687.14	0.29	6	0	0	50	No	Yes	No	Yes	10.0
Central African Republic	Yes	24	83.08	1.78	6	0	50	..	No	Yes	Yes	No	25.3
Chad	No	48	118.22	0.80	6	0	100	10	Yes	No	No	No	24.7
Chile	No	12	412.29	0.24	6	0	0	50	No	Yes	No	No	15.0
China (Beijing)	No	No limit	274.07	0.31	6	0	100	50	No	Yes	No	No	6.7
China (Shanghai)	No	No limit	348.96	0.39	6	34	100	50	No	Yes	No	No	6.7
Colombia	No	No limit	302.43	0.35	6	35	75	25	No	Yes	No	No	15.0
Comoros	No	36	0.00	0.00	6	28	0	25	No	Yes	Yes	No	22.0
Congo, Dem. Rep.	Yes	48	65.00	0.00	5	25	0	38	Yes	Yes	No	No	13.0

	Redundancy rules								Redundancy cost		Job quality							
Maximum length of probationary period (months)[d]	Dismissal due to redundancy allowed by law?	Third-party notification if one worker is dismissed?	Third-party approval if one worker is dismissed?	Third-party notification if nine workers are dismissed?	Third-party approval if nine workers are dismissed?	Retraining or reassignment compulsory before redundancy?	Priority rules for redundancies?	Priority rules for reemployment?	Notice period for redundancy dismissal (weeks of salary)[c]	Severance pay for redundancy dismissal (weeks of salary)[c]	Equal remuneration for work of equal value?*	Gender nondiscrimination in hiring?*	Paid or unpaid maternity leave mandated by law?**	Minimum length of maternity leave (calendar days)[f]*	Receive 100% of wages on maternity leave?*	Five fully paid days of sick leave a year?	Unemployment protection after one year of employment?	Minimum contribution period for unemployment protection (months)[g]
6.0	Yes	Yes	No	Yes	No	No	No	No	8.3	0.0	No	No	Yes	56	Yes	Yes	No	n.a.
3.0	No	n.a.	n.a.	n.a.	n.a.	n.a.	n.a.	n.a.	n.a.	n.a.	Yes	No	Yes	90	Yes	Yes	No	n.a.
6.0	Yes	No	No	Yes	No	Yes	No	Yes	2.0	7.2	Yes	Yes	Yes	365	No	Yes	Yes	8
3.0	Yes	Yes	No	Yes	No	No	Yes	Yes	4.9	16.8	No	No	Yes	84	No	Yes	No	n.a.
3.0	Yes	No	No	No	No	No	No	No	6.6	8.9	No	Yes	Yes	120	Yes	Yes	Yes	12
3.0	Yes	No	No	No	No	No	No	No	6.6	8.9	No	Yes	Yes	120	Yes	Yes	Yes	12
n.a.	Yes	No	No	No	No	No	No	No	3.0	0.0	No	No	Yes	91	Yes	Yes	No	n.a.
6.0	Yes	No	No	No	No	No	No	No	4.3	4.3	Yes	Yes	Yes	410	No	Yes	Yes	9
2.0	Yes	No	No	Yes	No	No	Yes	Yes	4.3	6.1	No	No	Yes	98	Yes	Yes	No	n.a.
6.0	Yes	No	No	Yes	No	No	Yes	Yes	8.7	7.2	No	No	Yes	84	Yes	..	No	n.a.
2.0	Yes	Yes	Yes	Yes	Yes	Yes	Yes	No	6.4	23.1	No	No	Yes	60	Yes	Yes	Yes	6
1.0	Yes	No	No	Yes	No	No	Yes	Yes	7.9	11.4	Yes	Yes	Yes	90	No	No	No	n.a.
2.0	Yes	Yes	Yes	Yes	Yes	No	Yes	Yes	11.6	8.3	No	No	Yes	98	Yes	Yes	No	n.a.
3.0	Yes	No	No	No	No	No	No	No	5.0	5.0	Yes	No	Yes	105	No	No	Yes	3.6
2.0	Yes	Yes	No	Yes	Yes	No	Yes	Yes	4.3	17.3	No	No	Yes	98	No	Yes	No	n.a.
3.0	Yes	Yes	No	Yes	No	No	Yes	Yes	7.2	5.8	Yes	Yes	Yes	98	No	Yes	No	n.a.
n.a.	Yes	Yes	No	Yes	No	No	No	No	4.3	23.1	No	No	Yes	126	Yes	No	Yes	12
6.0	Yes	Yes	No	Yes	No	Yes	Yes	Yes	4.3	23.1	No	Yes	Yes	98	Yes	Yes	Yes	12
6.0	Yes	Yes	No	Yes	No	Yes	Yes	Yes	4.3	23.1	No	Yes	Yes	128	Yes	Yes	Yes	12
2.0	Yes	No	No	No	No	No	No	No	0.0	16.7	Yes	No	Yes	98	Yes	Yes	Yes	12
6.0	Yes	Yes	No	Yes	No	No	Yes	Yes	8.7	5.0	Yes	Yes	Yes	98	Yes	..	No	n.a.
1.0	Yes	Yes	Yes	Yes	Yes	No	Yes	Yes	10.3	0.0	No	Yes	Yes	98	No	No	No	n.a.

LABOR MARKET REGULATION DATA

Economy	Hiring				Working hours								
	Fixed-term contracts prohibited for permanent tasks?	Maximum length of fixed-term contracts (months)[a]	Minimum wage for a full-time worker (US$/month)[b]	Ratio of minimum wage to value added per worker	Maximum number of working days per week	Premium for night work (% of hourly pay)	Premium for work on weekly rest day (% of hourly pay)	Premium for overtime work (% of hourly pay)	Restrictions on night work?	Nonpregnant and nonnursing women permitted to work same night hours as men?*	Restrictions on weekly holiday work?	Restrictions on overtime work?	Paid annual leave (working days)[c]
Congo, Rep.	Yes	24	231.81	0.59	6	0	0	14	No	Yes	Yes	Yes	29.7
Costa Rica	Yes	12	605.46	0.49	6	0	100	50	Yes	No	No	No	12.0
Côte d'Ivoire	No	24	110.51	0.51	6	38	0	24	No	Yes	No	No	27.4
Croatia	Yes	No limit	503.96	0.32	6	10	35	50	Yes	Yes	Yes	No	20.0
Cyprus	No	30	1,153.63	0.38	5.5	0	100	100	No	Yes	No	No	20.0
Czech Republic	No	108	545.05	0.24	6	10	10	25	No	Yes	No	No	20.0
Denmark	No	No limit	0.00	0.00	6	0	0	0	No	Yes	No	No	25.0
Djibouti	Yes	24	0.00	0.00	6	0	0	0	No	Yes	No	Yes	30.0
Dominica	No	No limit	349.02	0.42	6	0	100	50	No	Yes	No	No	13.3
Dominican Republic	Yes	No limit	311.87	0.39	5.5	0	100	35	No	Yes	Yes	No	16.7
Ecuador	Yes	No limit	418.09	0.54	5	25	100	50	No	Yes	No	Yes	12.0
Egypt, Arab Rep.	No	No limit	0.00	0.00	6	0	0	35	No	Yes	No	No	24.0
El Salvador	Yes	No limit	213.00	0.42	6	25	100	125	Yes	Yes	Yes	No	11.0
Equatorial Guinea	Yes	24	812.30	0.72	6	25	50	25	No	Yes	Yes	No	22.0
Eritrea	Yes	No limit	0.00	0.00	6	0	0	25	No	Yes	No	No	19.0
Estonia	Yes	120	520.44	0.22	5	25	0	50	Yes	Yes	No	No	24.0
Ethiopia	Yes	No limit	0.00	0.00	6	0	0	25	No	Yes	No	No	18.3
Fiji	No	No Limit	311.97	0.51	6	4	0	50	No	Yes	No	No	10.0
Finland	Yes	60	2,169.37	0.35	6	16	100	50	No	Yes	No	No	30.0
France	Yes	18	1,866.90	0.34	6	20	20	25	Yes	Yes	Yes	No	30.3
Gabon	No	48	299.00	0.23	6	0	0	10	No	Yes	No	No	24.0
Gambia, The	No	No limit	0.00	0.00	5	0	0	0	No	Yes	No	No	21.0

Redundancy rules									Redundancy cost		Job quality							
Maximum length of probationary period (months)[d]	Dismissal due to redundancy allowed by law?	Third-party notification if one worker is dismissed?	Third-party approval if one worker is dismissed?	Third-party notification if nine workers are dismissed?	Third-party approval if nine workers are dismissed?	Retraining or reassignment compulsory before redundancy?	Priority rules for redundancies?	Priority rules for reemployment?	Notice period for redundancy dismissal (weeks of salary)[c]	Severance pay for redundancy dismissal (weeks of salary)[c]	Equal remuneration for work of equal value?*	Gender nondiscrimination in hiring?*	Paid or unpaid maternity leave mandated by law?[e]*	Minimum length of maternity leave (calendar days)[f]*	Receive 100% of wages on maternity leave?*	Five fully paid days of sick leave a year?	Unemployment protection after one year of employment?	Minimum contribution period for unemployment protection (months)[g]
4.0	Yes	Yes	Yes	Yes	Yes	No	Yes	Yes	8.7	6.9	No	No	Yes	105	Yes	Yes	No	n.a.
3.0	Yes	No	No	No	No	No	No	No	4.3	14.4	No	No	Yes	120	Yes	Yes	No	n.a.
2.0	Yes	No	No	Yes	No	No	No	Yes	5.8	7.3	Yes	Yes	Yes	98	Yes	Yes	No	n.a.
6.0	Yes	Yes	No	Yes	No	No	Yes	Yes	7.9	7.2	Yes	No	Yes	208	Yes	Yes	Yes	9
24.0	Yes	Yes	No	Yes	No	Yes	No	Yes	5.7	0.0	Yes	Yes	Yes	126	No	No	Yes	6
3.0	Yes	No	No	No	No	No	No	No	8.7	11.6	Yes	Yes	Yes	196	No	No	Yes	12
3.0	Yes	No	No	No	No	No	No	No	0.0	0.0	Yes	No	Yes	126	No	Yes	Yes	12
2.0	Yes	Yes	No	Yes	No	No	No	Yes	4.3	0.0	Yes	Yes	Yes	98	Yes	Yes	No	n.a.
6.0	Yes	No	No	No	No	No	Yes	Yes	5.8	9.3	No	No	Yes	84	No	No	No	n.a.
3.0	Yes	No	No	No	No	No	No	No	4.0	22.2	No	No	Yes	84	Yes	No	No	n.a.
3.0	Yes	Yes	No	Yes	No	No	No	No	0.0	31.8	Yes	No	Yes	84	Yes	No	No	n.a.
3.0	Yes	Yes	Yes	Yes	Yes	No	Yes	No	10.1	26.7	No	No	Yes	90	Yes	No	Yes	6
1.0	Yes	No	No	No	No	No	No	No	0.0	22.9	No	No	Yes	112	Yes	No	No	n.a.
1.0	Yes	Yes	Yes	Yes	Yes	No	Yes	Yes	4.3	34.3	Yes	No	Yes	84	No	Yes	No	n.a
3.0	Yes	No	No	No	No	No	No	No	3.1	12.3	No	No	Yes	60	Yes	Yes	No	n.a.
4.0	Yes	No	No	No	No	Yes	Yes	No	8.6	4.3	No	Yes	Yes	140	Yes	No	Yes	12
1.5	Yes	No	No	Yes	No	Yes	Yes	No	8.7	10.5	No	No	Yes	90	Yes	Yes	No	n.a.
3.0	Yes	Yes	No	Yes	No	No	No	No	4.3	5.3	Yes	No	Yes	84	Yes	Yes	No	n.a.
6.0	Yes	Yes	No	Yes	No	Yes	No	Yes	10.1	0.0	Yes	Yes	Yes	105	No	Yes	Yes	6
2.0	Yes	No	No	Yes	No	Yes	Yes	Yes	7.2	4.6	Yes	Yes	Yes	112	No	No	Yes	4
6.0	Yes	Yes	Yes	Yes	Yes	No	Yes	Yes	14.4	4.3	No	No	Yes	98	Yes	Yes	No	n.a.
12.0	Yes	Yes	No	Yes	No	No	Yes	Yes	26.0	0.0	No	No	Yes	180	Yes	Yes	No	n.a.

LABOR MARKET REGULATION DATA

Economy	Hiring: Fixed-term contracts prohibited for permanent tasks?	Hiring: Maximum length of fixed-term contracts (months)[a]	Hiring: Minimum wage for a full-time worker (US$/month)[b]	Hiring: Ratio of minimum wage to value added per worker	Working hours: Maximum number of working days per week	Working hours: Premium for night work (% of hourly pay)	Working hours: Premium for work on weekly rest day (% of hourly pay)	Working hours: Premium for overtime work (% of hourly pay)	Working hours: Restrictions on night work?	Working hours: Nonpregnant and nonnursing women permitted to work same night hours as men?*	Working hours: Restrictions on weekly holiday work?	Working hours: Restrictions on overtime work?	Working hours: Paid annual leave (working days)[c]
Georgia	No	30	19.86	0.04	7	0	0	0	No	Yes	No	No	24.0
Germany	No	No limit	1,777.63	0.31	6	0	0	0	No	Yes	No	No	24.0
Ghana	No	No limit	51.86	0.24	5	0	0	0	No	Yes	No	No	15.0
Greece	Yes	No limit	740.67	0.28	6	25	75	28	No	Yes	Yes	No	22.3
Grenada	Yes	No limit	247.31	0.23	6	0	0	50	No	Yes	No	No	13.3
Guatemala	Yes	No limit	394.84	0.77	6	0	50	50	Yes	Yes	Yes	Yes	15.0
Guinea	No	24	56.43	0.78	6	20	0	30	No	Yes	Yes	No	30.0
Guinea-Bissau	Yes	12	0.00	0.00	6	25	50	0	No	No	No	No	21.0
Guyana	No	No limit	167.72	0.33	7	0	100	50	No	Yes	No	No	12.0
Haiti	No	No limit	137.23	1.24	6	50	50	50	No	Yes	No	No	13.0
Honduras	Yes	24	453.73	1.52	6	25	100	38	Yes	Yes	No	No	16.7
Hong Kong SAR, China	No	No limit	829.13	0.18	6	0	0	0	No	Yes	No	No	10.3
Hungary	No	60	437.42	0.27	5	15	50	50	No	Yes	No	No	21.3
Iceland	No	24	1,958.82	0.31	6	1	1	1	No	Yes	No	No	24.0
India (Delhi)	No	No limit	180.65	0.89	6	0	0	100	Yes	No	Yes	Yes	15.0
India (Mumbai)	No	No limit	136.06	0.67	6	0	0	100	Yes	No	Yes	Yes	21.0
Indonesia (Jakarta)	Yes	36	262.64	0.62	6	0	0	75	No	Yes	No	No	12.0
Indonesia (Surabaya)	Yes	36	241.91	0.57	6	0	0	75	No	Yes	No	No	12.0
Iran, Islamic Rep.	No	No limit	279.95	0.40	6	35	40	40	No	Yes	No	No	24.0
Iraq	Yes	No limit	123.55	0.15	6	0	50	50	Yes	No	No	No	22.0
Ireland	No	No limit	1,697.67	0.28	6	1	0	0	No	Yes	No	No	20.0
Israel	No	No limit	1,216.95	0.25	5.5	0	50	25	No	Yes	Yes	No	18.0

Redundancy rules									Redundancy cost		Job quality							
Maximum length of probationary period (months)[d]	Dismissal due to redundancy allowed by law?	Third-party notification if one worker is dismissed?	Third-party approval if one worker is dismissed?	Third-party notification if nine workers are dismissed?	Third-party approval if nine workers are dismissed?	Retraining or reassignment compulsory before redundancy?	Priority rules for redundancies?	Priority rules for reemployment?	Notice period for redundancy dismissal (weeks of salary)[c]	Severance pay for redundancy dismissal (weeks of salary)[c]	Equal remuneration for work of equal value?*	Gender nondiscrimination in hiring?*	Paid or unpaid maternity leave mandated by law?[e]*	Minimum length of maternity leave (calendar days)[f]*	Receive 100% of wages on maternity leave?*	Five fully paid days of sick leave a year?	Unemployment protection after one year of employment?	Minimum contribution period for unemployment protection (months)[g]
6.0	Yes	No	No	No	No	No	No	No	4.3	4.3	No	No	Yes	183	Yes	Yes	No	n.a.
6.0	Yes	Yes	No	Yes	No	Yes	Yes	No	10.0	11.6	No	No	Yes	98	Yes	Yes	Yes	12
6.0	Yes	Yes	Yes	Yes	Yes	No	No	No	3.6	46.2	No	No	Yes	84	Yes	No	No	n.a.
12.0	Yes	No	No	Yes	Yes	No	Yes	No	0.0	15.9	Yes	No	Yes	119	Yes	No	Yes	4
1.0	Yes	No	No	No	No	No	No	No	7.2	5.3	Yes	No	Yes	90	No	Yes	No	n.a.
2.0	Yes	No	No	No	No	No	No	No	0.0	27.0	No	No	Yes	84	Yes	Yes	No	n.a.
1.0	Yes	Yes	No	Yes	No	No	No	No	4.3	5.8	Yes	Yes	Yes	98	Yes	No	No	n.a.
3.0	Yes	Yes	Yes	Yes	Yes	No	Yes	Yes	0.0	26.0	No	No	Yes	60	Yes	Yes	No	n.a.
3.0	Yes	Yes	No	Yes	No	No	No	No	4.3	12.3	Yes	Yes	Yes	91	Yes	Yes	No	n.a.
0.0	Yes	No	No	No	No	No	No	No	10.1	0.0	No	No	Yes	42	Yes	Yes	No	n.a.
2.0	Yes	Yes	Yes	Yes	Yes	No	Yes	No	7.2	23.1	No	Yes	Yes	84	Yes	Yes	No	n.a.
1.0	Yes	No	No	No	No	No	No	No	4.3	1.4	No	Yes	Yes	70	No	No	Yes	0
3.0	Yes	No	No	No	No	No	No	No	6.2	7.2	Yes	Yes	Yes	168	No	Yes	Yes	12
3.0	Yes	No	No	No	No	No	No	No	13.0	0.0	Yes	Yes	Yes	90	No	Yes	Yes	3
3.0	Yes	Yes	No	Yes	No	No	Yes	Yes	4.3	11.4	No	Yes	Yes	84	Yes	No	No	n.a.
3.0	Yes	Yes	No	Yes	No	No	Yes	Yes	4.3	11.4	No	Yes	Yes	84	Yes	No	No	n.a.
3.0	Yes	Yes	Yes	Yes	Yes	Yes	No	No	0.0	57.8	No	No	Yes	90	Yes	Yes	No	n.a.
3.0	Yes	Yes	Yes	Yes	Yes	Yes	No	No	0.0	57.8	No	No	Yes	90	Yes	Yes	No	n.a.
1.0	Yes	Yes	Yes	Yes	Yes	No	No	No	0.0	23.1	No	No	Yes	180	No	No	Yes	6
3.0	Yes	Yes	No	Yes	No	No	No	No	0.0	0.0	No	No	Yes	72	Yes	Yes	..	..
12.0	Yes	No	No	Yes	No	No	No	No	3.7	10.7	Yes	Yes	Yes	182	No	No	No	24
n.a.	Yes	No	No	No	No	No	No	No	4.3	23.1	Yes	Yes	Yes	98	Yes	No	Yes	12

LABOR MARKET REGULATION DATA

Economy	Hiring				Working hours								
	Fixed-term contracts prohibited for permanent tasks?	Maximum length of fixed-term contracts (months)[a]	Minimum wage for a full-time worker (US$/month)[b]	Ratio of minimum wage to value added per worker	Maximum number of working days per week	Premium for night work (% of hourly pay)	Premium for work on weekly rest day (% of hourly pay)	Premium for overtime work (% of hourly pay)	Restrictions on night work?	Nonpregnant and nonnursing women permitted to work same night hours as men?*	Restrictions on weekly holiday work?	Restrictions on overtime work?	Paid annual leave (working days)[c]
Italy	No	36	2,083.94	0.49	6	15	30	15	No	Yes	No	No	26.0
Jamaica	No	No limit	229.40	0.37	6	0	100	0	No	Yes	No	No	11.7
Japan (Osaka)	No	No limit	1,332.36	0.27	6	25	35	25	No	Yes	No	Yes	15.3
Japan (Tokyo)	No	No limit	1,408.45	0.28	6	25	35	25	No	Yes	No	Yes	15.3
Jordan	No	No limit	256.83	0.40	6	0	50	25	Yes	No	No	Yes	18.7
Kazakhstan	No	No limit	121.21	0.08	6	50	100	50	No	Yes	No	No	18.0
Kenya	No	No limit	247.26	1.22	6	0	0	50	No	Yes	No	No	21.0
Kiribati	No	No limit	0.00	0.00	7	0	0	50	No	No	No	No	0.0
Korea, Rep.	No	24	927.49	0.30	6	50	50	50	No	Yes	No	No	17.0
Kosovo	No	No limit	158.32	0.33	6	30	50	30	No	Yes	No	No	21.0
Kuwait	No	No limit	251.08	0.06	6	0	50	25	No	No	Yes	Yes	30.0
Kyrgyz Republic	Yes	60	18.14	0.12	6	50	100	50	No	Yes	No	No	20.0
Lao PDR	No	36	111.10	0.47	6	15	150	50	No	Yes	No	No	15.0
Latvia	Yes	60	448.83	0.24	5.5	50	0	100	No	Yes	No	No	20.0
Lebanon	No	24	435.22	0.45	6	0	50	50	No	Yes	No	Yes	15.0
Lesotho	No	No limit	150.09	0.89	6	0	100	25	Yes	Yes	No	No	12.0
Liberia	No	No limit	141.44	0.03	5.5	0	0	50	No	Yes	No	Yes	16.5
Libya	No	48	392.86	0.51	6	0	0	50	Yes	Yes	No	No	30.0
Lithuania	No	60	427.34	0.23	5.5	50	100	50	No	Yes	No	No	20.7
Luxembourg	Yes	24	2,798.24	0.30	5.5	0	70	40	No	Yes	Yes	No	25.0
Macedonia, FYR	No	60	287.46	0.47	6	35	50	35	Yes	Yes	No	No	20
Madagascar	Yes	24	58.03	0.92	6	30	40	30	No	Yes	No	No	24.0

Redundancy rules									Redundancy cost		Job quality							
Maximum length of probationary period (months)[d]	Dismissal due to redundancy allowed by law?	Third-party notification if one worker is dismissed?	Third-party approval if one worker is dismissed?	Third-party notification if nine workers are dismissed?	Third-party approval if nine workers are dismissed?	Retraining or reassignment compulsory before redundancy?	Priority rules for redundancies?	Priority rules for reemployment?	Notice period for redundancy dismissal (weeks of salary)[c]	Severance pay for redundancy dismissal (weeks of salary)[c]	Equal remuneration for work of equal value?*	Gender nondiscrimination in hiring?*	Paid or unpaid maternity leave mandated by law?[e]*	Minimum length of maternity leave (calendar days)[f]*	Receive 100% of wages on maternity leave?*	Five fully paid days of sick leave a year?	Unemployment protection after one year of employment?	Minimum contribution period for unemployment protection (months)[g]
2.0	Yes	Yes	No	Yes	No	Yes	Yes	Yes	4.5	0.0	Yes	No	Yes	150	No	No	Yes	3
3.0	Yes	No	No	No	No	No	No	No	4.0	10.0	No	No	Yes	56	Yes	Yes	No	n.a.
n.a.	Yes	No	No	No	No	Yes	No	No	4.3	0.0	No	Yes	Yes	98	No	No	Yes	12
n.a.	Yes	No	No	No	No	Yes	No	No	4.3	0.0	No	Yes	Yes	98	No	No	Yes	12
3.0	Yes	Yes	Yes	Yes	Yes	No	No	Yes	4.3	0.0	No	No	Yes	70	Yes	Yes	No	36
3.0	Yes	Yes	No	Yes	No	No	No	No	4.3	4.3	No	Yes	Yes	126	Yes	Yes	Yes	0
12.0	Yes	Yes	No	Yes	No	No	Yes	No	4.3	2.1	Yes	No	Yes	90	Yes	Yes	No	n.a.
n.a.	Yes	Yes	Yes	Yes	Yes	No	No	No	4.3	0.0	Yes	No	Yes	84	No	..	No	n.a.
3.0	Yes	Yes	No	Yes	No	No	No	Yes	4.3	23.1	No	Yes	Yes	90	Yes	No	Yes	6
6.0	Yes	No	No	No	No	Yes	Yes	Yes	4.3	7.2	Yes	Yes	Yes	270	No	Yes	No	n.a.
3.0	Yes	No	No	No	No	No	No	No	13.0	15.1	No	No	Yes	70	Yes	Yes	No	n.a.
3.0	Yes	No	No	No	No	No	No	No	4.3	13.0	No	No	Yes	126	No	No	Yes	12
2.0	Yes	Yes	No	Yes	No	No	No	No	6.4	27.7	No	No	Yes	105	Yes	Yes	No	n.a.
3.0	Yes	No	No	No	No	Yes	Yes	No	4.3	8.7	Yes	No	Yes	112	No	No	Yes	9
3.0	Yes	Yes	No	Yes	No	No	Yes	Yes	8.7	0.0	No	No	Yes	70	Yes	Yes	No	n.a.
4.0	Yes	No	No	No	No	No	No	No	4.3	10.7	Yes	No	Yes	84	Yes	Yes	No	n.a.
3.0	Yes	Yes	No	Yes	No	No	Yes	Yes	4.3	21.3	Yes	No	Yes	98	Yes	Yes	No	n.a.
1.0	Yes	Yes	No	Yes	No	No	No	No	4.3	15.2	Yes	No	Yes	98	Yes	Yes	No	n.a.
3.0	Yes	No	No	No	No	Yes	Yes	No	8.7	15.9	Yes	No	Yes	126	Yes	Yes	No	18
6.0	Yes	Yes	No	Yes	No	No	No	Yes	17.3	4.3	Yes	No	Yes	112	Yes	Yes	Yes	6
6.0	Yes	No	No	No	No	No	No	No	4.3	8.7	No	Yes	Yes	270	Yes	Yes	Yes	12
3.0	Yes	No	No	Yes	Yes	No	Yes	Yes	5.8	8.9	No	No	Yes	98	Yes	Yes	No	n.a.

LABOR MARKET REGULATION DATA

Economy	Hiring				Working hours								
	Fixed-term contracts prohibited for permanent tasks?	Maximum length of fixed-term contracts (months)[a]	Minimum wage for a full-time worker (US$/month)[b]	Ratio of minimum wage to value added per worker	Maximum number of working days per week	Premium for night work (% of hourly pay)	Premium for work on weekly rest day (% of hourly pay)	Premium for overtime work (% of hourly pay)	Restrictions on night work?	Nonpregnant and nonnursing women permitted to work same night hours as men?*	Restrictions on weekly holiday work?	Restrictions on overtime work?	Paid annual leave (working days)[c]
Malawi	Yes	No limit	34.47	0.61	6	0	100	50	No	Yes	No	No	18.0
Malaysia	No	No limit	256.61	0.20	6	0	100	50	No	Yes	No	No	13.3
Maldives	No	24	0.00	0.00	6	0	50	25	No	Yes	No	No	30.0
Mali	Yes	72	74.17	0.56	6	0	0	10	No	Yes	No	No	22.0
Malta	No	48	813.07	0.33	6	0	0	50	No	Yes	No	No	24.0
Marshall Islands	No	No limit	416.00	0.66	7	0	0	0	No	Yes	No	No	0.0
Mauritania	No	24	99.50	0.56	6	0	0	15	No	Yes	No	No	18.0
Mauritius	No	24	292.99	0.26	6	0	100	50	No	Yes	No	No	17.0
Mexico (Mexico City)	Yes	No limit	168.32	0.14	6	0	25	100	No	Yes	No	Yes	12.0
Mexico (Monterrey)	Yes	No limit	168.32	0.14	6	0	25	100	No	Yes	No	Yes	12.0
Micronesia, Fed. Sts.	No	No limit	364.00	0.84	7	0	0	50	No	Yes	No	No	0.0
Moldova	Yes	No limit	115.81	0.47	6	50	100	50	Yes	No	Yes	No	20.0
Mongolia	No	No limit	103.47	0.22	5	0	50	50	No	No	No	Yes	16.0
Montenegro	No	24	235.36	0.26	6	40	0	40	No	Yes	No	No	21.0
Morocco	Yes	12	282.93	0.74	6	0	0	25	No	Yes	Yes	No	19.5
Mozambique	Yes	72	132.21	1.40	6	25	100	50	No	Yes	Yes	No	24.0
Myanmar	No	No limit	73.80	0.46	6	0	100	100	Yes	Yes	No	No	10.0
Namibia	No	No limit	0.00	0.00	5.5	6	100	50	No	Yes	No	No	20.0
Nepal	Yes	No limit	93.46	0.95	6	0	50	50	No	No	No	No	18.0
Netherlands	No	24	978.75	0.16	5.5	0	0	0	No	Yes	No	No	20.0
New Zealand	No	No limit	2,025.35	0.39	7	0	0	0	No	Yes	No	No	20.0
Nicaragua	No	No limit	214.50	0.86	6	0	100	100	Yes	Yes	Yes	No	30.0

	Redundancy rules								Redundancy cost		Job quality							
Maximum length of probationary period (months)[d]	Dismissal due to redundancy allowed by law?	Third-party notification if one worker is dismissed?	Third-party approval if one worker is dismissed?	Third-party notification if nine workers are dismissed?	Third-party approval if nine workers are dismissed?	Retraining or reassignment compulsory before redundancy?	Priority rules for redundancies?	Priority rules for reemployment?	Notice period for redundancy dismissal (weeks of salary)[c]	Severance pay for redundancy dismissal (weeks of salary)[c]	Equal remuneration for work of equal value?*	Gender nondiscrimination in hiring?*	Paid or unpaid maternity leave mandated by law?[e]*	Minimum length of maternity leave (calendar days)[f]*	Receive 100% of wages on maternity leave?*	Five fully paid days of sick leave a year?	Unemployment protection after one year of employment?	Minimum contribution period for unemployment protection (months)[g]
12.0	Yes	No	No	No	No	No	No	No	4.3	12.3	Yes	No	Yes	56	Yes	Yes	No	n.a.
n.a.	Yes	No	No	Yes	No	No	No	No	6.7	22.8	No	No	Yes	60	Yes	Yes	No	n.a.
3.0	Yes	No	No	No	No	No	No	No	7.2	0.0	No	Yes	Yes	60	Yes	Yes	No	n.a.
6.0	Yes	Yes	No	Yes	No	No	Yes	Yes	4.3	9.3	No	No	Yes	98	Yes	Yes	No	n.a.
6.0	Yes	No	No	No	No	No	Yes	Yes	7.3	0.0	Yes	Yes	Yes	126	No	Yes	Yes	6
n.a.	Yes	No	No	No	No	No	No	No	0.0	0.0	No	No	No	n.a.	n.a.	No	No	n.a.
1.0	Yes	Yes	No	Yes	No	No	Yes	Yes	4.3	6.1	No	Yes	Yes	98	Yes	Yes	No	n.a.
No limit	Yes	Yes	No	Yes	No	No	No	No	4.3	6.3	Yes	Yes	Yes	98	Yes	Yes	Yes	6
1.0	Yes	Yes	Yes	Yes	Yes	No	Yes	Yes	0.0	22.0	No	Yes	Yes	84	Yes	No	No	n.a.
1.0	Yes	Yes	Yes	Yes	Yes	No	Yes	Yes	0.0	22.0	No	Yes	Yes	84	Yes	No	No	n.a.
n.a.	Yes	No	No	No	No	No	No	No	0.0	0.0	No	No	No	n.a.	n.a.	No	No	n.a.
0.5	Yes	Yes	No	Yes	No	Yes	Yes	No	8.7	13.9	No	Yes	Yes	126	Yes	Yes	Yes	9
6.0	Yes	No	No	No	No	No	No	No	4.3	4.3	No	No	Yes	120	Yes	Yes	Yes	9
6.0	Yes	No	No	No	No	Yes	Yes	No	4.3	6.9	Yes	Yes	Yes	365	Yes	Yes	Yes	12
1.5	Yes	No	No	Yes	Yes	Yes	Yes	Yes	7.2	13.5	Yes	Yes	Yes	98	No	No	No	36
3.0	Yes	Yes	No	Yes	No	No	No	No	4.3	33.2	No	No	Yes	60	Yes	No	No	n.a.
n.a.	Yes	No	No	No	No	No	No	No	4.3	18.8	No	No	Yes	98	No	Yes	No	36
n.a.	Yes	Yes	No	Yes	No	No	No	No	4.3	5.3	Yes	Yes	Yes	84	Yes	Yes	No	n.a.
12.0	Yes	Yes	Yes	Yes	Yes	No	Yes	Yes	4.3	22.9	No	No	Yes	52	Yes	No	No	n.a.
2.0	Yes	Yes	Yes	Yes	Yes	Yes	Yes	No	8.7	7.2	Yes	Yes	Yes	112	Yes	No	Yes	6
3.0	Yes	No	No	No	No	Yes	No	No	0.0	0.0	No	Yes	Yes	112	No	Yes	No	n.a.
1.0	Yes	No	No	No	No	No	No	No	0.0	14.9	No	No	Yes	84	Yes	No	No	n.a.

LABOR MARKET REGULATION DATA

Economy	Hiring				Working hours								
	Fixed-term contracts prohibited for permanent tasks?	Maximum length of fixed-term contracts (months)[a]	Minimum wage for a full-time worker (US$/month)[b]	Ratio of minimum wage to value added per worker	Maximum number of working days per week	Premium for night work (% of hourly pay)	Premium for work on weekly rest day (% of hourly pay)	Premium for overtime work (% of hourly pay)	Restrictions on night work?	Nonpregnant and nonnursing women permitted to work same night hours as men?*	Restrictions on weekly holiday work?	Restrictions on overtime work?	Paid annual leave (working days)[c]
Niger	Yes	48	56.19	0.81	6	38	0	10	No	Yes	No	No	22.0
Nigeria (Kano)	No	No limit	100.47	0.23	6	0	0	0	No	Yes	No	No	6.0
Nigeria (Lagos)	No	No limit	100.47	0.23	6	0	0	0	No	Yes	No	No	6.0
Norway	No	48	3,582.00	0.30	6	0	0	40	Yes	Yes	Yes	No	21.0
Oman[h]	No	No limit	935.77	0.51	5	50	100	25	Yes	No	No	Yes	22.0
Pakistan (Karachi)	Yes	9	121.94	0.61	6	0	100	100	Yes	Yes	Yes	No	14.0
Pakistan (Lahore)	Yes	9	121.94	0.61	6	0	100	100	Yes	Yes	Yes	No	14.0
Palau	No	No limit	634.54	0.46	7	0	0	0	No	Yes	No	No	0.0
Panama	Yes	12	558.72	0.36	6	13	50	50	No	Yes	Yes	Yes	22.0
Papua New Guinea	No	No limit	231.41	0.79	6	0	0	50	No	No	No	No	11.0
Paraguay	Yes	No limit	376.81	0.68	6	30	100	50	Yes	Yes	No	Yes	20.0
Peru	Yes	60	280.28	0.35	6	35	100	25	No	Yes	No	No	13.0
Philippines	No	No limit	301.08	0.65	6	10	30	25	No	Yes	No	No	5.0
Poland	No	33	540.66	0.34	5.5	20	100	50	No	Yes	No	No	22.0
Portugal	Yes	36	748.46	0.29	6	25	50	31	No	Yes	Yes	No	22.0
Puerto Rico (U.S.)	No	No limit	1,256.67	0.52	7	0	100	100	No	Yes	No	No	15.0
Qatar	No	No limit	0.00	0.00	6	0	0	25	Yes	Yes	No	Yes	22.0
Romania	Yes	60	338.23	0.29	5	25	100	75	No	Yes	No	No	20.0
Russian Federation (Moscow)	Yes	60	367.24	0.27	6	20	100	50	No	Yes	Yes	No	22.0
Russian Federation (St. Petersburg)	Yes	60	248.36	0.18	6	20	100	50	No	Yes	Yes	No	22.0
Rwanda	No	No limit	0.00	0.00	6	0	0	0	No	Yes	No	No	19.3
Samoa	No	No limit	209.65	0.37	6	0	100	50	No	Yes	Yes	No	10.0

Redundancy rules									Redundancy cost		Job quality							
Maximum length of probationary period (months)[d]	Dismissal due to redundancy allowed by law?	Third-party notification if one worker is dismissed?	Third-party approval if one worker is dismissed?	Third-party notification if nine workers are dismissed?	Third-party approval if nine workers are dismissed?	Retraining or reassignment compulsory before redundancy?	Priority rules for redundancies?	Priority rules for reemployment?	Notice period for redundancy dismissal (weeks of salary)[c]	Severance pay for redundancy dismissal (weeks of salary)[c]	Equal remuneration for work of equal value?*	Gender nondiscrimination in hiring?*	Paid or unpaid maternity leave mandated by law?[e]*	Minimum length of maternity leave (calendar days)[f]*	Receive 100% of wages on maternity leave?*	Five fully paid days of sick leave a year?	Unemployment protection after one year of employment?	Minimum contribution period for unemployment protection (months)[g]
6.0	Yes	Yes	No	Yes	No	Yes	Yes	Yes	4.3	9.7	Yes	Yes	Yes	98	Yes	Yes	No	n.a.
3.0	Yes	No	No	Yes	No	No	Yes	No	3.2	0.0	No	No	Yes	84	No	Yes	No	n.a.
3.0	Yes	No	No	Yes	No	No	Yes	No	3.2	0.0	No	No	Yes	84	No	Yes	No	n.a.
6.0	Yes	No	No	No	No	Yes	Yes	Yes	8.7	0.0	Yes	Yes	Yes	343	Yes	Yes	Yes	0
3.0	No	n.a.	n.a.	n.a.	n.a.	n.a.	n.a.	n.a.	n.a.	n.a.	No	No	Yes	50	Yes	Yes	No	n.a.
3.0	Yes	No	No	No	No	Yes	Yes	Yes	4.3	22.9	No	No	Yes	84	Yes	Yes	No	n.a.
3.0	Yes	No	No	No	No	Yes	Yes	Yes	4.3	22.9	No	No	Yes	84	Yes	Yes	No	n.a.
n.a.	Yes	No	No	No	No	No	No	No	0.0	0.0	No	No	No	n.a.	n.a.	No	No	n.a.
3.0	Yes	Yes	Yes	Yes	Yes	No	Yes	No	0.0	18.1	No	No	Yes	98	Yes	Yes	No	n.a.
n.a.	Yes	No	No	No	No	No	No	No	3.3	9.2	No	No	Yes	0	n.a.	Yes	No	n.a.
1.0	Yes	Yes	Yes	Yes	Yes	No	No	Yes	10.8	18.6	Yes	No	Yes	98	No	Yes	No	n.a.
3.0	Yes	Yes	Yes	Yes	Yes	No	No	Yes	0.0	11.4	Yes	No	Yes	98	Yes	Yes	No	n.a.
6.0	Yes	Yes	No	Yes	No	No	Yes	No	4.3	23.1	Yes	No	Yes	60	Yes	No	No	n.a.
3.0	Yes	No	No	No	No	No	Yes	Yes	10.1	8.7	Yes	No	Yes	182	Yes	No	Yes	12
3.0	Yes	Yes	No	Yes	No	Yes	No	Yes	7.9	9.1	Yes	Yes	Yes	120	Yes	No	Yes	12
3.0	Yes	No	No	No	No	No	Yes	Yes	0.0	0.0	No	Yes	Yes	56	Yes	Yes	Yes	6
6.0	Yes	No	No	No	No	No	No	No	7.2	16.0	No	No	Yes	50	Yes	Yes	No	n.a.
3.0	Yes	No	No	No	No	No	Yes	Yes	4.0	0.0	Yes	Yes	Yes	126	No	Yes	Yes	12
3.0	Yes	Yes	No	Yes	No	Yes	Yes	No	8.7	8.7	No	No	Yes	140	Yes	Yes	Yes	0
3.0	Yes	Yes	No	Yes	No	Yes	Yes	No	8.7	8.7	No	No	Yes	140	Yes	Yes	Yes	0
6.0	Yes	Yes	No	Yes	No	No	Yes	No	4.3	8.7	No	No	Yes	84	No	Yes	No	n.a.
3.0	Yes	No	No	No	No	No	No	No	3.3	0.0	Yes	No	Yes	28	Yes	Yes	No	n.a.

LABOR MARKET REGULATION DATA

Economy	Hiring				Working hours								
	Fixed-term contracts prohibited for permanent tasks?	Maximum length of fixed-term contracts (months)[a]	Minimum wage for a full-time worker (US$/month)[b]	Ratio of minimum wage to value added per worker	Maximum number of working days per week	Premium for night work (% of hourly pay)	Premium for work on weekly rest day (% of hourly pay)	Premium for overtime work (% of hourly pay)	Restrictions on night work?	Nonpregnant and nonnursing women permitted to work same night hours as men?*	Restrictions on weekly holiday work?	Restrictions on overtime work?	Paid annual leave (working days)[c]
San Marino	Yes	18	2,369.93	0.40	6	35	0	26	No	Yes	No	No	26.0
São Tomé and Príncipe	Yes	36	72.43	0.31	6	25	100	38	No	No	Yes	No	26.0
Saudi Arabia	No	No limit	0.00	0.00	6	0	50	50	No	No	Yes	No	23.3
Senegal	Yes	24	175.04	1.12	6	38	0	10	No	Yes	Yes	Yes	24.3
Serbia	Yes	24	216.87	0.32	6	26	26	26	No	Yes	No	No	20.0
Seychelles	Yes	No limit	420.62	0.24	6	0	100	50	No	Yes	No	No	21.0
Sierra Leone	Yes	No limit	90.79	0.95	5.5	15	100	50	No	No	No	No	23.0
Singapore	No	No limit	0.00	0.00	6	0	100	50	No	Yes	No	No	10.7
Slovak Republic	No	24	498.83	0.25	6	20	0	25	No	Yes	No	No	25.0
Slovenia	Yes	24	966.65	0.35	6	75	100	30	No	Yes	No	No	22.0
Solomon Islands	No	No limit	116.23	0.41	6	0	0	50	No	No	No	No	15.0
Somalia	No	No limit	0.00	0.00	6	0	0	0	No	No	No	No	15.0
South Africa	Yes	No limit	287.39	0.37	6	0	100	50	Yes	Yes	No	No	18.33
South Sudan	No	48	0.00	0.00	6	0	0	50	No	No	No	No	23.3
Spain	Yes	48	1,054.47	0.29	5.5	7	0	0	No	Yes	No	No	22.0
Sri Lanka	No	No limit	78.53	0.16	5.5	0	0	50	Yes	Yes	No	No	14.0
St. Kitts and Nevis	No	No limit	557.23	0.31	7	0	0	50	No	Yes	No	No	14.0
St. Lucia	No	24	0.00	0.00	6	0	100	50	No	Yes	No	No	21.0
St. Vincent and the Grenadines	No	No limit	234.49	0.29	6	0	0	50	No	Yes	No	No	18.7
Sudan	No	48	63.70	0.23	6	0	0	50	No	No	No	No	23.3
Suriname	No	No limit	363.66	0.31	6	0	100	50	No	Yes	No	No	16.0
Swaziland	No	No limit	140.91	0.31	5.5	0	0	50	No	Yes	No	No	11.0

	Redundancy rules								Redundancy cost		Job quality						
Maximum length of probationary period (months)[d]	Dismissal due to redundancy allowed by law?	Third-party notification if one worker is dismissed?	Third-party approval if one worker is dismissed?	Third-party notification if nine workers are dismissed?	Third-party approval if nine workers are dismissed?	Retraining or reassignment compulsory before redundancy?	Priority rules for redundancies?	Priority rules for reemployment?	Notice period for redundancy dismissal (weeks of salary)[c]	Severance pay for redundancy dismissal (weeks of salary)[c]	Equal remuneration for work of equal value?*	Gender nondiscrimination in hiring?*	Paid or unpaid maternity leave mandated by law?[e]*	Minimum length of maternity leave (calendar days)[f]*	Receive 100% of wages on maternity leave?*	Five fully paid days of sick leave a year?	Unemployment protection after one year of employment?	Minimum contribution period for unemployment protection (months)[g]
1.6	Yes	Yes	Yes	Yes	Yes	No	Yes	Yes	0.0	0.0	No	No	Yes	150	Yes	Yes	Yes	..
1.0	Yes	Yes	Yes	Yes	Yes	No	No	Yes	4.3	26.0	No	No	Yes	90	Yes	No	No	n.a.
3.0	Yes	No	No	No	No	No	No	No	8.6	15.2	No	No	Yes	70	Yes	Yes	Yes	12
2.0	Yes	Yes	No	Yes	No	No	Yes	Yes	4.3	10.5	No	No	Yes	98	Yes	Yes	No	n.a.
6.0	Yes	No	No	No	No	Yes	No	Yes	0.0	7.7	No	Yes	Yes	135	Yes	No	Yes	12
6.0	Yes	Yes	Yes	Yes	Yes	No	No	No	4.3	7.6	No	No	Yes	98	Yes	Yes	No	n.a.
6.0	Yes	Yes	No	Yes	No	Yes	Yes	Yes	13.0	62.5	No	No	Yes	84	Yes	Yes	No	n.a.
6.0	Yes	No	No	No	No	No	No	No	3.0	0.0	No	No	Yes	105	Yes	Yes	No	n.a.
3.0	Yes	Yes	No	Yes	No	Yes	No	No	11.6	7.2	Yes	Yes	Yes	238	No	No	No	24
6.0	Yes	No	No	No	No	No	Yes	No	5.3	5.3	Yes	Yes	Yes	105	Yes	Yes	Yes	9
n.a.	Yes	Yes	No	Yes	No	No	No	No	4.3	10.7	No	No	Yes	42	No	Yes	No	n.a.
n.a	Yes	No	No	No	No	No	No	No	4.3	23.1	No	No	Yes	98	No	Yes	No	n.a
n.a.	Yes	Yes	No	Yes	No	Yes	No	No	4.0	5.3	Yes	No	Yes	120	No	Yes	Yes	0
3.0	Yes	Yes	Yes	Yes	Yes	No	No	No	4.3	21.7	No	No	Yes	56	Yes	Yes	No	n.a.
6.0	Yes	Yes	No	Yes	No	No	No	No	2.1	15.2	Yes	Yes	Yes	112	Yes	Yes	Yes	12
n.a.	Yes	Yes	Yes	Yes	Yes	No	Yes	No	4.3	54.2	No	No	Yes	84	Yes	Yes	No	n.a.
n.a.	Yes	No	No	No	No	No	No	Yes	8.7	0.0	No	No	Yes	91	No	No	No	n.a.
3.0	Yes	Yes	No	Yes	No	No	No	No	3.7	9.3	Yes	Yes	Yes	91	No	Yes	No	n.a.
6.0	Yes	No	No	Yes	No	No	No	Yes	4.0	10.0	No	No	Yes	91	No	Yes	No	n.a.
3.0	Yes	Yes	Yes	Yes	Yes	No	No	No	4.3	21.7	No	No	Yes	56	Yes	Yes	No	n.a.
2.0	Yes	Yes	Yes	Yes	Yes	No	No	No	0.0	8.8	No	No	No	n.a.	n.a.	No	No	n.a.
3.0	Yes	No	No	Yes	No	No	Yes	No	5.9	8.7	No	No	Yes	14	Yes	Yes	No	n.a.

LABOR MARKET REGULATION DATA

	Hiring				Working hours								
Economy	Fixed-term contracts prohibited for permanent tasks?	Maximum length of fixed-term contracts (months)[a]	Minimum wage for a full-time worker (US$/month)[b]	Ratio of minimum wage to value added per worker	Maximum number of working days per week	Premium for night work (% of hourly pay)	Premium for work on weekly rest day (% of hourly pay)	Premium for overtime work (% of hourly pay)	Restrictions on night work?	Nonpregnant and nonnursing women permitted to work same night hours as men?*	Restrictions on weekly holiday work?	Restrictions on overtime work?	Paid annual leave (working days)[c]
Sweden	No	24	0.00	0.00	5.5	0	0	50	No	Yes	Yes	No	25.0
Switzerland	No	120	0.00	0.00	6	25	50	25	Yes	Yes	Yes	No	20.0
Syrian Arab Republic	No	60	54.46	0.30	6	0	100	38	No	No	Yes	No	21.7
Taiwan, China	Yes	12	627.01	0.25	6	0	100	33	No	Yes	No	No	12.0
Tajikistan	Yes	No limit	45.37	0.27	6	50	100	100	Yes	No	No	No	23.3
Tanzania	Yes	No limit	61.94	0.42	6	5	100	50	No	Yes	No	No	20.0
Thailand	Yes	No limit	235.68	0.36	6	0	0	50	No	Yes	No	No	6.0
Timor-Leste	Yes	36	114.85	0.37	6	25	100	50	No	Yes	Yes	No	12.0
Togo	Yes	48	99.18	1.21	6	0	0	20	No	Yes	No	No	30.0
Tonga	No	No limit	0.00	0.00	6	0	0	0	No	Yes	Yes	No	0.0
Trinidad and Tobago	No	No limit	408.04	0.18	6	0	100	50	No	Yes	No	No	10.0
Tunisia	No	48	256.82	0.54	6	0	100	25	No	No	No	No	19.0
Turkey	Yes	No limit	669.00	0.54	6	0	100	50	Yes	No	No	No	18.0
Uganda	No	No limit	2.16	0.02	6	0	0	50	No	Yes	No	No	21.0
Ukraine	Yes	No limit	83.46	0.27	5.5	20	100	100	No	No	Yes	Yes	18.0
United Arab Emirates	No	No limit	0.00	0.00	6	0	50	25	No	No	Yes	No	26.0
United Kingdom	No	No limit	1,417.39	0.25	6	0	0	0	No	Yes	No	No	28.0
United States (Los Angeles)	No	No limit	1,687.97	0.24	6	0	0	50	No	Yes	No	No	0.0
United States (New York City)	No	No limit	1,519.17	0.22	6	0	0	50	No	Yes	No	No	0.0
Uruguay	Yes	No limit	579.80	0.28	6	0	100	100	No	Yes	No	No	21.0
Uzbekistan	Yes	60	124.41	0.46	6	50	100	100	Yes	Yes	No	No	15.0
Vanuatu	No	No limit	276.94	0.69	6	0	50	25	No	No	No	No	17.0

Redundancy rules									Redundancy cost		Job quality							
Maximum length of probationary period (months)[d]	Dismissal due to redundancy allowed by law?	Third-party notification if one worker is dismissed?	Third-party approval if one worker is dismissed?	Third-party notification if nine workers are dismissed?	Third-party approval if nine workers are dismissed?	Retraining or reassignment compulsory before redundancy?	Priority rules for redundancies?	Priority rules for reemployment?	Notice period for redundancy dismissal (weeks of salary)[c]	Severance pay for redundancy dismissal (weeks of salary)[c]	Equal remuneration for work of equal value?*	Gender nondiscrimination in hiring?*	Paid or unpaid maternity leave mandated by law?[e]*	Minimum length of maternity leave (calendar days)[f]*	Receive 100% of wages on maternity leave?*	Five fully paid days of sick leave a year?	Unemployment protection after one year of employment?	Minimum contribution period for unemployment protection (months)[g]
6.0	Yes	No	No	Yes	No	Yes	Yes	Yes	14.4	0.0	No	Yes	Yes	480	No	No	Yes	6
3.0	Yes	No	No	No	No	No	No	No	10.1	0.0	Yes	Yes	Yes	98	No	Yes	Yes	12
3.0	Yes	Yes	Yes	Yes	Yes	No	No	No	8.7	0.0	No	No	Yes	120	Yes	No	No	n.a.
n.a.	Yes	Yes	No	Yes	No	Yes	No	Yes	3.8	18.8	Yes	Yes	Yes	56	Yes	No	Yes	12
3.0	Yes	Yes	No	Yes	No	Yes	Yes	No	8.7	6.9	Yes	Yes	Yes	140	Yes	No	No	18
6.0	Yes	Yes	Yes	Yes	Yes	No	No	Yes	4.0	5.3	Yes	Yes	Yes	84	Yes	Yes	No	n.a.
4.0	Yes	No	No	No	No	No	No	No	4.3	31.7	No	No	Yes	90	Yes	Yes	Yes	6
1.0	Yes	Yes	No	Yes	No	No	No	No	3.6	0.0	No	Yes	Yes	84	Yes	Yes	No	n.a.
2.0	Yes	Yes	No	Yes	No	No	Yes	Yes	4.3	8.8	Yes	No	Yes	98	Yes	Yes	No	n.a.
n.a.	Yes	No	No	No	No	No	No	No	0.0	0.0	No	No	No	n.a.	n.a.	No	No	n.a.
n.a.	Yes	No	No	Yes	No	No	Yes	No	6.4	14.1	No	Yes	Yes	98	No	Yes	No	n.a.
6.0	Yes	Yes	Yes	Yes	Yes	Yes	Yes	Yes	4.3	17.2	No	No	Yes	30	No	Yes	No	n.a.
2.0	Yes	No	No	No	No	No	No	Yes	6.7	23.1	Yes	No	Yes	112	No	Yes	Yes	6
12.0	Yes	No	No	No	No	No	No	No	8.7	0.0	Yes	No	Yes	84	Yes	Yes	No	n.a.
3.0	Yes	No	No	No	No	Yes	Yes	Yes	8.7	4.3	No	Yes	Yes	126	Yes	Yes	Yes	6
6.0	Yes	No	No	No	No	No	No	No	4.3	0.0	No	No	Yes	45	Yes	Yes	No	n.a.
6.0	Yes	No	No	No	No	No	No	No	5.3	4.0	Yes	Yes	Yes	14	No	No	Yes	0
n.a.	Yes	No	No	No	No	No	No	No	0.0	0.0	No	Yes	Yes	0	n.a.	No	Yes	12
n.a.	Yes	No	No	No	No	No	No	No	0.0	0.0	No	Yes	Yes	0	n.a.	Yes	Yes	6
3.0	Yes	No	No	No	No	No	No	No	0.0	20.8	No	Yes	Yes	98	Yes	No	Yes	6
3.0	Yes	No	No	Yes	No	Yes	Yes	No	8.7	8.7	No	No	Yes	126	Yes	Yes	Yes	0
6.0	Yes	No	No	No	No	No	No	No	9.3	23.1	No	No	Yes	84	No	Yes	No	n.a.

LABOR MARKET REGULATION DATA

Economy	Hiring				Working hours								
	Fixed-term contracts prohibited for permanent tasks?	Maximum length of fixed-term contracts (months)[a]	Minimum wage for a full-time worker (US$/month)[b]	Ratio of minimum wage to value added per worker	Maximum number of working days per week	Premium for night work (% of hourly pay)	Premium for work on weekly rest day (% of hourly pay)	Premium for overtime work (% of hourly pay)	Restrictions on night work?	Nonpregnant and nonnursing women permitted to work same night hours as men?*	Restrictions on weekly holiday work?	Restrictions on overtime work?	Paid annual leave (working days)[c]
Venezuela, RB[h]	Yes	24	1,842.43	1.20	5	30	50	50	Yes	Yes	Yes	No	19.3
Vietnam	No	72	160.68	0.68	6	30	0	50	No	Yes	No	No	13.0
West Bank and Gaza	No	24	373.06	0.82	6	0	150	50	Yes	No	Yes	No	12.0
Yemen, Rep.	No	No limit	93.07	0.56	6	15	100	50	No	No	No	No	30.0
Zambia	Yes	No limit	211.71	0.87	6	4	100	50	No	Yes	No	No	24.0
Zimbabwe	No	No limit	261.75	2.05	6	0	0	50	No	Yes	No	No	22.0

Source: Doing Business database.

.. No *Doing Business* data available.

* Data were collected jointly with the World Bank Group's *Women, Business and the Law* team.

a. Including renewals.

b. Refers to the worker in the *Doing Business* case study: a cashier, age 19, with one year of work experience. Economies for which 0.0 is shown have no minimum wage in the private sector.

c. Average for workers with 1, 5 and 10 years of tenure.

d. Not applicable (n.a.) for economies with no statutory provision for a probationary period.

e. If no maternity leave is mandated by law, parental leave is measured if applicable.

f. The minimum number of days that legally have to be paid by the government, the employer or both.

g. Not applicable (n.a.) for economies with no unemployment protection scheme.

h. Some answers are not applicable (n.a.) for economies where dismissal due to redundancy is disallowed.

Redundancy rules									Redundancy cost		Job quality							
Maximum length of probationary period (months)[d]	Dismissal due to redundancy allowed by law?	Third-party notification if one worker is dismissed?	Third-party approval if one worker is dismissed?	Third-party notification if nine workers are dismissed?	Third-party approval if nine workers are dismissed?	Retraining or reassignment compulsory before redundancy?	Priority rules for redundancies?	Priority rules for reemployment?	Notice period for redundancy dismissal (weeks of salary)[c]	Severance pay for redundancy dismissal (weeks of salary)[c]	Equal remuneration for work of equal value?*	Gender nondiscrimination in hiring?*	Paid or unpaid maternity leave mandated by law?[e]*	Minimum length of maternity leave (calendar days)[f]*	Receive 100% of wages on maternity leave?*	Five fully paid days of sick leave a year?	Unemployment protection after one year of employment?	Minimum contribution period for unemployment protection (months)[g]
1.0	No	n.a.	n.a.	n.a.	n.a.	n.a.	n.a.	n.a.	n.a.	n.a.	No	Yes	Yes	182	Yes	Yes	Yes	12
1.0	Yes	No	No	Yes	Yes	Yes	No	No	0.0	24.6	Yes	Yes	Yes	180	Yes	Yes	Yes	12
6.0	Yes	Yes	No	Yes	No	No	No	No	4.3	23.1	No	No	Yes	84	Yes	Yes	No	n.a.
6.0	Yes	Yes	No	Yes	No	No	No	Yes	4.3	23.1	No	No	Yes	70	Yes	Yes	No	n.a.
n.a.	Yes	Yes	No	Yes	No	No	No	No	4.3	46.2	No	No	Yes	84	Yes	Yes	No	n.a.
3.0	Yes	Yes	Yes	Yes	Yes	Yes	No	No	13.0	12.3	Yes	Yes	Yes	98	Yes	Yes	No	n.a.

Acknowledgments

Data collection and analysis for *Doing Business 2017* were conducted by a team led by Rita Ramalho (Manager, *Doing Business*) under the general direction of Augusto Lopez-Claros (Director, Global Indicators Group, Development Economics). Overall guidance for the preparation of the report was provided by Kaushik Basu, Senior Vice President and Chief Economist of the World Bank. The project was managed with the support of Santiago Croci Downes, Carolin Geginat, Adrian Gonzalez and Hulya Ulku. Other team members included Nadine Abi Chakra, Jean Arlet, Yuriy Valentinovich Avramov, Rodrigo Sarmento de Beires, Erica Bosio, Emily Bourke, Edgar Chavez Sanchez, Maria Magdalena Chiquier, Selima Daadouche Crum, Baria Nabil Daye, Marcio Augusto De La Cruz Gómez, Christian De la Medina Soto, Marie Lily Delion, Laura Diniz, Varun Eknath, Faiza El Fezzazi El Maziani, Cécile Ferro, Felipe Abel Flores Meregote, Albina Gasanbekova, Dorina Georgieva, Anushavan Hambardzumyan, Volha Hrytskevich, Maksym Iavorskyi, Joyce Antoine Ibrahim, Nan Jiang, Hervé Kaddoura, Klaus Koch Saldarriaga, Olena Koltko, Magdalini Konidari, Khrystyna Kushnir, Mathilde Lugger, Frédéric Meunier, Haya Mortada, Joanna Nasr, Marie-Jeanne Ndiaye, Albert Nogués i Comas, Nadia Novik, Tigran Parvanyan, María Antonia Quesada Gámez, Parvina Rakhimova, Morgann Courtney Reeves, Anna Reva, Margarida Rodrigues, Julie Ryan, Valentina Saltane, Jayashree Srinivasan, Mihaela Stangu, Shraddha Suresh, Brandon Thompson, Erick Tjong, Camille Henri Vaillon, Yelizaveta Yanovich, Marilyne Youbi, Inés Zabalbeitia Múgica and Yasmin Zand. Thuraiya Alhashmi, Ahmad Famm AlKhuzam, Noimot Olaide Bakare, Kate Aoife Brolley, Ana Paula Cañedo Guichard, Imani Cherry, Adelaida Correa Miranda, Flavio Cesar Cultrera Munoz, Bidisha Das, Diane Davoine, Stephanie Desjardins, Imane Fahli, Emma Valentina Fernandez Diaz, Leo Forder, McSwain Pello Forkoh, Juan David Garcia Vidal, Albe Gjonbalaj, Baya Hariche, Dimitra Christina Heliotis, Fjolla Kondirolli, Gbogbo Nina Marie-Laure Kouadio, Margaux Veronica Roussel, Roxanne Moin-Safa, Aurelio Nascimento de Amaral, Albert D. Nyuangar Jr., Madwa-Nika Phanord-Cadet, Renaud Poizat, Lourdes Sabina Poma Canazaca, Katerina Louisa Roumeliotis, Tetyana Sydorenko, Alessandra Volpe Martinez, Yaxin Yan and Ana Maria Zárate Moreno assisted in the months before publication.

The *Doing Business* Advisory Board, which includes leading academics, corporate leaders and policy makers, provides guidance and advice on broader strategic opportunities for *Doing Business* and on areas for expansion and improvement. Its members are: Timothy Besley, Robert D. Cooter, Eleni Gabre-Madhin, Aart Kraay, Felipe Larraín Bascuñán, Ann-Marie Leroy, Anand Mahindra and Dani Rodrik.

The selling to the government data was collected by Elisabeth Danon, Natalia Del Valle Catoni, Maria Paula Gutierrez Casadiego, Raquel Mayer Cuesta, Sophie Pouget and Dima Rbeiz. The team was supervised by Tania Ghossein and Federica Saliola.

The online service of the *Doing Business* database is managed by Andres Baquero Franco, Varun Doiphode, Fengsheng Huang, Arun Chakravarthi Nageswaran, Kunal Patel, Jiawen Peng, Kamalesh Sengaonkar, Bishal Raj Thakuri and Hashim Zia. The *Doing Business 2017* outreach strategy is managed by Indira Chand, under the general direction of Phillip Jeremy Hay with support from World Bank Group communications colleagues around the world.

The team is grateful for the valuable comments provided by colleagues in the World Bank Group (both on the draft report and on the changes in the methodology) and outside the World Bank Group (on the changes in the methodology) and for the guidance provided by World Bank Group Executive Directors. The team would especially like to acknowledge the comments and guidance of Gabi Afram, Ahmad Ahsan, Ratchada Anantavrasilpa, Pedro Antmann, Leah April, Elmas Arisoy, Rajul Awasthi, Katherine Baer, Svetlana Bagaudinova, Amina A. Bajwa, Jennifer Barsky, Amjad Bashir, David Bridgman, Abel L. Caamano, James A. Brumby, Rodrigo Chaves, Simon Chirwa, Tamoya Christie, Anna Y. Chytla, Julian Clarke, Richard Damania, Thomas Dane, Arsala Deane, Jorge Familiar Calderon, Marianne Fay, Elsa Felipe, Ana Margarida Fernandes, Achim Fock, Vivien Foster, Charles Fox, Fabrizio Fraboni, Ernesto Franco-Temple, Indermit Gill, Anabel Gonzalez, Caren Grown, Eva Gutierrez, Faris Hadad-Zervos, Lucia Hanmer, Antony Bryan Hazeldon Lythgoe, Caroline Heider, Vivian Y.N. Hon, Mombert Hoppe, Neville Howlett, Yoichiro Ishihara, Melissa Johns, Michael Keen, Saida Khamidova, Arthur Kochnakyan, Aphichoke (Andy) Kotikula, Arvo Kuddo, Keith E. Hansen, Peter Ladegaard, John Litwack, Jean Michel Lobet, Gladys Lopez-Acevedo, Elaine MacEachern, Oscar Madeddu, Sanja Madzarevic-Sujster, William F. Maloney, Susan Maslen, Shabih Ali Mohib, Fredesvinda F. Montes Herraiz, Alejandro Moreno, Rafael Moreno, Khampao Nanthavong, Andrew Kazora Okello, Maria Beatriz Orlando, Victoria Perry, Carlos Pinerua, Alban Pruthi, Alvaro Quijandría, Martin Rama, Colin Ewell Wesley Raymond, Alberto Rodriguez, Luz Maria Salamina, Shalini Sankaranarayanan, Inka Schomer, Sudhir Shetty, Vannara Sok, Richard Spencer, Murat Sultanov, Laura Tuck, Joel A. Turkewitz, Aman Ullah, Mahesh Uttamchandani, Robert Utz, Jos Verbeek, Marijn Verhoeven and Justin O.S. Zake.

The paying taxes project was conducted in collaboration with PwC, led by Stef van Weeghel.

Bronwen Brown edited the manuscript. Corporate Visions, Inc. designed the report and the graphs.

Doing Business would not be possible without the expertise and generous input of a network of more than 12,500 local partners, including legal experts, business consultants, accountants, freight forwarders, government officials and other professionals routinely administering or advising on the relevant legal and regulatory requirements in the 190 economies covered. Contact details for local partners are available on the *Doing Business* website at http://www.doingbusiness.org.

The names of the local partners wishing to be acknowledged individually are listed below. The global and regional contributors listed are firms that have completed multiple questionnaires in their various offices around the world.

GLOBAL CONTRIBUTORS

Advocates for International Development

American Bar Association, Section of International Law

Baker & McKenzie

BDO

Colibri Law Firm

Deloitte

Dentons

DLA Piper

Ernst & Young

FIABCI, the International Real Estate Federation

GRATA Law Firm

Ius Laboris - Alliance of Labor, Employment, Benefits and Pensions Law Firms

KPMG

Law Society of England and Wales

Lex Mundi, Association of Independent Law Firms

Panalpina

PwC[1]

Russell Bedford International

SDV International Logistics

REGIONAL CONTRIBUTORS

A.P. Moller - Maersk Group

Arias & Muñoz

Ashurst LLP

Association of Consumer Credit Information Suppliers (ACCIS)

Boga & Associates

DFDL

García & Bodán

Garrigues

Gide Loyrette Nouel, member of Lex Mundi

Grant Thornton

Mayer Brown

John W. Ffooks & Co., member of Bowman Gilfillan Africa Group

Miranda & Associados

Norton Rose Fulbright

SORAINEN

Talal Abu-Ghazaleh Legal (TAG-Legal)

TransUnion International

White & Case

AFGHANISTAN

Icon Trading and Forwarding Company

Naseer Ahmad
Da Afghanistan Breshna Sherkat

Taqi Ahmad
A.F. Ferguson & Co., Chartered Accountants, a member firm of PwC network

Najibullah Ahmadi
Skywards Construction Company

Maroof Ahmadzai
Wahidqudrat Ltd.

Mirwais Alami
Da Afghanistan Breshna Sherkat

Sayed Farzad Alavi
European Technology Company

Ziaullah Astana
Afghan Land Consulting Organization (ALCO)

Shaheryar Aziz
A.F. Ferguson & Co., Chartered Accountants, a member firm of PwC network

Zalmai Bakhtyari
Bakhtar-e-Bastan Solar Wind

Mazhar Bangash
RIAA Barker Gillette

Nadia Bazidwal

Nooraqa Dawari
Stonecutter Company

Suleman Fatimie
Afghanistan Financial Services LLC

Sultan Maqsood Fazel
Qaderdan Electricity Company

Chantal Grut
Rosenstock Legal Services

Naheed Hababi
Da Afghanistan Bank

Sayed Jawid Hashemi
Masnad Legal Consultancy

Ahmad Khalid Hatam
RIAA Barker Gillette

Saduddin Haziq
Afghan United Bank

Hussain Ali Hekmat
Ikmal Engineering Construction Company

Conan Higgins
TSI Legal Enterprises, PC

Mohammad Homayoon
Da Afghanistan Breshna Sherkat

Rashid Ibrahim
A.F. Ferguson & Co., Chartered Accountants, a member firm of PwC network

Umaira Iqbal Raza
RIAA Barker Gillette

Ahmad Jawid Karimzada
Kabul Municipality

Mudassir Khan
Da Afghanistan Bank

Wisal Khan
Legal Oracles

Gaurav Lekh Raj Kukreja
Afghan Container Transport Company

Khalid Massoudi
Masnad Legal Consultancy

Tali Mohammad
Afghanistan Investment Support Agency

Abdul Qayoum Mohammadi
Skywards Construction Company

Saqib Naseer
A.F. Ferguson & Co., Chartered Accountants, a member firm of PwC network

Abdul Nasser Nazari
Rainbow Consulting Services

Tariq Nazarwall
Dehsabz City Development Authority, Independent Board of Kabul New City Development

Gul Pacha
Afghanistan Investment Support Agency

Essa Parwani
RIAA Barker Gillette

Habiburahman Qaderdan
Qaderdan Electricity Company

Tamsil Rashid
Afghanistan International Bank

Abdul Sami Saber
Da Afghanistan Bank

Ali Saberi
Ikmal Engineering Construction Company

Abdul Rahim Saeedi
Ministry of Commerce and Industry

Mohammad Ashoqullah Safi
Ensaf Block Construction Company

Zahid Safi
RIAA Barker Gillette

Abdul Nasser Sahak
Da Afghanistan Bank

Abdul Hanan Salam
Afghan Land Consulting Organization (ALCO)

Khalil Sediq
Afghanistan International Bank

Mohammad Ismail Shahid
Legal Oracles

Saeeq Shajjan
Shajjan & Associates

Asiyah Sharifi
Afghanistan Financial Services LLC

Sharifullah Shirzad
Da Afghanistan Bank

Nagina Sultani
Legal Oracles

Mohammad Mukhtar Tahwi
Win Kabul-Istanbul

M. Taimur Taimur
Da Afghanistan Bank

Gul Rahman Totakhail

Najibullah Wardak
Ministry of Finance

Maseeh Ahmad Wassil
Da Afghanistan Bank

Mohammadi Khan Yaqoobi
Da Afghanistan Bank

Nesar Ahmad Yosufzai
Da Afghanistan Bank

Mohammad Zarif
Kabul Municipality

Rohullah Zarif
ACCL International

ALBANIA

Wolf Theiss

Iris Ago
Abkons

Marsida Agolli
Abkons

Anjola Aliaj
OPTIMA Legal and Financial

Ermelinda Alimeri
Abkons

Enkelejda Alite
Enkelejda Alite Accountant

Artur Asllani
Tonucci & Partners

Ditjon Baboci
Urban Planning and Infrastructure

Redjan Basha
Abkons

Boiken Bendo
Bendo Law, Advocates & Legal Consultants

Jona Bica
Ernst & Young

Arben Bicoku
Albanian Association of Architects

Armando Bode
Boga & Associates

Genc Boga
Boga & Associates

Artan Bozo
Bozo & Associates Law Firm

Njazuela Braholli
Gjika & Associates

Jori Bregasi
Hoxha, Memi & Hoxha

Ledian Bregasi
Albanian Union of Architects

Denada Breshanaj
Abkons

Irma Cacaj
Boga & Associates

Megi Caushi
Avanntive Consulting Sh.p.k

Ilir Daci
OPTIMA Legal and Financial

Deniz Deralla
Bank of Albania

Eniana Dupi
AECO Consulting

Ana Dylgjeri
Bank of Albania

Sokol Elmazaj
Boga & Associates

Jonida Gaba
Ministry of Urban Development

Lorena Gega
PricewaterhouseCoopers Audit sh.p.k.

Aurela Gjokutaj
Al-Tax Center

Ermira Gjoncaj
Kuehne + Nagel Ltd.

Valbona Gjonçari
Boga & Associates

Shirli Gorenca
Kalo & Associates

Florian Hasko
Tashko Pustina - Attorneys

Maksim R. Haxhia
Haxhia & Hajdari

Enis Hoxha
Immovable Property Registration Office

Shpati Hoxha
Hoxha, Memi & Hoxha

Elona Hoxhaj
Boga & Associates

Jolita Hoxholli
Tashko Pustina - Attorneys

Elira Hroni
Kalo & Associates

Eris Hysi
Haxhia & Hajdari

---

1. *"PwC" refers to the network of member firms of PricewaterhouseCoopers International Limited (PwCIL), or, as the context requires, individual member firms of the PwC network. Each member firm is a separate legal entity and does not act as agent of PwCIL or any other member firm. PwCIL does not provide any services to clients. PwCIL is not responsible or liable for the acts or omissions of any of its member firms nor can it control the exercise of their professional judgment or bind them in any way. No member firm is responsible or liable for the acts or omissions of any other member firm nor can it control the exercise of another member firm's professional judgment or bind another member firm or PwCIL in any way.*

Brunilda Jegeni
Registry of Security Pledges

Ilir Johollari
Hoxha, Memi & Hoxha

Neritan Kallfa
Tonucci & Partners

Miranda Kapllani
Benimpex & Co.

Olta Kaziaj
Avanntive Consulting Sh.p.k

Aliel Kika
Kika sh.p.k.

Avenir Kika
Kika sh.p.k.

Merita Kola
Registry of Security Pledges

Evelina Koldashi
MCL sh.p.k. (Management Consulting & Law)

Dionis Kolila
Kalo & Associates

Ilir Korbi
Boga & Associates

Rudi Laze
Bozo & Associates Law Firm

Renata Leka
Boga & Associates

Arbër Lloshi
OPTIMA Legal and Financial

Ari Luarasi
OSHEE (Operatori i Shperndarjes se Energjise Elektrike)

Emirjon Marku
Boga & Associates

Rezarta Mataj
Tirana District Court

Arbjan Mazniku
Municipality of Tirana

Andi Memi
Hoxha, Memi & Hoxha

Eglon Metalia
Ernst & Young

Bora Muzhaqi
PricewaterhouseCoopers Audit sh.p.k.

Drini Nushi
Abkons

Albulen Pano
PricewaterhouseCoopers Audit sh.p.k.

Loreta Peci
PricewaterhouseCoopers Audit sh.p.k.

Ilda Perdhiku
ENKO Studio Kontabiliteti

Florian Piperi
OPTIMA Legal and Financial

Floran Pustina
Tashko Pustina - Attorneys

Krisela Qirushi
Gjika & Associates

Loriana Robo
Kalo & Associates

Jonida Skendaj
Boga & Associates

Ardjana Shehi
Kalo & Associates

Flonia Tashko-Borici
Tashko Pustina - Attorneys

Besa Tauzi
Boga & Associates

Ketrin Topçiu
Bozo & Associates Law Firm

Oltion Toro
Gjika & Associates

Fioralba Trebicka
Hoxha, Memi & Hoxha

Alketa Uruçi
Boga & Associates

Gerhard Velaj
Boga & Associates

Vasilika Vjero
Tirana Municipality Registration

Flavia Xhafo
Kalo & Associates

Elona Xhepa
Boga & Associates

Enida Zeneli
Bozo & Associates Law Firm

Lareda Zenuna
Gjika & Associates

ALGERIA

Amel Aiad
Accountant

Mohamed Nadir Aissani
PwC Algeria

Salima Aloui
Law Firm Goussanem & Aloui

Arab Aoudj
CACC - Cabinet d'Audit et de Contrôle des Comptes SARL

Djelloul Aouidette
Union Nationale des Transitaires et Commissionnaires Algériens (UNTCA)

Farid Arzani
Ministère des Finances - Direction Générale du Domaine National

Mohamed Atbi
Etude Notariale Mohamed Atbi

Hassan Djamel Belloula
Cabinet Belloula

Nabil Belloula
Cabinet Belloula

Tayeb Belloula
Cabinet Belloula

Farid Beloui
Studio A

Mohammed Tahar Benabid
Cabinet Mohammed Tahar Benabid

Abdelouahab Benali
Transit Mouhoub Kamal

Amina Bencharif
Sherca Concept

Mohamed Salah Benhammou
Accountant

Adnane Bouchaib
Bouchaib Law Firm

Mohamed Boudaoud
Sarl GCELEC

Hamid Boughenou
Become SCP

Rachida Boughenou
Become SCP

Hafida Bounefrat
Accountant

Merouane Chabane
Société Distribution de l'Electricité et du Gaz d'Alger (SDA)

Mohand Larbi Ikram Chikhi

Said Dib
Banque d'Algérie

Ahmed Djouadi
Law Firm Hadj-Hamou & Djouadi - associate office of Dentons

Mourad El Besseghi
Cabinet El Besseghi

Brahim Embouazza
MCD Consulting

Hamil Faidi
Studio A

Khaled Goussanem
Law Firm Goussanem & Aloui

Mohamed El-Amine Haddad
Cabinet de Maître Amine Haddad

Sakina Haddad
Crédit Populaire d'Algérie

Ali Hamadache
Conservation Foncière d'Alger

Samir Hamouda
Cabinet d'Avocats Samir Hamouda

Issaad M. Hand
Ministère des Finances - Direction Générale des Impôts

Halim Karabadji
Société Distribution de l'Electricité et du Gaz d'Alger (SDA)

Yamina Kebir
Law Office of Yamina Kebir

Abdelmalek Kherbachene
Bouchemla Lanouar & Associés

Bachir Khodja
SNC Khodja et Cie

Farouk Lakli
Lakelec

Samira Lalig
Global Assistance

Mohamed Lanouar
Bouchemla Lanouar & Associés

Vincent Lunel
DS Avocats

Harous Madjid
PwC Algeria

Mohamed Mokrane
Ministère des Finances - Direction Générale du Domaine National

Hamid Ould Hocine
Studio A

Malika Redouani
PwC Algeria

Lazhar Sahbani
PwC Algeria

Mourad Seghir
Bennani & Associés LLP

Leila Sellali
Cabinet Architecte Sellali

Rabah Tafighoult
Cabinet Tafighoult

Nourredine Yahi
Cabinet Yahi

Hachemi Yanat
Accountant

Amine Zerhouni
BDO

ANGOLA

Luís Andrade
PwC Angola

Filipa Faustino Arenga
ADCA Law Firm

Augusto Balaso
ENDE-EP

Guilherme Carreira
Edifer Angola

Luis Filipe Carvalho
ADCA Law Firm

Ricardo Cassenda
ENDE-EP

Irineu Chingala
Lourdes Caposso Fernandes & Associados (LCF)

Marie-Laurence Ciccarone
SDV Logistics

Nelson Couto-Cabral
3C International

Inês Cunha
PwC Portugal

Miguel de Avillez Pereira
Abreu Advogados

Alexandre Fernandes
AFBS Partners

Lourdes Caposso Fernandes
Lourdes Caposso Fernandes & Associados

Arnold Ferreira
FBL Advogados

Beatriz Ferreira de Andrade dos Santos
Banco Nacional de Angola

Luís Fraústo Varona
Abreu Advogados

Mafalda Granjo
PwC Portugal

José Helder da Conceição
Instituto de Planeamento e Gestão Urbana do Governo Provincial de Luanda

Guiomar Lopes
FBL Advogados

António Manuel da Silva
Instituto Regulador dos Serviços de Electricidade e Águas (IRSEA)

Arcelio Matias
Arcélio Inácio de Almeida Matias – Ardja-Prestação de Serviços e Consultoria, Lda

Marcos Neto
Banco Nacional de Angola

Luis Miguel Nunes
AVM Advogados

Júlio Pascoal
ENDE-EP

Alexandre Pegado
Alexandre Pegado - Escritório de Advogados

Joaquim Piedade
UNICARGAS

Laurinda Prazeres Cardoso
FBL Advogados

José Quarta
Instituto Regulador dos Serviços de Electricidade e Águas (IRSEA)

Maurilson Ramos
Gabinete Legal Angola – Advogados

Gonçalo Antunes Rita
Banco Nacional de Angola

João Robles
F. Castelo Branco & Associados

Sandra Saraiva
Gabinete Legal Angola – Advogados

Maikel Steve
Center for Entrepreneurship in Cazenga

Renata Valenti
Gabinete Legal Angola – Advogados

M.C. Vasnani
Consolidated Shipping Agencies Limited

Patrícia Viana
Abreu Advogados

Antônio Vicente Marques
AVM Advogados

Amaury Vrignaud
Bolloré Africa Logistics Angola

ANTIGUA AND BARBUDA

Antigua & Barbuda Intellectual Property & Commerce Office (ABIPCO)

Ministry of Labor

Roberts & Co.

Nicola Alleyne
CaribTrans

Neil Coates
Grant Thornton

Nicolette Doherty
Nicolette M. Doherty Attorney-at-Law and Notary Public

Terence Dornellas
Consolidated Maritime Services

Gilbert Findlay
Antigua Public Utility Authority

Ann Henry
Henry & Burnette

Ian Lewis
Antigua Public Utilities Authority (APUA)

Lisa M. John Weste
Thomas, John & Co.

Hugh C. Marshall
Marshall & Co.

Gloria Martin
Francis Trading Agency Limited

Jason Peters
Antigua Public Utility Authority

Girvan Pigott
Antigua Public Utility Authority

Jermaine C. Rhudd
Rhudd & Associates

Septimus A. Rhudd
Rhudd & Associates

Andrea Roberts
Roberts & Co.

Safiya Roberts
Roberts & Co.

Ivan Rodrigues
Antigua Public Utilities Authority (APUA)

Sharon Simmons
Land Registry

Eleanor R. Solomon
Clarke & Clarke

Frederick Southwell
Development Control Authority

Arthur Thomas
Thomas, John & Co.

Marietta Warren
Interfreight Ltd.

ARGENTINA

Petrobras

Martinica Abal Gallardon
Wiener Soto Caparrós

Ignacio Acedo
Gonzalez & Ferraro Mila

Sebastian Alvarez
Brons & Salas Abogados

Natalia Artmann
Alfaro Abogados

Alejo Baca Castex
G. Breuer

Vanesa Balda
Vitale, Manoff & Feilbogen

Gonzalo Carlos Ballester
J.P. O'Farrell Abogados

Néstor J. Belgrano
M. & M. Bomchil

Fiorella Belsito
Severgnini, Robiola, Grinberg & Tombeur

Pilar Etcheverry Boneo
Marval, O'Farrell & Mairal, member of Lex Mundi

Ignacio Fernández Borzese
Luna Requena & Fernández Borzese Tax Law Firm

Nicolás Bühler
Hope, Duggan & Silva

Adriana Paola Caballero
Wiener Soto Caparrós

Federico Carenzo
Leonhardt & Dietl

Gabriela Carissimo
Alfaro Abogados

Mariano E. Carricart
Badeni, Cantilo, Laplacette & Carricart

Luciano Cativa
Luna Requena & Fernández Borzese Tax Law Firm

Agustín Comastri
G. Breuer

Roberto H. Crouzel
Estudio Beccar Varela

Valeria D'Alessandro
Marval, O'Farrell & Mairal, member of Lex Mundi

Nicolás Debernardi
Hope, Duggan & Silva

Carola Del Rio
Severgnini, Robiola, Grinberg & Tombeur

Oscar Alberto del Río
Central Bank of Argentina

Noelia Aldana Di Stefano
J.P. O'Farrell Abogados

Andrés Edelstein
PwC Argentina

Joaquín Eppens Echague
Fiorito Murray & Diaz Cordero

Pablo Ferraro Mila
Gonzalez & Ferraro Mila

Diego M. Fissore
G. Breuer

Arq. Eduardo Galleazzi
Architect

Martín Gastaldi
Estudio Beccar Varela

Javier M. Gattó Bicain
Candioti Gatto Bicain & Ocantos

Giselle Rita Geuna
Alfaro Abogados

Juan Jose Glusman
PwC Argentina

Matías Grinberg
Severgnini, Robiola, Grinberg & Tombeur

Gonzalo Maria Gros
J.P. O'Farrell Abogados

José Guarracino
Hope, Duggan & Silva

Federico Guillermo
G. Breuer

Federico Guillermo Absi
G. Breuer

Gabriela Hidalgo
Gabriela Hidalgo

Daniel Intile
Russell Bedford Argentina - member of Russell Bedford International

Andrea Junquera
Candioti Gatto Bicain & Ocantos

Federico Leonhardt
Leonhardt, Dietl, Graf & von der Fecht

Pilar Lodewyckx Hardy
Estudio Beccar Varela

Tomás M. Fiorito
Fiorito Murray & Diaz Cordero

Juan Manuel Magadan
PwC Argentina

Julian Melis
Candioti Gatto Bicain & Ocantos

Maria Fernanda Mierez
Estudio Beccar Varela

José Oscar Mira
Central Bank of Argentina

Jorge Miranda
Clippers SA

Miguel P. Murray
Murray, Anguillesi, Guyot, Rossi & Sirito de Zavalía

Pablo Murray
Fiorito Murray & Diaz Cordero

Pedro Nicholson
Estudio Beccar Varela

Luciano Jose Nístico
J.P. O'Farrell Abogados

Alfredo Miguel O'Farrell
Marval, O'Farrell & Mairal, member of Lex Mundi

Gabriela E. Orsini
Sentido Común

Federico Jorge Panero
International Notary of Argentina

Javier M. Petrantonio
M. & M. Bomchil

Alejandro Poletto
Estudio Beccar Varela

María Clara Pujol
Wiener Soto Caparrós

Federico José Reibestein
Reibestein & Asociados

Sebastián Rodrigo
Alfaro Abogados

Teodoro Rodríguez Cáceres
G. Breuer

Juan Ignacio Ruiz
Alfaro Abogados

Luz María Salomón
J.P. O'Farrell Abogados

Ramiro Santurio
Leonhardt, Dietl, Graf & von der Fecht

Enrique Schinelli
Leonhardt, Dietl, Graf & von der Fecht

Liliana Cecilia Segade
Laprida, Goñi Moreno & González Urroz

Carolina Serra
Estudio Beccar Varela

Federico Sosa
Estudio Beccar Varela

Maria Florencia Sota Vazquez
Alfaro Abogados

Pablo Staszewski
Staszewski & Associates

Javier Tarasido
Severgnini, Robiola, Grinberg & Tombeur

Ricardo Tavieres
PwC Argentina

Adolfo Tombolini
Russell Bedford Argentina - member of Russell Bedford International

Marcos Torassa
Torassa & O'Donnel

Martín Torres Girotti
M. & M. Bomchil

María Paola Trigiani
Alfaro Abogados

Emilio Beccar Varela
Estudio Beccar Varela

Abraham Viera
Planosnet.com Consultoria Municipal

Roberto Wiman
Green Ingeniería

Joaquín Emilio Zappa
J.P. O'Farrell Abogados

ARMENIA

The State Committee of Real Property Cadastre of the Government of the Republic of Armenia

Urban Logistic Services

Sergey Aghinyan
Public Services Regulatory Commission of Armenia

Ani Alaverdyan
Avenue Consulting Group

Amalia Artemyan
Paradigma Armenia CJSC

Zaruhi Arzuamnyan
Legelata

Hayk Asatryan
Yerevan City Municipality

Narek Ashughatoyan
Legal Lab

Ella Atoyan
PwC Armenia

Sergey Avetisyan
Ministry of Economy

Aram Ayvazyan
Yerevan Municipality

Albert Babayan
Ministry of Economy

Karapet Badalyan
Prudence Legal CJSC

Sayad Badalyan
Investment Law Group LLC

Anush Baghdasaryan
Avenue Consulting Group

Vahagn Balyan
Avenue Consulting Group

Irina Belubekyan
Union of Manufacturers and Businessmen (Employers) of Armenia

Vartan Bezhanyan
Law Faculty, Yerevan State University

Aharon Chilingaryan
Paradigma Armenia CJSC

Azat Dunamalyan
Arshinbank CJSC

Ani Galstyan
Ministry of Justice

Avetis Gevorgyan
Public Administration Academy of the Republic of Armenia

Shoghik Gharibyan
KPMG

Arsen Ghazaryan
Union of Manufacturers and Businessmen (Employers) of Armenia

Mihran Grigoryan
Avenue Consulting Group

Sargis Grigoryan
GPartners

Tigran Grigoryan
Avenue Consulting Group

Alla Hakhnazaryan
Legelata

Anahit Hakhumyan
Ministry of Urban Development

Artak Hovakimyan
Big Energo LLC

Izabela Hovhannisyan
EBRD Business Support Office

Mariam Hovsepyan
Ter-Tachatyan Legal and Business Consulting

Angela Hovshannisyan
Ter-Tachatyan Legal and Business Consulting

Diana Javadyan
Central Bank of Armenia

Vahram Jotyan
Gosselin

Vahe G. Kakoyan
Investment Law Group LLC

Arshak Karapetyan
Investment Law Group LLC

Andranik Kasaryan
Yerevan Municipality

Georgi Khachatryan
Avenue Consulting Group

Rafik Khachatryan
KPMG

Vigen Khachatryan
Avenue Consulting Group

Stepan Khzrtian
Legal Lab

Nelli Kirakosyan
Central Bank of Armenia

Arayik Kurdyan
Yerevan Municipality

Hayk Mamajanyan
Arlex International CJSC

Sargis Manukyan
Yerevan City Municipality

Nshan Martirosyan
Ministry of Urban Development

Lilit Matevosyan
PwC Armenia

Vahagn Mikayelyan
HSBC Bank

Vahe Movsisyan
Investment Law Group LLC

Rajiv Nagri
Globalink Logistics Group

Narine Nersisyan
PwC Armenia

Nerses Nersisyan
PwC Armenia

Satenik Nubaryan
Legal Lab

Karen Petrosyan
Investment Law Group LLC

Naira Petrosyan
Paradigma Armenia CJSC

Sarhat Petrosyan
Urbanlab Yerevan

Suren Petrosyan
SP Consulting LLC

Hayk Pogosyan
Arsarqtex LLC

Nare Sahakyan
Arshinbank CJSC

Thomas Samuelian
Arlex International CJSC

Gor Shahbazyan
PwC Armenia

Ruben Shakhmuradyan
Comfort R&V

Hakob Tadevosyan
Grant Thornton LLP

Mikael Vardgesyan
HSBC Bank

Tserun Voskanyan
Electric Networks of Armenia

Emilia Yeghiazaryan
Central Bank of Armenia

Arman Yesayan
Alfa System Technologies

Liana Yordanyan
Ter-Tachatyan Legal and Business Consulting

Aram Zakaryan
ACRA Credit Bureau

AUSTRALIA

Attorney-General's Department

Ausgrid

Harold Bolitho
King & Wood Mallesons

Lynda Brumm
PwC Australia

Amanda Coneyworth
Ferrier Hodgson Limited

Mark Dalby
Office of State Revenue, NSW Treasury

Stephen Davis
Nexia Australia

Kristy Dixon
Marque Lawyers

Ali Dogan
M+K Lawyers

Steven Dowsley
Dowsley Electrical

Mike Gooley
McKenzie Group

Philip Harvey
King & Wood Mallesons

Owen Hayford
Clayton Utz, member of Lex Mundi

Ian Humphreys
Ashurst LLP

Jennifer Ingram
Clayton Utz, member of Lex Mundi

Eric Janssens
Veda (an Equifax Company)

Stephen Jauncey
Henry Davis York

James Johnston
Ashurst LLP

Onkar Kale
PwC Australia

John Karantonis
Clayton Utz, member of Lex Mundi

Morgan Kelly
Ferrier Hodgson Limited

Felicia Lal
Marque Lawyers

Peter Leonard
Gilbert + Tobin Lawyers

Angus Luffman
Veda (an Equifax Company)

John Martin
Thomson Geer

Nicholas Mavrakis
Clayton Utz, member of Lex Mundi

Mark Maxwell
Fusion Industries Pty Ltd.

Denis McCarthy
PwC Australia

Aaron McKenzie
Marque Lawyers

Des Mooney
Department of Finance, Services & Innovation

Patricia Muscat
PwC Australia

Garry Pritchard
Emil Ford Lawyers

Mitchell Robertson
Ashurst LLP

Cameron Robinson
Treasury of Australia

Dean Schiller
Fayman International Pty. Ltd.

Ruwan Senanayake

Damian Sturzaker
Marque Lawyers

Simon Truskett
Clayton Utz, member of Lex Mundi

Dilini Waidyanatha

AUSTRIA

Ministry for Science, Research and Economy

Thomas Bareder
Oesterreichische National Bank

Constantin Benes
Schoenherr

Nicole Bergsleitner
SCWP Schindhelm Austria

Georg Brandstetter
Brandstetter, Baurecht, Pritz & Partner Rechtsanwälte KG

Manfred Buric
Federal Ministry of Justice

Marta Chalupa
Revisionstreuhand - member of Russell Bedford International

Thomas Deutinger
Freshfields Bruckhaus Deringer

Martin Eckel
TaylorWessing e|n|w|c Natlacen Walderdorff Cancola Rechtsanwälte GmbH

Agnes Eigner
Brandstetter, Baurecht, Pritz & Partner Rechtsanwälte KG

Julius Ernst
BEV

Tibor Fabian
Binder Grösswang Rechtsanwälte GmbH

Julian Feichtinger
CHSH Cerha Hempel Spiegelfeld Hlawati, member of Lex Mundi

Leopold Ferch
Graf & Pitkowitz Rechtsanwälte GmbH

Martin Foerster
Graf & Pitkowitz Rechtsanwälte GmbH

Ferdinand Graf
Graf & Pitkowitz Rechtsanwälte GmbH

Andreas Hable
Binder Grösswang Rechtsanwälte GmbH

Sebastian Haensse
Graf & Pitkowitz Rechtsanwälte GmbH

Herbert Herzig
Austrian Chamber of Commerce

Verena Hitzinger
PwC Austria

Alexander Hofmann
RA Dr. Alexander Hofmann, LL.M.

Armin Immervoll
Ministry of Finance

Alexander Isola
Graf & Pitkowitz Rechtsanwälte GmbH

Rudolf Kaindl
Kaindl Duerr Schuller-Koehler Antenreiter & Partner Civil Law Notaries

Birgit Kettlgruber
Freshfields Bruckhaus Deringer

Alexander Klauser
Brauneis Klauser Prändl Rechtsanwälte GmbH

Christian Köttl
Ministry of Finance

Rudolf Krickl
PwC Austria

Michaela Krist
CHSH Cerha Hempel Spiegelfeld Hlawati, member of Lex Mundi

Peter Madl
Schoenherr

Mario Maier
Orrick, Herrington & Sutcliffe LLP

Gerald Mitteregger
International Logistic Gateway

Johannes Mrazek
Austrian Regulatory Authority

Gerhard Muggenhuber
BEV - Federal Office of Metrology & Surveying

Thomas Müller
Freshfields Bruckhaus Deringer

Elke Napokoj
bpv Hügel Rechtsanwälte OG

Nikolaus Neubauer
PwC Austria

Felix Neuwirther
Freshfields Bruckhaus Deringer

Martin Österreicher
Graf & Pitkowitz Rechtsanwälte GmbH

Christopher Peitsch
CHSH Cerha Hempel Spiegelfeld Hlawati, member of Lex Mundi

Angelika Prichystal
KSV 1870

Moritz Salzgeber
Binder Grösswang Rechtsanwälte GmbH

Johannes Samaan
Freshfields Bruckhaus Deringer

Edwin Scharf
SCWP Schindhelm Austria

Georg Schima
Kunz Schima Wallentin Rechtsanwälte OG, member of Ius Laboris

Stephan Schmalzl
Graf & Pitkowitz Rechtsanwälte GmbH

Ernst Schmidt
Halpern & Prinz

Alexander Schultmeyer
DLA Piper Weiss-Tessbach Rechtsanwälte GmbH

Helmut Sprongl
Austrian Regulatory Authority

Thomas Strassner
Orrick, Herrington & Sutcliffe LLP

Thomas Trettnak
CHSH Cerha Hempel Spiegelfeld Hlawati, member of Lex Mundi

Eugen Velicu
STRABAG SE

Birgit Vogt-Majarek
Kunz Schima Wallentin Rechtsanwälte OG, member of Ius Laboris

Matthias Wach
Graf & Pitkowitz Rechtsanwälte GmbH

Gerhard Wagner
KSV 1870

Lukas A. Weber
Brauneis Klauser Prändl Rechtsanwälte GmbH

Arno Weigand
Öffentlicher Notar MMag. Dr. Arno Weigand

Markus Winkler
CHSH Cerha Hempel Spiegelfeld Hlawati, member of Lex Mundi

Natalia Wolfschwenger
Schoenherr

Elisabeth Zehetner-Piewald
Austrian Chamber of Commerce

Anton Zeilinger
Ministry of Finance

Kathrin Zeller
Freshfields Bruckhaus Deringer

Jasna Zwitter-Tehovnik
DLA Piper Weiss-Tessbach Rechtsanwälte GmbH

AZERBAIJAN

Aygun Abasova
Michael Wilson & Partners Ltd.

Ophelia Abdulaeva
Dentons

Parviz Abdullayev
PwC Azerbaijan

Husniyye Abdullayeva
Ministry of Taxes

Chingiz Agarzaev
Chiza Architectural Bureau

Hamid Aghahuseynov
Ernst & Young

Ilham Ahmedov
Baku Administrative-Economical Court No. 1

Nigar Aimova
Ministry of Taxes

Eldar Abuzarovich Aliev
State Agency for the Control of Construction Safety

Jamil Alizada
Baker & McKenzie - CIS, Limited

Farid Amirov
Ministry of Economy and Industry

Aykhan Asadov
BM Morrison Partners Law Firm

Ismail Askerov
MGB Law Offices

Iftixar Axundov
Ministry of Taxes

Kamran Babayev
State Committee for Securities

Jamal Baghirov
BM Morrison Partners Law Firm

Shahin Bagirov
Azerbaijan Customs Committee

Farid Bakhshiyev
GRATA Law Firm

Erik Cahangir
ASNAF Group

Parviz Ilham Gasanov
EVRASCON

Arif Guliyev
PwC Azerbaijan

Konul Guliyeva
PwC Azerbaijan

Fatima Gurbanova
PwC Azerbaijan

Elchin Habibov
Central Bank of Azerbaijan

Arzu Hajiyeva
Ernst & Young

Kamala Hajiyeva
Ernst & Young

Nigar Hajiyeva
Baker & McKenzie - CIS, Limited

Shamkhal Hasanov
Baker & McKenzie - CIS, Limited

Qalib Hemidov
Azerishiq

Farid Huseynov
Ekvita

Zumrud Ibrahim
Baker & McKenzie - CIS, Limited

Elchin Ibrahimov
Ministry of Economy and Industry

Mehti Ilgar
Ekvita

Alakbar Ismayilzada
Central Bank of Azerbaijan

Ummi Jalilova
GRATA Law Firm

Elshad Khanalibayli
The State Committee on Property Issues

Umit Konyar
Azersun

Elena Lee
Michael Wilson & Partners Ltd.

Elnur Mammadov
PwC Azerbaijan

Elshad Mammadov
The State Committee on Property Issues

Sahib Mammadov
Citizens' Labour Rights Protection League

Zaur Mammadov
Ernst & Young

Kamal Mammadzada
Dentons

Safar Mehdiyev
Azerbaijan Customs Committee

Gumru Mehdiyeva
BHM Baku Law Centre LLC

Rauf Memmedov
Azerbaijan Customs Committee

Telman Memmedov
Ministry of Taxes

Farhad Mirzayev
BM Morrison Partners Law Firm

Ruslan Mukhtarov
BM Morrison Partners Law Firm

Farida Musayeva
Ministry of Justice

Altay Mustafayev
Baker & McKenzie - CIS, Limited

Turkan Mustafayeva
BHM Baku Law Centre LLC

Vusal Novruzov
Azerbaijan Customs Committee

Sabina Orujova
Dentons

Ramiz Rustamov
Sin RRG MMC

Leyla Safarova
Baker & McKenzie - CIS, Limited

Mustafa Salamov
BM Morrison Partners Law Firm

Elchin Shirinov
Azerbaijan Customs Committee

Sona Taghiyeva
Dentons

Anar A. Umudov
Alibi Professional Legal & Consulting Services

Ilkin Veliyev
Ministry of Taxes

Michael Wilson
Michael Wilson & Partners Ltd.

Aygun Zeynalova
MGB Law Offices

Ulvia Zeynalova-Bockin
Dentons

BAHAMAS, THE

APD Limited

Bryan A. Glinton
Glinton | Sweeting | O'Brien

Kevin Basden
Bahamas Electricity Corporation

Gowon Bowe
PwC Bahamas

Sonia Brown
Graphite Engineering Ltd.

Dayrrl Butler
Moore Stephens Butler & Taylor Chartered Accountants and Business Advisors

Jeremy Cafferata
Freeport Shipping Services

Anastasia Campbell
Graham, Thompson & Co.

Surinder Deal
Higgs & Johnson

Craig G. Delancy
Ministry of Works & Transport

Amos J. Ferguson Jr.
Ferguson Associates & Planners

Wendy Forsythe
Import Export Brokers Ltd.

Amanda John
Lennox Paton

Kenneth L. Lightbourne
Graham Thompson Attorneys

Ja'Ann Major
Higgs & Johnson

Simone Morgan-Gomez
Callenders & Co.

Lester J. Mortimer Jr.
Callenders & Co.

Michael Moss
Ministry of Finance

Andrea Moultrie
Higgs & Johnson

Portia Nicholson
Higgs & Johnson

Andrew G.S. O'Brien II
Glinton | Sweeting | O'Brien

Courtney Pearce-Hanna
Callenders & Co.

Lindsy Pinders
Pinders Customs Brokerage

Kamala Richardson
Glinton | Sweeting | O'Brien

Chad D. Roberts
Callenders & Co.

Alvan Rolle
Alvan K. Rolle & Associates Co. Ltd.

Sophie Rolle
Lennox Paton

Castino D. Sands
Lennox Paton

Rochelle Sealy
PwC Bahamas

Giahna Soles
Graham Thompson Attorneys

Merrit A. Storr
Chancellor Chambers

Burlington Strachan
Bahamas Electricity Corporation

Roy Sweeting
Glinton | Sweeting | O'Brien

Jody Wells
Lennox Paton

Dwayne Whylly
Lennox Paton

Nadia A. Wright
Chancellor Chambers

BAHRAIN

Ernst & Young

Keypoint Business Services W.L.L.

Ministry of Industry & Commerce & Tourism

Rana Abdulghaffar Al Alawi
Zu'bi & Partners Attorneys & Legal Consultants

Ahmed Abdullah
Ministry of Works, Municipalities and Urban Planning

Savio Aguiar
Panalpina World Transport LLP

Amel Al Aseeri
Zeenat Al Mansoori & Associates

Mahmood Al Asheeri
The BENEFIT Company

Zeenat Al Mansoori
Zeenat Al Mansoori & Associates

Salem Al Quti
Ministry of Works, Municipalities and Urban Planning

Reem Al Rayes
Zeenat Al Mansoori & Associates

Waleed Al Sabbagh
Bahrain Customs

Noor Al Taraif
Zu'bi & Partners Attorneys & Legal Consultants

Raju Alagarsamy
Hassan Radhi & Associates

Hazar Al-Sayed
Ministry of Works, Municipalities and Urban Planning

Sana Amin
Amin Law Firm

Nada Azmi
Bahrain Economic Development Board

Steven Brown
ASAR – Al Ruwayeh & Partners

Yousif Bubshait
Ports and Maritime Affairs - Ministry of Transportation

Samir Can'an
Gulf House Engineering S.P.C.

Laith Damer
Talal Abu-Ghazaleh Legal (TAG-Legal)

Qays H. Zu'bi
Zu'bi & Partners Attorneys & Legal Consultants

Najma Hassan
Ministry of Works, Municipalities and Urban Planning

Ken Healy
PwC Bahrain

Brian Howard
Trowers & Hamlins

Hessa Hussain
The BENEFIT Company

Noora Janahi
Hassan Radhi & Associates

Jawad Habib Jawad
BDO

Sara Jawahery
Elham Ali Hassan & Associates

Ronald Langat
Haya Rashed Al Khalifa

Saifuddin Mahmood
Hassan Radhi & Associates

Omar Manassaki
Zu'bi & Partners Attorneys & Legal Consultants

Hadeel Mohammed
Talal Abu-Ghazaleh Legal (TAG-Legal)

Eman Omar
Zu'bi & Partners Attorneys & Legal Consultants

Hassan Ali Radhi
Hassan Radhi & Associates

Najib F. Saade
ASAR – Al Ruwayeh & Partners

Naji Sabt
Survey and Land Registration Bureau

Oleg Shmal
PwC Bahrain

Esmond Hugh Stokes
Zu'bi & Partners Attorneys & Legal Consultants

Baiju Thomas
Agility Logistics

Aseel Zimmo
Supreme Judicial Council

BANGLADESH

Chittagong Water Supply and Sewerage Authority

Dhaka Electricity Supply Company Ltd. (DESCO)

Office of the Registrar of Joint Stock Companies and Firms

Rahman's Chambers

Mohammed Abu Sayed
Assurance Maritime Bangladesh Limited

Sumaiya Ifrit Binte Ahmed
Vertex Chambers

Shammi Ahsan
Vertex Chambers

Sayeed Abdullah Al Mamun Khan
A.S. & Associates

Intekhab-Ul Alam
A.S. & Associates

K. M. Tanjib-ul Alam
Tanjib Alam and Associates

Shajib Mahmood Alam
Counsels Law Partners CLP

M.D. Nurul Amin
Development Constructions Ltd.

Mehedy Amin
Development Constructions Ltd.

Saady Amin
Development Constructions Ltd.

Imran Anwar
Tanjib Alam and Associates

Mohammed Asaduzzaman
Syed Ishtiaq Ahmed & Associates

A.S.A. Bari
A.S. & Associates

Avijit Barua
Grihayan Limited

Kapil Basu
PricewaterhouseCoopers Pvt. Ltd.

Sushmita Basu
PricewaterhouseCoopers Pvt. Ltd.

Md. Halim Bepari
Hafiz and Haque Solicitors

Gouranga Chakraborty
Bangladesh Bank

Paavan Chhabra
Healy Consultants

Jamilur Reza Choudhury
University of Asia Pacific

Abu Naser Chowdhury
University of Asia Pacific

Arif Moinuddin Chowdhury
Munim & Associates

Md. Liaquat H. Chowdhury
M.L.H. Chowdhury & Co.

Prajna Roy Chowdhury
Karim & Co.

Junayed A. Chowdury
Vertex Chambers

Md Khademul Islam Choyon
Rahman's Chambers

Monjur Elahi
S.A. Khan & Associates

Dewan Faisal
A.S. & Associates

Sheikh Faisal Ziad
Tanjib Alam and Associates

Imitaz Farooq
Ahmed and Farooq LP

Abdullah Faruque
Faculty of Law, University of Chittagong

Osman Goni
OGR Legal

Simon Guidecoq
Healy Consultants

M. Rezwanul Haque

Rafinur Haque
Counsels Law Partners CLP

Rashedul Haque
Counsels Law Partners CLP

Mirza Quamrul Hasan
Adviser's Legal Alliance Firm

Muhammad Tanvir Hashem Munim
Munim & Associates

Anam Hossain
FM Associates

Farhana Hossain
FM Associates

Faria Huq
A.S. & Associates

Ashiq Imran
Fialka

Md Aminul Islam
City Apparel-Tex Co.

Rafiqul Islam
AMS & Associates

Aminul Islam Nazir
Assurance Maritime Bangladesh Limited

Abdul Jabbar
A.S. & Associates

Karishma Jahan
The Legal Circle

Md. Kamruzzaman
KPMG

Adnan M. L. Karim
Karim & Co.

Abdul Khaleque
Fialka

A. R. M. Ahsanul Haq Khan
The Legal Circle

Abdul Monem Khan
Vertex Chambers

Farhana Islam Khan
Syed Ishtiaq Ahmed & Associates

Hafizur Rahaman Khan
Counsels Law Partners CLP

Mashfiqul Haque Khan
Lex Juris

Narita Khan
The Legal Circle

Sarjean Rahman Lian
FM Associates

Kazi Mahboob
A. Wahab & Co.

Mohammad Moniruzzaman
The Law Counsel

Mehran Morshed
Huq and Co.

Sayedul Munim
Karim & Co.

Noushad Parvez
Counsels Law Partners CLP

Fahad Qader
Counsels Law Partners CLP

Tanvir Quader
Vertex Chambers

Md. Faysal Rahaman
KPMG

Al Amin Rahman
FM Associates

Anita Ghazi Rahman
The Legal Circle

Akther Rezvi
KPMG

Ridi Rubaiyat
Tanjib Alam and Associates

S M Golam Sahria
Karim & Co.

Toufiq Seraj
Sheltech (Pvt.) Ltd.

Mohd. Shariful Islam Shaheen
Bangladesh Energy Regulatory Commission

Sohail Shakoor
Pronayon

Imran Siddiq
The Law Counsel

Shakhawat Sumon
Shodesh Shipping & Logistic Company

Khander Tahmid Tishad
A.S. & Associates

Mahbub Uddin
Mahbub & Company

Rashid ul Haque
Sheltech (Pvt.) Ltd.

Ammatul Uzma
A.S. & Associates

Abdul Wahab
A. Wahab & Co.

Nurul Wahab
A. Wahab & Co.

Sabrina Zarin
FM Associates

BARBADOS

Clarke Gittens Farmer

PwC Barbados

Alicia Archer
Artemis Law

Patricia Boyce
Everson R. Elcock & Co. Ltd.

Andrew F. Brathwaite
KPMG Barbados

Kevin Burke
Rotherley Construction Inc.

Vincent Burnett
Ministry of Labor and Social Security and Human Resource Development

Rosalind Bynoe
BCF Attorneys-at-Law

Trevor A. Carmichael
Chancery Chambers

Adrian Carter
The Barbados Light and Power Company Ltd.

Berkeley Clark
BJS Customs Service Inc.

Andrew Cox
Ministry of Labor and Social Security and Human Resource Development

Adrian M. Elcock
Everson R. Elcock & Co. Ltd.

Antonio Elcock
Everson R. Elcock & Co. Ltd.

Marcel El-Daher
Daher & Associates

Andrew C. Ferreira
Chancery Chambers

Mark Franklin

Sharalee Gittens
Chancery Chambers

Anice C.N. Granville
LEX Caribbean

Liza A. Harridyal-Sodha
Harridyal-Sodha & Associates

Jomo Crowther McGlinne Hope
Artemis Law

Keisha N Hyde Porchetta
Harridyal-Sodha & Associates

Ruan C. Martinez
BCF Attorneys-at-Law

Jennivieve Maynard
Inn Chambers

Noel M. Nurse
The Booth Steamship Co. Barbados Ltd.

Karen Perreira
InterCaribbean Legal

Tony Selby
SRM Architects Ltd.

Heather Tull
David King & Co., Attorneys at Law

Stephen Worme
The Barbados Light and Power Company Ltd.

BELARUS

RUP BelEnergoSetProekt

SORAINEN Belarus

Anastasia Akulich
Borovtsov & Salei Legal Services

Natalia Aleksandrovna Vysotskaya
Association of International Road Carriers (BAMAP)

Aliaksandr Anisovich
PROMAUDIT

Dzmitry Barouka
Arzinger & Partners International Law Firm

Vladimir G. Biruk
Capital Group

Kiril Bizunok
Osipova, Koltunovich and Partners

Denis Bogdanov
Revera Consulting Group

Dmitry Bokhan
Verkhovodko & Partners LLC

Alexander Botian
Borovtsov & Salei Legal Services

Diana Bovdey
Grant Thornton

Eugenia Chetverikova
PwC Belarus

Sergey Chistyakov
Stepanovski, Papakul and Partners Ltd.

Aliaksandr Danilevich
Danilevich & Volozhinets

Alexey Daryin
Revera Consulting Group

Tatsiana Fadzeyeva
BNT Legal & Tax

Aliaksei Fidzek
PwC Belarus

Valentin Galich
SB-Global

Nikolai Gorelik
Arzinger & Partners International Law Firm

Elena Hmeleva
Verkhovodko & Partners LLC

Olga Vladimirovna Kakovka
Supreme Court of the Republic of Belarus

Ulyana Kavalionak
BNT Legal & Tax

Yurij Kazakevitch
Rödl & Partner, Belarus

Dmitry Khalimonchyk
Softclub LLC

Vitaly Khmelnitsky
Allford Morisson

Alexandre Khrapoutski
Sysouev, Bondar, Khrapoutski SBH Law Office

Sergey Khromov
Verkhovodko & Partners LLC

Siarhei Khvastovich
Legal Company Anticrisis Consulting Ltd.

Alexander Kirienko
Agency of Turnaround Technologies

Tatsiana Klochko
Aliance of Independent Legal Advisers

Nina Knyazeva
Verkhovodko & Partners LLC

Nadezhda Koroleva
Sysouev, Bondar, Khrapoutski SBH Law Office

Alexander Korsak
Arzinger & Partners International Law Firm

Mikhail E. Kostyukov
Attorney-at-Law

Dmitry Kovalchik
Stepanovski, Papakul and Partners Ltd.

Iryna Kozikava
Borovtsov & Salei Legal Services

Inna Leus
Ministry of Justice

Yulya Liashenko
Vlasova Mikhel & Partners

Alexander Ließem
BNT Legal & Tax

Valery Lovtsov
Lovtsov Klochko & Partners

Natalya Mahanek
Grant Thornton

Sergei Makarchuk
CHSH Cerha Hempel Spiegelfeld Hlawati

Sergey Mashonsky
Arzinger & Partners International Law Firm

Yuliya Matsiuk
Arzinger & Partners International Law Firm

Aleksandr Mironichenko
Ministry of Economy

Valentina Neizvestnaya
RSM Bel Audit

Sergey Odintsov
Schneider Group

Elena Orda
National Bank of the Republic of Belarus

Ekaterina Pedo
Revera Consulting Group

Dzina Pinchuk
PwC Belarus

Victor Pleonkin
National Bank of the Republic of Belarus

Tatyana Pozdneeva
Vlasova Mikhel & Partners

Pavel Pravdikov
JurZnak Law Firm LLC

Raman Ramanau
Minsk Cable (Electrical) Network

Aleksey Reneyskiy
FBK-Bel LLC - member of PKF

Olga Rybakovskaya
Ministry of Energy

Illia Salei
Borovtsov & Salei Legal Services

Vassili I. Salei
Borovtsov & Salei Legal Services

Elena Sapego
Stepanovski, Papakul and Partners Ltd.

Marianna Schimanowitsch
Rödl & Partner, Belarus

Dmitriy Igorevich Semenkevich
Ministry of Architecture and Construction

Vadzim Senkin
Minsk Cable (Electrical) Network

Liubov Sergeevna Boris
Goellner Spedition

Yuliya Shuba
Borovtsov & Salei Legal Services

Natalia Shulzhenko
Schneider Group

Valentina Silina
Grant Thornton

Anna Skorodulina
JurZnak Law Firm LLC

Maksim Slepitch
Arzinger & Partners International Law Firm

Vitaliy Sorokin
National Bank of the Republic of Belarus

Klim Stashevsky
Arzinger & Partners International Law Firm

Uladzimir Sukalo

Alla Sundukova
Ministry of Taxes and Duties

Elena Svirid
Software Applied System Institute

Dmitry Tihno
PwC Belarus

Nikita Tolkanitsa
CHSH Cerha Hempel Spiegelfeld Hlawati

Andrey Tolochko
Revera Consulting Group

Elizaveta Trakhalina
Arzinger & Partners International Law Firm

Nikita Nikolayevich Trosko
Vlasova Mikhel & Partners

Dennis Turovets
Egorov Pugisnky Afanasiev and Partners (EPA&P)

Alena Usenia
Arzinger & Partners International Law Firm

Irina Veremeichuk
Verkhovodko & Partners LLC

Igor Verkhovodko
Verkhovodko & Partners LLC

Dmitry Viltovsky
Arzinger & Partners International Law Firm

Ekaterina Zabello
Vlasova Mikhel & Partners

Vadzim Zakreuski
Ministry of Energy

Olga Zdobnova
Vlasova Mikhel & Partners

Dmitri Zikratski
Peterka & Partners

Ekaterina Zheltonoga
Verdict Law Office

Maksim Zhukov
Sysouev, Bondar, Khrapoutski SBH Law Office

Maksim Znak
Borovtsov & Salei Legal Services

BELGIUM

SPF Finances | Documentation Patrimoniale | Inspection Générale

Hubert André-Dumont
McGuireWoods LLP

Jan Bael
Notariskantoor Jan Bael - Ilse De Brauwere

Herlinde Baert
Notariskantoor Jan Bael - Ilse De Brauwere

Quentin Baudrihaye
NautaDutilh

Dennis Beyers
PwC Belgium

Thierry Bosly
White & Case

Hakim Boularbah
Liedekerke Wolters Waelbroeck Kirkpatrick, member of Lex Mundi

Stan Brijs
NautaDutilh

Laura Charlier
Stibbe

Karolien Coenen
PwC Belgium

Adriaan Dauwe
Altius

Martijn De Meulemeester
PwC Belgium

Kris De Schutter
Loyens & Loeff

Didier De Vliegher
NautaDutilh

Vincent Dieudonné
Sibelga

Eric Dirix
Cour de Cassation

Camille Dümm
National Bank of Belgium

Jürgen Egger
LAGA

Danaïs Fol
Loyens & Loeff

Alex Franchimont
Crowell & Moring

Alain François
Eubelius Attorneys

Pierre-Yves Gillet
Cabinet d'Architecte

Conny Grenson
Eubelius Attorneys

Sophie Jacmain
NautaDutilh

An Jacobs
Liedekerke Wolters Waelbroeck Kirkpatrick, member of Lex Mundi

Evelien Jamaels
Crowell & Moring

Stéphanie Kervyn de Meerendré
Deminor International SCRL

Laurent Lantonnois
White & Case

Marianne Laruelle
Conseil International du Notariat Belge

Stephan Legein
Federal Public Service Finance

Axel Maeterlinck
Simont Braun

Allan Magerotte
Eubelius Attorneys

Philippe Massart
Sibelga

Pascale Moreau
PwC Belgium

Sabrina Otten
PwC Belgium

Leo Peeters
Peeters Advocaten-Avocats

Emmanuel Plasschaert
Crowell & Moring

Johan Poedts
Sibelga

Julie Salteur
NautaDutilh

Eric Schmitz
PwC Belgium

Axel Smits
PwC Belgium

Frédéric Souchon
PwC Belgium

Timothy Speelman
McGuireWoods LLP

Bernard Thuysbaert
Deminor International SCRL

Hans Van Bavel
Stibbe

Jan Van Celst
DLA Piper UK LLP

Gill Van Damme
PwC Belgium

Bart Van Rossum
B.T.V.

Grégory Vandenbussche
Aren Architects and Engineers SPRL

Robert Vermetten
Transport & Project Logistics

Ivan Verougstraete
Cour de Cassation

Bart Volders
Stibbe

Katrien Vorlat
Stibbe

Bram Vuylsteke
Notary Bram Vuylsteke

Tom Wallyn
PwC Belgium

Luc Weyts
Conseil International du Notariat Belge

Dirk Wouters
Wouters, Van Merode & Co. Bedrijfsrevisoren BVBA - member of Russell Bedford International

BELIZE

W.H. Courtenay & Co.

Emil Arguelles
Arguelles & Company LLC

Jenny Armstrong
Belize Companies and Corporate Affairs Registry

Harry Bradley
Harry Bradley Customs Brokerage

Herbert Bradley
Herbert Bradley Custom House Brokers

Christopher Coye
Courtenay Coye LLP

Ana Maria Espat
Strukture Architects

Fred Lumor
Fred Lumor & Co.

Tania Moody
Barrow & Williams

Aldo Reyes
Reyes Retreage LLP

Wilfred Rhaburn
W. Rhaburn Consulting

Patricia Rodriguez
Belize Companies and Corporate Affairs Registry

Giacomo Sanchez
Grant Thornton LLP

Llewelyn Usher
International Financial Services Commission

Saidi Vaccaro
Arguelles & Company LLC

Darlene Margaret Vernon
Vernon & Lochan

Lisa Zayden
Horwath Belize LLP

BENIN

Agbantou Law Firm

BCEAO

Cabinet d'Huissier de Justice

Société Nationale des Eaux du Bénin

Eric Fadhil Adamon
Notaire Adamon

Abdou Kabir Adoumbou
Cabinet Maître Sakariyaou Nouro-Guiwa

Désiré H. Aïhou
FADESP/UAC

Rodolphe Kadoukpe Akoto
CBCT Sarl

Sybel Akuesson
Fiduciaire Conseil et Assistance (FCA)

Rafikou Agnila Alabi
Cabinet Maître Rafikou Alabi

Aum Rockas Amoussouvi
Cabinet Rafikou A. Alabi

Zachari Baba Body
Cabinet SPA Baba Body, Quenum et Sambaou

Charles Badou
Cabinet d'Avocats Charles Badou

Is-Dine Bouraima
Agence de Promotion des Importations et des Exportations (APIEX)

Sètondji Pierre Codjia
Cabinet d'Avocats Charles Badou

Johannès Dagnon
Groupe Helios Afrique

Bonaventure Dansou
Africa Handling and Logistics

Magloire Daoudou
Cabinet des Experts Associés - CEA SARL

Nadine Dossou Sakponou
Cabinet Robert M. Dossou

Rodrigue Dossou-Togbe

Franck Wilfried Fakeye
Agence de Promotion des Importations et des Exportations (APIEX)

Djakaridja Fofana
PwC Côte d'Ivoire

Nadege Honvo
Etude de Nadege Honvo

Cyprien Hounsounou
Société Béninoise d'Energie Electrique

Noel Kelembho
SDV Logistics

William Kodjoh-Kpakpassou
Tribunal de Première Instance de Cotonou

Monique Kotchofa
Etude Maître Kotchofa

Alain René Kpetehoto
Cabinet Artech

Adeline Messou Couassi-Blé
PwC Côte d'Ivoire

Sakariyaou Nourou-Guiwa
Cabinet Maître Sakariyaou Nouro-Guiwa

Arouna Oloulade
Société Béninoise d'Energie Electrique

Alexandrine Falilatou Saizonou-Bedie
Cabinet d'Avocats Alexandrine F. Saizonou-Bedie

Adegbindin Saliou
Cabinet des Experts Associés - CEA SARL

Hermann Senou
Entreprise Générale De Construction Mackho

Nelly Tagnon Gambor
Fiduciaire Conseil et Assistance (FCA)

Brice Allassane Tamba
La Mairie de Cotonou - Service des Affaires Domaniales

Dominique Taty
PwC Côte d'Ivoire

Gilles Togan
Maersk Benin SA

Fousséni Traoré
PwC Côte d'Ivoire

Adjété Fabrice O. Wilson
Cabinet Maître Rafikou Alabi

Victorin Yehouenou
Cabinet des Experts Associés - CEA SARL

BHUTAN

Bhutan Power Corporation Ltd.

Royal Monetary Authority of Bhutan

Sonam Chophel
Credit Information Bureau of Bhutan

Mukesh Dave
Druk PNB Bank

Bhim Dhungel
Zorig Consultancy Pvt Ltd.

Tashi Dorji
Judiciary of Bhutan

N.B. Gurung
Global Logistics

Tashi Penjor
Ministry of Economic Affairs

Dorji Phuntsho
Royal Securities Exchange of Bhutan Ltd.

Shrowan Pradhan
Niche Financial Services

Tenzin Rabgay
Royal Securities Exchange of Bhutan Ltd.

Jamyang Sherab
Garuda Legal Services

Karma Tshewang
Visit Asia

Kinley Wangdi
Credit Information Bureau of Bhutan Ltd.

Karma Yeshey
Ministry of Economic Affairs

BOLIVIA

Prime Technologies

PwC Bolivia

Fernando Aguirre
Bufete Aguirre Soc. Civ.

Carolina Aguirre Urioste
Bufete Aguirre Soc. Civ.

René Alcázar
Autoridad de Supervisión del Sistema Financiero

Richard Cesar Alcócer Garnica
Autoridad de Fiscalización y Control Social de Electricidad (AE)

Christian Amestegui
Asesores Legales CP

Daniela Aragones Cortez
Sanjinés & Asociados - Abogados

Johnny Arteaga Chavez
Dirección General de Tierras de Santa Cruz

Pedro Asturizaga
Autoridad de Supervisión del Sistema Financiero

Sergio Avendaño
Rigoberto Paredes & Associates

Rigoberto Paredes Ayllón
Rigoberto Paredes & Associates

Leonardo Azurduy Saunero
Quintanilla, Soria & Nishizawa Soc. Civ.

Raúl A. Baldivia
Baldivia Unzaga & Asociados

Mauricio Becerra de la Roca Donoso
Becerra de la Roca Donoso & Asociados

Hugo Berthin
BDO Berthin Amengual & Asociados

Andrea Bollmann-Duarte
Salazar Salazar & Asociados

Estefani Cabrera
Wbc Abogados SRL

Walter B. Calla Cardenas
Colegio Departamental de Arquitectos de La Paz

Grisset Carrasco
C.R. & F. Rojas Abogados, member of Lex Mundi

Ibling Chavarria
Becerra de la Roca Donoso & Asociados

Asdruval Columba Jofre
AC Consultores Legales

Carla De la Barra
Rigoberto Paredes & Associates

Jose Luis Diaz Romero
Servicios Generales en Electricidad y Construcción (SGEC)

Ivar Fernando Zabaleta Rioja
Sociedad de Ingenieros de Bolivia

Alejandra Guevara
Guevara & Gutiérrez SC

Primitivo Gutiérrez
Guevara & Gutiérrez SC

Jorge Luis Inchauste
Guevara & Gutiérrez SC

Jaime M. Jiménez Alvarez
Colegio de Ingenieros Electricistas y Electrónicos La Paz

Rodrigo Jimenez-Cusicanqui
Salazar Salazar & Asociados

Paola Justiniano Arias
Sanjinés & Asociados - Abogados

Julio César Landívar Castro
Guevara & Gutiérrez SC

Omar Martinez Velasquez
Autoridad de Fiscalización y Control Social de Electricidad (AE)

Alejandra Bernal Mercado
C.R. & F. Rojas Abogados, member of Lex Mundi

Ariel Morales Vasquez
C.R. & F. Rojas Abogados, member of Lex Mundi

Ana Carola Muñoz Añez
Indacochea & Asociados

Rocio Plata
Rigoberto Paredes & Associates

Oscar Antonio Plaza Ponte Sosa
Buro de Información Infocenter SA

Gerardo Quelca
Autoridad de Supervisión del Sistema Financiero

Joaquin Rodriguez
Autoridad de Fiscalización y Control Social de Electricidad (AE)

Patricio Rojas
C.R. & F. Rojas Abogados, member of Lex Mundi

Mariela Rojas de Hamel
Buro de Información Infocenter SA

Sergio Salazar-Arce
Salazar Salazar & Asociados

Sergio Salazar-Machicado
Salazar Salazar & Asociados

Sandra Salinas
C.R. & F. Rojas Abogados, member of Lex Mundi

Raúl Sanjinés Elizagoyen
Sanjinés & Asociados - Abogados

Claudio Sejas
Beraters

Rosa Serrano
Beraters

Jorge N. Serrate
Würth Bedoya Costa du Rels Abogados

Diego Tamayo
Würth Bedoya Costa du Rels Abogados

A. Mauricio Torrico Galindo
Quintanilla, Soria & Nishizawa Soc. Civ.

Ramiro Velasco
Colegio de Ingenieros Electricistas y Electrónicos La Paz

Vanessa Villarroel
Baldivia Unzaga & Asociados

BOSNIA AND HERZEGOVINA

Tajana Batlak
Marić & Co. Law Firm

Jesenko Behlilovic
Advokatsko društvo Spaho d.o.o. Sarajevo

Jasmin Bešo
FERK (Regulatory Commission for Electricity in the Federation of Bosnia and Herzegovina)

Bojana Bošnjak-London
Marić & Co. Law Firm

Mubera Brkovic
PwC Bosnia and Herzegovina

Femil Čurt
Law Office Femil Curt - part of DLA Piper Group

Naida Čustović
Law Office Custovic in association with Wolf Theiss

Mia Delić
Spaho Law office

Đorđe Dimitrijevic

Stevan Dimitrijevic

Višnja Dizdarević
Marić & Co. Law Firm

Amina Djugum
Marić & Co. Law Firm

Feđa Dupovac
Advokatsko društvo Spaho d.o.o. Sarajevo

Samra Hadžović
Wolf Theiss

Zijad Hasović
Komora Revizora FBiH

Lajla Hastor
Wolf Theiss

Ahmet Hukic
FERK (Regulatory Commission for Electricity in the Federation of Bosnia and Herzegovina)

Amir Husić
Lagermax AED Bosna i Herzegowina d.o.o.

Nusmir Huskić
Huskic Law Office

Emir Ibisevic
Deloitte Advisory Services d.o.o.

Arela Jusufbasić-Goloman
Lawyers Office Tkalcic-Dulic, Prebanic, Rizvic & Jusufbasic-Goloman

Admir Jusufbegovic
Advokatsko društvo Spaho d.o.o. Sarajevo

Harun Kahvedžić
University in Zenica

Selma Kahvedžić

Nedžada Kapidžić
Notary

Ilma Kasumagić
Law Office Custovic in association with Wolf Theiss

Sejda Kruščica-Fejzić
JP Elektroprivreda BiH Podružnica Elektrodistribucija Sarajevo

Emil Kučković
LRC Credit Bureau

Saša Lemez
Central Bank of Bosnia and Herzegovina

Muamer Mahmutovic
Chamber of Commerce of Canton Sarajevo - Legal Department

Branko Marić
Marić & Co. Law Firm

Davorin Marinković

Adnan Mataradžija
MERFI d.o.o.

Mejrima Memić-Drino
Public Employment Office of Zenica-Doboj Canton

Kristijan Meršpah
LRC Credit Bureau

Emir Naimkadić
JP Elektroprivreda BiH Podružnica Elektrodistribucija Sarajevo

Monija Nogulic
FERK (Regulatory Commission for Electricity in the Federation of Bosnia and Herzegovina)

Mehmed Omeragić
Čovjek i Prostor

Lejla Popara

Olodar Prebanić
Lawyers Office Tkalcic-Dulic, Prebanic, Rizvic & Jusufbasic-Goloman

Đorđe Racković
Central Bank of Bosnia and Herzegovina

Predrag Radovanović
Marić & Co. Law Firm

Branka Rajicic
PricewaterhouseCoopers Consulting d.o.o.

Nedzida Salihović-Whalen
CMS Reich-Rohrwig Hainz d.o.o.

Hasib Salkić
Jump Logistics d.o.o.

Lana Sarajlic

Adnan Sarajlić
Law Office Durakovic in association with Wolf Theiss

Jasmin Saric
Law Office Šarić in cooperation with Wolf Theiss

Arjana Selimić
JP Elektroprivreda BiH Podružnica Elektrodistribucija Sarajevo

Nihad Sijerčić

Ivona Soce
FERK (Regulatory Commission for Electricity in the Federation of Bosnia and Herzegovina)

Mehmed Spaho
Advokatsko društvo Spaho d.o.o. Sarajevo

Bojana Tkalčić-Djulić
Lawyers Office Tkalcic-Dulic, Prebanic, Rizvic & Jusufbasic-Goloman

Edin Zametica
DERK (State Electricity Regulatory Commission)

BOTSWANA

Botswana Unified Revenue Service (BURS)

Piyush Sharma Attorneys

TransUnion ITC (Pty) Ltd.

John Carr-Hartley
Armstrongs Attorneys

Alice Chiusiwa
Luke & Associates

One Damane
Modimo & Associates

Nigel Dixon-Warren
KPMG

Edward W. Fasholé-Luke II
Luke & Associates

Vasie Hager
PwC Botswana

Julius Mwaniki Kanja
Chibanda, Makgalemele & Co.

Queen Letshabo
Luke & Associates

Bokani Machinya
Collins Newman & Co.

City Mafa
Tectura International Botswana

Spokes Makabo
Botswana Power Corporation

Mercia Bonzo Makgalemele
Chibanda, Makgalemele & Co.

Jonathan Maphepa
Gaborone City Council

Kgaotsang Matthews
Moribame Matthews

Finola McMahon
Osei-Ofei Swabi & Co.

Rebecca M. Mgadla
Botswana Power Corporation

Neo Thelma Moatlhodi
Lawyer

Abel Walter Modimo
Modimo & Associates

Justice Moilwa
Zismo Engineering (Pty.) Ltd.

Mmatshipi Motsepe
Manica Africa Pty. Ltd.

Robert Mpabanga
TransUnion Botswana (Pty) Ltd.

Walter Mushi
Collins Newman & Co.

Godfrey N. Nthomiwa
Administration of Justice - High Court of Botswana

Benjamin Olebile
Zero Design Consulting Engineers Ltd.

Kwadwo Osei-Ofei
Osei-Ofei Swabi & Co.

Butler Phirie
PwC Botswana

Jacob Raleru
Botswana Power Corporation

Moemedi J. Tafa
Armstrongs Attorneys

Nilusha Weeraratne
PwC Botswana

BRAZIL

STIL - Sociedade Técnica de Instalações Ltda

Eduardo Abrantes
Souza, Cescon, Barrieu & Flesch Advogados

Marina Agueda
De Luca, Derenusson, Schuttoff e Azevedo Advogados

Antônio Aires
Demarest Advogados

Cleusa Almeida
Lefosse Advogados

Pedro Almeida
Souza, Cescon, Barrieu & Flesch Advogados

Guilherme Almeida de Oliveira
Vella Pugliese Buosi Guidoni

Maria Lúcia Almeida Prado e Silva
Demarest Advogados

Pedro Almeida Sampaio Lima
Vella Pugliese Buosi Guidoni

Franklin Alves de Oliveira Gomes Filho
Lobo & De Rizzo Advogados

Ivana Amorim de Coelho Bomfim
Machado, Meyer, Sendacz e Opice Advogados

Isabela Amorim Lobo
Machado, Meyer, Sendacz e Opice Advogados

Edinilson Apolinário
PwC Brazil

Gianvito Ardito
Pinheiro Neto Advogados

Amanda Arêas
Souza, Cescon, Barrieu & Flesch Advogados

Matheus Azevedo Bastos de Oliveira
Demarest Advogados

Josef Azulay
Barbosa, Müssnich & Aragão Advogados

Bruno Balduccini
Pinheiro Neto Advogados

Armando Balteiro
Vitor Costa Advogados

Rafael Baptista Baleroni
Souza, Cescon, Barrieu & Flesch Advogados

Priscyla Barbosa
Veirano Advogados

Marcus Phelipe Barbosa de Souza
Gasparini, De Cresci e Nogueira de Lima Advogados

Matheus Barcelos
Barbosa, Müssnich & Aragão Advogados

Fernanda Bastos
Souza, Cescon, Barrieu & Flesch Advogados

Leonardo Bastos Carvalho
Letech Engenharia

Júlio Henrique Batista
Guerra e Batista Advogados

Gilberto Belleza
Belleza & Batalha C. Do Lago Arquitetos Associados

David Benoliel
Noronha Advogados

Marcello Bernardes
Pinheiro Neto Advogados

Camila Biral Vieira da Cunha Martins
Demarest Advogados

Amir Bocayuva Cunha
Barbosa, Müssnich & Aragão Advogados

Joana Bontempo
Pinheiro Neto Advogados

Adriano Borges
De Vivo, Whitaker e Castro Advogados

Pedro Pio Borges
Machado, Meyer, Sendacz e Opice Advogados

Carlos Braga
Souza, Cescon, Barrieu & Flesch Advogados

Natalia Brasil Correa da Silva

Sergio Bronstein
Veirano Advogados

João Henrique Brum
Dominges E. Pinho Contadores

Marcus Brumano
Demarest Advogados

Ana Flávia Buck
Pinheiro Guimarães Advogados

Frederico Buosi
Vella Pugliese Buosi Guidoni

Fernanda Camarinha
Souza, Cescon, Barrieu & Flesch Advogados

Raíssa Campelo
Pinheiro Neto Advogados

Renato Canizares
Demarest Advogados

Luiz Henrique Capeli
Brazilian Electricity Regulatory Agency (ANEEL)

Paula Carlini
De Luca, Derenusson, Schuttoff e Azevedo Advogados

Angela Carvalho
Souza, Cescon, Barrieu & Flesch Advogados

David Carvalho
Kraft Advogados Associados

Marcos Carvalho
Lefosse Advogados

Thiago Carvalho Stob
Noronha Advogados

Mariana Castro
De Luca, Derenusson, Schuttoff e Azevedo Advogados

Roberto Castro
Machado, Meyer, Sendacz e Opice Advogados

Eduardo Chaves
Rayes & Fagundes Advogados

Ricardo E. Vieira Coelho
Pinheiro Neto Advogados

Roberta Coelho de Souza Batalha
Demarest Advogados

Vivian Coelho dos Santos Breder
Ulhôa Canto, Rezende e Guerra-Advogados

Jarbas Contin
PwC Brazil

Caroline Cordeiro
Costa e Tavares Paes Sociedade de Advogados

Luiz Felipe Cordeiro
Chediak, Lopes da Costa, Cristofaro, Menezes Côrtes, Rennó e Aragão Advogados

Marcel Cordeiro
PwC Brazil

Frederico Costa
Macedo & Costa Avaliações e Consultoria Técnica Ltda

Pedro Costa
Barbosa, Müssnich & Aragão Advogados

Bruno Henrique Coutinho de Aguiar
Rayes & Fagundes Advogados

Maria Cibele Crepaldi Affonso dos Santos
Costa e Tavares Paes Sociedade de Advogados

Juliana Cristina Ramos de Carvalho
Souza, Cescon, Barrieu & Flesch Advogados

Camilla Cunha
Barbosa, Müssnich & Aragão Advogados

Nathalia Cunha
Ernst & Young Serviços Tributários SS

Gabriel da Câmara de Queiroz
Demarest Advogados

Carlos da Costa e Silva Filho
Vieira, Rezende, Barbosa e Guerreiro Advogados

Gisela da Silva Freire
Porto Advogados

Adriana Daiuto
Demarest Advogados

João Luis Ribeiro de Almeida
Demarest Advogados

Ana Beatriz de Almeida Lobo
Veirano Advogados

Rodrigo de Castro
Veirano Advogados

Aldo de Cresci Neto
Gasparini, De Cresci e Nogueira de Lima Advogados

João Claudio De Luca Junior
De Luca, Derenusson, Schuttoff e Azevedo Advogados

Pedro Ivo de Menezes Cavalcante
Noronha Advogados

Beatriz Gross Bueno de Moraes Gomes de Sá
De Vivo, Whitaker e Castro Advogados

Dennis Christofer de Paula Silva
Companhia Docas do Estado de São Paulo

Daniela de Pontes Andrade
Lobo & De Rizzo Advogados

Gabriela Dell Agnolo de Carvalho
Zeigler e Mendonça de Barros Sociedade de Advogados (ZMB)

Eduardo Depassier
Loeser e Portela Advogados

Claudia Derenusson Riedel
De Luca, Derenusson, Schuttoff e Azevedo Advogados

Heloisa Bonciani Nader di Cunto
Duarte Garcia, Caselli Guimarães e Terra Advogados

Renata Dias
Souza, Cescon, Barrieu & Flesch Advogados

Rodrigo Yves Dias
Pinheiro Neto Advogados

Antonio Luiz Diniz
Diniz Instalações Elétricas e Hidráulicas Ltda

Wagner Douglas Dockhorn

José Ricardo dos Santos Luz Júnior
Duarte Garcia, Caselli Guimarães e Terra Advogados

Brigida Melo e Cruz Gama Filho
Pinheiro Neto Advogados

Marcelo Elias
Pinheiro Guimarães Advogados

João Paulo F.A. Fagundes
Rayes & Fagundes Advogados

Fabio Falkenburger
Machado, Meyer, Sendacz e Opice Advogados

Thomas Benes Felsberg
Felsberg Advogados

Iara Ferfoglia Gomes Dias Vilardi
Machado, Meyer, Sendacz e Opice Advogados

Alexsander Fernandes de Andrade
Duarte Garcia, Caselli Guimarães e Terra Advogados

João Guilherme Ferreira
Noronha Advogados

Marcelo Ferreira
Ernst & Young Serviços Tributários SS

Marilia Ferreira de Miranda
Tabeliã de Notas e Protesto de Santa Branca/SP

Gabriella Ferreira do Nascimento

Tatiane Ferreti
Lefosse Advogados

Guilherme Filardi
De Luca, Derenusson, Schuttoff e Azevedo Advogados

Silvia Rajsfeld Fiszman

Gabriel Fiuza
Chediak, Lopes da Costa, Cristofaro, Menezes Côrtes, Rennó e Aragão Advogados

Paulo Roberto Fogarolli Filho
Duarte Garcia, Caselli Guimarães e Terra Advogados

Leandro Amorim C. Fonseca
Costa e Tavares Paes Sociedade de Advogados

Alessandra Fonseca de Morais
Pinheiro Neto Advogados

Julian Fonseca Peña Chediak
Chediak, Lopes da Costa, Cristofaro, Menezes Côrtes, Rennó e Aragão Advogados

Renato G.R. Maggio
Machado, Meyer, Sendacz e Opice Advogados

Rafael Gagliardi
Demarest Advogados

Rodrigo Garcia da Fonseca
Fonseca e Salles Lima Advogados Associados

João Genesca
NCM Serviços Aduaneiros Ltda

Rafaella Gentil Gervaerd
Chediak, Lopes da Costa, Cristofaro, Menezes Côrtes, Rennó e Aragão Advogados

Murilo Germiniani
Machado, Meyer, Sendacz e Opice Advogados

Luiz Marcelo Gois
Barbosa, Müssnich & Aragão Advogados

Rodrigo Gomes Maia
Noronha Advogados

Diógenes Gonçalves
Pinheiro Neto Advogados

Renata Gonçalves
Halliburton Produtos Ltda

Maria Eduarda Goston Tisi Ferraz
Machado, Meyer, Sendacz e Opice Advogados

Gustavo Guedes
Pinheiro Guimarães Advogados

Eduardo Ferraz Guerra
Guerra e Batista Advogados

António Carlos Guidoni Filho
Vella Pugliese Buosi Guidoni

Ubiratan Pereira Guimarães
Colegio Notarial do Brasil-Conselho Federal

Bruno Habib Negreiros Barbosa
Veirano Advogados

Felipe Hanszmann
Vieira, Rezende, Barbosa e Guerreiro Advogados

Alexandre Herlin
Chediak, Lopes da Costa, Cristofaro, Menezes Côrtes, Rennó e Aragão Advogados

Luis Hiar
Lefosse Advogados

Jaili Isabel Santos Quinta Cunha
Pinheiro Guimarães Advogados

Ilie Jardim
Vieira, Rezende, Barbosa e Guerreiro Advogados

Rogério Jorge
AES Eletropaulo

Breno Kingma
Vieira, Rezende, Barbosa e Guerreiro Advogados

Dan Kraft
Kraft Advogados Associados

Everaldo Lacerda
Cartorio Maritimo

José Paulo Lago Alves Pequeno
Noronha Advogados

Daniel Lago Rodrigues
Registro de Imóveis de Taboão da Serra

Thomás Lampster
Pinheiro Neto Advogados

Juliano Lazzarini Moretti
Lazzarini Moretti Advogados

José Augusto Leal
Castro, Barros, Sobral, Gomes Advogados

Ana Flavia Leandro
Lazzarini Moretti Advogados

Alexandre Leite
Souza, Cescon, Barrieu & Flesch Advogados

Rodrigo Leite Moreira
Vieira, Rezende, Barbosa e Guerreiro Advogados

Alexandre Leite Ribeiro do Valle
VM&L Sociedade de Advogados

Karina Lerner
Barbosa, Müssnich & Aragão Advogados

Paloma Valeria Lima Martins
Machado, Meyer, Sendacz e Opice Advogados

Maury Lobo de Athayde
Chaves, Gelman, Machado, Gilberto e Barboza

Fernando Loeser
Loeser e Portela Advogados

Marcelo Lopes
Veirano Advogados

Maria Emilia Lopes
Ernst & Young Assessoria Empresarial Ltda.

Tiago Lopes
Souza, Cescon, Barrieu & Flesch Advogados

José Andrés Lopes da Costa Cruz
Chediak, Lopes da Costa, Cristofaro, Menezes Côrtes, Rennó e Aragão Advogados

Zora Lyra
Vieira, Rezende, Barbosa e Guerreiro Advogados

Marina Maccabelli
Demarest Advogados

Henrique Macedo
Macedo & Costa Avaliações e Consultoria Técnica Ltda

Pedro Maciel
Lefosse Advogados

Lucilena Madaleno
Ernst & Young Serviços Tributários SS

Alceu Maitino Junior
Companhia Docas do Estado de São Paulo

José Guilherme do Nascimento Malheiro
Souza, Cescon, Barrieu & Flesch Advogados

Estêvão Mallet
Mallet e Advogados Associados

Camila Mansur Haddad O. Santos
Lazzarini Moretti Advogados

Stephanie Manzi Lopes Schiavinato
Souza, Cescon, Barrieu & Flesch Advogados

Glaucia Mara Coelho
Machado, Meyer, Sendacz e Opice Advogados

Johnatan Maranhao
Pinheiro Neto Advogados

Juliana Marteli
Loeser e Portela Advogados

Stefania Martignago
De Luca, Derenusson, Schuttoff e Azevedo Advogados

Aldo Martinez
Souza, Cescon, Barrieu & Flesch Advogados

Vinicius Martins
Souza, Cescon, Barrieu & Flesch Advogados

Renata Martins de Oliveira
Machado, Meyer, Sendacz e Opice Advogados

Roberta R. Matheus
Lefosse Advogados

Eduardo Augusto Mattar
Pinheiro Guimarães Advogados

Gustavo Mattos
Vella Pugliese Buosi Guidoni

Marcelo Mattos
Veirano Advogados

Felipe Oliveira Mavignier
Gasparini, De Cresci e Nogueira de Lima Advogados

Thiago Medaglia
Felsberg Advogados

Davi Medina Vilela
Vieira, Rezende, Barbosa e Guerreiro Advogados

Aloysio Meirelles de Miranda
Ulhôa Canto, Rezende e Guerra-Advogados

Camila Mendes Vianna Cardoso
Kincaid | Mendes Vianna Advogados

Marianne Mendes Webber
Souza, Cescon, Barrieu & Flesch Advogados

Mônica Missaka
Noronha Advogados

Maria Eduarda Moog Rodrigues da Cunha
Castro, Barros, Sobral, Gomes Advogados

Renata M. Moreira Lima
Lazzarini Moretti Advogados

Gustavo Morel
Veirano Advogados

Vladimir Mucury Cardoso
Chediak, Lopes da Costa, Cristofaro, Menezes Côrtes, Rennó e Aragão Advogados

Ian Muniz
Veirano Advogados

Ana Carolina Musa
Vieira, Rezende, Barbosa e Guerreiro Advogados

Cássio S. Namur
Souza, Cescon, Barrieu & Flesch Advogados

Jorge Nemr
Leite, Tosto e Barros

Flavio Nicoletti Siqueira
STTAS

Walter Nimir
Zeigler e Mendonça de Barros Sociedade de Advogados (ZMB)

Sergio Niskier

Flavio Nunes

Michael O'Connor
Guerra e Batista Advogados

Daniel Oliveira
Souza, Cescon, Barrieu & Flesch Advogados

Evany Oliveira
PwC Brazil

Lidia Amalia Oliveira Ferranti
VM&L Sociedade de Advogados

Eduardo Ono Terashima
Demarest Advogados

Gyedre Palma Carneiro de Oliveira
Souza, Cescon, Barrieu & Flesch Advogados

Luis Filipe Pedro

Rogério Rabelo Peixoto
Banco Central do Brasil

Gabrielle Pelegrini
Vieira, Rezende, Barbosa e Guerreiro Advogados

Nivio Perez dos Santos
New-Link Com. Ext. Ltda

Leila Pigozzi Alves
De Luca, Derenusson, Schuttoff e Azevedo Advogados

Antonio Claudio Pinto da Fonseca
Construtora MG Ltda

Nelson Pires
Neltek Elétrica

Cássia Pizzotti
Demarest Advogados

Raphael Polito
Rayes & Fagundes Advogados

Renato Poltronieri
Demarest Advogados

Durval Araulo Portela Filho
PwC Brazil

Marcos Prado
Souza, Cescon, Barrieu & Flesch Advogados

Antonio Celso Pugliese
Vella Pugliese Buosi Guidoni

Marcelo Pupo
Felsberg Advogados

João Ramos
Souza, Cescon, Barrieu & Flesch Advogados

Carlos Alberto Ramos de Vasconcelos
Demarest Advogados

Ronaldo Rayes
Rayes & Fagundes Advogados

Gabriella Reao
Ulhôa Canto, Rezende e Guerra-Advogados

Marília Rennó
Chediak, Lopes da Costa, Cristofaro, Menezes Côrtes, Rennó e Aragão Advogados

Bruna Rey
Veirano Advogados

Elisa Rezende
Veirano Advogados

Eliane Ribeiro Gago
Duarte Garcia, Caselli Guimarães e Terra Advogados

Laura Ribeiro Vissotto
1° Cartório de Notas de São José dos Campos

Luis Fernando Riskalla
Leite, Tosto e Barros Advogados

Beatriz Roditi Lilenbaum
Noronha Advogados

Carolina Rodrigues
Machado, Meyer, Sendacz e Opice Advogados

Mariana Rodrigues
Souza, Cescon, Barrieu & Flesch Advogados

Viviane Rodrigues
Souza, Cescon, Barrieu & Flesch Advogados

Vitor Rogério da Costa
Vitor Costa Advogados

Suzanna Romero
Vieira, Rezende, Barbosa e Guerreiro Advogados

José Luiz Rossi
Serasa S.A.

Lia Roston
Rayes & Fagundes Advogados

Luis Augusto Roux Azevedo
De Luca, Derenusson, Schuttoff e Azevedo Advogados

Marcelo Saciotto
Rayes & Fagundes Advogados

Leandro Santos
Atos Soluções Técnicas

Thiago Santos Barroca
Noronha Advogados

Priscilla Saraiva
Ulhôa Canto, Rezende e Guerra-Advogados

Carolina Guerra Sarti
Costa e Tavares Paes Sociedade de Advogados

Anelise Maria Jircik Sasson
AES Eletropaulo

Julia Schulz Rotenberg
Demarest Advogados

Sabine Schuttoff
De Luca, Derenusson, Schuttoff e Azevedo Advogados

Lucas Seabra
Machado, Meyer, Sendacz e Opice Advogados

Fernando Semerdjian
Lobo & De Rizzo Advogados

Erik Sernik
Vella Pugliese Buosi Guidoni

Rafael Setoguti Julio Pereira
Gasparini, De Cresci e Nogueira de Lima Advogados

Donizetti Antonio Silva
DAS Consultoria

Sydney Simonaggio
AES Eletropaulo

Michel Siqueira Batista
Vieira, Rezende, Barbosa e Guerreiro Advogados

Isaque Soares Ribeiro
Colegio Notarial do Brasil-Conselho Federal

Livia Sousa Borges Leal
Demarest Advogados

Beatriz Souza
Souza, Cescon, Barrieu & Flesch Advogados

Guilherme Spinacé
Demarest Advogados

Walter Stuber
Walter Stuber Consultoria Jurídica

Daniel Szyfman
Machado, Meyer, Sendacz e Opice Advogados

Marcos Tabatschnic
PwC Brazil

Rodrigo Takano
Machado, Meyer, Sendacz e Opice Advogados

Bruno Tanus Job e Meira
Souza, Cescon, Barrieu & Flesch Advogados

Celina Teixeira
18° Oficio de Notas

Rodrigo Teixeira
Lobo & De Rizzo Advogados

Maurício Teixeira dos Santos
Souza, Cescon, Barrieu & Flesch Advogados

Milena Tesser
Rayes & Fagundes Advogados

Carlos Augusto Texeira da Silva

Gisele Trindade
Vella Pugliese Buosi Guidoni

Oswaldo Cesar Trunci de Oliveira
Machado, Meyer, Sendacz e Opice Advogados

Suslei Tufaniuk
AES Eletropaulo

Bruno Valente
PwC Brazil

Luiz Fernando Valente De Paiva
Pinheiro Neto Advogados

Guilherme Vaz
Pinheiro Guimarães Advogados

Ronaldo C. Veirano
Veirano Advogados

Anna Carolina Venturini
Pinheiro Neto Advogados

Ademilson Viana
Demarest Advogados

Marcelo Viegas
Mar & Mar Engenharia

Ana Cecilia Viegas Madasi
Pinheiro Neto Advogados

Eric Visini
Felsberg Advogados

Rafael Vitelli Depieri
1° Cartório de Notas de São José dos Campos

José Carlos Wahle
Veirano Advogados

Eduardo Guimarães Wanderley
Veirano Advogados

Thiago Wscieklica
Souza, Cescon, Barrieu & Flesch Advogados

Karin Yamauti Hatanaka
Souza, Cescon, Barrieu & Flesch Advogados

Natalia Yazbek
Veirano Advogados

BRUNEI DARUSSALAM

C H Williams Talhar & Wong Sdn Bhd

CCW Partnership

Eco Bumi Arkitek

Ledgerplus Services

Penggerak, Prime Minister's Office

Zainon Abang
Lands Department, Ministry of Development

Rena Azlina Abd Aziz
Ministry of Finance

Nur Shahreena Abdullah
Tabung Amanah Pekerja

Khairul Bariah Ahmad
Royal Customs and Excise Department

Erma Ali Rahman
Registry of Companies & Business Names

Najibah Aziz
Royal Customs and Excise Department

Khalid Bin HJ Awg Sirat
Kha Arkitek

Mahri Bin Hj Latif
Gemilang Latif Associates

HJ Abd Ghani Bin HJ Mohamed
A.G.A-Abdul Ghani Arkitek

Siti Norzainah Binti Azharan
Autoriti Monetari Brunei Darussalam

Jonathan Cheok
Cheok Advocates & Solicitors

Hajah Norajimah Haji Aji
Department of Labor, Ministry of Home Affairs

Mohammad Faizal Haji Ali
Brunei Methanol Company

Amal Hayati Haji Suhaili
Tabung Amanah Pekerja

Khalid Halim
Royal Customs and Excise Department

Hj Abdullah Hj Ahmad
Abdullah Ahmad Architects

Norizzah Hazirah Husin
Department of Labor, Ministry of Home Affairs

H. Jamin
Belait Shipping Co. (B) Sdn Bhd

Mohammed Roaizan bin Haji Johari
Autoriti Monetari Brunei Darussalam

Awangku Mohd Fikry Hardinie bin Pengiran Kassim
Prime Minister's Office

Zuleana Kassim
Lee Corporatehouse Associates

Farah Kong
Autoriti Monetari Brunei Darussalam

Cynthia Kong Bit Min
WKA & Associates

Susan Law
D'Sunlit Sdn Bhd

Kin Chee Lee
Lee Corporatehouse Associates

Simon Leong
KR Kamarulzaman & Associates

Muhammad Billy Lim Abdul Aziz
Arkitek Rekajaya

Will Meikle
Arkitek Ibrahim

Hajah Naimah Ali
Registry of Companies & Business Names

Harold Ng
CCW Partnership

Ahmad Norhayati
Sepakat Setia Perunding Engineering Consultant

Awangku Aziz Pengiran Ali Hassan
Energy and Industry Department

Amin Nuddin Mat Saruddin
Belait Shipping Co. (B) Sdn Bhd

Wong Shu Ah
BMS Engineering & Partners Sdn Bhd

Shran Singh
Glamco Aviation SDN

Karthigeyan Srinivasan
Autoriti Monetari Brunei Darussalam

Shazali Sulaiman
KPMG

Aidah Suleiman
Autoriti Monetari Brunei Darussalam

Wario Tacbad
Arkitek Haza

Bernard Tan Thiam Swee

Ting Tiu Pheng
Arkitek Ting

Cecilia Wong
Tricor (B) Sdn Bhd

Johnny Wong
BMS Engineering & Partners Sdn Bhd

Lucy Wong
Lucy Wong & Associates

Mahmoud Syaheer Yusoff
Tabung Amanah Pekerja

Zulina Zainal Abidin
Royal Customs and Excise Department

BULGARIA

Bulgarian National Bank

Svetlin Adrianov
Penkov, Markov & Partners

Leni Andonova
Schoenherr

Stefan Angelov
V Consulting Bulgaria

Rusalena Angelova
Djingov, Gouginski, Kyutchukov & Velichkov

Ina Bankovska
Kinkin & Partners

Ganka Belcheva
Belcheva & Karadjova LLP

Svilena Bogdantchova
Orbit

Marina Borisova
Kinkin & Partners

Christopher Christov
Penev LLP

Ralitza Damyanova
Delchev & Partners

Maria Danailova
Danailova, Todorov and Partners Law Firm

Emil Delchev
Delchev & Partners

Kostadinka Deleva
Gugushev & Partners

Valeria Dieva
Kalaidjiev & Georgiev

Irina Dilkinska
Penev LLP

George Dimitrov
Dimitrov, Petrov & Co.

Tzvetelina Dimitrova
Georgiev, Todorov & Co.

Nataliya Dimova
CEZ Distribution Bulgaria AD, member of CEZ Group

Ina Dobriyanova
CEZ Distribution Bulgaria AD, member of CEZ Group

Vasilena Goranova
Penkov, Markov & Partners

Ralitsa Gougleva
Djingov, Gouginski, Kyutchukov & Velichkov

Kristina Gouneva
Dobrev & Lyutskanov

Katerina Gramatikova
Dobrev & Lyutskanov

Hristian Gueorguiev
Dinova Rusev & Partners

Stefan Gugushev
Gugushev & Partners

Nadia Hadjov
Spasov & Bratanov Lawyers' Partnership

Vassil Hadjov
Spasov & Bratanov Lawyers' Partnership

Yassen Hristev
Kinkin & Partners

Hristina Hristova
DHL Express Bulgaria

Velyana Hristova
Penkov, Markov & Partners

Krasimira Ignatova
PwC Bulgaria

Iliya Iliev
Primorska Audit Company - member of Russell Bedford International

Ginka Iskrova
PwC Bulgaria

Vesela Kabatliyska
Dinova Rusev & Partners

Angel Kalaidjiev
Kalaidjiev & Georgiev

Vladi Kalinov
Sofia Municipality - Town Hall

Niya Kehayova
CEZ Distribution Bulgaria AD, member of CEZ Group

Stoina Kirazova
Penev LLP

Hristina Kirilova
Kambourov & Partners

Violeta Kirova
Boyanov & Co.

Donko Kolev
Address Real Estate JSCo

Ilya Komarevski
Tsvetkova Bebov Komarevski

Yavor Kostov
Arsov, Nachev, Ganeva

Yordan Kostov
Legalex Law Office

Zisis Kotsias
Orbit

Svetlin Krastanov
PwC Bulgaria

Tsvetan Krumov
Schoenherr

Stephan Kyutchukov
Djingov, Gouginski, Kyutchukov & Velichkov

Nina Lazarova
Registry Agency of Bulgaria

Ivan Linev
Spasov & Bratanov Lawyers' Partnership

Todor Manev
Dobrev & Lyutskanov

Ivan Marinov
Delchev & Partners

Dimitrinka Metodieva
Gugushev & Partners

Slavi Mikinski
Legalex Law Office

Yordanka Mravkova
Registry Agency of Bulgaria

Vladimir Natchev
Arsov, Nachev, Ganeva

Yordan Naydenov
Boyanov & Co.

Alexander Nikolov
Orbit

Elitsa Nikolova-Dimitrova
Orbit

Maria Pashalieva
Penkov, Markov & Partners

Mariya Pendeva
Georgiev, Todorov & Co.

Sergey Penev
Penev LLP

Ilian Petkov
ISPDD

Vladimir Popov
SANORA

Teodora Popova
Penev LLP

Bozkho Poryazov
Delchev & Partners

Maria Pramatarova
Sofia Municipality - Town Hall

Ina Raikova
Spasov & Bratanov Lawyers' Partnership

Konstantin Rizov
Gyurov & Rizov Law Office

Milen Rusev
Dinova Rusev & Partners

Aneta Sarafova
Danailova, Todorov and Partners Law Firm

Kalina Savova
Penkov, Markov & Partners

Boiko Sekiranov
Sofia Municipality - Town Hall

Gergana Shinikova
Kinkin & Partners

Vanya Shubelieva
Danailova, Todorov and Partners Law Firm

Georgi Slanchev
Dokovska, Atanasov & Partners Law Firm

Dimitar Slavchev
Penkov, Markov & Partners

Julian Spassov
McGregor & Partners

Krum Stanchev
ELIA Plc.

Teodor Stefanov
RUTEX

Nina Stoeva
Legalex Law Office

Tsvetelina Stoilova-Valkanova
Kinkin & Partners

Roman Stoyanov
Penkov, Markov & Partners

Vessela Tcherneva-Yankova
V Consulting Bulgaria

Yordan Terziev
Arsov, Nachev, Ganeva

Alexandrina Terziyska
Gugushev & Partners

Kaloyan Todorov
Danailova, Todorov and Partners Law Firm

Svilen Todorov
Todorov & Doykova Law Firm

Lyubomira Todorova
Kinkin & Partners

Georgi Tsonchev
Schoenherr

Irina Tsvetkova
PwC Bulgaria

Georgi Tzvetkov
Djingov, Gouginski, Kyutchukov & Velichkov

Miroslav Varnaliev
Unimasters Logistics Plc.

Siyana Veleva
Kinkin & Partners

Mariana Velichkova
Tsvetkova Bebov Komarevski

Nedyalka Vylcheva
Delchev & Partners

Monika Yaneva
Kalaidjiev & Georgiev

Iliyana Zhoteva
Registry Agency of Bulgaria

BURKINA FASO

BCEAO

Cabinet Kam et Some

GIFA Sarl

John W. Ffooks & Co., member of Bowman Gilfillan Africa Group

Pierre Abadie
Cabinet Pierre Abadie

Fortune Bicaba
Etude de Maître Fortune Bicaba

Dieudonne Bonkoungou
SCPA Themis-B

Roland Patrick Bouda
SCPA Consilium

Ilboudo Clovice
Maison de l'Entreprise

Bobson Coulibaly
Cabinet d'Avocats Barthélemy Kere

Denis Dawende
Office Notarial Me Jean Celestin Zoure

Sylvie Dembelé
SCPA Consilium

Paul Gnaleko
PwC Côte d'Ivoire

Pascal Hema
SONABEL

Brice Marie Valentin Ilboudo
Maison de l'Entreprise du Burkina Faso

Willermine Laurence Edwige Kabore
Cabinet Pierre Abadie

Olé Alain Kam
Dembs Associates Sarl

Sansan Césaire Kambou
Cabinet d'Architecture AGORA Burkina

Alain Gilbert Koala
Ordre des Architectes du Burkina

Vincent Armand Kobiané
ARDI – Architectes Conseils

Moumouny Kopiho
Cabinet d'Avocats Moumouny Kopiho

Armand Kpoda
SCPA Themis-B

Colette Lefebvre
Inspection du Travail

Abraham Liadan
PwC Côte d'Ivoire

Adeline Messou Couassi-Blé
PwC Côte d'Ivoire

Ali Neya
Cabinet d'Avocats Ali Neya

Sayouba Neya
Cabinet d'Avocats Ali Neya

Karim Ouedraogo
Ministere des Finances et du Budget

Madina Ouedraogo
Bureau d'Assistance à la Construction (BAC) SARL

Oumarou Ouedraogo
Cabinet Ouedraogo

Ousmane Honore Ouedraogo
Maison de l'Entreprise du Burkina Faso

Roger Omer Ouédraogo
Association Professionnelle des Transitaires & Commissionnaires en Douane Agrées

Assana Pare
Cabinet d'Avocats Moumouny Kopiho

Jean Georges Sanogoh
Movis Burkina Faso SA

Hermann Lambert Sanon
Groupe Hage

Emile Sawadogo
SONABEL

Moussa Ousmane Sawadogo
Direction Générale des Impôts

Dominique Taty
PwC Côte d'Ivoire

Alassane Tiemtore
Autorité de Régulation du Sous-secteur de l'Electricité (ARSE)

Fousséni Traoré
PwC Côte d'Ivoire

Yacouba Traoré
Commune de Ouagadougou

Bouba Yaguibou
SCPA Yaguibou & Associés

Raïssa Yo
Cabinet d'Avocats Ali Neya

Albert Zoma
Cabinet d'Avocats Ali Neya

BURUNDI

Agence de Promotion des Investissements

Banque de la République du Burundi

Ministère des Finances

OBR

PSD

Gahama Alain
FINABANK SA

Jean Marie Barambona
Université du Burundi

Cyprien Bigirimana
Ministère de la Justice

Remy Bigirimana
Guichet Unique de Burundi

Joseph Gitonyotsi
Joseph Gitonyotsi

Emmanuel Hakizimana
Cabinet d'Avocats-Conseils

Ange-Dorine Irakoze
Rubeya & Co Advocates

Arnold Issa
Freight in Time Rwanda

Jean-Marie Karitunze
Bujumbura Associated and Professional Advocates (BAPA)

Gloria Kubwimana
Kiyuku & Co. Advocates

Augustin Mabushi
A & JN Mabushi Cabinet d'Avocats

René-Claude Madebari
Legal Solution Chambers

Rodrigue Majambere
BNM & Co. Advocates

Stanislas Makoroka
Université du Burundi

Anatole Nahayo
Université du Burundi

Horace Ncutiyumuheto
Ncuti Law Firm & Consultancy

Charles Nihangaza
Consultant Charles Nihangaza

Mireille Niyongabo
Rubeya & Co. Advocates

Prosper Niyoyankana
Cabinet d'Avocat Prosper Niyoyankana

Janvier Nsengiyumva
REGIDESO

Jocelyne Ntibangana
Cabinet de Maître Ntibangana

Happy Ntwari
Legal Solution Chambers

Gilbert L.P. Nyatanyi
ENSafrica Burundi Limited

Déogratias Nzemba
Avocat à la Cour

Willy Rubeya
Rubeya & Co. Advocates

Fabien Segatwa
Etude Me Segatwa

Jérôme Vejuru
Transport and Trading Company, Agent of DSV Global Transport and Logistics

CABO VERDE

SAMP - Sociedades de Advogados

Tiago Albuquerque Dias
Deloitte

José Manuel Andrade
Núcleo Operacional da Sociedade de Informação

Luís Filipe Bernardo
Deloitte

Constantino Cabral
MTCV Cabo Verde

Nádia Cardoso
BTOC - Cabo Verde

Vasco Carvalho Oliveira Ramos
ENGIC Engenheiros Associados Lda

João Manuel Chantre
Câmara de Comércio Portugal Cabo Verde

Eurico Correia Monteiro
Advogados & Jurisconsultos

Geraldo da Cruz Almeida
Advogados e Consultores Associados

Dúnia Delgado
PwC Portugal

Jorge Lima Delgado Lopes
Núcleo Operacional da Sociedade de Informação

Vanda Evoara
Advogados & Jurisconsultos

Sofia Fonseca
Advogados & Jurisconsultos

Tomás Garcia Vasconcelos
Deloitte

António Gonçalves
CV Lexis Advogados

Teresa Livramento Monteiro
Dulce Lopes, Solange Lisboa Ramos, Teresa Livramento Monteiro-Sociedade de Advogados

Ana Cristina Lopes Semedo
Banco de Cabo Verde

Julio Martins Junior
Raposo Bernardo & Associados

Fernando Aguiar Monteiro
Advogados Associados

João Pereira
FPS

Eurico Pinto Monteiro
Advogados & Jurisconsultos

José Manuel Pinto Monteiro
Advogados & Jurisconsultos

Angela Rodrigues
Tiba Group

José Rui de Sena
Agência de Despacho Aduaneiro Ferreira e Sena Lda

Leida Santos
Advogados & Jurisconsultos

Tito Lívio Santos Oliveira Ramos
ENGIC Engenheiros Associados Lda

Arnaldo Silva
Arnaldo Silva & Associados

Armindo Sousa
FPS

José Spinola
FPS

Salvador Varela
Advocacia Consultoria Jurídica

Liza Helena Vaz
PwC Portugal

Leendert Verschoor
PwC Portugal

CAMBODIA

Credit Bureau (Cambodia) Co. Ltd.

Trois S (Cambodge) Logistics Solution

Borany Bon
Arbitration Council Foundation

Lam Bui
Maersk Line Cambodia

Seng Bun Huy
MAR Associates

Buth Bunsayha
Acleda Bank Plc.

Sreypeou Chaing
CSP & Associates Law Firm

Huot Channa
Koki Engineering Co., Ltd.

Chanthearith Chea
VDB Loi

Phanin Cheam
Municipality of Phnom Penh Bureau of Urban Affairs

Rithy Chey
BNG Legal

Heng Chhay
R&T Sok & Heng Law Office

Chea Chhaynora
HBS Law

Ouk Chittra
Electricité du Cambodge (EDC)

Om Dararith
Ministry of Commerce

Kun Dirang
Ministry of Commerce

Pha Eng Veng
General Department of Customs and Excise of Cambodia

Bradley J. Gordon
Edenbridge Asia

Viren Hak
DFDL Mekong (Cambodia) Co., Ltd.

Darwin Hem
BNG Legal

Sreysros Heng
PwC Cambodia

Charles Ngoc-Khoi Hoang
HBS Law

Sotheary Hout
R&T Sok & Heng Law Office

Seng Vuoch Hun
Asia Cambodia Law Group

Sujeet Karkala
BNG Legal

Sophorne Kheang
DFDL Mekong (Cambodia) Co., Ltd.

Taingpor Kheng
Arbitration Council Foundation

Robert M. King
Ernst & Young

Sieng Komira
Secured Transactions Filing Office

Alex Larkin
DFDL Mekong (Cambodia) Co., Ltd.

Vicheka Lay
Asia Century Law Office

Sok Leaksmy
General Department of Customs and Excise of Cambodia

Kang Leap
HML Law Firm & Consultants

Chanmakara Ly
DFDL Mekong (Cambodia) Co., Ltd.

Tayseng Ly
HBS Law

Nimmith Men
Arbitration Council Foundation

Tom Mizukoshi
Forval Cambodia

Eng Monyrith
HML Law Firm & Consultants

Koy Neam
KN Legal Consulting

Sovannith Nget
P&A Asia Law Firm

Vandeth Nguon
PwC Cambodia

Daniel Noonan

Clint O'Connell
DFDL Mekong (Cambodia) Co., Ltd.

Heng Pagnawat
P&A Asia Law Firm

Navy Pat
Arbitration Council Foundation

Piseth Path
BNG Legal

Keo Penta
General Department of Taxation

Ham Phea
The Glory Legal

Ham Pheamarina
The Glory Legal

Porchhay Phoung
Sciaroni & Associates

Blake Theo Porter
R&T Sok & Heng Law Office

Robert Porter
VDB Loi

Allen Prak
P&A Asia Law Firm

Vann Puthipol
General Department of Taxation

Borapyn Py
DFDL Mekong (Cambodia) Co., Ltd.

Sok Rattana
General Department of Customs and Excise of Cambodia

Paul Redfern
Red Furnesse Co. Ltd.

Chris Robinson
DFDL Mekong (Cambodia) Co., Ltd.

Kunthy Roy
KN Legal Consulting

Somarith Sam
Electricité du Cambodge (EDC)

Mar Samborana
MAR Associates

Kiri San
R&T Sok & Heng Law Office

Sokla San
P&A Asia Law Firm

Vathana Sar
DFDL Mekong (Cambodia) Co., Ltd.

Kem Saroeung
Secured Transactions Filing Office

Piseth Sea
PAT Professional Limited

Neak Seakirin
Neak Law Office

Prum Sear
Komnit Design

Dave L. Seibert
Edenbridge Asia

Leung Seng
KCP Cambodia Ltd.

Leung Seng
PYT & Associates

Vannak Seng
Municipality of Phnom Penh Bureau of Urban Affairs

Patrick Smith
Sciaroni & Associates

San Socheata
HBS Law Firm & Consultants

Lor Sok
Sok Xing & Hwang

Phany Sok
HBS Law

Sin Sokanha
Bun & Associates

Sum Sokhamphou

Sim Sokheng
Ministry of Commerce

Pheang Sokvirak
PwC Cambodia

Suon Sopha
Ministry of Land Management, Urban Planning and Construction

H.E. Sok Sopheak
Ministry of Commerce

Leng Sopheap
General Department of Customs and Excise of Cambodia

Tiv Sophonnora
R&T Sok & Heng Law Office

Samnangvathana Sor
DFDL Mekong (Cambodia) Co., Ltd.

Bou Sothearith
General Department of Customs and Excise of Cambodia

Tep Sotheavy
The FLAG Attorneys & Counselors at Law

Nika Sour
VDB Loi

Vannaroth Sovann
BNG Legal

Phin Sovath
Bun & Associates

Sochivy Suong
PAT Professional Limited

Chesda Teng
Arbitration Council Foundation

Mom Thana
Ministry of Commerce

Heng Thy
PwC Cambodia

Thavsothaly Tok
BNG Legal

Hem Tola
HR Inc. (Cambodia) Co., Ltd.

Reangsey Darith Touch
Ernst & Young

Vichan Nadeth Uy
R&T Sok & Heng Law Office

Bun Youdy
Bun & Associates

Potim Yun
VDB Loi

CAMEROON

Etude Me Etoke

Stanley Abane
The Abeng Law Firm

Armelle Silvana Abel
MOJUFISC Monde Juridique et Fiscal

Roland Abeng
The Abeng Law Firm

Tocke Adrien
DGI Cameroon (Direction Générale des Impots du Cameroun)

Oscar Alebga
The Abeng Law Firm

Rosine Pauline Amboa
MOJUFISC Monde Juridique et Fiscal

Abel Piskopanis Armelle Silvana
MOJUFISC Monde Juridique et Fiscal

Queenta Asibong
The Abeng Law Firm

Cyrano Atoka
Cabinet Francine Nyobe

Lolita Bakala Mpessa
SCPA Ngalle-Miano

Thomas Didier Remy Batoumbouck
CADIRE

Jean-Marie Bendégué
IG/MINDCAF

Pierre Bertin Simbafo
BICEC

Lilie Betsama Eloundou
Cabinet Francine Nyobe

Xavier Martial Biwoli Ayissi
Cabinet Francine Nyobe

Nah Christabel Achu
Barmi-Njoh Chambers

Paul Marie Djamen
Mobile Telephone Networks Cameroon (MTN)

Aurélien Djengue Kotte
Cabinet Ekobo

Joseph Djeuga
SOTRAFIC

Etienne Donfack
GIEA

Laurent Dongmo
Jing & Partners

Narcisse Ekome Essake
EKOME ESSAKE & Associés

Simon Ekotto Ndemba
Ville de Douala Communauté Urbaine de Douala

Ebot Elias Arrey
ARC Consultants Ltd.

Philippe Claude Elimbi Elokan

Marie Marceline Enganalim
Etude Me Enganalim Marceline

Etchu Epey Begona
Legal Power Law Firm

Joseph Evagle Dime
Conseil National du Crédit

Elvis Eyong
The Abeng Law Firm

Hyacinthe Clément Fansi Ngamou
SCP Ngassam Njike & Associes

Berlise Fimeni Djieya
Atanga Law Office

Isabelle Fomukong
Cabinet d'Avocats Fomukong

Georges Fopa
GIEA

Carine Danielle Fossey
MOJUFISC Monde Juridique et Fiscal

Philippe Fouda Fouda
BEAC Cameroon

Bertrand Gieangnitchoke
GIEA

Nicaise Ibohn
The Abeng Law Firm

Samuel Iyug Iyug
Groupement des Entreprises de Frêt et Messagerie du Cameroun (GEFMCAM)

Paul T. Jing
Jing & Partners

Thérese Joumessi
Atanga Law Office

Christian Kamdoum
PwC Cameroun

Denis Kengni
Transimex SA

Jean-Aime Kounga
The Abeng Law Firm

Merlin Arsene Kouogang
Société Quifeurou

Serge Madola

Tchande Magloire
PwC Cameroun

Augustin Yves Mbock Keked
CADIRE

Charles Melchior Moudouthe
Union de Consignataires et Armateurs du Cameroun

Danielle Moukouri
D. Moukouri & Partners

Arielle Christiane Marthe Mpeck
Atanga Law Office

Joan Landry Wilfried Mpeck
Atanga Law Office

Marie Agathe Ndeme
CADIRE

Bernard Ngaibe
The Abeng Law Firm

Ntah Charlote Ngara
Atanga Law Office

Virgile Ngassam Njiké
SCP Ngassam Njike & Associes

Dieu le Fit Nguiyan
Université de Douala

Urbain Nini Teunda
Cameroon Customs

Moliki Nitua Tabot
Legal Power Law Firm

Francine Nyobe
Cabinet Francine Nyobe

Jacob Oben
Jing & Partners

Ilias Poskipanis
MOJUFISC Monde Juridique et Fiscal

Paul-Gérard Pougoue

Olivier Priso
Ville de Douala Communauté Urbaine de Douala

Bolleri Pym
Université de Douala

Claude Simo
CL Audit et Consei

Linda Tatabod Amuteng

Hélène Florette Tchidjip Kapnang
Atanga Law Office

Emmanuel Tchiffo
Atanga Law Office

Pierre Morgant Tchuikwa
CADIRE

Nadine Tinen Tchadgoum
PricewaterhouseCoopers Tax & Legal SARL

Chrétien Toudjui
Afrique Audit Conseil Baker Tilly

Tamfu Ngarka Tristel Richard
Tamfu & Co. Law Firm

Bergerele Reine Tsafack Dongmo
MOJUFISC Monde Juridique et Fiscal

Tanwie Walson Emmanuel
UNICS PLC

Aghen Yannick Encho
Legal Power Law Firm

Philippe Zouna
PwC Cameroun

CANADA

Dineen Construction Corporation

TransUnion Canada

Jon A. Levin
Fasken Martineau DuMoulin LLP

Bekhzod Abdurazzakov
Borden Ladner Gervais LLP

David Bish
Torys LLP

Paul Boshyk
McMillan LLP

Richard Cantin
Nero Boutique Law Firm

John Craig
Fasken Martineau DuMoulin LLP

Rod Davidge
Osler, Hoskin & Harcourt LLP

Audrey Diamant
PwC Canada

Abe Dube
Amerinde Law Group

Esmat El-Bacha
PwC Canada

Michael Elder
Blake, Cassels & Graydon, member of Lex Mundi

Isabelle Foley
Corporations Canada

Paul Gasparatto
Ontario Energy Board

Attila Gaspardy
PwC Canada

Rachel April Giguère
McMillan LLP

Christopher Gillespsie
Gillespie-Munro Inc.

Yoine Goldstein
McMillan LLP

Talia Gordner
Blaney McMurtry, LLP

Mary Grozdanis
Fogler Rubinoff

Andrew Kent
McMillan LLP

Jordan Knowles
Blake, Cassels & Graydon, member of Lex Mundi

Joshua Kochath
Comage Container Lines

Adam Kurnik
PwC Canada

Catherine MacInnis
IBI Group Inc.

Alfred Page
Borden Ladner Gervais LLP

Meaghan Parry
Blake, Cassels & Graydon, member of Lex Mundi

Yonatan Petel
McMillan LLP

Martin Pinard
Corporations Canada

Zac Resnick
Blake, Cassels & Graydon, member of Lex Mundi

Gautam Rishi
PwC Canada

Jim Robson
Blake, Cassels & Graydon, member of Lex Mundi

Gaynor Roger
Shibley Righton LLP

Harris M. Rosen
Fogler Rubinoff

John Tobin
Torys LLP

Shane Todd
Fasken Martineau DuMoulin LLP

Sharon Vogel
Borden Ladner Gervais LLP

George Waggot
McMillan LLP

CENTRAL AFRICAN REPUBLIC

Guichet Unique de Formalités des Entreprises (GUFE)

Nirilala Antsa Andriantsoa
John W. Ffooks & Co., member of Bowman Gilfillan Africa Group

Jean Christophe Bakossa
L'Ordre Centrafricain des Architectes

Jean-Noël Bangue
Cour de Cassation de Bangui

Blaise Banguitoumba
ENERCA (Energie Centrafricaine)

Thierry Chaou
Sofia Credit

Maurice Dibert- Dollet
Ministère de la Justice

Emile Doraz-Serefessenet
Cabinet Notaire Doraz-Serefessenet

Jacques Eboule
SDV Logistics

Philippe Fouda Fouda
BEAC Cameroon

Cyr Gregbanda
Bamelec

Marious Guibaut Metongo
Bolloré Africa Logistics en République Centrafricaine

Laurent Hankoff
ENERCA (Energie Centrafricaine)

Théodore Lawson
Audit & Revision Comptable Cabinet Lawson & Associes

Jean Paul Maradas Nado
Ministère de l'Urbanisme

Serge Médard Missamou
Club OHADA République Centrafricaine

Richard Moulet
Sutter & Pearce (RCA) Ltd.

Jacob Ngaya
Ministère des Finances - Direction Générale des Impôts et des Domaines

Rigo-Beyah Parse
Cabinet Parse

Ghislain Samba Mokamanede
Bamelec

Bruno Sambia
Agence Centrafricaine pour la Formation Professionnelle et l'Emploi (A.C.F.P.E.)

Bandiba Max Symphorien
Club OHADA République Centrafricaine

CHAD

3ACE Commerce Energie et Etude

Ordre National des Architectes du Tchad

Dana Abdelkader Waya
Cabinet Notarial Bongoro

Abdelkerim Ahmat
Bolloré Logistics et Transport

Nirilala Antsa Andriantsoa
John W. Ffooks & Co., member of Bowman Gilfillan Africa Group

Théophile B. Bongoro
Cabinet Notarial Bongoro

Oscar d'Estaing Deffosso

Thomas Dingamgoto
Cabinet Thomas Dingamgoto

Philippe Fouda Fouda
BEAC Cameroon

Francis Kadjilembaye
Cabinet Thomas Dingamgoto

Prosper Kemayou
Transimex Tchad SA

Mahamat Kikigne

Abakar Adam Nassour
STMT (Groupe SNER)

Hayatte N'Djiaye
Profession Libérale

Guy Emmanuel Ngankam
PricewaterhouseCoopers Tax & Legal SARL

Abba Oumar Ngarbyo
Cabinet Notarial Bongoro

Issa Ngarmbassa
Etude Me Issa Ngar mbassa

Joseph Pagop Noupoué
Ernst & Young Juridique et Fiscal Tchad

Jean Bernard Padare
Cabinet Padare

Tchouafiene Pandare
Cabinet Notarial Bongoro

Anselme Patipéwé Njiakin
Ernst & Young Juridique et Fiscal Tchad

Claudia Randrianavory
John W. Ffooks & Co., member of Bowman Gilfillan Africa Group

Nastasja Schnorfeil-Pauthe

Nadine Tinen Tchadgoum
PricewaterhouseCoopers Tax & Legal SARL

Massiel Toudjoum Melyoel
Office Notarial

Masrangue Trahogra
Cabinet d'Avocats Associés

Sobdibé Zoua
Cabinet Sobdibé Zoua

CHILE

Boletín de Informaciones Comerciales

Leticia Acosta Aguirre
Redlines Group

Paula Aguilera
Urenda, Rencoret, Orrego y Dörr

Sergio Andreu
Colegio de Arquitectos de Chile

Jonathan Arendt
Albagli Zaliasnik Abogados

Jorge Arredondo
Albagli Zaliasnik Abogados

Luis Avello
PwC Chile

Angeles Barría
Philippi, Prietocarrizosa Ferrero DU & Uría

María José Bernal
Philippi, Prietocarrizosa Ferrero DU & Uría

Mario Bezanilla
Alcaíno Abogados

Rodrigo Cabrera Ortiz
Chilectra

Raimundo Camus Varas
Yrarrázaval, Ruiz-Tagle, Goldenberg, Lagos & Silva

Miguel Capo Valdes
Besalco SA

Héctor Carrasco
Superintendencia de Bancos y Instituciones Financieras Chile

Javier Carrasco
Nuñez Muñoz Verdugo & Cía Ltda Abogados

Isaac Cea
ICEA Proyectos e Instalaciones Electricas

Andrés Chirgwin
Chirgwin Larreta Peñafiel

Nury Clavería
Besalco SA

Manuel Concha Oyaneder
Colegio de Arquitectos de Chile

María Alejandra Corvalán
Yrarrázaval, Ruiz-Tagle, Goldenberg, Lagos & Silva

Gracia Curtze
Urenda, Rencoret, Orrego y Dörr

Andrés Dighero
Alessandri Abogados

Gloria Drogett
PwC Chile

Gonzalo Errázuriz
Urenda, Rencoret, Orrego y Dörr

Maira Esteban
Urenda, Rencoret, Orrego y Dörr

Peter Faille
Urenda, Rencoret, Orrego y Dörr

Raquel Frattini
Chirgwin Larreta Peñafiel

Cristobal Giogoux
Nuñez Muñoz Verdugo & Cía Ltda Abogados

Felipe González
Urenda, Rencoret, Orrego y Dörr

Maureen Grob
Guerrero, Olivos, Novoa & Errázuriz Abogados

Sofía Haupt
Alessandri Abogados

Cristian Hermansen Rebolledo
ACTIC Consultores

Jorge Hirmas
Albagli Zaliasnik Abogados

Daniela Hirsch
Albagli Zaliasnik Abogados

Javier Hurtado
Cámara Chilena de la Construcción

Fernando Jamarne
Alessandri Abogados

Rodrigo Jeria Selaive
Cariola Diez Perez-Cotapos & Cia

José Ignacio Jiménez
Guerrero, Olivos, Novoa & Errázuriz Abogados

Ignacio Larraín
Philippi, Prietocarrizosa Ferrero DU & Uría

Juan Ignacio León Lira
Reymond & Fleischmann Abogados

Jose Luis Letelier
Cariola Diez Perez-Cotapos & Cia

Nicole Lüer
Urenda, Rencoret, Orrego y Dörr

Nicolás Maillard
Maillard & Celis Abogados

Juan Pablo Matus
Cariola Diez Perez-Cotapos & Cia

Sebastian Melero
Philippi, Prietocarrizosa Ferrero DU & Uría

Nicolás Miranda Larraguibel
Alessandri Abogados

Rodrigo Muñoz
Nuñez Muñoz Verdugo & Cía Ltda Abogados

Fenanda Nash
Nuñez Muñoz Verdugo & Cía Ltda Abogados

Juan Pablo Navarrete
Carey y Cía Ltda

Sebastián Nieme
Urenda, Rencoret, Orrego y Dörr

Nicolás Ocampo
Carey y Cía Ltda

Alberto Oltra
DHL Global Forwarding

Sergio Orrego
Urenda, Rencoret, Orrego y Dörr

Gerardo Ovalle Mahns
Yrarrázaval, Ruiz-Tagle, Goldenberg, Lagos & Silva

Pablo Oyarce
Nuñez Muñoz Verdugo & Cía Ltda Abogados

Orlando Palominos
Morales, Besa & Cía. Ltda

Luis Parada Hoyl
Bahamondez, Alvarez & Zegers

Daniela Peña Fergadiott
Barros & Errázuriz

Andrés Pennycook Castro
Superintendencia de Insolvencia y Reemprendimiento

Alberto Pulido A.
Philippi, Prietocarrizosa Ferrero DU & Uría

Nina Radovic Fanta
Besalco SA

Gianfranco Raglianti
Carey y Cía Ltda

Felipe Rencoret
Urenda, Rencoret, Orrego y Dörr

Gonzalo Rencoret
Urenda, Rencoret, Orrego y Dörr

Alfonso Reymond Larrain
Reymond & Fleischmann Abogados

Ricardo Riesco
Philippi, Prietocarrizosa Ferrero DU & Uría

Constanza Rodriguez
Philippi, Prietocarrizosa Ferrero DU & Uría

Nelson Contador Rosales
Nelson Contador y Cia. Abogados

Alvaro Rosenblut
Albagli Zaliasnik Abogados

Bernardita Saez
Alessandri Abogados

Hugo Salinas
PwC Chile

Jaime Salinas
Philippi, Prietocarrizosa Ferrero DU & Uría

Andrés Sanfuentes
Philippi, Prietocarrizosa Ferrero DU & Uría

Martín Santa María O.
Guerrero, Olivos, Novoa & Errázuriz Abogados

Bernardita Schmidt
Urenda, Rencoret, Orrego y Dörr

Francisco Selamé
PwC Chile

Marcela Silva
Philippi, Prietocarrizosa Ferrero DU & Uría

Luis Fernando Silva Ibañez
Yrarrázaval, Ruiz-Tagle, Goldenberg, Lagos & Silva

Alan Smith
Smith y Cía

Consuelo Tarud
Urenda, Rencoret, Orrego y Dörr

Victor Tavera
Chilectra

Jorge Timmermann
Bahamondez, Alvarez & Zegers

Ricardo Tisi L.
Cariola Diez Perez-Cotapos & Cia

Carlos Torres
Redlines Group

Javier Ugarte Undurraga
Yrarrázaval, Ruiz-Tagle, Goldenberg, Lagos & Silva

Víctor Hugo Valenzuela Millán

Felipe Valle
Cariola Diez Perez-Cotapos & Cia

Nicolás Velasco Jenschke
Superintendencia de Insolvencia y Reemprendimiento

Santiago Verdugo
Urenda, Rencoret, Orrego y Dörr

Liliana Vergara
Colegio de Arquitectos de Chile

Javiera Vicuña
Urenda, Rencoret, Orrego y Dörr

Gonzalo Villazon
Nuñez Muñoz Verdugo & Cía Ltda Abogados

Kenneth Werner
Agencia de Aduana Jorge Vio y Cía Ltda

Sergio Yávar
Guerrero, Olivos, Novoa & Errázuriz Abogados

Arturo Yrarrázaval Covarrubias
Yrarrázaval, Ruiz-Tagle, Goldenberg, Lagos & Silva

Jean Paul Zalaquett
Chilectra

Matías Zegers
Bahamondez, Alvarez & Zegers

Barbara Zlatar Ayuso
Cariola Diez Perez-Cotapos & Cia

CHINA

King & Wood Mallesons Lawyers

Jacob Blacklock
Lehman, Lee & Xu

Russell Brown
LehmanBrown

Elliott Youchun Chen
JunZeJun Law Offices

Jie Chen
Jun He Law Office, member of Lex Mundi

Mingqing Chen
Jun He Law Office, member of Lex Mundi

Samuel Chen
BYC

Tao Chen
Jun He Law Office, member of Lex Mundi

Xinping Chen
Zhong Lun Law Firm

Michael Diaz Jr.
Diaz, Reus & Targ, LLP

Zhitong Ding
Credit Reference Center of People's Bank of China

Tina Dong
Lehman, Lee & Xu

Lijing Du
Jun He Law Office, member of Lex Mundi

Helen Feng
Angela Wang & Co.

Christopher Fung
Lehman, Lee & Xu

Shuai Gao
Aerospace Construction Company of China

Grace Geng
Zhong Lun Law Firm

Zichen Guo
Kunlun Law Firm

Huizhong Hu
Beijing Huanzhong & Partners

Sherry Hu
Hogan Lovells

Ziyan Huang
Jun He Law Office, member of Lex Mundi

Wilson Huo
Zhong Lun Law Firm

Shan Jin
King & Wood Mallesons Lawyers

Yiru Jin
Pudong Garments Import & Export Co. Ltd. Oie

Jiang Junlu
King & Wood Mallesons

Edward E. Lehman
Lehman, Lee & Xu

Jack Kai Lei
Kunlun Law Firm

Ian Lewis
Mayer Brown JSM

Audry Li
Zhong Lun Law Firm

Qing Li
Jun He Law Office, member of Lex Mundi

Ellen Liu
Mayer Brown JSM

Grace Liu
Russell Bedford Hua-Ander CPAs - member of Russell Bedford International

Jingjing Liu
Beijing Huanzhong & Partners

Ning Liu
Jun He Law Office, member of Lex Mundi

Sherry Liu
Noronha Advogados

Tony Liu
Kunlun Law Firm

Yanyan Liu
Kunlun Law Firm

Kuan Lu
Chance & Bridge Partners

Xiaomin Luo
Pengyuan Credit Services Co. Ltd.

Hongli Ma
Jun He Law Office, member of Lex Mundi

Jonathan Mok
Angela Wang & Co.

Matthew Mui
PwC China

Matthew Murphy
MMLC Group

Winnie Nie
Hogan Lovells

Lei Niu
Zhong Lun Law Firm

Peng Pan
King & Wood Mallesons

Giovanni Pisacane
GWA Greatway Advisory

Lori Qi
BYC

Long Rao
Jun He Law Office, member of Lex Mundi

Chen Rumeng
Fujian South Pharmaceutical Co. Ltd.

Tina Shi
Mayer Brown JSM

Peng Tan
Fangda Partners

John Thompson
Jones Lang LaSalle

Terence Tung
Mayer Brown JSM

Angela Wang
Angela Wang & Co.

Ariel Wang
Chance & Bridge Partners

Eileen Wang
Mayer Brown JSM

Guoqi Wang
Russell Bedford Hua-Ander CPAs - member of Russell Bedford International

Jinghua Wang
Jun He Law Office, member of Lex Mundi

Lihua Wang
Jun He Law Office, member of Lex Mundi

Thomas Wang
Shanghai Boss & Young

Xiaolei Wang
Credit Reference Center of People's Bank of China

Xuehua Wang
Beijing Huanzhong & Partners

Yu Wang
Lehman, Lee & Xu

Kent Woo
Guangda Law Firm

Vincent Wu
Mayer Brown JSM

Xiaohong Xiong
Pengyuan Credit Services Co. Ltd.

Di Xu
JunZeJun Law Offices

Sunny Xu
Lehman, Lee & Xu

Wenliang Xu
Sumavision

Qing (Christine) Yang
Kunlun Law Firm

Tiecheng Yang
Clifford Chance

Andy Yeo
Mayer Brown JSM

Nancy Yu
Mayer Brown JSM

Natalie Yu
Shanghai Li Yan Law Firm

Xia Yu
MMLC Group

Jianan Yuan
Jun He Law Office, member of Lex Mundi

Bonnie Zhang
Lehman, Lee & Xu

Sarah Zhang
Hogan Lovells

Xin Zhang
Global Law Office

George Zhao
King & Wood Mallesons

Xingjian Zhao
Diaz, Reus & Targ, LLP

Crys Zheng
Lehman, Lee & Xu

Fei Zheng
Jun He Law Office, member of Lex Mundi

Jianying Zheng
Jun He Law Office, member of Lex Mundi

Jiong Zhu

Ning Zhu
Chance & Bridge Partners

Simon Zhu
Simmons & Simmons

Roy Zou
Hogan Lovells

COLOMBIA

BIMBO

PwC Colombia

Enrique Alvarez
José Lloreda Camacho & Co.

Alexandra Arbeláez Cardona
Russell Bedford Colombia - member of Russell Bedford International

María Alejandra Arboleda
Posse Herrera Ruiz

Felipe Aristizabal
Nieto & Chalela

Patricia Arrázola-Bustillo
Gómez-Pinzón Zuleta Abogados SA

Cesar Barajas
Parra Rodríguez Abogados SAS

Luis Alfredo Barragán
Brigard & Urrutia, member of Lex Mundi

Aurora Barroso
Parra Rodríguez Abogados SAS

Claudia Benavides Galvis
Baker & McKenzie

Fernando Bermúdez Durana
Muñoz Tamayo & Asociados

Juan Pablo Bonilla
Posse Herrera Ruiz

Joe Ignacio Bonilla Gálvez
Muñoz Tamayo & Asociados

Jimmy Buenaventura
José Lloreda Camacho & Co.

Carolina Camacho
Posse Herrera Ruiz

Samuel Cano
José Lloreda Camacho & Co.

Darío Cárdenas
Cárdenas & Cárdenas

Natalia Caroprese
José Lloreda Camacho & Co.

Carlos Carvajal
José Lloreda Camacho & Co.

Luis Miguel Carvajal
Codensa SA ESP

Fernando Castañeda
Organización Corona

Alejandro Castilla
Parra Rodríguez Abogados SAS

Ernesto Jorge Clavijo Sierra
Curaduria Urbana 1

Juan Pablo Concha Delgado
Baker & McKenzie

Felipe Cuberos
Philippi Prietocarrizosa Ferrero DU & Uría

Lyana De Luca
Brigard & Urrutia, member of Lex Mundi

Juan Carlos Diaz
Genelec de Colombia SAS

Maria Fernanda Diaz Chacon
Baker & McKenzie

Maria Lucia Echandia
Posse Herrera Ruiz

Juan Camilo Fandiño-Bravo
Cárdenas & Cárdenas

Lina María Fernández
Parra Rodríguez Abogados SAS

Jairo Flechas
Genelec de Colombia SAS

Carlos Fradique-Méndez
Brigard & Urrutia, member of Lex Mundi

Luis Hernando Gallo Medina
Gallo Medina Abogados Asociados

Wilman Garzón
Codensa SA ESP

Julianna Giorgi
Posse Herrera Ruiz

Carlos Gómez Guzmán
Parra Rodríguez Abogados SAS

Sandra Liliana Gutiérrez
Russell Bedford Colombia - member of Russell Bedford International

Santiago Gutiérrez
José Lloreda Camacho & Co.

William Rene Gutierrez Oregon
Instituto Colombiano Agropecuario

Edwar Hernandez
Genelec de Colombia SAS

Susana Hidvegi
Brigard & Urrutia, member of Lex Mundi

Ana María Iregui
Philippi Prietocarrizosa Ferrero DU & Uría

Jhovanna Jiménez
Brigard & Urrutia, member of Lex Mundi

Juan Camilo Jiménez
Cárdenas & Cárdenas

Nubia Lamprea
Codensa SA ESP

Jorge Lara-Urbaneja
Arciniegas Lara Briceño Plana

Federico Lewin
Lewin & Wills Abogados

Alejandro Linares-Cantillo
Gómez-Pinzón Zuleta Abogados SA

William Marin
Productos Familia

Miguel Martinez
Genelec de Colombia SAS

Christoph Möller
Parra Rodríguez Abogados SAS

Luis Gabriel Morcillo-Méndez
Brigard & Urrutia, member of Lex Mundi

Francisco Javier Morón López
Parra Rodríguez Abogados SAS

Luis E. Nieto
Nieto & Chalela

Caterine Noriega Cardenas
Gestión Legal Colombia

Juan Sebastian Noriega Cardenas
Gestión Legal Colombia

Adriana Carolina Ospina Jiménez
Brigard & Urrutia, member of Lex Mundi

Juan Guillermo Otero Gonzalez
Baker & McKenzie

Juan Andres Palacios
Lewin & Wills Abogados

Alvaro Parra
Parra Rodríguez Abogados SAS

Santiago Parra Salazar
Parra Rodríguez Abogados SAS

Carlos Felipe Pinilla Acevedo
Pinilla González & Prieto Abogados

Estefanía Ponce Durán
Posse Herrera Ruiz

Carolina Posada
Posse Herrera Ruiz

Daniel Posse
Posse Herrera Ruiz

Natalia Eugenia Quijano Uribe
Codensa SA ESP

Santiago Renjifo Ortega
Confecamaras

Luisa Rico Sierra
Leyva Ontier

Andrés Rincón
Cárdenas & Cárdenas

Irma Isabel Rivera
Brigard & Urrutia, member of Lex Mundi

Luis Carlos Robayo Higuera
Russell Bedford Colombia - member of Russell Bedford International

Adrián Rodríguez
Lewin & Wills Abogados

Mauricio Rodriguez Gallego
Confecamaras

Bernardo Rodriguez Ossa
Parra Rodríguez Abogados SAS

Sonia Elizabeth Rojas Izaquita
Gallo Medina Abogados Asociados

Katherine Romero Hinestrosa
Parra Rodríguez Abogados SAS

Paula Samper Salazar
Gómez-Pinzón Zuleta Abogados SA

Diego Sastoque
Parra Rodríguez Abogados SAS

Cristina Stiefken
Lewin & Wills Abogados

Juan Reinaldo Suarez
Curaduria Urbana 1

Raúl Alberto Suárez Arcila
Suárez Arcila & Abogados Asociados

Diego Munoz Tamayo
Muñoz Tamayo & Asociados

Gustavo Tamayo Arango
José Lloreda Camacho & Co.

Olga Viviana Tapias
Russell Bedford Colombia - member of Russell Bedford International

Faunier David Toro Heredia
Codensa SA ESP

Jose Alejandro Torres
Posse Herrera Ruiz

Natalia Tovar Ibagos
Experian - Datacrédito

Juan Uribe-Holguin Borda
Parra Rodríguez Abogados SAS

Daniel Vargas Umaña
Experian - Datacrédito

Diana Vaughan
Lewin & Wills Abogados

Frank Velandia
Teclogic Ltda

Patricia Vergara-Gomez
Gómez-Pinzón Zuleta Abogados SA

Lilalba Vinasco
Instituto Colombiano Agropecuario

Alirio Virviescas
Notaría 41 de Bogotá

Adriana Zapata
Cavelier Abogados

Alberto Zuleta
Cárdenas & Cárdenas

Natalia Zuleta
Cárdenas & Cárdenas

COMOROS

Banque Centrale des Comores

Mohamed Abdallah Halifa
Groupe Hassanati Soilihi - Groupe Hasoil

Hilmy Aboudsaid
Comores Cargo International

Zainoudine Ahamada
Ministère de l'Économie et du Commerce

Bahassani Ahmed
Cabinet d'Avocat Bahassani

Aida Ahmed Yahaia
I2A Societe Immobiliere des Comores

Moissi Ali
Energie Comoros

Feissoili Ali Oubeidi
Cabinet Feissoili

Omar Said Allaoui
ECDI

Mouzaoui Amroine
Commission Nationale de Prévention et de Lutte contre la Corruption (CNPLC)

Said Ali Said Athouman
Union of the Chamber of Commerce

Youssoub Ibn Ismael Aticki
Barreau de Moroni

Daoud Saidali Toihiri
ANPI Invest in Comoros

Haroussi Idrissa
Tribunal de premiere instance de Moroni

Madiane Mohamed Issa
Cabinet d'Avocat Bahassani

Said Bacar Kaab
Préfecture Moroni

Faouzi Mohamed Lakj
Tribunal de Commerce Comoros

Mohamed Maoulida
Audit Conseil-International

Abdoulbastoi Moudjahidi
Cabinet d'Avocats Saïd Ibrahim

Farahati Moussa
Mouvement des Entrepreneurs Comoriens (MODEC)

Azad Mze
Cabinet d'Avocats Mze

Ibrahim A. Mzimba
Cabinet Mzimba Avocats

Halidi Ali Omar
Ministère de l'Économie et du Commerce

Marco Raymond

Salimou Yahaya
Tribunal de premiere instance de Moroni

CONGO, DEM. REP.

Albert-Blaise Akoka
Deloitte RDC

Salavatrice Bahindwa Bahati
Etude Kabinda - Cabinet d'Avocats

Boniface Baluti
Cabinet Ntoto

Nathalie Banza
SDV Logistics

Romain Battajon
Cabinet Battajon

Billy Batunzy
Cabinet Batunzy

Jean Timothée Bisimwa
Provincial Commission

Hugo Bolanshi
Yav & Associates

Deo Bukayafwa
MBM Conseil

Nicaise Chikuru Munyiogwarha
Chikuru & Associés

Siegfried Dibong
PwC Congo (Democratic Republic of)

Prosper Djuma Bilali
Cabinet Masamba

Holly Embonga Tomboli
Chikuru & Associés

Jose Engbanda Mananga
Guichet Unique de Creation d'Entreprise

Irénée Falanka
Cabinet Irénée Falanka

Safari Habibu
Cabinet d'Avocats

Amisi Herady
Guichet Unique de Creation d'Entreprise

Patou Ikoko Tangamu
Banque Centrale du Congo

Parfait-Didier Kabongo Mukadi
NTN & Partners SCRL

Cedrick Kala Konga
EGEC

Rene Kala Konga
EGEC

Vincent Kangulumba Mbambi
André & Vincent Avocats Associés

Benoit Kapila
SDV Logistics

Clément Mukendi Kashingi
Société Nationale d'Electricité (SNEL)

Gracia Kavumvula
Ministère des Affaires Foncières

Pixii Kazyumba
Cabinet Masamba

Dieu Donné Kfuma
Cabinet Khuma et Bekombe

Arly Khuty
Cabinet Emery Mukendi Wafwana & Associés

Dolores Sonia Kimpwene
Etude Kabinda - Cabinet d'Avocats

Baby Kitoko
Experts Freight - RDC

Marc Kongomayi Mulumba
Société Nationale d'Electricité (SNEL)

Phistian Kubangusu Makiese
Cabinet Masamba

Christ Kuty
Cabinet Emery Mukendi Wafwana & Associés

Fénelon Kyangaluka
Société de Techniques Spéciales (STS)

Jean-Marie Lepriya Molenge
Cabinet Ngaliema

Desiré Likolo
EGEC

Ilan Liongi Ilankaka
Cabinet Masamba

Jules Wemby Lofudu
Ministère de l'Enseignement Supérieur, Institut Supérieur d'Architecture et d'Urbanisme

Jean-Pierre Kevin Lofumbwa
Deloitte RDC

Francis Lugunda Lubamba
Cabinet Lukombe & Les Avocats

Carol Lutaladio
Direction Générale des Douanes et Accises

Brigitte Luyambuladio
EGEC

Aubin Mabanza
Klam & Partners Avocats

Béatrice Mabanza
Klam & Partners Avocats

Yves Madre
Deloitte RDC

Jimmy Mafamvula
Cabinet Emery Mukendi Wafwana & Associés

Robert Majambo
Yav & Associates

Andre Malangu Muabila
Cabinet Famille

Noel Mangala
Cabinet Certac

Serge Mangungu
DHL Global

Steve Manuana
Cabinet Emery Mukendi Wafwana & Associés

Rigobert Nzundu Mawunga
Emery Mukendi Wafwana & Associates

Aristide Mbayo Makyata
Direction Générale des Douanes et Accises

Gérard Mosolo
MBM Conseil

Christine Mpunga Tshim
Banque Centrale du Congo

Fabrice Muabila Mutamba
Cabinet Avocats Associes Andre et Vincent

Tarin Muhongo
PwC Congo (Democratic Republic of)

Céléstine Mukalay Kionde
Société Nationale d'Electricité (SNEL)

Emery Mukendi Wafwana
Cabinet Emery Mukendi Wafwana & Associés

Eliance Muloji Wa Mbuyi
Cabinet Ngaliema

Jacques Munday
Cabinet Ntoto

Yannick Muwawa
Banque Centrale du Congo

Jean-Pierre Muyaya
Emery Mukendi Wafwana & Associates

Philippe Mvita Kabasele
Banque Centrale du Congo

Jean-Paul Mvuni Malanda
Cabinet Ngaliema

Gabriel Mwepu Numbi
Direction Générale des Douanes et Accises

Nicaise Navanga
SDV Logistics

Eric Ngabo Kalesh
NTN & Partners SCRL

Emmanuel Ngalamulume Kalala
NTN & Partners SCRL

Placide Nkala Basadilua
Guichet Unique de Creation d'Entreprise

Bernard Nsimba Bilandu
Cabinet Masamba

Marcel Ntoto
Cabinet Ntoto

Jean-Bienvenu Ntwali Byavulwa
Etude Kabinda - Cabinet d'Avocats

Marlyne Nzailu
PwC Congo (Democratic Republic of)

Léon Nzimbi
PwC Congo (Democratic Republic of)

Destin Pelete
La Generale de Services la Fontaine

Gérard Pointe
KPMG

Freddy Mulamba Senene
Mulamba & Associates Law Firm

Christie Madudu Sulubika
Cabinet Madudu Sulubika

Moise Tangala
Cabinet Irénée Falanka

Mamie Gisèle Tshibalabala Banga

Christian Tshibanda Mulunda
NTN & Partners SCRL

Antoine Tshibuabua Mbuyi
Société Nationale d'Electricité (SNEL)

Seraphin Umba
Yav & Associates

Ngaliema Zephyrin
Cabinet Ngaliema

CONGO, REP.

Patrice Bazolo
PwC

Prosper Bizitou
PwC

Alexis Debi
PwC

Mathias Essereke
Cabinet d'Avocats Mathias Essereke

Philippe Fouda Fouda
BEAC Cameroon

Joe Pépin Foundoux
PwC

Gaston Gapo
Atelier d'Architecture et d'Urbanisme

Dieudonné Patrice Kitoto

Moïse Kokolo
PwC

Jay Makoundou
PwC

Ado Patricia Marlene Matissa
Cabinet Notarial Matissa

Benic Mbanwie Sarr
PwC

Françoise Mbongo
Cabinet Mbongo

Fortuné Mbouma Peya
Congo Terminal

Firmin Moukengue
Cabinet Moukengue

Prospèr K. Nzengue
Ministère de la Construction, de l'Urbanisme et Habitat

Aimé Pambou
Bolloré Africa Logistics Congo

Andre François Quenum
Cabinet Andre Francois Quenum

Sariaka Randrianarisoa
John W. Ffooks & Co., member of Bowman Gilfillan Africa Group

Jean Jacques Youlou
Ministère de la Construction, de l'Urbanisme et Habitat

Alpha Zinga Moko
PwC

COSTA RICA

Batalla Salto Luna

Servicios Eléctricos del Sur SA

TransUnion

Luis Acuna
Asesores Legales en Propiedad Industrial

Aisha Acuña
Lexincorp Costa Rica

Gloriana Alvarado
Pacheco Coto

Rocio Amador
Arias & Muñoz

Arnoldo André
Lexincorp Costa Rica

Alejandro Antillon
Pacheco Coto

Carlos Araya
Central Law - Quiros Abogados

Daniel Araya
Arias & Muñoz

Luis Diego Barahona
PwC Costa Rica

Alejandro Bettoni Traube
Doninelli & Doninelli - Asesores Jurídicos Asociados

Eduardo Calderón-Odio
BLP Abogados

Giorginella Carranza
G Logistics Costa Rica, SA

Monica Castillo Quesada
Cámara Costarricense de la Construcción

Adriana Castro
BLP Abogados

Leonardo Castro
Oller Abogados

Silvia Chacon
Soley, Saborio & Asociados

Margot Chinchilla
SOCIACO

Alejandra Dobles
Proyectos ICC SA

Andrey Dorado
Arias & Muñoz

Roberto Esquivel
Oller Abogados

Dieter Gallop Fernandez
G logistics Costa Rica, SA

Randall Zamora Hidalgo
Costa Rica ABC

Henry Lang
Lang & Asociados

Vicente Lines
Arias & Muñoz

Andres Mercado
Oller Abogados

Jaime Molina
Proyectos ICC SA

Jorge Montenegro
SCGMT Arquitectura y Diseño

Eduardo Montoya Solano
Superintendencia General de Entidades Financieras

Ana Cristina Mora
Expertis GHP Abogados

Magda Morales
Lang & Asociados

Ricardo Murillo
SOCIACO

Cecilia Naranjo
LEX Counsel

Pedro Oller
Oller Abogados

Mauricio Paris
Expertis GHP Abogados

Sergio Pérez
Lexincorp

Roger Petersen
P Law Group

Donato Rivas
Arias & Muñoz

Ricardo Rodriguez
Central Law - Quiros Abogados

Oscar Rodríguez
IPRA-CINDER

Manrique Rojas
Lexincorp

Mauricio Salas
BLP Abogados

Jose Luis Salinas
Grupo Inmobiliario del Parque

Luis Sánchez
Facio & Cañas, member of Lex Mundi

Adriana Segura
PwC Costa Rica

Ronny Michel Valverde Mena

Tracy Varela Calderón
Arias & Muñoz

Marianela Vargas
PwC Costa Rica

Diego Villalobos

Jonathan Villegas Alvarado
SOCIACO

Jafet Zúñiga Salas
Superintendencia General de Entidades Financieras

CÔTE D'IVOIRE

Autorité Nationale de Régulation du secteur de l'Electricité

BCEAO

Cabinet EXPERTISES

Société Civile Professionnelle d'Avocats (SCPA)

Imboua-Kouao-Tella (IKT) & Associés

Narcisse Aka
Cour Commune de Justice et d'Arbitrage (CCJA) de l'OHADA

Patricia Akpangni
FDKA

Claude Aman
Bolloré Africa Logistics

Nirilala Antsa Andriantsoa
John W. Ffooks & Co., member of Bowman Gilfillan Africa Group

Simplice Anougba
CIE

Oumar Bane
Jurifis Consult

Altiné Amadou Belko
Creditinfo VoLo

Abou Berte
Tieri

Binde Binde
Africa Trans-Logistics International

Michel Kizito Brizoua-Bi
Bile-Aka, Brizoua-Bi & Associés

Lassiney Kathann Camara
CLK Avocats

Thierry Court
Tieri

Arsène Dablé
SCPA Dogué-Abbé Yao & Associés

Zirignon Constant Delbe
Ministère de l'Agriculture et du Développement Rural

Issa Diabaté
Koffi & Diabaté

Lynn Diagou
SCPA Dogué-Abbé Yao & Associés

Aboubakar-Sidiki Diarrassouba
CLK Avocats

Cheick Diop
Cabinet du Docteur Cheick Diop Avocats

Aly Djiohou
IJF Conseils Juridiques

Marius Doh
CIE

Yannick Dossongui
Association des Cabinets d'Avocats d'Affaries Africains

Yolande Doukoure Séhinabou
DSY Architecte

Dorothée K. Dreesen
Etude Maître Dreesen

Stéphane Eholie
SIMAT

Ramatou Fall
Guichet Unique de l'Investissement en Côte d'Ivoire - CEPICI

Joseph Gbegnon
Creditinfo VoLo

Koupo Gnoleba
Ministère de la Construction, du Logement, de l'Assainissement et de l'Urbanisme

Fares Goli
Egei

Claude-Andrée Groga
Cabinet Jean-François Chauveau

Nanette Kaba Ackah
Bolloré Africa Logistics

Barnabe Kabore
NOVELEC SARL

Colette Kacoutié
FDKA

Charles Kakou Kande
Energie et Télécomunication de Côte d'Ivoire (ETEL-CI)

Kitifolo Kignaman- Soro
Webb Fontaine Côte d'Ivoire

Noël Koffi
Cabinet Noël Y. Koffi

Raymonf Koffi
SIMAT

François Komoin
Tribunal de Commerce

Antoine Kona Yoha
DSY Architecte

Grace Yocoli Konan
SCPA Dogué-Abbé Yao & Associés

Fatoumata Konate Toure-B.
Etude de Me Konate Toure-B. Fatoumata

Marc Arthur Kouacou
Mazars CI

Blaise Kouadio Blaise
Sield

Guillaume Kouame
Bolloré Africa Logistics

Gilles Kouamé
PwC Côte d'Ivoire

Sylvere Koyo
SABKA

Sidibé Lancina
Guichet Unique du Permis de Construire

Claude Lath
Universal Service Company

Marie Leonard
Webb Fontaine Côte d'Ivoire

Faty Balla Lo
Creditinfo VoLo

Cisse Mamadou
Tribunal de Commerce

Christian Marmignon
C C M - Audit & Conseil

Desire Racine M'Bengue
Atelier M-RAUD

Roger M'Bengue
Atelier M-RAUD

Adeline Messou Couassi-Blé
PwC Côte d'Ivoire

Sylla Mory
CIE

Xavier Edouard N'cho
Ministère de l'Agriculture et du Développement Rural

Jean-Charles N'Dri
SIMAT

Georges N'Goan
Cabinet N'Goan, Asman & Associés

Isabelle Niamkey
CLK Avocats

Odette N'zi
Cap Transit International

Madou Ouattara
Tieri

Nanakan Ouattara
Ministère de l'Agriculture et du Développement Rural

Paul-Gérard Pougoue

Sariaka Randrianarisoa
John W. Ffooks & Co., member of Bowman Gilfillan Africa Group

Athanase Raux
Cabinet Raux, Amien & Associés

Felix Sally
Universal Service Company

Adamou Sambaré
Creditinfo VoLo

Idrissa Seynou
Ministère de l'Agriculture et du Développement Rural

Fatoumata Sidibe-Diarra
FSD Conseils Law Firm

Serge Kouassy Siekouo
Creditinfo VoLo

Isabelle Sokolo-Boni
Bile-Aka, Brizoua-Bi & Associés

Mamadou Sylla
Laboratoire du batiment et des travaux publics

Souleymane Sylla
Creditinfo VoLo

Dominique Taty
PwC Côte d'Ivoire

Sandrine Tegnan
Guichet Unique de l'Investissement en Côte d'Ivoire - CEPICI

Gwénaelle Teruin
Cabinet Jean-François Chauveau

Mahamadou Traore
Avocat à la Cour

Fousséni Traoré
PwC Côte d'Ivoire

Pauline Traoré
SIMAT

Flora Vabry
SCPA Dogué-Abbé Yao & Associés

Eloi Kouakou Yao
CLK Avocats

Koffi Noël Yao
Cabinet YZAS Baker Tilly

Didier Yao Koffi Kan
AITM

Seydou Zerbo
SCPA Dogué-Abbé Yao & Associés

Tiede Robert Zizonhi
Ministère de l'Agriculture et du Développement Rural

CROATIA

HEP Distribution System Operator Ltd.

PwC Croatia

Gordana Adamović
Odvjetničko društvo Leko i Partneri

Sara Al Hamad
Divjak, Topić & Bahtijarević

Andrea August
Agency for Investments and Competitiveness

Milan Bandić
Central City Administration of Zagreb

Hrvoje Bardek
CMS Legal

Marija Bartoluci
Leko i Partneri Attorneys-at-Law

Nera Beroš
Odvjetničko društvo Leko i Partneri

Karmen Boban Jerolimov
Glinska & Mišković Ltd.

Zoran Bohaček
Croatian Banking Association

Maja Zadravec Boloban
Eugen Zadravec Law Firm

Ivana Bos
Zagreb Stock Exchange

Željka Bregeš
Commercial Court

Mijo Brković
HROK d.o.o.

Rajka Bunjevac
Croatian Chamber of Architects

Belinda Čačić
Čačić & Partners Law Firm

Vanja Caratan Krenedić
Law Office Vanja Caratan Krenedić

Vlatka Cikac
Law Office Cikac

Lucija Colak
Žurić i Partneri d.o.o.

Iva Crnogorac
Divjak, Topić & Bahtijarević

Ivan Ćuk
Vukmir & Asociates

Ivana Delalić
Božić and Partners

Saša Divjak
Divjak, Topić & Bahtijarević

Mladen Dragičević
Law Firm Dragičević & Partners

Renata Duka
Ministry of Justice

Mirta Dusparić
Croatian Bank for Reconstruction and Development

Bozidar Feldman
Matic, Feldman & Herman Law Firm

Tomislav Fridrich
Cargo-Partner d.o.o.

Tomislava Furčić
Law Office Furcic

Tonka Gjoić
Glinska & Mišković Ltd.

Ivan Gjurgjan
Gjurgjan & Šribar Radić Law Firm

Krešimir Golubiž
Golmax d.o.o.

Lidija Hanžek
HROK d.o.o.

Sonja Herceg
Croatian Bank for Reconstruction and Development

Branimir Ivekoviž
Iveković Law Office

Tina Jakupak
Commercial Court

Vinka Jelavić
Agency for Investments and Competitiveness

Irina Jelčić
Hanžeković & Partners Ltd., member of Lex Mundi

Saša Jovičić
Wolf Theiss

Josipa Jurčić
Praljak & Svić

Petra Jurković Mutabžija
Croatian Bank for Reconstruction and Development

Andrijana Kastelan
Žurić i Partneri d.o.o.

Filip Kocis
Agency for Investments and Competitiveness

Iva Kemec Kokot
Zagreb Civil Law Notary

Vesna Kadić Komadina
Customs Directorate of Croatia

Linda Križić
Divjak, Topić & Bahtijarević

Anita Krizmanić
Mačešić & Partners Ltd.

Dinko Lauš
LAURA d.o.o.

Sandra Lauš
LAURA d.o.o.

Ivan Ljubic
Croatian Chamber of Architects

Marko Lovrić
Divjak, Topić & Bahtijarević

Miran Mačešić
Mačešić & Partners Ltd.

Josip Madirazza
Madirazza & Partners

Mihaela Malenica
Vidan Attorneys-at-Law

Ivana Manovelo
Mačešić & Partners Ltd.

Josip Martinić
Wolf Theiss

Iva Masten
Vidan Attorneys-at-Law

Tin Matić
Tin Matić Law Office

Jan Mokos
Korper & Partneri Law Firm

Zeljana Muslim
Financial Agency - HITRO.HR Center

Harun Omerbasic
Central City Administration of Zagreb

Jadranka Orešković
Čačić & Partners Law Firm

Jelena Orlic
Wolf Theiss

Nataša Owens
Owens and Houška

Ana Padjen
Mačešić & Partners Ltd.

Andrea Pavlek
Gjurgjan & Šribar Radić Law Firm

Tomislav Pedišić
Vukmir & Asociates

Igor Periša
High Commercial Court of the Republic of Croatia

Miroslav Plašćar
Žurić i Partneri d.o.o.

Snježana Premus Baltić
Law Firm Dragičević & Partners

Hrvoje Radić
Gjurgjan & Šribar Radić Law Firm

Iva Rašić
Ministry of Justice

Anća Redžić
Ministry of Finance, Tax Administration

Hana Renić Heni
Divjak, Topić & Bahtijarević

Sanja Rodek
Odvjetničko društvo Leko i Partneri

Boris Šavorić
Šavorić & Partners

Slaven Šego
Šego Law Office

Dino Simonoski Bukovski
Žurić i Partneri d.o.o.

Dušanka Šimunović
Croatian Chamber of Architects

Andrej Skočić
MERVIS d.o.o. - correspondent of Russell Bedford International

Vladimir Skočić
MERVIS d.o.o. - correspondent of Russell Bedford International

Ana-Marija Skoko
CMS Legal

Alan Soric
Alan Soric & Aleksandra Tomekovic Dunda Law Office

Morena Šoštarić
Gjurgjan & Šribar Radić Law Firm

Irena Šribar Radić
Gjurgjan & Šribar Radić Law Firm

Marko Stilinović
Čačić & Partners Law Firm

Silva Stipić Kobali
Croatian Chamber of Economy

Vatroslav Subotic
Ministry of Labour and Pension System

Goranka Šumonja Laktić
Laktic & Partners Law Firm Ltd.

Marin Svić
Praljak & Svić

Branka Tabak Parascic
Central City Administration of Zagreb

Zoran Tasić
CMS Legal

Tin Težak
Madirazza & Partners

Marko Topiž
Croatian Bank for Reconstruction and Development

Aleksander Topol
Cargo-Partner d.o.o.

Jan Torjanac
Korper & Partneri Law Firm

Ana Udiljak
Praljak & Svić

Hrvoje Vidan
Vidan Attorneys-at-Law

Igor Vidra
Ministry of Justice

Laurenz Vuchetich
Vuchetich Law Office in cooperation with Specht & Partner

Mario Vukelić
High Commercial Court of the Republic of Croatia

Eugen Zadravec
Eugen Zadravec Law Firm

Boris Zelenika
Ministry of Justice

Inga Zic
Ministry of Labour and Pension System

Petar Živković
Divjak, Topić & Bahtijarević

Jelena Zjacic
Mačešić & Partners Ltd.

Bosiljko Zlopaša
Customs Directorate of Croatia

Andrej Žmikić
Divjak, Topić & Bahtijarević Law Firm

Ivan Zornada
Wolf Theiss

CYPRUS

Olga Adamidou
Antis Triantafyllides & Sons LLC

Alexandros Alexandrou
Tornaritis Law Firm

Achilleas Amvrosiou
Artemis Bank Information Systems Ltd.

Andreas Anagnostou
Harris Kyriakides LLC

Irene Anastasiou
Ministry of Interior

Anaxagoras Anaxagora
Demos Anaxagoras Ltd. Electrical Contractors

Marios Andreou
PwC Cyprus

Chryso Antoniou
Alexandros Economou LLC

Ioannis Antoniou
TMA Real Estate Ltd.

Ioanna Apostolidou
Ministry of Finance, Tax Department

Katia Argyridou
PwC Cyprus

Pavlos Aristodemou
Harneys Aristodemou Loizides Yiolitis LLC

Anita Boyadjian
Infocredit Group Ltd.

Antonis Charalambous
Limassol Municipality

Charalambos Charalambous
Ministry of Interior

Harry S. Charalambous
KPMG

Antonis Christodoulides
PwC Cyprus

Kypros Chrysostomides
Dr. K. Chrysostomides & Co. LLC

Chrysostomos Chrysostomou
Town Planning and Housing Department

Achilleas Demetriades
Lellos P. Demetriades Law Office LLC

Eleni Droussioti
Dr. K. Chrysostomides & Co. LLC

Alexandros Economou
Alexandros Economou LLC

Lefteris S. Eleftheriou
Cyprus Investment Promotion Agency

Elikkos Elia
Department of Lands and Surveys

Elena Frixou
Artemis Bank Information Systems Ltd.

Charis Georgakis
Electricity Authority of Cyprus

Demetris Georgiades
Harneys Aristodemou Loizides Yiolitis LLC

Phedra Gregoriou
Ministry of Justice and Public Order

Froso Gypsioti
Tornaritis Law Firm

Marios Hadjigavriel
Antis Triantafyllides & Sons LLC

Costas Hadjimarcou
Leptos Estates

Andreas Ioannides
Electricity Authority of Cyprus

Georgia Karamalli
Harris Kyriakides LLC

Georgios Karrotsakis
Insolvency Service, Department of Registrar of Companies and Official Receiver

Maria Katsikidou
Alexandros Economou LLC

Eleni Kitrou
Social Insurance Services, Ministry of Labour, Welfare and Social Insurance

Spyros G. Kokkinos
Department of Registrar of Companies and Official Receiver

Iacovos Kounnamas
Ministry of Finance

Kyriacos Kouros
Ministry of Interior - Technical Services

Theodoros Kringou
First Cyprus Credit Bureau

Nicholas Ktenas
Andreas Neocleous & Co. Legal Consultants

Michalis Kyriakides
Harris Kyriakides LLC

Olga Lambrou
Mouaimis & Mouaimis LLC

Andreas Lelekis
Chrysses Demetriades & Co. LLC

Margarita Liasi
KPMG

Stella Livadiotou
Ministry of Finance

Antonis Loizou
Antonis Loizou & Associates

Michalis Marcou
Electricity Authority of Cyprus

George V. Markides
KPMG

Pieris M. Markou
Deloitte

Joseph Merhi
AGC Contractors

Michalis Mouaimis
Mouaimis & Mouaimis LLC

Panayotis Mouaimis
Mouaimis & Mouaimis LLC

Loukia Mouskou
Ministry of Finance

Kyriaki Myrianthopoulou
Department of Customs & Excise

Demetris Nicolaou
Harneys Aristodemou Loizides Yiolitis LLC

Varnavas Nicolaou
PwC Cyprus

Andry Panteli
P.G. Economides & Co Limited - member of Russell Bedford International

Christos Papamarkides
Deloitte

Mikaella Papanicolaou
Presidency of the Republic of Cyprus

Andriana Patsalosavvi
Ministry of Interior - Technical Services

Marilou Pavlou
Antis Triantafyllides & Sons LLC

Chrysilios Pelekanos
PwC Cyprus

Costas Petrou
Electricity Authority of Cyprus

Ioanna Petrou
PwC Cyprus

Maria Petsa
Cyprus Stock Exchange

Chryso Pitsilli - Dekatris
Dr. K. Chrysostomides & Co. LLC

Haris Satsias
Lellos P. Demetriades Law Office LLC

Andreas Sokratous
Ministry of Interior

Rafaella Sordini
Harris Kyriakides LLC

George Soteriou
Cyprus Ports Authority

Costas Stasopoulos
Electricity Authority of Cyprus

Eliza Stasopoulou
Cyprus Stock Exchange

Athina Stephanou
Ministry of Finance, Tax Department

Anna Stylianou
Artemis Bank Information Systems Ltd.

Stelios Stylianou
Electricity Authority of Cyprus

Nayia Symeonidou
Ministry of Finance, Tax Department

Georgia Theodorou
PwC Cyprus

Criton Tornaritis
Tornaritis Law Firm

Stelios Triantafyllides
Antis Triantafyllides & Sons LLC

Alexandros Tsirides
Costas Tsirides & Co. LLC

Christiana Vassiliou Miliou
Antis Triantafyllides & Sons LLC

CZECH REPUBLIC

Ondrej Antoš
Squire Sanders v.o.s. Advokátní Kancelář

Denisa Assefová
Schoenherr

Lukáš Balada
Municipality of Prague 1, Trade Licensing Department

Libor Basl
Baker & McKenzie

Tomáš Běhounek
BNT Attorneys-at-Law s.r.o.

Rudolf Bicek
Schoenherr

Simona Bradáčová
Metropolitan Court of Prague

Tomas Brozek
Baker & McKenzie

David Bujgl
Squire Sanders v.o.s. Advokátní Kancelář

Jan Capek
Ernst & Young

Petra Cechova
PwC Czech Republic

Ivan Chalupa
Squire Sanders v.o.s. Advokátní Kancelář

Peter Chrenko
PwC Czech Republic

Pavel Cirek
Energy Regulator Office Czech Republic

Vladimír Čížek
Schoenherr

Martin Dančišin
Glatzová & Co.

Kamila Dankova
White & Case

Svatava Dokoupilova
Czech Office for Surveying, Mapping and Cadastre

Dagmar Dubecka
Kocián Šolc Balaštík, advokátní kancelář, s.r.o.

Jiří Dvořák
TH Energo

Tereza Erényi
PRK Partners s.r.o. advokátní kancelář, member of Lex Mundi

Jindřich Fuka
Glatzová & Co.

Michal Hanko
Bubnik, Myslil & Partners

Marie Hasíková
Schoenherr

Martin Hofman
CRIF - Czech Credit Bureau AS

Vít Horáček
LEGALITÉ Advokátní Kancelář s.r.o.

Ondřej Hromádko
Municipality of Prague 1, Trade Licensing Department

Lukáš Hron
Baker & McKenzie

Lucie Janouskova
Czech Association of Energy Sector Employers

Veronika Jašová
KPMG Česká republika, s.r.o.

Jan Klas
Czech Association of Energy Sector Employers

Martina Kneiflová
Ernst & Young

Filip Košťál
Wolf Theiss Rechtsanwälte GmbH & Co.

Jan Krampera
Dvořák Hager & Partners

Petr Kucera
CRIF - Czech Credit Bureau AS

Bohumil Kunc
Notary Chamber, Czech Republic

Petr Kusy
Ministry of Finance

Lukas Lejcek
BDP-Wakestone s.r.o.

Jakub Lichnovský
PRK Partners s.r.o. advokátní kancelář, member of Lex Mundi

Ondrej Lukas Machala
Attorney

Daniela Machova
Notarial Chamber of the Czech Republic

Peter Maysenhölder
BNT Attorneys-at-Law s.r.o.

Petr Měšťánek
Kinstellar

David Musil
PwC Czech Republic

Tereza Naučová
Kinstellar

Veronika Odrobinova
Dvořák Hager & Partners

Jakub Porod
Kocián Šolc Balaštík, advokátní kancelář, s.r.o.

Tomáš Procházka
Dvořák Hager & Partners

Štěpán Radkovský
Czech National Bank

Michal Rohacek
Financni Sprava - General Financial Directorate

Barbora Rovenská
White & Case

Mike Silin
DHL Czech Republic

Ivo Skolil
Glatzová & Co.

Dana Sládečková
Czech National Bank

Kristýna Solomonová
Municipality of Prague 1, Trade Licensing Department

Pavel Srb
Wolf Theiss Rechtsanwälte GmbH & Co.

Jana Stavjanova
Ministry of Finance

Tomas Strelecek
Ministry of Justice

Petra Stupkova
PRK Partners s.r.o. advokátní kancelář, member of Lex Mundi

Marek Švehlík
Švehlí & Mikuláš Advokáti s.r.o.

Sarka Tlaskova
Notarial Chamber of the Czech Republic

Růžena Trojánková
Kinstellar

Lenka Valesova
Vejmelka & Wünsch, s.r.o.

Zuzana Valoušková
Kinstellar

Daniel Vejsada
PRK Partners s.r.o. advokátní kancelář, member of Lex Mundi

Aneta Vermachová
Ministry of Justice

Jiri Vlastnik
Vejmelka & Wünsch, s.r.o.

Tomáš Volejník
BNT Attorneys-at-Law s.r.o.

Stanislav Votruba
PREdistribuce

Luděk Vrána
Vrána & Partners

DENMARK

Jumbo Transport A/S

Elsebeth Aaes-Jørgensen
Norrbom Vinding, member of Ius Laboris

Peter Bang
Plesner

Thomas Bang
Lett Law Firm

Ole Borch
Bech-Bruun Law Firm

Frants Dalgaard-Knudsen
Plesner

Sonny Gaarslev
Kromann Reumert, member of Lex Mundi

Anne Birgitte Gammeljord
Gammeljord Advokater

Line Geisler Havelund
Kromann Reumert, member of Lex Mundi

Henrik Groos
Accura Advokatpartnerselskab

Thomas Hansen
Plesner

Silan Harmankaya
PwC Denmark

Jens Steen Jensen
Kromann Reumert, member of Lex Mundi

Jacob C. Jørgensen
Lawyer

Lars Kjaer
Bech-Bruun Law Firm

Troels Kjersgaard
Lett Law Firm

Christian Kjølbye
Plesner

Ida Kjølbye
Bruun & Hjejle

Michael Krath
Kilting A/S

Mikkel Stig Larsen
Kromann Reumert, member of Lex Mundi

Susanne Schjølin Larsen
Kromann Reumert, member of Lex Mundi

Lise Lauridsen
Bech-Bruun Law Firm

Kasper Lykkegaard Sorensen
Spedman Global Logistics AB

Robert Mikelsons
Njord Law Firm

Morten Bang Mikkelsen
PwC Denmark

Jesper Mortensen
Plesner

Andreas Nielsen
Bruun & Hjejle

Michael Vilhelm Nielsen
Plesner

Susanne Norgaard
PwC Denmark

Jim Øksnebjerg
Advokatpartnerselskabet Horten

Carsten Pedersen
Bech-Bruun Law Firm

Lars Lindencrone Petersen
Bech-Bruun Law Firm

Sofie Precht Poulse
Bech-Bruun Law Firm

Tina Reissmann
Plesner

Tessa Maria Rosenberg
Bech-Bruun Law Firm

Christian Sander
COBE Architects

Louise Krarup Simonsen
Kromann Reumert, member of Lex Mundi

Thomas Christian Thune
Bech-Bruun Law Firm

Jens Zilstorff
Plesner

DJIBOUTI

Direction de l'Habitat et de l'Urbanisme

Mohamed Abayazid Houmed

Ouloufa Ismail Abdo
Office Djiboutien de la Propriété Industrielle et Commerciale (ODPIC)

Ahmed Abdourahman Cheik

Iwad Ali Mohamed

Idriss Assoweh
Cabinet Assoweh & Associés

Loubna Bawazir
Bank of Africa Mer Rouge

Sofia Curradi

Ali Dini
Avocat à la Cour

Félix Emok N'Dolo
Groupe CHD

Mourad Farah
Etude Maître Mourad Farah

Fahmi Fouad
SELECT

Tolmone A. Haid
Gobad Architects

Ramiss Houmed
Alephe-Consulting

Zeinab Kamil Ali
Cabinet ZK

Ismael Mahamoud
Université de Djibouti

Oubah Mohamed
Baraka Transit & Transport Service

Alsane Mohamed Elmi
Cabinet ZK

Ibrahim Mohamed Omar
Cabinet CECA

Abdallah Mohammed Kamil
Etude Maître Mohammed Kamil

Ayman Said
Ayman Said Law Firm

Aicha Youssouf Abdi
Cabinet CECA

DOMINICA

Kertist Augustus
Waterfront and Allied Workers Union

Jo-Anne Commodore
Supreme Court Registry

Gina Dyer
Dyer & Dyer

Evelina E-M. Baptiste
Magistrate Court

Marvlyn Estrado
KPB Chartered Accountants

Nathaniel George
DOMLEC

F. Adler Hamlet
Realco Company Limited

Rhoda Joseph
Invest Dominica Authority

Justinn Kase
Independent Regulatory Commission

Noelize Knight Didier
Harris & Harris

Frankie Lowe
DOMLEC

Michelle Matthew
National Co-operative Credit Union Limited

Bertilia Mckenzie
DOMLEC

Eric Mendes
House of Assembly

Richard Peterkin
Grant Thornton

Joan K.R. Prevost
Prevost & Roberts

Eugene G. Royer
Eugene G. Royer Chartered Architect

Anya Trim
Grant Thornton

Pearl Williams
Supreme Court Registry

Dawn Yearwood
Yearwood Chambers

DOMINICAN REPUBLIC

Maria Teresa Acta Morales
Headrick Rizik Alvarez & Fernández

Juan Alcalde
OMG

Melba Alcántara
Headrick Rizik Alvarez & Fernández

Merielin Almonte
Asociacion Dominicana de Constructores y Promotores de Vivienda (ACOPROVI)

Merielin Almonte
Merielin Almonte Estudio Legal

Patricia Alvarez
Medina Garrigó Abogados

Larry Azcona
Schad Consulting

Lissette Balbuena
Stewart Title Dominicana, SA

Jennifer Beauchamps
Jiménez Cruz Peña

Luis Eduardo Bernard
Gonzalez Tapia Abogados and Coiscou & Asociados

Laura Bobea
Medina Garrigó Abogados

Hector Breton
Asociacion Dominicana de Constructores y Promotores de Vivienda (ACOPROVI)

Ana Isabel Caceres
Troncoso y Caceres

Maité Camilo
Ernst & Young

Eileen Jimenez Cantisano
Headrick Rizik Alvarez & Fernández

Marvin Cardoza
Dirección General de Impuestos Internos

Roberto Carvajal Polanco
Carvajal Polanco & Asociados SRL

Milvio Coiscou Castro
Coiscou & Asociados

José Colón
EDESUR

Ludovino Colón
Ernst & Young

Pamela Contreras
JJ Roca & Associates

Leandro Corral
Estrella & Tupete

José Cruz Campillo
Jiménez Cruz Peña

Jean Louis de Boyrie
Asociación Dominicana de Agentes de Carga Aérea y Marítima, Inc., ADACAM

Caleb de la Rosa
Dynatec

Leonardo de la Rosa
Dynatec

Sarah de León Perelló
Headrick Rizik Alvarez & Fernández

Rosa Díaz
Jiménez Cruz Peña

Rafael Dickson Morales
Dickson Morales - Abogados | Consultores

Ruben Edmead
Marítima Dominicana

Michel El-Hage
Hageco Ingenieros & Arquitectos

Zenon Felipe
Marítima Dominicana

Ingrid Fermín-Terrero
Seibel Dargam Henríquez & Herrera

Maria Fernández A. de Pou
Russin, Vecchi & Heredia Bonetti

Alejandro Fernández de Castro
PwC Dominican Republic

Mary Fernández Rodríguez
Headrick Rizik Alvarez & Fernández

Milagros Figuereo
Job, Báez, Soto & Asociados - member of Russell Bedford International

Leoncio García
Electromecánica Garcia SRL

Gloria Gasso
OMG

Sandra Goico
Seibel Dargam Henríquez & Herrera

Pablo Gonzalez Tapia
Gonzalez Tapia Abogados

Fabio Guzmán-Ariza
Guzmán-Ariza

Marco Henriquez
Asociación Dominicana de Agentes de Carga Aérea y Marítima, Inc., ADACAM

Rosa Hernandez
Asociación Dominicana de Agentes de Carga Aérea y Marítima, Inc., ADACAM

María Hernández
Ernst & Young

Paula Hernández
Gonzalez Tapia Abogados

David Infante
Deloitte RD, SRL

Luis J. Jiménez
Jiménez Cruz Peña

Alejandro Lama
Headrick Rizik Alvarez & Fernández

Paola Manon Taveras
Seibel Dargam Henríquez & Herrera

Fernando Marranzini
Headrick Rizik Alvarez & Fernández

Carlos Marte
Agencia de Comercio Exterior CM

Jesús Geraldo Martínez Alcántara
Superintendencia de Bancos

Fabiola Medina
Medina Garrigó Abogados

Laura Medina
Jiménez Cruz Peña

Vitelio Mejia Ortiz
Pellerano & Herrera, member of Lex Mundi

Rodolfo Mesa Chavez
Mesa & Mesa Abogados

Natia Núñez
Headrick Rizik Alvarez & Fernández

Ramón Ortega
PwC El Salvador

Ricardo Pallerano Paradas
Pellerano & Herrera, member of Lex Mundi

Arvelyn Peña
Gonzalez Tapia Abogados and Coiscou & Asociados

Kaulynam Peralta
EDESUR

Yakaira Pérez
Ernst & Young

Luisa Ericka Pèrez Hernàndez
Superintendencia de Bancos

Edward Piña Fernandez
Biaggi & Messina

Julio Pinedo
PwC Dominican Republic

Aimee Prieto
Prieto Cabrera & Asociados

Martha Ramirez
Gonzalez Tapia Abogados and Coiscou & Asociados

Sayra J. Ramirez
Prieto Cabrera & Asociados

Alejandro Miguel Ramirez Suzaña
Ramirez Suzaña & Asoc.

Eduardo Ramos E.
Ramos Morel & Asocs.

Reynaldo Ramos Morel
Ramos Morel & Asocs.

Aida Ripoll
Guzmán-Ariza

Jaime Roca
JJ Roca & Associates

Solanyi Rodriguez
Schad Consulting

Naomi Rodríguez
Headrick Rizik Alvarez & Fernández

Mariel Romero
EDESUR

Katherine Rosa
Jiménez Cruz Peña

Juan Rosario
EDESUR

Wendy Sánchez
TransUnion Dominican Republic

Felicia Santana
JJ Roca & Associates

Victor Santana Díaz
Jiménez Cruz Peña

Jaime Senior
Headrick Rizik Alvarez & Fernández

Elizabeth Silfa
Headrick Rizik Alvarez & Fernández

Melissa Silie
Medina Garrigó Abogados

Manuel Silverio
Jiménez Cruz Peña

Llilda Solano
DMK Lawyers Santo Domingo

Juan Tejeda
PwC Dominican Republic

Laura Troncoso
OMG

Richard Troncoso
Deloitte RD, SRL

Paola Ureña
Gonzalez Tapia Abogados

Robert Valdez
Schad Consulting

Gisselle Valera Florencio
Jiménez Cruz Peña

Tony Vazquez
Asociación Dominicana de Agentes de Carga Aérea y Marítima, Inc., ADACAM

Vilma Veras Terrero
Jiménez Cruz Peña

Jeannerette Vergez Soto
Job, Báez, Soto & Asociados - member of Russell Bedford International

Pedro Vilas
EDESUR

Chery Zacarías
Medina Garrigó Abogados

ECUADOR

Claudio Mesias Agama Chiluisa
Empresa Eléctrica Quito SA

Pablo Aguirre
PwC Ecuador

Maria Isabel Aillon
Pérez, Bustamante y Ponce, member of Lex Mundi

Mario Armendáriz
DLL Law Office

Esteban Baquero
Ferrere Abogados

Alberto Brown
Ferrere Abogados

Maria Gabriela Cando
Ferrere Abogados

Daniela Cifuentes
CAMICON Cámara de la Industria de la Construcción

Lucía Cordero Ledergerber
Falconi Puig Abogados

David Cornejo
PwC Ecuador

Augusto Curillo
Empresa Eléctrica Quito SA

Juan Carlos Darquea
Ferrere Abogados

Pablo Davila Jaramillo
DLL Law Office

Miguel Falconi-Puig
Falconi Puig Abogados

Andrea Fernández de Córdova
Ferrere Abogados

Bolívar Figueroa
Ferrere Abogados

Paola Gachet
Ferrere Abogados

Martín Galarza Lanas
Puente Reyes & Galarza Attorneys-at-Law Cia. Ltda

Cristina García
Ferrere Abogados

Jaime Gordillo
PwC Ecuador

Arturo Griffin Valdivieso
Pérez, Bustamante y Ponce, member of Lex Mundi

Sebastián Jarrín
Equifax Ecuador Buró de Información Crediticia C.A.

María Isabel Machado
Falconi Puig Abogados

Francisco Javier Naranjo Grijalva
FedLex

Letty Ordoñez
Empresa Pública de Movilidad y Obras Públicas

Julian Pastor
Sempértegui Ontaneda

Andrea Pavon
Vicsan Logistics SA

Ciro Pazmiño Yánez
P&P Abogados

Ciro Pazmiño Zurita
P&P Abogados

Hernán Pérez Loose
Coronel y Pérez

Rodrigo Martin Pesantes Saenz
Pérez, Bustamante y Ponce, member of Lex Mundi

Daniel Pino Arroba
Coronel y Pérez

Clementina Pomar Anta
Bustamante & Bustamante

Patricia Ponce Arteta
Bustamante & Bustamante

Sandra Reed-Serrano
Pérez, Bustamante y Ponce, member of Lex Mundi

Santiago Reyes
DLL Law Office

Daniel Robalino-Orellana
Ferrere Abogados

Felipe Ron

Leonardo Sempértegui
Sempértegui Ontaneda

María Sol Sevilla
Sempértegui Ontaneda

Estefania Sigcha Orrico
DLL Law Office

Andrés Terán
Bustamante & Bustamante

Sebastián Yépez
PwC Ecuador

Manuel Zurita
MZ Sistemas Electricos y Electronicos

EGYPT, ARAB REP.

Assiut Court

Central Bank of Egypt

Egyptian Financial Supervisory Authority

Omar Abd el Salam
Al Kamel Law Office

Mohamed Abd El-Sadek
International Center for Law, Intellectual Property and Arbitration (ICLIPA)

Shereen Abdallah
Egyptian Electricity Utility and Consumer Protection

Ibrahim Mustafa Ibrahim Abdel Khalek
General Authority for Investment GAFI

Sara Abdelghafar
Youssry Saleh & Partners

Ahmed S. Abdelnabi
Youssry Saleh & Partners

Mostafa Abdel-Rahim
Helmy, Hamza & Partners, member firm of Baker & McKenzie International

Mohamed Abdul Aziz
South Cairo Electricity Distribution Company

Sherein Abdulla
Egyptian Electric Utility and Consumer Protection Regulatory Agency

Nour Mostafa Abo Elella
General Organization of Export & Import Control

Amr Abo Elfetouh
Ministry of Investment

Ahmed Abou Ali
Hassouna & Abou Ali

Gamal A. Abou Ali
Hassouna & Abou Ali

Ashraf Abou Elkheir
Alliance Law Firm

Sherief Abu Saree
Ministry of Housing and Urban Communities

Sayed Abuelkomsan
Ministry of Industry and Foreign Trade

Nermine Abulata
Ministry of Industry and Foreign Trade

Mona Adel Hussein
Talal Abu-Ghazaleh Legal (TAG-Legal)

Mohamed Reda Afifi
Engineering Consultancies Office

Ahmed Agami
Ibrachy & Partners

Mohamed Aggag
Ministry of Justice

Suzan Saad Ahmed
Al-Saad for Engineering Designs

Vivian Ahmed Hassan
Ministry of Housing and Urban Communities

Yulia V. Akinfieva
Youssry Saleh & Partners

Omnia Al Banna
Government services development program

Mahmoud AlFeki

Shaimaa Ali
Ministry of Industry and Foreign Trade

Ashraf Alkafrawy
Cairo Economic Court

Osama Abd Al-Monem
Ministry of Industry and Foreign Trade

Naser Al-Qormani
Office of the Minister of Justice for Real Estate Registration Affairs

Sayed Ammar
Al Kamel Law Office

Amr Ibrahim As Sarwy
MLSN Law Firm

Hoda Attia
Ministry of Transport

Khaled Balbaa
KPMG Hazem Hassan

Wagih Barakat
AAW Consulting Engineers

Mansour Boriek
Alexandria Port Authority, Ministry of Transportation

Mohamed Darwish
El Said Darwish & Partners

Amal Afifi Dawood
Dentons

Reham Eissa
Sharkawy & Sarhan Law Firm

Abdallah El Adly
PwC Egypt

Amany El Bagoury
Attorney-at-Law

Mohamed Refaat El Houshi
The Egyptian Credit Bureau I-Score

Hassan El Maraashly
AAW Consulting Engineers

Aly El Shalakany
Shalakany Law Office, member of Lex Mundi

Emad El Shalakany
Shalakany Law Office, member of Lex Mundi

Khaled El Shalakany
Shalakany Law Office, member of Lex Mundi

Sherry El Shalakany
Shalakany Law Office, member of Lex Mundi

Passant El Tabei
PwC Egypt

Menna Elabdeeny
Ministry of Industry and Foreign Trade

Salma ElAmir
Ibrachy & Dermarkar Law Firm

Soheir Elbanna
Ibrachy & Partners

Amr Eleish
General Authority for Investment GAFI

Naser Elfarmany
Office of the Minister of Justice for Real Estate Registration Affairs

Samir El-Gammal
Ministry of Industry and Foreign Trade

Ashraf Elibrachy
Ibrachy & Partners

Ihab El-Mahdy
Registering Property Project

Mohammad Elsayed
Ministry of Justice

Mostafa Elshafei
Ibrachy & Partners

Emad El-Tamawy
Office of the Minister of Justice for Real Estate Registration Affairs

Amany Elwessal
Ministry of Industry and Foreign Trade

Karim Emam
PwC Egypt

Shahdan Essam
Talal Abu-Ghazaleh Legal (TAG-Legal)

Mariam Fahmy
Shalakany Law Office, member of Lex Mundi

Hazem Fathi
Hassouna & Abou Ali

Osama Fathy
Laws Answer

Sheren Foad
Egyptian Electricity Holding Company

Tamim Foda
Al Kamel Law Office

Tarek Gadallah
Ibrachy & Partners

Mahmoud Gamal El-Din
Ministry of Industry and Foreign Trade

Merna George
Youssry Saleh & Partners

Mohamed Gomaa Ali
Ministry of Industry and Foreign Trade

Mohamed H. El Ehwany
Al Kamel Law Office

Dalia Habib
The Egyptian Credit Bureau I-Score

Farah Ahmed Haggag
Ministry of Industry and Foreign Trade

Hany Hanna
Ministry of Justice

Mahmoud Hany
Sharkawy & Sarhan Law Firm

Nafisa Mahmoud Hashem
Ministry of Housing and Urban Communities

Mohamed Hashish
Soliman, Hashish and Partners

Dina Hassan
Shalakany Law Office, member of Lex Mundi

Mohab Hassan
Helmy, Hamza & Partners, member firm of Baker & McKenzie International

Tarek Hassib
Al Kamel Law Office

Mostafa Helmy
Ibrachy & Partners

Omneia Helmy
Faculty of Economics and Political Science, Cairo University

Taher Helmy
Helmy, Hamza & Partners, member firm of Baker & McKenzie International

Mohamed Hisham Hassan
Ministry of Investment

Ramy Hussein
Ministry of Investment

Ahmed I. Hegazy
The Law Offices of Ibrahim Hegazy

Badawi Ibrahim
Ministry of Industry and Foreign Trade

Mohamed Kafafi
The Egyptian Credit Bureau I-Score

Ahmed Kamal
Government services development program

Omar Sherif Kamal El Din
Shalakany Law Office, member of Lex Mundi

Khaled Sherif Kamal El Dine
Shalakany Law Office, member of Lex Mundi

Mohamed Kamel
Al Kamel Law Office

Rasheed Kamel
Al Kamel Law Office

Mohanad Khaled
BDO Khaled & Co.

Taha Khaled
BDO Khaled & Co.

Gomaa M. Madny
Ministry of Trade and Industry

Lamia Mahgoub
PwC Egypt

Ahmed Makky
Shalakany Law Office, member of Lex Mundi

Mustafa Makram
BDO Khaled & Co.

Abdel Monam Mattar
Egyptian Tax Authority

Hassan Fahmy Mohamed
General Authority for Investment GAFI

Yasmin Mohamed Mahran
Talal Abu-Ghazaleh Legal (TAG-Legal)

Ola Mohammed Hassan
Talal Abu-Ghazaleh Legal (TAG-Legal)

Eman Mohey
Hassouna & Abou Ali

Alia Monieb
Ibrachy & Partners

Hossam Mostafa Ali
Hossam Avocat

Yousr Mounib
Ministry of Industry and Foreign Trade

Marina Mouris
Ibrachy & Dermarkar Law Firm

Youssef Nassef
Al Kamel Law Office

Shimaa Omar
Readymade Garments Export Council

Alya Rady
Ministry of Industry and Foreign Trade

Ahmad Bahaa Rashed
AM Law Firm

Ahmed Nour El-Din Rashed
Dentons

Mayar Rashed
Youssry Saleh & Partners

Mirna Saad
Youssry Saleh & Partners

Doaa Mohamed Ahmed Sangak
Egyptian Tax Authority

Karim Sarhan
Sharkawy & Sarhan Law Firm

Muhammad Omar Sarwy
Chubb

Mohamed Serry
Serry Law Office

Doaa M. Shabaan
International Center for Law, Intellectual Property and Arbitration (ICLIPA)

Mohamed Shafik
Ministry of Industry and Foreign Trade

Mohammad Shamroukh
Ministry of Justice

Sharif Shihata
Shalakany Law Office, member of Lex Mundi

Zeinab Shohdy
Khodeir, Nour, & Taha Law Firm (in association with Al Tamimi & Company)

Shaimaa Solaiman
Challenge Law Firm

Frédéric Soliman
Soliman, Hashish and Partners

Hesham Soliman
Medstar For Trading & Stevedoring Co. SAE

Ehab Taha
Ibrachy & Partners

Mamdouh Taha
General Organization of Export & Import Control

Hatem Waheed
Egyptian Electricity Utility and Consumer Protection

Nabil A.B. Yehia
Cairo University

Darah Zakaria
Shalakany Law Office, member of Lex Mundi

Mona Zobaa
General Authority for Investment GAFI

EL SALVADOR

León Sol Arquitectos

Miguel Angel Aguilar
Ale Cargo SA de CV

Francisco Armando Arias Rivera
Arias & Muñoz

Mauricio Bernal
AES El Salvador

Abraham Bichara
AES El Salvador

Rafael Burgos
Arias & Muñoz

Hazel Alexandra Cabezas
Aguilar Castillo Love

Juan Cabezas
JC Electricista

Alexander Cader
PwC El Salvador

Claudia Castellanos
La Oficina de Planificación del Área Metropolitana de San Salvador (OPAMSS)

Carlos Roberto Alfaro Castillo
Aguilar Castillo Love

Christian Castro
AES El Salvador

Armando Chacon
Lexincorp

Walter Chávez
Gold Service

Eduardo Iván Colocho Catota
Innovations & Integrated Solutions, SA de CV

Luis Alfredo Cornejo Martínez
Cornejo & Umaña, Ltda de CV - member of Russell Bedford International

Celina Cruz
La Oficina de Planificación del Área Metropolitana de San Salvador (OPAMSS)

Porfirio Díaz Fuentes
DLM, Abogados, Notarios & Consultores

Lorena Dueñas
Superintendencia del Sistema Financiero

David Ernesto Claros Flores
García & Bodán

Enrique Escobar
Lexincorp

Guillermo Escobar
Lexincorp

Pablo Espinoza
DLM, Abogados, Notarios & Consultores

Roberta Gallardo de Cromeyer
Arias & Muñoz

Edwin Gálvez
AES El Salvador

Raúl González
Consejo Nacional de Energía (CNE)

Antonio Guirola Moze
Lexincorp

America Hernandez
Ale Cargo SA de CV

Luis Roberto Hernández Arita
Hernández Arita Ingenieros

Sandra Hernandez de Cabezas
Central Law (El Salvador)

Hexiell Jarquin
DLM, Abogados, Notarios & Consultores

Thelma Dinora Lizama de Osorio
Superintendencia del Sistema Financiero

Martha de Jesús López Méndez
Guandique Segovia Quintanilla - LatamLex

Mario Lozano
Arias & Muñoz

Diego Martin-Menjivar
Consortium Centro América Abogados

Astrud María Meléndez
Asociación Protectora de Créditos de El Salvador (PROCREDITO)

Claudia Meléndez de Solis
Pacheco Coto

José Walter Meléndez Ramírez
Dirección General de Aduanas, Ministerio de Hacienda de El Salvador

Miriam Eleana Mixco Reyna
Gold Service

Fernando Montano
Arias & Muñoz

Maria Francisca Montenegro
García & Bodán

Jose Navas
All World Cargo, SA de CV

Luis Orlando Liévano
Instituto Salvadoreño de la Construcción - ISC

Geraldine Palma
AES El Salvador

Sergio Perez
AES El Salvador

Mónica Pineda Machuca
Pacheco Coto

Ana Patricia Portillo Reyes
Guandique Segovia Quintanilla - LatamLex

Carlos Roberto Rodriguez
Consortium Centro América Abogados

Otto Rodríguez Salazar
Benjamín Valdez & Asociados

Kelly Beatriz Romero
Nassar Abogados

Jaime Salinas
García & Bodán

Oscar Samour
Consortium Centro América Abogados

Ernesto Sánchez
Arias & Muñoz

Oscar Torres
García & Bodán

Mauricio Antonio Urrutia Urrutia
Superintendencia del Sistema Financiero

Julio Vargas
García & Bodán

EQUATORIAL GUINEA

Construcciones Vinguema

N.J. Ayuk
Centurion LLP

Irene Balaguer Delgado
L&S Abogados

Francisco Campos Braz
Solege

Keseena Chengadu
Centurion LLP

Gustavo Ndong Edu
Afri Logistics

Angel-Francisco Ela Ngomo Nchama
Juzgado de Instruccion de Bata

Philippe Fouda Fouda
BEAC Cameroon

Javier Iñiguez
PwC Equatorial Guinea

Marcel Jeutsop

Soraia Lacerda
Miranda Alliance

Sébastien Lechêne
PwC Equatorial Guinea

Marta López-Pena González
L&S Abogados

Angel Mba Abeso
Centurion LLP

Carl Mbeng
Centurion LLP

Paulino Mbo Obama
Oficina de estudieos - ATEG

Ponciano Mbomio Nvo
Gabinete Juridico

Jose Emilio Ndong
Abuy Asesores

Honorio Ndong Obama
Attorney-at-Law

Nanda Nzambi
PwC Equatorial Guinea

Jacinto Ona
Centurion LLP

Cristina Sánchez Cosme
Centurion LLP

Raquel Teresa Serón Calvo
L&S Abogados

ERITREA

Senai Andemariam
Berhane Gila-Michael Law Firm

Berhane Gilamichael
Berhane Gila-Michael Law Firm

Victor Majani
Parker Randall EA – Certified Public Accountants

Mewael Tekle
Department of Energy

ESTONIA

Angela Agur
NJORD Law Firm

Aet Bergmann
BNT Attorneys-at-Law Advokaadibüroo OÜ

Ülleke Eerik
Estonian Land Board

Kelli Eilart
Advokaadibüroo SORAINEN AS

Alger Ers
AE Projekti Insener

Carri Ginter
Advokaadibüroo SORAINEN AS

Janek Hamidžanov
Metaprint Ltd.

Kristjan Hänni
Kawe Kapital

Andres Juss
Estonian Land Board

Erica Kaldre
Hough, Hutt & Partners OÜ

Kadri Kallas
Advokaadibüroo SORAINEN AS

Katre Kasepold
Estonian Logistics and Freight Forwarding Association

Jevgeni Kazutkin
Hough, Hutt & Partners OÜ

Kätlin Klaos
PwC Estonia

Igor Kostjuk
Hough, Hutt & Partners OÜ

Villu Kõve
Estonian Supreme Court

Tanja Kriisa
PwC Estonia

Timo Kullerkupp
NJORD Law Firm

Paul Künnap
Advokaadibüroo SORAINEN AS

Siiri Kuusik
NJORD Law Firm

Martti Lemendik
Metaprint Ltd.

Hannes Lentsius
PwC Estonia

Tanel Lillesaar
Astorfi

Kerstin Linnart
Aliance of Independent Legal Advisers

Berit Loog
Ministry of Justice

Karin Madisson
Advokaadibüroo SORAINEN AS

Kaps Meelis
Elektrilevi OÜ

Veiko Meos
Krediidiinfo AS

Teele Mikk
Advokaadibüroo SORAINEN AS

Sandra-Kristin Noot
Raidla Ellex Advokaadibüroo OÜ

Arne Ots
Raidla Ellex Advokaadibüroo OÜ

Olavi Ottenson
Deloitte Advisory AS

Hanna Pahk
Advokaadibüroo SORAINEN AS

Kirsti Pent
Law Office FORT

Kaitti Persidski
Estonian Chamber of Notaries

Tõnu Roosve
Elektrilevi OÜ

Einar Rosin
KPMG Baltics OÜ

Kertu Ruus
Advokaadibüroo SORAINEN AS

Tuuli Saarits
BNT Attorneys-at-Law Advokaadibüroo OÜ

Piret Saartee
Centre of Registers & Information Systems

Katrin Sarap
NJORD Law Firm

Veronika Selge
Law Office FORT

Lisette Suik
Advokaadibüroo SORAINEN AS

Maria Teder
Raidla Ellex Advokaadibüroo OÜ

Triin Tigane
Advokaadibüroo SORAINEN AS

Triin Toom
Advokaadibüroo SORAINEN AS

Veikko Toomere
NJORD Law Firm

Neve Uudelt
Aliance of Independent Legal Advisers

Erle Uus
KPMG Baltics OÜ

Hannes Vallikivi
Law Office Tark Grunte Sutkiene

Ivo Vanasaun
Deloitte Advisory AS

Paul Varul
Primus Attorneys-at-Law

Anne Veerpalu
NJORD Law Firm

Peeter Viirsalu
Primus Attorneys-at-Law

ETHIOPIA

Ernst & Young

Dagnachew Tesfaye Abetew
Dagnachew Tesfaye and Mahlet Mesganaw Law Office

Abdella Ali
Abdella Ali Law Office

Dibaba Amensissa

Gebre Amlak
Tadesse Kiros Law Office

Hailemariam Tesfaye Asnake
Hailemariam Tesfaye Law Office

Yodit Assefa
The Motor & Engineering Company

Filipos Aynalem
Lawyer

Nega Binalfew
Binalfew Law Firm

Semere Wolde Bonger
National Bank of Ethiopia

Hailu Burayu
Lawyer

Marina Bwile
Teshome Gabre-Mariam Bokan Law Firm

Abinet Damtachew
Construction Proxy

Yonas Kidane Demiyesus
Dashen Bank S.C.

Fekadu Gebremeskel
Fekadu Petros Legal Service

Asheber Hailesilassie
Trans Ethiopia PLC - TEPLCO

Nuru Hassen
Trans Ethiopia PLC - TEPLCO

Yosef Kebede
Dashen Bank S.C.

Belay Ketema
Belay Ketema Law Office

Tadesse Kiros
Tadesse Kiros Law Office

Mehrteab Leul
Mehrteab Leul & Associates

Tamrat Assefa Liban
Tamrat Assefa Liban Law Offices

Getnet Yawkal Mebratu
Getnet Yawkal Mebratu

Alem Mengsteab
Ethiopian General Installation Supply

Mahlet Mesganaw Getu
Mahlet Mesganaw Legal Advisory Office

Getu Shiferaw
Mehrteab Leul & Associates

Mekdes Shiferaw
Green International Logistic Services

Ameha Sime
Ameha Sime B.C.

L.H. Solomon
Net Engineering Consultancy

Mesfin Tafesse
Mesfin Tafesse and Associates Law Office

Brook Tefera
Bigar Architecture and Engineering

Amanuel Teshome
Aman & Partners

Gizeshwork Tessema
Gize PLC

Wossenyeleh Tigu
Mesfin Tafesse and Associates Law Office

Shimelis Tilahun
Net Consult

Emebet Worku

Getahun Worku
Lawyer

Mekidem Yehiyes
Mesfin Tafesse and Associates Law Office

Sintayehu Zeleke
First Instance Federal Court

FIJI

David Aidney
Williams & Gosling Ltd.

Eddielin Almonte
PwC Fiji

Nicholas Barnes
Munro Leys

Nehla Basawaiya
Munro Leys

Suresh Chandra
MC Lawyers

William Wylie Clarke
Howards Lawyers

Lawrence Fung
Munro Leys

Jerome Kado
PwC Fiji

Viren Kapadia
Sherani & Co.

Netani Kau
Suva City Council

Mohammed Afzal Khan
Khan & Co Barristers & Solicitors

Emily King
Munro Leys

Peter Ian Knight
Cromptons Solicitors

Roneel Lal
Williams & Gosling Ltd.

Taina Leweny
TL Lawyers

Hemendra Nagin
Sherani & Co.

Jon Orton
Orton Architects

Pradeep Patel
BDO

Nilesh Prasad
Mitchell, Keil & Associates

Ramesh Prasad Lal
Carpenters Shipping

Mele Rakai
Sherani & Co.

Rahul Ral
Carpenters Shipping

Abhi Ram
Companies Registrar

Jagindar Singh
Carpenters Shipping

Shelvin Singh
Shelvin Singh Lawyers

Narotam Solanki
PwC Fiji

Eparama Tawake
Fiji Electricity Authority

Nancy Toganivalu
Toganivalu Valenitabua Barristers & Solicitors

Vulisere Tukama
Suva City Council

Jay Udit
Howards Lawyers

Eddie Yuen
Williams & Gosling Ltd.

FINLAND

Manne Airaksinen
Roschier Attorneys Ltd.

Timo Airisto
White & Case

Roope Apponen
Helen Sähköverkko Oy

Petri Avikainen
Asianajotoimisto White & Case Oy

Johanna Ellonen
Roschier Attorneys Ltd.

Marja Eskola
PwC Finland

Maria Fagerström-Ryder
Asianajotoimisto White & Case Oy

Elina Finnilä
PwC Finland

Oona Fromholdt
Castrén & Snellman Attorneys Ltd.

Emma Grönroos
Krogerus Attorneys Ltd.

Esa Halmari
Hedman Partners

Johanna Haltia-Tapio
Hannes Snellman Attorneys Ltd.

Joni Hatanmaa
Hedman Partners

Seppo Havia
Dittmar & Indrenius

Harri Hirvonen
PwC Finland

Lauri Ignatius
Roschier Attorneys Ltd.

Nina Isokorpi
Roschier Attorneys Ltd.

Lauri Jääskeläinen
Building Control Department of the City of Helsinki

Pekka Jaatinen
Castrén & Snellman Attorneys Ltd.

Sarianna Järviö
Asianajotoimisto White & Case Oy

Johanna Jarvinen
Panalpina AB

Juuso Jokela
Suomen Asiakastieto Oy

Vilja Juvonen
PwC Finland

Mika Karpinnen
Hannes Snellman Attorneys Ltd.

Milla Kokko-Lehtinen
PwC Finland

Kaisa Lamppu
PwC Finland

Ina Lehto
Finnish Energy Industries

Anna-Ilona Lehtonen
Roschier Attorneys Ltd.

Pertteri Leinonen

Jan Lilius
Hannes Snellman Attorneys Ltd.

Patrik Lindfors
Lindfors & Co., Attorneys-at-Law Ltd.

Patrick Lindgren
Law Office ADVOCARE

Olli Mäkelä
Hannes Snellman Attorneys Ltd.

Kimmo Mettälä
Krogerus Attorneys Ltd.

Linda Miettinen
Eversheds Attorneys Ltd.

Marta Monteiro
Hannes Snellman Attorneys Ltd.

Eeva-Leena Niemelä
Roschier Attorneys Ltd.

Jani Pitkänen
Eversheds Attorneys Ltd.

Mikko Rajala
Bird & Bird Attorneys Ltd.

Ingrid Remmelgas
Roschier Attorneys Ltd.

Jasse Ritakallio
Lindfors & Co, Attorneys-at-Law Ltd.

Peter Salovaara
Eversheds Attorneys Ltd.

Claus Schmidt
Panalpina World Transport

Petri Seppälä
PwC Finland

Nikolas Sjöberg
Krogerus Attorneys Ltd.

Aatos Solhagen
Asianajotoimisto White & Case Oy

Dina Stolt
Roschier Attorneys Ltd.

Petri Taivalkoski
Roschier Attorneys Ltd.

Tanja Törnkvist
Asianajotoimisto White & Case Oy

Tuuli Vapaavuori-Vartiainen
Eversheds Attorneys Ltd.

Seija Vartiainen
PwC Finland

Marko Vuori
Krogerus Attorneys Ltd.

Gunnar Westerlund
Roschier Attorneys Ltd.

FRANCE

Air Cargo International Group

Commission de Régulation de l'Energie

Eau de Paris

Mairie de Paris

Nadhia Ameziane
Dentons

Alexandre Avrillon
Gondran de Robert Avocats

Nicolas Barberis
Ashurst LLP

Julien Bellapianta
ATS International

Florence Bequet-Abdou
PwC Société d'Avocats

Sylvain Bergès
Paul Hastings

Vincent Berthat
SCP Berthat-Schihin-Duchanoy-Heritier

Pierre Binon
Banque de France

Andrew Booth
Andrew Booth Architect

Guillaume Bordier
Capstan

Isabelle-Victoria Carbuccia
IVCH Paris

Frédéric Cauvin
PwC Société d'Avocats

Georges Cavalier
PwC Société d'Avocats

Gwendal Chatain
PwC Société d'Avocats

Jean-Pierre Clavel
SCP Jean-Pierre Clavel

Jean-Paul Decorps
Etude Maître Jean-Paul Decorps

Marie d'Ocagne
DLA Piper France LLP

Florence Druesne
SCP Jean-Pierre Clavel

Segolene Dufetel
Mayer Brown International LLP

Jean-Marc Dufour
France eCommerce International

Philippe Durand
PwC Société d'Avocats

Olivier Everaere
Agence Epure SARL

Benoit Fauvelet
Banque de France

Ingrid Fauvelière
Jeantet AARPI

Ivan Féron
PwC Société d'Avocats

Lionel Galliez
Conseil Supérieur du Notariat (Paris)

Nassim Ghalimi
Veil Jourde

Jacques Gondran de Robert
Gondran de Robert Avocats

Pierre-Edouard Gondran de Robert
Gondran de Robert Avocats

Régine Goury
Mayer Brown International LLP

François Grenier

Frederic Gros
Jones Day

Kevin Grossmann
Cabinet Grossmann

Jérôme Halphen
DLA Piper France LLP

Karl Hepp de Sevelinges
Jeantet AARPI

Michael Jaffe
PwC Société d'Avocats

Marc Jobert
Jobert & Associés

Laurent Karila
Karila

Abdelmalek Kherbachene
Bouchemla Lanouar & Associés

Kaela Kim
Capstan

Paul Lafuste
Veil Jourde

Mohamed Lanouar
Bouchemla Lanouar & Associés

Daniel Arthur Laprès
Avocat à la Cour d'Appel de Paris

Vanessa Li
DLA Piper France LLP

Florian Linditch
Gondran de Robert Avocats

Olivier Lopez
Cohen & Gresser, AARPI

Elsa Lourdeau
Mayer Brown International LLP

Alexandre Majbruch
Dentons

Wladimir Mangel
Mayer Brown International LLP

Lucie Maurice
PwC Société d'Avocats

Frederic Mercier
Mathez Transports Internationaux S.A

Nathalie Morel
Mayer Brown International LLP

Thierry Morgant
PwC Société d'Avocats

Wye-Peygn Morter
Mayer Brown International LLP

Lamia Naamoune
Bouchemla Lanouar & Associés

Michel Nisse
PwC Société d'Avocats

Arnaud Pelpel
Pelpel Avocats

Thomas Philippe
Mayer Brown International LLP

Nathalène Pierard
Gondran de Robert Avocats

Vanessa Raindre
Transparence - member of Russell Bedford International

Pierre-Yves Rossignol
FIABCI, the International Real Estate Federation

Philippe Roussel Galle
Université Paris Descartes

Hugues Roux
Banque de France

Maxime Simonnet
Dentons

Johannes Singelnstein
Racine Avocats

Isabelle Smith Monnerville
Smith d'Oria

Camille Sparfel
Capstan

Jean Tarrade
Conseil Supérieur du Notariat (Paris)

Steven Theallier
Mayer Brown International LLP

Lucas Vergnaud
Gondran de Robert Avocats

François Vergne
Gide Loyrette Nouel, member of Lex Mundi

Ronène Zana
PwC Société d'Avocats

Mathias Zenou
PwC Société d'Avocats

Claire Zuliani
Transparence - member of Russell Bedford International

GABON

John W. Ffooks & Co., member of Bowman Gilfillan Africa Group

Jean-Pierre Bozec
Project Lawyers

Jean Paul Camus
Société d'Energie et d'Eau du Gabon (SEEG)

Myriam Diallo
Panalpina Transports Mondiaux Gabon

Anaïs Edzang Pouzere
PricewaterhouseCoopers Tax & Legal SA

Gilbert Erangah
Etude Maître Erangah

Augustin Fang
Cabinet Augustin Fang

Philippe Fouda Fouda
BEAC Cameroon

Athanase Ndoye Loury
Syndic Judiciaire

Pélagie Massamba Mouckocko
PricewaterhouseCoopers Tax & Legal SA

Jean-Joel Mebaley
Destiny Executives Architects - Agence du Bord de Mer

Célestin Ndelia
Etude Maître Ndelia Célestin

Clotaire N'dong
Ministère de l'Economie, du Commerce, de l'Industrie et du Tourisme

Ruben Mindonga Ndongo

Thierry Ngomo
ARCHi Pro International

Lubin Ntoutoume
Cabinet SCP Ntoutoume et Mezher

Josette Cadie Olendo

Fulgence Ongama
Tribunal de Première Instance de Libreville

Marie-Jose Ongo Mendou
Business Consulting

Laurent Pommera
PricewaterhouseCoopers Tax & Legal SA

Christophe Adrien Relongoué
PricewaterhouseCoopers Tax & Legal SA

Erwan Rouxel
Société d'Energie et d'Eau du Gabon (SEEG)

Fabien Tannhof
Société d'Energie et d'Eau du Gabon (SEEG)

GAMBIA, THE

Lamin A.K. Touray
Attorney General Chambers of Gambia

Victoria Andrews
Farage Andrews Law Practice

Malick Bah
National Environment Agency

Amie N.D. Bensouda
Amie Bensouda & Co.

Lamin B.S. Camara
Dandimayo Law Chambers

Ida Denise Drameh
Ida D. Drameh & Associates

Loubna Farage
Farage Andrews Law Practice

Dzidzedze Fiadjoe
PwC Ghana

Alexander Fiifi-Yankson
PwC Ghana

Sarane Hydara
Mahfous Engineering Consultants

Lamin S. Jatta
Accord Associates

Sulayman Jobe
DT Associates, Independent Correspondence Firm of Deloitte Touche Tohmatsu Limited

Sulayman M. Joof
S.M. Joof Agency

Abdoullah Konateh
Mahfous Engineering Consultants

George Kwatia
PwC Ghana

Omar Njie
Law Firm Omar Njie

Baboucarr Owl
National Water and Electricity Company Ltd.

Janet Ramatoulie Sallah-Njie
Torodo Chambers

Aji Penda B. Sankareh
DT Associates, Independent Correspondence Firm of Deloitte Touche Tohmatsu Limited

Bakary Sanneh
Department of Physical Planning and Housing

Yassin Senghore
Senghore Law Practice

Mama Fatima Singhateh
Attorney General Chambers of Gambia

Hawa Sisay-Sabally
Lawyer

Salieu Taal
Temple Legal Practitioners

Kimbeng T. Tah
Attorney General Chambers of Gambia

GEORGIA

Mgaloblishvili, Kipiani, Dzidziguri (MKD) Law Firm

Wakhtang Alania
SOFMAR Shipping Agency

Marekh Amirashvili
Amirashvili, Gogishvili & Shengelia AGS

Kakhaber Arabidze
Arco Ltd.

Niko Bakashvili
Bakashvili and Company

Nino Bakhia
National Agency of Public Registry

Mikheil Baliashvili
Architectural Bureau

Giorgi Begiashvili
Begiashvili & Co. Limited Law Offices

Lasha Beraia
Rustavi Metallurgical Plant

Tatia Berekashvili
Ministry of Justice

Revaz Beridze
Eristavi & Partners

Nino Bezhitashvili
Ministry of Economy and Sustainable Development

Temur Bolotashvili
Tbilisi Municipality City Hall

Aleksandre Cheishvili
JSC TBC Bank

Giorgi Chichinadze
Ministry of Economy and Sustainable Development

Mikheil Daushvili
Economic Council Administration (Government of Georgia)

Khatia Esebua
Alliance Group Holding

Mariam Gabashvili
Eristavi & Partners

Teymuraz Gamrekelashvili
Telasi

Teona Gaprindashvili
Nodia, Urumashvili & Partners

Rusudan Gergauli
Legal Partners Associated (LPA) LLC

Givi Giorgadze
Investors Council

Lasha Gogiberidze
BGI Legal

Alexander Gomiashvili
JSC Credit Info Georgia

Goga Gujejiani
Kaukasus Transport Logistik

Nana Gurgenidze
Legal Partners Associated (LPA) LLC

Batu Gvasalia
National Agency of Public Registry

David Javakhadze
Ministry of Economy and Sustainable Development

Revaz Javelidze
Colibri Law Firm

George Jugeli
Investors Council

David Kakabadze
Colibri Law Firm

Grigol Kakauridze
Ministry of Economy and Sustainable Development

Ana Kamkhadze
Eristavi & Partners

Nino Khachapuridze
Ministry of Economy and Sustainable Development

Mari Khardziani
National Agency of Public Registry

Nino Khoperia
Notary Chamber of Georgia

Dachi Kinkladze
Georgia Revenue Service

Sergi Kobakhidze
PwC Georgia

Aieti Kukava
Alliance Group Holding

Sophio Kurtauli
National Bureau of Enforcement

Nino Kvinikadze
Nodia, Urumashvili & Partners

Archil Lezhava
Legal Partners Associated (LPA) LLC

Tea Loladze
Ministry of Economy and Sustainable Development

Mirab-Dmitry Lomadze

Sofia Machaladze
Eristavi & Partners

Irakli Mamaladze
Tegeta Motors

Jaba Mamulashvili
Begiashvili & Co. Limited Law Offices

Marekh Merabishvili
Office of the Business Ombudsman of Georgia

Salome Meunargia
Legal Partners Associated (LPA) LLC

Roin Migriauli
Law Office Migriauli & Partners

Ia Mikhelidze
Georgia Revenue Service

Tamar Morchiladze
BGI Legal

Kakhaber Nariashvili

Sophie Natroshvili
BGI Legal

Levan Nikoladze
Legal Partners Associated (LPA) LLC

Gamkrelidze Nikoloz
CaucasTransExpress Ltd.

Lasha Nodia
Nodia, Urumashvili & Partners

Tamta Nutsubidze
Begiashvili & Co. Limited Law Offices

Maia Okruashvili
Georgian Legal Partnership

Papuna Papiashvili
National Bureau of Enforcement

Simon Parsons
PwC Georgia

Tamara Pkhakadze
The Universal Consulting

Tsisnami Sabadze
Ministry of Economy and Sustainable Development

Natia Sakhokia
National Bureau of Enforcement

Giorgi Salakaia
National Bureau of Enforcement

Joseph Salukvadze
Tbilisi State University

Manzoor Shah
Globalink Logistics Group

Tea Sonishvili
Ministry of Economy and Sustainable Development

Giorgi Tavartkiladze
Deloitte

Tamara Tevdoradze
BGI Legal

Antonina Tselovalnikova
Gianti Logistics

Khatuna Turmanidze
National Bureau of Enforcement

Samson Uridia
Georgia Revenue Service

Zviad Voshakidze
Telasi

GERMANY

Stromnetz Berlin GmbH

Vattenfall Berlin

Daja Apetz-Dreier

Judith Becker
Reed Smith LLP

Mark Bekker
Bekker Logistica

Henning Berger
White & Case

Eva Bergmann
SCHUFA Holding AG

Philipp Johannes Bergmann
Reed Smith LLP

Jennifer Bierly
GSK Stockmann + Kollegen

Tom Braegelmann
DLA Piper UK LLP

Jan Bunnemann
DLA Piper UK LLP

Thomas Büssow
PwC Germany

Andreas Eckhardt
PricewaterhouseCoopers Legal Aktiengesellschaft Rechtsanwaltsgesellschaft

Alexander Freiherr von Aretin
Graf von Westphalen Rechtsanwälte Partnerschaft

Andrea Gruss
Merget + Partner

Klaus Günther
Oppenhoff & Partner

Daniel Hacker
PricewaterhouseCoopers Legal Aktiengesellschaft Rechtsanwaltsgesellschaft

Marc Alexander Häger
Oppenhoff & Partner

Nadine Haubner
Mayer Brown LLP

Tina Hoffmann
Mayer Brown LLP

Götz-Sebastian Hök
Dr. Hök Stieglmeier & Partner

Ralph Hummel
Avocado Rechtsanwälte

Wiebke Jakob
DLA Piper UK LLP

Markus Jakoby
Jakoby Rechtsanwälte

Peter Jark
DLA Piper UK LLP

Helmuth Jordan
Jordan & Wagner Rechtsanwaltsgesellschaft mbH

Wladimir Kern
PwC Germany

Johann Klein
Beeh & Happich GmbH - member of Russell Bedford International

Artur Korn
Reed Smith LLP

Ernst-Otto Kuchenbrandt
Deutsche Bundesbank

Stefan Kuhl
Mayer Brown LLP

Baerbel Kuhlmann
Ernst & Young

Andreas Lange
Mayer Brown LLP

Sabine Läufer
SCHUFA Holding AG

Peter Limmer
Notare Dr. Limmer & Dr. Friederich

Rene Lochmann
Reed Smith LLP

Mario Maier
Orrick, Herrington & Sutcliffe LLP

Sabine Malik
SCHUFA Holding AG

Nora Matthaei
Avocado Rechtsanwälte

Jan Geert Meents
DLA Piper UK LLP

Werner Meier
King & Spalding LLP

Daniel Meier-Greve
PricewaterhouseCoopers Legal Aktiengesellschaft Rechtsanwaltsgesellschaft

Frank Mizera
Reed Smith LLP

Marius Moeller
PwC Germany

Wolfgang Nardi
Kirkland & Ellis LLP Germany Munich

Dirk Otto
Gobbers & Denk

John Piotrowski
Jakoby Rechtsanwälte

Sebastian Prügel
White & Case

Anselm Reinertshofer
Reed Smith LLP

Sebastian Reinsch
Janke & Reinsch

Carl Renner
DLA Piper UK LLP

Philipp Ruehland
PricewaterhouseCoopers Legal Aktiengesellschaft Rechtsanwaltsgesellschaft

Marvin Ruth
DLA Piper UK LLP

Jana Schlimgene
GSK Stockmann + Kollegen

Astrid Schnabel
DLA Piper UK LLP

Volker Schwarz
HEUSSEN Rechtsanwalts-gesellschaft mbH

Kirstin Schwedt
Linklaters LLP

Benjamin Siering
PricewaterhouseCoopers Legal Aktiengesellschaft Rechtsanwaltsgesellschaft

Stefanie Skoruppa
Mayer Brown LLP

Thomas Strassner
Orrick, Herrington & Sutcliffe LLP

Jürgen Streng

Dr. Tobias Taetzner
PwC Germany

Kévin Paul-Hervé Tanguy
PricewaterhouseCoopers Legal Aktiengesellschaft Rechtsanwaltsgesellschaft

Holger Thomas
WilmerHale

Heiko Vogt
Panalpina Welttransport GmbH

Bernd Weller
Heuking Kühn Lüer Wojtek

Hartmut Wicke
Notare Dr. Wicke und Herrler

Marco Wilhelm
Mayer Brown LLP

Thomas Winkler
DOMUS AG - member of Russell Bedford International

Gerlind Wisskirchen
CMS Hasche Sigle

Uwe Witt
PricewaterhouseCoopers Legal Aktiengesellschaft Rechtsanwaltsgesellschaft

Michael Wuebbeke
PricewaterhouseCoopers Legal Aktiengesellschaft Rechtsanwaltsgesellschaft

GHANA

Baker Tilly Andah+Andah Chartered Accountants

Ismael Andani Abdulai
Renaissance Law Chambers

Solomon Ackom
Grimaldi Ghana Ltd.

George Kingsley Acquah
Standard Chartered Bank Ghana Limited

Watkins Adamah
Ntrakwah & Co.

Victor Adjei
XDSDATA Ghana Ltd.

Sena Agbekoh
AB & David

Irene Agyenim-Boateng
AB & David

George Ahiafor
XDSDATA Ghana Ltd.

Kweku Ainuson
AB Lexmall & Associates

Cecilia Akyeampong
Town and Country Planning Department

Mellisa Amarteifio
Sam Okudzeto & Associates

Nene Amegatcher
Sam Okudzeto & Associates

Kennedy Paschal Anaba
Lawfields Consulting

Wilfred Kwabena Anim-Odame
Lands Commission

Ellis Arthur
Beyuo & Company

Kwabena Asante Offei
Bentsi-Enchill, Letsa & Ankomah, member of Lex Mundi

Akousa Akoma Asiama
Ntrakwah & Co.

Fred Asiamah-Koranteng
Bank of Ghana

Bridget Atta-Konadu
Ntrakwah & Co.

Nana Akwasi Awuah
AB Lexmall & Associates

Kwadwo Baafi
Sell Right Ghana Limited

Sena Bakar
Ntrakwah & Co.

Ayesha Bedwei
PwC Ghana

Kizito Beyuo
Beyuo & Company

Thomas Blankson
XDSDATA Ghana Ltd.

C. Kwesi Buckman
Archi-Dev Consult

Diana Asonaba Dapaah
Sam Okudzeto & Associates

Jerry Dei
Sam Okudzeto & Associates

Saviour Dzuali
Bollore Africa Logistics Ghana

Frank Fugar
College of Architecture and Planning

Christina Furler
Furler Architects Ltd.

Abeku Gyan-Quansah
PwC Ghana

Roland Horsoo
Bouygues Construction

Daniel Imadi
Bentsi-Enchill, Letsa & Ankomah, member of Lex Mundi

Adam Imoru Ayarna
Cadesmee International

Cynthia Jumu
CQ Legal & Consulting

Edem Kofi Penty
Renaissance Law Chambers

Rosa Kudoadzi
Bentsi-Enchill, Letsa & Ankomah, member of Lex Mundi

Mary Kwarteng
PwC Ghana

George Kwatia
PwC Ghana

Musah Masahudu
Archsyntax Consult

Eric Nii Yarboi Mensah
Sam Okudzeto & Associates

Paul Kobina Mensah
Mass Logistics Ghana Limited

Victor Mensah
Town and Country Planning Department

Kwadwo Ntrakwah
Ntrakwah & Co.

Nana Yaw Ntrakwah
Ntrakwah & Co.

Abena Ntrakwah-Mensah
Ntrakwah & Co.

Wordsworth Odame Larbi
Consultant

Kwaku D. Ofori
Ofori Law Firm, LLC

Sam Okudzeto
Sam Okudzeto & Associates

Rexford Assasie Oppong
KNUST

Mike Oppong Adusah
Bank of Ghana

Prince Oppong Boakye
Bentsi-Enchill, Letsa & Ankomah

Daniel Osei-Kufuor
Osei-Kufuor, Sohne & Partners

Patience Ose-Nyarko
Town and Country Planning Department

Vera Owusu Osei
AB & David

Benjamin Quaye
Ministry of Land and Natural Resources of the Republic of Ghana

Jacob Saah
Saah & Co.

Shirley Somuah
Ntrakwah & Co.

Ebenezer Teye Agawu
Consolidated Shipping Agencies Limited

Joyce Franklyn Thompson
Ntrakwah & Co.

Samuel Twerefour
Lawfields Consulting

M.C. Vasnani
Consolidated Shipping Agencies Limited

Kwadwo Yeboah
Town and Country Planning Department

GREECE

Sophia Ampoulidou
Drakopoulos Law Firm

Alexander Anagnostopoulos
Karatzas & Partners

Evangelos Angelopoulos
E Angelopoulos Law Office

Eve Athanasekou
Hellenic Notary Association

Anastasia Baka
Potamitis-Vekris

Amalia Balla
Potamitis-Vekris

Georgia Balopoulou
Kyriakides Georgopoulos Law Firm

George Bersis
Potamitis-Vekris

Theodora Betsi
Karatzas & Partners

Dimitris Bimpas
IME GSEVEE

Athanasia Braimi
Pantazis & Associates

Ira Charisiadou
Charisiadou Law Office

Viktoria Chatzara
IKRP Rokas & Partners

George Chousos
XCON Xousos Construction

Theodora Christodoulou
KLC Law Firm

Alkistis Marina Christofilou
IKRP Rokas & Partners

Evangelia Christopoulou-Stamelou
Notary

Vasiliki Christou
KLC Law Firm

Leda Condoyanni
Hellenic Corporate Gouvernance Council

Theodora D. Karagiorgou
Koutalidis Law Firm

Nikolaos Demiroglou
TaxExperts

Panagiota Dikaiou
Koutalidis Law Firm

Eleni Dikonimaki
Teiresias SA - Bank Information Systems

Sotirios Douklias
KG Law Firm

Anastasia Dritsa
Kyriakides Georgopoulos Law Firm

Elisabeth Eleftheriades
KG Law Firm

Katerina Filippatou
C. Papacostopoulos & Associates

Spyros Foulias
Vgenopoulos and Partners Law Firm

Sophia Fourlari
Court of First Instance

Stergios Frastanlis
Zepos & Yannopoulos Law Firm, member of Lex Mundi

Dionyssia I. Gamvrakis
Sarantitis Law Firm

Georgios Garoufis
PwC Greece

Dionysios Gavounelis
K | P Law Firm

Dimitra Georgaraki
TaxExperts

Antonis Giannakodimos
Zepos & Yannopoulos Law Firm, member of Lex Mundi

Antonios Gkiokas
PwC Greece

Christos Goulas
Kremalis Law Firm, member of Ius Laboris

Aikaterini Grivaki
PwC Greece

Dimitris V. Hatzihristidis
Electrical Engineer

Efthymios Kallitsis

Harry Karampelis
Kyriakides Georgopoulos Law Firm

Artemis Karathanassi
PwC Greece

Catherine Karatzas
Karatzas & Partners

Rita Katsoula
Potamitis-Vekris

Dionysis Kazaglis
Sarantitis Law Firm

Anna Kazantzidou
Vainanidis Economou & Associates Law Firm

Anastasia Kelveridou
Kyriakides Georgopoulos Law Firm

Eirini Kikarea
Karatzas & Partners

Efthymios Kleftogiannis
PwC Greece

Ioanna Kompou
PwC Greece

Alexandra Kondyli
Karatzas & Partners

Lena Kontogeorgou
Notary

Panos Koromantzos
Bahas, Gramatidis & Partners

Olga Koromilia
PwC Greece

Dimitrios Kotsionis
Michael Kyprianou & Co. LLC

Aggeliki Kounadi
TaxExperts

Dimitrios Kremalis
Kremalis Law Firm, member of Ius Laboris

Irene C. Kyriakides
Kyriakides Georgopoulos Law Firm

Domna Kyrzopoulou
K | P Law Firm

Antonis Mantonanakis
Panmonotiki Prostasia

Evangelos Margaritis
Drakopoulos Law Firm

Emmanuel Mastromanolis
Zepos & Yannopoulos Law Firm, member of Lex Mundi

John Mazarakos
Elias Paraskevas Attorneys 1933

Alexandros N. Metaxas
Sarantitis Law Firm

Effie G. Mitsopoulou
Kyriakides Georgopoulos Law Firm

Theodora G. Monochartzi
Sarantitis Law Firm

Athena Moraiti
Stratos - Moraiti - Stamelos Law Offices

Konstantinos Nanopoulos
TaxExperts

Anthony Narlis
Calberson SA

Effie Nestorides
EYDAP SA

Panagiota (Yiota) Ntassiou
Reed Smith LLP

Anastasia Oikonomopoulou
KLC Law Firm

Kyriakos Oikonomou
Ministry of Justice

Dionysios Pantazis
Pantazis & Associates

Stefanos Pantazis
Pantazis & Associates

Christina Papachristopoulou
K | P Law Firm

Kelly Papadaki
Potamitis-Vekris

Konstantinos Papadiamantis
Potamitis-Vekris

Dimitris Papamentzelopoulos
KLC Law Firm

Stavros Papantonis
Action Auditing SA - member of Russell Bedford International

Martha Papasotiriou
UnityFour

Alexios Papastavrou
Potamitis-Vekris

Dimitris E. Paraskevas
Elias Paraskevas Attorneys 1933

Marios Petropoulos
Kremalis Law Firm, member of Ius Laboris

Spiros Pilios
Phoenix

Katerina Politi
Kyriakides Georgopoulos Law Firm

Panagiotis Polychronopoulos
Kelemenis & Co.

Stathis Potamitis
Potamitis-Vekris

Anthony Poulopoulos
Reed Smith LLP

Vicky Psaltaki
Sarantitis Law Firm

Mary Psylla
PwC Greece

Terina Raptis
Sarantitis Law Firm

Kyriaki (Korina) Raptopoulou
Kyriakides Georgopoulos Law Firm

Eva Rodaki
PwC Greece

Ioannis Sarakinos
Ioannis A. Sarakinos (IAS) Law Office

Nikolaos Siakantaris
UnityFour

Ioannis Skandalis
PwC Greece

Fani Skartouli
Potamitis-Vekris

Ioanna Stamou
Karatzas & Partners

Natassa Stamou
Hellenic Exchanges SA

Alexia Stratou
Kremalis Law Firm, member of Ius Laboris

Evangelia Tasiopoulou
Sarantitis Law Firm

Georgios Thanopoulos
IME GSEVEE

Athanasios Thoedorou

Fotini Trigazi
Notary

John Tripidakis
John Tripidakis & Associates Law Firm

Kimon Tsakiris
KG Law Firm

Angeliki Tsatsi
Karatzas & Partners

Antonios Tsavdaridis
IKRP Rokas & Partners

Panagiota Tsinouli
Kyriakides Georgopoulos Law Firm

Chryssi Tsirogianni
Notary

Panagiota D. Tsitsa
Panagiota Tsitsa

Achillefs Tsoutsis
Sarantitis Law Firm

Katerina Tzamalouka
Kyriakides Georgopoulos Law Firm

Ioanna Tzinieri
Greek Land Registrars Association

Alexia Tzouni
Potamitis-Vekris

Spyros Valvis
PwC Greece

Aris Velentzas
Vgenopoulos and Partners Law Firm

Penny Vithoulka
C. Papacostopoulos & Associates

Konstantinos Vlachakis
Notary

Kalliopi Vlachopoulou
Kelemenis & Co.

Ioanna Vourvoulia
Kyriakides Georgopoulos Law Firm

Sofia Xanthoulea
John Tripidakis & Associates Law Firm

Panagiotis Xenitelis
Karatzas & Partners

Fredy Yatracou
PwC Greece

Stergios Zygouras
Koutalidis Law Firm

GRENADA

Danny Williams & Co.

Grenada Electricity Services Ltd.

W.R. Agostini
W. R. Agostini & Co.

Roger Archer
Scotiabank Grenada

James Bristol
Henry, Henry & Bristol

Linda Dolland
Seon & Associates

Ruggles Ferguson
Ciboney Chambers

Corland Forrester
Inland Revenue Department

Aubrey Garcia
Seon & Associates

Kim George
Kim George & Associates

Carlyle Glean Jr.
Glean's Construction & Engineering Co.

Annette Henry
Ministry of Legal Affairs

Keith Hosten
Hosten's (Electrical Services) Ltd.

Ernie James
Ministry of Economic Development, Planning, Trade, Cooperatives and International Business

Henry Joseph
PKF International

Michell Julien-Farray
Inland Revenue Department

Anselm LaTouche
Creative Design

Garvey Louison
Louison Consulting

Kelly Roberts
Scotiabank Grenada

Karen Samuel
Samuel Phillip & Associates

Safiya Sawney
Tradship International

Valentino Sawney
Tradship International

David R. Sinclair
Sinclair Enterprises Limited

Trevor St. Bernard
Lewis & Renwick

Shireen Wilkinson
Wilkinson, Wilkinson & Wilkinson

GUATEMALA

Empresa Eléctrica de Guatemala, S. A.

Protectora de Crèdito Comercial

Superintendencia de Administración Tributaria

Julio Aparicio
Lexincorp

Pedro Aragón
Aragón & Aragón

Mario R. Archila Cruz
Consortium - RACSA

Jorge Luis Arenales de la Roca
Arias & Munoz

José Alejandro Arévalo Alburez
Superintendencia de Bancos

Elías Arriaza Sáenz
Consortium - RACSA

María de los Angeles Barillas Buchhalter
Saravia & Muñoz

Nancy Barrera
PwC Guatemala

Jorge Rolando Barrios
Bonilla, Montano, Toriello & Barrios

Elmer Erasmo Beltetón Morales
Registro General de la Propiedad de Guatemala (RGP)

Roberto Bermejo Q.
Bermejo & Asociados

Axel Beteta
Carrillo y Asociados

Jean Paul Brichaux
Asociación de Exportadores de Café (ADEC)

Eva Cacacho González
QIL+4 Abogados, SA

Emanuel Callejas
Carrillo & Asociados

Rodrigo Callejas Aquino
Carrillo & Asociados

Delia Cantoral
Ernst & Young

Jorge Castañeda
SPEC

Raul Castañeda
SPEC

Francisco José Castillo Chacón
Aguilar Castillo Love

Juan Carlos Castillo Chacón
Aguilar Castillo Love

Maria Mercedes Castro
García & Bodán

Juan Carlos Chavarría
Ernst & Young

Juan Carlos Corona
Bermejo & Asociados

Rafael Garavito
Bufete Garavito

Jose Gonzalez
Precon

Carlos Guillermo Herrera
Registro General de la Propiedad de Guatemala (RGP)

Pamela Jimenez
Arias & Munoz

Eva Maria Lima
City Hall of Guatemala City

Alma Mejia
Ernst & Young

Edgar Mendoza
PwC Guatemala

Jorge Mario Mendoza Sandoval
FedEx

Gonzalo Menéndez González
Lexincorp

Jorge Meoño
Inproalegal

Enrique Moller
Ernst & Young

Edgar Montes
Registro General de la Propiedad de Guatemala (RGP)

Edvin Montoya
Lexincorp

María José Najera
Carrillo & Asociados

Anajoyce Oliva
City Hall of Guatemala City

Monica Ordoñez
Registro General de la Propiedad de Guatemala (RGP)

Hugo Rafael Oroxóm Mérida
Superintendencia de Bancos

Carlos Ortega
Mayora & Mayora, S.C.

Jorge Osoy
City Hall of Guatemala City

Roberto Ozaeta
PwC Guatemala

Marco Antonio Palacios
Palacios & Asociados

Maria Jose Pepio Pensabene
Cámara Guatemalteca de la Construcción

Claudia Pereira
Mayora & Mayora, S.C.

Patrocinio Pérez y Pérez
Superintendencia de Bancos

Mélida Pineda
Carrillo & Asociados

Manuel Ramírez
Ernst & Young

Diego Ramírez Bathen
Grupo ICC

Alfredo Rodríguez Mahuad
Consortium - RACSA

Luis Alfonso Ruano
CGW

Glendy Salguero
PwC Guatemala

Salvador Augusto Saravia Castillo
Saravia & Muñoz

José Augusto Toledo Cruz
Arias & Muñoz

Arelis Yariza Torres de Alfaro
Superintendencia de Bancos

Rodrigo Valladares
Registro Mercantil

Elmer Vargas
Pacheco Coto

GUINEA

Yves Constant Amani
Cabinet d'Avocats BAO & Fils

Pierre Kodjo Avode
Sylla & Partners

Ayelama Bah
Notaire Ayelama Bah

Aminata Bah Tall
Nimba Conseil SARL

Mohamed Aly Baldé
PwC Guinea

Mamadou Barry
Nimba Conseil SARL

Ismaila Camara
Maersk Logistics SA

Gabriel Curtis
Agence de Promotion des Investissments Privés

Abdelaziz Derrahi
Electricité de Guinée

Zakaria Diakité
Nimba Conseil SARL

Ahmadou Diallo
Chambre des Notaires

Youssouf Diallo
Chambre des Notaires

Housseyni Fofana
MERS

Naby Moussa Fofana
Banque Centrale de Guinée (BCRG)

Soukeina Fofana
Banque Centrale de Guinée (BCRG)

Joachim Gbilimou

Amadou Thidiane Kaba

Madigbe Kaba
Sylla & Partners

Mariama Ciré Keita Diallo
Nimba Conseil SARL

Fatoumata Koulibaly
Banque Centrale de Guinée (BCRG)

Nounké Kourouma
Administration et Contrôle des Grands Projets

Mohamed Lahlou
PwC Guinea

Augustin Lovichi
Electricité de Guinée

Souleymane Mariama Dalde
Orabank

Enang Odile Mboe Ntungwe
Nimba Conseil SARL

Stéphane Ntsogo Pana
Nimba Conseil SARL

Guy Piam Kaptue
Nimba Conseil SARL

Amadou Salif Kébé
Cabinet Avocat Salif Kébé

Soriba Sidibé
Electricité de Guinée

Mohamed Sidiki Sylla
Sylla & Partners

Paul Tchagna
PwC Guinea

Abdourahamane Tounkara
Guinée Consulting

Aboubacar Salimatou Toure
Banque de Développement de Guinée

Mohamed Lamine Touré
Banque Centrale de Guinée (BCRG)

GUINEA-BISSAU

BCEAO

Luís Antunes
LUFTEC – Técnicas Eléctricas, Lda.

Humiliano Alves Cardoso
Gabinete Advocacia

Rui Paulo Coutinho de Mascarenhas Ataíde
Professor of Law

Adelaida Mesa D'Almeida
Jurisconta SRL

Octávio Lopes
GB Legal - Miranda Alliance

Gregorio Malu
Transmar Services Lda

Miguel Mango
Audi - Conta Lda

Ismael Mendes de Medina
GB Legal - Miranda Alliance

Ruth Monteiro
TSK Legal Advogados e Jurisconsultos

Eduardo Pimentel
Centro de Formalização de Empresas

Fernando Resina da Silva
Vieira de Almeida & Associados Portugal

Marta Sampaio
Mediterranean Shipping Company Lisbon (MSC)

Fernando Tavares
Transmar Services Lda

Carlos Vamain
Gomes & Vamain Associados

GUYANA

Digicom

Noels Electrical and Engineering Service

Rodrigues Architects Ltd.

Tracey Bancroft
City Engineers Office Mayor & Councillors of City of Georgetown

Wiston Beckles
Correia & Correia Ltd.

Marcel Bobb
Fraser, Housty & Yearwood Attorneys-at-Law

Ronald Burch-Smith
Waldron & Burch-Smith

Julius Campbell
Correia & Correia Ltd.

Desmond Correia
Correia & Correia Ltd.

Lucia Desir-John
D & J Shipping Services

Orin Hinds
Orin Hinds & Associates Arch. Ltd.

Renford Homer
Guyana Power & Light Inc.

Teni Housty
Fraser, Housty & Yearwood Attorneys-at-Law

Kalam Azad Juman-Yassin
Guyana Olympic Association

Kashir Khan
Attorney-at-Law

Rakesh Latchana
Ram & McRae Chartered Accountants

Harry Noel Narine
PKF International

Charles Ogle
Ministry of Labour, Human Services and Social Security

Carolyn Paul
Amice Legal Consultants Inc.

Deryck Phyll
Guyana Power & Light Inc.

Christopher Ram
Ram & McRae Chartered Accountants

Vishwamint Ramnarine
PFK Barcellos, Narine & Co.

Reginald Roach
R&D Engineering Services

Ryan Ross
Guyana Power & Light Inc.

Shantel Scott
Fraser, Housty & Yearwood Attorneys-at-Law

Judy Semple-Joseph
Creditinfo Guyana

Terry Singh
Galaxy Electrical Sales and Service

Leslie Sobers
Attorney-at-Law

Gidel Thomside
National Shipping Corporation Ltd.

Allyson West
PricewaterhouseCoopers Limited

Tonika Wilson-Gabriel
PricewaterhouseCoopers Limited

Horace Woolford
Guyana Power & Light Inc.

HAITI

Banque de la République d'Haiti

Mérové-Pierre - Cabinet d'Experts-Comptables

Ministère des Travaux Publics, Transports et Communications

Theodore Achille III
UNOPS

Marc Kinson Antoine
ADEKO Enterprises

Marie-Alice Belisaire
Syndicat des Notaires d'Haiti

Michelle Bien-Aimé
Cabinet Lissade

Erica Bouchereau Godefroy
Brown Legal Group

Jean Baptiste Brown
Brown Legal Group

Djacaman Charles
Cabinet Gassant

Karine Chenet

Martine Chevalier
Cabinet Leblanc & Associés

Karl B. Couba

Rigaud Duplan

Lucien Fresnel
Cabinet Gassant

Enerlio Gassant
Cabinet Gassant

Nadyne M. Joseph
Unibank

Ronald Laraque
AAU

Camille Leblanc
Cabinet Leblanc & Associés

Ludwig Leblanc
Cabinet Leblanc & Associés

Roberson Louis
Cabinet Gassant

Kathia Magloire
Cabinet Gassant

Dieuphète Maloir
Sam Construction

Jean Paul Nazon
Haiti Shipping SA

Joel Nexil
Air Courrier & Shipping

Jean Yves Noël
Noël, Cabinet d'Experts-Comptables

Joseph Paillant
BUCOFISC

Micosky Pompilus
Cabinet d'Avocats Chalmers

Margarette Antoine Sanon
Cabinet Margarette Antoine Sanon

Michel Succar
Cabinet Lissade

Salim Succar
Cabinet Lissade

Sibylle Theard Mevs
Theard & Associes

Jean Vandal
Vandal & Vandal

HONDURAS

CNBS - Comisión Nacional de Bancos y Seguros

Comisión Nacional de Energía

Mario Aguero
Arias & Muñoz

Vanessa Aguilera
Transcoma

Juan José Alcerro Milla
Aguilar Castillo Love

Karla Andino Peñalva
Consortium Centro América Abogados

Valmir Araujo
Operadora Portuaria Centroamericana

José Simón Azcona
Inmobiliaria Alianza SA

Andrea Casco
Bufete Casco & Asociados

Jorge Omar Casco
Bufete Casco & Asociados

Tania Vanessa Casco
Bufete Casco & Asociados

Freddy Castillo
García & Bodán

Carlos Chavarria
Consortium Centro América Abogados

Jaime Alberto Colindres Rosales
DYCELES S de R.L.

Kenia Cortés
ACZALAW

Graciela Cruz
García & Bodán

Heidy Cruz
García & Bodán

Terencio Garcia Montenegro
García & Bodán

Dennis Emilio Hércules Rosa
Aguilar Castillo Love

Evangelina Lardizábal
Arias & Muñoz

Armida María López de Arguello
ACZALAW

Rafael Enrique Medina Elvir
Cámara de Comercio e Industria de Tegucigalpa

Juan Carlos Mejía Cotto
Instituto de la Propiedad

Vanessa Oquelí
García & Bodán

José Ramón Paz
Consortium Centro América Abogados

Dino Rietti
Arquitecnic

Julio Rivera
García & Bodán

Milton Rivera
PwC Honduras

José Rafael Rivera Ferrari
Consortium Centro América Abogados

Enrique Rodriguez Burchard
Aguilar Castillo Love

Fanny Rodríguez del Cid
Arias & Muñoz

René Serrano
Arias & Muñoz

Godofredo Siercke
García & Bodán

Mariano Turnes
Operadora Portuaria Centroamericana

Daysi Gricelda Urquía Hernández
TransUnion

Armando Urtecho López
COHEP (Consejo Hondureño de la Empresa Privada)

Hilsy Villalobos
García & Bodán

Mauricio Villeda
Gutierrez Falla & Asociados

Jose Emilio Zablah Ulloa
PwC Honduras

Mario Rubén Zelaya
Energía Integral S. de RL de CV

Carlos F. Zúniga
Irías & Asociados S. de RL - correspondent of Russell Bedford International

HONG KONG SAR, CHINA

AECOM Asia Company Limited

Atrix Business Services Limited

TransUnion Limited

Albert P.C. Chan
The Hong Kong Polytechnic University

Leonard Chan
JLA-Asia

Nick Chan
Squire Sanders

Jacqueline Chiu
Mayer Brown JSM

Selraniy Chow
PwC Hong Kong

Robert Chu
Economic Analysis and Business Facilitation Unit

Tony Chu
Victon Registrations Ltd.

Jimmy Chung
Russell Bedford Hong Kong - member of Russell Bedford International

Victor Dawes
Temple Chambers

Vickie Fan
Fan, Chan & Co.

Wilson Fung
Mayer Brown JSM

Dominic Gregory
Ashurst Hong Kong

Keith Man Kei Ho
Wilkinson & Grist

Reynold Hung
PwC Hong Kong

Denise Jong
Reed Smith Richards Butler

Peter Kwon
Ashurst Hong Kong

Billy Lam
Mayer Brown JSM

Christie Lam
Hong Kong Financial Secretary

Kai Chiu Lam
CLP Power Hong Kong Limited

Ka Shi Lau
BCT Financial Limited (BCTF) / Bank Consortium Trust Company Limited (BCTC)

John Robert Lees
JLA-Asia

Camille Leung
Squire Patton Boggs LLC

Clara Leung
Reed Smith Richards Butler

Terry LK Kan
Shinewing Specialist Advisory Services Limited

Psyche S.F. Luk
Fairbairn Catley Low & Kong

Louise Ng
Squire Sanders

Mat Ng
JLA-Asia

James Ngai
Russell Bedford Hong Kong - member of Russell Bedford International

Kok Leong Ngan
CLP Power Hong Kong Limited

Yeung Or
Inland Revenue Department, HKSAR

Martinal Quan
Metopro Associates Limited

Matthias Schemuth
Ashurst Hong Kong

Holden Slutsky
Pacific Chambers

Keith Tam
Dun & Bradstreet (HK) Ltd.

Tammie Tam
Mayer Brown JSM

Eric Tang
Asia Business Service Limited

Anita Tsang
PwC Hong Kong

William Tsang
Y H Tsang & Co.

Cliff Tsui
JLA-Asia

Paul Tsui
Hong Kong Association of Freight Forwarding & Logistics Ltd. (HAFFA)

Christopher Whiteley
Ashurst Hong Kong

Agnes Wong
Companies Registry

Danny Wong
Dun & Bradstreet (HK) Ltd.

Fergus Wong
PwC Hong Kong

Kwok Kuen Yu
Companies Registry

HUNGARY

Pallér Csarnok Kft.

Balázs Balog
Reti, Antall and Partners Law Firm

Bela Banati
Bánáti + Hartvig Építész Iroda Kft.

Sándor Békési
Partos & Noblet Hogan Lovells

Blanka Börzsönyi
Siegler Law Office / Weil, Gotshal & Manges

Hédi Bozsonyik
Szecskay Attorneys-at-Law

Sárosi Csanád
Obuda-Ujalk

Zsuzsanna Cseri
Cseri & Partners Law Offices

Gábor Dohány
Partos & Noblet Hogan Lovells

Peter Eles
Bánáti + Hartvig Építész Iroda Kft.

Tamás Esze
BPV | Jádi Németh Attorneys-at-Law

Zsuzsa File
Partos & Noblet Hogan Lovells

Veronika Francis-Hegedűs
BPV | Jádi Németh Attorneys-at-Law

Gyula Gábriel
Bogsch & Partners

Anna Gáspár
Build-Econ Ltd.

Ervin Gombos
GMBS Kft.

Zoltán Gurszky
ELMŰ Hálózati Kft.

Tamas Halmos
Partos & Noblet Hogan Lovells

Dóra Horváth
Reti, Antall and Partners Law Firm

Andrea Jádi Németh
BPV | Jádi Németh Attorneys-at-Law

Atilla Jambor
Dr. Jámbor Attila Law Office

Ferenc Kalla
GTF Kft

Veronika Kiss
Partos & Noblet Hogan Lovells

Andrea Kladiva
Cseri & Partners Law Offices

Andrea Kocziha
PricewaterhouseCoopers Hungary Ltd.

Dóra Máthé
PricewaterhouseCoopers Hungary Ltd.

Mariann Miskovics
Sándor Szegedi Szent-Ivány Komáromi Eversheds

László Mohai
Mohai Law Office

Orsolya Molnar
Partos & Noblet Hogan Lovells

Tibor Molnár
CEF Invest

Noemi Nacsa
GMBS Kft.

Aniko Nagy
BPV | Jádi Németh Attorneys-at-Law

Viktor Nagy
BISZ Central Credit Information PLC

Sándor Németh
Szecskay Attorneys-at-Law

Christopher Noblet
Partos & Noblet Hogan Lovells

Örs Pénzes

Rita Rado
Cseri & Partners Law Offices

Richard Safcsak
BISZ Central Credit Information PLC

István Sándor
Kelemen, Meszaros, Sandor & Partners

Konrád Siegler
Siegler Law Office / Weil, Gotshal & Manges

Tamas Sotet
International Logistic Gateway

Botond Szalma
Hungarian Shipbrokers & Shipping Agents Association

Gábor Szanka
BISZ Central Credit Information PLC

Rita Szarva
Partos & Noblet Hogan Lovells

Szilvia Szeleczky
Budapest 1st District Municipality

Ágnes Szent-Ivány
Sándor Szegedi Szent-Ivány Komáromi Eversheds

Gergely Szoboszlai
Siegler Law Office / Weil, Gotshal & Manges

Ádám Tóth
Dr. Tóth Ádám Közjegyzői Iroda

Annamária Tóth
Partos & Noblet Hogan Lovells

Gábor Zoltán Szabó
Siegler Law Office / Weil, Gotshal & Manges

ICELAND

Reykjavik Municipal Building Control Officer

Ásta Sólveig Andrésdóttir
Registers Iceland

Benedikt Egill Árnason
LOGOS, member of Lex Mundi

Ragnar Tomas Árnason
LOGOS, member of Lex Mundi

Heiðar Ásberg Atlason
LOGOS, member of Lex Mundi

Stefán Árni Auðólfsson
Lögmenn Bárugötu - LMB

Margrét Berg Sverrisdóttir
Court of Arbitration of the Iceland Chamber of Commerce

Karen Bragadóttir
Tollstjóri - Directorate of Customs

Eymundur Einarsson
CPA.is Endurskoðun og Ráðgjöf ehf

Ólafur Eiríksson
LOGOS, member of Lex Mundi

Sigríður Anna Ellerup
Registers Iceland

Björg Finnbogadóttir
Registers Iceland

Anna Björg Guðjónsdóttir
BBA Legal

Gudrun Gudmundsdottir
Jónar Transport

Halldor Karl Halldorsson
Fjeldsted & Blöndal Legal Services

Reynir Haraldsson
Jónar Transport

Hörður Davíð Harðarson
Tollstjóri - Directorate of Customs

Burkni Maack Helgason
Creditinfo Iceland

Jón Ingi Ingibergsson
PwC Iceland

Aðalsteinn E. Jónasson
LEX Law Offices

Dagbjört Oddsdóttir
BBA Legal

Helga Melkorka Óttarsdóttir
LOGOS, member of Lex Mundi

Kristján Pálsson
Jónar Transport

Ásgeir Á. Ragnarsson
BBA Legal

Arna Sigurjónsdóttir
Lögmenn Bárugötu - LMB

Eyvindur Sólnes
CATO Lögmenn

Gunnar Sturluson
LOGOS, member of Lex Mundi

Rúnar Svavar Svavarsson
Orkuveita Reykjavíkur, Distribution-Electrical System

Helgi Þór Þorsteinsson
LEX Law Offices

SteinÞór Þorsteinsson
Tollstjóri - Directorate of Customs

Runólfur Vigfússon
PwC Iceland

Jon Vilhjalmsson
EFLA Consulting Engineers

INDIA

Ashok Dhingra Associates

Aum Architects

M.D. Architects

Ajay Abad
SKP Business Consulting LLP

Jolly Abraham
Desai & Diwanji

Alfred Adebare
LexCounsel

Amit Agarwal
Equifax Credit Information Services Pvt. Ltd.

Anil Agarwal
DUA Associates

Ca Surabhi Agarwal
SS Kothari Mehta & Co.

Kritika Agarwal
Majmudar & Partners

Uday Agarwal
SS Kothari Mehta & Co.

Nishant Ahlawat
Technolegals

Jotinder Ahluwalia
Reliance Infrastructure Ltd.

Aqil Ahmed
South Delhi Municipal Corporation

Deepti Ahuja
SKP Business Consulting LLP

Praveen Alok
Khaitan and Company

Bhushan Amrute
Law and Judiciary Department, Government of Maharashtra

Krishan Arora
Grant Thornton India LLP

Saurabh Babulkar
Seth Dua & Associates

Aditi Bagri
Juris Corp

Mantul Bajpai
Juris Corp

P. V. Balasubramaniam
BFS Legal

Shrenik N. Bamb
Shrenik N. Bamb & Associates

Anupam Bansal
ABRD Architects

Raghav Bansal
RSB League Consultants, Attorneys & Solicitors

Shashwat Bansal
RSB League Consultants, Attorneys & Solicitors

Subhash Bansal
RSB League Consultants, Attorneys & Solicitors

Sumitava Basu
Juris Corp

Sanjay Bhagwat
The Brihan Mumbai Electric Supply & Transport Undertaking

M.L. Bhakta
Kanga & Co.

Pradeep Bhandari
Intuit Management Consultancy

Gopal Bhansali
Law and Judiciary Department, Government of Maharashtra

M P Bharucha
Bharucha & Partners

Deepak Bhaskar
Trilegal

Moksha Bhat
Trilegal

Rachita Bhat
Lex Mundi Association of Law Firms

Gurpriya Bhatia
I.L.A. Pasrich & Company

Anirban Bhattacharya
Luthra & Luthra

Saurav Bhattacharya
PwC India

Sukanya Bhattacharya
Luthra & Luthra

Mona Bhide
Dave & Girish & Co.

Kajal Bhimani
Axon Partners LLP

Ujwal Bhole
UV Architects

Hetal Bilaye
Nishith Desai Associates

Nidhi Bothra
Vinod Kothari & Co. Practicing Company Secretaries

Leena Chacko

Shubhabrata Chakraborti
Juris Corp

Biswadeep Chakravarty
Dave & Girish & Co.

Harshala Chandorkar
Credit Information Bureau (India) Ltd.

Jyoti Chaudhari
Legasis Services Private Limited

Aseem Chawla
MPC Legal, Solicitors & Advocates

Manjula Chawla
Phoenix Legal

Prem Chhatpar

Vinita Chhatwal
I.L.A. Pasrich & Company

Arzineh Chinoy
Desai & Diwanji

Vinod Chithore
Municipal Corporation of Greater Mumbai

Sachin Chugh
Singhi Chugh & Kumar, Chartered Accountants

Chetan Daga
Sudit K. Parekh and Co.

Hitesh Darji
Yes Bank

Detty Davis
Juris Corp

Amin Dayani

Rhuta Deobagkar
Trilegal

Vishwang Desai
Desai & Diwanji

Kaustubh Deshpande
Equifax Credit Information Services Pvt. Ltd.

Saratha Devi
BFS Legal

Manish Dhingra
Dhingra & Singh - Attorneys-at-Law

Farida Dholkawala
Desai & Diwanji

Samir D'Monte
SDMArchitects

Anagha Dongre
Sudit K. Parekh and Co.

Rajesh Dongre
ABRD Architects

Jigar Doshi
SKP Business Consulting LLP

Maulik Doshi
SKP Business Consulting LLP

Atul Dua
Seth Dua & Associates

Rahul Dubey
Infini Juridique

Ferdinand Duraimanickam
BFS Legal

Shweta Dutta
Trilegal

Shanha Farah
Infini Juridique

Sreya Ganguly
Juris Corp

Sushmita Ganguly
Trilegal

Ritika Ganju
Phoenix Legal

Anuj Garg
India Law Offices

Manoj Gidwani
SKP Business Consulting LLP

Mukund Godbole
GodboleMukadam and Associates

Rakesh Goel
New Delhi Municipal Council

A. D. Gosavi
Municipal Corporation of Greater Mumbai

Niranjan Govindekar
BSR & Associates LLP

Anil Kumar Gulati
Department of Justice, Ministry of Law and Justice

Arun Gupta
Factum Legal

Atul Gupta
Trilegal

N K Gupta
SS Kothari Mehta & Co.

Parika Gupta
Diwan Advocates

Rajeev Gupta
New Delhi Municipal Council

Ruchira Gupta
The Juris Socis

Sunil K. Gupta
TCF Consulting Services (India) Private Limited

Surabhi Handa
Tata Power Delhi Distribution Limited

Parma Nand Hans
MNC Management Solutions & Kapson Law

Anil Harish
D. M. Harish & Co.

Akil Hirani
Majmudar & Partners

Michael Holland
FIABCI, the International Real Estate Federation

Akshaya Iyer
Majmudar & Partners

Jomy Jacob
Office of Chief Commissioner of Customs

Paraag Jaiin Nainuttia
Maharashtra Sales Tax Department

Anshul Jain
Luthra & Luthra

Radhika Jain
Walker Chandiok & Co. LLP

Sarul Jain
K N J Partners

Rajiv Jalota
Maharashtra Sales Tax Department

N.J. Jamadar
Law and Judiciary Department, Government of Maharashtra

Haresh Jani
Haresh Jani & Associates

Rajat Jariwal
Khaitan & Co.

H. Jayesh
Juris Corp

Saloni Jhaveri
SKP Business Consulting LLP

Abhijit Joglekar
Reliance Infrastructure Ltd.

Kunal Juneja
MPC Legal, Solicitors & Advocates

Manmohan Juneja
Ministry of Corporate Affairs

Sumeet Kachwaha
Kachwaha & Partners

Ravi Kaimal
Kaimal Chatterjee and Associates

Ashish Kalia
Debts Recovery Tribunal Mumbai

Jilas Kannappan
Pioneer Electricals

Atul Kansal
Indus Environmental Services Pvt. Ltd.

Apurva Kanvinde
Juris Corp

Aditi Kapoor
Trilegal

Vishal Kapoor
Ministry of Power

Kripi Kathuria
Phoenix Legal

Charandeep Kaur
Trilegal

Mitalee Kaushal
KNM & Partners

Sanjay Kesari
Employee's Provident Fund Organisation

Giridhar Kesavan
Vinzas Solutions India Private Limited

Gautam Khaitan
O.P. Khaitan & Co.

Farrukh Khan
Diwan Advocates

Salar M Khan
Diwan Advocates

Durgesh Khanapurkar
Juris Corp

Pooja Khanna
Phoenix Legal

Shinjni Kharbanda
Phoenix Legal

Tanya Khare
Khaitan and Company

Rajeev Kharyal
Tata Power Delhi Distribution Limited

Gautam Khurana
India Law Offices

Ankit Khushu
Kachwaha & Partners

Ravinder Komaragiri
The Tata Power Company Limited

Shinoj Koshy
Luthra & Luthra

Vinod Kothari
Vinod Kothari & Co. Practicing Company Secretaries

Gordhan Kukreja
Lawyer

Ajai Kumar

Mihir Kumar
Department of Financial Services, Ministry of Finance

Mrinal Kumar
Lex Mundi Association of Law Firms

Mrityunjay Kumar
Dhingra & Singh - Attorneys-at-Law

Mukesh Kumar
KNM & Partners

S. Kumar
Central Board of Excise & Customs

Shrutikirti Kumar
Lex Mundi Association of Law Firms

Shreedhar T. Kunte
Sharp & Tannan Group - member of Russell Bedford International

Samira Lalani
Phoenix Legal

Harjeet Lall
Axon Partners LLP

Minhaz Lokhandwala
Desai & Diwanji

Rajiv K. Luthra
Luthra & Luthra

Manish Madhukar
Infini Juridique

Ruchi Mahajan
Shardul Amarchand Mangaldas & Co. Advocates & Solicitors

Divya Malcolm
Kochhar & Co.

Neeraj Mandloi
Ministry of Urban Development

Shilpa Mankar Ahluwalia
Shardul Amarchand Mangaldas & Co. Advocates & Solicitors

Vipender Mann
KNM & Partners

Ajoy Mehta
Municipal Corporation of Greater Mumbai

Amrit Mehta
Majmudar & Partners

K.S. Mehta
SS Kothari Mehta & Co.

Pankaj Mehta
Fortune Legal Advocates & Legal Consultants

Preeti G. Mehta
Kanga & Co.

Sushil Mehta
Seth Dua & Associates

Sachin Menon
KPMG

Dhiraj Mhetre
Desai & Diwanji

Avinash Mishra
Shetty Infra Services Pvt.

Gunjan Mishra
Luthra & Luthra

Sushmit Mishra
Axon Partners LLP

Saurabh Misra
Saurabh Misra & Associates, International Lawyers

Ajay Mital
South Delhi Municipal Corporation

Hemal Modi
Sharp & Tannan Group - member of Russell Bedford International

Priyanka Mongia
MPC Legal, Solicitors & Advocates

Avikshit Moral
Juris Corp

Jitendra Mukadam
GodboleMukadam and Associates

Aaheree Mukherjee
Juris Corp

Rajat Mukherjee
Khaitan & Co.

Aanchal Mulick
Axon Partners LLP

KVR Murty
Ministry of Corporate Affairs - Registrar

Ramaswami N.
Department of Registration and Stamps

Ramesh Nair
FIABCI, the International Real Estate Federation

Aseem Nanda
Central Board of Excise & Customs

Nikhil Narayanan
Khaitan & Co.

Vaibhav Nautiyal
Indus Environmental Services Pvt. Ltd.

Harshakumar Nikam
Maharashtra Sales Tax Department

Sanjay Nirmal
Municipal Corporation of Greater Mumbai

Shubham Paliwal
KNM & Partners

Janak Pandya
Nishith Desai Associates

Ajay Pant
Indus Environmental Services Pvt. Ltd.

Amir Z. Singh Pasrich
I.L.A. Pasrich & Company

Supriya Patange
Law and Judiciary Department, Government of Maharashtra

Sameer Patel
Desai & Diwanji

Latik Patil
UV Architects

Sanjay Patil
BDH Industries Limited

Soumya Patnaik
J. Sagar Associates, Advocates & Solicitors

Sunil Kumar Pillai
Equifax Credit Information Services Pvt. Ltd.

Nitin Potdar
J. Sagar Associates, Advocates & Solicitors

M. Prabhakaran
Consulta Juris

Rashmi Pradeep
Cyril Amarchand Mangaldas

Anush Raajan
Bharucha & Partners

Ajay Raghavan
Trilegal

Ravishankar Raghavan
Majmudar & Partners

Faridi Saifur Rahman
Shardul Amarchand Mangaldas & Co. Advocates & Solicitors

Hafeez Rahman
I.L.A. Pasrich & Company

Vasanth Rajasekeran
Seth Dua & Associates

Madhav Raman
Anagram Architects

Yomesh Rao
YMS Consultants Ltd.

Siva Rathinam
Vinzas Solutions India Private Limited

Ankita Ray
Cyril Amarchand Mangaldas

C.K. Reejonia
Department of Justice, Ministry of Law and Justice

Suparna Sachar
O.P. Khaitan & Co.

Shamik Saha
MPC Legal, Solicitors & Advocates

Priyanka Sahi
Walker Chandiok & Co. LLP

Keshav Saini
KNM & Partners

Abhishek Saket
Infini Juridique

Sirisha Sampat
Kanga & Co.

Hitesh Sanghvi
Hitesh Sanghvi Law Offices

Piyush Sangoi
BSR & Associates LLP

Rakesh Saraf
Power Post

Navneet Sehdev
Axon Partners LLP

Manu Sehgal
Equifax Credit Information Services Pvt. Ltd.

Sukrit Seth
Seth Dua & Associates

Dilip S. Shah
Reliance Infrastructure Ltd.

Manish Shah
Sudit K. Parekh and Co.

Parag Shah
Parag G Shah and Associates

Pratik Shah
Sudit K. Parekh and Co.

Raj Shah
Nina Electrical Corporation

Avnish Sharma
Lex Mundi Association of Law Firms

Himani Sharma
Axon Partners LLP

Kartika Sharma
Axon Partners LLP

Manoranjan Sharma
KNM & Partners

Pramod Sharma
New Delhi Municipal Council

Rupali Sharma
Kochhar & Co.

Saumya Sharma
LexCounsel

Sunil Dutt Sharma
Khalsha Consultancy Services

K.M. Aasim Shehzad
BFS Legal

Amit Shetye
Luthra & Luthra

Arjun Shiv
Trilegal

Vishnu Shriram
Phoenix Legal

Prabhat Shroff
Shroff & Company

Vikram Shroff
Nishith Desai Associates

Aakarsh Singh
Universal Legal

Sajai Singh
J. Sagar Associates, Advocates & Solicitors

Sandeep Singh
Harting India Pvt. Ltd.

Shakti Singh Champawat
Desai & Diwanji

Mukesh Singhal
KNM & Partners

Neha Sinha
Luthra & Luthra

Praveer Sinha
Tata Power Delhi Distribution Limited

Sanjay Sinha
Ministry of Labour & Employment

Vineet Sinha
KNM & Partners

Vinay Sirohia
Axon Partners LLP

Veena Sivaramakrishnan
Juris Corp

Preetha Soman
Nishith Desai Associates

Rajeev Sood
New Delhi Municipal Council

Akash Suri
Yes Bank

Manpreet Singh Suri
KNM & Partners

Medha Tamhanekar
Universal Legal

Rajesh Tayal
KNM & Partners

Praveen Teotia
Grant Thornton India LLP

Chetan Thakkar
Kanga & Co.

Pooja Thomas
Phoenix Legal

Anurag Tomar
Anurag Tomar & Associates

Tanya Uppal
Khaitan & Co.

Uday Y. Vajandar
The Brihan Mumbai Electric Supply & Transport Undertaking

Chahat Varma
India Law Offices

Dipankar Vig
MPC Legal, Solicitors & Advocates

Sameep Vijayvergiya
Dhingra & Singh - Attorneys-at-Law

Neetu Vinayek
BSR & Associates LLP

Rajiv Wadhwa
PLVK Power Engineers & Consultants

Vasant Walavalkar
Navrang Electricals

Abhijeet Yadav
The Tata Power Company Limited

Kuldeep Yadav
Anurag Tomar & Associates

Neha Yadav
LexCounsel

Sanjay Yadav
South Delhi Municipal Corporation

Mohammad Yunus
Infini Juridique

INDONESIA

Abdibangun Buana

Ernst & Young

FIABCI, the International Real Estate Federation

Zamro Law Firm

Wiba Abdul Habib
PT Pembina Jaya

Hizban Achmad
Indo Karya Senior

Adhika Aditya
Oentoeng Suria & Partners

Shamy Adrian
Land Data and Information Center

Nafis Adwani
Ali Budiardjo, Nugroho, Reksodiputro, member of Lex Mundi

Widiarahmi Afiandari
Nurjadin Sumono Mulyadi & Partners

Monica Agnes
Markus Sajogo & Associates

Bambang Agus Mulyono
CJ Korea Express Indonesia

Eko Agus Supiadi
UPTSA (Unit Pelayanan Terpadu Satu Atap) Surabaya Timur (One-Stop Shop)

Andri Alfian
PT Papua Utama Mitra

Musdig Ali Suhudi
UKL/UPL

Lia Alizia
Makarim & Taira S.

Irina Anindita
Makarim & Taira S.

Charles Antoine Morgan
Ludovic Guinot
OnlinePajak

Karina Antonio
Nurjadin Sumono Mulyadi & Partners

Almer Apon
IWA Logistics (Indonesia)

Sasibi Ardi Hersubeno
PT PLN (Persero), East Java Distribution

Hizkia Ardianto
Ernst & Young

Cucu Asmawati
Simbolon & Partners Law Firm

Surja Teruna Bahari
PT Kredit Biro Indonesia Jaya (KBIJ)

Hamud M. Balfas
Law Office of HBP & Partners

Dimas Bimo
Melli Darsa & Co.

Fabian Buddy Pascoal
Hanafiah Ponggawa & Partners

Ita Budhi
PwC Indonesia

Tony Budidjaja
Budidjaja & Associates

Noor Budiwan
PT Terminal Petikemas Surabaya

Heru Chandra
BPJS Ketenagakerjaan

Juni Dani
Budidjaja & Associates

Melli Darsa
Melli Darsa & Co.

Nawangwulan Dilla Savitri
Rivai Triprasetio & Partners

Mita Djajadiredja
MD & Partners

Natasha Djamin
Oentoeng Suria & Partners

Bama Djokonugroho
Budidjaja & Associates

Kristen Natalia Doloksaribu
Budidjaja & Associates

Lukman Efendi
Wilmar Nabati Indonesia

Asma El Moufti
PT Terminal Petikemas Surabaya

Goesyen Erinda Resti
Leks&Co Lawyers

Ahmad Fadli
Brigitta I. Rahayoe & Partners

Nurulita Fauzie
Brigitta I. Rahayoe & Partners

Edly Febrian Widjaja
Budidjaja & Associates

Ahmad Fikri Assegaf
Assegaf Hamzah & Partners

Aprilda Fiona Butarbutar
Aprilda Fiona & Partners Law Firm

Widigdya Gitaya
WSG & Company

S. Hadaris
Ministry of Law and Human Rights

Michael Hadi
PT Kredit Biro Indonesia Jaya (KBIJ)

Retno Hadi
PT Tiga Bintang Berkarya

Didik S. Hadiwidodo
PT Nasio Karya Pratama

Mohammad Iqbal Hadromi
Hadromi & Partners

Eko Haidi Prasetyo
Samudera Logistics

Melanie Sri Handayani
Bank Indonesia

Siti Harni Harahap
PT PAM Lyonnaise Jaya

Dedet Hardiansyah
Budiman and Partners

Abdul Haris M. Rum
Himpunan Konsultan Hukum Pasar Modal

Soeko Hartoyo
PT Sukoi Teknik Jaya

Stefanus Haryanto
Adnan Kelana Haryanto & Hermanto

Ibnu Hasan
TNB & Partners

Anang Hidayat
PT GPI Logistics

Brigitta Imam Rahayoe
Brigitta I. Rahayoe & Partners

Adiwidya Imam Rahayu
Brigitta I. Rahayoe & Partners

Deshaputra Intanperdana
Hadromi & Partners

Isnavodiar Jatmiko
BPJS Ketenagakerjaan

Virgo Eresta Jaya
Ministry of Agrarian and Spatial Planning / National Land Agency

Edy Junaedi
Badan Pelayanan Terpadu Satu Pintu (BPTS)

Fitra Kadarina
Kementerian Hukum dan ham, Direktorat jenderal administrasi hukum

Brinanda Lidwina Kaliska
Makarim & Taira S.

Iswahjudi A. Karim
KarimSyah Law Firm

Mirza Karim
KarimSyah Law Firm

Othman Karim
KarimSyah Law Firm

Shakuntala Kartika
PTI Architects

Anita Lucia Kendarto
Notaris & Pejabat Pembuat Akta Tanah

Theo Kumaat
Indonesian Logistics and Forwarders Association

Herry N. Kurniawan
Ali Budiardjo, Nugroho, Reksodiputro, member of Lex Mundi

Winita E. Kusnandar
Kusnandar & Co.

Diana Kusumasari
Budidjaja & Associates

Jatmiko Adi Kusumo
Interiors & Co.

Andrew L. Las Marias
Heint Logistics

Eddy M. Leks
Leks&Co Lawyers

Noorfina Luthfiany
Bank Indonesia

Syamsul Ma'Arif
Mahkamah Agung RI

Marvin Mahendra
Markus Sajogo & Associates

Benny Marbun
PT PLN (Persero) Indonesia State Electricity Corporation

Roni Marpaung
Oentoeng Suria & Partners

Mario Maurice Sinjal
Nurjadin Sumono Mulyadi & Partners

Amalia Mayasari
Simbolon & Partners Law Firm

Ella Melany
Hanafiah Ponggawa & Partners

Any Miami
PwC Indonesia

Sri Mulyati
Rivai Tripasetio & Partners

Alexander Nainggolan
Hadromi & Partners

Alfin Nainggolan
Mataram Partners

Dimas Nandaraditya
Hadiputranto, Hadinoto & Partners

Adam Nasution
Oentoeng Suria & Partners

Chandra Nataadmadja
Suria Nataadmadja & Associates

Suria Nataadmadja
Suria Nataadmadja & Associates

Ratih Nawangsari
Oentoeng Suria & Partners

Mia Noni Yuniar
Brigitta I. Rahayoe & Partners

Reza Nurtjahja
PT Urbane Indonesia

Oza Olavia
Ministry of Finance

Inta Oviyantari
PTI Architects

Heru Pambudi
Ministry of Finance

Ay Tjhing Phan
PwC Indonesia

Abraham Pierre
KPMG

Deni Prasetyo
Land Data and Information Center

Erwin Prasetyo
PDAM Surya Sembada Surabaya

Lila Pratiwi
Markus Sajogo & Associates

Njoto Rachmat
Architect

Atiek Rahayu
Welgrow

Tantia Rahmadhina
Rivai Triprasetio & Partners

Ilman Rakhmat
KarimSyah Law Firm

Dhamma Ratna
Notaris & Pejabat Pembuat Akta Tanah

Sophia Rengganis
PwC Indonesia

Rengganis Renngganis
Hadromi & Partners

Natalia Rizky
Leks&Co Lawyers

Mahesa Rumondor
Adnan Kelana Haryanto & Hermanto

Valdano Ruru
Makarim & Taira S.

Indra Safitri
Himpunan Konsultan Hukum Pasar Modal

Ayundha Sahar
Oentoeng Suria & Partners

Markus Sajogo
Markus Sajogo & Associates

Rika Salim
Oentoeng Suria & Partners

Darma Saputra
Bank Indonesia

Perdana Saputro
Melli Darsa & Co.

Mahardikha K. Sardjana
Hadiputranto, Hadinoto & Partners

Brimanti Sari
Makarim & Taira S.

Nur Asyura Anggini Sari
Bank Indonesia

Erwin Setiawan
Ernst & Young

Indra Setiawan
Ali Budiardjo, Nugroho, Reksodiputro, member of Lex Mundi

Agatha Sherly
Leks&Co Lawyers

Taji M. Sianturi

Bonar Sidabukke
Sidabukke Clan & Associates

Bernard Sihombing
Budidjaja & Associates

Obed Simamora
Land Office of Surabaya

Ricardo Simanjuntak
Ricardo Simanjuntak & Partners

Berlian Dumaris Simbolon
Suria Nataadmadja & Associates

Yudianta Medio N. Simbolon
Simbolon & Partners Law Firm

Kristian Takasdo Simorangkir
Budidjaja & Associates

Fransisca Sintia
Leks&Co Lawyers

Nadia Soraya
TNB & Partners

Selvana Stella Oviona
Budidjaja & Associates

Fath Armada Sukardi
Hanafiah Ponggawa & Partners

Debby Sulaiman
Oentoeng Suria & Partners

Iwan Supriadi
Ministry of Law and Human Rights

Bambang Suprijanto
Ernst & Young

Atik Susanto
Oentoeng Suria & Partners

Otje Sutedi
PTI Architects

Teuku Anggra Syahreza
Ali Budiardjo, Nugroho, Reksodiputro, member of Lex Mundi

Hefli Syarifuddin
Communication and Information Agency

Kurniawan Tanzil
Makarim & Taira S.

Doddy Tjahjadi
PTI Architects

Bapak Tjahjadi Aquasa
Wisma

Gatot Triprasetio
Rivai Triprasetio & Partners

Wahyu Tunggono
Aramex International Indonesia

Runi Tusita
PwC Indonesia

Trina Uli
Simbolon & Partners Law Firm

Francine E.V. W.
Budidjaja & Associates

Ilham Wahyu
Ali Budiardjo, Nugroho, Reksodiputro, member of Lex Mundi

A.R. Kendista Wantah
Frans Winarta & Partners

Tjuk Winarjo
PT Caturpilar Perkasatangguh

Frans Winarta
Frans Winarta & Partners

Garry Wood
PT Kredit Biro Indonesia Jaya (KBIJ)

Pelopor Yanto
Land Data and Information Center

Jono Yeo
Budidjaja & Associates

Akbar Zainuri
KarimSyah Law Firm

Andi Zulfikar
Mataram Partners

Jacob Zwaan
KPMG

IRAN, ISLAMIC REP.

Sadid Bar International Transport

Morteza Adab
Registration Companies Office

Ali Ahmadi
Tehran Chamber of Commerce, Industries and Mines

Mousa Ahmadi
Islamic Azad University of Abhar Branch

Nazem Ahmadian Nasr Abadi
Morteza

Behrooz Akhlaghi
International Law Office of Dr. Behrooz Akhlaghi & Associates

Ali Amani
Daya-Rahyaft Auditing & Management Services

Mohammad Amin
Sahra Ruby Co.

Hassan Amirshahi
Law Offices of Dr. Hassan Amirshahi

Gholam Ali Asghari
Great Tehran Electricity Distribution Company (GTEDC)

Fatemeh Bagherzadeh
Farjam Law Office

Rambod Barandoust
Consultant

Hamid Berenjkar
Office of Hamid Berenjkar

Pouyan Bohloul
Bohloul & Associates Law Office

Gholam-Hossein Davani
Daya-Rahyaft Auditing & Management Services

Morteza Dezfoulian
Morteza

Meysam Doaei
Securities and Exchange Organization of Iran

Sepideh Dowlatshahi
Bartar Associates Law Firm

Mahmoud Ebadi Tabrizi
Law Offices M. Ebadi Tabrizi & Associates Attorneys-at-Law

Maryam Ebrahimi
Tehran Stock Exchange (TSE)

Shirin Ozra Entezari
Dr. Shirin O. Entezari & Associates

Mahmoud Eskandari

Seyyed Amir Hossein Etesami
Securities and Exchange Organization of Iran

Maryam Farah Bakhsh
Trade Promotion of Iran

Zahra Farzalian
Morteza

Hosein Hashemi
Azin Samand Petrochemical Complex

Rahman Hassani
Australian Green Management & Services

S. Hamid Hosseini
Meraat International Group

Nasim Jahanbani
Great Tehran Electricity Distribution Company (GTEDC)

Mohammad Jalili
Iran Credit Scoring

Jafar Jamali

Majid Amin Javahery
Architect

Seyed Hamid Jelveh Tabaei
Registration Companies Office

Tannaz Jourabchi-Eisenhut
Amereller Legal Consultants

Majid Mahallati
A.M. Mahallati & Co.

Gholam Reza Malekshoar
Central Bank of the Islamic Republic of Iran

Mahdi Mas'oudnia
Pasak Enduring Design

Seyed Ali Mirshafiei
Tehran Chamber of Commerce, Industries and Mines

Fatemeh Sadat Mirsharifi
Ministry of Commerce

Ali Mirzaie
State Organization for Registration of Deeds & Properties

Hamidreza Mokhtarian
Mehr International Law Firm

Mehdi Mousavi
PERSOL Corporation

Rasoul Nowrouzi

Zohreh Papi
Central Bank of the Islamic Republic of Iran

Farmand Pourkarim
Tehran Municipality - Fanavaran Shahr Co.

Mohsen Rahimi
Ministry of Commerce

Mehdi Ranjkesh
Zagros Petrochemical Company

Yahya Rayegani
Farjam Law Office

Atiyeh Rezaei
Dr. Shirin O. Entezari & Associates

Mohammad Rezayi Mazrae
Central Bank of the Islamic Republic of Iran

Mohammadali Rezvani
Azin Samand Petrochemical Complex

Jamal Seifi
Dr. Jamal Seifi & Associates

Amin Setayesh
State Organization for Registration of Deeds & Properties

Encyeh Seyed Sadr
International Law Office of Dr. Behrooz Akhlaghi & Associates

Ahmad Shabanifard
Azin Samand Petrochemical Complex

Mir Shahbiz Shafe'e
Dr. Jamal Seifi & Associates

Farzan Shirvanbeigi
Tehran Municipality - Fanavaran Shahr Co.

Rajat Ratan Sinha
RCS Pvt. Ltd. Business Advisors Group

Pedram Soltani
PERSOL Corporation

Mohammad Reza Talischi
PERSOL Corporation

Ebrahim Tavakoli
Bartar Associates Law Firm

Vrej Torossian
Torossian, Avanessian & Associate

Gholam Hossein Vahidi

Hamid Vakili
Ofoghe Sabz Idalat

Ahmad Yousefi
Attorney-at-Law

Azadeh Zarei

IRAQ

Ernst & Young

Ministry of Electricity

Hussam Arzooqi Abbas
Hussam Arzooqi Abbas Firm for Legal and Investment Services and Real Estate Development

Nisreen Abdul Hadi Al-Hamiri
Nisreen Abdul Hadi Al-Hamiri Law Office

Omar Abidi
OHA Group

Riyadh Adnan Al-Haidary
USAID-Tarabot

Ammar Al Rubaye
Infrastructure Associates

Abdulhussein Alanbaki
Office of the Prime Minister

Ibrahim Al-Baghdadi
Al-Baraka Group

Rashid Al-Khouri
Rashid Al-Khouri

Adil Al-Lami
Management Systems International

Zuhair Al-Maliki
Al-Maliki & Associates Law Firm

Azhar Al-Rubaie
Ministry of Planning

Meervat Altaie
University of Baghdad

Hussam Arzoky
Hussam Arzoky Law Firm

Munther B. Hamoudi
Al-Buraq Engineering Co. Ltd.

Majid Botrous
Legal Consultations

Ahmed Dawood
BHC Law Firm LLC

Kamal Field Al-Basri
Iraqi Institute for Economic Reform

Ali Fikiki
Management Systems International

Ahmed J. Hammoodi
BHC Law Firm LLC

Alain Hannouche
Hannouche Associates

Ihsan Jaseem
Ministry of Planning

Firas Jawhari
BHC Law Firm LLC

Deepak John
Skybridge Freight Solutions LLC

Sham Kadem
Ministry of Planning

Zaid Mahdi
Trade Finance

Mzahim Mahmud Al-Jubouri
Sanad Law Firm

Rasha Nadeem
BHC Law Firm LLC

Ammar Naji
Confluent Law Group

Rukaya Sabaah
Ministry of Planning

Kareem Salim Kamash
General Commission for Taxes

Haider Salman
BHC Law Firm LLC

Zuhair Jassim Shahad
BHC Law Firm LLC

Stephan Stephan
PwC Jordan

Khaled Yaseen
Al-Saqer Advisers & Legal Services

Haythem Zayed
PwC Jordan

Dawood Zayer
Dawwod

IRELAND

ESB International

John Comerford
Cooney Carey Consulting Ltd., member of Russell Bedford International

Miranda Cox
PwC Ireland

Majella Crennan
Philip Lee Solicitors

Kiara Daly
Daniel Murphy Solicitors

Helen Dixon
Companies Registration Office

Emma Doherty
Matheson

Gavin Doherty
Eugene F. Collins Solicitors

Eoghan Doyle
Philip Lee Solicitors

Jamie Ensor
Dillon Eustace

Garret Farrelly
Matheson

Frank Flanagan
Mason Hayes & Curran

Paul Gough
Eugene F. Collins Solicitors

Orla Hegarty
University College Dublin - Richview

Thomas Johnson
Irish Building Control Institute

William Johnston
Arthur Cox, member of Lex Mundi

Eamonn Madden
Cooney Carey Consulting Ltd., member of Russell Bedford International

Mary Liz Mahony
Arthur Cox, member of Lex Mundi

Joseph Maxwell
Mason Hayes & Curran

Bernadette McArdle
Irish Building Control Institute

Brid McCoy
Amoss Solicitors

Thomas McGovern
Companies Registration Office

Eddie Meaney
DHL Express

Kevin Meehan
Compass Maritime Ltd.

Heather Murphy
Matheson

James O'Boyle
The Property Registration Authority

Brian O'Malley
A&L Goodbody

David O'Shea
Dillon Eustace

Laura O'Sullivan
Mason Hayes & Curran

Maurice Phelan
Mason Hayes & Curran

Kevin Quinn
PwC Ireland

Laura Rafferty
Arthur Cox, member of Lex Mundi

Geoffrey Rooney
Amoss Solicitors

Gavin Simons
Amoss Solicitors

Mark Traynor
A&L Goodbody

Joe Tynan
PwC Ireland

Maeve Walsh
Amoss Solicitors

Patrick Walshe
Philip Lee Solicitors

Emma Weld-Moore
Daniel Murphy Solicitors

Maura Young
Irish Credit Bureau

ISRAEL

Erez Ben-Arii
PwC Israel

Jacob Ben-Chitrit
Yigal Arnon & Co.

Jeremy Benjamin
Goldfarb Seligman & Co.

Roy Caner
Erdinast Ben Nathan & Co. Advocates

Doron Cohen
Raveh, Ravid & Co. CPAs - member of Russell Bedford International

Clifford Davis
S. Horowitz & Co., member of Lex Mundi

Danny Dilbary
Goldfarb Seligman & Co.

Jonathan Finklestone
Erdinast Ben Nathan & Co. Advocates

Shmulik Fried
Goldfarb Seligman & Co.

Viva Gayer
Erdinast Ben Nathan & Co. Advocates

Tuvia Geffen
Naschitz, Brandes & Co.

Yael Gershon Gobernik
Erdinast Ben Nathan & Co. Advocates

Ido Gonen
Goldfarb Seligman & Co.

Amos Hacmun
Heskia-Hacmun Law Firm

Liron HaCohen
Yigal Arnon & Co.

Tova Hilman
Hilman & Co. CPAs (Isr.)

Tali Hirsch-Sherman
Ministry of Construction and Housing

Zeev Katz
PwC Israel

Vered Kirshner
PwC Israel

Adam Klein
Goldfarb Seligman & Co.

Gideon Koren
Gideon Koren & Co. Law Offices

Hadas Lavi
S. Horowitz & Co., member of Lex Mundi

Michelle Liberman
S. Horowitz & Co., member of Lex Mundi

Liron Mendelevitz
Krief Albatros Ltd.

Mirit Reif
Dave Wolf & Co. Law Firm

Doron Sadan
PwC Israel

Dan Sharon
Dan Sharon - Consulting Engineers 2002 Ltd.

Daniel Singerman
COFACEBDI

Yoav Tal
Erdinast Ben Nathan & Co. Advocates

Eran Taussig
Balter, Guth, Aloni LLP

Eylam Weiss
Weiss-Porat & Co.

Zeev Weiss
Weiss-Porat & Co.

Ita Yarmish
Dave Wolf & Co. Law Firm

Liora Zaaidman
Ministry of Construction and Housing

ITALY

Fabrizio Acerbis
PwC Italy

Giuseppe Alemani
Alemani e Associati

Iacopo Aliverti Piuri
Dentons

Alberto Angeloni
DLA Piper

Federico Antich
Studio dell'Avvocato Antich

Umberto Antonelli
Studio Legale Associato ad Ashurst LLP

Gea Arcella
Civil Law Notary, Lawyer

Claudia Adele Aresu
PwC - Tax and Legal Services

Roberto Argeri
Cleary Gottlieb Steen & Hamilton LLP

Gaetano Arnò
PwC - Tax and Legal Services

Romina Ballanca
PwC - Tax and Legal Services

Gianluigi Baroni
PwC - Tax and Legal Services

Alvise Becker
PwC - Tax and Legal Services

Susanna Beltramo
Studio Legale Beltramo

Marta Bianchi
PwC - Tax and Legal Services

Edoardo Augusto Bononi
Studio Legale Associato ad Ashurst LLP

Gianluca Borraccia
PwC - Tax and Legal Services

Giampaolo Botta
Spediporto - Associazione Spedizionieri Corrieri e Trasportatori di Genova

Giuseppe Broccoli
BDA Studio Legale

Carlo Andrea Bruno
Gitti Raynaud and Partners - Studio Legale

Alice Buonafede
Court of Appeal of Rome

Raffaele Buono
DLA Piper

Claudio Burello
PwC - Tax and Legal Services

Sergio Calderara
Almaviva S.p.A. - Direzione Affari Legali

Federico Calloni
Studio Corno - member of Russell Bedford International

Flavia Caltagirone
Pirola Pennuto Zei & Associati

Claudia Caluori
Studio dell'Avvocato Antich

Gianluca Cambareri
Tonucci & Partners

Antonio Campagnoli
Il Punto Real Estate Advisor

Paolo Canal
Orsingher Ortu – Avvocati Associati

Stefano Cancarini
PwC - Tax and Legal Services

Gianni Carfì Pavia
PwC - Tax and Legal Services

Cecilia Carrara
Legance Avvocati Associati

Fausto Caruso
NCTM - Studio Legale Associato

Maria Castiglione Minischetti
PwC - Tax and Legal Services

Sandro Cecili
Acea S.p.A.

Nicla Cimmino
PwC Italy

Ludovica Citarella
BDA Studio Legale

Michela Cocchi
Lady Lawyer Foundation

Domenico Colella
Orsingher Ortu – Avvocati Associati

Stefano Colla
PwC - Tax and Legal Services

Mattia Colonnelli de Gasperis
Colonnelli de Gasperis Studio Legale

Marianna Concordia
Portolano Cavallo Studio Legale

Barbara Corsetti
Portolano Cavallo Studio Legale

Filippo Corsini
Chiomenti Studio Legale

Barbara Cortesi
Studio Legale Guasti

Marco Cosa
NCTM - Studio Legale Associato

Salvatore Cuzzocrea
PwC - Tax and Legal Services

Carlo Andrea D'Addetta
Studio Legale Ghia

Mariano Davoli
Pirola Pennuto Zei & Associati

Antonio De Martinis
Spasaro De Martinis Law Firm

Raffaella De Martinis
Spasaro De Martinis Law Firm

Francesca De Paolis
Studio Legale Salvatore De Paolis

Rosa Del Sindaco
Abbatescianni Studio Legale e Tributario

Claudio Di Falco
Cleary Gottlieb Steen & Hamilton LLP

Federica Di Mario
Studio Legale Associato ad Ashurst LLP

Alessio Di Pietro
Court of Appeal of Rome

Silvia Digregorio
Court of Appeal of Rome

Giampiero Ferrante
Court of Appeal of Rome

Maddalena Ferrari
Studio Notarile Ferrari

Guiseppe Ferrelli
Studio Legale Sinatra

Barbara Mirta Ferri
PwC - Tax and Legal Services

Gianclaudio Fischetti
PwC - Tax and Legal Services

Emanuele Franchi
PwC Italy

Pier Andrea Fré Torelli Massini
Carabba & Partners

Filippo Frigerio
Portolano Cavallo Studio Legale

Marialaura Frittella
Cocuzza e Associati

Bruno Frugis
Italian Revenue Agency

Paolo Gallarati
NCTM - Studio Legale Associato

Luca Gambini
Portolano Cavallo Studio Legale

Andrea Gangemi
Portolano Cavallo Studio Legale

Daniele Geronzi
Legance Avvocati Associati

Carlo Ghia
Studio Legale Ghia

Enrica Maria Ghia
Studio Legale Ghia

Lucio Ghia
Studio Legale Ghia

Vincenzo Fabrizio Giglio
Giglio & Scofferi Studio Legale del Lavoro

Antonio Grieco
Grieco e Associati

Valentino Guarini
PwC - Tax and Legal Services

Federico Guasti
Studio Legale Guasti

Francesco Iodice
Cleary Gottlieb Steen & Hamilton LLP

Alberto Irace
Acea S.p.A.

Giovanni Izzo
Abbatescianni Studio Legale e Tributario

Ignazio La Candia
Pirola Pennuto Zei & Associati

Carlo Lanfranchi
Bank of Italy

Cecilia Laporta
BDA Studio Legale

Luca Lavazza
PwC Italy

Francesco Liberatori
Cleary Gottlieb Steen & Hamilton LLP

Stefano Liotta
Acea S.p.A.

Alessandra Livreri
A. Hartrodt Italiana SRL

Agostina Lodde
Italian Revenue Agency

Enrico Lodi
CRIF S.p.A.

Stefano Macchi di Cellere

Federico Magi
PwC - Tax and Legal Services

Marta Magistrelli
PwC - Tax and Legal Services

Luigi Fabrizio Mancuso
Court of Appeal of Rome

Roberta Marconi
Italian Revenue Agency

Anna Chiara Margottini
Orsingher Ortu – Avvocati Associati

Fabrizio Mariotti
Studio Legale Beltramo

Donatella Martinelli
Studio Legale Associato Tommasini e Martinelli

Dania Marzo
De Gayardon Bureau

Gennaro Mazzuoccolo
Norton Rose Fulbright

Carloandrea Meacci
Studio Legale Associato ad Ashurst LLP

Gilberto Melchiorri
United Nations Economic Commission for Europe

Michele Melchiorri
United Nations Economic Commission for Europe

Laura Mellone
Bank of Italy

Priscilla Merlino
Nunziante Magrone

Flavia Messina
PwC - Tax and Legal Services

Marco Monaco Sorge
Tonucci & Partners

Luisa Monti
CRIF S.p.A.

Micael Montinari
Portolano Cavallo Studio Legale

Davide Moretti
Bank of Italy

Valeria Morosini
Toffoletto e Soci Law Firm, member of Ius Laboris

Gianmatteo Nunziante
Nunziante Magrone

Luca Occhetta
Pirola Pennuto Zei & Associati

Fabiana Padroni
Ristuccia & Tufarelli

Marcella Panucci
Confindustria (National Business Association)

Luciano Panzani
Court of Appeal of Rome

Giovanni Patti
Abbatescianni Studio Legale e Tributario

Fabio Pazzini
Shearman & Sterling LLP

Yan Pecoraro
Portolano Cavallo Studio Legale

Federica Periale
Studio Legale Associato ad Ashurst LLP

Davide Petris
Portolano Cavallo Studio Legale

Annamaria Pinzuti
Studio Legale Associato ad Ashurst LLP

Emanuele Plini
Court of Appeal of Rome

Carlo Pozzi
Aprile S.p.A.

Maria Progida
PwC - Tax and Legal Services

Daniele Raynaud
Gitti Raynaud and Partners - Studio Legale

Consuelo Rigo
CRIF S.p.A.

Marianna Ristuccia
Ristuccia & Tufarelli

Filippo Maria Riva
PwC - Tax and Legal Services

Carlo Romano
PwC Italy

Cinzia Romano
Studio Legale Salvatore De Paolis

Carlo Umberto Rossi
Rossi & Rossi Law Firm

Michele Salemo
StudioCredit

Francesca Salerno
Legance Avvocati Associati

Chiara Sannasardo
Portolano Cavallo Studio Legale

Giuseppe Santarelli
Tonucci & Partners

Arturo Santoro
Pirola Pennuto Zei & Associati

Marzio Scaglioni
PwC - Tax and Legal Services

Alice Scotti
Studio Legale Guasti

Lidia Maria Sella
Studio Corno - member of Russell Bedford International

Susanna Servi
Carabba & Partners

Ginevra Sforza
Portolano Cavallo Studio Legale

Massimiliano Silvetti
Legália

Carlo Sinatra
Studio Legale Sinatra

Manlio Carlo Soldani

Luca Spallarossa
Aprile S.p.A.

Piervincenzo Spasaro
Spasaro De Martinis Law Firm

Luca Sportelli
Cleary Gottlieb Steen & Hamilton LLP

Elisa Sulcis
Studio Legale Sinatra

Maria Antonietta Tanico
Studio Legale Tanico

Andrea Tedioli
Studio legale Tedioli

Roberto Tirone
Cocuzza e Associati

Francesca Tironi
PwC - Tax and Legal Services

Giacinto Tommasini
Studio Legale Associato Tommasini e Martinelli

Nicola Toscano
Studio Legale Associato ad Ashurst LLP

Stefano Tresca
iSeed

Luca Tufarelli
Ristuccia & Tufarelli

Valentina Turco
Portolano Cavallo Studio Legale

Rachele Vacca de Dominicis
Grieco e Associati

Mario Valentini
Pirola Pennuto Zei & Associati

Elisabetta Ventrella
BDA Studio Legale

Francesco Vitali
Orsingher Ortu – Avvocati Associati

Emilio Zendri
Acea S.p.A.

Domenico Zuccaro
Cleary Gottlieb Steen & Hamilton LLP

Filippo Zucchinelli
PwC - Tax and Legal Services

JAMAICA

PwC Jamaica

Rattray Patterson Rattray

Rollin Alveranga
Ministry of Water, Land, Environment and Climate Change

Althea Anderson
LEX Caribbean

Danielle Archer
The Law Practice of Danielle S. Archer & Associates

Christopher Bovell
DunnCox

Raymond Campbell
KPMG

Errington Case
Jamaica Public Service Company Limited

Terrence Cooper
CRIF NM Credit Assure Limited

Angela Cousins-Robinson
Robinson & Clarke

Sixto P. Coy
Mair Russell Grant Thornton

Jemelia Davis
The Supreme Court of Jamaica

Everald Dewar
BDO

Natalie Farrell-Ross
Myers, Fletcher & Gordon, member of Lex Mundi

Joan Ferreira-Dallas
ABTAX Limited

Nicole Foga
Foga Daley

Lecia Gaye Taylor
Hylton & Hylton

Gavin Goffe
Myers, Fletcher & Gordon, member of Lex Mundi

Narda Graham
DunnCox

Herbert Winston Grant
Grant, Stewart, Phillips & Co.

Inger Hainsley-Bennett
Companies Office

Howard Harris
Foga Daley

Marsha Henry-Martin
Ministry of Local Government & Community Development

Michael Hylton
Hylton Powell

Donovan Jackson
Nunes, Scholefield DeLeon & Co.

Beverly Johnson
JLB International Ltd.

Jeniffer Johnson
Mair Russell Grant Thornton

Andrea Kinach
Patterson Mair Hamilton

Michael Lake
Michael Lake & Associates Architects

Joan Lawla
University of Technology

Kenneth Lewis
Mair Russell Grant Thornton

Melinda Lloyd
Jamaica Public Service Company Limited

Marlon Lowe
Jamaica Customs Department

Zaila McCalla
The Supreme Court of Jamaica

Raynold McFarlane
BDO

Sonia McFarlane
BDO

Karlene McKenzie
Cabinet Office of the Government of Jamaica

Andrine McLaren
Kingston and St. Andrew Corporation

Horace Messado
Jamaica Public Service Company Limited

Alton Morgan
Legis-Alton E. Morgan & Co. Attorneys-at-Law

Sharon Neil Smith
Patterson Mair Hamilton

Shyvonne Osborne
Foga Daley

Gina Phillipps Black
Myers, Fletcher & Gordon, member of Lex Mundi

Kevin Powell
Hylton Powell

Norman Rainford
KPMG

Judith Ramlogan
Companies Office

Paul Randall
Creditinfo Jamaica Limited

Hilary Reid
Myers, Fletcher & Gordon, member of Lex Mundi

Natasha Richards
Myers, Fletcher & Gordon, member of Lex Mundi

Alexis Robinson
Myers, Fletcher & Gordon, member of Lex Mundi

Camile Rose
Jamaica Public Service Company Limited

Judy Schoenbein
LTN Logistics International Co. Ltd.

Norman Shand
Kingston and St. Andrew Corporation

Stephen Shelton
Myers, Fletcher & Gordon, member of Lex Mundi

Jacqueline Simmonds
Jamaica Public Service Company Limited

John Sinclair
Sinco's Electrical Co. Ltd.

Tana'ania Small Davis
Livingston, Alexander & Levy Attorneys-at-Law

Hakon Stefansson
Creditinfo Jamaica Limited

Craig Stephen
Creditinfo Jamaica Limited

Danielle Stiebel
Myers, Fletcher & Gordon, member of Lex Mundi

Douglas Stiebel
Stiebel & Company Limited

Stuart Stimpson
Hart Muirhead Fatta Attorneys at Law

Marlene Street Forrest
Jamaica Stock Exchange

Paul Tai
Nunes, Scholefield DeLeon & Co.

Humprey Taylor
Taylor Construction Ltd.

Marvalyn Taylor-Wright
Taylor-Wright & Company

Lorraine Thomas-Harris
LTN Logistics International Co. Ltd.

Lori-Ann Thompson
National Land Agency

Cheriese Walcott
National Land Agency

Maxine Whyte
Transworld Shipping Services

Dominic Williams
Jamaica Public Service Company Limited

Lisa Williams
Livingston, Alexander & Levy Attorneys-at-Law

Anna-Kay Wilson
KPMG

Kelley C. Wong
Livingston, Alexander & Levy

Anwar Wright
Taylor-Wright & Company

Scott Wright
Taylor-Wright & Company

Angelean Young-Daley
Jamaica Public Service Company Limited

JAPAN

Osaka Business and Investment Center

Daiki Akahane
Law Office of Daiki Akahane

Takashi Asakura
Credit Information Center Corp.

Takuya Eguchi
Mori Hamada & Matsumoto - Osaka

Toyoki Emoto
Atsumi & Sakai

Miho Fujita
Adachi, Henderson, Miyatake & Fujita

Tatsuya Fukui
Atsumi & Sakai

Shinnosuke Fukuoka
Nishimura & Asahi

Tomoko Goto
Nishimura & Asahi

Norio Harasawa
Ishikawa-Gumi Ltd.

Miyu Harashima
Atsumi & Sakai

Yuichi Hasegawa
Adachi, Henderson, Miyatake & Fujita

Shunsuke Honda
Anderson Mori & Tomotsune

Hiroshi Inagaki
Hankyu Hanshin Express Co. Ltd.

Katsunori Irie

Akiko Isoyama
PwC Tax Japan

Jun Ito
Kintetsu World Express, Inc.

Ruriko Iwase
Atsumi & Sakai

Saki Kamiya
Anderson Mori & Tomotsune

Hiroshi Kasuya
Baker & McKenzie

Yuijro Katayama
Nishimura & Asahi

Takahiro Kato
Nishimura & Asahi

Toriuchi Kazuki
Alps Logistics Co. Ltd.

Takumi Kiriyama
Nishimura & Asahi

Akemi Kito
PwC Tax Japan

Akiko Kobayashi
Credit Information Center Corp.

Masayoshi Kobayashi
Baker & McKenzie

Kazushige Koide
KPMG Tax Corporation

Yasuyuki Kuribayashi
City-Yuwa Partners

Xiquan Li
Kansai Electric Power

Takafumi Masukata
Nippon Express Co., Ltd.

Torahiko Masutani
Anderson Mori & Tomotsune

Hiroaki Matsui
Nishimura & Asahi

Naoki Matsuo
City-Yuwa Partners

Nobuaki Matsuoka
Osaka International Law Offices

Nakano Michiaki
South Toranomon Law Offices

Hideaki Mitani
Mitani CPA Office

Kumi Mitani
Mitani CPA Office

Kazuya Miyakawa
PwC Tax Japan

Toshio Miyatake
Adachi, Henderson, Miyatake & Fujita

Teppei Mogi
Oh-Ebashi LPC & Partners

Michihiro Mori
Nishimura & Asahi

Hirosato Nabika
City-Yuwa Partners

Hideto Nakai
Kinden Corp.

Miho Niunoya
Atsumi & Sakai

Takeshi Ogura
Ogura Accounting Office

Kotaro Okamoto
Ernst & Young

Takashi Saito
City-Yuwa Partners

Yuka Sakai
City-Yuwa Partners

Tetsumichi Sakaki
White & Case

Sara Sandford
Garvey Schubert Barer Law Firm

Noriyuki Sano
Maersk Line

Hitoshi Saruwatari
Kinki Tsukan Co. Ltd.

Kei Sasaki
Anderson Mori & Tomotsune

Tetsuro Sato
Baker & McKenzie

Takashi Shinbo
Ishikawa-Gumi Ltd.

Yuri Sugano
Nishimura & Asahi

Sachiko Sugawara
Atsumi & Sakai

Junya Suzuki
Baker & McKenzie

Yasuyuki Suzuki
Standard Chartered Bank

Yoshimasa Takagi
Ernst & Young

Hiroaki Takahashi
Anderson Mori & Tomotsune

Y. Takahashi
Sankyu Inc.

Junichi Tobimatsu
Mori Hamada & Matsumoto

Yamamoto Tomohide
Kinden Corp.

Takaharu Totsuka
Anderson Mori & Tomotsune

Naohiro Toyoda
AEON Financial Service Co. Ltd.

Yoshito Tsuji
Obayashi Corporation

Shougo Tsuruta
PwC Tax Japan

Shino Uenuma
South Toranomon Law Offices

Kengo Watanabe
Ishikawa-Gumi Ltd.

Tatsuya Yagishita
Daito Koun Co. Ltd.

Michi Yamagami
Anderson Mori & Tomotsune

Akio Yamamoto
Kajima Corporation

JORDAN

Ernst & Young

Nayef Abu Alim
Premier Law Firm LLP

Ibrahim Akel
Saed Karajah & Partners LLP

Rawan Alameddin
Hammouri & Partners

Eman M. Al-Dabbas
International Business Legal Associates

Mazen Abu Alghanam
Webb Fontaine

Omar Aljazy
Aljazy & Co. Advocates & Legal Consultants

Sabri S. Al-Khassib
Amman Chamber of Commerce

Faris Allouzi
Khalifeh & Partners Lawyers

Naser Al-Mughrabi
PwC Jordan

Nisreen Alsayed
Amman Chamber of Commerce

Essa Amawi
Amawi & Co. Advocates & Legal Consultants

Mohammed Amawi
Amawi & Co. Advocates & Legal Consultants

Khaled Asfour
Ali Sharif Zu'bi, Advocates & Legal Consultants, member of Lex Mundi

Jafar Barham
Jordan Customs

Rasha Dabbouri
Nathan Inc.

Michael T. Dabit
Michael T. Dabit & Associates

Tariq Hammouri
Hammouri & Partners

Nadim Hattar
Saed Karajah & Partners LLP

George Hazboun
International Consolidated for Legal Consultations

Reem Hazboun
International Consolidated for Legal Consultations

Farah Jaradat
Hammouri & Partners

Emad Karkar
PwC Jordan

Basel Kawar
Kawar Transport & Transit Kargo

Rakan Kawar
Ali Sharif Zu'bi, Advocates & Legal Consultants, member of Lex Mundi

Ahmed Khalifeh
Hammouri & Partners

Ola Khalil
Central Bank of Jordan

Hussein Kofahy
Central Bank of Jordan

Rasha Laswi
Zalloum & Laswi Law Firm

Firas Malhas
International Business Legal Associates

Suhail Mjalli
Jordan Customs

Omar B. Naim
National Construction Company

Khaldoun Nazer
Khalifeh & Partners Lawyers

Majd Nemeh
International Consolidated for Legal Consultations

Main Nsair
Nsair & Partners - Lawyers

Mutasem Nsair
Nsair & Partners - Lawyers

Yotta Pantoula-Bulmer
Hammouri & Partners

Ahmad Quandour
Khalifeh & Partners Lawyers

Hala Qutteineh
Ali Sharif Zu'bi, Advocates & Legal Consultants, member of Lex Mundi

Majdi Salaita
Ali Sharif Zu'bi, Advocates & Legal Consultants, member of Lex Mundi

Omar Sawadha
Hammouri & Partners

Nour Staitieh
Saed Karajah & Partners LLP

Stephan Stephan
PwC Jordan

Azzam Zalloum
Zalloum & Laswi Law Firm

Kareem Zureikat

KAZAKHSTAN

Almaty Bar Association

Keden Customs

Municipal State Enterprise - Almaty Department of Architecture and Urban Planning

Emil Halilyevich Abdrashitov
Notary Association of the Almaty City

Sardar Inarovich Abdysadykov
Notary Association of the Almaty City

Zhanar Abuova
Olympex Advisers

Kuben Abzhanov
GRATA Law Firm

Gaukhar Alibekova
Ministry of National Economy

Nurtay Almashov
Supreme Court of the Republic of Kazakhstan

Andrey Artyushenko
Artyushenko & Partners

Samat Aryshev
Almaty Energo Zbyt

Yermek Aubakirov
Michael Wilson & Partners Ltd.

Zarina Baikenzhina
White & Case

Yuriy Bakulin
Aequitas Law Firm

Samal Bapinova
Ministry of Finance

Aliya Baysenova
Assistance, LLC Law Firm

Ruslan Bayshev
Almaty City Court

Jypar Beishenalieva
Michael Wilson & Partners Ltd.

Madiyar Bekturganov
ORIS Law Firm

Arman Berdalin
Sayat Zholshy & Partners

Berik Berkimbayev
Ministry of Justice

Aidyn Bikebayev
Sayat Zholshy & Partners

Arailym Bisembayeva
Ministry of National Economy

Dmitriy Chumakov
Sayat Zholshy & Partners

Dariga Dairanbek
GRATA Law Firm

Saltanat Dauletova
KPMG Kazakhstan

Aigerim Dyussembekova
Ministry of Justice

Inara Elemanova
Colibri Law Firm

Sungat Essimkhanov
Nuclear and Energy Supervision and Control Committee of the Ministry of Energy

Abzhani Gali
Ministry of Justice

Alexander Giros
Paradigm Projects Kazakhstan

Umigul Gubasheva
Ministry of National Economy

Ardak Idayatova
Aequitas Law Firm

Majra Iskakova
Almaty Energo Zbyt

Yerlan Ismailov
The National Bank of Kazakhstan

Kamil Jambakiyev
Norton Rose Fulbright

Galiya Joldybayeva
Ministry of National Economy

Mariyash Kabikenova
Rehabilitation Manager

Elena Kaeva
PwC Kazakhstan

Marina Kahiani
GRATA Law Firm

Aelita Kakimova
Ministry of National Economy

Assel Kalmagambetova
Synergy Partners Law Firm

Aybek Kambaliyev
GRATA Law Firm

Mira Kamzina
The National Bank of Kazakhstan

Maksud Karaketov
Linkage & Mind LLP

Madina Kazhimova
Ministry of National Economy

Saltanat Kemalova
Signum Law Firm

Aigoul Kenjebayeva
Dentons Kazakhstan LLP

Altynay Kenzhegaliyeva
State Revenue Committee

Yekaterina Khamidullina
Aequitas Law Firm

Olga Kim
Colibri Law Firm

Stanislav Kocherov
Geoderm+

Marina Kolesnikova
GRATA Law Firm

Askar Konysbayev
GRATA Law Firm

Alexander Korobeinikov
Baker & McKenzie

Nurlan Kubenov
KPMG Kazakhstan

Gaukhar Kudaibergenova
Signum Law Firm

Tair Kulteleev
Aequitas Law Firm

Meruert Kulzhabaeva
Tigrohaud LLP

Asset Kussaiyn
Michael Wilson & Partners, Ltd.

Elena Lee
Michael Wilson & Partners Ltd.

Kenneth Mack
Dechert

Aituar Madin
ORIS Law Firm

Madina Makanova

Yerzhan Manasov
Linkage & Mind LLP

Marzhan Mardenova
PwC Kazakhstan

Yessen Massalin
Olympex Advisers

Assel Meiramgaliyeva
Colibri Law Firm

Nurhan Mermankulov
Supreme Court of the Republic of Kazakhstan

Victor Mokrousov
Dechert Kazakhstan LLP

Elena Motovilova
Ministry of Finance

Assel Mukhambekova
GRATA Law Firm

Daniyar Mussakhan
Norton Rose Fulbright

Oxana Neplokhova
Transatlantic Lone Star

Yevgeniya Nossova
Dechert

Kulzhiyan Nurbayeva
Ministry of Justice

Kulbatyrov Nurlan
Economic Research Institute Kazakhstan

Perizat Nurlankyzy
Signum Law Firm

Kanat Olzhabayev
Ministry of National Economy

Ruslan Omarov
First Credit Bureau

Sergazy Omash
Supreme Court of the Republic of Kazakhstan

Nadezhda Oparina
Chadbourne & Parke LLP

Kazieva Orynkul
State Revenue Committee

Andrey Yuriyevich Ponomarenko
Almaty Branch of the RSE Research and Production Center of Land Cadastre

Adilbek Primbetov
State Revenue Committee

Darya Ryapissova
GRATA Law Firm

Berikbol Samenov
Ministry of Justice

Gaukhar Sapina
Ministry of National Economy

Talgat Sariev
Signum Law Firm

Yerlan Serikbayev
Michael Wilson & Partners Ltd.

Aida Shadirova
Dechert Kazakhstan LLP

Abai Shaikenov
Dentons Kazakhstan LLP

Zhanel Shakenova
Colibri Law Firm

Elmira Shamayeva
White & Case

Sofia Shaykhrazieva
Colibri Law Firm

Yerzhan Shermakhanbetov
The National Bank of Kazakhstan

Alzhan Stamkulov
Synergy Partners Law Firm

Nurzhan Stamkulov
Synergy Partners Law Firm

Ulan Stybayev
Signum Law Firm

Otabek Suleimanov
Colibri Law Firm

Yerzhan Suleimenov
APK Olzha Holding LLP

Zhaslan Alimgazinovich Sultanbekov
Firma Paritet Ltd.

Zarina Syzdykova
GRATA Law Firm

Nurysh Tasbulatov
Supreme Court of the Republic of Kazakhstan

Olzhas Taubayev
JSC State Credit Bureau

Zhandos Taukenov
Olympex Advisers

Lyailya S. Tleulina
Aequitas Law Firm

Dana Tokmurzina
PwC Kazakhstan

Yerzhan Toktarov
Sayat Zholshy & Partners

Botanova Totynur
State Revenue Committee

Victoriya Trofimovich
Signum Law Firm

Aigul Turetayeva
GRATA Law Firm

Amir Tussupkhanov
ORIS Law Firm

Alexandr Tyo
KPMG Kazakhstan

Aigerim Tyurebayeva
KPMG Kazakhstan

Azim Usmanov
Colibri Law Firm

Tim Ussen
Assistance, LLC Law Firm

Zhaniya Ussen
Assistance, LLC Law Firm

Aliya Utegaliyeva
PwC Kazakhstan

Nikita Sergeevich Vasilchuk
EnergoPromStroiProekt LLC

Sergei Vataev
Dechert Kazakhstan LLP

Vitaliy Vodolazkin
Sayat Zholshy & Partners

Michael Wilson
Michael Wilson & Partners Ltd.

Olga Olegovna Yershova
Notary Association of the Almaty City

Yerzhan Yessimkhanov
GRATA Law Firm

Saken Zhailauov
SAEN Engineering Group

Gulzat Zhanzukova
Supreme Court of the Republic of Kazakhstan

Birzhan Zharasbayev
Dentons Kazakhstan, LLP

Bolat Zhulamanov
Supreme Court of the Republic of Kazakhstan

Daniyar Zhumabekuly
Colibri Law Firm

Liza Zhumakhmetova
Signum Law Firm

Sofiya Zhylkaidarova
Signum Law Firm

Anton Zinoviev
Booz Allen Hamilton

Egor Zudilin
Stela Electric LLC

KENYA

Metropol Corporation Ltd.

Pyramid Builders

Job Achoki
Daly & Figgis Advocates

Simon B. Luseno
Kenya Revenue Authority

Mohammed A. Bhatti
Bhatti Electrical Limited

Philip Coulson
Coulson Harney Advocates

Oliver Fowler
Kaplan & Stratton

Bernice Gachagu
Companies Registry

Peter Gachuhi
Kaplan & Stratton

Victor Gatahi
Africa Legal Network

Roy Gathecha
Daly & Figgis Advocates

Agnes Nicole Gichuhi
Anjarwalla & Khanna Advocates

Francis Gichuhi Kamau
A4 Architect

Doris Githau
Companies Registry

Ben Githinji
APT Design Solutions

R.M. Hirani
Mangat I.B. Patel & Partners

Milly Jalega
Iseme, Kamau & Maema Advocates

Isaac Kalua
Honda Motorcycle Kenya Ltd

Kenneth Kamaitha
Kaplan & Stratton

Martha Kamanu-Mutugi
Kenya Power

Reuben Njoroge Kamau Kabbau
Dreams Architects

Apollo Karumba
PwC Kenya

Ronald Khavagali
B.M. Musau & Co. Advocates

Njoroge Kibatia
Kibatia & Company Advocates

Alan Kigen
Kamotho Maiyo & Mbatia Advocates

Nancy Kinyanjui
Credit Reference Bureau Africa Ltd.

Calystus Kisaka
B.M. Musau & Co. Advocates

Owen Koimburi
Mazars Kenya

Evelyn Kyania
B.M. Musau & Co. Advocates

David Lekerai
Iseme, Kamau & Maema Advocates

Eric Lukoye
Kenya Trade Network Agency (KENTRADE)

Jacob Malelu
B.M. Musau & Co. Advocates

Nicholas Malonza
Sisule Munyi Kilonzo & Associates

James Mburu Kamau
Iseme, Kamau & Maema Advocates

Ken Melly
Iseme Kamau & Maema Advocates

Peter Momanyi
Mazars Kenya

Bernard Muange
Anjarwalla & Khanna Advocates

George Muchiri
Daly & Figgis Advocates

Titus Mukora
PwC Kenya

John Muoria
Waruhiu K'owade & Ng'ang'a Advocates

Murigu Murithi
ARCS Africa

Benjamin Musau
B.M. Musau & Co. Advocates

Susan Mutinda
B.M. Musau & Co. Advocates

Joshua Mutua
Kenya Power

Jane Mutulili
La Femme Engineering Services Ltd.

Jacob W. Mwangi
The Architectural Association of Kenya

Angela Namwakira
Axis Kenya

James Ndegwa
Kenya Power

Sammy Ndolo
Hamilton Harrison & Mathews (Incorporating Oraro & Co.)

Christina Nduba-Banja
Coulson Harney Advocates

Mbage Nganga
Kenya Law Reform

Mbage Ng'ang'a
Waruhiu K'owade & Ng'ang'a Advocates

Victor Njenga
Kaplan & Stratton

Alex Nyagah
Archbuild Limited

Conrad Nyukuri
Chunga Associates

Desmond Odhiambo
Daly & Figgis Advocates

John Ojwang
Nairobi City County Government

James Okeyo
Muthoga, Gaturu & Company Advocates

Esther Omulele
Muriu Mungai & Co. Advocates

Richard Omwela
Hamilton Harrison & Mathews (Incorporating Oraro & Co.)

Andrew Ondieki
PwC Kenya

Belinda Ongonga
Coulson Harney Advocates

Phillip Onyango
Kaplan & Stratton

Tony Osambo
University of Nairobi

Cephas Osoro
Horwath Erastus & Co. Member, Crowe Horwarth International

Charles Osundwa
Kaplan & Stratton

Ishwarlal B. Patel
Mangat I.B. Patel & Partners

Charlotte Patrick-Patel
Anjarwalla & Khanna Advocates

Andrew Ragui
PwC Kenya

Dominic Rebelo
Anjarwalla & Khanna Advocates

Sonal Sejpal
Anjarwalla & Khanna Advocates

Deepen Shah
Walker Kontos Advocates

Elizabeth Tanui
Milimani Law Courts in Nairobi

Joseph Taracha
Central Bank of Kenya

Angela Waki
Coulson Harney Advocates

Eugene Waluvengo
Kenya Trade Network Agency (KENTRADE)

Margaret Wangu
Companies Registry

Angela Waweru
Kaplan & Stratton

John Wekesa
Kenya Power

Edmond Wesonga
B.M. Musau & Co. Advocates

KIRIBATI

Ministry of Public Works and Utilities

Public Utilities Board

Kibae Akaaka
Ministry of Finance

Arian Arintetaake Vai
High Court of Kiribati

Kenneth Barden
Attorney-at-Law

Susan Barrie
Tobaraoi Travel

Rengaua Bauro
Ministry of Finance

Raweita Beniata
OLP Kiribati

Taake Cama
Ministry of Finance

Sister Bernadette Eberi
High Court of Kiribati

Tomitiana Eritama
Ministry of Labour & Human Resources Development

Anthony Frazier

Jarrod Harrington
Asian Development Bank

Pesega Iaribwebwe
Ministry of Commerce, Industry and Cooperatives

Motiti Moriati Koae
Development Bank of Kiribati

Iaokiri Koreaua
Ministry of Finance

Aaron Levine
Asian Development Bank

Tion Neemia
Shipping Agency of Kiribati

Tetiro Semilota
High Court of Kiribati

Batitea Tekanito

Tauniu Teraoi Moy
Tobaraoi Travel

Reei Tioti
Ministry of Environment, Lands & Agriculture Development (MELAD)

KOREA, REP.

Korea Credit Bureau

Kyoung Soo Chang
Shin & Kim

Seung Hee Grace Chang
Shinhan Customs Service Inc.

Yoonyoung Chang
Hwang Mok Park PC

Hyeong-Tae Cho
Samil PricewaterhouseCoopers

Junghoon Cho
Korean Electrical Contractors Association

Sung-Min Cho
Joyang Logistics

Young-Dae Cho
Kim & Chang

Jinhyuk Choi
Barun Law LLC

Kyung-Joon Choi
Kim, Change & Lee

Paul Choi
Barun Law LLC

Sung-Soo Choi
Kim & Chang

Jin Yeong Chung
Kim & Chang

Robert Flemer
Kim & Chang

Mark Goodrich
White & Case LLC

Jason Ha
Barun Law LLC

Sang Hoon Han
Shin & Kim

Sang-goo Han
Yoon & Yang LLC

Ji-Sang Hur
Korea Customs Service

C.W. Hyun
Kim & Chang

James I.S. Jeon
Sojong Partners

Changho Jo
Samil PricewaterhouseCoopers

Bo Moon Jung
Kim & Chang

Haeng Chang Jung
Hanaro TNS

Hyukjun Jung
Barun Law LLC

Jinku Kang
Lee & Ko

Kyung-won Kang
Samil PricewaterhouseCoopers

Young Seok Ki
Shin & Kim

Byung-Tae Kim
Shin & Kim

Hyo-Sang Kim
Kim & Chang

Jennifer Min Sun Kim
Sojong Partners

Jeong Ho Kim
Kim & Chang

Ju-mi Kim
Samil PricewaterhouseCoopers

Kwang Soo Kim
Woosun Electric Company Ltd.

Rieu Kim
Barun Law LLC

Sang-jin Kim
KEPCO

Seong Won (David) Kim
Hanaro TNS

Wonhyung Kim
Yoon & Yang LLC

Yoon Young Kim
Hwang Mok Park PC

Youn Jong Kim
Shinhan Customs Service Inc.

Seong-Cheon Ko
Samil PricewaterhouseCoopers

Joonghoon Kwak
Lee & Ko

Alex Joong-Hyun Lee
Samil PricewaterhouseCoopers

Ann Seung-Eun Lee
Kim & Chang

Hongyou Lee
Panalpina Korea Ltd.

Jae-Hahn Lee
Kim, Change & Lee

Kyu Wha Lee
Lee & Ko

Moonsub Lee
Sojong Partners

Seung Yoon Lee
Kim & Chang

Young Shin Lee
Hwang Mok Park PC

Yunseok Lim
Supreme Court of Korea

David MacArthur
Bae, Kim & Lee LLC

Young Min Kim
Yoon & Yang LLC

Yon Kyun Oh
Kim & Chang

Jihye Park
Lee & Ko

Sang Il Park
Hwang Mok Park PC

Yong Seok Park
Shin & Kim

Sang-ug Ryu
Supreme Court of Korea

Jeong Seo
Kim & Chang

Minah Seo
Hwang Mok Park PC

Sungjean Seo
Kim & Chang

Changho Seong
Seoul Central District Court

Mi-Jin Shin
Kim & Chang

Philippe Shin
Shin & Kim

Ahn Sooyoung
Hwang Mok Park PC

Jiwon Suh
Ministry of Strategy and Finance

Kiwon Suh
Cheonji Accounting Corporation

Jae Wook Oh
Barun Law LLC

Sou Hee Sophie Yang
White & Case LLC

Catherine J. Yeo
Kim & Chang

Elizabeth Shinwon Yoon
Shinhan Customs Service Inc.

Jae-Yoon Yoon
Korea Customs Service

KOSOVO

KPMG Albania shpk

Ministry of Economic Development (MED)

Flamur Abdullahu
Boga & Associates

Shaqir Behrami
N.P.SH Tomi Elektro

Genc Boga
Boga & Associates Tirana

Alexander Borg Olivier
Interlex Associates LLC

Shyqiri Bytyqi
VALA Consulting

Amir Dërmala
BDO Kosova LLC

Naim Devetaku
VALA Consulting

Agon Dula
Ministry of Trade and Industry

Sokol Elmazaj
Boga & Associates Tirana

Mirjeta Emini
Boga & Associates

Yllka Emini
Tax Administration of Kosovo

Haxhi Gashi
University of Prishtina, Law Faculty

Lorena Gega
PricewaterhouseCoopers Audit sh.p.k.

Besmir F. Grezda
Grezda Trade N. T. Sh

Valon Hasani
Interlex Associates LLC

Rrahim Hoxha
ISARS

Rifat Hyseni
Tax Administration of Kosovo

Bejtush Isufi
Interlex Associates LLC

Nijazi Jakupi
Audit Check

Liresa Kadriu
VALA Consulting

Besarta Kllokoqi
Boga & Associates

Kreshnik Kurtishi

Sabina Lalaj
Boga & Associates

Abedin Matoshi
Interlex Associates LLC

Leonik Mehmeti
Deloitte

Gazmend Mejzini
Ministry of Trade and Industry

Fitore Mekaj
Boga & Associates

Christian Mikosch
Wolf Theiss Rechtsanwälte GmbH & Co KG

Delvina Nallbani
Boga & Associates

Driton Nikaj

Besim Osmani
Interlex Associates LLC

Valdet Osmani
Architect Association of Kosovo

Naxhije Pajaziti-Arifaj
KEDS

Loreta Peci
PricewaterhouseCoopers Audit sh.p.k.

Naser Prapashtica
Crimson Capital

Vigan Rogova
Ethem Rogova Law Firm

Ariana Rozhaja
VALA Consulting

Shendrit Sadiku
PricewaterhouseCoopers Kosovo

Sami Salihu
Tax Administration of Kosovo

Arbena Shehu
Notary Chamber of the Republic of Kosovo

Teki Shehu
The USAID Contract Law Enforcement (CLE) Program

Lukas Slameczka
Wolf Theiss Rechtsanwälte GmbH & Co KG

Fatmir Stublla

Arbresha Tuhina
Baker Tilly Kosovo

Valon Uka
TLW

Agime Spahiu Vrainca
A&GJ – Shped

Gëzim Xharavina
Architectural, Design and Engineering

Arta Xhema
Baker Tilly Kosovo

Lulzim Zeka
Baker Tilly Kosovo

Petrit Zeka
Baker Tilly Kosovo

Shpend Zeka
PricewaterhouseCoopers Kosovo

Ruzhdi Zenelaj
Deloitte

Ruzhdi Zeqiri
Crimson Capital

Shaha Zylfiu
Central Bank of the Republic of Kosovo

KUWAIT

Al Hamad Legal Group

Labeed Abdal
The Law Firm of Labeed Abdal

Nader Abdelaziz
ASAR – Al Ruwayeh & Partners

Abdulrazzaq Abdullah
Abdulrazzaq Abdullah & Partners Law Firm

Hossam Abdullah

Lina A.K. Adlouni

Hossam Afify
PricewaterhouseCoopers Al-Shatti & Co.

Basma Akbar
Capital Market Authority of Kuwait

Lamia Al Abbasi
Ministry of Justice

Ghada Al Ajami
Ministry of Justice

Khaldah Al Ali
Ministry of Finance

Hanan Al Gharabally
Capital Market Authority of Kuwait

Jasim Mohammad Al Habib
Kuwait Municipality

Amina Al India
Ministry of Justice

Faisal Al Jihayem
Kuwait Municipality

Hamad M. Al Mashaan
Al-Ahlia Contracting Group

Waleed Al Nasser
Customs - General Administration

Hanaa Al Razzouqi
Credit Information Network

Shuruq Al Zayed
Ministry of Justice

Fahad Al Zumai
Kuwait University

Aiman Alaraj
KEO International Consultants

Waleed Al-Awadhi
Central Bank of Kuwait

Abdullah Al-Ayoub
Abdullah Kh. Al-Ayoub & Associates, member of Lex Mundi

Waleed Al-Ayoub
Abdullah Kh. Al-Ayoub & Associates, member of Lex Mundi

Anwar Al-Bisher
AlBisher Legal Group

Omar Hamad Yousuf Al-Essa
The Law Office of Al-Essa & Partners

Nada F.A. Al-Fahad
GEC DAR Gulf Engineers Consultants

Nora Al-Haoun
Capital Market Authority of Kuwait

Fahid Almari
Kuwait Municipality

Rasha Al-Naibar
Capital Market Authority of Kuwait

Aisha Al-Nusf
Capital Market Authority of Kuwait

Waleed Alowaiyesh
Capital Market Authority of Kuwait

Yousef Alroumi
Capital Market Authority of Kuwait

Akusa Batwala
ASAR – Al Ruwayeh & Partners

Waleed BenHassan
Credit Information Network

Kevin J. Burke
The Law Office of Bader Saud Al-Bader & Partners

Maysaa Mousa Bushihri
Kuwait Municipality

Twinkle Anie Chacko
Abdulrazzaq Abdullah & Partners Law Firm

Alok Chugh
Ernst & Young

Luis Nene Cunha
ASAR – Al Ruwayeh & Partners

Bader Ali Dashti
Customs - General Administration

Fouad Douglas
PricewaterhouseCoopers Al-Shatti & Co.

Sulaiman Al Fahad
Customs - General Administration

Michel Ghanem
Meysan Partners

Sam Habbas
ASAR – Al Ruwayeh & Partners

Yousef Hamadh
Ministry of Finance

Hussein Hassan
Abdullah Kh. Al-Ayoub & Associates, member of Lex Mundi

Jad Jabre
ASAR – Al Ruwayeh & Partners

Dany Labaky
The Law Office of Al-Essa & Partners

Ahmed Labib
ASAR – Al Ruwayeh & Partners

Areej Marwan Al Dulimi
Ministry of Justice

Anju Menon
Abdullah Kh. Al-Ayoub & Associates, member of Lex Mundi

Abdulrahman Mohamad
Capital Market Authority of Kuwait

Ayman Nada
Al Markaz Law Firm

Mohammed Ramadan
Al Markaz Law Firm

Ganesh Ramanath
PricewaterhouseCoopers Al-Shatti & Co.

Abdul Qayyum Saeed
GH Law Firm

Mohamed Saeed
ASAR – Al Ruwayeh & Partners

Nadyn Saleh
Al Markaz Law Firm

Ibrahim Sattout
ASAR – Al Ruwayeh & Partners

Sherif Shawki
PricewaterhouseCoopers Al-Shatti & Co.

Prateek Shete
Abdullah Kh. Al-Ayoub & Associates, member of Lex Mundi

David Walker
ASAR – Al Ruwayeh & Partners

KYRGYZ REPUBLIC

Globalink Logistics Group

Almaz Abdiev
Department of Cadastre and Registration of Rights on Immovable Property

Yulia Abdumanapova
Baker Tilly Bishkek LLC

Alexander Ahn
Kalikova & Associates Law Firm

Myrzagul Aidaralieva
Koan Lorenz

Gulnara Akhmatova
Lawyer

Atabek Akhmedov
GRATA Law Firm, Tajikistan

Niyazbek Aldashev
Koan Lorenz

Sanzhar Aldashev
GRATA Law Firm, Tajikistan

Elena Babitskaya
Veritas Law Agency

Omurgul Balpanova
Arte Law Firm

Bayansulu Bassepova
PwC Kazakhstan

Kerim Begaliev
Colibri Law Firm

Elena Bit-Avragim
Veritas Law Agency

Daria Bulatova
Koan Lorenz

Elmira Chikieva
Severelektro

Samara Dumanaeva
Koan Lorenz

Bakytbek Dzhusupbekov
Department of Cadastre and Registration of Rights on Immovable Property

Akjoltoi Elebesova
Credit Information Bureau Ishenim

Askar Eshimbekov
Severelektro

Albina Fakerdinova
Deloitte

Kymbat Ibakova
Koan Lorenz

Indira Ibraimova
Mega Stroy LLC

Aidaraliev Erkin Isagalievich
Alternativa Garant Law Firm

Elena Kaeva
PwC Kazakhstan

Gulnara Kalikova
Kalikova & Associates Law Firm

Amanbek Kebekov
Department of Cadastre and Registration of Rights on Immovable Property

Sultan Khalilov
Kalikova & Associates Law Firm

Evgeny Kim
Koan Lorenz

Kuttubai Marzabaev
Orion Construction Company

Asel Momoshova
Kalikova & Associates Law Firm

Umtul Muratkyzy
Koan Lorenz

Mariya Nazarova
PwC Kazakhstan

Aidar Oruzbaev
Koan Lorenz

Myktybek Osmonaliev
Analytical Center Bizexpert

Karlygash Ospankulova
IGroup, Public Association

Nargiz Sabyrova
Veritas Law Agency

Aisanat Safarbek kyzy
GRATA Law Firm

Kanat Seidaliev
GRATA Law Firm

Temirbek Shabdanaliev
Freight Operators Association of Kyrgyzstan

Saodat Shakirova
Arte Law Firm

Anna Shirshova
Customs Cargo Service Ltd.

Maksim Smirnov
Kalikova & Associates Law Firm

Anvar Suleimanov
PwC Kazakhstan

Zhyldyz Tagaeva
Kalikova & Associates Law Firm

Meerim Talantbek kyzy
Kalikova & Associates Law Firm

Guljan Tashimova
Orion Construction Company

Jibek Tenizbaeva
Koan Lorenz

Gulnara Uskenbaeva
Audit Plus

Gulnara Uskenbaeva
Supplier Association - Committee Member of CCI

Mansur Usmanov
Mega Stroy LLC

Lydia Vasilyeva
Veritas Law Agency

LAO PDR

Vinay Ahuja
DFDL

Chonchanok Akarakitkasem
LS Horizon Limited (Lao)

Anthony Assassa
VDB Loi

Kate Baillie
Arion Legal (Lao) Sole Company Limited

Thatsnachone Bounthanh
Xanglao Engineering Consultants

Ciela Marie Cantuba
PricewaterhouseCoopers (Lao) Ltd.

Xaynari Chanthala
LS Horizon Limited (Lao)

Lasonexay Chanthavong
DFDL

Rawat Chomsri
Lao Premier International Law Office

Agnès Couriol
DFDL

Bounyong Dalasone
Lao Premier International Law Office

Bounyasith Daopasith
Lao Premier International Law Office

Aristotle David
ZICOlaw (Laos) Sole Co., Ltd.

Simeuang Douangbouddy
Xanglao Engineering Consultants

Daodeuane Duangdara
VDB Loi

Valyna Keochomsi
LS Horizon Limited (Lao)

Kan Khuprasert
Lao Premier International Law Office

Natchar Leedae
Lao Premier International Law Office

Soulignasack Liemphrachanh
Arion Legal (Lao) Sole Company Limited

Anna Linden
Sciaroni & Associates

Phayboun Nampanya
ZICOlaw (Laos) Sole Co., Ltd.

Souvanno S. Phabmixay
SV Legal Advocate (Lao) Co. Ltd.

Somphone Phasavath
Lao Freight Forwarder Co. Ltd.

Komonchanh Phet-asa
Electricite Du Laos

Vassana Phetlamphanh
Electricite Du Laos

Khamphaeng Phochanthilath
ZICOlaw (Laos) Sole Co., Ltd.

Ketsana Phommachanh
Ministry of Justice

Phompasit Sadettan
VDB Loi

Aparat Sanpibul
ZICOlaw (Laos) Sole Co., Ltd.

Prachith Sayavong
Societe Mixte de Transport (SMT)

Sivath Sengdouangchanh
Allen & Gledhill Co. Ltd.

Phonexay Southiphong
Design Group

Manilin Souvannakham
Lao Premier International Law Office

Latsamy Sysamouth
Ministry of Justice

Somsack Taybounlack
The People's Central High Court

Danyel Thomson
DFDL

Arpon Tunjumras
Lao Premier International Law Office

LATVIA

AB Ways

Baltic Legal

Colliers International

Martins Aljens
Aliance of Independent Legal Advisers

Ilona Bauda
Loze & Partners

Marija Berdova
COBALT Attorneys

Raivis Busmanis
State Labour Inspectorate

Andis Čonka
Latvijas Banka

Ainis Dabols
Latvian Association of Tax Advisers

Andris Dimants
COBALT Attorneys

Valters Diure
Klavins Ellex, member of Lex Mundi

Edvīns Draba
SORAINEN

Jānis Dreimanis
Court Administration

Zlata Elksniņa-Zaščirinska
PwC Latvia

Kristīne Gailīte
COBALT Attorneys

Janis Gavars
Klavins Ellex, member of Lex Mundi

Andris Ignatenko
Estma Ltd.

Viesturs Kadiķis
Public Utilities Commission

Valters Kalme
Public Utilities Commission

Snezhina Kazakova
DHL Express Latvia

Anna Kontere
Loze & Partners

Irina Kostina
Klavins Ellex, member of Lex Mundi

Dainis Leons
Sadales Tīkls AS

Indriķis Liepa
COBALT Attorneys

Dainis Locs
Court Administration

Janis Loze
Loze & Partners

Kristaps Loze
Loze & Partners

Rolands Lūsveris
Sadales Tīkls AS

Zane Markvarte
Markvarte Lexchange Law Office

Ivo Maskalans
COBALT Attorneys

Linda Matisane
State Labour Inspectorate

Alexey Melsitov
MTA Maritime Transport & Agencies

Baiba Orbidane
Klavins Ellex, member of Lex Mundi

Guna Paidere
Register of Enterprises

Kristine Parsonse
ECB SIA

Kristine Patmalniece
Aliance of Independent Legal Advisers

Galina Pilutina
ECB SIA

Anastasija Pimenova
Zoom Room

Baiba Plaude
Law Offices Blueger & Plaude

Ilze Rauza
PwC Latvia

Lelde Rozentale
State Land Service of the Republic of Latvia

Elīna Rožulapa
Latvian Association of Architects (LAA)

Sandra Stipniece
Chamber of Sworn Notaries of Latvia

Darja Tagajeva
PwC Latvia

Ruta Teresko
AZ Service Ltd.

Jānis Timermanis
AS Kredītinformācijas Birojs

Edgars Timpa
State Labour Inspectorate

Ingus Užulis
Public Utilities Commission

Maris Vainovskis
Eversheds Bitāns

Elina Vilde
Eversheds Bitāns

Krista Zariņa
Klavins Ellex, member of Lex Mundi

Agate Ziverte
PwC Latvia

Daiga Zivtina
Klavins Ellex, member of Lex Mundi

LEBANON

Nadim Abboud
Law Office of A. Abboud & Associates

Nada Abdelsater-Abusamra
AbdelSater AbuSamra & Associates - ASAS LAW

Marie Abi-Antoun
AbdelSater AbuSamra & Associates - ASAS LAW

Riham Al Ali
Smayra Law Office

Zeina Azzi
Obeid & Medawar Law Firm

Corinne Baaklini
MENA City Lawyers

Jean Baroudi
Baroudi & Associates

Boutros Bou Lattouf
EBL Bureau in Beirut

Constantin Calliondji
MENA City Lawyers

Nayla Chemaly
MENA City Lawyers

Najib Choucair
Central Bank of Lebanon

Alice Choueiri
MENA City Lawyers

Lina El Cheikh
MENA City Lawyers

Mario El Cheikh
AGC SAL

Hanadi El Hajj
MENA City Lawyers

Amanda El Madani
MENA City Lawyers

Richard El Mouallem
PwC Lebanon

Nada Elsayed
PwC Lebanon

Jenny Fares
Hyam G. Mallat Law Firm

Hadi Fathallah
ESCO Fathallah & Co.

Izzat Fathallah
ESCO Fathallah & Co.

Wafic Fathallah
ESCO Fathallah & Co.

Ribal Fattal
Law Office of A. Abboud & Associates

Lea Ferzli
Baroudi & Associates

Samir Francis
Freight Leader SARL

Serena Ghanimeh
AbdelSater AbuSamra & Associates - ASAS LAW

Ghassan Haddad
Badri and Salim El Meouchi Law Firm, member of Interleges

Abdallah Hayek
Hayek Group

Nicolas Hayek
Hayek Group

Walid Honein
Badri and Salim El Meouchi Law Firm, member of Interleges

Maher Jaber
MENA City Lawyers

Fady Jamaleddine
MENA City Lawyers

Mohammad Joumaa
PwC Lebanon

Georges Jureidini
Coserv sarl - Panalpina Agents

Elie Kachouh
ELC Transport Services SAL

Georges Kadige
Kadige & Kadige Law Firm

Michel Kadige
Kadige & Kadige Law Firm

Hussein Kazan
MENA City Lawyers

Tatiana Kehdy
Baroudi & Associates

Najib Khattar
Khattar Associates

Abdo Maatouk
Smayra Law Office

Fady Mahfouz
HBD-T Law Firm

Georges Mallat
Hyam G. Mallat Law Firm

Nabil Mallat
Hyam G. Mallat Law Firm

Rachad Medawar
Obeid & Medawar Law Firm

Mario Mohanna
Patrimoine Conseil SARL

Romanos Mouawad
MENA City Lawyers

Mirvat Moustapha
MENA City Lawyers

Andre Nader
Nader Law Office

Rana Nader
Nader Law Office

Toufic Nehme
Law Offices of Toufic Nehme

Nehman Rhayem
Electricité du Liban

Mireille Richa
Tyan & Zgheib Law Firm

Jihan Rizk Khattar
Khattar Associates

Jihad Rizkallah
Badri and Salim El Meouchi Law Firm, member of Interleges

Mustafa Saadeh
Tyan & Zgheib Law Firm

Nisrine Mary Salhab
Hyam G. Mallat Law Firm

Rached Sarkis
Consultant

Antoine Sfeir
Badri and Salim El Meouchi Law Firm, member of Interleges

Mona Sfeir
Hyam G. Mallat Law Firm

Rami Smayra
Smayra Law Office

Ida Elise Tommerup
MENA City Lawyers

Nady Tyan
Tyan & Zgheib Law Firm

Alaa Zeineddine
EMEA Legal Counsels

LESOTHO

Bidvest Panalpina Logistics

Khatleli Tomane Moteane (KTM) Architects

Maseru Municipal Council

Mahashe Chaka
Land Administration Authority

Emile du Toit
Ernst & Young

Jacobus J. Eksteen
Compuscan Lesotho

Corne Fourie
Compuscan South Africa

Motselisi Khiba
Harley & Morris

Mannete Khotle
Compuscan Lesotho

Albertus Kleingeld
Webber Newdigate

Makali Lepholisa
Lesotho Revenue Authority

Qhalehang Letsika
Mei & Mei Attorneys Inc.

Thakane Makume
Lesotho Electricity Company (Pty) Ltd.

Tlhobohano Matela
National Environment Secretariat

Veronica Matiea

Denis Molyneaux
Webber Newdigate

Ntlatlapa Mosae
Sello-Mafatle Attorneys

Molupe Mothepu
Lesotho Revenue Authority

Mothae Nonyana
Lesotho Electricity Company (Pty) Ltd.

Bafokeng Noosi
Central Bank of Lesotho

Duduzile Seamatha
Sheeran & Associates

Tiisetso Sello-Mafatle
Sello-Mafatle Attorneys

Lindiwe Sephomolo
Association of Lesotho Employers and Business

Starford Sharite
High Court

Mooresi Tau Thabane

James J. Tesele
Compuscan Lesotho

Marorisang Thekiso
Sheeran & Associates

Phoka Thene
Letšeng Diamonds

George Thokoa
Maseru Electro Services Pty Ltd.

Mark Frederick Webber
Harley & Morris

LIBERIA

Joseph Anim
International Bank of Liberia

Francis Baiden
International Bank of Liberia

Yafar Baikeph
Heritage Partner & Associates, Inc.

F. Augustus Caesar Jr.
Caesar Architects, Inc.

Jenkins Charles
PwC

Henry Reed Cooper
Cooper & Togbah Law Office

John Davis
Liberia Bank for Development and Investment

Jamal Dehtho
PwC

Valery Djamby
Bolloré Africa Logistics

Fonsia Donzo
Central Bank of Liberia

Christine Sonpon Freeman
Cooper & Togbah Law Office

Robert Freeman
Cooper & Togbah Law Office

Peter Graham
Liberia Electricity Corporation

Cyril Jones
Jones & Jones

Theophilus Dekonty Joseph
Baker Tilly Liberia

Abu Kamara
Liberia Business Registry

Sophie Kayemba Mutebi
PwC

Bob Weetol Livingstone

Barnabas Norris
Center for National Documents & Records (National Archives)

Philomena Bloh Sayeh
Center for National Documents & Records (National Archives)

Robert Smallwood
PwC

Justin Tengbeh
National Custom Brokers Association of Liberia

Emmanuel Total
Heritage Partner & Associates, Inc.

J. Awia Vankan
Heritage Partner & Associates, Inc.

Taweh J Veikai
PwC

Madlyne Wah
Center for National Documents & Records (National Archives)

T. Negbalee Warner
Heritage Partner & Associates, Inc.

Mustapha Wesseh
Center for National Documents & Records (National Archives)

LIBYA

Zahaf & Partners Law Firm

Ahmed Abdulaziz
Mukhtar, Kelbash & Elgharabli

Wael Al-Shagagi
Alteraz Engineering Consultants

Abdudayem Elgharabli
Mukhtar, Kelbash & Elgharabli

Abdul Salam El-Marghani
PwC

Husam Elnaili
PwC

Mahmoud ELSheikh
University of Tripoli

Ahmed Ghattour
Ahmed Ghattour & Co.

Bahloul Kelbash
Mukhtar, Kelbash & Elgharabli

Belkasem Magid Obadi
General Electricity Company of Libya (GECOL)

Ibrahim Maher
DLA Matouk Bassiouny (part of DLA Piper Group)

Mahmud Mukhtar
Mukhtar, Kelbash & Elgharabli

Ali Naser
Libyan Credit Information Center

Abuejila Saif Annaser
Saif Annaser Law Office

Muftah Saif Annaser
Saif Annaser Law Office

Abdulkarim Tayeb
Libyan Credit Information Center

Mazen Tumi
Tumi Law Firm

Raif Wafa

LITHUANIA

Loreta Andziulyte
ECOVIS ProventusLaw Law Firm

Asta Avizaite
Ministry of Justice

Greta Bagdonavičūtėl
Primus Attorneys-at-Law

Liutauras Baikštys
Primus Attorneys-at-Law

Pavel Balbatunov

Petras Baltusevičius
DSV Transport UAB

Donatas Baranauskas
Vilniaus Miesto 14 - Asis Notaru Biuras

Šarūnas Basijokas
Glimstedt

Vilius Bernatonis
Tark Grunte Sutkiene

Andrius Bogdanovičius
JSC Creditinfo Lietuva

Kornelija Bogniukaitė
Glimstedt

Alina Burlakova
Law Firm Valiunas Ellex, member of Lex Mundi

Monika Casado
Amerinde Consolidated, Inc.

Robertas Čiočys
Law Firm Valiunas Ellex, member of Lex Mundi

Justas Ciomanas
Lithuanian Chamber of Notaries

Giedre Dailidenaite
Primus Attorneys-at-Law

Ignas Dargužas
Law Firm SORAINEN & Partners

Aurelija Daubaraitė
Law Firm SORAINEN & Partners

Gintaras Daugela
Bank of Lithuania

Darius Dieckus
Bank of Lithuania

Giedre Domkute
AAA Baltic Service Company - Law Firm

Reda Gabrilavičiūtė
Ministry of Justice

Karolina Gasparke
BNT Attorneys-at-Law

Yvonne Goldammer
BNT Attorneys-at-Law

Joana Gramakovaitė
PwC Lithuania

Dovile Greblikiene
Valiunas Ellex

Tania Griškienė
Ministry of Economy

Arturas Gutauskas
Primus Attorneys-at-Law

Frank Heemann
BNT Attorneys-at-Law

Robert Juodka
Primus Attorneys-at-Law

Ieva Kairytė
PwC Lithuania

Inga Karulaityte-Kvainauskiene
ECOVIS ProventusLaw Law Firm

Romualdas Kasperavičius
State Enterprise Centre of Registers

Aušra Keniausytė
Ministry of Economy

Ieva Krivickaitė
Law Firm SORAINEN & Partners

Egidijus Kundelis
PwC Lithuania

Žilvinas Kvietkus
Raidla Lejins & Norcous

Linas Liktorius
KPMG Lithuania

Odeta Maksvytytė
Primus Attorneys-at-Law

Linas Margevicius
Legal Bureau of Linas Margevicius

Vilius Martišius
Law Firm of Reda Zaboliene

Laura Matuizaite
Law Firm SORAINEN & Partners

Jolita Meškelytė
Ministry of Justice

Bronislovas Mikūta
State Enterprise Centre of Registers

Donata Montvydaitė
Law Firm Valiunas Ellex, member of Lex Mundi

Nerijus Nedzinskas
PwC Lithuania

Greta Obadauskaite
AAA Baltic Service Company - Law Firm

Michail Parchimovič
Motieka & Audzevičius

Algirdas Pekšys
Law Firm SORAINEN & Partners

Nicolai Portelli
Baltic Freight Services

Justina Rakauskaitė
Glimstedt

Lina Ramanauskaite

Liudas Ramanauskas
Law Firm SORAINEN & Partners

Vytautas Sabalys
Law Firm SORAINEN & Partners

Simona Šarkauskaitė
Law Firm Zabiela, Zabielaite & Partners

Arvydas Sedekerskis
Lithuanian Electric Energy Association

Aušra Sičiūnienė
Vilnius City Municipality

Justina Šilinskaitė
Eversheds Saladzius

Mingailė Šilkūnaitė
Glimstedt

Rimantas Simaitis
COBALT

Donatas Šliora
Tark Grunte Sutkiene

Agneska Stanulevic
PwC Lithuania

Marius Stračkaitis
Lithuanian Chamber of Notaries

Alina Streckytė
Valiunas Ellex

Arnoldas Tomasevicius
Ministry of Justice

Daiva Ušinskaitė-Filonovienė
Tark Grunte Sutkiene

Irma Vagulytė
Ministry of Economy

Vilija Vaitkutė Pavan
Valiunas Ellex

Adrijus Vegys
Bank of Lithuania

Agnietė Venckiene
Law Firm SORAINEN & Partners

Tomas Venckus
Primus Attorneys-at-Law

Darius Zabiela
Law Firm Zabiela, Zabielaite & Partners

Ernesta Žiogienė
Primus Attorneys-at-Law

Povilas Žukauskas
Law Firm Valiunas Ellex, member of Lex Mundi

Audrius Žvybas
Glimstedt

LUXEMBOURG

IPRA-CINDER

PwC Luxembourg

Tom Baumert
Chamber of Commerce of the Grand-Duchy of Luxembourg

Louis Berns
Arendt & Medernach SA

Sébastien Binard
Arendt & Medernach SA

Eleonora Broman
Loyens & Loeff Luxembourg S. à r.l.

Raymond Dhur
Administration de l'Enregistrement et des Domaines

Gérard Eischen
Chamber of Commerce of the Grand-Duchy of Luxembourg

Thomas Feider
Administration de l'Enregistrement et des Domaines

Peggy Goossens
Pierre Thielen Avocats

Andreas Heinzmann
GSK Stockmann + Kollegen

Vincent Hieff
Chamber of Commerce of the Grand-Duchy of Luxembourg

Véronique Hoffeld
Loyens & Loeff Luxembourg S. à r.l.

François Kremer
Arendt & Medernach SA

Paul Lanois

Tom Loesch
Law Firm Loesch

Evelyne Lordong
Arendt & Medernach SA

Jeannot Medinger
Creos Luxembourg SA

Philipp Metzchke
Arendt & Medernach SA

Marc Meyer
Creos Luxembourg SA

Marco Peters
Creos Luxembourg SA

Elisa Ragazzoni
Paul Wurth Geprolux SA

Judith Raijmakers
Loyens & Loeff Luxembourg S. à r.l.

Jean-Luc Schaus
Pierre Thielen Avocats

Roger Schintgen
Paul Wurth Geprolux SA

Phillipe Schmit
Arendt & Medernach SA

Alex Schmitt
Bonn & Schmitt

Valerio Scollo
GSK Stockmann + Kollegen

Marielle Stevenot
MNKS Law Firm

Jill Thinnes
Institut Luxembourgeois de Régulation

Candice Wiser
Bonn & Schmitt

MACEDONIA, FYR

Apostolska & Aleksandrovski

Dom - Dizajn

IKRP Rokas & Partners

Ljubinka Andonovska
Central Registry of the Republic of Macedonia

Natasha Andreeva
National Bank of the Republic of Macedonia

Zlatko Antevski
Lawyers Antevski

Dina Apostolovska
Emil Miftari Law Office

Maja Atanasova
Georgi Dimitrov Attorneys

Dragan Blažev
Timelproject Engineering

Slavica Bogoeva
Macedonian Credit Bureau AD Skopje

Nebojsa Cvetanovski
Intereuropa

Ljupco Cvetkovski
DDK Attorneys-at-Law

Dragan Dameski
DDK Attorneys-at-Law

Irene Dimitrievikj
Cakmakova Advocates

Zorica Dimitrovska
Law Office Nikolovski

Elena Dimova
Cakmakova Advocates

Ana Georgievska
DIMA Forwarders

Dimche Georgievski
DIMA Forwarders

Katarina Ginoska
Georgi Dimitrov Attorneys

Marijana Gjoreska
Central Registry of the Republic of Macedonia

Verica Hadzi Vasileva-Markovska
AAG - Analysis and Advisory Group

Ana Hadzieva-Angelovska
DDK Attorneys-at-Law

Aleksandar Ickovski

Maja Jakimovska
Cakmakova Advocates

Aneta Jovanoska Trajanovska
Lawyers Antevski

Ana Kapceva
Donevski Law Firm

Emilija Kelesoska Sholjakovska
DDK Attorneys-at-Law

Risto Kitev
MEPOS Operativa Ltd.

Dejan Knezović
Law Office Knezovic & Associates

Stanko Korunoski
Central Registry of the Republic of Macedonia

Ivana Lekic
PwC Macedonia

Georgi Markov
PwC Macedonia

Emil Miftari
Emil Miftari Law Office

Vlatko Mihailov
Emil Miftari Law Office

Petra Mihajlovska
Cakmakova Advocates

Oliver Mirchevski
EVN Macedonia

Irena Mitkovska
Lawyers Antevski

Biljana Mladenovska Dimitrova
Lawyers Antevski

Martin Monevski
Monevski Law Firm

Vojdan Monevski
Monevski Law Firm

Marijana Naumovska
Central Registry of the Republic of Macedonia

Svetlana Neceva
Law Office Pepeljugoski

Ilija Nedelkoski
Cakmakova Advocates

Elena Nikodinovska
Emil Miftari Law Office

Marina Nikoloska
Cakmakova Advocates

Vesna Nikolovska
Law Office Nikolovski

Goran Nikolovski
Law Office Nikolovski

Nino Noveski
Law Office Nikolovski

Martin Odzaklieski
Ministry of Transport and Communications

Bojana Paneva
Law Firm Trpenoski

Aleksandar Penovski
Law Firm Trpenoski

Ana Pepeljugoska
Law Office Pepeljugoski

Valentin Pepeljugoski
Law Office Pepeljugoski

Iva Petrovska
Cakmakova Advocates

Andrea Popovski
Central Registry of the Republic of Macedonia

Ljubica Ruben
Mens Legis Law Firm

Sasho Saltirovski
EVN Macedonia

Radovan Sanclic
Law Firm Trpenoski

Lidija Sarafimova-Danevska
National Bank of the Republic of Macedonia

Tatjana Siskovska
Polenak Law Firm

Sonja Stojcevska
Cakmakova Advocates

Blagoj Stojevski
EVN Macedonia

Ana Stojilovska
Analytica MK

Dragica Tasevska
National Bank of the Republic of Macedonia

Borjanka Todorovska
Donevski Law Firm

Dragan Trajkovski
Eltek

Stefan Trost
EVN Macedonia

Natasha Trpenoska Trenchevska
Law Firm Trpenoski

Slavce Trpeski
Agency for Real Estate Cadastre

Vladimir Vasilevski
BETASPED d.o.o.

Metodija Velkov
Polenak Law Firm

Ivana Velkovska
PwC Macedonia

Tome Velkovski
AAG - Analysis and Advisory Group

Sladjana Zafirova
TIVA-AS D.O.O.E.L. - Valandovo

Dragisa Zlatkovski
Siskon Ltd.

MADAGASCAR

Natacha Adrianjakamanarivo
Cabinet Mazars Fivoarana

Serge Andretseheno
Cabinet AS Architecte

Liva Harisoa Andriamahady
Madagascar Law Offices

Tsiry Andriamisamanana

Aimée Andrianasolo
Office de Regulation Électricité

Rivo Andrianirina-Ratsialonana
Observatoire du Foncier

Sarah Andrianjatovo
PricewaterhouseCoopers Tax & Legal Madagascar - PwC Madagascar

Jocelyn Marie Claude Andrianoasy
Ordre des Architectes

Nirilala Antsa Andriantsoa
John W. Ffooks & Co., member of Bowman Gilfillan Africa Group

Cedric Catheline
Bureau de Liaison SGS

Yves Duchateau
Bolloré Africa Logistics Madagascar

Raphaël Jakoba
Madagascar Conseil International

Rakotomalala Mamy Njatoson
Registre du Commerce et des Sociétés (RNCS)

Clara Michel Nala
Commune Urbaine d'Antananarivo

Namindranasoa Ny Haja
SMR & HR Associates SA

Pascaline R. Rabearisoa
Delta Audit Deloitte

Rija Rabeharisoa
Cabinet Mazars Fivoarana

Ketakandriana Rabemananjara
Office de Regulation Électricité

Sahondra Rabenarivo
Madagascar Law Offices

Jeannot Julien Padoue Rafanomezana
Etude de Me Jeannot Rafanomezana

Andry Rajaona
Cabinet SIGMA Consulting

Tahina Rajaona
Madagascar Law Offices

Pierrette Rajaonarisoa
SDV Logistics

Manantsoa Rakoto
John W. Ffooks & Co., member of Bowman Gilfillan Africa Group

Fetrahanta Sylviane Rakotomanana
PricewaterhouseCoopers Tax & Legal Madagascar - PwC Madagascar

Harivola Joan Rakotomanjaka

Corinne Holy Rakotoniaina
PricewaterhouseCoopers Tax & Legal Madagascar - PwC Madagascar

Ralidera Junior Rakotoniaina
John W. Ffooks & Co., member of Bowman Gilfillan Africa Group

Fidèle Armand Rakotonirina
Cabinet Mazars Fivoarana

Heritiana Rakotosalama
Legislink Consulting

Harotsilavo Rakotoson
SMR & HR Associates SA

Lanto Tiana Ralison
PricewaterhouseCoopers Tax & Legal Madagascar - PwC Madagascar

Aviva Ramanitra
Lexel Juridique & Fiscal

Roland Ramarijaona
Delta Audit Deloitte

Laingo Ramarimbahoaka
Madagascar Conseil International

André Randranto
Randranto

Desire Marcel Randrianarisoa
Jiro Sy Rano Malagasy (JIRAMA)

Sariaka Randrianarisoa
John W. Ffooks & Co., member of Bowman Gilfillan Africa Group

William Randrianarivelo
PricewaterhouseCoopers Tax & Legal Madagascar - PwC Madagascar

Fanja Ranisamananjaralala
DHL Danzas

Sylvia Rasoarilala
Banque Centrale de Madagascar

Sahondra Rasoarisoa
Delta Audit Deloitte

Rivaharilala Rasolojaona
Office de Regulation Électricité

Ramarolanto Ratiaray
Universite d'Antananarivo

Henintsoa Ratiarison
Madagascar Law Offices

Hasina Ratsimanarisoa
Kaliana Corporation

Mialy Ratsimba
PricewaterhouseCoopers Tax & Legal Madagascar - PwC Madagascar

Princy Raveloharison
PricewaterhouseCoopers Tax & Legal Madagascar - PwC Madagascar

Andriamisa Ravelomanana
PricewaterhouseCoopers Tax & Legal Madagascar - PwC Madagascar

Landy Raveloson
Commune Urbaine d'Antananarivo

Jean Marcel Razafimahenina
Delta Audit Deloitte

Chantal Razafinarivo
Cabinet Razafinarivo

Parson Harivel Razafindrainibe
Etude Razafindrainibe / Ravoajanahary

Lisiniaina Razafindrakoto
Bureau de Liaison SGS

Olivier Ribot
Lexel Juridique & Fiscal

Ida Soamiliarimana
Madagascar Conseil International

Hariniaina Soloarivelo
Commune Urbaine d'Antananarivo

MALAWI

Marshal Chilenga
TF & Partners

Andrew Chimpololo
University of Malawi (The Polytechnic)

Ricky Chingota
Savjani & Co.

Alan Chinula
William Faulkner

Gautoni D. Kainja
Kainja & Dzonzi

Chimwemwe Kalua
Golden & Law

Griffin Kamanga
Spine Cargo Co.

Dannie J. Kamwaza
Kamwaza Design Partnership

Frank Edgar Kapanda
Supreme Court of Appeal

Kalekeni Kaphale
Kalekeni Kaphale

Andrews Katuya
Dowell & Jones, Attorneys-at-Law

Mabvuto Khoza
Bolloré Logistics - Malawi

James Masumbu
Tembenu, Masumbu & Co.

Raphael Mhone
Racane Associates

Noel Misanjo
Savjani & Co.

Vyamala Aggriel Moyo
PwC Malawi

Modecai Msisha
Nyirenda & Msisha Law Offices

Misheck Msiska
Ernst & Young

Arthur Alick Msowoya
Wilson & Morgan

Charles Mvula
DUMA Electrics Ltd. - Control Systems and Energy Management

Patricia Mwase
Credit Data Credit Reference Bureau Ltd.

Grant Nyirongo
Elemech Designs

Ted Roka
Kalekeni Kaphale

Krishna Savjani
Savjani & Co.

Donns Shawa
RD Consultants

Samuel Tembenu
Tembenu, Masumbu & Co.

MALAYSIA

Bank Negara Malaysia

Ernst & Young

Worldgate Express Services Sdn Bhd

Aniza Abd Manaf
Credit Bureau Malaysia Sdn Bhd

Abu Daud Abd Rahim
Azmi & Associates

Azura Abd Rahman
Land & Mines Office

Nor Azimah Abdul Aziz
Companies Commission

Ahmad Danial Abdul Rahim
Azmi & Associates

Sonia Abraham
Azman, Davidson & Co.

Wilfred Abraham
Zul Rafique & Partners, Advocate & Solicitors

Zarina Alias
Malaysia Department of Insolvency

Nur Sajati Binti Asan Mohamed
Azmi & Associates

Ahmad Hafiz Abdul Aziz
Ministry of International Trade and Industry

Muhamad Azizul Bin Zahidin
Westports Malaysia Sdn Bhd

Anita Balakrishnan
Shearn Delamore & Co.

Shamsuddin Bardan
Malaysian Employers Federation

Mohd Nawawi bin Hj Said Abdullah
Tenaga Nasional Berhad

Ahmad Fuad bin Md Kasim
Tenaga Nasional Berhad

Hosni Hussen Bin MD Saat
Royal Malaysian Customs Department

Che Adnan Bin Mohamad
Nadi Consult Era Sdn Bhd

Tahir bin Mohd Deni
Tenaga Nasional Berhad

Shamsol Zakri bin Zakaria Pengarah
Malaysia Department of Insolvency

YM Tengku Rohana Binti Tengku Nawawi
Land & Mines Office

KC Chan
Freight Transport Network Sdn. Bhd.

Hong Yun Chang
Tay & Partners

Ar. Teoh Chee Wui
Archicentre Sdn Bhd

Chow Keng Chin
Indra Gandhi & Co.

Eric Chin
CTOS Data Systems Sdn Bhd

Michelle Choo
Dun & Bradstreet (D&B) Malaysia Sdn Bhd

Jack Chor
Christopher Lee & Co.

Melinda Marie D'Angelus
Azmi & Associates

Ruzaida Daud
Energy Commission

J. Wilfred Durai
Zain & Co.

Indra Gandhi
Indra Gandhi & Co.

Mohammed Rhiza Ghazi
Rhiza & Richard

Dato Zainal Abidin Haji Kamarudin
Pejabat Ketua Pendaftar

Ar. Ezumi Harzani Ismail
Arkitek MAA

Khalid Hashim
Azmi & Associates

Hasniza Ahmad Hassan
Zain & Co.

Andrew Heng
Ferrier Hodgson Limited

Abdul Hafiz Bin Hidzir
Tenaga Nasional Berhad

Wong Hin Loong
Azman, Davidson & Co.

Ivan Yue Chan Ho
Shook Lin & Bok

Mohamad Ali Abdul Husain
North Port (Malaysia) Bhd.

Ahmad Hafiz bin Hussin
Customs Westport

Mazrina Mohd Ibramsah
MPC

Dato' Dr. Sallehudin Ishak
Land & Mines Office

Rohani Ismail
Sessions Court Kuala Lumpur

Rosnani Ismail
Inland Revenue Department Lembaga Hasil Dalam Negeri (LHDN)

Kumarakuru Jai
Ferrier Hodgson Limited

Hisamuddin Bin Jarudy
Royal Malaysian Customs Department

Norhaiza Jemon
Companies Commission

Dato' Dr. Ir. Andy K. H. Seo

Amos Kok
Jeff Leong, Poon & Wong

Richard Kok
Rhiza & Richard

LOH Kok Leong
Russell Bedford LC & Company - member of Russell Bedford International

Dawn Lai
RAM Credit Information Sdn Bhd

Christopher Lee
Christopher Lee & Co.

Cing-Cing Lee
Azmi & Associates

Marc Lee
Rahmat Lim & Partners

Jeff Leong
Jeff Leong, Poon & Wong

Alex Lian
Jeff Leong, Poon & Wong

Anne Liew
RAM Credit Information Sdn Bhd

Lim Lift
Ferrier Hodgson Limited

Joo Ho Lim
Azman, Davidson & Co.

Koon Huan Lim
Skrine, member of Lex Mundi

Ahmad Lutfi Abdull Mutalip
Azmi & Associates

Ir. Bashir Ahamed Maideen
Nadi Consult Era Sdn Bhd

John Matthew
Christopher Lee & Co.

Khairon Niza Md Akhir
Companies Commission

Arvind Menon
Ranhill Bersekutu Sdn Bhd

Hanani Hayati Mohd Adhan
Azmi & Associates

Azmi Mohd Ali
Azmi & Associates

Nik Mohd Fadhil Bin Salleh
Fire and Rescue Department of Kuala Lumpur

Suzana Mohd Razali
Companies Commission

Zuhaidi Mohd Shahari
Azmi & Associates

Rohaizad Mohd Yusof
North Port (Malaysia) Bhd.

Shameen Mohd. Haaziq Pillay
Wong & Partners

Mohd Yusoff Mokhzani Aris
Malaysia Productivity Corporation

Nanthakumar Murokana
Westport Malaysia

Marina Nathan
Companies Commission

Henry Ng
Jeff Leong, Poon & Wong

Oy Moon Ng
CTOS Data Systems Sdn Bhd

Swee Kee Ng
Shearn Delamore & Co.

Hock An Ong
BDO

Allison Ong Lee Fong
Azman, Davidson & Co.

Tamilmaran A/L Palaniappan
North Port (Malaysia) Bhd.

Kim Yong Pang
Ferrier Hodgson Limited

Tan Kar Peng
Kamaruddin Wee & Co. Advocates & Solicitors

Aurobindo Ponniah
PwC Malaysia

Aminah Bt Abd Rahman
Ministry of Urban Wellbeing, Housing and Local Government

Nirmala Ramadass
Companies Commission

Nurul Lidya Razali
Indah Water Home

Siti Zurina Sabarudin
Azmi & Associates

Muzawipah Bt Md. Salim
Tenaga Nasional Berhad

Sugumar Saminathan
Malaysia Productivity Corporation

Victor Saw Seng Kee
PricewaterhouseCoopers Advisory Services Sdn Bhd

Sharifah Marina Sayeid
Malaysia Department of Insolvency

Zamzuri Selamat
Syarikat Bekalan Air Selangor Sdn. Bhd (SYABAS)

Thong Ming Sen
Shook Lin & Bok

Fiona Sequerah
Christopher Lee & Co.

Thirilogachandran Shanmugasundaram
TLC Architect

Devi Sheela
Norliza, Sheela, Param & Co.

Jagdev Singh
PwC Malaysia

Noeline Chanan Singh
Malaysia Productivity Corporation

Adeline Thor Sue Lyn
Russell Bedford LC & Company - member of Russell Bedford International

Nor Fajariah Sulaiman
City Hall of Kuala Lumpur

Muhendaran Suppiah
Muhendaran Sri

Jamilah Haji Mohd Taib
Companies Commission

Ee Ling Tan
Tay & Partners

Esther Tan
Zul Rafique & Partners, Advocate & Solicitors

Emilia Tee
Bursa Malaysia

Hemant Thakore
Ranhill Bersekutu Sdn Bhd

Lim Liu Ting
Azman, Davidson & Co.

Sahrom Ujang
Kuala Lumpur City Hall

Siti Wahida binti Sheikh Hussien
Credit Bureau Malaysia Sdn Bhd

Anne Wai Yee Wong
Jeff Leong, Poon & Wong

Sue Wan
Wong & Partners

Tuan Wan Zaid
Sessions Court Kuala Lumpur

Chee Lin Wong
Skrine, member of Lex Mundi

Justin Wong
Azmi & Associates

Wei Kwang Woo
Wong & Partners

Yeo Yao Huang
Wong & Partners

Elaine Yap
Wong & Partners

Moy Pui Yee
Rahmat Lim & Partners

MALDIVES

Avant-Garde Lawyers

Maldives Monetary Authority

Asna Ahmed
Bank of Maldives PLC

Izuan Ahmed
Amin Construction Pvt. Ltd.

Junaina Ahmed
Shah, Hussain & Co. Barristers & Attorneys

Mohamed Shahdy Anwar
Suood Anwar & Co. - Attorneys-at-Law

Jatindra Bhattray
PwC Maldives

Asma Chan-Rahim
Shah, Hussain & Co. Barristers & Attorneys

Aishath Haifa
Shah, Hussain & Co. Barristers & Attorneys

Mohamed Hameed
Antrac Maldives Pvt. Ltd.

Dheena Hussain
Shah, Hussain & Co. Barristers & Attorneys

Yudhishtran Kanagasabai
PwC Sri Lanka

Prasanta Misra
PwC Maldives

Abdulla Muizzu
Praxis Law Firm

Sulakshan Ramanan
Ernst & Young

Aishath Samah
Bank of Maldives PLC

Mohamed Shafaz Wajeeh
Praxis Law Firm

Shuaib M. Shah
Shah, Hussain & Co. Barristers & Attorneys

Mizna Shareef
Shah, Hussain & Co. Barristers & Attorneys

Manal Shihab
Suood Anwar & Co. - Attorneys-at-Law

A. Shimhaz
A. Ahmed Legal Chambers

Tyronne Soza
John Keells Logistics

Mariyam Visam
Ministry of Economic Development

Sumudu Wijesundara
Ernst & Young

MALI

BCEAO

Assadeck Allasane
Direction Générale des Douanes

Nirilala Antsa Andriantsoa
John W. Ffooks & Co., member of Bowman Gilfillan Africa Group

Faradji Baba
Tribunal de Grande Instance de la Commune III de Bamako

Oumar Bane
Jurifis Consult

Altiné Amadou Belko
Creditinfo VoLo

Nadia Biouelé
Hera Conseils

Mariam Bocoum
Matrans

Amadou Camara
SCP Camara Traoré

Boubacar Coulibaly
Matrans

Elvis Danon
PwC Côte d'Ivoire

Sekou Dembele
Etude Maître Sekou Dembele

Abou Diallo
API Mali

Aboubacar S. Diarra
Hera Conseils

Mamadou Diarra
Cabinet Juri-Partner

Almahamoud Ibrahima Dicko
Hera Conseils

Mariama Doumbia
Matrans

Abdoulaye Fofana
Matrans

Joseph Gbegnon
Creditinfo VoLo

Djibril Guindo
Jurifis Consult

Baba Haidara
Etude Gaoussou Haidara

Mansour Haidara
API Mali

Abdoul Karim Samba Timbo Konaté
Agence d'Architecture CADET

Mamadou Ismaïla Konate
Jurifis Consult

Gaoussou A.G. Konaté
Agence d'Architecture Cadet

Abdoul Karim Kone
Cabinet Berth - Kone - Avocats Associés

Faty Balla Lo
Creditinfo VoLo

Celestin Maiga
SYTRAM

Adeline Messou Couassi-Blé
PwC Côte d'Ivoire

Bérenger Y. Meuke
Jurifis Consult

Claudia Randrianavory
John W. Ffooks & Co., member of Bowman Gilfillan Africa Group

Bourema Sagara
Jurifis Consult

Adamou Sambaré
Creditinfo VoLo

Alassane T. Sangaré
Notary

Oumar Sanogo
Direction de l'Inspection du Travail

Fatoumata Sidibe-Diarra
FSD Conseils Law Firm

Serge Kouassy Siekouo
Creditinfo VoLo

Mamadou Moustapha Sow
Cabinet Sow & Associés

Souleymane Sylla
Creditinfo VoLo

Dominique Taty
PwC Côte d'Ivoire

Cheick Oumar Tounkara
Hera Conseils

Abdoulaye Toure
Cellule Technique des reformes et du climat des Affaires

Moctar Toure
Commission de Regulation de l'Electricite et de l'Eau

Imirane A. Touré
Direction Nationale de l'Urbanisme et de l'Habitat

Lasseni Touré
Etude Gaoussou Haidara

Mahamadou Traore
Avocat à la Cour

Alassane Traoré
ICON SARL

Fousséni Traoré
PwC Côte d'Ivoire

MALTA

Central Bank of Malta

Christabelle Agius
CSB International

Shawn Agius
Inland Revenue Department

Yasmine Aquilina
GVZH Advocates

Matthew Attard
Ganado Advocates

Nicole Attard
GVZH Advocates

Carla Barthet
GVZH Advocates

Leonard Bonello
Ganado Advocates

Kris Borg
Dr. Kris Borg & Associates - Advocates

Mario Raymond Borg
Inland Revenue Department

Martina Borg Steven
GVZH Advocates

Josianne Brimmer
Fenech & Fenech Advocates

Joseph Buhagiar
Malta Enterprise

Brian Camilleri
Malta Enterprise

Simon Camilleri
CreditInfo

Joseph Caruana
Malta Financial Services Authority (MFSA)

Kirsten Cassar
Camilleri Preziosi

Sandro Chetcuti
Malta Developers Association

Claude Cuschieri
Ministry of Finance

David Felice
Architecture Project

Neville Gatt
PwC Malta

Joseph Ghio
Fenech & Fenech Advocates

Steve Gingell
PwC Malta

Paul Gonzi
Fenech & Fenech Advocates

Cain Grech
Malta Enterprise

Karl Grech Orr
Ganado Advocates

Roberta Gulic Hammett
PwC Malta

Kurt Hyzler
GVZH Advocates

Henri Mizzi
Camilleri Preziosi

John Paris
CreditInfo

Claude Sapiano
Land Registry

Jonathan Scerri
Enemalta Corporation

Jude Schembri
PwC Malta

Joseph Scicluna
Scicluna & Associates

Ian Stafrace
Ian Stafrace Legal

Pierre Theuma
Malta Enterprise

Carina Vasallo
GVZH Advocates

Simone Vella Lenicker
Architecture Project

Quentin Zahra
Eurofreight

Andrew J. Zammit
GVZH Advocates

MARSHALL ISLANDS

Marshalls Energy Company

Helkena Anni
Marshall Islands Registry

Kenneth Barden
Attorney-at-Law

Tune Carlos
Pacific International, Inc.

Tatyana E. Cerullo
Marshall Islands Lawyers

Melvin Dacillo
Ministry of Public Works

Raquel De Leon
Marshall Islands Social Security Administration

William Fife
Micronesian Legal Services Corporation

Anthony Frazier

Kenneth Gideon
PII Shipping

Avelino R. Gimao Jr.
Marshall Islands Social Security Administration

Don Hess
College of the Marshall Islands

Jerry Kramer
Pacific International, Inc.

Aaron Levine
Asian Development Bank

Lani Milne
Environmental Protection Agency - Marshall Islands

Steve Philip
Chamber of Commerce

Dennis James Reeder
Reeder & Simpson

Michael Slinger
Chamber of Commerce

Scott H. Stege
Law Offices of Scott Stege

David M. Strauss
Chamber of Commerce

Bori Ysawa
Majuro Marine

MAURITANIA

Mohamed Abdallahi Belil

Mohamed Yahya Abdel Ghahar

Wane Abdelaziz
Chambre de Commerce, d'Industrie et d'Agriculture de Mauritanie

Sid'Ahmed Abeidna
SOGECO Mauritania

Kane Aly
Guichet Unique Mauritania

Mohamed Lemine Ould Babiye
Banque Centrale de Mauritanie

Dieng Adama Boubou
Banque Centrale de Mauritanie

Mohamed Marouf Bousbe

Moulaye Ahmed Boussabou
Banque Centrale de Mauritanie

Hadrami Boydia
THB

Mohamed Cheikh Abdallah
AFACOR - Audit Finance Assistance Comptable Organisation SARL

Demba Diawara
Damco

Abdoulaye Dieng Yaré
Etablissement Dieng Yaré

Hamath Diop
Assurim Consulting

Brahim Ebety

Moulaye El Hassen Kamara
Socere Lambert Somec Mauritanie (SLSM)

Fadel Elaoune
Ministère des Affaires Economiques et du Développement

Sidi Mohamed Elemine
Conex

Mame Fall
GHA Mauritanie

Abdallah Gah
Etude Gah

Amadou Hamady Ndiaye
Direction Générale des Douanes

Hamoud Ismail
SMPN

Cheikhany Jules

Oumar Sada Kelly
Assurim Consulting

Mohamed Koum Maloum
BETEEM Ingenieries de l'Energie et de l'Eau

Mohamed Lemine Selmane
Ministère des Affaires Economiques et du Développement

Taleb Mohamed Lemrabott
Somecompt

Abraham Liadan
PwC Côte d'Ivoire

Bah Elbar M'beirik
Tribunal de Commerce de Nouakchott

Abdou M'Bodj

Mohamed M'Boyrick
Société de Développement des Infrastructures Portuaires (SDIP)

Mazar Mohamed Mahmoud Hmettou
Société Mauritanienne d'Electricité (SOMELEC)

Layti Ndiaye
SOGECO Mauritania

Mine Ould Abdoullah
Cabinet d'Avocat Ould Abdoullah

Jemal Ould Ahmed
Direction Générale des Douanes

Ishagh Ould Ahmed Miské
Cabinet Ishagh Miske

Moustapha Ould Bilal
Tribunal de Commerce de Nouakchott

M'Hamed Ould Bouboutt
Ministère des Affaires Economiques et du Développement

Abdellahi Ould Charrouck
Atelier Architecture et Design

Mohamed Yeslem Ould El Vil
Réseau des Petites et Moyennes Entreprises Mauritaniennes

Hassena Ould Ely
Port Autonome de Nouakchott

Mohamed Ould Hanine
Ministère du Commerce

Moulaye El Ghali Ould Moulaye Ely
Avocat

Ahmed Ould Radhi
Banque Centrale de Mauritanie

Haimoud Ould Ramdan
Ministère de la Justice

Abdel Fettah Ould Sidi Mohamed
Société Mauritanienne d'Electricité (SOMELEC)

Abdelkader Said

Aliou Sall
Etude Me Aliou Sall & Associés

Abdellahi Seyidi

Souleimane Sidi Mohamed El Haiba
Direction Générale des Impôts

Sophie Teffahi
Port Autonome de Nouakchott

Zakaria Thiam
Tribunal de Commerce de Nouakchott

Mohamed Mokhtar O. Yahevdhou
Bureau CAUPID

Mohamed Yahia Eba
Société Mauritanienne d'Electricité (SOMELEC)

Mohamed Yarguett
Ministère du Pétrole, de l'Energie et des Mines

MAURITIUS

Daygarasen Amoomoogum
Mauritius Chamber of Commerce and Industry

Fabrice Aza
Banymandhub Boolell Chambers

Wasoudeo Balloo
KPMG

Ambareen Beebeejaun
BLC Chambers

Valerie Bisasur
BLC Chambers

Urmila Boolell
Banymandhub Boolell Chambers

Poonam Calcutteea
BLC Chambers

Nicolas Carcasse
Dagon Ingenieur Conseil Ltée

D.P. Chinien
Registrar of Companies and Businesses, Corporate and Business Registration Department

Stephanie Chong Mei Lin Ah Tow
MCB Group Limited

Jenifer Chung
PwC Mauritius

Chandansingh Chutoori
VYYAASS Consulting Engineer Ltd.

Jessen Coolen
MCB Group Limited

Asmaa Coowar
PwC Mauritius

Amritraj Dassyne
Chambers of Notaries of Mauritius

Martine de Fleuriot de la Colinière
De Comarmond & Koenig

Catherine de Rosnay
Legis & Partners

Shalinee Dreepaul-Halkhoree
Juristconsult Chambers

Gavin Glover
The Chambers of Gavin Glover, SC

J. Gilbert Gnany
MCB Group Limited

Tilotma Gobin Jhurry
Bank of Mauritius

Yandraduth Googoolye
Bank of Mauritius

Darmalingum Goorriah
Etude Me Darmalingum Goorriah

Gopaul Gupta
Velogic Ltd.

Arvin Halkhoree
Juristconsult Chambers

Arzeenah Hassunally
PwC Mauritius

Raymond Marie Marc Hein
Juristconsult Chambers

Elodie Hermelin
Legis & Partners

Nitish Hurnaum
The Chambers of Gavin Glover, SC

Yhesma Jankee Chukoory
Acutus Management Ltd.

Nalini Jhowry
Central Electricity Board

Navin Jowaheer
Wastewater Management Authority

Nishi Kichenin
JurisTax

Thierry Koenig
De Comarmond & Koenig

Anthony Leung Shing
PwC Mauritius

Jayram Luximon
Central Electricity Board

Antish Maroam
PwC Mauritius

Jean Pierre Montocchio

Bala Moonsamy
CMT International Ltd.

Ramdas Mootanah
Architecture & Design Ltd.

Ashwin Mudhoo
Juristconsult Chambers

Mushtaq Namdarkhan
BLC Chambers

Khemila Narraidoo
Juristconsult Chambers

Daniel Ng Cheong Hin
Mauritius Cargo Community Services Ltd.

Stéphanie Odayen
Juristconsult Chambers

Cristelle Parsooramen
Banymandhub Boolell Chambers

Ashwina Pittea
Banymandhub Boolell Chambers

Iqbal Rajahbalee
BLC Chambers

Vidoula Ramkurrun-Mohungoo
City Council of Port Louis

Jayshen Rammah
Merits Consulting Engineers Ltd.

Annabelle Ribet
Juristconsult Chambers

Nicolas Richard
Juristconsult Chambers

André Robert
Etude André Robert

Keeranlallsing Santokhee
City Council of Port Louis

Wenda Sawmynaden
Cabinet de Notaire Sawmynaden

Shailesh Seebaruth
The Chambers of Gavin Glover, SC

Hurrydeo Seebchurrun
Central Electricity Board

Geetanjali Seewoosurrun
Central Electricity Board

Gilbert Seeyave
BDO Financial Services Ltd.

Deviantee Sobarun
Ministry of Finance & Economic Development

Menzie Sunglee
Central Electricity Board

Dhanesswurnath Vikash Thakoor
Bank of Mauritius

Natasha Towokul Jiagoo
Acutus Management Ltd.

Muhammad R.C. Uteem
Uteem Chambers

Amy Vaulbert de Chantilly
Juristconsult Chambers

Aynur Visram
Banymandhub Boolell Chambers

Nashenta Vuddamalay
De Comarmond & Koenig

Bobby Yerkiah
KPMG

MEXICO

Comisión Reguladora de Energía

Victoria Acosta Torres
Comisión Federal de Electricidad

Andrea Melissa Alanís Ochoa
Pena Mouret Abogados, S.C.

Rogelio Alanis Robles
Littler Employment and Labor Law Solutions Worldwide

Jaime Alejandro Gutiérrez Vidal
Instituto Federal de Especialistas de Concursos Mercantiles

Frida Alonso
Mexican Construction Chamber (CMIC)

José Manuel Arce Ruíz
Standard Go

Francisco Samuel Arias González
Notary Public 28

Francisco Javier Arias Vazque
Ministry of Finance

José Alejandro Astorga Hilbert
Instituto Federal de Especialistas de Concursos Mercantiles

Rodrigo Avendano
White & Case SC

Alberto Avila
Federation of Interamerican Construction Industry (FIIC)

Ana Rosa Avila
Cruz Abrego Consorcio Juridico S.C.

Juan Guillermo Avila Sarabia
Avila & Lozano S.C.

Elsa Regina Ayala Gómez
Secretaría de Economía, Dirección General de Normatividad Mercantil (RUG)

Alfonso Azcona Anaya
ZityMerka SA de CV

Antonio Barrera Ríos
Sánchez DeVanny Eseverri SC

Jorge Barrero Stahl
Santamarina y Steta SC

Rodrigo Barros
Ministry of Finance

Jose Franscisco Caballero Garcia
SEDECO

Gilberto Calderon Lachino
Galaz, Yamazaki, Ruiz Urquiza SC, member of Deloitte Touche Tohmatsu Limited

Adrian Martin Camacho Fernandez
Comisión Federal de Electricidad

Samuel Campos Leal
Gonzalez Calvillo SC

Carlos Cano
PwC Mexico

Tomás Cantú González
Cantu Estrada y Martinez (CEM Abogados)

Fernando Antonio Cardenas Gonzalez
Notary Public #44

Pedro Carreon
PwC Mexico

María Casas López
Baker & McKenzie

José Luis Castellanos Pérez
Colegio de Ingenieros Mecánicos y Electricistas (CIME)

Kathalina Chapa Peña
CAF-SIAC Contadores

Carlos Chávez
Galicia Abogados SC

Carlos A. Chávez Pereda
J.A. Treviño Abogados SA de CV

Rodrigo Conesa
Ritch Mueller, Heather y Nicolau, S.C.

Lic. Samanta Cornu Sandoval
Secretaria de Desarrollo Urbano (SEDUE) - Secretariat for Urban Development and Ecology

Francisco Coronado
Santamarina y Steta SC

Nancy Mireya Coronado Perez
Direccion de Proteccion Civil (Civil Protection Agency)

Abel Cotoñeto
Notaria 7, D.F.

Jose Covarrubias-Azuela
Solórzano, Carvajal, González y Pérez-Correa, S.C

Victor Cruz
Kundiso RedLogistica

Maria Teresa Cruz Abrego
Cruz Abrego Consorcio Juridico S.C.

Sergio Cuevas Villalobos
Notaria 197

Carlos De la Garza
Martinez, Algaba, De Haro, Curiel y Galvan-Duque SC

Arq. Jorge Armando Jose De Los Santos
Secretaria de Servicios Publicos (Public Services Agency)

Jorge de Presno
Basham, Ringe y Correa, member of Ius Laboris

María del Carmen Cercós
Kundiso RedLogistica

Jose Manuel del Rio Zolezzi
SEDECO

María del Rocío Romero Meza
Registro Público de la Propiedad y del Comercio del Distrito Federal

Franco Alberto Del Valle Prado
P&A Legal Services, S.C.

Tracy Delgadillo Miranda
J.A. Treviño Abogados SA de CV

Carlos Ramon Diaz Sordo
Lopez Velarde, Heftye y Soria SC

Carlos Diez Garcia
Gonzalez Calvillo SC

Felipe Dominguez P.
Moore Stephens Orozco Medina, S.C.

Mariana Eguiarte Morett
Sánchez Devanny Eseverri SC

Ivonne A. Elizondo de la Garza
Cantu Estrada y Martinez (CEM Abogados)

Dolores Enriquez
PwC Mexico

David Escalante
KPMG Cardenas Dosal, S.C.

Natalia Espinoza
Basham, Ringe y Correa, member of Ius Laboris

Miguel Espitia
Bufete Internacional

Victor Fernandez Sanchez
Comisión Federal de Electricidad

Othón Flores
Ritch Mueller, Heather y Nicolau, S.C.

Pedro Flores Carillo
Moore Stephens Orozco Medina, S.C.

Julio Flores Luna
Goodrich, Riquelme y Asociados

Juan Francisco Galarza
PwC Mexico

Manuel Galicia
Galicia Abogados SC

Maria Antonieta Galvan Carriles
Tribunal Superior de Justicia del Distrito Federal

Mauricio Gamboa
TransUnion de Mexico SA SIC

Brenda Garcia
PwC Mexico

Emilio García
Sánchez DeVanny Eseverri SC

Jorge García
Goodrich, Riquelme y Asociados

Jose Martin Garcia Bautista
Galaz, Yamazaki, Ruiz Urquiza SC, member of Deloitte Touche Tohmatsu Limited

Lic. Blanca Garcia Camargo
Sistema de Aguas de la Ciudad de Mexico (Mexico City Water Services Agency)

Eduardo Garcia Fraschetto
Sánchez DeVanny Eseverri SC

Francisco García Lerma
Sánchez Devanny Eseverri SC

Ing. Carlos Garcia Salazar
Servicios de Agua y Drenaje de Monterrey (Water and Sewage Services Agency)

Heriberto Garza
Santamarina y Steta SC

Mauricio Garza Bulnes
J.A. Treviño Abogados SA de CV

Nohemi Gpe. Garza Olguin
Instituto Registral y Catastral del Estado de Nuevo León

Jose Alberto Gonzalez
KPMG Cardenas Dosal, S.C.

Ricardo Gonzalez Orta
Galaz, Yamazaki, Ruiz Urquiza SC, member of Deloitte Touche Tohmatsu Limited

Jesús Martín González Rodríguez
Poder Judicial del Estado de Nuevo León

Alvaro Gonzalez-Schiaffino
PwC Mexico

James Graham
3CT

Adrian Guarneros
Servicio de Administración Tributaria

Andres Guerra Gomez
Guerra Gomez Abogados

Antonio Guerra Gomez
Guerra Gomez Abogados

Benito Ivan Guerra Silla
Notaria 7, D.F.

Ignacio Oswaldo Guillén Ángel
Lopez Velarde, Heftye y Soria SC

Mario Alberto Gutiérrez
PwC Mexico

Arq. Miguel Angel Gutierrez Garcia
Mexican Construction Chamber (CMIC)

Yves Hayaux-du-Tilly
Nader, Hayaux & Goebel

Francisco Abimael Hernández
Solórzano, Carvajal, González y Pérez-Correa, S.C

Lic. Jose Antonio Hernandez Balbuena
Mexican Construction Chamber (CMIC)

Roberto Hernandez Garcia
COMAD SC

Angel Herrera Gonzalez
Raigosa Consultores

Oscar Octavio Hinojosa Guerra
Hinojosa Abogados

Zita Horvath
Leah Isla Horvath

Mauricio Hurtado
PwC Mexico

Ricardo Ibarra
Servicio de Administración Tributaria

Jose Ricardo Ibarra Cordova
Sánchez Devanny Eseverri SC

Carlos Marco Iga
Arizpe, Valdés & Marcos Abogados - San Pedro Garza García

Ivan Imperial
KPMG Cardenas Dosal, S.C.

María Concepción Isoard Viesca
Ritch Mueller, Heather y Nicolau, S.C.

Daniela Jara
Cruz Abrego Abogados

Jorge Jiménez
Lopez Velarde, Heftye y Soria SC

Jorge Jiménez
Russell Bedford México - member of Russell Bedford International

Diana Juárez Martínez
Baker & McKenzie

Alfredo Kupfer-Dominguez
Sánchez DeVanny Eseverri SC

Luis Lavalle Moreno
Galaz, Yamazaki, Ruiz Urquiza SC, member of Deloitte Touche Tohmatsu Limited

Daniel Antonio Del Rio Loiza
Basham, Ringe y Correa, member of Ius Laboris

Carlos Leal-Isla Garza
Leah Isla Horvath

Josue Lee
Iñaki Echeverria Arquitectos

Ricardo León-Santacruz
Sánchez DeVanny Eseverri SC

Lic. Rafael Licea Alvarez
Mexican Construction Chamber (CMIC)

Giovanna Lizárraga Osuna
Sánchez DeVanny Eseverri SC

Leonor Llamas
Goodrich, Riquelme y Asociados

Eduardo Lobatón Guzmán
Baker & McKenzie

Alfonso López Lajud
Sánchez DeVanny Eseverri SC

Cesar Inaki Lorda Dumont
Hinojosa Abogados

Miguel Ángel Loredo Gutiérrez
Comisión Federal de Electricidad

Jose Antonio Lozada Capetillo
Tribunal Superior de Justicia del Distrito Federal

Arturo Lozano Guerrero
Cantu Estrada y Martinez (CEM Abogados)

Laura Macarty Cortes
Cruz Abrego Abogados

Alejandro Madero
Sánchez Devanny Eseverri SC

Gerardo Maltos
Grupo Sys

Gabriel Manrique
Russell Bedford México - member of Russell Bedford International

Roberto Márquez Arjona
Poder Judicial del Estado de Nuevo León

José Antonio Marquez González
Notary Public #2

Ing. Adrian Martinez Arzarte
Sistema de Aguas de la Ciudad de Mexico (Mexico City Water Services Agency)

Lic. Patricia Martinez Ayala
Sistema de Aguas de la Ciudad de Mexico (Mexico City Water Services Agency)

Juan Sergio Alfonso Martínez González
Comisión Federal de Electricidad

Griselda Martínez Vázquez
Registro Público de la Propiedad y del Comercio del Distrito Federal

Mariana Maxinez Hernández
Galaz, Yamazaki, Ruiz Urquiza SC, member of Deloitte Touche Tohmatsu Limited

Arq. Fernando Mendez Bernal
Direccion General de Adminsitracion Urbana de la Ciudad de Mexico

Carla E. Mendoza Pérez
Baker & McKenzie

Tania Paola Miranda Reyes
Delegación de Azcapotzalco

Daniela Montero
PwC Mexico

Angel Humberto Montiel Trujano
Tribunal Superior de Justicia del Distrito Federal

Ing. Alma Elisa Montoya Rodriguez
Servicios de Agua y Drenaje de Monterrey (Water and Sewage Services Agency)

Erika Mora
Sánchez DeVanny Eseverri SC

Ignacio R. Morales Lechuga
Notaria 116

Ricardo Morales Salazar
EMEESA

Ruben Morales Zamora
CYMIMEX

Daniel Moran
Gonzalez Calvillo SC

Guillermo Moran Franco
Galaz, Yamazaki, Ruiz Urquiza SC, member of Deloitte Touche Tohmatsu Limited

Giovanni Moreno
CAF-SIAC Contadores

Eloy F. Muñoz M.
IMEYEL Soluciones Integrales SA de CV

Juan Nájera
NDA Najera Danieli & Asocs.

Jorge Narváez Hasfura
Baker & McKenzie

Marco Nava
PwC Mexico

Octavio Gerardo Navarro Gómez del Campo
Instituto Registral y Catastral del Estado de Nuevo León

Javier Luis Navarro Velasco
Baker & McKenzie

Pablo Nosti Herrera
Miranda & Estavillo SC

Juan Manuel Ochoa
Rivadeneyra, Trevino & De Campo SC

María José Ortiz Haro
Galicia Abogados SC

Gilberto Osio
Solórzano, Carvajal, González y Pérez-Correa, S.C

Raúl Paniahua
Nader, Hayaux & Goebel

Gabriel Peña Mouret
Pena Mouret Abogados, S.C.

Sergio Peña Zazueta
TransUnion de Mexico SA SIC

Oscar Peralta
Wuma Integral Cargo

Arturo Perdomo
Galicia Abogados SC

Eduardo Perez Armienta
Moore Stephens Orozco Medina, S.C.

Luis Uriel Pérez Delgado
Goodrich, Riquelme y Asociados

José Jacinto Pérez Silva
Ke Desarrolladora SA de CV

Pablo Perezalonso Eguía
Ritch Mueller, Heather y Nicolau, S.C.

Fernando Perez-Correa
Solórzano, Carvajal, González y Pérez-Correa, S.C

Guillermo Piecarchic
PMC & Asociados

Federico Pineda
Hub Logistics Mexico

Ricardo Platt
Federation of Interamerican Construction Industry (FIIC)

David Puente-Tostado
Sánchez Devanny Eseverri SC

Eric Quiles Gutierrez
White & Case LLP

Arq. Olga Cristina Ramirez Acosta
Secretaria de Desarrollo Urbano (SEDUE) - Secretariat for Urban Development and Ecology

David Ramírez Ramírez
D&J Ingeniería y Servicios, SA de CV

Juan Carlos Ramirez Vertiz
Secretaria de Desarrollo Urbano y Vivienda

Alberto Revilla
PwC Mexico

Brindisi Reyes Delgado
Ritch Mueller, Heather y Nicolau, S.C.

Eduardo Reyes Díaz-Leal
Bufete Internacional

Héctor Reyes Freaner
Baker & McKenzie

Lic. Hector Francisco Reyes Lopez
Secretaria de Desarrollo Urbano (SEDUE) - Secretariat for Urban Development and Ecology

Claudia Ríos
PwC Mexico

Fernando Rivadeneyra
Rivadeneyra, Trevino & De Campo SC

Blanca Berenice Rivas Penilla
Galaz, Yamazaki, Ruiz Urquiza SC, member of Deloitte Touche Tohmatsu Limited

Jose Ignacio Rivero
Gonzalez Calvillo SC

Beatriz A. Robles Acosta
CAF-SIAC Contadores

Irazu Rodríguez Garza
Comisión Federal de Electricidad

Oscar Rodriguez Loera
Secretaria de Desarrollo Urbano (SEDUE) - Secretariat for Urban Development and Ecology

Alejandro Rodríguez Montemayor
Poder Judicial del Estado de Nuevo León

Victor Mauricio Rodriguez Ramos
Ministry of Finance

Cecilia Rojas
Galicia Abogados SC

Héctor Rosas
Goodrich, Riquelme y Asociados

Luis Enrique Ruiz Chirinos
Secretaria de Desarrollo Urbano y Vivienda

Raúl Sahagun
Bufete Internacional

Pedro Said Nader
Basham, Ringe y Correa, member of Ius Laboris

Juan Pablo Sainz
Nader, Hayaux & Goebel

José Roberto Salinas
Salinas Padilla & Associates Law Firm

Javier Sanchez
Subestaciones, SA de CV

Lucero Sánchez de la Concha
Baker & McKenzie

Juan Pablo Sanchez Enriquez
Secretaria de Desarrollo Urbano y Vivienda

Luis Sanchez Galguera
Galaz, Yamazaki, Ruiz Urquiza SC, member of Deloitte Touche Tohmatsu Limited

Jorge Sanchez Hernández
Galaz, Yamazaki, Ruiz Urquiza SC, member of Deloitte Touche Tohmatsu Limited

Rodrigo Sanchez Mejorada
Sánchez-Mejorada, Velasco y Ribé

Arq. Alberto Sanchez Rodriguez
Direccion de Proteccion Civil (Civil Protection Agency)

Cristina Sanchez Vebber
Sánchez DeVanny Eseverri SC

Cristina Sánchez-Urtiz
Miranda & Estavillo SC

Jose Antonio Sandoval
SEDECO

Quetzalcoatl Sandoval Mata
Velez y Sandoval S.C.

Ricardo Sandoval Ortega
Comisión Federal de Electricidad

María Esther Sandoval Salgado
Instituto Federal de Especialistas de Concursos Mercantiles

José Santiago
Grupo IMEV, SA de CV

Monica Schiaffino Pérez
Littler Mexico

Francisco Serna Báez
Colegio de Ingenieros Mecánicos Electricistas y Electrónicos de Nuevo León (CIME-NL)

Daniel Sosa
Skynet

Arturo Suárez
KPMG Cardenas Dosal, S.C.

Yazbek Taja
Rivadeneyra, Trevino & De Campo SC

Miguel Téllez
Creel, García-Cuéllar, Aiza y Enriquez SC

Juan Francisco Torres Landa Ruffo
Hogan Lovells

Cesar Treviño
J.A. Treviño Abogados SA de CV

Jaime A. Treviño
J.A. Treviño Abogados

Magda Treviño Morales
Instituto Registral y Catastral del Estado de Nuevo León

Roberto Treviño Ramos
Poder Judicial del Estado de Nuevo León

Maribel Trigo Aja
Goodrich, Riquelme y Asociados

Yeny Trinidad Orduño
Registro Público de la Propiedad y del Comercio del Distrito Federal

Favio Camilo Vazquez Lopez
Santamarina y Steta SC

Denise Carla Vazquez Wallach
Secretaría de Economía, Dirección General de Normatividad Mercantil (RUG)

José Luis Vega Garrido
Goodrich, Riquelme y Asociados

Luis Miguel Velasco Lizárraga
Sánchez DeVanny Eseverri SC

Alejandra Velazquez
COMAD SC

Jose Vidana
Trade Up

Adrian Roberto Villagomez Aleman
COMAD SC

Rafael Villamar-Ramos
Sánchez Devanny Eseverri SC

Guillermo Villaseñor
Sánchez DeVanny Eseverri SC

Claudio Villavicencio
Galaz, Yamazaki, Ruiz Urquiza SC, member of Deloitte Touche Tohmatsu Limited

Eloy Zambrano
Russell Bedford Monterrey SC

Mayela E. Zapata Cisneros
Instituto Registral y Catastral del Estado de Nuevo León

Jose I. Zertuche Guerrero
Zertuche Abogados

Antonio Zuazua
KPMG Cardenas Dosal, S.C.

MICRONESIA, FED. STS.

Marcelino Actouka
Pohnpei Utilities Corporation

Nixon Anson
Pohnpei Utilities Corporation

Kenneth Barden
Attorney-at-Law

Lam Dang
Congress of the FSM

Erick Divinagracia
Ramp & Mida Law Firm

Mark Heath
Micronesia Registration Advisors, Inc.

Eric Iban
Office of the Attorney General

Douglas Nelber
Pohnpei State Department of Lands and Natural Resources

Ronald Pangelinan
A&P Enterprises Inc.

Sam Peterson
Pohnpei Export Association

Salomon Saimon
Micronesian Legal Services Corporation

Nora Sigrah
FSM Development Bank

Brad Soram
Pohnpei State Environmental Protection Agency

Mike Thomas
MicroPC

Joseph Vitt
Pohnpei Transfer & Storage, Inc.

Larry Wentworth
FSM Supreme Court

MOLDOVA

Union Fenosa

Veronica Bradautanu
ACI Partners Law Office

Daniel Cobzac
Cobzac & Partners

Stanislav Copetchi
ACI Partners Law Office

Anastasia Dereveanchina
PwC Moldova

Silviu Foca
Biroul de Credit - Moldova

Iulia Furtuna
Turcan Cazac

Ana Galus
Turcan Cazac

Roger Gladei
Gladei & Partners

Victoria Goncearuc
Cobzac & Partners

Andrian Guzun
Schoenherr

Ana Iovu
Cobzac & Partners

Vladimir Iurkovski
Schoenherr

Roman Ivanov
Vernon David & Associates

Ciubaciuc Ludmila
PwC Moldova

Cristina Martin
ACI Partners Law Office

Mihaela Mitroi
PwC Romania

Alexandru Munteanu
PwC Moldova

Oxana Novicov
National Union of Judicial Officers

Vladimir Palamarciuc
Turcan Cazac

Bodiu Pantelimon
SRL Reconscivil

Carolina Parcalab
ACI Partners Law Office

Vladimir Plehov

Dumitru Popescu
PwC Moldova

Laura Şambra
Cobzac & Partners

Olga Saveliev
Turcan Cazac

Alexandru Savva
Chemonics International Inc. Representative Office in Moldova

Alexandru Sipitca
ICS Ernst and Young SRL

Adrian Sorocean
ACI Partners Law Office

Mariana Stratan
Turcan Cazac

Lilia Tapu
PwC Moldova

Cristina Tiscul-Diaconu
ACI Partners Law Office

Alexander Tuceac
Turcan Cazac

Alexander Turcan
Turcan Cazac

Irina Verhovetchi
ACI Partners Law Office

Carolina Vieru
IM PAA SRL

Marina Zanoga
ACI Partners Law Office

MONGOLIA

Amarmurun Amartuvshin
Lehman, Lee & Xu

Odgerel Amgalan
Monlogistics Worldwide LLC

Tumurkhuyag Azjargal
Mongolian National Construction Association

Hishigtaya B.
Tsast Construction LLC

Telenged Baast
Monlogistics Worldwide LLC

Lkhagvasuren Baigal
Mongolian National Construction Association

Molor Bakhdal
Tsets LLP

Nandinchimeg Banzragch
Tsogt & Nandin

Uranzaya Batdorj
Tsets LLP

Javkhlant Batmunkh
Anand Advocates Law Firm

Azzaya Batsuuri
Electrosetiproject, LLC

Solongo Battulga
GTs Advocates LLP

Altanduulga Bazarragchaa
UBEDN

David Beckstead
Lehman, Lee & Xu

Jacob Blacklock
Lehman, Lee & Xu

Bayar Budragchaa
ELC LLP Advocates

Tsendmaa Choijamts
PwC Mongolia

Khatanbat Dashdarjaa
Arlex Consulting Services

Zoljargal Dashnyam
GTs Advocates LLP

Onchinsuren Dendevsambuu
Deloitte

Gerel Enebish
Lehman, Lee & Xu

Tsolmonchimeg Enkhbat
GTs Advocates LLP

Naranchimeg Erdembileg
Arlex Consulting Services

Tsewegrash Erdenechuluun
Mongolian National Construction Association

Oyunbold Ganchimeg
The Bank of Mongolia

Selenge Gantulga
Mahoney Liotta LLP

Tuvshin Javkhlant
Deloitte

Bat-Ulzii Lkhaasuren
Monsar LLC

Ganzorig Luvsan
UBEDN

Daniel Mahoney
Mahoney Liotta LLP

Bayarmanla Manljav
Mongolyn Alt (MAK) Corporation

Christopher Melville
Hogan Lovells

Tsogt Natsagdorj
Tsogt & Nandin

Enkhtsetseg Nergui
Anand Advocates Law Firm

Bayarsaikhan Nyamragchaa
Tsast Construction LLC

Munkhsoyombo Nyamsuren
GTs Advocates LLP

Nomindari Otgonbayar
Mahoney Liotta LLP

Oyuntseren Oyunbat
Mongolian National Construction Association

Ariuntuya Rentsen
Mahoney Liotta LLP

Gandolgor Sambuu
Erdenet Tex Corporation

Tumurkhuu Sukgbaatar
UBEDN

Oyun Surenjav
Anderson and Anderson LLP

Bolortungalag Tsedendamba
PwC Mongolia

Enkhtuvshin Tsetsegmaa
Anderson and Anderson LLP

Ganzaya Tsogtgerel
Anderson and Anderson LLP

Dudgen Turbat
The Bank of Mongolia

Bolormaa Volodya
GRATA Law Firm

Khosbayar Zorig
Arlex Consulting Services

MONTENEGRO

Anja Abramovic
Prelević Law Firm

Veselin Anđjušić
Business Center Čelebić

Asheet Awasthi
Amerinde Consolidated, Inc.

Tara Bogdan
Amerinde Consolidated, Inc.

Marija Bojović
Bojovic & Partners

Bojana Bošković
Ministry of Finance

Jelena Brajković
BDK Advokati Attorneys-at-Law

Dragoljub Cibulić
BDK Advokati Attorneys-at-Law

Ognjen Cipovic
Harrisons Solicitors

Milan Dakic
BDK Advokati Attorneys-at-Law

Vladimir Dasić
BDK Advokati Attorneys-at-Law

Mesud Delagić
Law Office Vujačić

Savo Djurović
Adriatic Marinas d.o.o.

Dragan Draca
PricewaterhouseCoopers Consulting d.o.o.

Veselin Dragićević
Chamber of Economy of Montenegro, Sector for Associations and Economic Development

Sladana Dragović
Normal Company

Dragana Filipovic
Ministry of Sustainable Development and Tourism

Mile Gujić
Normal Company

Danilo Gvozdenović
Ministry of Sustainable Development and Tourism

Ana Jankov
BDK Advokati Attorneys-at-Law

Maja Jokanović
Ministry of Economy

Nada Jovanovic
Central Bank of Montenegro

Jelena Jovetic
Ministry of Finance

Milica Jovicevic
Montenomax

Radoš-Lolo Kastratović
Advokatska Kancelarija

Bojana Krkovic
Business Center Čelebić

Ana Krsmanović
Ministry of Finance

Elma Kurtanovic
Harrisons Solicitors

Nikola Martinović
Advokatska Kancelarija

Milomir Matovic
Bojovic & Partners

Edita Mehović
Law Office Vujačić

Milica Milanovic
PricewaterhouseCoopers Consulting d.o.o.

Novica Pesic
Pesic & Bajceta

Zorica Pesic Bajceta
Pesic & Bajceta

Luka Popovic
BDK Advokati Attorneys-at-Law

Dragana Radević
CEED

Radovan Radulovic
Montenomax

Ivan Radulović
Ministry of Finance

Dražen Raičković
FinancePlus

Branka Rajicic
PricewaterhouseCoopers Consulting d.o.o.

Sead Salkovic
FinancePlus

Slaven Šćepanović
Legal Consultant

Marko Tintor
Central Bank of Montenegro

Danka Tošković
Law Office Vujačić

Vera Vucelic
Harrisons Solicitors

Saša Vujačić
Law Office Vujašić

Jelena Vujisić
Law Office Vujašić

Tatjana Vujosevic
Ministry of Sustainable Development and Tourism

Lana Vukmirovic Misic
Harrisons Solicitors

Sandra Zdravkovic
Montecco INC d.o.o.

Djordje Zejak
BDK Advokati Attorneys-at-Law

Jelena Zivkovic
Eurofast Global

MOROCCO

PortNet SA

Idriss Abou Mouslim
Bhirat

Sidimohamed Abouchikhi
Creditinfo Maroc

Abdelkrim Karim Adyel
Cabinet Adyel

Amina Ammor
Creditinfo Maroc

Maïlis Andrieu
Chassany Watrelot & Associés

Redouane Assakhen
Centre Régional d'Investissement

Salima Bakouchi
Bakouchi & Habachi - HB Law Firm LLP

Fassi-Fihri Bassamat
Cabinet Bassamat & Associée

Maria Belafia
Etude Maître Belafia

Toufiq Benali
Ministère de l'Urbanisme et de l'Aménagement du Territoire

Meriem Benis
Hajji & Associés

Azel-Arab Benjelloun
Agence d'Architecture d'Urbanisme et de Decoration

Badria Benjelloun
Ministère de l'Urbanisme et de l'Aménagement du Territoire

Meriem Benzakour
Cabinet d'Avocats Morsad

Oussama Boualam
Lydec

Ali Bougrine
UGGC Law Firm

Khalid Boumichi
Tecnomar

Richard Cantin
Nero Boutique Law Firm

Bouchaib Chahi
Agence Nationale de la Conservation Foncière du Cadastre et de la Cartographie (ANCFCC)

Abdallah Chater
Centre Régional d'Investissement

Mahat Chraibi
PwC Advisory Maroc

Driss Debbagh
Kettani Law Firm

Hamid Errida
Accounthink Maroc SARLAU

Driss Ettaki
Administration des Douanes et Impots Indirects

Nadia Fajr
Avocate au Barreau de Casablanca

Youssef Fassi Fihri
FYBA Lawyers

Houda Habachi
Bakouchi & Habachi - HB Law Firm LLP

Kamal Habachi
Bakouchi & Habachi - HB Law Firm LLP

Amin Hajji
Hajji & Associés

Djamila Hamel
Oulamine Law Group

Mehdi Kettani
DLA Piper

Nadia Kettani
Kettani Law Firm

Rita Kettani
Kettani Law Firm

Yassir Khalil
Yassir Studio

Mhammed Lahlou
Etude de Notariat Moderne

Nabyl Lakhdar
Administration des Douanes et Impots Indirects

Zineb Laraqui
Cabinet Zineb Laraqui

Mohamed Amine Mahboub
Etude de Me Mahboub

Amine Mahfoud
Amine Mahfoud Notaire

Noureddine Marzouk
PwC Advisory Maroc

Kenza Mejbar
Creditinfo Maroc

Abdelkhalek Merzouki
Administration des Douanes et Impots Indirects

Adil Morsad
Cabinet d'Avocats Morsad

Ahmed Morsad
Cabinet d'Avocats Morsad

Réda Oulamine
Oulamine Law Group

Mohamed Oulkhouir
Chassany Watrelot & Associés

Abderrahim Outass
Fonction libérale

Hassane Rahmoun
Etude Notariale Hassane Rahmoun

Mohamed Rifi
PwC Advisory Maroc

Nesrine Roudane
Nero Boutique Law Firm

Kenza Yamani
Chassany Watrelot & Associés

Meryem Zoubir
Chassany Watrelot & Associés

MOZAMBIQUE

AVM Advogados Mozambique

Luís Antunes
LUFTEC – Técnicas Eléctricas, Lda.

Henrique Castro Amaro Arqto Castro Amaro
Amaro Arquitectos e Associados Lda

Carolina Balate
PwC Mozambique

Ebrahim Bhikhá
PwC Mozambique

Abubacar Calú
Electrovisao Lda

Eduardo Calú
Sal & Caldeira Advogados Lda

Adelia Canda
Silva Garcia Advogados & Consultores

Alexandra Carvalho Monjardino
Attorney-at-Law

Natércio Chambule
Maputo City Court (Commercial Chamber)

Pedro Chilengue
Mott MacDonald PDNA Moçambique, Lda

Pedro Couto
CGA - Couto, Graça e Associados, Sociedade de Advogados

Avelar da Silva
Intertek International Ltd.

Thera Dai
CGA - Couto, Graça e Associados, Sociedade de Advogados

Carla de Sousa
Fernanda Lopes & Associados Advogados, Lda

Alferio Dgedge
Fernanda Lopes & Associados Advogados, Lda

Fulgêncio Dimande
Manica Freight Services SARL

Vanessa Fernandes
CGA - Couto, Graça e Associados, Sociedade de Advogados

Telmo Ferreira
CGA - Couto, Graça e Associados, Sociedade de Advogados

Maria Fatima Fonseca
Maputo City Court (Commercial Chamber)

Jorge Graça
CGA - Couto, Graça e Associados, Sociedade de Advogados

Nilza Guivala
Fernanda Lopes & Associados Advogados

Abdul Satar Hamid
BDO Mozambique

Fabricia Henriques
Henriques, Rocha & Associados (Mozambique Legal Circle Advogados)

Zara Jamal
Ferreira Rocha & Advogados

Adriano João
PwC Mozambique

Katia Jussub
CM&A - Carlos Martines & Associados

Gimina Langa
Sal & Caldeira, Advogados, LDA.

Rui Loforte
CGA - Couto, Graça e Associados, Sociedade de Advogados

Fernanda Lopes
Fernanda Lopes & Associados Advogados, Lda

Mara Lopes
Henriques, Rocha & Associados (Mozambique Legal Circle Advogados)

Yussuf Mahomed
KPMG Auditores e Consultores SA

Carlos Martins
CM&A - Carlos Martines & Associados

João Martins
PwC Mozambique

Jean-Louis Neves Mandelli
Shearman & Sterling LLP

Ilidio Nhamahango
BDO Mozambique

Diana Ramalho
Sal & Caldeira Advogados Lda

Malaika Ribeiro
PwC Mozambique

Liana Utxavo
Manica Freight Services SARL

Cesar Vamos Ver
Sal & Caldeira, Advogados, LDA.

Joaquim Vilanculos
Fernanda Lopes & Associados Advogados, Lda

MYANMAR

AGX Logistics Myanmar Co. Ltd.

Department of Agricultural Land Management and Statistics

Myanmar Global Law Firm

PricewaterhouseCoopers Myanmar Co. Ltd.

Tilleke & Gibbins Myanmar Ltd.

Win Thin & Associates

Quamruddin Ahmed
Bay Line Shipping Pte Ltd.

Viacheslav Baksheev
DFDL

Juergen Baur
Rödl & Partner Co. Ltd.

Sam Britton
ZICOlaw Myanmar Ltd.

Jaime Casanova
DFDL

Francesco Cassinerio
DFDL

Thomas Chan
KPMG (Advisory) Myanmar Ltd.

Stefan Chapman
Berwin Leighton Paisner Myanmar

Mark D'Alelio
Selvam & Partners

William Greenlee
DFDL

Daw Mary Htwe
Hitachi Soe Electric & Machinery Co., Ltd.

Kyawt Kay Khaing
United Amara Bank Limited

Yu Lin Khoo
ZICOlaw Myanmar Ltd.

Nay Myo Myat Ko
Care Freight Services Ltd.

U Nyein Kyaw

U Moe Kyaw Aye
Myanmar Customs

Yan Lin
Yangon City Electricity Supply Boards

Zaw Lin Aung
KBZ Bank (Kanbawza Bank Ltd.)

Moe Lwin
Moe Lwin Moe & Tun Associates Limited

Oliver Thant Lwin
Fifth Generation Co. Ltd.

Yu Lwin
Myawaddy Bank Limited

Marlar Mala Dutta
Bay Line Shipping Pte Ltd.

Mar Mar Aung
DFDL

Ah Lonn Maung
DFDL

Aye Chan Maung
Hitachi Soe Electric & Machinery Co., Ltd.

U Khin Mg Soe
Electric Mfg. Co. Ltd.

Alex Minn Thu Aung
Helio Business Corporation

Yee Mon Mon
Yangon City Electricity Supply Boards

Cho Cho Myint
Interactive Co. Ltd.

Kyaw Swa Myint
Rödl & Partner Co. Ltd.

Si Thu Myint Swe
S T & T Architects

Win Naing
Lucy Wayne & Associates Limited

Minn Naing Oo
Allen & Gledhill LLP

Ursus-Mortimer Negenborn
Rödl & Partner Co. Ltd.

Sa Sa Nyunt
Interactive Co. Ltd.

Wint Thandar Oo
Polastri Wint & Partners

Hiroyuki Ota

Sebastian Pawlita
Lincoln Legal Services (Myanmar) Ltd.

Claudia Petrat
Rajah & Tann LLP

Su Wai Phyo
ZICOlaw Myanmar Ltd.

Alessio Polastri
Polastri Wint & Partners

Key Pwint Phoo Wai
Care Freight Services Ltd.

San Lwin
JLPW Legal Services

Kyaw Soe Min
Myanma Apex Bank

Kevin Thant Aung
Fifth Generation Co. Ltd.

Min Thein

U Myint Thein
Myint Thein & Son

U Tet Htut Aung
Ministry of Finance

Hnin Thet Wai
ZICOlaw Myanmar Ltd.

Lucy Wayne Mbe
Lucy Wayne & Associates Limited

Htut Khaung Win
Yangon City Development Committee

Zaw Win
Yangon City Development Committee

Cho Cho Wynn
Ministry of National Planning and Economic Development

NAMIBIA

Gino Absa
KPMG Advisory Services (Namibia) (Pty) Ltd.

Joos Agenbach
Koep & Partners

Tiaan Bazuin
Namibian Stock Exchange

Adeline Beukes
KPMG Advisory Services (Namibia) (Pty) Ltd.

Clifford Bezuidenhout
Engling, Stritter & Partners

Benita Blume
H.D. Bossau & Co.

Hanno D. Bossau
H.D. Bossau & Co.

Dirk Hendrik Conradie
Conradie & Damaseb

Myra Craven
ENS

André Davids
Maersk Line

Luziem Diergaardt
Transworld Cargo Pty. Ltd.

Britt du Plessis
Standard Bank Namibia

Marcha Erni
TransUnion

Johann Espag
Clarke Architects

Ulrich Etzold
Etzold-Duvenhage Firm

Ismeralda Hangue
Deeds Office

Stefan Hugo
PwC Namibia

Stefan Hyman
H.D. Bossau & Co.

Rochelle Kandjella
Köpplinger Boltman

Edward Kawesha
City of Windhoek Electricity Department

Frank Köpplinger
Köpplinger Boltman

Cameron Kotze
Ernst & Young

Norbert Liebich
Transworld Cargo Pty. Ltd.

Prisca Mandimika
Ministry of Lands and Resettlement

Marie Mandy
MMM Consultancy

Johan Nel
PwC Namibia

Mari-Nelia Nieuwoudt
PwC Namibia

Tim Parkhouse
Namibian Employer's Federation

Lukas Siremo
City of Windhoek Electricity Department

Johny M. Smith
Walvis Bay Corridor Group

Helmut Stolze
Conradie & Damaseb

Axel Stritter
Engling, Stritter & Partners

Andre Swanepoel
Dr. Weder, Kauta & Hoveka Inc.

Erentia Tromp
Institute of Chartered Accountants of Namibia

Hugo Van den Berg
Koep & Partners

Stefan van Zijl
Koep & Partners

Nevadia van Zyl
Dr. Weder, Kauta & Hoveka Inc.

NEPAL

Lalit Aryal
LA & Associates Chartered Accountants

Narayan Bajaj
Narayan Bajaj & Associates

Jaya Raj Bhandari
Nepal Electricity Authority

Tulasi Bhatta
Unity Law Firm & Consultancy

BM Dhungana
B&B Associates - correspondent of Russell Bedford International

Naresh Giri
Asian Development Bank

Sunil Gupta
Gupta Counsel

Gourish K. Kharel
KTO Inc.

Parsuram Koirala
Koirala & Associates

Amir Maharjan
SAFE Consulting Architects & Engineers Pvt. Ltd.

Bikash Malla Thakuri
Unity Law Firm & Consultancy

Anjan Neupane
Neupane Law Associates

Matrika Niraula
Niraula Law Chamber & Co.

Arun Pant
Design Cell Ltd.

Dev Raj Paudyal
University of Southern Queensland

Purnachitra Pradhan
Karja Suchana Kendra Ltd. (CIB)

Sakar Pradhan
Inter-space Design Group

Anup Raj Upreti
Pioneer Law Associates

Rajan Sharma
Nepal Freight Forwarders Association

Deepak K. Shrestha
Nepal Investment Bank

P. L. Shrestha
Evergreen Cargo Services Pvt. Ltd.

Rajeshwor Shrestha
Sinha Verma Law Concern

Suman Lal Shrestha
H.R. Logistic Pvt. Ltd.

Mahesh Kumar Thapa
Sinha Verma Law Concern

NETHERLANDS

Joost Achterberg
Kennedy Van der Laan

Maarten Appels
Van Doorne NV

Mieke Bestebreurtje
Leeman Verheijden Huntjens Advocaten

Reint Bolhuis
AKD Lawyers & Civil Law Notaries

Matthijs Bolkenstein
Eversheds B.V.

Sytso Boonstra
PwC Netherlands

Peter Bouterse
OceanExpress Netherlands BV

Roland Brandsma
PwC Netherlands

Mirjam de Blecourt
Baker & McKenzie Amsterdam NV

Margriet de Boer
Just Litigation Advocatuur B.V.

Wyneke de Gelder
PwC Netherlands

Taco de Lange
AKD Lawyers & Civil Law Notaries

Rolef de Weijs
Houthoff Buruma

Noël Ellens
Fruytier Lawyers in Business

Arjan Enneman
Expatax BV

Ingrid Greveling
NautaDutilh Attorneys

Jan Hockx
Lexence

Niels Huurdeman
Houthoff Buruma

Alfred Kers
BDO CampsObers Accountants & Belastingadviseurs

Ilse Kersten
Baker & McKenzie Amsterdam NV

Marcel Kettenis
PwC Netherlands

Edwin M.A.J. Kleefstra
Stolp+KAB Adviseurs en Accountants BV

Christian Koedam
PwC Netherlands

Gerard Koster
Baker & McKenzie Amsterdam NV

Thomas Kraan
Stichting Bureau Krediet Registratie

Andrej Kwitowski
Akadis BV

Lucas Lustermans
Eversheds B.V.

Jan-Joost Mak
PwC Netherlands

Danique Meijer
HVK Stevens Legal B.V.

Sharon Neven
PwC Netherlands

Jeroen Postma
Kennedy Van der Laan

Peter Radema
Merzario

Hugo Reumkens
Van Doorne NV

Jan Willem Schenk
HVK Stevens Legal B.V.

Rutger Schimmelpenninck
Houthoff Buruma

Jack Schrijver
Baker & McKenzie Amsterdam NV

Fedor Tanke
Baker & McKenzie Amsterdam NV

Jaap Jan Trommel
NautaDutilh Attorneys

Manon Ultee
PwC Netherlands

Gert-Jan van Gijs
VAT Logistics (Ocean Freight) BV

Sjaak van Leeuwen
Stichting Bureau Krediet Registratie

Jan van Oorschot
Liander

IJsbrand Van Straten
Stibbe

Frédéric Verhoeven
Houthoff Buruma

Reinout Vriesendorp
De Brauw Blackstone Westbroek

Stephan Westera
Lexence

Marcel Willems
Kennedy Van der Laan

Bianco Witjes
Liander

Marleen Zandbergen
NautaDutilh Attorneys

NEW ZEALAND

Michael Brosnahan
Ministry of Business, Innovation & Employment

Paul Chambers
Anderson Creagh Lai Limited

Philip Coombe
Panalpina World Transport LLP

John Cuthbertson
PwC New Zealand

Corey Dixon
PwC New Zealand

Igor Drinkovic
Minter Ellison Rudd Watts

Ashton Dunn
Astech Electrical Ltd.

Ian Gault
Bell Gully

Andy Glenie
Bell Gully

Lucy Harris
Simpson Grierson, member of Lex Mundi

James Hawes
Simpson Grierson, member of Lex Mundi

Paul Heaslip
Paul Heaslip Lawyer

Arun Jain
Minter Ellison Rudd Watts

Paul Jennings
Jackson Russell

Matthew Kersey
Russell McVeagh

Bernard Lagane
SDV Logistics

Jeffrey Lai
Anderson Creagh Lai Limited

Kate Lane
Minter Ellison Rudd Watts

Michael Langdon
Minter Ellison Rudd Watts

Dan Lowe
Grant Thornton Auckland Limited

Himmy Lui
Bell Gully

Mandy McDonald
Ministry of Business, Innovation & Employment

Andrew Minturn
Qualtech International Ltd.

Nick Moffatt
Bell Gully

Phillipa Muir
Simpson Grierson, member of Lex Mundi

Robert Muir
Land Information New Zealand

Geof Nightingale
PwC New Zealand

Ian Page
BRANZ

Chris Park
PwC New Zealand

Mihai Pascariu
Minter Ellison Rudd Watts

Jose Paul
Auckland City Council

David Quigg
Quigg Partners

John Rooney
Simpson Grierson, member of Lex Mundi

Silvana Schenone
Minter Ellison Rudd Watts

Andrew Tetzlaff
Simpson Grierson, member of Lex Mundi

Murray Tingey
Bell Gully

Ben Upton
Simpson Grierson, member of Lex Mundi

Simon Vannini

Richard Wilson
Jackson Russell

NICARAGUA

ProNicaragua

Elias Alvarez
PwC Nicaragua

Roberto Octavio Arguello Villavicencio
Arias & Muñoz

Alfredo Artiles
KPMG

Maria Alejandra Aubert Carcamo
García & Bodán

Juan Ramon Aviles Molina
Lawyer

Soledad Balladares
Superintendencia de Bancos

Ana Carolina Baquero Urroz
Latin Alliance

Minerva Adriana Bellorín Rodríguez
Pacheco Coto

Flavio Andrés Berríos Zepeda
Multiconsult & Cia Ltda

Blanca Buitrago
García & Bodán

Rodolfo Cano
DISNORTE-DISSUR

Orlando Cardoza
Bufete Juridico Obregon y Asociados

Thelma Carrion
Aguilar Castillo Love

Tito Castillo
INNICSA

Francisco Castro
PwC Nicaragua

Jorge Cubillo
INGSERSA Ingenieria y Servicios SA

Brenda Darce
CETREX

Miriam Espinosa
Pacheco Coto

Ana Gabriel Espinoza
Arias & Muñoz

Diana Fonseca
Arias & Muñoz

Luis Fuentes Balladares
Arquitectura Fuentes

Terencio Garcia Montenegro
García & Bodán

Claudia Guevara
Aguilar Castillo Love

Federico Gurdian
García & Bodán

Eduardo Gutierrez
Pacheco Coto

Marianela Gutierrez
Aguilar Castillo Love

Denisse Gutiérrez Rayo
García & Bodán

Gerardo Hernandez
Consortium Legal

Rodrigo Ibarra Rodney
Arias & Muñoz

Myriam Jarquín
IPRA-CINDER

Eduardo Lacayo
TransUnion

Brenda Ninoska Martínez Aragón
Consortium Legal

Jose Ivan Mejia Miranda
García & Bodán

Alvaro Molina
Molina & Asociados Central Law

Soraya Montoya Herrera
Molina & Asociados Central Law

Norma Elena Morales Barquero
Arias & Muñoz

Jeanethe Morales Núñez
Superintendencia de Bancos

Tania Muñoz
KPMG

Alonso Porras
Pacheco Coto

Jessica Porras Martinez
García & Bodán

Olga Renee Torres
Latin Alliance

Erwin Rodriguez
PwC Nicaragua

Ricardo Trillos Rodriguez
Multitrans

Patricia Rodríguez
Multiconsult & Cia Ltda

Hansel Saborio
García & Bodán

Alfonso José Sandino Granera
Consortium Legal

Oscar A. Silva Peter
Delaney & Abogados

Maryeling Suyen Guevara Sequeira
Arias & Muñoz

Rodrigo Taboada
Consortium Legal

Carlos Téllez
García & Bodán

Joe Henry Thompson

Diógenes Velásquez V.
Pacheco Coto

Gustavo Viales

NIGER

BCEAO

Ministère de l'Energie et du Petrole

Projet Sécurité des Installations Electriques Intérieures au Niger (SIEIN)

Kassoum Abarry
Ville de Niamey

Abdallah Abdoulati
Banque Centrale des Etats de l'Afrique de l'Ouest

Issoufou Adamou
NIGELEC

Moumouni Ali Ousseini
Etude Notariale Ousseini Ali Moumouni

Mamoudou Aoula
Ministère de l'Urbanisme et du Logement

Sidi Sanoussi Baba Sidi
Cabinet d'Avocats Souna-Coulibaly

Issouf Baco
Société Nigérienne de Transit (NITRA)

Altiné Amadou Belko
Creditinfo VoLo

Amadou Boukar
Cellule de Partenariat Public Privé

Moustapha Boukari
Cabinet Boukari

Moussa Coulibaly
Cabinet d'Avocats Souna-Coulibaly

Moussa Dantia
Maison de l'Entreprise Niger

Aïssatou Djibo
Etude de Maître Djibo Aïssatou

Mai Moussa Ellhadji Basshir
Tribunal de Grande Instance hors classe de Niamey

Ismael Ganda
Chambre Nationale des Notaires du Niger

Joseph Gbegnon
Creditinfo VoLo

Abder Rhamane Halidou Abdoulaye
Chambre Nationale des Notaires du Niger

Souley Hammi Illiassou
Cabinet Kouaovi

Moussa Douma Hmidou
Ministère de la Justice

Diori Maïmouna Idi Malé
Laitière du Sahel SARL

Ali Idrissa Sounna
Toutelec Niger SA

Seybou Issifi
Urbamed Consult

Habibou Kane Kadoure
Agence Projedis Afrique

Bernar-Oliver Kouaovi
Cabinet Kouaovi

Faty Balla Lo
Creditinfo VoLo

Boubaca Mai Aiki
Ministère de l'Urbanisme et du Logement

Sabiou Mamane Naissa
Tribunal de Commerce de Niamey

Adeline Messou Couassi-Blé
PwC Côte d'Ivoire

André Abboh Joseph Monso
PwC Côte d'Ivoire

Sadou Mounkaila
Haské Solaire

Yayé Mounkaïla
Cabinet d'Avocats Mounkaila-Niandou

Ali Hamidou Nafissatou
Cellule de Partenariat Public Privé

Insa Abary Noufou
Cellule de Partenariat Public Privé

Mamoudou Ousseini
NIGELEC

Adamou Sambaré
Creditinfo VoLo

Serge Kouassy Siekouo
Creditinfo VoLo

Souleymane Sylla
Creditinfo VoLo

Dominique Taty
PwC Côte d'Ivoire

Idrissa Tchernaka
Etude d'Avocats Marc Le Bihan & Collaborateurs

Fousséni Traoré
PwC Côte d'Ivoire

Ramatou Wankoye
Office Notarial Etude Wankoye

Hamadou Yacouba
Etude de Maître Dodo Dan Gado Haoua

Wouro Yahia
Etude d'Avocats Marc Le Bihan & Collaborateurs

Souleymane Yankori
Societe Civile Professionnelle d'Avocats Yankori et Associés

Ali Yeya
Direction Générale des Impôts

NIGERIA

De Splendor Solicitors

Reason Abajuo
Olaniwun Ajayi LP

Ijeoma Abalogu
Gbenga Biobaku & Co.

Abdullateef Abdul
Ikeyi & Arifayan

Ismail Abdulaziz
Pointblank Attorneys

Lateefah Abdulkareem
Lateef O. Fagbemi San & Co.

Fariha Abdullahi
Dikko and Mahmoud Solicitors and Advocates

Innocent Abidoye
Nnenna Ejekam Associates

Lemea Abina
Sterling Partnership

Oluseyi Abiodun Akinwunmi
Akinwunmi & Busari Legal Practitioners

Alhaji Garba Abubakar
Corporate Affairs Commission

Olaleye Adebiyi
WTS Adebiyi & Associates

Kunle Adegbite
Canaan Solicitors

Bode Adegoke
Bloomfield Law Practice

Steve Adehi
Steve Adehi and Co.

Oni-Orisan Aderemi Ademola
Ministry of Physical Planning and Urban Development

Adekunle Adewale
Jackson, Etti & Edu

Agbolade Adeyemi
Udo Udoma & Belo-Osagie

Mary Adeyi
Dikko and Mahmoud Solicitors and Advocates

Albert Adu
Alliance Law Firm

Dayo Adu
Bloomfield Law Practice

Daniel Agbor
Udo Udoma & Belo-Osagie

Nura Ahmad
Kano Urban Planning and Development Authority

Halimah Ahmed
PwC Nigeria

Michael Ajaegbo
Alliance Law Firm

Kunle Ajagbe
Perchstone & Graeys

Olaoluwa Ajala
Gbenga Biobaku & Co.

Ayodele Ajayi
SPA Ajibade & Co.

Konyin Ajayi
Olaniwun Ajayi LP

Babatunde Ajibade
SPA Ajibade & Co.

Blessing Ajunwo
Alliance Law Firm

Ahmed Akanbi
Akanbi & Wigwe Legal Practitioners

Raodat Akanji-Aderibigbe
KPMG

Olatoye Akinboro
KPMG

Dafe Akpeneye
PwC Nigeria

Folake Alabi
Olaniwun Ajayi LP

Ezinne Alajemba
Akanbi & Wigwe Legal Practitioners

Usman Aliyu Mahmud
Nigerian Communications Commission

Jonathan Aluju
Olaniwun Ajayi LP

Chioma Amadi
Akanbi & Wigwe Legal Practitioners

Nnenna Anowai
KPMG

Sola Arifayan
Ikeyi & Arifayan

Temitayo Arikenbi
CRC Credit Bureau Limited

Oluseye Arowolo
Deloitte

Oluwapelumi Asiwaju
G. Elias & Co. Solicitors and Advocates

Popoola Atilola Omosanya
Lateef O. Fagbemi San & Co.

Ebunoluwa Awosika
Ajumogobia & Okeke

Zainab Babalola
Akinwunmi & Busari Legal Practitioners

Bisola Babington
Perchstone & Graeys

Gilbert Benson-Oladeinbo
G. Elias & Co. Solicitors and Advocates

Aliyu Yusuf Dada
Kano Urban Planning and Development Authority

Matthias Dawodu
SPA Ajibade & Co.

Obinna Dike
Alliance Law Firm

Haliru Dikko
Nigerian Electricity Regulatory Commission (NERC)

Rebecca Dokun
Aluko & Oyebode

Emmanuel Egwuagu
Obla & Co.

Oyindamola Ehiwere
Udo Udoma & Belo-Osagie

Nnenna Ejekam
Nnenna Ejekam Associates

Ijezie Emedosi
Aluko & Oyebode

Harrison Emmanuel
Abdulai, Taiwo & Co.

Samuel Etuk
1st Attorneys

Chibuzo Ezegamba
Obla & Co.

Anse Agu Ezetah
Chief Law Agu Ezetah & Co.

Lateef O. Fagbemi San
Lateef O. Fagbemi San & Co.

Babatunde Fagbohunlu
Aluko & Oyebode

Olubunmi Fayokun
Aluko & Oyebode

Yetunde Filani
WTS Adebiyi & Associates

Fatai Folarin
Deloitte

Bolaji Gabari
SPA Ajibade & Co.

Abba Galadima
Kano Urban Planning and Development Authority

Sagir Gezawa
S. S. Gezawa & Co.

Lateefat Hakeem-Bakare
Ajumogobia & Okeke

Aminu Isa Hashim

Ibrahim Hashim
Electromech Prime Utility Resources Ltd.

Tokunbo Ibrahim
PwC Nigeria

Ezinne Igbokwe
Akanbi & Wigwe Legal Practitioners

Chidinma Ihemedu
Alliance Law Firm

Bukola Iji
SPA Ajibade & Co.

Emmanuel Ikeakonwu
Deloitte

Nduka Ikeyi
Ikeyi & Arifayan

Meshach Ikpe
Abubakar D. Sani & Co.

Olalekan Ikuomola
SPA Ajibade & Co.

Ifedayo Iroche
Perchstone & Graeys

Maryam Jaji
Dikko and Mahmoud Solicitors and Advocates

Okorie Kalu
Punuka Attorneys & Solicitors

Babatunde Kolawole
HLB Z.O. Ososanya & Co.

Mobolaji Ladapo
Olaniwun Ajayi LP

Habibat Iadeniran
Ikeyi & Arifayan

Temisan lOtis-Amurun
Jackson, Etti & Edu

Obinna Maduako
Olaniwun Ajayi LP

Abubakar Mahmoud
Dikko and Mahmoud Solicitors and Advocates

Bello Mahmud
Corporate Affairs Commission

Tosanbami Mene-Afejuku
Akanbi & Wigwe Legal Practitioners

Victor Munis
TRLP Law

Ugochi Ndebbio
KPMG

Juliet Ndoh
IMO State University

Justine Nidiya
Corporate Affairs Commission

Victor Nwakasi
Olisa Agbakoba & Associates

Victor Obaro
Libra Law Office

V. Uche Obi
Alliance Law Firm

Godwin Obla
Obla & Co.

Chijioke Odo
Deloitte

Onyinye Odogwu
Punuka Attorneys & Solicitors

Oluwakemi Oduntan
Jade & Stone Solicitors

Anthony Ogbuanu
PwC Nigeria

Nelson Ogbuanya
Nocs Consults

Godson Ogheneochuko
Udo Udoma & Belo-Osagie

Ozofu Ogiemudia
Udo Udoma & Belo-Osagie

Alayo Ogunbiyi
Abdulai, Taiwo & Co.

Peter Ogundele
Elektrint (Nigeria) Limited

Yvonne Ogunoiki
Ikeyi & Arifayan

Adebola Ogunsanya
Olaniwun Ajayi LP

Oladimeji Ojo
Aluko & Oyebode

Cindy Ojogbo
Olaniwun Ajayi LP

Chudi Ojukwu
Infrastructure Consulting Partnership

Ikenna Okafor
Perchstone & Graeys

Ngo-Martins Okonmah
Aluko & Oyebode

Chidubem Okoye
Olaniwun Ajayi LP

Oluwatosin Okunrinboye
Ajumogobia & Okeke

Dozie Okwuosah
Central Bank of Nigeria

Stephen Ola Jagun
Jagun Associates

Moshood Olajide
PwC Nigeria

Olayimika Olasewere
SPA Ajibade & Co.

Ajibola Olomola
KPMG

Afolasade Olowe
Jackson, Etti & Edu

Uma Olugo
1ST ATTORNEYS

Adanna Omaka
1ST ATTORNEYS

Tolulope Omidiji
PWC NIGERIA

Emmanuel Omoju
WTS ADEBIYI & ASSOCIATES

David Omoloye
KANO DISTRIBUTION ELECTRICITY COMPANY

Chris Erhi Omoru
ORBIS CHANCERY SOLICITORS

Ekundayo Onajobi
UDO UDOMA & BELO-OSAGIE

Adefunke Onakoya
AKINWUNMI & BUSARI LEGAL PRACTITIONERS

Gabriel Onojason
ALLIANCE LAW FIRM

Kelechi Onouha
AKANBI & WIGWE LEGAL PRACTITIONERS

Joseph Onugwu
OLISA AGBAKOBA & ASSOCIATES

Fred Onuobia
G. ELIAS & CO. SOLICITORS AND ADVOCATES

Emmanuela Onyilofor
OLANIWUN AJAYI LP

Kola Osholeye
ELEKTRINT (NIGERIA) LIMITED

Olufemi Ososanya
HLB Z.O. OSOSANYA & CO.

Ignatius Nwosu Owelle
HOMELUX CONSTRUCTION & EQUIPMENT CO. LTD.

Maryam Oyebode
OLANIWUN AJAYI LP

Olajumoke Oyebode
PWC NIGERIA

Taiwo Oyedele
PWC NIGERIA

Bukola Oyeneyin
AKANBI & WIGWE LEGAL PRACTITIONERS

Feyisola Oyeti
SPA AJIBADE & CO.

Femi Oyetosho
BIOS 2 LIMITED

Tunde Popoola
CRC CREDIT BUREAU LIMITED

Temitope Salami
AKANBI & WIGWE LEGAL PRACTITIONERS

Simisola Salu
PWC NIGERIA

Abubakar Sani
ABUBAKAR D. SANI & CO.

Isiaku Sani
DIGIBITS CONTROLS NIGERIA LTD.

Yewande Senbore
OLANIWUN AJAYI LP

Eric Sesu
PWC NIGERIA

Jameelah Sharrieff-Ayedun
CREDIT REGISTRY SERVICES (CREDIT BUREAU) PLC

Taofeek Shittu
IKEYI & ARIFAYAN

Christine Sijuwade
UDO UDOMA & BELO-OSAGIE

Olugbenga Sodipo
IKEYI & ARIFAYAN

Ololade Sowemimo
SPA AJIBADE & CO.

Adeola Sunmola
UDO UDOMA & BELO-OSAGIE

Rafiu Sunmonu
DELMORE ENGINEERING AND CONSTRUCTION COMPANY LIMITED

Kelechi Ugbeva
KCU LEGAL

Uchenna Ugonabo
OBLA & CO.

Ovie E. Ukiri
AJUMOGOBIA & OKEKE

Aniekan Ukpanah
UDO UDOMA & BELO-OSAGIE

Adamu M. Usman
F.O. AKINRELE & CO.

Ebere Uzum
UDO UDOMA & BELO-OSAGIE

Uchechukwu Wigwe
AKANBI & WIGWE LEGAL PRACTITIONERS

Kamaluddeen Yahaya
KAMALUDDEEN YAHAYA & CO.

Umar Bala Yahaya
KANO URBAN PLANNING AND DEVELOPMENT AUTHORITY

Olufunke Yesufu
AKINWUNMI & BUSARI LEGAL PRACTITIONERS

Isma'ila M. Zakari
AHMED ZAKARI & CO.

NORWAY

EXPERIAN NORWAY

JÓNAR TRANSPORT

NORWEGIAN BUILDING AUTHORITY

Marianne Aronsen
NORWEGIAN SEAFOOD COUNCIL

Nanette Arvesen
ADVOKATFIRMAET THOMMESSEN AS

Jan L. Backer
WIKBORG, REIN & CO.

Guro Bakke Haga
PWC NORWAY

Eli Beck Nilsen
PWC NORWAY

Stig Berge
ADVOKATFIRMAET THOMMESSEN AS

John Ole Bjørnerud
HAFSLUND

Trine Blix
THE BRONNOYSUND REGISTER CENTER

Carl Christiansen
RAEDER DA

Per Arne Dæhli
ADVOKATFIRMAET SELMER DA

Tron Dalheim
ARNTZEN DE BESCHE ADVOKATFIRMA AS

Lars Davidsen
HAFSLUND

Lill Egeland
ADVOKATFIRMA SIMONSEN VOGT WIIG

Knut Ekern
PWC NORWAY

Turid Ellingsen
STATENS KARTVERK

Marius Moursund Gisvold
WIKBORG, REIN & CO.

Katrine Gjestemoen
PWC NORWAY

Erlend Haaskjold
ARNTZEN DE BESCHE ADVOKATFIRMA AS

Johan Astrup Heber
WIKBORG, REIN & CO.

Hilde Høksnes
ADVOKATFIRMAET SELMER DA

Heidi Holmelin
ADVOKATFIRMAET SELMER DA

Odd Hylland
PWC NORWAY

Anette Istre
ADVOKATFIRMA SIMONSEN VOGT WIIG

Andreas Jarbø
ADVOKATFIRMAET SELMER DA

Kyrre Width Kielland
ADVOKATFIRMA RÆDER DA

Bente Langsrud
ARNTZEN DE BESCHE ADVOKATFIRMA AS

Per Einar Lunde
PWC NORWAY

Leif Petter Madsen
WIKBORG, REIN & CO.

Bjørn Rustad Nilssen
STATENS KARTVERK

William Peter Nordan
ADVOKATFIRMA SIMONSEN VOGT WIIG

Tore Tosse Notoy
PWC NORWAY

Hege Oftedal
PWC NORWAY

Ole Kristian Olsby
HOMBLE OLSBY ADVOKATFIRMA AS

Haldis Framstad Skaare
STATENS KARTVERK

Ståle Skutle Arneson
ADVOKATFIRMA SIMONSEN VOGT WIIG

Fredrik Sparre-Enger
ADVOKATFIRMAET SELMER DA

Carina Strom
HOMBLE OLSBY ADVOKATFIRMA AS

Svein Sulland
ADVOKATFIRMAET SELMER DA

Liss Sunde
ADVOKATFIRMA RÆDER DA

Ragnar Ulsund
HAFSLUND

Kai Sølve Urke
WIKBORG, REIN & CO.

Oyvind Vagan
THE BRONNOYSUND REGISTER CENTER

Øystein Valanes
NORWEGIAN SEAFOOD COUNCIL

OMAN

AL BUSAIDY MANSOOR JAMAL & CO.

MUSCAT ELECTRICITY DISTRIBUTION COMPANY

Malcolm Abaza
CURTIS MALLET - PREVOST, COLT & MOSLE LLP

Zubaida Fakir Mohammed Al Balushi
CENTRAL BANK OF OMAN (CBO)

Dali Al Habboub
SNR DENTON & CO.

Hamed Amur Al Hajri
OMAN CABLES INDUSTRY (SAOG)

Ahmed Al Khatib
SASLO - SAID AL SHAHRY & PARTNERS

Al Waleed Al Kiyumi
SNR DENTON & CO.

Shariffa Al Maskary
INFORMATION TECHNOLOGY AUTHORITY

Hamood Al Rawahi
SALEGAL

Eman Al Shahry
SASLO - SAID AL SHAHRY & PARTNERS

Majid Al Toky
TROWERS & HAMLINS

Fatima Al-Sabahi
TROWERS & HAMLINS

Mohammed Alshahri
MOHAMMED ALSHAHRI & ASSOCIATES

Umaima Al-Wahaibi
SNR DENTON & CO.

Ahmed Amor Al Esry
ERNST & YOUNG

Sahar Askalan
SALEGAL

Sadaf Buchanan
SNR DENTON & CO.

Francis D'Souza

Raza Elahi
SALEGAL

Jamie Gibson
TROWERS & HAMLINS

Sarah Glover
PWC OMAN

Justine Harding
SNR DENTON & CO.

Davis Kallukaran
HORWATH MAK GHAZALI LLC

O.A. Kuraishy
HASAN JUMA BACKER TRADING & CONTRACTING

P.E. Lalachen MJ
KHALIFA AL HINAI ADVOCATES & LEGAL CONSULTANCY

Pushpa Malani
PWC OMAN

Yashpal Mehta

Githa Nair
CURTIS MALLET - PREVOST, COLT & MOSLE LLP

Ali Naveed Arshad
SASLO - SAID AL SHAHRY & PARTNERS

Ahmed Naveed Farooqui
OMAN CABLES INDUSTRY (SAOG)

Farah Ourabah
SALEGAL

Bruce Palmer
CURTIS MALLET - PREVOST, COLT & MOSLE LLP

Raghavendra Pangala
SEMAC & PARTNERS LLC

Dhanalakshmi Pillai Perumal
SNR DENTON & CO.

Maria Mariam Rabeaa Petrou
SASLO - SAID AL SHAHRY & PARTNERS

Paul Sheridan
SNR DENTON & CO.

Nick Simpson
SNR DENTON & CO.

Yasser Taqi
SNR DENTON & CO.

Roy Thomas
OMAN CABLES INDUSTRY (SAOG)

Rajesh Vaidyanathan
KHIMJI RAMDAS

PAKISTAN

MAERSK LINE

PORT LINE SHIPPING & LOGISTIC

PUNJAB BAR COUNCIL

Ghulam Abbas
LAND REGISTRY

Zaheer Abbas Chughtai
QAISER & ABBAS ATTORNEYS & CORPORATE COUNSELLORS

Mahmood Abdul Ghani
MAHMOOD ABDUL GHANI & CO.

Umer Abdullah
ABDULLAH & HUSSAIN

Imran Ahmad
STATE BANK OF PAKISTAN

Khalil Ahmad
KARIM CHAMBER

Nadeem Ahmad
ORR, DIGNAM & CO. ADVOCATES

Taqi Ahmad
A.F. FERGUSON & CO., CHARTERED ACCOUNTANTS, A MEMBER FIRM OF PWC NETWORK

Zahra Ahmad
EBRAHIM HOSAIN, ADVOCATES AND CORPORATE COUNSEL

Munir Ahmad Bhatti
MUNIR BHATTI LAW ASSOCIATES

Akhtiar Ahmed
STATE BANK OF PAKISTAN

Ijaz Ahmed
IJAZ AHMED & ASSOCIATES

Mansoor Ahmed
BOARD OF REVENUE SCANNING UNIT

Salahuddin Ahmed
MCAS&W LAW ASSOCIATES

Waqar Ahmed

Jamil Ahmed Khan
ERECTION ENGINEERS AND CONTRACTORS

Majid Ahmed Khan
ERECTION ENGINEERS AND CONTRACTORS

Abbas Ali
ERNST & YOUNG

Ashraf Ali
ABRAHAM & SARWANA

Tabassum Ali
TMT LAW SERVICES

Liaqat Ali Dolla
SECURITIES AND EXCHANGE COMMISSION

Ayoob Ali Pathan
EXCISE, TAXATION & NARCOTICS DEPARTMENT

Syed Ali Zafar
MANDVIWALLA & ZAFAR

Ali Ameel Malik
PARVEZ & COMPANY

Armughan Ashfaq
SURRIDGE & BEECHENO

Ejaz Ashraf
ASHRAF & ASHRAF LAW FIRM

Shahzad Ashraf
ASHRAF & ASHRAF LAW FIRM

Zeeshan Ashraf Meer
Meer & Hasan

Jam Asif Mejmood
Ahmed & Qazi

Zarina Aslam
Abraham & Sarwana

Ambreen Atta

Jahanzeb Awan
Khalid Anwer & Co.

Anum Azhar
Saad Rasool Law Associates

Shaheryar Aziz
A.F. Ferguson & Co., Chartered Accountants, a member firm of PwC network

Nadeem Babar
Babar Builders & Developers

Fawad Baluch
Khalid Anwer & Co.

Hasan Hameed Bhatti

Huzaima Bukhari
Huzaima & Ikram

Waheed Chaudhary
Legis Inn Attorneys & Corporate Consultants

Muhammad Saifullah Chaudhry
Development Impact Solutions (SMC-PVT) Ltd.

Salman Chima
Chima & Ibrahim

Khurram Shehzad Chughtai
Jus & Rem

Faisal Daudpota
Khalid Daudpota & Co.

Junaid Daudpota
Khalid Daudpota & Co.

Diana Dsouza
Datacheck Pvt. Ltd.

Huma Ejaz Zaman
Mandviwalla & Zafar

Mahwish Elahi
Abraham & Sarwana

Hashim Arshad Faruqui
Surridge & Beecheno

Aman Ghanchi
Unilever Pakistan Limited

Asma Ghayoor
Sindh Building Control Authority

Syed Yadullah Haider
Meinhardt Pakistan Pvt. Ltd.

Asma Hameed Khan
Surridge & Beecheno

Ikramul Haq
Huzaima & Ikram

Salman Haq
Ernst & Young

Qamar Hashmat
Hashmat Law Associates

Khalil Hashmi
Synthetic Products Enterprises Limited

Saim Hashmi
Ahmed & Qazi

Faiz Hassan
Land Record Management Information System

Jawad Hassan
Hassan, Qureshi & Mamdot

Mohammad Hassan Bakshi
Association of Builders and Developers of Pakistan (ABAD)

Dilawar Hussain
DS Engineering Services

Muhammad Hussain
LESCO

Riaz Hussain Rizvi
Mass Consultant

Ahmad Hyder
Lahore Chamber of Commerce and Industry (LCCI)

Rashid Ibrahim
A.F. Ferguson & Co., Chartered Accountants, a member firm of PwC network

Saman Rafat Imtiaz
The Law Offices of Saman R. Imtiaz

Zafar Iqbal
Azimuddin Law Associates

Fiza Islam
Legis Inn Attorneys & Corporate Consultants

Muzaffar Islam
Legis Inn Attorneys & Corporate Consultants

Sidrah Jameel
Mandviwalla & Zafar

Saila Jamshaid
Securities and Exchange Commission

Tariq Nasim Jan
Datacheck Pvt. Ltd.

Assad Ullah Jaral
AUJ Lawyers

Majid Jehangir
FAM & Partners

Bilal Kashmiri
Adil & Bilal

Nadim Kausar
Lali, Morris Sr. Nadim & Co.

Habib Kazi
Khalid Anwer & Co.

Aftab Ahmed Khan
Surridge & Beecheno

Haider Ali Khan
Rizvi and Rizvi

Mudassir Khan
Da Afghanistan Bank

Fariyal Khizar

Yousaf Khosa
RIAA Barker Gillette

Misbah Kokab
TMT Law Services

Ali Abbas Lali
Saad Rasool Law Associates

Husnain Lotia
SLA Associates

Faisal Mahmood
Mahmood Abdul Ghani & Co.

Jawwad Rafique Malik
Punjab Board of Revenue

Mohsin Malik
Builders Associates Pvt. Ltd.

Arshad Malik Awan
Malik Noor Muhammad Awan & AMA Law Associates

Abdul Manan
RIAA Barker Gillette

Zara Mandiwalla
Mandviwalla & Zafar

Sidra Mansur
Securities and Exchange Commission

Shahbano Masud
Hassan, Qureshi & Mamdot

Rashid Rahman Mir
Rahman Sarfaraz Rahim Iqbal Rafiq - member of Russell Bedford International

Waqqas Mir
Mohsin Tayabaly & Co.

Abdul Moeez
Meinhardt Pakistan Pvt. Ltd.

Atif Mufassir
Deloitte Yousuf Adil, Chartered Accountants

Rana Muhammad
Rana Ijaz & Partners

Syed Muhammad Ijaz
Huzaima & Ikram

Anwar Kashif Mumtaz
Saiduddun & Co.

Faiza Muzaffar
Legis Inn Attorneys & Corporate Consultants

Naeemuddin N. A. Siddiqui
ZCL-Ziauddin Ahmed & Company (Pvt) Limited

Saqib Naseer
A.F. Ferguson & Co., Chartered Accountants, a member firm of PwC network

Faryal Nazir
Ebrahim Hosain, Advocates and Corporate Counsel

Shahid Bhatti Orion
Orion

Nawaz Osmani
A. Nawaz Osmani Law Associates

Owais Patel
Datacheck Pvt. Ltd.

Anees Ahmed Pechuho
Abraham & Sarwana

Ahmad Pervez Mizra
Architects Afilliation

Khushbakht Qaiser
Qaiser & Abbas Attorneys & Corporate Counsellors

Zarfishan Qaiser
Qaiser & Abbas Attorneys & Corporate Counsellors

Fayez Qamar Rasheed
CKR & Zia

Adnan Qureshi
Qureshi Law Associates

Haider Qureshi
Hassan, Qureshi & Mamdot

Khalid A. Rahman
Surridge & Beecheno

Zaki Rahman
Ebrahim Hosain, Advocates and Corporate Counsel

Rai Muhammad Saleh Azam
Azam & Rai Advocates & Legal Consultants

Ameeruddin Rana
Abraham & Sarwana

Bilal Rana
Kazmi and Rana

Mobeen Rana

Mazar Iqbal Ranja

Saad Rasool
Saad Rasool Law Associates

Khurram Raza
CKR & Zia

Tayyab Raza
TMT Law Services

Abdur Razzaq
Qamar Abbas & Co.

Taffazul Haider Rizvi
Rizvi and Rizvi

Saad Saboor
Ernst & Young

Ahmed Saeed
Saad Rasool Law Associates

Farooq Saeed
Fajar Inc.

Rana Sajjad
Rana Ijaz & Partners

Aftab Salahuddin
Ernst & Young

Muhammad Saleem Iqbal
Winston & Saleem

Jawad A. Sarwana
Abraham & Sarwana

Hafiz Adnan Sarwar
Winston & Saleem

Mohammad Ali Seena
Surridge & Beecheno

Syed Mansoor Ali Sha
High Court

Huma Shah
Sheikh Shah Rana & Ijaz

Zulfiqar Shah
Land Record Management Information System

Muhammad Shahid
Synthetic Products Enterprises Limited

Arshad Shehzad
Taxperts

Adnan Sheikh
Akram Sheikh Law Associates

Muneeb Admed Sheikh
Mandviwalla & Zafar

Barrister Sherjeel
Akram Sheikh Law Associates

Zafar Sherwani
Sindh High Court

Muhammad Siddique
Securities and Exchange Commission

Mian Hamdoon Subhani
M.H.S. Associates

Namdar Subhani
Punjab Law & Parliamentary Affairs Department

Fawad Sufi
Fawad Sufi and Associates

Khaled Suleman Chima
Chima & Ibrahim

Waqas Ahmed Tamimi
Deloitte Yousuf Adil, Chartered Accountants

Mahmood Masood Tammana
TMA

Ahmed Tauqueer
Environmental Protection Agency

Saud ul-Hassan
Ernst & Young

Chaudhary Usman
Ebrahim Hosain, Advocates and Corporate Counsel

Hafiz Waqar Ahmed
Ernst & Young

Mehek Zafar
Mandviwalla & Zafar

Muneeb Zafar
Zafar & Associates LLP

Murtaza Zahoor
CKR & Zia

Hussain Tahir Zaidi
Abdullah & Hussain

Syed Zeeshan Ali
Ernst & Young

PALAU

Western Caroline Trading Co.

Alfia Alfonso
Small Business Development Center (SBDC)

Kenneth Barden
Attorney-at-Law

Kassi Berg
The Pacific Development Law Group

Tito Cabunagan
Palau Public Utility Corporation

Anthony Frazier

Ltelatk LT Fritz
Small Business Development Center (SBDC)

Larry Goddard
The Pacific Development Law Group

Wilbert Kamerang
Palau Shipping Company, Inc.

Mouias Kangichi
Koror State Government

Ramsey Ngiraibai
Koror Planning and Zoning Office

David O'Brien
Senate of the Republic of Palau

William L. Ridpath
William L. Ridpath, Attorney-at-Law (AMCIT)

V. Tikei Sbal
Financial Institutions Commission

Ken Sugiyama
Palau Public Utility Corporation

Sylcerius Tewalei
Bureau of Labour

Lynna Thomas
Palau Environmental Quality Protection Board

Ann Tirso
Palau Land Registry

PANAMA

De Obaldia y Garcia de Paredes

Alejandro Alemán
Alfaro, Ferrer & Ramírez

Aristides Anguizola
Morgan & Morgan

Mercedes Araúz de Grimaldo
Morgan & Morgan

Francisco Arias G.
Morgan & Morgan

Khatiya Asvat
Patton, Moreno & Asvat

Francisco A. Barrios G.
PwC Panama

Gustavo Adolfo Bernal
ETESA

Klaus Bieberach Schriebl
Ernst & Young

Luis Carlos Bustamante
Panamá Soluciones Logísticas Int. - PSLI

Giovanna Cardellicchio
APC Buró SA

José Carrizo Durling
Morgan & Morgan

Luis Chalhoub
Icaza, Gonzalez-Ruiz & Aleman

Julio Cesar Contreras III
Arosemena Noriega & Contreras

Gonzalo Córdoba
APC Buró SA

Juan Carlos Croston
Manzanillo International Terminal Operator MIT

Eduardo De Alba
Arias, Fábrega & Fábrega

Claudio De Castro
Arias, Fábrega & Fábrega

Felipe Escalona
Galindo, Arias & López

Michael Fernandez
CAPAC (Cámara Panameña de la Construcción)

Enna Ferrer
Alfaro, Ferrer & Ramírez

Angie Guzmán
Morgan & Morgan

Edgar Herrera
Galindo, Arias & López

Cristina Lewis de la Guardia
Galindo, Arias & López

Ivette Elisa Martínez Saenz
Patton, Moreno & Asvat

Olmedo Miranda B.
Arosemena Noriega & Contreras

Erick Rogelio Muñoz
Sucre, Arias & Reyes

Hassim Patel
PwC Panama

Mario Rognoni
Arosemena Noriega & Contreras

Nelson E. Sales
Alfaro, Ferrer & Ramírez

Mayte Sánchez González
Morgan & Morgan

Daniel Sessa
Galindo, Arias & López

Yinnis Solís de Amaya
Union Fenosa - EDEMET - EDECHI

Natasha Sucre
FIABCI, the International Real Estate Federation

Hermes Tello
Electromechanical Consulting Group

Ramón Varela
Morgan & Morgan

Gabriela Vasquez
Galindo, Arias & López

Jorge Ventre
Patton, Moreno & Asvat

PAPUA NEW GUINEA

Credit & Data Bureau Limited

PNG Ports Corporation Ltd.

PwC Papua New Guinea

Paul Barker
Consultative Implementation & Monitoring Council

Simon Bendo
Department of Lands and Physical Planning

Ian Clarke
Gadens Lawyers

Greta Cooper
Gadens Lawyers

Paul Cullen
Gadens Lawyers

Anthony Frazier

Gibson Geroro
Leahy Lewin Nutley Sullivan

Lea Henao
Steamships Trading Company Ltd.

Clarence Hoot
Investment Promotion Authority

Joshua Hunt
Gadens Lawyers

Samuel James
Investment Promotion Authority

Thompson Kama
Master Freelance Services

Steven Kami
S & L Kami Consultants Ltd.

Jack Kariko
Investment Promotion Authority

Timothy Koris
PNG Power Ltd.

Kristophe Kup
Ninai Lawyers

John Leahy
Leahy Lewin Nutley Sullivan

Doug Mageo
PNG Power Ltd.

Greg Manda
Greg Manda Lawyers

Stephen Massa
Gadens Lawyers

Steve Patrick
Gadens Lawyers

Daroa Peter
Investment Promotion Authority

Lou Pipi
NCDC Municipality

Nancy Pogla
Allens Linklaters

Ivan Pomaleu
Investment Promotion Authority

Greg Runnegar
Pacific Architects Consortium

Ian Shepherd
Ashurst LLP

Lilian Sukot
PNG Power Ltd.

Thomas Taberia
Leahy Lewin Nutley Sullivan

Thomas Tarabu
Investment Promotion Authority

Alex Tongayu
Investment Promotion Authority

Stuart Wilson
LCS Electrical & Mechanical Contractors

Veronica Yobone Randy
Greg Manda Lawyers

PARAGUAY

Magalí Rodríguez Alcalá
Berkemeyer, Attorneys & Counselors

Perla Alderete
Vouga Abogados

Enrique Benitez
BDO Auditores Consultores

Maximo Gustavo Benitez Gimenez
Superintendencia de Bancos - BCP

Alex Berkemeyer
Berkemeyer, Attorneys & Counselors

Hugo T. Berkemeyer
Berkemeyer, Attorneys & Counselors

Esteban Burt
Peroni, Sosa, Tellechea, Burt & Narvaja, member of Lex Mundi

Carlos Cañete
BDO Auditores Consultores

Pedro Cuevas
Administración Nacional de Electricidad

Sergio Dejesus
Kemper – Dejesus & Pangrazio Abogados y Consultores

Paolo Doria
Peroni, Sosa, Tellechea, Burt & Narvaja, member of Lex Mundi

Natalia Enciso Benitez
Notary Public

Bruno Fiorio Carrizosa
Fiorio, Cardozo & Alvarado

Juan Bautista Fiorio Gimenez
Fiorio, Cardozo & Alvarado

Edgardo Fleitas
ABC Consultores

Néstor Gamarra
Servimex SACI

Liliana Maria Giménez de Castillo
Dirección General de los Registros Públicos

Jorge Guillermo Gomez
PwC Paraguay

Lourdes Gonzalez
Dirección General de los Registros Públicos

Nadia Gorostiaga
PwC Paraguay

Sigfrido Gross Brown
Estudio Juridico Gross Brown

Carl Gwynn
Gwynn & Gwynn - Legal Counsellors

Norman Gwynn
Supreme Court of Justice

Manfred Heyn
Ferrere Abogados

Christian Kemper
Kemper – Dejesus & Pangrazio Abogados y Consultores

Gabriel Lamas
Onix SACI Consulting + Engineering

Pablo Livieres Guggiari
Estudio Jurídico Livieres Guggiari

Nestor Loizaga
Ferrere Abogados

Oscar A. Mersan Galli
Mersan Abogados

María Esmeralda Moreno Rodríguez Alcalá
Moreno Ruffinelli & Asociados

Gustavo Olmedo
Olmedo Abogados

Anibal Pangrazio
Kemper – Dejesus & Pangrazio Abogados y Consultores

Rocío Penayo
Moreno Ruffinelli & Asociados

Yolanda Pereira
Berkemeyer, Attorneys & Counselors

María Antonia Ramírez de Gwynn
Gwynn & Gwynn - Legal Counsellors

Adolfo Rautenberg
Fiorio, Cardozo & Alvarado

Veronica Recalde
Kemper – Dejesus & Pangrazio Abogados y Consultores

Mauricio Salgueiro
Vouga Abogados

Ruben Taboada
PwC Paraguay

Ninfa Rolanda Torres de Paredes
Agencia Paredes

Maria Gloria Triguis Gonzalez
Berkemeyer, Attorneys & Counselors

Emmanuel Trulls
Ferrere Abogados

Andres Vera
Vouga Abogados

Walter Vera
Vouga Abogados

Carlos Vouga
Vouga Abogados

Rodolfo Vouga Muller
Vouga Abogados

Roberto Vuyk
Codas Vuyk SA

PERU

Guillermo Acuña Roeder
Rubio Leguía Normand

Fanny Aguirre
Estudio Alvarez Calderon

Walter Aguirre
Aguirre Abogados & Asesores

Marco Antonio Alarcón Piana
Estudio Luis Echecopar García SRL

Alfonso Alvarez Calderón
Estudio Alvarez Calderon

Guilhermo Auler
Forsyth Abogados

Brian Avalos
Payet, Rey, Cauvi, Pérez Abogados

Arelis Avila Tagle
CONUDFI

Maritza Barzola
Russell Bedford Perú - member of Russell Bedford International

Stephany Giovanna Bravo de Rueda Arce
Ransa Comercial SA

Cristian Calderon
ADEX

Renzo Camaiora
Gallo Barrios Pickmann

Maria Alejandra Cano Mujica
Aguirre Abogados & Asesores

Alfredo Cardona
Experian Perú SAC

Ursula Caro
Rubio Leguía Normand

Norka Chirinos La Torre
SUNARP

Alvaro Chuquipiondo
Barrios & Fuentes Abogados

Sandra Copacondori
Barrios & Fuentes Abogados

Tomas Cosco
Russell Bedford Perú - member of Russell Bedford International

Ricardo de la Piedra
Estudio Olaechea, member of Lex Mundi

Jose Dedios
Payet, Rey, Cauvi, Pérez Abogados

Pierre Alexander Duobert Abarca
Pizarro, Botto & Escobar Abogados

Alex Espinoza
PwC Peru

Maria del Pilar Falcon Castro
Estudio Llona & Bustamante Abogados

Fiama Fernandez Saldamando
CONUDFI

Luis Fuentes
Barrios & Fuentes Abogados

Julio Gallo
Gallo Barrios Pickmann

Alfredo Gastañeta
García Sayán Abogados

Maria Alejandra Giufra Chavez
Estudio Llona & Bustamante Abogados

Diego Gomez
Barrios & Fuentes Abogados

Rafael Gonzales
Barrios & Fuentes Abogados

Carlos Hernández Ladera
Ransa Comercial SA

Jose Antonio Honda
Estudio Olaechea, member of Lex Mundi

Diego Huertas del Pino
Barrios & Fuentes Abogados

César Ballón Izquierdo
Ransa Comercial SA

Alexandra Lemke
Barrios & Fuentes Abogados

Gonzalo Leo
Barrios & Fuentes Abogados

Juan Carlos Leon Siles
ADEX

Luigi Lindley
Experian Perú SAC

German Lora
Payet, Rey, Cauvi, Pérez Abogados

Cesar Luna Victoria
Rubio Leguía Normand

Milagros Maravi Sumar
Rubio Leguía Normand

Orlando Marchesi
PwC Peru

Jesús Matos
Estudio Olaechea, member of Lex Mundi

Alejandro Medina
Superintendency of Banking, Insurance and Private Pension Fund Administrator

Gino Menchola
PwC Peru

Hugo Mendez
Aguirre Abogados & Asesores

Juan Antonio Morales Bermudes
CONUDFI

Diego Muñiz
Estudio Olaechea, member of Lex Mundi

Alexandra Orbezo
Rebaza, Alcázar & De Las Casas Abogados Financieros

Ariel Orrego-Villacorta
Barrios & Fuentes Abogados

Cristina Oviedo
Payet, Rey, Cauvi, Pérez Abogados

Max Panay Cuya
SUNARP

Verónica Perea
Barrios & Fuentes Abogados

Lucianna Polar
Estudio Olaechea, member of Lex Mundi

Juan Manuel Prado Bustamante
Estudio Llona & Bustamante Abogados

Maribel Príncipe Hidalgo
Rubio Leguía Normand

María José Puertas
Gallo Barrios Pickmann

Rafael Puiggros
Delmar Ugarte Abogados

Cesar Puntriano
PwC Peru

Bruno Marchese Quintana
Rubio Leguía Normand

Fernando M. Ramos
Barrios & Fuentes Abogados

Alonso Rey Bustamante
Payet, Rey, Cauvi, Pérez Abogados

José Miguel Reyes
Barrios & Fuentes Abogados

Andrea Rieckhof
Gallo Barrios Pickmann

Rossana Rodriguez
García Sayán Abogados

Erick Rojas
Cámara Peruana de la Construcción

Martin Ruggiero
Payet, Rey, Cauvi, Pérez Abogados

Felix Arturo Ruiz Sanchez
Rubio Leguía Normand

Carolina Sáenz
Rubio Leguía Normand

Carolina Salcedo
Estudio Muñiz, Ramirez, Perez-Taiman & Olaya

Adolfo Sanabria Mercado
García Sayán Abogados

Raúl Sanchez
Barrios & Fuentes Abogados

Victor Scarsi
Luz del Sur

Martin Serkovic
Estudio Olaechea, member of Lex Mundi

Claudia Sevillano
Pizarro, Botto & Escobar Abogados

Hugo Silva
Rodrigo, Elías, Medrano Abogados

Ricardo P. Silva
Estudio Muñiz, Ramirez, Perez-Taiman & Olaya

Carla Sinchi
Payet, Rey, Cauvi, Pérez Abogados

Mario Solari Zerpa
SUNARP

Enrique Soto
ADEX

Jose Steck
NPG Abogados

Edmundo Taboada
Barrios & Fuentes Abogados

Carlos Tapia
NPG Abogados

Xenia Tello
Estudio Olaechea, member of Lex Mundi

Jack Vainstein
Vainstein & Ingenieros SA

Mitchell Alex Valdiviezo Del Carpio
Rubio Leguía Normand

Evelyn Vargas
Estudio Olaechea, member of Lex Mundi

Rosa Vera
Aguirre Abogados & Asesores

Manuel Villa-García
Estudio Olaechea, member of Lex Mundi

Rafael Villaran
Estudio Luis Echecopar García SRL

Agustín Yrigoyen
García Sayán Abogados

Sabino Zaconeta Torres
Asociación Peruana de Agentes Marítimos

PHILIPPINES

Arveen Agunday
Castillo Laman Tan Pantaleon & San Jose

Rosario Carmela Asutria
SEC

Francis Avellana
BAP Credit Bureau, Inc.

Juan B. Santos
Republic of the Philippines Social Security System

Joanne Babon
Follosco Morallos & Herce

Manuel Batallones
BAP Credit Bureau, Inc.

Vera Marie Bautista
SyCip Salazar Hernandez & Gatmaitan

Paolo Bernardo
Romulo, Mabanta, Buenaventura, Sayoc & de los Angeles, member of Lex Mundi

Jose A. Bernas
Bernas Law

Pearl Grace Cabali
Puyat Jacinto Santos Law Office

Juan Arturo Iluminado Cagampang de Castro
De Castro & Cagampang-de Castro Law Firm

Brian Calinao
Texas Instruments

Justina Callangan
SEC

Mylene Capangcol
Department of Energy

Ruben Gerald Capones
SyCip Salazar Hernandez & Gatmaitan

Domingo Castillo
SyCip Salazar Hernandez & Gatmaitan

Joseph Omar A. Castillo
Puyat Jacinto Santos Law Office

Kenneth L. Chua
Quisumbing Torres, member firm of Baker & McKenzie International

Roselle Craig
Isla Lipana & Co.

Diwata D. de Leon
Castillo Laman Tan Pantaleon & San Jose

Emerico O. de Guzman
Angara Abello Concepcion Regala & Cruz Law Offices (ACCRALAW)

Richard De La Cruz
Ultralite Electrical Company Inc.

Emilio S. De Quiros Jr.
Republic of the Philippines Social Security System

Anthony Dee
SyCip Salazar Hernandez & Gatmaitan

Rafael del Rosario
Romulo, Mabanta, Buenaventura, Sayoc & de los Angeles, member of Lex Mundi

Mark Kevin Dellosa
SyCip Salazar Hernandez & Gatmaitan

Jenny Jean Domino
SyCip Salazar Hernandez & Gatmaitan

Colonel Jesus Fernandez
Local Government of Quezon City

Francis Ferrer
EMS Components Assembly, Inc.

Rachel Follosco
Follosco Morallos & Herce

Florida Fomaneg
Isla Lipana & Co.

Catherine Franco
Quisumbing Torres, member firm of Baker & McKenzie International

Pablito Lito Freo
Powerloops

Enrique Galang
Castillo Laman Tan Pantaleon & San Jose

Geraldine S. Garcia
Follosco Morallos & Herce

Vicente Gerochi IV
SyCip Salazar Hernandez & Gatmaitan

George Matthew Habacon
SyCip Salazar Hernandez & Gatmaitan

Judy Hao
Angara Abello Concepcion Regala & Cruz Law Offices (ACCRALAW)

Tadeo F. Hilado
Angara Abello Concepcion Regala & Cruz Law Offices (ACCRALAW)

Nancy Joan M. Javier
Javier Law

Rafael Khan
Siguion Reyna Montecillo & Ongsiako

Hiyasmin Lapitan
SyCip Salazar Hernandez & Gatmaitan

Everlene Lee
Angara Abello Concepcion Regala & Cruz Law Offices (ACCRALAW)

Innah Lim
Romulo, Mabanta, Buenaventura, Sayoc & de los Angeles, member of Lex Mundi

Herbert M. Bautista
Local Government of Quezon City

Katrina Michelle Mancao
Quasha Ancheta Pena & Nolasco

Enriquito J. Mendoza
Romulo, Mabanta, Buenaventura, Sayoc & de los Angeles, member of Lex Mundi

Maria Teresa Mercado-Ferrer
SyCip Salazar Hernandez & Gatmaitan

Marianne Miguel
SyCip Salazar Hernandez & Gatmaitan

Jose Salvador Mirasol
Romulo, Mabanta, Buenaventura, Sayoc & de los Angeles, member of Lex Mundi

Jesusito G. Morallos
Follosco Morallos & Herce

Maria Christina Ortua
SyCip Salazar Hernandez & Gatmaitan

Ma. Milagros Padernal
Uy Singson Abella & Co.

Nicanor N. Padilla
Siguion Reyna Montecillo & Ongsiako

Ma. Patricia Paz
SyCip Salazar Hernandez & Gatmaitan

Maybellyn Pinpin-Malayo
Isla Lipana & Co.

Revelino Rabaja
Isla Lipana & Co.

Frederika Rentoy
Local Government of Quezon City

Elaine Patricia S. Reyes-Rodolfo
Angara Abello Concepcion Regala & Cruz Law Offices (ACCRALAW)

Ruben Gerald Ricasata
Puyat Jacinto Santos Law Office

Ricardo J. Romulo
Romulo, Mabanta, Buenaventura, Sayoc & de los Angeles, member of Lex Mundi

Patrick Henry Salazar
Quisumbing Torres, member firm of Baker & McKenzie International

Rowena Fatima Salonga
Puyat Jacinto Santos Law Office

Neptali Salvanera
Angara Abello Concepcion Regala & Cruz Law Offices (ACCRALAW)

Ethel San Juan
EMS Components Assembly, Inc.

Amando Tetangco Jr.
Bangko Sentral ng Pilipinas

Roland Glenn Tuazon
Romulo, Mabanta, Buenaventura, Sayoc & de los Angeles, member of Lex Mundi

Isagani, Jr. Versoza
Local Government of Quezon City

Priscela Verzonilla
Local Government of Quezon City

Redentor C. Zapata
Quasha Ancheta Pena & Nolasco

Gil Roberto Zerrudo
Quisumbing Torres, member firm of Baker & McKenzie International

POLAND

Bank Zachodni WBK SA

ECE Projektmanagement Polska Sp. z o.o.

Energy Regulatory Office

Naprawa Kabli Energetycznych Andrzej Rogowski

Wojciech Andrzejewski
Kancelaria Prawna Piszcz, Norek i Wspólnicy sp.k.

Katarzyna Jadwiga Babicka
Windmill Gąsiewski & Roman Law Office

Andrzej Balicki
DLA Piper Wiater sp.k.

Michał Barłowski
Wardyński & Partners

Justyna Bartnik
Morawski & Partners Law Firm

Michal Białobrzeski
Hogan Lovells (Warszawa) LLP

Paulina Blukacz
Ministry of Finance

Joanna Bugajska
JAMP

Rafał Burda
DLA Piper Wiater sp.k.

Małgorzata Chruściak
CMS Cameron McKenna

Agnieszka Czarnecka
KPT Tax Advisors

Katarzyna Czwartosz
White & Case

Michał Dąbrowski
Ministry of Justice

Aleksandra Danielewicz
DLA Piper Wiater sp.k.

Andrzej Dmowski
Russell Bedford Poland Sp. z o.o. - member of Russell Bedford International

Bartosz Draniewicz
Kancelaria Prawa Gospodarczego i Ekologicznego dr Bartosz Draniewicz

Patryk Filipiak
Zimmerman Filipiak Restrukturyzacja SA

Marek Firlej
Ministry of Finance

Maciej Geromin
Allerhand Institute

Michał Gliński
Wardyński & Partners

Rafał Godlewski
Wardyński & Partners

Rafał Góralczyk
BNT Neupert Zamorska & Partnerzy sp.j.

Jaromir Grabowski
Wojewódzki Inspektorat Nadzoru Budowlanego w Warszawie

Bartosz Groele
Allerhand Institute

Dominik Gruca
Windmill Gąsiewski & Roman Law Office

Andrzej Grześkiewicz
Gridnet

Maciej Grzeszczyk
KPT Tax Advisors

Monika Hartung
Wardyński & Partners

Mariusz Hildebrand
BIG InfoMonitor SA

Marcin Hołówka
Marcin Hołówka

Łukasz Iwański
Ergonomix

Michal Jadwisiak
White & Case

Jakub Jędrzejak
WKB Wiercinski, Kwiecinski, Baehr

Magdalena Kalińska
WKB Wiercinski, Kwiecinski, Baehr

Mateusz Kalinski
Kancelaria Prawa Restrukturyzacyjnego i Upadlosciowego Tatara i Wspolpracownicy

Karolina Kalucka
DLA Piper Wiater sp.k.

Aleksandra Kaminska
Dentons

Tomasz Kański
Sołtysiński Kawecki & Szlęzak

Iwona Karasek-Wojciechowicz
Jagiellonian University

Mariusz Każuch
Ministry of Finance

Zbigniew Korba
Deloitte Doradztwo Podatkowe Sp. z o.o.

Jacek Korzeniewski
Baker & McKenzie

Aleksandra Kozlowska
DLA Piper Wiater sp.k.

Adam Krolik
Kancelaria Prawa Restrukturyzacyjnego i Upadlosciowego Tatara i Wspolpracownicy

Iga Kwasny
Moore Stephens Central Audit Sp. z o.o.

Ewa Łachowska - Brol

Wojciech Langowski
Miller Canfield

Katarzyna Lawinska
Baker & McKenzie

Konrad Piotr Lewandowski
Maurice Ward & Co. Sp.z.o.o.

Agnieszka Lisiecka
Wardyński & Partners

Tomasz Listwan
Moore Stephens Central Audit Sp. z o.o.

Paweł Ludwiniak
Eltech

Jarosław Malicki
RWE Stoen Operator Sp.

Ewa Malinowska
Regional Commercial Court

Wojciech Marchwicki
Wardyński & Partners

Konrad Marciniuk
Miller Canfield

Marta Marczak
Marcin Hołówka

Adam Marszałek
DLA Piper Wiater sp.k.

Agnieszka Marzec
BIK

Pawel Meus
Gide Loyrette Nouel Poland Warsaw

Tomasz Michalak
Ministry of Finance

Tomasz Michalik
MDDP Michalik Dłuska Dziedzic i Partnerzy

Anna Miernik
Clifford Chance

Tomasz Milewski
Miller Canfield

Aleksandra Minkowicz-Flanek
Dentons

Joanna Młot
CMS Cameron McKenna

Marcin Moj
Marcin Hołówka

Adam Morawski
Morawski & Partners Law Firm

Grzegorz Namiotkiewicz
Clifford Chance

Michal Niemirowicz-Szczytt
LEX IUVAT Kancelaria Radcy Prawnego Michal Niemirowicz-Szczytt

Zygmunt Niewiadomski
Warsaw School of Economics

Dominika Nowak
DLA Piper Wiater sp.k.

Filip Opoka
DLA Piper Wiater sp.k.

Tomasz Ostrowski
White & Case

Mateusz Palian
Kancelaria Prawa Restrukturyzacyjnego i Upadlosciowego Tatara i Wspolpracownicy

Krzysztof Pawlak
Sołtysiński Kawecki & Szlęzak

Agata Pawlak-Jaszczak
Kancelaria Prawna Piszcz, Norek i Wspólnicy sp.k.

Tomasz Pietrzak
Hogan Lovells (Warszawa) LLP

Malgorzata Pietrzak-Paciorek
Baker & McKenzie

Kamilla Piotrowska-Król
Terramar Ltd.

Mariusz Purgał
Tomasik, Pakosiewicz, Groele Adwokaci i Radcowie Prawni sp. p.

Bartłomiej Raczkowski
Raczkowski Paruch

Piotr Sadownik
Gide Loyrette Nouel Poland Warsaw

Marek Sawicki
DLA Piper Wiater sp.k.

Karol Skibniewski
Sołtysiński Kawecki & Szlęzak

Michał Słoniewicz
BIK

Michal Snitko-Pleszko
Blackstones

Marek Sosnowski
Gide Loyrette Nouel Poland Warsaw

Agnieszka Stodolna
Windmill Gąsiewski & Roman Law Office

Małgorzata Studniarek
DLA Piper Wiater sp.k.

Michał Subocz
White & Case

Michal Suska
Ergonomix

Jadwiga Szabat
ECOVIS System Rewident SP. Z O.O.

Emil Szczepanik
Ministry of Justice

Łukasz Szegda
Wardyński & Partners

Marcelina Szwed
DLA Piper Wiater sp.k.

Maciej Szwedowski
Squire Sanders Święcicki Krześniak sp.k.

Paulina Szymczak-Kamińska
Raczkowski Paruch

Anna Tarasiuk
Hogan Lovells (Warszawa) LLP

Karol Tatara
Kancelaria Prawa Restrukturyzacyjnego i Upadlosciowego Tatara i Wspolpracownicy

Dariusz Tokarczuk
Gide Loyrette Nouel Poland Warsaw

Ryszard Trykosko
Polish Association of Civil Engineers

Mateusz Tusznio
Wardyński & Partners

Dominika Wagrodzka
BNT Neupert Zamorska & Partnerzy sp.j.

Jakub Warnieło
KPT Tax Advisors

Emilia Waszkiewicz
Baker & McKenzie

Cezary Wernic
Ministry of Finance

Jacek Wesołowski
Immofinanz Services Poland Ltd.

Maciej Wesołowski
DLA Piper Wiater sp.k.

Sebastian Wieczorek
Dentons

Anna Wietrzyńska-Ciołkowska
DLA Piper Wiater sp.k.

Patrick Wilhelmsen
Marcin Hołówka

Robert Windmill
Windmill Gąsiewski & Roman Law Office

Anna Wojciechowska
WKB Wiercinski, Kwiecinski, Baehr

Steven Wood
Blackstones

Anna Wyrzykowska
WKB Wiercinski, Kwiecinski, Baehr

Edyta Zalewska
Gide Loyrette Nouel Poland Warsaw

Małgorzata Zamorska
BNT Neupert Zamorska & Partnerzy sp.j.

Agnieszka Ziółek
CMS Cameron McKenna

Katarzyna Zukowska
Wardyński & Partners

PORTUGAL

João Jacinto Tomé SA

Victor Abrantes
Victor Abrantes - International Sales Agent

Bruno Andrade Alves
PwC Portugal

Joana Andrade Correia
Raposo Bernardo & Associados

Luís Antunes
LUFTEC – Técnicas Eléctricas, Lda.

Filipa Arantes Pedroso
Morais Leitão, Galvão Teles, Soares da Silva & Associados, member of Lex Mundi

Miguel Azevedo
Garrigues Portugal SLP - Sucursal

João Banza
PwC Portugal

Manuel P. Barrocas
Barrocas Advogados

Mark Bekker
Bekker Logistica

Antonio Belmar da Costa
Associação dos Agentes de Navegação de Portugal (AGEPOR)

Andreia Bento Simões
Morais Leitão, Galvão Teles, Soares da Silva & Associados, member of Lex Mundi

João Bettencourt da Camara
Credinformações - Equifax

João Cadete de Matos
Banco de Portugal

Susana Caetano
PwC Portugal

Inês Calor
Santarem Municipality

Vitor Campos
National Laboratory for Civil Engineering - LNEC

Rui Capote
PLEN - Sociedade de Advogados, RL

Fernando Cardoso da Cunha
Gali Macedo & Associados

João Carneiro
Miranda & Associados

Petra Carreira
Garrigues Portugal SLP - Sucursal

Jaime Carvalho Esteves
PwC Portugal

Filipa Castanheira de Almeida
Morais Leitão, Galvão Teles, Soares da Silva & Associados, member of Lex Mundi

Tiago Castanheira Marques
Abreu Advogados

Joana Correia
Raposo Bernardo & Associados

Joaquim Correia Teixeira
EDP Distribuição - Energia, SA

Maria de Lancastre Valente
SRS Advogados

João Duarte de Sousa
Garrigues Portugal SLP - Sucursal

Sara Ferraz Mendonça
Morais Leitão, Galvão Teles, Soares da Silva & Associados, member of Lex Mundi

Ana Luisa Ferreira
Abreu Advogados

Sofia Ferreira Enriquez
Raposo Bernardo & Associados

Rita Ferreira Lopes
Morais Leitão, Galvão Teles, Soares da Silva & Associados, member of Lex Mundi

Nuno Gundar da Cruz
Morais Leitão, Galvão Teles, Soares da Silva & Associados, member of Lex Mundi

Tiago Lemos
PLEN - Sociedade de Advogados, RL

Jorge Pedro Lopes
Polytechnic Institute of Bragança

Tiago Gali Macedo
Gali Macedo & Associados

Francisco Magalhães
PwC Portugal

Ana Margarida Maia
Miranda & Associados

Carlos Pedro Marques
EDP Distribuição - Energia, SA

Frederica Marques-Pinto
Raposo Bernardo & Associados

Catarina Medeiros
PwC Portugal

Francisco Melo
SGOC Sousa Guedes, Oliveira Couto & Associados, Soc. Advogados R.L.

Patricia Melo Gomes
Morais Leitão, Galvão Teles, Soares da Silva & Associados, member of Lex Mundi

Joaquim Luís Mendes
Grant Thornton LLP

Andreia Morins
PwC Portugal

Rita Nogueira Neto
Garrigues Portugal SLP - Sucursal

Catarina Nunes
PwC Portugal

Eduardo Paulino
Morais Leitão, Galvão Teles, Soares da Silva & Associados, member of Lex Mundi

João Branco Pedro
National Laboratory for Civil Engineering - LNEC

Pedro Pereira Coutinho
Garrigues Portugal SLP - Sucursal

Pedro Catão Pinheiro
Gali Macedo & Associados

Acácio Pita Negrão
PLEN - Sociedade de Advogados, RL

Margarida Ramalho
Associação de Empresas de Construção, Obras Públicas e Serviços

Ana Cláudia Rangel
Raposo Bernardo & Associados

Sara Reis
Miranda & Associados

Maria João Ricou
Cuatrecasas, Gonçalves Pereira, RL (Portugal)

Ana Robin de Andrade
Morais Leitão, Galvão Teles, Soares da Silva & Associados, member of Lex Mundi

Filomena Rosa
Instituto dos Registos e do Notariado

Pedro Rosa
Garrigues Portugal SLP - Sucursal

César Sá Esteves
SRS Advogados

Francisco Salgueiro
Neville de Rougemont & Associados

José Santos Afonso
EDP Distribuição - Energia, SA

Filipe Santos Barata
Gómez-Acebo & Pombo Abogados, SLP Sucursal em Portugal

Ana Sofia Silva
Cuatrecasas, Gonçalves Pereira, RL (Portugal)

Rui Silva
PwC Portugal

João Silva Pereira
Barrocas Advogados

Inês Sousa Godinho
Gómez-Acebo & Pombo Abogados, SLP Sucursal em Portugal

Carmo Sousa Machado
Abreu Advogados

PUERTO RICO (U.S.)

TransUnion De Puerto Rico

Alfredo Alvarez-Ibañez
O'Neill & Borges

Vicente Antonetti
Goldman Antonetti & Córdova LLC

Hermann Bauer
O'Neill & Borges

Nicole Berio
O'Neill & Borges

Jorge Capó Matos
O'Neill & Borges

Delia Castillo de Colorado
Registro de la Propiedad de Puerto Rico

Solymar Castillo-Morales
Goldman Antonetti & Córdova LLC

Odemaris Chacon
Estrella, LLC

Manuel De Lemos
Manuel de Lemos Aia Arquitectos

Alfonso Fernández
Ivy Group

Julio A. Galíndez
FPV & Galíndez CPAs, PSC - member of Russell Bedford International

Nelson William Gonzalez
Colegio de Notarios de Puerto Rico

Alexis González-Pagani
Ferraiuoli, LLC

Yarot Lafontaine-Torres
Ferraiuoli, LLC

Luis Marini
O'Neill & Borges

Oscar O. Meléndez-Sauri
Malley Tamargo & Meléndez-Sauri LLC

Juan Carlos Méndez

Antonio Molina
Pietrantoni Méndez & Alavrez LLC

Luis Mongil-Casasnovas
Martinez Odell & Calabria

Jose Armando Morales Rodriguez
JAM Cargo Sales Inc.

Lucy Navarro Rosado
Colegio de Notarios de Puerto Rico

Jhansel Núñez
Attorney

Jose O. Esquerdo
PwC Puerto Rico

Francisco Pérez-Betancourt
Ferraiuoli, LLC

Marta Ramirez
O'Neill & Borges

Jesus Rivera
Banco Popular de Puerto Rico

Thelma Rivera
Goldman Antonetti & Córdova LLC

Kenneth Rivera-Robles
FPV & Galíndez CPAs, PSC - member of Russell Bedford International

Victor Rodriguez
Multitransport & Marine Co.

Victor Rodriguez
PwC Puerto Rico

Antonio Roig
O'Neill & Borges

Edgardo Rosa-Ortiz
FPV & Galíndez CPAs, PSC - member of Russell Bedford International

José Fernando Rovira-Rullán
Ferraiuoli, LLC

Jorge M. Ruiz Montilla
McConnell Valdés LLC

Jaime Santos
Pietrantoni Méndez & Alavrez LLC

Tania Vazquez Maldonado
Banco Popular de Puerto Rico

Raúl Vidal y Sepúlveda
Omnia Economic Solutions LLC

Nayuan Zouairabani
O'Neill & Borges

QATAR

Dentons

Hani Al Naddaf
Al Tamimi & Company Advocates & Legal Consultants

Abdulla Mohamed Al Naimi
Qatar Credit Bureau

Grace Alam
Badri and Salim El Meouchi Law Firm, member of Interleges

Rashed Albuflasa
Noble Global Logistics

Maryam Al-Thani
Qatar Credit Bureau

Dina Al-Wahabit
Al Tamimi & Company Advocates & Legal Consultants

Jason Arnedo
Noble Global Logistics

Imran Ayub
KPMG Qatar

Monita Barghachieh
Pinsent Masons LLP

Alexis Coleman
Pinsent Masons LLP

Michael Earley
Sultan Al-Abdulla & Partners

Fouad El Haddad
LALIVE LLC

Ahmed Eljaale
Al Tamimi & Company Advocates & Legal Consultants

James Elwen
Pinsent Masons LLP

Mohammed Fouad
Sultan Al-Abdulla & Partners

Sharifah Hamzah
Al Tamimi & Company Advocates & Legal Consultants

Conan Higgins
TSI Legal Enterprises, PC

Walid Honein
Badri and Salim El Meouchi Law Firm, member of Interleges

Rafiq Jaffer
Al Tamimi & Company Advocates & Legal Consultants

Kristen M. Jarvis Johnson
Squire Patton Boggs (MEA) LLP

Mohamed Jeffery
Noble Global Logistics

Tamsyn Jones
KPMG Qatar

Dani Kabbani
Eversheds

Upuli Kasthuriarachchi
PwC Qatar

Pradeep Kumar
Diamond Shipping Services

Frank Lucente
Al Tamimi & Company Advocates & Legal Consultants

Seem Maleh
Al Tamimi & Company Advocates & Legal Consultants

Julie Menhem
Eversheds

Sara Milne
Pinsent Masons LLP

Shejeer Muhammed
Noble Global Logistics

Sujani Nisansala
PwC Qatar

Neil O'Brien
PwC Qatar

Ferdie Ona
Noble Global Logistics

Michael Palmer
Squire Patton Boggs (MEA) LLP

Sony Pereira
National Shipping and Marine Services Company WLL

Jihane Rizk
Badri and Salim El Meouchi Law Firm, member of Interleges

Sohaib Rubbani
PwC Qatar

Lilia Sabbagh
Badri and Salim El Meouchi Law Firm, member of Interleges

David Salt
Clyde & Co.

Zain Al Abdin Sharar
Qatar International Court and Dispute Resolution Centre

Tabara Sy
LALIVE LLC

Mohammed Tawfeek M. Ahmed
Squire Patton Boggs (MEA) LLP

Richard Ward
Eversheds

ROMANIA

ARHIPAR S.R.L.

Cosmin Anghel
Clifford Chance Badea SCA

Mihai Anghel
Ţuca Zbârcea & Asociaţii

Gabriela Anton
Ţuca Zbârcea & Asociaţii

Francesco Atanasio
ENEL

Ioana Avram
Dentons Europe

Anca Băiţan
Maravela & Asociaţii

Georgiana Balan
D&B Davidşi Baias Law Firm

Florina Balanescu
ENEL

Irina Elena Bănică
POP & Partners SCA Attorneys-at-Law

Monica Biciusca
Adghel Stabb & Partners

Sandra Cahu
DLA Piper Dinu SCA

Maria Cambien
PwC Romania

Ioana Cercel
D&B David Şi Baias Law Firm

Vlad Cercel
Ţuca Zbârcea & Asociaţii

Marius Chelaru
STOICA & Asociaţii - Societate Civilă de Avocaţi

Teodor Chirvase
Maravela & Asociaţii

Alin Chitu
Ţuca Zbârcea & Asociaţii

Andreea Ciorapciu
Dentons Europe

Veronica Cocârlea
Jinga & Asociaţii

Valentin Cocean
Drakopoulos Law Firm

Smaranda Cojocaru
Eversheds Lina & Guia SCA

Raluca Coman
Clifford Chance Badea SCA

Ileana Constantin
Dentons Europe

Razvan Constantinescu
Dentons Europe

Paula Corban
DLA Piper Dinu SCA

Anamaria Corbescu
Dentons Europe

Oana Cornescu
Ţuca Zbârcea & Asociaţii

Dorin Coza
Sulica Protopopescu Vonica

Sergius Creţu
Ţuca Zbârcea & Asociaţii

Tiberiu Csaki
Dentons Europe

Radu Damaschin
Nestor Nestor Diculescu Kingston Petersen

Anca Danilescu
Zamfirescu Racoţi & Partners Attorneys-at-Law

Dan Dascalu
D&B David Şi Baias Law Firm

Adrian Deaconu
Taxhouse SRL

Luminita Dima
Nestor Nestor Diculescu Kingston Petersen

Rodica Dobre
PwC Romania

Monia Dobrescu
Muşat & Asociaţii

Laura Adina Duca
Nestor Nestor Diculescu Kingston Petersen

Emil Duhnea
Dentons Europe

Geanina Dumitru
Enel (former Electrica Muntenia Sud)

Nastasia Dumitru
DLA Piper Dinu SCA

Lidia Dutu-Carstea
DLA Piper Dinu SCA

Serban Epure
Biroul de Credit

Sonia Fedorovici
Maravela & Asociații

Iulia Ferăstrău-Grigore
Maravela & Asociații

Adriana Gaspar
Nestor Nestor Diculescu Kingston Petersen

George Ghitu
Mușat & Asociații

Fanizzi Giuseppe
ENEL

Laurentiu Gorun
Drakopoulos Law Firm

Laura Gradinescu
DLA Piper Dinu SCA

Daniela Gramaticescu
Nestor Nestor Diculescu Kingston Petersen

Magda Grigore
Maravela & Asociații

Emilian-Victor Grigoriu
SC Arhi Grup Impex Srl

Adina Grosu
Dentons Europe

Argentina Hincu
Dentons Europe

Ana-Maria Hrituc
Sulica Protopopescu Vonica

Camelia Iantuc
Clifford Chance Badea SCA

Alexandra Ichim
Maravela & Asociații

Ilinca Iliescu
Radu Tărăcilă Pădurari Retevoescu SPRL in association with Allen & Overy

Diana Emanuela Ispas
Nestor Nestor Diculescu Kingston Petersen

Horia Ispas
Țuca Zbârcea & Asociații

Madalina Ivan
Zamfirescu Racoți & Partners Attorneys-at-Law

Mihai Jelea
Eversheds Lina & Guia SCA

Aurimas Kacinskas
Creditinfo Romania

Cristian Lina
Eversheds Lina & Guia SCA

Edita Lovin
Retired Judge of Romanian Supreme Court of Justice

Bogdan Lucan
Drakopoulos Law Firm

Ileana Lucian
Mușat & Asociații

Madalina Mailat
Clifford Chance

Smaranda Mandrescu
POP & Partners SCA Attorneys-at-Law

Gelu Titus Maravela
Maravela & Asociații

Neil McGregor
McGregor & Partners S.C.A.

Mirela Metea
Maravela & Asociații

Maria Cristina Metelet
POP & Partners SCA Attorneys-at-Law

Cătălina Mihăilescu
Țuca Zbârcea & Asociații

Stefan Mihartescu
D&B Davidși Baias Law Firm

Mihaela Mitroi
PwC Romania

Geanina Moraru
Clifford Chance Badea SCA

Mona Musat
Mușat & Asociații

Adriana Neagoe
National Bank of Romania

Larisa Negoias
DLA Piper Dinu SCA

Manuela Marina Nestor
Nestor Nestor Diculescu Kingston Petersen

Andreea Nica
DLA Piper Dinu SCA

Theodor Catalin Nicolescu
Nicolescu & Perianu Law Firm

Raluca Onufreiciuc
Săvescu & Asociații

Gabriela Oprea
Clifford Chance Badea SCA

Andrei Ormenean
Mușat & Asociații

Alexandra Ovedenie
DLA Piper Dinu SCA

Delia Paceagiu
Nestor Nestor Diculescu Kingston Petersen

Bogdan Papandopol
Dentons Europe

Mircea Parvu
SCPA Parvu si Asociatii

Marius Pătrășcanu
Maravela & Asociații

Laurentiu Petre
Săvescu & Asociații

Sergiu Petrea
SC Tecto Arhitectura Srl

Ana Maria Placintescu
Mușat & Asociații

Carolina Pletniuc
Lina & Guia SCA

Claudiu Pop
POP & Partners SCA Attorneys-at-Law

Alina Elena Popescu
Maravela & Asociații

Iulian Popescu
Mușat & Asociații

Mariana Popescu
National Bank of Romania

Tiberiu Potyesz
Bitrans Ltd.

Olga Preda
POP & Partners SCA Attorneys-at-Law

Cristian Radu
Țuca Zbârcea & Asociații

Laura Radu
STOICA & Asociații - Societate Civilă de Avocați

Raluca Radu
Dentons Europe

Magdalena Raducanu
Dentons Europe

Alexandra Radulescu
DLA Piper Dinu SCA

Eugen Radulescu
National Bank of Romania

Argentina Rafail
Dentons Europe

Lavinia Rasmussen
Nestor Nestor Diculescu Kingston Petersen

Corina Ricman
Clifford Chance Badea SCA

Bogdan Riti
Mușat & Asociații

Ioan Roman
Maravela & Asociații

Angela Rosca
Taxhouse SRL

Cristina Sandu
Taxhouse SRL

Raluca Sanucean
Țuca Zbârcea & Asociații

Andrei Săvescu
Săvescu & Asociații

Corina Simion
PwC Romania

Alina Solschi
Mușat & Asociații

Oana Soviani
Dentons Europe

David Stabb
Adghel Stabb & Partners

Georgiana Stan
DLA Piper Dinu SCA

Ionut Stancu
Nestor Nestor Diculescu Kingston Petersen

Oana-Lavinia Stancu
Drakopoulos Law Firm

Marie-Jeanna Stefanescu
RATEN-CITON

Tania Stefanita
Taxhouse SRL

Andrei Stoica
DLA Piper Dinu SCA

Izabela Stoicescu
Țuca Zbârcea & Asociații

Sorin Corneliu Stratula
Stratula Mocanu & Asociatii

Cătălina Sucaciu
Maravela & Asociații

Alina Tacea
Mușat & Asociații

Diana Tatulescu
Nestor Nestor Diculescu Kingston Petersen

Amelia Teis
D&B David și Baias Law Firm

Anda Todor
Dentons Europe

Adela Topescu
PwC Romania

Madalina Trifan
Dentons Europe

Ada Țucâ
Jinga & Asociații

Cristina Tutuianu
PwC Romania

Anca Maria Ulea
Mușat & Asociații

Andrei Vartires
Dentons Europe

Cristina Vedel
POP & Partners SCA Attorneys-at-Law

Luigi Vendrami
DHL International Romania

Maria Vlad
Jinga & Asociații

Stefan Zamfirescu
Zamfirescu Racoți & Partners Attorneys-at-Law

Ana Zaporojan
Maravela & Asociații

RUSSIAN FEDERATION

Arbitrazh Court of the City of Moscow

Defis-99

Federal Service for State Registration Cadastre and Cartography

Mosenergosbyt

Saint Petersburg Supply Company

Schneider Group SPb

Svyatoslav Abramov
Ministry of Economic Development

Andrei Afanasiev
Baker & McKenzie - CIS, Limited

Elena Agaeva
Egorov Puginsky Afanasiev & Partners Law Offices

Timur Akhmetshin
ALRUD Law Firm

Vera Akimkina

Anatoly E. Andriash
Norton Rose Fulbright (Central Europe) LLP

Olga Anikina
Baker & McKenzie

Natalya Antipina
Ministry of Construction and Communal Infrastructure

Vitaly Antonov
ESPRO Real Estate

Irina Anyukhina
ALRUD Law Firm

Suren Avakov
Avakov Tarasov & partners

Irina Babyuk
Committee on Investments

Marc Bartholomy
Clifford Chance

Gleb Bazurin
Lidings Law Firm

Elena Beier
Beier & Partners

Dennis Bekker
ALRUD Law Firm

Evgenia Belokon
Norton Rose Fulbright (Central Europe) LLP

Victoria Belykh
OKB - United Credit Bureau

Artem Berlin
Kachkin & Partners

Mikhail Beshtoyev

Dmitry Bessolitsyn
PricewaterhouseCoopers Russia BV

Egor Bogdanov
Gide Loyrette Nouel, member of Lex Mundi

Julia Borozdna
Pepeliaev Group

Thomas Brand
Brand & Partner

Maria Bykovskaya
Gide Loyrette Nouel, member of Lex Mundi

Lidiya Charikova
Liniya Prava Law Firm

Anna Chaykina
Capital Legal Services

Elena Chernishova
Interexpertiza LLC, member of AGN International

Alexander Chizhov
Ernst & Young

Dmitry Churin
Capital Legal Services

Vladimir Domashin
Gide Loyrette Nouel, member of Lex Mundi

Olga Duchenko
Kachkin & Partners

Anastasia Dukhina
Capital Legal Services

Arslan Dyakiev
PricewaterhouseCoopers Russia BV

Olga Egorova
Dentons

Vasina Ekaterina
ALRUD Law Firm

Ekaterina Ekimova
Yust Law Firm

Victoria Feleshtin
LEVINE Bridge

Evgenia Fomicheva
Mosinzhproekt OJSC

Ilya Fomin
Golsblat BLP

Elizaveta Fursova
Lidings Law Firm

Magomed Gasanov
ALRUD Law Firm

Vladimir Vladimirovich Golobokov
Center for Innovation and Information Technology Foundation

Vladimir Gorbunov
TSRRN (Center for Real Estate Development)

Igor Gorokhov
Capital Legal Services

Andrei Gusev
Borenius Attorneys

George Gutiev
Golsblat BLP

Roman Ibriyev
MOESK

Ekaterina Ilina
DS Law

Anton Isakov
Golsblat BLP

Anton Kabakov
Awara Group

Polina Kachkina
Kachkin & Partners

Maxim Kalinin
Baker & McKenzie

Nadezhda Karavanova
Department of Urban Planning Policy of Moscow

Kamil Karibov
Beiten Burkhardt Rechtsanwälte (Attorneys-at-Law)

Pavel Karpunin
Capital Legal Services

Ekaterina Karunets
Baker & McKenzie - CIS, Limited

Ivan Khaydurov
Hough Trofimov & Partners

Denis Khlopushin
Russin & Vecchi

Snezhana Kitaeva
Lenenergo

Alexander Kleschev
ALRUD Law Firm

Konstantin Kochetkov
Morgan Lewis

Vadim Kolomnikov
Debevoise & Plimpton LLP

Aleksey Konevsky
Pepeliaev Group

Daria Konoplina
Liniya Prava Law Firm

Anastasia Konovalova
Norton Rose Fulbright (Central Europe) LLP

Vadim Konyushkevich
Liniya Prava Law Firm

Vladislav Korablin
Pepeliaev Group

Alexander Korkin
Pepeliaev Group

Sergey Korolyov
Egorov Puginsky Afanasiev & Partners Law Offices

Igor Kostennikov
Yust Law Firm

Tatiana Kovalkova
Dentons

Alyona Kozyreva
Norton Rose Fulbright (Central Europe) LLP

Elena Krestyantseva
Pepeliaev Group

Anna Kruglova
Baker & McKenzie

Ekaterina Krylova
Agency for Strategic Initiatives

Anna Kukli
Egorov Puginsky Afanasiev & Partners Law Offices

Maria Kulikova
ASB Audit Company

Dmitry Kunitsa
Morgan Lewis

Irina Kuyantseva
ALRUD Law Firm

Roman Kuzmin
Liniya Prava Law Firm

Elena Kvartnikova
Egorov Puginsky Afanasiev & Partners Law Offices

David Lasfargue
Gide Loyrette Nouel, member of Lex Mundi

Ekaterina Lazorina
PwC Russia

Sergei Lee
Castrén & Snellman International Ltd.

Elena Lepneva
Capital Legal Services

Sergey Likhachev
Golsblat BLP

Anastasiya Likhanova
Geometriya

Yulia Litovtseva
Pepeliaev Group

Maxim Losik
Castrén & Snellman International Ltd.

Aleksandr Luboserdov
All Law Center

Anton Luzhanin
Russin & Vecchi

Igor N. Makarov
Baker & McKenzie - CIS, Limited

Alexei Yurievich Makarovsky
MOESK

Bagel Maksim Anatolyevich
Garant Energo

Sofya Mamonova
Norton Rose Fulbright (Central Europe) LLP

Alisa Manaka
MOESK

Grigory Marinichev
Morgan Lewis

Igor Marmalidi
Pepeliaev Group

Anna Maximenko
Debevoise & Plimpton LLP

Olga Mazina
Accountor Russia

Maxim Mezentsev
Yust Law Firm

Anastasia Mikhailova
Morgan Lewis

Michael Morozov
KPMG Russia

Ekaterina Motyvan
Yust Law Firm

Niyaz Muhametdinov
ZF KAMA

Anastasia Murzinova
DLA Piper

Andrey Naberezhniy
Liniya Prava Law Firm

Tatiana Nikolayevna Nekrasova
MOESK

Dmitry Nekrestyanov
Kachkin & Partners

Tatyana Neveeva
Egorov Puginsky Afanasiev & Partners

Natalie Neverovskaya
UNICOMLEGAL Russia

Alexey Nikitin
Borenius Attorneys

Gennady Odarich
PricewaterhouseCoopers Russia BV

Elena Odud
Awara Group

Elena Ogawa
LEVINE Bridge

Irina Onikienko
Capital Legal Services

Svetlana Panfilova
Debevoise & Plimpton LLP

Sergey Patrakeev
Lidings Law Firm

Sergey Petrachkov
ALRUD Law Firm

Maya Petrova
Borenius Attorneys

Sergei Pikin
Energy Development Fund

Ivan Podbereznyak
Debevoise & Plimpton LLP

Anna Ponomareva
Golsblat BLP

Sergei Vladimirovich Popov
OOO Skiv

Irina Potasova
OOO Nefteks

Ivan Potekhin
ESPRO Real Estate

Ilya Povetkin
Lenenergo

Natalia Prisekina
Russin & Vecchi

Svetlana Prokofieva
Lenenergo

Alexandr Pyatigor
MOESK

Alexander Rostovsky
Castrén & Snellman International Ltd.

Ekaterina Rudova
Capital Legal Services

Alexander Rudyakov
Yust Law Firm

Anna Rybalko
Deloitte & Touche CIS

Gudisa Sakania
MOESK

Artem Samoylov
Liniya Prava Law Firm

Kirill Saskov
Kachkin & Partners

Elena Sevastianova
Debevoise & Plimpton LLP

Alexei Shcherbakov
TsDS Group of Companies

Yulia Aleksandrovna Shirokova
MOESK

Victoria Sivachenko
ALRUD Law Firm

Nadezhda Sizikova
OOO Nefteks

Yury Smolin
De Berti Jacchia Franchini Forlani Studio Legale

Mihail Sergeevich Smolko
GSP Group

Alexander Sokolov
Arendt

Julia Solomkina
LEVINE Bridge

Ksenia Soloschenko
Castrén & Snellman International Ltd.

Elena Solovyeva
Agency for Strategic Initiatives

Sergey Sosnovsky
Pepeliaev Group

Alexandra Stelmakh
Egorov Puginsky Afanasiev & Partners Law Offices

Vladimir Stepanov
Egorov Puginsky Afanasiev & Partners Law Offices

Elena Subocheva
Russin & Vecchi

Evgeny Sumin
Accountor Russia

Dagadina Svetlana
Cliff Legal Services

Dmitry Tarasov
Avakov Tarasov & partners

Vladlena Terekhina
PricewaterhouseCoopers Russia BV

Tatiana Tereshchenko
Prime Advice St. Petersburg Law Office

Evgeny Timofeev
Golsblat BLP

Ksenia Tomilina
Gide Loyrette Nouel, member of Lex Mundi

Artem Toropov
Golsblat BLP

Sergei Tribus
Hough Trofimov & Partners

Alexander Tsakoev
Norton Rose Fulbright (Central Europe) LLP

Liubov Tsvetkova
Agency for Strategic Initiatives

Ilya Tur
Egorov Puginsky Afanasiev & Partners Law Offices

Aleksandra Ulezko
Kachkin & Partners

Anastasia Vasilieva
Beiten Burkhardt Rechtsanwälte (Attorneys-at-Law)

Igor Vasilyev
JSC MR Group

Artem Vasyutin
Deloitte & Touche CIS

Inna Vavilova
Prime Advice St. Petersburg Law Office

Polina Vodogreeva
LEVINE Bridge

Aleksei Volkov
National Bureau of Credit Histories

Taisiya Vorotilova
Baker & McKenzie

Viktoria Aleksandrovna Vostrosablina
MOESK

Andrey Yakushin
Central Bank of Russia

Vadim Yudenkov
OOO Geotechnic

Vladislav Zabrodin
Capital Legal Services

Andrey Zelenin
Lidings Law Firm

Roman Zhavner
Egorov Puginsky Afanasiev & Partners

Artem Zhavoronkov
Dentons

Evgeny Zhilin
Yust Law Firm

Maria Zhilina
Kachkin & Partners

RWANDA

Bolloré Africa Logistics

National Bank of Rwanda

Ray Amusengeri
PwC

Alberto Basomingera
Cabinet Zénith Law Firm

Flavia Busingye
East African Community Secretariat

Louis de Gonzague Mukerangabo
Vision Technologies Company

Paul Frobisher Mugambwa
PwC

Charles Gahima Nkusi
Bureau d'Etudes Charles Gahima Architecture

Claver Gakwavu
Rwanda Energy Group

Patrick Gashagaza
GPO Partners Rwanda

Ange D'arc Habeshahomungu
Ange D'arc Habeshahomungu - Notary

Jean Havugimana
ECODESEP Ltd.

Samuel Havugimana
Samuel Havugimana - Notary Public

Domina Izabayo
Izabayo Domina - Notary Public

Kabera Johnson
Kigali Allied Advocates

Francois Xavier Kalinda
University of Rwanda

Assiel Kamanzi
Assiel Kamanzi - Notary Public

Désiré Kamanzi
ENSafrica Rwanda

Tushabe Karim
Rwanda Development Board

Julien Kavaruganda
K-Solutions and Partners

Didas Kayihura
Fountain Advocates

Eudes Kayumba
Landmark Studio

Théophile Kazeneza
Cabinet d'Avocats Kazeneza

Patrice Manirakiza
Repro Ltd.

Lewis Manzi Rugema
Ecobank

Isaïe Mhayimana
Cabinet d'Avocats Mhayimana

Calvin Mitali
Equity Juris Chambers

Merard Mpabwanamaguru
City of Kigali - One Stop Center for Construction

Alex Mugire
Rwanda Customs

Esperance Mukamana
Rwanda Natural Resources Authority, Office of the Registrar of Land Titles

Léopold Munderere
Cabinet d'Avocats-Conseils

Alloys Mutabingwa
Aims Capital Attorneys

Pothin Muvara
Rwanda Natural Resources Authority, Office of the Registrar of Land Titles

Sylvain Muyombano
Rwanda Natural Resources Authority, Office of the Registrar of Land Titles

Geoffrey Mwine
GM Corporate Consult Limited (GMCC)

Apollinaire Ndabategereje
Ndabategereje Apollinaire - Notary Public

Egide Niyigena
Niyigena Egide - Notary Public

Innocent Nizeyimana
Nizeyimana Innocent - Notary Public

Aimable Nkuranga
TransUnion Rwanda

Emmanuel Nkurunziza

Martin Nkurunziza
GPO Partners Rwanda

Emile Nzabamwita
Case Consultants

Dieudonne Nzafashwanayo
ENSafrica Rwanda

Richard Rwihandagaza
R & Partners Law Firm

Fred Rwihunda
RFM Engineering Ltd.

Yves Sangano
Rwanda Development Board, Office of the Registrar General of Rwanda

Sandrali Sebakara
Bureau d'Etudes CAEDEC

Pierre Valery Singizumukiza
Singizumukiza Pierre Valery - Notary Public

Asante Twagira
ENSafrica Rwanda

Maureen Wamahiu
TransUnion Rwanda

SAMOA

Betham Brothers Enterprises Ltd.

Lesa Ma Penn

Alatina Ioelu
Small Business Enterprise Centre

Treena F. Atoa
Atoa Law Firm Lawyers & Notary Public

Ferila Brown
Planning and Urban Management Agency

Lawrie Burich
Quantum Contrax Ltd.

Shelley Burich
Quantum Contrax Ltd.

Lyndon Chu-Ling
Ministry of Commerce, Industry and Labour

Ruby Drake
Drake & Co.

Fiona Ey
Clarke Ey Lawyers

Patrick Fepuleai
Fepuleai & Roma

Anthony Frazier

Anne Godinet-Milbank
Ministry of Works, Transport & Infrastructure

Filisita Ikenasio-Heather
Ministry of Natural Resources & Environment

Misa Ioane Esoto
Misa Electrical

Komisi Koria
Clarke Ey Lawyers

Uputaua Lauvi
Ministry of Commerce, Industry and Labour

Tima Leavai
Leavai Law

Tuala Pat Leota
Public Accountant

Aaron Levine
Asian Development Bank

Peseta Margaret Malua
Ministry of Commerce, Industry and Labour

Albert Meredith
Ministry of Commerce, Industry and Labour

Atuaisaute Misipati
Small Business Enterprise Centre

Ameperosa Roma
Fepuleai & Roma

Peato Sam Ling
Samoa Shipping Services Ltd.

Faiiletasi Elaine Seuao
Ministry of Commerce, Industry and Labour

Sala Theodore Sialau Toalepai
Samoa Shipping Services Ltd.

Keilani Soloi
Soloi Survey Services

Ladesha Stevenson
Stevensons Lawyers

Grace Stowers
Stevensons Lawyers

Tessa Tone
Samoa Shipping Corporation

Helen Uiese
Ministry of Commerce, Industry and Labour

SAN MARINO

Simone Arcangeli
Avvocato e Notaio

Renzo Balsimelli
Ufficio Urbanistica

Dennis Beccari
Avv. Erika Marani

Gian Luca Belluzzi
Studio Commerciale Belluzzi

Gianna Burgagni
Studio Legale e Notarile

Cecilia Cardogna
Studio Legale e Notarile

Vincent Cecchetti
Cecchetti, Albani & Associati

Debora Cenni
Studio Legale e Notarile Lonfernini

Alberto Chezzi
Studio Chezzi

Sara Cupioli
Ufficio Tributario della Repubblica di San Marino

Alessandro de Mattia
Azienda Autonoma di Stato per i Servizi Pubblici

Laura Ferretti
Segreteria di Stato Industria Artigianato e Commercio Trasporti e Ricerca - Dipartimento Economia

Marcello Forcellini
Studio Chezzi

Davide Gasperoni
Ufficio Tributario della Repubblica di San Marino

Simone Gatti
World Line

Cinzia Guerretti
World Line

Anna Maria Lonfernini
Studio Legale e Notarile Lonfernini

Erika Marani
Avv. Erika Marani

Lucia Mazza
Ufficio Tecnico del Catasto

Daniela Mina

Gianlucca Minguzzi
Antao Progetti S.P.A.

Alfredo Nicolini
Lawyer

Fabio Pazzini
Shearman & Sterling LLP

Sara Pelliccioni
Studio Legale e Notarile Avv. Matteo Mularoni - in Associazione con Bussoletti Nuzzo & Associati

Cesare Pisani
Telecom Italia San Marino S.p.A.

Giuseppe Ragini
Studio Legale e Notarile Giuseppe Ragini

Daniela Reffi
Ufficio Tecnico del Catasto

Daniela Tombeni
S.M. Studio Sped

SÃO TOMÉ AND PRÍNCIPE

António de Barros A. Aguiar
SOCOGESTA

Eudes Aguiar
Aguiar & Pedronho Studio

Adelino Amado Pereira
Amado Pereira & Associados, Sociedade de Advogados

Ilza Amado Vaz
Direcção das Alfândegas

Luisenda Andrade
Direcção das Alfândegas

Joana Andrade Correia
Raposo Bernardo & Associados

Nuno Barata
Miranda & Associados

Nuria Brinkmann
Miranda & Associados

Paula Caldeira Dutschmann
Miranda Correia Amendoeira & Associados

Jaime Carvalho Esteves
PwC Portugal

Tânia Cascais
Miranda & Associados

Elísio Cruz
L.J. Cruz

Celiza Deus Lima
ODL & Associados

Cláudia do Carmo Santos
Miranda & Associados

Maria Figueiredo
Miranda & Associados

Saul Fonseca
Miranda & Associados

Abdulay Godinho
Direcção dos Registos e Notariado de São Tomé

Filipa Gonçalves
STP Counsel, member of the Miranda Alliance

Pedro Guiomar
Supermaritime São Tomé

Fernando Lima da Trindade
Ministry of Publics Works, Geographical-Cadastre, Natural Resources, and Environment

Sofia Martins
STP Counsel, member of the Miranda Alliance

Julio Martins Junior
Raposo Bernardo & Associados

Virna Neves
STP Counsel, member of the Miranda Alliance

Zerna Nezef
STP Counsel, member of the Miranda Alliance

Catarina Nunes
PwC Portugal

Guilherme Posser da Costa
Posser da Costa Advogados Associados

Miguel Bento Ribeiro
PwC Portugal

Cosme Bonfim Afonso Rita
Câmara de Comércio, Agricultura e Serviços

Hugo Rita
Terra Forma

Ilma Salvaterra
Guiché Único Para Empresas

Cláudia Santos Malaquias
Miranda & Associados

Daniel Vaz
Direcção das Alfândegas

Leendert Verschoor
PwC Portugal

Antônio Vicente Marques
AVM Advogados

SAUDI ARABIA

AlGasim Zamakhchary

Electricity & Co-Generation Regulatory Authority

Saudi Arabian General Investment Authority

Asad Abedi
The Law Firm of Hatem Abbas Ghazzawi & Co.

Fayyaz Ahmad
Jones Lang LaSalle

Omar Al Ansari
Legal Advisors, Abdulaziz I. Al-Ajlan & Partners in Association with Baker & McKenzie Limited

Mai Al Ashgar
Baker & McKenzie

Bassam Al Bassam
Al-Bassam

Fayez Al Debs
PwC Saudi Arabia

Majed Al Hedayan
Chamber of Commerce & Industry

Joza Al Rasheed
Baker & McKenzie

Khalid Al-Abdulkareem
Clifford Chance

Saud Al-Ammari
Blake, Cassels & Graydon LLP

Nizar Al-Awwad
Saudi Credit Bureau - SIMAH

Noura AlFahad
Baker & McKenzie

Nasser Alfaraj
Legal Advisors, Abdulaziz I. Al-Ajlan & Partners in Association with Baker & McKenzie Limited

Abdulaziz Alharthy
Dhabaan and Partners

Fatima Alhasan
Legal Advisors, Abdulaziz I. Al-Ajlan & Partners in Association with Baker & McKenzie Limited

Omar AlHoshan
AlHoshan CPAs & Consultants - member of Russell Bedford International

Yousef A. Al-Joufi
Al-Joufi Law Firm

Fahad I. Al-Khudairy
Fadha Engineering Consultants

Nabil Abdullah Al-Mubarak
Saudi Credit Bureau - SIMAH

Abdullah Aloqla
Dhabaan and Partners

Sultan Alqudiry
Saudi Credit Bureau - SIMAH

Wisam AlSindi
AlSindi Law Firm

Mohammed Al-Soaib
Al-Soaib Law Firm

Mashhour Altubaishi
Riyadh Municipality

Wicki Andersen
Baker Botts LLP

Haifa Bahaian
Baker & McKenzie

John Balouziyeh
Dentons

Nada Bashammakh
AlSindi Law Firm

Emad El-Hout
Alfanar Precast

Aisha Gondal
Baker & McKenzie

Fehem Hashmi
Clifford Chance

Amgad Husein
Dentons

Caroline Long
Legal Advisors, Abdulaziz I. Al-Ajlan & Partners in Association with Baker & McKenzie Limited

Zaid Mahayni
SEDCO Holding

Rukn Eldeen Mohammed
Omrania & Associates

Humaid Mudhaffr
Saudi Credit Bureau - SIMAH

Karim Nassar
Legal Advisors, Abdulaziz I. Al-Ajlan & Partners in Association with Baker & McKenzie Limited

Michael Quigley
Blake, Cassels & Graydon LLP

Mohammad Arif Saeed
Dhabaan and Partners

Muhammad Anum Saleem
Dhabaan and Partners

Ayman Salem
Vague Consultant Company

Rehana Shukkur
The Law Firm of Hatem Abbas Ghazzawi & Co.

Fouad Sindi
Clifford Chance

Faisal Tabbaa
Dhabaan and Partners

Zahi Younes
Baker & McKenzie

Soudki Zawaydeh
PwC Saudi Arabia

SENEGAL

BCEAO

Chambre des Notaires du Senegal

Senelec

Khaled Abou El Houda
Cabinet Kanjo Koita

Baba Aly Barro
PricewaterhouseCoopers Tax & Legal SA

Altiné Amadou Belko
CreditInfo VoLo

Mamadou Berthe
Atelier D' Architecture

Ibrahima Beye
Présidence de la République du Togo

Yolande Boissy Kabou
Etude Me Patricia Lake Diop

Ibrahima Diagne
Gainde 2000

Amadou Diouldé Diallo
Ministère de l'Urbanisme et de l'Assainissement

Maciré Diallo
SCP Ndiaye Diagne & Diallo Notaires Associés

Abdoul Aziz Dieng
Centre de Gestion Agrée de Dakar

Aziz Dieye
Cabinet Aziz Dieye

Mohamed Dieye
Tax & Legal Service Afrique SA

Abdou Birahim Diop
Direction du Developpement Urbain

Alioune Badara Diop
ONAS

Amadou Diop
Gainde 2000

Angelique Pouye Diop
APIX Agence Chargée de la Promotion de l'Investissement et des Grands Travaux

Andrée Diop-Depret
Ga 2 D

Medieumbe Diouf
ONAS

Yoro Diouf

Abdoulaye Drame
Cabinet Abdoulaye Drame

Bathilde Diouf Fall
Tax & Legal Service Afrique SA

Cheikh Fall
Cabinet d'Avocat Cheikh Fall

Fama de Sagama Fall Gueye
ONAS

Mor Talla Faye
Société Civile Professionnelle d'Avocats François Sarr & Associés

Moustapha Faye
Société Civile Professionnelle d'Avocats François Sarr & Associés

Catherine Faye Diop
Ordre des Architectes du Sénégal

Joseph Gbegnon
CreditInfo VoLo

Abdoulaye Gningue
Direction Générale des Impôts et Domaines

Antoine Gomis
SCP Senghor & Sarr, Notaires Associés

Papa Bathie Gueye
RMA Sénégal

Matthias Hubert
PricewaterhouseCoopers Tax & Legal SA

Alioune Ka
Étude SCP Mes Ka

Abdou Kader Konaté
Architecte DPLG

Oumy Kalsoum Gaye
Chambre de Commerce d'Industrie et d'Agriculture de Dakar

Abdou Dialy Kane
Cabinet Maître Abdou Dialy Kane

Mahi Kane
PricewaterhouseCoopers Tax & Legal SA

Ousseynou Lagnane
BDS

Patricia Lake Diop
Etude Me Patricia Lake Diop

Malick Lamotte
Tribunal de Grande Instance de Dakar

Armel Lane Zogning
Cabinet d'Avocat Cheikh Fall

Faty Balla Lo
CreditInfo VoLo

Moussa Mbacke
Etude Notariale Moussa Mbacke

Ngouda Mbaye
Hecto Energy

Saliou Mbaye
Hecto Energy

Birame Mbaye Seck
Direction du Developpement Urbain

Lamine Mboup
Socestra

Aly Mar Ndiaye
Commission de Régulation du Secteur de l'Electricité

Amadou Ndiaye
Cabinet d'Avocat Cheikh Fall

Amadou Moustapha Ndiaye
SCP Ndiaye Diagne & Diallo Notaires Associés

Elodie Dagneaux Ndiaye
APIX Agence Chargée de la Promotion de l'Investissement et des Grands Travaux

Francois Ndiaye
Direction Générale des Impôts et Domaines

Sadel Ndiaye
SCP Ndiaye & Mbodj

Macodou Ndour
Cabinet Macodou Ndour

Moustapha Ndoye
Cabinet Maitre Moustapha Ndoye

Macoumba Niang
Registre du Commerce et du Credit Mobilier

Maître Ibrahima Niang
Etude de Maître Ibrahima Niang

Souleymane Niang
Etude de Maître Ibrahima Niang

Babacar Sall
BDS

Mouhamadou Abass A. Sall
Lamtoro Studios

Adamou Sambaré
CreditInfo VoLo

Abdou Ben J. Sambou
Direction Générale des Impôts et Domaines

François Sarr
Société Civile Professionnelle d'Avocats François Sarr & Associés

Daniel-Sédar Senghor
SCP Senghor & Sarr, Notaires Associés

Serge Kouassy Siekouo
CreditInfo VoLo

Souleymane Sylla
CreditInfo VoLo

Ndèye Khoudia Tounkara
Etude Me Mayacine Tounkara et Associés

SERBIA

Senka Anđelković
National Alliance for Local Economic Development

Milos Anđelkovic
Wolf Theiss

Aleksandar Andrejic
Prica & Partners Law Office

Luka Andric
Andric Law Office

Aleksandar Arsic
PricewaterhouseCoopers Consulting d.o.o.

Bojana Arsic
Tebodin Consultants and Engineers

Vlado Babic
Air Speed

Marija Beljic
Advokatska Kancelarija Olјačić & Todorovic

Slavko Bingulac
Erste Group Immorent Serbia d.o.o.

Jelena Bojovic
National Alliance for Local Economic Development

Bojana Bregovic
Wolf Theiss

Milan Brkovic
Association of Serbian Banks

Marina Bulatovic
Wolf Theiss

Marija Čabarkapa
AVS Legal

Ana Čalić Turudija
Prica & Partners Law Office

Dejan Certic
Advokatska Kancelarija

Dragoljub Cibulić
BDK Advokati Attorneys-at-Law

Vladimir Dabić
The International Center for Financial Market Development

Marina Dacija
Belgrade Commercial Court

Milan Dakic
BDK Advokati Attorneys-at-Law

Jovica Damnjanovic
Development Consulting Group

Tanja Danojevic
Živković & Samardžić Law Office

Vladimir Dasić
BDK Advokati Attorneys-at-Law

Simon Dayes
CMS Cameron McKenna

Gili Dekel
Direct Capital S d.o.o.

Lidija Djeric
Law Offices Popovic, Popovic & Partners

Uroš Djordjević
Živković & Samardžić Law Office

Zeljko Djuric
Continental Wind

Jelena Kuveljic Dmitric
Law Offices Zecevic & Lukic

Stefan Dobrić
Law Offices Janković, Popović & Mitić

Veljko Dostanic
Marić, Mališić & Dostanić o.a.d.

Dragan Draca
PricewaterhouseCoopers Consulting d.o.o.

Ilija Drazic
Dražić, Beatović & Partners Law Office

Jovana Gavrilovic
Prica & Partners Law Office

Jelena Gazivoda
Law Offices Janković, Popović & Mitić

Danica Gligorijevic
Prica & Partners Law Office

Marko Janicijevic
Tomic Sindjelic Groza Law Office

Ana Jankov
BDK Advokati Attorneys-at-Law

Branko Jovičić
Advokatska Kancelarija

Nemanja Kačavenda
A.D. InterEuropa, Belgrade

Irena Kalmić
BDK Advokati Attorneys-at-Law

Dušan Karalić
DMK Tax & Finance

Marija Karalić
DMK Tax & Finance

Miodrag Klančnik
Marić, Mališić & Dostanić o.a.d.

Tijana Kojovic
BDK Advokati Attorneys-at-Law

Ivana Kopilovic
Kopilovic & Kopilovic

Milica Košutić
Law Offices Janković, Popović & Mitić

Filip Kovacevic
Deloitte d.o.o.

Vidak Kovacevic
Wolf Theiss

Ivan Krsikapa
Ninković Law Office

Zach Kuvizić
Kuvizic & Tadic Law Office

Kosta D. Lazic
Kosta D. Lazic

Milan Lazić
KN Karanović & Nikolić

Ružica Mačukat
Serbian Business Registers Agency

Miladin Maglov
Serbian Business Registers Agency

Rastko Malisic
Marić, Mališić & Dostanić o.a.d.

Aleksandar Mančev
Prica & Partners Law Office

Dragana Markovic
Development Consulting Group

Djordje Mijatov
Law Office Ilić

Predrag Milenković
Dražić, Beatović & Partners Law Office

Nenad Milić
PD Elektrodistribucija Beograd d.o.o.

Branko Milovanovic
Tebodin d.o.o.

Milena Mitić
KN Karanović & Nikolić

Aleksandar Mladenović
Rokas International Law Firm

Dejan Mrakovic
Deloitte d.o.o.

Veljko Nešić
Prica & Partners Law Office

Ivan Nikolic
BDK Advokati Attorneys-at-Law

Marija Nikolic
Kopilovic & Kopilovic

Dimitrije Nikolić
Gebruder Weiss d.o.o.

Djurdje Ninković
Ninković Law Office

Bojana Noskov
Wolf Theiss

Zvonko Obradović
Serbian Business Registers Agency

Darija Ognjenović
Prica & Partners Law Office

Igor Oljačić
Advokatska Kancelarija Oljačić & Todorovic

Stefan Pavlovic
Rokas International Law Firm

Vladimir Perić
Prica & Partners Law Office

Milan Petrović
Advokatska Kancelarija

Ms. Jasmina Petrović
City of Belgrade, Urbanism Department

Mihajlo Prica
Prica & Partners Law Office

Branka Rajicic
PricewaterhouseCoopers Consulting d.o.o.

Branimir Rajsic
Karanovic & Nikolic Law Firm

Adela Ristic
Marić, Mališić & Dostanić o.a.d.

Adrianae Ristic
Marić, Mališić & Dostanić o.a.d.

Branislav Ristić
Advokatska Kancelarija

Sonja Sehovac
Živković & Samardžić Law Office

Neda Spajić
Živković & Samardžić Law Office

Radmila Spasic
Delta Real Estate

Marko Srdanović
Municipality of Surcin

Mirjana Stankovic
Development Consulting Group

Dragana Stanojević
USAID Business Enabling Project - by Cardno Emerging Markets USA

Milica Stojanović
Law Offices Janković, Popović & Mitić

Petar Stojanović
Joksovic, Stojanović and Partners

Robert Sundberg
Development Consulting Group

Marko Tesanovic
Wolf Theiss

Ana Tomic
Joksovic, Stojanović and Partners

Jovana Tomić
Živković & Samardžić Law Office

Snežana Tosić
Serbian Business Registers Agency

Tanja Unguran
Karanovic & Nikolic Law Firm

Srećko Vujaković
Moravčević, Vojnović & Zdravković u saradnji sa Schönherr

Tanja Vukotić Marinković
Serbian Business Registers Agency

Milena Vuković Buha
Ajilon Solutions

Miloš Vulić
Prica & Partners Law Office

Djordje Zejak
BDK Advokati Attorneys-at-Law

Miloš Živković
Živković & Samardžić Law Office

Igor Živkovski
Živković & Samardžić Law Office

SEYCHELLES

Office of the Attorney General

Public Utilities Corporation

Seychelles Ports Authority

Seychelles Revenue Commission

Fanette Albert
Seychelles Planning Authority

Laura A. Alcindor Valabhji

Justin Bacharie
Electrical Consultant Seychelles

Wasoudeo Balloo
KPMG

Karishma Beegoo
Appleby

Terry Biscornet
Seychelles Planning Authority

Juliette Butler
Appleby

Alex Ellenberger
Add Locus Architects Ltd.

Bernard Georges
Georges & Georges

Fred Hoareau
Company and Land Registry

Gerard Hoareau
Seychelles Planning Authority

Durai Karunakaran
Judiciary of the Seychelles

Conrad Lablache
Pardiwalla Twomey Lablache

Carlos Loizeau
Central Bank of Seychelles

Malcolm Moller
Appleby

Margaret Nourice
Stamp Duty Commission

Brian Orr
MEJ Electrical

Zara Pardiwalla
Pardiwalla Twomey Lablache

Wendy Pierre
Company and Land Registry

Lucie Antoinette Pool
Attorney

Divino Sabino
Pardiwalla Twomey Lablache

Brohnsonn Winslow
Winslow Naya Consulting

SIERRA LEONE

Amos Odame Adjei
PwC Ghana

Alfred Akibo-Betts
National Revenue Authority

Gideon Ayi-Owoo
PwC Ghana

Isiaka Balogun
KPMG

Mallay F. Bangura
Electricity Distribution and Supply Authority

Ayesha Bedwei
PwC Ghana

Anthony Y Brewah
Brewah & Co.

Sonia Browne
CLAS Consult Ltd.

David Carew
Freetown Nominees

Solade Carpenter
BDO

Beatrice Chaytor
Chariot Eight

Siman Mans Conteh
Income Tax Board of Appellate Commissioners

Kwesi Amo Dadson
PwC Ghana

Ibrahim Musa Dumbuya
Bank of Sierra Leone

Mariama Dumbuya
Renner Thomas & Co., Adele Chambers

Momoh Dumbuya
Electricity Distribution and Supply Authority

Joseph Fofanah
Office of the Administrator and Registrar General (OARG)

Manilius Garber
Jarrett-Yaskey, Garber & Associates: Architects (JYGA)

Emilia Gbomor
CLAS Consult Ltd.

Ahmed Yassin Jallo - Jamboria
National Revenue Authority

Cyril Jalloh
National Social Security and Insurance Trust

Ransford Johnson
Lambert & Partners, Premiere Chambers

Henrietta Johnston
CLAS Consult Ltd.

Donald Jones
Ministry of Lands, Country Planning and the Environment

Mariama Seray Kallay
Office of the Administrator and Registrar General, Government of Sierra Leone

Jerrie Kamara
KPMG

Mohamed Kamara
Freetown Nominees

Melvin Khabenje
CLAS Consult Ltd.

George Kwatia
PwC Ghana

Peter Larvai
Bank of Sierra Leone

Millicent Lewis-Ojumu
CLAS Consult Ltd.

Chrispina Luke
BDO

Michala Mackay
Corporate Affairs Commission of Sierra Leone

Sahada Mahama
PwC Ghana

Ibrahim Mansaray
Fast Track Commercial Court

Clifford Marcus-Roberts
KPMG

Corneleius Max-Williams
Destiny Shipping Agencies Ltd.

Mohamed Pa Momoh Fofanah
Edrina Chambers

Tamba P. Ngegba
Ministry of Works Housing and Infrastructure (MWH&I)

Samuel Abayomi Noldred
BDO

Francis Nyama
Electricity Distribution and Supply Authority

Sidney Ojumu
CLAS Consult Ltd.

John Dudley Okrafo-Smart
CLAS Consult Ltd.

Afolabi Oluwole
Customerworth

Eduard Parkinson
Electricity Distribution and Supply Authority

Christopher J. Peacock
Serpico Trading Enterprises

Edward Siaffa
National Revenue Authority

Alvin Tamba
KPMG

Rodney O. Temple
EROD Construction & Engineering Services

Valisius Thomas
Advent Chambers

Donald Samuel Williams
National Revenue Authority (NRA) Large Taxpayers Office (LTO), Domestic Tax Department (DTD)

Prince Williams
Corporate Affairs Commission of Sierra Leone

Yada Williams
Yada Williams and Associate

SINGAPORE

Allen & Gledhill LLP

EY Singapore

Insolvency and Public Trustee's Office

State Courts

Lim Ah Kuan
SP PowerGrid Ltd.

Patrick Ang
Rajah & Tann Singapore LLP

Yvonne Ang
Public Utilities Board

Caroline Berube
HJM Asia Law & Co. LLC

YC Chee
RSM Chio Lim LLP

Jennifer Chia
TSMP Law Corporation

Hooi Yen Chin
Polaris Law Corporation

Koon Fun Chin
Urban Redevelopment Authority

Ng Chin Lock
SP PowerGrid Ltd.

Chee Beow Chng
Chip Eng Seng Corporation Ltd.

Kit Min Chye
Tan Peng Chin LLC

Kamil Dada
TetraFlow Pte Ltd.

Charmaine Deng
Building & Construction Authority

Eric Eio
Paul Hype Page Management Service Pte. Ltd.

Miah Fok
Credit Bureau Singapore Pte. Ltd.

Joseph Foo
The National Environment Agency

Sandy Foo
Drew & Napier LLC

Don Ho
Don Ho & Associates

Kaiwei Ho
Ministry of Manpower

Jay Jay
Just R. Transport Enterprise Pte Ltd.

Chong Kah Kheng
Rajah & Tann Singapore LLP

Lam Fong Kiew
Nexia TS Tax Services Pte. Ltd.

Soo How Koh
PwC Singapore

Wong Kum Hoong
Energy Market Authority

K. Latha
Accounting & Corporate Regulatory Authority, ACRA

Dave Lau
Accounting & Corporate Regulatory Authority, ACRA

Yvonne Lay
Inland Revenue Authority of Singapore

Lee Lay See
Rajah & Tann Singapore LLP

Eng Beng Lee
Rajah & Tann Singapore LLP

Yuan Lee
Wong Tan & Molly Lim LLC

Yik Wee Liew
Wong Partnership LLP

Peng Hong Lim
PH Consulting Pte. Ltd.

William Lim
Credit Bureau Singapore Pte. Ltd.

Wai Hui Ling
Building & Construction Authority

Joseph Liow
Straits Law

Eugene Luah
Drew Napier

Renu Rajan Menon
Drew Napier

Madan Mohan
MDR Ltd.

Girish Naik
PwC Singapore

Beng Hong Ong
Wong Tan & Molly Lim LLC

Muthu Palanivelu
Cyclect Electrical Engineering Pte. Ltd.

Lilian Quah
Ministry of Manpower

Teck Beng Quek
Land Transport Authority

Meera Rajah
Rajah & Tann Singapore LLP

Lim Bok Hwa Sandy
Just R. Transport Enterprise Pte Ltd.

Kwan Kiat Sim
Rajah & Tann Singapore LLP

Hak Khoon Tan
Energy Market Authority

Tay Lek Tan
PwC Singapore

Siu Ing Teng
Singapore Land Authority

Elaine Teoh
Ministry of Trade & Industry

Siew Kwong Wong
Energy Market Authority

Elaine Yeo
Singapore Customs

Jennifer Yeo
MDR Ltd.

Jennifer Yip Yoke Fun
Building & Construction Authority

Isaac Yong
Fire Safety & Shelter Department

SLOVAK REPUBLIC

Zárecký Zeman

Ján Budinský
CRIF - Slovak Credit Bureau, s.r.o.

Peter Čavojský
CLS Čavojský & Partners, s.r.o.

Katarína Čechová
Čechová & Partners s. r. o.

Tomas Cermak
Weinhold Legal

Tomáš Cibuía
White & Case s.r.o.

Peter Drenka
Hamala Kluch Víglaský s.r.o.

Jan Dvorecky
Green Integrated Logistics (Slovakia) s.r.o.

Sona Farkasova
Monarex Audit Consulting

Matúš Fojtl
Geodesy, Cartography and Cadastre Authority

Roman Hamala
Hamala Kluch Víglaský s.r.o.

Tatiana Hlušková
Ministry of Economy

Peter Hodál
White & Case s.r.o.

Barbora Hrabcakova
White & Case s.r.o.

Veronika Hrušovská
PRK Partners s.r.o.

Miroslav Jalec
Západoslovenská Distribučná AS

Jakub Jura
DEDÁK & Partners

Mária Juraševská
PwC Slovakia

Michaela Jurková
Čechová & Partners s. r. o.

Tomáš Kamenec
DEDÁK & Partners

Marián Kapec
Západoslovenská Distribučná AS

Kristina Klenova
White & Case s.r.o.

Martin Kluch
Hamala Kluch Víglaský s.r.o.

Roman Konrad
Profinam, s.r.o.

Miroslav Kopac
National Bank of Slovakia

Peter Kovac
Ministry of Economy

Jakub Kováčik
CLS Čavojský & Partners, s.r.o.

Soňa Lehocká
Aliancia advokátov ak, s.r.o.

Frantisek Lipka
ULC Čarnogurský s.r.o.

Jakub Malý
Detvai Ludik Malý Udvaros

Nina Molcanova
PwC Slovakia

Tomáš Morochovič
White & Case s.r.o.

Miloš Nagy
Západoslovenská Distribučná AS

Andrea Olšovská
PRK Partners s.r.o.

Peter Ondrejka
Ministry of Economy

Ladislav Pompura
Monarex Audit Consulting

Simona Rapavá
White & Case s.r.o.

Katarina Rohacova
Monarex Audit Consulting

Gerta Sámelová-Flassiková
Aliancia advokátov ak, s.r.o.

Zuzana Satkova
PwC Slovakia

Christiana Serugova
PwC Slovakia

Jakub Skaloš
Ministry of Economy

Jaroslav Škubal
PRK Partners s.r.o.

Otakar Weis
PwC Slovakia

Katarina Zaprazna
PwC Slovakia

Michal Zathurecky
White & Case s.r.o.

Miroslav Zaťko
Čechová & Partners s. r. o.

SLOVENIA

Law Firm Neffat

Gregor Berkopec
Deloitte

Nina Bogataj
Supreme Court Land Registry Department

Miodrag Dordevic
Supreme Court of the Republic of Slovenia

Maša Drkušič
ODI Law Firm

Andrej Ekart
Ministry of Justice

Luka Fabiani

Mojca Fakin
CMS Legal

Aleksander Ferk
PwC Svetovanje d.o.o.

Ana Filipov
Filipov o.p.d.o.o. in cooperation with Schoenherr Rechtsanwalte GmbH

Pavle Flere

Tina Fuchs
Bank of Slovenia

Tajka Golob
Gross & Golob

Alenka Gorenčič
Deloitte

Mia Gostinčar
Law Firm Miro Senica and Attorneys Ltd.

Eva Gostisa
Jadek & Pensa d.o.o. - o.p.

Hermina Govekar Vičič
Banka Slovenije - Credit Register SISBON

Teja Grad
Odvetniki Šelih & partnerji, o.p., d.n.o

Damijan Gregorc
Law Firm Miro Senica and Attorneys Ltd.

Damjana Iglič
Bank of Slovenia

Branko Ilić
ODI Law Firm

Andraž Jadek

Matjaž Jan
ODI Law Firm

Andrej Jarkovič
Law Firm Janežič & Jarkovič Ltd.

Jernej Jeraj
CMS Legal

Sabina Jereb
Ministry for Environmental and Spatial Planning

Boris Kastelic
Financial Institution of the Republic of Slovenia

Lovro Kleindienst
Transocean Shipping

Miro Košak
Notary Office Košak

Brigita Kraljič
CMS Legal

Nina Kristarič
Jadek & Pensa d.o.o. - o.p.

Sabina Lamut
Lamuts d.o.o

Borut Leskovec
Jadek & Pensa d.o.o. - o.p.

Jera Majzelj
Odvetniki Šelih & Partnerji

Miroslav Marchev
PwC Svetovanje d.o.o.

Matjaž Miklavčič
SODO d.o.o.

Bojan Mlaj
Energy Agency of the Republic of Slovenia

Mojca Muha
Law Firm Miro Senica and Attorneys Ltd.

Jože Murko
Dodoma d.o.o.

Ela Omersa
CMS Legal

Sonja Omerza
Deloitte

Aljaz Perme
Ministry of Justice

Miroslav Pikovnik
UNIJA računovodska hiša d.d.

Nataša Pipan-Nahtigal
Odvetniki Šelih & Partnerji

Petra Plevnik
Law Firm Miro Senica and Attorneys Ltd.

Bojan Podgoršek
Notariat

Anka Pogačnik
PwC Svetovanje d.o.o.

Luka Pregelj

Jasmina Rešidović
Notary Office Košak

Konstanca Rettinger
Banka Slovenije - Credit Register SISBON

Ema Rode
Ministry of Finance

Patricija Rot

Sanja Savic
Deloitte

Bostjan Sedmak
Odvetnik Sedmak

Branka Sedmak
Jadek & Pensa d.o.o. - o.p.

Jaka Simončič
Jadek & Pensa d.o.o. - o.p.

Andreja Škofič Klanjšček
Deloitte

Nives Slemenjak
Schoenherr

Petra Smolnikar
Schoenherr

Rok Starc
Notary Office Košak

Gregor Strojin
Supreme Court of the Republic of Slovenia

Tilen Terlep
Odvetniki Šelih & Partnerji

Nevenka Tory
Notary Nevenka Tory

Ana Vran
Law firm Fabiani, Petrovic, Jeraj, Ltd.

Sara Vrhunc
Jadek & Pensa d.o.o. - o.p.

Nina Žefran
Deloitte

Nina Zupan
Supreme Court of the Republic of Slovenia

Tina Žvanut Mioč

SOLOMON ISLANDS

Company Haus - Registrar of Companies

Credit & Data Bureau Limited

Rodney Begley
TRADCO Shipping

Don Boykin
Pacific Architects Ltd.

Anthony Frazier

Julie Haro
Premiere Group of Companies Ltd.

Jarrod Harrington
Asian Development Bank

Douglas Hou

Sebastian Ilala
BJS Agencies Ltd.

John Katahanas
Sol - Law

Aaron Levine
Asian Development Bank

Wayne Morris
Morris & Sojnocki Chartered Accountants

Maurice Nonipitu
Kramer Ausenco

Megan Praeger
Honiara City Council

Livingston Saepio
Honiara City Council

Gregory Joseph Sojnocki
Morris & Sojnocki Chartered Accountants

John Sullivan
Sol - Law

Gabriel Suri
Suri's Law Practice

Makario Tagini
Global Lawyers, Barristers & Solicitor

Cindrella Vunagi
Honiara City Council

Pamela Wilde
Ministry for Justice and Legal Affairs

Yolande Yates

John Zama
Light Lawyers

SOMALIA

Hafsa Aamin
Ministry of Foreign Affairs

Mohamed A. Abdi
Galmudug Chamber of Commerce and Industry

Abdulwahab Hassan Abdullahi
CXC Company

Ismail Abdullahi
Ministry of Labour and Social Affairs

Zainab Adam
Mogadishu Chamber of Commerce & Industry

Abdisalam Mohamed Addow
Ministry of Commerce & Industry

Abdikarin Mohamed Ahmed
Horn Legal Consulting Services

Tahlil H. Ahmed
Horn Legal Consulting Services

Osman Ahmed Ali
SOMTECH Construction

Maryan Ahmed Harun
Horn Legal Consulting Services

Mohamed Ali
Simatech International - Sima Marine Ltd.

Raage Mohamed Ali
Ministry of Commerce & Industry

Abdullahir Ali Adow
Mayor's Office at the Municipality of Mogadishu

Saiid Ali Osoble
Mogadishu Public Notary

Dhoore Bile
East Africa Modern Engineering Company (EAMECO)

Abdi Abshir Dorre
Mogadishu Chamber of Commerce & Industry

Mohamed Dubad
East Africa Modern Engineering Company (EAMECO)

Hassan Mohammed Farah
Holac Construction Company

Suldan Farah

Omar Faruq Sheikh
Howlson Forwarding and Clearance

Abdullahi Ahmed Gutale
Somali Chamber of Commerce & Industry

Abdiwahid Osman Haji
Mogadishu Law Office

Mahdi Hassan
Daryeel Shipping and Forwarding

Mohamed Ali Hassan
Ministry of Commerce & Industry

Mohamed Jackub Hassan
Ministry of Commerce & Industry

Abdirahman Hassan Wardere
Mogadishu University

Mohamed Ahmed Hussein
Ministry of Labour and Social Affairs

Said Mohamed Hussein
Ministry of Commerce & Industry

Ahmed Jaura Ehure
Adami General Service

Abdulqadir Omar Kaatib
Kaatib Public Notary

Godfrey Kleuna Macharia

Abdukadir Osman Mohamed
Ministry of Commerce & Industry

Sadia Hassan Mohamed
Sima Marine Somalia

Hassan Mohamed Ali
Mogadishu Law Office

Bashir Mohamed Sheikh
Mogadishu University

Abdiwahad Mohamud
Mogadishu Chamber of Commerce & Industry

Abdullahi Ahmed Mohed
Ministry of Commerce & Industry

Sabriye Moallim Musse
Ministry of Commerce & Industry

Hassan Noor
Hanvard Africa

Hilal Osman
FSO Insurance

Koshir Osman
Sima Marine Somalia

Samia Saciid
East Africa Modern Engineering Company (EAMECO)

Hassan Yussuf
International Bank of Somalia

SOUTH AFRICA

Norton Rose Fulbright South Africa

Gerhard Badenhorst
ENS

Claire Barclay
Cliffe Dekker Hofmeyr Inc.

Lauren Becker
Werksmans Inc.

Ashley Kim Biggs
Bid Corporation Limited

Kobus Blignaut
Attorney

Tony Bolton
Tony Bolton Architect

Brendon Christian
Business Law BC

Haydn Davies
Webber Wentzel

Gretchen de Smit
ENS

Heather Dodd
Savage + Dodd Architects

Kim Goss
Bowman Gilfillan Inc.

Anine Greeff
TransUnion

Wesley Grimm
Webber Wentzel

Njabulo Hlophe
Werksmans Inc.

Tobie Jordaan
Cliffe Dekker Hofmeyr Inc.

J. Michael Judin
Judin Combrinck Inc. Attorneys

Lisa Koenig
TransUnion

Leza Marie Kotzé
Shepstone & Wylie

Lloyd Langenhoven
Bowman Gilfillan Inc.

Paul Lategan
Shepstone & Wylie

Johnathan Leibbrandt
Webber Wentzel

Eric Levenstein
Werksmans Inc.

Shoayb Loonat
Enumerate Consulting

Kyle Mandy
PwC South Africa

Mahomed Monga
Grosskopff Lombart Huyberechts & Associates Architects

Kacey Moses
African Seas Freight Forwarders

Callum O'Connor
Baker & McKenzie

Graeme Palmer
Garlicke & Bousfield Inc.

Kwanele Radebe
The Standard Bank of South Africa Limited

Binayka Rama
Activate Architecture (Pty) Ltd.

Malope Ramagaga
CityPower

Lucinde Rhoodie
Cliffe Dekker Hofmeyr Inc.

Shirley Salvoldi
Eskom

Chelsea Efrat Shar
Bowman Gilfillan Inc.

Richard Shein
Bowman Gilfillan Inc.

Yondela Silimela
City of Johannesburg - Building Development Management

Rajat Ratan Sinha
RCS Pvt. Ltd. Business Advisors Group

Ian Statham
BDO

Riaan Stipp
PwC South Africa

Danie Strachan
Adams & Adams

Jane Strydom
TransUnion

Anastasia Vatalidis
Werksmans Inc.

Paul Vermulan
CityPower

Jean Visagie
PwC South Africa

Rory Voller
Companies and Intellectual Property Commission (CIPC)

Anthony Whittaker
CityPower

Gareth Williams-Wynn
Karter Margub & Associates

Colin Wolfsohn
Wolfsohn and Associates

Sicelo Xulu
CityPower

SOUTH SUDAN

Ministry of Electricity and Dams

Mufti Othaneil Akum
Ministry of Justice

Mutakhul Ali

Roda Allison Dokolo
Lomoro & Co. Advocates

Monyluak Alor Kuol
Liberty Advocates LLP

Jimmy Araba Parata
Engineering Council of South Sudan

Gabriel Isaac Awow
Ministry of Justice

Martijn Breedveld
Recon FM International

Christo Jada
RCB Consulting Co. Ltd.

Jimmy Kato
Jireh Services Company Limited

Kamba Kenyi
Department of Housing

Biju Kumar MS
Bolloré Africa Logistics

Hellen Achiro Lotara
Central Equatoria Ministry of Labor, Public Service & Human Resources

Robert Lwoki
South Sudan Land Commission

Petro Maduk Deng
Qatar National Bank South Sudan

Ramadhan A.M. Mogga
Ramadhan & Law Associates

Issa Muzamil
Juba Associated Advocates

Peter Atem Ngor
Rhino Stars

Peter Pitya
Ministry of Housing

Lomoro Robert Bullen
Lomoro & Co. Advocates

Emmanuel Sadaraka
U.V.

Jeremaih Sauka
Ministry of Justice

Sara Seyoum
X-REME Architects

James Tadiwe
National Consultants Association

Paul Wanambuko
Accountant

Daniel Wani
Engineering Council of South Sudan

SPAIN

Basilio Aguirre
Registro de la Propiedad de España

Inigo Alejandre
Ashurst LLP

Angel Alonso Hernández
Uría & Menéndez, member of Lex Mundi

Alfonso Alvarado Planas
Dirección General de Industria, Energía y Minas

Javier Álvarez
J&A Garrigues SLP

Elena Álvarez Fernández
Addient

José Ignacio Antón
DLA Piper Spain SLU

Jacobo Archilla Martín-Sanz
Asociacion/Colegio Nacional de Ingenieros del ICAI

Irene Arévalo
White & Case

Serena Argente Escartín
Raposo Bernardo & Associados

Nuria Armas
Banco de España

Ana Armijo
Ashurst LLP

Ana Galán Arquiaga
Cleanergetic SEERS Solutions SLU

Antonio Bautista
Cleanergetic SEERS Solutions SLU

Denise Bejarano
Pérez - Llorca

Andrés Berral
Clifford Chance

Henar Bocigas Arias
J&A Garrigues SLP

Vicente Bootello
J&A Garrigues SLP

Agustín Bou
Jausas

Héctor Bouzo Cortejosa
Solcaisur S.L.

Antonio Bravo
Evershed Nicea

Laura Camarero
Baker & McKenzie

Laura Lanos Camarero
DLA Piper Spain SLU

Rosalia Cambronero
Dirección General del Espacio Público, Ayuntamiento de Madrid

Lola Cano
Banco de España

Clotilde Abascal Cánovas
DLA Piper Spain SLU

Adriana Carrasco
DLA Piper Spain SLU

Alvaro Cid-Luna
DLA Piper Spain SLU

Lorenzo Clemente Naranjo
J&A Garrigues SLP

Miguel Cruz Amorós
PwC Spain

Leonardo Felice Cultrera Munoz
Aster Abogados

Pelayo de Salvador Morell
DeSalvador Real Estate Lawyers

Iván Delgado González
Pérez - Llorca

Rossanna D'Onza
Baker & McKenzie

Iván Escribano
J&A Garrigues SLP

Antonio Fernández
J&A Garrigues SLP

Adriadna Galimany
Gómez-Acebo & Pombo Abogados

Patricia Garcia
Baker & McKenzie

Valentín García González
Cuatrecasas, Gonçalves Pereira

Ignacio García Silvestre
Baker & McKenzie

Borja García-Alamán
J&A Garrigues SLP

Héctor Gómez Ferrero
DLA Piper Spain SLU

Juan Ignacio Gomeza Villa
Notario de Bilbao

Carlos Rueda Gómez-Calcerrada
Gómez-Acebo & Pombo Abogados

Flaminia González-Barba Bolza
White & Case

David Grasa Graell
Monereo, Meyer & Marinel-Lo Abogados SLP

Juan Miguel Hernandez Herrera
Uría & Menéndez, member of Lex Mundi

Gabriele Hofmann
Fourlaw Abogados

Alejandro Huertas León
J&A Garrigues SLP

Tatiana Llorente
Uría Menéndez

Juan Carlos Bleda López
DLA Piper Spain SLU

Marina Lorente
J&A Garrigues SLP

Alberto Lorenzo
Banco de España

Joaquin Macias
Ashurst LLP

Alberto Manzanares
Ashurst LLP

Daniel Marín
Gómez-Acebo & Pombo Abogados

Sergio Martin
Equifax Iberica

Ignacio Martín Martín Fernández
Cazorla Abogados, SLP

Bartolomé Martín Fernéndez
DLA Piper Spain SLU

Jorge Martín-Fernández
Clifford Chance

Alberto Mata
The Spain American Bar Association

José Manuel Mateo
J&A Garrigues SLP

María Jesús Mazo Venero
Consejo General del Notariado

José María Menéndez Sánchez
Asociacion/Colegio Nacional de Ingenieros del ICAI

Valentin Merino Lopez
Valentin Merino Arquitectos SL

Alberto Monreal Lasheras
PwC Spain

Pedro Moreira dos Santos
SCA Legal

Eva Mur Mestre
PwC Spain

Pedro Neira
Cazorla Abogados, SLP

Àlex Nistal Vázquez
Monereo, Meyer & Marinel-Lo Abogados SLP

Alejandro Nuñez Jimenez
Cleanergetic SEERS Solutions SLU

Rafael Núñez-Lagos
Uría & Menéndez, member of Lex Mundi

Álvaro Felipe Ochoa Pinzón
J&A Garrigues SLP

Francisco Pablo
DHL Express

Isabel Palacios
Clifford Chance

Carla Palau Segura
Gómez-Acebo & Pombo Abogados

Daniel Parejo Ballesteros
J&A Garrigues SLP

Julio Peralta de Arriba
White & Case

María José Plaza
Asociacion/Colegio Nacional de Ingenieros del ICAI

Carlos Pol
Jausas

Ignacio Quintana
PwC Spain

Nelson Raposo Bernardo
Raposo Bernardo & Associados

Fátima Rico-Villademoros González
DLA Piper Spain SLU

Álvaro Rifá
Uría Menéndez

Eduardo Rodríguez-Rovira
Uría & Menéndez, member of Lex Mundi

Álvaro Rojo
J&A Garrigues SLP

Javier Romeu
TIBA Internacional SA

Irene Rueda Liñares
Gómez-Acebo & Pombo Abogados

Mireia Sabate
Baker & McKenzie

Jaime Salvador
Russell Bedford España Auditores y Consultores SL - member of Russell Bedford International

José Sánchez
Eversheds Nicea

Eduardo Santamaría Moral
J&A Garrigues SLP

Pablo Santos Fita
Deloitte Abogados

Miguel Sarabia
DLA Piper Spain SLU

Aída Sevillano
DLA Piper Spain SLU

Raimon Tagliavini
Uría Menéndez

Francisco Téllez de Gregorio
Fourlaw Abogados

Adrián Thery
J&A Garrigues SLP

Roberto Tojo Thomas de Carranza
Clifford Chance

Victoriano Travieso
Stepinlaw S.L.P.

Alejandro Valls
Baker & McKenzie

Adrián Vázquez
Uría & Menéndez, member of Lex Mundi

Juan Verdugo
J&A Garrigues SLP

Fernando Vives Ruiz
J&A Garrigues SLP

Marta Zarco
Eversheds Nicea

Natalia Zumárraga
DLA Piper Spain SLU

SRI LANKA

Asanka Abeysekera
Tiruchelvam Associates

Nihal Sri Ameresekere
Consultants 21 Ltd.

Surangi Arawwawala
PwC Sri Lanka

Peshala Attygalle
Nithya Partners

Harsha Cabral
Chamber's of Harsha Cabral

Senajith Dasanayake
Ceylon Electricity Board

Chamari de Silva
F.J. & G. De Saram

Nilmini Ediriweera
Julius & Creasy

Manjula Ellepola
F.J. & G. De Saram

Amila Fernando
Julius & Creasy

Anjali Fernando
F.J. & G. De Saram

Ayomi Fernando
Employers' Federation of Ceylon

Bimal Fernando
Project Services Ltd.

P.N.R. Fernando
Colombo Municipal Council

Saman Gamage
Ceylon Electricity Board

Thuwaraka Ganeshan
Tiruchelvam Associates

Thambippillai Gobalasingam
Deloitte

Jivan Goonetilleke
D.L. & F. De Saram

Naomal Goonewardena
Nithya Partners

Ramal Gunasekera
LAN Management Development Service

Shehara Gunasekera
F.J. & G. De Saram

Anandhiy Gunawardhana
Julius & Creasy

Thilanka Namalie Haputhanthrie
Julius & Creasy

Dharshika Herath Gunaratne
Sudath Perera Associates

M. Basheer Ismail
Deloitte

Sonali Jayasuriya-Rajapakse
D.L. & F. De Saram

Shamalie Jayatunge
Attorney-at-Law

Keerthi Jayawardana
LAN Management Development Service

Sanjaya Jayawardene
Progressive Design Associates

Niral Kadawatharatchie
Freight Links International (Pte.) Ltd.

Yudhishtran Kanagasabai
PwC Sri Lanka

Charana Kanankegamage
F.J. & G. De Saram

H.E.I. Karunarathna
Colombo Municipal Council

Sankha Karunaratne
F.J. & G. De Saram

Uma Kitulgoda
F.J. & G. De Saram

Janaka Lakmal
Credit Information Bureau Ltd.

Ishara Madarasinghe
F.J. & G. De Saram

Kandiah Neelakandan
Neelakandan & Neelakandan

Abirami Nithiananthan
Tiruchelvam Associates

Nirosha Peiris
Tiruchelvam Associates

Priyantha Peiris
Colombo Municipal Council

Dayaratne Perera
Colombo Municipal Council

K.L.G. Thilak Perera
Department of Customs

Nissanka Perera
PwC Sri Lanka

Sudath Perera
Sudath Perera Associates

Nishan Premathiratne
Chamber's of Harsha Cabral

M. Puviharan
Department of Customs

S. Rajendran
Department of Customs

Rasheedha Ramjani
Tiruchelvam Associates

Hiranthi Ratnayake
PwC Sri Lanka

Sanjeewanie Ratnayake
Credit Information Bureau Ltd.

Mohamed Rizni
Speed International Freight Systems Ltd.

Heshika Rupasinghe
Tiruchelvam Associates

Achithri Silva
Sudath Perera Associates

Shane Silva
Julius & Creasy

Priya Sivagananathan
Julius & Creasy

A.H. Sumathipala
Neelakandan & Neelakandan

Harshana Suriyapperuma
Securities & Exchange Commission

J.M. Swaminathan
Julius & Creasy

Bandula S. Tilakasena
Ceylon Electricity Board

Shehara Varia
F.J. & G. De Saram

G.G. Weerakkody
Colombo Municipal Council

Sheanda Wijetunge
Nithya Partners

Jagath P. Wijeweera
Department of Customs

John Wilson
John Wilson Partners

ST. KITTS AND NEVIS

Kelsick, Wilkin and Ferdinand

Scotiabank

Michella Adrien
The Law Offices of Michella Adrien

Rublin Audain
Audain & Associates

Neil Coates
Grant Thornton

Jan Dash
Liburd and Dash

Rayana Dowden
Webster Law Firm

Barbara L. Hardtman
Hardtman & Associates

Dahlia Joseph
Joseph Rowe Attorneys-at-Law

Te Andre Joseph
Creative Designs

Sherry-Ann Liburd-Charles
Gonsalves Parry

Fonsonia O'Garro-Lewis
Brisbane O'Garro Alvaranga

Shaunette Pemberton
Grant Thornton

Tony Scatliffe II
R & T Design-Build Consultants Group Ltd.

Marva Thompson
St. Kitts Electricity Department

Sanshe N.N. Thompson
St. Kitts Electricity Department

Deborah Tyrell
Halix Corporation

Leonora Walwyn
WalwynLaw

Charles Wilkin QC
Kelsick Wilkin & Ferdinand

Rodney Wilson
Home Designs

ST. LUCIA

Lucelec

Clive Antoine
Ministry of Sustainable Development, Energy, Science and Technology

Thaddeus M. Antoine
TM Antoine Partners

Natalie Augustin
Glitzenhirn Augustin & Co.

Judge Francis Belle
Eastern Caribbean Supreme Court

Vincent Boland
Bank of Saint Lucia Limited

Sardia Cenac- Prospere
Floissac Fleming & Associates

Glenn Charlemagne
Superior Shipping Services

Geoffrey Duboulay
Floissac Fleming & Associates

Michael Duboulay
Floissac Fleming & Associates

Barbara Eloi
Carribean Cargo DC

Brenda Floissac-Fleming
Floissac Fleming & Associates

Peter I. Foster
Peter I. Foster & Associates

Carol J. Gedeon
Chancery Chambers

Garth George
St. Lucia Electricity Services Ltd.

Trudy O. Glasgow
Trudy O. Glasgow & Associates

Cheryl Goddard-Dorville
Floissac Fleming & Associates

Claire Greene-Malaykhan
Peter I. Foster & Associates

Adrian Hilaire
St. Lucia Air and Seaport Authority

Natasha James
Eastern Caribbean Supreme Court

Cuthbert McDiarmed
Ministry of Physical Development, Housing, and Urban Renewal

Richard Peterkin
Grant Thornton

Joanna Raynold Arthurton
Ministry of Physical Development, Housing, and Urban Renewal

Martin S. Renee
Renee's Construction Company

Matthew T. Sargusingh
Tri-Finity Associates

Catherine Sealys
Procurement Services International

Anya Trim
Grant Thornton

Avery Trim
Ministry of Physical Development, Housing, and Urban Renewal

Leandra Gabrielle Verneuil
Chambers of Jennifer Remy & Associates

ST. VINCENT AND THE GRENADINES

St. Vincent Electricity Services Ltd.

Michaela N. Ambrose
Baptiste & Co. Law Firm

Kay R.A. Bacchus-Browne
Kay Bacchus-Browne Chambers

Rene M. Baptiste
Baptiste & Co. Law Firm

Odelinda Barbour
Baptiste & Co. Law Firm Inc.

Anthony Bowman
Ministry of Housing, Informal Human Settlements, Lands and Surveys

Mikhail A.X. Charles
Baptiste & Co. Law Firm

Syran Clarke
The Bank of Nova Scotia - St. Vincent and the Grenadines

Stanley DeFreitas
DeFreitas & Associates

Vilma Diaz de Gonsalves
BDO Eastern Caribbean

Theona R. Elizee-Stapleton
Commerce & Intellectual Property Office (CIPO)

Ralph Henry
Scotiabank

Zhinga Horne Edwards
Law Chambers of Zhinga Horne Edwards

Stanley John
Elizabeth Law Chambers

Moulton Mayers
Moulton Mayers Architects

Michael Richards
Globalink Logistics Group

Martin Sheen
Commerce & Intellectual Property Office (CIPO)

Shelford Stowe
Ministry of Housing, Informal Human Settlements, Lands and Surveys

Trevor Thompson
TVA Consultant

Carlos Williams
Williams Custom & Shipping Agency

SUDAN

Omer Abdel Ati
Omer Abdelati Law Firm

Ali Abdelrahman Khalil
Shami, Khalil & Siddig Advocates

Mustafa Abdelwahab
CIASA

Mohammed Abdullah Mohammed
SDV Logistics

Abdalla Abuzeid
Abdalla A. Abuzeid & Associates

Mohamed Ibrahim Adam
Dr. Adam & Associates

Al Fadel Ahmed Al Mahdi
Al Mahdi Law Office

Emtinan Ali
CIASA

Mohamed Alobodi
CIASA

Ahmed M. Elhillali
American Sudanese Consulting Inc.

Hiba Elsayed Abdo
Mahmoud Elsheikh Omer & Associates Advocates

Hatim Elshoush
El Barkal Engineering Company

Asma Hamad Abdullatif Ali
Mahmoud Elsheikh Omer & Associates Advocates

Amr Hamad Omar
Emirates Islamic Bank

Elwaleed Hussein
CIASA

Hind Hussein
Aramex International For Services Co. Ltd.

Ahmed Mahdi
Mahmoud Elsheikh Omer & Associates Advocates

Tarig Mahmoud Elsheikh Omer
Mahmoud Elsheikh Omer & Associates Advocates

Amel Mohamed Shrif
Mahmoud Elsheikh Omer & Associates Advocates

Tarig Monim
TM Advisory

Abdulhakim Omar
SDV Logistics

Nafisa Omer
Omer Abdelati Law Firm

Rayan Omer
Omer Abdelati Law Firm

Razan Saif Eldin Abdalla
Mahmoud Elsheikh Omer & Associates Advocates

Sara Saif Elislam Abbas
Mahmoud Elsheikh Omer & Associates Advocates

Enas Salih
Shami, Khalil & Siddig Advocates

Wafa Shami
Shami, Khalil & Siddig Advocates

Marwa Taha
Shami, Khalil & Siddig Advocates

Abdel Gadir Warsama Ghalib
Dr. Abdel Gadir Warsama Ghalib & Associates Legal Firm

Mohamed Zain
KAYAN Consultancy

SURINAME

Notariaat Blom

Sieglien Burleson
Competitiveness Unit Suriname

G. Clide Cambridge
Paramaribo Custom Broker & Packer

Dennis Chandansingh
DCA Accountants & Consultants

Anneke Chin-A-Lin
Notariaat J.A. Jadnanansing

Joanne Danoesemito
VSH Shipping

Anoeschka Debipersad
A.E. Debipersad & Associates

Norman Doorson
Management Institute GLIS

Marcel K. Eyndhoven
N.V. Energiebedrijven Suriname

Johan Kastelein
Kastelein Design

Henk Naarendorp
Chamber of Commerce & Industry

Joanne Pancham
Chamber of Commerce & Industry

Frank E. M. Raijmann
BDO

Adiel Sakoer
N.V. Global Expedition

Martha P. Schaap
Hakrinbank N.V.

Prija Soechitram
Chamber of Commerce & Industry

Albert D. Soedamah
Lawfirm Soedamah & Associates

Radjen A. Soerdjbalie
Notariaat R.A. Soerdjbalie

Maureen Tjon Jaw Chong

Silvano Tjong-Ahin
Management Institute GLIS

Carol-Ann Tjon-Pian-Gi
Lawyer & Sworn Translator

Andy B. Wong
N.V. Energiebedrijven Suriname

Anthony Wong
General Contractors Association of Suriname

SWAZILAND

Federation of Swaziland Employers and Chamber of Commerce

TransUnion ITC (Pty) Ltd.

Deon Appelcryn
DHL

Lucas Bhembe
Ezulwini Municipality

Tenele Dhladhla
Swaziland Electricity Company

Musa Dlamini
M.L. Dlamini Attorneys

Veli Dlamini
Interfreight Pty. Ltd.

Chris Forte
Swazi Surveys

Bonginkosi Ginindza
DHL

Ncamsile Hlanze
DHL

Fisokuhle Hlope
M.L. Dlamini Attorneys

Zwelethu Desmond Jele
Robinson Bertram

Andrew Linsey
PwC Swaziland

Muzi Imasina
Mbabane Town Council

Mangaliso Magagula
Magagula & Hlophe

Nhlanhla Maphanga
Lang Mitchell Associates

Nontombi Maphanga
Swaziland Water Services Corporation

Tshidi Masisi-Hlanze
Masisi-Hlanze Attorneys

Theo Mason
PwC Swaziland

Sabelo Masuku
Howe Masuku Nsibande Attorneys

Steve Mitchell
MMA

Mandla Mkhwanazi
Mandla Z. Mkhwanazi and Associates

George Mzungu
M&E Consulting Engineers

Jerome Ndzimandze
FJ Building Construction

Kobla Quashie
Kobla Quashie and Associates

José Rodrigues
Rodrigues & Associates

Zweli T. Shabangu
Magagula & Hlophe

Bongani Simelane
Municipal Council of Mbabane

Muzi Simelane
Waring Simelane

Pieter Smoor
Integrated Development Consultants (IDC)

Caroline Sullivan
KPMG

John Thomson
Mormond Electrical Contractors

Manene Thwala
Thwala Attorneys

Bradford Mark Walker
Brad Walker Architects

SWEDEN

Charles Andersson
Ashurst Advokatbyrå AB

Therese Andersson
Öhrlings PricewaterhouseCoopers AB

Mats Berter
MAQS Law Firm

Emil Bertfelt
Öhrlings PricewaterhouseCoopers AB

Caroline Bogemyr
Hammarskiöld & Co.

Helena Brännvall
Advokatfirman Vinge KB, member of Lex Mundi

Alexander Broch
Öresunds Redovisning AB

Laura Carlson
Stockholm University, Department of Law

Åke Dahlqvist
UC

Mia Edlund
Baker & McKenzie

Mia Fogelberg
Ashurst Advokatbyrå AB

Ylva Forsberg
Roschier Sweden

Peder Hammarskiöld
Hammarskiöld & Co.

Lars Hartzell
Elmzell Advokatbyrå AB, member of Ius Laboris

Elisabeth Heide
Ashurst Advokatbyrå AB

Camilla Holmkvist
Ashurst Advokatbyrå AB

James Hope
Advokatfirman Vinge KB, member of Lex Mundi

Erik Hygrell
Wistrand Advokatbyrå

Rickard Jansson
Panalpina AB

Jenny Jilmstad
Ashurst Advokatbyrå AB

Kim Jokinen
Öhrlings PricewaterhouseCoopers AB

Rikard Lindahl
Advokatfirman Vinge KB, member of Lex Mundi

Dennis Linden
Lantmäteriet

Inger Lindhe
Lantmäteriet

Heléne Lindqvist
Bolagsverket - Swedish Companies Registration Office (SCRO)

Thomas Lindqvist
Hammarskiöld & Co.

Christoffer Monell
Mannheimer Swartling Advokatbyrå

Malin Nordin
MAQS Law Firm

Karl-Arne Olsson
Gärde Wesslau Advokatbyrå

Felix Rudberg
Roschier Sweden

Therese Säde
Advokatfirman Vinge KB, member of Lex Mundi

Bojana Saletic
Hammarskiöld & Co.

Jesper Schönbeck
Advokatfirman Vinge KB, member of Lex Mundi

Albert Wällgren
Advokatfirman Vinge KB, member of Lex Mundi

Carl Johan Wallnerström
Swedish Energy Markets Inspectorate (Energimarknadsinspektionen)

Petter Wenehult
Elmzell Advokatbyrå AB, member of Ius Laboris

Camilla Westerlund
AlphaGlobe Logistics

SWITZERLAND

Rashid Bahar
Bär & Karrer AG

Beat M. Barthold
Froriep

Marc Bernheim
Staiger, Schwald & Partner Ltd.

Myriam Büchi-Bänteli
PwC Switzerland

Lukas Bühlmann
PwC Switzerland

Martin Burkhardt
Lenz & Staehelin

Andrea Cesare Canonica
Swiss Customs

Boudry Charles
LALIVE

Stefan Eberhard
Oberson Abels SA

Suzanne Eckert
Wenger Plattner

Jana Essebier
VISCHER AG

Claudio Fischer
Ernst & Young

Robert Furter
Pestalozzi, member of Lex Mundi

Gaudenz Geiger
Staiger, Schwald & Partner Ltd.

Debora Ghilardotti
MAG Legis SA

Thomas H. Henle
IL Industrie-Leasing Ltd.

Nicolas Herzog
Niedermann Rechtsanwälte

Anouk Hirt
Bär & Karrer AG

Jakob Hoehn
Pestalozzi, member of Lex Mundi

Ani Homberger
LALIVE

Patrick Hünerwadel
Lenz & Staehelin

Sara Ianni
VISCHER AG

David Jenny
VISCHER AG

Mattias Johnson
Froriep

Cyrill Kaeser
Lenz & Staehelin

Michael Kramer
Pestalozzi, member of Lex Mundi

Yury Kudryavtsev
Audiconsult SA - member of Russell Bedford International

Cédric Lenoir
LALIVE

Beat Luescher
AZ Elektro AG

Mario Maier
Orrick, Herrington & Sutcliffe LLP

Andrea Molino
MAG Legis SA

Konrad Moor
Bürgi Nägeli Lawyers

Roman Rinderknecht
Ernst & Young

Charlotte Sophie Rüegg
Lenz & Staehelin

Ueli Schindler
AECOM/URS

Daniel Schmitz
PwC Switzerland

Walter Sommer
Ernst & Young

Thomas Strassner
Orrick, Herrington & Sutcliffe LLP

Corinne Studer
Handelsregisteramt des Kantons

Jean-Paul Vulliéty
LALIVE

Patrick Weber
EKZ Elektrizitätswerke des Kantons Zürich

Stefan Zangger
Belglobe International LLC

Marc Zimmermann
Lenz & Staehelin

SYRIAN ARAB REPUBLIC

Wadih Abou Nasr
PwC Lebanon

Alaa Ahmad
Syrian Strategic Think Tank Research Center

Hanan Alhomse
Central Bank of Syria

Abir Alkadi
Syrian Strategic Think Tank Research Center

Jamil Ammar
Rutgers Law School

Ghada Armali
Sarkis & Associates

Richard El Mouallem
PwC Lebanon

Nada Elsayed
PwC Lebanon

Anas Ghazi
Meethak - Lawyers & Consultants

Gordon Gray
National U.S.-Arab Chamber of Commerce

Mohammad Joumaa
PwC Lebanon

Fadi Kardous
Kardous Law Office

Mamon Katbeh
Central Bank of Syria

Guevara Mihoub
Hekmieh Group

Randa Moftah
Central Bank of Syria

Alaa Nizam

Gabriel Oussi
Oussi Law Firm

Ramez Raslan
Commerce & Engineering Consultants

Danny Saada
United Company For Electrical Projects

Housam Safadi
Safadi Bureau

Fadi Sarkis
Sarkis & Associates

Arem Taweel
Ebraheem Taweel Law Office

Ebraheem Taweel
Ebraheem Taweel Law Office

TAIWAN, CHINA

Mark Brown
Winkler Partners

Jack Chang
Yangming Partners

Joyce Chang
Yangming Partners

Kuo-ming Chang
Joint Credit Information Center

Victor I. Chang
LCS & Partners

Christine Chen
Winkler Partners

Daniel Chen
Winkler Partners

Edgar Y. Chen
Tsar & Tsai Law Firm, member of Lex Mundi

Emily Chen
LCS & Partners

Nicholas V. Chen
Pamir Law Group

Romy Chen
National Development Council

Yo-Yi Chen
Formosa Transnational

Ben Cheng
Tsar & Tsai Law Firm, member of Lex Mundi

Chun-Yih Cheng
Formosa Transnational

Chih-Hung Chiang
Ministry of Interior

Tiffany Fan
Winkler Partners

Philip T. C. Fei
Fei & Cheng Associates

Mark Harty
LCS & Partners

Sophia Hsieh
Tsar & Tsai Law Firm, member of Lex Mundi

Barbara Hsu
SDV Logistics

Robert Hsu
SDV Logistics

Theresa Hu
National Development Council

Margaret Huang
LCS & Partners

T.C. Huang
Huang & Partners

Charles Hwang
Yangming Partners

Howard Kuo
PwC Taiwan

Wei-Ping Lai
Yu-Ding Law Firm

En Fan Lan
Primordial Law Firm

Jenny Lee
Pamir Law Group

Max Lee
Tsar & Tsai Law Firm, member of Lex Mundi

Vivian Lee
Huang & Partners

John Li
LCS & Partners

Justin Liang
Baker & McKenzie

Angela Lin
Lexcel Partners

Frank Lin
Rexmed Industries Co. Ltd.

Jeffrey Lin
Joint Credit Information Center

Kien Lin
Joint Credit Information Center

Ming-Yen Lin
Deep & Far, Attorneys-at-Law

Nelson J. Lin
Huang & Partners

Rich Lin
LCS & Partners

Sheau Chyng Lin
Primordial Law Firm

You-Jing Lin
Chi-Sheng Law Firm

Kang-Shen Liu
Lexcel Partners

Wanyi Liu
Financial Supervisory Commission, Banking Bureau

Stacy Lo
Lexcel Partners

Joseph Ni
Good Earth CPA

Patrick Pai-Chiang Chu
Lee and Li, Attorneys-at-Law

Ching-Ping Shao
National Taiwan University

Tanya Y. Teng
Huang & Partners

Bee Leay Teo
Baker & McKenzie

David Tien
Lee and Li, Attorneys-at-Law

C.F. Tsai
Deep & Far, Attorneys-at-Law

David Tsai
Lexcel Partners

Felix Y. Wang
Yangming Partners

Richard Watanabe
PwC Taiwan

Huang William
Gibsin Electrical Consultancy

Ja-Lin Wu
National Development Council

Pei-Yu Wu
Baker & McKenzie

Alex Yeh
LCS & Partners

TAJIKISTAN

Association of Banks of Tajikistan

Baker Tilly Tajikistan

Tax Committee under Government of the Republic of Tajikistan

Zarrina Adham
CJSC MDO Humo

Zulfiya Akchurina
GRATA Law Firm

Khujanazar Aslamshoev
Colibri Law Firm

Dzhamshed Asrorov
CJSC MDO Humo

Gulanor Atobek
Deloitte & Touche, LLC

Amirbek Azizov
Ministry of Labor, Migration and Employment of Population

Abdulbori Baybabaev
Law Firm Lex

Jienshoh Bukhoriev
Asian Development Bank

Firuz Bulbulov
BDO Tajikistan

Akhror Edgarov
CJSC MDO Humo

Mirali Kadyrov
Centre for Entreprenurship Development Support in Dushanbe

Elena Kaeva
PwC Kazakhstan

Assel Khamzina
PwC Kazakhstan

Alisher Khoshimov
Colibri Law Firm

Shirinbek Milikbekov
Colibri Law Firm

Kamoliddin Mukhamedov
GRATA Law Firm

Rustam Mukhtarov
CIBT - Credit Information Bureau in Tajikistan

Rustam Nazrisho
Nazrisho & Mirzoev Law Firm LLC

Temirlan Nildibayev
PwC Kazakhstan

Jamshed Nurmahmadzoda
National Bank of Faizali Rajabov

Association of Constructors of
Firdavs S. Mirzoev
Nazrisho & Mirzoev Law Firm LLC

Aisanat Safarbek kyzy
GRATA Law Firm

Emin Sanginzoda
Ministry of Labor, Migration and Employment of Population

Kanat Seidaliev
GRATA Law Firm

Marina Shamilova
Legal Consulting Group

Takdir Sharifov
Association of Anti Crisis Managers

Abdujabbor Shirinov
National Bank of Tajikistan

Sherzod Sodatkadamov
Nazrisho & Mirzoev Law Firm LLC

Farzona Tilavova

Aliya Utegaliyeva
PwC Kazakhstan

Abdurakhmon Yuldoshev
Ministry of Labor, Migration and Employment of Population

TANZANIA

Said Athuman
Tanzania Revenue Authority

Albina Burra

Aggrey Ernest
ATZ Law Chambers

Hanif Habib
Hanif Habib & Co. - correspondent of Russell Bedford International

Asma Hilal
CRB Africa Legal

Sophia D. Issa
ATZ Law Chambers

Sujata Jaffer
Nexia SJ Tanzania

Davith Kahwa
Creditinfo Tanzania Limited

Njerii Kanyama
ENSafrica Tanzania Attorneys

Adam Lovett
Norton Rose Fulbright

Nkanwa Magina
Bank of Tanzania

Hyacintha Benedict Makileo
National Construction Council

Siri A. Malai
Malai Freight Forwarders Ltd.

Sunil Maru
Sumar Varma Associates

Umaiya Masoli
Bank of Tanzania

Henry Sato Massaba
M&A Attorneys

Lydia Massawe

Deogratius Mmasy
PwC Tanzania

Freddy Moshy
Tanzania Revenue Authority

Mirumbe Mseti
PwC Tanzania

Ayoub Mtafya
Nexlaw Advocates

Ilvin Mugeta
Judiciary of Tanzania

Jonathan Mugila
FB Attorneys

Mzumbe Musa

Deogratias Myamani
Bank of Tanzania

Stella Ndikimi
East African Law Chambers

Raymond Ngatuni
ENSafrica Tanzania Attorneys

Alex Thomas Ngluma
ENSafrica Tanzania Attorneys

Sweetbert Nkuba
Sweet and Conrad LLP

Shamiza Ratansi
ATZ Law Chambers

Katarina T. Revocati
Judiciary of Tanzania

Van Reynders
Creditinfo Tanzania Limited

Charles R.B. Rwechungura
CRB Africa Legal

Nabihah Seif
East African Law Chambers

Pendo Shamte
CRB Africa Legal

John Shimbala
PwC Tanzania

Amb. Mwanaidi Sinare Maajar
ENSafrica Tanzania Attorneys

Miriam Sudi
PwC Tanzania

David Tarimo
PwC Tanzania

Regis Tissier
Bolloré Africa Logistics

THAILAND

Metropolitan Electricity Authority

Tilleke & Gibbins

Panida Agkavikai
Bangkok Global Law Offices Limited

Somsak Anakkasela
PwC Thailand

Vatcharin Ariyanuntaka
Bangkok Global Law Offices Limited

Roi Bak
Dej-Udom & Associates

Amara Bhuwanawat
Siam Premier International Law Office Limited

Rujira Bunnang
Marut Bunnang International Law Office

Narumon Burapachayanont
DHL Express (Thailand) Ltd.

Thanakorn Busarasopitkul
PwC Thailand

Panotporn Chalodhorn
Office of the Judiciary

Aye Chananan
Panu & Partners

Isorn Chandrawong
Bangkok Jurist Ltd.

Benyapa Changpradit
PwC Thailand

Anan Chankuptarat
Aero-Marine Transworld Co.

Pavinee Channuntapipat
PwC Thailand

Udomphan Chantana
Department of Lands

Cheewin Chiangkane
Baker & McKenzie

Chinnavat Chinsangaram
Weerawong, Chinnavat & Peangpanor Ltd.

Weerawong Chittmittrapap
Weerawong, Chinnavat & Peangpanor Ltd.

Suwanna Chuerboonchai
Securities and Exchange Commission

Karnjanick Chutima
Thanathip & Partners Counsellors Limited

Paul Connelly
International Legal Counsellors Thailand Limited (ILCT)

Monnira Danwiwat
Bangkok Global Law Offices Limited

Thanathat Ghonkaew
Comin Thai Engineering Solutions Co. Ltd.

Thirapa Glinsukon
PwC Thailand

Manita Hengriprasopchoke
Thanathip & Partners Counsellors Limited

Suradech Hongsa
DFDL

Monthcai Itisurasing
LEED AP

Kanok Jullamon
The Supreme Court of Thailand

Nuttinee Kaewsa-ard
National Credit Bureau Co. Ltd.

Praorujee Kanthasorn
Legal Execution Department

Amnart Khongsakda
Bangkok Global Law Offices Limited

Chaiyut Kumkun
Customs Standard Procedure and Valuation Division

William Lehane
Siam Premier International Law Office Limited

Woraphong Leksakulchai
Hughes Krupica

Sakchai Limsiripothong
Weerawong, Chinnavat & Peangpanor Ltd.

Chotika Lurponglukana
ZICOlaw

Arunee Mahathorn
Thanathip & Partners Counsellors Limited

Douglas D. Mancill
Deacons

Ploy Maneepaksin
Thanathip & Partners Counsellors Limited

Dittaporn Munsri
Siam Premier International Law Office Limited

Anuwat Ngamprasertkul
PwC Thailand

Bowornsith Nitiyavanich
Hughes Krupica

Patthanawach Nuntawowart
Chandler & Thong-ek

Surapol Opasatien
National Credit Bureau Co. Ltd.

Wynn Padeejit
Baker & McKenzie

Natchapon Padungkittimal
Clifford Chance

Nipa Pakdeechanuan
Dej-Udom & Associates

Pisut Pakwong
Silk Legal Company Ltd.

Tussanee Pao-In
Legal Execution Department

Panu Patani
Panu & Partners

Wisitchai Phasuk
Siam Premier International Law Office Limited

Pakinee Pipatpoka
National Credit Bureau Co. Ltd.

Viroj Piyawattanametha
Baker & McKenzie

Alexander Polgar
Antares Advisory Ltd.

Harit Na Pombejra
Silk Legal Company Ltd.

Ratana Poonsombudlert
Chandler & Thong-ek

Ruengrit Pooprasert
ZICOlaw

Kavita Pradoemkulchai
DFDL

Predee Pravichpaibul
Weerawong, Chinnavat & Peangpanor Ltd.

Rangsima Rattana
Legal Execution Department

Vunnipa Ruamrangsri
PwC Thailand

Sawat Sangkavisit
Siam Premier International Law Office Limited

Alexander James Seeley
International Legal Counsellors Thailand Limited (ILCT)

Treetip Siripreechapong
Thanathip & Partners Counsellors Limited

Chawaluck Sivayathorn Araneta
Thanathip & Partners Counsellors Limited

Ratanavadee Somboon
Legal Execution Department

Kowit Somwaiya
LawPlus Ltd.

Kaittipat Sonchareon
Bangkok Metropolitan Administration

Audray Souche
DFDL

Picharn Sukparangsee
Bangkok Global Law Offices Limited

Apinan Suntharanan
Sukhumvit Asset Management Co., Ltd.

Tanachol Suthasuwan
Panu & Partners

Ruanvadee Suwanmongkol
Legal Execution Department

Naddaporn Suwanvajukkasikij
LawPlus Ltd.

Hunt Talmage
Chandler & Thong-ek

Jeffery Tan
Tricharoen Engineering Co., Ltd.

Ornjira Tangwongyodying
PwC Thailand

Omanong Tesabamroong
S.J. International Legal Consulting and Advisory Co., Ltd.

Noppramart Thammateeradaycho
Siam Premier International Law Office Limited

Norarat Theeranukoon
Bangkok Global Law Offices Limited

Atitaya Thongboon
Legal Execution Department

V. Joseph Tisuthiwongse
Clifford Chance

Nitchaya Vaneesorn
Thanathip & Partners Counsellors Limited

Kanokkorn Viriyasutum
Chandler & Thong-ek

Auradee P. Wongsaroj
Chandler & Thong-ek

Somchai Yungkarn
Chandler & Thong-ek

Yada Yuwataepakorn
Baker & McKenzie

TIMOR-LESTE

Nur Aini Djafar Alkatiri
Banco Central de Timor-Leste

Rui Amendoeira
Vieira de Almeida & Associados (Atlas Lda)

Brendan Bilston
ANL Timor, Unipessoal Lda

José Borges Guerra
Miranda & Associados

Paula Caldeira Dutschmann
Miranda Correia Amendoeira & Associados

Luis Carvalho
Engipro

Patrick Chan
ANL Timor, Unipessoal Lda

João Cortez Vaz
Vieira de Almeida & Associados (Atlas Lda)

Octaviana Da S.A. Maxanches
Banco Central de Timor-Leste

Pascoela M.R. da Silva
Banco Central de Timor-Leste

Francisco de Deus Maia
Banco Central de Timor-Leste

Anthony Frazier

João Galamba de Oliveira
Abreu and C&C Advogados

Tereza Garcia André
Miranda & Associados

Eusebio Guterres
UNIDO Business Regulatory Consultant

João Leite
Miranda & Associados

Carolina Letra
Caixa Geral de Depositos (CGD)

Alexander Lukito
PwC Indonesia

João Mayer Moreira
Vieira de Almeida & Associados (Atlas Lda)

Vega Ramadhan
PwC Indonesia

Ettore Rulli
Elettro 2000 S.r.l.

Gaurav Sareen
Deloitte

Filipa Serra
Vieira de Almeida & Associados (Atlas Lda)

Ricardo Silva
Miranda & Associados

Pedro Sousa Uva
Miranda & Associados

Erik Stokes
RMS Engineering and Construction

Christiara Tiffani
PwC Indonesia

Fernando Torrão Alves
Caixa Geral de Depositos (CGD)

Tim Robert Watson
PwC Indonesia

TOGO

BCEAO

John W. Ffooks & Co., member of Bowman Gilfillan Africa Group

Tribunal de Lome

A. M. Abbi Toyi
Direction des Affaires Domaniales et Cadastrales

Abbas Aboulaye
Autorité de Réglementation du Secteur de l'Electricité (ARSE)

Claude Adama
Aquereburu and Partners Cabinet d'Avocats

Jean-Marie Adenka
Cabinet Adenka

Djifa Emefa Adjale Suku
SCP Dogbeavou & Associes

Mensah Adje
Aquereburu and Partners Cabinet d'Avocats

Komi Adjivon Kowuvi
Société Togolaise des Eaux

Sylvia Adjoa Hundt Aquereburu
Office Notarial Sylvia Adjoa Hundt Aquereburu

Komi Agbeli
Compagnie Energie Electrique du Togo (CEET)

Koudzo Mawuéna Agbemaple
Autorité de Réglementation du Secteur de l'Electricité (ARSE)

Ayétsé Modeste Agbo
Archimod - Cabinet d'Architecture Moderne

Martial Akakpo
Martial Akakpo et Associés

Nicolas Kossi Akidjetan
Ordre National des Architectes du Togo (ONAT)

Bamaze Akilam
Etude Bamaze

Yves Yaovi Akoue
ETINSEL

Eklu Patrick Amendah
Ordre National des Architectes du Togo (ONAT)

Koezi Ankou
Tribunal de 1ere Instance de Lome

Coffi Alexis Aquereburu
Aquereburu and Partners Cabinet d'Avocats

Cécile Assogbavi
Etude Notariale Assogbavi

Antoine Ayiv
Ligue des Genies

Sandrine Badjili
Martial Akakpo et Associés

Awa Beleyi
Seguce Togo

Ibrahima Beye
Présidence de la République du Togo

Assiom Kossi Bokodjin
Cabinet d'Avocats Me Toble Gagnon

Cedric Chalvon
Seguce Togo

Essenouwa Degla
Compagnie Energie Electrique du Togo (CEET)

Kofimessa Devotsou
Cabinet d'Avocat

Kokou Djegnon
Ministère de l'Urbanisme et de l'habitat

Sédjro Koffi Dogbeavou
SCP Dogbeavou & Associes

Essiame Koko Dzoka
Lawyer

Bassimsouwe Edjam-Etchaki
Direction des Services Technique de la Mairie

Mathias A. Edorh-Komahe
Lawyer

Ayaovi Gbedevi Egloh
Office Togolais des Recettes

Désiré K. Ekpe
DAS-Togo

Bérenger Ette
PwC Côte d'Ivoire

Akossiwa Fonouvi
Cabinet de Maître Galolo Soedjede

Ayélé Annie Gbadoe Deckon
Aquereburu and Partners Cabinet d'Avocats

Mèmèssilé Dominque Gnazo
Cabinet de Notaire Gnazo

Tchakoura Gnon
OTR – Commissariat des Douanes

Tino Hoffer
Aquereburu and Partners Cabinet d'Avocats

Odadje Hounnake
Lawyer

Atchroe Leonard Johnson
SCP Aquereburu & Partners

Gilbert Josias
Chambre de Commerce et d'Industrie du Togo (CCIT)

Molgah Kadjaka-Abougnima
Cabinet de Notaire Kadjaka-Abougnima

Yentroudjoa Kantati
Tribunal de 1ere Instance de Lome

Komivi Kassegne
Compagnie Energie Electrique du Togo (CEET)

Folydze Kofi Zobinu
Boswell Consulting Group

Philippe Kokou Tchodie
Office Togolais des Recettes

Agbéwonou Koudasse
Cabinet de Maître Galolo Soedjede

Hokaméto Kpenou
Autorité de Réglementation du Secteur de l'Electricité (ARSE)

Emmanuel Mamlan
Martial Akakpo et Associés

Koffi Sylvain Mensah Attoh
Cabinet Maître Mensah-Attoh

Adeline Messou Couassi-Blé
PwC Côte d'Ivoire

Ophélie Pokou Mivedor
SCP Dogbeavou & Associes

Laname Nayante
Calafi

Dissadama Ouro-Bodi
Office Togolais des Recettes

Nourou Sama
Compagnie Energie Electrique du Togo (CEET)

Samuel Sanwogou
Chambre de Commerce et d'Industrie du Togo (CCIT)

Galolo Soedjede
Cabinet de Maître Galolo Soedjede

Hoédjéto Tonton Soedjede
Cabinet de Maître Galolo Soedjede

Lazare Sossoukpe
SCP Dogbeavou & Associes

Dominique Taty
PwC Côte d'Ivoire

Tchitchao Tchalim
Lawyer

Mouhamed Tchassona Traore
Etude Me Mouhamed Tchassona Traore

Gagnon Yawo Toble
Cabinet d'Avocats Me Toble Gagnon

Fousséni Traoré
PwC Côte d'Ivoire

Komi Tsakadi
Cabinet De Me Tsakadi

Thierry Verdier
Seguce Togo

Senyo Komla Wozufia
Comelec Électricité

Edem Zotchi
Martial Akakpo et Associés

TONGA

Tukio Afeaki
A&S Electrical and Painting

Kulu Bloomfield
Inland Revenue Tonga

Delores Elliott
Data Bureau Limited

Taniela Fonna
Kramer Ausenco Tonga

Anthony Frazier

Lopeti Heimuli
Ministry of Infrastructure

Taaniela Kula
Ministry of Lands, Survey, Natural Resources & Environment

Fisilau Leone
Ministry of Infrastructure

James Lutui
Crown Law

Salesi Mataele
Oceantranz Tonga Ltd.

Sione Tomasi Naite Fakahua
Fakahua-Fa'otusia & Associates

Laki M. Niu
Laki Niu Offices

Ralph Stephenson
Stephenson Associates

Tuipulotu Taufoou
Dateline Trans-Am Shipping

Vaimoana Taukolo
Ministry of Commerce, Tourism and Labour

Alisi Numia Taumoepeau
TMP Law

Fine Tohi
Dateline Trans-Am Shipping

Lesina Tonga
Lesina Tonga Law Firm

Pesalili Tuiano
Ministry of Infrastructure

Distquaine P. Tu'ihalamaka
Ministry of Commerce, Tourism and Labour

Petunia Tupou
Fungateiki Law Office

Lepaola B. Vaea
Inland Revenue Tonga

Malakai Vakasiuola
ITS Pacific Engineering Consultants

Fotu Veikune
Ministry of Infrastructure

Dianne Warner
Skip's Custom Joinery Ltd.

TRINIDAD AND TOBAGO

Regulated Industries Commission

Christopher Alexander
Phoenix Logistics (Trinidad) Ltd.

Ashmead Ali
Ashmead Ali & Co.

Donna Chin Asiong
LEX Caribbean

Clyde Roach
Rotech Services Ltd.

Luis Dini
HSMDT Ltd.

Thomas Escalante
TransUnion

Nicole Ferreira-Aaron
M. Hamel-Smith & Co., member of Lex Mundi

Glenn Hamel-Smith
M. Hamel-Smith & Co., member of Lex Mundi

Marie Hinds
Town and Country Planning Division

Melissa Inglefield
M. Hamel-Smith & Co., member of Lex Mundi

Sunil Lalloo
Raymond and Pierre Limited

Mariella Lange
HSMDT Ltd.

Orrisha Maharajh
Johnson, Camacho & Singh

Kevin Maraj
PricewaterhouseCoopers Limited

Imtiaz Mohammed
Delta Electrical Contractors, Ltd.

David Montgomery
HLB Montgomery & Co.

Sheldon Mycoo
Synovations Limited

Marjorie Nunez
LEX Caribbean

Gregory Pantin
M. Hamel-Smith & Co., member of Lex Mundi

Yolander Persaud
Ashmead Ali & Co.

Sonji Pierre Chase
Johnson, Camacho & Singh

Fanta Punch
M. Hamel-Smith & Co., member of Lex Mundi

Catherine Ramnarine
M. Hamel-Smith & Co., member of Lex Mundi

Deoraj Ramtahal
Ministry of Local Government

Krystal Richardson
M. Hamel-Smith & Co., member of Lex Mundi

Andre Rudder
J.D. Sellier & Co.

Alana T.G. Russell
Ashmead Ali & Co.

Arun Seenath
Deloitte

Stephen A. Singh
Johnson, Camacho & Singh

Tammy Timal-Toonday
Grant Thornton ORBIT Solutions Limited

Jonathan Walker
M. Hamel-Smith & Co., member of Lex Mundi

Turkessa Warwick
Brokerage Solution

Allyson West
PricewaterhouseCoopers Limited

Tonika Wilson-Gabriel
PricewaterhouseCoopers Limited

TUNISIA

Kamel Abdel Khalek
Société Tunisienne de l'Elecricité et du Gaz (STEG)

Ilhem Abderrahim
Société Tunisienne de l'Elecricité et du Gaz (STEG)

Adly Bellagha
Adly Bellagha & Associates

Hend Ben Achour
Adly Bellagha & Associates

Thouraya Ben Ghenia
Tribunal Immobilier - Tunisie

Wassim Ben Mahmoud
Bureau Wassem Ben Mahmoud

Amel Ben Rahal
Banque Centrale de Tunisie

Abdelfetah Benahji
Ferchiou & Associés

Slah-Eddine Bensaid
SCET-Tunisie

Peter Bismuth
Tunisie Electro Technique

Omar Boukhdir
Bolloré Africa Logistics

Mongi Bousbia
Société Tunisienne de l'Elecricité et du Gaz (STEG)

Salaheddine Caid Essebsi
Caid Essebsi and Partners Law Firm

Elyes Chafter
Chafter Raouadi LLP

Zine el Abidine Chafter
Chafter Raouadi LLP

Faouzi Cheikh
Banque Centrale de Tunisie

Mona Cherif
Gide Loyrette Nouel, member of Lex Mundi

Abdelmalek Dahmani
Dahmani Transit International

Mohamed Derbel
BDO

Mohamed Lotfi El Ajeri
El Ajeri Lawyers EAL

Abderrahmen Fendri
CAF Membre du Réseau International PwC

Noureddine Ferchiou
Ferchiou & Associés

Rym Ferchiou
Ferchiou & Associés

Amina Fradi
CAF Membre du Réseau International PwC

Slim Gargouri
CPA

Imen Guettat
CAF Membre du Réseau International PwC

Anis Jabnoun
Gide Loyrette Nouel, member of Lex Mundi

Badis Jedidi
Meziou Knani & Associés

Sami Kallel
Kallel & Associates

Mabrouk Maalaoui
CAF Membre du Réseau International PwC

Slim Malouche
Malouche Avocats-Conseils

Mohamed Mgazzen
Société Tunisienne de l'Elecricité et du Gaz (STEG)

Mohamed Taieb Mrabet
Banque Centrale de Tunisie

Hichem M'rabet
Société Tunisienne de l'Elecricité et du Gaz (STEG)

Imen Nouira
Conservation Foncière Tunisia

Olfa Othmane
Banque Centrale de Tunisie

Habiba Raouadi
Chafter Raouadi LLP

Raoudha Sammoudi
Ministry of Justice

Ferid Smida
Office de la Topographie et du Cadastre - Tunisie

Hafedeh Trabelsi
Cabinet d'Architecture Hafedeh Trabelsi

Anis Wahabi
AWT Audit & Conseil

TURKEY

Boğaziçi Elektik Dağitim A.Ş. (Bedaş)

Gunduz Simsek Gago Avukatlik Ortakligi

INLAWCO Law Firm

Metin Abut
Moroglu Arseven

Burcu Acartürk Yıldız
KarataşYildizBorovali

Cansu Ak
Pekin & Pekin

Deniz Akbaş
Serap Zuvin Law Offices

Mehmet Ali Akgün
Serap Zuvin Law Offices

Doğacan Akören
KarataşYildizBorovali

Simge Akyüz
Devres Law Office

Cansu Alparman
ADMD - Mavioglu & Alkan Law Office

Ali Alsirt
Yenigün Construction Company

Ekin Altıntaş
PwC Turkey

Çisem Altundemir
Kolcuoğlu Demirkan Attorneys-at-Law

Selin Barlin Aral
Paksoy Law Firm

Melsa Ararat
Corporate Governance Forum of Turkey, Sabanci University

Ergun Benan Arseven
Moroglu Arseven

Banu Aslan
Bezen & Partners

Oğuz Aslaner
Central Bank of the Republic of Turkey

Melis Atamer
Ministry of Economy

Melis Atasagun
Pekin & Bayar Law Firm

Damla Aybar
Tarlan – Baksi Law Firm

Aybike Aygün
Aygün Özterzi Karoğlu Law Office

Murat Ayyıldız
Eryürekli Law Office

Elvan Aziz
Paksoy Law Firm

Burak Babacan
KPMG

Derya Baksı
Tarlan – Baksi Law Firm

Aslihan Balci
Somay Hukuk Bürosu

Z. İlayda Balkan
ADMD - Mavioglu & Alkan Law Office

Naz Bandik Hatipoglu
Çakmak Avukatlik Bürosu

Sedef Başcı
Devres Law Office

Erdem Basgul
Çakmak Avukatlik Bürosu

Kaan Batum
Cerrahoğlu Law Firm

Ayça Bayburan
ADMD - Mavioglu & Alkan Law Office

Burak Baydar
Moroglu Arseven

Harun Bayramoglu
ITKIB Istanbul Textile and Apparel Exporters' Association

Imge Besenk
Pekin & Pekin

Serdar Bezen
Bezen & Partners

Yeşim Bezen
Bezen & Partners

Ahmet Biçer
Central Bank of the Republic of Turkey

Ayşe Eda Biçer
Çakmak Avukatlik Bürosu

Aysegul Bogrun
Ersoy Bilgehan Lawyers and Consultants

Guley Bor
YükselKarkinKüçük Avukatlik Ortakliği

Sinan Borovalı
KarataşYildizBorovali

Miray Merve Bozkurt
Sariibrahimoğlu Law Office

Başak Bumin
PERA Construction

Esin Çamlıbel
Turunç Law Office

Uraz Canbolat
Cerrahoğlu Law Firm

Ifakat Merve Çaparoğlu
Yuka Law Office

Maria Lianides Çelebi
Bener Law Office, member of Ius Laboris

Ezgi Celik
Turkish Industry and Business Association

M. Fadlullah Cerrahoğlu
Cerrahoğlu Law Firm

Meline Cilingir
Bezen & Partners

Sertaç Coşgun
PwC Turkey

Ipek Coşkun
Pekin & Pekin

Yavuz Dayıoğlu
PwC Turkey

Sabiha Busra Demir
Moroglu Arseven

Ebru Demirhan
Taboglu & Demirhan

Rüçhan Derici
3e Danişmanlik Ltd. Şti.

Emine Devres
Devres Law Office

Ebru Dicle
Turkish Industry and Business Association

Şule Dilek Çelik
Cerrahoğlu Law Firm

Deniz Dinçer Öner
PwC Turkey

Melis Dogac
Sariibrahimoğlu Law Office

Orkun Dokener
3e Danişmanlik Ltd. Şti.

Onur Dönmez
Orhaner Law Office

Dilara Duman
Duman Law Office

Safa Mustafa Durakoğlu
Çakmak Avukatlik Bürosu

Hakan Durusel
Pekin & Pekin

Diler Emiroğlu Özterzi
Aygün Özterzi Karoğlu Law Office

Hüseyin Emre Eney
Çakmak Avukatlik Bürosu

Gökben Erdem Dirican
Pekin & Pekin

Muzaffer Eroğlu
Kocaeli University, Hukuk Fakültesi

Deniz Zeynep Erverdi
ADMD - Mavioglu & Alkan Law Office

Naz Esen
Turunç Law Office

Merve Evrim
Moroglu Arseven

Özgür Can Geçim
Ernst & Young

Tuba Gedik
PwC Turkey

Oya Gencay
Central Bank of the Republic of Turkey

Alev Güçlüer
Moroglu Arseven

Serkan Gul
Herguner Bilgen Ozeke

Selin Gül
Barlas Law

Kenan Güler
Güler Dinamik Gümrük Müşavirliği A.Ş.

Stj Av. Bahadir Gultekin
Moroglu Arseven

Omer Gumusel
Pekin & Bayar Law Firm

Arzum Gunalcin
Günalçin Hukuk Bürosu

Cangur Gunaydin
Serap Zuvin Law Offices

Nurettin Gündoğmuş
Aktif Investment Bank AS

Zeki Gündüz
PwC Turkey

Remzi Orkun Guner
ADMD - Mavioglu & Alkan Law Office

Burcu Güray
Moroglu Arseven

E. Nazlı Gürdal
Turunç Law Office

Ayşegül Gürsoy
Cerrahoğlu Law Firm

Özhan Güven
Eroglu Yapi

Ece İlçi
Bezen & Partners

Aslı Işık
Turunç Law Office

Pelin Işık
Turkish Industry and Business Association

Sevi Islamagec
Moroglu Arseven

Ali Can Kahya
Ministry of Economy

Ilker Karabulut
3e Danişmanlik Ltd. Şti.

Irmak Karabulut
YükselKarkinKüçük Avukatlik Ortakliği

Nihat Karadirek
3e Danişmanlik Ltd. Şti.

Ahmet Karahan
Herguner Bilgen Ozeke

Ayfer Basac Karakoc
Moroglu Arseven

Özge Kavasoğlu
The Banks Association of Turkey

Betül Kencebay
TUYID - Turkish IR Society

Burak Kepkep
Paksoy Law Firm

Simge Selef Kiliçi
PwC Turkey

Duygu Ece Kındır
Kolcuoğlu Demirkan Attorneys-at-Law

Süleyman Kısaç
Turk Telekom

Özlem Kızıl Voyvoda
Çakmak Avukatlik Bürosu

Çağla Koç
Yuka Law Office

Serhan Koçaklı
Kolcuoğlu Demirkan Attorneys-at-Law

Korhan Kocali
Cerrahoğlu Law Firm

Galya Kohen
Taboglu & Demirhan

Bahadır Köksal
Sariibrahimoğlu Law Office

Bukle Korkmaz
Sariibrahimoğlu Law Office

Cumhur Köseoğlu
Kentsel Group Machinery

Nazım Olcay Kurt
Herguner Bilgen Ozeke

Aybala Kurtuldu
Serap Zuvin Law Offices

Mert Kutlar
ADMD - Mavioglu & Alkan Law Office

Dilara Leventoğlu
Taboglu & Demirhan

Francesca Maran
Pekin & Pekin

Orhan Yavuz Mavioğlu
ADMD - Mavioglu & Alkan Law Office

Günes Mermer
Çakmak Avukatlik Bürosu

Maral Minasyan
Kolcuoğlu Demirkan Attorneys-at-Law

Gokhan Mirahmetoglu
Union of Chambers and Commodity Exchanges of Turkey

Erhan Seyfi Moroglu
Moroglu Arseven

Ayça Mustafa
ADMD - Mavioglu & Alkan Law Office

Vedia Nihal Koyuncu
Tarlan – Baksi Law Firm

Vakkas Nohut
Bezen & Partners

Zumbul Odaman Taskin
Odaman and Taskin Law Firm

Pelin Oguzer
Moroglu Arseven

Neşe Taşdemir Onder
Onder Legal Law Firm

Mert Oner
KPMG

Yavus Oner
KPMG

Volkan Oray
Güler Dinamik Gümrük Müşavirliği A.Ş.

Çağlayan Orhaner Dündar
Orhaner Law Office

Begum Durukan Ozaydin
Birsel Law Offices

Kaan Ozaydin
Serap Zuvin Law Offices

Yusuf Mansur Özer
Ersoy Bilgehan Lawyers and Consultants

Can Özilhan
Bezen & Partners

Afife Nazlıgül Özkan
ADMD - Mavioglu & Alkan Law Office

Funda Özsel
Bener Law Office, member of Ius Laboris

Özlem Özyiğit
YASED - International Investors Association

Ahmed Pekin
Pekin & Pekin

Ferhat Pekin
Pekin & Bayar Law Firm

İlknur Peksen
Ersoy Bilgehan Lawyers and Consultants

Ecem Pirler
Çakmak Avukatlik Bürosu

Erenalp Rençber
Pekin & Pekin

Dilara Saatçioğlu
PwC Turkey

Batuhan Şahmay
Bener Law Office, member of Ius Laboris

Ece Salman
Moroglu Arseven

Selim Sarıibrahimoğlu
Sariibrahimoğlu Law Office

Gulce Saydam
Paksoy Law Firm

Uğur Sebzeci
Bezen & Partners

Mustafa Sevgin
YükselKarkinKüçük Avukatlik Ortakliği

Ömer Kayhan Seyhun
Central Bank of the Republic of Turkey

Irmak Seymen
ADMD - Mavioglu & Alkan Law Office

Sinan Sigva
General Directorate of Land Registry and Cadastre

Sezil Simsek
PwC Turkey

Bilgehan Şimşek
Barlas Law

Zafer Ertunç Şirin
Istanbul University

Ayse Ülkü Solak
Moroglu Arseven

Ilke Isin Süer
Çakmak Avukatlik Bürosu

Çağıl Sünbül
PwC Turkey

Esin Taboğlu
Taboglu & Demirhan

Gönül Talu
DOĞUŞ İnşaat ve Ticaret A.Ş.

Dilara Tamtürk
ADMD - Mavioglu & Alkan Law Office

Serhat Tanrıverdi
Jones Lang LaSalle

Bekir Tarik Yigit
General Directorate of Land Registry and Cadastre

Aylin Tarlan Tüzemen
Tarlan – Baksi Law Firm

Mehmet Ali Taskin
Odaman and Taskin Law Firm

Selen Terzi Özsoylu
Paksoy Law Firm

Güneş Ece Topbaş
Duman Law Office

Elif Tulunay
Turunç Law Office

Oguz Tumis
3e Danişmanlik Ltd. Şti.

Ceren Hazal Tunçay
Moroglu Arseven

Yigit Turker
Serap Zuvin Law Offices

Noyan Turunç
Turunç Law Office

Ibrahim Tutar
Penetra Consulting and Auditing

Burcu Tuzcu Ersin
Moroglu Arseven

Ürün Ülkü
ADMD - Mavioglu & Alkan Law Office

Leyla Ulucan
Ersoy Bilgehan Lawyers and Consultants

Furkan Ünal
Aktif Investment Bank AS

Ü. Barış Urhan
TÜSİAD

Doğa Usluel
Çakmak Avukatlik Bürosu

Onur Yalçin
YükselKarkinKüçük Avukatlik Ortakliği

Ufuk Yalçın
Herguner Bilgen Ozeke

Ayşegül Yalçınmani
Cerrahoğlu Law Firm

Cansu Yazıcı
Pekin & Pekin

Cüneyt Yetgin
Güler Dinamik Gümrük Müşavirliği A.Ş.

Muhammet Yiğit
Bener Law Office, member of Ius Laboris

A. Çağrı Yıldız
ADMD - Mavioglu & Alkan Law Office

Beste Yıldızili
Turunç Law Office

Bilge Yilmaz
ADMD - Mavioglu & Alkan Law Office

Senay Yilmaz
TOBB - The Union of Chambers and Commodity Exchanges of Turkey

Simal Yilmaz
PwC Turkey

Murat Yülek
PGlobal Global Advisory and Training Services Ltd.

Çağlar Yurttürk
Yuka Law Office

Izzet Zakuto
Somay Hukuk Bürosu

Serap Zuvin
Serap Zuvin Law Offices

UGANDA

Bank of Uganda

Byenkya, Kihika & Co. Advocates

Rodney Adakakin
DHL Global Forwarding (U) Ltd.

Rose Mary Brenda Aeko
Uganda Electricty Generation Company Limited

Michael Akampurira
Akampurira & Partners, Advocates & legal consultants

Daniel Angualia
Angualia, Busiku & Co. Advocates

Robert Apenya
Engoru, Mutebi Advocates

Leria Arinaitwe
Sebalu & Lule Advocates

Edward Balaba
Ernst & Young

Joseph Baliddawa

Robert Bbosa
KSK Associates

Didymus Byenkya
Global 6C Star Logistics Ltd.

Matovu Emmy
Marma Technical Services

Ivan Engoru
Engoru, Mutebi Advocates

Sarfaraz Jiwani
Seyani Brothers & Co. (U) Ltd.

Lwanga John Bosco
Marma Technical Services

Nicholas Kabonge
PwC Uganda

Francis Kamulegeya
PwC Uganda

Ali Kankaka
Kyazze, Kankaka & Co. Advocates

Doreen Kansiime
Sebalu & Lule Advocates

John Fisher Kanyemibwa
Kateera & Kagumire Advocates

Stephen Kasenge
KSK Associates

Vincent Katutsi
Kateera & Kagumire Advocates

Enoch Kibamu
Uganda Society of Architects

Innocent Kihika
Shonubi, Musoke & Co.

Arthur Kwesiga
Uganda Registration Services Bureau

Mercy Kyomugasho-Kainobwisho
Uganda Registration Services Bureau

Arnold Lule
Engoru, Mutebi Advocates

John Magezi
Magezi, Ibale & Co. Advocates

Michael Malan
Compuscan CRB Ltd.

Alex Mbonye Manzi
Uganda Shippers Council

Paul Moores
FBW Group

Naboth Muhairwe
Agaba Muhairwe & Co. Advocates

Albert Mukasa
Kanduho & Co. Advocates

Cornelius Mukiibi
C. Mukiibi Sentamu & Co. Advocates

Paul Mukiibi
Mukiibi and Kyeyune Advocates

Isaac Mumfumbiro
UMEME Limited

Rachel Mwanje Musoke
MMAKS Advocates

Priscilla Mutebi
Engoru, Mutebi Advocates

Harriet Nakaddu
PwC Uganda

Victoria Nakaddu
Sebalu & Lule Advocates

Hellen Nakiryowa
Shonubi, Musoke & Co.

Matthias Nalyanya
LEX Uganda Advocates & Solicitors

Nusula Kizito Nassuna
Capital Markets Authority

Doreen Nawaali
MMAKS Advocates

Martin Ngugi
Brosban Consultants Architecture and Planning

Florence Nsubuga
UMEME Limited

Kefa Nsubuga
Lawyer

John Ntende
UMEME Limited

Patricia Ocan
UMEME Limited

Charles Odere
LEX Uganda Advocates & Solicitors

Jane Okot P' Bitek Langoya
Uganda Registration Services Bureau

Denis Omodi Alyela
Kampala Capital City Authority (KCCA)

Kenneth Rutaremwa
Kateera & Kagumire Advocates

Moses Segawa
Sebalu & Lule Advocates

Stephen Serunjogi
Kateera & Kagumire Advocates

Alan Shonubi
Shonubi, Musoke & Co.

Charles Lwanga Ssemanda
Mukwano Industries (U) Limited

Ambrose Turyahabwe
DHL Global Forwarding (U) Ltd.

Bemanya Twebaze
Uganda Registration Services Bureau

Remmy George Wamimbi
Akampurira & Partners, Advocates & legal consultants

William Were
Capital Law Partners & Advocates

UKRAINE

Yaroslav Abramov
Integrites

Denis Absalyamov
JSC Ukrenergochermet

Rotov Alexander
Confederation of Builders of Ukraine

Yuliya Atamanova
LCF Law Group

Anna Babych
AEQUO

Anastasia Belkina
PwC

Gleb Bialyi
Egorov Puginsky Afanasiev & Partners

Daniel Bilak
CMS Cameron McKenna LLC

Julia Bilonozhko
Dentons

Aleksandr Biryukov
LCF Law Group

Oleg Boichuk
Egorov Puginsky Afanasiev & Partners

Yulia Bondar
HLB Ukraine

Timur Bondaryev
Arzinger & Partners

Alexander Borodkin
Vasil Kisil & Partners

Pavlo Byelousov
AEQUO

Kateryna Chechulina
CMS Cameron McKenna

Iaroslav Cheker
KPMG

Serhiy Chorny
Baker & McKenzie

Sergey Chulkov
Kievenergo

Borys Danevych
Marchenko Danevych

Ivan Demtso
KPMG

Aleksandr Deputat
Elit Group

Olga Dubanevych
KPMG

Mariana Dudnyk
PwC

Igor Dykunskyy
DLF Attorneys-at-Law

Oleksandr Fomenko
Kievenergo

Oleksandr Frolov
CMS Cameron McKenna LLP

Ivan Nikolaevich Gelyukh
Kievenergo

Leonid Gilevich
Ilyashev & Partners

Leonid Gorshenin
Konnov & Sozanovsky

Yaroslav Guseynov
PwC

Vitalii Hamalii
PwC

Pavlo Iamko
HLB Ukraine

Oksana Ilchenko
Egorov Puginsky Afanasiev & Partners

Jon Johannesson
IBCH

Andrei Kaminsky
IBCH

Oleg Kanikovskyi
Proxen & Partners

Yuriy Katser
KPMG

Tatiana Kheruvimova
KPMG

Pavlo Khodakovsky
Arzinger & Partners

Halyna Khomenko
Ernst & Young LLC

Ruslan Kim
Kibenko, Onika & Partners Law Firm

Maryana Kolyada
PwC

Maksym Kopeychykov
Ilyashev & Partners

Andrey Kosharny
Elit Group

Vladimir Kotenko
Ernst & Young LLC

Inna Koval
Inyurpolis Law Firm

Anton Kozlov
AiG Law Firm

Oksana Krasnokutskaya
AEQUO

Khrystyna Krukivska
Marchenko Danevych

Alina Kuksenko
Asters

Vitaliy Kulinich
Egorov Puginsky Afanasiev & Partners

Tatyana Kuzmenko
AiG Law Firm

Oles Kvyat
Asters

Oleksii Latsko
Egorov Puginsky Afanasiev & Partners

Yaroslav Lepko
AEQUO

Maksym Libanov
National Securities and Stock Market Commission

Arsenyy Milyutin
Egorov Puginsky Afanasiev & Partners

Ivan Mustanien
Ernst & Young LLC

Tetiana Mykhailenko
CMS Cameron McKenna LLP

Artem Naumov
Inyurpolis Law Firm

Yuriy Nechayev
Avellum

Alina Nedilko
Egorov Puginsky Afanasiev & Partners

Olena Ohonovska
Egorov Puginsky Afanasiev & Partners Law Offices

Kateryna Oliynyk
Egorov Puginsky Afanasiev & Partners

Liliya Palko
KPMG

Alesya Pavlynska
Arzinger

Konstantin Pilkov
Cai & Lenard

Sergiy Popov
KPMG

Viktoriia Prokharenko
Aurora PJSC

Anatolii Rybak-Sikorskiy
KPMG

Vadym Samoilenko
Asters

Iuliia Savchenko
Asters

Maryana Sayenko
Asters

Viktor Semenyuta
Kievenergo

Olga Serbul
Law Firm IP & C. Consult, LLC

Victor Shekera
KPMG

Olga Shenk
CMS Cameron McKenna

Bohdan Shmorgun
Arzinger & Partners

Hanna Shtepa
Baker & McKenzie

Dmitry Sichkar
Konnov & Sozanovsky

Anton Sintsov
Egorov Puginsky Afanasiev & Partners

Anna Sisetska
Vasil Kisil & Partners

Anastasia Sotir
AEQUO

Natalia Spiridonova
Egorov Puginsky Afanasiev & Partners

Roman Stepanenko
Egorov Puginsky Afanasiev & Partners

Andriy Stetsenko
CMS Cameron McKenna

Mykola Stetsenko
Avellum

Dmitriy Sukhin
Kievenergo

Dmitriy Sykaluk
DLF Attorneys-at-Law

Dmytro Symanov
Cai & Lenard

Vitaliy Tertytsia
LCF Law Group

Svitlana Teush
Arzinger & Partners

Anna Tkachenko
Dentons

Andriy Tsvyetkov
Attorneys' Association Gestors

Serhii Uvarov
Avellum

Camiel van der Meij
PwC

Yuriy Volovnik
Egorov Puginsky Afanasiev & Partners

Elena Volyanskaya
LCF Law Group

Bohdan Yakymenko
Arzinger & Partners

Olexiy Yanov
Law Firm IP & C. Consult, LLC

Yulia Yashenkova
AiG Law Firm

Aleksandra Yevstafyeva
Egorov Puginsky Afanasiev & Partners

Vasyl Yurmanovych
Integrites

Tatiana Zamorska
KPMG

Marina V. Zarina
Private Notary

Anna Zorya
Arzinger & Partners

Kateryna Zviagina
Arzinger & Partners

UNITED ARAB EMIRATES

Al Etihad Credit Bureau

Nadia Abdulrazagh
Nadia Abdulrazagh Advocacy & Legal Consultations

Laith Abuqauod
Talal Abu-Ghazaleh Legal (TAG-Legal)

Firas Adi
Kaanan Advocates and Legal Consultants

Paul Afif
Al Suwaidi & Company

Hesam Aghaloui
OHM Electromechanic

Sultan Al Akraf
Dubai Land Department

Laila Al Asbahi
Tamleek Real Estate Registration Trustee

Mahmood Al Bastaki
Dubai Trade

Khalifa Al Falasi
General Pensions and Social Securities Authority

Obaid Saif Atiq Al Falasi
Dubai Electricity and Water Authority

Eman Al Hosani
Ministry of Human Resources and Emiratisation

Habib M. Al Mulla
Baker & McKenzie

Salah El Dien Al Nahas
Hadef & Partners

Abdullah Al Nasser

Buti Al Subosi
Tamleek Real Estate Registration Trustee

Mohammad Al Suwaidi
Al Suwaidi & Company

Essam Al Tamimi
Al Tamimi & Company Advocates & Legal Consultants

Humam Al Zaqqa
Adnan Saffarini Consultants

Saeed Al-Hamiz
Central Bank of the United Arab Emirates

Amir H. Aljord
Abdullah Alzarooni Advocates and Legal Consultants

Hussain Almatrood
Al Tamimi & Company Advocates & Legal Consultants

Mohammed AlSuboosi
Dubai Courts

Yousaf Al-Suwaidi
Dubai Courts

Wicki Andersen
Baker Botts LLP

Charlotte Attfield
Herbert Smith Freehills

Mahmoud Awad
Hadef & Partners

Elmugtaba Bannaga
Bin Suwaidan Advocates & Legal Consultants

Mounther Barakat
Emirates Securities and Commodities Authority

Piyush Bhandari
Intuit Management Consultancy

Rashid Bin Humaidan
Dubai Electricity and Water Authority

Maryam BinLahej AlFalasi
Dubai Courts

Aed Bouchakra
Huqooq Legal Practice

Mazen Boustany
Baker & McKenzie

Simone Brown
Reed Smith

Omar Bushahab
Business Registration in Department of Economic Development

Joe Carrol
Dentons

Maggie Chang
PwC United Arab Emirates

Pooja Dabir
PwC United Arab Emirates

Rahat Dar
Afridi & Angell, member of Lex Mundi

Mohammed El Ghul
Baker & McKenzie

Michael George
Dar Al-Handasah

Jamal Guzlan
Al Ajmi Engineering Consultants

Nazim Hashim
Afridi & Angell, member of Lex Mundi

Ahmed Hegazy
Tamleek Real Estate Registration Trustee

Conan Higgins
TSI Legal Enterprises, PC

Ashraf Hossain
Summer Sky Electromechanical

Sameer Huda
Hadef & Partners

Rita Jaballah
Al Tamimi & Company Advocates & Legal Consultants

Edger Larose Joseph
Amptec Electromechanical LLC

Gul Kalam
OHM Electromechanic

Kristine Kalnina
Reed Smith

Jonia Kashalaba
PwC United Arab Emirates

George Khoury
Hadef & Partners

Vipul Kothari
Kothari Auditors & Accountants

Ravi Kumar
Dubai Trade

Charles S. Laubach
Afridi & Angell, member of Lex Mundi

Abdulla M. Al Mannaei
Emirates Auction

Christine Maksoud
Baroudi & Associates

Arslan Malik
OHM Electromechanic

Helen Martin
Addleshaw Goddard LLP

Peter Michelmore
Reed Smith

Omar Mohammad

Tarig Monim
TM Advisory

Badih Moukarzel
Huqooq Legal Practice

Saeed Nageeb

Mohamad Nizam
Al Tamimi & Company Advocates & Legal Consultants

Rakesh Pardasani
RSM UAE

Motaz Qaoud
Al Khawaja Engineering Consultancy

Samer Qudah
Al Tamimi & Company Advocates & Legal Consultants

Yusuf Rafiudeen
Dubai Electricity and Water Authority

Ashraf M. Rahman
Adam Global

Johnson Rajan
Intuit Management Consultancy

Mehul Rajyaguru
Al Hili Star ElectroMechanical Works L.L.C

Chatura Randeniya
Afridi & Angell, member of Lex Mundi

Jochem Rossel
PwC United Arab Emirates

Mohammad Safwan
Al Hashemi Planners, Architects, Engineers

Shoeb Saher
Baker & McKenzie

Said Said
Dubai Trade

Mohammed Ahmed Saleh
Dubai Municipality

Osama Shabaan
Talal Abu-Ghazaleh Legal (TAG-Legal)

Hassan Shakrouf
Global Team Décor & Maintenance LLC

Duvvuri Gangadhara Shastry
Elemec Electromechanical Contracting LLC

Mashair Shazli

Craig C. Shepherd
Herbert Smith Freehills

Douglas Smith
Baker & McKenzie

Izabella Szadkowska
Al Tamimi & Company Advocates & Legal Consultants

Hamad Thani Mutar
Dubai Courts

Nitin Tirath
Dubai Trade

Mohsen Tomh
Options Engineering Consultants

Stuart Walker
Afridi & Angell, member of Lex Mundi

Gary Watts
Al Tamimi & Company Advocates & Legal Consultants

Alan Wood
PwC United Arab Emirates

Baher Yousef
Engineering Consultants Group (ECG)

Rania Yousseph
Baker & McKenzie

UNITED KINGDOM

Companies House

DHL Aviation (UK) Ltd.

Dodd Group

Alexandra Adams
Clyde & Co.

Philip Allenby
DLA Piper UK LLP

Paul Bagon
Weil, Gotshal & Manges LLP

Corina Barsa
Clyde & Co.

Ravi Basra
Lubbock Fine - member of Russell Bedford International

Marie Batchelor
Birketts LLP

Andrew Booth
Andrew Booth Architect

Kerri Bridges
Reed Smith LLP

Rob Briggs
CMS Cameron McKenna LLP

Howard Bushell
Her Majesty's Land Registry

Brendon Christian
Business Law BC

Michael Collard
5 Pump Court Chambers

Aisling Connaughton
Clyde & Co.

Elouisa Crichton
Shepherd & Wedderburn

James Cross
Reed Smith LLP

Robert Davies
CMS Cameron McKenna LLP

Michael Dawes
Memery Crystal LLP

Vivien De Melo
Baker & McKenzie

Zaki Ejaz
Right Legal Advice

Nick Francis
PwC United Kingdom

Robert Franklin
Clyde & Co.

Jack Gardener
Clyde & Co.

Camilla Graham
Milbank, Tweed, Hadley & McCloy LLP

Donald Gray
Darwin Gray LLP

Rakesh Grubb-Sharma
Morrison & Foerster LLP

Andrew Haywood
Penningtons Manches LLP

Nicky Heathcote
Her Majesty's Land Registry

Conan Higgins
TSI Legal Enterprises, PC

Robert Hillhouse
Clyde & Co.

Daden Hunt
Birketts LLP

Hannah Jones
Sherrards Solicitors

Michael Josypenko
Institute of Export

Bradley Kilbane
Experian Ltd.

Monika Kuzelova
Reed Smith LLP

Pascal Lalande
Her Majesty's Land Registry

Bob Ledsome
Department for Communities and Local Government

Gemma Lodge
DLA Piper UK LLP

Sandra Lou
Skadden, Arps, Slate, Meagher & Flom LLP

Joanna Macintosh
Latham & Watkins LLP

Neil Maclean
Shepherd & Wedderburn

Neil Magrath
UK Power Networks

Christopher Mallon
Skadden, Arps, Slate, Meagher & Flom LLP

Paul Marmor
Sherrards Solicitors

Mark McGarry
Saffery Champness

Seán McGuinness
Milbank, Tweed, Hadley & McCloy LLP

Antoinette McManus
PwC United Kingdom

Victoria Miller
Memery Crystal LLP

Charlotte Moller
Reed Smith LLP

Howard Morris
Morrison & Foerster LLP

Phil Moss
Lubbock Fine - member of Russell Bedford International

Peter Newman
Milbank, Tweed, Hadley & McCloy LLP

Kevin Nicholson
PwC United Kingdom

Phil Norton
Clyde & Co.

Steve Parker
DHL Global Forwarding

Stewart Perry
Clyde & Co.

Samantha Pigden
Department for Communities and Local Government

Ross Pooley
Latham & Watkins LLP

Helena Potts
Latham & Watkins LLP

Naomi Prashker
Weil, Gotshal & Manges LLP

Alex Rogan
Skadden, Arps, Slate, Meagher & Flom LLP

Angela Shaw
Her Majesty's Land Registry

Sandra Simoni
Department for Communities and Local Government

Lance Terry
Glanvilles Solicitors

Rebecca Thorp
Reed Smith LLP

Julia Vaynzof
Clyde & Co.

Jasmine Wall
Air Sea Worldwide (U.K.) Limited

Alistair White
DLA Piper UK LLP

Christopher Wigley
London Building Control Ltd.

Geoff Wilkinson
Wilkinson Construction Consultants

Alexandra Wood
Clyde & Co.

David Ziyambi
Latham & Watkins LLP

UNITED STATES

Sam J. Alberts
Dentons

Manish Antani
Eisner Jaffe PC

Pamy J. S. Arora
Cornell Group, Inc.

Asheet Awasthi
Amerinde Consolidated, Inc.

David Bartlett
Amerinde Consolidated, Inc.

Eve Brackmann
Stuart Kane

Diane Carter
Dentons

Steven Clark
Clark Firm PLLC

María Amalia Cruz

Federico Cryz

Vilas Dhar
Dhar Law, LLP

Joshua L. Ditelberg
Seyfarth Shaw LLP

Motsa Dubois
FIABCI, the International Real Estate Federation

Michael Dyll
Texas International Freight

David Elden
Parker, Milliken, Clark, O'Hara & Samuelian

Robert Goethe
Cornell Group, Inc.

Peter Gordon
Peter D. Gordon and Associates

William Gould
TroyGould PC

Boris Grosman
L & B Electrical International

Javier Gutierrez
Stuart Kane

Tony Hadley
Experian

Thomas Halket
Halket Weitz LLP

Donald Hamman
Stuart Kane

Dennis Harber
Miami Legal, Title & Remediation

Conan Higgins
TSI Legal Enterprises, PC

Sanford Hillsberg
TroyGould PC

Nancy Israel
Law Office of Nancy D. Israel

Neil Jacobs
NI Jacobs & Associates

Christopher Kelleher
Seyfarth Shaw LLP

Charles L. Kerr
Morrison & Foerster LLP

Joshua Kochath
Comage Container Lines

John LaBar
Henry, McCord, Bean, Miller, Gabriel & LaBar PLLC

Jen Leary
CliftonLarsonAllen LLP

Wen-Ching Lin
Law Offices of Wen-Ching Lin

Bradford L. Livingston
Seyfarth Shaw LLP

Samuel L. Lovitch
PwC United States

Aline Matta
Talal Abu-Ghazaleh Legal (TAG-Legal)

Alene McMahon
Crown Agents Ltd.

Dietrick Miller
TroyGould PC

Kelly J. Murray
PwC United States

David Newberg
Collier, Halpern, Newberg, Nolletti, LLP

Christopher O'Connell
Parker, Milliken, Clark, O'Hara & Samuelian

Richard O'Neill
Consolidated Edison Co. of NY, Inc.

Eric Pezold
Snell & Wilmer

Darrell Pierce
Dykema

Shanen Prout
Law Office of Shanen R. Prout

Stephen Raslavich
United States Bankruptcy Court

Janet Reid
Crown Agents Ltd.

Kenneth Rosen
University of Alabama School of Law

Joshua Roy
Morrison & Foerster LLP

Manuel Santiago
Milrose Consultants, Inc.

Mayer Sasson
Consolidated Edison Co. of NY, Inc.

William Shawn
ShawnCoulson LLP

E. Lee Smith
Dentons

Leonard Smith
Rucci, Bardaro & Falzone, PC

Joseph Tannous
JT Construction

Michael Temin
Fox Rothschild LLP

Steve Thomas
Crown Agents Ltd.

Frederick Turner
Turner & Turner

Robert James Voetsch
Crown Agents Ltd.

Robert Wallace
Stuart Kane

Ann Marie Zaletel
Seyfarth Shaw LLP

Olga Zalomiy
Law Offices of Olga Zalomiy, PC

URUGUAY

Graetz Nuñez

Marta Alvarez
Administración Nacional de Usinas y Transmisión Eléctrica (UTE)

Bernardo Amorín
Amorin Larrañaga

Alfredo Arocena
Ferrere Abogados

Leticia Barrios
Bergstein Abogados

Virginia Brause
Jiménez de Aréchaga, Viana & Brause

Luis Burastero Servetto
Luis Burastero & Asoc.

Valeria Cabrejos
Amorin Larrañaga

Lucia Carbajal
Posadas, Posadas & Vecino

Federico Caresani
Galante & Martins

Pablo Chocho
Russell Bedford International

Augusto Cibils
PwC Uruguay

Victoria Costa
Hughes & Hughes

Leonardo Couto
Jose Maria Facal & Co.

Hernán de la Fuente
Escribanía de la Fuente

Juan Angel de la Fuente
Escribanía de la Fuente

Fernando De Posadas
Posadas, Posadas & Vecino

Rosana Díaz
Superintendencia de Servicios Financieros - Banco Central del Uruguay

Carolina Diaz De Armas
Guyer & Regules, member of Lex Mundi

Maria Jose Echinope
Jiménez de Aréchaga, Viana & Brause

Analía Fernández
Bergstein Abogados

Javier Fernández Zerbino
Bado, Kuster, Zerbino & Rachetti

Mario Ferrari Rey
PwC Uruguay

Hector Ferreira
Hughes & Hughes

Juan Federico Fischer
Fischer & Schickendantz

Federico Florin
Guyer & Regules, member of Lex Mundi

Bruno Foggiato
Russell Bedford International

Sergio Franco
PwC Uruguay

Diego Galante
Galante & Martins

Alejandra García
Ferrere Abogados

Daniel García
PwC Uruguay

Enrique Garcia Pini
Administración Nacional de Usinas y Transmisión Eléctrica (UTE)

Rodrigo Goncalvez
Guyer & Regules, member of Lex Mundi

Renato Guerrieri
Guyer & Regules, member of Lex Mundi

Andrés Hessdörfer
Olivera Abogados

Marcela Hughes
Hughes & Hughes

Ariel Imken
Superintendencia de Servicios Financieros - Banco Central del Uruguay

Alfredo Inciarte Blanco
Estudio Inciarte

Richard Iturria
Bado, Kuster, Zerbino & Rachetti

Jimena Lanzani
Guyer & Regules, member of Lex Mundi

Santiago Madalena
Guyer & Regules, member of Lex Mundi

Leandro Marques
PwC Uruguay

Leonardo Melos
Bergstein Abogados

Alejandro Miller Artola
Guyer & Regules, member of Lex Mundi

Federico Moares
Russell Bedford International

Daniel Ignacio Mosco Gómez
Guyer & Regules, member of Lex Mundi

Pablo Mosto
Administración Nacional de Usinas y Transmisión Eléctrica (UTE)

Javier Noblega
Jiménez de Aréchaga, Viana & Brause

Mateo Noseda
Guyer & Regules, member of Lex Mundi

Lucía Patrón
Ferrere Abogados

Mariana Pisón
Bergstein Abogados

Walter Planells
Ferrere Abogados

Maria Clara Porro
Ferrere Abogados

Pilar Posada
Superintendencia de Servicios Financieros - Banco Central del Uruguay

María Macarena Rachetti
PwC Uruguay

Agustín Rachetti Pérez
Bado, Kuster, Zerbino & Rachetti

Cecilia Ricciardi
Fischer & Schickendantz

Mariana Saracho
Guyer & Regules, member of Lex Mundi

Eliana Sartori
PwC Uruguay

Leonardo Slinger
Guyer & Regules, member of Lex Mundi

Fabiana Steinberg
Hughes & Hughes

Alejandro Taranto
Estudio Taranto

Lucia Techera
Guyer & Regules, member of Lex Mundi

Diego Tognazzolo
PwC Uruguay

Juan Ignacio Troccoli
Fischer & Schickendantz

Silvina Vila
Bergstein Abogados

María Eugenia Yavarone
Ferrere Abogados

UZBEKISTAN

Advokat-Himoya Law Office

Avent Advocat

Credit Bureau Credit Informational-Analytical Centre LLC

Department of Land Resources and State Cadastre of Tashkent

International Legal Group

Jahongir Abdurasulov
Charges Registry of the Central Bank of Uzbekistan

Ravshan Adilov
Colibri Law Firm

Mels Akhmedov
BAS Law Firm

Umid Aripdjanov
Colibri Law Firm

Elvina Asanova
GRATA Law Firm

Umarzhon Usmanalievich Egamberdiev
Uzgosenergonadzor

Azamat Fayzullaev
Leges Advokat Law Firm

Mansurkhon Kamalov
Foreign Enterprise of Huawei Tech Investment of Tashkent

Shurhat Ummatovich Kambarov
Administration on State Expertise of Architecture

Mouborak Kambarova
Dentons

Dilshad Khabibullaev
Colibri Law Firm

Kamilla Khamraeva
Colibri Law Firm

Sergey Mayorov
Simay Kom

Sabdulla Shukhratovich Muhtarkhodzhaev
State Committee of the Republic of Uzbekistan on Architecture and Construction

Jamol Ryskiyev
GRATA Law Firm

Alisher Shaihov
Chamber of Commerce and Industry Uzbekistan

Nizomiddin Shakhabutdinov
Leges Advokat Law Firm

Sofia Shaykhrazieva
Colibri Law Firm

Otabek Suleimanov
Colibri Law Firm

Asomiddin Tadjiev
State Committee of the Republic of Uzbekistan on Architecture and Construction

Atabek Tollehoojaev
Administration for Quality Control

Nargiza Turgunova
GRATA Law Firm

Nodir Yuldashev
GRATA Law Firm

Shuhrat Yunusov
BAS Law Firm

VANUATU

Barrett & Partners

Utilities Regulatory Authority of Vanuatu

Vanuatu Financial Services Commission

Tony Joel Alvos
UNELCO

Barry Amoss
South Sea Shipping (Vanuatu) Ltd.

Loïc Bernier
Caillard & Kaddour

George Boar
Pacific Lawyers

Alan Brown
Fletcher Construction

Frederic Derousseau
Vate Electrics

Delores Elliott
Data Bureau Limited

Anthony Frazier

Angèle Jacquier
UNELCO

Remy Janet
UNELCO

Bill Jimmy
Fr8 Logistics Ltd.

David Lefevre
UNELCO

Aaron Levine
Asian Development Bank

Edward Nalyal
Edward Nalyal & Partners

Mark Pardoe
South Sea Shipping (Vanuatu) Ltd.

Harold Qualao
Qualao Consulting Ltd. QCL

Martin St-Hilaire
Cabinet AJC, an independent correspondent member of DFK International

Pierre Zaccuri
Cabinet AJC, an independent correspondent member of DFK International

VENEZUELA, RB

Claudia Abreu
Baker & McKenzie

Tamara Adrian
Adrian & Adrian

Yanet Aguiar
Despacho de Abogados miembros de Norton Rose Fulbright SC

Juan Enrique Aigster
Hoet Pelaez Castillo & Duque

Francisco Aleman Planchart
Tinoco, Travieso, Planchart & Nuñez

Servio T. Altuve Jr.
Servio T. Altuve R. & Asociados

Aixa Añez
D'Empaire Reyna & Asociados

Pedro Azpurua
Pack Engenieros C.A.

Carlos Bachrich Nagy
De Sola Pate & Brown, Abogados - Consultores

Marian Basciani
De Sola Pate & Brown, Abogados - Consultores

Francesco Castiglione
Baker & McKenzie

Geraldine d'Empaire
D'Empaire Reyna & Asociados

Dalí Rojas
Cámara de Construccion de Venezuela

Oscar de Lima G.
deBarr C.A.

Arturo De Sola Lander
De Sola Pate & Brown, Abogados - Consultores

Maria Gabriela Galavis
Hoet Pelaez Castillo & Duque

Jose Javier Garcia
PwC Venezuela

Luis Ignacio Gil Palacios
Palacios, Ortega y Asociados

Lynne H. Glass
Despacho de Abogados miembros de Norton Rose Fulbright SC

Adriana Goncalves
Baker & McKenzie

Andres Gonzalez Crespo

Diego Gonzalez Crespo

Enrique Gonzalez Crespo

Alfredo Hurtado
Hurtado Esteban y Asociados - member of Russell Bedford International

Enrique Itriago
Rodriguez & Mendoza

Daniela Jaimes
Despacho de Abogados miembros de Norton Rose Fulbright, S.C.

Pedro Jedlicka
Imery Urdaneta Calleja Itriago Flamarique

Gabriela Longo
Palacios, Ortega y Asociados

Greta Marazzi
Adrian & Adrian

Pedro Mendoza
Mendoza Davila Toledo

Maritza Meszaros
Baker & McKenzie

Lorena Mingarelli Lozzi
De Sola Pate & Brown, Abogados - Consultores

José Manuel Ortega
Palacios, Ortega y Asociados

Pedro Pacheco
PwC Venezuela

Ruth Paz
PwC Venezuela

Bernardo Pisani
Rodriguez & Mendoza

Eduardo Porcarelli
CONAPRI

Juan Carlos Pró-Rísquez
Despacho de Abogados miembros de Norton Rose Fulbright SC

José Alberto Ramirez
Hoet Pelaez Castillo & Duque

Andreína Rondón
CONAPRI

Pedro Saghy
Despacho de Abogados miembros de Norton Rose Fulbright SC

Eva Marina Santos
Hoet Pelaez Castillo & Duque

Laura Silva Aparicio
Hoet Pelaez Castillo & Duque

Oscar Ignacio Torres
Travieso Evans Arria Rengel & Paz

Arnoldo Troconis
D'Empaire Reyna & Asociados

John Tucker
Hoet Pelaez Castillo & Duque

Pedro Urdaneta
Imery Urdaneta Calleja Itriago Flamarique

Jose Valecillos
D'Empaire Reyna & Asociados

Indhira Vivas
Imery Urdaneta Calleja Itriago Flamarique

VIETNAM

Grant Thornton LLP

Ho Chi Minh City Power Corporation (EVN HCMC)

Pham Nghiem Xuan Bac
Vision & Associates

Frederick Burke
Baker & McKenzie (Vietnam) Ltd.

Hung Phat Chau
Honor Partnership Law Company Limited

Tran Cong Quoc
Bizconsult Law Firm

Giles Thomas Cooper
Duane Morris LLC

Nhung Dang
LVN & Associates

Phuong Dzung Dang
Vision & Associates

Trong Hieu Dang
Vision & Associates

Nguyen Dang Viet
Bizconsult Law Firm

Phan Thanh Dat
Russin & Vecchi

Linh Doan
LVN & Associates

Dang The Duc
Indochine Counsel

Tran Duc Hoai
Vietbid Law Firm

Thanh Long Duong
Aliat Legal

Tieng Thu Duong
Vision & Associates

Vu Thu Hang
Honor Partnership Law Company Limited

Le Hong Phong
Bizconsult Law Firm

Nguyen Huong
Rajah & Tann LCT Lawyers

Dai Thang Huynh
DFDL

Milton Lawson
Freshfields Bruckhaus Deringer

Anh Tuan Le
The National Credit Information Centre - The State Bank of Vietnam

Nguyen Huy Thuy Le
Indochine Counsel

Nhan Le
Duane Morris LLC

Loc Le Thi
YKVN

Uyen Le Thi Canh
LuatViet - Advocates & Solicitors

Logan Leung
Rajah & Tann LCT Lawyers

Tien Ngoc Luu
Vision & Associates

Duy Minh Ngo
VB Law

Hoang Anh Nguyen
Mayer Brown LLP

Hoang Kim Oanh Nguyen
Baker & McKenzie (Vietnam) Ltd.

Huong Nguyen
Mayer Brown JSM

Minh Tuan Nguyen
Viet Premier Law Ltd.

Oanh Nguyen
Baker & McKenzie (Vietnam) Ltd.

Q. Anh Nguyen
Group Counsel

Quoc Phong Nguyen
Aliat Legal

Quynh Hoa Nguyen
DFDL

Thanh Hai Nguyen
Baker & McKenzie (Vietnam) Ltd.

Thi Minh Ngoc Nguyen
The National Credit Information Centre - The State Bank of Vietnam

Thi Phuong Lan Nguyen
Vietnam Credit Information J.S.C. (PCB)

Thi Phuong Thao Nguyen
Vietnam Credit Information J.S.C. (PCB)

Tram Nguyen
LVN & Associates

Tram Nguyen
YKVN

Trang Kim Nguyen
Indochine Counsel

Van Anh Nguyen
Vietbid Law Firm

Anh Phuong Pham
Honor Partnership Law Company Limited

Huong Pham
YKVN

Phuong Phan
Rajah & Tann LCT Lawyers

Viet D. Phan
LuatPVD

Vu Anh Phan
Indochine Counsel

Kim Cuong Phung
Honor Partnership Law Company Limited

Dang Anh Quan
Russin & Vecchi

Chau Quang
Rajah & Tann LCT Lawyers

Vu Que
Rajah & Tann LCT Lawyers

Nguyen Que Tam
CSP Legal LLC

Nguyen Thi Hong Thang
Rajah & Tann LCT Lawyers

Dinh The Phuc
Electricity Regulatory Authority of Vietnam

Tan Heng Thye
CSP Legal LLC

Chi Anh Tran
Baker & McKenzie (Vietnam) Ltd.

Nam Hoai Truong
Indochine Counsel

Vo Huu Tu
Indochine Counsel

Nguyen Anh Tuan
DP Consulting Ltd.

Thuy Duong Van
Baker & McKenzie (Vietnam) Ltd.

Dzung Vu
LVN & Associates

Hong Hanh Vu
Mayer Brown LLP

Phuong Vu
LVN & Associates

Quoc Vuong
Group Counsel

Son Ha Vuong
Vision & Associates

WEST BANK AND GAZA

Nidal Abu Lawi
Palestine Real Estate Investment Co.

Saleh Ahmaid
Al Kamal Shipping and Clearing Co. (Ltd.)

Tareq Al Masri
Ministry of National Economy

Shadi Al-Haj
PwC

Raja Al-Shafi'i
Engineers Association

Sharhabeel Al-Zaeem
Sharhabeel Al-Zaeem and Associates

Haytham L. Al-Zubi
Al-Zubi Law Office

Mohammad Amarneh
EU Police Mission in the Palestinian Territories (EUPOL COPPS)

Moayad Amouri
PwC

Thaer Amro
Amro & Associates Law Office

Hazem Anabtawi
Alliance Consulting Services

Muhanad Assaf
Ittqan Law Firm

Hanna Atrash
AEG

Firas Attereh
Hussam Attereh Group for Legal Services

Mohammad A. Dahadha
Mohammad A. Dahadha Lawyer

Ashraf Far
Ittqan Law Firm

Ali Faroun
Palestinian Monetary Authority

Philip Farrage
Baker Tilly International

Hussein Habbab
Palestine Ijara Company

Osama Hamdeh
Ramallah Municipality

Yousef Hammodeh
Palestine Auditing & Accounting Co.

Hanna N. Hanania
Hanania Law Office

Maher Hanania
Equity Legal Group

Hiba I. Husseini
Husseini & Husseini

Rula Izz
Ramallah Engineering Office

Bilal Kamal
Ittqan Attorneys-at-Law

Rasem Kamal
Kamal & Associates - Attorneys and Counsellors-at-Law

Lubna S. Katbeh
Equity Legal Group

Mohamed Khader
Lausanne Trading Consultants

Deena Khalaf
Al Kamal Shipping and Clearing Co. (Ltd.)

Spiro Khoury
Ramallah Engineering Office

Raja Khwialed
Palestine Company Control

Ahmad Madi
Land Registration

Dima Saad Mashaqi
Ramallah Municipality

Nabil A. Mushahwar
Law Offices of Nabil A. Mushahwar

Tony H. Nassar
A.F. & R. Shehadeh Law Office

Mark-George Nesnas
Ittqan Law Firm

Rami Rabah
DAI

Raed Rajab

Wael Saadi
PwC

Samir Sahhar
HLB Samir B. Sahhar Certified Public Accountants

Maysa Sarhan
Palestinian Monetary Authority

Kareem Fuad Shehadeh
A.F. & R. Shehadeh Law Office

Nadeem Shehadeh
A.F. & R. Shehadeh Law Office

Thaer Sheikh
Ittqan Law Firm

Hatem Sirhan
Companies Registry, Ministry of Economy and Trade-Industry, Palestinian National Authority

Raed Tharf
Raed Tharf Law Office

Mazin Theeb
Shahd Electrical Engineering Consultants

Tareq Z. Touqan
Equity Legal Group

Odeh Zaghmori
Palestinian Federation of Industries

YEMEN, REP.

Khalid Abdullah
Sheikh Mohammed Abdullah Sons (est. 1927)

Ghazi Shaif Al Aghbari
Al Aghbari & Partners Law Firm

Noura Yahya H. Al-Adhhi
Central Bank of Yemen

Yaser Al-Adimi
Abdul Gabar A. Al-Adimi for Construction & Trade

Khaled Al-Buraihi
Khaled Al-Buraihi for Advocacy & Legal Services

Ahmed Al-Gharasi
Al-Ghasari Trading

Mohamed Taha Hamood Al-Hashimi
Mohamed Taha Hamood & Co.

Abdulkader Al-Hebshi
Advocacy and Legal Consultations Office (ALCO)

Ali Al-Hebshi
Advocacy and Legal Consultations Office (ALCO)

Omar Al-Qatani
Central Bank of Yemen

Mahmood Abdulaziz Al-Shurmani
Lawyer

Abdulla Farouk Luqman
Luqman Legal Advocates & Legal Consultants

Amani Hail
Central Bank of Yemen

Ejlal Mofadal
Central Bank of Yemen

Esam Nadeesh
Advocacy and Legal Consultations Office (ALCO)

Khaled Mohammed Salem Ali
Luqman Legal Advocates & Legal Consultants

Walid Shawafee
Yemen International for Construction and Trading Co. Ltd.

Saeed Sohbi
Saeed Hassan Sohbi

Nigel Truscott
Damac Group

ZAMBIA

Atherstone & Cook

Energy Management Services

Azizhusein Adam
AD Adams & Co.

Aditya
DSV Swift Freight International Ltd (Zambia)

Dingani C. Banda
Zambia Revenue Authority

Pricilla C. Banda
Zambia Revenue Authority

Salome Banda
KPMG

Wilson Banda
Patents and Companies Registration Agency (PACRA)

Judith Beene
Lusaka City Council

Dickson Bwalya
Lisulo + Bwalya

Lewis K. Bwalya
ZESCO Ltd.

Anthony Bwembya
Patents and Companies Registration Agency (PACRA)

Kazimbe Chenda
Simeza, Sangwa and Associates

Tafara Chenda
Corpus Legal Practioners

Bonaventure Chibamba Mutale
Ellis & Co.

Mwelwa Chibesakunda
Chibesakunda & Company, member of DLA Piper Group

Abigail Chimuka
Musa Dudhia and Co.

Alick Chirwa
Sinok Logistics Ltd.

Sydney Chisenga
Corpus Legal Practitioners

Kennedy Chishimba
Lusaka City Council

Bradley Choonga
PwC Zambia

John Chowa
Digital Wave

Chisanga Chungu
Deloitte

Nelson H. Mwila
EY Zambia

Lynn Habanji
Ministry of Lands, Natural Resources and Environmental Protection

Edgar Hamuwele
Grant Thornton Zambia

Diane Harrington
SDV Logistics

Andrew Howard
Sharpe Howard & Mwenye

Malcolm G.G. Jhala
Deloitte

Mwiche Kabwe
Zambia Environmental Management Agency

Chishimba Kachasa
Chibesakunda & Company, member of DLA Piper Group

Charles Kafunda
High Court

John K. Kaite
John Kaite Legal Practitioners

Kelly Kalumba
Green Cold Architects

Momba M. Kalyabantu
Malambo & Company

Peter S. Kang'ombe
Musa Dudhia & Company

Moono I.M. Kanjelesa
Zambia Environmental Management Agency

Arnold Kasalwe
EY Zambia

Lubinda Linyama
Eric Silwamba, Jalasi & Linyama Legal Practitioners

Walusiku Lisulo
Lisulo + Bwalya

Johan Lombaard
Manica Africa Pty. Ltd.

Mwangala Lubinda
Sharpe Howard & Mwenye

Vincent Malambo
Malambo and Company

Christopher Mapani
Patents and Companies Registration Agency (PACRA)

Tiziana Marietta
Sharpe & Howard

Ernest Mate
PwC Zambia

Bonaventure Mbewe
Barclays Bank

Chosani Mbewe
PwC Zambia

Bekithemba Mbuyisa
Lusaka City Council

Harriet Mdala
Musa Dudhia & Company

Jyoti Mistry
PwC Zambia

Gerald Mkandawire
SDV Logistics

Mukuka Mubanga
ZESCO Ltd.

Monde Mukela
Entry Point Africa

Chintu Y. Mulendema
CYMA

Mwasa Mulenga
Lusaka City Council

Alex Muluwe
Digital Wave

Sara Mulwanda
Ministry of Lands, Natural Resources and Environmental Protection

Muchinda Muma
Corpus Legal Practitioners

Henry Musonda
Kiran & Musonda Associates

Chanda Musonda-Chiluba
Africa Legal Network (ALN)

Francis Mwape
WorldSkills Zambia

Paul Mwiksa
Mwikisa and Company

Brian H. Namachila
Lusaka City Council

Nchima Nchito
Nchito and Nchito Advocates

Francis K. Ngomba
Lusaka City Council

Brenda Ngulube
BCN Consultants

Annette Nkhowani
Musa Dudhia & Company

Aleksandar Perunicic
SDV Logistics

Ezekiel Phiri
Zambia Revenue Authority

Michael Phiri
KPMG

Lydia Pwadura
PwC Zambia

Miriam Sabi
ZRA - Taxpayer Services

Edward Sampa
Chibesakunda & Company, member of DLA Piper Group

Valerie Sesia
Customized Clearing and Forwarding Ltd.

Namakuzu Shandavu
Corpus Legal Practitioners

Abigail Shansonga
Corpus Legal Practitioners

Clavel M. Sianodo
Malambo and Company

Sharon K. Sichilongo
Zambia Development Agency

Ngosa Simachela
Nchito and Nchito Advocates

Chitembo Simwanza
ZESCO Ltd.

Mutengo Sindano
Ministry of Lands, Natural Resources and Environmental Protection

Mildred Stephenson
Credit Reference Bureau Africa Limited T/A TransUnion

Dumisani Tembo
AB & David, Zambia

Liu Yang
SDV Logistics

Inutu Zaloumis
PAM Golding Properties

Patson Zulu
Zambia Environmental Management Agency

ZIMBABWE

Atherstone & Cook

Ministry of Energy and Power Development

Richard Beattie
The Stone/Beattie Studio

Tim Boulton
Manica Africa

Peter Cawood
PwC Zimbabwe

Regina Chadya
Manica Africa

Grant Davies
Manica Africa

Beloved Dhlakama
Dhlakama B. Attorneys

Paul Fraser
Lofty & Fraser

Daniel Garwe
Planet

Norman Gombera
Manica Africa

Alan Goodrich
Financial Clearing Bureau

Obert Chaurura Gutu
Gutu & Chikowero

Trust Jeferson
Clear Horizons (Private) Limited

Prince Kanokanga
Kanokanga & Partners

Manuel Lopes
PwC Zimbabwe

Charity Machiridza
BDO Tax & Advisory Services Pvt. Ltd.

Faro Mahere
Gill, Godlonton & Gerrans

Rita Makarau
High Court Zimbabwe

Zanudeen Makorie
Coghlan, Welsh & Guest

Chatapiwa Malaba
Kantor and Immerman

Gertrude Maredza
Gutu & Chikowero

Tsungirirai Marufu
Gutu & Chikowero

Norman Mataruka
Reserve Bank of Zimbabwe

Gloria Mawarire
Mawere & Sibanda Legal Practitioners

Thembiwe Mazingi
Coghlan, Welsh & Guest

Jim McComish
Pearce McComish Architects

Roselyn Mhlanga
Kanokanga & Partners

Kundai Msemburi
Securities & Exchange Commission

Sithembinkosi Msipa
Judicial Services Commission

T. Muringani
Speartec

Lina Mushanguri
Zimbabwe Stock Exchange

Eldard Mutasa
High Court Zimbabwe

Alec Tafadzwa Muza
Mawere & Sibanda Legal Practitioners

Christina Muzerengi
Grant Thornton Zimbabwe

Duduzile Ndawana
Gill, Godlonton & Gerrans

Maxwell Ngorima
BDO Tax & Advisory Services Pvt. Ltd.

Tatenda Nhemachena
Mawere & Sibanda Legal Practitioners

Dorothy Pasipanodya
Gill, Godlonton & Gerrans

John Ridgewell
BCHOD and Partners

Edward Rigby
Casling, Rigby, McMahon

Unity Sakhe
Kantor & Immerman

Reggie Saruchera
Grant Thornton Zimbabwe

Bellina Sigauke
Reserve Bank of Zimbabwe

Edward Siwela
Institute of Directors of Zimbabwe (IoDZ)

Takoleza Takoleza
Zimbabwe Investment Authority

Murambiwa Tarabuku
Pearce McComish Architects

Sonja Vas
Scanlen & Holderness

Adam Bongani Wenyimo
Gutu & Chikowero

Ruvimbo Zakeo
Gill, Godlonton & Gerrans